K. L. Knickerbocker
University of Tennessee

H. Willard Reninger
University of Northern Iowa

Interpreting Literature

Preliminaries to Literary Judgment

Shorter Edition

Holt, Rinehart and Winston

New York Chicago San Francisco Atlanta Dallas Montreal Toronto

Library of Congress Cataloging in Publication Data

Knickerbocker, Kenneth Leslie, ed.
Interpreting literature.
Includes index.
1. Literature—Collections. I. Reninger, Harry Willard, II. Title.
PN6014.K572 808.8 78-6444

ISBN: 0-03-043821-7

Printed in the United States of America

2 3 4 0 7 4 1 0 9 8 7 6 5

ACKNOWLEDGMENTS

For permission to reprint materials in this book, the editors are indebted to the following sources:

Almo Music Corp. for permission to reprint lyrics of "Crucifixion" and "Nobody's Buying Flowers from the Flower Lady," lyrics and music by Phil Ochs, both copyright © 1966 by Barricade Music, Inc.; all rights administered by Almo Music Corp. (ASCAP); all rights reserved; international copyright secured.

Wallace L. Anderson for permission to reprint "An Analysis of 'Mr. Flood's Party'."

Atheneum Publishers, Inc., for permission to reprint "The Dover Bitch" from *The Hard Hours* by Anthony Hecht (appeared originally in the *Partisan Review*); "From a Litany" from *Darker* by Mark Strand, copyright © 1968, 1969, 1970 by Mark Strand; and "An Annual and Perennial Problem," originally published in *A Time of Bees,* which is now included in *Merciful Disguises* by Mona Van Duyn, copyright © 1964, 1973 by Mona Van Duyn.

James Baldwin for permission to reprint "Exodus."

The Bobbs-Merrill Company, Inc., for "A Poem for Black Hearts" from *Black Magic Poetry 1961–1967,* copyright © 1969 by LeRoi Jones (Imamu Amiri Baraka).

Broadside Press for permission to reprint "Kidnap Poem" from *Re: Creation* by Nikki Giovanni; "Booker T. and W. E. B." and "Black Poet, White Critic" by Dudley Randall; and "For Malcolm X" by Margaret A. Walker.

Calder & Boyers, Ltd., for permission to reprint "what would I do without this world faceless incurious" from *Collected Poems in English and French* by Samuel Beckett, copyright © 1961 by Samuel Beckett.

Cambridge University Press for permission to reprint *Hamlet* from *Shakespearian Tragedy* by H. B. Charlton.

Jonathan Cape, Ltd., and the Estate of Elizabeth Bowen for permission to reprint "The Demon Lover" from *Ivy Gripped the Steps and Other Stories* by Elizabeth Bowen, copyright © 1946, renewed 1974.

Charing Cross Music for permission to reprint the lyrics of "The Sound of Silence," © 1964 by Paul Simon.

City Lights Books for permission to reprint "Last Night in Calcutta" by Allen Ginsberg from *Planet News,* copyright 1968 by Allen Ginsberg.

(Acknowledgments are continued on page 719.)

Interpreting Literature

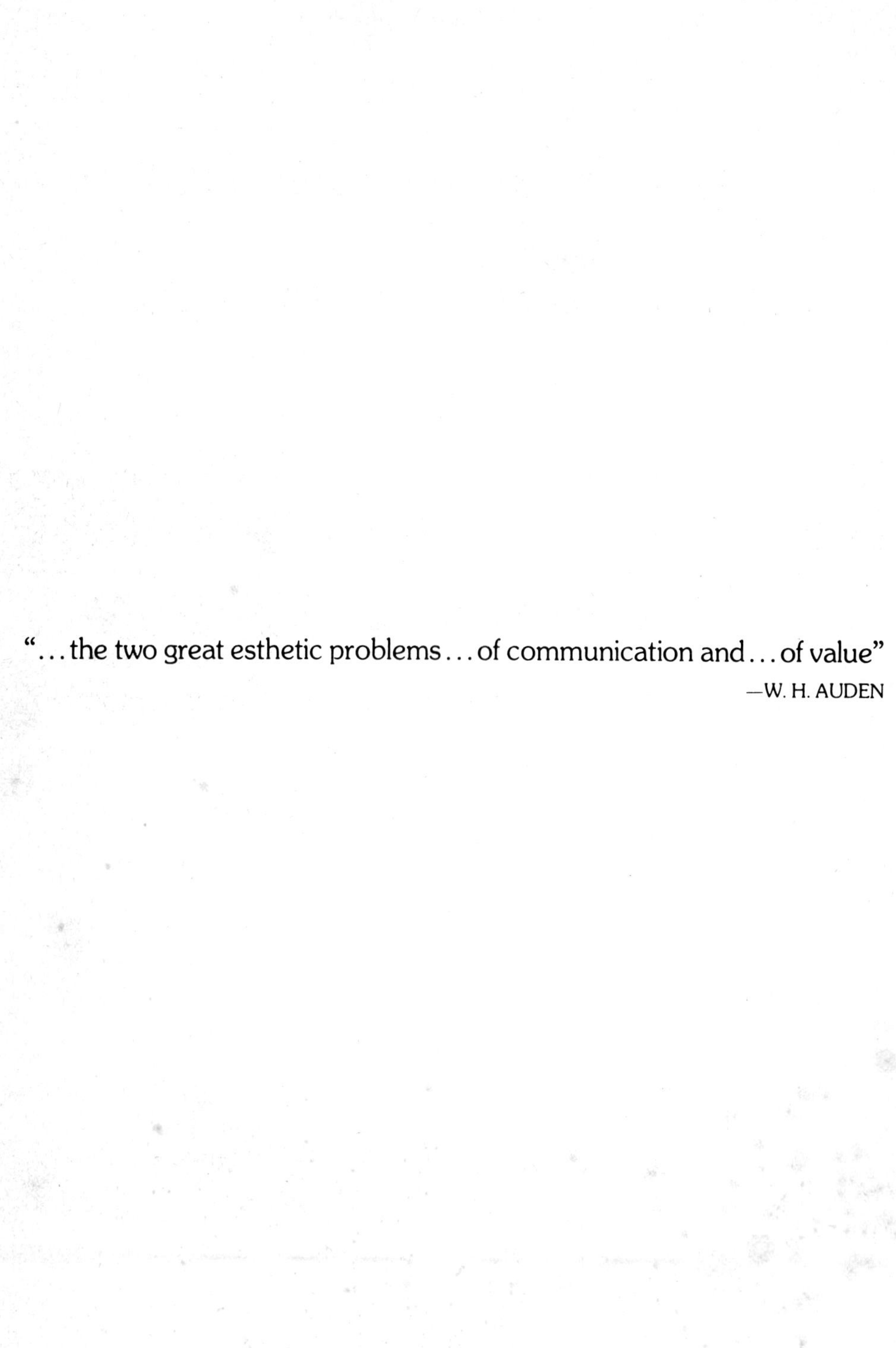

"... the two great esthetic problems ... of communication and ... of value"

—W. H. AUDEN

Preface

Have you practis'd so long
to learn to read?
Have you felt so proud
to get at the meaning
of poems?
WALT WHITMAN, "Song of Myself"*

This volume retains, intact, the sections on Fiction, Poetry, and Drama as they appear in the Sixth Edition of *Interpreting Literature*, 1978. A half dozen critical essays have been placed in the Appendix. All of Biography and the remaining essays have been dropped in order to focus full attention on the creative genres.

Editorial devices and selection of material have been guided by concentration on both the abilities and limitations of students when they are faced with a piece of imaginative writing. Many students regard imaginative literature as a conspiracy against their mental and emotional peace. Their minds are accustomed to function best at a literal—that is, a servile—level. They are in a very real sense shackled. Can such fetters be removed? We think so. A key figure in this process of liberation is the instructor, and a book's effectiveness—ours or anyone else's—must depend in great part upon the wisdom and enthusiasm of those who teach. It has been our chief purpose to provide a readily teachable book.

Several principles have guided our editorial work. First of all, we have as far as possible allowed literature to speak for itself. In "General Preliminaries," for example, we call on literature to define itself so that the reader may see and know what literature is and not simply be told what it is. In "Fiction: Preliminaries," instead of laying down rules for short stories, we present a story that shows many of the rules in action. The same procedure is followed in the Preliminaries to the sections on Poetry and Drama.

The second guiding principle—a corollary of the first—was to delay comment on a literary technique or characteristic until a demonstration actually appeared in one of the selections. Robert Frost's "Stopping by Woods on a Snowy Evening," John Galsworthy's "Quality," and Eugene O'Neill's *Ile* are analyzed thoroughly as specimens of the major creative literary genres: poetry, fiction, and drama. Our procedure in this respect accounts for our use of the term "Preliminaries" instead of "Introductions." Each section as a whole—"Preliminaries," selections, comments, and questions—constitutes an introduction to the type of literature it contains.

The third principle was that all technical terms should be explained or defined as soon as used.

* See p. 328, ll. 31–32.

Furthermore, since sections of this book may be studied out of the order given, we have not hesitated to repeat definitions of terms that recur in the various sections.

Finally, we have included in each section a relatively small number of selections without comments or questions. We have done this so that students independently may apply whatever they have learned.

Teachers will note that in addition to the regular Table of Contents and Index, selections have been organized according to theme. This sort of cross-referencing will suggest many ideas for writing and class discussions. Although the Thematic Contents is extensive, the controlling topics are clearly subject to modification. Numerous selections illustrate more than one theme. Instructors and students are free, of course, to create other topics and to rearrange ours in any way.

We have been concerned with "relevance," but not when the word is interpreted to mean "recent." The older literature has something to say to our times, and the best of the younger literature also speaks to us. We have avoided fads, causes, and biases and have sought a balance between the new and the old.

The section on fiction features the storytellers of our century largely because short narratives are a relatively recent form. The upsurge of interest in science fiction and fantasy has led us to include stories by Ray Bradbury, Elizabeth Bowen, Walter Van Tilburg Clark, E. B. White, and Donald Barthelme. Joseph Conrad's masterpiece, "Heart of Darkness," is included along with tales by Sherwood Anderson, Colette, Kurt Vonnegut, Jr., and Edgar Allan Poe.

The poetry section, after "Preliminaries" and some illustrative verses, goes on to "Story Ballads," followed by "New Folk and Country Ballads." A subsection called "Four Modern Classics" places in sequence W. B. Yeats's "Among School Children," Robert Frost's "A Masque of Reason," Wallace Stevens's "Sunday Morning," and T. S. Eliot's "The Love Song of J. Alfred Prufrock." Diverse in subject matter and style, these four poems speak in universals that transcend the contemporary. Living poets with potentially lasting appeal are represented by a large group, including James Dickey, Mona Van Duyn, Donald Justice, Adrienne Rich, Richard Rackstraw, Diane Wakoski, Erica Jong, Nikki Giovanni, Ted Hughes, James Wright, Gary Snyder, Mark Strand, and James Tate. We have included others who are writing the latest poetic word, such as Samuel Beckett, J. V. Cunningham, and Allen Ginsberg. George Santayana, Dorothy Parker, and Edna St. Vincent Millay are of this century but wrote in a more traditional style. A remote "contemporary," Michelangelo, in three short poems, identifies himself as a "modern." Archibald MacLeish's "America Was Promises" adds significantly to the longer poems in this book. Traditional poets are, of course, heavily represented.

The Drama section, in addition to *Ile,* includes two tragedies, *Antigone* (classical) and *Hamlet* (neoclassical); two naturalistic, common-man tragedies, *Ghosts* and *Miss Julie;* a light comedy, *The Playboy of the Western World;* two melodramas, *The Visit* and *Caligula;* and two farces, *The Physician in Spite of Himself* and *The Sunshine Boys.*

The Appendix contains an excerpt from Aristotle's *Poetics* and six other critical essays: Stephen Spender's "On Teaching Modern Poetry," Wallace L. Anderson's "An Analysis of 'Mr. Flood's Party'," Peter J. Stanlis's "Robert Frost's 'A Masque of Reason': An Analysis," Grover Smith's "A Critique of 'The Love Song of J. Alfred Prufrock'," H. G. Charlton's *Hamlet,* and A. Alvarez's *August Strindberg.* These selections provide insights into works in this text and are models of how to write about literature.

We are grateful for help from a number of individuals. Our colleagues at the University of Northern Iowa and the University of Tennessee at Knoxville have made a number of useful suggestions. We particularly thank James Hearst (U.N.I.), a poet himself, for advising in the selection of recent poets deserving of inclusion. We are indebted to Professor Edward Bratton (U.T.K.) for leading us to some of the best science fiction and fantasy stories, no mean feat when one considers the welter of possibilities. Some off-hand but good suggestions by Professor Bob J. Leggett (U.T.K.) we have accepted and are glad to acknowledge. Alzada Forbes gave valuable assistance in several editorial tasks, chief among them the preparation of the notes for *Hamlet.*

Outside readers have carefully scanned all six editions of *Interpreting Literature* and have offered numerous suggestions. The editors are impressed by the care and thoroughness of these critics for the Sixth Edition: Faith Gardner, Texas Southern University; Richard Lewis, Sandhills Community College; David A. Loscalzo, Jr., Mercer County Community College; LeRoy J. Mottla, William Rainey Harper College; Irma Murphy, Scottsdale Community College; Byron J. Patterson, American River College; Charles M. Rankin, Georgia College; Earl F. Schrock, Jr., Arkansas Polytechnic College; Donald Schultz, Wayne State; Wilma Washburn, Lynchburg College; Martha Weathers, Houston Community College; Frederick Winter, Southeastern Massachusetts University.

Mrs. Bonita Bryant, Bibliographer of the University of Northern Iowa, and the Reference Staff at the University of Tennessee have solved many stubborn problems for us.

The *Instructor's Manual* for the Sixth Edition supplements the editorial matter of this Shorter Edition. It provides comments, interpretations, ways to present the material in class, and suggestions for writing. The *Manual* may be obtained through a local Holt representative or by writing to English Editor, College Department, Holt, Rinehart and Winston, 383 Madison Avenue, New York, N.Y. 10017.

Knoxville, Tennessee
Cedar Falls, Iowa
January 1979

K.L.K.
H.W.R.

Contents

THE DIMENSIONS OF POETIC EXPERIENCE 313

Thematic Contents*

THE INDIVIDUAL: THE PSYCHOLOGICAL PROBLEM

The Worth of the Individual

* The editors recognize the difficulty of classifying works of literature, especially imaginative literature that by its very nature is suggestive, connotative, and fictional. This thematic classification is meant only to suggest clusters of works each of which has the same general theme approached from differing points of view. We have resisted the temptation to place some works in more than one category feeling that overclassification could be more confusing than helpful to some readers. We leave that interesting project to the resourceful reader to enjoy in his own way and on his own responsibility.

Self-Love and Self-Delusion

Love Between Man and Woman

Love as Healer and Destroyer

Toward Self-Knowledge and the Search for One's Identity

Problems of the Sexes

Humor, Wit, and the Delight of the Senses

Satirical Thrusts at Human Foibles or Social Inequities

THE INDIVIDUAL, SOCIETY, AND THE STATE: THE SOCIAL PROBLEM

The Conflict of Human and Material Values

Conflict and Reconciliation of the Individual and Society

Morality and Justice: The Dignity of the Individual and the Preservation of His Rights and Responsibilities

"What Man Has Made of Man"*

* Taken from Wordsworth's "Lines Written in Early Spring," page 290.

The Conflict of Freedom and Authoritarianism

The Inhumanity of Human Beings

The Spiritual Degeneration of the Age

The Debate over Values: What Will the Future Bring?

The Necessary Identification of the Individual with Humanity

THE INDIVIDUAL, NATURE, AND THE UNIVERSE: PHILOSOPHICAL AND RELIGIOUS PROBLEMS

Nature and the Universe as Sources of Religious Feeling and Knowledge

The Struggle with the Nature of Faith, Truth, and the Unknown

Human Responses to Deity

Attitudes Toward Death, Judgment Day, Immortality, and Paradise

Attitudes Toward the Meaning of Life

THE FUNCTIONS OF LITERATURE

Critical Theories and Individual Attitudes

Attitudes Toward the Artist

Interpreting Literature

General Preliminaries

"... we may come to realize that the two essential facts about a work of art, that it is contemporary with its own time and that it is contemporary with ours, are not opposed but complementary facts."

NORTHROP FRYE

We are concerned here with three basic questions: (1) What is the difference between utilitarian and creative literature? (2) What are the devices used by writers to create the forms of creative literature? (3) What kind of truth, or reality, do we find in creative literature, and how is such truth created? The purpose of this introductory essay is to explore the elemental answers to these questions as preparation for understanding the nature and uses of literature.

It is possible to find many of the answers to such basic questions in the literature itself. We have a classic precedent in Aristotle to support us. As preparation for writing his *Poetics** (often regarded as the fountainhead of all criticism of tragedy), Aristotle attended the Greek theater, analyzed the plays *and* the spectators' reactions, and used his observations to give us his theory of the ideal, or best, structure of tragedy in his *Poetics*. In other words, the Greek plays helped Aristotle to answer his questions about the nature and uses of tragedy.

Let us adopt a similar method. In a very real sense let us ask the kinds of literature to define themselves. In doing so we shall acquire some common ground and common literary vocabulary to help us understand and savor the literary experiences as we move through this volume. Only confusion will result if we use terms like *imagery, symbol,* and *creative literature* before they are defined as they emerge from the literature itself.

UTILITARIAN LITERATURE: LITERAL TRUTH

As sound is the medium of music and color the medium of painting, language is the medium of literature. The only purpose of language is to communicate something—anything—from one person to another. Throughout the centuries the various literary forms—poem, essay, short story—have been invented by writers to serve their needs. There the simplicity ends because men and their lives can be very complex. But whether simple or complex, whether impersonal or personal, every writer is communicating whatever is real to him, and this reality is *his* truth. As we shall see in the extracts on the next few pages, the kind of reality, or truth, varies with the literary form, and from writer to writer.

Here is an example of utilitarian literature written by Thomas Henry Huxley in his essay "The Nature of an Hypothesis":

> When our means of observation of any natural fact fail to carry us beyond a certain point, it is perfectly legitimate, and often extremely useful, to make a supposition as to what we should see, if we could carry direct observation a step farther. A supposition of this kind is called an *hypothesis,* and the value of any hypothesis depends upon the extent to which reasoning upon the assumption that it is true enables us to account for the phenomena with which it is concerned.

What has Huxley done, and how has he done it? His subject is the hypothesis, sometimes called an assumption, used to explain a group of established facts. Huxley's paragraph is a definition, or explanation, of the nature and value of an hypothesis. The remainder of his essay demonstrates, by example, how the hypothesis is used. The essay is a useful definition for anyone interested in the nature of an hypothesis, and is therefore utilitarian literature.

To communicate his information Huxley has used a series of literal, abstract, declarative sentences; except for the words *carry* and *step* the paragraph is barren of imagery. These sentences are called propositions, statements embodying practical experience and observation. Their truth is called scientific or empirical, and these propositions *about* such experience are sometimes defined as "anything which can be said to be true or false." Such literature is called utilitarian because it is useful in the practical affairs of men. It was invented to present information objectively and impersonally. Let us keep in mind that a proposition is truth *about* something: we shall return to this idea later.

THE TRANSITION TO CREATIVE LITERATURE

One way to learn why Huxley's essay is called utilitarian literature is to compare it with a different kind of essay, Emerson's "Self-Reliance." Here are a few of Emerson's sentences:

> To believe your own thought, to believe that what is true for you in your private heart is true for all men,—that is genius. Speak your latent conviction, and it shall be the

* See p. 680.

universal sense; for the inmost in due time becomes the outmost, and our first thought is rendered back to us by the trumpets of the Last Judgment. Familiar as the voice of the mind is to each, the highest merit we ascribe to Moses, Plato and Milton is that they set at naught books and traditions, and spoke not what men, but what *they* thought. A man should learn to detect and watch that gleam of light which flashes across his mind from within, more than the lustre of the firmament of bards and sages. Yet he dismisses without notice his thought, because it is his. In every work of genius we recognize our own rejected thoughts; they come back to us with a certain alienated majesty. . . . Trust thyself: every heart vibrates to that iron string.

Again we ask our questions: What has Emerson done, and how has he done it? His tone, or his attitude toward his subject, suggests that he is offering more than information for some utilitarian purpose. We feel that his attitudes are deeply involved with something of supreme importance to him. Emerson's subject is the importance of self-reliance as a human value, and for Emerson this subject is far more important than a material value.* Unlike Huxley, his purpose is not only to inform, but also to arouse and persuade: he urges us to embrace the doctrine of self-reliance and to participate in its consequences.

To communicate his meaning Emerson, like Huxley, has used a series of propositions, but he has used something more, and *in that more lies Emerson's approach into creative literature.* This something more is Emerson's personal, urgent tone, mentioned before, his imagery and allusions, figures of speech, symbols, and sentence rhythms. These are the devices of poetry, and we therefore call Emerson's essay *poetic prose.* Indeed, practiced readers of Emerson know he thinks like a poet, as the complete "Self-Reliance" will testify. Note Emerson's use of images:

> A man should learn to detect and watch that gleam of light which flashes across his mind from within, more than the lustre of the firmament of bards and sages.

Paraphrased literally, the sentence could read as Huxley might have written it:

> A man should learn to rely on his own intuitive perception more than on the notable ideas of the past.

This literal, abstract paraphrase speaks ***about*** something, but Emerson's poetic imagery requires us to *experience* the little scene in concrete, lifelike terms, and we therefore participate in the scene. The "intuitive perception" becomes a "gleam of light which flashes across his mind," and we see the lighted revelation which is brighter than the "lustre of the firmament of bards and sages." Emerson's allusions to "Moses, Plato and Milton" are rich in suggestion, as is the figure (personification) of our rejected thoughts coming back to us with "alienated majesty." The image of the "iron string" becomes a symbol that *stands for* the integrity of the self which Emerson never tires of celebrating. Many of Emerson's sentences fall naturally into free-verse units, as this one:

> In every work of genius
> We recognize our own rejected thoughts;
> They come back to us
> With a certain alienated majesty. . . .

Unlike Huxley's *abstract* impersonal prose, Emerson's *concrete* poetic prose translates his abstract ideas into imagery, and we identify ourselves personally with his own experiences and values. We shall again see poetry at work in another kind of situation when we later examine *Hamlet.* (For further discussion of the poet's method, see "Poetry: Preliminaries," p. 218. See also MacLeish's poem, "Ars Poetica," p. 270, for his belief that poetry is not true as a theory or a proposition is true, but that poetry should be its own witness for its own kind of truth by presenting experience as *experience.*)

The essay as a form, then, can look in either direction: it can present impersonal truth and empirical experience (one kind of reality for the writer) in abstract propositions as Huxley does, or it can present personal convictions (another kind of reality for the writer) in poetic prose as Emerson does. Reading an essay like "Self-Reliance" is our first step into understanding and enjoying creative literature.

Our next step is reading biography. Whether in a full-length work or in a brief anecdote, a biographer comments on the human situation. To do so, he uses the devices of action (narrative), character, scene, and dialogue, and a touch of

* See p. 283 for a discussion of human and material values.

symbolism. These are the devices of creative literature, but nevertheless biography is not fiction, and the reasons therefor will help us to understand the exact nature of both biography and creative literature.

The subject of a biography is an actual person, and a biography's truth lies (1) in the accuracy of empirical fact collected about the person, and (2) in the interpretation made of those facts. Biography, then, is a form of history, *subject to its methods and limitations.* The value of both biography and history lies in their truthfulness to actual life; neither has any other serious reason for existing. The biographer collects the facts of a person's life from birth to death: these facts constitute empirical truth—objective, impersonal information. The biographer's selection and arrangement of these facts constitute an *interpretation* which is subjective truth. In five biographies of Walt Whitman we therefore have five somewhat different Whitmans.

We are now prepared to make a careful distinction between biography and creative literature, especially fiction and drama.

The biographer may—and most legitimately does—use some of the devices of fiction or drama, and yet write neither. If the biographer possesses integrity, he is limited by the nature of his subject—his character—as dictated by the known facts. He can, of course, select a few facts of a life, write a biography in the form of a novel, and emerge with neither biography nor fiction. Ordinarily he strives to portray a particular and unique character, to delineate the qualities which make that personality different from any other. The great biographies of men and women have followed this pattern. If a biographer's subject becomes a symbol or the epitome of a whole generation or class of men, it is usually accidental, not purposely designed. Further, the biographer is not bound to explain cause and effect in the action of his subject; he is bound by a time sequence only. Indeed, some of the most extraordinary actions of extraordinary men seem to be inexplicable. The biographer may offer solutions and apparent reasons, but his successor is likely to offer different ones. And finally, the biographer is not bound by credibility. It's all very well for us to exclaim about an act of, say, Charles II, "I don't see how it *really* happened!"—but the biographer can ignore our skepticism by pointing to the documents which verify the act. Indeed, the very incredibility of some of his acts helped to make Charles II what he was.

The story writer and dramatist, however, are (1) *not* limited by known facts. These writers create facts and characters for their own purposes. (2) The creative writer *is* bound to explain cause and effect if his characters' motives are to mean anything. (3) A creative writer's violation of credibility *would* vitiate the impact of his story.

CREATIVE LITERATURE: SYMBOLIC TRUTH

What would happen if a writer depended solely on invented characters and events and not on impersonal, historical facts? Suppose he created (hence the term *creative literature*) the whole poem, story, or play, from beginning to end? What truth would exist? The practical man devoted to empirical facts and the search for useful information is likely to answer, "None at all" —but let us follow our original plan by investigating for ourselves.

Except for certain descriptive and lyric poems, the very essence of creative literature is *character* involved either in external action (outside himself) or internal action (within himself). What this character *is* and *why* he does what he does mark the distinction between creative and noncreative literature (informational literature based on verifiable empirical facts). Let us test this statement by examining *Hamlet.**

As the play begins we learn that King Hamlet, Hamlet's father, has recently died; Claudius, brother of the late king, has succeeded him by denying the throne to Hamlet, and has married Hamlet's mother, Gertrude, very soon after her husband's funeral. By marrying her former husband's brother, Gertrude has, according to the moral law of the time, committed incest, a burden almost too great for Hamlet to bear. In the second scene, when the court has cleared, Hamlet, a virtual prisoner, finds himself alone and speaks his first soliloquy in the play.

* See p. 428 for the complete play.

O that this too too solid flesh would melt,
Thaw, and resolve itself into a dew!
Or that the Everlasting had not fix'd
His canon 'gainst self-slaughter! Oh, God! God!
How weary, stale, flat, and unprofitable
Seem to me all the uses of this world!
Fie on't! ah, fie! 'Tis an unweeded garden
That grows to seed; things rank and gross in nature
Possess it merely. That it should come to this!
But two months dead! Nay, not so much, not two.
So excellent a King, that was to this,
Hyperion to a satyr; so loving to my mother
That he might not beteem the winds of heaven
Visit her face too roughly. Heaven and earth!
Must I remember? Why, she would hang on him
As if increase of appetite had grown
By what it fed on; and yet, within a month—
Let me not think on't! Frailty, thy name is woman!—
A little month, or ere those shoes were old
With which she followed my poor father's body
Like Niobe, all tears—why she, even she
(O God! a beast that wants discourse of reason
Would have mourn'd longer) married with my uncle;
My father's brother, but no more like my father
Than I to Hercules. Within a month,
Ere yet the salt of most unrighteous tears
Had left the flushing in her galled eyes,
She married. O, most wicked speed, to post
With such dexterity to incestuous sheets!
It is not, nor it cannot, come to good.
But break, my heart, for I must hold my tongue!

(I: ii, 129–159)

What has Shakespeare accomplished with this passage, especially with Hamlet's cry of the heart? Unlike the essayist and biographer who, with occasional exceptions, make literal statements about people, Shakespeare has Hamlet present himself, giving the reader (or observer at the play) the opportunity to identify himself with Hamlet. Why in poetry? Because poetry is a language capable of saying some things unsayable in any other way. (See "The Language of Poetry," p. 253.) The soliloquy provides an opportunity for Hamlet to summarize the depth of his emotional concern for his mother whom he has loved and honored, for his own future role as the son of a noble king, and perhaps most important, for the immediate future of Denmark. We see as the play progresses that Hamlet does not suffer from thwarted worldly ambition; his problem is personal and related to the honor of his country. Hamlet's world is in a state of collapse, and he ends with a cry of the heart:

It is not, nor it cannot, come to good.
But break, my heart, for I must hold my tongue!

Our participation in this poetic soliloquy, created through imagery, rhythm, and emotion, is active, not passive. As we read, we can imagine the gestures and facial expressions; we can feel the collapse of Hamlet's soul; we participate in Hamlet's inner world. To cause us to do so is a basic function of creative literature.

We still have to answer our final question, what kind of reality, or truth, is to be found in creative literature, and how is it created? *Symbolic truth* is the customary label, although such labels as representative truth, universal truth, and artistic truth are used, and each label describes an element of the nature of this kind of truth. *The creation of this kind of truth is a unique and fascinating phenomenon in creative literature and, however labeled, it is the fundamental justification for all serious literary art.*

The careful examination of almost any work of creative literature (poem, story, or play) will uncover its literal truth and its symbolic truth, often called its literal and symbolic levels of meaning. This distinction means that the writer has used the literal truth, or literal sense, to *stand for*—to express by implication or indirection—something more universal in place and time than the literal sense of his work.* For ex-

* Perhaps more technically stated, symbolic truth is philosophical, generalized truth dramatized through the particulars of human personality. Surely Aristotle is talking about a similar idea when he says that poetry, or creative literature, "is a more philosophical and higher thing than history; for poetry tends to express the universal, history the particular. By the universal I mean how a person of a certain type will on occasion speak or act, according to the law of probability or necessity; and it is this universality at which poetry aims. . . ." See *Poetics,* IX, p. 683.

ample: William Allen White is supposed to have said, "I was never a Socialist in my youth so as not to be a Republican in my old age." Frost wrote:

> I never dared be radical when young
> For fear it would make me conservative when
> old.

White's timely statement in political terms has been converted by Frost to a timeless comment on the nature of human beings. Socialist and Republican in White's sense could and undoubtedly will pass away, but human nature as Frost conceives it is likely to remain constant. Symbolic truth is thus constant—true yesterday, today, and tomorrow. In fiction and drama symbolic truth can emerge from the setting, exposition, characters, action, and poetry if any, but the essential symbolic truth usually comes from the characters in action, and because such action expresses more than its literal meaning, it has been called *symbolic action*.

To explain these matters we return to some of the differences between biography and *Hamlet*. The biographer's facts and characters are empirically true: they exist in an actual way in an actual locality in actual time. The biographer *starts* with the collected facts about an actual person and works *toward* an interpretation of that person's life. The empirical (verifiable) facts sternly dictate the kind of person who emerges from the biography.

Hamlet, on the other hand, is a "fiction," the result of Shakespeare's imagination, shaped by a theme perhaps as old as civilization. Creative literature is also called imaginative literature because the writer, to dramatize the theme and to make it articulate in terms of lifelike action, may begin with a controlling theme and then imagine (create) a situation and characters governed by certain motives. An older technique as found in Aesop's fables was used to "illustrate" an abstract truth to make the truth, or lesson, arresting and palatable.** But dramatic technique invites (actually requires?) us to *participate* in the consequences of the theme for the human soul by creating an *illusion of reality* that can be more real than much of life itself. Here lies the unique paradox of symbolic truth: How can an illusion of reality be more real than reality itself? As some wit has put it, truth may be stranger than fiction, but fiction can be truer than [literal] truth.

Unlike the biographer who is limited to actual facts about an actual person, Shakespeare was free to shape the nature of the plot, characters, and poetry around a theme. Suppose we say that the general theme of *Hamlet* is man's eternal attempt to fight injustice with justice—to avoid the temptation to fight one injustice with another, piling evil upon evil in nothing more than revenge.*** But the play cannot be read as a fable by Aesop is read. Shakespeare has qualified and sharpened this theme by creating a specific situation with well-defined characters controlled by specific human motives. From these dramatized qualifications of the theme emerges the symbolic truth. How is this accomplished?

The literal level of *Hamlet* is found in the story's facts, the kind of story offered in handbooks such as Marchette Chute's *Stories from Shakespeare*.**** But the "story" of *Hamlet* is, emphatically, not the play because we cannot *experience* the story as poetic drama, and we therefore miss most of the symbolic action. The question is, then, how does Shakespeare take us from the literal to the symbolic level of meaning?

We can look first at the setting and atmosphere. As he often does, Shakespeare involves us immediately with the prevailing atmosphere. At midnight with Horatio and the officers of the watch on a platform with cannon mounted, the ghost of Hamlet's father appears for the third time. Horatio determines that Hamlet must confront the Ghost, and later when he does, the Ghost tells Hamlet:

> The serpent that did sting thy father's life
> Now wears his crown. . . .
> Ay, that incestuous, that adulterate beast,
> With witchcraft of his wit, with traitorous
> gifts—
> O wicked wit and gifts, that have the power
> So to seduce!—won to his shameful lust
> The will of my most seeming-virtuous queen.
> O Hamlet, what a falling-off was there. . . .
> (I: v, 39–46)

** Aesop's "The Fox and the Grapes" promotes the moral, "too much cunning overreaches itself."

*** We do not say that another reading of the play would not locate a different theme. For a thoughtful interpretation of *Hamlet* see Charlton's essay, p. 706.

**** New York: Mentor Books, 1959.

Murder and adultery have now been added to incest, evil piled upon evil, as represented by Claudius who, having usurped the throne, now has the power to spread evil throughout Denmark.

Shakespeare has shaped the characters of Hamlet, Claudius, and others for his own purposes, making them dramatic symbols. Actually the characters do not exist, but they represent types of people who do exist. The point is this: Shakespeare has taken an abstract concept of two kinds of human beings, and by the devices of poetry and drama he has presented the characters of Hamlet and Claudius so realistically that they come to life in our imagination as symbols of something in the real world.

As the play unfolds, the principal characters make moral choices which bring certain consequences. On the literal level these characters are the agents of Shakespeare's will, but on the symbolic level of action (hence, symbolic truth) they represent certain human tendencies or moral and immoral currents of human action. Once Shakespeare had constructed his total action and had determined the final consequences of that action, his problem was to make the play credible (probable, not merely possible*) and representative of the human situation. Shakespeare solves his problem by the inevitability of his plot, which depends on cause and effect, life*like* characters, and poetry which reveals each soul's depth, nobility, or degradation.

Therefore the literal facts, the characters, and the action in *Hamlet* are true if we believe they represent a situation that *could* be true. We ask, would two personalities like Hamlet and Claudius, with their motives, confronted with their kind of situation, have acted as they did? If we answer yes, *Hamlet* is true, and its truth we call symbolic truth, which has emerged from all the symbols working together to rise above the play's literal, surface action. (For further discussion of the creative writer's method, see Fiction: Preliminaries," p. 10; for the story writer's method, and for the dramatist's method, see "Drama: Preliminaries," p. 396.)

The reader who wishes to explore the concepts of creative literature more fully may want to investigate the critics whose essays appear in the Appendix of this book. However, in approaching either literature or critical evaluations of literature, no student should ever forget the advice of Aldous Huxley in his essay "Music at Night." Using Shakespeare as an example he says, "Nobody's 'own words,' except those of Shakespeare himself, can possibly 'express' what Shakespeare meant. The substance of a work of art is inseparable from its form: its truth and beauty are two and yet, mysteriously one."** In a very real sense the burden of Huxley's sentence is one of the basic burdens of this book.

* See Aristotle's *Poetics,* IX, p. 683 for a discussion of this distinction.

** From *Music at Night* by Aldous Huxley (New York: Harper & Row, 1931).

Fiction

"The meagre satisfaction that [man] can extract from reality leaves him starving."
SIGMUND FREUD

"As usual truth is a surprise."
KENNETH CLARK

PRELIMINARIES

The storyteller is the perennial delight of mankind. As he begins, we are immediately confronted with people—characters, the most interesting thing in the world. We may be entertained by the unusual turn of events (plot); we may be given a fresh insight into human personality (character); or we may be offered a penetrating comment on the human situation (theme). The meaning of plot, character, and theme is determined, we shall later discover, by the storyteller's *attitude* toward the facts he relates.

But why should we take seriously a story whose characters and action have never existed? We accept as authentic most biography and history, but why should we attend to something invented, made up? This is a fair question, most often asked by the practical, hardheaded person who gives his devotion to facts. We shall search for the answer by employing one of the basic principles of this book: We shall ask a few storytellers to provide the answer as we examine their work. We begin with John Galsworthy.

JOHN GALSWORTHY
1867–1933

Quality

I knew him from the days of my extreme youth, because he made my father's boots; inhabiting with his elder brother two little shops let into one, in a small by-street—now no more, but then most fashionably placed in the West End.

That tenement had a certain quiet distinction; there was no sign upon its face that he made for any of the Royal Family—merely his own German name of Gessler Brothers; and in the window a few pairs of boots. I remember that it always troubled me to account for those unvarying boots in the window, for he made only what was ordered, reaching nothing down, and it seemed so inconceivable that what he made could ever have failed to fit. Had he bought them to put there? That, too, seemed inconceivable. He would never have tolerated in his house leather on which he had not worked himself. Besides, they were too beautiful—the pair of pumps, so inexpressibly slim, the patent leathers with cloth tops, making water come into one's mouth, the tall brown riding-boots with marvellous sooty glow, as if, though new, they had been worn a hundred years. Those pairs could only have been made by one who saw before him the Soul of Boot—so truly were they prototypes incarnating the very spirit of all footgear. These thoughts, of course, came to me later, though even when I was promoted to him, at the age of perhaps fourteen, some inkling haunted me of the dignity of himself and brother. For to make boots—such boots as he made—seemed to me then, and still seems to me, mysterious and wonderful.

I remember well my shy remark, one day, while stretching out to him my youthful foot: "Isn't it awfully hard to do, Mr. Gessler?"

And his answer, given with a sudden smile from out of the sardonic redness of his beard: "Id is an Ardt!"

Himself, he was a little as if made from leather, with his yellow crinkly face, and crinkly reddish hair and beard, and neat folds slanting down his cheeks to the corners of his mouth, and his guttural and one-toned voice; for leather is a sardonic substance, and stiff and slow of purpose. And that was the character of his face, save that his eyes, which were grey-blue, had in them the simple gravity of one secretly possessed by the Ideal. His elder brother was so very like him—though watery, paler in every way, with a great industry—that sometimes in early days I was not quite sure of him until the interview was over. Then I knew that it was he, if the words, "I will ask my brudder," had not been spoken; and that, if they had, it was his elder brother.

When one grew old and wild and ran up bills, one somehow never ran them up with Gessler Brothers. It would not have seemed becoming to go in there and stretch out one's foot to that blue iron-spectacled glance, owing him for more than—say—two pairs, just the comfortable reassurance that one was still his client.

For it was not possible to go to him very often—his boots lasted terribly, having something beyond the temporary—some, as it were, essence of boot stitched into them.

One went in, not as into most shops, in the mood of: "Please serve me, and let me go!" but restfully, as one enters a church; and, sitting on the single wooden chair, waited—for there was never anybody there. Soon, over the top edge of that sort of well—rather dark, and smelling soothingly of leather—which formed the shop, there would be seen his face, or that of his elder brother, peering down. A guttural sound, and the tip-tap of bast slippers beating the narrow wooden stairs, and he would stand before one without coat, a little bent, in leather apron, with sleeves turned back, blinking—as if awakened from some dream of boots, or like an owl surprised in daylight and annoyed at this interruption.

And I would say: "How do you do, Mr. Gessler? Could you make me a pair of Russia leather boots?"

Without a word he would leave me, retiring whence he came, or into the other portion of the shop, and I would continue to rest in the wooden chair, inhaling the incense of his trade. Soon he would come back, holding in his thin, veined hand a piece of gold-brown leather. With eyes fixed on it, he would remark: "What a beautiful biece!" When I, too, had admired it, he would speak again. "When do you wand dem?" And I would answer: "Oh! As soon as you conveniently can." And he would say: "To-morrow fordnighd?" Or if he were his elder brother: "I will ask my brudder!"

Then I would murmur: "Thank you! Good-morning, Mr. Gessler." "Goot-morning!" he would reply, still looking at the leather in his hand. And as I moved to the door, I would hear the tip-tap of his bast slippers restoring him, up the stairs, to his dream of boots. But if it were some new kind of footgear that he had not yet made me, then indeed he would observe ceremony—divesting me of my boot and holding it long in his hand, looking at it with eyes at once critical and loving, as if recalling the glow with which he had created it, and rebuking the way in which one had disorganized this masterpiece. Then, placing my foot on a piece of paper, he would two or three times tickle the outer edges with a pencil and pass his nervous fingers over my toes, feeling himself into the heart of my requirements.

I cannot forget that day on which I had occasion to say to him: "Mr. Gessler, that last pair of town walking-boots creaked, you know."

He looked at me for a time without replying, as if expecting me to withdraw or qualify the statement, then said:

"Id shouldn'd 'ave greaked."

"It did, I'm afraid."

"You goddem wed before dey found demselves?"

"I don't think so."

At that he lowered his eyes, as if hunting for memory of those boots, and I felt sorry I had mentioned this grave thing.

"Zend dem back!" he said; "I will look at dem."

A feeling of compassion for my creaking boots surged up in me, so well could I imagine the sorrowful long curiosity of regard which he would bend on them.

"Zome boods," he said slowly, "are bad from birdt. If I can do noding wid dem, I dake dem off your bill."

Once (once only) I went absently-mindedly into his shop in a pair of boots bought in an emergency at some large firm's. He took my order without showing me any leather, and I could feel his eyes penetrating the inferior integument of my foot. At last he said:

"Dose are nod my boods."

The tone was not one of anger, nor of sorrow, not even of contempt, but there was in it something quiet that froze the blood. He put his hand down and pressed a finger on the place where the left boot, endeavoring to be fashionable, was not quite comfortable.

"Id 'urds you dere," he said. "Dose big virms 'ave no self-respect. Drash!" And then, as if something had given way within him, he spoke long and bitterly. It was the only time I ever heard him discuss the conditions and hardships of his trade.

"Dey get id all," he said, "dey get id by adverdisement, nod by work. Dey dake it away from us, who lofe our boods. Id gomes to this—bresently I haf no work. Every year id gets less—you will see." And looking at his lined face I saw things I had never noticed before, bitter things and bitter struggle—and what a lot of grey hairs there seemed suddenly in his red beard!

As best I could, I explained the circumstances of the purchase of those ill-omened boots. But his face and voice made so deep an impression that during the next few minutes I ordered many pairs. Nemesis fell! They lasted more terribly than ever. And I was not able conscientiously to go to him for nearly two years.

When at last I went I was surprised to find that outside one of the two little windows of his shop another name was painted, also that of a bootmaker—making, of course, for the Royal Family. The old familiar boots, no longer in dignified isolation, were huddled in the single window. Inside, the now contracted well of the one little shop was more scented and darker than ever. And it was longer than usual, too, before a face peered down, and the tip-tap of the bast slippers began. At last he stood before me, and gazing through those rusty iron spectacles, said:

"Mr. ——, isn'd it?"

"Ah! Mr. Gessler," I stammered, "but your boots are really *too* good, you know! See, these are quite decent still!" And I stretched out to him my foot. He looked at it.

"Yes," he said, "beople do nod wand good boods, id seems."

To get away from his reproachful eyes and voice I hastily remarked: "What have you done to your shop?"

He answered quietly: "Id was too exbensif. Do you wand some boods?"

I ordered three pairs, though I had only wanted two, and quickly left. I had, I do not know quite what feeling of being part, in his mind, of a conspiracy against him; or not perhaps so much against him as against his idea of boot. One does not, I suppose, care to feel like that; for it was again many months before my next visit to his shop, paid, I remember, with the feeling: "Oh! well, I can't leave the old boy—so here goes! Perhaps it'll be his elder brother!"

For his elder brother, I knew, had not character enough to reproach me, even dumbly.

And, to my relief, in the shop there did appear to be his elder brother, handling a piece of leather.

"Well, Mr. Gessler," I said, "how are you?"

He came close, and peered at me.

"I am breddy well," he said slowly, "but my elder brudder is dead."

And I saw that it was indeed himself—but how aged and wan! And never before had I heard him mention his brother. Much shocked, I murmured: "Oh! I am sorry!"

"Yes," he answered, "he was a good man, he made a good bood; but he is dead." And he touched the top of his head, where the hair had suddenly gone as thin as it had been on that of his poor brother, to indicate, I suppose, the cause of death. "He could nod ged over losing de oder shop. Do you wand any boods?" And he held up the leather in his hand: "Id's a beaudiful biece."

I ordered several pairs. It was very long before they came—but they were better than ever. One simply could not wear them out. And soon after that I went abroad.

It was over a year before I was again in London. And the first shop I went to was my old friend's. I had left a man of sixty, I came back to one of seventy-five, pinched and worn and tremulous, who genuinely, this time, did not at first know me.

"Oh! Mr. Gessler," I said, sick at heart; "how splendid your boots are! See, I've been wearing this pair nearly all the time I've been abroad; and they're not half worn out, are they?"

He looked long at my boots—a pair of Russia leather, and his face seemed to regain steadiness. Putting his hand on my instep, he said:

"Do dey vid you here? I 'ad drouble wid dat bair, I remember."

I assured him that they had fitted beautifully.

"Do you wand any boods?" he said. "I can make dem quickly; id is a slack dime."

I answered: "Please, please! I want boots all round—every kind!"

"I will make a vresh model. Your food must be bigger." And with utter slowness, he traced round my foot, and felt my toes, only once looking up to say:

"Did I dell you my brudder was dead?"

To watch him was painful, so feeble had he grown; I was glad to get away.

I had given those boots up, when one evening they came. Opening the parcel, I set the four pairs out in a row. Then one by one I tried them on. There was no doubt about it. In shape and fit, in finish and quality of leather, they were the best he had ever made me. And in the mouth of one of the town walking-boots I found his bill. The amount was the same as usual, but it gave me quite a shock. He had never before sent it in till quarter day. I flew downstairs and wrote a cheque, and posted it at once with my own hand.

A week later, passing the little street, I thought I would go in and tell him how splendidly the new boots fitted. But when I came to where his shop had been, his name was gone. Still there, in the window, were the slim pumps, the patent leathers with cloth tops, the sooty riding boots.

I went in, very much disturbed. In the two little shops—again made into one—was a young man with an English face.

"Mr. Gessler in?" I said.

He gave me a strange, ingratiating look.

"No, sir," he said, "no. But we can attend to anything with pleasure. We've taken the shop over. You've seen our name, no doubt, next door. We make for some very good people."

"Yes, yes," I said; "but Mr. Gessler?"

"Oh!" he answered; "dead."

"Dead! But I only received these boots from him last Wednesday week."

"Ah!" he said; 'a shockin' go. Poor old man starved 'imself."

"Good God!"

"Slow starvation, the doctor called it! You see he went to work in such a way! Would keep the shop on; wouldn't have a soul touch his boots except himself. When he got an order, it took him such a time. People won't wait. He lost everybody. And there he'd sit, goin' on and on—I will say that for him—not a man in London made a better boot! But look at the competition! He never advertised! Would 'ave the best leather, too, and do it all 'imself. Well, there it is. What could you expect with his ideas?"

"But starvation—!"

"That may be a bit flowery, as the sayin' is—but I know myself he was sittin' over his boots day and night, to the very last. You see I used to watch him. Never gave 'imself time to eat; never had a penny in the house. All went in rent and leather. How he lived so long I don't know. He regular let his fire go out. He was a character. But he made good boots."

"Yes," I said, "he made good boots."

FIRST IMPRESSIONS

Perhaps our first question about this or any other story is, do we like it? Our immediate answer comes from our first impressions and can be called a *natural* response. But experience has taught us that our first impressions about life, people, and literature can be exceedingly misleading, and thoughtful men have therefore devised many ways of critically examining their impressions. To examine anything we must have a framework of ideas about its nature and function: the buyer of a used car, for example, better have a pretty sound notion of the structure of the automobile before he determines its real value. Likewise, the reader of fiction should have a sound notion of the structure and function of the short story or novel before he accepts its influence on his life. Both the buyer of a car and the reader of fiction should have a method of analysis to confirm or reject first impressions, particularly emotional ones.

The chief reason for analyzing a story is to assure us that our total reading experience has been *provided by the story*. Our analysis tests the accuracy of our response; it protects us against uncritical stock responses (p. 225); and it helps us to suspend judgment until the story is understood as a complete whole.

With the suggested method of analysis found below, we can test our first impressions of "Quality," and better still we can, in the process, be developing a method of analysis of our own. One reason, surely, for analyzing literature is finally to make every reader his own qualified critic.

THE BASIC QUESTION

We can begin our exploration, or analysis, of Galsworthy's story by asking the question, what happens to whom and why? This question directs our attention to the fundamental matters of fiction. *What happens?* asks for a consideration of *plot,* or the structure of action; *to whom?* asks for a consideration of the *characters;* and *why?* requires us to investigate the story's *theme,* which controls and shapes the meaning of the characters' action. To keep this basic question constantly in mind will show us how Galsworthy has worked to achieve his final meaning, and of course that meaning is precisely what we are after.

THE FACTS OF THE STORY

To think clearly about the story we must first have a firm command of the facts of the story—we must know what happens to whom on the literal level. Unless the literal facts of the story are clearly understood before further analysis begins, we are likely to misconstrue the story's total meaning. This book will repeatedly emphasize this principle because its violation misinterprets imaginative literature. At the moment we shall postpone asking why these things happened to the Gessler brothers—let us take one thing at a time to be sure of our ground. The facts of the story can be stated as follows.

> For many years Gessler Brothers had made and sold boots in "two little shops let into one," a tenement which had "a certain quiet distinction." Because the younger brother dealt with the customers, it is through him that we see the character and integrity of these brothers as men and bootmakers. For him the making of boots was an ideal and an art, and the boots were therefore both utilitarian and aesthetic masterpieces. They "lasted terribly" long, and their beauty was "mysterious and wonderful."
>
> But now the big firms of bootmakers were diminishing Gesslers' trade by advertising, according to the younger brother, and not by good work. They were forced to abandon one of their two shops to another bootmaker who represented the new regime of advertising and quick service. This blow brought death to the elder brother, but the younger brother doggedly refused to meet the new "competition" and continued to use the best leather and to produce boots of supreme quality. He finally died of "slow starvation" and his shop was taken over by his brisk competitor. It is significant that the last boots he made immediately before his death were, according to the narrator, "the best he had ever made me."

The basic facts of any story may be made more manageable by the use of a device called an *action line* (see the chart at page bottom) which clearly shows their sequence.

The account of the facts of the story, which resembles a newspaper notice of the troubles and failure of Gessler Brothers, is known as a *paraphrase* on the literal level. But in making the paraphrase we have raised some questions. Unless Galsworthy's story means more than the paraphrase includes, does the story deserve further consideration? The paraphrase has omitted a good deal, and we sense that the real meaning will be found in these omissions. Why has Galsworthy caused these facts to move in this sequence? What is Galsworthy's *attitude* toward the failure of the Gessler brothers? In short, to know the *surface* action is not enough: what is the *symbolic* action, or the artistic truth of the story—the kind of truth we contemplated in "General Preliminaries"?

WARNINGS

Because no single method of analysis will reveal the meaning of all stories, each one must be attacked on its own grounds and interpreted within its own terms of construction. There are, of course, certain principles of fiction which do

For years Gessler Brothers had made fine boots. For	Big firms now furnish new competition.	They give up part of their shop to a new firm.	Surviving Gessler refuses	He dies of slow
them bootmaking was an art.	Gesslers' trade is diminished.	Elder Gessler dies of the blow.	to compromise his art.	starvation.

remain constant, but even these must be applied with tact and discrimination by the reader as interpreter. We should greet with skepticism such dogmatic doctrines as, "All stories must have a plot," or "The conflicts in stories must always be resolved," or "Virtue should always be rewarded, and evil punished." We may finally accept such doctrines, but we must not begin with them. Let us begin by discussing a story. Let us look first for the basic devices by which Galsworthy has transformed the facts of his story into a piece of fictional art with meaning.

Like other writers of fiction, Galsworthy has created his own characters, placed them on his own fictional stage, and caused them to act to some purpose. But in doing so he was forced to make some decisions which can be found embodied in his story. If we can locate these decisions and determine *why* he made them, the meaning of the story should become clear.

Suppose we try to get at the matter this way: if we were to set up a motion-picture camera on a busy, city-street intersection and shoot the scene for half an hour, we would have a documentary film, but no art. Why? Because the action and characters would be purely accidental, without purpose, form, and specific meaning. Since Galsworthy's story does have these characteristics, we know he must have made certain decisions regarding the course his story was to take. His story was no accident.

AUTHOR'S CONTROLLING THEME

Every good story is shaped by a controlling theme, or idea. This controlling theme selects and arranges everything which goes into the story—the characters, the action, the resolution of the conflict, and anything else used by the writer to dramatize his total meaning. As we read a story, its theme is usually revealed to us by degrees as the story moves to its conclusion.

We find our first clue to Galsworthy's theme in his title: his general theme or subject is quality. But as the story unfolds, the theme becomes more sharply defined. Whose quality? How does it shape the story's action? What are its consequences in the lives of the principal characters? To answer these questions Galsworthy begins to dramatize his theme through the actions and responses of Gessler, and the story is on its way.

It is apparent that Galsworthy has written a serious story, a thoughtful interpretation of an aspect of humanity. In a serious writer such an interpretation emerges from his world view, or his philosophy of life, which is his accounting of the meaning of existence. He has therefore a scale of values, and above all he makes a distinction between quantitative and qualitative values. The artist, regardless of his medium, is deeply involved with the quality of experience. His general subject is the quality of human nature, and his evaluation of any specific human experience is his truth or, if you disagree with him, his bias. As we move on through our examination of Galsworthy's story we shall observe the influence of his scale of values, or his attitude toward the facts of the story.

THE SHAPING DEVICES OF FICTION

Plot, or the Structure of Action

We have said before that Galsworthy has created his own characters, placed them on his own stage, and caused them to act to some purpose. Here, we are especially concerned with that word *act*. Whatever else a storywriter does, he must present characters in action, an action which is designed to dramatize a fully realized theme, a situation, a character—in fact, anything the writer wishes to dramatize, or to make concrete in terms of action. This action can take more than one form: it can be violent and obvious like Othello's murder of Desdemona; it can be a lovers' embrace like Romeo and Juliet's; or it can be the inward action of lovers' affection like Queen Victoria's and Albert's. Whatever form the action takes, its function is to dramatize the event for the reader.

The word *plot* has been used to indicate almost any kind of action found in a story, including the closed plot, the open plot, and straight narrative with little or no serious complication. (For further discussion of plot, see p. 21.) Generally, whatever means is used to dramatize the writer's purpose is called plot, or the structure of action.

Most stories emphasize plot, character, or theme, and we shall later meet stories which are notable for one of the three. What of Galsworthy's "Quality"? Let us refer again to the story's action line (p. 14). Galsworthy has used a rather slight, closed plot which runs the customary course of complication, conflict, climax, and denouement (resolution). The story's external action can be described in this way: the complication appears when the Gesslers' trade is diminished; the conflict appears between the Gesslers and the big firm when they lose one of their two shops; the climax arrives when the surviving Gessler can no longer make a living; and the denouement, or resolution, comes with Gessler's death and the success of the big firm. The story does depend on plot, but we see that the significant action and conflict actually lie within Gessler himself—which means that Galsworthy is using his plot to reveal character. He is doing even more: he is using plot and character to reveal his theme. The story is an excellent example, as we shall see more fully later, of how the basic elements of a story work together harmoniously to produce a significant interpretation of some phase of life.

Before leaving this matter of plot, we can profitably clarify the uses of the word *dramatic*. It can mean one of three things. One sense of the word has been implied directly above: it is used to make a distinction between the essay which presents abstract ideas and the story which presents a theme concretely through characters in action. Students often refer to Professor ——who dramatizes his ideas in the classroom, meaning that he illustrates the sense of his abstract ideas with concrete examples in action. All stories by their very nature have this kind of dramatic quality. The word *dramatic* is used also to mean the dramatic method used in a scene where characters present themselves with their own words. Hemingway's "A Clean, Well-Lighted Place" (p. 40) uses the dramatic scene almost exclusively. And finally, the word is used to indicate the tension created by the conflict of the characters in action. The action is dramatic, we say, when we are stirred emotionally and suspended in a state of expectancy.

Character

We return once more to our statement that Galsworthy has created his characters and has caused them to act to some purpose. This time we are especially interested in that word *character*. The nature and use of characters in any story are determined by the purpose of the writer.

Galsworthy presents a conflict over quality, and his characters therefore represent in one way or another the terms of the conflict. This conflict, as we have seen, is both external and internal: external, between Gessler Brothers and the big firm; and internal, within the younger Gessler himself. The external conflict could have been represented by type characters only, but, because Galsworthy chose to dramatize an inner conflict as well, at least one character had to be individualized to make the inner conflict understandable and credible.

In a serious story like Galsworthy's one of the uses of character is to dramatize the moral choices made by the author. When Gessler is faced with a declining trade, he is forced to make a decision. Shall he maintain his ideal of making boots or shall he cheapen his product and meet the new competition? Gessler has uncommon personal integrity and his boots must not represent merely a price on the open market; they must represent him as a workman. His boots in a very real sense are Gessler. Gessler's choice must therefore be basically a moral choice, not merely a profit-and-loss choice. Galsworthy has created a character who is required by his very nature to make the moral choice he made. That is, the choice is motivated by the created character, which means, of course, that Galsworthy made the choice when he created Gessler who helps to dramatize Galsworthy's theme. We have here a concrete example of what is meant by the parts of a story working harmoniously to reveal meaning,

Any story's credibility depends on the consistency of each one of its characters. This is more true of the short story than of the novel because there is rarely time enough in the former to permit the development of, or changes in, characters. Once Galsworthy has defined the terms of the conflict over quality and has established the meaning or temper of each character, the action moves to its inevitable conclusion. Suppose that Gessler had compromised his art and had met the new competition. Would that action have been inevitable or credible? Had he done so, the story's structure would have collapsed.

Symbolism

As we continue to penetrate beneath the surface of Galsworthy's story we see that the meaning of his symbolism must not escape us. His basic symbols are his characters, the finished boots, and even the raw leather itself. In fact, Gessler, his boots, and his leather are actually a compound symbol which stands for an uncompromising ideal. Speaking of the boots on display in Gessler's window, Galsworthy says,

> Those pairs could only have been made by one who saw before him the Soul of Boot—so truly were they prototypes incarnating the very spirit of all footgear.

This is a reference, of course, to Plato's idealism, and Galsworthy is saying in effect that Gessler attempted to make copies of the Ideal Boot. If we recall Matthew Arnold's saying that culture is *"a study of perfection,"* Gessler becomes a symbol of a rich philosophical and literary tradition. When a character is used as a symbol, regardless of how much of an individual he may be, he represents more than himself, and in that more lie the richness and universality of the story. The truth of this statement will be demonstrated when we discuss the full, or symbolic, meaning of "Quality."

Narrator's Point of View: Who Shall Tell the Story?

To make the story credible as fiction the author must establish some authority outside himself who will objectify and make a representative truth of the author's theme or personal bias. The author must disentangle himself from the web of his personal experience and not permit his personality to stand between the representative truth (p. 5) of the story and the reader. Writers have devised ways of establishing an authority outside themselves, one of which is to create a narrator whose point of view controls the entire story. What he knows, sees, and feels dominates everything. The "I" in a story may, of course, be the author, but nevertheless the author must make it appear as if the "I" were the authority for the story.

Galsworthy has used a first-person narrator who speaks in the past tense and who tells only what he has seen and experienced. Because he says in effect, "I saw it all," this point of view carries a good deal of authority. And by confronting us with a witness, Galsworthy helps to achieve his illusion of reality.

This witness has observed the Gessler brothers since his boyhood. He first bought boots from them "at the age of perhaps fourteen," and years later saw them meet defeat and disappear in death. Moreover, he seems to be sensitive to human values, and he understands the ideal which motivates Gessler. Could Galsworthy's credibility and the illusion of reality have been so convincingly achieved by another kind of narrator? Suppose the "young man with the English face" had told the story? Or the president of the "big firm"? To tell so much with so few words apparently required a visible witness whose authority is implicit in his presence and his basic understanding of Gessler.

Panorama and Scene

The narrator's point of view focuses our attention on whatever the author wishes us to hear and see. Joseph Conrad has said, "My task which I am trying to achieve is, by the power of the written word to make you hear, to make you feel—it is, before all, to make you *see*." To make us see, most writers of fiction use a blend of panorama and scene. Panorama gives us the comprehensive, extensive view, and scene gives us the close-up, or intensive view. Henry James calls them *pictorial* and *picture*. The movies use these two views constantly to focus our attention one way or the other.

The *panoramic* view is usually presented through exposition and description, and it greatly helps to establish the atmosphere and tone (see p. 19) of the story. Here are Galsworthy's opening sentences:

> I knew him from the days of my extreme youth, because he made my father's boots; inhabiting with his elder brother two little shops let into one; in a small by-street—now no more, but then most fashionably placed in the West End.
>
> That tenement had a certain quiet distinction; there was no sign upon its face that he made for any of the Royal Family—merely his own German name of Gessler Brothers; and in the window a few pairs of boots. . . . Had he bought them to put there? . . . He would never have tolerated in his house leather on which he had not worked himself.

The focus here is comprehensive: The West End of London, the street, the two shops, the window, the shoes, and finally a suggestion of the character of the younger brother. This description of the Gesslers' environment does at least three things almost simultaneously: it describes the Gesslers' character; it establishes the tone of the story—Galsworthy's attitude toward the facts of the story; and it establishes the authority of the narrator. These three things together help to create the atmosphere which will guide our interpretation of every character and action to follow.

When we are to meet Gessler face to face, the narrator shifts the focus from panorama to scene:

> I remember well my shy remark, one day, while stretching out to him my youthful foot:
>
> "Isn't it awfully hard to do, Mr. Gessler?"
>
> And his answer, given with a sudden smile from out of the sardonic redness of his beard: "Id is an Ardt!"

The focus here is the close-up, like the focus of a scene in drama. Through dialogue the characters present and interpret themselves with little or no comment by the narrator. Galsworthy uses dialogue and scene whenever he wishes us to feel and hear the intense quality of Gessler's idealism and his scorn for shoddy workmanship. Examining a pair of boots made by a large firm, Gessler reveals himself:

> "Id 'urds you dere," he said. "Dose big virms 'ave no self-respect. Drash!" And then as if something had given away within him, he spoke long and bitterly. . . .
>
> "Dey get id all," he said, "dey get id by adverdisement, nod by work."

If the devices of panorama and scene seem to be pretty obvious, perhaps the effects achieved by them are not. Good art is usually deceivingly simple until we examine it closely.

Closely related to focus is a factor known as *aesthetic distance,* sometimes called *psychic,* or *artistic, distance,* which helps to control the intensity and kind of attention the reader is asked to give to the story, especially to its dramatic scenes (close-ups). It helps to determine how near the author should bring the reader to the scene. Art is not life: art re-creates a phase of life for a specific purpose. Art selects, emphasizes, and interprets a phase of life to direct the observer's attention to it in some significant way. The question of how close the observer should be brought into the dramatic scenes of a story (or of a play) becomes very important if the author is to make the story credible—and if he fails to make it credible, all is lost (see "Credibility and the Illusion of Reality," p. 19). The good author desires the reader to participate in the story's action but not to the extent of losing himself in his emotional reaction. The reader must be able to contemplate and feel the action almost simultaneously. If the distance between him and the action is too great, he cannot participate in the feeling; if the distance is too little, he cannot contemplate the intellectual content of the action. He must neither stand off to smile at pure invention, nor must he wallow in the intense emotional experience of the characters. Aesthetic distance, in short, contributes to making a story art. A good story is not a slice of emotional life dramatized to overwhelm us, to give us "a good cry," or to violate our sensibilities as was done in one moving picture. In the final scene a character dies in childbirth, but the movie's focus was so close and detailed that some observers were forced to leave the theater before the scene ran its course. This focus was a gross violation of aesthetic distance, and the scene as art was therefore shattered. The scene did have life, but it was not credible as art. It is entirely reasonable, of course, for a writer to violate this principle to achieve some desirable effect necessary to realize his total purpose, as Shakespeare does in *King Lear* when Gloucester's eyes are plucked out. But for Shakespeare to have included this mutilation scene as a shocker and end in itself would have been artistically false.

Aesthetic distance is also the distance the author himself keeps from the action and characters in his story. He designs his form to permit the action and characters to speak for themselves, to obliterate himself as a person. Such writing is sometimes called *objective* as opposed to *subjective* writing in which the person and personality of the author are clearly apparent. Such objectivity is one of the tenets of naturalism in fiction, and is identified with the dramatic method as we see it operating in Hemingway's "A Clean, Well-Lighted Place" (p. 40). The point to be made here for our purposes is that whether aesthetic distance is used to name the distance the author himself keeps from the story's action, or to name the distance the reader is kept from the action, the result is likely to be the same: to represent life *in art*, not to reproduce life's bare actualism.

THE RESULTS OF THE SHAPING DEVICES

Credibility and the Illusion of Reality

We now return to a question asked at the beginning of this section: why do we read and take seriously, or accept as authentic, a story whose characters and action have never existed? Some answers will be suggested in this section, but one thing is incontestably clear: regardless of the writer's brilliance and depth, regardless of the dexterity used in employing the devices of fiction already mentioned, if the writer fails to make the story credible, the story will fail. Many philosophers of art (aestheticians) have made similar comments about all art. For example: "There is . . . absolutely no test of good drawing or painting except the capacity of the artist to make us believe. . . . So . . . we demand of every novel and play, every dramatic and narrative poem, that it create the semblance of reality." *

When we approach a story we must, in Coleridge's words, exercise a "willing suspension of disbelief." We do not ask, did this thing really happen? When we demand something that really happened, we go to history and biography. When we begin a story we suspend our skepticism of its actual, literal truth, and ask at the story's end, *could* this thing have happened? The tests for the truth of history and biography are irrelevant for the truth of fiction. This distinction has been enunciated at least since Aristotle (384–322 B.C.) observed

> that it is not the function of the poet [the imaginative writer] to relate what has happened, but what may happen,—what is possible according to the law of probability or necessity. . . . Poetry [imaginative literature], therefore, is more philosophical and a higher thing than history: for poetry tends to express the universal, history the particular . . . and it is this universality at which poetry aims. . . .
> (*Poetics*, IX, see page 683.)

* DeWitt H. Parker, *The Analysis of Art*, New Haven, Conn.: Yale University Press, 1926, p. 6.

The key words here are *probability* and *universality*. (See "General Preliminaries," p. 5, for a discussion of symbolic truth.) To dramatize some specific truth found universally in mankind or in a given civilization—not the truth of an isolated occurrence—the writer is free to be false to the actual in order to be true to the general, the universal. But in devising his fiction he must make it probable, *not* merely possible; within its own terms of construction it must be credible, believable. The story must create the illusion of reality from beginning to end. How is this done?

How does Galsworthy do it? In many ways with many devices. By using a first-person narrator who has witnessed the actions of the Gesslers, and who has worn their boots; by confronting us with characters who present themselves in their own characteristic words; but most of all by properly motivating the actions of the characters to make the plot, or the structure of action, move to its *probable* and inevitable conclusion. That is, Galsworthy is saying, given these characters including the Gesslers in this situation according to these circumstances, it is entirely probable that this story would happen in this way.

Is all this so mysterious? Hardly. What do we mean by saying "Truth is stranger than fiction"? We simply mean that any story whose aim is universal truth based on "the law of probability or necessity" cannot rely on the strange, isolated occurrence. If the story relied on such, no sane reader would believe what happens in the story even though it could be proved true in life. We confirm the accuracy of this point of view whenever we read a newspaper account of a strange occurrence and find ourselves saying, "If it hadn't happened, I wouldn't believe it. Incredible, isn't it?" It may seem to be incredible, but it is true. *In fiction, however, a situation must seem to be credible or it cannot be accepted as true.*

Tone and Atmosphere

We remind ourselves again that the basic, shaping force of Galsworthy's story is his attitude toward the story's literal facts. Gessler makes fine boots; he refuses to compromise his ideal; he dies of slow starvation; the big firm takes over his shops. What does Galsworthy think of all this? Where shall we look beyond the matters already discussed above to find out? We can examine his tone and atmosphere, less tangible than plot, characters, theme, and symbolism, but perhaps the most potent and revealing of all.

In a very real sense Galsworthy's tone *is* his attitude toward the facts of the story. When someone in real life speaks, we attend not only to what he says, but also to the tone or attitude he takes toward what he is saying. In a story we listen for the tone of the author's voice in the same way. "Written words," said Joseph Conrad, "have their accent, too."

What does Galsworthy think about Gessler's ideal, and what is his attitude toward his fate? Gessler is treated with the most sensitive consideration, as if Galsworthy were exhibiting something very uncommon in the human scene. For example:

> But if it were some new kind of footgear that he had not yet made me, then indeed he would observe ceremony—divesting me of my boot and holding it long in his hand, looking at it with eyes at once critical and loving, as if recalling the glow with which he had created it, and rebuking the way in which one had disorganized this masterpiece.

In an interesting and instructive way Galsworthy has demonstrated how important it is to maintain a consistent tone throughout a story. When "Quality" was first published, the last sentence read:

> And I turned and went out quickly, for I did not want that youth to know that I could hardly see.

Later, this sentence was eliminated. Why? Apparently because it violated the story's tone by introducing sentimentality in the narrator for which there is no motivation.

Atmosphere is sometimes used to mean the setting of a story, or the physical environment in which the action takes place. In many stories, including Galsworthy's, atmosphere means psychological as well as physical environment. The two opening paragraphs of Galsworthy's story provide this psychological atmosphere which gives direction to his attitudes and values.

The value of tone and atmosphere working together lies in their powerful and subtle suggestiveness. Galsworthy's tone and atmosphere come through mostly by indirection, and we know without his ever saying so that Gessler's fate is more than a personal tragedy. We feel, as we say, the enveloping tragedy, and we know it will spread, not end, with Gessler's death.

Tone is then, as we shall see again in the section on poetry, a figure of speech because it permeates the entire story and helps to interpret the symbolic action as distinguished from the mere surface action of the plot. We are now prepared to examine the symbolic action of "Quality."

The Meaning of the Story: The Parts and the Whole

The unremitting quality of Gessler Brothers moves through three actions which approximate three scenes in a one-act play. Galsworthy's attitude toward the three actions is established early by the title and the two opening paragraphs. The references to "quality," to the Gesslers' tenement that had a "certain quiet distinction," and to "those unvarying boots in the window" that "could only have been made by one who saw before him the Soul of Boot," all clearly reveal Galsworthy's respect for the Gessler "Ideal."

The first action presents the Gesslers pursuing their " 'Ardt,' " exercising extreme care with their customers' needs, and at peace with their world except for the complication introduced by the new competition of the big firms. Gessler Brothers had been for years the symbol of quality and persevering workmanship. These men had fused making a *living* with making a *life*, and their boots therefore represented their intrinsic character. When they offered a pair of boots to a customer, they offered themselves. When the narrator complains about a pair that creaked, Gessler says, " 'Zome boods . . . are bad from birdt. If I can do noding wid dem, I dake dem off your bill.' " There were no written guarantees carefully modified in small print: there was only Gessler Brothers, and that was enough.

The second action presents the pivotal event, the crisis in Gessler when he is forced by the big firms to decide whether to maintain his quality or meet the new competition. For Gessler this problem is basically moral, not economic. He does not make a living with his left hand and moral decisions with his right. The whole man makes all decisions, and his decision to maintain his quality followed from his moral integrity as the night the day. He knew in advance of their coming what the consequences of his decision would be: his business would decline, it would finally fail—but he would not compromise his Ideal. The quality was maintained to the end, and the last boots he made for the narrator were "in shape and fit, in finish and quality of leather . . . the best he had ever made me."

The third action presents the resolution of the crisis, or the consequence of Gessler's decision: his economic failure, his death, and the success of the new firm that bought his shops. Perhaps the basic question to be answered is, what was defeated? Two men or what they stood for?

To answer these questions we move to the symbolic level of meaning in the story. Because Gessler refused to compromise his ideal, he won a personal, moral victory, but his death symbolizes the defeat of something larger than himself, a defeat which constitutes a tragedy more far-reaching than his personal end. His death symbolizes a blow against the preindustrial practice of combining making a living with making a life. It symbolizes an attack on the personal responsibility taken by the artisan for his work. For Gessler there was no such thing as an economic morality apart from a personal morality. Gessler symbolizes the absorption of material values by human values. (For a brief discussion of these two kinds of value, see "Human Values and the Criticism of Experience," p. 283.) The larger tragedy of the story appears when the symbol is reversed, when human values are absorbed by material values, when boots are made to sell, as Gessler himself says, " 'by adverdisement, nod by work,' " instead of being a joy to both the maker as artist and the buyer.

Comment on Further Fictional Practices

The examination of "Quality" has not, of course, revealed all the standard devices and practices used by short-story writers, to say nothing of the many unconventional ones. Galsworthy has used the devices of first-person narrator and closed plot, but there are other kinds of narrators and plots which produce results quite different from Galsworthy's. While we review the steps already taken to analyze "Quality," we shall investigate other fictional practices as appropriate. Before we begin, one principle should be fixed in mind: *No device or practice in a story is good or bad except as its use makes it so; any device should be judged according to its effectiveness in the story.* Wharton's "Roman Fever" (p. 24) is radically different from "Quality," and to judge Wharton's story by Galsworthy's technique would be unspeakably insensitive to the entire cause-and-effect problem in fiction.

1. THE FACTS OF THE STORY. Our first step was to locate the facts of "Quality" to understand its literal level. All analysis begins there if we wish to be clearheaded about the rest of it. This act freed us to examine Galsworthy's devices, to see what he had done with the facts, to define his attitude toward them, and to discover what symbolic meaning he had derived from them. To locate the literal facts is, then, the initial step into almost any story. If the exception appears in the form of pure symbolism (see 5, p. 22), it will be revealed as an exception because in looking for the literal facts we shall find none.

2. AUTHOR'S CONTROLLING THEME. Theme has been defined as the controlling idea which has determined everything Galsworthy has done in his story. Theme may mean a definite intellectual concept, as it does in Kafka's "A Hunger Artist," or it may indicate a highly complex situation, as for example in Faulkner's "A Rose for Emily." In general, the value of a story does not lie in its theme but rather in what the writer has done with it. The same general theme of the growing pains experienced by young people is used by Flannery O'Connor and Anderson, yet both stories (in this volume) develop and dramatize the theme in different ways. The theme of a story can usually be defined in a crisp abstraction, but the abstraction should never be accepted as the total meaning of a substantial story.

3. PLOT, OR THE STRUCTURE OF ACTION. Although "Quality" has a closed plot, Galsworthy uses plot chiefly to reveal character. Many other writers, however, use closed plots for other reasons. This type of plot, with its definite resolution of conflict, is usually found in mystery stories and in stories, such as Maupassant's "La Mère Sauvage," which have an obvious thesis whose truth the writer attempts to demonstrate.

The open plot has little or no resolution. Certain writers of serious stories, such as Chekhov in "On the Road," may believe that resolutions cannot be found for many of our basic conflicts; they may refuse the formula of the closed plot because they reject on philosophical grounds a finished interpretation of a complicated world.

Steinbeck rejects it in "The Chrysanthemums," and Hemingway in "A Clean, Well-Lighted Place" simply ignores it in favor of the dramatic, simple narrative. Except when a reader is looking for sheer entertainment and amusement, he has good reason to suspect a story which relies heavily on plot, especially the story with a trick ending whose plot machinery grinds audibly.

4. CHARACTER. "Quality" is a judicious blend of plot, character, and theme, but many, if not most, stories rely mainly on one of the three. Character studies rely chiefly, of course, on fully drawn characters and very little on plot or theme.

At the other extreme, in a story predominantly of plot, the characters may be little more than types, sometimes no more than pawns, used to create suspense or horror or a situation. Likewise, sometimes in a story predominantly of theme, the characters resemble counters moved about in such a way as to prove the theme. Does Kafka's "A Hunger Artist" entirely avoid the use of characters as pawns?

There is, of course, always the middle ground, occupied, for example, by Gessler in "Quality" and by Liharev in Chekhov's "On the Road." These characters, rounded individuals, are types of humanity in the symbolic sense: they stand for groups of individuals and therefore achieve universality.

5. SYMBOLISM. Symbolism can appear almost anywhere in fiction: in characters, plots, natural objects, man-made objects, and situations. When a symbol is worked through an entire story, it can be used as an integrating device by which many facts are fused and made meaningful in some basic and comprehensive way. Characters are used to symbolize abstract ideas, as Gessler symbolizes quality, or a psychological state such as we find in Ellison's "King of the Bingo Game." As we have seen in "General Preliminaries," the symbol is in a sense the basic device of most imaginative literature.

6. NARRATOR'S POINT OF VIEW. In "Quality" the authority for telling the story is vested in the narrator by Galsworthy to convert the facts of the story into a credible, universal truth. The many kinds of narrators have been variously named and classified, but the basic kinds can perhaps be reduced to four.

First, there is the *first-person narrator,* as used by Galsworthy, who has the authority of an intimate witness, one who is himself involved in the action. In some stories the narrator is the principal character, who describes with unchallenged authority his own sensations and ideas. Such a narrator can invest a story with uncommon credibility, but the device has its obvious limitations because the narrator can know and understand only what his temperament and talent permit.

Second, there is the *dramatic narrator* who effaces himself almost completely, as he does in Hemingway's "A Clean, Well-Lighted Place." This narrator resembles the playwright whose characters present themselves with little or no comment by the narrator. Modified in one way or another, this narrative device is very popular in current fiction because, perhaps, it gives the effect of impersonal objectivity and appeals to the scientific temper of our time.

Third, there is the *third-person limited narrator* who comes by his knowledge through natural means only, as he does in Maupassant's "La Mère Sauvage," Steinbeck's "The Chrysanthemums," and many others. Such a narrator is sometimes called a *roving narrator* who can be anywhere at any time except within the minds of the characters. In a sense he is omniscient with his omniscience artfully concealed.

And last, there is the *third-person omniscient narrator* who knows everything and can be at any place at any time without having to explain his presence. Such a device gives the author extraordinary flexibility, particularly because he can look into the minds of his characters and report their thoughts and sensations. Maugham's "The Colonel's Lady" uses such a narrator in a very special and effective manner.

Is there a best kind of narrator? The best narrator best fulfills the purposes of the author, and we judge the efficacy of a narrator as we judge all other elements in a story—according to the consequences he produces in the story.

7. PANORAMA AND SCENE. The function of these two devices is to permit a necessary shift in focus. "Quality" uses both as appropriate to the purpose, but some stories rely on one or the other almost exclusively. The use of panorama is sometimes much more subtle than readers may recognize, including as it does setting and atmosphere. In "Heart of Darkness," Conrad's panoramic use of nature becomes a method of

interpreting the meaning of the story's action.

Scene, as we found in "Quality," is the focus of the close-up. Perhaps no story in this volume uses scenes quite so effectively as Chekhov's "On the Road," unless it is Hemingway's "A Clean, Well-Lighted Place." Chekhov's use of scene seems to have more depth than Hemingway's because, perhaps, his understanding of the motives of humanity is more penetrating.

8. CREDIBILITY AND THE ILLUSION OF REALITY. There are various levels of credibility, in fact, about five. "Quality" is credible on the realistic level, chiefly because the plot, characters, theme, setting, and atmosphere are all entirely probable on natural grounds. The meaning of this statement should become clearer as we examine the remaining levels.

Hughes's mixture of fantasy and realism in "On the Road" is one step removed from the realistic level.

A story like Kafka's "A Hunger Artist" is another step away from the realistic level because it veers toward, but does not seriously enter, the supernatural level.

The fourth and fifth levels of credibility are at times so closely merged in the same story as to make them appear as one level, although the use of one is possible without the other. We shall call them the symbolic and the supernatural levels. Poe's "Ligeia" is an example of the merger, an uncommonly successful one.

A story (or poem such as Yeats's "The Second Coming") which uses the symbolic level exclusively, or almost so, is incomprehensible unless the symbols are clearly understood. When symbols are used in a story told on the realistic level of credibility, they are defined by the context of the story; this is not necessarily true of a story which is credible only on the symbolic level. Such a story is credible if its theme is comprehensible and its tone consistent, but to attempt to apply the test of the realistic level to such a story is to misconceive the nature of the story's art.

9. TONE AND ATMOSPHERE. Consistency of tone and atmosphere is without question one of the basic necessities of a good story, especially if the story is satiric or ironic. If satire and irony are revealed by broad exaggeration, tone and atmosphere may seem to make only a minor contribution; but if the satire and irony are subtle and perhaps profound, consistency of tone and atmosphere is indispensable. A close study of Chekhov's "On the Road" reveals how delicately yet positively he has worked to maintain an especially consistent tone: one major slip could have reduced the story to confusion.

10. THE MEANING OF THE STORY: THE PARTS AND THE WHOLE. A reader may be acute and discriminating, but his real test centers in this area. Like any organism, the meaning of a story is always more than the sum of its parts. One of the cardinal errors in the interpretation of imaginative literature is accepting a part for the whole. The meaning of "Quality" does not lie in Gessler alone: it lies in the interaction of Gessler with everything else in the story. This principle of interpretation is often violated, and unless the principle is carefully observed, Tolstoy's "Three Deaths," for example, can be easily misinterpreted and some of the symbolism in this story may escape all except the most discriminating readers.

First, master all the facts of a story, and then determine what has been done with *all* of them. There is no short cut to the precise interpretation of fiction, poetry, or drama, but there is tremendous pleasure in mastering the approaches to them.

A Note on the Novel

Most of the preceding observations concerning the structure of the short story can also be applied to the novel. Although the greater length of the novel gives the reader increased responsibilities, particularly in fusing all the parts of the novel to make the complete whole of his focus and comprehension, the basic devices in both forms remain much the same. Like the short story, the novel uses the devices already discussed to transform the facts of the story into a piece of fictional art with meaning. The basic reading problem, then, is quite the same for both the short story and the novel, namely, to learn to read the forms. (See p. 169 for observations on the novella.)

What Makes a Good Story?

Fortunately, there is no single formula to guarantee excellence. Fortunately indeed, because if there were, the fascinating variety in stories would be lost, and the formula would quickly bring boredom. Some readers demand entertainment of stories; other readers demand ideas, or interesting characters, or action, plot, and suspense. All such demands are reasonable, but if a reader demands, say, suspense and finds none, the story is not necessarily a failure. Suspense would have been quite ridiculous in Galsworthy's "Quality"; indeed, he dissipated all hope for it in his opening paragraph.

In our search for excellence, we may begin with one fairly stable assumption: *We should judge all the elements in a story according to the consequences they produce in the story.* Plot, character, theme, suspense—none of these things is good or bad except as its use makes it so. All good creative writers seek to use the right means to bring the desired ends. We therefore ask of every story, has it been told well? Is it a piece of *literary art* whose technique and subject matter are fused to produce a meaningful whole? Such questions will at least reduce the temptation to condemn escape literature for its want of philosophy, and parable literature for its want of sheer entertainment. There are twenty-nine stories in this volume and twenty-nine ways of telling them. Let us begin by judging every story within its own terms of construction, within its own frame of accomplishment. Some tellings may be better than others, and we shall look to this matter as we go along. We shall look to another ingredient also, a final and indispensable matter: Having decided how well a story has been told, we shall ask about its value and its truth to humanity.

EDITH WHARTON
1862–1937

Roman Fever

Edith Wharton's "Roman Fever" differs from Galsworthy's "Quality" in many ways. Meaning in stories can be controlled and made manifest variously—through plot, character, theme, symbol, irony, tone, and so on. "Quality" is a blend of plot, character, and theme, but our analysis above has shown the basic importance to Galsworthy of theme, as the story's title indicates. "Roman Fever" is quite a different matter. Readers who look exclusively for philosophical ideas may find too few, and other readers who look for subtle character analysis may find too little, but readers who enjoy the revelation of character and theme through plot will be richly rewarded. The sudden revelation of character made credible is perhaps Wharton's chief technical achievement here.

1

From the table at which they had been lunching two American ladies of ripe but well-cared-for middle age moved across the lofty terrace of the Roman restaurant and, leaning on its parapet, looked first at each other, and then down on the outspread glories of the Palatine[1] and the Forum, with the same expression of vague but benevolent approval.

As they leaned there a girlish voice echoed up gaily from the stairs leading to the court below. "Well, come along, then," it cried, not to them but to an invisible companion, "and let's leave the young things to their knitting"; and a voice as fresh laughed back: "Oh, look here, Babs, not actually *knitting*—" "Well, I mean figuratively," rejoined the first. "After all, we haven't left our poor parents much else to do . . ." and at that point the turn of the stairs engulfed the dialogue.

The two ladies looked at each other again, this time with a tinge of smiling embarrassment, and the smaller and paler one shook her head and coloured slightly.

"Barbara!" she murmured, sending an unheard rebuke after the mocking voice in the stairway.

The other lady, who was fuller, and higher in colour, with a small determined nose supported by vigorous black eyebrows, gave a good-humoured laugh. "That's what our daughters think of us!"

Her companion replied by a deprecating gesture. "Not of us individually. We must remember that. It's just the collective modern idea of Mothers. And you see—" Half guiltily she drew

[1] Palace of the Roman Caesars.

from her handsomely mounted black handbag a twist of crimson silk run through by two fine knitting needles. "One never knows," she murmured. "The new system has certainly given us a good deal of time to kill; and sometimes I get tired just looking—even at this." Her gesture was now addressed to the stupendous scene at their feet.

The dark lady laughed again, and they both relapsed upon the view, contemplating it in silence, with a sort of diffused serenity which might have been borrowed from the spring effulgence of the Roman skies. The luncheon-hour was long past, and the two had their end of the vast terrace to themselves. At its opposite extremity a few groups, detained by a lingering look at the outspread city, were gathering up guidebooks and fumbling for tips. The last of them scattered, and the two ladies were alone on the air-washed height.

"Well, I don't see why we shouldn't just stay here," said Mrs. Slade, the lady of the high colour and energetic brows. Two derelict basket-chairs stood near, and she pushed them into the angle of the parapet, and settled herself in one, her gaze upon the Palatine. "After all, it's still the most beautiful view in the world."

"It always will be, to me," assented her friend Mrs. Ansley, with so slight a stress on the "me" that Mrs. Slade, though she noticed it, wondered if it were not merely accidental, like the random underlinings of old-fashioned letter-writers.

"Grace Ansley was always old-fashioned," she thought; and added aloud, with a retrospective smile: "It's a view we've both been familiar with for a good many years. When we first met here we were younger than our girls are now. You remember?"

"Oh, yes, I remember," murmured Mrs. Ansley, with the same undefinable stress.—"There's that head-waiter wondering," she interpolated. She was evidently far less sure than her companion of herself and of her rights in the world.

"I'll cure him of wondering," said Mrs. Slade, stretching her hand toward a bag as discreetly opulent-looking as Mrs. Ansley's. Signing to the head-waiter, she explained that she and her friend were old lovers of Rome, and would like to spend the end of the afternoon looking down on the view—that is, if it did not disturb the service? The head-waiter, bowing over her gratuity, assured her that the ladies were most welcome, and would be still more so if they would condescend to remain for dinner. A full-moon night, they would remember. . . .

Mrs. Slade's black brows drew together, as though references to the moon were out-of-place and even unwelcome. But she smiled away her frown as the head-waiter retreated. "Well, why not? We might do worse. There's no knowing, I suppose, when the girls will be back. Do you even know back from *where?* I don't!"

Mrs. Ansley again coloured slightly. "I think those young Italian aviators we met at the Embassy invited them to fly to Tarquinia[2] for tea. I suppose they'll want to wait and fly back by moonlight."

"Moonlight—moonlight! What a part it still plays. Do you suppose they're as sentimental as we were?"

"I've come to the conclusion that I don't in the least know what they are," said Mrs. Ansley. "And perhaps we didn't know much more about each other."

"No; perhaps we didn't."

Her friend gave her a shy glance. "I never should have supposed you were sentimental, Alida."

"Well, perhaps I wasn't." Mrs. Slade drew her lids together in retrospect; and for a few moments the two ladies, who had been intimate since childhood, reflected how little they knew each other. Each one, of course, had a label ready to attach to the other's name; Mrs. Delphin Slade, for instance, would have told herself, or any one who asked her, that Mrs. Horace Ansley, twenty-five years ago, had been exquisitely lovely—no, you wouldn't believe it, would you? . . . though, of course, still charming, distinguished. . . . Well, as a girl she had been exquisite; far more beautiful than her daughter Barbara, though certainly Babs, according to the new standards at any rate, was more effective—had more *edge,* as they say. Funny where she got it, with those two nullities as parents. Yes; Horace Ansley was—well, just the duplicate of his wife. Museum specimens of old New York. Good-looking, irreproachable, ex-

[2] Town in central Italy.

emplary. Mrs. Slade and Mrs. Ansley had lived opposite each other—actually as well as figuratively—for years. When the drawing-room curtains in No. 20 East 73rd Street were renewed, No. 23, across the way, was always aware of it. And of all the movings, buyings, travels, anniversaries, illnesses—the tame chronicle of an estimable pair. Little of it escaped Mrs. Slade. But she had grown bored with it by the time her husband made his big *coup* in Wall Street, and when they bought in upper Park Avenue had already begun to think: "I'd rather live opposite a speak-easy for a change; at least one might see it raided." The idea of seeing Grace raided was so amusing that (before the move) she launched it at a woman's lunch. It made a hit, and went the rounds—she sometimes wondered if it had crossed the street, and reached Mrs. Ansley. She hoped not, but didn't much mind. Those were the days when respectability was at a discount, and it did the irreproachable no harm to laugh at them a little.

A few years later, and not many months apart, both ladies lost their husbands. There was an appropriate exchange of wreaths and condolences, and a brief renewal of intimacy in the half-shadow of their mourning; and now, after another interval, they had run across each other in Rome, at the same hotel, each of them the modest appendage of a salient daughter. The similarity of their lot had again drawn them together, lending itself to mild jokes, and the mutual confession that, if in old days it must have been tiring to "keep up" with daughters, it was now, at times, a little dull not to.

No doubt, Mrs. Slade reflected, she felt her unemployment more than poor Grace ever would. It was a big drop from being the wife of Delphin Slade to being his widow. She had always regarded herself (with a certain conjugal pride) as his equal in social gifts, as contributing her full share to the making of the exceptional couple they were: but the difference after his death was irremediable. As the wife of the famous corporation lawyer, always with an international case or two on hand, every day brought its exciting and unexpected obligation: the impromptu entertaining of eminent colleagues from abroad, the hurried dashes on legal business to London, Paris or Rome, where the entertaining was so handsomely reciprocated; the amusement of hearing in her wake: "What, that handsome woman with the good clothes and the eyes is Mrs. Slade—*the* Slade's wife? Really? Generally the wives of celebrities are such frumps."

Yes; being *the* Slade's widow was a dullish business after that. In living up to such a husband all her faculties had been engaged; now she had only her daughter to live up to, for the son who seemed to have inherited his father's gifts had died suddenly in boyhood. She had fought through that agony because her husband was there, to be helped and to help; now, after the father's death, the thought of the boy had become unbearable. There was nothing left but to mother her daughter; and dear Jenny was such a perfect daughter that she needed no excessive mothering. "Now with Babs Ansley I don't know that I *should* be so quiet," Mrs. Slade sometimes half-enviously reflected; but Jenny, who was younger than her brilliant friend, was that rare accident, an extremely pretty girl who somehow made youth and prettiness seem as safe as their absence. It was all perplexing—and to Mrs. Slade a little boring. She wished that Jenny would fall in love—with the wrong man, even; that she might have to be watched, outmanoeuvred, rescued. And instead, it was Jenny who watched her mother, kept her out of draughts, made sure that she had taken her tonic. . . .

Mrs. Ansley was much less articulate than her friend, and her mental portrait of Mrs. Slade was slighter, and drawn with fainter touches. "Alida Slade's awfully brilliant; but not as brilliant as she thinks," would have summed it up; though she would have added, for the enlightenment of strangers, that Mrs. Slade had been an extremely dashing girl; much more so than her daughter, who was pretty, of course, and clever in a way, but had none of her mother's —well, "vividness," some one had once called it. Mrs. Ansley would take up current words like this, and cite them in quotation marks, as unheard-of audacities. No; Jenny was not like her mother. Sometimes Mrs. Ansley thought Alida Slade was disappointed; on the whole she had had a sad life. Full of failures and mistakes; Mrs. Ansley had always been rather sorry for her. . . .

So these two ladies visualized each other, each through the wrong end of her little telescope.

2

For a long time they continued to sit side by side without speaking. It seemed as though, to both, there was a relief in laying down their somewhat futile activities in the presence of the vast Memento Mori[3] which faced them. Mrs. Slade sat quite still, her eyes fixed on the golden slope of the Palace of the Caesars, and after a while Mrs. Ansley ceased to fidget with her bag, and she too sank into meditation. Like many intimate friends, the two ladies had never before had occasion to be silent together, and Mrs. Ansley was slightly embarrassed by what seemed, after so many years, a new stage in their intimacy, and one with which she did not yet know how to deal.

Suddenly the air was full of that deep clangour of bells which periodically covers Rome with a roof of silver. Mrs. Slade glanced at her wristwatch. "Five o'clock already," she said, as though surprised.

Mrs. Ansley suggested interrogatively: "There's bridge at the Embassy at five." For a long time Mrs. Slade did not answer. She appeared to be lost in contemplation, and Mrs. Ansley thought the remark had escaped her. But after a while she said, as if speaking out of a dream: "Bridge, did you say? Not unless you want to. . . . But I don't think I will, you know."

"Oh, no," Mrs. Ansley hastened to assure her. "I don't care to at all. It's so lovely here; and so full of old memories, as you say." She settled herself in her chair, and almost furtively drew forth her knitting. Mrs. Slade took sideway note of this activity, but her own beautifully cared-for hands remained motionless on her knee.

"I was just thinking," she said slowly, "what different things Rome stands for to each generation of travellers. To our grandmothers, Roman fever; to our mothers, sentimental dangers—how we used to be guarded!—to our daughters, no more dangers than the middle of Main Street. They don't know it—but how much they're missing!"

The long golden light was beginning to pale, and Mrs. Ansley lifted her knitting a little closer to her eyes. "Yes; how we were guarded!"

"I always used to think," Mrs. Slade continued, "that our mothers had a much more difficult job than our grandmothers. When Roman fever stalked the streets it must have been comparatively easy to gather in the girls at the danger hour; but when you and I were young, with such beauty calling us, and the spice of disobedience thrown in, and no worse risk than catching cold during the cool hour after sunset, the mothers used to be put to it to keep us in—didn't they?"

She turned again toward Mrs. Ansley, but the latter had reached a delicate point in her knitting. "One, two, three—slip two; yes, they must have been," she assented, without looking up.

Mrs. Slade's eyes rested on her with a deepened attention. "She can knit—in the face of *this!* How like her. . . ."

Mrs. Slade leaned back, brooding, her eyes ranging from the ruins which faced her to the long green hollow of the Forum, the fading glow of the church fronts beyond it, and the outlying immensity of the Colosseum. Suddenly she thought: "It's all very well to say that our girls have done away with sentiment and moonlight. But if Babs Ansley isn't out to catch that young aviator—the one who's a Marchese—then I don't know anything. And Jenny has no chance beside her. I know that too. I wonder if that's why Grace Ansley likes the two girls to go everywhere together? My poor Jenny as a foil —!" Mrs. Slade gave a hardly audible laugh, and at the sound Mrs. Ansley dropped her knitting.

"Yes?"

"I—oh, nothing. I was only thinking how your Babs carries everything before her. That Campolieri boy is one of the best matches in Rome. Don't look so innocent, my dear—you know he is. And I was wondering, ever so respectfully, you understand . . . wondering how two such exemplary characters as you and Horace had managed to produce anything quite so dynamic." Mrs. Slade laughed again, with a touch of asperity.

Mrs. Ansley's hands lay inert across her needles. She looked straight out at the great accumulated wreckage of passion and splendour at her feet. But her small profile was almost expressionless. At length she said: "I think you overrate Babs, my dear."

Mrs. Slade's tone grew easier. "No; I don't. I appreciate her. And perhaps envy you. Oh, my

[3] An object, usually emblematic, used as a reminder of death.

girl's perfect; if I were a chronic invalid I'd—well, I think I'd rather be in Jenny's hands. There must be times . . . but there! I always wanted a brilliant daughter . . . and never quite understood why I got an angel instead."

Mrs. Ansley echoed her laugh in a faint murmur. "Babs is an angel too."

"Of course—of course! But she's got rainbow wings. Well, they're wandering by the sea with their young men; and here we sit . . . and it all brings back the past a little too acutely."

Mrs. Ansley had resumed her knitting. One might almost have imagined (if one had known her less well, Mrs. Slade reflected) that, for her also, too many memories rose from the lengthening shadows of those august ruins. But no; she was simply absorbed in her work. What was there for her to worry about? She knew that Babs would almost certainly come back engaged to the extremely eligible Campolieri. "And she'll sell the New York house, and settle down near them in Rome, and never be in their way . . . she's much too tactful. But she'll have an excellent cook, and just the right people in for bridge and cocktails . . . and a perfectly peaceful old age among her grandchildren."

Mrs. Slade broke off this prophetic flight with a recoil of self-disgust. There was no one of whom she had less right to think unkindly than of Grace Ansley. Would she never cure herself of envying her? Perhaps she had begun too long ago.

She stood up and leaned against the parapet, filling her troubled eyes with the tranquillizing magic of the hour. But instead of tranquillizing her the sight seemed to increase her exasperation. Her gaze turned toward the Colosseum. Already its golden flank was drowned in purple shadow, and above it the sky curved crystal clear, without light or colour. It was the moment when afternoon and evening hang balanced in mid-heaven.

Mrs. Slade turned back and laid her hand on her friend's arm. The gesture was so abrupt that Mrs. Ansley looked up, startled.

"The sun's set. You're not afraid, my dear?"

"Afraid—?"

"Of Roman fever or pneumonia? I remember how ill you were that winter. As a girl you had a very delicate throat, hadn't you?"

"Oh, we're all right up here. Down below, in the Forum, it does get deathly cold, all of a sudden . . . but not here."

"Ah, of course you know because you had to be so careful." Mrs. Slade turned back to the parapet. She thought: "I must make one more effort not to hate her." Aloud she said: "Whenever I look at the Forum from up here, I remember that story about a great-aunt of yours, wasn't she? A dreadfully wicked great-aunt?"

"Oh, yes; Great-aunt Harriet. The one who was supposed to have sent her young sister out to the Forum after sunset to gather a night-blooming flower for her album. All our great-aunts and grandmothers used to have albums of dried flowers."

Mrs. Slade nodded. "But she really sent her because they were in love with the same man—"

"Well, that was the family tradition. They said Aunt Harriet confessed it years afterward. At any rate, the poor little sister caught the fever and died. Mother used to frighten us with the story when we were children."

"And you frightened *me* with it, that winter when you and I were here as girls. The winter I was engaged to Delphin."

Mrs. Ansley gave a faint laugh. "Oh, did I? Really frightened you? I don't believe you're easily frightened."

"Not often; but I was then. I was easily frightened because I was too happy. I wonder if you know what that means?"

"I—yes. . . ." Mrs. Ansley faltered.

"Well, I suppose that was why the story of your wicked aunt made such an impression on me. And I thought: 'There's no more Roman fever, but the Forum is deathly cold after sunset—especially after a hot day. And the Colosseum's even colder and damper.' "

"The Colosseum—?"

"Yes. It wasn't easy to get in, after the gates were locked for the night. Far from easy. Still, in those days it could be managed; it *was* managed, often. Lovers met there who couldn't meet elsewhere. You knew that?"

"I—I daresay. I don't remember."

"You don't remember? You don't remember going to visit some ruins or other one evening, just after dark, and catching a bad chill? You were supposed to have gone to see the moon rise. People always said that expedition was what caused your illness."

There was a moment's silence; then Mrs. Ansley rejoined: "Did they? It was all so long ago."

"Yes. And you got well again—so it didn't matter. But I suppose it struck your friends—the reason given for your illness, I mean—because everybody knew you were so prudent on account of your throat, and your mother took such care of you. . . . You *had* been out late sight-seeing, hadn't you, that night?"

"Perhaps I had. The most prudent girls aren't always prudent. What made you think of it now?"

Mrs. Slade seemed to have no answer ready. But after a moment she broke out: "Because I simply can't bear it any longer—!"

Mrs. Ansley lifted her head quickly. Her eyes were wide and very pale. "Can't bear what?"

"Why—your not knowing that I've always known why you went."

"Why I went—?"

"Yes. You think I'm bluffing, don't you? Well, you went to meet the man I was engaged to—and I can repeat every word of the letter that took you there."

While Mrs. Slade spoke Mrs. Ansley had risen unsteadily to her feet. Her bag, her knitting and gloves, slid in a panic-stricken heap to the ground. She looked at Mrs. Slade as though she were looking at a ghost.

"No, no—don't," she faltered out.

"Why not? Listen, if you don't believe me. 'My one darling, things can't go on like this. I must see you alone. Come to the Colosseum immediately after dark tomorrow. There will be somebody to let you in. No one whom you need fear will suspect'—but perhaps you've forgotten what the letter said?"

Mrs. Ansley met the challenge with an unexpected composure. Steadying herself against the chair she looked at her friend, and replied: "No; I know it by heart too."

"And the signature? 'Only *your* D.S.' Was that it? I'm right, am I? That was the letter that took you out that evening after dark?"

Mrs. Ansley was still looking at her. It seemed to Mrs. Slade that a slow struggle was going on behind the voluntarily controlled mask of her small quiet face. "I shouldn't have thought she had herself so well in hand," Mrs. Slade reflected, almost resentfully. But at this moment Mrs. Ansley spoke. "I don't know how you knew. I burnt that letter at once."

"Yes; you would, naturally—you're so prudent!" The sneer was open now. "And if you burnt the letter you're wondering how on earth I know what was in it. That's it, isn't it?"

Mrs. Slade waited, but Mrs. Ansley did not speak.

"Well, my dear, I know what was in that letter because I wrote it!"

"You wrote it?"

"Yes."

The two women stood for a minute staring at each other in the last golden light. Then Mrs. Ansley dropped back into her chair. "Oh," she murmured, and covered her face with her hands.

Mrs. Slade waited nervously for another word or movement. None came, and at length she broke out: "I horrify you."

Mrs. Ansley's hands dropped to her knee. The face they uncovered was streaked with tears. "I wasn't thinking of you. I was thinking—it was the only letter I ever had from him!"

"And I wrote it. Yes; I wrote it! But I was the girl he was engaged to. Did you happen to remember that?"

Mrs. Ansley's head drooped again. "I'm not trying to excuse myself . . . I remembered. . . ."

"And still you went?"

"Still I went."

Mrs. Slade stood looking down on the small bowed figure at her side. The flame of her wrath had already sunk, and she wondered why she had ever thought there would be any satisfaction in inflicting so purposeless a wound on her friend. But she had to justify herself.

"You do understand? I'd found out—and I hated you, hated you. I knew you were in love with Delphin—and I was afraid; afraid of you, of your quiet ways, your sweetness . . . your . . . well, I wanted you out of the way, that's all. Just for a few weeks; just till I was sure of him. So in a blind fury I wrote that letter . . . I don't know why I'm telling you now."

"I suppose," said Mrs. Ansley slowly, "it's because you've always gone on hating me."

"Perhaps. Or because I wanted to get the whole thing off my mind." She paused. "I'm glad you destroyed the letter. Of course I never thought you'd die."

Mrs. Ansley relapsed into silence, and Mrs.

Slade, leaning above her, was conscious of a strange sense of isolation, of being cut off from the warm current of human communion. "You think me a monster!"

"I don't know. . . . It was the only letter I had, and you say he didn't write it?"

"Ah, how you care for him still!"

"I cared for the memory," said Mrs. Ansley.

Mrs. Slade continued to look down on her. She seemed physically reduced by the blow—as if, when she got up, the wind might scatter her like a puff of dust. Mrs. Slade's jealousy suddenly leapt up again at the sight. All these years the woman had been living on that letter. How she must have loved him, to treasure the mere memory of its ashes! The letter of the man her friend was engaged to. Wasn't it she who was the monster?

"You tried your best to get him away from me, didn't you? But you failed; and I kept him. That's all."

"Yes. That's all."

"I wish now I hadn't told you. I'd no idea you'd feel about it as you do; I thought you'd be amused. It all happened so long ago, as you say; and you must do me the justice to remember that I had no reason to think you'd ever taken it seriously. How could I, when you were married to Horace Ansley two months afterward? As soon as you could get out of bed your mother rushed you off to Florence and married you. People were rather surprised—they wondered at its being done so quickly; but I thought I knew. I had an idea you did it out of *pique*—to be able to say you'd got ahead of Delphin and me. Girls have such silly reasons for doing the most serious things. And your marrying so soon convinced me that you'd never really cared."

"Yes. I suppose it would," Mrs. Ansley assented.

The clear heaven overhead was emptied of all its gold. Dusk spread over it, abruptly darkening the Seven Hills. Here and there lights began to twinkle through the foliage at their feet. Steps were coming and going on the deserted terrace—waiters looking out of the doorway at the head of the stairs, then reappearing with trays and napkins and flasks of wine. Tables were moved, chairs straightened. A feeble string of electric lights flickered out. Some vases of faded flowers were carried away, and brought back replenished. A stout lady in a dust-coat suddenly appeared, asking in broken Italian if any one had seen the elastic band with her stick under the table at which she had lunched, the waiters assisting.

The corner where Mrs. Slade and Mrs. Ansley sat was still shadowy and deserted. For a long time neither of them spoke. At length Mrs. Slade began again: "I suppose I did it as a sort of joke—"

"A joke?"

"Well, girls are ferocious sometimes, you know. Girls in love especially. And I remember laughing to myself all that evening at the idea that you were waiting around there in the dark, dodging out of sight, listening for every sound, trying to get in—. Of course I was upset when I heard you were ill afterward."

Mrs. Ansley had not moved for a long time. But now she turned slowly toward her companion. "But I didn't wait. He'd arranged everything. He was there. We were let in at once," she said.

Mrs. Slade sprang up from her leaning position. "Delphin there? They let you in? Ah, now you're lying!" she burst out with violence.

Mrs. Ansley's voice grew clearer, and full of surprise. "But of course he was there. Naturally he came—"

"Came? How did he know he'd find you there? You must be raving!"

Mrs. Ansley hesitated, as though reflecting. "But I answered the letter. I told him I'd be there. So he came."

Mrs. Slade flung her hands up to her face. "Oh, God—you answered! I never thought of your answering. . . ."

"It's odd you never thought of it, if you wrote the letter."

"Yes. I was blind with rage."

Mrs. Ansley rose, and drew her fur scarf about her. "It is cold here. We'd better go. . . . I'm sorry for you," she said, as she clasped the fur about her throat.

The unexpected words sent a pang through Mrs. Slade. "Yes; we'd better go." She gathered up her bag and cloak. "I don't know why you should be sorry for me," she muttered.

Mrs. Ansley stood looking away from her toward the dusky secret mass of the Colosseum. "Well—because I didn't have to wait that night."

Mrs. Slade gave an unquiet laugh. "Yes; I was beaten there. But I oughtn't to begrudge it to you, I suppose. At the end of all these years. After all, I had everything; I had him for twenty-five years. And you had nothing but that one letter that he didn't write."

Mrs. Ansley was again silent. At length she turned toward the door of the terrace. She took a step, and turned back, facing her companion.

"I had Barbara," she said, and began to move ahead of Mrs. Slade toward the stairway.

Comments and Questions

"Roman Fever" is in the tradition of the well-made story characterized by a highly compressed structure of action which moves to its inevitable conclusion without author comment, without interruption of any kind, and providing no more intensity than the situation will bear. Wharton has chosen a single subject and has embodied it in a dramatic situation to permit the characters to develop and speak for themselves. The resolution of the story is reserved for the final sentence, and if credibility is therefore not to be violated, the plot structure must be logically impeccable. Yet, the plot seems not to be contrived—as such plots so often are—to guarantee the final surprise. The story relies, then, on plot to reveal character, theme, and final meaning. What does Wharton accomplish with this technique?

The story, if nothing more, is good entertainment. Mrs. Ansley's triumph comes as a dramatic surprise which is itself a subtle kind of humor and delight, and we may be tempted to classify the story as escape literature, enjoyed once and then dismissed. But a little reflection may prove otherwise. There is something arresting in the story's tone—Wharton's implied attitude toward the dramatic situation of the two women. If we are delighted with the final sentence, we are sympathetic with Mrs. Ansley, as Wharton intended us to be. But why? Hardly because our sportsmanship relishes a victory of the demure little Grace Ansley over the aggressive, self-assured Alida Slade. Surely Wharton has provided us with something more than a game—her tone tells us that.

It is often remarked that a second or third reading of a story is one test of its excellence. We may have been taken in by the excitement of the first reading; or we may have missed basic implications which give the story substantial status. As we read Wharton's story again, some statements become more arresting. Mrs. Slade to Mrs. Ansley: " 'I was wondering, ever so respectfully, you understand . . . wondering how two such exemplary characters as you and Horace had managed to produce anything quite so dynamic [as Barbara].' Mrs. Slade laughed again, with a touch of asperity." Mrs. Slade again: " 'I always wanted a brilliant daughter . . . and never quite understood why I got an angel instead.' " The serious aspect of the story appears, of course, in Mrs. Slade's self-assumed superiority over Mrs. Ansley, and yet she cannot quite endure the paradox (see "Figure and Symbol," p. 266) of Mrs. Ansley's inferiority producing the brilliant Barbara while her own superiority produces only Jenny. The story's final sentence therefore accomplishes a good deal. This revelation releases the irony (see "The Misreading of Poems," p. 222) which now envelops Mrs. Slade whose sense of superiority crashes before the real superiority of Mrs. Ansley—and the irony is compounded because Mrs. Slade, as well as the reader, experiences the irony.

1. This brief interpretation has omitted many important aspects of the story. Despite the humor found in the final sentence, the story has its measure of pathos. Consider Mrs. Slade's final speech, and then describe what her sensations must have been after the final blow.

2. Any story that relies chiefly on plot must stand or fall on the author's ability to achieve credibility. Do you find any serious flaws? Why did Mrs. Slade write the letter to Mrs. Ansley? How does Wharton make Mrs. Ansley's having Barbara credible?—does Aunt Harriet help to explain matters?

FLANNERY O'CONNOR
1925–1964

Everything That Rises Must Converge

This story provides, among other things, a challenge to one's ability to read fiction as imaginative literature, as an art. Two basic questions confront most readers. Is the title ironic? Is the race problem central to the story or only peripheral? The answers to these questions have generated a good deal of critical debate.

Because of O'Connor's multiple interests, her Southern experience and background, and her deeply religious nature and readings in theology, the meaning of her stories has become uncommonly controversial. As one sympathetic critic points out, some readers find "her as another member of the Southern Gothic School"; some "Roman Catholic critics . . . were often pleased to claim this staunch daughter of their Communion as their own especial property . . . in the tradition of 'modern Catholic writers' "; while other critics, "declining to tag Miss O'Connor with such convenient labels, and conceding her gift for the comic, expressed distaste for what seemed her undue emphasis on the grotesque . . . and the unnecessary theological intrusions into the body of her fiction." Instead of such excursions by critics into the extrinsic causes of her fiction, what she really needed, according to this critic, "was a good liberating from literary critics unwilling to grant her the primary concession, according to Henry James, due any artist—an acceptance by the reader of her *donnée,"** or the set of assumptions upon which her fiction proceeds. That is, it is time that she be regarded first as an artist and that her stories be examined as works of art instead of as veiled religious or Southern doctrine.

The excursions into the causes of O'Connor's fiction have been plentiful as readers have looked for the meaning of "Everything That Rises Must Converge." O'Connor offers us some help: "Justice is justice and should not be appealed to along racial lines. The problem is not abstract for the Southerner, it's concrete; he sees it in terms of persons, not races—which way of seeing does away with easy answers. I have tried to touch this subject by way of fiction only once—in a story called 'Everything That Rises Must Converge.' "**

She leaves no doubt about the kind of personal and public world Mrs. Chestny lives in as contrasted with her son Julian's personal and public world. "She lived," says the narrator, "according to the laws of her own fantasy world, outside of which [Julian] had never seen her set foot." Julian is determined to avoid her fantasy world and to come to grips with the reality of his own existence. The conflict between him and his mother brings tragedy to both of them. So the question remains, what is the nature of their "convergence"? Is it ironic or otherwise?

Her doctor had told Julian's mother that she must lose twenty pounds on account of her blood pressure, so on Wednesday nights Julian had to take her downtown on the bus for a reducing class at the Y. The reducing class was designed for working girls over fifty, who weighed from 165 to 200 pounds. His mother was one of the slimmer ones, but she said ladies did not tell their age or weight. She would not ride the buses by herself at night since they had been integrated, and because the reducing class was one of her few pleasures, necessary for her health, and *free,* she said Julian could at least put himself out to take her, considering all she did for him. Julian did not like to consider all she did for him, but every Wednesday night he braced himself and took her.

She was almost ready to go, standing before the hall mirror, putting on her hat, while he, his hands behind him, appeared pinned to the door frame, waiting like Saint Sebastian for the arrows to begin piercing him. The hat was new and had cost her seven dollars and a half. She kept saying, "Maybe I shouldn't have paid that for it. No, I shouldn't have. I'll take it off and return it tomorrow. I shouldn't have bought it."

Julian raised his eyes to heaven. "Yes, you should have bought it," he said. "Put it on and let's go." It was a hideous hat. A purple velvet

* Robert Drake, *Flannery O'Connor, A Critical Essay,* Grand Rapids, Mich.: William B. Eerdmans, Publisher, 1966, p. 6.

** From a letter to Sister M. Bernetta Quinn, July 27, 1963.

flap came down on one side of it and stood up on the other; the rest of it was green and looked like a cushion with the stuffing out. He decided it was less comical than jaunty and pathetic. Everything that gave her pleasure was small and depressed him.

She lifted the hat one more time and set it down slowly on top of her head. Two wings of gray hair protruded on either side of her florid face, but her eyes, sky-blue, were as innocent and untouched by experience as they must have been when she was ten. Were it not that she was a widow who had struggled fiercely to feed and clothe and put him through school and who was supporting him still, "until he got on his feet," she might have been a little girl that he had to take to town.

"It's all right, it's all right," he said. "Let's go." He opened the door himself and started down the walk to get her going. The sky was a dying violet and the houses stood out darkly against it, bulbous liver-colored monstrosities of a uniform ugliness though no two were alike. Since this had been a fashionable neighborhood forty years ago, his mother persisted in thinking they did well to have an apartment in it. Each house had a narrow collar of dirt around it in which sat, usually, a grubby child. Julian walked with his hands in his pockets, his head down and thrust forward and his eyes glazed with the determination to make himself completely numb during the time he would be sacrificed to her pleasure.

The door closed and he turned to find the dumpy figure, surmounted by the atrocious hat, coming toward him. "Well," she said, "you only live once and paying a little more for it, I at least won't meet myself coming and going."

"Some day I'll start making money," Julian said gloomily—he knew he never would—"and you can have one of those jokes whenever you take the fit." But first they would move. He visualized a place where the nearest neighbors would be three miles away on either side.

"I think you're doing fine," she said, drawing on her gloves. "You've only been out of school a year. Rome wasn't built in a day."

She was one of the few members of the Y reducing class who arrived in hat and gloves and who had a son who had been to college. "It takes time," she said, "and the world is in such a mess. This hat looked better on me than any of the others, though when she brought it out I said, 'Take that thing back. I wouldn't have it on my head,' and she said, 'Now wait till you see it on,' and when she put it on me, I said, 'We-ull,' and she said, 'If you ask me, that hat does something for you and you do something for the hat, and besides,' she said, 'with that hat, you won't meet yourself coming and going.' "

Julian thought he could have stood his lot better if she had been selfish, if she had been an old hag who drank and screamed at him. He walked along, saturated in depression, as if in the midst of his martyrdom he had lost his faith. Catching sight of his long, hopeless, irritated face, she stopped suddenly with a grief-stricken look, and pulled back on his arm. "Wait on me," she said. "I'm going back to the house and take this thing off and tomorrow I'm going to return it. I was out of my head. I can pay the gas bill with that seven-fifty."

He caught her arm in a vicious grip. "You are not going to take it back," he said. "I like it."

"Well," she said, "I don't think I ought . . ."

"Shut up and enjoy it," he muttered, more depressed than ever.

"With the world in the mess it's in," she said, "it's a wonder we can enjoy anything. I tell you, the bottom rail is on the top."

Julian sighed.

"Of course," she said, "if you know who you are, you can go anywhere." She said this every time he took her to the reducing class. "Most of them in it are not our kind of people," she said, "but I can be gracious to anybody. I know who I am."

"They don't give a damn for your graciousness," Julian said savagely. "Knowing who you are is good for one generation only. You haven't the foggiest idea where you stand now or who you are."

She stopped and allowed her eyes to flash at him. "I most certainly do know who I am," she said, "and if you don't know who you are, I'm ashamed of you."

"Oh hell," Julian said.

"Your great-grandfather was a former governor of this state," she said. "Your grandfather was a prosperous landowner. Your grandmother was a Godhigh."

"Will you look around you," he said tensely, "and see where you are now?" and he swept his arm jerkily out to indicate the neighborhood, which the growing darkness at least made less dingy.

"You remain what you are," she said. "Your great-grandfather had a plantation and two hundred slaves."

"There are no more slaves," he said irritably.

"They were better off when they were," she said. He groaned to see that she was off on that topic. She rolled onto it every few days like a train on an open track. He knew every stop, every junction, every swamp along the way, and knew the exact point at which her conclusion would roll majestically into the station: "It's ridiculous. It's simply not realistic. They should rise, yes, but on their own side of the fence."

"Let's skip it," Julian said.

"The ones I feel sorry for," she said, "are the ones that are half white. They're tragic."

"Will you skip it?"

"Suppose we were half white. We would certainly have mixed feelings."

"I have mixed feelings now," he groaned.

"Well let's talk about something pleasant," she said. "I remember going to Grandpa's when I was a little girl. Then the house had double stairways that went up to what was really the second floor—all the cooking was done on the first. I used to like to stay down in the kitchen on account of the way the walls smelled. I would sit with my nose pressed against the plaster and take deep breaths. Actually the place belonged to the Godhighs but your grandfather Chestny paid the mortgage and saved it for them. They were in reduced circumstances," she said, "but reduced or not, they never forgot who they were."

"Doubtless that decayed mansion reminded them," Julian muttered. He never spoke of it without contempt or thought of it without longing. He had seen it once when he was a child before it had been sold. The double stairways had rotted and been torn down. Negroes were living in it. But it remained in his mind as his mother had known it. It appeared in his dreams regularly. He would stand on the wide porch, listening to the rustle of oak leaves, then wander through the high-ceilinged hall into the parlor that opened onto it and gaze at the worn rugs and faded draperies. It occurred to him that it was he, not she, who could have appreciated it. He preferred its threadbare elegance to anything he could name and it was because of it that all the neighborhoods they had lived in had been a torment to him—whereas she had hardly known the difference. She called her insensitivity "being adjustable."

"And I remember the old darky who was my nurse, Caroline. There was no better person in the world. I've always had a great respect for my colored friends," she said. "I'd do anything in the world for them and they'd . . ."

"Will you for God's sake get off that subject?" Julian said. When he got on a bus by himself, he made it a point to sit down beside a Negro, in reparation as it were for his mother's sins.

"You're mighty touchy tonight," she said. "Do you feel all right?"

"Yes I feel all right," he said. "Now lay off."

She pursed her lips. "Well, you certainly are in a vile humor," she observed. "I just won't speak to you at all."

They had reached the bus stop. There was no bus in sight and Julian, his hands still jammed in his pockets and his head thrust forward, scowled down the empty street. The frustration of having to wait on the bus as well as ride on it began to creep up his neck like a hot hand. The presence of his mother was borne in upon him as she gave a pained sigh. He looked at her bleakly. She was holding herself very erect under the preposterous hat, wearing it like a banner of her imaginary dignity. There was in him an evil urge to break her spirit. He suddenly unloosened his tie and pulled it off and put it in his pocket.

She stiffened. "Why must you look like *that* when you take me to town?" she said. "Why must you deliberately embarrass me?"

"If you'll never learn where you are," he said, "you can at least learn where I am."

"You look like a—thug," she said.

"Then I must be one," he murmured.

"I'll just go home," she said. "I will not bother you. If you can't do a little thing like that for me . . ."

Rolling his eyes upward, he put his tie back on. "Restored to my class," he muttered. He thrust his face toward her and hissed, "True culture is in the mind, the *mind*," he said, and tapped his head, "the mind."

"It's in the heart," she said, "and in how you do things and how you do things is because of who you *are*."

"Nobody in the damn bus cares who you are."

"I care who I am," she said icily.

The lighted bus appeared on top of the next hill and as it approached, they moved out into the street to meet it. He put his hand under her elbow and hoisted her up on the creaking step. She entered with a little smile, as if she were going into a drawing room where everyone had been waiting for her. While he put in the tokens, she sat down on one of the broad front seats for three which faced the aisle. A thin woman with protruding teeth and long yellow hair was sitting on the end of it. His mother moved up beside her and left room for Julian beside herself. He sat down and looked at the floor across the aisle where a pair of thin feet in red and white canvas sandals were planted.

His mother immediately began a general conversation meant to attract anyone who felt like talking. "Can it get any hotter?" she said and removed from her purse a folding fan, black with a Japanese scene on it, which she began to flutter before her.

"I reckon it might could," the woman with the protruding teeth said, "but I know for a fact my apartment couldn't get no hotter."

"It must get the afternoon sun," his mother said. She sat forward and looked up and down the bus. It was half filled. Everybody was white. "I see we have the bus to ourselves," she said. Julian cringed.

"For a change," said the woman across the aisle, the owner of the red and white canvas sandals. "I come on one the other day and they were thick as fleas—up front and all through."

"The world is in a mess everywhere," his mother said. "I don't know how we've let it get in this fix."

"What gets my goat is all those boys from good families stealing automobile tires," the woman with the protruding teeth said. "I told my boy, I said you may not be rich but you been raised right and if I ever catch you in any such mess, they can send you on to the reformatory. Be exactly where you belong."

"Training tells," his mother said. "Is your boy in high school?"

"Ninth grade," the woman said.

"My son just finished college last year. He wants to write but he's selling typewriters until he gets started," his mother said.

The woman leaned forward and peered at Julian. He threw her such a malevolent look that she subsided against the seat. On the floor across the aisle there was an abandoned newspaper. He got up and got it and opened it out in front of him. His mother discreetly continued the conversation in a lower tone but the woman across the aisle said in a loud voice, "Well that's nice. Selling typewriters is close to writing. He can go right from one to the other."

"I tell him," his mother said, "that Rome wasn't built in a day."

Behind the newspaper Julian was withdrawing into the inner compartment of his mind where he spent most of his time. This was a kind of mental bubble in which he established himself when he could not bear to be a part of what was going on around him. From it he could see out and judge but in it he was safe from any kind of penetration from without. It was the only place where he felt free of the general idiocy of his fellows. His mother had never entered it but from it he could see her with absolute clarity.

The old lady was clever enough and he thought that if she had started from any of the right premises, more might have been expected of her. She lived according to the laws of her own fantasy world, outside of which he had never seen her set foot. The law of it was to sacrifice herself for him after she had first created the necessity to do so by making a mess of things. If he had permitted her sacrifices, it was only because her lack of foresight had made them necessary. All of her life had been a struggle to act like a Chestny without the Chestny goods, and to give him everything she thought a Chestny ought to have; but since, said she, it was fun to struggle, why complain? And when you had won, as she had won, what fun to look back on the hard times! He could not forgive her that she had enjoyed the struggle and that she thought *she* had won.

What she meant when she said she had won was that she had brought him up successfully and had sent him to college and that he had turned out so well—good looking (her teeth had gone unfilled so that his could be straightened), intelligent (he realized he was too intelligent to be a success), and with a future ahead of him (there was of course no future ahead of him). She excused his gloominess on the grounds that he was still growing up and his radical ideas on his lack of practical experience. She said he didn't yet know a thing about "life," that he hadn't even entered the real world—when already he was as disenchanted with it as a man of fifty.

The further irony of all this was that in spite of her, he had turned out so well. In spite of going to only a third-rate college, he had, on his own initiative, come out with a first-rate education; in spite of growing up dominated by a small mind, he had ended up with a large one; in spite of all her foolish views, he was free of prejudice and unafraid to face facts. Most miraculous of all, instead of being blinded by love for her as she was for him, he had cut himself emotionally free of her and could see her with complete objectivity. He was not dominated by his mother.

The bus stopped with a sudden jerk and shook him from his meditation. A woman from the back lurched forward with little steps and barely escaped falling in his newspaper as she righted herself. She got off and a large Negro got on. Julian kept his paper lowered to watch. It gave him a certain satisfaction to see injustice in daily operation. It confirmed his view that with a few exceptions there was no one worth knowing within a radius of three hundred miles. The Negro was well dressed and carried a briefcase. He looked around and then sat down on the other end of the seat where the woman with the red and white canvas sandals was sitting. He immediately unfolded a newspaper and obscured himself behind it. Julian's mother's elbow at once prodded insistently into his ribs. "Now you see why I won't ride on these busses by myself," she whispered.

The woman with the red and white canvas sandals had risen at the same time the Negro sat down and had gone further back in the bus and taken the seat of the woman who had got off. His mother leaned forward and cast her an approving look.

Julian rose, crossed the aisle, and sat down in the place of the woman with the canvas sandals. From this position, he looked serenely across at his mother. Her face had turned an angry red. He stared at her, making his eyes the eyes of a stranger. He felt his tension suddenly lift as if he had openly declared war on her.

He would have liked to get in conversation with the Negro and to talk with him about art or politics or any subject that would be above the comprehension of those around them, but the man remained entrenched behind his paper. He was either ignoring the change of seating or had never noticed it. There was no way for Julian to convey his sympathy.

His mother kept her eyes fixed reproachfully on his face. The woman with the protruding teeth was looking at him avidly as if he were a type of monster new to her.

"Do you have a light?" he asked the Negro.

Without looking away from his paper, the man reached in his pocket and handed him a packet of matches.

"Thanks," Julian said. For a moment he held the matches foolishly. A NO SMOKING sign looked down upon him from over the door. This alone would not have deterred him; he had no cigarettes. He had quit smoking some months before because he could not afford it. "Sorry," he muttered and handed back the matches. The Negro lowered the paper and gave him an annoyed look. He took the matches and raised the paper again.

His mother continued to gaze at him but she did not take advantage of his momentary discomfort. Her eyes retained their battered look. Her face seemed to be unnaturally red, as if her blood pressure had risen. Julian allowed no glimmer of sympathy to show on his face. Having got the advantage, he wanted desperately to keep it and carry it through. He would have liked to teach her a lesson that would last her a while, but there seemed no way to continue the point. The Negro refused to come out from behind his paper.

Julian folded his arms and looked stolidly before him, facing her but as if he did not see her, as if he had ceased to recognize her existence. He visualized a scene in which, the bus having reached their stop, he would remain in his seat and when she said, "Aren't you going to get off?" he would look at her as at a stranger who had rashly addressed him. The corner they got off on was usually deserted, but it was well lighted and it would not hurt her to walk by herself the four blocks to the Y. He decided to wait until the time came and then decide whether or not he would let her get off by herself. He would have to be at the Y at ten to bring her back, but he could leave her wondering if he was going to show up. There was no reason for her to think she could always depend on him.

He retired again into the high-ceilinged room sparsely settled with large pieces of antique furniture. His soul expanded momentarily but then he became aware of his mother across from him and the vision shriveled. He studied her coldly. Her feet in little pumps dangled like a child's and did not quite reach the floor. She was training on him an exaggerated look of reproach. He felt completely detached from her. At that moment he could with pleasure have slapped her as he would have slapped a particularly obnoxious child in his charge.

He began to imagine various unlikely ways by which he could teach her a lesson. He might make friends with some distinguished Negro professor or lawyer and bring him home to spend the evening. He would be entirely justified but her blood pressure would rise to 300. He could not push her to the extent of making her have a stroke, and moreover, he had never been successful at making any Negro friends. He had tried to strike up an acquaintance on the bus with some of the better types, with ones that looked like professors or ministers or lawyers. One morning he had sat down next to a distinguished-looking dark brown man who had answered his questions with a sonorous solemnity but who had turned out to be an undertaker. Another day he had sat down beside a cigar-smoking Negro with a diamond ring on his finger, but after a few stilted pleasantries, the Negro had rung the buzzer and risen, slipping two lottery tickets into Julian's hand as he climbed over him to leave.

He imagined his mother lying desperately ill and his being able to secure only a Negro doctor for her. He toyed with that idea for a few minutes and then dropped it for a momentary vision of himself participating as a sympathizer in a sit-in demonstration. This was possible but he did not linger with it. Instead, he approached the ultimate horror. He brought home a beautiful suspiciously Negroid woman. Prepare yourself, he said. There is nothing you can do about it. This is the woman I've chosen. She's intelligent, dignified, even good, and she's suffered and she hasn't thought it *fun*. Now persecute us, go ahead and persecute us. Drive her out of here, but remember, you're driving me too. His eyes were narrowed and through the indignation he had generated, he saw his mother across the aisle, purple-faced, shrunken to the dwarf-like proportions of her moral nature, sitting like a mummy beneath the ridiculous banner of her hat.

He was tilted out of his fantasy again as the bus stopped. The door opened with a sucking hiss and out of the dark a large, gaily dressed, sullen-looking colored woman got on with a little boy. The child, who might have been four, had on a short plaid suit and a Tyrolean hat with a blue feather in it. Julian hoped that he would sit down beside him and that the woman would push in beside his mother. He could think of no better arrangement.

As she waited for her tokens, the woman was surveying the seating possibilities—he hoped with the idea of sitting where she was least wanted. There was something familiar-looking about her but Julian could not place what it was. She was a giant of a woman. Her face was set not only to meet opposition but to seek it out. The downward tilt of her large lower lip was like a warning sign: DON'T TAMPER WITH ME. Her bulging figure was encased in a green crepe dress and her feet overflowed in red shoes. She had on a hideous hat. A purple velvet flap came down on one side of it and stood up on the other; the rest of it was green and looked like a cushion with the stuffing out. She carried a mammoth red pocketbook that bulged throughout as if it were stuffed with rocks.

To Julian's disappointment, the little boy climbed up on the empty seat beside his mother. His mother lumped all children, black and white, into the common category, "cute," and she thought little Negroes were on the whole cuter than little white children. She smiled at the little boy as he climbed on the seat.

Meanwhile the woman was bearing down upon the empty seat beside Julian. To his annoyance, she squeezed herself into it. He saw his mother's face change as the woman settled herself next to him and he realized with satisfaction that this was more objectionable to her than it was to him. Her face seemed almost gray and there was a look of dull recognition in her eyes, as if suddenly she had sickened at some awful confrontation. Julian saw that it was because she and the woman had, in a sense, swapped sons. Though his mother would not realize the symbolic significance of this, she would feel it. His amusement showed plainly on his face.

The woman next to him muttered something unintelligible to herself. He was conscious of a kind of bristling next to him, a muted growling like that of an angry cat. He could not see anything but the red pocketbook upright on the bulging green thighs. He visualized the woman as she had stood waiting for her tokens—the ponderous figure, rising from the red shoes upward over the solid hips, the mammoth bosom, the haughty face, to the green and purple hat.

His eyes widened.

The vision of the two hats, identical, broke upon him with the radiance of a brilliant sunrise. His face was suddenly lit with joy. He could not believe that Fate had thrust upon his mother such a lesson. He gave a loud chuckle so that she would look at him and see that he saw. She turned her eyes on him slowly. The blue in them seemed to have turned a bruised purple. For a moment he had an uncomfortable sense of her innocence, but it lasted only a second before principle rescued him. Justice entitled him to laugh. His grin hardened until it said to her as plainly as if he were saying aloud: Your punishment exactly fits your pettiness. This should teach you a permanent lesson.

Her eyes shifted to the woman. She seemed unable to bear looking at him and to find the woman preferable. He became conscious again of the bristling presence at his side. The woman was rumbling like a volcano about to become active. His mother's mouth began to twitch slightly at one corner. With a sinking heart, he saw incipient signs of recovery on her face and realized that this was going to strike her suddenly as funny and was going to be no lesson at all. She kept her eyes on the woman and an amused smile came over her face as if the woman were a monkey that had stolen her hat. The little Negro was looking up at her with large fascinated eyes. He had been trying to attract her attention for some time.

"Carver!" the woman said suddenly. "Come heah!"

When he saw that the spotlight was on him at last, Carver drew his feet up and turned himself toward Julian's mother and giggled.

"Carver!" the woman said. "You heah me? Come heah!"

Carver slid down from the seat but remained squatting with his back against the base of it, his head turned slyly around toward Julian's mother, who was smiling at him. The woman reached a hand across the aisle and snatched him to her. He righted himself and hung backwards on her knees, grinning at Julian's mother. "Isn't he cute?" Julian's mother said to the woman with the protruding teeth.

"I reckon he is," the woman said without conviction.

The Negress yanked him upright but he eased out of her grip and shot across the aisle and scrambled, giggling wildly, onto the seat beside his love.

"I think he likes me," Julian's mother said, and smiled at the woman. It was the smile she used when she was being particularly gracious to an inferior. Julian saw everything lost. The lesson had rolled off her like rain on a roof.

The woman stood up and yanked the little boy off the seat as if she were snatching him from contagion. Julian could feel the rage in her at having no weapon like his mother's smile. She gave the child a sharp slap across his leg. He howled once and then thrust his head into her stomach and kicked his feet against her shins. "Be-have," she said vehemently.

The bus stopped and the Negro who had been reading the newspaper got off. The woman moved over and set the little boy down with a thump between herself and Julian. She held him firmly by the knee. In a moment he put his hands in front of his face and peeped at Julian's mother through his fingers.

"I see yoooooooo!" she said and put her hand in front of her face and peeped at him.

The woman slapped his hand down. "Quit yo'

foolishness," she said, "before I knock the living Jesus out of you!"

Julian was thankful that the next stop was theirs. He reached up and pulled the cord. The woman reached up and pulled it at the same time. Oh my God, he thought. He had the terrible intuition that when they got off the bus together, his mother would open her purse and give the little boy a nickel. The gesture would be as natural to her as breathing. The bus stopped and the woman got up and lunged to the front, dragging the child, who wished to stay on, after her. Julian and his mother got up and followed. As they neared the door, Julian tried to relieve her of her pocketbook.

"No," she murmured, "I want to give the little boy a nickel."

"No!" Julian hissed. "No!"

She smiled down at the child and opened her bag. The bus door opened and the woman picked him up by the arm and descended with him, hanging at her hip. Once in the street she set him down and shook him.

Julian's mother had to close her purse while she got down the bus step but as soon as her feet were on the ground, she opened it again and began to rummage inside. "I can't find but a penny," she whispered, "but it looks like a new one."

"Don't do it!" Julian said fiercely between his teeth. There was a streetlight on the corner and she hurried to get under it so that she could better see into her pocketbook. The woman was heading off rapidly down the street with the child still hanging backward on her hand.

"Oh little boy!" Julian's mother called and took a few quick steps and caught up with them just beyond the lamppost. "Here's a bright new penny for you," and she held out the coin, which shone bronze in the dim light.

The huge woman turned and for a moment stood, her shoulders lifted and her face frozen with frustrated rage, and stared at Julian's mother. Then all at once she seemed to explode like a piece of machinery that had been given one ounce of pressure too much. Julian saw the black fist swing out with the red pocketbook. He shut his eyes and cringed as he heard the woman shout, "He don't take nobody's pennies!" When he opened his eyes, the woman was disappearing down the street with the little boy staring wide-eyed over her shoulder. Julian's mother was sitting on the sidewalk.

"I told you not to do that," Julian said angrily. "I told you not to do that!"

He stood over her for a minute, gritting his teeth. Her legs were stretched out in front of her and her hat was on her lap. He squatted down and looked her in the face. It was totally expressionless. "You got exactly what you deserved," he said. "Now get up."

He picked up her pocketbook and put what had fallen out back in it. He picked the hat up off her lap. The penny caught his eye on the sidewalk and he picked that up and let it drop before her eyes into the purse. Then he stood up and leaned over and held his hands out to pull her up. She remained immobile. He sighed. Rising above them on either side were black apartment buildings, marked with irregular rectangles of light. At the end of the block a man came out of a door and walked off in the opposite direction. "All right," he said, "suppose somebody happens by and wants to know why you're sitting on the sidewalk?"

She took the hand and, breathing hard, pulled heavily up on it and then stood for a moment, swaying slightly as if the spots of light in the darkness were circling around her. Her eyes, shadowed and confused, finally settled on his face. He did not try to conceal his irritation. "I hope this teaches you a lesson," he said. She leaned forward and her eyes raked his face. She seemed trying to determine his identity. Then, as if she found nothing familiar about him, she started off with a headlong movement in the wrong direction.

"Aren't you going on to the Y?" he asked.

"Home," she muttered.

"Well, are we walking?"

For answer she kept going. Julian followed along, his hands behind him. He saw no reason to let the lesson she had had go without backing it up with an explanation of its meaning. She might as well be made to understand what had happened to her. "Don't think that was just an uppity Negro woman," he said. "That was the whole colored race which will no longer take your condescending pennies. That was your black double. She can wear the same hat as you, and to be sure," he added gratuitously (because he thought it was funny), "it looked better on her than it did on you. What all this means," he said, "is that the old world is gone. The old manners are obsolete and your graciousness is not worth a damn." He thought bitterly of the house that had been lost for him. "You aren't who you think you are," he said.

She continued to plow ahead, paying no attention to him. Her hair had come undone on one side. She dropped her pocketbook and took no notice. He stooped and picked it up and handed it to her but she did not take it.

"You needn't act as if the world had come to an end," he said, "because it hasn't. From now on you've got to live in a new world and face a few realities for a change. Buck up," he said, "it won't kill you."

She was breathing fast.

"Let's wait on the bus," he said.

"Home," she said thickly.

"I hate to see you behave like this," he said. "Just like a child. I should be able to expect more of you." He decided to stop where he was and make her stop and wait for a bus. "I'm not going any farther," he said, stopping. "We're going on the bus."

She continued to go on as if she had not heard him. He took a few steps and caught her arm and stopped her. He looked into her face and caught his breath. He was looking into a face he had never seen before. "Tell Grandpa to come get me," she said.

He stared, stricken.

"Tell Caroline to come get me," she said.

Stunned, he let her go and she lurched forward again, walking as if one leg were shorter than the other. A tide of darkness seemed to be sweeping her from him. "Mother!" he cried. "Darling, sweetheart, wait!" Crumpling, she fell to the pavement. He dashed forward and fell at her side, crying, "Mamma, Mamma!" He turned her over. Her face was fiercely distorted. One eye, large and staring, moved slightly to the left as if it had become unmoored. The other remained fixed on him, raked his face again, found nothing and closed.

"Wait here, wait here!" he cried and jumped up and began to run for help toward a cluster of lights he saw in the distance ahead of him. "Help, help!" he shouted, but his voice was thin, scarcely a thread of sound. The lights drifted farther away the faster he ran and his feet moved numbly as if they carried him nowhere. The tide of darkness seemed to sweep him back to her, postponing from moment to moment his entry into the world of guilt and sorrow.

ERNEST HEMINGWAY
1899–1961

A Clean, Well-Lighted Place

It was late and everyone had left the café except an old man who sat in the shadow the leaves of the tree made against the electric light. In the day time the street was dusty, but at night the dew settled the dust and the old man liked to sit late because he was deaf and now at night it was quiet and he felt the difference. The two waiters inside the café knew that the old man was a little drunk, and while he was a good client they knew that if he became too drunk he would leave without paying, so they kept watch on him.

"Last week he tried to commit suicide," one waiter said.

"Why?"

"He was in despair."

"What about?"

"Nothing."

"How do you know it was nothing?"

"He has plenty of money."

They sat together at a table that was close against the wall near the door of the café and looked at the terrace where the tables were all empty except where the old man sat in the shadow of the leaves of the tree that moved slightly in the wind. A girl and a soldier went by in the street. The street light shone on the brass number on his collar. The girl wore no head covering and hurried beside him.

"The guard will pick him up," one waiter said.

"What does it matter if he gets what he's after?"

"He had better get off the street now. The guard will get him. They went by five minutes ago."

The old man sitting in the shadow rapped on his saucer with his glass. The younger waiter went over to him.

"What do you want?"

The old man looked at him. "Another brandy," he said.

"You'll be drunk," the waiter said. The old man looked at him. The waiter went away.

"He'll stay all night," he said to his colleague. "I'm sleepy now. I never get into bed before three o'clock. He should have killed himself last week."

The waiter took the brandy bottle and another saucer from the counter inside the café and marched out to the old man's table. He put down the saucer and poured the glass full of brandy.

"You should have killed yourself last week," he said to the deaf man. The old man motioned with his finger. "A little more," he said. The waiter poured on into the glass so that the brandy slopped over and ran down the stem into the top saucer of the pile. "Thank you," the old man said. The waiter took the bottle back inside the café. He sat down at the table with his colleague again.

"He's drunk now," he said.

"He's drunk every night."

"What did he want to kill himself for?"

"How should I know."

"How did he do it?"

"He hung himself with a rope."

"Who cut him down?"

"His niece."

"Why did they do it?"

"Fear for his soul."

"How much money has he got?"

"He's got plenty."

"He must be eighty years old."

"Anyway I should say he was eighty."

"I wish he would go home. I never get to bed before three o'clock. What kind of hour is that to go to bed?"

"He stays up because he likes it."

"He's lonely. I'm not lonely. I have a wife waiting in bed for me."

"He had a wife once too."

"A wife would be no good to him now."

"You can't tell. He might be better with a wife."

"His niece looks after him. You said she cut him down."

"I know."

"I wouldn't want to be that old. An old man is a nasty thing."

"Not always. This old man is clean. He drinks without spilling. Even now, drunk. Look at him."

"I don't want to look at him. I wish he would go home. He has no regard for those who must work."

The old man looked from his glass across the square, then over at the waiters.

"Another brandy," he said, pointing to his glass. The waiter who was in a hurry came over.

"Finished," he said, speaking with that omission of syntax stupid people employ when talking to drunken people or foreigners. "No more tonight. Close now."

"Another," said the old man.

"No. Finished." The waiter wiped the edge of the table with a towel and shook his head.

The old man stood up, slowly counted the saucers, took a leather coin purse from his pocket and paid for the drinks, leaving half a peseta tip.

The waiter watched him go down the street, a very old man walking unsteadily but with dignity.

"Why didn't you let him stay and drink?" the unhurried waiter asked. They were putting up the shutters. "It is not half-past two."

"I want to go home to bed."

"What is an hour?"

"More to me than to him."

"An hour is the same."

"You talk like an old man yourself. He can buy a bottle and drink at home."

"It's not the same."

"No, it is not," agreed the waiter with a wife. He did not wish to be unjust. He was only in a hurry.

"And you? You have no fear of going home before your usual hour?"

"Are you trying to insult me?"

"No, hombre, only to make a joke."

"No," the waiter who was in a hurry said, rising from pulling down the metal shutters. "I have confidence. I am all confidence."

"You have youth, confidence, and a job," the older waiter said. "You have everything."

"And what do you lack?"

"Everything but work."

"You have everything I have."

"No. I have never had confidence and I am not young."

"Come on. Stop talking nonsense and lock up."

"I am of those who like to stay late at the café," the older waiter said. "With all those who do not want to go to bed. With all those who need a light for the night."

"I want to go home and into bed."

"We are of two different kinds," the older waiter said. He was now dressed to go home. "It is not only a question of youth and confidence although those things are very beautiful. Each night I am reluctant to close up because there may be some one who needs the café."

"Hombre, there are bodegas open all night long."

"You do not understand. This is a clean and pleasant café. It is well lighted. The light is very good and also, now, there are shadows of the leaves."

"Good night," said the younger waiter.

"Good night," the other said. Turning off the electric light he continued the conversation with himself. It is the light of course but it is necessary that the place be clean and pleasant. You do not want music. Certainly you do not want music. Nor can you stand before a bar with dignity although that is all that is provided for these hours. What did he fear? It was not fear or dread. It was a nothing that he knew too well. It was all a nothing and a man was nothing too. It was only that and light was all it needed and a certain cleanness and order. Some lived in it and never felt it but he knew it all was nada y pues nada y nada y pues nada.[1] Our nada who art in nada, nada be thy name thy kingdom nada thy will be nada in nada as it is in nada. Give us this nada our daily nada and nada us our nada as we nada our nadas and nada us not into nada but deliver us from nada; pues nada. Hail nothing full of nothing, nothing is with thee.[2] He smiled and stood before a bar with a shining steam pressure coffee machine.

"What's yours?" asked the barman.

"Nada."

"Otro loco mas,"[3] said the barman and turned away.

"A little cup," said the waiter.

The barman poured it for him.

"The light is very bright and pleasant but the bar is unpolished," the waiter said.

The barman looked at him but did not answer. It was too late at night for conversation.

"You want another copita?"[4] the barman asked.

"No, thank you," said the waiter and went out. He disliked bars and bodegas. A clean, well-lighted café was a very different thing. Now, without thinking further, he would go home to his room. He would lie in the bed and finally, with daylight, he would go to sleep. After all, he said to himself, it is probably only insomnia. Many must have it.

Comments

The problem here, as found in so many Hemingway stories, is to discover how he manages to make apparently so little come to so much. A basic concern of every literary artist is to devise a technique, a literary form, to fashion the meaning of the situation he is exploring. No modern writer has worked more diligently to develop such a literary technique than Hemingway.

Ralph Ellison, author of the story "King of the Bingo Game" (p. 53) and the celebrated novel *Invisible Man* (1952), says about Hemingway: "In the end . . . it is the quality of his art which is primary. . . . And it was through this struggle with form that he became the master, the culture hero, whom we have come to know and admire." In a letter (February 4, 1930) to one of the editors of this book Hemingway comments on that struggle: "I have some 40 drafts of the last chapter [of *A Farewell to Arms*]—may have destroyed others. This process proves nothing as far as I know except that I worked over and over it to get it right. . . . This process of transmitting your sensations and imagination, etc. from yourself, complete, to the person reading is what constitutes the discipline of prose."

What disciplines has Hemingway used to create "A Clean, Well-Lighted Place," one of the shortest stories in the English language and one of Hemingway's favorites?

[1] "nada y pues nada . . .": nothing and then nothing . . . [2] "Our nada who art in nada. . . . nothing is with thee.": an ironic prayer. [3] One more crazy person.

[4] Usually a small drink of wine.

On the surface level we have a simple tale with three principal characters, but its implications, like those in Hemingway's *The Old Man and the Sea* (1952), can be as profound as the reader has insight. The scene is a Spanish cafe very late at night where an old man is having a drink while an old waiter and a young one discuss him. Except when the old waiter closes the cafe and goes to a bar for a drink, there is no action, much less suspense, whatever.

The story is a triumph of meaning expressed through dramatic tone and symbolism. Hemingway uses the dramatic method (see "Plot," p. 15) to permit the characters to present themselves. The story is actually a little one-act play with the author's comment almost totally absent. Further, most of the customary exposition and author comment are embodied in the dialogue (for which Hemingway is justly famous), and the key facts are merely touched upon, rarely accented. The story is highly compressed: hardly a wasted word and every word counts. All this means that the reader participates in a drama which requires him to contribute to its understanding. Whatever tension the story possesses is created by the conflict between the old and young waiter as they regard the old man drinking in his loneliness. The symbolism? Each character represents a value system, a basic attitude toward life, and the word *nada,* or *nothing,* finally becomes the basic symbol upon which the meaning of the story turns.

It is easy to say, as one critic has said, "The story is about nothing, and we know that from the start. . . . the style itself tells us that there is no meaning in life." But this peremptory judgment hardly considers the importance of the cafe as a substitute for home as understood by the old waiter. And he understands even more: the value of affection, of communication among men, and that love is necessary to self-realization and simple dignity to the end. These things are precisely what the young waiter does not understand, and the old waiter's *ironic* prayer makes perfectly clear that the story is about Something very important to sensitive men and women. How else account for the final paragraph where the old waiter says to himself, "After all . . . it is probably only insomnia. Many must have it." Insomnia? Surely, an ironic name for loneliness and loss of identity, as Hemingway means it to be.

FRANK O'CONNOR[1]
1903–1966

The Drunkard

It was a terrible blow to Father when Mr. Dooley on the terrace died. Mr. Dooley was a commercial traveller with two sons in the Dominicans and a car of his own, so socially he was miles ahead of us, but he had no false pride. Mr. Dooley was an intellectual, and, like all intellectuals the thing he loved best was conversation, and in his own limited way Father was a well-read man and could appreciate an intelligent talker. Mr. Dooley was remarkably intelligent. Between business acquaintances and clerical contacts, there was very little he didn't know about what went on in town, and evening after evening he crossed the road to our gate to explain to Father the news behind the news. He had a low, palavering voice and a knowing smile, and Father would listen in astonishment, giving him a conversational lead now and again, and then stump triumphantly in to Mother with his face aglow and ask: "Do you know what Mr. Dooley is after telling me?" Ever since, when somebody has given me some bit of information off the record I have found myself on the point of asking: "Was it Mr. Dooley told you that?"

Till I actually saw him laid out in his brown shroud with the rosary beads entwined between his waxy fingers I did not take the report of his death seriously. Even then I felt there must be a catch and that some summer evening Mr. Dooley must reappear at our gate to give us the low-down on the next world. But Father was very upset, partly because Mr. Dooley was about one age with himself, a thing that always gives a distinctly personal turn to another man's demise; partly because now he would have no one to tell him what dirty work was behind the latest scene at the Corporation. You could count on your fingers the number of men in Blarney Lane

[1] Pen name for Michael O'Donovan.

who read the papers as Mr. Dooley did, and none of these would have overlooked the fact that Father was only a labouring man. Even Sullivan, the carpenter, a mere nobody, thought he was a cut above Father. It was certainly a solemn event.

"Half past two to the Curragh," Father said meditatively, putting down the paper.

"But you're not thinking of going to the funeral?" Mother asked in alarm.

" 'Twould be expected," Father said, scenting opposition. "I wouldn't give it to say to them."

"I think," said Mother with suppressed emotion, "it will be as much as anyone will expect if you go to the chapel with him."

("Going to the chapel," of course, was one thing, because the body was removed after work, but going to a funeral meant the loss of a half-day's pay.)

"The people hardly know us," she added.

"God between us and all harm," Father replied with dignity, "we'd be glad if it was our own turn."

To give Father his due, he was always ready to lose a half day for the sake of an old neighbour. It wasn't so much that he liked funerals as that he was a conscientious man who did as he would be done by; and nothing could have consoled him so much for the prospect of his own death as the assurance of a worthy funeral. And, to give Mother her due, it wasn't the half-day's pay she begrudged, badly as we could afford it.

Drink, you see, was Father's great weakness. He could keep steady for months, even for years, at a stretch, and while he did he was as good as gold. He was first up in the morning and brought the mother a cup of tea in bed, stayed at home in the evenings and read the paper; saved money and bought himself a new blue serge suit and bowler hat. He laughed at the folly of men who, week in week out, left their hard-earned money with the publicans; and sometimes, to pass an idle hour, he took pencil and paper and calculated precisely how much he saved each week through being a teetotaller. Being a natural optimist he sometimes continued this calculation through the whole span of his prospective existence and the total was breathtaking. He would die worth hundreds.

If I had only known it, this was a bad sign; a sign he was becoming stuffed up with spiritual pride and imagining himself better than his neighbours. Sooner or later, the spiritual pride grew till it called for some form of celebration. Then he took a drink—not whisky, of course; nothing like that—just a glass of some harmless drink like lager beer. That was the end of Father. By the time he had taken the first he already realized that he had made a fool of himself, took a second to forget it and a third to forget that he couldn't forget, and at last came home reeling drunk. From this on it was "The Drunkard's Progress," as in the moral prints. Next day he stayed in from work with a sick head while Mother went off to make his excuses at the works, and inside a fortnight he was poor and savage and despondent again. Once he began he drank steadily through everything down to the kitchen clock. Mother and I knew all the phases and dreaded all the dangers. Funerals were one.

"I have to go to Dunphy's to do a half-day's work," said Mother in distress. "Who's to look after Larry?"

"I'll look after Larry," Father said graciously. "The little walk will do him good."

There was no more to be said, though we all knew I didn't need anyone to look after me, and that I could quite well have stayed at home and looked after Sonny, but I was being attached to the party to act as a brake on Father. As a brake I had never achieved anything, but Mother still had great faith in me.

Next day, when I got home from school, Father was there before me and made a cup of tea for both of us. He was very good at tea, but too heavy in the hand for anything else; the way he cut bread was shocking. Afterwards, we went down the hill to the church, Father wearing his best blue serge and a bowler cocked to one side of his head with the least suggestion of the masher. To his great joy he discovered Peter Crowley among the mourners. Peter was another danger signal, as I knew well from certain experiences after Mass on Sunday morning: a mean man, as Mother said, who only went to funerals for the free drinks he could get at them. It turned out that he hadn't even known Mr. Dooley! But Father had a sort of contemptuous regard for him as one of the foolish people who wasted their good money in public-houses when they could be saving it. Very little of his own money Peter Crowley wasted!

It was an excellent funeral from Father's point of view. He had it all well studied before we set off after the hearse in the afternoon sunlight.

"Five carriages!" he exclaimed. "Five carriages and sixteen covered cars! There's one alderman, two councillors and 'tis unknown how many priests. I didn't see a funeral like this from the road since Willie Mack, the publican, died."

"Ah, he was well liked," said Crowley in his husky voice.

"My goodness, don't I know that?" snapped Father. "Wasn't the man my best friend? Two nights before he died—only two nights—he was over telling me the goings-on about the housing contract. Them fellows in the Corporation are night and day robbers. But even I never imagined he was as well connected as that."

Father was stepping out like a boy, pleased with everything: the other mourners, and the fine houses along Sunday's Well. I knew the danger signals were there in full force: a sunny day, a fine funeral, and a distinguished company of clerics and public men were bringing out all the natural vanity and flightiness of Father's character. It was with something like genuine pleasure that he saw his old friend lowered into the grave; with the sense of having performed a duty and the pleasant awareness that however much he would miss poor Mr. Dooley in the long summer evenings, it was he and not poor Mr. Dooley who would do the missing.

"We'll be making tracks before they break up," he whispered to Crowley as the grave-diggers tossed in the first shovelfuls of clay, and away he went, hopping like a goat from grassy hump to hump. The drivers, who were probably in the same state as himself, though without months of abstinence to put an edge on it, looked up hopefully.

"Are they nearly finished, Mick?" bawled one.

"All over now bar the last prayers," trumpeted Father in the tone of one who brings news of great rejoicing.

The carriages passed us in a lather of dust several hundred yards from the public-house, and Father, whose feet gave him trouble in hot weather, quickened his pace, looking nervously over his shoulder for any sign of the main body of mourners crossing the hill. In a crowd like that a man might be kept waiting.

When we did reach the pub the carriages were drawn up outside, and solemn men in black ties were cautiously bringing out consolation to mysterious females whose hands reached out modestly from behind the drawn blinds of the coaches. Inside the pub there were only the drivers and a couple of shawly women. I felt if I was to act as a brake at all, this was the time, so I pulled Father by the coattails.

"Dadda, can't we go home now?" I asked.

"Two minutes now," he said, beaming affectionately. "Just a bottle of lemonade and we'll go home."

This was a bribe, and I knew it, but I was always a child of weak character. Father ordered lemonade and two pints. I was thirsty and swallowed my drink at once. But that wasn't Father's way. He had long months of abstinence behind him and an eternity of pleasure before. He took out his pipe, blew through it, filled it, and then lit it with loud pops, his eyes bulging above it. After that he deliberately turned his back on the pint, leaned one elbow on the counter in the attitude of a man who did not know there was a pint behind him, and deliberately brushed the tobacco from his palms. He had settled down for the evening. He was steadily working through all the important funerals he had ever attended. The carriages departed and the minor mourners drifted in till the pub was half full.

"Dadda," I said, pulling his coat again, "can't we go home now?"

"Ah, your mother won't be in for a long time yet," he said benevolently enough. "Run out in the road and play, can't you?"

It struck me as very cool, the way grown-ups assumed that you could play all by yourself on a strange road. I began to get bored as I had so often been bored before. I knew Father was quite capable of lingering there till nightfall. I knew I might have to bring him home, blind drunk, down Blarney Lane, with all the old women at their doors, saying: "Mick Delaney is on it again." I knew that my mother would be half crazy with anxiety; that next day Father wouldn't go out to work; and before the end of the week she would be running down to the pawn with the clock under her shawl. I could never get over the lonesomeness of the kitchen without a clock.

I was still thirsty. I found if I stood on tiptoe I could just reach Father's glass, and the idea occurred to me that it would be interesting to know what the contents were like. He had his back to it and wouldn't notice. I took down the glass and sipped cautiously. It was a terrible disappointment. I was astonished that he could even drink such stuff. It looked as if he had never tried lemonade.

I should have advised him about lemonade but he was holding forth himself in great style. I heard him say that bands were a great addition to a funeral. He put his arms in the position of someone holding a rifle in reverse and hummed a few bars of Chopin's Funeral March. Crowley nodded reverently. I took a longer drink and began to see that porter might have its advantages. I felt pleasantly elevated and philosophic. Father hummed a few bars of the Dead March in *Saul.* It was a nice pub and a very fine funeral, and I felt sure that poor Mr. Dooley in Heaven must be highly gratified. At the same time I thought they might have given him a band. As Father said, bands were a great addition.

But the wonderful thing about porter was the way it made you stand aside, or rather float aloft like a cherub rolling on a cloud, and watch yourself with your legs crossed, leaning against a bar counter, not worrying about trifles but thinking deep, serious, grown-up thoughts about life and death. Looking at yourself like that, you couldn't help thinking after a while how funny you looked, and suddenly you got embarrassed and wanted to giggle. But by the time I had finished the pint, that phase too had passed; I found it hard to put back the glass, the counter seemed to have grown so high. Melancholia was supervening again.

"Well," Father said reverently, reaching behind him for his drink, "God rest the poor man's soul, wherever he is!" He stopped, looked first at the glass, and then at the people round him. "Hello," he said in a fairly good-humoured tone, as if he were just prepared to consider it a joke, even if it was in bad taste, "who was at this?"

There was silence for a moment while the publican and the old women looked first at Father and then at his glass.

"There was no one at it, my good man," one of the women said with an offended air. "Is it robbers you think we are?"

"Ah, there's no one here would do a thing like that, Mick," said the publican in a shocked tone.

"Well, someone did it," said Father, his smile beginning to wear off.

"If they did, they were them that were nearer it," said the woman darkly, giving me a dirty look; and at the same moment the truth began to dawn on Father. I suppose I must have looked a bit starry-eyed. He bent and shook me.

"Are you all right, Larry?" he asked in alarm.

Peter Crowley looked down at me and grinned.

"Could you beat that?" he exclaimed in a husky voice.

I could, and without difficulty. I started to get sick. Father jumped back in holy terror that I might spoil his good suit, and hastily opened the back door.

"Run! run! run!" he shouted.

I saw the sunlit wall outside with the ivy overhanging it, and ran. The intention was good but the performance was exaggerated, because I lurched right into the wall, hurting it badly, as it seemed to me. Being always very polite, I said "Pardon" before the second bout came on me. Father, still concerned for his suit, came up behind and cautiously held me while I got sick.

"That's a good boy!" he said encouragingly. "You'll be grand when you get that up."

Begor, I was not grand! Grand was the last thing I was. I gave one unmerciful wail out of me as he steered me back to the pub and put me sitting on the bench near the shawlies. They drew themselves up with an offended air, still sore at the suggestion that they had drunk his pint.

"God help us!" moaned one, looking pityingly at me, "isn't it the likes of them would be fathers?"

"Mick," said the publican in alarm, spraying sawdust on my tracks, "that child isn't supposed to be in here at all. You'd better take him home quick in case a bobby would see him."

"Merciful God!" whimpered Father, raising his eyes to heaven and clapping his hands silently as he only did when distraught, "what misfortune was on me? Or what will his mother say? . . . If women might stop at home and look after their children themselves!" he added in a snarl for the benefit of the shawlies. "Are them carriages all gone, Bill?"

"The carriages are finished long ago, Mick," replied the publican.

"I'll take him home," Father said despairingly. . . . "I'll never bring you out again," he threatened me. "Here," he added, giving me the clean handkerchief from his breast pocket, "put that over your eye."

The blood on the handkerchief was the first indication I got that I was cut, and instantly my temple began to throb and I set up another howl.

"Whisht, whisht, whisht!" Father said testily, steering me out the door. "One'd think you were killed. That's nothing. We'll wash it when we get home."

"Steady now, old scout!" Crowley said, taking the other side of me. "You'll be all right in a minute."

I never met two men who knew less about the effects of drink. The first breath of fresh air and the warmth of the sun made me groggier than ever and I pitched and rolled between wind and tide till Father started to whimper again.

"God Almighty, and the whole road out! What misfortune was on me didn't stop at my work! Can't you walk straight?"

I couldn't. I saw plain enough that, coaxed by the sunlight, every woman old and young in Blarney Lane was leaning over her half-door or sitting on her doorstep. They all stopped gabbling to gape at the strange spectacle of two sober, middle-aged men bringing home a drunken small boy with a cut over his eye. Father, torn between the shamefast desire to get me home as quick as he could, and the neighbourly need to explain that it wasn't his fault, finally halted outside Mrs. Roche's. There was a gang of old women outside a door at the opposite side of the road. I didn't like the look of them from the first. They seemed altogether too interested in me. I leaned against the wall of Mrs. Roche's cottage with my hands in my trousers pockets, thinking mournfully of poor Mr. Dooley in his cold grave on the Curragh, who would never walk down the road again, and, with great feeling, I began to sing a favourite song of Father's.

Though lost to Mononia and cold in the grave
He returns to Kincora no more.

"Wisha, the poor child!" Mrs. Roche said. "Haven't he a lovely voice, God bless him!"

That was what I thought myself, so I was the more surprised when Father said "Whisht!" and raised a threatening finger at me. He didn't seem to realize the appropriateness of the song, so I sang louder than ever.

"Whisht, I tell you!" he snapped, and then tried to work up a smile for Mrs. Roche's benefit. "We're nearly home now. I'll carry you the rest of the way."

But, drunk and all as I was, I knew better than to be carried home ignominiously like that.

"Now," I said severely, "can't you leave me alone? I can walk all right. 'Tis only my head. All I want is a rest."

"But you can rest at home in bed," he said viciously, trying to pick me up, and I knew by the flush on his face that he was very vexed.

"Ah, Jasus," I said crossly, "what do I want to go home for? Why the hell can't you leave me alone?"

For some reason the gang of old women at the other side of the road thought this very funny. They nearly split their sides over it. A gassy fury began to expand in me at the thought that a fellow couldn't have a drop taken without the whole neighbourhood coming out to make game of him.

"Who are ye laughing at?" I shouted, clenching my fists at them. "I'll make ye laugh at the other side of yeer faces if ye don't let me pass."

They seemed to think this funnier still; I had never seen such ill-mannered people.

"Go away, ye bloody bitches!" I said.

"Whisht, whisht, whisht, I tell you!" snarled Father, abandoning all pretence of amusement and dragging me along behind him by the hand. I was maddened by the women's shrieks of laughter. I was maddened by Father's bullying. I tried to dig in my heels but he was too powerful for me, and I could only see the women by looking back over my shoulder.

"Take care or I'll come back and show ye!" I shouted. "I'll teach ye to let decent people pass. Fitter for ye to stop at home and wash yeer dirty faces."

" 'Twill be all over the road," whimpered Father. "Never again, never again, not if I lived to be a thousand!"

To this day I don't know whether he was forswearing me or the drink. By way of a song suitable to my heroic mood I bawled "The Boys of Wexford," as he dragged me in home. Crowley, knowing he was not safe, made off and Father undressed me and put me to bed. I couldn't sleep because of the whirling in my head. It was very unpleasant, and I got sick again. Father came in with a wet cloth and mopped up after me. I lay in a fever, listening to him chopping sticks to start a fire. After that I heard him lay the table.

Suddenly the front door banged open and Mother stormed in with Sonny in her arms, not her usual gentle, timid self, but a wild, raging woman. It was clear that she had heard it all from the neighbours.

"Mick Delaney," she cried hysterically, "what did you do to my son?"

"Whisht, woman, whisht, whisht!" he hissed, dancing from one foot to the other. "Do you want the whole road to hear?"

"Ah," she said with a horrifying laugh, "the road knows all about it by this time. The road knows the way you filled your unfortunate innocent child with drink to make sport for you and that other rotten, filthy brute."

"But I gave him no drink," he shouted, aghast at the horrifying interpretation the neighbours had chosen to give his misfortune. "He took it while my back was turned. What the hell do you think I am?"

"Ah," she replied bitterly, "everyone knows what you are now. God forgive you, wasting our hard-earned few ha'pence on drink, and bringing up your child to be a drunken corner-boy like yourself."

Then she swept into the bedroom and threw herself on her knees by the bed. She moaned when she saw the gash over my eye. In the kitchen Sonny set up a loud bawl on his own, and a moment later Father appeared in the bedroom door with his cap over his eyes, wearing an expression of the most intense self-pity.

"That's a nice way to talk to me after all I went through," he whined. "That's a nice accusation, that I was drinking. Not one drop of drink crossed my lips the whole day. How could it when he drank it all? I'm the one that ought to be pitied, with my day ruined on me, and I after being made a show for the whole road."

But next morning, when he got up and went out quietly to work with his dinner-basket, Mother threw herself on me in the bed and kissed me. It seemed it was all my doing, and I was being given a holiday till my eye got better.

"My brave little man!" she said with her eyes shining. "It was God did it you were there. You were his guardian angel."

JOHN STEINBECK
1902–1968
The Chrysanthemums

The high grey-flannel fog of winter closed off the Salinas Valley from the sky and from all the rest of the world. On every side it sat like a lid on the mountains and made of the great valley a closed pot. On the broad, level land floor the gang plows bit deep and left the black earth shining like metal where the shares had cut. On the foothill ranches across the Salinas River, the yellow stubble fields seemed to be bathed in pale cold sunshine, but there was no sunshine in the valley now in December. The thick willow scrub along the river flamed with sharp and positive yellow leaves.

It was a time of quiet and of waiting. The air was cold and tender. A light wind blew up from the southwest so that the farmers were mildly hopeful of a good rain before long; but fog and rain do not go together.

Across the river, on Henry Allen's foothill ranch there was little work to be done, for the hay was cut and stored and the orchards were plowed up to receive the rain deeply when it should come. The cattle on the higher slopes were becoming shaggy and rough-coated.

Elisa Allen, working in her flower garden, looked down across the yard and saw Henry, her husband, talking to two men in business suits. The three of them stood by the tractor shed, each man with one foot on the side of the little Fordson. They smoked cigarettes and studied the machine as they talked.

Elisa watched them for a moment and then went back to her work. She was thirty-five. Her face was lean and strong and her eyes were as clear as water. Her figure looked blocked and heavy in her gardening costume, a man's black hat pulled low down over her eyes, clodhopper shoes, a figured print dress almost completely covered by a big corduroy apron with four big pockets to hold the snips, the trowel and scratcher, the seeds and the knife she worked with. She wore heavy leather gloves to protect her hands while she worked.

She was cutting down the old year's chrysanthemum stalks with a pair of short and powerful scissors. She looked down toward the men by the tractor shed now and then. Her face was eager and mature and handsome; even her work with the scissors was over-eager, over-powerful. The chrysanthemum stems seemed too small and easy for her energy.

She brushed a cloud of hair out of her eyes with the back of her glove, and left a smudge of earth on her cheek in doing it. Behind her stood the neat white farm house with red geraniums close-banked around it as high as the windows. It was a hard-swept looking little house, with hard-polished windows, and a clean mud-mat on the front steps.

Elisa cast another glance toward the tractor shed. The strangers were getting into their Ford coupe. She took off a glove and put her strong fingers down into the forest of new green chrysanthemum sprouts that were growing around the old roots. She spread the leaves and looked down among the close-growing stems. No aphids were there, no sowbugs or snails or cutworms. Her terrier fingers destroyed such pests before they could get started.

Elisa started at the sound of her husband's voice. He had come near quietly, and he leaned over the wire fence that protected her flower garden from cattle and dogs and chickens.

"At it again," he said. "You've got a strong new crop coming."

Elisa straightened her back and pulled on the gardening glove again. "Yes. They'll be strong this coming year." In her tone and on her face there was a little smugness.

"You've got a gift with things," Henry observed. "Some of those yellow chrysanthemums you had this year were ten inches across. I wish you'd work out in the orchard and raise some apples that big."

Her eyes sharpened. "Maybe I could do it, too. I've a gift with things, all right. My mother had it. She could stick anything in the ground and make it grow. She said it was having planters' hands that knew how to do it."

"Well, it sure works with flowers," he said.

"Henry, who were those men you were talking to?"

"Why, sure, that's what I came to tell you. They were from the Western Meat Company. I sold those thirty head of three-year-old steers. Got nearly my own price, too."

"Good," she said. "Good for you."

"And I thought," he continued, "I thought how it's Saturday afternoon, and we might go into Salinas for dinner at a restaurant, and then to a picture show—to celebrate, you see."

"Good," she repeated. "Oh, yes. That will be good."

Henry put on his joking tone. "There's fights tonight. How'd you like to go to the fights?"

"Oh, no," she said breathlessly. "No, I wouldn't like fights."

"Just fooling, Elisa. We'll go to a movie. Let's see. It's two now. I'm going to take Scotty and bring down those steers from the hill. It'll take us maybe two hours. We'll go in town about five and have dinner at the Cominos Hotel. Like that?"

"Of course I'll like it. It's good to eat away from home."

"All right, then. I'll go get up a couple of horses."

She said, "I'll have plenty of time to transplant some of these sets, I guess."

She heard her husband calling Scotty down by the barn. And a little later she saw the two men ride up the pale yellow hillside in search of the steers.

There was a little square sandy bed kept for rooting the chrysanthemums. With her trowel she turned the soil over and over, and smoothed it and patted it firm. Then she dug ten parallel trenches to receive the sets. Back at the chrysanthemum bed she pulled out the little crisp shoots, trimmed off the leaves of each one with her scissors and laid it on a small orderly pile.

A squeak of wheels and plod of hoofs came from the road. Elisa looked up. The country road ran along the dense bank of willows and cottonwoods that bordered the river, and up this road came a curious vehicle, curiously drawn. It was an old spring-wagon, with a round canvas top on it like the cover of a prairie schooner. It was drawn by an old bay horse and a little grey-and-white burro. A big stubble-bearded man sat between the cover flaps and drove the crawling team. Underneath the wagon, between the hind wheels, a lean and rangy mongrel dog walked sedately. Words were painted on the canvas, in clumsy, crooked letters. "Pots, pans, knives, sisors, lawn mores, Fixed." Two rows of articles, and the triumphantly definitive "Fixed" below. The black paint had run down in little sharp points beneath each letter.

Elisa, squatting on the ground, watched to see the crazy, loose-jointed wagon pass by. But it didn't pass. It turned into the farm road in front of her house, crooked old wheels skirling and squeaking. The rangy dog darted from between the wheels and ran ahead. Instantly the two ranch shepherds flew out at him. Then all three stopped, and with stiff and quivering tails, with taut straight legs, with ambassadorial dignity, they slowly circled, sniffing daintily. The caravan pulled up to Elisa's wire fence and stopped. Now the newcomer dog, feeling outnumbered, lowered his tail and retired under the wagon with raised hackles and bared teeth.

The man on the wagon seat called out, "That's a bad dog in a fight when he gets started."

Elisa laughed. "I see he is. How soon does he generally get started?"

The man caught up her laughter and echoed it heartily. "Sometimes not for weeks and weeks," he said. He climbed stiffly down, over the wheel. The horse and the donkey drooped like unwatered flowers.

Elisa saw that he was a very big man. Although his hair and beard were greying, he did not look old. His worn black suit was wrinkled and spotted with grease. The laughter had disappeared from his face and eyes the moment his laughing voice ceased. His eyes were dark, and they were full of the brooding that gets in the eyes of teamsters and of sailors. The calloused hands he rested on the wire fence were cracked, and every crack was a black line. He took off his battered hat.

"I'm off my general road, ma'am," he said. "Does this dirt road cut over across the river to the Los Angeles highway?"

Elisa stood up and shoved the thick scissors in her apron pocket. "Well, yes, it does, but it winds around and then fords the river. I don't think your team could pull through the sand."

He replied with some asperity, "It might surprise you what them beasts can pull through."

"When they get started?" she asked.

He smiled for a second. "Yes. When they get started."

"Well," said Elisa, "I think you'll save time if you go back to the Salinas road and pick up the highway there."

He drew a big finger down the chicken wire and made it sing. "I ain't in any hurry, ma'am. I go from Seattle to San Diego and back every year. Takes all my time. About six months each way. I aim to follow nice weather."

Elisa took off her gloves and stuffed them in the apron pocket with the scissors. She touched the under edge of her man's hat, searching for fugitive hairs. "That sounds like a nice kind of a way to live," she said.

He leaned confidentially over the fence. "Maybe you noticed the writing on my wagon. I mend pots and sharpen knives and scissors. You got any of them things to do?"

"Oh, no," she said quickly. "Nothing like that." Her eyes hardened with resistance.

"Scissors is the worst thing," he explained. "Most people just ruin scissors trying to sharpen 'em, but I know how. I got a special tool. It's a little bobbit kind of thing, and patented. But it sure does the trick."

"No. My scissors are all sharp."

"All right, then. Take a pot," he continued earnestly, "a bent pot, or a pot with a hole. I can make it like new so you don't have to buy no new ones. That's a saving for you."

"No," she said shortly. "I tell you I have nothing like that for you to do."

His face fell to an exaggerated sadness. His voice took on a whining undertone. "I ain't had a thing to do today. Maybe I won't have no supper tonight. You see I'm off my regular road. I know folks on the highway clear from Seattle to San Diego. They save their things for me to sharpen up because they know I do it so good and save them money."

"I'm sorry," Elisa said irritably. "I haven't anything for you to do."

His eyes left her face and fell to searching the ground. They roamed about until they came to the chrysanthemum bed where she had been working. "What's them plants, ma'am?"

The irritation and resistance melted from Elisa's face. "Oh, those are chrysanthemums, giant whites and yellows. I raise them every year, bigger than anybody around here."

"Kind of a long-stemmed flower? Looks like a quick puff of colored smoke?" he asked.

"That's it. What a nice way to describe them."

"They smell kind of nasty till you get used to them," he said.

"It's a good bitter smell," she retorted, "not nasty at all."

He changed his tone quickly. "I like the smell myself."

"I had ten-inch blooms this year," she said.

The man leaned farther over the fence. "Look. I know a lady down the road a piece, has got the nicest garden you ever seen. Got nearly every kind of flower but no chrysantheums. Last time I was mending a copper-bottom wash-tub for her (that's a hard job but I do it good), she said to me, 'If you ever run acrost some nice chrysantheums I wish you'd try to get me a few seeds.' That's what she told me."

Elisa's eyes grew alert and eager. "She couldn't have known much about chrysanthemums. You can raise them from seed, but it's much easier to root the little sprouts you see there."

"Oh," he said. "I s'pose I can't take none to her, then."

"Why yes you can," Elisa cried. "I can put some in damp sand, and you can carry them right along with you. They'll take root in the pot if you keep them damp. And then she can transplant them."

"She'd sure like to have some, ma'am. You say they're nice ones?"

"Beautiful," she said. "Oh, beautiful." Her eyes shone. She tore off the battered hat and shook out her dark pretty hair. "I'll put them in a flower pot, and you can take them right with you. Come into the yard."

While the man came through the picket gate Elisa ran excitedly along the geranium-bordered path to the back of the house. And she returned carrying a big red flower pot. The gloves were forgotten now. She kneeled on the ground by the starting bed and dug up the sandy soil with her fingers and scooped it into the bright new flower pot. Then she picked up the little pile of shoots she had prepared. With her strong fingers she pressed them into the sand and tamped around them with her knuckles. The man stood over her. "I'll tell you what to do," she said. "You remember so you can tell the lady."

"Yes, I'll try to remember."

"Well, look. These will take root in about a month. Then she must set them out, about a foot apart in good rich earth like this, see?" She lifted a handful of dark soil for him to look at. "They'll grow fast and tall. Now remember this: In July tell her to cut them down, about eight inches from the ground."

"Before they bloom?" he asked.

"Yes, before they bloom." Her face was tight with eagerness. "They'll grow right up again. About the last of September the buds will start."

She stopped and seemed perplexed. "It's the budding that takes the most care," she said hesitantly. "I don't know how to tell you." She looked deep into his eyes, searchingly. Her mouth opened a little, and she seemed to be listening. "I'll try to tell you," she said. "Did you ever hear of planting hands?"

"Can't say I have, ma'am."

"Well, I can only tell you what it feels like. It's when you're picking off the buds you don't want. Everything goes right down into your fingertips. You watch your fingers work. They do it themselves. You can feel how it is. They pick and pick the buds. They never make a mistake. They're with the plant. Do you see? Your fingers and the plant. You can feel that, right up your arm. They know. They never make a mistake. You can feel it. When you're like that you can't do anything wrong. Do you see that? Can you understand that?"

She was kneeling on the ground looking up at him. Her breast swelled passionately.

The man's eyes narrowed. He looked away self-consciously. "Maybe I know," he said. "Sometimes in the night in the wagon there——"

Elisa's voice grew husky. She broke in on him, "I've never lived as you do, but I know what you mean. When the night is dark—why, the stars are sharp-pointed and there's quiet. Why, you rise up and up! Every pointed star gets driven into your body. It's like that. Hot and sharp and—lovely."

Kneeling there, her hand went out toward his legs in the greasy black trousers. Her hesitant fingers almost touched the cloth. Then her hand dropped to the ground. She crouched low like a fawning dog.

He said, "It's nice, just like you say. Only when you don't have no dinner, it ain't."

She stood up then, very straight, and her face was ashamed. She held the flower pot out to him and placed it gently in his arms. "Here. Put it in your wagon, on the seat, where you can watch it. Maybe I can find something for you to do."

At the back of the house she dug in the can pile and found two old and battered aluminum saucepans. She carried them back and gave them to him. "Here, maybe you can fix these."

His manner changed. He became professional. "Good as new I can fix them." At the back of his wagon he set a little anvil, and out of an oily tool box dug a small machine hammer. Elisa came through the gate to watch him while he pounded out the dents in the kettles. His mouth grew sure and knowing. At a difficult part of the work he sucked his under-lip.

"You sleep right in the wagon?" Elisa asked.

"Right in the wagon, ma'am. Rain or shine I'm dry as a cow in there."

"It must be nice," she said. "It must be very nice. I wish women could do such things."

"It ain't the right kind of a life for a woman."

Her upper lip raised a little, showing her teeth. "How do you know? How can you tell?" she said.

"I don't know, ma'am," he protested. "Of course I don't know. Now here's your kettles, done. You don't have to buy no new ones."

"How much?"

"Oh, fifty cents'll do. I keep my prices down and my work good. That's why I have all them satisfied customers up and down the highway."

Elisa brought him a fifty-cent piece from the house and dropped it in his hand. "You might be surprised to have a rival some time. I can sharpen scissors, too. And I can beat the dents out of little pots. I could show you what a woman might do."

He put his hammer back in the oily box and shoved the little anvil out of sight. "It would be a lonely life for a woman, ma'am, and a scarey life, too, with animals creeping under the wagon all night." He climbed over the singletree, steadying himself with a hand on the burro's white rump. He settled himself in the seat, picked up the lines. "Thank you kindly, ma'am," he said. "I'll do like you told me; I'll go back and catch the Salinas road."

"Mind," she called, "if you're long in getting there, keep the sand damp."

"Sand, ma'am? . . . Sand? Oh, sure. You mean around the chrysantheums. Sure I will." He clucked his tongue. The beasts leaned luxuriously into their collars. The mongrel dog took his place between the back wheels. The wagon turned and crawled out the entrance road and back the way it had come, along the river.

Elisa stood in front of her wire fence watching the slow progress of the caravan. Her shoulders were straight, her head thrown back, her eyes half-closed, so that the scene came vaguely into them. Her lips moved silently, forming the words "Good-bye—good-bye." Then she whispered, "That's a bright direction. There's a glowing there." The sound of her whisper startled her. She shook herself free and looked about to see whether anyone had been listening. Only the dogs had heard. They lifted their heads toward her from their sleeping in the dust, and then stretched out their chins and settled asleep again. Elisa turned and ran hurriedly into the house.

In the kitchen she reached behind the stove and felt the water tank. It was full of hot water from the noonday cooking. In the bathroom she tore off her soiled clothes and flung them into the corner. And then she scrubbed herself with a little block of pumice, legs and thighs, loins and chest and arms, until her skin was scratched and red. When she had dried herself she stood in front of a mirror in her bedroom and looked at her body. She tightened her stomach and threw out her chest. She turned and looked over her shoulder at her back.

After a while she began to dress, slowly. She put on her newest underclothing and her nicest stockings and the dress which was the symbol of her prettiness. She worked carefully on her hair, penciled her eyebrows and rouged her lips.

Before she was finished she heard the little thunder of hoofs and the shouts of Henry and his helper as they drove the red steers into the corral. She heard the gate bang shut and set herself for Henry's arrival.

His step sounded on the porch. He entered the house calling, "Elisa, where are you?"

"In my room, dressing. I'm not ready. There's hot water for your bath. Hurry up. It's getting late."

When she heard him splashing in the tub, Elisa laid his dark suit on the bed, and shirt and socks and tie beside it. She stood his polished shoes on the floor beside the bed. Then she went to the porch and sat primly and stiffly down. She looked toward the river road where the willow-line was still yellow with frosted leaves so that under the high grey fog they seemed a thin band of sunshine. This was the only color in the grey afternoon. She sat unmoving for a long time. Her eyes blinked rarely.

Henry came banging out of the door, shoving his tie inside his vest as he came. Elisa stiffened and her face grew tight. Henry stopped short and looked at her. "Why—why, Elisa. You look so nice!"

"Nice? You think I look nice? What do you mean by 'nice'?"

Henry blundered on. "I don't know. I mean you look different, strong and happy."

"I am strong? Yes, strong. What do you mean 'strong'?"

He looked bewildered. "You're playing some kind of a game," he said helplessly. "It's a kind of a play. You look strong enough to break a calf over your knee, happy enough to eat it like a watermelon."

For a second she lost her rigidity. "Henry! Don't talk like that. You didn't know what you said." She grew complete again. "I'm strong," she boasted. "I never knew before how strong."

Henry looked down toward the tractor shed, and when he brought his eyes back to her, they were his own again. "I'll get out the car. You can put on your coat while I'm starting."

Elisa went into the house. She heard him drive to the gate and idle down his motor, and then she took a long time to put on her hat. She pulled it here and pressed it there. When Henry turned the motor off she slipped into her coat and went out.

The little roadster bounced along on the dirt road by the river, raising the birds and driving the rabbits into the brush. Two cranes flapped heavily over the willow-line and dropped into the river-bed.

Far ahead on the road Elisa saw a dark speck. She knew.

She tried not to look as they passed it, but her eyes would not obey. She whispered to herself sadly, "He might have thrown them off the road. That wouldn't have been much trouble, not very much. But he kept the pot," she explained. "He had to keep the pot. That's why he couldn't get them off the road."

The roadster turned a bend and she saw the caravan ahead. She swung full around toward her husband so she could not see the little covered wagon and the mismatched team as the car passed them.

In a moment it was over. The thing was done. She did not look back.

She said loudly, to be heard above the motor, "It will be good, tonight, a good dinner."

"Now you're changed again," Henry complained. He took one hand from the wheel and patted her knee. "I ought to take you in to dinner oftener. It would be good for both of us. We get so heavy out on the ranch."

"Henry," she asked, "could we have wine at dinner?"

"Sure we could. Say! That will be fine."

She was silent for a while; then she said, "Henry, at those prize fights, do the men hurt each other very much?"

"Sometimes a little, not often. Why?"

"Well, I've read how they break noses, and blood runs down their chests. I've read how the fighting gloves get heavy and soggy with blood."

He looked around at her. "What's the matter, Elisa? I didn't know you read things like that." He brought the car to a stop, then turned to the right over the Salinas River bridge.

"Do any women ever go to the fights?" she asked.

"Oh, sure, some. What's the matter, Elisa? Do you want to go? I don't think you'd like it, but I'll take you if you really want to go."

She relaxed limply in the seat. "Oh, no. No. I don't want to go. I'm sure I don't." Her face was turned away from him. "It will be enough if we can have wine. It will be plenty." She turned up her coat collar so he could not see that she was crying weakly—like an old woman.

RALPH ELLISON
1914–

King of the Bingo Game

This story was published in 1944 when Ellison was thirty years old, and it preceded his celebrated novel, *Invisible Man* (1952), by eight years. In 1965 the magazine *Book Week* asked 200 authors, critics, and editors to determine according to their collective judgment the most distinguished writers and the most distinguished novel published in America between 1945 and 1965. Of the more than 10,000 novels, *Invisible Man* was judged to be "the most distinguished single work," and Ellison was given sixth place among novelists, one place above Norman Mailer and two above Hemingway. Concerning *Invisible Man* Ellison wrote: "Indeed, if I were asked in all seriousness just what I considered to be the chief significance of *Invisible Man* as a fiction, I would reply: Its experimental attitude, and its attempt to return to the mood of personal moral responsibility for democracy which typified the best of our nineteenth-century fiction. . . . I came to believe that the writers of that period took a much greater responsibility for the condition of democracy and, indeed, their works were imaginative projections of the conflicts within the human heart which arose when the sacred principles of the Constitution and the Bill of Rights clashed with the practical exigencies of human greed and fear, hate and love. . . . Whenever we as Americans have faced serious crises we have returned to fundamentals; this, in brief, is what I have tried to do."* Undoubtedly Ellison's basic concern in this statement is that writers should take a personal moral responsibility for the condition of democracy, as Ellison has done himself.

"King of the Bingo Game" and "Flying Home" (1944) are often said to be his best short stories, and in them he clearly accepts his moral responsibility for the condition of democracy. The larger, deeper issue in "King of the Bingo Game" is the condition and place of the black in American democracy, an issue that permeates most of black American literature.** The desperate young black who tries to win the bingo game of life as arranged by the whites is defeated, and the consequences of this defeat are, as Ellison dramatizes here and in *Invisible Man,* a violation of the Constitution and the Bill of Rights. Just who is the King of the bingo game? Ellison provides his answer.

The woman in front of him was eating roasted peanuts that smelled so good that he could barely contain his hunger. He could not even sleep and wished they'd hurry and begin the bingo game. There, on his right, two fellows were drinking wine out of a bottle wrapped in a paper bag, and he could hear soft gurgling in the dark. His stomach gave a low, gnawing growl. "If this was down South," he thought, "all I'd have to do is lean over and say, 'Lady, gimme a few of those peanuts, please ma'am,' and she'd pass me the bag and never think nothing of it." Or he could ask the fellows for a drink in the same way. Folks down South stuck together that way; they didn't even have to know you. But up here it was different. Ask somebody for something, and they'd think you were crazy. Well, I ain't crazy. I'm just broke, 'cause I got no birth certificate to get a job, and Laura 'bout to die 'cause we got no money for a doctor. But I ain't crazy. And yet a pinpoint of doubt was focused in his mind as he glanced toward the screen and saw the hero stealthily entering a dark room and sending the beam of a flashlight along a wall of bookcases. This is where he finds the trapdoor, he remembered. The man would pass abruptly through the wall and find the girl tied to a bed, her legs and arms spread wide, and her clothing torn to rags. He laughed softly to himself. He had seen the picture three times, and this was one of the best scenes.

On his right the fellow whispered wide-eyed to his companion, "Man, look a-yonder!"

"Damn!"

"Wouldn't I like to have her tied up like that . . ."

"Hey! That fool's letting her loose!"

"Aw, man, he loves her."

"Love or no love!"

The man moved impatiently beside him, and he tried to involve himself in the scene. But Laura was on his mind. Tiring quickly of watching the picture he looked back to where the white beam filtered from the projection room above the balcony. It started small and grew large, specks of dust dancing in its whiteness as it reached the screen. It was strange how the beam always landed right on the screen and didn't mess up and fall somewhere else. But they had it all fixed. Everything was fixed. Now suppose when they showed that girl with her dress torn the girl started taking off the rest of her clothes, and when the guy came in he didn't untie her but kept her there and went to taking off his own clothes? *That* would be something to see. If a picture got out of hand like

* From *Shadow and Act* by Ralph Ellison (New York: Random House, 1964), copyright © 1963, 1964 by Ralph Ellison.

** See stories by Langston Hughes (p. 112) and James Baldwin (p. 140).

that those guys up there would go nuts. Yeah, and there'd be so many folks in here you couldn't find a seat for nine months? A strange sensation played over his skin. He shuddered. Yesterday he'd seen a bedbug on a woman's neck as they walked out into the bright street. But exploring his thigh through a hole in his pocket he found only goose pimples and old scars.

The bottle gurgled again. He closed his eyes. Now a dreamy music was accompanying the film and train whistles were sounding in the distance, and he was a boy again walking along a railroad trestle down South, and seeing the train coming, and running back as fast as he could go, and hearing the whistle blowing, and getting off the trestle to solid ground just in time, with the earth trembling beneath his feet, and feeling relieved as he ran down the cinder-strewn embankment onto the highway, and looking back and seeing with terror that the train had left the track and was following him right down the middle of the street, and all the white people laughing as he ran screaming . . .

"Wake up there, buddy! What the hell do you mean hollering like that? Can't you see we trying to enjoy this here picture?"

He stared at the man with gratitude.

"I'm sorry, old man, he said. "I musta been dreaming."

"Well, here, have a drink. And don't be making no noise like that, damn!"

His hands trembled as he tilted his head. It was not wine, but whiskey. Cold rye whiskey. He took a deep swoller, decided it was better not to take another, and handed the bottle back to its owner.

"Thanks, old man," he said.

Now he felt the cold whiskey breaking a warm path straight through the middle of him, growing hotter and sharper as it moved. He had not eaten all day, and it made him light-headed. The smell of the peanuts stabbed him like a knife, but he got up and found a seat in the middle aisle. But no sooner did he sit than he saw a row of intense-faced young girls, and he got up again, thinking, "You chicks musta been Lindy-hopping somewhere." He found a seat several rows ahead as the lights came on, and he saw the screen disappear behind a heavy red and gold curtain; then the curtain rising, and the man with the microphone and a uniformed attendant coming on the stage.

He felt for his bingo cards, smiling. The guy at the door wouldn't like it if he knew about his having *five* cards. Well, not everyone played the bingo game; and even with five cards he didn't have much of a chance. For Laura, though, he had to have faith. He studied the cards, each with its different numerals, punching the free center hole in each and spreading them neatly across his lap; and when the light faded he sat slouched in his seat so that he could look from his cards to the bingo wheel with but a quick shifting of his eyes.

Ahead, at the end of the darkness, the man with the microphone was pressing a button attached to a long cord and spinning the bingo wheel and calling out the number each time the wheel came to rest. And each time the voice rang out his finger raced over the cards for the number. With five cards he had to move fast. He became nervous; there were too many cards, and the man went too fast with his grating voice. Perhaps he should just select one and throw the others away. But he was afraid. He became warm. Wonder how much Laura's doctor would cost? Damn that, watch the cards! And with despair he heard the man call three in a row which he missed on all five cards. This way he'd never win. . .

When he saw the row of holes punched across the third card, he sat paralyzed and he heard the man call three more numbers before he stumbled forward, screaming.

"Bingo! Bingo!"

"Let that fool up there," someone called.

"Get up there, man!"

He stumbled down the aisle and up the steps to the stage into a light so sharp and bright that for a moment it blinded him, and he felt that he had moved into the spell of some strange, mysterious power. Yet it was as familiar as the sun, and he knew it was the perfectly familiar bingo.

The man with the microphone was saying something to the audience as he held out his card. A cold light flashed from the man's finger as the card left his hand. His knees trembled. The man stepped closer, checking the card against the numbers chalked on the board. Suppose he had made a mistake? The pomade on the man's hair made him feel faint, and he backed away. But the man was checking the card over the microphone now, and he had to stay. He stood tense, listening.

"Under the O, forty-four," the man chanted. Under the I, seven. Under the G, three. Under the B, ninety-six. Under the N, thirteen!"

His breath came easier as the man smiled at the audience.

"Yessir, ladies and gentlemen, he's one of the chosen people!"

The audience rippled with laughter and applause.

"Step right up to the front of the stage."

He moved slowly forward, wishing that the light was not so bright.

"To win tonight's jackpot of $36.90 the wheel must stop between the double zero, understand?"

He nodded, knowing the ritual from the many days and nights he had watched the winners march across the stage to press the button that controlled the spinning wheel and receive the prizes. And now he followed the instructions as though he'd crossed the slippery stage a million prize-winning times.

The man was making some kind of a joke, and he nodded vacantly. So tense had he become that he felt a sudden desire to cry and shook it away. He felt vaguely that his whole life was determined by the bingo wheel; not only that which would happen now that he was at last before it, but all that had gone before, since his birth, and his mother's birth and the birth of his father. It had always been there, even though he had not been aware of it, handing out the unlucky cards and numbers of his days. The feeling persisted, and he started quickly away. I better get down from here before I make a fool of myself, he thought.

"Here, boy," the man called. "You haven't started yet."

Someone laughed as he went hesitantly back.

"Are you all reet?"

He grinned at the man's jive talk, but no words would come, and he knew it was not a convincing grin. For suddenly he knew that he stood on the slippery brink of some terrible embarrassment.

"Where are you from, boy?" the man asked.

"Down South."

"He's from down South, ladies and gentlemen," the man said. "Where from? Speak right into the mike."

"Rocky Mont," he said. "Rock' Mont, North Car'lina."

"So you decided to come down off the mountain to the U.S.," the man laughed. He felt that the man was making a fool of him, but then something cold was placed in his hand, and the lights were no longer behind him.

Standing before the wheel he felt alone, but that was somehow right, and he remembered his plan. He would give the wheel a short quick twirl. Just a touch of the button. He had watched it many times, and always it came close to double zero when it was short and quick. He steeled himself; the fear had left, and he felt a profound sense of promise, as though he were about to be repaid for all the things he'd suffered all his life. Trembling, he pressed the button. There was a whirl of lights, and in a second he realized with finality that though he wanted to, he could not stop. It was as though he held a high-powered line in his naked hand. His nerves tightened. As the wheel increased its speed it seemed to draw him more and more into his power, as though it held his fate; and with it came a deep need to submit, to whirl, to lose himself in its swirl of color. He could not stop it now, he knew. So let it be.

The button rested snugly in his palm where the man had placed it. And now he became aware of the man beside him, advising him through the microphone, while behind the shadowy audience hummed with noisy voices. He shifted his feet. There was still that feeling of helplessness within him, making part of him desire to turn back, even now that the jackpot was right in his hand. He squeezed the button until his fist ached. Then, like the sudden shriek of a subway whistle, a doubt tore through his head. Suppose he did not spin the wheel long enough? What could he do, and how could he tell? And then he knew, even as he wondered, that as long as he pressed the button, he could control the jackpot. He and only he could determine whether or not it was to be his. Not even the man with the microphone could do anything about it now. He felt drunk. Then, as though he had come down from a high hill into a valley of people, he heard the audience yelling.

"Come down from there, you jerk!"

"Let somebody else have a chance . . ."

"Ole Jack thinks he done found the end of the rainbow . . ."

The last voice was not unfriendly, and he turned and smiled dreamily into the yelling mouths. Then he turned his back squarely on them.

"Don't take too long, boy," a voice said.

He nodded. They were yelling behind him. Those folks did not understand what had happened to him. They had been playing the bingo game day in and night out for years, trying to win rent money or hamburger change. But not one of those wise guys had discovered this wonderful thing. He watched the wheel whirling past the numbers and experienced a burst of exaltation: This is God! This is the really truly God! He said it aloud, "This is God!"

He said it with such absolute conviction that he feared he would fall fainting into the footlights. But the crowd yelled so loud that they could not hear. Those fools, he thought. I'm here trying to tell them the most wonderful secret in the world, and they're yelling like they gone crazy. A hand fell upon his shoulder.

"You'll have to make a choice now, boy. You've taken too long."

He brushed the hand violently away.

"Leave me alone, man. I know what I'm doing!"

The man looked surprised and held on to the microphone for support. And because he did not wish to hurt the man's feelings he smiled, realizing with a sudden pang that there was no way of explaining to the man just why he had to stand there pressing the button forever.

"Come here," he called tiredly.

The man approached, rolling the heavy microphone across the stage.

"Anybody can play this bingo game, right?" he said.

"Sure, but . . ."

He smiled, feeling inclined to be patient with this slick looking white man with his blue sport shirt and his sharp gabardine suit.

"That's what I thought," he said. "Anybody can win the jackpot as long as they get the lucky number, right?"

"That's the rule, but after all . . ."

"That's what I thought," he said. "And the big prize goes to the man who knows how to win it?"

The man nodded speechlessly.

"Well then, go on over there and watch me win like I want to. I ain't going to hurt nobody," he said, "and I'll show you how to win. I mean to show the whole world how it's got to be done."

And because he understood, he smiled again to let the man know that he held nothing against him for being white and impatient. Then he refused to see the man any longer and stood pressing the button, the voices of the crowd reaching him like sounds in distant streets. Let them yell. All the Negroes down there were just ashamed because he was black like them. He smiled inwardly, knowing how it was. Most of the time he was ashamed of what Negroes did himself. Well, let them be ashamed for something this time. Like him. He was like a long thin black wire that was being stretched and wound upon the bingo wheel; wound until he wanted to scream; wound, but this time himself controlling the winding and the sadness and the shame, and because he did, Laura would be all right. Suddenly the lights flickered. He staggered backwards. Had something gone wrong? All this noise. Didn't they know that although he controlled the wheel, it also controlled him, and unless he pressed the button forever and forever and ever it would stop, leaving him high and dry, dry and high on this hard high slippery hill and Laura dead? There was only one chance; he had to do whatever the wheel demanded. And gripping the button in despair, he discovered with surprize that it imparted a nervous energy. His spine tingled. He felt a certain power.

Now he faced the raging crowd with defiance, its screams penetrating his eardrums like trumpets shrieking from a juke-box. The vague faces glowing in the bingo lights gave him a sense of himself that he had never known before. He was running the show, by God! They had to react to him, for he was their luck. This is *me*, he thought. Let the bastards yell. Then someone was laughing inside him, and he realized that somehow he had forgotten his own name. It was a sad, lost feeling to lose your name, and a crazy thing to do. That name had been given him by the white man who had owned his grandfather a long lost time ago down South. But maybe those wise guys knew his name.

"Who am I?" he screamed.

"Hurry up and bingo, you jerk!"

They didn't know either, he thought sadly. They didn't even know their own names, they were all poor nameless bastards. Well, he didn't need that old name; he was reborn. For as long as he pressed the button he was The-man-who-pressed-the-button-who-held-the-prize-who-was-the-King-of-Bingo. That was the way it was, and he'd have to press the button even if nobody understood, even though Laura did not understand.

"Live!" he shouted.

The audience quieted like the dying of a huge fan.

"Live, Laura, baby. I got holt of it now, sugar. Live!"

He screamed it, tears streaming down his face. "I got nobody but YOU!"

The screams tore from his very guts. He felt as though the rush of blood to his head would burst out in baseball seams of small red droplets, like a head beaten by police clubs. Bending over he saw a trickle of blood splashing the toe of his shoe. With his free hand he searched his head. It was his nose. God, suppose something has gone wrong? He felt that the whole audience had somehow entered him and was stamping his feet in his stomach and he was unable to throw them out. They wanted the prize, that was it. They wanted the secret for themselves. But they'd never get it; he would keep the bingo wheel whirling forever, and Laura would be safe in the wheel. But would she? It had to be, because if she were not safe the wheel would cease to turn; it could not go on. He had to get away, *vomit* all, and his mind formed an image of himself running with Laura in his arms down the tracks of the subway just ahead of an A train, running desperately *vomit* with people screaming for him to come out but knowing no way of leaving the tracks because to stop would bring the train crushing down upon him and to attempt to leave across the other tracks would mean to run into a hot third rail as high as his waist which threw blue sparks that blinded his eyes until he could hardly see.

He heard singing and the audience was clapping its hands.

Shoot the liquor to him, Jim, boy!
Clap-clap-clap
Well a-calla the cop
He's blowing his top!
Shoot the liquor to him, Jim, boy!

Bitter anger grew within him at the singing. They think I'm crazy. Well let 'em laugh. I'll do what I got to do.

He was standing in an attitude of intense listening when he saw that they were watching something on the stage behind him. He felt weak. But when he turned he saw no one. If only his thumb did not ache so. Now they were applauding. And for a moment he thought that the wheel had stopped. But that was impossible, his thumb still pressed the button. Then he saw them. Two men in uniform beckoned from the end of the stage. They were coming toward him, walking in step, slowly, like a tap-dance team returning for a third encore. But their shoulders shot forward, and he backed away, looking wildly about. There was nothing to fight them with. He had only the long black cord which led to a plug somewhere back stage, and he couldn't use that because it operated the bingo wheel. He backed slowly, fixing the men with his eyes as his lips stretched over his teeth in a tight, fixed grin; moved toward the end of the stage and realizing that he couldn't go much further, for suddenly the cord became taut and he couldn't afford to break the cord. But he had to do something. The audience was howling. Suddenly he stopped dead, seeing the men halt, their legs lifted as in an interrupted step of a slow-motion dance. There was nothing to do but run in the other direction and he dashed forward, slipping and sliding. The men fell back, surprised. He struck out violently going past.

"Grab him!"

He ran, but all too quickly the cord tightened, resistingly, and he turned and ran back again. This time he slipped them, and discovered by running in a circle before the wheel he could keep the cord from tightening. But this way he had to flail his arms to keep the men away. Why couldn't they leave a man alone? He ran, circling.

"Ring down the curtain," someone yelled. But they couldn't do that. If they did the wheel flashing from the projection room would be cut off. But they had him before he could tell them so, trying to pry open his fist, and he was wrestling and trying to bring his knees into the fight and holding on to the button, for it was his life. And now he was down, seeing a foot coming down, crushing his wrist cruelly, down, as he saw the wheel whirling serenely above.

"I can't give up," he screamed. Then quietly,

in a confidential tone, "Boys, I really can't give it up."

It landed hard against his head. And in the blank moment they had it away from him, completely now. He fought them trying to pull him up from the stage as he watched the wheel spin slowly to a stop. Without surprise he saw it rest at double-zero.

"You see," he pointed bitterly.

"Sure, boy, sure, it's O. K.," one of the men said smiling.

And seeing the man bow his head to someone he could not see, he felt very, very happy; he would receive what all the winners received.

But as he warmed in the justice of the man's tight smile he did not see the man's slow wink, nor see the bow-legged man behind him step clear of the swiftly descending curtain and set himself for a blow. He only felt the dull pain exploding in his skull, and he knew even as it slipped out of him that his luck had run out on the stage.

SHERWOOD ANDERSON
1876–1941

I'm a Fool

It was a hard jolt for me, one of the most bitterest I ever had to face. And it all came about through my own foolishness, too. Even yet sometimes, when I think of it, I want to cry or swear or kick myself. Perhaps, even now, after all this time, there will be a kind of satisfaction in making myself look cheap by telling of it.

It began at three o'clock one October afternoon as I sat in the grand stand at the fall trotting and pacing meet at Sandusky, Ohio.

To tell the truth, I felt a little foolish that I should be sitting in the grand stand at all. During the summer before I had left my home town with Harry Whitehead and, with a nigger named Burt, had taken a job as swipe with one of the two horses Harry was campaigning through the fall race meets that year. Mother cried and my sister Mildred, who wanted to get a job as a school teacher in our town that fall, stormed and scolded about the house all during the week before I left. They both thought it was something disgraceful that one of our family should take a place as a swipe with race horses. I've an idea Mildred thought my taking the place would stand in the way of her getting the job she'd been working so long for.

But after all I had to work, and there was no other work to be got. A big lumbering fellow of nineteen couldn't just hang around the house and I had got too big to mow people's lawns and sell newspapers. Little chaps who could get next to people's sympathies by their sizes were always getting jobs away from me. There was one fellow who kept saying to everyone who wanted a lawn mowed or a cistern cleaned, that he was saving money to work his way through college, and I used to lay awake nights thinking up ways to injure him without being found out. I kept thinking of wagons running over him and bricks falling on his head as he walked along the street. But never mind him.

I got the place with Harry and I liked Burt fine. We got along splendid together. He was a big nigger with a lazy sprawling body and soft, kind eyes, and when it came to a fight he could hit like Jack Johnson. He had Bucephalus, a big black pacing stallion that could do 2.09 or 2.10, if he had to, and I had a little gelding named Doctor Fritz that never lost a race all fall when Harry wanted him to win.

We set out from home late in July in a box car with the two horses and after that, until late November, we kept moving along to the race meets and the fairs. It was a peachey time for me, I'll say that. Sometimes now I think that boys who are raised regular in houses, and never have a fine nigger like Burt for best friend, and go to high schools and college, and never steal anything, or get drunk a little, or learn to swear from fellows who know how, or come walking up in front of a grand stand in their shirt sleeves and with dirty horsy pants on when the races are going on and the grand stand is full of people all dressed up—What's the use of talking about it? Such fellows don't know nothing at all. They've never had no opportunity.

But I did. Burt taught me how to rub down a horse and put the bandages on after a race and steam a horse out and a lot of valuable things for any man to know. He could wrap a bandage on a horse's leg so smooth that if it had been the same color you would think it was his skin, and I guess he'd have been a big driver, too, and got to the top like Murphy and Walter Cox and the others if he hadn't been black.

Gee whizz, it was fun. You got to a county seat town, maybe say on a Saturday or Sunday, and the fair began the next Tuesday and lasted until Friday afternoon. Doctor Fritz would be, say in the 2.25 trot on Tuesday afternoon and on Thursday afternoon Bucephalus would knock 'em cold in the "free-for-all" pace. It left you a lot of time to hang around and listen to horse talk, and see Burt knock some yap cold that got too gay, and you'd find out about horses and men and pick up a lot of stuff you could use all the rest of your life, if you had some sense and salted down what you heard and felt and saw.

And then at the end of the week when the race meet was over, and Harry had run home to tend up to his livery stable business, you and Burt hitched the two horses to carts and drove slow and steady across country, to the place for the next meeting, so as to not overheat the horses, etc., etc., you know.

Gee whizz, Gosh amighty, the nice hickorynut and beechnut and oaks and other kinds of trees along the roads, all brown and red, and the good smells, and Burt singing a song that was called Deep River, and all the country girls at the windows of houses and everything. You can stick your colleges up your nose for all me. I guess I know where I got my education.

Why, one of those little burgs of towns you come to on the way, say now on a Saturday afternoon, and Burt says, "let's lay up here." And you did.

And you took the horses to a livery stable and fed them, and you got your good clothes out of a box and put them on.

And the town was full of farmers gaping, because they could see you were race horse people, and the kids maybe never see a nigger before and was afraid and run away when the two of us walked down their main street.

And that was before prohibition and all that foolishness, and so you went into a saloon, the two of you, and all the yaps come and stood around, and there was always someone pretended he was horsy and knew things and spoke up and began asking questions, and all you did was to lie and lie all you could about what horses you had, and I said I owned them, and then some fellow said, "Will you have a drink of whiskey" and Burt knocked his eye out the way he could say, offhand like, "Oh well, all right, I'm agreeable to a little nip. I'll split a quart with you." Gee whizz.

But that isn't what I want to tell my story about. We got home late in November and I promised mother I'd quit the race horses for good. There's a lot of things you've got to promise a mother because she don't know any better.

And so, there not being any work in our town any more than when I left there to go to the races, I went off to Sandusky and got a pretty good place taking care of horses for a man who owned a teaming and delivery and storage and coal and real estate business there. It was a pretty good place with good eats, and a day off each week, and sleeping on a cot in a big barn, and mostly just shovelling in hay and oats to a lot of big good-enough skates of horses, that couldn't have trotted a race with a toad. I wasn't dissatisfied and I could send money home.

And then, as I started to tell you, the fall races come to Sandusky and I got the day off and I went. I left the job at noon and had on my good clothes and my new brown derby hat, I'd just bought the Saturday before, and a stand-up collar.

First of all I went down-town and walked about with the dudes. I've always thought to myself, "put up a good front" and so I did it. I had forty dollars in my pocket and so I went into the West House, a big hotel, and walked up to the cigar stand. "Give me three twenty-five cent cigars," I said. There was a lot of horsemen and strangers and dressed-up people from other towns standing around in the lobby and in the bar, and I mingled amongst them. In the bar there was a fellow with a cane and a Windsor tie on, that it made me sick to look at him. I like a man to be a man and dress up, but not to go put on that kind of airs. So I pushed him aside, kind of rough, and had me a drink of whiskey. And then he looked at me, as though he thought maybe he'd get gay, but he changed his mind and didn't say anything. And then I had another drink of whiskey, just to show him something, and went out and had a hack out to the races, all to myself, and when I got there I bought myself the best seat I could get up in the grand stand, but didn't go in for any of these boxes. That's putting on too many airs.

And so there I was, sitting up in the grand stand as gay as you please and looking down on the swipes coming out with their horses, and with their dirty horsy pants on and the horse blankets swung over their shoulders, same as I had been doing all the year before. I liked one thing about the same as the other, sitting up there and feeling grand and being down there and looking up at the yaps and feeling grander and more important, too. One thing's about as good as another, if you take it just right. I've often said that.

Well, right in front of me, in the grand stand that day, there was a fellow with a couple of girls and they was about my age. The young fellow was a nice guy all right. He was the kind maybe that goes to college and then comes to be a lawyer or maybe a newspaper editor or something like that, but he wasn't stuck on himself. There are some of that kind are all right and he was one of the ones.

He had his sister with him and another girl and the sister looked around over his shoulder, accidental at first, not intending to start anything—she wasn't that kind—and her eyes and mine happened to meet.

You know how it is. Gee, she was a peach! She had on a soft dress, kind of a blue stuff and it looked carelessly made, but was well sewed and made and everything. I knew that much. I blushed when she looked right at me and so did she. She was the nicest girl I've ever seen in my life. She wasn't stuck on herself and she could talk proper grammar without being like a school teacher or something like that. What I mean is, she was O.K. I think maybe her father was well-to-do, but not rich to make her chesty because she was his daughter, as some are. Maybe he owned a drug store or a drygoods store in their home town, or something like that. She never told me and I never asked.

My own people are all O.K. too, when you come to that. My grandfather was Welsh and over in the old country, in Wales he was— But never mind that.

The first heat of the first race come off and the young fellow setting there with the two girls left them and went down to make a bet. I knew what he was up to, but he didn't talk big and noisy and let everyone around know he was a sport, as some do. He wasn't that kind. Well, he come back and I heard him tell the two girls what horse he'd bet on, and when the heat trotted they all half got to their feet and acted in the excited, sweaty way people do when they've got money down on a race, and the horse they bet on is up there pretty close at the end, and they think maybe he'll come on with a rush, but he never does because he hasn't got the old juice in him, come right down to it.

And then, pretty soon, the horses came out for the 2.18 pace and there was a horse in it I knew. He was a horse Bob French had in his string but Bob didn't own him. He was a horse owned by a Mr. Mathers down at Marietta, Ohio.

This Mr. Mathers had a lot of money and owned some coal mines or something and he had a swell place out in the country, and he was stuck on race horses, but was a Presbyterian or something, and I think more than likely his wife was one, too, maybe a stiffer one than himself. So he never raced his horses hisself, and the story round the Ohio race tracks was that when one of his horses got ready to go to the races he turned him over to Bob French and pretended to his wife he was sold.

So Bob had the horses and he did pretty much as he pleased and you can't blame Bob, at least, I never did. Sometimes he was out to win and sometimes he wasn't. I never cared much about that when I was swiping a horse. What I did want to know was that my horse had the speed and could go out in front, if you wanted him to.

And, as I'm telling you, there was Bob in this race with one of Mr. Mathers' horses, was named "About Ben Ahem"[1] or something like that, and was fast as a streak. He was a gelding and had a mark of 2.21, but could step in .08 or .09.

Because when Burt and I were out, as I've told you, the year before, there was a nigger, Burt knew, worked for Mr. Mathers and we went out there one day when we didn't have no race on at the Marietta Fair and our boss Harry was gone home.

And so everyone was gone to the fair but just this one nigger and he took us all through Mr. Mathers' swell house and he and Burt tapped a bottle of wine Mr. Mathers had hid in his bedroom, back in a closet, without his wife knowing, and he showed us this Ahem horse. Burt

[1] Intentional misspelling for "Abou Ben Adhem," a poem by Leigh Hunt, whose "name led all the rest."

was always stuck on being a driver but didn't have much chance to get to the top, being a nigger, and he and the other nigger gulped the whole bottle of wine and Burt got a little lit up.

So the nigger let Burt take this About Ben Ahem and step him a mile in a track Mr. Mathers had all to himself, right there on the farm. And Mr. Mathers had one child, a daughter, kinda sick and not very good looking, and she came home and we had to hustle and get About Ben Ahem stuck back in the barn.

I'm only telling you to get everything straight. At Sandusky, that afternoon I was at the fair, this young fellow with the two girls was fussed, being with the girls and losing his bet. You know how a fellow is that way. One of them was his girl and the other his sister. I had figured that out.

"Gee whizz," I says to myself, "I'm going to give him the dope."

He was mighty nice when I touched him on the shoulder. He and the girls were nice to me right from the start and clear to the end. I'm not blaming them.

And so he leaned back and I give him the dope on About Ben Ahem. "Don't bet a cent on this first heat because he'll go like an oxen hitched to a plow, but when the first heat is over go right down and lay on your pile." That's what I told him.

Well, I never saw a fellow treat any one sweller. There was a fat man sitting beside the little girl, that had looked at me twice by this time, and I at her, and both blushing, and what did he do but have the nerve to turn and ask the fat man to get up and change places with me so I could set with his crowd.

Gee whizz, craps amighty. There I was. What a chump I was to go and get gay up there in the West House bar, and just because that dude was standing there with a cane and that kind of a necktie on, to go and get all balled up and drink that whiskey, just to show off.

Of course she would know, me sitting right beside her and letting her smell of my breath. I could have kicked myself right down out of that grand stand and all around that race track and made a faster record than most of the skates of horses they had there that year.

Because that girl wasn't any mutt of a girl. What wouldn't I have give right then for a stick of chewing gum to chew, or a lozenger, or some licorice, or most anything. I was glad I had those twenty-five cent cigars in my pocket and right away I give that fellow one and lit one myself. Then that fat man got up and we changed places and there I was, plunked right down beside her.

They introduced themselves and the fellow's best girl, he had with him, was named Miss Elinor Woodbury, and her father was a manufacturer of barrels from a place called Tiffin, Ohio. And the fellow himself was named Wilbur Wessen and his sister was Miss Lucy Wessen.

I suppose it was their having such swell names that got me off my trolley. A fellow just because he has been a swipe with a race horse, and works taking care of horses for a man in the teaming, delivery, and storage business isn't any better or worse than any one else. I've often thought that, and said it too.

But you know how a fellow is. There's something in that kind of nice clothes, and the kind of nice eyes she had, and the way she had looked at me, awhile before, over her brother's shoulder, and me looking back at her, and both of us blushing.

I couldn't show her up for a boob, could I?

I made a fool of myself, that's what I did. I said my name was Walter Mathers from Marietta, Ohio, and then I told all three of them the smashingest lie you ever heard. What I said was that my father owned the horse About Ben Ahem and that he had let him out to this Bob French for racing purposes, because our family was proud and had never gone into racing that way, in our own name, I mean. Then I had got started and they were all leaning over and listening, and Miss Lucy Wessen's eyes were shining, and I went the whole hog.

I told about our place down at Marietta, and about the big stables and the grand brick house we had on a hill, up above the Ohio River, but I knew enough not to do it in no bragging way. What I did was to start things and then let them drag the rest out of me. I acted just as reluctant to tell as I could. Our family hasn't got any barrel factory, and since I've known us, we've always been pretty poor, but not asking anything of any one at that, and my grandfather, over in Wales—but never mind that.

We set there talking like we had known each

other for years and years, and I went and told them that my father had been expecting maybe this Bob French wasn't on the square, and had sent me up to Sandusky on the sly to find out what I could.

And I bluffed it through. I had found out all about the 2.18 pace, in which About Ben Ahem was to start.

I said he would lose the first heat by pacing like a lame cow and then he would come back and skin 'em alive after that. And to back up what I said I took thirty dollars out of my pocket and handed it to Mr. Wilbur Wessen and asked him, would he mind, after the first heat, to go down and place it on About Ben Ahem for whatever odds he could get. What I said was that I didn't want Bob French to see me and none of the swipes.

Sure enough the first heat come off and About Ben Ahem went off his stride, up the back stretch, and looked like a wooden horse or a sick one, and come in to be last. Then this Wilbur Wessen went down to the betting place under the grand stand and there I was with the two girls, and when that Miss Woodbury was looking the other way once, Lucy Wessen kinda, with her shoulder you know, kinda touched me. Not just tucking down, I don't mean. You know how a woman can do. They get close, but not getting gay either. You know what they do. Gee whizz.

And then they give me a jolt. What they had done, when I didn't know, was to get together, and they had decided Wilbur Wessen would bet fifty dollars, and the two girls had gone and put in ten dollars each, of their own money, too. I was sick then, but I was sicker later.

About the gelding, About Ben Ahem, and their winning their money, I wasn't worried a lot about that. It come out O.K. Ahem stepped the next three heats like a bushel of spoiled eggs going to market before they could be found out, and Wilbur Wessen had got nine to two for the money. There was something else eating at me.

Because Wilbur come back, after he had bet the money, and after that he spent most of his time talking to that Miss Woodbury, and Lucy Wessen and I was left alone together like on a desert island. Gee, if I'd only been on the square or if there had been any way of getting myself on the square. There ain't any Walter Mathers, like I said to her and them, and there hasn't ever been one, but if there was, I bet I'd go to Marietta, Ohio, and shoot him tomorrow.

There I was, big boob that I am. Pretty soon the race was over, and Wilbur had gone down and collected our money, and we had a hack downtown, and he stood us a swell supper at the West House, and a bottle of champagne beside.

And I was with that girl and she wasn't saying much, and I wasn't saying much either. One thing I know. She wasn't stuck on me because of the lie about my father being rich and all that. There's a way you know. . . . Craps amighty. There's a kind of girl, you see just once in your life, and if you don't get busy and make hay, then you're gone for good and all, and might as well go jump off a bridge. They give you a look from inside of them somewhere, and it ain't no vamping, and what it means is—you want that girl to be your wife, and you want nice things around her like flowers and swell clothes, and you want her to have the kids you're going to have, and you want good music played and no ragtime. Gee whizz.

There's a place over near Sandusky, across a kind of bay, and it's called Cedar Point. And after we had supper we went over to it in a launch, all by ourselves. Wilbur and Miss Lucy and that Miss Woodbury had to catch a ten o'clock train back to Tiffin, Ohio, because, when you're out with girls like that you can't get careless and miss any trains and stay out all night, like you can with some kinds of Janes.

And Wilbur blowed himself to the launch and it cost him fifteen cold plunks, but I wouldn't never have knew if I hadn't listened. He wasn't no tin horn kind of a sport.

Over at the Cedar Point place, we didn't stay around where there was a gang of common kind of cattle at all.

There was big dance halls and dining places for yaps, and there was a beach you could walk along and get where it was dark, and we went there.

She didn't talk hardly at all and neither did I, and I was thinking how glad I was my mother was all right, and always made us kids learn to eat with a fork at table, and not swill soup, and not be noisy and rough like a gang you see around a race track that way.

Then Wilbur and his girl went away up the

beach and Lucy and I sat down in a dark place, where there was some roots of old trees, the water had washed up, and after that the time, till we had to go back in the launch and they had to catch their trains, wasn't nothing at all. It went like winking your eye.

Here's how it was. The place we were setting in was dark, like I said, and there was the roots from that old stump sticking up like arms, and there was a watery smell, and the night was like —as if you could put your hand out and feel it—so warm and soft and dark and sweet like an orange.

I most cried and I most swore and I most jumped up and danced, I was so mad and happy and sad.

When Wilbur come back from being alone with his girl, and she saw him coming, Lucy she says, "we got to go to the train now," and she was most crying too, but she never knew nothing I knew, and she couldn't be so all busted up. And then, before Wilbur and Miss Woodbury got up to where we was, she put her face up and kissed me quick and put her head up against me and she was all quivering and—Gee whizz.

Sometimes I hope I have cancer and die. I guess you know what I mean. We went in the launch across the bay to the train like that, and it was dark, too. She whispered and said it was like she and I could get out of the boat and walk on the water, and it sounded foolish, but I knew what she meant.

And then quick we were right at the depot, and there was a big gang of yaps, the kind that goes to the fairs, and crowded and milling around like cattle, and how could I tell her? "It won't be long because you'll write and I'll write to you." That's all she said.

I got a chance like a hay barn afire. A swell chance I got.

And maybe she would write me, down at Marietta that way, and the letter would come back, and stamped on the front of it by the U. S. A. "there ain't any such guy," or something like that, whatever they stamp on a letter that way.

And me trying to pass myself off for a bigbug and a swell—to her, as decent a little body as God ever made. Craps amighty—a swell chance I got!

And then the train come in, and she got on it, and Wilbur Wessen, he come and shook hands with me, and that Miss Woodbury was nice too and bowed to me, and I at her, and the train went and I busted out and cried like a kid.

Gee, I could have run after that train and made Dan Patch look like a freight train after a wreck but, socks amighty, what was the use? Did you ever see such a fool?

I'll bet you what—if I had an arm broke right now or a train had run over my foot—I wouldn't go to no doctor at all. I'd go set down and let her hurt and hurt—that's what I'd do.

I'll bet you what—if I hadn't drunk that booze I'd never been such a boob as to go tell such a lie—that couldn't never be made straight to a lady like her.

I wish I had that fellow right here that had on a Windsor tie and carried a cane. I'd smash him for fair. Gosh darn his eyes. He's a big fool —that's what he is.

And if I'm not another you just go find me one and I'll quit working and be a bum and give him my job. I don't care nothing for working, and earning money, and saving it for no such boob as myself.

Comments and Questions

There are many things to be considered in this story, among them method, style, and meaning. The quality of the story can be easily underestimated, for here is an outstanding example of art that conceals its art. In most of his short stories and novels Anderson is interested in the drama of the inner life. It is one thing to dramatize external action; it is quite another to dramatize the inner life, and in his many stories Anderson had devised more than one way of doing it. In "I'm a Fool" he uses a first-person participating narrator by which he creates the atmosphere of the confessional. After reading the story we see how thoroughly well designed the first paragraph is to set the stage for the action to follow. It opens the story with a sort of plunging intensity which is retained to the end.

1. The story is told in dramatic monologue. What are the advantages of this method in this story? Compare Anderson's method with that used in Browning's "My Last Duchess" (p.

226) and in Eliot's "The Love Song of J. Alfred Prufrock" (p. 390).

2. The story is an example, not common in fiction, of psychological *self*-analysis. By what devices does Anderson permit the narrator to achieve it?

3. In what sense is the story dramatic? Is it told in the dramatic past or present? Do not be too sure of your first answers.

4. It has been suggested that Anderson helped "to free American short-story writers from the tyranny of mechanical plots." Explain.

5. Anderson's style obviously makes a basic contribution to the meaning of his story. Comment on the diction, sentence structure, and especially the rhythm of the narrator's speech.

6. It has been said that the story contains a good deal of poetry. Is there some truth in the comment? Do you believe that a young man like the narrator would speak so "naturally" in figures of speech? Select a few figures from the story and discuss them.

7. To what extent does the story achieve credibility? How real is this young man? Do we *feel* the tugs and quiet desperation of his inner struggle, or is the whole story mostly a tour de force?

8. Has Anderson dramatized some universal truth? Does the story have a theme of any kind beyond the young man's struggle with himself?

JOYCE CAROL OATES
1938–

In the Region of Ice

Sister Irene was a tall, deft woman in her early thirties. What one could see of her face made a striking impression—serious, hard gray eyes, a long slender nose, a face waxen with thought. Seen at the right time, from the right angle, she was almost handsome. In her past teaching positions she had drawn a little upon the fact of her being young and brilliant and also a nun, but she was beginning to grow out of that.

This was a new university and an entirely new world. She had heard—of course it was true—that the Jesuit administration of this school had hired her at the last moment to save money and to head off the appointment of a man of dubious religious commitment. She had prayed for the necessary energy to get her through this first semester. She had no trouble with teaching itself; once she stood before a classroom she felt herself capable of anything. It was the world immediately outside the classroom that confused and alarmed her, though she let none of this show—the cynicism of her colleagues, the indifference of many of the students, and, above all, the looks she got that told her nothing much would be expected of her because she was a nun. This took energy, strength. At times she had the idea that she was on trial and that the excuses she made to herself about her discomfort were only the common excuses made by guilty people. But in front of a class she had no time to worry about herself or the conflicts in her mind. She became, once and for all, a figure existing only for the benefit of others, an instrument by which the facts were communicated.

About two weeks after the semester began, Sister Irene noticed a new student in her class. He was slight and fair-haired, and his face was blank, but not blank by accident, blank on purpose, suppressed and restricted into a dumbness that looked hysterical. She was prepared for him before he raised his hand, and when she saw his arm jerk, as if he had at last lost control of it, she nodded to him without hesitation.

"Sister, how can this be reconciled with Shakespeare's vision in *Hamlet?* How can these opposing views be in the same mind?"

Students glanced at him, mildly surprised. He did not belong in the class, and this was mysterious, but his manner was urgent and blind.

"There is no need to reconcile opposing views," Sister Irene said, leaning forward against the podium. "In one play Shakespeare suggests one vision, in another play another; the plays are not simultaneous creations, and even if they were, we never demand a logical—"

"We must demand a logical consistency," the young man said. "The idea of education is itself predicated upon consistency, order, sanity—"

He had interrupted her, and she hardened her face against him—for his sake, not her own, since she did not really care. But he noticed nothing. "Please see me after class," she said.

After class the young man hurried up to her.

"Sister Irene, I hope you didn't mind my visiting today. I'd heard some things, interesting things," he said. He stared at her, and something in her face allowed him to smile. "I . . . could we talk in your office? Do you have time?"

They walked down to her office. Sister Irene sat at her desk, and the young man sat facing her; for a moment they were self-conscious and silent.

"Well, I suppose you know—I'm a Jew," he said.

Sister Irene stared at him. "Yes?" she said.

"What am I doing at a Catholic university, huh?" He grinned. "That's what you want to know."

She made a vague movement of her hand to show that she had no thoughts on this, nothing at all, but he seemed not to catch it. He was sitting on the edge of the straight-backed chair. She saw that he was young but did not really look young. There were harsh lines on either side of his mouth, as if he had misused that youthful mouth somehow. His skin was almost as pale as hers, his eyes were dark and not quite in focus. He looked at her and through her and around her, as his voice surrounded them both. His voice was a little shrill at times.

"Listen, I did the right thing today—visiting your class! God, what a lucky accident it was; some jerk mentioned you, said you were a good teacher—I thought, what a laugh! These people know about good teachers here? But yes, listen, yes, I'm not kidding—you are good. I mean that."

Sister Irene frowned. "I don't quite understand what all this means."

He smiled and waved aside her formality, as if he knew better. "Listen, I got my B. A. at Columbia, then I came back here to this crappy city. I mean, I did it on purpose, I wanted to come back. I wanted to. I have my reasons for doing things. I'm on a three-thousand-dollar fellowship," he said, and waited for that to impress her. "You know, I could have gone almost anywhere with that fellowship, and I came back home here—my home's in the city—and enrolled here. This was last year. This is my second year. I'm working on a thesis, I mean I was, my master's thesis—but the hell with that. What I want to ask you is this: Can I enroll in your class, is it too late? We have to get special permission if we're late."

Sister Irene felt something nudging her, some uneasiness in him that was pleading with her not to be offended by his abrupt, familiar manner. He seemed to be promising another self, a better self, as if his fair, childish, almost cherubic face were doing tricks to distract her from what his words said.

"Are you in English studies?" she asked.

"I was in history. Listen," he said, and his mouth did something odd, drawing itself down into a smile that made the lines about it deepen like knives, "listen, they kicked me out."

He sat back, watching her. He crossed his legs. He took out a package of cigarettes and offered her one. Sister Irene shook her head, staring at his hands. They were small and stubby and might have belonged to a ten-year-old, and the nails were a strange near-violet color. It took him awhile to extract a cigarette.

"Yeah, kicked me out. What do you think of that?"

"I don't understand."

"My master's thesis was coming along beautifully, and then this bastard—I mean, excuse me, this professor, I won't pollute your office with his name—he started making criticisms, he said some things were unacceptable, he—" The boy leaned forward and hunched his narrow shoulders in a parody of secrecy. "We had an argument. I told him some frank things, things only a broad-minded person could hear about himself. That takes courage, right? He didn't have it! He kicked me out of the master's program, so now I'm coming into English. Literature is greater than history; European history is one big pile of garbage. Sky-high. Filth and rotting corpses, right? Aristotle says that poetry is higher than history; he's right; in your class today I suddenly realized that this is my field, Shakespeare, only Shakespeare is—"

Sister Irene guessed that he was going to say that only Shakespeare was equal to him, and she caught the moment of recognition and hesitation, the half-raised arm, the keen, frowning forehead, the narrowed eyes; then he thought better of it and did not end the sentence. "The students in your class are mainly negligible, I can tell you that. You're new here, and I've been here a year—I would have finished my studies last year but my father got sick, he was hospitalized, I couldn't take exams and it was a mess —but I'll make it through English in one year or drop dead. I can do it, I can do anything. I'll take six courses at once—" He broke off, breathless. Sister Irene tried to smile. "All right then, it's settled? You'll let me in? Have I missed anything so far?"

He had no idea of the rudeness of his question. Sister Irene, feeling suddenly exhausted, said, "I'll give you a syllabus of the course."

"Fine! Wonderful!"

He got to his feet eagerly. He looked through the schedule, muttering to himself, making favorable noises. It struck Sister Irene that she was making a mistake to let him in. There were these moments when one had to make an intelligent decision. . . . But she was sympathetic with him, yes. She was sympathetic with something about him.

She found out his name the next day: Allen Weinstein.

After this she came to her Shakespeare class with a sense of excitement. It became clear to her at once that Weinstein was the most intelligent student in her class. Until he had enrolled, she had not understood what was lacking, a mind that could appreciate her own. Within a week his jagged, protean mind had alienated the other students, and though he sat in the center of the class, he seemed totally alone, encased by a miniature world of his own. When he spoke of the "frenetic humanism of the High Renaissance," Sister Irene dreaded the raised eyebrows and mocking smiles of the other students, who no longer bothered to look at Weinstein. She wanted to defend him, but she never did, because there was something rude and dismal about his knowledge; he used it like a weapon, talking passionately of Nietzsche and Goethe and Freud until Sister Irene would be forced to close discussion.

In meditation, alone, she often thought of him. When she tried to talk about him to a young nun, Sister Carlotta, everything sounded gross. "But no, he's an excellent student," she insisted. "I'm very grateful to have him in class. It's just that . . . he thinks ideas are real." Sister Carlotta, who loved literature also, had been forced to teach grade-school arithmetic for the last four years. That might have been why she said, a little sharply, "You don't think ideas are real?"

Sister Irene acquiesced with a smile, but of course she did not think so: only reality is real.

When Weinstein did not show up for class on the day the first paper was due, Sister Irene's heart sank, and the sensation was somehow a familiar one. She began her lecture and kept waiting for the door to open and for him to hurry noisily back to his seat, grinning an apology toward her—but nothing happened.

If she had been deceived by him, she made herself think angrily, it was as a teacher and not as a woman. He had promised her nothing.

Weinstein appeared the next day near the steps of the liberal arts building. She heard someone running behind her, a breathless exclamation: "Sister Irene!" She turned and saw him, panting and grinning in embarrassment. He wore a dark-blue suit with a necktie, and he looked, despite his childish face, like a little old man; there was something oddly precarious and fragile about him. "Sister Irene, I owe you an apology, right?" He raised his eyebrows and smiled a sad, forlorn, yet irritatingly conspiratorial smile. "The first paper—not in on time, and I know what your rules are. . . . You won't accept late papers, I know—that's good discipline, I'll do that when I teach too. But, unavoidably, I was unable to come to school yesterday. There are many—many—" He gulped for breath, and Sister Irene had the startling sense of seeing the real Weinstein stare out at her, a terrified prisoner behind the confident voice. "There are many complications in family life. Perhaps you are unaware—I mean—"

She did not like him, but she felt this sympathy, something tugging and nagging at her the way her parents had competed for her love so many years before. They had been whining, weak people, and out of their wet need for affection, the girl she had been (her name was Yvonne) had emerged stronger than either of them, contemptuous of tears because she had seen so many. But Weinstein was different; he was not simply weak—perhaps he was not weak at all—but his strength was confused and hysterical. She felt her customary rigidity as a teacher begin to falter. "You may turn your paper in today if you have it," she said, frowning.

Weinstein's mouth jerked into an incredulous grin. "Wonderful! Marvelous!" he said. "You are very understanding, Sister Irene, I must say. I must say . . . I didn't expect, really . . ." He was fumbling in a shabby old briefcase for the paper. Sister Irene waited. She was prepared for another of his excuses, certain that he did not have the paper, when he suddenly straightened up and handed her something. "Here! I took the liberty of writing thirty pages instead of just fifteen," he said. He was obviously quite excited; his cheeks were mottled pink and white. "You may disagree violently with my interpretation—I expect you to, in fact I'm counting on it—but let me warn you, I have the exact proof, right here in the play itself!" He was thumping at a book, his voice growing louder and shriller. Sister Irene, startled, wanted to put her hand over his mouth and soothe him.

"Look," he said breathlessly, "may I talk with you? I have a class now I hate, I loathe, I can't bear to sit through! Can I talk with you instead?"

Because she was nervous, she stared at the title page of the paper: " 'Erotic Melodies in *Romeo and Juliet*' by Allen Weinstein, Jr."

"All right?" he said. "Can we walk around here? Is it all right? I've been anxious to talk with you about some things you said in class."

She was reluctant, but he seemed not to notice. They walked slowly along the shaded campus paths. Weinstein did all the talking, of course, and Sister Irene recognized nothing in his cascade of words that she had mentioned in class. "The humanist must be committed to the totality of life," he said passionately. "This is the failing one finds everywhere in the academic world! I found it in New York and I found it here and I'm no ingénu, I don't go around with my mouth hanging open—I'm experienced, look, I've been to Europe, I've lived in Rome! I went everywhere in Europe except Germany, I don't talk about Germany . . . Sister Irene, think of the significant men in the last century, the men who've changed the world! Jews, right? Marx, Freud, Einstein! Not that I believe Marx, Marx is a madman . . . and Freud, no, my sympathies are with spiritual humanism. I believe that the Jewish race is the exclusive . . . the exclusive, what's the word, the exclusive means by which humanism will be extended. . . . Humanism begins by excluding the Jew, and now," he said with a high, surprised laugh, "the Jew will perfect it. After the Nazis, only the Jew is authorized to understand humanism, its limitations and its possibilities. So, I say that the humanist is committed to life in its totality and not just to his profession! The religious person is totally religious, he is his religion! What else? I recognize in you a humanist and a religious person—"

But he did not seem to be talking to her or even looking at her.

"Here, read this," he said. "I wrote it last night." It was a long free-verse poem, typed on a typewriter whose ribbon was worn out.

"There's this trouble with my father, a wonderful man, a lovely man, but his health—his strength is fading, do you see? What must it be to him to see his son growing up? I mean, I'm a man now, he's getting old, weak, his health is bad—it's hell, right? I sympathize with him. I'd do anything for him, I'd cut open my veins, anything for a father—right? That's why I wasn't in school yesterday," he said, and his voice dropped for the last sentence, as if he had been dragged back to earth by a fact.

Sister Irene tried to read the poem, then pretended to read it. A jumble of words dealing with "life" and "death" and "darkness" and "love." "What do you think?" Weinstein said nervously, trying to read it over her shoulder and crowding against her.

"It's very . . . passionate," Sister Irene said.

This was the right comment; he took the poem back from her in silence, his face flushed with excitement. "Here, at this school, I have few people to talk with. I haven't shown anyone else that poem." He looked at her with his dark, intense eyes, and Sister Irene felt them focus upon her. She was terrified at what he was trying to do—he was trying to force her into a human relationship.

"Thank you for your paper," she said, turning away.

When he came the next day, ten minutes late, he was haughty and disdainful. He had nothing to say and sat with his arms folded. Sister Irene took back with her to the convent a feeling of betrayal and confusion. She had been hurt. It was absurd, and yet— She spent too much time thinking about him, as if he were somehow a kind of crystallization of her own loneliness; but she had no right to think so much of him. She did not want to think of him or of her loneliness. But Weinstein did so much more than think of his predicament; he embodied it, he acted it out, and that was perhaps why he fascinated her. It was as if he were doing a dance for her, a dance of shame and agony and delight, and so long as he did it, she was safe. She felt embarrassment for him, but also anxiety; she wanted to protect him. When the dean of the graduate school questioned her about Weinstein's work, she insisted that he was an "excellent" student, though she knew the dean had not wanted to hear that.

She prayed for guidance, she spent hours on her devotions, she was closer to her vocation than she had been for some years. Life at the convent became tinged with unreality, a misty distortion that took its tone from the glowering skies of the city at night, identical smokestacks ranged against the clouds and giving to the sky the excrement of the populated and successful earth. This city was not her city, this world was not her world. She felt no pride in knowing this, it was a fact. The little convent was not like an island in the center of this noisy world, but rather a kind of hole or crevice the world did not bother with, something of no interest. The convent's rhythm of life had nothing to do with the world's rhythm, it did not violate or alarm it in any way. Sister Irene tried to draw together the fragments of her life and synthesize them somehow in her vocation as a nun: she was a nun, she was recognized as a nun and had given herself happily to that life, she had a name, a place, she had dedicated her superior intelligence to the Church, she worked without pay and without expecting gratitude, she had given up pride, she did not think of herself but only of her work and her vocation, she did not think of anything external to these, she saturated herself daily in the knowledge that she was involved in the mystery of Christianity.

A daily terror attended this knowledge, however, for she sensed herself being drawn by that student, that Jewish boy, into a relationship she was not ready for. She wanted to cry out in fear that she was being forced into the role of a Christian, and what did that mean? What could her studies tell her? What could the other nuns tell her? She was alone, no one could help; he was making her into a Christian, and to her that was a mystery, a thing of terror, something others slipped on the way they slipped on their clothes, casually and thoughtlessly, but to her a magnificent and terrifying wonder.

For days she carried Weinstein's paper, marked A, around with her; he did not come to class. One day she checked with the graduate office and was told that Weinstein had called in to say his father was ill and that he would not be able to attend classes for a while. "He's strange, I remember him," the secretary said. "He missed all his exams last spring and made a lot of trouble. He was in and out of here every day."

So there was no more of Weinstein for a while, and Sister Irene stopped expecting him to hurry into class. Then, one morning, she found a letter from him in her mailbox.

He had printed it in black ink, very carefully, as if he had not trusted handwriting. The return address was in bold letters that, like his voice, tried to grab onto her: Birchcrest Manor. Somewhere north of the city. "Dear Sister Irene," the block letters said, "I am doing well here and have time for reading and relaxing. The Manor is delightful. My doctor here is an excellent, intelligent man who has time for me, unlike my former doctor. If you have time, you might drop in on my father, who worries about me too much, I think, and explain to him what my condition is. He doesn't seem to understand. I feel about this new life the way that boy, what's his name, in *Measure for Measure,* feels about the prospects of a different life; you remember what he says to his sister when she visits him in prison, how he is looking forward to an escape into another world. Perhaps you could *explain* this to my father and he would stop worrying." The letter ended with the father's name and address, in letters that were just a little too big. Sister Irene, walking slowly down the corridor as she read the letter, felt her eyes cloud over with tears. She was cold with fear, it was something she had never experienced before. She knew what Weinstein was trying to tell her, and the desperation of his attempt made it all the more pathetic; he did not deserve this, why did God allow him to suffer so?

She read through Claudio's speech to his sister, in *Measure for Measure:*[1]

Ay, but to die, and go we know not where;
To lie in cold obstruction[2] *and to rot;*
This sensible warm motion[3] *to become*
A kneaded clod;[4] *and the delighted spirit*
To bathe in fiery floods, or to reside
In thrilling[5] *region of thick-ribbèd ice,*
To be imprison'd in the viewless[6] *winds*
And blown with restless violence round about
The pendent world; or to be worse than worst
Of those that lawless and incertain thought
Imagine howling! 'Tis too horrible!
The weariest and most loathed worldly life
That age, ache, penury, and imprisonment
Can lay on nature is a paradise
To what we fear of death.

Sister Irene called the father's number that day. "Allen Weinstein residence, who may I say is calling?" a woman said, bored. "May I speak to Mr. Weinstein? It's urgent—about his son," Sister Irene said. There was a pause at the other end. "You want to talk to his mother, maybe?" the woman said. "His mother? Yes, his mother, then. Please. It's very important."

She talked with this strange, unsuspected woman, a disembodied voice that suggested absolutely no face, and insisted upon going over that afternoon. The woman was nervous, but Sister Irene, who was a university professor, after all, knew enough to hide her own nervousness. She kept waiting for the woman to say, "Yes, Allen has mentioned you . . ." but nothing happened.

She persuaded Sister Carlotta to ride over with her. This urgency of hers was something they were all amazed by. They hadn't suspected that the set of her gray eyes could change to this blurred, distracted alarm, this sense of mission that seemed to have come to her from nowhere. Sister Irene drove across the city in the late afternoon traffic, with the high whining noises from residential streets where trees were being sawed down in pieces. She understood now the secret, sweet wildness that Christ must have felt, giving himself for man, dying for the billions of men who would never know of him and never understand the sacrifice. For the first time she approached the realization of that great act. In her troubled mind the city traffic was jumbled and yet oddly coherent, an image of the world that was always out of joint with what was happening in it, its inner history struggling with its external spectacle. This sacrifice of Christ's, so mysterious and legendary now, almost lost in time—it was that by which Christ transcended both God and man at one moment, more than man because of his fate to do what no other man could do, and more than God because no god could suffer as he did. She felt a flicker of something close to madness.

She drove nervously, uncertainly, afraid of missing the street and afraid of finding it too, for while one part of her rushed forward to confront these people who had betrayed their son, another part of her would have liked nothing so much as to be waiting as usual for the summons to dinner, safe in her room. . . . When she found the street and turned onto it, she was in a state of breathless excitement. Here lawns were bright green and marred with only a few leaves, magically clean, and the houses were enormous and pompous, a mixture of styles: ranch houses, colonial houses, French country houses, white-bricked wonders with curving glass and clumps of birch trees somehow encircled by white concrete. Sister Irene stared as if she had blundered into another world. This was a kind of heaven, and she was too shabby for it.

The Weinstein's house was the strangest one of all: it looked like a small Alpine lodge, with an inverted-V-shaped front entrance. Sister Irene drove up the black-topped driveway and let the car slow to a stop; she told Sister Carlotta she would not be long.

At the door she was met by Weinstein's mother, a small, nervous woman with hands like her son's. "Come in, come in," the woman said. She had once been beautiful, that was clear, but now in missing beauty she was not handsome or even attractive but looked ruined and perplexed, the misshapen swelling of her white-blond professionally set hair like a cap lifting up from her surprised face. "He'll be right in. Allen?" she called, "our visitor is here." They went into the living room. There was a grand piano at one end and an organ at the other. In between were scatterings of brilliant

[1] III. i. 118–132. [2] Obstruction: i.e., stiff and cold. [3] This sensible warm motion: this feeling, living body. [4] Kneaded clod; i.e., turned into earth. [5] Thrilling: freezing. [6] Viewless: invisible.

modern furniture in conversational groups, and several puffed-up white rugs on the polished floor. Sister Irene could not stop shivering.

"Professor, it's so strange, but let me say when the phone rang I had a feeling—I had a feeling," the woman said, with damp eyes. Sister Irene sat, and the woman hovered about her. "Should I call you Professor? We don't . . . you know . . . we don't understand the technicalities that go with—Allen, my son, wanted to go here to the Catholic school; I told my husband why not? Why fight? It's the thing these days, they do anything they want for knowledge. And he had to come home, you know. He couldn't take care of himself in New York, that was the beginning of the trouble. . . . Should I call you Professor?"

"You can call me Sister Irene."

"Sister Irene?" the woman said, touching her throat in awe, as if something intimate and unexpected had happened.

Then Weinstein's father appeared, hurrying. He took long, impatient strides. Sister Irene stared at him and in that instant doubted everything—he was in his fifties, a tall, sharply handsome man, heavy but not fat, holding his shoulders back with what looked like an effort, but holding them back just the same. He wore a dark suit and his face was flushed, as if he had run a long distance.

"Now," he said, coming to Sister Irene and with a precise wave of his hand motioning his wife off, "now, let's straighten this out. A lot of confusion over that kid, eh?" He pulled a chair over, scraping it across a rug and pulling one corner over, so that its brown underside was exposed. "I came home early just for this, Libby phoned me. Sister, you got a letter from him, right?"

The wife looked at Sister Irene over her husband's head as if trying somehow to coach her, knowing that this man was so loud and impatient that no one could remember anything in his presence.

"A letter—yes—today—"

"He says what in it? You got the letter, eh? Can I see it?"

She gave it to him and wanted to explain, but he silenced her with a flick of his hand. He read through the letter so quickly that Sister Irene thought perhaps he was trying to impress her with his skill at reading. "So?" he said, raising his eyes, smiling, "so what is this? He's happy out there, he says. He doesn't communicate with us any more, but he writes to you and says he's happy—what's that? I mean, what the hell is that?"

"But he isn't happy. He wants to come home," Sister Irene said. It was so important that she make him understand that she could not trust her voice; goaded by this man, it might suddenly turn shrill, as his son's did. "Someone must read their letters before they're mailed, so he tried to tell me something by making an allusion to—"

"What?"

"—an allusion to a play, so that I would know. He may be thinking suicide, he must be very unhappy—"

She ran out of breath. Weinstein's mother had begun to cry, but the father was shaking his head jerkily back and forth. "Forgive me, Sister, but it's a lot of crap, he needs the hospital, he needs help—right? It costs me fifty a day out there, and they've got the best place in the state, I figure it's worth it. He needs help, that kid, what do I care if he's unhappy? He's unbalanced!" he said angrily. "You want us to get him out again? We argued with the judge for two hours to get him in, an acquaintance of mine. Look, he can't control himself—he was smashing things here, he was hysterical. They need help, lady, and you do something about it fast! You do something! We made up our minds to do something and we did it! This letter—what the hell is this letter? He never talked like that to us!"

"But he means the opposite of what he says—"

"Then he's crazy! I'm the first to admit it." He was perspiring, and his face had darkened. "I've got no pride left this late. He's a little bastard, you want to know? He calls me names, he's filthy, got a filthy mouth—that's being smart huh? They give him a big scholarship for his filthy mouth? I went to college too, and I got out and knew something, and I for Christ's sake did something with it; my wife is an intelligent woman, a learned woman, would you guess she does book reviews for the little newspaper out here? Intelligent isn't crazy—crazy isn't intelligent. Maybe for you at the school he writes nice papers and gets an A, but out here, around the house, he can't control himself, and we got him committed!"

"But—"

"We're fixing him up, don't worry about it!" He turned to his wife. "Libby, get out of here, I mean it. I'm sorry, but get out of here, you're making a fool of yourself, go stand in the kitchen or something, you and the goddamn maid can cry on each other's shoulders. That one in the kitchen is nuts too, they're all nuts. Sister," he said, his voice lowering, "I thank you immensely for coming out here. This is wonderful, your interest in my son. And I see he admires you—that letter there. But what about that letter? If he did want to get out, which I don't admit—he was willing to be committed, in the end he said okay himself—if he wanted out I wouldn't do it. Why? So what if he wants to come back? The next day he wants something else, what then? He's a sick kid, and I'm the first to admit it."

Sister Irene felt that sickness spread to her. She stood. The room was so big it seemed it must be a public place; there had been nothing personal or private about their conversation. Weinstein's mother was standing by the fireplace, sobbing. The father jumped to his feet and wiped his forehead in a gesture that was meant to help Sister Irene on her way out. "God, what a day," he said, his eyes snatching at hers for understanding, "you know—one of those days all day long? Sister, I thank you a lot. There should be more people in the world who care about others, like you. I mean that."

On the way back to the convent, the man's words returned to her, and she could not get control of them; she could not even feel anger. She had been pressed down, forced back, what could she do? Weinstein might have been watching her somehow from a barred window, and he surely would have understood. The strange idea she had had on the way over, something about understanding Christ, came back to her now and sickened her. But the sickness was small. It could be contained.

About a month after her visit to his father, Weinstein himself showed up. He was dressed in a suit as before, even the necktie was the same. He came right into her office as if he had been pushed and could not stop.

"Sister," he said, and shook her hand. He must have seen fear in her because he smiled ironically. "Look, I'm released. I'm let out of the nut house. Can I sit down?"

He sat. Sister Irene was breathing quickly, as if in the presence of an enemy who does not know he is an enemy.

"So, they finally let me out. I heard what you did. You talked with him, that was all I wanted. You're the only one who gave a damn. Because you're a humanist and a religious person, you respect . . . the individual. Listen," he said, whispering, "it was hell out there! Hell Birchcrest Manor! All fixed up with fancy chairs and *Life* magazines lying around—and what do they do to you? They locked me up, they gave me shock treatments! Shock treatments, how do you like that, it's discredited by everybody now—they're crazy out there themselves, sadists. They locked me up, they gave me hypodermic shots, they didn't treat me like a human being! Do you know what that is," Weinstein demanded savagely, "not to be treated like a human being? They made me an animal—for fifty dollars a day! Dirty filthy swine! Now I'm an outpatient because I stopped swearing at them. I found somebody's bobby pin, and when I wanted to scream I pressed it under my fingernail and it stopped me—the screaming went inside and not out—so they gave me good reports, those sick bastards. Now I'm an outpatient and I can walk along the street and breathe in the same filthy exhaust from the buses like all you normal people! Christ," he said, and threw himself back against the chair.

Sister Irene stared at him. She wanted to take his hand, to make some gesture that would close the aching distance between them. "Mr. Weinstein—"

"Call me Allen!" he said sharply.

"I'm very sorry—I'm terribly sorry—"

"My own parents committed me, but of course they didn't know what it was like. It was hell," he said thickly, "and there isn't any hell except what other people do to you. The psychiatrist out there, the main shrink, he hates Jews, too, some of us were positive of that, and he's got a bigger nose than I do, a real beak." He made a noise of disgust. "A dirty bastard, a sick, dirty, pathetic bastard—all of them. Anyway, I'm getting out of here, and I came to ask you a favor."

"What do you mean?"

"I'm getting out. I'm leaving. I'm going up to Canada and lose myself. I'll get a job, I'll forget everything, I'll kill myself maybe—what's the difference? Look, can you lend me some money?"

"Money?"

"Just a little! I have to get to the border, I'm going to take a bus."

"But I don't have any money—"

"No money?" He stared at her. "You mean—you don't have any? Sure you have some!"

She stared at him as if he had asked her to do something obscene. Everything was splotched and uncertain before her eyes.

"You must . . . you must go back," she said, "you're making a—"

"I'll pay it back. Look, I'll pay it back, can you go to where you live or something and get it? I'm in a hurry. My friends are sons of bitches: one of them pretended he didn't see me yesterday—I stood right in the middle of the sidewalk and yelled at him, I called him some appropriate names! So he didn't see me, huh? You're the only one who understands me, you understand me like a poet, you—"

"I can't help you, I'm sorry—I . . ."

He looked to one side of her and flashed his gaze back, as if he could control it. He seemed to be trying to clear his vision.

"You have the soul of a poet," he whispered, "you're the only one. Everybody else is rotten! Can't you lend me some money, ten dollars maybe? I have three thousand in the bank, and I can't touch it! They take everything away from me, they make me into an animal. . . . You know I'm not an animal, don't you? Don't you?"

"Of course," Sister Irene whispered.

"You could get money. Help me. Give me your hand or something, touch me, help me—please. . . ." He reached for her hand and she drew back. He stared at her and his face seemed about to crumble, like a child's. "I want something from you, but I don't know what—I want something!" he cried. "Something real! I want you to look at me like I was a human being, is that too much to ask? I have a brain, I'm alive, I'm suffering—what does that mean? Does that mean nothing? I want something real and not this phony Christian love garbage—it's all in the books, it isn't personal—I want something real—look. . . ."

He tried to take her hand again, and this time she jerked away. She got to her feet. "Mr. Weinstein," she said, "please—"

"You! You nun!" he said scornfully, his mouth twisted into a mock grin. "You nun! There's nothing under that ugly outfit, right? And you're not particularly smart even though you think you are; my father has more brains in his foot than you—"

He got to his feet and kicked the chair.

"You bitch!" he cried.

She shrank back against her desk as if she thought he might hit her, but he only ran out of the office.

Weinstein: the name was to become disembodied from the figure, as time went on. The semester passed, the autumn drizzle turned into snow, Sister Irene rode to school in the morning and left in the afternoon, four days a week, anonymous in her black winter cloak, quiet and stunned. University teaching was an anonymous task, each day dissociated from the rest, with no necessary sense of unity among the teachers: they came and went separately and might for a year miss a colleague who left his office five minutes before they arrived, and it did not matter.

She heard of Weinstein's death, his suicide by drowning, from the English Department secretary, a handsome white-haired woman who kept a transistor radio on her desk. Sister Irene was not surprised; she had been thinking of him as dead for months. "They identified him by some special television way they have now," the secretary said. "They're shipping the body back. It was up in Quebec. . . ."

Sister Irene could feel a part of herself drifting off, lured by the plains of white snow to the north, the quiet, the emptiness, the sweep of the Great Lakes up to the silence of Canada. But she called that part of herself back. She could only be one person in her lifetime. That was the ugly truth, she thought, that she could not really regret Weinstein's suffering and death; she had only one life and had already given it to someone else. He had come too late to her. Fifteen years ago, perhaps, but not now.

She was only one person, she thought, walking down the corridor in a dream. Was she safe in this single person, or was she trapped? She had only one identity. She could make only one choice. What she had done or hadn't done was the result of that choice, and how was she guilty? If she could have felt guilt, she thought, she might at least have been able to feel something.

SHIRLEY JACKSON
1919–1965
The Lottery

Although this story was published before the appearance of what has come to be known as the literature of the absurd,* nevertheless the temptation to read "The Lottery" as part of this literary movement is compelling. In discussing the military draft lottery** Max Lerner says, "It is a game in which a third of the players are bound to lose, another third to win and the in-between third sentenced for a spell to uncertainty. I am speaking of the lottery drawing which pulled all 366 possible birthdays out of a big jar in a random sequence that decided the draft future of over 800,000 young Americans." And then Lerner adds a philosophical note: "We go through life on the assumption that it makes some sort of rational sense, but constantly we have to face the element of the absurd in it. To all the absurdities of the human condition the young men must now add this wild absurdity of having their fate decided by a random drawing of a birthdate which was accidental to start with." Lerner's comments serve as an appropriate way of identifying Jackson's "The Lottery" with the literature of the absurd.

The morning of June 27th was clear and sunny, with the fresh warmth of a full-summer day; the flowers were blossoming profusely and the grass was richly green. The people of the village began to gather in the square, between the post office and the bank, around ten o'clock; in some towns there were so many people that the lottery took two days and had to be started on June 26th, but in this village, where there were only about three hundred people, the whole lottery took less than two hours, so it could begin at ten o'clock in the morning and still be through in time to allow the villagers to get home for noon dinner.

The children assembled first, of course. School was recently over for the summer, and the feeling of liberty sat uneasily on most of them; they tended to gather together quietly for a while before they broke into boisterous play, and their talk was still of the classroom and the teacher, of books and reprimands. Bobby Martin had already stuffed his pockets full of stones, and the other boys soon followed his example, selecting the smoothest and roundest stones; Bobby and Harry Jones and Dickie Delacroix—the villagers pronounced this name "Dellacroy"—eventually made a great pile of stones in one corner of the square and guarded it against the raids of the other boys. The girls stood aside, talking among themselves, looking over their shoulders at the boys, and the very small children rolled in the dust or clung to the hands of their older brothers or sisters.

Soon the men began to gather, surveying their own children, speaking of planting and rain, tractors and taxes. They stood together, away from the pile of stones in the corner, and their jokes were quiet and they smiled rather than laughed. The women, wearing faded house dresses and sweaters, came shortly after their menfolk. They greeted one another and exchanged bits of gossip as they went to join their husbands. Soon the women, standing by their husbands, began to call to their children, and the children came reluctantly, having to be called four or five times. Bobby Martin ducked under his mother's grasping hand and ran, laughing, back to the pile of stones. His father spoke up sharply, and Bobby came quickly and took his place between his father and his oldest brother.

The lottery was conducted—as were the square dances, the teen-age club, the Halloween program—by Mr. Summers, who had time and energy to devote to civic activities. He was a round-faced, jovial man and he ran the coal business, and people were sorry for him, because he had no children and his wife was a

* For a definition and discussion of the literature of the absurd, see the headnote to Sartre's "The Wall" (p. 130). This story is identified with the literature of the absurd as is Kafka's story "A Hunger Artist" (p. 125). Camus's play "Caligula" (p. 619) exemplifies the theater of the absurd.

** *Miami Herald,* December 5, 1969.

scold. When he arrived in the square, carrying a black wooden box, there was a murmur of conversation among the villagers, and he waved and called, "Little late today, folks." The postmaster, Mr. Graves, followed him, carrying a three-legged stool, and the stool was put in the center of the square and Mr. Summers set the black box down on it. The villagers kept their distance, leaving a space between themselves and the stool, and when Mr. Summers said, "Some of you fellows want to give me a hand?" there was a hesitation before two men, Mr. Martin and his oldest son, Baxter, came forward to hold the box steady on the stool while Mr. Summers stirred up the papers inside it.

The original paraphernalia for the lottery had been lost long ago, and the black box now resting on the stool had been put into use even before Old Man Warner, the oldest man in town, had been born. Mr. Summers spoke frequently to the villagers about making a new box, but no one liked to upset even as much tradition as there was represented by the black box. There was a story that the present box had been made with some pieces of the box that had preceded it, the one that had been constructed when the first people settled down to make a village here. Every year, after the lottery, Mr. Summers began talking again about a new box, but every year the subject was allowed to fade off without anything's being done. The black box grew shabbier each year; by now it was no longer completely black but splintered badly along one side to show the original wood color, and in some places faded or stained.

Mr. Martin and his oldest son, Baxter, held the black box securely on the stool until Mr. Summers had stirred the papers thoroughly with his hand. Because so much of the ritual had been forgotten or discarded, Mr. Summers had been successful in having slips of paper substituted for the chips of wood that had been used for generations. Chips of wood, Mr. Summers had argued, had been all very well when the village was tiny, but now that the population was more than three hundred and likely to keep on growing, it was necessary to use something that would fit more easily into the black box. The night before the lottery, Mr. Summers and Mr. Graves made up the slips of paper and put them in the box, and it was then taken to the safe of Mr. Summers' coal company and locked up until Mr. Summers was ready to take it to the square next morning. The rest of the year, the box was put away, sometimes one place, sometimes another: it had spent one year in Mr. Graves's barn and another year underfoot in the post office, and sometimes it was set on a shelf in the Martin grocery and left there.

There was a great deal of fussing to be done before Mr. Summers declared the lottery open. There were the lists to make up—of heads of families, heads of households in each family, members of each household in each family. There was the proper swearing-in of Mr. Summers by the postmaster, as the official of the lottery; at one time, some people remembered, there had been a recital of some sort, performed by the official of the lottery, a perfunctory, tuneless chant that had been rattled off duly each year; some people believed that the official of the lottery used to stand just so when he said or sang it, others believed that he was supposed to walk among the people, but years and years ago this part of the ritual had been allowed to lapse. There had been, also, a ritual salute, which the official of the lottery had had to use in addressing each person who came up to draw from the box, but this also changed with time, until now it was felt necessary only for the official to speak to each person approaching. Mr. Summers was very good at all this; in his clean white shirt and blue jeans, with one hand resting carelessly on the black box, he seemed very proper and important as he talked interminably to Mr. Graves and the Martins.

Just as Mr. Summers finally left off talking and turned to the assembled villagers, Mrs. Hutchinson came hurriedly along the path to the square, her sweater thrown over her shoulders, and slid into place in the back of the crowd. "Clean forgot what day it was," she said to Mrs. Delacroix, who stood next to her, and they both laughed softly. "Thought my old man was out back stacking wood," Mrs. Hutchinson went on, "and then I looked out the window and the kids was gone, and then I remembered it was the twenty-seventh and came a-running." She dried her hands on her apron, and Mrs. Delacroix said, "You're in time though. They're still talking away up there."

Mrs. Hutchinson craned her neck to see through the crowd and found her husband and children standing near the front. She tapped

Mrs. Delacroix on the arm as a farewell and began to make her way through the crowd. The people separated good-humoredly to let her through; two or three people said, in voices just loud enough to be heard across the crowd, "Here comes your Missus, Hutchinson," and "Bill, she made it after all." Mrs. Hutchinson reached her husband, and Mr. Summers, who had been waiting, said cheerfully, "Thought we were going to have to get on without you, Tessie." Mrs. Hutchinson said, grinning, "Wouldn't have me leave m'dishes in the sink, now, would you, Joe?" and soft laughter ran through the crowd as the people stirred back into position after Mrs. Hutchinson's arrival.

"Well, now," Mr. Summers said soberly, "guess we better get started, get this over with, so's we can go back to work. Anybody ain't here?"

"Dunbar," several people said, "Dunbar, Dunbar."

Mr. Summers consulted his list. "Clyde Dunbar," he said. "That's right. He's broke his leg, hasn't he. Who's drawing for him?"

"Me, I guess," a woman said, and Mr. Summers turned to look at her. "Wife draws for her husband," Mr. Summers said. "Don't you have a grown boy to do it for you, Janey?" Although Mr. Summers and everyone else in the village knew the answer perfectly well, it was the business of the official of the lottery to ask such questions formally. Mr. Summers waited with an expression of polite interest while Mrs. Dunbar answered.

"Horace's not but sixteen yet," Mrs. Dunbar said regretfully. "Guess I gotta fill in for the old man this year."

"Right," Mr. Summers said. He made a note on the list he was holding. Then he asked, "Watson boy drawing this year?"

A tall boy in the crowd raised his hand. "Here," he said. "I'm drawing for m'mother and me." He blinked his eyes nervously and ducked his head as several voices in the crowd said things like "Good fellow, Jack," and "Glad to see your mother's got a man to do it."

"Well," Mr. Summers said, "guess that's everyone. Old Man Warner make it?"

"Here," a voice said, and Mr. Summers nodded.

A sudden hush fell on the crowd as Mr. Summers cleared his throat and looked at the list. "All ready?" he called. "Now, I'll read the names—heads of families first—and the men come up and take a paper out of the box. Keep the paper folded in your hand without looking at it until everyone has had a turn. Everything clear?"

The people had done it so many times that they only half listened to the directions; most of them were quiet, wetting their lips, not looking around. Then Mr. Summers raised one hand high and said, "Adams." A man disengaged himself from the crowd and came forward. "Hi, Steve," Mr. Summers said, and Mr. Adams said, "Hi, Joe." They grinned at one another humorlessly and nervously. Then Mr. Adams reached into the black box and took out a folded paper. He held it firmly by one corner as he turned and went hastily back to his place in the crowd, where he stood a little apart from his family, not looking down at his hand.

"Allen," Mr. Summers said. "Anderson . . . Bentham."

"Seems like there's no time at all between lotteries any more," Mrs. Delacroix said to Mrs. Graves in the back row. "Seems like we got through with the last one only last week."

"Time sure goes fast," Mrs. Graves said.

"Clark. . . . Delacroix."

"There goes my old man." Mrs. Delacroix said. She held her breath while her husband went forward.

"Dunbar," Mr. Summers said, and Mrs. Dunbar went steadily to the box while one of the women said, "Go on, Janey," and another said, "There she goes."

"We're next," Mrs. Graves said. She watched while Mr. Graves came around from the side of the box, greeted Mr. Summers gravely, and selected a slip of paper from the box. By now, all through the crowd there were men holding the small folded papers in their large hands, turning them over and over nervously. Mrs. Dunbar and her two sons stood together, Mrs. Dunbar holding the slip of paper.

"Harburt. . . . Hutchinson."

"Get up there, Bill," Mrs. Hutchinson said, and the people near her laughed.

"Jones."

"They do say," Mr. Adams said to Old Man Warner, who stood next to him, "that over in the north village they're talking of giving up the lottery."

Old Man Warner snorted. "Pack of crazy fools," he said. "Listening to the young folks, nothing's good enough for *them*. Next thing you know, they'll be wanting to go back to living in caves, nobody work any more, live *that* way for a while. Used to be a saying about 'Lottery in June, corn be heavy soon.' First thing you know, we'd all be eating stewed chickweed and acorns. There's *always* been a lottery," he added petulantly. "Bad enough to see young Joe Summers up there joking with everybody."

"Some places have already quit lotteries," Mrs. Adams said.

"Nothing but trouble in *that*," Old Man Warner said stoutly. "Pack of young fools."

"Martin." And Bobby Martin watched his father go forward. "Overdyke. . . . Percy."

"I wish they'd hurry," Mrs. Dunbar said to her older son. "I wish they'd hurry."

"They're almost through," her son said.

"You get ready to run tell Dad," Mrs. Dunbar said.

Mr. Summers called his own name and then stepped forward precisely and selected a slip from the box. Then he called, "Warner."

"Seventy-seventh year I been in the lottery," Old Man Warner said as he went through the crowd. "Seventy-seventh time."

"Watson." The tall boy came awkwardly through the crowd. Someone said, "Don't be nervous, Jack," and Mr. Summers said, "Take your time, son."

"Zanini."

After that, there was a long pause, a breathless pause, until Mr. Summers, holding his slip of paper in the air, said, "All right, fellows." For a minute, no one moved and then all the slips of paper were opened. Suddenly, all the women began to speak at once, saying, "Who is it?" "Who's got it?" "Is it the Dunbars?" "Is it the Watsons?" Then the voices began to say, "It's Hutchinson. It's Bill." "Bill Hutchinson's got it."

"Go tell your father," Mrs. Dunbar said to her older son.

People began to look around to see the Hutchinsons. Bill Hutchinson was standing quiet, staring down at the paper in his hand. Suddenly, Tessie Hutchinson shouted to Mr. Summers, "You didn't give him time enough to take any paper he wanted. I saw you. It wasn't fair!"

"Be a good sport, Tessie," Mrs. Delacroix called, and Mrs. Graves said, "All of us took the same chance."

"Shut up, Tessie." Bill Hutchinson said.

"Well, everybody," Mr. Summers said, "that was done pretty fast, and now we've got to be hurrying a little more to get done in time." He consulted his next list. "Bill," he said, "you draw for the Hutchinson family. You got any other households in the Hutchinsons?"

"There's Don and Eva," Mrs. Hutchinson yelled. "Make *them* take their chance!"

"Daughters draw with their husbands' families, Tessie," Mr. Summers said gently. "You know that as well as anyone else."

"It wasn't *fair*," Tessie said.

"I guess not, Joe," Bill Hutchinson said regretfully. "My daughter draws with her husband's family, that's only fair. And I've got no other family except the kids."

"Then, as far as drawing for families is concerned, it's you," Mr. Summers said in explanation, "and as far as drawing for households is concerned, that's you, too. Right?"

"Right," Bill Hutchinson said.

"How many kids, Bill?" Mr. Summers asked formally.

"Three," Bill Hutchinson said. "There's Bill, Jr., and Nancy, and little Dave. And Tessie and me."

"All right, then," Mr. Summers said. "Harry, you got their tickets back?"

Mr. Graves nodded and held up the slips of paper. "Put them in the box, then," Mr. Summers directed. "Take Bill's and put it in."

"I think we ought to start over," Mrs. Hutchinson said, as quietly as she could. "I tell you it wasn't *fair*. You didn't give him time enough to choose. Everybody saw that."

Mr. Graves had selected the five slips and put them in the box, and he dropped all the papers but those onto the ground, where the breeze caught them and lifted them off.

"Listen, everybody," Mrs. Hutchinson was saying to the people around her.

"Ready, Bill?" Mr. Summers asked, and Bill Hutchinson, with one quick glance around at his wife and children, nodded.

"Remember," Mr. Summers said, "take the slips and keep them folded until each person has taken one. Harry, you help little Dave." Mr. Graves took the hand of the little boy, who came willingly with him up to the box. "Take a paper out of the box, Davy," Mr. Summers said. Davy put his hand into the box and laughed. "Take just *one* paper," Mr. Summers said. "Harry, you hold it for him." Mr. Graves took the child's hand and removed the folded paper from the tight fist and held it while little Dave stood next to him and looked up at him wonderingly.

"Nancy next," Mr. Summers said. Nancy was twelve, and her school friends breathed heavily as she went forward, switching her skirt, and took a slip daintily from the box. "Bill, Jr.," Mr. Summers said, and Billy, his face red and his feet overlarge, nearly knocked the box over as he got a paper out. "Tessie," Mr. Summers said. She hesitated for a minute, looking around defiantly, and then set her lips and went up to the box. She snatched a paper out and held it behind her.

"Bill," Mr. Summers said, and Bill Hutchinson reached into the box and felt around, bringing his hand out at last with the slip of paper in it.

The crowd was quiet. A girl whispered. "I hope it's not Nancy," and the sound of the whisper reached the edges of the crowd.

"It's not the way it used to be," Old Man Warner said clearly. "People ain't the way they used to be."

"All right," Mr. Summers said. "Open the papers. Harry, you open little Dave's."

Mr. Graves opened the slip of paper and there was a general sigh through the crowd as he held it up and everyone could see that it was blank. Nancy and Bill, Jr., opened theirs at the same time, and both beamed and laughed, turning around to the crowd and holding their slips of paper above their heads.

"Tessie," Mr. Summers said. There was a pause, and then Mr. Summers looked at Bill Hutchinson, and Bill unfolded his paper and showed it. It was blank.

"It's Tessie," Mr. Summers said, and his voice was hushed. "Show us her paper, Bill."

Bill Hutchinson went over to his wife and forced the slip of paper out of her hand. It had a black spot on it, the black spot Mr. Summers had made the night before with the heavy pencil in the coal-company office. Bill Hutchinson held it up, and there was a stir in the crowd.

"All right, folks," Mr. Summers said. "Let's finish quickly."

Although the villagers had forgotten the ritual and lost the original black box, they still remembered to use stones. The pile of stones the boys had made earlier was ready; there were stones on the ground with the blowing scraps of paper that had come out of the box. Mrs. Delacroix selected a stone so large she had to pick it up with both hands and turned to Mrs. Dunbar. "Come on," she said. "Hurry up."

Mrs. Dunbar had small stones in both hands, and she said, gasping for breath, "I can't run at all. You'll have to go ahead and I'll catch up with you."

The children had stones already, and someone gave little Davy Hutchinson a few pebbles.

Tessie Hutchinson was in the center of a cleared space by now, and she held her hands out desperately as the villagers moved in on her. "It isn't fair," she said. A stone hit her on the side of the head.

Old Man Warner was saying, "Come on, come on, everyone." Steve Adams was in the front of the crowd of villagers, with Mrs. Graves beside him.

"It isn't fair, it isn't right," Mrs. Hutchinson screamed, and then they were upon her.

WILLIAM FAULKNER
1897–1962

A Rose for Emily

1

When Miss Emily Grierson died, our whole town went to her funeral: the men through a sort of respectful affection for a fallen monument, the women mostly out of curiosity to see the inside of her house, which no one save an old manservant—a combined gardener and cook—had seen in at least ten years.

It was a big, squarish frame house that had once been white, decorated with cupolas and spires and scrolled balconies in the heavily lightsome style of the seventies, set on what had once been our most select street. But garages and cotton gins had encroached and obliterated even the august names of that neighborhood; only Miss Emily's house was left, lifting its stubborn and coquettish decay above the cotton wagons and the gasoline pumps—an eyesore among eyesores. And now Miss Emily had gone to join the representatives of those august names where they lay in the cedar-bemused cemetery among the ranked and anonymous graves of Union and Confederate soldiers who fell at the battle of Jefferson.[1]

Alive, Miss Emily had been a tradition, a duty and a care; a sort of hereditary obligation upon the town, dating from that day in 1894 when Colonel Sartoris, the mayor—he who fathered the edict that no Negro woman should appear on the streets without an apron—remitted her taxes, the dispensation dating from the death of her father on into perpetuity. Not that Miss Emily would have accepted charity. Colonel Sartoris invented an involved tale to the effect that Miss Emily's father had loaned money to the town, which the town, as a matter of business, preferred this way of repaying. Only a man of Colonel Sartoris' generation and thought could have invented it, and only a woman could have believed it.

When the next generation, with its more modern ideas, became mayors and aldermen, this arrangement created some little dissatisfaction. On the first of the year they mailed her a tax notice. February came, and there was no reply. They wrote her a formal letter, asking her to call at the sheriff's office at her convenience. A week later the mayor wrote her himself, offering to call or send his car for her and received in reply a note on paper of an archaic shape, in a thin flowing calligraphy in faded ink, to the effect that she no longer went out at all. The tax notice was also enclosed, without comment.

They called a special meeting of the Board of Aldermen. A deputation waited upon her, knocked at the door through which no visitor had passed since she ceased giving china-painting lessons eight or ten years earlier. They were admitted by the old Negro into a dim hall from which a stairway mounted into still more shadow. It smelled of dust and disuse—a close, dank smell. The Negro led them into the parlor. It was furnished in heavy, leather-covered furniture. When the Negro opened the blinds of one window, they could see that the leather was cracked; and when they sat down, a faint dust rose sluggishly about their thighs, spinning with slow motes in the single sun-ray. On a tarnished gilt easel before the fireplace stood a crayon portrait of Miss Emily's father.

They rose when she entered—a small, fat woman in black, with a thin gold chain descending to her waist and vanishing into her belt, leaning on an ebony cane with a tarnished gold head. Her skeleton was small and spare; perhaps that was why what would have been merely plumpness in another was obesity in her. She looked bloated, like a body long submerged in motionless water, and of that pallid hue. Her eyes, lost in the fatty ridges of her face, looked like two small pieces of coal pressed into a lump of dough as they moved from one face to another while the visitors stated their errand.

She did not ask them to sit. She just stood in the door and listened quietly until the spokesman came to a stumbling halt. Then they could hear the invisible watch ticking at the end of the gold chain.

Her voice was dry and cold. "I have no taxes in Jefferson. Colonel Sartoris explained it to me. Perhaps one of you can gain access to the city records and satisfy yourselves."

"But we have. We are the city authorities, Miss Emily. Didn't you get a notice from the sheriff, signed by him?"

"I received a paper, yes," Miss Emily said. "Perhaps he considers himself the sheriff . . . I have no taxes in Jefferson."

"But there is nothing on the books to show that, you see. We must go by the—"

"See Colonel Sartoris. I have no taxes in Jefferson."

"But, Miss Emily—"

"See Colonel Sartoris." (Colonel Sartoris had been dead almost ten years.) "I have no taxes in Jefferson. Tobe!" The Negro appeared. "Show these gentlemen out."

2

So she vanquished them, horse and foot, just as she had vanquished their fathers thirty years before about the smell. That was two years after her father's death and a short time after her sweetheart—the one we believed would marry her—had deserted her. After her father's death she went out very little; after her sweetheart went away, people hardly saw her at all. A few of the ladies had the temerity to call, but were not received, and the only sign of life about the

[1] Faulkner's name for Oxford, Mississippi.

place was the Negro man—a young man then—going in and out with a market basket.

"Just as if a man—any man—could keep a kitchen properly," the ladies said; so they were not surprised when the smell developed. It was another link between the gross, teeming world and the high and mighty Griersons.

A neighbor, a woman, complained to the mayor, Judge Stevens, eighty years old.

"But what will you have me do about it, madam?" he said.

"Why, send her word to stop it," the woman said. "Isn't there a law?"

"I'm sure that won't be necessary," Judge Stevens said. "It's probably just a snake or a rat that nigger of hers killed in the yard. I'll speak to him about it."

The next day he received two more complaints, one from a man who came in diffident deprecation. "We really must do something about it, Judge. I'd be the last one in the world to bother Miss Emily, but we've got to do something." That night the Board of Aldermen met—three graybeards and one younger man, a member of the rising generation.

"It's simple enough," he said. "Send her word to have her place cleaned up. Give her a certain time to do it in, and if she don't . . ."

"Dammit, sir," Judge Stevens said, "will you accuse a lady to her face of smelling bad?"

So the next night, after midnight, four men crossed Miss Emily's lawn and slunk about the house like burglars, sniffing along the base of the brickwork and at the cellar openings while one of them performed a regular sowing motion with his hand out of a sack slung from his shoulder. They broke open the cellar door and sprinkled lime there, and in all the outbuildings. As they recrossed the lawn, a window that had been dark was lighted and Miss Emily sat in it, the light behind her, and her upright torso motionless as that of an idol. They crept quietly across the lawn and into the shadow of the locusts that lined the street. After a week or two the smell went away.

That was when people had begun to feel really sorry for her. People in our town, remembering how old lady Wyatt, her great-aunt, had gone completely crazy at last, believed that the Griersons held themselves a little too high for what they really were. None of the young men were quite good enough for Miss Emily and such. We had long thought of them as a tableau, Miss Emily a slender figure in white in the background, her father a spraddled silhouette in the foreground, his back to her and clutching a horsewhip, the two of them framed by the back-flung front door. So when she got to be thirty and was still single, we were not pleased exactly, but vindicated; even with insanity in the family she wouldn't have turned down all of her chances if they had really materialized.

When her father died, it got about that the house was all that was left to her; and in a way, people were glad. At last they could pity Miss Emily. Being left alone, and a pauper, she had become humanized. Now she too would know the old thrill and the old despair of a penny more or less.

The day after his death all the ladies prepared to call at the house and offer condolence and aid, as is our custom. Miss Emily met them at the door, dressed as usual and with no trace of grief on her face. She told them that her father was not dead. She did that for three days, with the ministers calling on her, and the doctors, trying to persuade her to let them dispose of the body. Just as they were about to resort to law and force, she broke down, and they buried her father quickly.

We did not say she was crazy then. We believed she had to do that. We remembered all the young men her father had driven away, and we knew that with nothing left, she would have to cling to that which had robbed her, as people will.

3

She was sick for a long time. When we saw her again, her hair was cut short, making her look like a girl, with a vague resemblance to those angels in colored church windows—sort of tragic and serene.

The town had just let the contracts for paving the sidewalks, and in the summer after her father's death they began the work. The construction company came with niggers and mules and machinery, and a foreman named Homer Barron, a Yankee—a big, dark, ready man, with a big voice and eyes lighter than his face. The little boys would follow in groups to hear him cuss the niggers, and the niggers singing in time to the rise and fall of picks. Pretty soon he knew everybody in town. Whenever you heard a lot of laughing anywhere about the square, Homer Barron would be in the center of the group. Presently we began to see him and Miss Emily on Sunday afternoons driving in the yellow-wheeled buggy and the matched team of bays from the livery stable.

At first we were glad that Miss Emily would have an interest, because the ladies all said, "Of course a Grierson would not think seriously of a Northerner, a day laborer." But there were still others, older people, who said that even grief could not cause a real lady to forget *noblesse oblige*[2]—without calling it *noblesse oblige*. They just said, "Poor Emily. Her kinsfolk should come to her." She had some kin in Alabama; but years ago her father had fallen out with them over the estate of old lady Wyatt, the crazy woman, and there was no communication between the two families. They had not even been represented at the funeral.

And as soon as the old people said, "Poor Emily," the whispering began. "Do you suppose it's really so?" they said to one another. "Of course it is. What else could . . ." This behind their hands; rustling of craned silk and satin behind jalousies closed upon the sun of Sunday afternoon as the thin, swift clop-clop-clop of the matched team passed: "Poor Emily."

She carried her head high enough—even when we believed that she was fallen. It was as if she demanded more than ever the recognition of her dignity as the last Grierson; as if it had wanted that touch of earthiness to reaffirm her imperviousness. Like when she bought the rat poison, the arsenic. That was over a year after they had begun to say "Poor Emily," and while the two female cousins were visiting her.

"I want some poison," she said to the druggist. She was over thirty then, still a slight woman, though thinner than usual, with cold, haughty black eyes in a face the flesh of which was strained across the temples and about the eye-sockets as you imagine a lighthouse-keeper's face ought to look. "I want some poison," she said.

"Yes, Miss Emily. What kind? For rats and such? I'd recom—"

"I want the best you have. I don't care what kind."

The druggist named several. "They'll kill anything up to an elephant. But what you want is—"

"Arsenic," Miss Emily said. "Is that a good one?"

"Is . . . arsenic? Yes, ma'am. But what you want—"

"I want arsenic."

The druggist looked down at her. She looked back at him, erect, her face like a strained flag. "Why, of course," the druggist said. "If that's what you want. But the law requires you to tell what you are going to use it for."

Miss Emily just stared at him, her head tilted back in order to look him eye for eye, until he looked away and went and got the arsenic and wrapped it up. The Negro delivery boy brought her the package; the druggist didn't come back. When she opened the package at home there was written on the box, under the skull and bones: "For rats."

4

So the next day we all said, "She will kill herself"; and we said it would be the best thing. When she had first begun to be seen with Homer Barron, we had said, "She will marry him." Then we said, "She will persuade him yet," because Homer himself had remarked—he liked men, and it was known that he drank with the younger men in the Elks' Club—that he was not a marrying man. Later we said, "Poor Emily" behind the jalousies as they passed on Sunday afternoon in the glittering buggy, Miss Emily with her head high and Homer Barron with his hat cocked and a cigar in his teeth, reins and whip in a yellow glove.

Then some of the ladies began to say that it was a disgrace to the town, and a bad example to the young people. The men did not want to interfere, but at last the ladies forced the Baptist minister—Miss Emily's people were Episcopal—to call upon her. He would never divulge what happened during that interview, but he refused to go back again. The next Sunday they again drove about the streets, and the following day the minister's wife wrote to Miss Emily's relations in Alabama.

So she had blood-kin under her roof again and we sat back to watch developments. At first

2 The obligation of the noble.

nothing happened. Then we were sure that they were to be married. We learned that Miss Emily had been to the jeweler's and ordered a man's toilet set in silver, with the letters H. B. on each piece. Two days later we learned that she had bought a complete outfit of men's clothing, including a nightshirt, and we said, "They are married." We were really glad. We were glad because the two female cousins were even more Grierson than Miss Emily had ever been.

So we were not surprised when Homer Barron—the streets had been finished some time since—was gone. We were a little disappointed that there was not a public blowing-off, but we believed that he had gone on to prepare for Miss Emily's coming, or to give her a chance to get rid of the cousins. (By that time it was a cabal, and we were all Miss Emily's allies to help circumvent the cousins). Sure enough. after another week they departed. And, as we had expected all along, within three days Homer Barron was back in town. A neighbor saw the Negro man admit him at the kitchen door at dusk one evening.

And that was the last we saw of Homer Barron. And of Miss Emily for some time. The Negro man went in and out with the market basket, but the front door remained closed. Now and then we would see her at a window for a moment, as the men did that night when they sprinkled the lime, but for almost six months she did not appear on the streets. Then we knew that this was to be expected too; as if that quality of her father which had thwarted her woman's life so many times had been too virulent and too furious to die.

When we next saw Miss Emily, she had grown fat and her hair was turning gray. During the next few years it grew grayer and grayer until it attained an even pepper-and-salt iron-gray, when it ceased turning. Up to the day of her death at seventy-four it was still that vigorous iron-gray, like the hair of an active man.

From that time on her front door remained closed, save for a period of six or seven years, when she was about forty, during which she gave lessons in china-painting. She fitted up a studio in one of the downstairs rooms, where the daughters and grand-daughters of Colonel Sartoris' contemporaries were sent to her with the same regularity and in the same spirit that they were sent to church on Sundays with a twenty-five cent piece for the collection plate. Meanwhile her taxes had been remitted.

The newer generation became the backbone and the spirit of the town, and the painting pupils grew up and fell away and did not send their children to her with boxes of color and tedious brushes and pictures cut from the ladies' magazines. The front door closed upon the last one and remained closed for good. When the town got free postal delivery, Miss Emily alone refused to let them fasten the metal numbers above her door and attach a mailbox to it. She would not listen to them.

Daily, monthly, yearly we watched the Negro grow grayer and more stooped, going in and out with the market basket. Each December we sent her a tax notice, which would be returned by the post office a week later, unclaimed. Now and then we would see her in one of the downstairs windows—she had evidently shut up the top floor of the house—like the carven torso of an idol in a niche, looking or not looking at us, we could never tell which. Thus she passed from generation to generation—dear, inescapable, impervious, tranquil, and perverse.

And so she died. Fell ill in the house filled with dust and shadows, with only a doddering Negro man to wait on her. We did not even know she was sick; we had long since given up trying to get any information from the Negro. He talked to no one, probably not even to her, for his voice had grown harsh and rusty, as if from disuse.

She died in one of the downstairs rooms, in a heavy walnut bed with a curtain, her gray head propped on a pillow yellow and moldy with age and lack of sunlight.

5

The Negro met the first of the ladies at the front door and let them in, with their hushed, sibilant voices and their quick, curious glances, and then he disappeared. He walked right through the house and out the back and was not seen again.

The two female cousins came at once. They held the funeral on the second day, with the town coming to look at Miss Emily beneath a mass of bought flowers, with the crayon face of her father musing profoundly above the bier and the ladies sibilant and macabre; and the very old men—some in their brushed Confederate uniforms—on the porch and the lawn, talking of Miss Emily as if she had been a contemporary of theirs, believing that they had danced with her and courted her perhaps, confusing time with its mathematical progression, as the old do, to whom all the past is not a diminishing road but, instead, a huge meadow which no winter ever quite touches, divided from them now by the narrow bottleneck of the most recent decade of years.

Already we knew that there was one room in that region above stairs which no one had seen in forty years, and which would have to be forced. They waited until Miss Emily was decently in the ground before they opened it.

The violence of breaking down the door seemed to fill this room with pervading dust. A thin, acrid pall as of the tomb seemed to lie everywhere upon this room decked and furnished as for a bridal: upon the valance curtains of faded rose color, upon the rose-shaded lights, upon the dressing table, upon the delicate array of crystal and the man's toilet things backed with tarnished silver, silver so tarnished that the monogram was obscured. Among them lay a collar and tie, as if they had just been removed, which, lifted, left upon the surface a pale crescent in the dust. Upon a chair hung the suit, carefully folded; beneath it the two mute shoes and the discarded socks.

The man himself lay in the bed.

For a long while we just stood there, looking down at the profound and fleshless grin. The body had apparently once lain in the attitude of an embrace, but now the long sleep that outlasts love, that conquers even the grimace of love, had cuckolded him. What was left of him, rotted beneath what was left of the nightshirt, had become inextricable from the bed in which he lay; and upon him and upon the pillow beside him lay that even coating of the patient and biding dust.

Then we noticed that in the second pillow was the indentation of a head. One of us lifted something from it, and leaning forward, that faint and invisible dust dry and acrid in the nostrils, we saw a long strand of iron-gray hair.

GUY DE MAUPASSANT
1850–1893

La Mère Sauvage[1]

Like most of Maupassant's stories, this one has been praised for its compression and suggestiveness, and for the management of detail and economy of means. Indeed, the author's objective, matter-of-fact tone, and simple narrative technique may trap the reader on the literal level until he examines the meaning of the rabbit and the stone, especially the meaning of the final sentence, "And I picked up a little stone, still blackened by the flames," which not only explains the transformation of the mother but also reveals Maupassant's universal theme of the effect of the brutality of war on human beings.

I had not been at Virelogne for fifteen years. I went back there in the autumn, to shoot with my friend Serval, who had at last rebuilt his château, which had been destroyed by the Prussians.

I loved that district very much. It is one of those corners of the world which have a sensuous charm for the eyes. You love it with a bodily love. We, whom the country seduces, we keep tender memories for certain springs, for certain woods, for certain pools, for certain hills, seen very often, and which have stirred us like joyful events. Sometimes our thoughts turn back towards a corner in a forest, or the end of a bank, or an orchard powdered with flowers, seen but a single time, on some gay day; yet remaining in our hearts like the images of certain women met in the street on a spring morning, with bright transparent dresses; and leaving in soul and body an unappeased desire which is not to be forgotten, a feeling that you have just rubbed elbows with happiness.

At Virelogne I loved the whole countryside, dotted with little woods, and crossed by brooks which flashed in the sun and looked like veins, carrying blood to the earth. You fished in them

[1] The Savage Mother.

for crawfish, trout, and eels! Divine happiness! You could bathe in places, and you often found snipe among the high grass which grew along the borders of these slender watercourses.

I was walking, lightly as a goat, watching my two dogs ranging before me. Serval, a hundred metres to my right, was beating a field of lucern. I turned the thicket which forms the boundary of the wood of Sandres, and I saw a cottage in ruins.

All of a sudden, I remembered it as I had seen it the last time, in 1869, neat, covered with vines, with chickens before the door. What is sadder than a dead house, with its skeleton standing upright, bare and sinister?

I also remembered that in it, one very tiring day, the good woman had given me a glass of wine to drink, and that Serval had then told me the history of its inhabitants. The father, an old poacher, had been killed by the gendarmes. The son, whom I had once seen, was a tall, dry fellow who also passed for a ferocious destroyer of game. People called them *"les Sauvage."*

Was that a name or a nickname?

I hailed Serval. He came up with his long strides like a crane.

I asked him:

"What's become of those people?"

And he told me this story:

When war was declared, the son Sauvage, who was then thirty-three years old, enlisted, leaving his mother alone in the house. People did not pity the old woman very much because she had money; they knew it.

But she remained quite alone in that isolated dwelling so far from the village, on the edge of the wood. She was not afraid, however, being of the same strain as her menfolk; a hardy old woman, tall and thin, who laughed seldom, and with whom one never jested. The women of the fields laugh but little in any case; that is men's business, that! But they themselves have sad and narrowed hearts, leading a melancholy, gloomy life. The peasants learn a little boisterous merriment at the tavern, but their helpmates remain grave, with countenances which are always severe. The muscles of their faces have never learned the movements of the laugh.

La Mère Sauvage continued her ordinary existence in her cottage, which was soon covered by the snows. She came to the village once a week, to get bread and a little meat; then she returned into her house. As there was talk of wolves, she went out with a gun upon her back —her son's gun, rusty, and with the butt worn by the rubbing of the hand; and she was strange to see, the tall "Sauvage," a little bent, going with slow strides over the snow, the muzzle of the piece extending beyond the black headdress, which pressed close to her head and imprisoned her white hair, which no one had ever seen.

One day a Prussian force arrived. It was billeted upon the inhabitants, according to the property and resources of each. Four were allotted to the old woman, who was known to be rich.

They were four great boys with blond skin, with blond beards, with blue eyes, who had remained stout notwithstanding the fatigues which they had endured already, and who also, though in a conquered country, had remained kind and gentle. Alone with this aged woman, they showed themselves full of consideration, sparing her, as much as they could, all expenses and fatigue. They would be seen, all four of them, making their toilet around the well, of a morning, in their shirt-sleeves, splashing with great swishes of water, under the crude daylight of the snowy weather, their pink-white Northman's flesh, while La Mère Sauvage went and came, making ready the soup. Then they would be seen cleaning the kitchen, rubbing the tiles, splitting wood, peeling potatoes, doing up all the housework, like four good sons about their mother.

But the old woman thought always of her own, so tall and thin, with his hooked nose and his brown eyes and his heavy mustache which made a roll of black hairs upon his lip. She asked each day of each of the soldiers who were installed beside her hearth:

"Do you know where the French Marching Regiment No. 23 was sent? My boy is in it."

They answered, "No, not know, not know at all." And, understanding her pain and her uneasiness (they, who had mothers too, there at home), they rendered her a thousand little services. She loved them well, moreover, her four enemies, since the peasantry feels no patriotic hatred; that belongs to the upper class alone. The humble, those who pay the most, because they are poor, and because every new burden crushes them down; those who are killed in masses, who make the true cannon's-meat, because they are so many; those, in fine, who suffer most cruelly the atrocious miseries of war, because they are the feeblest, and offer least resistance—they hardly understand at all those bellicose ardors, that excitable sense of honor, or those pretended political combinations which in six months exhaust two nations, the conqueror with the conquered.

They said on the countryside in speaking of the Germans of La Mère Sauvage:

"There are four who have found a soft place."

Now, one morning, when the old woman was alone in the house, she perceived far off on the plain a man coming towards her dwelling. Soon she recognized him; it was the postman charged to distribute the letters. He gave her a folded paper, and she drew out of her case the spectacles which she used for sewing; then she read:

MADAME SAUVAGE,—The present letter is to tell you sad news. Your boy Victor was killed yesterday by a shell which near cut him in two. I was just by, seeing that we stood next each other in the company, and he would talk to me about you to let you know on the same day if anything happened to him.

I took his watch, which was in his pocket, to bring it back to you when the war is done.

I salute you very friendly.

CÉSAIRE RIVOT

Soldier of the 2nd class, March. Reg. No. 23

The letter was dated three weeks back.

She did not cry at all. She remained motionless, so seized and stupefied that she did not even suffer as yet. She thought: "V'la Victor who is killed now." Then little by little the tears mounted to her eyes, and the sorrow caught her heart. The ideas came to her, one by one, dreadful, torturing. She would never kiss him again, her child, her big boy, never again! The gendarmes had killed the father, the Prussians had killed the son. He had been cut in two by a cannon-ball. She seemed to see the thing, the horrible thing: the head falling, the eyes open, while he chewed the corner of his big mustache as he always did in moments of anger.

What had they done with his body afterwards? If they had only let her have her boy back as they had given her back her husband—with the bullet in the middle of his forehead!

But she heard a noise of voices. It was the Prussians returning from the village. She hid her letter very quickly in her pocket, and she received them quietly, with her ordinary face, having had time to wipe her eyes.

They were laughing, all four, delighted, since they brought with them a fine rabbit—stolen, doubtless—and they made signs to the old woman that there was to be something good to eat.

She set herself to work at once to prepare breakfast; but when it came to killing the rabbit, her heart failed her. And yet it was not the first. One of the soldiers struck it down with a blow of his fist behind the ears.

The beast once dead, she separated the red body from the skin; but the sight of the blood which she was touching, and which covered her hands, of the warm blood which she felt cooling and coagulating, made her tremble from head to foot; and she kept seeing her big boy cut in two, and quite red also, like this still-palpitating animal.

She set herself at table with the Prussians, but she could not eat, not even a mouthful. They devoured the rabbit without troubling themselves about her. She looked at them askance, without speaking, ripening a thought, and with a face so impassible that they perceived nothing.

All of a sudden she said: "I don't even know your names, and here's a whole month that we've been together." They understood, not without difficulty, what she wanted, and told their names. That was not sufficient; she had them written for her on a paper, with the addresses of their families, and, resting her spectacles on her great nose, she considered that strange handwriting, then folded the sheet and put it in her pocket, on top of the letter which told her of the death of her son.

When the meal was ended, she said to the men:

"I am going to work for you."

And she began to carry up hay into the loft where they slept.

They were astonished at her taking all this trouble; she explained to them that thus they would not be so cold; and they helped her. They heaped the trusses of hay as high as the straw roof; and in that manner they made a sort of great chamber with four walls of fodder, warm and perfumed, where they should sleep splendidly.

At dinner, one of them was worried to see

that La Mère Sauvage still ate nothing. She told him that she had the cramps. Then she kindled a good fire to warm herself up, and the four Germans mounted to their lodging-place by the ladder which served them every night for this purpose.

As soon as they closed the trap, the old woman removed the ladder, then opened the outside door noiselessly, and went back to look for more bundles of straw, with which she filled her kitchen. She went barefoot in the snow, so softly that no sound was heard. From time to time she listened to the sonorous and unequal snoring of the four soldiers who were fast asleep.

When she judged her preparations to be sufficient, she threw one of the bundles into the fireplace, and when it was alight she scattered it all over the others. Then she went outside again and looked.

In a few seconds the whole interior of the cottage was illumined with a violent brightness and became a dreadful brasier, a gigantic fiery furnace, whose brilliance spouted out of the narrow window and threw a glittering beam upon the snow.

Then a great cry issued from the summit of the house; it was a clamor of human shriekings, heart-rending calls of anguish and of fear. At last, the trap having fallen in, a whirlwind of fire shot up into the loft, pierced the straw roof, rose to the sky like the immense flame of a torch; and all the cottage flared.

Nothing more was heard therein but the crackling of the fire, the crackling sound of the walls, the falling of the rafters. All of a sudden the roof fell in, and the burning carcass of the dwelling hurled a great plume of sparks into the air, amid a cloud of smoke.

The country, all white, lit up by the fire, shone like a cloth of silver tinted with red.

A bell, far off, began to toll.

The old 'Sauvage" remained standing before her ruined dwelling, armed with her gun, her son's gun, for fear lest one of those men might escape.

When she saw that it was ended, she threw her weapon into the brasier. A loud report rang back.

People were coming, the peasants, the Prussians.

They found the woman seated on the trunk of a tree, calm and satisfied.

A German officer, who spoke French like a son of France, demanded of her:

"Where are your soldiers?"

She extended her thin arm towards the red heap of fire which was gradually going out, and she answered with a strong voice:

"There!"

They crowded round her. The Prussian asked:

"How did it take fire?"

She said:

"It was I who set it on fire."

They did not believe her, they thought that the sudden disaster had made her crazy. So, while all pressed round and listened, she told the thing from one end to the other, from the arrival of the letter to the last cry of the men who were burned with her house. She did not forget a detail of all which she had felt, nor of all which she had done.

When she had finished, she drew two pieces of paper from her pocket, and, to distinguish them by the last glimmers of the fire, she again adjusted her spectacles; then she said, showing one: "That, that is the death of Victor." Showing the other, she added, indicating the red ruins with a bend of the head: "That, that is their names, so that you can write home." She calmly held the white sheet out to the officer, who held her by the shoulders, and she continued:

"You must write how it happened, and you must say to their mothers that it was I who did that, Victoire Simon, la Sauvage! Do not forget."

The officer shouted some orders in German. They seized her, they threw her against the walls of her house, still hot. Then twelve men drew quickly up before her, at twenty paces. She did not move. She had understood; she waited.

An order rang out, followed instantly by a long report. A belated shot went off by itself, after the others.

The old women did not fall. She sank as though they had mowed off her legs.

The Prussian officer approached her. She was almost cut in two, and in her withered hand she held her letter bathed with blood.

My friend Serval added:

"It was by way of reprisal that the Germans destroyed the château of the district, which belonged to me."

As for me, I thought of the mothers of those

four gentle fellows burned in the house; and of the atrocious heroism of that other mother shot against the wall.

And I picked up a little stone, still blackened by the flames.

ANTON CHEKHOV
1860–1904

On the Road

"Upon the breast of a gigantic crag,
A golden cloudlet rested for one night."

—LERMONTOV[1]

In the room which the tavern keeper, the Cossack Semyon Tchistopluy, called the "travellers' room," that is kept exclusively for travellers, a tall, broad-shouldered man of forty was sitting at the big unpainted table. He was asleep with his elbows on the table and his head leaning on his fist. An end of tallow candle, stuck into an old pomatum pot, lighted up his light brown beard, his thick, broad nose, his sunburnt cheeks and the thick, black eyebrows overhanging his closed eyes. . . . The nose and the cheeks and the eyebrows, all the features, each taken separately, were coarse and heavy, like the furniture and the stove in the "travellers' room," but taken all together they gave the effect of something harmonious and even beautiful. Such is the lucky star, as it is called, of the Russian face: the coarser and harsher its features the softer and more good-natured it looks. The man was dressed in a gentleman's reefer jacket, shabby, but bound with wide new braid, a plush waistcoat, and full black trousers thrust into big high boots.

On one of the benches, which stood in a continuous row along the wall, a girl of eight, in a brown dress and long black stockings, lay asleep on a coat lined with fox. Her face was pale, her hair was flaxen, her shoulders were narrow, her whole body was thin and frail, but her nose stood out as thick and ugly a lump as the man's. She was sound asleep, and unconscious that her semicircular comb had fallen off her head and was cutting her cheek.

The "travellers' room" had a festive appearance. The air was full of the smell of freshly scrubbed floors, there were no rags hanging as usual on the line that ran diagonally across the room, and a little lamp was burning in the corner over the table, casting a patch of red light on the ikon of St. George the Victorious.[2] From the ikon stretched on each side of the corner a row of cheap oleographs, which maintained a strict and careful gradation in the transition from the sacred to the profane. In the dim light of the candle end and the red ikon lamp the pictures looked like one continuous stripe, covered with blurs of black. When the tiled stove, trying to sing in unison with the weather, drew in the air with a howl, while the logs, as though waking up, burst into bright flame and hissed angrily, red patches began dancing on the log walls, and over the head of the sleeping man could be seen first the Elder Seraphim,[3] then the Shah Nasir-ed-Din,[4] then a fat, brown baby with goggle eyes, whispering in the ear of a young girl with an extraordinarily blank, and indifferent face. . . .

Outside a storm was raging. Something frantic and wrathful, but profoundly unhappy, seemed to be flinging itself about the tavern with the ferocity of a wild beast and trying to break in. Banging at the doors, knocking at the windows and on the roof, scratching at the walls, it alternately threatened and besought, then subsided for a brief interval, and then with a gleeful, treacherous howl burst into the chimney, but the wood flared up, and the fire, like a chained dog, flew wrathfully to meet its foe, a battle began, and after it—sobs, shrieks howls of wrath. In all of this there was the sound of angry misery and unsatisfied hate, and the mortified impatience of something accustomed to triumph.

Bewitched by this wild, inhuman music the "travellers' room" seemed spellbound forever, but all at once the door creaked and the potboy, in a new print shirt, came in. Limping on one leg, and blinking his sleepy eyes, he snuffed the candle with his fingers, put some more wood on the fire and went out. At once from the church, which was three hundred paces from the tavern, the clock struck midnight. The wind played

[1] Mikhail Yurievich Lermontov (1814–1841), Russian poet and novelist, was called the "poet of the Caucasus" because he was twice exiled there.

[2] Historical and mythological religious character.
[3] Literally, Elder Angel.
[4] Famous jester of Turkish legend.

with the chimes as with the snowflakes; chasing the sounds of the clock it whirled them round and round over a vast space, so that some strokes were cut short or drawn out in long, vibrating notes, while others were completely lost in the general uproar. One stroke sounded as distinctly in the room as though it had chimed just under the window. The child, sleeping on the foxskin, started and raised her head. For a minute she stared blankly at the dark window, at Nasir-ed-Din over whom a crimson glow from the fire flickered at that moment, then she turned her eyes upon the sleeping man.

"Daddy," she said.

But the man did not move. The little girl knitted her brow angrily, lay down, and curled up her legs. Someone in the tavern gave a loud, prolonged yawn. Soon afterwards there was the squeak of the swing door and the sound of indistinct voices. Someone came in, shaking the snow off, and stamping in felt boots which made a muffled thud.

"What is it?" a woman's voice asked languidly.

"Mademoiselle Ilovaisky has come, . . ." answered a bass voice.

Again there was the squeak of the swing door. Then came the roar of the wind rushing in. Someone, probably the lame boy, ran to the door leading to the "travellers' room," coughed deferentially, and lifted the latch.

"This way, lady, please," said a woman's voice in dulcet tones. "It's clean in here, my beauty. . . ."

The door was opened wide and a peasant with a beard appeared in the doorway, in the long coat of a coachman, plastered all over with snow from head to foot, and carrying a big trunk on his shoulder. He was followed into the room by a feminine figure, scarcely half his height, with no face and no arms, muffled and wrapped up like a bundle and also covered with snow. A damp chill, as from a cellar, seemed to come to the child from the coachman and the bundle, and the fire and the candles flickered.

"What nonsense!" said the bundle angrily. "We could go perfectly well. We have only nine more miles to go, mostly by the forest, and we should not get lost. . . ."

"As for getting lost, we shouldn't, but the horses can't go on, lady!" answered the coachman. "And it is Thy Will, O Lord! As though I had done it on purpose!"

"God knows where you have brought me. . . . Well, be quiet. . . . There are people asleep here, it seems. You can go. . . ."

The coachman put the portmanteau on the floor, and as he did so, a great lump of snow fell off his shoulders. He gave a sniff and went out.

Then the little girl saw two little hands come out from the middle of the bundle, stretch upwards and begin angrily disentangling the network of shawls, kerchiefs, and scarves. First a big shawl fell on the ground, then a hood, then a white knitted kerchief. After freeing her head, the traveller took off her pelisse and at once shrank to half the size. Now she was in a long, grey coat with big buttons and bulging pockets. From one pocket she pulled out a paper parcel, from the other a bunch of big, heavy keys, which she put down so carelessly that the sleeping man started and opened his eyes. For some time he looked blankly round him as though he didn't know where he was, then he shook his head, went to the corner and sat down. . . . The newcomer took off her greatcoat, which made her shrink to half her size again, she took off her big felt boots, and sat down, too.

By now she no longer resembled a bundle: she was a thin little brunette of twenty, as slim as a snake, with a long white face and curly hair. Her nose was long and sharp, her chin, too, was long and sharp, her eyelashes were long, the corners of her mouth were sharp, and, thanks to this general sharpness, the expression of her face was biting. Swathed in a closely fitting black dress with a mass of lace at her neck and sleeves, with sharp elbows and long pink fingers, she recalled the portraits of mediaeval English ladies. The grave concentration of her face increased this likeness.

The lady looked round at the room, glanced sideways at the man and the little girl, shrugged her shoulders, and moved to the window. The dark windows were shaking from the damp west wind. Big flakes of snow glistening in their whiteness lay on the window frame, but at once disappeared, borne away by the wind. The savage music grew louder and louder. . . .

After a long silence the little girl suddenly turned over, and said angrily, emphasizing each word:

"Oh, goodness, goodness, how unhappy I am! Unhappier than anyone!"

The man got up and moved with little steps to the child with a guilty air, which was utterly out of keeping with his huge figure and big beard.

"You are not asleep, dearie?" he said, in an apologetic voice. "What do you want?"

"I don't want anything, my shoulder aches! You are a wicked man, Daddy, and God will punish you! You'll see He will punish you."

"My darling, I know your shoulder aches, but what can I do, dearie?" said the man, in the tone in which men who have been drinking excuse themselves to their stern spouses. "It's the journey has made your shoulder ache, Sasha. To-morrow we shall get there and rest, and the pain will go away. . . ."

"To-morrow, to-morrow. . . . Every day you say to-morrow. We shall be going on another twenty days."

"But we shall arrive to-morrow, dearie, on your father's word of honour. I never tell a lie, but if we are detained by the snowstorm it is not my fault."

"I can't bear any more, I can't, I can't!"

Sasha jerked her leg abruptly and filled the room with an unpleasant wailing. Her father made a despairing gesture, and looked hopelessly toward the young lady. The latter shrugged her shoulders, and hesitatingly went up to Sasha.

"Listen, my dear," she said, "it is no use crying. It's really naughty; if your shoulder aches it can't be helped."

"You see, Madam," said the man quickly, as though defending himself, "we have not slept for two nights, and have been travelling in a revolting conveyance. Well, of course, it is natural she should be ill and miserable, . . . and then, you know, we had a drunken driver, our portmanteau has been stolen . . . the snowstorm all the time, but what's the use of crying, Madam? I am exhausted, though, by sleeping in a sitting position, and I feel as though I were drunk. Oh, dear! Sasha, and I feel sick as it is, and then you cry!"

Then man shook his head, and with a gesture of despair sat down.

"Of course you mustn't cry," said the young lady. "It's only little babies cry. If you are ill, dear, you must undress and go to sleep. . . Let us take off your things!"

When the child had been undressed and pacified a silence reigned again. The young lady seated herself at the window, and looked round wonderingly at the room of the inn, at the ikon, at the stove. . . . Apparently the room and the little girl with the thick nose, in her short boy's nightgown, and the child's father, all seemed strange to her. This strange man was sitting in a corner; he kept looking about him helplessly, as though he were drunk, and rubbing his face with the palm of his hand. He sat silent, blinking, and judging from his guilty-looking figure it was difficult to imagine that he would soon begin to speak. Yet he was the first to begin. Stroking his knees, he gave a cough, laughed, and said:

"It's a comedy, it really is. . . . I look and I cannot believe my eyes: for what devilry has destiny driven us to this accursed inn? What did she want to show by it? Life sometimes performs such '*salto mortale*,'[5] one can only stare and blink in amazement. Have you come from far, Madam?"

"No, not from far," answered the young lady. "I am going from our estate, fifteen miles from here, to our farm, to my father and brother. My name is Ilovaisky, and the farm is called Ilovaiskoe. It's nine miles away. What unpleasant weather!"

"It couldn't be worse."

The lame boy came in and stuck a new candle in the pomatum pot.

"You might bring us the samovar, boy," said the man, addressing him.

"Who drinks tea now?" laughed the boy. "It is a sin to drink tea before mass. . . ."

"Never mind, boy, you won't burn in hell if we do. . . ."

Over the tea the new acquaintances got into conversation.

Mlle. Ilovaisky learned that her companion was called Grigory Petrovitch Liharev, that he was the brother of the Liharev who was Marshal of Nobility in one of the neighbouring districts, and he himself had once been a landowner, but had "run through everything in his time." Li-

[5] Mortal leap; deadly jump.

harev learned that her name was Marya Mihailovna, that her father had a huge estate, but that she was the only one to look after it as her father and brother looked at life through their fingers, were irresponsible, and were too fond of harriers.

"My father and brother are all alone at the farm," she told him, brandishing her fingers (she had the habit of moving her fingers before her pointed face as she talked, and after every sentence moistened her lips with her sharp little tongue). "They, I mean men, are an irresponsible lot, and don't stir a finger for themselves. I can fancy there will be no one to give them a meal after the fast! We have no mother, and we have such servants that they can't lay the tablecloth properly when I am away. You can imagine their condition now! They will be left with nothing to break their fast, while I have to stay here all night. How strange it all is."

She shrugged her shoulders, took a sip from her cup, and said:

"There are festivals that have a special fragrance: at Easter, Trinity and Christmas there is a peculiar scent in the air. Even unbelievers are fond of those festivals. My brother, for instance, argues that there is no God, but he is the first to hurry to Matins at Easter."

Liharev raised his eyes to Mlle. Ilovaisky and laughed.

"They argue that there is no God," she went on, laughing too, "but why is it, tell me, all the celebrated writers, the learned men, clever people generally, in fact, believe towards the end of their life?"

"If man does not know how to believe when he is young, Madam, he won't believe in his old age if he is ever so much of a writer."

Judging from Liharev's cough he had a bass voice, but, probably from being afraid to speak aloud, or from exaggerated shyness, he spoke in a tenor. After a brief pause he heaved a sigh and said:

"The way I look at it is that faith is a faculty of the spirit. It is just the same as a talent, one must be born with it. So far as I can judge by myself, by the people I have seen in my time, and by all that is done around us, this faculty is present in Russians in its highest degree. Russian life presents us with an uninterrupted succession of convictions and aspirations, and if you care to know, it has not yet the faintest notion of lack of faith or scepticism. If a Russian does not believe in God, it means he believes in something else."

Liharev took a cup of tea from Mlle. Ilovaisky, drank off half in one gulp, and went on:

"I will tell you about myself. Nature has implanted in my breast an extraordinary faculty for belief. Whisper it not to the night, but half my life I was in the ranks of the Atheists and Nihilists,[6] but there was not one hour in my life in which I ceased to believe. All talents, as a rule, show themselves in early childhood, and so my faculty showed itself when I could still walk upright under the table. My mother liked her children to eat a great deal, and when she gave me food she used to say: 'Eat! Soup is the great thing in life!' I believed, and ate the soup ten times a day, ate like a shark, ate till I was disgusted and stupefied. My nurse used to tell me fairy tales, and I believed in house-spirits, in wood-elves, and in goblins of all kinds. I used sometimes to steal corrosive sublimate from my father, sprinkle it on cakes, and carry them up to the attic that the house-spirits, you see, might eat them and be killed. And when I was taught to read and understand what I read, then there was a fine to-do. I ran away to America and went off to join the brigands, and wanted to go into a monastery, and hired boys to torture me for being a Christian. And note that my faith was always active, never dead. If I was running away to America I was not alone, but seduced someone else, as great a fool as I was, to go with me, and was delighted when I was nearly frozen outside the town gates and when I was thrashed; if I went to join the brigands I always came back with my face battered. A most restless childhood, I assure you! And when they sent me to the high school and pelted me with all sorts of truths—that is, that the earth goes round the sun, or that white light is not white, but is made up of seven colours—my poor little head began to go round! Everything was thrown into a whirl in me: Navin who made the sun stand still, and my

[6] Believer in Nihilism (Lat. *nihil,* nothing), a movement that appeared in Russia about 1850 aimed at the annihilation of many beliefs and institutions; happiness was to be the only law.

mother who in the name of the Prophet Elijah[7] disapproved of lightning conductors, and my father who was indifferent to the truths I had learned. My enlightenment inspired me. I wandered about the house and stables like one possessed, preaching my truths, was horrified by ignorance, glowed with hatred for anyone who saw in white light nothing but white light. . . . But all that's nonsense and childishness. Serious, so to speak, manly enthusiasms began only at the university. You have, no doubt, Madam, taken your degree somewhere?"

"I studied at Novotcherkask at the Don Institute."

"Then you have not been to a university? So you don't know what science means. All the sciences in the world have the same passport, without which they regard themselves as meaningless . . . the striving towards truth! Every one of them, even pharmacology, has for its aim not utility, not the alleviation of life, but truth. It's remarkable! When you set to work to study any science, what strikes you first of all is its beginning. I assure you there is nothing more attractive and grander, nothing is so staggering, nothing takes a man's breath away like the beginning of any science. From the first five or six lectures you are soaring on wings of the brightest hopes, you already seem to yourself to be welcoming truth with open arms. And I gave myself up to science, heart and soul, passionately, as to the woman one loves. I was its slave; I found it the sun of my existence, and asked for no other. I studied day and night without rest, ruined myself over books, wept when before my eyes men exploited science for their own personal ends. But my enthusiasm did not last long. The trouble is that every science has a beginning but not an end, like a recurring decimal. Zoology has discovered 35,000 kinds of insects, chemistry reckons 60 elements. If in time tens of noughts can be written after these figures, zoology and chemistry will be just as far from their end as now, and all contemporary scientific work consists in increasing these numbers. I saw through this trick when I discovered the 35,001st and felt no satisfaction. Well, I had no time to suffer from disillusionment, as I was soon possessed by a new faith. I plunged into Nihilism, with its manifestoes, its 'black divisions,' and all the rest of it. I 'went to the people,' worked in factories, worked as an oiler, as a barge hauler. Afterwards, when wandering over Russia, I had a taste of Russian life, I turned into a fervent devotee of that life. I loved the Russian people with poignant intensity, I loved their God and believed in Him, and in their language, their creative genius. . . . And so on, and so on. . . . I have been a Slavophile[8] in my time, I used to pester Aksakov[9] with letters, and I was a Ukrainophile, and an archaeologist, and a collector of specimens of peasant art. . . . I was enthusiastic over ideas, people, events, places . . . my enthusiasm was endless! Five years ago I was working for the abolition of private property; my last creed was non-resistance to evil."

Sasha gave an abrupt sigh and began moving. Liharev got up and went to her.

"Won't you have some tea, dearie?" he asked tenderly.

"Drink it yourself," the child answered rudely.

Liharev was disconcerted, and went back to the table with a guilty step.

"Then you have had a lively time," said Mlle. Ilovaisky; "you have something to remember."

"Well, yes, it's all very lively when one sits over tea and chatters to a kind listener, but you should ask what that liveliness has cost me! What price have I paid for the variety of my life? You see, Madam, I have not held my convictions like a German doctor of philosophy, *zierlichmännerlich*,[10] I have not lived in solitude, but every conviction I have had has bound my back to the yoke, has torn my body to pieces. Judge, for yourself. I was wealthy like my brothers, but now I am a beggar. In the delirium of my enthusiasm I smashed up my own fortune and my wife's—a heap of other people's money. Now I am forty-two, old age is close upon me, and I am homeless, like a dog that has dropped behind its waggon at night. All my life I have

[7] See *I Kings*, 18, especially verse 38: "Then the fire of the Lord fell. . . ." The point here is that Liharev's mother disapproved of lightning rods because they distorted God's purposes.

[8] Lover of Slav civilization. [9] Sergei Aksakov (1791–1859), a Russian novelist. [10] Elegantly man-like, or in a culturally mannered way.

not known what peace meant, my soul has been in continual agitation, distressed even by its hopes . . . I have been wearied out with heavy irregular work, have endured privation, have five times been in prison, have dragged myself across the provinces of Archangel and of Toblosk . . . it's painful to think of it! I have lived, but in my fever I have not even been conscious of the process of life itself. Would you believe it, I don't remember a single spring, I never noticed how my wife loved me, how my children were born. What more can I tell you? I have been a misfortune to all who have loved me. . . . My mother has worn mourning for me all these fifteen years, while my proud brothers, who have had to wince, to blush, to bow their heads, to waste their money on my account, have come in the end to hate me like poison."

Liharev got up and sat down again.

"If I were simply unhappy I should thank God," he went on without looking at his listener. "My personal unhappiness sinks into the background when I remember how often in my enthusiasms I have been absurd, far from the truth, unjust, cruel, dangerous! How often I have hated and despised those whom I ought to have loved, and *vice versa.* I have changed a thousand times. One day I believe, fall down and worship, the next I flee like a coward from the gods and friends of yesterday, and swallow in silence the 'scoundrel!' they hurl after me. God alone has seen how often I have wept and bitten my pillow in shame for my enthusiasms. Never once in my life have I intentionally lied or done evil, but my conscience is not clear! I cannot even boast, Madam, that I have no one's life upon my conscience, for my wife died before my eyes, worn out by my reckless activity. Yes, my wife! I tell you they have two ways of treating women nowadays. Some measure women's skulls to prove woman is inferior to man, pick out her defects to mock at her, to look original in her eyes, and to justify their sensuality. Others do their utmost to raise women to their level, that is, force them to learn by heart the 35,000 species, to speak and write the same foolish things as they speak and write themselves."

Liharev's face darkened.

"I tell you that woman has been and always will be the slave of man," he said in a bass voice, striking his fist on the table. "She is soft, tender wax which a man always moulds into anything he likes. . . . My God! for the sake of some trumpery masculine enthusiasm she will cut off her hair, abandon her family, die among strangers! . . . among the ideas for which she has sacrificed herself there is not a single feminine one. . . . An unquestioning, devoted slave! I have not measured skulls, but I say this from hard, bitter experience: the proudest, most independent women, if I have succeeded in communicating to them my enthusiasm, have followed me without criticism, without question, and have done anything I chose; I have turned a nun into a Nihilist who, as I heard afterwards, shot a gendarme; my wife never left me for a minute in my wanderings, and like a weather-cock changed her faith in step with my changing enthusiasms."

Liharev jumped up and walked up and down the room.

"A noble, sublime slavery!" he said, clasping his hands. "It is just in it that the highest meaning of woman's life lies! Of all the fearful medley of thoughts and impressions accumulated in my brain from my association with women my memory, like a filter, has retained no ideas, no clever saying, no philosophy, nothing but that extraordinary resignation to fate, that wonderful mercifulness, forgiveness of everything."

Liharev clenched his fists, stared at a fixed point, and with a sort of passionate intensity, as though he were savouring each word as he uttered it, hissed through his clenched teeth:

"That . . . that great-hearted fortitude, faithfulness unto death, poetry of the heart. . . . The meaning of life lies in just that unrepining martyrdom, in the tears which would soften a stone, in the boundless, all-forgiving love which brings light and warmth into the chaos of life. . . ."

Mlle. Ilovaisky got up slowly, took a step towards Liharev, and fixed her eyes upon his face. From the tears that glittered on his eyelashes, from his quivering, passionate voice, from the flush on his cheeks, it was clear to her that women were not a chance, not a simple subject of conversation. They were the object of his new enthusiasm, or, as he said himself, his new faith! For the first time in her life she saw a man carried away, fervently believing. With his gesticulations, with his flashing eyes he seemed to her mad, frantic, but there was a feeling of such beauty in the fire of his eyes, in his words, in all the movements of his huge body, that without noticing what she was doing she stood facing him as though rooted to the spot, and gazed into his face with delight.

"Take my mother," he said, stretching out his hand to her with an imploring expression on his face, "I poisoned her existence, according to her ideas disgraced the name of Liharev, did her as much harm as the most malignant enemy, and what do you think? My brothers give her little sums for holy bread and church services, and outraging her religious feelings, she saves that money and sends it in secret to her erring Grigory. This trifle alone elevates and ennobles the soul far more than all the theories, all the clever sayings and the 35,000 species. I can give you thousands of instances. Take you, even, for instance! With tempest and darkness outside you are going to your father and your brother to cheer them with your affection in the holiday, though very likely they have forgotten and are not thinking of you. And, wait a bit, and you will love a man and follow him to the North Pole. You would, wouldn't you?"

"Yes, if I loved him."

"There, you see," cried Liharev delighted, and he even stamped with his foot. "Oh dear! How glad I am that I have met you! Fate is kind to me, I am always meeting splendid people. Not a day passes but one makes acquaintance with somebody one would give one's soul for. There are ever so many more good people than bad in this world. Here, see, for instance, how openly and from our hearts we have been talking as though we had known each other a hundred years. Sometimes, I assure you, one restrains oneself for ten years and holds one's tongue, is reserved with one's friends and one's wife, and meets some cadet in a train and babbles one's whole soul out to him. It is the first time I have the honour of seeing you, and yet I have confessed to you as I have never confessed in my life. Why is it?"

Rubbing his hands and smiling good-humouredly Liharev walked up and down the room, and fell to talking about women again. Meanwhile they begin ringing for matins.

"Goodness," wailed Sasha. "He won't let me sleep with his talking!"

"Oh, yes!" said Liharev, startled. "I am sorry, darling, sleep, sleep. . . . I have two boys besides her," he whispered. "They are living with their uncle, Madam, but this one can't exist a day without her father. She's wretched, she complains, but she sticks to me like a fly to honey. I have been chattering too much, Madam, and it would do you no harm to sleep. Wouldn't you like me to make up a bed for you?"

Without waiting for permission he shook the wet pelisse, stretched it on a bench, fur side upwards, collected various shawls and scarves, put the overcoat folded up into a roll for a pillow, and all this he did in silence with a look of devout reverence, as though he were not handling a woman's rags, but the fragments of holy vessels. There was something apologetic, embarrassed about his whole figure, as though in the presence of a weak creature he felt ashamed of his height and strength. . . .

When Mlle. Ilovaisky had lain down, he put out the candle and sat down on a stool by the stove.

"So, Madam," he whispered, lighting a fat cigarette and puffing the smoke into the stove. "Nature has put into the Russian an extraordinary faculty for belief, a searching intelligence, and the lift of speculation, but all that is reduced to ashes by irresponsibility, laziness, and dreamy frivolity. . . . Yes. . . ."

She gazed wonderingly into the darkness, and saw only a spot of red on the ikon and the flicker of the light of the stove on Liharev's face. The darkness, the chime of the bells, the roar of the storm, the lame boy, Sasha with her fretfulness, unhappy Liharev and his sayings—all this was mingled together, and seemed to grow into one huge impression, and God's world seemed to her fantastic, full of marvels and magical forces. All that she had heard was ringing in her ears, and human life presented itself to her as a beautiful poetic fairy tale without an end.

The immense impression grew and grew, clouded consciousness, and turned into a sweet dream. She was asleep, though she saw the little ikon lamp and a big nose with the light playing on it.

She heard the sound of weeping.

"Daddy, darling," a child's voice was tenderly entreating, "let's go back to uncle! There is a Christmas-tree there! Styopa and Kolya are there!"

"My darling, what can I do?" a man's bass

persuaded softly. "Understand me! Come, understand!"

And the man's weeping blended with the child's. This voice of human sorrow, in the midst of the howling of the storm, touched the girl's ear with such sweet human music that she could not bear the delight of it, and wept too. She was conscious afterwards of a big, black shadow coming softly up to her, picking up a shawl that had dropped on to the floor and carefully wrapping it round her feet.

Mlle. Ilovaisky was awakened by a strange uproar. She jumped up and looked about her in astonishment. The deep blue dawn was looking in at the window half-covered with snow. In the room there was a grey twilight, through which the stove and the sleeping child and Nasir-ed-Din stood out distinctly. The stove and the lamp were both out. Through the wide-open door she could see the big tavern room with a counter and chairs. A man, with a stupid, gipsy face and astonished eyes, was standing in the middle of the room in a puddle of melting snow, holding a big red star on a stick. He was surrounded by a group of boys, motionless as statues, and plastered over with snow. The light shone through the red paper of the star, throwing a glow of red on their wet faces. The crowd was shouting in disorder, and from its uproar Mlle. Ilovaisky could make out only one couplet:

> "Hi, you little Russian lad,
> Bring your sharp knife,
> We will kill the Jew, we will kill him,
> The son of tribulation. . . ."

Liharev was standing near the counter, looking feelingly at the singers and tapping his feet in time. Seeing Mlle. Ilovaisky, he smiled all over his face and came up to her. She smiled too.

"A happy Christmas!" he said. "I saw you slept well."

She looked at him, said nothing, and went on smiling.

After the conversation in the night he seemed to her not tall and broad shouldered, but little, just as the biggest steamer seems to us a little thing when we hear that it has crossed the ocean.

"Well, it is time for me to set off," she said. "I must put on my things. Tell me where you are going now?

"I? To the station of Klinushki, from there to Sergievo, and from Sergievo, with horses, thirty miles to the coal mines that belong to a horrid man, a general called Shashkovsky. My brothers have got me the post of superintendent there. . . . I am going to be a coal miner."

"Stay, I know those mines. Shashkovsky is my uncle, you know. But . . . what are you going there for?" asked Mlle. Ilovaisky, looking at Liharev in surprise.

"As superintendent. To superintend the coal mines."

"I don't understand!" she shrugged her shoulders. "You are going to the mines. But you know, it's the bare steppe, a desert, so dreary that you couldn't exist a day there! It's horrible coal, no one will buy it, and my uncle's a maniac, a despot, a bankrupt. . . . You won't get your salary!"

"No matter," said Liharev, unconcernedly. "I am thankful even for coal mines."

She shrugged her shoulders, and walked about the room in agitation.

"I don't understand, I don't understand," she said, moving her fingers before her face. "It's impossible, and . . . and irrational! You must understand that it's . . . it's worse than exile. It is a living tomb! O Heavens!" she said hotly, going up to Liharev and moving her fingers before his smiling face; her upper lip was quivering, and her sharp face turned pale, "Come, picture it, the bare steppe, solitude. There is no one to say a word to there, and you . . . are enthusiastic over women! Coal mines . . . and women!"

Mlle. Ilovaisky was suddenly ashamed of her heat and, turning away from Liharev, walked to the window.

"No, no, you can't go there," she said, moving her fingers rapidly over the pane.

Not only in her heart, but even in her spine she felt that behind her stood an infinitely unhappy man, lost and outcast, while he, as though he were unaware of his unhappiness, as though he had not shed tears in the night, was looking at her with a kindly smile. Better he should go on weeping! She walked up and down the room several times in agitation, then stopped short in a corner and sank into thought. Liharev was saying something, but she did not hear him. Turning her back on him she took out of her purse a money note, stood for a long time crumpling it in her hand, and looking round at Liharev, blushed and put it in her pocket.

The coachman's voice was heard through the door. With a stern concentrated face she began putting on her things in silence. Liharev wrapped her up, chatting gaily, but every word he said lay on her heart like a weight. It is not cheering to hear the unhappy or the dying jest.

When the transformation of a live person into a shapeless bundle had been completed, Mlle. Ilovaisky looked for the last time round the "travellers' room," stood a moment in silence, and slowly walked out. Liharev went to see her off. . . .

Outside, God alone knows why, the winter was raging still. Whole clouds of big soft snowflakes were whirling restlessly over the earth, unable to find a resting-place. The horses, the sledge, the trees, a bull tied to a post, all were white and seemed soft and fluffy.

"Well, God help you," muttered Liharev, tucking her into the sledge. "Don't remember evil against me. . . ."

She was silent. When the sledge started, and had to go round a huge snowdrift, she looked back at Liharev with an expression as though she wanted to say something to him. He ran up to her, but she did not say a word to him, she only looked at him through her long eyelashes with little specks of snow on them.

Whether his finely intuitive soul were really able to read that look, or whether his imagination deceived him, it suddenly began to seem to him that with another touch or two that girl would have forgiven him his failures, his age, his desolate position, and would have followed him without question or reasonings. He stood a long while as though rooted to the spot, gazing at the tracks left by the sledge runners. The snowflakes greedily settled on his hair, his beard, his shoulders. . . . Soon the track of the runners had vanished, and he himself covered with snow, began to look like a white rock, but still his eyes kept seeking something in the clouds of snow.

Comments and Questions

As we continue with our study of the short story, we must not lose sight of the basic matters while we, of necessity, move among the technical matters of story construction. We recall our earlier statement that although we are giving a good deal of attention to form, we must never lose sight of our ultimate goal, which is *to comprehend the values and reality explored by any piece of writing.*

We still keep in mind our question, what makes a good short story? As we look back —Galsworthy, Hemingway, Steinbeck, Faulkner—have we found a *great* short story? How would we make the distinction between a good and a great one? Perhaps we can help ourselves to find that distinction by trying to answer questions like these about Chekhov's story:

1. What are the principal devices used by Chekhov to transform the facts of his story into a piece of fictional art with meaning? Has he relied chiefly on plot, character, or theme? Panorama or scene? What kind of a narrator? Does the symbolism, if any, help to give the story its most fundamental meaning? In what ways do the tone and atmosphere help to make clear Chekhov's meaning? These questions concern technique and form; they are ways of getting into a discussion of the story's meaning. To know the answers to the questions is not to know very much, but to know the *meaning* of the answers is to know a great deal about the meaning of the story.

2. Let us drive more deeply into the heart of our problem: Is the story a good or a great one? Is Chekhov a mechanic only who can fit parts together, or is he an artist? To put the question another way: Is the story a satisfactory technical performance or is the technique *used* to dramatize a penetrating interpretation of life? Have you ever heard a pianist or violinist who gave a brilliant technical performance, yet left you unmoved—a technician but no artist? How would you classify Chekhov?

3. It has been said that the whole purpose of art is to get below the surface meaning of life. Does Chekhov get there? Does the story have two or three dimensions? Support your opinion by evidence from the story.

4. Is Chekhov unusually sensitive to hu-

man personality and character? Do we *know* Liharev and Mlle. Ilovaisky?

5. What is the significance of the snowstorm? The story begins and ends with the storm. Is this an accident, decoration, or symbolism?

W. SOMERSET MAUGHAM
1874–1965

The Colonel's Lady

All this happened two or three years before the outbreak of the war.

The Peregrines were having breakfast. Though they were alone and the table was long they sat at opposite ends of it. From the walls George Peregrine's ancestors, painted by the fashionable painters of the day, looked down upon them. The butler brought in the morning post. There were several letters for the Colonel, business letters, *The Times* and a small parcel for his wife Evie. He looked at his letters and then, opening *The Times,* began to read it. They finished breakfast and rose from the table. He noticed that his wife hadn't opened the parcel.

"What's that?" he asked.

"Only some books."

"Shall I open it for you?"

"If you like."

He hated to cut string and so with some difficulty untied the knots.

"But they're all the same," he said when he had unwrapped the parcel. "What on earth d'you want six copies of the same book for?" He opened one of them. "Poetry." Then he looked at the title page. *When Pyramids Decay,* he read, by E. K. Hamilton. Eva Katherine Hamilton: that was his wife's maiden name. He looked at her with smiling surprise. "Have you written a book, Evie? You are a slyboots."

"I didn't think it would interest you very much. Would you like a copy?"

"Well, you know poetry isn't much in my line, but—yes, I'd like a copy; I'll read it. I'll take it along to my study. I've got a lot to do this morning."

He gathered up *The Times,* his letters and the book and went out. His study was a large and comfortable room, with a big desk, leather armchairs and what he called "trophies of the chase" on the walls. In the bookshelves were works of reference, books on farming, gardening, fishing and shooting, and books on the last war, in which he had won an M.C. and a D.S.O. For before his marriage he had been in the Welsh Guards. At the end of the war he retired and settled down to the life of a country gentleman in the spacious house, some twenty miles from Sheffield, which one of his forebears had built in the reign of George III. George Peregrine had an estate of some fifteen hundred acres which he managed with ability; he was a justice of the peace and performed his duties conscientiously. During the season he rode to hounds two days a week. He was a good shot, a golfer and though now a little over fifty could still play a hard game of tennis. He could describe himself with propriety as an all-round sportsman.

He had been putting on weight lately, but was still a fine figure of a man; tall, with grey curly hair, only just beginning to grow thin on the crown, frank blue eyes, good features and a high colour. He was a public-spirited man, chairman at any number of local organizations and, as became his class and station, a loyal member of the Conservative party. He looked upon it as his duty to see to the welfare of the people on his estate and it was a satisfaction to him to know that Evie could be trusted to tend the sick and succour the poor. He had built a cottage hospital on the outskirts of the village and paid the wages of a nurse out of his own pocket. All he asked of the recipients of his bounty was that at elections, county or general, they should vote for his candidate. He was a friendly man, affable to his inferiors, considerate with his tenants and popular with the neighbouring gentry. He would have been pleased and at the same time slightly embarrassed if someone had told him he was a jolly good fellow. That was what he wanted to be. He desired no higher praise.

It was hard luck that he had no children. He would have been an excellent father, kindly but strict, and would have brought up his sons as a gentleman's sons should be brought up, sent them to Eton, you know, taught them to fish, shoot and ride. As it was, his heir was a nephew, son of his brother killed in a motor accident, not a bad boy, but not a chip off the old block, no, sir, far from it; and would you believe it, his fool of a mother was sending him to a co-educational school. Evie had been a sad disappointment to him. Of course she was a lady, and she had a bit of money of her own; she managed the house uncommonly well and she was a good hostess. The village people adored her. She had been a pretty young thing when he married her, with a creamy skin, light brown hair and a trim figure, healthy, too, and not a bad tennis player; he couldn't understand why she'd had no children; of course she was faded now, she must be getting on for five and forty; her skin was drab, her hair had lost its sheen and she was as thin as a rail. She was always neat and suitably dressed, but she didn't seem to bother how she looked; she wore no makeup and didn't even use lipstick; sometimes at night when she dolled herself up for a party you could tell that once she'd been quite attractive, but ordinarily she was—well, the sort of woman you simply didn't notice. A nice woman, of course, a good wife, and it wasn't her fault if she was barren, but it was tough on a fellow who wanted an heir of his own loins; she hadn't any vitality, that's what was the matter with her. He supposed he'd been in love with her when he asked her to marry him, at least sufficiently in love for a man who wanted to marry and settle down, but with time he discovered that they had nothing much in common. She didn't care about hunting, and fishing bored her. Naturally they'd drifted apart. He had to do her the justice to admit that she'd never bothered him. There'd been no scenes. They had no quarrels. She seemed to take it for granted that he should go his own way. When he went up to London now and then she never wanted to come with him. He had a girl there, well, she wasn't exactly a girl, she was thirty-five if she was a day, but she was blonde and luscious and he only had to wire ahead of time and they'd dine, do a show and spend the night together. Well, a man, a healthy normal man had to have some fun in his life. The thought crossed his mind that if Evie hadn't been such a good woman she'd have been a better wife; but it was not the sort of thought that he welcomed and he put it away from him.

George Peregrine finished his *Times* and being a considerate fellow rang the bell and told the butler to take the paper to Evie. Then he looked at his watch. It was half-past ten and at eleven he had an appointment with one of his tenants. He had half an hour to spare.

"I'd better have a look at Evie's book," he said to himself.

He took it up with a smile. Evie had a lot of highbrow books in her sitting-room, not the sort of books that interested him, but if they amused her he had no objection to her reading them. He noticed that the volume he now held in his hand contained no more than ninety pages. That was all to the good. He shared Edgar Allan Poe's opinion that poems should be short. But as he turned the pages he noticed that several of Evie's had long lines of irregular length and didn't rhyme. He didn't like that. At his first school, when he was a little boy, he remembered learning a poem that began: *The boy stood on the burning deck*, and later, at Eton, one that started: *Ruin seize thee, ruthless king;* and then there was Henry V; they'd had to take that one half. He stared at Evie's pages with consternation.

"That's not what I call poetry," he said.

Fortunately it wasn't all like that. Interspersed with the pieces that looked so odd, lines of three or four words and then a line of ten or fifteen, there were little poems, quite short, that rhymed, thank God, with the lines all the same length. Several of the pages were just headed with the word *Sonnet*, and out of curiosity he counted the lines; there were fourteen of them. He read them. They seemed all right, but he didn't quite know what they were all about. He repeated to himself: *Ruin seize thee, ruthless king*.

"Poor Evie," he sighed.

At that moment the farmer he was expecting was ushered into the study, and putting the book down he made him welcome. They embarked on their business.

"I read your book, Evie," he said as they sat down to lunch. "Jolly good. Did it cost you a packet to have it printed?"

"No, I was lucky. I sent it to a publisher and he took it."

"Not much money in poetry, my dear," he said in his good-natured, hearty way.

"No, I don't suppose there is. What did Bannock want to see you about this morning?"

Bannock was the tenant who had interrupted

his reading of Evie's poems.

"He's asked me to advance the money for a pedigree bull he wants to buy. He's a good man and I've half a mind to do it."

George Peregrine saw that Evie didn't want to talk about her book and he was not sorry to change the subject. He was glad she had used her maiden name on the title page; he didn't suppose anyone would ever hear about the book, but he was proud of his own unusual name and he wouldn't have liked it if some damned penny-a-liner had made fun of Evie's effort in one of the papers.

During the few weeks that followed he thought it tactful not to ask Evie any questions about her venture into verse and she never referred to it. It might have been a discreditable incident that they had silently agreed not to mention. But then a strange thing happened. He had to go to London on business and he took Daphne out to dinner. That was the name of the girl with whom he was in the habit of passing a few agreeable hours whenever he went to town.

"Oh, George," she said, "is that your wife who's written a book they're all talking about?"

"What on earth d'you mean?"

"Well, there's a fellow I know who's a critic. He took me out to dinner the other night and he had a book with him. 'Got anything for me to read?' I said. 'What's that?' 'Oh, I don't think that's your cup of tea,' he said, 'It's poetry, I've just been reviewing it.' 'No poetry for me,' I said. 'It's about the hottest stuff I ever read, he said. 'Selling like hot cakes. And it's damned good.' "

"Who's the book by?" asked George.

"A woman called Hamilton. My friend told me that wasn't her real name. He said her real name was Peregrine. 'Funny,' I said, 'I know a fellow called Peregrine.' 'Colonel in the army,' he said. 'Lives near Sheffield.' "

"I'd just as soon you didn't talk about me to your friends," said George with a frown of vexation.

"Keep your shirt on, dearie. Who'd you take me for? I just said, 'It's not the same one.' " Daphne giggled. "My friend said: 'They say he's a regular Colonel Blimp.' "

George had a keen sense of humour.

"You could tell them better than that," he laughed. "If my wife had written a book I'd be the first to know about it, wouldn't I?"

"I suppose you would."

Anyhow the matter didn't interest her and when the Colonel began to talk of other things she forgot about it. He put it out of his mind too. There was nothing to it, he decided, and that silly fool of a critic had just been pulling Daphne's leg. He was amused at the thought of her tackling that book because she had been told it was hot stuff and then finding it just a lot of stuff cut up into unequal lines.

He was a member of several clubs and next day he thought he'd lunch at one in St. James's Street. He was catching a train back to Sheffield early in the afternoon. He was sitting in a comfortable armchair having a glass of sherry before going into the dining-room when an old friend came up to him.

"Well, old boy, how's life?" he said. "How d'you like being the husband of a celebrity?"

George Peregrine looked at his friend. He thought he saw an amused twinkle in his eyes.

"I don't know what you're talking about," he answered.

"Come off it, George. Everyone knows E. K. Hamilton is your wife. Not often a book of verse has a success like that. Look here, Henry Dashwood is lunching with me. He'd like to meet you."

"Who the devil is Henry Dashwood and why should he want to meet me?"

"Oh, my dear fellow, what do you do with yourself all the time in the country? Henry's about the best critic we've got. He wrote a wonderful review on Evie's book. D'you mean to say she didn't show it to you?"

Before George could answer his friend had called a man over. A tall, thin man, with a high forehead, a beard, a long nose and a stoop, just the sort of man whom George was prepared to dislike at first sight. Introductions were effected. Henry Dashwood sat down.

"Is Mrs. Peregrine in London by any chance? I should very much like to meet her," he said.

"No, my wife doesn't like London. She prefers the country," said George stiffly.

"She wrote me a very nice letter about my review. I was pleased. You know, we critics get more kicks than halfpence. I was simply bowled over by her book. It's so fresh and original, very modern without being obscure. She seems to be as much at her ease in free verse as in classical metres." Then because he was a critic he thought he should criticize. "Sometimes her ear is a trifle at fault, but you can say the same of Emily Dickinson. There are several of those short lyrics of hers that might have been written by Landor."

All this was gibberish to George Peregrine. The man was nothing but a disgusting highbrow. But the Colonel had good manners and he answered with proper civility. Henry Dashwood went on as though he hadn't spoken.

"But what makes the book so outstanding is the passion that throbs in every line. So many of these young poets are so anaemic, cold, bloodless, dully intellectual, but here you have real naked, earthy passion; of course deep, sincere emotion like that is tragic—ah, my dear Colonel, how right Heine was when he said that the poet makes little songs out of his great sorrows. You know, now and then, as I read and re-read those heart-rending pages I thought of Sappho."

This was too much for George Peregrine and he got up.

"Well, it's jolly nice of you to say such nice things about my wife's little book. I'm sure she'll be delighted. But I must bolt, I've got to catch a train and I want to get a bite of lunch."

"Damned fool," he said irritably to himself as he walked upstairs to the dining-room.

He got home in time for dinner and after Evie had gone to bed he went into his study and looked for her book. He thought he'd just glance through it again to see for himself what they were making such a fuss about, but he couldn't find it. Evie must have taken it away.

"Silly," he muttered.

He'd told her he thought it jolly good. What more could a fellow be expected to say? Well, it didn't matter. He lit his pipe and read the *Field* till he felt sleepy. But a week or so later it happened that he had to go into Sheffield for the day. He lunched there at his club. He had nearly finished when the Duke of Haverel came in. This was the great local magnate and of course the Colonel knew him, but only to say how d'you do to; and he was surprised when the Duke stopped at his table.

"We're so sorry your wife couldn't come to us for the week-end," he said, with a sort of shy cordiality. "We're expecting rather a nice lot of people."

George was taken aback. He guessed that the Haverels had asked him and Evie over for the week-end and Evie, without saying a word to him about it, had refused. He had the presence of mind to say he was sorry too.

"Better luck next time," said the Duke pleasantly and moved on.

Colonel Peregrine was very angry and when he got home he said to his wife:

"Look here, what's this about our being asked over to Haverel? Why on earth did you say we couldn't go? We've never been asked before and it's the best shooting in the county."

"I didn't think of that. I thought it would only bore you."

"Damn it all, you might at least have asked me if I wanted to go."

"I'm sorry."

He looked at her closely. There was something in her expression that he didn't quite understand. He frowned.

"I suppose *I* was asked?" he barked.

Evie flushed a little.

"Well, in point of fact you weren't."

"I call it damned rude of them to ask you without asking me."

"I suppose they thought it wasn't your sort of party. The Duchess is rather fond of writers and people like that, you know. She's having Henry Dashwood, the critic, and for some reason he wants to meet me."

"It was damned nice of you to refuse, Evie."

"It's the least I could do," she smiled. She hesitated a moment. "George, my publishers want to give a little dinner party for me one day towards the end of the month and of course they want you to come too."

"Oh, I don't think that's quite my mark. I'll come up to London with you if you like. I'll find someone to dine with."

Daphne.

"I expect it'll be very dull, but they're making rather a point of it. And the day after, the American publisher who's taken my book is giving a cocktail party at Claridge's. I'd like you to come to that if you wouldn't mind."

"Sounds like a crashing bore, but if you really want me to come I'll come."

"It would be sweet of you."

George Peregrine was dazed by the cocktail party. There were a lot of people. Some of them didn't look so bad, a few of the women were decently turned out, but the men seemed to him pretty awful. He was introduced to everybody as Colonel Peregrine, E. K. Hamilton's husband, you know. The men didn't seem to have anything to say to him, but the women gushed.

"You *must* be proud of your wife. Isn't it *wonderful?* You know, I read it right through at a sitting, I simply couldn't put it down, and when I'd finished I started again at the beginning and read it right through a second time. I was simply *thrilled*."

The English publisher said to him:

"We've not had a success like this with a book of verse for twenty years. I've never seen such reviews."

The American publisher said to him:

"It's swell. It'll be a smash hit in America. You wait and see."

The American publisher had sent Evie a great spray of orchids. Damned ridiculous, thought George. As they came in, people were taken up to Evie and it was evident that they said flattering things to her, which she took with a pleasant smile and a word or two of thanks. She seemed a trifle flushed with excitement, but seemed quite at her ease. Though he thought the whole thing a lot of stuff and nonsense, George noted with approval that his wife was carrying it off in just the right way.

"Well, there's one thing," he said to himself, "you can see she's a lady and that's a damned sight more than you can say of anyone else here."

He drank a good many cocktails. But there was one thing that bothered him. He had a notion that some of the people he was introduced to looked at him in a rather funny sort of way, he couldn't quite make out what it meant, and once when he strolled by two women who were sitting together on a sofa he had the impression that they were talking about him and after he passed he was almost certain they tittered. He was very glad when the party came to an end.

In the taxi on their way back to their hotel Evie said to him:

"You were wonderful, dear. You made quite a hit. The girls simply raved about you; they thought you so handsome."

"Girls," he said bitterly. "Old hags."

"Were you bored, dear?"

"Stiff."

She pressed his hand in a gesture of sympathy.

"I hope you won't mind if we wait and go down by the afternoon train. I've got some things to do in the morning."

"No, that's all right. Shopping?"

"I do want to buy one or two things, but I've got to go and be photographed. I hate the idea, but they think I ought to be. For America, you know."

He said nothing. But he thought. He thought it would be a shock to the American public when they saw the portrait of the homely, dessicated little woman who was his wife. He'd always been under the impression that they liked glamour in America.

He went on thinking and next morning when Evie had gone out he went to his club and up to the library. There he looked up recent numbers of *The Times Literary Supplement,* the *New Statesman* and the *Spectator*. Presently he found reviews of Evie's book. He didn't read them very carefully, but enough to see that they were extremely favourable. Then he went to the bookseller's in Piccadilly where he occasionally bought books. He'd made up his mind that he had to read this damned thing of Evie's properly, but he didn't want to ask her what she'd done with the copy she'd given him. He'd buy one for himself. Before going in he looked in the window and the first thing he saw was a display of *When Pyramids Decay*. Damned silly title! He went in. A young man came forward and asked if he could help him.

"No, I'm just having a look round." It embarrassed him to ask for Evie's book and he thought he'd find it for himself and then take it to the salesman. But he couldn't see it anywhere and at last, finding the young man near him, he said in a carefully casual tone: "By the way, have you got a book called *When Pyramids Decay?*"

"The new edition came in this morning. I'll get a copy."

In a moment the young man returned with it. He was a short, rather stout young man, with a shock of untidy carroty hair and spectacles. George Peregrine, tall, upstanding, very military, towered over him.

"Is this a new edition then?" he asked.

"Yes, sir. The fifth. It might be a novel the way it's selling."

George Peregrine hesitated a moment.

"Why d'you suppose it's such a success? I've always been told no one reads poetry."

"Well, it's good, you know. I've read it meself." The young man, though obviously cultured, had a slight Cockney accent, and George quite instinctively adopted a patronizing attitude. "It's the story they like. Sexy, you know, but tragic."

George frowned a little. He was coming to the conclusion that the young man was rather impertinent. No one had told him anything about there being a story in the damned book and he had not gathered that from reading the reviews. The young man went on.

"Of course it's only a flash in the pan, if you know what I mean. The way I look at it, she was sort of inspired like by a personal experience, like Housman was with *The Shropshire Lad*. She'll never write anything else."

"How much is the book?" said George coldly to stop his chatter. "You needn't wrap it up, I'll just slip it in my pocket."

The November morning was raw and he was wearing a greatcoat.

At the station he bought the evening papers and magazines and he and Evie settled themselves comfortably in opposite corners of a first-class carriage and read. At five o'clock they went along to the restaurant car to have tea and chatted a little. They arrived. They drove home in the car which was waiting for them. They bathed, dressed for dinner, and after dinner Evie, saying she was tired out, went to bed. She kissed him, as was her habit, on the forehead. Then he went into the hall, took Evie's book out of his greatcoat pocket and going into the study began to read it. He didn't read verse very easily and though he read with attention, every word of it, the impression he received was far from clear. Then he began at the beginning again and read it a second time. He read with increasing malaise, but he was not a stupid man and when he had finished he had a distinct understanding of what it was all about. Part of the book was in free verse, part in conventional metres, but the story it related was coherent and plain to the meanest intelligence. It was the story of a passionate love affair between an older woman, married, and a young man. George Peregrine made out the steps of it as easily as if he had been doing a sum in simple addition.

Written in the first person, it began with the tremulous surprise of the woman, past her youth, when it dawned upon her that the young man was in love with her. She hesitated to believe it. She thought she must be deceiving herself. And she was terrified when on a sudden she discovered that she was passionately in love with him. She told herself it was absurd; with the disparity of age between them nothing but unhappiness could come to her if she yielded to her emotion. She tried to prevent him from speaking, but the day came when he told her that he loved her and forced her to tell him that she loved him too. He begged her to run away with him. She couldn't leave her husband, her home; and what life could they look forward to, she an ageing woman, he so young? How could she expect his love to last? She begged him to have mercy on her. But his love was impetuous. He wanted her, he wanted her with all his heart, and at last trembling, afraid, desirous, she yielded to him. Then there was a period of ecstatic happiness. The world, the dull, humdrum world of every day, blazed with glory. Love songs flowed from her pen. The woman worshipped the young, virile body of her lover. George flushed darkly when she praised his broad chest and slim flanks, the beauty of his legs and the flatness of his belly.

Hot stuff, Daphne's friend had said. It was that all right. Disgusting.

There were sad little pieces in which she lamented the emptiness of her life when, as must happen, he left her, but they ended with a cry that all she had to suffer would be worth it for the bliss that for a while had been hers. She wrote of the long, tremulous nights they passed together and the languor that lulled them to sleep in one another's arms. She wrote of the rapture of brief stolen moments when, braving all danger, their passion overwhelmed them and they surrendered to its call.

She thought it would be an affair of a few weeks, but miraculously it lasted. One of the poems referred to three years having gone by without lessening the love that filled their hearts. It looked as though he continued to press her to go away with him, far away, to a hill town in Italy, a Greek island, a walled city in Tunisia, so that they could be together always, for in another of the poems she besought him to let things be as they were. Their happiness was precarious. Perhaps it was owing to the difficulties they had to encounter and the rarity of their meetings that their love had retained for so long its first enchanting ardour. Then on a sudden the young man died. How, when or where George could not discover. There followed a long, heartbroken cry of bitter grief, grief she could not indulge in, grief that had to be hidden. She had to be cheerful, give dinner parties and go out to dinner, behave as she had always behaved, though the light had gone out of her life and she was bowed down with anguish. The last poem of all was a set of four short stanzas in which the writer, sadly resigned to her loss, thanked the dark powers that rule man's destiny that she had been privileged at least for a while to enjoy the greatest happiness that we poor human beings can ever hope to know.

It was three o'clock in the morning when George Peregrine finally put the book down. It had seemed to him that he heard Evie's voice in every line; over and over again he came upon turns of phrase he had heard her use, there were details that were as familiar to him as to her; there was no doubt about it; it was her own story she had told, and it was as plain as anything could be that she had had a lover and her lover had died. It was not anger so much that he felt, nor horror or dismay, though he was dismayed and he was horrified, but amazement. It was as inconceivable that Evie should have had a love affair, and a wildly passionate one at that, as that the trout in a glass case over the chimney piece in his study, the finest he had ever caught, should suddenly wag its tail. He understood now the meaning of the amused look he had seen in the eyes of that man he had spoken with at the club, he understood why Daphne when she was talking about the book had seemed to be enjoying a private joke, and why those two women at the cocktail party had tittered when he strolled past them.

He broke out into a sweat. Then on a sudden he was seized with fury and he jumped up to go and awake Evie and ask her sternly for an explanation. But he stopped at the door. After all what proof had he? A book. He remembered that he'd told Evie he thought it jolly good. True, he hadn't read it, but he'd pretended he had. He would look a perfect fool if he had to admit that.

"I must watch my step," he muttered.

He made up his mind to wait for two or three days and think it all over. Then he'd decide what to do. He went to bed, but he couldn't sleep for a long time.

"Evie," he kept on saying to himself, "Evie, of all people."

They met at breakfast next morning as usual. Evie was as she always was, quiet, demure and self-possessed, a middle-aged woman who made no effort to look younger than she was, a woman who had nothing of what he still called It. He looked at her as he hadn't looked at her for years. She had her usual placid serenity. Her pale blue eyes were untroubled. There was no sign of guilt on her candid brow. She made the same little casual remarks she always made.

"It's nice to get back to the country again after those two hectic days in London. What are you going to do this morning?"

It was incomprehensible.

Three days later he went to see his solicitor. Henry Blane was an old friend of George's as well as his lawyer. He had a place not far from Peregrine's and for years they had shot over one another's preserves. For two days a week he was a busy country gentleman and for the other five a busy lawyer in Sheffield. He was a tall, robust fellow, with a boisterous manner and a jovial laugh, which suggested that he liked to be looked upon essentially as a sportsman and a good fellow and only incidentally as a lawyer. But he was shrewd and worldly-wise.

"Well, George, what's brought you here today?" he boomed as the Colonel was shown into his office. "Have a good time in London? I'm taking my missus up for a few days next week. How's Evie?"

"It's about Evie I've come to see you," said Peregrine, giving him a suspicious look. "Have you read her book?"

His sensitivity had been sharpened during those last days of troubled thought and he was conscious of a faint change in the lawyer's expression. It was as though he were suddenly on his guard.

"Yes, I've read it. Great success, isn't it? Fancy Evie breaking out into poetry. Wonders will never cease."

George Peregrine was inclined to lose his temper.

"It's made me look a perfect damned fool."

"Oh, what nonsense, George! There's no harm in Evie's writing a book. You ought to be jolly proud of her."

"Don't talk such rot. It's her own story. You know it and everyone else knows it. I suppose I'm the only one who doesn't know who her lover was."

"There is such a thing as imagination, old boy. There's no reason to suppose the whole thing isn't just made up."

"Look here, Henry, we've known one another all our lives. We've had all sorts of good times together. Be honest with me. Can you look me in the face and tell me you believe it's a made-up story?"

Henry Blane moved uneasily in his chair. He was disturbed by the distress in old George's voice.

"You've got no right to ask me a question like that. Ask Evie."

"I daren't," George answered after an anguished pause. "I'm afraid she'd tell me the truth."

There was an uncomfortable silence.

"Who was the chap?"

Henry Blane looked at him straight in the eye.

"I don't know, and if I did I wouldn't tell you."

"You swine. Don't you see what a position I'm in? Do you think it's very pleasant to be made absolutely ridiculous?"

The lawyer lit a cigarette and for some moments silently puffed it.

"I don't see what I can do for you," he said at last.

"You've got private detectives you employ, I suppose. I want you to put them on the job and let them find everything out."

"It's not very pretty to put detectives on one's wife, old boy; and besides, taking for granted for a moment that Evie had an affair, it was a good many years ago and I don't suppose it would be possible to find a thing. They seem to have covered their tracks pretty carefully."

"I don't care. You put the detectives on. I want to know the truth."

"I won't, George. If you're determined to do that you'd better consult someone else. And look here, even if you got evidence that Evie had been unfaithful to you what would you do with it? You'd look rather silly divorcing your wife because she'd committed adultery ten years ago."

"At all events I could have it out with her."

"You can do that now, but you know just as well as I do that if you do she'll leave you. D'you want her to do that?"

George gave him an unhappy look.

"I don't know. I always thought she'd been a damned good wife to me. She runs the house perfectly, we never have any servant trouble; she's done wonders with the garden and she's splendid with all the village people. But damn it, I have my self-respect to think of. How can I go on living with her when I know that she was grossly unfaithful to me?"

"Have you always been faithful to her?"

"More or less, you know. After all we've been married for nearly twenty-four years and Evie was never much for bed."

The solicitor slightly raised his eyebrows, but George was too intent on what he was saying to notice.

"I don't deny that I've had a bit of fun now and then. A man wants it. Women are different."

"We only have men's word for that," said Henry Blane, with a faint smile.

"Evie's absolutely the last woman I'd have suspected of kicking over the traces. I mean, she's a very fastidious, reticent woman. What on earth made her write the damned book?"

"I suppose it was a very poignant experience and perhaps it was a relief to her to get it off her chest like that."

"Well, if she had to write it why the devil didn't she write it under an assumed name?"

"She used her maiden name. I suppose she thought that was enough and it would have been if the book hadn't had this amazing boom."

George Peregrine and the lawyer were sitting opposite one another with a desk between them. George, his elbow on the desk, his cheek resting on his hand, frowned at his thought.

"It's so rotten not to know what sort of a chap he was. One can't even tell if he was by way of being a gentleman. I mean, for all I know he may have been a farmhand or a clerk in a lawyer's office."

Henry Blane did not permit himself to smile and when he answered there was in his eyes a kindly, tolerant look.

"Knowing Evie so well I think the probabilities are that he was all right. Anyhow I'm sure he wasn't a clerk in my office."

"It's been such a shock to me," the Colonel sighed. "I thought she was fond of me. She couldn't have written that book unless she hated me."

"Oh, I don't believe that. I don't think she's capable of hatred."

"You're not going to pretend that she loves me."

"No."

"Well, what does she feel for me?"

Henry Blane leaned back in his swivel chair and looked at George reflectively.

"Indifference, I should say."

The Colonel gave a little shudder and reddened.

"After all, you're not in love with her, are you?"

George Peregrine did not answer directly.

"It's been a great blow to me not to have any children, but I've never let her see that I think she's let me down. I've always been kind to her. Within reasonable limits I've tried to do my duty by her."

The lawyer passed a large hand over his mouth to conceal the smile that trembled on his lips.

"It's been such an awful shock to me," Peregrine went on. "Damn it all, even ten years ago Evie was no chicken, and God knows she wasn't much to look at. It's so ugly." He sighed deeply. "What would *you* do in my place?"

"Nothing."

George Peregrine drew himself bolt upright in his chair and he looked at Henry with the stern, set face that he must have worn when he inspected his regiment.

"I can't overlook a thing like this. I've been made a laughing-stock. I can never hold up my head again."

"Nonsense," said the lawyer sharply, and then in a pleasant, kindly manner: "Listen, old boy: the man's dead; it all happened a long while back. Forget it. Talk to people about Evie's book, rave about it, tell 'em how proud you are of her. Behave as though you had so much confidence in her, you *knew* she could never have been unfaithful to you. The world moves so quickly and people's memories are so short. They'll forget."

"I shan't forget."

"You're both middle-aged people. She probably does a great deal more for you than you think and you'd be awfully lonely without her. I don't think it matters if you don't forget. It'll be all to the good if you can get it into that thick head of yours that there's a lot more in Evie than you ever had the gumption to see."

"Damn it all, you talk as if *I* was to blame."

"No, I don't think you were to blame, but I'm not so sure that Evie was either. I don't suppose she wanted to fall in love with this boy. D'you remember those verses right at the end? The impression they gave me was that though she was shattered by his death, in a strange sort of way she welcomed it. All through she'd been aware of the fragility of the tie that bound them. He died in the full flush of his first love and had never known that love so seldom endures; he'd only known its bliss and beauty. In her own bitter grief she found solace in the thought that he'd been spared all sorrow."

"All that's a bit above my head, old boy. I see more or less what you mean."

George Peregrine stared unhappily at the inkstand on the desk. He was silent and the lawyer looked at him with curious, yet sympathetic eyes.

"Do you realize what courage she must have had never by a sign to show how dreadfully unhappy she was?" he said gently.

Colonel Peregrine sighed.

"I'm broken. I suppose you're right; it's no good crying over spilt milk and it would only make things worse if I made a fuss."

"Well?"

George Peregrine gave a pitiful little smile. "I'll take your advice. I'll do nothing. Let them think me a damned fool and to hell with them. The truth is, I don't know what I'd do without Evie. But I'll tell you what, there's one thing I shall never understand till my dying day: What in the name of heaven did the fellow ever see in her?"

Comments and Questions

It is uncommonly profitable to compare the method and results of Chekhov's "On the Road" (p. 87) with those of Maugham's story. Each writer has a method and subject quite different from the other's. Maugham is critical of Chekhov's method and results, particularly because Chekhov does not rely on plot, because, from Maugham's point of view, he tells no story. "If you try to tell one of his stories," says Maugham, "you will find that there is nothing to tell." For Maugham, apparently Chekhov's stories have a middle, but no beginning or end. Here, Maugham could be commenting about "On the Road": "If you could take two or three persons, describe their mutual relations and leave it at that, why then it wasn't hard to write a story. . . ." Both Chekhov and Maugham have had a tremendous influence on the short story, and it would be naive to conclude that one is right, the other wrong. As Henry James said, "The House of Fiction has . . . not one window, but a million. . . ."

1. The tone and atmosphere of "On the Road" and "The Colonel's Lady" are quite different. How does each writer achieve them, and with what results? This is a large question, and it requires a comprehensive, thoughtful answer. Perhaps the answers to the following questions will help.

2. In what ways does Maugham comment on the action of the story? Consider especially his *indirect* comments; for example, the scene in which Peregrine meets the critic Dashwood. We seem to have a clear idea about Maugham's attitude toward his characters—are we so clear about Chekhov's attitude?

3. Assuming that you enjoyed both stories, describe what you enjoyed about each one. Does the word *enjoy* exactly describe your reaction to *both* stories?

4. We recognize that Chekhov's structure of action differs considerably from Maugham's. Is one better than the other or is each one designed to produce different and *justifiable* results?

5. Is one author more serious than the other, or is it simply that one is Russian and the other British? If the latter part of this question is quite meaningless to you, state your case. Did you laugh at all as you read either story? If we laugh at a serious story, do we discredit it?

LEO TOLSTOY
1828–1910

Three Deaths

1

It was autumn. Two carriages were driving at a rapid trot along the highroad. In the foremost sat two women. One was a lady, thin and pale; the other, her maid, was plump, with shining, red cheeks. Her short, coarse hair stood out under her faded hat; her red hand, in a torn glove, kept hurriedly putting it tidy; her high bosom, covered with a tapestry kerchief, was eloquent of health; her quick, black eyes watched out of the window the fields flying past, then glanced timidly at her mistress, then shifted uneasily about the corners of the carriage. Just before the maid's nose swung the lady's hat, hanging from the rack above; on her lap lay a puppy. Her feet were kept from the floor by the boxes that stood on the carriage floor, and could be faintly heard knocking on them through the shaking of the springs and the rattling of the windows.

With her hands clasped on her knees and her eyes closed, the lady swayed feebly to and fro on the cushions that had been put at her back, and with a slight frown she coughed inwardly. On her head she wore a white nightcap, and a light blue kerchief was tied on her soft, white neck. A straight parting, retreating under her cap, divided her fair, pomaded, exceedingly flat hair, and there was a dry, deathlike look about the whiteness of the skin of this wide parting. The faded, yellowish skin hung loose on her delicate and beautiful features and was flushed on her cheeks. Her lips were dry and restless, her eyelashes were thin and straight, and her cloth travelling cloak fell in straight folds over her sunken bosom. Though her eyes were closed, the lady's face expressed fatigue, irritation, and habitual suffering. A footman was dozing on the box, one elbow on the rail of the seat. The driver, hired from the posting-station, shouted briskly to the four sturdy, sweating horses, and looked round now and then at the other driver, who called to him from behind on the coach. Smoothly and rapidly the wheels made their broad, parallel tracks along the chalky mud of the road. The sky was gray and cold; a damp mist was falling over the fields and the road. The carriage was close, and smelt of eau de Cologne and dust. The sick woman stretched her head back and slowly opened her eyes. Her large, handsome, dark eyes were very bright.

"Again," she said, her beautiful, thin hand nervously thrusting away a corner of the maid's cloak which was just brushing against her knees, and her mouth twitched painfully. Matryosha gathered up her cloak in both hands, lifted it up on her lap, and edged further away. Her blooming face flushed bright red. The sick woman's fine dark eyes kept eager watch on the servant's actions. She leaned with both hands on the seat and tried to raise herself, so as to be sitting higher; but her strength failed her. Her mouth twitched and her whole face worked with an expression of helpless, wrathful irony. "You might at least help me! . . . Ah, you needn't! I can do it myself, only be so good as not to lay your bundles, bags, or whatever they are behind me, please! You had better not touch me if you're so awkward!"

The lady shut her eyes, and rapidly raising her eyelids again glanced at the maid. Matryosha was staring at her and biting her red underlip. A heavy sigh rose from the sick woman's chest, but changed to a cough before it was uttered. She turned away, frowning, and clutched at her chest with both hands. When the cough was over, she closed her eyes again and sat without stirring. The carriage and the coach drove into a village. Matryosha put her stout arm out from under her kerchief and crossed herself.

"What is it?" asked the lady.

"A station, madam."

"What do you cross yourself for, I ask?"

"A church, madam."

The sick woman turned towards the window, and began slowly crossing herself, her great eyes fastened on the big village church as the carriage drove by it.

The two carriages stopped together at the station. The sick woman's husband and the doctor got out of the other carriage and came up to her.

"How do you feel?" asked the doctor, taking her pulse.

"Well, how are you, my dear—not tired?" asked her husband, in French. "Wouldn't you like to get out?"

Matryosha, gathering up her bundles, squeezed into a corner so as not to be in their way as they talked.

"Just the same," answered the lady. "I won't get out."

Her husband stayed a little while beside the carriage, then went into the station-house. Matryosha got out of the carriage and ran on tiptoe through the mud to the gates.

"If I am ill, it's no reason you shouldn't have your lunch," the invalid said with a faint smile to the doctor, who was standing at the carriage window.

"None of them care anything about me," she added to herself, as soon as the doctor had moved with sedate step away from her and run at a trot up the steps of the station-house. "They are all right, so they don't care. O my God!"

"Well, Eduard Ivanovich," said her husband, meeting the doctor and rubbing his hands, with a cheery smile. "I've ordered the case of wine to be brought in. What do you say to a bottle?"

"I shouldn't say no," answered the doctor.

"Well, how is she?" the husband asked with a sigh, lifting his eyebrows and dropping his voice.

"I have told you she can't possibly get as far as Italy; if she reaches Moscow it will be a wonder, especially in this weather."

"What are we to do! Oh my God! my God!" The husband put his hand over his eyes. "Put it here," he added to the servant who brought in the case of wine.

"You should have kept her at home," the doctor answered, shrugging his shoulders.

"But tell me, what could I do?" protested the husband. "I did everything I could, you know, to keep her. I talked to her of our means, and of the children whom we should have to leave behind, and of my business—she won't hear a word of anything. She makes plans for her life abroad as though she were strong and well. And to tell her of her position would be the death of her."

"But death has hold of her already, you ought

to know it, Vasily Dmitrich. A person can't live without lungs, and the lungs can't grow again. It's distressing and terrible, but what's one to do? My duty and yours is simply to see that her end should be as easy as possible. It's the priest who is needed now."

"O my God! But conceive my position, having to speak to her of the last sacrament. Come what will, I can't tell her. You know how good she is."

"You must try, all the same, to persuade her to wait till the roads are frozen," said the doctor, shaking his head significantly, "or we may have a disaster on the road."

"Aksyusha, hey, Aksyusha!" shrieked the stationmaster's daughter, flinging a jacket over her head, and stamping on the dirty back steps of the station; "let's go and have a look at the lady from Shirkin; they say she's being taken abroad for her lungs. I've never seen what people look like in consumption."

Aksyusha darted out at the doorway, and arm in arm they ran by the gate. Slackening their pace, they walked by the carriage, and peeped in at the lowered window. The sick woman turned her head towards them, but noticing their curiosity, she frowned and turned away.

"My gra-a-cious!" said the stationmaster's daughter, turning her head away quickly. "Such a wonderful beauty as she was, and what does she look like now. Enough to frighten one, really. Did you see, did you see, Aksyusha?"

"Yes, she is thin!" Aksyusha assented. "Let's go by and get another look at her, as though we were going to the well. She turned away before I'd seen her properly. I am sorry for her, Masha!"

"And the mud's awful!" answered Masha, and both ran back to the gate.

"I've grown frightful, it seems," thought the invalid. "Ah, to make haste, to make haste to get abroad, then I shall soon be better!"

"Well, how are you, my dear?" said her husband, still munching as he came up to the carriage.

"Always that invariable question," thought the sick woman, "and he goes on eating too!"

"Just the same," she muttered through her teeth.

"Do you know, my dear, I'm afraid the journey will be bad for you in this weather, and Eduard Ivanovich says so too. Hadn't we better turn back?"

She kept wrathfully silent.

"The weather will change, and the roads perhaps will be hard, and that would make it better for you; and then we would all go together."

"Excuse me. If I hadn't listened to you long ago, I should be in Berlin by now and should be quite well."

"That couldn't be helped, my angel; it was out of the question, as you know! But now, if you would wait for a month, you would be ever so much better. I should have settled my business, and we could take the children."

"The children are quite well, and I am not."

"But consider, my dear, with this weather if you get worse on the road . . . there, at any rate, you're at home."

"And if I am at home? . . . To die at home?" the sick woman answered hotly. But the word "die" evidently terrified her; she bent an imploring, questioning look upon her husband. He dropped his eyes and did not speak. The sick woman's mouth puckered all at once like a child's, and tears dropped from her eyes. Her husband buried his face in his handkerchief, and walked away from the carriage without speaking.

"No, I am going," said the sick woman, lifting her eyes towards heaven, and she fell to whispering disconnected words. "My God, what for?" she said, and the tears flowed more freely. For a long while she prayed fervently, but there was still the same pain and tightness on her chest. The sky, the fields, and the road were just as gray and cheerless; and the same autumn mist, neither thicker nor clearer, hung over the mud of the road, the roofs of the huts, the carriage and the sheepskin coats of the drivers, who were greasing and harnessing a carriage, chatting together in their vigorous, merry voices.

2

The horses were put in the shafts; but the driver lingered. He went into the drivers' hut. It was hot and stifling, dark and oppressive in the hut; there was a smell of human beings, baking bread, and cabbage, and sheepskins. There were several drivers in the room: the cook was busy at the stove; on the top of the stove lay a sick man wrapped in sheepskins.

"Uncle Fyodor! hey, Uncle Fyodor!" said the

driver as he came into the room. He was a young fellow, in a sheepskin coat with a whip stuck in his belt, and he was addressing the sick man.

"What do you want Fedya for, you windbag?" one of the drivers interposed. "They are waiting for you in the carriage.

"I want to ask him for his boots; I've worn mine out," answered the young fellow, tossing back his hair and straightening the gloves in his belt. "Is he asleep? Hey, Uncle Fyodor?" he repeated, going up to the stove.

"What?" a weak voice was heard in reply, and a thin face with a red beard bent over from the stove. A big, wasted, white hand, covered with hair, pulled up a coat on the bony shoulder in the dirty shirt. "Give me a drink, brother; what do you want?"

The young man handed him a dipper of water.

"Well, Fedya," he said, hesitating, "you won't be wanting your new boots now; give them to me; you won't be going out, you know."

Pressing his weary head to the shining dipper, and wetting his scanty, hanging mustaches in the turbid water, the sick man drank feebly and eagerly. His tangled beard was not clean, his sunken, lusterless eyes were lifted with an effort to the young man's face. When he had finished drinking he tried to lift his hand to wipe his wet lips, but he could not, and he wiped them on the sleeve of the coat. Without uttering a sound, but breathing heavily through his nose, he looked straight into the young man's eyes, trying to rally his strength.

"Maybe you've promised them to someone already?" said the young man; "if so, never mind. The thing is, it's soaking wet outside, and I've got to go out on a job; and I said to myself, why, I'll ask Fedya for his boots, he'll not need them, for sure. If you are likely to need them yourself, say so."

There was a gurgle and a rattle in the sick man's throat; he bent over and was choked by a deep, stifling cough.

"He need them!" the cook cried out in sudden anger, filling the whole hut with her voice. "He's not got off the stove these two months! Why, he coughs fit to split himself; it makes me ache inside simply to hear him. How could he want boots? He won't wear new boots to be buried! And time he was, too, long ago—God forgive me the sin! Why, he coughs fit to split himself. He ought to be moved into another hut, or somewhere! There are hospitals, I've heard say, for such in the town; he takes up the whole place, and what's one to do? One hasn't room to turn around. And then they expect me to keep the place clean!"

"Hi, Seryoga! go and take your seat; the gentry are waiting," the stationmaster shouted at the door.

Seryoga would have gone away without waiting for an answer, but the sick man's eyes, while he was coughing, had told him he wanted to answer.

"You take the boots, Seryoga," said he, stifling the cough and taking breath a minute. "Only buy me a stone when I die, do you hear?" he added huskily.

"Thanks, uncle, so I'll take them; and as to the stone, ay, ay, I'll buy it."

"There, lads, you hear?" the sick man managed to articulate, and again he bent over and began choking.

"All right, we heard," said one of the drivers. "Go along, Seryoga, or the overseer will be running after you again. The lady from Shirkin is ill."

Seryoga quickly pulled off his torn boots, which were much too large for him, and thrust them under a bench. Uncle Fyodor's new boots fitted his feet perfectly, and Seryoga went out to the carriage looking at them.

"What grand boots! let me grease them for you," said a driver with the greasepot in his hand, as Seryoga got on the box and picked up the reins. "Did he give them to you for nothing?"

"Why, are you jealous?" answered Seryoga, getting up and shaking down the skirts of his coat about his legs. "Hi, get up, my darlings!" he shouted to the horses, brandishing the whip, and the two carriages, with their occupants, boxes, and baggage, rolled swiftly along the wet road, and vanished into the gray autumn mist.

The sick driver remained lying on the stove in the stifling hut. Unrelieved by coughing, he turned over on the other side with an effort, and was quiet. All day till evening, men were coming and going and dining in the hut; there was no sound from the sick man. At nightfall, the cook clambered up onto the stove and reached across his legs to get a sheepskin. "Don't you be angry with me, Nastasya," said the sick man; "I shall soon clear out of your place."

"That's all right, that's all right; why, I didn't mean it," muttered Nastasya. "But what is it that's wrong with you, uncle? Tell me about it."

"All my inside's wasted away. God knows what it is."

"My word! and does your throat hurt when you cough!"

"It hurts me all over. My death is at hand—that's what it is. Oh, oh, oh!" moaned the sick man.

"Cover your legs up like this," said Nastasya, pulling a coat over him as she crept off the stove.

A night-light glimmered dimly all night in the hut. Nastasya and some ten drivers lay on the floor and the benches asleep, and snoring loudly. The sick man alone moaned faintly, coughed, and turned over on the stove. Towards morning he became quite still.

"A queer dream I had in the night," said the cook, stretching next morning in the half-light. "I dreamed that Uncle Fyodor got down from the stove and went out to chop wood. 'Nastasya,' says he, 'I'll split you some'; and I says to him, 'How can you chop wood?' and he snatches up the axe and starts chopping so fast, so fast that the chips were flying. 'Why,' says I, 'you were ill, weren't you?' 'No,' says he, 'I'm all right,' and he swings the axe, so that it gave me quite a fright. I screamed out and waked up. Isn't he dead, perhaps? Uncle Fyodor! Hey, uncle!"

Fyodor made no sound in reply.

"May be he is dead. I'll get up and see," said one of the drivers who was awake.

A thin hand, covered with reddish hairs, hung down from the stove; it was cold and pale.

"I'll go and tell the overseer. He's dead, seemingly," said the driver.

Fyodor had no relations—he had come from distant parts. The next day he was buried in the new graveyard beyond the copse, and for several days after Nastasya told every one of the dream she had had, and how she had been the first to discover that Uncle Fyodor was dead.

3

Spring had come. Streams of water hurried gurgling between the frozen dung-heaps in the wet streets of the town. The people moving to and fro were gayly dressed and gayly chattering. Behind the fences of the little gardens the buds on the trees were swelling, and their branches rustled faintly in the fresh breeze. Everywhere there was a running and a dripping of clear drops. . . . The sparrows chattered incoherently, and fluttered to and fro on their little wings. On the sunny side, on fences, trees, and houses, all was movement. There was youth and gladness in the sky and on the earth and in the heart of man. In one of the principal streets there was straw lying in front of a large house; in the house lay the dying woman who had been hastening abroad.

At the closed door of her room stood the patient's husband and her cousin, an elderly woman; on a sofa sat a priest with downcast eyes, holding something wrapped up in his stole. In a corner an old lady, the patient's mother, lay in an armchair, weeping bitterly. Near her stood a maid holding a clean pocket-handkerchief in readiness for the old lady when she should ask for it. Another maid was rubbing the old lady's temples with something and blowing on her gray head under her cap.

"Well, Christ be with you, my dear," said the husband to the elderly woman who was standing with him at the door; "she has such confidence in you, you know so well how to talk to her; go in, and have a good talk with her." He would have opened the door; but the cousin restrained him, put her handkerchief several times to her eyes, and shook her head.

"Come, now, I don't look as if I had been crying, I think," she said, and opening the door herself, she went into the sickroom.

The husband was in great excitement, and seemed utterly distraught. He walked towards the old lady, but stopped short a few paces from her, turned, walked about the room, and went up to the priest. The priest looked at him, raised his eyebrows heavenwards, and sighed. His thick, grizzled beard turned upwards too, and then sank again.

"My God! my God!" said the husband.

"There is nothing one can do," said the priest, and again his brows and his beard were elevated and drooped again.

"And her mother here!" the husband said, almost in despair. "She will never be able to bear this! She loves her, she loves her so that she . . . I don't know. If you, father, would attempt to soothe her and to persuade her to go out of this room."

The priest rose and went to the old lady.

"True it is, that none can sound the depths of a mother's heart," said he; "but God is merciful."

The old lady's face began suddenly twitching, and she sobbed hysterically.

"God is merciful," the priest went on, when she was a little calmer. "In my parish, I must tell you, there was a man ill, much worse than Marya Dmitryevna, and a simple artisan cured him with herbs in a very short time. And this same artisan is in Moscow now, indeed. I told Vasily Dmitryevich—he might try him. Any way, it would be a comfort to the sick woman. To God all things are possible."

"No, she can't live," said the old lady; "if it could have been me, but God takes her." And her hysterics grew so violent that she fainted.

The sick woman's husband hid his face in his hands, and ran out of the room.

The first person that met him in the corridor was a boy of six, who was running at full speed after a little girl younger than himself.

"Shouldn't I take the children to see their mamma?" asked the nurse.

"No, she doesn't want to see them. It upsets her."

The boy stood still for a moment, staring intently into his father's face, then suddenly kicking up his foot, with a merry shriek he ran on.

"I'm pretending she's my black horse, papa!" shouted the boy, pointing to his sister.

Meanwhile in the next room the cousin was sitting by the sick woman's bedside, and trying by skillfully leading up to the subject to prepare her for the idea of death. The doctor was at the other window mixing a draught.

The sick woman, in a white dressing-gown, sat propped up with pillows in bed, and gazed at the cousin without speaking.

"Ah, my dear," she said, suddenly interrupting her, "don't try to prepare me. Don't treat me as a child. I am a Christian. I know all about it. I know I haven't long to live; I know that if my husband would have listened to me sooner, I should have been in Italy, and perhaps, most likely indeed, should have been quite well. Everyone told him so. But it can't be helped, it seems that it was God's will. We are all great sinners, I know that; but I put my trust in God's mercy: He will forgive all, surely, all. I try to understand myself. I, too, have sinned greatly, my dear. But, to make up, how I have suffered. I have tried to bear my sufferings with patience. . . ."

"Then may I send for the priest, my dear? You will feel all the easier after the sacrament," said the cousin. The sick woman bowed her head in token of assent. "God forgive me, a sinner!" she murmured.

The cousin went out and beckoned to the priest.

"She is an angel!" she said to the husband with tears in her eyes. The husband began to weep; the priest went in at the door; the old lady was still unconscious, and in the outer room there was a complete stillness. Five minutes later the priest came out, and taking off his stole smoothed back his hair.

"Thank God, the lady is calmer now," he said; "she wants to see you."

The cousin and the husband went in. The sick woman was weeping quietly, gazing at the holy picture.

"I congratulate you, my dear," said her husband.

"Thank you! How happy I am now, what unspeakable joy I am feeling!" said the sick woman, and a faint smile played about her thin lips. "How merciful is God! Is it not true? Is He not merciful and almighty?" And again with eyes full of tears she gazed at the holy picture in eager prayer.

Then suddenly something seemed to recur to her mind. She beckoned her husband to her.

"You never will do what I ask," she said in a weak, irritable voice.

Her husband, craning his neck forward, listened submissively.

"What is it, my dear?"

"How often I've told you those doctors don't know anything; there are plain women healers, who work cures. . . . The priest told me . . . an artisan . . . send for him."

"For whom, my dear?"

"My God, he won't understand anything!" . . .

And the sick woman frowned and covered her eyes. The doctor went up and took her hand. The pulse was growing perceptibly weaker and weaker. He made a sign to the husband. The sick woman noticed this gesture and looked around in alarm. The cousin turned away, and burst into tears.

"Don't cry, don't torture yourself and me," said the sick woman. "That destroys all the calm left me."

"You are an angel!" said the cousin, kissing her hand.

"No, kiss me here, it's only the dead who are kissed on the hand. My God! my God!"

The same evening the sick woman was a corpse, and the corpse lay in a coffin in the drawing-room of the great house. The doors of the big room were closed, and in it a deacon sat alone, reading the Psalms of David aloud in a rhythmic, nasal tone. The bright light of the wax candles in the tall silver candlesticks fell on the pale brow of the dead woman, on the heavy, waxen hands and the stonelike folds of the shroud, that jutted up horribly at the knees and toes. The deacon read on rhythmically without taking in the meaning of his own words, and the words echoed and died away strangely in the still room. From time to time the sounds of children's voices and the tramp of their feet came from a far-away room.

" 'Hidest thou thy face, they are troubled,' " the psalm-reader boomed; " 'thou takest away their breath, they die and return to their dust. Thou sendest forth thy spirit, they are created; and thou renewest the face of the earth. The glory of the Lord shall endure for ever.' "

The face of the dead woman was stern and solemn. Nothing stirred the pure, cold brow and the firmly set lips. She was all attention. But did she even now understand those grand words?

4

A month later a stone chapel was raised over the dead woman's grave. But there was still no stone over the driver's grave, and there was nothing but the bright green grass over the mound, which was the only sign of a man's past existence.

"You will be sinning, Seryoga," the cook at the station said one day, "if you don't buy a stone for Fyodor. You were always saying it was winter, but now why don't you keep your word? I was by at the time. He's come back once already to ask you for it; if you don't buy it, he'll come again and stifle you."

"Why, did I say I wasn't going to?" answered Seryoga; "I'll buy a stone as I said I would; I'll buy one for a silver rouble and a half. I've not forgotten, but it must be fetched, you know. As soon as I've a chance to go to the town I'll buy it."

"You might put a cross up anyway," put in an old driver, "or else it's a downright shame. You're wearing the boots.'

"Where's one to get a cross? You wouldn't cut one out of a log of firewood?"

"What are you talking about? You can't hew it out of a log. You take an axe and go early in the morning into the copse; you can cut a cross there. An aspen or something you can fell. And it'll make a fine wooden monument too. Or else you'll have to go and stand the forester a drink of vodka. One doesn't want to have to give him a drink for every trifle. The other day I broke a splinter-bar; I cut myself a first-rate new one, and no one said a word to me."

In the early morning, when it was hardly light, Seryoga took his axe and went into the wood. Over all lay a chill, even-colored veil of still-falling dew, not lighted up by the sun. The east was imperceptibly growing clearer, reflecting its faint light on the arch of sky covered with fine clouds. Not a blade of grass below, not a leaf on the topmost twig stirred. The stillness of the forest was only broken at intervals by the sound of wings in a tree or a rustle on the ground. Suddenly a strange sound, not one of nature's own, rang out and died away on the edge of the forest. But again the sound was heard, and began to be repeated at regular intervals near the trunk of the motionless trees. One of the treetops began shaking in a strange way; its sappy leaves whispered something; and a warbler that had been perched on one of its branches fluttered round it twice, and uttering a whistle and wagging its tail, settled on another tree.

The sound of the axe was more and more muffled, the sappy, white chips flew out on the dewy grass, and a faint crackling sound followed each blow. The tree shuddered all over, bowed, and quickly stood up straight again, trembling in dismay on its roots. For a moment all was still, but again the tree bent; a crack was heard in its trunk, and with a snapping of twigs its branches dropped, and it crashed down with its top on the damp earth. The sound of the axe and of steps died away. The warbler whistled and flew up higher. The branch in which it had caught its wings shook for a little while in all its leaves, then became still like the rest. The trees displayed their motionless branches more gladly than ever in the newly opened space.

The first beams of the sun, piercing the delicate cloud, shone out in the sky and darted over the earth. The mist began rolling in waves in the hollows; the dew glittered sparkling on the green grass; the translucent clouds turned white, and floated in haste across the blue sky. The birds flitted to and fro in the thickets and twittered some happy song, like mad things. The sappy leaves whispered joyously and calmly on the treetops, and the branches of the living trees, slowly, majestically, swayed above the fallen dead tree.

LANGSTON HUGHES 1902–1967

On the Road

Hughes, often regarded as "America's senior black professional literary man," believed that his purpose as a writer was "to explain and illuminate the Negro condition in America." One of Hughes's most knowledgeable critics and a black poet (see p. 362 for one of his poems), James A. Emanuel, believes that " 'On the Road' is artistically among the top five or six of Hughes's many stories" and "is a richly symbolic fusion of dream and reality, using well over two hundred precisely patterned images." In talking to the writer Kay Boyle about the story, Hughes commented:

> All I had in mind was cold, hunger, a strange town at night . . . and a black vagabond named Sargeant against white snow, cold people, hard doors, trying to go somewhere, but too tired and hungry to make it—hemmed in on the ground by the same people who hemmed Christ in by rigid rituals surrounding a man-made cross. It developed as a kind of visual picture-story out of night, snow, man, church, police, cross, doors becoming bars, then ending with a man shaking the bars, but Christ at least free on the precarious road—His destination Kansas City, being a half-way point across the country. . . .
>
> I was writing of the little man. . . . I was writing, too, of Jesus as a human being whose meaning sometimes has been lost through the organization of the church. . . . The function of religion in daily life, as the Reverend [Martin Luther] King has made it function, is what I was talking about. . . . Sargeant had done as much for Jesus in getting Him down off the cross as Jesus had done for Sargeant in showing him that even the Saviour of men had nowhere to go except to push on. . . .*

He was not interested in the snow. When he got off the freight, one early evening during the depression, Sargeant never even noticed the snow. But he must have felt it seeping down his neck, cold, wet, sopping in his shoes. But if you had asked him, he wouldn't have known it was snowing. Sargeant didn't see the snow, not even under the bright lights of the main street, falling white and flaky against the night. He was too hungry, too sleepy, too tired.

The Reverend Mr. Dorset, however, saw the snow when he switched on his porch light, opened the front door of his parsonage, and found standing there before him a big black man with snow on his face, a human piece of night with snow on his face—obviously unemployed.

Said the Reverend Mr. Dorset before Sargeant even realized he'd opened his mouth: "I'm sorry. No! Go right on down this street four blocks and turn to your left, walk up seven and you'll see the Relief Shelter. I'm sorry. No!" He shut the door.

Sargeant wanted to tell the holy man that he had already been to the Relief Shelter, been to hundreds of relief shelters during the depression years, the beds were always gone and supper was over, the place was full, and they drew the color line anyhow. But the minister said, "No," and shut the door. Evidently he didn't

* Quoted in James A. Emanuel, *Langston Hughes.* New York: Twayne Publishers, Inc., 1967, pp. 93–94.

want to hear about it. And he *had* a door to shut.

The big black man turned away. And even yet he didn't see the snow, walking right into it. Maybe he sensed it, cold, wet, sticking to his jaws, wet on his black hands, sopping in his shoes. He stopped and stood on the sidewalk hunched over—hungry, sleepy, cold—looking up and down. Then he looked right where he was—in front of a church. Of course! A church! Sure, right next to a parsonage, certainly a church.

It had *two* doors.

Broad, white steps in the night all snowy white. Two high arched doors with slender stone pillars on either side. And way up, a round lacy window with a stone crucifix in the middle and Christ on the crucifix in stone. All this was pale in the street lights, solid and stony pale in the snow.

Sargeant blinked. When he looked up the snow fell into his eyes. For the first time that night he *saw* the snow. He shook his head. He shook the snow from his coat sleeves, felt hungry, felt lost, felt not lost, felt cold. He walked up the steps of the church. He knocked at the door. No answer. He tried the handle. Locked. He put his shoulder against the door and his long black body slanted like a ramrod. He pushed. With loud rhythmic grunts, like the grunts in a chain-gang song, he pushed against the door.

"I'm tired . . . Huh! . . . Hongry . . . Uh! . . . I'm sleepy . . . Huh! I'm cold . . . I got to sleep somewheres," Sargeant said. "This here is a church, ain't it? Well, uh!"

He pushed against the door.

Suddenly, with an undue cracking and squeaking, the door began to give way to the tall black Negro who pushed ferociously against the door.

By now two or three white people had stopped in the street, and Sargeant was vaguely aware of some of them yelling at him concerning the door. Three or four more came running, yelling at him.

"Hey!" they said. "Hey!"

"Un-huh," answered the big tall Negro, "I know it's a white folks' church, but I got to sleep somewhere." He gave another lunge at the door. "Huh!"

And the door broke open.

But just when the door gave way, two white cops arrived in a car, ran up the steps with their clubs and grabbed Sargeant. But Sargeant for once had no intention of being pulled or pushed away from the door.

Sargeant grabbed, but not for anything so weak as a broken door. He grabbed for one of the tall stone pillars beside the door, grabbed at it and caught it. And held it. The cops pulled and Sargeant pulled. Most of the people in the street got behind the cops and helped them pull.

"A big black unemployed Negro holding onto our church!" thought the people. "The idea!"

The cops began to beat Sargeant over the head, and nobody protested. But he held on.

And then the church fell down.[1]

Gradually, the big stone front of the church fell down, the walls and the rafters, the crucifix and the Christ. Then the whole thing fell down, covering the cops and the people with bricks and stones and debris. The whole church fell down in the snow.

Sargeant got out from under the church and went walking on up the street with the stone pillar on his shoulder. He was under the impression that he had buried the parsonage and the Reverend Mr. Dorset who said, "No!" So he laughed, and threw the pillar six blocks up the street and went on.

Sargeant thought he was alone, but listening to the crunch, crunch, crunch on the snow of his own footsteps, he heard other footsteps, too, doubling his own. He looked around and there was Christ walking along beside him, the same Christ that had been on the cross on the church—still stone with a rough stone surface, walking along beside him just like he was broken off the cross when the church fell down.

"Well, I'll be dogged," said Sargeant. "This here's the first time I ever seed you off the cross."

"Yes," said Christ, crunching his feet in the snow. "You had to pull the church down to get me off the cross."

"You glad?" said Sargeant.

"I sure am," said Christ.

They both laughed.

"I'm a hell of a fellow, ain't I?" said Sargeant.

[1] Reminiscent of Samson's pulling down the pillars of the temple where the great feast of the Philistine god Dagon was held. See *Judges*, 16:28–31.

"Done pulled the church down!"

"You did a good job," said Christ. "They have kept me nailed on a cross for nearly two thousand years."

"Whee-ee-e!" said Sargeant. "I know you are glad to get off."

"I sure am," said Christ.

They walked on in the snow. Sargeant looked at the man of stone.

"And you been up there two thousand years?"

"I sure have," Christ said.

"Well, if I had a little cash," said Sargeant, "I'd show you around a bit."

"I been around," said Christ.

"Yeah, but that was a long time ago."

"All the same," said Christ, "I've been around."

They walked on in the snow until they came to the railroad yards. Sargeant was tired, sweating and tired.

"Where you goin'?" Sargeant said, stopping by the tracks. He looked at Christ. Sargeant said, "I'm just a bum on the road. How about you? Where you goin'?"

"God knows," Christ said, "but I'm leavin' here."

They saw the red and green lights of the railroad yard half veiled by the snow that fell out of the night. Away down the track they saw a fire in a hobo jungle.

"I can go there and sleep," Sargeant said.

"You can?"

"Sure," said Sargeant. "That place ain't got no doors."

Outside the town, along the tracks, there were barren trees and bushes below the embankment, snow-gray in the dark. And down among the trees and bushes there were makeshift houses made out of boxes and tin and old pieces of wood and canvas. You couldn't see them in the dark, but you knew they were there if you'd ever been on the road, if you had ever lived with the homeless and hungry in a depression.

"I'm side-tracking," Sargeant said. "I'm tired."

"I'm gonna make it on to Kansas City," said Christ.

"O.K.," Sargeant said. "So long!"

He went down into the hobo jungle and found himself a place to sleep. He never did see Christ no more. About six A.M. a freight came by. Sargeant scrambled out of the jungle with a dozen or so more hoboes and ran along the track, grabbing at the freight. It was dawn, early dawn, cold and gray.

"Wonder where Christ is by now?" Sargeant thought. "He must-a gone on way on down the road. He didn't sleep in this jungle."

Sargeant grabbed the train and started to pull himself up into a moving coal car, over the edge of a wheeling coal car. But strangely enough, the car was full of cops. The nearest cop rapped Sargeant soundly across the knuckles with his night stick. Wham! Rapped his big black hands for clinging to the top of the car. Wham! But Sargeant did not turn loose. He clung on and tried to pull himself into the car. He hollered at the top of his voice, "Damn it, lemme in this car!"

"Shut up," barked the cop. "You crazy coon!" He rapped Sargeant across the knuckles and punched him in the stomach. "You ain't out in no jungle now. This ain't no train. You in jail."

Wham! across his bare black fingers clinging to the bars of his cell. Wham! between the steel bars low down against his shins.

Suddenly Sargeant realized that he really was in jail. He wasn't on no train. The blood of the night before had dried on his face, his head hurt terribly, and a cop outside in the corridor was hitting him across the knuckles for holding onto the door, yelling and shaking the cell door.

"They must-a took me to jail for breaking down the door last night," Sargeant thought, "that church door."

Sargeant went over and sat on a wooden bench against the cold stone wall. He was emptier than ever. His clothes were wet, clammy cold wet, and shoes sloppy with snow water. It was just about dawn. There he was, locked up behind a cell door, nursing his bruised fingers.

The bruised fingers were his, but not the *door*.

Not the *club*, but the fingers.

"You wait," mumbled Sargeant, black against the jail wall. "I'm gonna break down this door, too."

"Shut up—or I'll paste you one," said the cop.

"I'm gonna break down this door," yelled Sargeant as he stood up in his cell.

Then he must have been talking to himself because he said, "I wonder where Christ's gone? I wonder if he's gone to Kansas City?"

BERNARD MALAMUD
1914–

The Magic Barrel

Not long ago there lived in uptown New York, in a small, almost meager room, though crowded with books, Leo Finkle, a rabbinical student in the Yeshivah University. Finkle, after six years of study, was to be ordained in June and had been advised by an acquaintance that he might find it easier to win himself a congregation if he were married. Since he had no present prospects of marriage, after two tormented days of turning it over in his mind, he called in Pinye Salzman, a marriage broker whose two-line advertisement he had read in the *Forward*.

The matchmaker appeared one night out of the dark fourth-floor hallway of the graystone rooming house where Finkle lived, grasping a black, strapped portfolio that had been worn thin with use. Salzman, who had been long in the business, was of slight but dignified build, wearing an old hat, and an overcoat too short and tight for him. He smelled frankly of fish, which he loved to eat, and although he was missing a few teeth, his presence was not displeasing because of an amiable manner curiously contrasted with mournful eyes. His voice, his lips, his wisp of beard, his bony fingers were animated, but gave him a moment of repose and his mild blue eyes revealed a depth of sadness, a characteristic that put Leo a little at ease although the situation, for him, was inherently tense.

He at once informed Salzman why he had asked him to come, explaining that his home was in Cleveland, and that but for his parents, who had married comparatively late in life, he was alone in the world. He had for six years devoted himself almost entirely to his studies, as a result of which, understandably, he had found himself without time for a social life and the company of young women. Therefore he thought it the better part of trial and error—of embarrassing fumbling—to call in an experienced person to advise him on these matters. He remarked in passing that the function of the marriage broker was ancient and honorable, highly approved in the Jewish community, because it made practical the necessary without hindering joy. Moreover, his own parents had been brought together by a matchmaker. They had made, if not a financially profitable marriage—since neither had possessed any worldly goods to speak of—at least a successful one in the sense of their everlasting devotion to each other. Salzman listened in embarrassed surprise, sensing a sort of apology. Later, however, he experienced a glow of pride in his work, an emotion that had left him years ago, and he heartily approved of Finkle.

The two went to their business. Leo had led Salzman to the only clear place in the room, a table near a window that overlooked the lamplit city. He seated himself at the matchmaker's side but facing him, attempting by an act of will to suppress the unpleasant tickle in his throat. Salzman eagerly unstrapped his portfolio and removed a loose rubber band from a thin packet of much-handled cards. As he flipped through them, a gesture and sound that physically hurt Leo, the student pretended not to see and gazed steadfastly out the window. Although it was still February, winter was on its last legs, signs of which he had for the first time in years begun to notice. He now observed the round white moon, moving high in the sky through a cloud menagerie, and watched with half-open mouth as it penetrated a huge hen, and dropped out of her like an egg laying itself. Salzman, though pretending through eyeglasses he had just slipped on, to be engaged in scanning the writing on the cards, stole occasional glances at the young man's distinguished face, noting with pleasure the long, severe scholar's nose, brown eyes heavy with learning, sensitive yet ascetic lips, and a certain, almost hollow quality of the dark cheeks. He gazed around at shelves upon shelves of books and let out a soft, contented sigh.

When Leo's eyes fell upon the cards, he counted six spread out in Salzman's hand.

"So few?" he asked in disappointment.

"You wouldn't believe me how much cards I got in my office," Salzman replied. "The drawers are already filled to the top, so I keep them now in a barrel, but is every girl good for a new rabbi?"

Leo blushed at this, regretting all he had revealed of himself in a curriculum vitae he had sent to Salzman. He had thought it best to acquaint him with his strict standards and specifications, but in having done so, felt he had told the marriage broker more than was absolutely necessary.

He hesitantly inquired, "Do you keep photographs of your clients on file?"

"First comes family, amount of dowry, also what kind promises," Salzman replied, unbuttoning his tight coat and settling himself in the chair. "After comes pictures, rabbi."

"Call me Mr. Finkle. I'm not yet a rabbi."

Salzman said he would, but instead called him doctor, which he changed to rabbi when Leo was not listening too attentively.

Salzman adjusted his horn-rimmed spectacles, gently cleared his throat and read in an eager voice the contents of the top card:

"Sophie P. Twenty-four years. Widow one year. No children. Educated high school and two years college. Father promises eight thousand dollars. Has wonderful wholesale business. Also real estate. On the mother's side comes teachers, also one actor. Well known on Second Avenue."

Leo gazed up in surprise. "Did you say a widow?"

"A widow don't mean spoiled, rabbi. She lived with her husband maybe four months. He was a sick boy she made a mistake to marry him."

"Marrying a widow has never entered my mind."

"This is because you have no experience. A widow, especially if she is young and healthy like this girl, is a wonderful person to marry. She will be thankful to you the rest of her life. Believe me, if I was looking now for a bride, I would marry a widow."

Leo reflected, then shook his head.

Salzman hunched his shoulders in an almost imperceptible gesture of disappointment. He placed the card down on the wooden table and began to read another:

"Lily H. High school teacher. Regular. Not a substitute. Has savings and new Dodge car. Lived in Paris one year. Father is successful dentist thirty-five years. Interested in professional man. Well Americanized family. Wonderful opportunity."

"I knew her personally," said Salzman. "I wish you could see this girl. She is a doll. Also very intelligent. All day you could talk to her about books and theyater and what not. She also knows current events."

"I don't believe you mentioned her age?"

"Her age?" Salzman said, raising his brows. "Her age is thirty-two years."

Leo said after a while, "I'm afraid that seems a little too old."

Salzman let out a laugh. "So how old are you, rabbi?"

"Twenty-seven."

"So what is the difference, tell me, between twenty-seven and thirty-two? My own wife is seven years older than me. So what did I suffer? —Nothing. If Rothschild's a daughter wants to marry you, would you say on account of her age, no?"

"Yes," Leo said dryly.

Salzman shook off the no in the yes. "Five years don't mean a thing. I give you my word that when you will live with her for one week you will forget her age. What does it mean five years—that she lived more and knows more than somebody who is younger? On this girl, God bless her, years are not wasted. Each one that it comes makes better the bargain."

"What subject does she teach in high school?"

"Languages. If you heard the way she speaks French, you will think it is music. I am in the business twenty-five years, and I recommend her with my whole heart. Believe me, I know what I'm talking, rabbi."

"What's on the next card?" Leo said abruptly.

Salzman reluctantly turned up the third card:

"Ruth K. Nineteen years. Honor student. Father offers thirteen thousand cash to the right bridegroom. He is a medical doctor. Stomach specialist with marvelous practice. Brother in law owns own garment business. Particular people."

Salzman looked as if he had read his trump card.

"Did you say nineteen?" Leo asked with interest.

"On the dot."

"Is she attractive?" He blushed. "Pretty?"

Salzman kissed his finger tips. "A little doll. On this I give you my word. Let me call the father tonight and you will see what means pretty."

But Leo was troubled. "You're sure she's that young?"

"This I am positive. The father will show you the birth certificate."

"Are you positive there isn't something wrong with her?" Leo insisted.

"Who says there is wrong?"

"I don't understand why an American girl her age should go to a marriage broker."

A smile spread over Salzman's face.

"So for the same reason you went, she comes."

Leo flushed. "I am pressed for time."

Salzman, realizing he had been tactless, quickly explained. "The father came, not her. He wants she should have the best, so he looks around himself. When we will locate the right boy he will introduce him and encourage. This makes a better marriage than if a young girl without experience takes for herself. I don't have to tell you this."

"But don't you think this young girl believes in love?" Leo spoke uneasily.

Salzman was about to guffaw but caught himself and said soberly, "Love comes with the right person, not before."

Leo parted dry lips but did not speak. Noticing that Salzman had snatched a glance at the next card, he cleverly asked, "How is her health?"

"Perfect," Salzman said, breathing with difficulty. "Of course, she is a little lame on her right foot from an auto accident that it happened to her when she was twelve years, but nobody notices on account she is so brilliant and also beautiful."

Leo got up heavily and went to the window. He felt curiously bitter and upbraided himself for having called in the marriage broker. Finally, he shook his head.

"Why not?" Salzman persisted, the pitch of his voice rising.

"Because I detest stomach specialists."

"So what do you care what is his business? After you marry her do you need him? Who says he must come every Friday night in your house?"

Ashamed of the way the talk was going, Leo dismissed Salzman, who went home with heavy, melancholy eyes.

Though he had felt only relief at the marriage broker's departure, Leo was in low spirits the next day. He explained it as arising from Salzman's failure to produce a suitable bride for him. He did not care for his type of clientele. But when Leo found himself hesitating whether to seek out another matchmaker, one more polished than Pinye, he wondered if it could be—his protestations to the contrary, and although he honored his father and mother—that he did not, in essence, care for the matchmaking institution? This thought he quickly put out of mind yet found himself still upset. All day he ran around in the woods—missed an important appointment, forgot to give out his laundry, walked out of a Broadway cafeteria without paying and had to run back with the ticket in his hand; had even not recognized his landlady in the street when she passed with a friend and courteously called out, "A good evening to you, Doctor Finkle." By nightfall, however, he had regained sufficient calm to sink his nose into a book and there found peace from his thoughts.

Almost at once there came a knock on the door. Before Leo could say enter, Salzman, commercial cupid, was standing in the room. His face was gray and meager, his expression hungry, and he looked as if he would expire on his feet. Yet the marriage broker managed, by some trick of the muscles, to display a broad smile.

"So good evening. I am invited?"

Leo nodded, disturbed to see him again, yet unwilling to ask the man to leave.

Beaming still, Salzman laid his portfolio on the table. "Rabbi, I got for you tonight good news."

"I've asked you not to call me rabbi. I'm still a student."

"Your worries are finished. I have for you a first-class bride."

"Leave me in peace concerning this subject." Leo pretended lack of interest.

"The world will dance at your wedding."

"Please, Mr. Salzman, no more."

"But first must come back my strength," Salzman said weakly. He fumbled with the portfolio straps and took out of the leather case an oily paper bag, from which he extracted a hard, seeded roll and a small, smoked white fish. With a quick motion of his hand he stripped the fish out of its skin and began ravenously to chew. "All day in a rush," he muttered.

Leo watched him eat.

"A sliced tomato you have maybe?" Salzman hesitantly inquired.

"No."

The marriage broker shut his eyes and ate.

When he had finished he carefully cleaned up the crumbs and rolled up the remains of the fish, in the paper bag. His spectacled eyes roamed the room until he discovered, amid some piles of books, a one-burner gas stove. Lifting his hat he humbly asked, "A glass tea you got, rabbi?"

Conscience-stricken, Leo rose and brewed the tea. He served it with a chunk of lemon and two cubes of lump sugar, delighting Salzman.

After he had drunk his tea, Salzman's strength and good spirits were restored.

"So tell me, rabbi," he said amiably, "you considered some more the three clients I mentioned yesterday?"

"There was no need to consider."

"Why not?"

"None of them suits me."

"What then suits you?"

Leo let it pass because he could give only a confused answer.

Without waiting for a reply, Salzman asked, "You remember this girl I talked to you—the high school teacher?"

"Age thirty-two?"

But, surprisingly, Salzman's face lit in a smile. "Age twenty-nine."

Leo shot him a look. "Reduced from thirty-two?"

"A mistake," Salzman avowed. "I talked today with the dentist. He took me to his safety deposit box and showed me the birth certificate. She was twenty-nine years last August. They made her a party in the mountains where she went for her vacation. When her father spoke to me the first time I forgot to write the age and I told you thirty-two, but now I remember this was a different client, a widow."

"The same one you told me about? I thought she was twenty-four?"

"A different. Am I responsible that the world is filled with widows?"

"No, but I'm not interested in them, nor for that matter, in school teachers."

Salzman pulled his clasped hands to his breast. Looking at the ceiling he devoutly exclaimed, "Yiddishe kinder, what can I say to somebody that he is not interested in high school teachers? So what then you are interested?"

Leo flushed but controlled himself.

"In what else will you be interested," Salzman went on, "if you not interested in this fine girl that she speaks four languages and has personally in the bank ten thousand dollars? Also her father guarantees further twelve thousand. Also she has a new car, wonderful clothes, talks on all subjects, and she will give you a first-class home and children. How near do we come in life to paradise?"

"If she's so wonderful, why wasn't she married ten years ago?"

"Why?" said Salzman with a heavy laugh. "—Why? Because she is *partikiler*. That is why. She wants the *best*."

Leo was silent, amused at how he had entangled himself. But Salzman had aroused his interest in Lily H., and he began seriously to consider calling on her. When the marriage broker observed how intently Leo's mind was at work on the facts he had supplied, he felt certain they would soon come to an agreement.

Late Saturday afternoon, conscious of Salzman, Leo Finkle walked with Lily Hirschorn along Riverside Drive. He walked briskly and erectly, wearing with distinction the black fedora he had that morning taken with trepidation out of the dusty hat box on his closet shelf, and the heavy black Saturday coat he had thoroughly whisked clean. Leo also owned a walking stick, a present from a distant relative, but quickly put temptation aside and did not use it. Lily, petite and not unpretty, had on something signifying the approach of spring. She was au courant, animatedly, with all sorts of subjects, and he weighed her words and found her surprisingly sound—score another for Salzman, whom he uneasily sensed to be somewhere around, hiding perhaps high in a tree along the street, flashing the lady signals with a pocket mirror; or perhaps a cloven-hoofed Pan, piping nuptial ditties as he danced his invisible way before them, strewing wild buds on the wall and purple grapes in their path, symbolizing fruit of a union, though there was of course still none.

Lily startled Leo by remarking, "I was thinking of Mr. Salzman, a curious figure, wouldn't you say?"

Not certain what to answer, he nodded.

She bravely went on, blushing. "I for one am grateful for his introducing us. Aren't you?"

He courteously replied, "I am."

"I mean," she said with a little laugh—and it was all in good taste, or at least gave the effect of being not in bad—"do you mind that we came together so?"

He was not displeased with her honesty, recognizing that she meant to set the relationship aright, and understanding that it took a certain amount of experience in life, and courage, to want to do it quite that way. One had to have some sort of past to make that kind of beginning.

He said that he did not mind. Salzman's function was traditional and honorable—valuable for what it might achieve, which, he pointed out, was frequently nothing.

Lily agreed with a sigh. They walked on for a while and she said after a long silence, again with a nervous laugh, "Would you mind if I asked you something a little bit personal? Frankly, I find the subject fascinating." Although Leo shrugged, she went on half embarrassedly, "How was it that you came to your calling? I mean was it a sudden passionate inspiration?"

Leo, after a time, slowly replied, "I was always interested in the Law."

"You saw revealed in it the presence of the Highest?"

He nodded and changed the subject. "I understand that you spent a little time in Paris, Miss Hirschorn?"

"Oh, did Mr. Salzman tell you, Rabbi Finkle?" Leo winced but she went on, "It was ages ago and almost forgotten. I remember I had to return for my sister's wedding."

And Lily would not be put off. "When," she asked in a trembly voice, "did you become enamored of God?"

He stared at her. Then it came to him that she was talking not about Leo Finkle, but of a total stranger, some mystical figure, perhaps even passionate prophet that Salzman had dreamed up for her—no relation to the living or dead. Leo trembled with rage and weakness. The trickster had obviously sold her a bill of goods, just as he had him, who'd expected to become acquainted with a young lady of twenty-nine, only to behold, the moment he laid eyes upon her strained and anxious face, a woman past thirty-five and aging rapidly. Only his self control had kept him this long in her presence.

"I am not," he said gravely, "a talented religious person," and in seeking words to go on, found himself possessed by shame and fear. "I think," he said in a strained manner, "that I came to God not because I loved Him, but because I did not."

This confession he spoke harshly because its unexpectedness shook him.

Lily wilted. Leo saw a profusion of loaves of bread go flying like ducks high over his head, not unlike the winged loaves by which he had counted himself to sleep last night. Mercifully, then, it snowed, which he would not put past Salzman's machinations.

He was infuriated with the marriage broker and swore he would throw him out of the room the minute he reappeared. But Salzman did not come that night, and when Leo's anger had subsided, an unaccountable despair grew in its place. At first he thought this was caused by his disappointment in Lily, but before long it became evident that he had involved himself with Salzman without a true knowledge of his own intent. He gradually realized—with an emptiness that seized him with six hands—that he had called in the broker to find him a bride because he was incapable of doing it himself. This terrifying insight he had derived as a result of his meeting and conversation with Lily Hirschorn. Her probing questions had somehow irritated him into revealing—to himself more than her—the true nature of his relationship to God, and from that it had come upon him, with shocking force, that apart from his parents, he had never loved anyone. Or perhaps it went the other way, that he did not love God so well as he might, because he had not loved man. It seemed to Leo that his whole life stood starkly revealed and he saw himself for the first time as he truly was—unloved and loveless. This bitter but somehow not fully unexpected revelation brought him to a point of panic, controlled only by extraordinary effort. He covered his face with his hands and cried.

The week that followed was the worst of his life. He did not eat and lost weight. His beard darkened and grew ragged. He stopped attending seminars and almost never opened a book. He seriously considered leaving the Yeshivah, although he was deeply troubled at the thought of the loss of all his years of study—saw them like pages torn from a book, strewn over the city—and at the devastating effect of this decision upon his parents. But he had lived without knowledge of himself, and never in the Five

Books[1] and all the Commentaries—mea culpa[2] —had the truth been revealed to him. He did not know where to turn, and in all this desolating loneliness there was no *to whom*, although he often thought of Lily but not once could bring himself to go downstairs and make the call. He became touchy and irritable, especially with his landlady, who asked him all manner of personal questions; on the other hand, sensing his own disagreeableness, he waylaid her on the stairs and apologized abjectly, until mortified, she ran from him. Out of this, however, he drew the consolation that he was a Jew and that a Jew suffered. But gradually, as the long and terrible week drew to a close, he regained his composure and some idea of purpose in life: to go on as planned. Although he was imperfect, the ideal was not. As for his quest for a bride, the thought of continuing afflicted him with anxiety and heartburn, yet perhaps with this new knowledge of himself he would be more successful than in the past. Perhaps love would now come to him and a bride to that love. And for this sanctified seeking who needed a Salzman?

The marriage broker, a skeleton with haunted eyes, returned that very night. He looked, withal, the picture of frustrated expectancy—as if he had steadfastly waited the week at Miss Lily Hirschorn's side for a telephone call that never came.

Casually coughing, Salzman came immediately to the point: "So how did you like her?"

Leo's anger rose and he could not refrain from chiding the matchmaker: "Why did you lie to me, Salzman?"

Salzman's pale face went dead white, the world had snowed on him.

"Did you not state that she was twenty- nine?" Leo insisted.

"I give you my word—"

"She was thirty-five, if a day. *At least* thirty-five."

"Of this don't be too sure. Her father told me—"

"Never mind. The worst of it was that you lied to her."

"How did I lie to her, tell me?"

"You told her things about me that weren't true. You made me out to be more, consequently less than I am. She had in mind a totally different person, a sort of semi-mystical Wonder Rabbi."

"All I said, you was a religious man."

"I can imagine."

Salzman sighed. "This is my weakness that I have," he confessed. "My wife says to me I shouldn't be a salesman, but when I have two fine people that they would be wonderful to be married, I am so happy that I talk too much." He smiled wanly. "This is why Salzman is a poor man."

Leo's anger left him. "Well, Salzman, I'm afraid that's all."

The marriage broker fastened hungry eyes on him.

"You don't want any more a bride?"

"I do," said Leo, "but I have decided to seek her in a different way. I am no longer interested in an arranged marriage. To be frank, I now admit the necessity of premarital love. That is, I want to be in love with the one I marry."

"Love?" said Salzman, astounded. After a moment he remarked, "For us, our love is our life, not for the ladies. In the ghetto they—"

"I know, I know," said Leo. "I've thought of it often. Love, I have said to myself, should be a by-product of living and worship rather than its own end. Yet for myself I find it necessary to establish the level of my need and fulfill it."

Salzman shrugged but answered, "Listen, rabbi, if you want love, this I can find for you also. I have such beautiful clients that you will love them the minute your eyes will see them."

Leo smiled unhappily. "I'm afraid you don't understand."

But Salzman hastily unstrapped his portfolio and withdrew a manila packet from it.

"Pictures," he said, quickly laying the envelope on the table.

Leo called after him to take the pictures away, but as if on the wings of the wind, Salzman had disappeared.

March came. Leo had returned to his regular routine. Although he felt not quite himself yet —lacked energy—he was making plans for a more active social life. Of course it would cost something, but he was an expert in cutting corners; and when there were no corners left he would make circles rounder. All the while Salz-

[1] The *Megilloth:* Song of Solomon, Ruth, Lamentations. Ecclesiastes, and Esther. [2] Through my fault.

man's pictures had lain on the table, gathering dust. Occasionally as Leo sat studying, or enjoying a cup of tea, his eyes fell on the manila envelope, but he never opened it.

The days went by and no social life to speak of developed with a member of the opposite sex —it was difficult, given the circumstances of his situation. One morning Leo toiled up the stairs to his room and stared out the window at the city. Although the day was bright his view of it was dark. For some time he watched the people in the street below hurrying along and then turned with a heavy heart to his little room. On the table was the packet. With a sudden relentless gesture he tore it open. For a half-hour he stood by the table in a state of excitement, examining the photographs of the ladies Salzman had included. Finally, with a deep sigh he put them down. There were six, of varying degrees of attractiveness, but look at them long enough and they all became Lily Hirschorn: all past their prime, all starved behind bright smiles, not a true personality in the lot. Life, despite their frantic yoohooings, had passed them by; they were pictures in a brief case that stank of fish. After a while, however, as Leo attempted to return the photographs into the envelope, he found in it another, a snapshot of the type taken by a machine for a quarter. He gazed at it a moment and let out a cry.

Her face deeply moved him. Why, he could at first not say. It gave him the impression of youth—spring flowers, yet age—a sense of having been used to the bone, wasted; this came from the eyes, which were hauntingly familiar, yet absolutely strange. He had a vivid impression that he had met her before, but try as he might he could not place her although he could almost recall her name, as if he had read it in her own handwriting. No, this couldn't be; he would have remembered her. It was not, he affirmed, that she had an extraordinary beauty—no, though her face was attractive enough; it was that *something* about her moved him. Feature for feature, even some of the ladies of the photographs could do better; but she leaped forth to his heart —had *lived,* or wanted to—more than just wanted, perhaps regretted how she had lived—had somehow deeply suffered: it could be seen in the depths of those reluctant eyes, and from the way the light enclosed and shone from her, and within her, opening realms of possibility: this was her own. Her he desired. His head ached and eyes narrowed with the intensity of his gazing, then as if an obscure fog had blown up in the mind, he experienced fear of her and was aware that he had received an impression, somehow, of evil. He shuddered, saying softly, it is thus with us all. Leo brewed some tea in a small pot and sat sipping it without sugar, to calm himself. But before he had finished drinking, again with excitement he examined the face and found it good: good for Leo Finkle. Only such a one could understand him and help him seek whatever he was seeking. She might, perhaps, love him. How she had happened to be among the discards in Salzman's barrel he could never guess, but he knew he must urgently go find her.

Leo rushed downstairs, grabbed up the Bronx telephone book, and searched for Salzman's home address. He was not listed, nor was his office. Neither was he in the Manhattan book. But Leo remembered having written down the address on a slip of paper after he had read Salzman's advertisement in the "personals" column of the *Forward.* He ran up to his room and tore through his papers, without luck. It was exasperating. Just when he needed the matchmaker he was nowhere to be found. Fortunately Leo remembered to look in his wallet. There on a card he found his name written and a Bronx address. No phone number was listed, the reason—Leo now recalled—he had originally communicated with Salzman by letter. He got on his coat, put a hat on over his skull cap and hurried to the subway station. All the way to the far end of the Bronx he sat on the edge of his seat. He was more than once tempted to take out the picture and see if the girl's face was as he remembered it, but he refrained, allowing the snapshot to remain in his inside coat pocket, content to have her so close. When the train pulled into the station he was waiting at the door and bolted out. He quickly located the street Salzman had advertised.

The building he sought was less than a block from the subway, but it was not an office building, nor even a loft, nor a store in which one could rent office space. It was a very old tenement house. Leo found Salzman's name in pencil on a soiled tag under the bell and climbed three dark flights to his apartment. When he knocked, the door was opened by a thin, asthmatic, gray-haired woman, in felt slippers.

"Yes?" she said, expecting nothing. She listened without listening. He could have sworn he had seen her, too, before but knew it was an illusion.

"Salzman—does he live here? Pinye Salzman," he said, "the matchmaker?"

She stared at him a long minute. "Of course."

He felt embarrassed. "Is he in?"

"No." Her mouth, though left open, offered nothing more.

"The matter is urgent. Can you tell me where his office is?"

"In the air." She pointed upward.

"You mean he has no office?" Leo asked.

"In his socks."

He peered into the apartment. It was sunless and dingy, one large room divided by a half-open curtain, beyond which he could see a sagging metal bed. The near side of a room was crowded with rickety chairs, old bureaus, a three-legged table, racks of cooking utensils, and all the apparatus of a kitchen. But there was no sign of Salzman or his magic barrel, probably also a figment of the imagination. An odor of frying fish made Leo weak to the knees.

"Where is he?" he insisted. "I've got to see your husband."

At length she answered, "So who knows where he is? Every time he thinks a new thought he runs to a different place. Go home, he will find you."

"Tell him Leo Finkle."

She gave no sign she had heard.

He walked downstairs, depressed.

But Salzman, breathless, stood waiting at his door.

Leo was astounded and overjoyed. "How did you get here before me?"

"I rushed."

"Come inside."

They entered. Leo fixed tea, and a sardine sandwich for Salzman. As they were drinking he reached behind him for the packet of pictures and handed them to the marriage broker.

Salzman put down his glass and said expectantly, "You found somebody you like?"

"Not among these."

The marriage broker turned away.

"Here is the one I want." Leo held forth the snapshot.

Salzman slipped on his glasses and took the picture into his trembling hand. He turned ghastly and let out a groan.

"What's the matter?" cried Leo.

"Excuse me. Was an accident this picture. She isn't for you."

Salzman frantically shoved the manila packet into his portfolio. He thrust the snapshot into his pocket and fled down the stairs.

Leo, after momentary paralysis, gave chase and cornered the marriage broker in the vestibule. The landlady made hysterical outcries but neither of them listened.

"Give me back the picture, Salzman."

"No." The pain in his eyes was terrible.

"Tell me who she is then."

"This I can't tell you. Excuse me."

He made to depart, but Leo, forgetting himself, seized the matchmaker by his tight coat and shook him frenziedly.

"Please," sighed Salzman. "*Please.*"

Leo ashamedly let him go. "Tell me who she is," he begged. "It's very important for me to know."

"She is not for you. She is a wild one—wild, without shame. This is not a bride for a rabbi."

"What do you mean wild?"

"Like an animal. Like a dog. For her to be poor was a sin. This is why to me she is dead now."

"In God's name, what do you mean?"

"Her I can't introduce to you," Salzman cried.

"Why are you so excited?"

"Why, he asks," Salzman said, bursting into tears. "This is my baby, my Stella, she should burn in hell."

Leo hurried up to bed and hid under the covers. Under the covers he thought his life was through. Although he soon fell asleep he could not sleep her out of his mind. He woke, beating his breast. Though he prayed to be rid of her, his prayers went unanswered. Through days of torment he endlessly struggled not to love her; fearing success, he escaped it. He then concluded to convert her to goodness, himself to God. The idea alternately nauseated and exalted him.

He perhaps did not know that he had come to a final decision until he encountered Salzman in a Broadway cafeteria. He was sitting alone at a rear table, sucking the bony remains of a fish. The marriage broker appeared haggard, and transparent to the point of vanishing.

Salzman looked up at first without recognizing him. Leo had grown a pointed beard and his eyes were weighted with wisdom.

"Salzman," he said, "love has at last come to my heart."

"Who can love from a picture?" mocked the marriage broker.

"It is not impossible."

"If you can love her, then you can love anybody. Let me show you some new clients that they just sent me their photographs. One is a little doll."

"Just her I want," Leo murmured.

"Don't be a fool, doctor. Don't bother with her."

"Put me in touch with her, Salzman," Leo said humbly. "Perhaps I can be of service."

Salzman had stopped eating and Leo understood with emotion that it was now arranged.

Leaving the cafeteria, he was, however, afflicted by a tormenting suspicion that Salzman had planned it all to happen this way.

Leo was informed by letter that she would meet him on a certain corner, and she was there one spring night, waiting under a street lamp. He appeared, carrying a small bouquet of violets and rosebuds. Stella stood by the lamp post, smoking. She wore white with red shoes, which fitted his expectations, although in a troubled moment he had imagined the dress red, and only the shoes white. She waited uneasily and shyly. From afar he saw that her eyes—clearly her father's—were filled with desperate innocence. He pictured, in her, his own redemption. Violins and lit candles revolved in the sky. Leo ran forward with flowers outthrust.

Around the corner, Salzman, leaning against a wall, chanted prayers for the dead.

COLETTE[1]
1873–1954

The Bitch

When the sergeant arrived in Paris on leave, he found his mistress not at home. He was nevertheless greeted with tremulous cries of surprise and joy, embraced and covered with wet kisses. His bitch, Vorace, the sheep-dog whom he had left with his young sweetheart, enveloped him like a flame and licked him with a tongue pale with emotion. Meanwhile, the charwoman was making as much noise as the dog and kept exclaiming:

"Of all the bad luck! Madame's just gone to Marlotte for a couple of days to shut up her house there. Madame's tenants have just left and she's going through the inventory of the furniture. Fortunately, it isn't all that far away! Will Monsieur write out a telegram for Madame? If it goes immediately, Madame will be here tomorrow morning before lunch. Monsieur must sleep here. Shall I turn on the geyser?"[2]

"My good Lucie, I had a bath at home. Soldiers on leave are pretty good at washing!"

He eyed his reflection in the glass; he was both bluish and ruddy, like the granite rocks of Brittany. The Briard sheep-dog, standing close to him in a reverent silence, was trembling in every hair. He laughed because she looked so like him, gray and blue and shaggy.

"Vorace!"

She raised her head and looked lovingly at her master, and the sergeant's heart turned over as he suddenly thought of his mistress Jeannine, so young and so gay—a little too young and often too gay.

During dinner the dog faithfully observed all the ritual of their former life, catching the pieces of bread he tossed for her and barking at certain words. So ardent was the worship in which she was rooted that the moment of return abolished for her the months of absence.

"I've missed you a lot," he told her in a low voice. "Yes, you too!"

He was smoking now, half lying on the divan. Crouching like a grayhound on a tombstone, the dog was pretending to be asleep, her ears quite still. Only her eyebrows, twitching at the slightest noise, revealed that she was on the alert.

Worn out as he was, the silence gradually lulled the man, until his hand which held the cigarette slid down the cushion, scorching the silk. He roused himself, opened a book, fingered a few new knick-knacks and a photograph, which he had not seen before, of Jeannine in a short skirt, with bare arms, in the country.

[1] Pen name for Sidonie Gabrielle Claudine Colette.

[2] An apparatus for heating water rapidly with a gas flame, as for a bath.

"An amateur snapshot . . . How charming she looks!"

On the back of the unmounted print he read:

"'June the fifth 1916.' Where was I on June the fifth? . . . Oh, I know, over in the direction of Arras. June the fifth. I don't know the writing."

He sat down again and was overcome by a sleep which drove all thought away. Ten o'clock struck; he was still just sufficiently awake to smile at the rich and solemn sound of the little clock whose voice, Jeannine used to say, was bigger than its stomach. But as it struck ten the dog got up.

"Quiet!" said the sleepy sergeant. "Lie down!"

But Vorace did not lie down. She snorted and stretched her paws which, for a dog, is the same as putting on a hat to go out. She went up to her master and her yellow eyes asked plainly:

"Well?"

"Well," he answered, "what's the matter with you?"

Out of respect she dropped her ears while he was speaking, raising them again immediately.

"Oh, what a bore you are!" sighed the sergeant. "You're thirsty. D'you want to go out?"

At the words "go out," Vorace grinned and began to pant gently, showing her beautiful teeth and the fleshy petal of her tongue.

"All right, then, we'll go out. But not for long, because I'm absolutely dropping with sleep."

In the road Vorace was so excited that she barked like a wolf, jumped right up to her master's neck, charged a cat and spun round playing "inner circle" with her tail. Her master scolded her tenderly and she did all her tricks for him. Finally, she sobered down again and walked along sedately. The sergeant suited his pace to hers, enjoying the warm night and making a little song out of two or three idle thoughts:

"I'll see Jeannine tomorrow morning . . . I'm going to sleep in a comfy bed . . . I've got seven more days to spend here . . ."

He became aware that his dog, who had trotted ahead, was waiting for him under a gas lamp with the same look of impatience. Her eyes, her wagging tail and her whole body asked:

"Well? Are you coming?"

As soon as he caught up with her, she turned the corner at a determined trot. It was then that he realized she was going somewhere.

"Perhaps," he thought to himself, "the charwoman usually . . . Or Jeannine . . ."

He stood still for a moment, then went on again, following the dog, without even noticing that he had, all at once, stopped feeling tired, and sleepy, and happy. He quickened his pace and the delighted dog went before, like a good guide.

"Go on, go on!" ordered the sergeant from time to time.

He looked at the name of a road, then went on again. They passed gardens with lodges at the gates; the road was dimly lit and they met no one. In her excitement, the dog pretended to bite the hand that hung at his side, and he had to restrain a brutal impulse, which he could not explain, in order not to beat her.

At last she stopped, as though saying: "Well, here we are!" before an old, broken-down railing protecting the garden of a little low house smothered in vines and bignonia, a timid shrouded little house.

"Well, why don't you open it?" said the dog, who had taken up a position before the wooden wicket-gate.

The sergeant lifted his hand to the latch and let it fall again. He bent down to the dog, pointed with his finger to a thread of light along the closed shutters, and asked her in a low voice:

"Who's there? . . . Jeannine?"

The dog gave a shrill "Hi!" and barked.

"Shhh!" breathed the sergeant, clapping his hands over her cool wet mouth.

Once more he stretched out a hesitant arm towards the door and the dog bounded forward. But he held her back by her collar and led her to the opposite pavement, whence he gazed at the unknown house and the thread of rosy light. He sat down on the pavement beside the dog. He had not yet gathered together all those images and thoughts which spring up round a possible betrayal, but he felt singularly alone, and weak.

"Do you love me?" he murmured in the dog's ear.

She licked his cheek.

"Come on; let's go away."

They set off, he in front this time. And when they were once more in the little sitting-room, she saw that he was putting his linen and slippers in a sack that she knew well. Desperate but respectful, she followed all his movements, while tears, the color of gold, trembled in her yellow eyes. He laid his hand on her neck to reassure her:

"You're coming too. You're not going to leave me any more. Next time you won't be able to tell me what happened 'after.' Perhaps I'm mistaken. Perhaps I haven't understood you properly. But you mustn't stay here. Your soul wasn't meant to guard any secrets but mine."

And while the dog shivered, still uncertain, he held her head in his hands, saying to her in a low voice:

"Your soul . . . Your doggy soul . . . Your beautiful soul . . ."

FRANZ KAFKA
1883–1924
A Hunger Artist

This story is an allegory in the sense that the symbols which are embodied in characters, events, and natural objects represent ideas. In most allegory, as for example John Bunyan's *The Pilgrim's Progress,* 1678, the symbols can be translated into equivalents which remain constant throughout the story. But in "A Hunger Artist" Kafka has used his symbols to produce more than one level of meaning, each one used to dramatize a different theme. Is the story "about" the artist in an alien society, "about" religion—or possibly both and even more? On the problem of reading Kafka, Albert Camus offers some help: "The whole art of Kafka consists in forcing the reader to reread. . . . Sometimes there is a double possibility of interpretation. . . . This is what the author wanted. But it would be wrong to try to interpret everything in Kafka in detail. A symbol is always in general and, however precise its translation, an artist can restore to it only its movement: there is no word-for-word rendering" (*The Myth of Sisyphus,* 1955).

During these last decades the interest in professional fasting has markedly diminished. It used to pay very well to stage such great performances under one's own management, but today that is quite impossible. We live in a different world now. At one time the whole town took a lively interest in the hunger artist; from day to day of his fast the excitement mounted; everybody wanted to see him at least once a day; there were people who bought season tickets for the last few days and sat from morning till night in front of his small barred cage; even in the nighttime there were visiting hours, when the whole effect was heightened by torch flares; on fine days the cage was set out in the open air, and then it was the children's special treat to see the hunger artist; for their elders he was often just a joke that happened to be in fashion, but the children stood open-mouthed, holding each other's hands for greater security, marveling at him as he sat there pallid in black tights, with his ribs sticking out so prominently, not even on a seat but down among straw on the ground, sometimes giving a courteous nod, answering questions with a constrained smile, or perhaps stretching an arm through the bars so that one might feel how thin it was, and then again withdrawing deep into himself, paying no attention to anyone or anything, not even to the all-important striking of the clock that was the only piece of furniture in his cage, but merely staring into vacancy with half-shut eyes, now and then taking a sip from a tiny glass of water to moisten his lips.

Besides casual onlookers there were also relays of permanent watchers selected by the public, usually butchers, strangely enough, and it was their task to watch the hunger artist day and night, three of them at a time, in case he should have some secret recourse to nourishment. This was nothing but a formality, instituted to reassure the masses, for the initiates knew well enough that during his fast the artist would never in any circumstances, not even under forcible compulsion, swallow the smallest morsel of food; the honor of his profession forbade it. Not every watcher, of course, was capable of understanding this, there were often groups of night watchers who were very lax in carrying out their duties and deliberately huddled together in a retired corner to play cards with great absorption, obviously intending to give the hunger artist the chance of a little refreshment, which they supposed he could draw from some private hoard. Nothing annoyed the artist more than such watchers; they made him miserable; they made his fast seem unendurable; sometimes he mastered his feebleness sufficiently to sing during their watch for as long as he could keep going, to show them how unjust their suspicions were. But that was of little use; they only wondered at his cleverness in being able to fill his mouth even while singing. Much more to his taste were the watchers who sat close up to the bars, who were not content with the dim night lighting of the hall but focused him in the full glare of the electric pocket torch given them by the impresario. The harsh light did not trouble him at all. In any case he could never sleep properly, and he could always drowse a little, whatever the light, at any hour, even when the hall was thronged with noisy onlookers. He was quite happy at the prospect of spending a sleepless night with such watchers; he was ready to exchange jokes with them, to tell them stories out of his nomadic life, anything at all to keep them awake and demonstrate to them again that he had no eatables in his cage and that he was fasting as not one of them could fast. But his happiest moment was when the morning came and an enormous breakfast was brought them, at his expense, on which they flung themselves with the keen appetite of healthy men after a weary night of wakefulness. Of course there were people who argued that this breakfast was an unfair attempt to bribe the watchers, but that was going rather too far, and when they were invited to take on a night's vigil without a breakfast, merely for the sake of the cause, they made themselves scarce, although they stuck stubbornly to their suspicions.

Such suspicions, anyhow, were a necessary accompaniment to the profession of fasting. No one could possibly watch the hunger artist continuously, day and night, and so no one could produce first-hand evidence that the fast had really been rigorous and continuous; only the artist himself could know that; he was therefore bound to be the sole completely satisfied spectator of his own fast. Yet for other reasons he was never satisfied; it was not perhaps mere fasting that had brought him to such skeleton thinness that many people had regretfully to keep away from his exhibitions, because the sight of him was too much for them, perhaps it was dissatisfaction with himself that had worn him down. For he alone knew, what no other initiate knew, how easy it was to fast. It was the easiest thing in the world. He made no secret of this, yet people did not believe him; at the best they set him down as modest, most of them, however, thought he was out for publicity or else was some kind of cheat who found it easy to fast because he had discovered a way of making it easy, and then had the impudence to admit the fact, more or less. He had to put up with all that, and in the course of time had got used to it, but his inner dissatisfaction always rankled, and never yet, after any term of fasting—this must be granted to his credit—had he left the cage of his own free will. The longest period of fasting was fixed by his impresario at forty days, beyond that term he was not allowed to go, not even in great cities, and there was good reason for it, too. Experience had proved that for about forty days the interest of the public could be stimulated by a steadily increasing pressure of advertisement, but after that the town began to lose interest, sympathetic support began notably to fall off; there were of course local variations as between one town and another or one country and another, but as a general rule forty days marked the limit. So on the fortieth day the flower-bedecked cage was opened, enthusiastic spectators filled the hall, a military band played, two doctors entered the cage to measure the results of the fast, which were announced through a megaphone, and finally two young ladies appeared, blissful at having been selected for the honor, to help the hunger artist down the few steps leading to a small table on which was spread a carefully chosen invalid repast. And at this very moment the artist always turned stubborn. True, he would entrust his bony arms to the outstretched helping hands of the ladies bending over him, but stand up he would not. Why stop fasting at this particular moment, after forty days of it? He had held out for a long time, an illimitably long time; why stop now, when he was in his best fasting form, or rather, not quite in his best fasting form? Why should he be cheated of the fame he would get for fasting longer, for being not only the record hunger artist of all time, which presumably he was already, but for beating his own record by a performance beyond human imagination, since he felt that there were no limits to his capacity for fasting? His public pretended to admire him so much, why should it have so little patience with him; if he could endure fasting longer, why shouldn't the public endure it? Besides, he was tired, he was comfortable sitting in the straw, and now he was supposed to lift himself to his full height and go down to a meal the very thought of which gave him a nausea that only the presence of the ladies kept him from betraying, and even that with an effort. And he looked up into the eyes of the ladies who were apparently so friendly and in reality so cruel, and shook his head, which felt too heavy on its strengthless neck. But then there happened yet again what always happened. The impresario came forward, without a word—for the band made speech impossible—lifted his arms in the air above the artist, as if inviting Heaven to look down upon its creature here in the straw, this suffering martyr, which indeed he was, although in quite another sense; grasped him round the emaciated waist, with exaggerated caution, so that the frail condition he was in might be appreciated; and committed him to the care of the blenching ladies, not without secretly giving him a shaking so that his legs and body tottered and swayed. The artist now submitted completely; his head lolled on his breast as if it had landed there by chance; his body was hollowed out; his legs in a spasm of self-preservation clung close to each other at the knees, yet scraped on the ground as if it were not really solid ground, as if they were only trying to find solid ground; and the whole weight of his body, a featherweight after all, relapsed onto one of the ladies, who, looking round for help and panting a little—this post of honor was not at all what she had expected it to be—first stretched her neck as far as she could to keep her face at least free from contact with the artist, then finding this impossible, and her more fortunate companion not coming to her aid but merely holding extended on her own trembling hand the little bunch of knucklebones that was the artist's, to the great delight of the spectators burst into tears and had to be replaced by an attendant who had long been stationed in readiness. Then came the food, a little of which the impresario managed to get between the artist's lips, while he sat in a kind of half-fainting trance, to the accompaniment of cheerful patter designed to distract the public's attention from the artist's condition; after that, a toast was drunk to the public, supposedly prompted by a whisper from the artist in the impresario's ear; the band confirmed it with a mighty flourish, the spectators melted away, and no one had any cause to be dissatisfied with the proceedings, no one except the hunger artist himself, he only, as always.

So he lived for many years, with small regular intervals of recuperation, in visible glory, honored by the world, yet in spite of that troubled in spirit, and all the more troubled because no one would take his trouble seriously. What comfort could he possibly need? What more could he possibly wish for? And if some good-natured person, feeling sorry for him, tried to console him by pointing out that his melancholy was probably caused by fasting, it could happen, especially when he had been fasting for some time, that he reacted with an outburst of fury and to the general alarm began to shake the bars of his cage like a wild animal. Yet the impresario had a way of punishing these outbreaks which he rather enjoyed putting into operation. He would apologize publicly for the artist's behavior, which was only to be excused, he admitted, because of the irritability caused by fasting; a condition hardly to be understood by well-fed people; then by natural transition he went on to mention the artist's equally incomprehensible boast that he could fast for much longer than he was doing; he praised the high ambition, the good will, the great self-denial undoubtedly implicit in such a statement; and then quite simply countered it by bringing out photographs, which were also on sale to the public, showing the artist on the fortieth day of a fast lying in bed almost dead from exhaustion. This perversion of the truth, familiar to the artist though it was, always unnerved him afresh and proved too much for him. What was a consequence of the premature ending of his fast was here presented as the cause of it! To fight against this lack of understanding, against a whole world of non-understanding, was impossible. Time and again in good faith he stood by the bars listening to the impresario, but as soon as the photographs appeared he always let go and sank with a groan back on to his straw, and the reassured public could once more come close and gaze at him.

A few years later when the witnesses of such scenes called them to mind, they often failed to understand themselves at all. For meanwhile the aforementioned change in public interest had set in; it seemed to happen almost overnight; there may have been profound causes for it, but who was going to bother about that; at any rate the pampered hunger artist suddenly found himself deserted one fine day by the amusement seekers, who went streaming past him to other more favored attractions. For the last time the impresario hurried him over half Europe to discover whether the old interest might still survive here and there; all in vain; everywhere, as if by secret agreement, a positive revulsion from professional fasting was in evidence. Of course it could not really have sprung up so suddenly as all that, and many premonitory symptoms which had not been sufficiently remarked or suppressed during the rush and glitter of success now came retrospectively to mind, but it was now too late to take any countermeasures. Fasting would surely come into fashion again at some future date, yet that was no comfort for those living in the present. What, then, was the hunger artist to do? He had been applauded by thousands in his time and could hardly come down to showing himself in a street booth at village fairs, and as for adopting another profession, he was not only too old for that but too fanatically devoted to fasting. So he took leave of the impresario, his partner in an unparalleled career, and hired himself to a large circus; in order to spare his own feelings he avoided reading the conditions of his contract.

A large circus with its enormous traffic in replacing and recruiting men, animals and apparatus can always find a use for people at any time, even for a hunger artist, provided of course that he does not ask too much, and in this particular case anyhow it was not only the artist who was taken on but his famous and long-known name as well; indeed considering the peculiar nature of his performance, which was not impaired by advancing age, it could not be objected that here was an artist past his prime, no longer at the height of his professional skill, seeking a refuge in some quiet corner of a circus; on the contrary, the hunger artist averred that he could fast as well as ever, which was entirely credible; he even alleged that if he were allowed to fast as he liked, and this was at once promised him without more ado, he could astound the world by establishing a record never yet achieved, a statement which certainly provoked a smile among the other professionals, since it left out of account the change in public opinion, which the hunger artist in his zeal conveniently forgot.

He had not, however, actually lost his sense of the real situation and took it as a matter of course that he and his cage should be stationed, not in the middle of the ring as a main attraction, but outside, near the animal cages, on a site that was after all easily accessible. Large and gaily painted placards made a frame for the cage and announced what was to be seen inside it. When the public came thronging out in the intervals to see the animals, they could hardly avoid passing the hunger artist's cage and stopping there for a moment, perhaps they might even have stayed longer had not those pressing behind them in the narrow gangway, who did not understand why they should be held up on their way towards the excitements of the menagerie, made it impossible for anyone to stand gazing quietly for any length of time. And that was the reason why the hunger artist, who had of course been looking forward to these visiting hours as the main achievement of his life, began instead to shrink from them. At first he could hardly wait for the intervals; it was exhilarating to watch the crowds come streaming his way, until only too soon—not even the most obstinate self-deception, clung to almost consciously, could hold out against the fact—the conviction was borne in upon him that these people, most of them, to judge from their actions, again and again, without exception, were all on their way to the menagerie. And the first sight of them from the distance remained the best. For when they reached his cage he was at once deafened by the storm of shouting and abuse that arose from the two contending factions, which renewed themselves continuously, of those who wanted to stop and stare at him—he soon began to dislike them more than the others—not out of real interest but only out of obstinate self-assertiveness, and those who wanted to go straight on to the animals. When the first great rush was past, the stragglers came along, and these, whom nothing could have prevented from stopping to look at him as long as they had breath, raced past with long strides, hardly even glancing at him, in their haste to get to the menagerie in time. And all too rarely did it happen that he had a stroke of luck, when some father of a family fetched up before him with his children, pointed a finger at the hunger artist and explained at length what the phenomenon meant, telling stories of earlier years when he himself had watched similar but much more thrilling performances, and the children, still rather uncomprehending, since neither inside nor outside school had they been sufficiently prepared for this lesson—what did they care about fasting?—yet showed by the brightness of their intent eyes that new and better times might be coming. Perhaps, said the hunger artist to himself many a time, things would be a little better if his cage were set not quite so near the menagerie. That made it too easy for people to make their choice, to say nothing of what he suffered from the stench of the menagerie, the animals' restlessness by night, the carrying past of raw lumps of flesh for the beasts of prey, the roaring at feeding times, which depressed him continually. But he did not dare to lodge a complaint with the management; after all, he had the animals to thank for the troops of people who passed his cage, among whom there might always be one here and there to take an interest in him, and who could tell where they might seclude him if he called attention to his existence and thereby to the fact that, strictly speaking, he was only an impediment on the way to the menagerie.

A small impediment, to be sure, one that grew steadily less. People grew familiar with the strange idea that they could be expected, in times like these, to take an interest in a hunger artist, and with this familiarity the verdict went out against him. He might fast as much as he could, and he did so; but nothing could save him now, people passed him by. Just try to explain to anyone the art of fasting! Anyone who has no feeling for it cannot be made to understand it. The fine placards grew dirty and illegible, they were torn down; the little notice board telling the number of fast days achieved, which at first was changed carefully every day, had long stayed at the same figure, for after the first few weeks even this small task seemed pointless to the staff; and so the artist simply fasted on and on, as he had once dreamed of doing, and it was no trouble to him, just as he had always foretold, but no one counted the days, no one, not even the artist himself, knew what records he was already breaking, and his heart grew heavy. And when once in a time some leisurely passer-by stopped, made merry over the old figure on the board and spoke of swindling, that was in its way the stupidest lie ever invented by indifference and inborn malice, since it was not the hunger artist who was cheating; he was working honestly, but the world was cheating him of his reward.

Many more days went by, however, and that too came to an end. An overseer's eye fell on the cage one day and he asked the attendants why this perfectly good stage should be left standing there unused with dirty straw inside it; nobody knew, until one man, helped out by the notice board, remembered about the hunger artist. They poked into the straw with sticks and found him in it. "Are you still fasting?" asked the overseer. "When on earth do you mean to stop?" "Forgive me, everybody," whispered the hunger artist; only the overseer, who had his ear to the bars, understood him. "Of course," said the overseer, and tapped his forehead with a finger to let the attendants know what state the man was in, "we forgive you." "I always wanted you to admire my fasting," said the hunger artist. "We do admire it," said the overseer, affably. "But you shouldn't admire it," said the hunger artist. "Well, then we don't admire it," said the overseer, "but why shouldn't we admire it?" "Because I have to fast, I can't help it," said the hunger artist. "What a fellow you are," said the overseer, "and why can't you help it?" "Because," said the hunger artist, lifting his head a little and speaking, with his lips pursed, as if for a kiss, right into the overseer's ear, so that no syllable might be lost, "because I couldn't find the food I liked. If I had found it, believe me, I should have made no fuss and stuffed myself like you or anyone else." These were his last words, but in his dimming eyes remained the firm though no longer proud persuasion that he was still continuing to fast.

"Well, clear this out now!" said the overseer, and they buried the hunger artist, straw and all. Into the cage they put a young panther. Even the most insensitive felt it refreshing to see this wild creature leaping around the cage that had so long been dreary. The panther was all right. The food he liked was brought him without hesitation by the attendants; he seemed not even to miss his freedom; his noble body, furnished almost to the bursting point with all that it needed, seemed to carry freedom around with it too; somewhere in his jaws it seemed to lurk; and the joy of life streamed with such ardent passion from his throat that for the onlookers it was not easy to stand the shock of it. But they braced themselves, crowded round the cage, and did not want ever to move away.

JEAN-PAUL SARTRE
1905–

The Wall

Sartre's story is commonly read as a dramatization of some basic aspects of existentialism,* a theory of existence which emerged in France after World War II and helped to generate the literature of the absurd of the new lost generation. Existentialism is essentially a philosophy of revolt against nineteenth-century rationalism that perceived and understood reality through the intellect. It rejects such speculation about reality and finds reality in the experience of the individual. It finds no purpose or meaning inherent in the universe, and leaves morality to the individual who must arrive at his own code through experience. As Albert Camus observes, "The fact that certain great novelists have chosen to write in terms of images rather than of arguments reveals a great deal about a certain kind of thinking common to them all, a conviction of the futility of all explanatory principles, and of the instructive message of sensory impressions." And Sartre, sometimes referred to as the High Priest of existentialism, speaking of Camus, says he "is very much at peace within disorder. Nature's obstinate blindness probably irritates him, but it comforts him as well. Its irrationality is only a negative thing. The absurd man is a humanist; he knows only the good things in the world." These two quotations put together seem to arrive at the heart of existentialism: the futility of trying to explain life through reason, and the irrationality of nature and the universe. (See Frost's "The Trial by Existence," p. 311, and "A Masque of Reason," p. 376; and Hardy's "Hap," p. 310.)

The setting of "The Wall" is the Spanish Civil War of 1936–1939. The story belongs to Pablo Ibbieta, the narrator, who is probably the voice of Sartre. The question is, why is Pablo prepared to die differently from Tom Steinbock and Juan Mirbal? He could have probably saved his life by betraying Ramon Gris. Why does Pablo finally say, "I laughed so hard the tears came to my eyes"? The answer lies, of course, in the kind of absurd world Pablo has experienced, the kind the existentialist rejects.

For two commentaries on values in modern literature, see Archibald MacLeish's *The Continuing Journey* (Boston: Houghton Mifflin, 1967) and Joseph Wood Krutch's *The Modern Temper* (New York: Harcourt Brace Jovanovich, 1929).

* The serious student who wishes to explore existentialism will find these sources helpful: Jean-Paul Sartre, *Existentialism,* New York: Philosophical Library; London: Methuen and Company, 1947. Walter Kaufmann, *Existentialism from Dostoevsky to Sartre,* Cleveland and New York: Meridian Books, 1956, pp. 287–311. Martin Esslin's *The Theatre of the Absurd,* New York: Doubleday & Company, 1969, shows the influence of existentialism on drama, especially through Sartre and Camus.

They pushed us into a large white room and my eyes began to blink because the light hurt them. Then I saw a table and four fellows seated at the table, civilians, looking at some papers. The other prisoners were herded together at one end and we were obliged to cross the entire room to join them. There were several I knew, and others who must have been foreigners. The two in front of me were blond with round heads. They looked alike. I imagine they were French. The smaller one kept pulling at his trousers, out of nervousness.

This lasted about three hours. I was dog-tired and my head was empty. But the room was well-heated, which struck me as rather agreeable; we had not stopped shivering for twenty-four hours. The guards led the prisoners in one after the other in front of the table. Then the four fellows asked them their names and what they did. Most of the time that was all—or perhaps from time to time they would ask such questions as: "Did you help sabotage the munitions?" or,

"Where were you on the morning of the ninth and what were you doing?" They didn't even listen to the replies, or at least they didn't seem to. They just remained silent for a moment and looked straight ahead, then they began to write. They asked Tom if it was true he had served in the International Brigade. Tom couldn't say he hadn't because of the papers they had found in his jacket. They didn't ask Juan anything, but after he told them his name, they wrote for a long while.

"It's my brother José who's the anarchist," Juan said. "You know perfectly well he's not here now. I don't belong to any party. I never did take part in politics." They didn't answer.

Then Juan said, "I didn't do anything. And I'm not going to pay for what the others did."

His lips were trembling. A guard told him to stop talking and led him away. It was my turn.

"Your name is Pablo Ibbieta?"

I said yes.

The fellow looked at his papers and said, "Where is Ramon Gris?"

"I don't know."

"You hid him in your house from the sixth to the nineteenth."

"I did not."

They continued to write for a moment and the guards led me away. In the hall, Tom and Juan were waiting between two guards. We started walking. Tom asked one of the guards, "What's the idea?" "How do you mean?" the guard asked. "Was that just the preliminary questioning, or was that the trial?" "That was the trial," the guard said. "So now what? What are they going to do with us?" The guard answered drily, "The verdict will be told you in your cell."

In reality, our cell was one of the cellars of the hospital. It was terribly cold there because it was very drafty. We had been shivering all night long and it had hardly been any better during the day. I had spent the preceding five days in a cellar in the archbishop's palace, a sort of dungeon that must have dated back to the Middle Ages. There were lots of prisoners and not much room, so they housed them just anywhere. But I was not homesick for my dungeon. I hadn't been cold there, but I had been alone, and that gets to be irritating. In the cellar I had company. Juan didn't say a word; he was afraid, and besides, he was too young to have anything to say. But Tom was a good talker and knew Spanish well.

In the cellar there were a bench and four straw mattresses. When they led us back we sat down and waited in silence. After a while Tom said, "Our goose is cooked."

"I think so too," I said. "But I don't believe they'll do anything to the kid."

Tom said, "They haven't got anything on him. He's the brother of a fellow who's fighting, and that's all."

I looked at Juan. He didn't seem to have heard.

Tom continued, "You know what they do in Saragossa? They lay the guys across the road and then they drive over them with trucks. It was a Moroccan deserter who told us that. They say it's just to save ammunition."

I said, "Well, it doesn't save gasoline."

I was irritated with Tom; he shouldn't have said that.

He went on, "There are officers walking up and down the roads with their hands in their pockets, smoking, and they see that it's done right. Do you think they'd put 'em out of their misery? Like hell they do. They just let 'em holler. Sometimes as long as an hour. The Moroccan said the first time he almost puked."

"I don't believe they do that here," I said, "unless they really are short of ammunition."

The daylight came in through four air vents and a round opening that had been cut in the ceiling, to the left, and which opened directly onto the sky. It was through this hole, which was ordinarily closed by means of a trapdoor, that they unloaded coal into the cellar. Directly under the hole, there was a big pile of coal dust; it had been intended for heating the hospital, but at the beginning of the war they had evacuated the patients and the coal had stayed there unused; it even got rained on from time to time, when they forgot to close the trapdoor.

Tom started to shiver. "God damn it," he said, "I'm shivering. There, it is starting again."

He rose and began to do gymnastic exercises. At each movement, his shirt opened and showed his white, hairy chest. He lay down on his back, lifted his legs in the air and began to do the scissors movement. I watched his big buttocks tremble. Tom was tough, but he had too much fat on him. I kept thinking that soon bullets and bayonet points would sink into that mass of tender flesh as though it were a pat of butter.

I wasn't exactly cold, but I couldn't feel my shoulders or my arms. From time to time, I had the impression that something was missing and I began to look around for my jacket. Then I would suddenly remember they hadn't given me a jacket. It was rather awkward. They had taken our clothes to give them to their own soldiers and had left us only our shirts and these cotton trousers the hospital patients wore in mid-summer. After a moment, Tom got up and sat down beside me, breathless.

"Did you get warmed up?"

"Damn it, no. But I'm all out of breath."

Around eight o'clock in the evening, a Major came in with two falangists.[1]

"What are the names of those three over there?" he asked the guard.

"Steinbock, Ibbieta and Mirbal," said the guard.

The Major put on his glasses and examined his list.

"Steinbock—Steinbock . . . Here it is. You are condemned to death. You'll be shot tomorrow morning."

He looked at his list again.

"The other two, also," he said.

"That's not possible," said Juan. "Not me."

The Major looked at him with surprise. "What's your name?"

"Juan Mirbal."

"Well, your name is here," said the Major, "and you're condemned to death."

"I didn't do anything," said Juan.

The Major shrugged his shoulders and turned toward Tom and me.

"You are both Basque?"[2]

"No, nobody's Basque."

He appeared exasperated.

"I was told there were three Basques. I'm not going to waste my time running after them. I suppose you don't want a priest?"

We didn't even answer.

Then he said, "A Belgian doctor will be around in a little while. He has permission to stay with you all night."

He gave a military salute and left.

"What did I tell you?" Tom said. "We're in for something swell."

"Yes," I said. "It's a damned shame for the kid."

I said that to be fair, but I really didn't like the kid. His face was too refined and it was disfigured by fear and suffering, which had twisted all his features. Three days ago, he was just a kid with a kind of affected manner some people like. But now he looked like an aging fairy, and I thought to myself he would never be young again, even if they let him go. It wouldn't have been a bad thing to show him a little pity, but pity makes me sick, and besides, I couldn't stand him. He hadn't said anything more, but he had turned gray. His face and hands were gray. He sat down again and stared, round-eyed, at the ground. Tom was good-hearted and tried to take him by the arm, but the kid drew himself away violently and made an ugly face. "Leave him alone," I said quietly. "Can't you see he's going to start to bawl?" Tom obeyed regretfully. He would have liked to console the kid; that would have kept him occupied and he wouldn't have been tempted to think about himself. But it got on my nerves. I had never thought about death, for the reason that the question had never come up. But now it had come up, and there was nothing else to do but think about it.

Tom started talking. "Say, did you ever bump anybody off?" he asked me. I didn't answer. He started to explain to me that he had bumped off six fellows since August. He hadn't yet realized what we were in for, and I saw clearly he didn't *want* to realize it. I myself hadn't quite taken it in. I wondered if it hurt very much. I thought about the bullets; I imagined their fiery hail going through my body. All that was beside the real question; but I was calm, we had all night in which to realize it. After a while Tom stopped talking and I looked at him out of the corner of my eye. I saw that he, too, had turned gray and that he looked pretty miserable. I said to myself, "It's starting." It was almost dark, a dull light filtered through the air vents across the coal pile and made a big spot under the sky. Through the hole in the ceiling I could already see a star. The night was going to be clear and cold.

The door opened and two guards entered. They were followed by a blond man in a tan uniform. He greeted us.

"I'm the doctor," he said. "I've been author-

[1] A member of the Spanish Phalanx, a fascist organization. [2] One of a people of obscure origin inhabiting the western Pyrenees on the Bay of Biscay.

ized to give you any assistance you may require in these painful circumstances."

He had an agreeable, cultivated voice.

I said to him, "What are you going to do here?"

"Whatever you want me to do. I shall do everything in my power to lighten these few hours."

"Why did you come to us? There are lots of others: the hospital's full of them."

"I was sent here," he answered vaguely. "You'd probably like to smoke, wouldn't you?" he added suddenly. "I've got some cigarettes and even some cigars."

He passed around some English cigarettes and some *puros*,[3] but we refused them. I looked him straight in the eye and he appeared uncomfortable.

"You didn't come here out of compassion," I said to him. "In fact, I know who you are. I saw you with some fascists in the barracks yard the day I was arrested."

I was about to continue, when all at once something happened to me which surprised me: the presence of this doctor had suddenly ceased to interest me. Usually, when I've got hold of a man I don't let go. But somehow the desire to speak had left me. I shrugged my shoulders and turned away. A little later, I looked up and saw he was watching me with an air of curiosity. The guards had sat down on one of the mattresses. Pedro, the tall thin one, was twiddling his thumbs, while the other one shook his head occasionally to keep from falling asleep.

"Do you want some light?" Pedro suddenly asked the doctor. The other fellow nodded, "Yes." I think he was not over-intelligent, but doubtless he was not malicious. As I looked at his big, cold, blue eyes, it seemed to me the worst thing about him was his lack of imagination. Pedro went out and came back with an oil lamp which he set on the corner of the bench. It gave a poor light, but it was better than nothing; the night before we had been left in the dark. For a long while I stared at the circle of light the lamp threw on the ceiling. I was fascinated. Then, suddenly, I came to, the light circle paled, and I felt as if I were being crushed under an enormous weight. It wasn't the thought of death, and it wasn't fear; it was something anonymous. My cheeks were burning hot and my head ached.

I roused myself and looked at my two companions. Tom had his head in his hands and only the fat, white nape of his neck was visible. Juan was by far the worst off; his mouth was wide open and his nostrils were trembling. The doctor came over to him and touched him on the shoulder, as though to comfort him; but his eyes remained cold. Then I saw the Belgian slide his hand furtively down Juan's arm to his wrist. Indifferent, Juan let himself be handled. Then, as though absent-mindedly, the Belgian laid three fingers over his wrist; at the same time, he drew away somewhat and managed to turn his back to me. But I leaned over backward and saw him take out his watch and look at it a moment before relinquishing the boy's wrist. After a moment, he let the inert hand fall and went and leaned against the wall. Then, as if he had suddenly remembered something very important that had to be noted down immediately, he took a notebook from his pocket and wrote a few lines in it. "The son-of-a-bitch," I thought angrily. "He better not come and feel my pulse; I'll give him a punch in his dirty jaw."

He didn't come near me, but I felt he was looking at me. I raised my head and looked back at him. In an impersonal voice, he said, "Don't you think it's frightfully cold here?"

He looked purple with cold.

"I'm not cold," I answered him.

He kept looking at me with a hard expression. Suddenly I understood, and I lifted my hands to my face. I was covered with sweat. Here, in this cellar, in mid-winter, right in a draft, I was sweating. I ran my fingers through my hair, which was stiff with sweat; at the same time, I realized my shirt was damp and sticking to my skin. I had been streaming with perspiration for an hour, at least, and had felt nothing. But this fact hadn't escaped that Belgian swine. He had seen the drops rolling down my face and had said to himself that it showed an almost pathological terror; and he himself had felt normal and proud of it because he was cold. I wanted to get up and go punch his face in, but I had hardly started to make a move before my shame and anger had disappeared. I dropped back into the bench with indifference.

I was content to rub my neck with my handkerchief because now I felt the sweat dripping

[3] A cigar.

from my hair onto the nape of my neck and that was disagreeable. I soon gave up rubbing myself, however, for it didn't do any good; my handkerchief was already wringing wet and I was still sweating. My buttocks, too, were sweating, and my damp trousers stuck to the bench.

Suddenly, Juan said, "You're a doctor, aren't you?"

"Yes," said the Belgian.

"Do people suffer—very long?"

"Oh! When . . . ? No, no," said the Belgian, in a paternal voice, "it's quickly over."

His manner was as reassuring as if he had been answering a paying patient.

"But I . . . Somebody told me—they often have to fire two volleys."

"Sometimes," said the Belgian, raising his head, "it just happens that the first volley doesn't hit any of the vital organs."

"So then they have to reload their guns and aim all over again?" Juan thought for a moment, then added hoarsely, "But that takes time!"

He was terribly afraid of suffering. He couldn't think about anything else, but that went with his age. As for me, I hardly thought about it any more and it certainly was not fear of suffering that made me perspire.

I rose and walked toward the pile of coal dust. Tom gave a start and looked at me with a look of hate. I irritated him because my shoes squeaked. I wondered if my face was as putty-colored as his. Then I noticed that he, too, was sweating. The sky was magnificent; no light at all came into our dark corner and I had only to lift my head to see the Big Bear. But it didn't look the way it had looked before. Two days ago, from my cell in the archbishop's palace, I could see a big patch of sky and each time of day brought back a different memory. In the morning, when the sky was a deep blue, and light, I thought of beaches along the Atlantic; at noon, I could see the sun, and I remembered a bar in Seville where I used to drink manzanilla[4] and eat anchovies and olives; in the afternoon, I was in the shade, and I thought of the deep shadow which covers half of the arena while the other half gleams in the sunlight: it really gave me a pang to see the whole earth reflected in the sky like that. Now, however, no matter how much I looked up in the air, the sky no longer recalled anything. I liked it better that way. I came back and sat down next to Tom. There was a long silence.

Then Tom began to talk in a low voice. He had to keep talking, otherwise he lost his way in his own thoughts. I believe he was talking to me, but he didn't look at me. No doubt he was afraid to look at me, because I was gray and sweating. We were both alike and worse than mirrors for each other. He looked at the Belgian, the only one who was alive.

"Say, do you understand? I don't."

Then I, too, began to talk in a low voice. I was watching the Belgian.

"Understand what? What's the matter?"

"Something's going to happen to us that I don't understand."

There was a strange odor about Tom. It seemed to me that I was more sensitive to odors than ordinarily. With a sneer, I said, "You'll understand, later."

"That's not so sure," he said stubbornly. "I'm willing to be courageous, but at least I ought to know . . . Listen, they're going to take us out into the courtyard. All right. The fellows will be standing in line in front of us. How many of them will there be?"

"Oh, I don't know. Five, or eight. Not more."

"That's enough. Let's say there'll be eight of them. Somebody will shout 'Shoulder arms!' and I'll see all eight rifles aimed at me. I'm sure I'm going to feel like going through the wall. I'll push against the wall as hard as I can with my back, and the wall won't give in. The way it is in a nightmare. . . . I can imagine all that. Ah, if you only knew how well I can imagine it!"

"Skip it!" I said. "I can imagine it too."

"It must hurt like the devil. You know they aim at your eyes and mouth so as to disfigure you," he added maliciously. "I can feel the wounds already. For the last hour I've been having pains in my head and neck. Not real pains —it's worse still: They're the pains I'll feel tomorrow morning. And after that, then what?"

I understood perfectly well what he meant, but I didn't want to seem to understand. As for the pains, I, too, felt them all through my body, like a lot of little gashes. I couldn't get used to them, but I was like him, I didn't think they were very important.

"After that," I said roughly, "you'll be eating daisies."

[4] A pale aromatic dry Spanish sherry wine.

He started talking to himself, not taking his eyes off the Belgian, who didn't seem to be listening to him. I knew what he had come for, and that what we were thinking didn't interest him. He had come to look at our bodies, our bodies which were dying alive.

"It's like in a nightmare," said Tom. "You want to think of something, you keep having the impression you've got it, that you're going to understand, and then it slips away from you, it eludes you and it's gone again. I say to myself, afterwards, there won't be anything. But I don't really understand what that means. There are moments when I almost do—and then it's gone again. I start to think of the pains, the bullets, the noise of the shooting. I am a materialist, I swear it; and I'm not going crazy, either. But there's something wrong. I see my own corpse. That's not hard, but it's *I* who see it, with *my* eyes. I'll have to get to the point where I think —where I think I won't see anything more. I won't hear anything more, and the world will go on for the others. We're not made to think that way, Pablo. Believe me, I've already stayed awake all night waiting for something. But this is not the same thing. This will grab us from behind, Pablo, and we won't be ready for it."

"Shut up," I said. "Do you want me to call a father confessor?"

He didn't answer. I had already noticed that he had a tendency to prophesy and call me "Pablo" in a kind of pale voice. I didn't like that very much, but it seems all the Irish are like that. I had a vague impression that he smelled of urine. Actually, I didn't like Tom very much, and I didn't see why, just because we were going to die together, I should like him any better. There are certain fellows with whom it would be different—with Ramon Gris, for instance. But between Tom and Juan, I felt alone. In fact, I liked it better that way. With Ramon I might have grown soft. But I felt terribly hard at that moment, and I wanted to stay hard.

Tom kept on muttering, in a kind of absent-minded way. He was certainly talking to keep from thinking. Naturally, I agreed with him, and I could have said everything he was saying. It's not *natural* to die. And since I was going to die, nothing seemed natural any more: neither the coal pile, nor the bench, nor Pedro's dirty old face. Only it was disagreeable for me to think the same things Tom thought. And I knew perfectly well that all night long, within five minutes of each other, we would keep on thinking things at the same time, sweating or shivering at the same time. I looked at him sideways and, for the first time, he seemed strange to me. He had death written on his face. My pride was wounded. For twenty-four hours I had lived side by side with Tom, I had listened to him, I had talked to him, and I knew we had nothing in common. And now we were as alike as twin brothers, simply because we were going to die together. Tom took my hand without looking at me.

"Pablo, I wonder . . . I wonder if it's true that we just cease to exist."

I drew my hand away.

"Look between your feet, you dirty dog."

There was a puddle between his feet and water was dripping from his trousers.

"What's the matter?" he said, frightened.

"You're wetting your pants," I said to him.

"It's not true," he said furiously. "I can't be . . . I don't feel anything."

The Belgian had come closer to him. With an air of false concern, he asked, "Aren't you feeling well?"

Tom didn't answer. The Belgian looked at the puddle without comment.

"I don't know what that is," Tom said savagely, "but I'm not afraid. I swear to you, I'm not afraid."

The Belgian made no answer. Tom rose and went to a corner. He came back, buttoning his fly, and sat down, without a word. The Belgian was taking notes.

We were watching the doctor. Juan was watching him too. All three of us were watching him because he was alive. He had the gestures of a living person, the interests of a living person; he was shivering in this cellar the way living people shiver; he had an obedient, well-fed body. We, on the other hand, didn't feel our bodies any more—not the same way, in any case. I felt like touching my trousers, but I didn't dare to. I looked at the Belgian, well-planted on his two legs, master of his muscles—and able to plan for tomorrow. We were like three shadows deprived of blood; we were watching him and sucking his life like vampires.

Finally he came over to Juan. Was he going to lay his hand on the nape of Juan's neck for some professional reason, or had he obeyed a charitable impulse? If he had acted out of charity, it was the one and only time during the whole night. He fondled Juan's head and the nape of his neck. The kid let him do it, without taking his eyes off him. Then, suddenly, he took hold of the doctor's hand and looked at it in a funny way. He held the Belgian's hand between his own two hands and there was nothing pleasing about them, those two gray paws squeezing that fat red hand. I sensed what was going to happen and Tom must have sensed it, too. But all the Belgian saw was emotion, and he smiled paternally. After a moment, the kid lifted the big red paw to his mouth and started to bite it. The Belgian drew back quickly and stumbled toward the wall. For a second, he looked at us with horror. He must have suddenly understood that we were not men like himself. I began to laugh, and one of the guards started up. The other had fallen asleep with his eyes wide open, showing only the whites.

I felt tired and over-excited at the same time. I didn't want to think any more about what was going to happen at dawn—about death. It didn't make sense, and I never got beyond just words, or emptiness. But whenever I tried to think about something else I saw the barrels of rifles aimed at me. I must have lived through my execution twenty times in succession; one time I thought it was the real thing; I must have dozed off for a moment. They were dragging me toward the wall and I was resisting; I was imploring their pardon. I woke with a start and looked at the Belgian. I was afraid I had cried out in my sleep. But he was smoothing his mustache; he hadn't noticed anything. If I had wanted to, I believe I could have slept for a while. I had been awake for the last forty-eight hours, and I was worn out. But I didn't want to lose two hours of life. They would have had to come and wake me at dawn. I would have followed them, drunk with sleep, and I would have gone off without so much as "Gosh!" I didn't want it that way, I didn't want to die like an animal. I wanted to understand. Besides, I was afraid of having nightmares. I got up and began to walk up and down and, so as to think about something else, I began to think about my past life. Memories crowded in on me, helter-skelter. Some were good and some were bad—at least that was how I had thought of them *before*. There were faces and happenings. I saw the face of a little *novillero*[5] who had gotten himself horned during the *Feria*,[6] in Valencia. I saw the face of one of my uncles, of Ramon Gris. I remembered all kinds of things that had happened: how I had been on strike for three months in 1926, and had almost died of hunger. I recalled a night I had spent on a bench in Granada; I hadn't eaten for three days, I was nearly wild, I didn't want to give up the sponge. I had to smile. With what eagerness I had run after happiness, and women, and liberty! And to what end? I had wanted to liberate Spain, I admired Py Margall, I had belonged to the anarchist movement, I had spoken at public meetings. I took everything as seriously as if I had been immortal.

At that time I had the impression that I had my whole life before me, and I thought to myself, "It's all a god-damned lie." Now it wasn't worth anything because it was finished. I wondered how I had ever been able to go out and have a good time with girls. I wouldn't have lifted my little finger if I had ever imagined that I would die like this. I saw my life before me, finished, closed, like a bag, and yet what was inside was not finished. For a moment I tried to appraise it. I would have liked to say to myself, "It's been a good life." But it couldn't be appraised, it was only an outline. I had spent my life writing checks on eternity, and had understood nothing. Now, I didn't miss anything. There were a lot of things I might have missed: the taste of manzanilla, for instance, or the swims I used to take in summer in a little creek near Cadiz. But death had taken the charm out of everything.

Suddenly the Belgian had a wonderful idea. "My friends," he said to us, "if you want me to—and providing the military authorities give their consent—I could undertake to deliver a word or some token from you to your loved ones. . . ."

Tom growled, "I haven't got anybody."

I didn't answer. Tom waited for a moment, then he looked at me with curiosity. "Aren't you going to send any message to Concha?"

"No."

I hated that sort of sentimental conspiracy. Of course, it was my fault, since I had mentioned

[5] An aspiring bullfighter who has not yet attained the rank of matador. [6] A local religious holiday.

Concha the night before, and I should have kept my mouth shut. I had been with her for a year. Even as late as last night, I would have cut my arm off with a hatchet just to see her again for five minutes. That was why I had mentioned her. I couldn't help it. Now I didn't care any more about seeing her. I hadn't anything more to say to her. I didn't even want to hold her in my arms. I loathed my body because it had turned gray and was sweating—and I wasn't even sure that I didn't loathe hers too. Concha would cry when she heard about my death; for months she would have no more interest in life. But still it was I who was going to die. I thought of her beautiful, loving eyes. When she looked at me something went from her to me. But I thought to myself that it was all over; if she looked at me *now* her gaze would not leave her eyes, it would not reach out to me. I was alone.

Tom too, was alone, but not the same way. He was seated astride his chair and had begun to look at the bench with a sort of smile, with surprise, even. He reached out his hand and touched the wood cautiously, as though he were afraid of breaking something, then he drew his hand back hurriedly, and shivered. I wouldn't have amused myself touching that bench, if I had been Tom, that was just some more Irish play-acting. But somehow it seemed to me too that the different objects had something funny about them. They seemed to have grown paler, less massive than before. I had only to look at the bench, the lamp or the pile of coal dust to feel I was going to die. Naturally, I couldn't think clearly about my death, but I saw it everywhere, even on the different objects, the way they had withdrawn and kept their distance, tactfully, like people talking at the bedside of a dying person. It was *his own death* Tom had just touched on the bench.

In the state I was in, if they had come and told me I could go home quietly, that my life would be saved, it would have left me cold. A few hours, or a few years of waiting are all the same, when you've lost the illusion of being eternal. Nothing mattered to me any more. In a way, I was calm. But it was a horrible kind of calm —because of my body. My body—I saw with its eyes and I heard with its ears, but it was no longer I. It sweat and trembled independently, and I didn't recognize it any longer. I was obliged to touch it and look at it to know what was happening to it, just as if it had been someone else's body. At times I still felt it, I felt a slipping, a sort of headlong plunging, as in a falling airplane, or else I heard my heart beating. But this didn't give me confidence. In fact, everything that came from my body had something damned dubious about it. Most of the time it was silent, it stayed put and I didn't feel anything other than a sort of heaviness, a loathsome presence against me. I had the impression of being bound to an enormous vermin.

The Belgian took out his watch and looked at it.

"It's half-past-three," he said.

The son-of-a-bitch! He must have done it on purpose. Tom jumped up. We hadn't yet realized the time was passing. The night surrounded us like a formless, dark mass; I didn't even remember it had started.

Juan started to shout. Wringing his hands, he implored, "I don't want to die! I don't want to die!"

He ran the whole length of the cellar with his arms in the air, then he dropped down onto one of the mattresses, sobbing. Tom looked at him with dismal eyes and didn't even try to console him any more. The fact was, it was no use; the kid made more noise than we did, but he was less affected, really. He was like a sick person who defends himself against his malady with a high fever. When there's not even any fever left, it's much more serious.

He was crying. I could tell he felt sorry for himself; he was thinking about death. For one second, one single second, I too felt like crying, crying out of pity for myself. But just the contrary happened. I took one look at the kid, saw his thin, sobbing shoulders, and I felt I was inhuman. I couldn't feel pity for these others or for myself. I said to myself, "I want to die decently."

Tom had gotten up and was standing just under the round opening looking out for the first signs of daylight. I was determined, I wanted to die decently, and I only thought about that. But underneath, ever since the doctor had told us the time, I felt time slipping, flowing by, one drop at a time.

It was still dark when I heard Tom's voice.

"Do you hear them?"

"Yes."

People were walking in the courtyard.

"What the hell are they doing? After all, they

can't shoot in the dark."

After a moment, we didn't hear anything more. I said to Tom, "There's the daylight."

Pedro got up yawning, and came and blew out the lamp. He turned to the man beside him. "It's hellish cold."

The cellar had grown gray. We could hear shots at a distance.

"It's about to start," I said to Tom. "That must be in the back courtyard."

Tom asked the doctor to give him a cigarette. I didn't want any; I didn't want either cigarettes or alcohol. From that moment on, the shooting didn't stop.

"Can you take it in?" Tom said.

He started to add something, then he stopped and began to watch the door. The door opened and a lieutenant came in with four soldiers. Tom dropped his cigarette.

"Steinbock?"

Tom didn't answer. Pedro pointed him out.

"Juan Mirbal?"

"He's the one on the mattress."

"Stand up," said the Lieutenant.

Juan didn't move. Two soldiers took hold of him by the armpits and stood him up on his feet. But as soon as they let go of him he fell down.

The soldiers hesitated a moment.

"He's not the first one to get sick," said the Lieutenant. "You'll have to carry him, the two of you. We'll arrange things when we get there." He turned to Tom. "All right, come along."

Tom left between two soldiers. Two other soldiers followed, carrying the kid by his arms and legs. He was not unconscious; his eyes were wide open and tears were rolling down his cheeks. When I started to go out, the Lieutenant stopped me.

"Are you Ibbieta?"

"Yes."

"You wait here. They'll come and get you later on."

They left. The Belgian and the two jailers left too, and I was alone. I didn't understand what had happened to me, but I would have liked it better if they had ended it all right away. I heard the volleys at almost regular intervals; at each one, I shuddered. I felt like howling and tearing my hair. But instead, I gritted my teeth and pushed my hands deep into my pockets, because I wanted to stay decent.

An hour later, they came to fetch me and took me up to the first floor in a little room which smelt of cigar smoke and was so hot it seemed to me suffocating. Here there were two officers sitting in comfortable chairs, smoking, with papers spread out on their knees.

"Your name is Ibbieta?"

"Yes."

"Where is Ramon Gris?"

"I don't know."

The man who questioned me was small and stocky. He had hard eyes behind his glasses.

"Come nearer," he said to me.

I went nearer. He rose and took me by the arms, looking at me in a way calculated to make me go through the floor. At the same time he pinched my arms with all his might. He didn't mean to hurt me; it was quite a game; he wanted to dominate me. He also seemed to think it was necessary to blow his fetid breath right into my face. We stood like that for a moment, only I felt more like laughing than anything else. It takes a lot more than that to intimidate a man who's about to die: it didn't work. He pushed me away violently and sat down again.

"It's your life or his," he said. "You'll be allowed to go free if you tell us where he is."

After all, these two bedizened fellows with their riding crops and boots were just men who were going to die one day. A little later than I, perhaps, but not a great deal. And there they were, looking for names among their papers, running after other men in order to put them in prison or do away with them entirely. They had their opinions on the future of Spain and on other subjects. Their petty activities seemed to me to be offensive and ludicrous. I could no longer put myself in their place. I had the impression they were crazy.

The little fat fellow kept looking at me, tapping his boots with his riding crop. All his gestures were calculated to make him appear like a spirited, ferocious animal.

"Well? Do you understand?"

"I don't know where Gris is," I said. "I thought he was in Madrid."

The other officer lifted his pale hand indolently. This indolence was also calculated. I saw through all their little tricks, and I was dumbfounded that men should still exist who took pleasure in that kind of thing.

"You have fifteen minutes to think it over," he said slowly. "Take him to the linen-room, and bring him back here in fifteen minutes. If he continues to refuse, he'll be executed at once."

They knew what they were doing. I had spent the night waiting. After that, they had made me wait another hour in the cellar, while they shot Tom and Juan, and now they locked me in the linen-room. They must have arranged the whole thing the night before. They figured that sooner or later people's nerves wear out and they hoped to get me that way.

They made a big mistake. In the linen-room I sat down on a ladder because I felt very weak, and I began to think things over. Not their proposition, however. Naturally I knew where Gris was. He was hiding in his cousins' house, about two miles outside of the city. I knew, too, that I would not reveal his hiding place, unless they tortured me (but they didn't seem to be considering that). All that was definitely settled and didn't interest me in the least. Only I would have liked to understand the reasons for my own conduct. I would rather die than betray Gris. Why? I no longer liked Ramon Gris. My friendship for him had died shortly before dawn along with my love for Concha, along with my own desire to live. Of course I still admired him —he was hard. But it was not for that reason I was willing to die in his place; his life was no more valuable than mine. No life was of any value. A man was going to be stood up against a wall and fired at till he dropped dead. It didn't make any difference whether it was I or Gris or somebody else. I knew perfectly well he was more useful to the Spanish cause than I was, but I didn't give a God damn about Spain or anarchy, either; nothing had any importance now. And yet, there I was. I could save my skin by betraying Gris and I refused to do it. It seemed more ludicrous to me than anything else; it was stubbornness.

I thought to myself, "Am I hard-headed!" And I was seized with a strange sort of cheerfulness.

They came to fetch me and took me back to the two officers. A rat darted out under our feet and that amused me. I turned to one of the falangists and said to him, "Did you see that rat?"

He made no reply. He was gloomy, and took himself very seriously. As for me, I felt like laughing, but I restrained myself because I was afraid that if I started, I wouldn't be able to stop. The falangist wore mustaches. I kept after him, "You ought to cut off those mustaches, you fool."

I was amused by the fact that he let hair grow all over his face while he was still alive. He gave me a kind of half-hearted kick, and I shut up.

"Well," said the fat officer, "have you thought things over?"

I looked at them with curiosity, like insects of a very rare species.

"I know where he is," I said. "He's hiding in the cemetery. Either in one of the vaults, or in the gravediggers' shack."

I said that just to make fools of them. I wanted to see them get up and fasten their belts and bustle about giving orders.

They jumped to their feet.

"Fine. Moles, go ask Lieutenant Lopez for fifteen men. And as for you," the little fat fellow said to me, "if you've told the truth, I don't go back on my word. But you'll pay for this, if you're pulling our leg."

They left noisily and I waited in peace, still guarded by the falangists. From time to time I smiled at the thought of the face they were going to make. I felt dull and malicious. I could see them lifting up the gravestones, or opening the doors of the vaults one by one. I saw the whole situation as though I were another person: the prisoner determined to play the hero, the solemn falangists with their mustaches and the men in uniform running around among the graves. It was irresistibly funny.

After half an hour, the little fat fellow came back alone. I thought he had come to give the order to execute me. The others must have stayed in the cemetery.

The officer looked at me. He didn't look at all foolish.

"Take him out in the big courtyard with the others," he said. "When military operations are over, a regular tribunal will decide his case."

I thought I must have misunderstood.

"So they're not—they're not going to shoot me?" I asked.

"Not now, in any case. Afterwards, that doesn't concern me."

I still didn't understand.

"But why?" I said to him.

He shrugged his shoulders without replying, and the soldiers led me away. In the big courtyard there were a hundred or so prisoners, women, children and a few old men. I started to walk around the grass plot in the middle. I felt absolutely idiotic. At noon we were fed in the dining hall. Two or three fellows spoke to me. I must have known them, but I didn't answer. I didn't even know where I was.

Toward evening, about ten new prisoners were pushed into the courtyard. I recognized Garcia, the baker.

He said to me, "Lucky dog! I didn't expect to find you alive."

"They condemned me to death," I said, "and then they changed their minds. I don't know why."

"I was arrested at two o'clock," Garcia said.

"What for?"

Garcia took no part in politics.

"I don't know," he said. "They arrest everybody who doesn't think the way they do."

He lowered his voice.

"They got Gris."

I began to tremble.

"When?"

"This morning. He acted like a damned fool. He left his cousins' house Tuesday because of a disagreement. There were any number of fellows who would have hidden him, but he didn't want to be indebted to anybody any more. He said, 'I would have hidden at Ibbieta's, but since they've got him, I'll go hide in the cemetery.' "

"In the cemetery?"

"Yes. It was the god-damnedest thing. Naturally they passed by there this morning; that had to happen. They found him in the gravediggers' shack. They opened fire at him and they finished him off."

"In the cemetery!"

Everything went around in circles, and when I came to I was sitting on the ground. I laughed so hard the tears came to my eyes.

JAMES BALDWIN
1924–
Exodus

James Baldwin has written in a variety of literary forms, using an even greater variety of subjects, all investigated with a moral force and sincerity not entirely common in our time. It is difficult to read any work of his without feeling the authenticity woven into the fabric of his essays, short stories, and novels. The essays of *Notes of a Native Son* (1955) and *Nobody Knows My Name* (1961) emerge from the depth of his personal experience in black life. More recently he has published a far-ranging commentary on the struggle of blacks in general, but most specifically of himself, to find his identity. The title, *No Name in the Street* (1972), is taken from *Job,* 18:17–18:

> His remembrance shall perish from the earth,
> And he shall have no name in the street.
> He shall be driven from light into darkness,
> And chased out of the world.

Baldwin's "Exodus" is the story of Florence's determination, almost regardless of the cost, to free herself of the white psychology that has dominated her people. Her dilemma, to remain with her mother, Rachel, until her mother dies or to leave the South for New York to escape her mother's fate, is the key symbol of the story. It is Florence's Exodus that hangs in the balance. The background of her mother's life is well-known to Florence—entirely too well-known—, and almost a story in itself. Baldwin's low-key method of telling the story could be a powerful influence on any sensitve reader who expects a condemnation of the Southern whites tinged with hatred. But since every fact of the mother's life is easily documented, we find the artist exploring the psychological effects of those facts instead of writing propaganda. If the reader feels as Florence feels, the artist in Baldwin is probably soberly content.

I

She had always seemed to Florence the oldest woman in the world—for she often spoke of Florence and Gabriel as the children of her old age; and she had been born, innumerable years ago, during slavery, on a plantation in another state. On this plantation she had grown up, one of the field workers, for she was very tall and strong; and by-and-by she had married, and raised children, all of whom had been taken from her, one by sickness, and two by auction, and one whom she had not been allowed to call her own, who had been raised in the master's house. When she was a woman grown, well past thirty as she reckoned it, with one husband buried—but the master had given her another—armies, plundering and burning, had come from the North to set them free. This was in answer to the prayers of the faithful, who had never ceased, both day and night, to cry out for deliverance.

For it had been the will of God that they should hear, and pass it, thereafter, one to another, the story of the Hebrew children, who had been held in bondage in the land of Egypt;[1] and how the Lord had heard their groaning, and how His heart was moved; and how He bid them wait but a little season till He should send deliverance. She had known this story, so it seemed, from the day that she was born. And while life ran, rising in the morning before the sun came up, standing and bending in the fields when the sun was high, crossing the fields homeward while the sun went down at the gates of heaven far away—hearing the whistle of the foreman, and his eerie cry across the fields; in the whiteness of winter when hogs and turkeys and geese were slaughtered, and lights burned bright in the big house, and Bathsheba, the cook, sent over in a napkin bits of ham and chicken and cakes left over by the white folks; in all that befell, in her joys—her pipe in the evening, her man at night, the children she suckled, and guided on their first short steps—and in her tribulations, death, and parting, and the lash; she did not forget that deliverance was promised, and would surely come. She had only to endure and trust in God. She knew that the big house, the house of pride where the white folks lived, would come down: it was written in the Word of God. And they, who walked so proudly now, yet had not fashioned, for themselves, or their children, so sure a foundation as was hers. They walked on the edge of a steep place and their eyes were sightless—God would cause them to rush down, as the herd of swine had once rushed down, into the sea. For all that they were so beautiful, and took their ease, she knew them, and she pitied them, who would have no covering in the great day of His wrath.

Yet, she told her children, God was just, and He struck no people without first giving many warnings. God gave men time, but all the times were in His hand, and, one day, the time to forsake evil and do good would all be finished: then only the whirlwind, death riding on the whirlwind, awaited those people who had forgotten God. In all the days that she was growing up, signs failed not, but none heeded. *Slaves done riz,* was whispered in the cabin, and at the master's gate: slaves in another county had fired the master's house and fields, and dashed their children to death against the stones. *Another slave in hell,* Bethsheba might say one morning, shooing the pickaninnies away from the great porch: a slave had killed his master, or his overseer, and had gone down to hell to pay for it. *I ain't got long to stay here,* someone crooned beside her in the fields: who would be gone by morning on his journey North. All these signs, like the plagues with which the Lord had afflicted Egypt, only hardened the hearts of these people against the Lord. They thought the lash would save them, and they used the lash; or the knife, or the gallows, or the auction block; they thought that kindness would save them, and the master and mistress came down, smiling, to the cabins, making much of the pickaninnies, and bearing gifts. These were great days, and they all, black and white, seemed happy together. But when the Word has gone forth from the mouth of God nothing can turn it back.

The word was fulfilled one morning before she was awake. Many of the stories her mother told meant nothing to Florence, she knew them for what they were, tales told by an old black woman in a cabin in the evening to distract her children from their cold and hunger. But the story of this day she was never to forget, it was a day like the day for which she lived. There was a great running and shouting, said her mother, everywhere outside, and, as she opened her eyes to the light of that day, so bright, she said, and cold, she was certain that the judgment trump had sounded. While she still sat, amazed, and wondering what, on the judgment day, would be the best behavior, in rushed Bathsheba, and behind her many tumbling children, and field hands, and house niggers, all together, and Bath-

[1] See *Exodus,* Israel in bondage: 1:1–22; 2:1–25. God delivers His people from Egypt: 3:1–14.

sheba shouted, "Rise up, rise up, Sister Rachel, and see the Lord's deliverance! He done brought us out of Egypt, just like He promised, and we's free at last!"

Bathsheba grabbed her, tears running down her face, she, dressed in the clothes in which she had slept, walked to the door to look out on the new day God had given them.

On that day she saw the proud house humbled, green silk and velvet blowing out of windows, and the garden trampled by many horsemen, and the big gates open. The master and mistress, and their kin, and one child she had borne were in that house—which she did not enter. Soon it occurred to her that there was no reason any more to tarry here. She tied her things in a cloth, which she put on her head, and walked out through the big gate, never to see that country any more.

And this, as Florence grew, became her deep ambition: to walk out one morning through the cabin door, never to return. . . .

II

In 1900, when she was twenty-six, Florence walked out through the cabin door. She had thought to wait until her mother, who was so ill now that she no longer stirred out of bed, should be buried—but suddenly she knew that she would wait no longer, the time had come. She had been working as cook and serving girl for a large white family in town, and it was on the day that her master proposed that she become his concubine that she knew that her life among these wretched had come to its destined end. She left her employment that same day (leaving behind her a most vehement conjugal bitterness) and with part of the money which, with cunning, cruelty, and sacrifice, she had saved over a period of years, bought a railroad ticket to New York. When she bought it, in a kind of scarlet rage, she held, like a talisman at the back of her mind, the thought: "I can give it back, I can sell it. This don't mean I got to go." But she knew that nothing could stop her.

And it was this leave-taking which came to stand, in Florence's latter days, and with many another witness, at her bedside. Gray clouds obscured the sun that day, and outside the cabin window she saw that mist still covered the ground. Her mother lay in bed, awake; she was pleading with Gabriel,[2] who had been out drinking the night before, and who was not really sober now, to mend his ways and come to the Lord. And Gabriel, full of the confusion, and pain, and guilt which were his whenever he thought of how he made his mother suffer, but which became nearly insupportable when she taxed him with it, stood before the mirror, head bowed, buttoning his shirt. Florence knew that he could not unlock his lips to speak; he could not say Yes to his mother, and to the Lord; and he could not say No.

"Honey," their mother was saying, "don't you *let* your old mother die without you look her in the eye and tell her she going to see you in glory. You hear me, boy?"

In a moment, Florence thought with scorn, tears would fill his eyes, and he would promise to "do better." He had been promising to "do better" since the day he had been baptized.

She put down her bag in the center of the hateful room.

"Ma," she said, "I'm going. I'm a-going this morning."

Now that she had said it, she was angry with herself for not having said it the night before, so that they would have had time to be finished with their weeping and their arguments. She had not trusted herself to withstand, the night before; but now there was almost no time left. The center of her mind was filled with the image of the great, white clock at the railway station, on which the hands did not cease to move.

"You going where?" her mother asked, sharply. But she knew that her mother had understood, had, indeed, long before this moment, known that this moment would come. The astonishment with which she stared at Florence's bag was not altogether astonishment, but a startled, wary attention. A danger imagined had

[2] It is significant that the mother's (Rachel's) son is given the biblical name Gabriel, meaning "God is mighty," but her daughter is given the name Florence, which is customarily identified with bloom and prosperity. His mother had named him Gabriel apparently with great hope, a hope later dashed by his sins, giving his name an ironical twist. For Gabriel see *Luke,* 1:19, 26–38.

become present and real, and her mother was already searching for a way to break Florence's will. All this Florence, in a moment, knew, and it made her stronger. She watched her mother, waiting.

But at the tone of his mother's voice, Gabriel, who had scarcely heard Florence's announcement, so grateful had he been that something had occurred to distract from him his mother's attention, dropped his eyes, and saw Florence's traveling bag. And he repeated his mother's question in a stunned, angry voice, understanding it only as the words hit the air:

"Yes, girl. Where you think you going?"

"I'm going," she said, "to New York. I got my ticket."

And her mother watched her. For a moment no one said a word. Then, Gabriel, in a changed and frightened voice, asked:

"And when you done decide that?

She did not look at him, nor answer his question. She continued to watch her mother. "I got my ticket," she repeated. "I'm going on the morning train."

"Girl," asked her mother, quietly, "is you sure you know what you's doing?"

She stiffened, seeing in her mother's eyes a mocking pity. "I'm a woman grown," she said. "I know what I'm doing."

"And you going," cried Gabriel, "this morning—just like that? And you going to walk off and leave your mother—just like that?"

"You hush," she said, turning to him for the first time; "she got you, ain't she?"

This was indeed, she realized, as he dropped his eyes, the bitter, troubling point. He could not endure the thought of being left alone with his mother, with nothing whatever to put between himself and his guilty love. With Florence gone, time would have swallowed up all his mother's children, except himself; and *he*, then, must make amends for all the pain that she had borne, and sweeten her last moments with all his proofs of love. And his mother required of him one proof only, that he tarry no longer in sin. With Florence gone, his stammering time, his playing time, contracted with a bound to the sparest interrogative second; when he must stiffen himself, and answer to his mother, and all the host of heaven, Yes, or No.

Florence smiled inwardly a small, malicious smile, watching his slow bafflement, and panic, and rage; and she looked at her mother again. "She got you," she repeated. "She don't need me."

"You going North," her mother said, then. "And when you reckon on coming back?"

"I don't reckon on coming back," she said.

"You come crying back soon enough," said Gabriel, with malevolence, "soon as they whip your butt up there four or five times."

She looked at him again. "Just don't you try to hold your breath till then, you hear?"

"Girl," said her mother, "you mean to tell me the devil's done made your heart so hard you can just leave your mother on her dying bed, and you don't care if you don't never see her in this world no more? Honey, you can't tell me you done got so evil as all that?"

She felt Gabriel watching her to see how she would take this question—the question, which, for all her determination, she had dreaded most to hear. She looked away from her mother, and straightened, catching her breath, looking outward through the small, cracked window. There, outside, beyond the slowly rising mist, and farther off than her eyes could see, her life awaited her. The woman on the bed was old, her life was fading as the mist rose. She thought of her mother as already in the grave; and she would not let herself be strangled by the hands of the dead.

"I'm going, Ma," she said. "I got to go."

Her mother leaned back, face upward to the light, and began to cry. Gabriel moved to Florence's side and grabbed her arm. She looked up into his face and saw that his eyes were full of tears.

"You can't go," he said. "You can't go. You can't go and leave your mother thisaway. She need a woman, Florence, to help look after her. What she going to do here, all alone with me?"

She pushed him from her and moved to stand over her mother's bed.

"Ma," she said, "don't be like that. Ain't a blessed thing for you to cry about so. Ain't a thing can happen to me up North can't happen to me here. God's everywhere, Ma. Ain't no need to worry."

She knew that she was mouthing words; and she realized suddenly that her mother scorned to dignify these words with her attention. She had granted Florence the victory—with a promptness which had the effect of making Florence, however dimly and unwillingly, wonder if her victory was real; and she was not weeping for her daughter's future; she was weeping for the past, and weeping in an anguish in which Florence had no part. And all of this filled Florence with a terrible fear, which was immediately transformed into anger.

"Gabriel can take care of you," she said, her voice shaking with malice; "Gabriel ain't never going to leave you. Is you, boy?" and she looked at him. He stood, stupid with bewilderment and grief, a few inches from the bed. "But me," she said, "I got to go." She walked to the center of the room again, and picked up her bag.

"Girl," Gabriel whispered, "ain't you got no feelings at *all?*"

"*Lord!*" her mother cried; and at the sound her heart turned over; she and Gabriel, arrested, stared at the bed. "Lord, Lord, Lord! Lord, have mercy on my sinful daughter! Stretch out your hand and hold her back from the lake that burns forever! Oh, my Lord, my Lord!" and her voice dropped, and broke, and tears ran down her face. "Lord, I done my best with all the children what you give me. Lord, have mercy on my children, and my children's children."

"Florence,' said Gabriel, "please don't go. Please don't go. You ain't really fixing to go and leave her like this?"

Tears stood suddenly in her own eyes, though she could not have said what she was crying for. "Leave me be," she said to Gabriel, and picked up her bag again. She opened the door; the cold morning air came in. "Good-by," she said. And then to Gabriel: "Tell her I said good-by." She walked through the cabin door and down the short steps into the frosty yard. Gabriel watched her, standing magnetized between the door and the weeping bed. Then, as her hand was on the gate, he ran before her, and slammed the gate shut.

"Girl, where you going? What you doing? You reckon on finding some men up North to dress you in pearls and diamonds?"

Violently, she opened the gate and moved out into the road. He watched her with his jaw hanging, until the dust and the distance swallowed her up.

EDGAR ALLAN POE
1809–1849

Ligeia

Like some other stories by Poe, this one has been variously interpreted. Historically it belongs to the Romantic movement, which often associated beauty with death. Victor Hugo (1802–1885), an early leader of French Romanticism, called them "two sisters" with the "same enigma," and Poe thought "the death . . . of a beautiful woman is, unquestionably, the most poetical topic in the world —and equally it is beyond doubt that the lips best suited for such a topic are those of a bereaved lover" ("The Philosophy of Composition"). In his *The Romantic Agony,* 1933 (*La Carne, La Morte, e il Diavolo*—The Flesh, Death, and the Devil), the Italian critic Mario Praz argues that the theme of many of Poe's stories is the "thirst for unrealizable love" and "the desire for that complete fusion with the beloved being which ends in vampirism." D. H. Lawrence finds that "Ligeia is still the old-fashioned woman. Her will is still to submit. She wills to submit to the vampire of her husband's consciousness. Even death. . . . It is the ghostly Ligeia who pours poison into Rowena's cup. It is the spirit of Ligeia, leagued with the spirit of the husband, that now lusts in the slow destruction of Rowena. The two vampires, dead wife and living husband."

And the will therein lieth, which dieth not. Who knoweth the mysteries of the will, with its vigor? For God is but a great will pervading all things by nature of its intentness. Man doth not yield himself to the angels, nor unto death utterly, save only through the weakness of his feeble will.[1]

[1] Supposedly taken from Joseph Glanvill (1636–1680), the English clergyman and philosopher who defended the preexistence of souls and belief in witchcraft. Apparently Poe devised the passage himself. D. H. Lawrence called it "a profound saying: and a deadly one."

I cannot, for my soul, remember how, when, or even precisely where, I first became acquainted with the lady Ligeia. Long years have since elapsed, and my memory is feeble through much suffering. Or, perhaps, I cannot *now* bring these points to mind, because in truth the character of my beloved, her rare learning, her singular yet placid cast of beauty, and the thrilling and enthralling eloquence of her low musical language, made their way into my heart by paces so steadily and stealthily progressive that they have been unnoticed and unknown. Yet I believe that I met her first and most frequently in some large, old, decaying city near the Rhine. Of her family I have surely heard her speak. That it is of a remotely ancient date cannot be doubted. Ligeia! Ligeia! Buried in studies of a nature more than all else adapted to deaden impressions of the outward world, it is by that sweet word alone—by Ligeia—that I bring before mine eyes in fancy the image of her who is no more. And now, while I write, a recollection flashes upon me that I have *never known* the paternal name of her who was my friend and my betrothed, and who became the partner of my studies, and finally the wife of my bosom. Was it a playful charge on the part of my Ligeia? or was it a test of my strength of affection, that I should institute no inquiries upon this point? or was it rather a caprice of my own—a wildly romantic offering on the shrine of the most passionate devotion? I but indistinctly recall the fact itself—what wonder that I have utterly forgotten the circumstances which originated or attended it? And, indeed, if ever that spirit which is entitled *Romance*—if ever she, the wan and the misty-winged Ashtophet[2] of idolatrous Egypt, presided, as they tell, over marriages ill-omened, then most surely she presided over mine.

There is one dear topic, however, on which my memory fails me not. It is the *person* of Ligeia. In stature she was tall, somewhat slender, and, in her latter days, even emaciated. I would in vain attempt to portray the majesty, the quiet ease, of her demeanor, or the incomprehensible lightness and elasticity of her footfall. She came and departed as a shadow. I was never made aware of her entrance into my closed study, save by the dear music of her low sweet voice, as she placed her marble hand upon my shoulder. In beauty of face no maiden ever equalled her. It was the radiance of an opium-dream—an airy and spirit-lifting vision more wildly divine than the fantasies which hovered about the slumbering souls of the daughters of Delos. Yet her features were not of that regular mould which we have been falsely taught to worship in the classical labors of the heathen. "There is no exquisite beauty," says Bacon, Lord Verulam, speaking truly of all the forms and genera of beauty, "without some *strangeness* in the proportion." Yet, although I saw that the features of Ligeia were not of a classic regularity—although I perceived that her loveliness was indeed "exquisite," and felt that there was much of "strangeness" pervading it, yet I have tried in vain to detect the irregularity and to trace home my own perception of "the strange." I examined the contour of the lofty and pale forehead: it was faultless—how cold indeed that word when applied to a majesty so divine!—the skin rivalling the purest ivory, the commanding extent and repose, the gentle prominence of the regions above the temples; and then the raven-black, the glossy, the luxuriant and naturally-curling tresses, setting forth the full force of the Homeric epithet, "hyacinthine!" I looked at the delicate outlines of the nose—and nowhere but in the graceful medallions of the Hebrews had I beheld a similar perfection. There were the same luxurious smoothness of surface, the same scarcely perceptible tendency to the aquiline, the same harmoniously curved nostrils speaking the free spirit. I regarded the sweet mouth. Here was indeed the triumph of all things heavenly—the magnificent turn of the short upper lip—the soft, voluptuous slumber of the under—the dimples which sported, and the color which spoke—the teeth glancing back, with a brilliance almost startling, every ray of the holy light which fell upon them in her serene and placid, yet most exultingly radiant of all smiles. I scrutinized the formation of the chin: and here, too, I found the gentleness of breadth, the softness and the majesty, the fulness and the spirituality, of the Greek—the contour which the god Apollo revealed but

[2] Apparently Poe means Ashtoreth or Ashtaroth, the goddess of fertility among the Canaanites and Phoenicians; Babylonian Ishtar (Venus), and Greek Astarte. She may be the "queen of heaven" as in *Jeremiah*, 7:18; 44:17, 25.

in a dream to Cleomenes, the son of the Athenian. And then I peered into the large eyes of Ligeia.

For eyes we have no models[3] in the remotely antique. It might have been, too, that in these eyes of my beloved lay the secret to which Lord Verulam alludes. They were, I must believe, far larger than the ordinary eyes of our own race. They were even fuller than the fullest of the gazelle eyes of the tribe of the valley of Nourjahad. Yet it was only at intervals—in moments of intense excitement—that this peculiarity became more than slightly noticeable in Ligeia. And at such moments was her beauty—in my heated fancy thus it appeared perhaps—the beauty of beings either above or apart from the earth, the beauty of the fabulous Houri of the Turk. The hue of the orbs was the most brilliant of black, and, far over them, hung jetty lashes of great length. The brows, slightly irregular in outline, had the same tint. The "strangeness," however, which I found in the eyes, was of a nature distinct from the formation, or the color, or the brilliancy of the features, and must, after all, be referred to the *expression*. Ah, word of no meaning! behind whose vast latitude of mere sound we intrench our ignorance of so much of the spiritual. The expression of the eyes of Ligeia! How for long hours have I pondered upon it! How have I, through the whole of a midsummer night, struggled to fathom it! What was it—that something more profound than the well of Democritus—which lay far within the pupils of my beloved? What *was* it? I was possessed with a passion to discover. Those eyes! those large, those shining, those divine orbs! they became to me twin stars of Leda, and I to them devoutest of astrologers.

There is no point, among the many incomprehensible anomalies of the science of mind, more thrillingly exciting than the fact—never, I believe, noticed in the schools—that in our endeavors to recall to memory something long forgotten, we often find ourselves *upon the very verge* of remembrance, without being able, in the end, to remember. And thus how frequently, in my intense scrutiny of Ligeia's eyes, have I felt approaching the full knowledge of their expression—felt it approaching, yet not quite be mine, and so at length entirely depart! And (strange, oh strangest mystery of all!) I found, in the commonest objects of the universe, a circle of analogies to that expression. I mean to say that, subsequently to the period when Ligeia's beauty passed into my spirit, there dwelling as in a shrine, I derived, from many existences in the material world, a sentiment such as I felt always around, within me, by her large and luminous orbs. Yet not the more could I define that sentiment, or analyze, or even steadily view it. I recognized it, let me repeat, sometimes in the survey of a rapidly-growing vine—in the contemplation of a moth, a butterfly, a chrysalis, a stream of running water. I have felt it in the ocean; in the falling of a meteor. I have felt it in the glances of unusually aged people. And there are one or two stars in heaven, (one especially, a star of the sixth magnitude, double and changeable, to be found near the large star in Lyra,) in a telescopic scrutiny of which I have been made aware of the feeling. I have been filled with it by certain sounds from stringed instruments, and not unfrequently by passages from books. Among innumerable other instances, I well remember something in a volume of Joseph Glanvill, which (perhaps merely from its quaintness—who shall say?) never failed to inspire me with the sentiment: "And the will therein lieth, which dieth not. Who knoweth the mysteries of the will, with its vigor? For God is but a great will pervading all things by nature of its intentness. Man doth not yield him to the angels, nor unto death utterly, save only through the weakness of his feeble will."

Length of years and subsequent reflection have enabled me to trace, indeed, some remote connection between this passage in the English moralist and a portion of the character of Ligeia. An *intensity* in thought, action, or speech, was possibly, in her, a result, or at least an index, of that gigantic volition which, during our long intercourse, failed to give other and more immediate evidence of its existence. Of all the women whom I have ever known, she, the outwardly calm, the ever-placid Ligeia, was the most violently a prey to the tumultuous vultures of stern passion. And of such passion I could form no estimate, save by the miraculous expansion of those eyes which at once so delighted and ap-

[3] For eyes we have no models: apparently a reference to the proverb of the Greek philosopher Democritus, "Truth lies at the bottom of the well." The "well of Democritus" is referred to immediately below.

palled me—by the almost magical melody, modulation, distinctness, and placidity of her very low voice—and by the fierce energy (rendered doubly effective by contrast with her manner of utterance) of the wild words which she habitually uttered.

I have spoken of the learning of Ligeia: it was immense—such as I have never known in woman. In the classical tongues was she deeply proficient, and as far as my own acquaintance extended in regard to the modern dialects of Europe, I have never known her at fault. Indeed upon any theme of the most admired, because simply the most abstruse of the boasted erudition of the academy, have I *ever* found Ligeia at fault? How singularly, how thrillingly, this one point in the nature of my wife has forced itself, at this late period only, upon my attention! I said her knowledge was such as I have never known in woman—but where breathes the man who has traversed, and successfully, *all* the wide areas of moral, physical, and mathematical science? I saw not then what I now clearly perceive, that the acquisitions of Ligeia were gigantic, were astounding; yet I was sufficiently aware of her infinite supremacy to resign myself, with a child-like confidence, to her guidance through the chaotic world of metaphysical investigation at which I was most busily occupied during the earlier years of our marriage. With how vast a triumph, with how vivid a delight, with how much of all that is ethereal in hope, did I *feel*, as she bent over me in studies but little sought—but less known, that delicious vista by slow degrees expanding before me, down whose long, gorgeous, and all untrodden path, I might at length pass onward to the goal of a wisdom too divinely precious not to be forbidden!

How poignant, then, must have been the grief with which, after some years, I beheld my well-grounded expectations take wings to themselves and fly away! Without Ligeia I was but as a child groping benighted. Her presence, her readings alone, rendered vividly luminous the many mysteries of the transcendentalism in which we were immersed. Wanting the radiant lustre of her eyes, letters, lambent and golden, grew duller than Saturnian lead. And now those eyes shone less and less frequently upon the pages over which I pored. Ligeia grew ill. The wild eyes blazed with a too-too glorious effulgence; the pale fingers became of the transparent waxen hue of the grave; and the blue veins upon the lofty forehead swelled and sank impetuously with the tides of the most gentle emotion. I saw that she must die—and I struggled desperately in spirit with the grim Azrael. And the struggles of the passionate wife were, to my astonishment, even more energetic than my own. There had been much in her stern nature to impress me with the belief that, to her, death would have come without its terrors; but not so. Words are impotent to convey any just idea of the fierceness of resistance with which she wrestled with the Shadow. I groaned in anguish at the pitiable spectacle. I would have soothed—I would have reasoned; but, in the intensity of her wild desire for life—for life—*but* for life—solace and reason were alike the uttermost of folly. Yet not until the last instance, amid the most convulsive writhings of her fierce spirit, was shaken the external placidity of her demeanor. Her voice grew more gentle—grew more low—yet I would not wish to dwell upon the wild meaning of the quietly uttered words. My brain reeled as I hearkened, entranced, to a melody more than mortal—to assumptions and aspirations which mortality had never before known.

That she loved me I should not have doubted; and I might have been easily aware that, in a bosom such as hers, love would have reigned no ordinary passion. But in death only was I fully impressed with the strength of her affection. For long hours, detaining my hand, would she pour out before me the overflowing of a heart whose more than passionate devotion amounted to idolatry. How had I deserved to be so blessed by such confessions? how had I deserved to be so cursed with the removal of my beloved in the hour of her making them? But upon this subject I cannot bear to dilate. Let me say only, that in Ligeia's more than womanly abandonment to a love, alas! all unmerited, all unworthily bestowed, I at length recognized the principle of her longing, with so wildly earnest a desire, for the life which was now fleeing so rapidly away. It is this wild longing, it is this eager vehemence of desire for life—*but* for life, that I have no power to portray, no utterance capable of expressing.

At high noon of the night in which she departed, beckoning me peremptorily to her side, she bade me repeat certain verses composed by herself not many days before. I obeyed her. They were these:[4]

Lo! 't is a gala night
  Within the lonesome latter years.
An angel throng, bewinged, bedight
  In veils, and drowned in tears,
Sit in a theatre to see
  A play of hopes and fears,
While the orchestra breathes fitfully
  The music of the spheres.

Mimes, in the form of God on high,
  Mutter and mumble low,
And hither and thither fly;
  Mere puppets they, who come and go
At bidding of vast formless things
  That shift the scenery to and fro,
Flapping from out their condor wings
  Invisible Woe.

That motley drama—oh, be sure
  It shall not be forgot!
With its Phantom chased for evermore,
  By a crowd that seize it not,
Through a circle that ever returneth in
  To the self-same spot;
And much of Madness, and more of Sin,
  And Horror the soul of the plot.

But see, amid the mimic rout[5]
  A crawling shape intrude:
A blood-red thing that writhes from out
  The scenic solitude!
It writhes—it writhes! with mortal pangs
  The mimes become its food,
And seraphs sob at vermin fangs
  In human gore imbued.

Out—out are the lights—out all!
  And over each quivering form
The curtain, a funeral pall,
  Comes down with the rush of a storm,
While the angels, all pallid and wan,
  Uprising, unveiling, affirm
That the play is the tragedy, "Man,"
  And its hero, the Conqueror Worm.

"O God!" half shrieked Ligeia, leaping to her feet and extending her arms aloft with a spasmodic movement, as I made an end of these lines—"O God! O Divine Father! shall these things be undeviatingly so? shall this conqueror be not once conquered? Are we not part and parcel in Thee? Who—who knoweth the mysteries of the will with its vigor? 'Man doth not yield him to the angels, *nor unto death utterly,* save only through the weakness of his feeble will.' "

And now, as if exhausted with emotion, she suffered her white arms to fall, and returned solemnly to her bed of death. And as she breathed her last sighs, there came mingled with them a low murmur from her lips. I bent to them my ear, and distinguished, again, the concluding words of the passage in Glanvill: "*Man doth not yield him to the angels, nor unto death utterly, save only through the weakness of his feeble will.*"

She died: and I, crushed into the very dust with sorrow, could no longer endure the lonely desolation of my dwelling in the dim and decaying city by the Rhine. I had no lack of what the world calls wealth. Ligeia had brought me far more, very far more, than ordinarily falls to the lot of mortals. After a few months, therefore, of weary and aimless wandering, I purchased, and put in some repair, an abbey, which I shall not name, in one of the wildest and least frequented portions of fair England. The gloomy and dreary grandeur of the building, the almost savage aspect of the domain, the many melancholy and time-honored memories connected with both, had much in unison with the feelings of utter abandonment which had driven me into that remote and unsocial region of the country. Yet although the external abbey, with its verdant decay hanging about it, suffered but little alteration, I gave way with a child-like perversity, and perchance with a faint hope of alleviating my sorrows, to a display of more than regal magnificence within. For such follies, even in childhood, I had imbibed a taste, and now they came back to me as if in the dotage of grief. Alas, I feel how much even of incipient madness might have been discovered in the gorgeous and fantastic draperies, in the solemn carvings of Egypt, in the wild cornices and furniture, in the Bedlam[6] patterns of the carpets of tufted gold! I had become a bounden slave in the trammels of opium, and my labors and my orders had taken a coloring from my dreams. But these absurdities I must not pause to detail. Let me speak

[4] Known as "The Conqueror Worm" as first published in *Graham's Magazine,* Jan. 1843. The poem does not appear in the first version of the story, Sept. 1838. [5] **Masked dance.**

[6] Insane.

only of that one chamber ever accursed, whither, in a moment of mental alienation, I led from the altar as my bride—as the successor of the unforgotten Ligeia—the fair-haired and blue-eyed Lady Rowena Trevanion, of Tremaine.

There is no individual portion of the architecture and decoration of that bridal chamber which is not now visibly before me. Where were the souls of the haughty family of the bride, when, through thirst of gold, they permitted to pass the threshold of an apartment *so* bedecked, a maiden and a daughter so beloved? I have said that I minutely remember the details of the chamber—yet I am sadly forgetful on topics of deep moment; and here there was no system, no keeping, in the fantastic display, to take hold upon the memory. The room lay in a high turret of the castellated abbey, was pentagonal in shape, and of capacious size. Occupying the whole southern face of the pentagon was the sole window—an immense sheet of unbroken glass from Venice—a single pane, and tinted of a leaden hue, so that the rays of either the sun or moon, passing through it, fell with a ghastly lustre on the objects within. Over the upper portion of this huge window extended the trellis-work of an aged vine, which clambered up the massy walls of the turret. The ceiling, of gloomy-looking oak, was excessively lofty, vaulted, and elaborately fretted with the wildest and most grotesque specimens of a semi-Gothic, semi-Druidical device. From out the most central recess of this melancholy vaulting depended, by a single chain of gold with long links, a huge censer of the same metal, Saracenic in pattern, and with many perforations so contrived that there writhed in and out of them, as if endued with a serpent vitality, a continual succession of party-colored[7] fires.

Some few ottomans and golden candelabra, of Eastern figure, were in various stations about; and there was the couch, too—the bridal couch—of an Indian model, and low, and sculptured of solid ebony, with a pall-like canopy above. In each of the angles of the chamber stood on end a gigantic sarcophagus of black granite, from the tombs of the kings over against Luxor, with their aged lids full of immemorial sculpture. But in the draping of the apartment lay, alas! the chief fantasy of all. The lofty walls, gigantic in height, even unproportionably so, were hung from summit to foot, in vast folds, with a heavy and massive-looking tapestry—tapestry of a material which was found alike as a carpet on the floor, as a covering for the ottomans and the ebony bed, as a canopy for the bed, and as the gorgeous volutes of the curtains which partially shaded the window. The material was the richest cloth of gold. It was spotted all over, at irregular intervals, with arabesque figures, about a foot in diameter, and wrought upon the cloth in patterns of the most jetty black. But these figures partook of the true character of the arabesque only when regarded from a single point of view. By a contrivance now common, and indeed traceable to a very remote period of antiquity, they were made changeable in aspect. To one entering the room, they bore the appearance of simple monstrosities; but upon a farther advance, this appearance gradually departed; and, step by step, as the visitor moved his station in the chamber, he saw himself surrounded by an endless succession of the ghastly forms which belong to the superstition of the Norman,[8] or arise in the guilty slumbers of the monk. The phantasmagoric effect was vastly heightened by the artificial introduction of a strong continual current of wind behind the draperies, giving a hideous and uneasy animation to the whole.

In halls such as these, in a bridal chamber such as this, I passed, with the Lady of Tremaine, the unhallowed hours of the first month of our marriage—passed them with but little disquietude. That my wife dreaded the fierce moodiness of my temper—that she shunned me, and loved me but little—I could not help perceiving; but it gave me rather pleasure than otherwise. I loathed her with a hatred belonging more to demon than to man. My memory flew back (oh, with what intensity of regret!) to Ligeia, the beloved, the august, the beautiful, the entombed. I revelled in recollections of her purity, of her wisdom, of her lofty, her ethereal nature, of her passionate, her idolatrous love. Now, then, did my spirit fully and freely burn with more than all the fires of her own. In the excitement of my opium dreams, (for I was habitually fettered in the shackles of the drug,) I would call aloud upon her name, during the

[7] An obsolete spelling for *parti-colored:* many colored.

[8] *Northman* in a later version of the story.

silence of the night, or among the sheltered recesses of the glens by day, as if, through the wild eagerness, the solemn passion, the consuming ardor of my longing for the departed, I could restore her to the pathway she had abandoned—ah, *could* it be forever?—upon the earth.

About the commencement of the second month of the marriage, the Lady Rowena was attacked with sudden illness, from which her recovery was slow. The fever which consumed her, rendered her nights uneasy; and in her perturbed state of half-slumber, she spoke of sounds and of motions, in and about the chamber of the turret, which I concluded had no origin save in the distemper of her fancy, or perhaps in the phantasmagoric influences of the chamber itself. She became at length convalescent—finally, well. Yet but a brief period elapsed, ere a second more violent disorder again threw her upon a bed of suffering; and from this attack her frame, at all times feeble, never altogether recovered. Her illnesses were, after this epoch, of alarming character, and of more alarming recurrence, defying alike the knowledge and the great exertions of her physicians. With the increase of the chronic disease, which had thus apparently taken too sure hold upon her constitution to be eradicated by human means, I could not fail to observe a similar increase in the nervous irritation of her temperament, and in her excitability by trivial causes of fear. She spoke again, and now more frequently and pertinaciously, of the sounds—of the slight sounds—and of the unusual motions among the tapestries, to which she had formerly alluded.

One night, near the closing in of September, she pressed this distressing subject with more than usual emphasis upon my attention. She had just awakened from an unquiet slumber, and I had been watching, with feelings half of anxiety, half of vague terror, the workings of her emaciated countenance. I sat by the side of her ebony bed, upon one of the ottomans of India. She partly arose, and spoke, in an earnest low whisper, of sounds which she *then* heard, but which I could not hear—of motions which she *then* saw, but which I could not perceive. The wind was rushing hurriedly behind the tapestries, and I wished to show her (what, let me confess it, I could not *all* believe) that those almost inarticulate breathings, and those very gentle variations of the figures upon the wall, were but the natural effects of that customary rushing of the wind. But a deadly pallor, overspreading her face, had proved to me that my exertions to reassure her would be fruitless. She appeared to be fainting, and no attendants were within call. I remembered where was deposited a decanter of light wine which had been ordered by her physicians, and hastened across the chamber to procure it. But, as I stepped beneath the light of the censer, two circumstances of a startling nature attracted my attention. I had felt that some palpable although invisible object had passed lightly by my person; and I saw that there lay upon the golden carpet, in the very middle of the rich lustre thrown from the censer, a shadow—a faint, indefinite shadow of angelic aspect—such as might be fancied for the shadow of a shade. But I was wild with the excitement of an immoderate dose of opium, and heeded these things but little, nor spoke of them to Rowena. Having found the wine, I recrossed the chamber, and poured out a gobletful, which I held to the lips of the fainting lady. She had now partially recovered, however, and took the vessel herself, while I sank upon an ottoman near me, with my eyes fastened upon her person. It was then that I became distinctly aware of a gentle footfall upon the carpet, and near the couch; and in a second thereafter, as Rowena was in the act of raising the wine to her lips, I saw, or may have dreamed that I saw, fall within the goblet, as if from some invisible spring in the atmosphere of the room, three or four large drops of a brilliant and ruby-colored fluid. If this I saw—not so Rowena. She swallowed the wine unhesitatingly, and I forbore to speak to her of a circumstance which must after all, I considered, have been but the suggestion of a vivid imagination, rendered morbidly active by the terror of the lady, by the opium, and by the hour.

Yet I cannot conceal it from my own perception that, immediately subsequent to the fall of the ruby-drops, a rapid change for the worst took place in the disorder of my wife; so that, on the third subsequent night, the hands of her menials prepared her for the tomb, and on the fourth, I sat alone, with her shrouded body, in that fantastic chamber which had received her as my bride. Wild visions, opium-engendered, flitted shadow-like before me. I gazed with unquiet eye upon the sarcophagi in the angles of the room, upon the varying figures of the drapery, and upon the writhing of the party-colored fires in the censer overhead. My eyes then fell, as I called to mind the circumstances of a former night, to the spot beneath the glare of the censer where I had seen the faint traces of the shadow. It was there, however, no longer; and breathing with greater freedom, I turned my glances to the pallid and rigid figure upon the bed. Then rushed upon me a thousand memories of Ligeia—and then came back upon my heart, with the turbulent violence of a flood, the whole of that unutterable woe with which I had regarded *her* thus enshrouded. The night waned; and still, with a bosom full of bitter thoughts of the one only and supremely beloved, I remained gazing upon the body of Rowena.

It might have been midnight, or perhaps earlier, or later, for I had taken no note of time, when a sob, low, gentle, but very distinct, startled me from my revery. I *felt* that it came from the bed of ebony—the bed of death. I listened in an agony of superstitious terror—but there was no repetition of the sound. I strained my vision to detect any motion in the corpse—but there was not the slightest perceptible. Yet I could not have been deceived. I *had* heard the noise, however faint, and my soul was awakened within me. I resolutely and perseveringly kept my attention riveted upon the body. Many minutes elapsed before any circumstances occurred tending to throw light upon the mystery. At length it became evident that a slight, a very feeble, and barely noticeable tinge of color had flushed up within the cheeks, and along the sunken small veins of the eyelids. Through a species of unutterable horror and awe, for which the language of mortality has no sufficiently energetic expression, I felt my heart cease to beat, my limbs grow rigid where I sat. Yet a sense of duty finally operated to restore my self-possession. I could no longer doubt that we had been precipitate in our preparations—that Rowena still lived. It was necessary that some immediate exertion be made; yet the turret was altogether apart from the portion of the abbey tenanted by the servants—there were none within call—I had no means of summoning them to my aid without leaving the room for many minutes—and this I could not venture to do. I therefore struggled alone in my endeavors to call back the spirit still hovering. In a short period it was certain, however, that a relapse had taken place; the color disappeared from both eyelid and cheek, leaving a wanness even more than that of marble; the lips became doubly shrivelled and pinched up in the ghastly expression of death; a repulsive clamminess and coldness overspread rapidly the surface of the body; and all the usual rigorous stiffness immediately supervened. I fell back with a shudder upon the couch from which I had been so startlingly aroused, and again gave myself up to passionate waking visions of Ligeia.

An hour thus elapsed, when (could it be possible?) I was a second time aware of some vague sound issuing from the region of the bed. I listened—in extremity of horror. The sound came again—it was a sigh. Rushing to the corpse, I saw—distinctly saw—a tremor upon the lips. In a minute afterwards they relaxed, disclosing a bright line of the pearly teeth. Amazement now struggled in my bosom with the profound awe which had hitherto reigned there alone. I felt that my vision grew dim, that my reason wandered; and it was only by a violent effort that I at length succeeded in nerving myself to the task which duty thus once more had pointed out. There was now a partial glow upon the forehead and upon the cheek and throat; a perceptible warmth pervaded the whole frame; there was even a slight pulsation at the heart. The lady *lived;* and with redoubled ardor I betook myself to the task of restoration. I chafed and bathed the temples and the hands, and used every exertion which experience, and no little medical reading, could suggest. But in vain. Suddenly, the color fled, the pulsation ceased, the lips resumed the expression of the dead, and, in an instant afterward, the whole body took upon itself the icy chilliness, the livid hue, the intense rigidity, the sunken outline, and all the loathsome peculiarities of that which has been, for many days, a tenant of the tomb.

And again I sunk into visions of Ligeia—and again, (what marvel that I shudder while I write?) *again* there reached my ears a low sob from the region of the ebony bed. But why shall I minutely detail the unspeakable horrors of that night? Why shall I pause to relate how, time after time, until near the period of the gray dawn, this hideous drama of revivification was repeated; how each terrific relapse was only into a sterner and apparently more irredeemable death; how each agony wore the aspect of a struggle with some invisible foe; and how each struggle was succeeded by I know not what of wild change in the personal appearance of the corpse? Let me hurry to a conclusion.

The greater part of the fearful night had worn away, and she who had been dead, once again stirred—and now more vigorously than hitherto, although arousing from a dissolution more appalling in its utter helplessness than any. I had long ceased to struggle or to move, and remained sitting rigidly upon the ottoman, a helpless prey to a whirl of violent emotions, of which extreme awe was perhaps the least terrible, the least consuming. The corpse, I repeat, stirred, and now more vigorously than before. The hues of life flushed up with unwonted energy into the countenance—the limbs relaxed—and, save that the eyelids were yet pressed heavily together, and that the bandages and draperies of the grave still imparted their charnel character to the figure, I might have dreamed that Rowena had indeed shaken off, utterly, the fetters of Death. But if this idea was not, even then, altogether adopted, I could at least doubt no longer, when, arising from the bed, tottering, with feeble steps, with closed eyes, and with the manner of one bewildered in a dream, the thing that was enshrouded advanced bodily and palpably into the middle of the apartment.

I trembled not—I stirred not—for a crowd of unutterable fancies connected with the air, the stature, the demeanor of the figure, rushing hurriedly through my brain, had paralyzed—had chilled me into stone. I stirred not—but gazed upon the apparition. There was a mad disorder in my thoughts—a tumult unappeasable. Could it, indeed, be the *living* Rowena who confronted me? Could it indeed be Rowena *at all*—the fair-haired, the blue-eyed Lady Rowena Trevanion of Tremaine? Why, *why* should I doubt it? The bandage lay heavily about the mouth—but then might it not be the mouth of the breathing Lady of Tremaine? And the cheeks—there were the roses as in her noon of life—yes, these might indeed be the fair cheeks of the living Lady of Tremaine. And the chin, with its dimples, as in health, might it not be hers? but *had she then grown taller since her malady?* What inexpressible madness seized me with that thought? One bound, and I had reached her feet! Shrinking from my touch, she let fall from her head the ghastly cerements which had confined it, and there streamed forth, into the rushing atmosphere of the chamber, huge masses of long and dishevelled hair; *it was blacker than the wings of the midnight!* And now slowly opened *the eyes* of the figure which stood before me. "Here then, at least," I shrieked aloud, "can I never—can I never be mistaken—these are the full, and the black, and the wild eyes—of my lost love—of the Lady—of the LADY LIGEIA."

RAY BRADBURY
1920–

There Will Come Soft Rains

This story is taken from Ray Bradbury's *The Martian Chronicles.* In his introduction to that book, Clifton Fadiman comments on Bradbury's basic point of view: "he is telling us . . . that human beings are still mental and moral children who cannot be trusted with the terrifying toys they have by some tragic accident invented. *The Martian Chronicles* is on one level a kind of Planetary Nights' Entertainment. But on a deeper level it is as grave and troubling as one of Hawthorne's fancy-filled allegories."

In the living room the voice-clock sang, *Tick-tock, seven o'clock, time to get up, time to get up, seven o'clock!* as if it were afraid that nobody would. The morning house lay empty. The clock ticked on, repeating and repeating its sounds into the emptiness. *Seven-nine, breakfast time, seven-nine!*

In the kitchen the breakfast stove gave a hissing sigh and ejected from its warm interior eight pieces of perfectly browned toast, eight eggs sunnyside up, sixteen slices of bacon, two coffees, and two cool glasses of milk.

"Today is August 4, 2026," said a second voice from the kitchen ceiling, "in the city of Allendale, California." It repeated the date three times for memory's sake. "Today is Mr. Featherstone's birthday. Today is the anniversary of Tilita's marriage. Insurance is payable, as are the water, gas, and light bills."

Somewhere in the walls, relays clicked, memory tapes glided under electric eyes.

Eight-one, tick-tock, eight-one o'clock, off to school, off to work, run, run, eight-one! But no doors slammed, no carpets took the soft tread of rubber heels. It was raining outside. The weather box on the front door sang quietly: "Rain, rain, go away; rubbers, raincoats for today . . ." And the rain tapped on the empty house, echoing.

Outside, the garage chimed and lifted its door to reveal the waiting car. After a long wait the door swung down again.

At eight-thirty the eggs were shriveled and the toast was like stone. An aluminum wedge scraped them into the sink, where hot water whirled them down a metal throat which digested and flushed them away to the distant sea. The dirty dishes were dropped into a hot washer and emerged twinkling dry.

Nine-fifteen, sang the clock, *time to clean.*

Out of warrens in the wall, tiny robot mice darted. The rooms were acrawl with the small cleaning animals, all rubber and metal. They thudded against chairs, whirling their mustached runners, kneading the rug nap, sucking gently at hidden dust. Then, like mysterious invaders, they popped into their burrows. Their pink electric eyes faded. The house was clean.

Ten o'clock. The sun came out from behind the rain. The house stood alone in a city of rubble and ashes. This was the one house left standing. At night the ruined city gave off a radioactive glow which could be seen for miles.

Ten-fifteen. The garden sprinklers whirled up in golden founts, filling the soft morning air with scatterings of brightness. The water pelted windowpanes, running down the charred west side where the house had been burned evenly free of its white paint. The entire west face of the house was black, save for five places. Here the silhouette in paint of a man mowing a lawn. Here, as in a photograph, a woman bent to pick flowers. Still farther over, their images burned on wood in one titanic instant, a small boy, hands flung into the air; higher up, the image of a thrown ball, and opposite him a girl, hands raised to catch a ball which never came down.

The five spots of paint—the man, the woman, the children, the ball—remained. The rest was a thin charcoaled layer.

The gentle sprinkler rain filled the garden with falling light.

Until this day, how well the house had kept its peace. How carefully it had inquired, "Who goes there? What's the password?" and, getting no answer from lonely foxes and whining cats, it had shut up its windows and drawn shades in an old-maidenly preoccupation with self-protection which bordered on a mechanical paranoia.

It quivered at each sound, the house did. If a sparrow brushed a window, the shade snapped up. The bird, startled, flew off! No, not even a bird must touch the house!

The house was an altar with ten thousand attendants, big, small, servicing, attending, in choirs. But the gods had gone away, and the ritual of the religion continued senselessly, uselessly.

Twelve noon.

A dog whined, shivering, on the front porch.

The front door recognized the dog voice and opened. The dog, once huge and fleshy, but now gone to bone and covered with sores, moved in and through the house, tracking mud. Behind it whirred angry mice, angry at having to pick up mud, angry at inconvenience.

For not a leaf fragment blew under the door but what the wall panels flipped open and the copper scrap rats flashed swiftly out. The offending dust, hair, or paper, seized in miniature steel jaws, was raced back to the burrows. There, down tubes which fed into the cellar, it was dropped into the sighing vent of an incinerator which sat like evil Baal[1] in a dark corner.

The dog ran upstairs, hysterically yelping to each door, at last realizing, as the house realized, that only silence was here.

It sniffed the air and scratched the kitchen door. Behind the door, the stove was making pancakes which filled the house with a rich baked odor and the scent of maple syrup.

The dog frothed at the mouth, lying at the door, sniffing, its eyes turned to fire. It ran wildly in circles, biting at its tail, spun in a frenzy, and died. It lay in the parlor for an hour.

Two o'clock, sang a voice.

[1] Baal (pl. Baalim) is a general name for the Syrian gods, as Ashtaroth is for the goddesses. Baal was a false god; Baalim, a form of worship that Hosea and other prophets denounced as heathenism. *Matthew* 12:24 refers to Beelzebub (Baalzebub) as "the prince of devils." Milton's *Paradise Lost* places him next in rank to Satan:

> One next himself in power, and next in crime,
> Long after known in Palestine, and nam'd
> Beelzebub. (I. 79–81)

Delicately sensing decay at last, the regiments of mice hummed out as softly as blown gray leaves in an electrical wind.

Two-fifteen.

The dog was gone.

In the cellar, the incinerator glowed suddenly and a whirl of sparks leaped up the chimney.

Two thirty-five.

Bridge tables sprouted from patio walls. Playing cards fluttered onto pads in a shower of pips.[2] Martinis manifested on an oaken bench with egg-salad sandwiches. Music played.

But the tables were silent and the cards untouched.

At four o'clock the tables folded like great butterflies back through the paneled walls..

Four-thirty.

The nursery walls glowed.

Animals took shape: yellow giraffes, blue lions, pink antelopes, lilac panthers cavorting in crystal substance. The walls were glass. They looked out upon color and fantasy. Hidden films clocked through well-oiled sprockets, and the walls lived. The nursery floor was woven to resemble a crisp, cereal meadow. Over this ran aluminum roaches and iron crickets, and in the hot still air butterflies of delicate red tissue wavered among the sharp aroma of animal spoors![3] There was the sound like a great matted yellow hive of bees within a dark bellows, the lazy bumble of a purring lion. And there was the patter of okapi[4] feet and the murmur of a fresh jungle rain, like other hoofs, falling upon the summer-starched grass. Now the walls dissolved into distances of parched weed, mile on mile, and warm endless sky. The animals drew away into thorn brakes and water holes.

It was the children's hour.

Five o'clock. The bath filled with clear hot water.

Six, seven, eight o'clock. The dinner dishes manipulated like magic tricks, and in the study a *click.* In the metal stand opposite the hearth where a fire now blazed up warmly, a cigar popped out, half an inch of soft gray ash on it, smoking, waiting.

Nine o'clock. The beds warmed their hidden circuits, for nights were cool here.

Nine-five. A voice spoke from the study ceiling:

"Mrs. McClellan, which poem would you like this evening?"

The house was silent.

The voice said at last, "Since you express no preference, I shall select a poem at random." Quiet music rose to back the voice. "Sara Teasdale. As I recall, your favorite. . . .

"There will come soft rains and the smell of the ground,
And swallows circling with their shimmering sound;

And frogs in the pools singing at night,
And wild plum-trees in tremulous white;

Robins will wear their feathery fire
Whistling their whims on a low fence-wire;

And not one will know of the war, not one
Will care at last when it is done.

Not one would mind, either bird nor tree
If mankind perished utterly;

And Spring herself, when she woke at dawn,
Would scarcely know that we were gone."[5]

The fire burned on the stone hearth and the cigar fell away into a mound of quiet ash on its tray. The empty chairs faced each other between the silent walls, and the music played.

At ten o'clock the house began to die.

The wind blew. A falling tree bough crashed through the kitchen window. Cleaning solvent, bottled, shattered over the stove. The room was ablaze in an instant!

"Fire!" screamed a voice. The house lights flashed, water pumps shot water from the ceilings. But the solvent spread on the linoleum, licking, eating under the kitchen door, while the voices took it up in chorus: "Fire, fire, fire!"

The house tried to save itself. Doors sprang tightly shut, but the windows were broken by the heat and the wind blew and sucked upon the fire.

[2] Spots. [3] Droppings. [4] African animal related to the giraffe.

[5] " 'There Will Come Soft Rains,' " in Sara Teasdale, ***Flame and Shadow*** **(New York: Macmillan, 1920).**

The house gave ground as the fire in ten billion angry sparks moved with flaming ease from room to room and then up the stairs. While scurrying water rats squeaked from the walls, pistoled their water, and ran for more. And the wall sprays let down showers of mechanical rain.

But too late. Somewhere, sighing, a pump shrugged to a stop. The quenching rain ceased. The reserve water supply which had filled baths and washed dishes for many quiet days was gone.

The fire crackled up the stairs. It fed upon Picassos and Matisses[6] in the upper halls, like delicacies, baking off the oily flesh, tenderly crisping the canvases into black shavings.

Now the fire lay in beds, stood in windows, changed the colors of drapes!

And then, reinforcements.

From attic trapdoors, blind robot faces peered down with faucet mouths gushing green chemical.

The fire backed off, as even an elephant must at the sight of a dead snake. Now there were twenty snakes whipping over the floor, killing the fire with a clear cold venom of green froth.

But the fire was clever. It had sent flame outside the house, up through the attic to the pumps there. An explosion! The attic brain which directed the pumps was shattered into bronze shrapnel on the beams.

The fire rushed back into every closet and felt of the clothes hung there.

The house shuddered, oak bone on bone, its bared skeleton cringing from the heat, its wire, its nerves revealed as if a surgeon had torn the skin off to let the red veins and capillaries quiver in the scalded air. Help, help! Fire! Run, run! Heat snapped mirrors like the first brittle winter ice. And the voices wailed Fire, fire, run, run, like a tragic nursery rhyme, a dozen voices, high, low, like children dying in a forest, alone, alone. And the voices fading as the wires popped their sheathings like hot chestnuts. One, two, three, four, five voices died.

In the nursery the jungle burned. Blue lions roared, purple giraffes bounded off. The panthers ran in circles, changing color, and ten million animals, running before the fire, vanished off toward a distant steaming river. . . .

Ten more voices died. In the last instant under the fire avalanche, other choruses, oblivious, could be heard announcing the time, playing music, cutting the lawn by remote-control mower, or setting an umbrella frantically out and in the slamming and opening front door, a thousand things happening, like a clock shop when each clock strikes the hour insanely before or after the other, a scene of maniac confusion, yet unity; singing, screaming, a few last cleaning mice darting bravely out to carry the horrid ashes away! And one voice, with sublime disregard for the situation, read poetry aloud in the fiery study, until all the film spools burned, until all the wires withered and the circuits cracked.

The fire burst the house and let it slam flat down, puffing out skirts of spark and smoke.

In the kitchen, an instant before the rain of fire and timber, the stove could be seen making breakfasts at a psychopathic rate, ten dozen eggs, six loaves of toast, twenty dozen bacon strips, which, eaten by fire, started the stove working again, hysterically hissing!

The crash. The attic smashing into kitchen and parlor. The parlor into cellar, cellar into sub-cellar. Deep freeze, armchair, film tapes, circuits, beds, and all like skeletons thrown in a cluttered mound deep under.

Smoke and silence. A great quantity of smoke.

Dawn showed faintly in the east. Among the ruins, one wall stood alone. Within the wall, a last voice said, over and over again and again, even as the sun rose to shine upon the heaped rubble and steam:

"Today is August 5, 2026, today is August 5, 2026, today is . . ."

ELIZABETH BOWEN
1899–1973

The Demon Lover[1]

Towards the end of her day in London Mrs. Drover went round to her shut-up house

[6] That is, valuable paintings by the Spaniard, Pablo Picasso, and the Frenchman, Henri Matisse.

[1] See "The Daemon Lover," a Scottish ballad with a similar theme, p. 236.

to look for several things she wanted to take away. Some belonged to herself, some to her family, who were by now used to their country life. It was late August; it had been a steamy, showery day: at the moment the trees down the pavement glittered in an escape of humid yellow afternoon sun. Against the next batch of clouds, already piling up ink-dark, broken chimneys and parapets stood out. In her once familiar street, as in any unused channel, an unfamiliar queerness had silted up; a cat wove itself in and out of railings, but no human eye watched Mrs. Drover's return. Shifting some parcels under her arm, she slowly forced her latchkey in an unwilling lock, then gave the door, which had warped, a push with her knee. Dead air came out to meet her as she went in.

The staircase window having been boarded up, no light came down into the hall. But one door, she could just see, stood ajar, so she went quickly through into the room and unshuttered the big window in there. Now the prosaic woman, looking about her, was more perplexed than she knew by everything that she saw, by traces of her long former habit of life—the yellow smoke-stain up the white marble mantelpiece, the ring left by a vase on the top of the escritoire;[2] the bruise in the wallpaper where, on the door being thrown open widely, the china handle had always hit the wall. The piano, having gone away to be stored, had left what looked like claw-marks on its part of the parquet. Though not much dust had seeped in, each object wore a film of another kind; and, the only ventilation being the chimney, the whole drawing-room smelled of the cold hearth. Mrs. Drover put down her parcels on the escritoire and left the room to proceed upstairs; the things she wanted were in a bedroom chest.

She had been anxious to see how the house was—the part-time caretaker she shared with some neighbors was away this week on his holiday, known to be not yet back. At the best of times he did not look in often, and she was never sure that she trusted him. There were some cracks in the structure, left by the last bombing, on which she was anxious to keep an eye. Not that one could do anything—

A shaft of refracted daylight now lay across the hall. She stopped dead and stared at the hall table—on this lay a letter addressed to her.

She thought first—then the caretaker *must* be back. All the same, who, seeing the house shuttered, would have dropped a letter in at the box? It was not a circular, it was not a bill. And the post office redirected, to the address in the country, everything for her that came through the post. The caretaker (even if he *were* back) did not know she was due in London to-day—her call here had been planned to be a surprise—so his negligence in the manner of this letter, leaving it to wait in the dusk and the dust, annoyed her. Annoyed, she picked up the letter, which bore no stamp. But it cannot be important, or they would know . . . She took the letter rapidly upstairs with her, without a stop to look at the writing till she reached what had been her bedroom, where she let in light. The room looked over the garden and other gardens: the sun had gone in; as the clouds sharpened and lowered, the trees and rank lawns seemed already to smoke with dark. Her reluctance to look again at the letter came from the fact that she felt intruded upon—and by someone contemptuous of her ways. However, in the tenseness preceding the fall of rain she read it: it was a few lines.

DEAR KATHLEEN,

You will not have forgotten that to-day is our anniversary, and the day we said. The years have gone by at once slowly and fast. In view of the fact that nothing has changed, I shall rely upon you to keep your promise. I was sorry to see you leave London, but was satisfied that you would be back in time. You may expect me, therefore, at the hour arranged.

Until Then . . .

K.

Mrs. Drover looked for the date: it was to-day's. She dropped the letter on to the bed-springs, then picked it up to see the writing again—her lips, beneath the remains of lipstick, beginning to go white. She felt so much the change in her own face that she went to the mirror, polished a clear patch in it and looked at once urgently and stealthily in. She was confronted by a woman of forty-four, with eyes starting out under a hat-brim that had been rather carelessly pulled down. She had not put on any more powder since she left the shop where she ate

[2] A writing table or desk.

her solitary tea. The pearls her husband had given her on their marriage hung loose round her now rather thinner throat, slipping into the V of the pink wool jumper her sister knitted last autumn as they sat round the fire. Mrs. Drover's most normal expression was one of controlled worry, but of assent. Since the birth of the third of her little boys, attended by a quite serious illness, she had had an intermittent muscular flicker to the left of her mouth, but in spite of this she could always sustain a manner that was at once energetic and calm.

Turning from her own face as precipitately as she had gone to meet it, she went to the chest where the things were, unlocked it, threw up the lid and knelt to search. But as rain began to came crashing down she could not keep from looking over her shoulder at the stripped bed on which the letter lay. Behind the blanket of rain the clock of the church that still stood struck six—with rapidly heightening apprehension she counted each of the slow strokes. "The hour arranged . . . My God," she said, "*what* hour? How should I . . . ? After twenty-five years. . . ."

The young girl talking to the soldier in the garden had not ever completely seen his face. It was dark; they were saying good-bye under a tree. Now and then—for it felt, from not seeing him at this intense moment, as though she had never seen him at all—she verified his presence for these few moments longer by putting out a hand, which he each time pressed, without very much kindness, and painfully, on to one of the breast buttons of his uniform. That cut of the button on the palm of her hand was, principally, what she was to carry away. This was so near the end of a leave from France that she could only wish him already gone. It was August 1916. Being not kissed, being drawn away from and looked at intimidated Kathleen till she imagined spectral glitters in the place of his eyes. Turning away and looking back up the lawn she saw, through branches of trees, the drawing-room window alight: she caught a breath for the moment when she could go running back there into the safe arms of her mother and sister, and cry: "What shall I do, what shall I do? He has gone."

Hearing her catch her breath, her fiancé said, without feeling: "Cold?"

"You're going away such a long way."

"Not so far as you think."

"I don't understand?"

"You don't have to," he said. "You will. You know what we said."

"But that was—suppose you—I mean, suppose."

"I shall be with you," he said, "sooner or later. You won't forget that. You need do nothing but wait."

Only a little more than a minute later she was free to run up the silent lawn. Looking in through the window at her mother and sister, who did not for the moment perceive her, she already felt that unnatural promise drive down between her and the rest of all human kind. No other way of having given herself could have made her feel so apart, lost and foresworn. She could not have plighted a more sinister troth.

Kathleen behaved well when, some months later, her fiancé was reported missing, presumed killed. Her family not only supported her but were able to praise her courage without stint because they could not regret, as a husband for her, the man they knew almost nothing about. They hoped she would, in a year or two, console herself—and had it been only a question of consolation things might have gone much straighter ahead. But her trouble, behind just a little grief, was a complete dislocation from everything. She did not reject other lovers, for these failed to appear: for years she failed to attract men—and with the approach of her 'thirties she became natural enough to share her family's anxiousness on this score. She began to put herself out, to wonder; and at thirty-two she was very greatly relieved to find herself being courted by William Drover. She married him, and the two of them settled down in this quiet, arboreal part of Kensington: in this house the years piled up, her children were born and they all lived till they were driven out by the bombs of the next war. Her movements as Mrs. Drover were circumscribed, and she dismissed any idea that they were still watched.

As things were—dead or living the letter-writer sent her only a threat. Unable, for some minutes, to go on kneeling with her back exposed to the empty room, Mrs. Drover rose from the chest to sit on an upright chair whose back was firmly against the wall. The desuetude of her former bedroom, her married London home's whole air of being a cracked cup from which memory, with its reassuring power, had either evaporated or leaked away, made a crisis—and at just this crisis the letter-writer had, knowledgeably, struck. The hollowness of the house this evening cancelled years on years of voices, habits and steps. Through the shut windows she only heard rain fall on the roofs around. To rally herself, she said she was in a mood—and, for two or three seconds shutting her eyes, told herself that she had imagined the letter. But she opened them—there it lay on the bed.

On the supernatural side of the letter's entrance she was not permitting her mind to dwell. Who, in London, knew she meant to call at the house to-day? Evidently, however, this had been known. The caretaker, *had* he come back, had had no cause to expect her: he would have taken the letter in his pocket, to forward it, at his own time, through the post. There was no other sign that the caretaker had been in—but, if not? Letters dropped in at doors of deserted houses do not fly or walk to tables in halls. They do not sit on the dust of empty tables with the air of certainty that they will be found. There is needed some human hand—but nobody but the caretaker had a key. Under circumstances she did not care to consider, a house can be entered without a key. It was possible that she was not alone now. She might be being waited for, downstairs. Waited for—until when? Until "the hour arranged." At least that was not six o'clock: six has struck.

She rose from the chair and went over and locked the door.

The thing was, to get out. To fly? No, not that: she had to catch her train. As a woman whose utter dependability was the keystone of her family life she was not willing to return to the country, to her husband, her little boys and her sister, without the objects she had come up to fetch. Resuming work at the chest she set about making up a number of parcels in a rapid, fumbling-decisive way. These, with her shopping parcels, would be too much to carry; these meant a taxi—at the thought of the taxi her heart went up and her normal breathing resumed. I will ring up the taxi now; the taxi cannot come too soon: I shall hear the taxi out there running its engine, till I walk calmly down to it through the hall. I'll ring up— But no: the telephone is cut off . . . She tugged at a knot she had tied wrong.

The idea of flight . . . He was never kind to me, not really. I don't remember him kind at all. Mother said he never considered me. He was set on me, that was what it was—not love. Not love, not meaning a person well. What did he do, to make me promise like that? I can't remember— But she found that she could.

She remembered with such dreadful acuteness that the twenty-five years since then dissolved like smoke and she instinctively looked for the weal left by the button on the palm of her hand. She remembered not only all that he said and did but the complete suspension of *her* existence during that August week. I was not myself—they all told me so at the time. She remembered—but with one white burning blank as where acid has dropped on a photograph: *under no conditions* could she remember his face.

So, wherever he may be waiting, I shall not know him. You have no time to run from a face you do not expect.

The thing was to get to the taxi before any clock struck what could be the hour. She would slip down the street and round the side of the square to where the square gave on the main road. She would return in the taxi, safe, to her own door, and bring the solid driver into the house with her to pick up the parcels from room to room. The idea of the taxi driver made her decisive, bold: she unlocked her door, went to the top of the staircase and listened down.

She heard nothing—but while she was hearing nothing the *passé*[3] air of the staircase was disturbed by a draught that travelled up to her face. It emanated from the basement: down there a door or window was being opened by someone who chose this moment to leave the house.

The rain had stopped; the pavements steamily shone as Mrs. Drover let herself out by inches from her own front door into the empty street. The unoccupied houses opposite continued to meet her look with their damaged stare. Making towards the thoroughfare and the taxi, she tried not to keep looking behind. Indeed, the silence was so intense—one of those creeks of London silence exaggerated this summer by

[3] Stale, dead.

the damage of war—that no tread could have gained on hers unheard. Where her street debouched on the square where people went on living she grew conscious of and checked her unnatural pace. Across the open end of the square two buses impassively passed each other; women, a perambulator, cyclists, a man wheeling a barrow signalized, once again, the ordinary flow of life. At the square's most populous corner should be—and was—the short taxi rank. This evening, only one taxi—but this, although it presented its blank rump, appeared already to be alertly waiting for her. Indeed, without looking round the driver started his engine as she panted up from behind and put her hand on the door. As she did so, the clock struck seven. The taxi faced the main road: to make the trip back to her house it would have to turn —she had settled back on the seat and the taxi *had* turned before she, surprised by its knowing movement, recollected that she had not "said where." She leaned forward to scratch at the glass panel that divided the driver's head from her own.

The driver braked to what was almost a stop, turned round and slid the glass panel back: the jolt of this flung Mrs. Drover forward till her face was almost into the glass. Through the aperture driver and passenger, not six inches between them, remained for an eternity eye to eye. Mrs. Drover's mouth hung open for some seconds before she could issue her first scream. After that she continued to scream freely and to beat with her gloved hands on the glass all round as the taxi, accelerating without mercy, made off with her into the hinterland of deserted streets.

E. B. WHITE
1899–

The Hour of Letdown

When the man came in, carrying the machine, most of us looked up from our drinks, because we had never seen anything like it before. The man set the thing down on top of the bar near the beerpulls. It took up an ungodly amount of room and you could see the bartender didn't like it any too well, having this big, ugly-looking gadget parked right there.

"Two rye-and-water," the man said.

The bartender went on puddling an Old-Fashioned that he was working on, but he was obviously turning over the request in his mind.

"You want a double?" he asked, after a bit.

"No," said the man. "Two rye-and-water, please." He stared straight at the bartender, not exactly unfriendly but on the other hand not affirmatively friendly.

Many years of catering to the kind of people that come into saloons had provided the bartender with an adjustable mind. Nevertheless, he did not adjust readily to this fellow, and he did not like the machine—that was sure. He picked up a live cigarette that was idling on the edge of the cash register, took a drag out of it, and returned it thoughtfully. Then he poured two shots of rye whiskey, drew two glasses of water, and shoved the drinks in front of the man. People were watching. When something a little out of the ordinary takes place at a bar, the sense of it spreads quickly all along the line and pulls the customers together.

The man gave no sign of being the center of attention. He laid a five-dollar bill down on the bar. Then he drank one of the ryes and chased it with water. He picked up the other rye, opened a small vent in the machine (it was like an oil cup) and poured the whiskey in, and then poured the water in.

The bartender watched grimly. "Not funny," he said in an even voice. "And furthermore, your companion takes up too much room. Why'n you put it over on that bench by the door, make more room here."

"There's plenty of room for everyone here," replied the man.

"I ain't amused," said the bartender. "Put the goddam thing over near the door like I say. Nobody will touch it."

The man smiled. "You should have seen it this afternoon," he said. "It was magnificent. Today was the third day of the tournament. Imagine it—three days of continuous brainwork! And against the top players in the country, too. Early in the game it gained an advantage; then for two hours it exploited the advantage brilliantly, ending with the opponent's king backed in a corner. The sudden capture of a knight, the neutralization of a bishop, and it was all over. You know how much money it won, all told, in three days of playing chess?"

"How much?" asked the bartender.

"Five thousand dollars," said the man. "Now it wants to let down, wants to get a little drunk."

The bartender ran his towel vaguely over some wet spots. "Take it somewheres else and get it drunk there!" he said firmly. "I got enough troubles."

The man shook his head and smiled. "No, we like it here." He pointed at the empty glasses. "Do this again, will you, please?"

The bartender slowly shook his head. He seemed dazed but dogged. "You stow the thing away," he ordered. "I'm not ladling out whiskey for jokestersmiths."

" 'Jokesmiths,' " said the machine. "The word is 'jokesmiths.' "

A few feet down the bar, a customer who was on his third highball seemed ready to participate in this conversation to which we had all been listening so attentively. He was a middle-aged man. His necktie was pulled down away from his collar, and he had eased the collar by unbuttoning it. He had pretty nearly finished his third drink, and the alcohol tended to make him throw his support in with the underprivileged and the thirsty.

"If the machine wants another drink, give it another drink," he said to the bartender. "Let's not have haggling."

The fellow with the machine turned to his new-found friend and gravely raised his hand to his temple, giving him a salute of gratitude and fellowship. He addressed his next remark to him, as though deliberately snubbing the bartender.

"You know how it is when you're all fagged out mentally, how you want a drink?"

"Certainly do," replied the friend. "Most natural thing in the world."

There was a stir all along the bar, some seeming to side with the bartender, others with the machine group. A tall, gloomy man standing next to me spoke up.

"Another whiskey sour, Bill," he said. "And go easy on the lemon juice."

"Picric acid,"[1] said the machine, sullenly. "They don't use lemon juice in these places."

"That does it!" said the bartender, smacking his hand on the bar. "Will you put that thing away or else beat it out of here. I ain't in the mood, I tell you. I got this saloon to run and I don't want lip from a mechanical brain or whatever the hell you've got there."

The man ignored this ultimatum. He addressed his friend, whose glass was not empty.

"It's not just that it's all tuckered out after three days of chess," he said amiably. "You know another reason it wants a drink?"

"No," said the friend. "Why?"

"It cheated," said the man.

At this remark, the machine chuckled. One of its arms dipped slightly, and a light glowed in a dial.

The friend frowned. He looked as though his dignity had been hurt, as though his trust had been misplaced. "Nobody can cheat at chess," he said. "Simpossible. In chess, everything is open and above the board. The nature of the game of chess is such that cheating is impossible."

"That's what I used to think, too," said the man. "But there *is* a way."

"Well, it doesn't surprise me any," put in the bartender. "The first time I laid my eyes on that crummy thing I spotted it for a crook."

"Two rye-and-water," said the man.

"You can't have the whiskey," said the bartender. He glared at the mechanical brain. "How do I know it ain't drunk already?"

"That's simple. Ask it something," said the man.

The customers shifted and stared into the mirror. We were all in this thing now, up to our necks. We waited. It was the bartender's move.

"Ask it what? Such as?" said the bartender.

"Makes no difference. Pick a couple big figures, ask it to multiply them together. You couldn't multiply big figures together if you were drunk, could you?"

The machine shook slightly, as though making internal preparations.

"Ten thousand eight hundred and sixty-two, multiply it by ninety-nine," said the bartender, viciously. We could tell that he was throwing in the two nines to make it hard.

The machine flickered. One of its tubes spat, and a hand changed position, jerkily.

[1] A bitter, toxic acid sometimes used in medicine.

"One million seventy-five thousand three hundred and thirty-eight," said the machine.

Not a glass was raised all along the bar. People just stared gloomily into the mirror; some of us studied our own faces, others took carom shots at the man and the machine.

Finally, a youngish, mathematically minded customer got out a piece of paper and pencil and went into retirement. "It works out," he reported after some minutes of calculating. "You can't say the machine is drunk."

Everyone now glared at the bartender. Reluctantly he poured two shots of rye, drew two glasses of water. The man drank his drink. Then he fed the machine its drink. The machine's light grew fainter. One of its cranky little arms wilted.

For a while the saloon simmered along like a ship at sea in calm weather. Every one of us seemed to be trying to digest the situation, with the help of liquor. Quite a few glasses were refilled. Most of us sought help in the mirror—the court of last appeal.

The fellow with the unbuttoned collar settled his score. He walked stiffly over and stood between the man and the machine. He put one arm around the man, the other arm around the machine. "Let's get out of here and go to a good place," he said.

The machine glowed slightly. It seemed to be a little drunk now.

"All right," said the man. "That suits me fine. I've got my car outside."

He settled for the drinks and put down a tip. Quietly and a trifle uncertainly he tucked the machine under his arm, and he and his companion of the night walked to the door and out into the street.

The bartender stared fixedly, then resumed his light housekeeping. "So he's got his car outside," he said, with heavy sarcasm. "Now isn't that nice!"

A customer at the end of the bar near the door left his drink, stepped to the window, parted the curtains, and looked out. He watched for a moment, then returned to his place and addressed the bartender. "It's even nicer than you think," he said. "It's a Cadillac. And which one of the three of them d'ya think is doing the driving?"

WALTER VAN TILBURG CLARK 1909–

The Portable Phonograph

The red sunset, with narrow, black cloud strips like threats across it, lay on the curved horizon of the prairie. The air was still and cold, and in it settled the mute darkness and greater cold of night. High in the air there was wind, for through the veil of the dusk the clouds could be seen gliding rapidly south and changing shapes. A sensation of torment, of two-sided, unpredictable nature, arose from the stillness of the earth air beneath the violence of the upper air. Out of the sunset, through the dead, matted grass and isolated weed stalks of the prairie, crept the narrow and deeply rutted remains of a road. In the road, in places, there were crusts of shallow, brittle ice. There were little islands of an old oiled pavement in the road too, but most of it was mud, now frozen rigid. The frozen mud still bore the toothed impress of great tanks, and a wanderer on the neighboring undulations might have stumbled, in this light, into large, partially filled-in and weed-grown cavities, their banks channeled and beginning to spread into badlands. These pits were such as might have been made by falling meteors, but they were not. They were the scars of gigantic bombs, their rawness already made a little natural by rain, seed and time. Along the road there were rakish remnants of fence. There was also, just visible, one portion of tangled and multiple barbed wire still erect, behind which was a shelving ditch with small caves, now very quiet and empty, at intervals in its back wall. Otherwise there was no structure or remnant of a structure visible over the dome of the darkling earth, but only, in sheltered hollows, the darker shadows of young trees trying again.

Under the wuthering arch of the high wind a V of wild geese fled south. The rush of their pinions sounded briefly, and the faint, plaintive notes of their expeditionary talk. Then they left a still greater vacancy. There was the smell and expectation of snow, as there is likely to be when the wild geese fly south. From the remote distance, toward the red sky, came faintly the protracted howl and quick yap-yap of a prairie wolf.

North of the road, perhaps a hundred yards, lay the parallel and deeply intrenched course of a small creek, lined with leafless alders and willows. The creek was already silent under ice. Into the bank above it was dug a sort of cell, with a single opening, like the mouth of a mine tunnel. Within the cell there was a little red of fire, which showed dully through the opening, like a reflection or a deception of the imagination. The light came from the chary burning of four blocks of poorly aged peat, which gave off a petty warmth and much acrid smoke. But the precious remnants of wood, old fence posts and timbers from the long-deserted dugouts, had to be saved for the real cold, for the time when a man's breath blew white, the moisture in his nostrils stiffened at once when he stepped out, and the expansive blizzards paraded for days over the vast open, swirling and settling and thickening, till the dawn of the cleared day when the sky was a thin blue-green and the terrible cold, in which a man could not live for three hours unwarmed, lay over the uniformly drifted swell of the plain.

Around the smoldering peat four men were seated cross-legged. Behind them, traversed by their shadows, was the earth bench, with two old and dirty army blankets, where the owner of the cell slept. In a niche in the opposite wall were a few tin utensils which caught the glint of the coals. The host was rewrapping in a piece of daubed burlap, four fine, leather-bound books. He worked slowly and very carefully, and at last tied the bundle securely with a piece of grass-woven cord. The other three looked intently upon the process, as if a great significance lay in it. As the host tied the cord, he spoke. He was an old man, his long, matted beard and hair gray to nearly white. The shadows made his brows and cheekbones appear gnarled, his eyes and cheeks deeply sunken. His big hands, rough with frost and swollen by rheumatism, were awkward but gentle at their task. He was like a prehistoric priest performing a fateful ceremonial rite. Also his voice had in it a suitable quality of deep, reverent despair, yet perhaps, at the moment, a sharpness of selfish satisfaction.

"When I perceived what was happening," he said, "I told myself, 'It is the end. I cannot take much; I will take these.'

"Perhaps I was impractical," he continued. "But for myself, I do not regret, and what do we know of those who will come after us? We are the doddering remnant of a race of mechanical fools. I have saved what I love; the soul of what was good in us here; perhaps the new ones will make a strong enough beginning not to fall behind when they become clever."

He rose with slow pain and placed the wrapped volumes in the niche with his utensils. The others watched him with the same ritualistic gaze.

"Shakespeare, the Bible, *Moby Dick, The Divine Comedy,*" one of them said softly. "You might have done worse; much worse."

"You will have a little soul left until you die," said another harshly. "That is more than is true of us. My brain becomes thick, like my hands." He held the big, battered hands, with their black nails, in the glow to be seen.

"I want paper to write on," he said. "And there is none."

The fourth man said nothing. He sat in the shadow farthest from the fire, and sometimes his body jerked in its rags from the cold. Although he was still young, he was sick, and coughed often. Writing implied a greater future than he now felt able to consider.

The old man seated himself laboriously, and reached out, groaning at the movement, to put another block of peat on the fire. With bowed heads and averted eyes, his three guests acknowledged his magnanimity.

"We thank you, Doctor Jenkins, for the reading," said the man who had named the books.

They seemed then to be waiting for something. Doctor Jenkins understood, but was loath to comply. In an ordinary moment he would have said nothing. But the words of *The Tempest,* which he had been reading, and the religious attention of the three, made this an unusual occasion.

"You wish to hear the phonograph," he said grudgingly.

The two middle-aged men stared into the fire, unable to formulate and expose the enormity of their desire.

The young man, however, said anxiously, between suppressed coughs, "Oh, please," like an excited child.

The old man rose again in his difficult way, and went to the back of the cell. He returned and placed tenderly upon the packed floor, where the firelight might fall upon it, an old, portable phonograph in a black case. He smoothed the top with his hand, and then opened it. The lovely green-felt-covered disk became visible.

"I have been using thorns as needles," he said. "But tonight, because we have a musician among us"—he bent his head to the young man, almost invisible in the shadow—"I will use a steel needle. There are only three left."

The two middle-aged men stared at him in speechless adoration. The one with the big hands, who wanted to write, moved his lips, but the whisper was not audible.

"Oh, don't," cried the young man, as if he were hurt. "The thorns will do beautifully."

"No," the old man said. "I have become accustomed to the thorns, but they are not really good. For you, my young friend, we will have good music tonight.

"After all," he added generously, and beginning to wind the phonograph, which creaked, "they can't last forever."

"No, nor we," the man who needed to write said harshly. "The needle, by all means."

"Oh, thanks," said the young man. "Thanks," he said again, in a low, excited voice, and then stifled his coughing with a bowed head.

"The records, though," said the old man when he had finished winding, "are a different matter. Already they are very worn. I do not play them more than once a week. One, once a week, that is what I allow myself.

"More than a week I cannot stand it; not to hear them," he apologized.

"No, how could you?" cried the young man. "And with them here like this."

"A man can stand anything," said the man who wanted to write, in his harsh, antagonistic voice.

"Please, the music," said the young man.

"Only the one," said the old man. "In the long run we will remember more that way."

He had a dozen records with luxuriant gold and red seals. Even in that light the others could see that the threads of the records were becoming worn. Slowly he read out the titles, and the tremendous, dead names of the composers and the artists and the orchestras. The three worked upon the names in their minds, carefully. It was difficult to select from such a wealth what they would at once most like to remember. Finally the man who wanted to write named Gershwin's "New York."

"Oh, no," cried the sick young man, and then could say nothing more because he had to cough. The others understood him, and the harsh man withdrew his selection and waited for the musician to choose.

The musician begged Doctor Jenkins to read the titles again, very slowly, so that he could remember the sounds. While they were read, he lay back against the wall, his eyes closed, his thin, horny hand pulling at his light beard, and listened to the voices and the orchestras and the single instruments in his mind.

When the reading was done he spoke despairingly. "I have forgotten," he complained. "I cannot hear them clearly.

"There are things missing," he explained.

"I know," said Doctor Jenkins. "I thought that I knew all of Shelley by heart. I should have brought Shelley."

"That's more soul than we can use," said the harsh man. "*Moby Dick* is better.

"By God, we can understand that," he emphasized.

The doctor nodded.

"Still," said the man who had admired the books, "we need the absolute if we are to keep a grasp on anything.

"Anything but these sticks and peat clods and rabbit snares," he said bitterly.

"Shelley desired an ultimate absolute," said the harsh man. "It's too much," he said. "It's no good; no earthly good."

The musician selected a Debussy nocturne. The others considered and approved. They rose to their knees to watch the doctor prepare for the playing, so that they appeared to be actually in an attitude of worship. The peat glow showed the thinness of their bearded faces, and the deep lines in them, and revealed the condition of their garments. The other two continued to kneel as the old man carefully lowered the needle onto the spinning disk, but the musician suddenly drew back against the wall again, with his knees up, and buried his face in his hands.

At the first notes of the piano the listeners were startled. They stared at each other. Even the musician lifted his head in amazement, but then quickly bowed it again, strainingly, as if he were suffering from a pain he might not be able to endure. They were all listening deeply, without movement. The wet, blue-green notes tinkled forth from the old machine, and were individual, delectable presences in the cell. The individual, delectable presences swept into a sudden tide of unbearably beautiful dissonance, and then continued fully the swelling and ebbing of that tide, the dissonant inpourings, and the resolutions, and the diminishments, and the little, quiet wavelets of interlude lapping between. Every sound was piercing and singularly sweet. In all the men except the musician, there occurred rapid sequences of tragically heightened recollection. He heard nothing but what was there. At the final, whispering disappearance, but moving quietly, so that the others would not hear him and look at him, he let his head fall back in agony, as if it were drawn there by the hair, and clenched the fingers of one hand over his teeth. He sat that way while the others were silent, and until they began to breathe again normally. His drawn-up legs were trembling violently.

Quickly Doctor Jenkins lifted the needle off, to save it, and not to spoil the recollection with scraping. When he had stopped the whirling of the sacred disk, he courteously left the phonograph open and by the fire, in sight.

The others, however, understood. The musician rose last, but then abruptly, and went quickly out at the door without saying anything. The others stopped at the door and gave their thanks in low voices. The doctor nodded magnificently.

"Come again," he invited, "in a week. We will have the 'New York.' "

When the two had gone together, out toward the rimed road, he stood in the entrance, peering and listening. At first there was only the resonant boom of the wind overhead, and then, far over the dome of the dead, dark plain, the wolf cry lamenting. In the rifts of clouds the doctor saw four stars flying. It impressed the doctor that one of them had just been obscured by the beginning of a flying cloud at the very moment he heard what he had been listening for, a sound of suppressed coughing. It was not near by, however. He believed that down against the pale alders he could see the moving shadow.

With nervous hands he lowered the piece of canvas which served as his door, and pegged it at the bottom. Then quickly and quietly, looking at the piece of canvas frequently, he slipped the records into the case, snapped the lid shut, and carried the phonograph to his couch. There, pausing often to stare at the canvas and listen, he dug earth from the wall and disclosed a piece of board. Behind this there was a deep hole in the wall, into which he put the phonograph. After a moment's consideration, he went over and reached down his bundle of books and inserted it also. Then, guardedly, he once more sealed up the hole with the board and the earth. He also changed his blankets, and the grass-stuffed sack which served as a pillow, so that he could lie facing the entrance. After carefully placing two more blocks of peat on the fire, he stood for a long time watching the stretched canvas, but it seemed to billow naturally with the first gusts of a lowering wind. At last he prayed, and got in under his blankets, and closed his smoke-smarting eyes. On the inside of the bed, next the wall, he could feel with his hand the comfortable piece of lead pipe.

KURT VONNEGUT, JR.
1922–

Harrison Bergeron[1]

The year was 2081, and everybody was finally equal. They weren't only equal before God and the law. They were equal every which way. Nobody was smarter than anybody else. Nobody was better looking than anybody else. Nobody was stronger or quicker than anybody else. All this equality was due to the 211th, 212th, and 213th Amendments to the Constitution, and to the unceasing vigilance of agents of the United States Handicapper General.

Some things about living still weren't quite right, though. April, for instance, still drove people crazy by not being springtime. And it was in that clammy month that the H-G men took George and Hazel Bergeron's fourteen-year-old son, Harrison, away.

It was tragic, all right, but George and Hazel

[1] Jeffers's poem "Science" (p. **344**) can be read as a companion piece to this story because both find human beings the victims of their own science and technology. Bradbury's story "There Will Come Soft Rains" (p. **152**) has a similar theme.

couldn't think about it very hard. Hazel had a perfectly average intelligence, which meant she couldn't think about anything except in short bursts. And George, while his intelligence was way above normal, had a little mental handicap radio in his ear. He was required by law to wear it at all times. It was tuned to a government transmitter. Every twenty seconds or so, the transmitter would send out some sharp noise to keep people like George from taking unfair advantage of their brains.

George and Hazel were watching television. There were tears on Hazel's cheeks, but she'd forgotten for the moment what they were about.

On the television screen were ballerinas.

A buzzer sounded in George's head. His thoughts fled in panic, like bandits from a burglar alarm.

"That was a real pretty dance, that dance they just did," said Hazel.

"Huh?" said George.

"That dance—it was nice," said Hazel.

"Yup," said George. He tried to think a little about the ballerinas. They weren't really very good—no better than anybody else would have been, anyway. They were burdened with sashweights and bags of birdshot, and their faces were masked, so that no one, seeing a free and graceful gesture or a pretty face, would feel like something the cat drug in. George was toying with the vague notion that maybe dancers shouldn't be handicapped. But he didn't get very far with it before another noise in his ear radio scattered his thoughts.

George winced. So did two out of the eight ballerinas.

Hazel saw him wince. Having no mental handicap herself, she had to ask George what the latest sound had been.

"Sounded like somebody hitting a milk bottle with a ball peen hammer," said George.

"I'd think it would be real interesting, hearing all the different sounds," said Hazel, a little envious. "All the things they think up."

"Um," said George.

"Only, if I was Handicapper General, you know what I would do?" said Hazel. Hazel, as a matter of fact, bore a strong resemblance to the Handicapper General, a woman named Diana Moon Glampers. "If I was Diana Moon Glampers," said Hazel, "I'd have chimes on Sunday—just chimes. Kind of in honor of religion."

"I could think, if it was just chimes," said George.

"Well—maybe make 'em real loud," said Hazel. "I think I'd make a good Handicapper General."

"Good as anybody else," said George.

"Who knows better'n I do what normal is?" said Hazel.

"Right," said George. He began to think glimmeringly about his abnormal son who was now in jail, about Harrison, but a twenty-one-gun salute in his head stopped that.

"Boy!" said Hazel, "that was a doozy, wasn't it?"

It was such a doozy that George was white and trembling, and tears stood on the rims of his red eyes. Two of the eight ballerinas had collapsed to the studio floor, were holding their temples.

"All of a sudden you look so tired," said Hazel. "Why don't you stretch out on the sofa, so's you can rest your handicap bag on the pillows, honeybunch." She was referring to the forty-seven pounds of birdshot in a canvas bag, which was padlocked around George's neck. "Go on and rest the bag for a little while," she said. "I don't care if you're not equal to me for a while."

George weighed the bag with his hands. "I don't mind it," he said. "I don't notice it any more. It's just a part of me."

"You been so tired lately—kind of wore out," said Hazel. "If there was just some way we could make a little hole in the bottom of the bag, and just take out a few of them lead balls. Just a few."

"Two years in prison and two thousand dollars fine for every ball I took out," said George. "I don't call that a bargain."

"If you could just take a few out when you came home from work," said Hazel. "I mean—you don't compete with anybody around here. You just set around."

"If I tried to get away with it," said George, "then other people'd get away with it—and pretty soon we'd be right back to the dark ages again, with everybody competing against everybody else. You wouldn't like that, would you?"

"I'd hate it," said Hazel.

"There you are," said George. "The minute people start cheating on laws, what do you think happens to society?"

If Hazel hadn't been able to come up with an

answer to this question, George couldn't have supplied one. A siren was going off in his head.

"Reckon it'd fall all apart," said Hazel.

"What would?" said George blankly.

"Society," said Hazel uncertainly. "Wasn't that what you just said?"

"Who knows?" said George.

The television program was suddenly interrupted for a news bulletin. It wasn't clear at first as to what the bulletin was about, since the announcer, like all announcers, had a serious speech impediment. For about half a minute, and in a state of high excitement, the announcer tried to say, "Ladies and gentlemen—"

He finally gave up, handed the bulletin to a ballerina to read.

"That's all right—" Hazel said of the announcer, "he tried. That's the big thing. He tried to do the best he could with what God gave him. He should get a nice raise for trying so hard."

"Ladies and gentlemen—" said the ballerina, reading the bulletin. She must have been extraordinarily beautiful, because the mask she wore was hideous. And it was easy to see that she was the strongest and most graceful of all the dancers, for her handicap bags were as big as those worn by two-hundred-pound men.

And she had to apologize at once for her voice, which was a very unfair voice for a woman to use. Her voice was a warm, luminous, timeless melody. "Excuse me—" she said, and she began again, making her voice absolutely uncompetitive.

"Harrison Bergeron, age fourteen," she said in a grackle squawk, "has just escaped from jail, where he was held on suspicion of plotting to overthrow the government. He is a genius and an athlete, is under-handicapped, and should be regarded as extremely dangerous."

A police photograph of Harrison Bergeron was flashed on the screen upside down, then sideways, upside down again, then right side up. The picture showed the full length of Harrison against a background calibrated in feet and inches. He was exactly seven feet tall.

The rest of Harrison's appearance was Halloween and hardware. Nobody had ever borne heavier handicaps. He had outgrown hindrances faster than the H-G men could think them up. Instead of a little ear radio for a mental handicap, he wore a tremendous pair of earphones, and spectacles with thick wavy lenses. The spectacles were intended to make him not only half blind, but to give him whanging headaches besides.

Scrap metal was hung all over him. Ordinarily, there was a certain symmetry, a military neatness to the handicaps issued to strong people, but Harrison looked like a walking junkyard. In the race of life, Harrison carried three hundred pounds.

And to offset his good looks, the H-G men required that he wear at all times a red rubber ball for a nose, keep his eyebrows shaved off, and cover his even white teeth with black caps at snaggle-tooth random.

"If you see this boy," said the ballerina, "do not—I repeat, do not—try to reason with him."

There was the shriek of a door being torn from its hinges.

Screams and barking cries of consternation came from the television set. The photograph of Harrison Bergeron on the screen jumped again and again, as though dancing to the tune of an earthquake.

George Bergeron correctly identified the earthquake, and well he might have—for many was the time his own home had danced to the same crashing tune. "My God—" said George, "that must be Harrison!"

The realization was blasted from his mind instantly by the sound of an automobile collision in his head.

When George could open his eyes again, the photograph of Harrison was gone. A living, breathing Harrison filled the screen.

Clanking, clownish, and huge, Harrison stood in the center of the studio. The knob of the uprooted studio door was still in his hand. Ballerinas, technicians, musicians, and announcers cowered on their knees before him, expecting to die.

"I am the Emperor!" cried Harrison. "Do you hear? I am the Emperor! Everybody must do what I say at once!" He stamped his foot and the studio shook.

"Even as I stand here—" he bellowed, "crippled, hobbled, sickened—I am a greater ruler than any man who ever lived! Now watch me become what I *can* become!"

Harrison tore the straps of his handicap harness like wet tissue paper, tore straps guaranteed to support five thousand pounds.

Harrison's scrap-iron handicaps crashed to the floor.

Harrison thrust his thumbs under the bar of the padlock that secured his head harness. The bar snapped like celery. Harrison smashed his headphones and spectacles against the wall.

He flung away his rubber-ball nose, revealed a man that would have awed Thor, the god of thunder.

"I shall now select my Empress!" he said, looking down on the cowering people. "Let the first woman who dares rise to her feet claim her mate and her throne!"

A moment passed, and then a ballerina arose, swaying like a willow.

Harrison plucked the mental handicap from her ear, snapped off her physical handicaps with marvelous delicacy. Last of all, he removed her mask.

She was blindingly beautiful.

"Now—" said Harrison, taking her hand, "shall we show the people the meaning of the word dance? Music!" he commanded.

The musicians scrambled back into their chairs, and Harrison stripped them of their handicaps, too. "Play your best," he told them, "and I'll make you barons and dukes and earls."

The music began. It was normal at first—cheap, silly, false. But Harrison snatched two musicians from their chairs, waved them like batons as he sang the music as he wanted it played. He slammed them back into their chairs.

The music began again and was much improved.

Harrison and his Empress merely listened to the music for a while—listened gravely, as though synchronizing their heartbeats with it.

They shifted their weights to their toes.

Harrison placed his big hands on the girl's tiny waist, letting her sense the weightlessness that would soon be hers.

And then, in an explosion of joy and grace, into the air they sprang!

Not only were the laws of the land abandoned, but the law of gravity and the laws of motion as well.

They reeled, whirled, swiveled, flounced, capered, gamboled, and spun.

They leaped like deer on the moon.

The studio ceiling was thirty feet high, but each leap brought the dancers nearer to it.

It became their obvious intention to kiss the ceiling.

They kissed it.

And then, neutralizing gravity with love and pure will, they remained suspended in air inches below the ceiling, and they kissed each other for a long, long time.

It was then that Diana Moon Glampers, the Handicapper General, came into the studio with a double-barreled ten-gauge shotgun. She fired twice, and the Emperor and the Empress were dead before they hit the floor.

Diana Moon Glampers loaded the gun again. She aimed it at the musicians and told them they had ten seconds to get their handicaps back on.

It was then that the Bergerons' television tube burned out.

Hazel turned to comment about the blackout to George. But George had gone out into the kitchen for a can of beer.

George came back in with a beer, paused while a handicap signal shook him up. And then he sat down again. "You been crying?" he said to Hazel.

"Yup," she said.

"What about?" he said.

"I forget," she said. "Something real sad on television."

"What was it?" he said.

"It's all kind of mixed up in my mind," said Hazel.

"Forget sad things," said George.

"I always do," said Hazel.

"That's my girl," said George. He winced. There was the sound of a rivetting gun in his head.

"Gee—I could tell that one was a doozy," said Hazel.

"You can say that again," said George.

"Gee—" said Hazel, "I could tell that one was a doozy."

DONALD BARTHELME
1931–
A City of Churches

"Yes," Mr. Phillips said, "ours is a city of churches all right."

Cecelia nodded, following his pointing hand. Both sides of the street were solidly lined with churches, standing shoulder to shoulder in a variety of architectural styles. The Bethel Baptist stood next to the Holy Messiah Free Baptist,

St. Paul's Episcopal next to Grace Evangelical Covenant. Then came the First Christian Science, the Church of God, All Souls, Our Lady of Victory, the Society of Friends, the Assembly of God, and the Church of the Holy Apostles. The spires and steeples of the traditional buildings were jammed in next to the broad imaginative flights of the "contemporary" designs.

"Everyone here takes a great interest in church matters," Mr. Phillips said.

Will I fit in? Cecelia wondered. She had come to Prester to open a branch office of a car-rental concern.

"I'm not especially religious," she said to Mr. Phillips, who was in the real-estate business.

"Not *now*," he answered. "Not *yet*. But we have many fine young people here. You'll get integrated into the community soon enough. The immediate problem is, where are you to live? Most people," he said, "live in the church of their choice. All of our churches have many extra rooms. I have a few belfry apartments that I can show you. What price range were you thinking of?"

They turned a corner and were confronted with more churches. They passed St. Luke's, the Church of the Epiphany, All Saints Ukrainian Orthodox, St. Clement's, Fountain Baptist, Union Congregational, St. Anargyri's, Temple Emanuel, the First Church of Christ Reformed. The mouths of all the churches were gaping open. Inside, lights could be seen dimly.

"I can go up to a hundred and ten," Cecelia said. "Do you have any buildings here that are *not* churches?"

"None," said Mr. Phillips. "Of course many of our fine church structures also do double duty as something else." He indicated a handsome Georgian façade. "That one," he said, houses the United Methodist and the Board of Education. The one next to it, which is Antioch Pentecostal, has the barbershop."

It was true. A red-and-white striped barber pole was attached inconspicuously to the front of the Antioch Pentecostal.

"Do many people rent cars here?" Cecelia asked. "Or would they, if there was a handy place to rent them?"

"Oh, I don't know," said Mr. Phillips. "Renting a car implies that you want to go somewhere. Most people are pretty content right here. We have a lot of activities. I don't think I'd pick the car-rental business if I was just starting out in Prester. But you'll do fine." He showed her a small, extremely modern building with a severe brick, steel, and glass front. "That's St. Barnabas. Nice bunch of people over there. Wonderful spaghetti suppers."

Cecelia could see a number of heads looking out of the windows. But when they saw that she was staring at them, the heads disappeared.

"Do you think it's healthy for so many churches to be gathered together in one place?" she asked the guide. "It doesn't seem . . . *balanced,* if you know what I mean."

"We are famous for our churches," Mr. Phillips replied. "They are harmless. Here we are now."

He opened a door and they began climbing many flights of dusty stairs. At the end of the climb they entered a good-sized room, square, with windows on all four sides. There was a bed, a table, and two chairs, lamps, a rug. Four very large bronze bells hung in the exact center of the room.

"What a view!" Mr. Phillips exclaimed. "Come here and look."

"Do they actually ring these bells?" Cecelia asked.

"Three times a day," Mr. Phillips said, smiling. "Morning, noon, and night. Of course when they're rung you have to be pretty quick at getting out of the way. You get hit in the head by one of these babies and that's all she wrote."

"God Almighty," said Cecelia involuntarily. Then she said, "Nobody lives in the belfry apartments. That's why they're empty."

"You think so?" Mr. Phillips said.

"You can only rent them to new people in town," she said accusingly.

"I wouldn't do that," Mr. Phillips said. "It would go against the spirit of Christian fellowship."

"This town is a little creepy, you know that?"

"That may be, but it's not for you to say, is it? I mean, you're new here. You should walk cautiously, for a while. If you don't want an upper apartment I have a basement over at Central Presbyterian. You'd have to share it. There are two women in there now."

"I don't want to share," Cecelia said. "I want a place of my own."

"Why?" the real-estate man asked curiously. "For what purpose?"

"Purpose?" asked Cecelia. "There is no particular purpose. I just want—"

"That's not usual here. Most people live with other people. Husbands and wives. Sons with their mothers. People have roommates. That's the usual pattern."

"Still, I prefer a place of my own."

"It's very unusual."

"Do you have any such places? Besides bell towers, I mean?"

"I guess there are a few," Mr. Phillips said, with clear reluctance. "I can show you one or two, I suppose."

He paused for a moment.

"It's just that we have different values, maybe, from some of the surrounding communities," he explained. "We've been written up a lot. We had four minutes on the C.B.S. Evening News one time. Three or four years ago. 'A City of Churches,' it was called."

"Yes, a place of my own is essential," Cecelia said, "if I am to survive here."

"That's kind of a funny attitude to take," Mr. Phillips said. "What denomination are you?"

Cecelia was silent. The truth was, she wasn't anything.

"I said, what denomination are you?" Mr. Phillips repeated.

"I can will my dreams," Cecelia said. "I can dream whatever I want. If I want to dream that I'm having a good time, in Paris or some other city, all I have to do is go to sleep and I will dream that dream. I can dream whatever I want."

"What do you dream, then, mostly?" Mr. Phillips said, looking at her closely.

"Mostly sexual things," she said. She was not afraid of him.

"Prester is not that kind of a town," Mr. Phillips said, looking away.

They went back down the stairs.

The doors of the churches were opening, on both sides of the street. Small groups of people came out and stood there, in front of the churches, gazing at Cecelia and Mr. Phillips.

A young man stepped forward and shouted, "*Everyone in this town already has a car! There is no one in this town who doesn't have a car!*"

"Is that true?" Cecelia asked Mr. Phillips.

"Yes," he said. "It's true. No one would rent a car here. Not in a hundred years."

"Then I won't stay," she said. "I'll go somewhere else."

"You must stay," he said. "There is already a car-rental office for you. In Mount Moriah Baptist, on the lobby floor. There is a counter and a telephone and a rack of car keys. And a calendar."

"I won't stay," she said. "Not if there's not any sound business reason for staying."

"We want you," said Mr. Phillips. "We want you standing behind the counter of the car-rental agency, during regular business hours. It will make the town complete."

"I won't," she said. "Not me."

"You must. It's essential."

"I'll dream," she said. "Things you won't like."

"We are discontented," said Mr. Phillips. "Terribly, terribly discontented. Something is wrong."

"I'll dream the Secret," she said. "You'll be sorry."

"We are like other towns, except that we are perfect," he said. "Our discontent can only be held in check by perfection. We need a car-rental girl. Someone must stand behind that counter."

"I'll dream the life you are most afraid of," Cecelia threatened.

"You are ours," he said, gripping her arm. "Our car-rental girl. Be nice. There is nothing you can do."

"Wait and see," Cecelia said.

THE NOVELLA: A MODERN CLASSIC

Literary theory and literary criticism are often plagued by imprecise terms because literature and the other arts defy exact classification and description, especially abstract description. The basic forms of fiction are usually referred to as the short story, the short novel, and the novel. But the very word *short* raises many questions. How short, or limited, must a novel be to be a short novel? And how much shorter to be a short story? Surely the number of pages involved can hardly be the only answer, for who is to determine the dividing lines? Is Hemingway's *The*

Old Man and the Sea a long short story, a short novel, or a novel? Melville's *Benito Cereno,* which was gathered into his *Piazza Tales,* has been labeled all three over the years, yet Melville called it a tale, which may be the right simplifying solution after all.

These three classifications—the short story, the short novel, and the novel—are perhaps better defined by the scope, or range, of the work instead of by counting the number of words or pages. Scope involves such matters as the amount of time represented in the work, the number of characters, the philosophical content, and perhaps above all the complexity of the situation in the work. Ordinarily the more complex the situation the more detail is required to present the complexity, and detail requires space that lengthens the work. Under these circumstances Conrad's "Heart of Darkness" is a short novel, and Hemingway's "A Clean, Well-Lighted Place" (p. 40) and Hughes's "On the Road" (p. 112) are short stories. These are rather clear-cut decisions, but how to classify, say, Hemingway's *The Old Man and the Sea*?

In recent years the term *novella* has been revived, especially by departments of English, to represent the short novel, and novella courses and novella anthologies have flourished by the dozen. We are often told that the term *novella* is used to represent the early collected tales of the Italian and French writers as, for example, Boccaccio's *Decameron* and Marguerite of Valois' *Heptameron.* Our term *novel* emerged from this usage, and our present use of *novella* can be explored in Conrad's "Heart of Darkness."

JOSEPH CONRAD
1857–1924

Heart of Darkness

I

The *Nellie,* a cruising yawl, swung to her anchor without a flutter of the sails, and was at rest. The flood had made, the wind was nearly calm, and being bound down the river, the only thing for it was to come to and wait for the turn of the tide.

The sea-reach of the Thames stretched before us like the beginning of an interminable waterway. In the offing the sea and the sky were welded together without a joint, and in the luminous space the tanned sails of the barges drifting up with the tide seemed to stand still in red clusters of canvas sharply peaked, with gleams of varnished sprits. A haze rested on the low shores that ran out to sea in vanishing flatness. The air was dark above Gravesend, and farther back still seemed condensed into a mournful gloom, brooding motionless over the biggest, and the greatest, town on earth.

The Director of Companies was our captain and our host. We four affectionately watched his back as he stood in the bows looking to seaward. On the whole river there was nothing that looked half so nautical. He resembled a pilot, which to a seaman is trustworthiness personified. It was difficult to realize his work was not out there in the luminous estuary, but behind him, within the brooding gloom.

Between us there was, as I have already said somewhere, the bond of the sea. Besides holding our hearts together through long periods of separation, it had the effect of making us tolerant of each other's yarns—and even convictions. The Lawyer—the best of old fellows—had, because of his many years and many virtues, the only cushion on deck, and was lying on the only rug. The Accountant had brought out already a box of dominoes, and was toying architecturally with the bones. Marlow sat cross-legged right aft, leaning against the mizzen-mast. He had sunken cheeks, a yellow complexion, a straight back, an ascetic aspect, and, with his arms dropped, the palms of hands outwards, resembled an idol. The director, satisfied the anchor had good hold, made his way aft and sat down amongst us. We exchanged a few words lazily. Afterwards there was silence on board the yacht. For some reason or other we did not begin that game of dominoes. We felt meditative, and fit for nothing but placid staring. The day was ending in a serenity of still and exquisite brilliance. The water shone pacifically; the sky, without a speck, was a benign immensity of unstained light; the very mist on the Essex marshes was like a gauzy and radiant fabric, hung from the wooded rises inland, and draping the low shores in diaphanous folds. Only the gloom to the west, brooding over the upper reaches, became more somber every minute, as if angered by the approach of the sun.

And at last, in its curved and imperceptible fall, the sun sank low, and from glowing white changed to a dull red without rays and without heat, as if about to go out suddenly, stricken to death by the touch of that gloom brooding over a crowd of men.

Forthwith a change came over the waters, and the serenity became less brilliant but more profound. The old river in its broad reach rested unruffled at the decline of day, after ages of good service done to the race that peopled its banks, spread out in the tranquil dignity of a waterway leading to the uttermost ends of the earth. We looked at the venerable stream not in the vivid flush of a short day that comes and departs forever, but in the august light of abiding memories. And indeed nothing is easier for a man who has, as the phrase goes, "followed the sea" with reverence and affection, than to evoke the great spirit of the past upon the lower reaches of the Thames. The tidal current runs to and fro in its unceasing service, crowded with memories of men and ships it had borne to the rest of home or to the battles of the sea. It had known and served all the men of whom the nation is proud, from Sir Francis Drake[1] to Sir John Franklin,[2] knights all, titled and untitled—the knights-errant of the sea. It had borne all the ships whose names are like jewels flashing in the night of time, from the *Golden Hind*[3] returning with her round flanks full of treasure, to be visited by the Queen's Highness and thus pass out of the gigantic tale, to the *Erebus* and *Terror,*[4] bound on other conquests—and that never returned. It had known the ships and the men. They had sailed from Deptford, from Greenwich, from Erith—the adventurers and the settlers; kings' ships and the ships of men on 'Change; captains, admirals, the dark "interlopers" of the Eastern trade, and the commissioned "generals" of East India fleets. Hunters for gold or pursuers of fame, they all had gone out on that stream, bearing the sword, and often the torch, messengers of the might within the land, bearers of a spark from the sacred fire. What greatness had not floated on the ebb of that river into the mystery of an unknown earth! . . . The dreams of men, the seed of commonwealths, the germs of empires.

The sun set; the dusk fell on the stream, and lights began to appear along the shore. The Chapman lighthouse, a three-legged thing erect on a mud-flat, shone strongly. Lights of ships moved in the fairway—a great stir of lights going up and going down. And farther west on the upper reaches the place of the monstrous town was still marked ominously on the sky, a brooding gloom in sunshine, a lurid glare under the stars.

"And this also," said Marlow suddenly, "has been one of the dark places on the earth."

He was the only man of us who still "followed the sea." The worst that could be said of him was that he did not represent his class. He was a seaman, but he was a wanderer, too, while most seamen lead, if one may so express it, a sedentary life. Their minds are of the stay-at-home order, and their home is always with them—the ship; and so is their country—the sea. One ship is very much like another, and the sea is always the same. In the immutability of their surroundings the foreign shores, the foreign faces, the changing immensity of life, glide past, veiled not by a sense of mystery but by a slightly disdainful ignorance; for there is nothing mysterious to a seaman unless it be the sea itself, which is the mistress of his existence and as inscrutable as Destiny. For the rest, after his hours of work, a casual stroll or a casual spree on shore suffices to unfold for him the secret of a whole continent, and generally he finds the secret not worth knowing. The yarns of seamen have a direct simplicity, the whole meaning of which lies within the shell of a cracked nut. But Marlow was not typical (if his propensity to spin yarns be excepted), and to him the meaning of an episode was not inside like a kernel but outside, enveloping the tale which brought it out only as a glow brings out a haze, in the likeness of one of these misty halos that sometimes are made visible by the spectral illumination of moonshine.

[1] Early English perennial sea explorer (1540?–1596).

[2] English Arctic explorer (1786–1847); started his last voyage in 1845, but never returned having been locked in ice for eighteen months.

[3] Originally named the *Pelican,* a ship of 100 tons in which Drake rounded the Cape of Good Hope and circled the world.

[4] The ships of Franklin's expedition, which searched for the North-West Passage, a route from the Atlantic to the Pacific around the north coast of the American continent.

His remark did not seem at all surprising. It was just like Marlow. It was accepted in silence. No one took the trouble to grunt even; and presently he said, very slow—

"I was thinking of very old times, when the Romans first came here, nineteen hundred years ago—the other day. . . . Light came out of this river since—you say Knights? Yes; but it is like a running blaze on a plain, like a flash of lightning in the clouds. We live in the flicker—may it last as long as the old earth keeps rolling! But darkness was here yesterday. Imagine the feelings of a commander of a fine—what d'ye call 'em?—trireme[5] in the Mediterranean, ordered suddenly to the north; run overland across the Gauls in a hurry; put in charge of one of these craft the legionaries—a wonderful lot of handy men they must have been, too—used to build, apparently by the hundred, in a month or two, if we may believe what we read. Imagine him here—the very end of the world, a sea the color of lead, a sky the color of smoke, a kind of ship about as rigid as a concertina—and going up this river with stores, or orders, or what you like. Sandbanks, marshes, forests, savages,—precious little to eat fit for a civilized man, nothing but Thames water to drink. No Falernian wine here, no going ashore. Here and there a military camp lost in a wilderness, like a needle in a bundle of hay—cold, fog, tempests, disease, exile, and death,—death skulking in the air, in the water, in the bush. They must have been dying like flies here. Oh, yes—he did it. Did it very well, too, no doubt, and without thinking much about it either, except afterwards to brag of what he had gone through in his time, perhaps. They were men enough to face the darkness. And perhaps he was cheered by keeping his eye on a chance of promotion to the fleet at Ravenna by and by, if he had good friends in Rome and survived the awful climate. Or think of a decent young citizen in a toga—perhaps too much dice, you know—coming out here in the train of some prefect, or tax-gatherer, or trader even, to mend his fortunes. Land in a swamp, march through the woods, and in some inland post feel the savagery, the utter savagery, had closed round him,—all that mysterious life of the wilderness that stirs in the forest, in the jungles, in the hearts of wild men. There's no initiation either into such mysteries. He has to live in the midst of the incomprehensible, which is also detestable. And it has a fascination, too, that goes to work upon him. The fascination of the abomination—you know, imagine the growing regrets, the longing to escape, the powerless disgust, the surrender, the hate."

He paused.

"Mind," he began again, lifting one arm from the elbow, the palm of the hand outwards, so that, with his legs folded before him, he had the pose of a Buddha preaching in European clothes and without a lotus-flower—"Mind, none of us would feel exactly like this. What saves us is efficiency—the devotion to efficiency. But these chaps were not much account, really. They were no colonists; their administration was merely a squeeze, and nothing more, I suspect. They were conquerors, and for that you want only brute force—nothing to boast of, when you have it, since your strength is just an accident arising from the weakness of others. They grabbed what they could get for the sake of what was to be got. It was just robbery with violence, aggravated murder on a great scale, and men going at it blind—as is very proper for those who tackle a darkness. The conquest of the earth, which mostly means the taking it away from those who have a different complexion or slightly flatter noses than ourselves, is not a pretty thing when you look into it too much. What redeems it is the idea only. An idea at the back of it; not a sentimental pretense but an idea; and an unselfish belief in the idea—something you can get set up, and bow down before, and offer a sacrifice to. . . ."

He broke off. Flames glided in the river, small green flames, red flames, white flames, pursuing, overtaking, joining, crossing each other—then separating slowly or hastily. The traffic of the great city went on in the deepening night upon the sleepless river. We looked on, waiting patiently—there was nothing else to do till the end of the flood; but it was only after a long silence, when he said, in a hesitating voice, "I suppose you fellows remember I did once turn fresh-water sailor for a bit," that we knew we were fated, before the ebb began to run, to hear one of Marlow's inconclusive experiences.

"I don't want to bother you much with what happened to me personally," he began, showing in this remark the weakness of many tellers of

[5] Galley with three banks of oars.

tales who seem so often unaware of what their audience would best like to hear; "yet to understand the effect of it on me you ought to know how I got out there, what I saw, how I went up that river to the place where I first met the poor chap. It was the farthest point of navigation and the culminating point of my experience. It seemed somehow to throw a kind of light on everything about me—and into my thoughts. It was somber enough, too—and pitiful—not extraordinary in any way—not very clear either. No, not very clear. And yet it seemed to throw a kind of light.

"I had then, as you remember, just returned to London after a lot of Indian Ocean, Pacific, China Seas—a regular dose of the East—six years or so, and I was loafing about, hindering you fellows in your work and invading your homes, just as though I had got a heavenly mission to civilize you. It was very fine for a time, but after a bit I did get tired of resting. Then I began to look for a ship—I should think the hardest work on earth. But the ships wouldn't even look at me. And I got tired of that game, too.

"Now when I was a little chap I had a passion for maps. I would look for hours at South America, or Africa, or Australia, and lose myself in all the glories of exploration. At that time there were many blank spaces on the earth, and when I saw one that looked particularly inviting on a map (but they all look that) I would put my finger on it and say, When I grow up I will go there. The North Pole was one of these places, I remember. Well, I haven't been there yet, and shall not try now. The glamour's off. Other places were scattered about the Equator, and in every sort of latitude all over the two hemispheres. I have been in some of them, and . . . well, we won't talk about that. But there was one yet—the biggest, the most blank, so to speak—that I had a hankering after.

"True, by this time it was not a blank space any more. It had got filled since my childhood with rivers and lakes and names. It had ceased to be a blank space of delightful mystery—a white patch for a boy to dream gloriously over. It had become a place of darkness. But there was in it one river especially, a mighty big river, that you could see on the map, resembling an immense snake uncoiled, with its head in the sea, its body at rest curving afar over a vast country, and its tail lost in the depths of the land. And as I looked at the map of it in a shop-window, it fascinated me as a snake could a bird—a silly little bird. Then I remembered there was a big concern, a Company for trade on that river. Dash it all! I thought to myself, they can't trade without using some kind of craft on that lot of fresh water—steamboats! Why shouldn't I try to get charge of one? I went on along Fleet Street, but could not shake off the idea. The snake had charmed me.

"You understand it was a Continental concern, that Trading society; but I have a lot of relations living on the Continent, because it's cheap and not so nasty as it looks, they say.

"I am sorry to own I began to worry them. This was already a fresh departure for me. I was not used to getting things that way, you know. I always went my own road and on my own legs where I had a mind to go. I wouldn't have believed it of myself; but, then—you see—I felt somehow I must get there by hook or by crook. So I worried them. The men said 'My dear fellow,' and did nothing. Then—would you believe it?—I tried the women. I, Charlie Marlow, set the women to work—to get a job. Heavens! Well, you see, the notion drove me. I had an aunt, a dear enthusiastic soul. She wrote: 'It will be delightful. I am ready to do anything, anything for you. It is a glorious idea. I know the wife of a very high personage in the Administration, and also a man who has lots of influence with,' etc., etc. She was determined to make no end of fuss to get me appointed skipper of a river steamboat, if such was my fancy.

"I got my appointment—of course; and I got it very quick. It appears the Company had received news that one of their captains had been killed in a scuffle with the natives. This was my chance, and it made me the more anxious to go. It was only months and months afterwards, when I made the attempt to recover what was left of the body, that I heard the original quarrel arose from a misunderstanding about some hens. Yes, two black hens. Fresleven—that was the fellow's name, a Dane—thought himself wronged somehow in the bargain, so he went ashore and started to hammer the chief of the village with a stick. Oh, it didn't surprise me in the least to hear this, and at the same time to be told that Fresleven was the gentlest, quietest creature that ever walked on two legs. No doubt he was; but he had been a couple of years already out there engaged in the noble cause, you know, and he probably felt the need at last of asserting his self-respect in some way. Therefore he whacked the old nigger mercilessly, while a big crowd of his people watched him, thunderstruck, till some man—I was told the chief's son—in desperation at hearing the old chap yell, made a tentative jab with a spear at the white man—and of course it went quite easy between the shoulderblades. Then the whole population cleared into the forest, expecting all kinds of calamities to happen, while, on the other hand, the steamer Fresleven commanded left also in a bad panic, in charge of the engineer, I believe. Afterwards nobody seemed to trouble much about Fresleven's remains, till I got out and stepped into his shoes. I couldn't let it rest, though; but when an opportunity offered at last to meet my predecessor, the grass growing through his ribs was tall enough to hide his bones. They were all there. The supernatural being had not been touched after he fell. And the village was deserted, the huts gaped black, rotting, all askew within the fallen enclosures. A calamity had come to it, sure enough. The people had vanished. Mad terror had scattered them, men, women, and children, through the bush, and they had never returned. What became of the hens I don't know either. I should think the cause of progress got them, anyhow. However, through this glorious affair I got my appointment, before I had fairly begun to hope for it.

"I flew around like mad to get ready, and before forty-eight hours I was crossing the Channel to show myself to my employers, and sign the contract. In a very few hours I arrived in a city that always makes me think of a whited sepulchre. Prejudice no doubt. I had no difficulty in finding the Company's offices. It was the biggest thing in the town, and everybody I met was full of it. They were going to run an over-sea empire, and make no end of coin by trade.

"A narrow and deserted street in deep shadow, high houses, innumerable windows with venetian blinds, a dead silence, grass sprouting between the stones, imposing carriage archways right and left, immense double doors standing ponderously ajar. I slipped through one of these cracks, went up a swept and ungarnished staircase, as arid as a desert, and opened the first door I came to. Two women, one fat and the other slim, sat on straw-bottomed chairs, knitting black wool. The slim one got up and walked straight at me—still knitting with down-cast eyes—and only just as I began to think of getting out of her way, as you would for a somnambulist, stood still, and looked up. Her dress was as plain as an umbrella-cover, and she turned round without a word and preceded me into a waiting-room. I gave my name, and looked about. Deal table in the middle, plain chairs all round the walls, on one end a large shining map, marked with all the colors of a rainbow. There was a vast amount of red—good to see at any time, because one knows that some real work is done in there, a deuce of a lot of blue, a little green, smears of orange, and, on the East Coast, a purple patch, to show where the jolly pioneers of progress drink the jolly lager-beer. However, I wasn't going into any of these. I was going into the yellow. Dead in the center. And the river was there—fascinating—deadly—like a snake. Ough! A door opened, a white-haired secretarial head, but wearing a compassionate expression, appeared, and a skinny forefinger beckoned me into the sanctuary. Its light was dim, and a heavy writing-desk squatted in the middle. From behind that structure came out an impression of pale plumpness in a frock-coat. The great man himself. He was five feet six, I should judge, and had his grip on the handle-end of ever so many millions. He shook hands, I fancy, murmured vaguely, was satisfied with my French. *Bon voyage.*

"In about forty-five seconds I found myself again in the waiting-room with the compassionate secretary, who, full of desolation and sympathy, made me sign some document. I believe I undertook amongst other things not to disclose any trade secrets. Well, I am not going to.

"I began to feel slightly uneasy. You know I am not used to such ceremonies, and there was something ominous in the atmosphere. It was just as though I had been let into some conspiracy—I don't know—something not quite right; and I was glad to get out. In the outer room the two women knitted black wool feverishly. People were arriving, and the younger one was walking back and forth introducing them. The old one sat on her chair. Her flat cloth slippers were propped up on a foot-warmer, and a cat reposed on her lap. She wore a starched white affair on her head, had a wart on one cheek, and silver-rimmed spectacles hung on the tip of her nose. She glanced at me above the glasses. The swift and indifferent placidity of that look troubled me. Two youths with foolish and cheery countenances were being piloted over, and she threw at them the same quick glance of unconcerned wisdom. She seemed to know all about them and about me, too. An eerie feeling came over me. She seemed uncanny and fateful. Often far away there I thought of these two, guarding the door of Darkness, knitting black wool as for a warm pall, one introducing, introducing continuously to the unknown, the other scrutinizing the cheery and foolish faces with unconcerned old eyes. *Ave!* Old knitter of black wool. *Morituri te salutant.*[6] Not many of those she looked at ever saw her again—not half, by a long way.

"There was yet a visit to the doctor. 'A simple formality,' assured me the secretary, with an air of taking an immense part in all my sorrows. Accordingly, a young chap wearing his hat over the left eyebrow, some clerk I suppose,—there must have been clerks in the business, though the house was as still as a house in a city of the dead—came from somewhere upstairs, and led me forth. He was shabby and careless, with inkstains on the sleeves of his jacket, and his cravat was large and billowy, under a chin shaped like the toe of an old boot. It was a little too early for the doctor, so I proposed a drink, and thereupon he developed a vein of joviality. As we sat over our vermouths he glorified the Company's business, and by and by I expressed casually my surprise at him not going out there. He became very cool and collected all at once. 'I am not such as fool as I look, quoth Plato to his disciples,' he said sententiously, emptied his glass with great resolution, and we rose.

"The old doctor felt my pulse, evidently thinking of something else the while. 'Good, good for there,' he mumbled, and then with a certain eagerness asked me whether I would let him measure my head. Rather surprised, I said Yes, when he produced a thing like calipers and got the dimensions back and front and every way, taking notes carefully. He was an unshaven little man in a threadbare coat like a gaberdine, with his feet in slippers, and I thought him a harmless fool. 'I always ask leave, in the interests of science, to measure the crania of those going out there,' he said. 'And when they come back, too?' I asked. 'Oh, I never see them,' he remarked; 'and, moreover, the changes take place inside, you know.' He smiled, as if at some quiet joke. 'So you are going out there. Famous. Interesting, too.' He gave me a searching glance, and made another note. 'Ever any madness in your family?' he asked, in a matter-of-fact tone. I felt very annoyed. 'Is that question in the interests of science, too?' 'It would be,' he said, without taking notice of my irritation, 'interesting for science to watch the mental changes of individuals, on the spot, but . . .' 'Are you an alienist?' I interrupted. 'Every doctor should be—a little,' answered that original, imperturbably. 'I have a little theory which you Messieurs who go out there must help me to prove. This is my share in the advantages my country shall reap from the possession of such a magnificent dependency. The mere wealth I leave to others. Pardon my questions, but you are the first Englishman coming under my observation. . . .' I hastened to assure him I was not in the least typical. 'If I were,' said I, 'I wouldn't be talking like this with you.' 'What you say is rather profound, and probably erroneous,' he said, with a laugh. 'Avoid irritation more than exposure to the sun. Adieu. How do you English say, eh? Good-bye. Ah! Good-bye. Adieu. In the tropics one must before everything keep calm.' . . . He lifted a warning forefinger. . . . *'Du calme, du calme. Adieu.'*[7]

"One thing more remained to do—say goodbye to my excellent aunt. I found her triumphant. I had a cup of tea—the last decent cup of tea for many days—and in a room that most soothingly looked just as you would expect a lady's drawing-room to look, we had a long quiet chat by the fireside. In the course of these confidences it became quite plain to me I had been represented to the wife of the high dignitary, and goodness knows to how many more people besides, as an exceptional and gifted creature—a piece of good fortune for the Company—a man you don't get hold of every day.

[6] "Those who are about to die salute you," the words with which gladiators in the ring greeted the Emperor.

[7] "Calm, take it easy. Good-bye."

Good heavens! and I was going to take charge of a two-penny-half-penny river-steamboat with a penny whistle attached! It appeared, however, I was also one of the Workers, with a capital—you know. Something like an emissary of light, something like a lower sort of apostle. There had been a lot of such rot let loose in print and talk just about that time, and the excellent woman, living right in the rush of all that humbug, got carried off her feet. She talked about 'weaning those ignorant millions from their horrid ways,' till, upon my word, she made me quite uncomfortable. I ventured to hint that the Company was run for profit.

" 'You forget, dear Charlie, that the labourer is worthy of his hire,' she said, brightly. It's queer how out of touch with truth women are. They live in a world of their own, and there has never been anything like it, and never can be. It is too beautiful altogether, and if they were to set it up it would go to pieces before the first sunset. Some confounded fact we men have been living contentedly with ever since the day of creation would start up and knock the whole thing over.

"After this I got embraced, told to wear flannel, be sure to write often, and so on—and I left. In the street—I don't know why—a queer feeling came to me that I was an imposter. Odd thing that I, who used to clear out for any part of the world at twenty-four hours' notice, with less thought than most men give to the crossing of a street, had a moment—I won't say of hesitation, but of startled pause, before this commonplace affair. The best way I can explain it to you is by saying that, for a second or two, I felt as though, instead of going to the center of a continent, I were about to set off for the center of the earth.

"I left in a French steamer, and she called in every blamed port they have out there, for, as far as I could see, the sole purpose of landing soldiers and custom-house officers. I watched the coast. Watching a coast as it slips by the ship is like thinking about an enigma. There it is before you—smiling, frowning, inviting, grand, mean, insipid, or savage, and always mute with an air of whispering, Come and find out. This one was almost featureless, as if still in the making, with an aspect of monotonous grimness. The edge of a colossal jungle, so dark-green as to be almost black, fringed with white surf, ran straight, like a ruled line, far, far away along a blue sea whose glitter was blurred by a creeping mist. The sun was fierce, the land seemed to glisten and drip with steam. Here and there grayish-whitish specks showed up clustered inside the white surf, with a flag flying above them perhaps. Settlements some centuries old, and still no bigger than pinheads on the untouched expanse of their background. We pounded along, stopped, landed soldiers; went on, landed custom-house clerks to levy toll in what looked like a God-forsaken wilderness, with a tin shed and a flag-pole lost in it; landed more soldiers—to take care of the custom-house clerks, presumably. Some, I heard, got drowned in the surf; but whether they did or not, nobody seemed particularly to care. They were just flung out there, and on we went. Every day the coast looked the same, as though we had not moved; but we passed various places—trading places—with names like Gran' Bassam, Little Popo; names that seemed to belong to some sordid farce acted in front of a sinister backcloth. The idleness of a passenger, my isolation amongst all these men with whom I had no point of contact, the oily and languid sea, the uniform somberness of the coast, seemed to keep me away from the truth of things, within the toil of a mournful and senseless delusion. The voice of the surf heard now and then was a positive pleasure, like the speech of a brother. It was something natural, that had its reason, that had a meaning. Now and then a boat from the shore gave one a momentary contact with reality. It was paddled by black fellows. You could see from afar the white of their eyeballs glistening. They shouted, sang; their bodies streamed with perspiration; they had faces like grotesque masks—these chaps; but they had bone, muscle, a wild vitality, an intense energy of movement, that was as natural and true as the surf along their coast. They wanted no excuse for being there. They were a great comfort to look at. For a time I would feel I belonged still to a world of straightforward facts; but the feeling would not last long. Something would turn up to scare it away. Once, I remember, we came upon a man-of-war anchored off the coast. There wasn't even a shed there, and she was shelling the bush. It appears the French had one of their wars going on thereabouts. Her ensign dropped limp like a rag; the muzzles of the long six-inch guns stuck out all over the low hull; the greasy, slimy swell swung her up lazily and let her down, swaying her thin masts. In the empty immensity of earth, sky, and water, there she was, incomprehensible, firing into a continent. Pop, would go one of the six-inch guns; a small flame would dart and vanish, a little white smoke would disappear, a tiny projectile would give a feeble screech—and nothing happened. Nothing could happen. There was a touch of insanity in the proceeding, a sense of lugubrious drollery in the sight; and it was not dissipated by somebody on board assuring me earnestly there was a camp of natives—he called them enemies!—hidden out of sight somewhere.

"We gave her her letters (I heard the men in that lonely ship were dying of fever at the rate of three a day) and went on. We called at some more places with farcical names, where the merry dance of death and trade goes on in a still and earthy atmosphere as of an overheated catacomb; all along the formless coast bordered by dangerous surf, as if Nature herself had tried to ward off intruders; in and out of rivers, streams of death in life whose banks were rotting into mud, whose waters, thickened into slime, invaded the contorted mangroves, that seemed to writhe at us in the extremity of an impotent despair. Nowhere did we stop long enough to get a particularized impression, but the general sense of vague and oppressive wonder grew upon me. It was like a weary pilgrimage amongst hints for nightmares.

"It was upward of thirty days before I saw the mouth of the big river. We anchored off the seat of the government. But my work would not begin till some two hundred miles farther on. So as soon as I could I made a start for a place thirty miles higher up.

"I had my passage on a little sea-going steamer. Her captain was a Swede, and knowing me for a seaman, invited me on the bridge. He was a young man, lean, fair, and morose, with lanky hair and a shuffling gait. As we left the miserable little wharf, he tossed his head contemptuously at the shore. 'Been living there?' he asked. I said, 'Yes.' 'Fine lot these government chaps—are they not?' he went on, speaking English with great precision and considerable bitterness. 'It is funny what some people will do for a few francs a month. I wonder what becomes of that kind when it goes up country?' I said to him I expected to see that soon. 'So-o-o!' he exclaimed. He shuffled athwart, keeping one eye ahead vigilantly. 'Don't be too sure,' he continued. 'The other day I took up a man who hanged himself on the road. He was a Swede, too.' 'Hanged himself! Why, in God's name?' I cried. He kept on looking out watchfully. 'Who knows? The sun was too much for him, or the country perhaps.'

"At last we opened a reach. A rocky cliff appeared, mounds of turned-up earth by the shore, houses on a hill, others with iron roofs, amongst a waste of excavations, or hanging to the declivity. A continuous noise of the rapids above hovered over his scene of inhabited devastation. A lot of people, mostly black and naked, moved about like ants. A jetty projected into the river. A blinding sunlight drowned all this at times in a sudden recrudescence of glare. 'There's your Company's station,' said the Swede, pointing to three wooden barrack-like structures on the rocky slope. 'I will send your things up. Four boxes did you say? So. Farewell.'

"I came upon a boiler wallowing in the grass, then found a path leading up the hill. It turned aside for the boulders, and also for an undersized railway-truck lying there on its back with its wheels in the air. One was off. The thing looked as dead as the carcass of some animal. I came upon more pieces of decaying machinery, a stack of rusty rails. To the left a clump of trees made a shady spot, where dark things seemed to stir feebly. I blinked, the path was steep. A horn tooted to the right, and I saw the black people run. A heavy and dull detonation shook the ground, a puff of smoke came out of the cliff, and that was all. No change appeared on the face of the rock. They were building a railway. The cliff was not in the way of anything; but this objectless blasting was all the work going on.

"A slight clinking behind me made me turn my head. Six black men advanced in a file, toiling up the path. They walked erect and slow, balancing small baskets full of earth on their heads, and the clink kept time with their footsteps. Black rags were wound round their loins, and the short ends behind waggled to and fro like tails. I could see every rib, the joints of their limbs were like knots in a rope; each had an iron collar on his neck, and all were connected together with a chain whose bights swung between them, rhythmically clinking. Another report from the cliff made me think suddenly of that ship of war I had seen firing into a continent. It was the same kind of ominous voices; but these men could by no stretch of imagination be called enemies. They were called criminals, and the outraged law, like the bursting shells, had come to them, an insoluble mystery from the sea. All their meager breasts panted together, the violently dilated nostrils quivered, the eyes stared stonily up-hill. They passed me within six inches, without a glance, with that complete, deathlike indifference of unhappy savages. Behind this raw matter one of the reclaimed, the product of the new forces at work, strolled despondently, carrying a rifle by its middle. He had a uniform jacket with one button off, and seeing a white man on the path, hoisted his weapon to his shoulder with alacrity. This was simple prudence, white men being so much alike at a distance that he could not tell who I might be. He was speedily reassured, and with a large, white, rascally grin, and a glance at his charge, seemed to take me into partnership in his exalted trust. After all, I also was a part of the great cause of these high and just proceedings.

"Instead of going up, I turned and descended to the left. My idea was to let that chain-gang get out of sight before I climbed the hill. You know I am not particularly tender; I've had to strike and to fend off. I've had to resist and to attack sometimes—that's only one way of resisting—without counting the exact cost, according to the demands of such sort of life as I had blundered into. I've seen the devil of violence, and the devil of greed, and the devil of hot desire; but by all the stars! these were strong, lusty, red-eyed devils, that swayed and drove men—men, I tell you. But as I stood on this hillside, I foresaw that in the blinding sunshine of that land I would become acquainted with a flabby, pretending, weak-eyed devil of a rapacious and pitiless folly. How insidious he could be, too, I was only to find out several months later and a thousand miles farther. For a moment I stood appalled, as though by a warning. Finally I descended the hill, obliquely, towards the trees I had seen.

"I avoided a vast artificial hole somebody had been digging on the slope, the purpose of which I found it impossible to divine. It wasn't a quarry or a sandpit anyhow. It was just a hole. It might have been connected with the philanthropic desire of giving the criminals something to do. I don't know. Then I nearly fell into a very narrow ravine, almost no more than a scar in the hillside. I discovered that a lot of imported drainage-pipes for the settlement had been tumbled in there. There wasn't one that was not broken. It was a wanton smash-up. At last I got under the trees. My purpose was to stroll into the shade for a moment; but no sooner within than it seemed to me I had stepped into the gloomy circle of some Inferno. The rapids were near, and an uninterrupted, uniform, headlong, rushing noise filled the mournful stillness of the grove, where not a breath stirred, not a leaf moved, with a mysterious sound—as though the tearing pace of the launched earth had suddenly become audible.

"Black shapes crouched, lay, sat between the trees, leaning against the trunks, clinging to the earth, half coming out, half effaced within the dim light, in all the attitudes of pain, abandonment, and despair. Another mine on the cliff went off, followed by a slight shudder of the soil under my feet. The work was going on. The work! And this was the place where some of the helpers had withdrawn to die.

"They were dying slowly—it was very clear. They were not enemies, they were not criminals, they were nothing earthly now,—nothing but black shadows of disease and starvation, lying confusedly in the greenish gloom. Brought from all the recesses of the coast in all the legality of time contracts, lost in uncongenial surroundings, fed on unfamiliar food, they sickened, became inefficient, and were then allowed to crawl away and rest. These moribund shapes were free as air—and nearly as thin. I began to distinguish the gleam of the eyes under the trees. Then, glancing down, I saw a face near my hand. The black bones reclined at full length with one shoulder against the tree, and slowly the eyelids rose and the sunken eyes looked up at me, enormous and vacant, a kind of blind, white flicker in the depths of the orbs, which died out slowly. The man seemed young—almost a boy—but you know with them it's hard to tell. I found nothing else to do but to offer him one of my good Swede's ship's biscuits I had in my pocket. The fingers closed slowly on it and held—there was no other movement and no other glance. He had tied a bit of white worsted round his neck—Why? Where did he get it? Was it a badge—an ornament—a charm—a propitiatory act? Was there any idea at all connected with it? It looked startling round his black neck, this bit of white thread from beyond the seas.

"Near the same tree two more bundles of acute angles sat with their legs drawn up. One, with his chin propped on his knees, stared at nothing, in an intolerable and appalling manner: his brother phantom rested its forehead, as if overcome with a great weariness; and all about others were scattered in every pose of contorted collapse, as in some picture of a massacre or a pestilence. While I stood horror-struck, one of these creatures rose to his hands and knees, and went off on all-fours towards the river to drink. He lapped out of his hand, then sat up in the sunlight, crossing his shins in front of him, and after a time let his wooly head fall on his breastbone.

"I didn't want any more loitering in the shade, and I made haste towards the station. When near the buildings I met a white man, in such an unexpected elegance of get-up that in the first moment I took him for a sort of vision. I saw a high starched collar, white cuffs, a light alpaca jacket, snowy trousers, a clean necktie, and varnished boots. No hat. Hair parted, brushed, oiled, under a green-lined parasol held in a big white hand. He was amazing, and had a penholder behind his ear.

"I shook hands with this miracle, and I learned he was the Company's chief accountant, and that all the book-keeping was done at this station. He had come out for a moment, he said, 'to get a breath of fresh air.' The expression sounded wonderfully odd, with its suggestion of sedentary desk-life. I wouldn't have mentioned the fellow to you at all, only it was from his lips that I first heard the name of the man who is so indissolubly connected with the memories of that time. Moreover, I respected the fellow. Yes; I respected his collars, his vast cuffs, his brushed hair. His appearance was certainly that of a hairdresser's dummy; but in the great demoralization of the land he kept up his appearance. That's backbone. His starched collars and got-up shirt-fronts were achievements of character. He had been out nearly three years; and, later, I could not help asking him how he managed to sport such linen. He had just the faintest blush, and said modestly, 'I've been teaching one of the native women about the station. It was difficult. She had a distaste for the work.' Thus this man had verily accomplished something. And he was devoted to his books, which were in apple-pie order.

"Everything else in the station was in a muddle,—heads, things, buildings. Strings of dusty niggers with splay feet arrived and departed; a stream of manufactured goods, rubbishy cottons, beads, and brass-wire set into the depths of darkness, and in return came a precious trickle of ivory.

"I had to wait in the station for ten days—an eternity. I lived in a hut in the yard, but to be out of the chaos I would sometimes get into the accountant's office. It was built of horizontal planks, and so badly put together that, as he bent over his high desk, he was barred from neck to heels with narrow strips of sunlight. There was no need to open the big shutter to see. It was hot there, too; big flies buzzed fiendishly, and did not sting, but stabbed. I sat generally on the floor, while, of faultless appearance (and even slightly scented), perching on a high stool, he wrote, he wrote. Sometimes he stood up for exercise. When a trucklebed with a sick man (some invalid agent from up-country) was put in there, he exhibited a gentle annoyance. 'The groans of this sick person,' he said, 'distract my attention. And without that it is extremely difficult to guard against clerical errors in this climate.'

"One day he remarked, without lifting his head, 'In the interior you will no doubt meet Mr. Kurtz.' On my asking who Mr. Kurtz was, he said he was a first-class agent; and seeing my disappointment at this information, he added slowly, laying down his pen, 'He is a very remarkable person.' Further questions elicited from him that Mr. Kurtz was at present in charge of a trading post, a very important one, in the true ivory-country, at 'the very bottom of there. Sends in as much ivory as all the others put together . . .' He began to write again. The sick man was too ill to groan. The flies buzzed in a great peace.

"Suddenly there was a growing murmur of voices and a great tramping of feet. A caravan had come in. A violent babble of uncouth sounds burst out on the other side of the planks. All the carriers were speaking together, and in the midst of the uproar the lamentable voice of the chief agent was heard 'giving it up' tearfully for the twentieth time that day. . . . He rose slowly. 'What a frightful row,' he said. He crossed the room gently to look at the sick man, and returning, said to me, 'He does not hear.' 'What! Dead?' I asked, startled. 'No, not yet,' he answered, with great composure. Then, alluding with a toss of the head to the tumult in the station-yard, 'When one has got to make correct entries, one comes to hate those savages —hate them to the death.' He remained thoughtful for a moment. 'When you see Mr. Kurtz,' he went on, 'tell him for me that everything here' —he glanced at the desk—'is very satisfactory. I don't like to write to him—with those messengers of ours you never know who may get hold of your letter—at that Central Station.' He stared at me for a moment with his mild, bulging eyes. 'Oh, he will go far, very far,' he began again. 'He will be a somebody in the Administration before long. They, above—the Council in Europe, you know—mean him to be.'

"He turned to his work. The noise outside had ceased, and presently in going out I stopped at the door. In the steady buzz of flies the homeward-bound agent was lying flushed and insensible; the other, bent over his books, was making correct entries of perfectly correct transactions; and fifty feet below the doorstep I could see the still tree-tops of the grove of death.

"Next day I left that station at last, with a caravan of sixty men, for a two hundred-mile tramp.

"No use telling you much about that. Paths, paths, everywhere; a stamped-in network of paths spreading over the empty land, through long grass, through burnt grass, through thickets, down and up chilly ravines, up and down stony hills ablaze with heat; and a solitude, a solitude, nobody, not a hut. The population had cleared out a long time ago. Well, if a lot of mysterious niggers armed with all kinds of fearful weapons suddenly took to traveling on the road between Deal and Gravesend, catching the yokels right and left to carry heavy loads for them, I fancy every farm and cottage thereabouts would get empty very soon. Only here the dwellings were gone, too. Still I passed through several abandoned villages. There's something pathetically childish in the ruins of grass walls. Day after day, with the stamp and shuffle of sixty pair of bare feet behind me, each pair under a sixty-lb. load. Camp, cook, sleep, strike camp, march. Now and then a carrier dead in harness, at rest in the long grass near the path, with an empty water-gourd and his long staff lying by his side. A great silence around and above. Perhaps on some quiet night the tremor of far-off drums, sinking, swelling, a tremor vast, faint; a sound weird, appealing, suggestive, and wild—and perhaps with as profound a meaning as the sound of bells in a Christian country. Once a white man in an unbuttoned uniform, camping on the path with an armed escort of lank Zanzibaris, very hospitable and festive—not to say drunk. Was looking after the upkeep of the road, he declared. Can't say I saw any road or any upkeep, unless the body of a middle-aged negro, with a bullet-hole in the forehead, upon which I absolutely stumbled three miles farther on, may be considered as a permanent improvement. I had a white companion, too, not a bad chap, but rather too fleshy and with the exasperating habit of fainting on the hot hillsides, miles away from the least bit of shade and water. Annoying, you know, to hold your own coat like a parasol over a man's head while he is coming-to. I couldn't help asking him once what he meant by coming there at all. 'To make money, of course. What do you think?' he said, scornfully. Then he got fever, and had to be carried in a hammock slung under a pole. As he weighed sixteen stone[8] I had no end of rows with the carriers. They jibbed,[9] ran away, sneaked off with their loads in the night—quite a mutiny. So, one evening, I made a speech in English with gestures, not one of which was lost to the sixty pairs of eyes before me, and the next morning I started the hammock off in front all right. An hour afterwards I came upon the whole concern wrecked in a bush—man, hammock, groans, blankets, horrors. The heavy pole had skinned his poor nose. He was very anxious for me to kill somebody, but there wasn't the shadow of a carrier near. I remembered the old doctor— 'It would be interesting for science to watch the mental changes of individuals, on the spot.' I felt I was becoming scientifically interesting. However, all that is to no purpose. On the fif-

[8] An official British unit equal to fourteen pounds; hence the dead man weighed 224 pounds.

[9] Refused to go farther.

teenth day I came in sight of the big river again, and hobbled into the Central Station. It was on a back water surrounded by scrub and forest, with a pretty border of smelly mud on one side, and on the three others enclosed by a crazy fence of rushes. A neglected gap was all the gate it had, and the first glance at the place was enough to let you see the flabby devil was running that show. White men with long staves in their hands appeared languidly from amongst the buildings, strolling up to take a look at me, and then retired out of sight somewhere. One of them, a stout, excitable chap with black mustaches, informed me with great volubility and many digressions, as soon as I told him who I was, that my steamer was at the bottom of the river. I was thunderstruck. What, how, why? Oh, it was 'all right.' The 'manager himself' was there. All quite correct. 'Everybody had behaved splendidly! splendidly!'—'you must,' he said in agitation, 'go and see the general manager at once. He is waiting!'

"I did not see the real significance of that wreck at once. I fancy I see it now, but I am not sure—not at all. Certainly the affair was too stupid—when I think of it—to be altogether natural. Still . . . But at the moment it presented itself simply as a confounded nuisance. The steamer was sunk. They had started two days before in a sudden hurry up the river with the manager on board, in charge of some volunteer skipper, and before they had been out three hours they tore the bottom out of her on stones, and she sank near the south bank. I asked myself what I was to do there, now my boat was lost. As a matter of fact, I had plenty to do in fishing my command out of the river. I had to set about it the very next day. That, and the repairs when I brought the pieces to the station, took some months.

"My first interview with the manager was curious. He did not ask me to sit down after my twenty-mile walk that morning. He was commonplace in complexion, in feature, in manners, and in voice. He was of middle size and of ordinary build. His eyes, of the usual blue, were perhaps remarkably cold, and he certainly could make his glance fall on one as trenchant and heavy as an ax. But even at these times the rest of his person seemed to disclaim the intention. Otherwise there was only an indefinable, faint expression of his lips, something stealthy—a smile—not a smile—I remember it, but I can't explain. It was unconscious, this smile was, though just after he had said something it got intensified for an instant. It came at the end of his speeches like a seal applied on the words to make the meaning of the commonest phrase appear absolutely inscrutable. He was a common trader, from his youth up employed in these parts—nothing more. He was obeyed, yet he inspired neither love nor fear, nor even respect. He inspired uneasiness. That was it! Uneasiness. Not a definite mistrust—just uneasiness—nothing more. You have no idea how effective such a . . . a . . . faculty can be. He had no genius for organizing, for initiative, or for order even. That was evident in such things as the deplorable state of the station. He had no learning, and no intelligence. His position had come to him—why? Perhaps because he was never ill. . . . He had served three terms of three years out there. . . . Because triumphant health in the general rout of constitutions is a kind of power in itself. When he went home on leave he rioted on a large scale—pompously. Jack ashore —with a difference—in externals only. This one could gather from his casual talk. He originated nothing, he could keep the routine going—that's all. But he was great. He was great by this little thing that it was impossible to tell what could control such a man. He never gave that secret away. Perhaps there was nothing within him. Such a suspicion made one pause—for out there there were no external checks. Once when various tropical diseases had laid low almost every 'agent' in the station, he was heard to say, 'Men who come out here should have no entrails.' He sealed the utterance with that smile of his, as though it had been a door opening into a darkness he had in his keeping. You fancied you had seen things—but the seal was on. When annoyed at meal-times by the constant quarrels of the white men about precedence, he ordered an immense round table to be made, for which a special house had to be built. This was the station's mess-room. Where he sat was the first place—the rest were nowhere. One felt this to be his unalterable conviction. He was neither civil nor uncivil. He was quiet. He allowed his 'boy'—an overfed young negro from the coast—to treat the white men, under his very eyes, with provoking insolence.

"He began to speak as soon as he saw me.

I had been very long on the road. He could not wait. Had to start without me. The up-river stations had to be relieved. There had been so many delays already that he did not know who was dead and who was alive, and how they got on—and so on, and so on. He paid no attention to my explanations, and, playing with a stick of sealing-wax, repeated several times that the situation was 'very grave, very grave.' There were rumors that a very important station was in jeopardy, and its chief, Mr. Kurtz, was ill. Hoped it was not true. Mr. Kurtz was . . . I felt weary and irritable. Hang Kurtz, I thought. I interrupted him by saying I had heard of Mr. Kurtz on the coast. 'Ah! So they talk of him down there,' he murmured to himself. Then he began again, assuring me Mr. Kurtz was the best agent he had, an exceptional man, of the greatest importance to the Company; therefore I could understand his anxiety. He was, he said, 'very, very uneasy.' Certainly he fidgeted on his chair a good deal, exclaimed, 'Ah, Mr. Kurtz!' broke the stick of sealing-wax and seemed dumfounded by the accident. Next thing he wanted to know 'how long it would take to' . . . I interrupted him again. Being hungry, you know, and kept on my feet too, I was getting savage. 'How can I tell?' I said. 'I haven't even seen the wreck yet—some months, no doubt.' All this talk seemed to me so futile. 'Some months,' he said. 'Well, let us say three months before we can make a start. Yes. That ought to do the affair.' I flung out of his hut (he lived all alone in a clay hut with a sort of veranda) muttering to myself my opinion of him. He was a chattering idiot. Afterwards I took it back when it was borne in upon me startlingly with what extreme nicety he had estimated the time requisite for the 'affair.'

"I went to work the next day, turning, so to speak, my back on that station. In that way only it seemed to me I could keep my hold on the redeeming facts of life. Still, one must look about sometimes; and then I saw this station, these men strolling aimlessly about in the sunshine of the yard. I asked myself sometimes what it all meant. They wandered here and there with their absurd long staves in their hands, like a lot of faithless pilgrims bewitched inside a rotten fence. The word 'ivory' rang in the air, was whispered, was sighed. You would think they were praying to it. A taint of imbecile rapacity blew through it all, like a whiff from some corpse. By Jove! I've never seen anything so unreal in my life. And outside, the silent wilderness surrounding this cleared speck on the earth struck me as something great and invincible, like evil or truth, waiting patiently for the passing away of this fantastic invasion.

"Oh, these months! Well, never mind. Various things happened. One evening a grass shed full of calico, cotton prints, beads, and I don't know what else, burst into a blaze so suddenly that you would have thought the earth had opened to let an avenging fire consume all that trash. I was smoking my pipe quietly by my dismantled steamer, and saw them all cutting capers in the light, with their arms lifted high, when the stout man with mustaches came tearing down to the river, a tin pail in his hand, assured me that everybody was 'behaving splendidly, splendidly,' dipped about a quart of water and tore back again. I noticed there was a hole in the bottom of his pail.

"I strolled up. There was no hurry. You see the thing had gone off like a box of matches. It had been hopeless from the very first. The flame had leaped high, driven everybody back, lighted up everything—and collapsed. The shed was already a heap of embers glowing fiercely. A nigger was being beaten near by. They said he had caused the fire in some way; be that as it may, he was screeching most horribly. I saw him, later, for several days, sitting in a bit of shade looking very sick and trying to recover himself: afterwards he arose and went out—and the wilderness without a sound took him into its bosom again. As I approached the glow from the dark I found myself at the back of two men, talking. I heard the name of Kurtz pronounced, then the words, 'take advantage of this unfortunate accident.' One of the men was the manager. I wished him a good evening. 'Did you ever see anything like it—eh? it is incredible,' he said, and walked off. The other man remained. He was a first-class agent, young, gentlemanly, a bit reserved, with a forked little beard and a hooked nose. He was standoffish with the other agents, and they on their side said he was the manager's spy upon them. As to me, I had hardly ever spoken to him before. We got into talk, and by and by we strolled away from the hissing ruins. Then he asked me to his room, which was in the main building of the station. He struck a match, and I perceived that this young aristocrat had not only a silver-mounted dressing-case but also a whole candle all to himself. Just at that time the manager was the only man supposed to have any right to candles. Native mats covered the clay walls; a collection of spears, assegais, shields, knives was hung up in trophies. The business intrusted to this fellow was the making of bricks—so I had been informed; but there wasn't a fragment of a brick anywhere in the station, and he had been there more than a year—waiting. It seems he could not make bricks without something, I don't know what—straw, maybe. Anyway, it could not be found there, and as it was not likely to be sent from Europe, it did not appear clear to me what he was waiting for. An act of special creation perhaps. However, they were all waiting—all the sixteen or twenty pilgrims of them —for something; and upon my word it did not seem an uncongenial occupation, from the way they took it, though the only thing that ever came to them was disease—as far as I could see. They beguiled the time by backbiting and intriguing against each other in a foolish kind of way. There was an air of plotting about that station, but nothing came of it, of course. It was as unreal as everything else—as the philanthropic pretense of the whole concern, as their talk, as their government, as their show of work. The only real feeling was a desire to get appointed to a trading-post where ivory was to be had, so that they could earn percentages. They intrigued and slandered and hated each other only on that account,—but as to effectually lifting a little finger—oh, no. By heavens! There is something after all in the world allowing one man to steal a horse while another must not look at a halter. Steal a horse straight out. Very well. He has done it. Perhaps he can ride. But there is a way of looking at a halter that would provoke the most charitable of saints into a kick.

"I had no idea why he wanted to be sociable, but as we chatted in there it suddenly occurred to me the fellow was trying to get at something —in fact, pumping me. He alluded constantly to Europe, to the people I was supposed to know there—putting leading questions as to my acquaintances in the sepulchral city, and so on. His little eyes glittered like mica discs—with curiosity—though he tried to keep up a bit of superciliousness. At first I was astonished, but very soon I became awfully curious to see what he would find out from me. I couldn't possibly imagine what I had in me to make it worth his while. It was very pretty to see how he baffled himself, for in truth my body was full only of chills, and my head had nothing in it but that wretched steamboat business. It was evident he took me for a perfectly shameless prevaricator. At last he got angry, and, to conceal a movement of furious annoyance, he yawned. I rose. Then I noticed a small sketch in oils, on a panel, representing a woman, draped and blindfolded, carrying a lighted torch. The background was somber—almost black. The movement of the woman was stately, and the effect of the torchlight on the face was sinister.

"It arrested me, and he stood by civilly, holding an empty half-pint champagne bottle (medical comforts) with the candle stuck in it. To my question he said Mr. Kurtz had painted this—in this very station more than a year ago—while waiting for means to go to his trading-post. 'Tell me, pray,' said I, 'who is this Mr. Kurtz?'

" 'The chief of the Inner Station,' he answered in a short tone, looking away. 'Much obliged,' I said, laughing. 'And you are the brickmaker of the Central Station. Everyone knows that.' He was silent for a while. 'He is a prodigy,' he said at last. 'He is an emissary of pity, and science, and progress, and devil knows what else. We want,' he began to declaim suddenly, 'for the guidance of the cause intrusted to us by Europe, so to speak, higher intelligence, wide sympathies, a singleness of purpose.' 'Who says that?' I asked. 'Lots of them,' he replied. 'Some even write that; and so *he* comes here, a special being, as you ought to know.' 'Why ought I to know?' I interrupted, really surprised. He paid no attention. 'Yes. To-day he is chief of the best station, next year he will be assistant-manager, two years more and . . . but I daresay you know what he will be in two years' time. You are of the new gang—the gang of virtue. The same people who sent him specially also recommended you. Oh, don't say no. I've my own eyes to trust.' Light dawned upon me. My dear aunt's influential acquaintances were producing an unexpected effect upon that young man. I nearly burst into a laugh. 'Do you read the Company's confidential correspondence?' I asked. He hadn't a word to say. It was great fun. 'When Mr. Kurtz,' I continued, severely, 'is General Manager, you won't have the opportunity.'

"He blew the candle out suddenly, and we went outside. The moon had risen. Black figures strolled about listlessly, pouring water on the glow, whence proceeded a sound of hissing; steam ascended in the moonlight, the beaten nigger groaned somewhere. 'What a row the brute makes!' said the indefatigable man with the mustaches, appearing near us. 'Serves him right. Transgression—punishment—bang! Pitiless, pitiless. That's the only way. This will prevent all conflagrations for the future. I was just telling the manager. . . .' He noticed my companion, and became crestfallen all at once. 'Not in bed yet,' he said, with a kind of servile heartiness; 'it's so natural. Ha! Danger—agitation.' He vanished. I went on to the river-side, and the other followed me. I heard a scathing murmur at my ear, 'Heap of muffs—go to.' The pilgrims could be seen in knots gesticulating, discussing. Several had still their staves in their hands. I verily believe they took these sticks to bed with them. Beyond the fence the forest stood up spectrally in the moonlight, and through the dim stir, through the faint sounds of that lamentable courtyard, the silence of the land went home to one's very heart—its mystery, its greatness, the amazing reality of its concealed life. The hurt nigger moaned feebly somewhere near by, and then fetched a deep sigh that made me mend my pace away from there. I felt a hand introducing itself under my arm. 'My dear sir,' said the fellow, 'I don't want to be misunderstood, and especially by you, who will see Mr. Kurtz long before I can have that pleasure. I wouldn't like him to get a false idea of my disposition. . . .'

"I let him run on, this papier-mâché Mephistopheles,[10] and it seemed to me that if I tried I could poke my forefinger through him, and would find nothing inside but a little loose dirt, maybe. He, don't you see, had been planning to be assistant-manager by and by under the present man, and I could see that the coming of that Kurtz had upset them both not a little. He talked precipitately, and I did not try to stop him. I had my shoulder against the wreck of my steamer, hauled up on the slope like a carcass of some big river animal. The smell of mud, of primeval mud, by Jove! was in my nostrils, the high stillness of primeval forest was before my eyes; there were shiny patches on the black creek. The moon had spread over everything a thin layer of silver—over the rank grass, over the mud, upon the wall of matted vegetation standing higher than the wall of a temple, over the great river I could see through a somber gap glittering, glittering, as it flowed broadly by without a murmur. All this was great, expectant, mute, while the man jabbered about himself. I wondered whether the stillness on the face of the immensity looking at us two were meant as an appeal or as a menace. What were we who had strayed in here? Could we handle that dumb thing, or would it handle us? I felt how big, how confoundedly big, was that thing that couldn't talk, and perhaps was deaf as well. What was in there? I could see a little ivory coming out from there, and I had heard Mr. Kurtz was in there. I had heard enough about it, too—God knows! Yet somehow it didn't bring any image with it—no more than if I had been told an angel or a fiend was in there. I believed it in the same way one of you might believe there are inhabitants in the planet Mars. I knew once a Scotch sailmaker who was certain, dead sure, there were people in Mars. If you asked him for some idea how they looked and behaved, he would get shy and mutter something about 'walking on all-fours.' If you as much as smiled, he would—though a man of sixty—offer to fight you. I would not have gone so far as to fight for Kurtz, but I went for him near enough to a lie. You know I hate, detest, and can't bear a lie, not because I am straighter than the rest of us, but simply because it appalls me. There is a taint of death, a flavor of mortality in lies—which is exactly what I hate and detest in the world—what I want to forget. It makes me miserable and sick, like biting something rotten would do. Temperament, I suppose. Well, I went near enough to it by letting the young fool there believe anything he liked to imagine as to my influence in Europe. I became in an instant as much of a pretense as the rest of the bewitched pilgrims. This simply because I had a notion it somehow would be of help to that Kurtz whom at the time I did not see—you understand. He was just a word for me. I did not see the man in the name any more than you

[10] Papier-mâché: waste paper pulped with glue. Mephistopheles: a chief devil in the Faust legend. Faust sells his soul to the Devil in return for twenty-four years of further life complete with every pleasure and all knowledge. Mephistopheles, the evil angel of Faust, supplies all of Faust's desires. A papier-mâché Mephistopheles is, then, a fraud incapable of supplying anything.

do. Do you see him? Do you see the story? Do you see anything? It seems to me I am trying to tell you a dream—making a vain attempt, because no relation of a dream can convey the dream-sensation, that commingling of absurdity, surprise, and bewilderment in a tremor of struggling revolt, that notion of being captured by the incredible which is of the very essence of dreams. . . ."

He was silent for a while.

". . . No, it is impossible; it is impossible to convey the life-sensation of any given epoch of one's existence—that which makes its truth, its meaning—its subtle and penetrating essence. It is impossible. We live, as we dream—alone. . . ."

He paused again as if reflecting, then added—

"Of course in this you fellows see more than I could then. You see me, whom you know. . . ."

It had become so pitch dark that we listeners could hardly see one another. For a long time already he, sitting apart, had been no more to us than a voice. There was not a word from anybody. The others might have been asleep, but I was awake. I listened, I listened on the watch for the sentence, for the word, that would give me the clew to the faint uneasiness inspired by this narrative that seemed to shape itself without human lips in the heavy night-air of the river.

". . . Yes—I let him run on," Marlow began again, "and think what he pleased about the powers that were behind me. I did! And there was nothing behind me! There was nothing but that wretched, old, mangled steamboat I was leaning against, while he talked fluently about 'the necessity for every man to get on.' 'And when one comes out here, you conceive, it is not to gaze at the moon.' Mr. Kurtz was a 'universal genius,' but even a genius would find it easier to work with 'adequate tools—intelligent men.' He did not make bricks—why, there was a physical impossibility in the way—as I was well aware; and if he did secretarial work for the manager, it was because 'no sensible man rejects wantonly the confidence of his superiors.' Did I see it? I saw it. What more did I want? What I really wanted was rivets, by heaven! Rivets. To get on with the work—to stop the hole. Rivets I wanted. There were cases of them down at the coast—cases—piled up—burst—split! You kicked a loose rivet at every second step in that station yard on the hillside. Rivets had rolled into the grove of death. You could fill your pockets with rivets for the trouble of stooping down—and there wasn't one rivet to be found where it was wanted. We had plates that would do, but nothing to fasten them with. And every week the messenger, a lone negro, letter-bag on shoulder and staff in hand, left our station for the coast. And several times a week a coast caravan came in with trade goods—ghastly glazed calico that made you shudder only to look at it; glass beads, valued about a penny a quart, confounded spotted cotton handkerchiefs. And no rivets. Three carriers could have brought all that was wanted to set that steamboat afloat.

"He was becoming confidential now, but I fancy my unresponsive attitude must have exasperated him at last, for he judged it necessary to inform me he feared neither God nor devil, let alone any mere man. I said I could see that very well, but what I wanted was a certain quantity of rivets—and rivets were what really Mr. Kurtz wanted, if he had only known it. Now letters went to the coast every week. . . . 'My dear sir,' he cried, 'I write from dictation.' I demanded rivets. There was a way—for an intelligent man. He changed his manner; became very cold, and suddenly began to talk about a hippopotamus; wondered whether sleeping on board the steamer (I stuck to my salvage night and day) I wasn't disturbed. There was an old hippo that had the bad habit of getting out on the bank and roaming at night over the station grounds. The pilgrims used to turn out in a body and empty every rifle they could lay hands on at him. Some even had sat up o' nights for him. All this energy was wasted, though. 'That animal has a charmed life,' he said; 'but you can say this only of brutes in this country. No man—you apprehend me?—no man here bears a charmed life.' He stood there for a moment in the moonlight with his delicate hooked nose set a little askew, and his mica eyes glittering without a wink, then, with a curt good night, he strode off. I could see he was disturbed and considerably puzzled, which made me feel more hopeful than I had been for days. It was a great comfort to turn from that chap to my influential friend, the battered, twisted, ruined, tin-pot steamboat. I clambered on board. She rang under my feet like an empty Huntley & Palmer biscuit-tin kicked along a gutter; she was nothing so solid in make, and rather less pretty in shape, but I had expended enough hard work on her to make me love her. No influential friend would have served me better. She had given me a chance to come out a bit—to find out what I could do. No, I don't like work. I had rather laze about and think of all the fine things that can be done. I don't like work—no man does—but I like what is in the work,—the chance to find yourself. Your own reality—for yourself, not for others—what no other man can ever know. They can only see the mere show, and never can tell what it really means.

"I was not surprised to see somebody sitting aft, on the deck, with his legs dangling over the mud. You see I rather chummed with the few mechanics there were in that station, whom the other pilgrims naturally despised—on account of their imperfect manners, I suppose. This was the foreman—a boiler-maker by trade—a good worker. He was a lank, bony, yellow-faced man, with big intense eyes. His aspect was worried, and his head was as bald as the palm of my hand; but his hair in falling seemed to have stuck to his chin, and had prospered in the new locality, for his beard hung down to his waist. He was a widower with six young children (he had left them in charge of a sister of his to come out there), and the passion of his life was pigeon-flying. He was an enthusiast and a connoisseur. He would rave about pigeons. After work hours he used sometimes to come over from his hut for a talk about his children and his pigeons; at work, when he had to crawl in the mud under the bottom of the steamboat, he would tie up that beard of his in a kind of white serviette he brought for the purpose. It had loops to go over his ears. In the evening he could be seen squatted on the bank rinsing that wrapper in the creek with great care, then spreading it solemnly on a bush to dry.

"I slapped him on the back and shouted, 'We shall have rivets!' He scrambled to his feet exclaiming, 'No! Rivets!' as though he couldn't believe his ears. Then in a low voice, 'You . . . eh?' I don't know why we behaved like lunatics. I put my finger to the side of my nose and nodded mysteriously. 'Good for you!' he cried, snapped his fingers above his head, lifting one foot. I tried a jig. We capered on the iron deck. A frightful clatter came out of that hulk, and the virgin forest on the other bank of the creek sent it back in a thundering roll upon the sleeping station. It must have made some of the pilgrims sit up in their hovels. A dark figure obscured the lighted doorway of the manager's hut, vanished, then, a second or so after, the doorway itself vanished, too. We stopped, and the silence driven away by the stamping of our feet flowed back again from the recesses of the land. The great wall of vegetation, an exuberant and entangled mass of trunks, branches, leaves, boughs, festoons, motionless in the moonlight, was like a rioting invasion of soundless life, a rolling wave of plants, piled up, crested, ready to topple over the creek, to sweep every little man of us out of his little existence. And it moved not. A deadened burst of mighty splashes and snorts reached us from afar, as though an ichthyosaurus had been taking a bath of glitter in the great river. 'After all,' said the boiler-maker in a reasonable tone, 'why shouldn't we get the rivets?' Why not, indeed! I did not know of any reason why we shouldn't. 'They'll come in three weeks,' I said, confidently.

"But they didn't. Instead of rivets there came an invasion, an infliction, a visitation. It came in sections during the next three weeks, each section headed by a donkey carrying a white man in new clothes and tan shoes, bowing from that elevation right and left to the impressed pilgrims. A quarrelsome band of footsore sulky niggers trod on the heels of the donkeys; a lot of tents, campstools, tin boxes, white cases, brown bales would be shot down in the courtyard, and the air of mystery would deepen a little over the muddle of the station. Five such installments came, with their absurd air of disorderly flight with the loot of innumerable outfit shops and provision stores, that, one would think, they were lugging, after a raid, into the wilderness for equitable division. It was an inextricable mess of things decent in themselves but that human folly made look like the spoils of thieving.

"This devoted band called itself the Eldorado Exploring Expedition, and I believe they were sworn to secrecy. Their talk, however, was the talk of sordid buccaneers: it was reckless without hardihood, greedy without audacity, and cruel without courage; there was not an atom of foresight or of serious intention in the whole batch of them, and they did not seem aware these things are wanted for the work of the world. To tear treasure out of the bowels of the land was their desire, with no more moral purpose at the back of it than there is in burglars breaking into a safe. Who paid the expenses of the noble enterprise I don't know; but the uncle of our manager was leader of that lot.

"In exterior he resembled a butcher in a poor neighborhood, and his eyes had a look of sleepy cunning. He carried his fat paunch with ostentation on his short legs, and during the time his gang infested the station spoke to no one but his nephew. You could see these two roaming about all day long with their heads close together in an everlasting confab.

"I had given up worrying myself about the rivets. One's capacity for that kind of folly is more limited than you would suppose. I said Hang!—and let things slide. I had plenty of time for meditation, and now and then I would give some thought to Kurtz. I wasn't very interested in him. No. Still, I was curious to see whether this man, who had come out equipped with moral ideas of some sort, would climb to the top after all and how he would set about his work when there."

II

"One evening as I was lying flat on the deck of my steamboat, I heard voices approaching—and there were the nephew and the uncle strolling along the bank. I laid my head on my arm again, and had nearly lost myself in a doze, when somebody said in my ear, as it were: 'I am as harmless as a little child, but I don't like to be dictated to. Am I the manager—or am I not? I was ordered to send him there. It's incredible.' . . . I became aware that the two were standing on the shore alongside the forepart of the steamboat, just below my head. I did not move; it did not occur to me to move: I was sleepy. 'It *is* unpleasant,' grunted the uncle. 'He has asked the Administration to be sent there,' said the other, 'with the idea of showing what he could do; and I was instructed accordingly. Look at the influence that man must have. Is it not frightful?' They both agreed it was frightful, then made several bizarre remarks: 'Make rain and fine weather—one man—the Council—by the nose'—bits of absurd sentences that got the better of my drowsiness, so that I had pretty near the whole of my wits about me when the uncle said, 'The climate may do away with this difficulty for you. Is he alone there?' 'Yes,' answered the manager; 'he sent his assistant down the river with a note to me in these terms: "Clear this poor devil out of the country, and don't bother sending more of that sort. I had rather be alone than have the kind of men you can dispose of with me." It was more than a year ago. Can you imagine such impudence!' 'Anything since then?' asked the other, hoarsely. 'Ivory,' jerked the nephew; 'lots of it—prime sort—lots—most annoying, from him.' 'And with that?' questioned the heavy rumble. 'Invoice,' was the reply fired out, so to speak. Then silence. They had been talking about Kurtz.

"I was broad awake by this time, but, lying perfectly at ease, remained still, having no inducement to change my position. 'How did that ivory come all this way?' growled the elder man, who seemed very vexed. The other explained that it had come with a fleet of canoes in charge of an English half-caste clerk Kurtz had with him; that Kurtz had apparently intended to return himself, the station being by that time bare of goods and stores, but after coming three hundred miles, had suddenly decided to go back, which he started to do alone in a small dugout with four paddlers, leaving the half-caste to continue down the river with the ivory. The two fellows there seemed astounded at anybody attempting such a thing. They were at a loss for an adequate motive. As to me, I seemed to see Kurtz for the first time. It was a distinct glimpse: the dugout, four paddling savages, and the lone white man turning his back suddenly on the headquarters, on relief, on thoughts of home—perhaps; setting his face towards the depths of the wilderness, towards his empty and desolate station. I did not know the motive. Perhaps he was just simply a fine fellow who stuck to his work for its own sake. His name, you understand, had not been pronounced once. He was 'that man.' The half-caste, who, as far as I could see, had conducted a difficult trip with great prudence and pluck, was invariably alluded to as 'that scoundrel.' The 'scoundrel' had reported that the 'man' had been very ill—had recovered imperfectly. . . . The two below me moved away then a few paces, and strolled back and forth at some little distance. I heard: 'Military post—doctor—two hundred miles—quite alone now—unavoidable delays—nine months—no news—strange rumors.' They approached again, just as the manager was saying, 'No one, as far as I know, unless a species of wandering trader—a pestilential fellow, snapping ivory from the natives.' Who was it they were talking about now? I gathered in snatches that this was some man supposed to be in Kurtz's district, and of whom the manager did not approve. 'We will not be free from unfair competition till one of these fellows is hanged for an example,' he said. 'Certainly,' grunted the other; 'get him hanged! Why not? Anything—anything can be done in this country. That's what I say; nobody here, you understand, *here,* can endanger your position. And why? You stand the climate—you outlast them all. The danger is in Europe; but there before I left I took care to—' They moved off and whispered, then their voices rose again. 'The extraordinary series of delays is not my fault. I did my best.' The fat man sighed. 'Very sad.' 'And the pestiferous absurdity of his talk,' continued the other; 'he bothered me enough when he was here. "Each station should be like a beacon on the road towards better things, a center for trade, of course, but also for humanizing, improving, instructing." Conceive you—that ass! And he wants to be manager! No, it's—' Here he got choked by excessive indignation, and I lifted my head the least bit. I was surprised to see how near they were—right under me. I could have spat upon their hats. They were looking on the ground, absorbed in thought. The manager was switching his leg with a slender twig: his sagacious relative lifted his head. 'You have been well since you came out this time?' he asked. The other gave a start. 'Who? I? Oh! Like a charm—like a charm. But the rest—oh, my goodness! All sick. They die so quick, too, that I haven't the time to send them out of the country—it's incredible!' 'H'm. Just so,' grunted the uncle. 'Ah! my boy, trust to this—I say, trust to this.' I saw him extend his short flipper of an arm for a gesture that took in the forest, the creek, the mud, the river,—seemed to beckon with a dishonoring flourish before the sunlit face of the land a treacherous appeal to the lurking death, to the hidden evil, to the profound darkness of its heart. It was so startling that I leaped to my feet and looked back at the edge of the forest, as though I had expected an answer of some sort to that black display of confidence. You know the foolish notions that come to one sometimes. The high stillness confronted these two figures with its ominous patience, waiting for the passing away of a fantastic invasion.

"They swore aloud together—out of sheer fright, I believe—then pretending not to know anything of my existence, turned back to the station. The sun was low; and leaning forward side by side, they seemed to be tugging painfully uphill their two ridiculous shadows of unequal length, that trailed behind them slowly over the tall grass without bending a single blade.

"In a few days the Eldorado Expedition went into the patient wilderness, that closed upon it as the sea closes over a diver. Long afterwards the news came that all the donkeys were dead. I know nothing as to the fate of the less valuable animals. They, no doubt, like the rest of us, found what they deserved. I did not inquire. I was then rather excited at the prospect of meeting Kurtz very soon. When I say very soon I mean it comparatively. It was just two months from the day we left the creek when we came to the bank below Kurtz's station.

"Going up that river was like traveling back to the earliest beginnings of the world, when vegetation rioted on the earth and the big trees were kings. An empty stream, a great silence, an impenetrable forest. The air was warm, thick, heavy, sluggish. There was no joy in the brilliance of sunshine. The long stretches of the waterway ran on, deserted, into the gloom of overshadowed distances. On silvery sandbanks hippos and alligators sunned themselves side by side. The broadening waters flowed through a mob of wooded islands; you lost your way on that river as you would in a desert, and butted all day long against shoals, trying to find the channel, till you thought yourself bewitched and cut off forever from everything you had known once—somewhere—far away—in another existence perhaps. There were moments when one's past came back to one, as it will sometimes when you have not a moment to spare to yourself; but it came in the shape of an unrestful and noisy dream, remembered with wonder amongst the overwhelming realities of this strange world of plants, and water, and silence. And this stillness of life did not in the least resemble a peace. It was the stillness of an implacable force brooding over an inscrutable intention. It looked at you with a vengeful aspect. I got used to it afterwards; I did not see it any more; I had no time. I had to keep guessing at the channel; I had to discern, mostly by inspiration, the signs of hidden banks; I watched for sunken stones; I was learning to clap my teeth smartly before my heart flew out, when I shaved by a fluke some infernal sly old snag that would have ripped the life out of the tin-pot steamboat and drowned all the pilgrims; I had to keep a look-out for the signs of dead wood we could cut up in the night for the next day's steaming. When you have to attend to things of that sort, to the mere incidents of the surface, the reality —the reality, I tell you—fades. The inner truth is hidden—luckily, luckily. But I felt it all the same; I felt often its mysterious stillness watching me at my monkey tricks, just as it watches you fellows performing on your respective tight-ropes for—what is it? half-a-crown a tumble—"

"Try to be civil, Marlow," growled a voice, and I knew there was at least one listener awake besides myself.

"I beg your pardon. I forgot the heartache which makes up the rest of the price. And indeed what does the price matter, if the trick be well done? You do your tricks very well. And I didn't do badly either, since I managed not to sink that steamboat on my first trip. It's a wonder to me yet. Imagine a blindfolded man set to drive a van over a bad road. I sweated and shivered over that business considerably, I can tell you. After all, for a seaman, to scrape the bottom of the thing that's supposed to float all the time under his care is the unpardonable sin. No one may know of it, but you never forget the thump—eh? A blow on the very heart. You remember it, you dream of it, you wake up at night and think of it—years after—and go hot and cold all over. I don't pretend to say that steamboat floated all the time. More than once she had to wade for a bit, with twenty cannibals splashing around and pushing. We had enlisted some of these chaps on the way for a crew. Fine fellows—cannibals—in their place. They were men one could work with, and I am grateful to them. And, after all, they did not eat each other before my face: they had brought along a provision of hippo-meat which went rotten, and made the mystery of the wilderness stink in my nostrils. Phoo! I can sniff it now. I had the manager on board and three or four pilgrims with their staves—all complete. Sometimes we came upon a station close by the bank, clinging to the skirts of the unknown, and the white men rushing out of a tumble-down hovel, with great gestures of joy and surprise and welcome, seemed very strange—had the appearance of being held there captive by a spell. The word ivory would ring in the air for a while—and on we went again into the silence, along empty reaches, round the still bends, between the high walls of our winding way, reverberating in hollow claps the ponderous beat of the stern-wheel. Trees, trees, millions of trees, massive, immense, running up high; and at their foot, hugging the bank against the stream, crept the little begrimed steamboat, like a sluggish beetle crawling on the floor of a lofty portico. It made you feel very small, very lost, and yet it was not altogether depressing, that feeling. After all, if you were small, the grimy beetle crawled on—which was just what you wanted it to do. Where the pilgrims imagined it crawled to I don't know. To some place where they expected to get something, I bet! For me it crawled towards Kurtz—exclusively; but when the steampipes started leaking we crawled very slow. The reaches opened before us and closed behind, as if the forest had stepped leisurely across the water to bar the way for our return. We penetrated deeper and deeper into the heart of darkness. It was very quiet there. At night sometimes the roll of drums behind the curtain of trees would run up the river and remain sustained faintly, as if hovering in the air high over our heads, till the first break of day. Whether it meant war, peace, or prayer we could not tell. The dawns were heralded by the descent of a chill stillness; the woodcutters slept, their fires burned low; the snapping of a twig would make you start. We were wanderers on a prehistoric earth, on an earth that wore the aspect of an unknown planet. We could have fancied ourselves the first of men taking possession of an accursed inheritance, to be subdued at the cost of profound anguish and of excessive toil. But suddenly, was we struggled round a bend, there would be a glimpse of rush walls, of peaked grass-roofs, a burst of yells, a whirl of black limbs, a mass of hands clapping, of feet stamping, of bodies swaying, of eyes rolling, under the droop of heavy and motionless foliage. The steamer toiled along slowly on the edge of a black and incomprehensible frenzy.

The prehistoric man was cursing us, praying to us, welcoming us—who could tell? We were cut off from the comprehension of our surroundings; we glided past like phantoms, wondering and secretly appalled, as sane men would be before an enthusiastic outbreak in a madhouse. We could not understand because we were too far and could not remember, because we were traveling in the night of first ages, of those ages that are gone, leaving hardly a sign—and no memories.

"The earth seemed unearthly. We are accustomed to look upon the shackled form of a conquered monster, but there—there you could look at a thing monstrous and free. It was unearthly, and the men were—No, they were not inhuman. Well, you know, that was the worst of it—this suspicion of their not being inhuman. It would come slowly to one. They howled and leaped, and spun, and made horrid faces; but what thrilled you was just the thought of their humanity—like yours—the thought of your remote kinship with this wild and passionate uproar. Ugly. Yes, it was ugly enough; but if you were man enough you would admit to yourself that there was in you just the faintest trace of a response to the terrible frankness of that noise, a dim suspicion of there being a meaning in it which you—you so remote from the night of first ages—could comprehend. And why not? The mind of man is capable of anything—because everything is in it, all the past as well as all the future. What was there after all? Joy, fear, sorrow, devotion, valor, rage—who can tell?—but truth—truth stripped of its cloak of time. Let the fool gape and shudder—the man knows, and can look on without a wink. But he must at least be as much of a man as these on the shore. He must meet that truth with his own true stuff—with his own inborn strength. Principles won't do. Acquisitions, clothes, pretty rags—rags that would fly off at the first good shake. No; you want a deliberate belief. An appeal to me in this fiendish row—is there? Very well; I hear; I admit, but I have a voice, too, and for good or evil mine is the speech that cannot be silenced. Of course, a fool, what with sheer fright and fine sentiments, is always safe. Who's that grunting? You wonder I didn't go ashore for a howl and a dance? Well, no—I didn't. Fine sentiments, you say? Fine sentiments, be hanged! I had no time. I had to mess about with white-lead and strips of woollen blanket helping to put bandages on those leaky steam-pipes—I tell you. I had to watch the steering, and circumvent those snags, and get the tin-pot along by hook or by crook. There was surface-truth enough in these things to save a wiser man. And between whiles I had to look after the savage who was fireman. He was an improved specimen; he could fire up a vertical boiler. He was there below me, and, upon my word, to look at him was as edifying as seeing a dog in a parody of breeches and a feather hat, walking on his hind-legs. A few months of training had done for that really fine chap. He squinted at the steam-gauge and at the water-gauge with an evident effort of intrepidity—and he had filed teeth, too, the poor devil, and the wool of his pate shaved into queer patterns, and three ornamental scars on each of his cheeks. He ought to have been clapping his hands and stamping his feet on the bank, instead of which he was hard at work, a thrall to strange witchcraft, full of improving knowledge. He was useful because he had been instructed; and what he knew was this—that should the water in that transparent thing disappear, the evil spirit inside the boiler would get angry through the greatness of his thirst, and take a terrible vengeance. So he sweated and fired up and watched the glass fearfully (with an impromptu charm, made of rags, tied to his arm, and a piece of polished bone, as big as a watch, stuck flatways through his lower lip), while the wooden banks slipped past us slowly, the short noise was left behind, the interminable miles of silence—and we crept on, towards Kurtz. But the snags were thick, the water was treacherous and shallow, the boiler seemed indeed to have a sulky devil in it, and thus neither that fireman nor I had any time to peer into our creepy thoughts.

"Some fifty miles below the Inner Station we came upon a hut of reeds, an inclined and melancholy pole, with the unrecognizable tatters of what had been a flag of some sort flying from it, and a neatly stacked woodpile. This was unexpected. We came to the bank, and on the stack of firewood found a flat piece of board with some faded pencil-writing on it. When deciphered it said: 'Wood for you. Hurry up. Approach cautiously.' There was a signature, but it was illegible—not Kurtz—a much longer word. 'Hurry up.' Where? Up the river? 'Approach cautiously.' We had not done so. But the warning could not have been meant for the place where it could be only found after approach. Something was wrong above. But what —and how much? That was the question. We commented adversely upon the imbecility of that telegraphic style. The bush around said nothing, and would not let us look very far, either. A torn curtain of red twill hung in the doorway of the hut, and flapped sadly in our faces. The dwelling was dismantled; but we could see a white man had lived there not very long ago. There remained a rude table—a plank on two posts; a heap of rubbish reposed in a dark corner, and by the door I picked up a book. It had lost its covers, and the pages had been thumbed into a state of extremely dirty softness; but the back had been lovingly stitched afresh with white cotton thread, which looked clean yet. It was an extraordinary find. Its title was, *An Inquiry into some Points of Seamanship*, by a man Towser, Towson—some such name—Master in his Majesty's Navy. The matter looked dreary reading enough, with illustrative diagrams and repulsive tables of figures, and the copy was sixty years old. I handled this amazing antiquity with the greatest possible tenderness, lest it should dissolve in my hands. Within, Towson or Towser was inquiring earnestly into the breaking strain of ships' chains and tackle, and other such matters. Not a very enthralling book; but at the first glance you could see there a singleness of intention, an honest concern for the right way of going to work, which made these humble pages, thought out so many years ago, luminous with another than a professional light. The simple old sailor, with his talk of chains and purchases, made me forget the jungle and the pilgrims in a delicious sensation of having come upon something unmistakably real. Such a book being there was wonderful enough; but still more astounding were the notes penciled in the margin, and plainly referring to the text. I couldn't believe my eyes! They were in cipher! Yes, it looked like cipher. Fancy a man lugging with him a book of that description into this nowhere and studying it—and making notes —in cipher at that! It was an extravagant mystery.

"I had been dimly aware for some time of a worrying noise, and when I lifted my eyes I saw the wood pile was gone, and the manager, aided by all the pilgrims, was shouting at me from the river-side. I slipped the book into my pocket. I assure you to leave off reading was like tearing myself away from the shelter of an old and solid friendship.

"I started the lame engine ahead. 'It must be this miserable trader—this intruder,' exclaimed the manager, looking back malevolently at the place we had left. 'He must be English,' I said. 'It will not save him from getting into trouble if he is not careful,' muttered the manager darkly. I observed with assumed innocence that no man was safe from trouble in this world.

"The current was more rapid now, the steamer seemed at her last gasp, the stern-wheel flopped languidly, and I caught myself listening on tiptoe for the next beat of the boat, for in sober truth I expected the wretched thing to give up every moment. It was like watching the last flickers of a life. But still we crawled. Sometimes I would pick out a tree a little way ahead to measure our progress toward Kurtz by, but I lost it invariably before we got abreast. To keep the eyes so long on one thing was too much for human patience. The manager displayed a beautiful resignation. I fretted and fumed and took to arguing with myself whether or no I would talk openly with Kurtz; but before I could come to any conclusion it occurred to me that my speech or my silence, indeed any action of mine, would be a mere futility. What did it matter what any one knew or ignored? What did it matter who was manager? One gets sometimes such a flash of insight. The essentials of this affair lay deep under the surface, beyond my reach, and beyond my power of meddling.

"Towards the evening of the second day we judged ourselves about eight miles from Kurtz's station. I wanted to push on; but the manager looked grave, and told me the navigation up there was so dangerous that it would be advisable, the sun being very low already, to wait where we were till next morning. Moreover, he pointed out that if the warning to approach cautiously were to be followed, we must approach in daylight—not at dusk, or in the dark. This was sensible enough. Eight miles meant nearly three hours' steaming for us, and I could also see suspicious ripples at the upper end of the reach. Nevertheless, I was annoyed beyond expression at the delay, and most unreasonably, too, since one night more could not matter much after so many months. As we had plenty of wood, and caution was the word, I brought up in the middle of the stream. The reach was narrow, straight, with high sides like a railway cutting. The dusk came gliding into it long before the sun had set. The current ran smooth and swift, but a dumb immobility sat on the banks. The living trees, lashed together by the creepers and every living bush of the undergrowth, might have been changed into stone, even to the slenderest twig, to the lightest leaf. It was not sleep—it seemed unnatural, like a state of trance. Not the faintest sound of any kind could be heard. You looked on amazed, and began to suspect yourself of being deaf—then the night came suddenly, and struck you blind as well. About three in the morning some large fish leaped, and the loud splash made me jump as though a gun had been fired. When the sun rose there was a white fog, very warm and clammy, and more blinding than the night. It did not shift or drive; it was just there, standing all round you like something solid. At eight or nine, perhaps, it lifted as a shutter lifts. We had a glimpse of the towering multitude of trees, of the immense matted jungle, with the blazing little ball of the sun hanging over it—all perfectly still—and then the white shutter came down again, smoothly, as if sliding in greased grooves. I ordered the chain, which we had begun to heave in, to be paid out again. Before it stopped running with a muffled rattle, a cry, a very loud cry, as of infinite desolation, soared slowly in the opaque air. It ceased. A complaining clamor, modulated in savage discords, filled our ears. The sheer unexpectedness of it made my hair stir under my cap. I don't know how it struck the others: to me it seemed as though the mist had screamed, so suddenly, and apparently from all sides at once, did this tumultuous and mournful uproar arise. It culminated in a hurried outbreak of almost intolerably excessive shrieking, which stopped short, leaving us stiffened in a variety of silly attitudes, and obstinately listening to the nearly as appalling and excessive silence. 'Good God! What is the meaning—' stammered at my elbow one of the pilgrims,—a little fat man, with sandy hair and red whiskers, who wore side-spring boots, and pink pajamas tucked into his socks. Two others remained open-mouthed a whole minute, then dashed into the little cabin, to rush out incontinently and stand darting scared glances, with Winchesters at 'ready' in their hands. What we could see was just the steamer we were on, her outlines blurred as though she had been on the point of dissolving, and a misty strip of water, perhaps two feet broad, around her—and that was all. The rest of the world was nowhere, as far as our eyes and ears were concerned. Just nowhere. Gone, disappeared; swept off without leaving a whisper or a shadow behind.

"I went forward, and ordered the chain to be hauled in short, so as to be ready to trip the anchor and move the steamboat at once if necessary. 'Will they attack?' whispered an awed voice. 'We will be all butchered in this fog,' murmured another. The faces twitched with the strain, the hands trembled slightly, the eyes forgot to wink. It was very curious to see the contrast of expressions of the white men and of the black fellows of our crew, who were as much strangers to that part of the river as we, though their homes were only eight hundred miles away. The whites, of course, greatly discomposed, had besides a curious look of being painfully shocked by such an outrageous row. The others had an alert, naturally interested expression; but their faces were essentially quiet, even those of the one or two who grinned as they hauled at the chain. Several exchanged short, grunting phrases, which seemed to settle the matter to their satisfaction. Their headman, a young, broad-chested black, severely draped in dark-blue fringed cloths, with fierce nostrils and his hair all done up artfully in oily ringlets, stood near me. 'Aha!' I said, just for good fellowship's sake. 'Catch 'im,' he snapped, with a bloodshot widening of his eyes and a flash of sharp teeth—'catch 'im. Give 'im to us.' 'To you, eh?' I asked; 'what would you do with them?' 'Eat 'im!' he said, curtly, and, leaning his elbow on the rail, looked out into the fog in a dignified and profoundly pensive attitude. I would no doubt have been properly horrified, had it not occurred to me that he and his chaps must be very hungry: that they must have been growing increasingly hungry for at least this month past. They had been engaged for six months (I don't think a single one of them had any clear idea of time, as we at the end of countless ages have. They still belonged to the beginnings of time—had no inherited experience to teach them as it were), and of course, as long as there was a piece of paper written over in accordance with some farcical law or other made down the river, it didn't enter anybody's head to trouble how they would live. Certainly they had brought with them some rotten hippo-meat, which couldn't have lasted very long, anyway, even if the pilgrims hadn't, in the midst of a shocking hullabaloo, thrown a considerable quantity of it overboard. It looked like a high-handed proceeding; but it was really a case of legitimate self-defense. You can't breathe dead hippo waking, sleeping, and eating, and at the same time keep your precarious grip on existence. Besides that, they had given them every week three pieces of brass wire, each about nine inches long; and the theory was they were to buy their provisions with that currency in river-side villages. You can see how *that* worked. There were either no villages, or the people were hostile, or the director, who like the rest of us fed out of tins, with an occasional old he-goat thrown in, didn't want to stop the steamer for some more or less recondite reason. So, unless they swallowed the wire itself, or made loops of it to snare the fishes with, I don't see what good their extravagant salary could be to them. I must say it was paid with a regularity worthy of a large and honorable trading company. For the rest, the only thing to eat—though it didn't look eatable in the least—I saw in their possession was a few lumps of some stuff like half-cooked dough, of a dirty lavender color, they kept wrapped in leaves, and now and then swallowed a piece of, but so small that it seemed done more for the looks of the thing than for any serious purpose of sustenance. Why in the name of all the gnawing devils of hunger they didn't go for us—they were thirty to five—and have a good tuck-in for once, amazes me now when I think of it. They were big powerful men, with not much capacity to weigh the consequences, with courage, with strength, even yet, though their skins were no longer glossy and their muscles no longer hard. And I saw that something restraining, one of those human secrets that baffle probability, had come into play there. I looked at them with a swift quickening of interest—not because it occurred to me I might be eaten by them before very long, though I own to you that just then I perceived—in a new light, as it were—how unwholesome the pilgrims looked, and I hoped, yes, I positively hoped, that my aspect was not so—what shall I say?—so—unappetizing: a touch of fantastic vanity which fitted well with the dream-sensation that pervaded all my days at that time. Perhaps I had a little fever, too. One can't live with one's finger everlastingly on one's pulse. I had often 'a little fever,' or a little touch of other things—the playful pawstrokes of the wilderness, the preliminary trifling before the more serious onslaught which came in due course. Yes; I looked at them as you would on any human being, with a curiosity in their impulses, motives, capacities, weaknesses, when brought to the test of an inexorable physical necessity. Restraint! What possible restraint? Was it superstition, disgust, patience, fear—or some kind of primitive honor? No fear can stand up to hunger, no patience can wear it out, disgust simply does not exist where hunger is; and as to superstition, beliefs, and what you may call principles, they are less than chaff in a breeze. Don't you know the devilry of lingering starvation, its exasperating torment, its black thoughts, its somber and brooding ferocity? Well, I do. It takes a man all his inborn strength to fight hunger properly. It's really easier to face bereavement, dishonor, and the perdition of one's soul—than this kind of prolonged hunger. Sad, but true. And these chaps, too, had no earthly reason for any kind of scruple. Restraint! I would just as soon have expected restraint from a hyena prowling amongst the corpses of a battlefield. But there was the fact facing me—the fact dazzling, to be seen, like the foam on the depths of the sea, like a ripple on an unfathomable enigma, a mystery greater—when I thought of it—than the curious, inexplicable note of desperate grief in this savage clamor that had swept by us on the river-bank, behind the blind whiteness of the fog.

"Two pilgrims were quarreling in hurried whispers as to which bank. 'Left.' 'No, no; how can you? Right, right, of course.' 'It is very serious,' said the manager's voice behind him; 'I would be desolated if anything should happen to Mr. Kurtz before we came up.' I looked at him, and had not the slightest doubt he was sincere. He was just the kind of man who would wish to preserve appearances. That was his restraint. But when he muttered something about going on at once, I did not even take the trouble to answer him. I knew, and he knew, that it was impossible. Were we to let go our hold of the bottom, we would be absolutely in the air—in space. We wouldn't be able to tell where we were going to—whether up or down stream, or across—till we fetched against one bank or the other,—and then we wouldn't know at first which it was. Of course I made no move. I had no mind for a smash-up. You couldn't imagine a more deadly place for a shipwreck. Whether drowned at once or not, we were sure to perish speedily in one way or another. 'I authorize you to take all the risks,' he said, after a short silence. 'I refuse to take any,' I said, shortly; which was just the answer he expected, though its tone might have surprised him. 'Well, I must defer to your judgment. You are captain,' he said, with marked civility. I turned my shoulder to him in sign of my appreciation, and looked into the fog. How long would it last? It was the most hopeless look-out. The approach to this Kurtz grubbing for ivory in the wretched bush was beset by as many dangers as though he had been an enchanted princess sleeping in a fabulous castle. 'Will they attack, do you think?' asked the manager, in a confidential tone.

"I did not think they would attack, for several obvious reasons. The thick fog was one. If they left the bank in their canoes they would get lost in it, as we would be if we attempted to move. Still, I had also judged the jungle of both banks quite impenetrable—and yet eyes were in it, eyes that had seen us. The river-side bushes were certainly very thick; but the undergrowth behind was evidently penetrable. However, during the short lift I had seen no canoes anywhere in the reach—certainly not abreast of the steamer. But what made the idea of attack inconceivable to me was the nature of the noise—of the cries we had heard. They had not the fierce character boding immediate hostile intention. Unexpected, wild, and violent as they had been, they had given me an irresistible impression of sorrow. The glimpse of the steamboat had for some reason filled those savages with unrestrained grief. The danger, if any, I expounded, was from our proximity to a great human passion let loose. Even extreme grief may ultimately vent itself in violence—but more generally takes the form of apathy. . . .

"You should have seen the pilgrims stare! They had no heart to grin, or even to revile me: but I believe they thought me gone mad—with fright, maybe. I delivered a regular lecture. My dear boys, it was no good bothering. Keep a look-out? Well, you may guess I watched the fog for the signs of lifting as a cat watches a mouse; but for anything else our eyes were of no more use to us than if we had been buried miles deep in a heap of cotton-wool. It felt like it, too—choking, warm, stifling. Besides, all I said, though it sounded extravagant, was absolutely true to fact. What we afterwards alluded to as an attack was really an attempt at repulse. The action was very far from being aggressive—it was not even defensive, in the usual sense: it was undertaken under the stress of desperation, and in its essence was purely protective.

"It developed itself, I should say, two hours after the fog lifted, and its commencement was at a spot, roughly speaking, about a mile and a half below Kurtz's station. We had just floundered and flopped round a bend, when I saw an islet, a mere grassy hummock of bright green, in the middle of the stream. It was the only thing of the kind; but as we opened the reach more, I perceived it was the head of a long sandbank, or rather of a chain of shallow patches stretching down the middle of the river. They were discolored, just awash, and the whole lot was seen just under the water, exactly as a man's backbone is seen running down the middle of his back under the skin. Now, as far as I did see, I could go to the right or to the left of this. I didn't know either channel, of course. The banks looked pretty well alike, the depth appeared the same; but as I had been informed the station was on the west side, I naturally headed for the western passage.

"No sooner had we fairly entered it than I became aware it was much narrower than I had supposed. To the left of us there was the long uninterrupted shoal, and to the right a high, steep bank heavily overgrown with bushes. Above the bush the trees stood in serried ranks. The twigs overhung the current thickly, and from distance to distance a large limb of some tree projected rigidly over the stream. It was then well on in the afternoon, the face of the forest was gloomy, and a broad strip of shadow had already fallen on the water. In this shadow we steamed up—very slowly, as you may imagine. I sheered her well inshore—the water being deepest near the bank, as the sounding-pole informed me.

"One of my hungry and forbearing friends

was sounding in the bows just below me. This steamboat was exactly like a decked scow. On the deck, there were two little teak-wood houses, with doors and windows. The boiler was in the fore-end, and the machinery right astern. Over the whole there was a light roof, supported on stanchions. The funnel projected through that roof, and in front of the funnel a small cabin built of light planks served for a pilot-house. It contained a couch, two camp-stools, a loaded Martini-Henry[11] leaning in one corner, a tiny table, and the steering-wheel. It had a wide door in front and a broad shutter at each side. All these were always thrown open, of course. I spent my days perched up there on the extreme fore-end of that roof, before the door. At night I slept, or tried to, on the couch. An athletic black belonging to some coast tribe, and educated by my poor predecessor, was the helmsman. He sported a pair of brass earrings, wore a blue cloth wrapper from the waist to the ankles, and thought all the world of himself. He was the most unstable kind of fool I had ever seen. He steered with no end of a swagger while you were by; but if he lost sight of you, he became instantly the prey of an abject funk, and would let that cripple of a steamboat get the upper hand of him in a minute.

"I was looking down at the sounding-pole, and feeling much annoyed to see at each try a little more of it stick out of that river, when I saw my poleman give up the business suddenly, and stretch himself flat on the deck, without even taking the trouble to haul his pole in. He kept hold on it though, and it trailed in the water. At the same time the fireman, whom I could also see below me, sat down abruptly before his furnace and ducked his head. I was amazed. Then I had to look at the river mighty quick, because there was a snag in the fairway. Sticks, little sticks, were flying about—thick: they were whizzing before my nose, dropping below me, striking behind me against my pilot-house. All this time the river, the shore, the woods, were very quiet—perfectly quiet. I could only hear the heavy splashing thump of the sternwheel and the patter of these things. We cleared the snag clumsily. Arrows, by Jove! We were being shot at! I stepped in quickly to close the shutter on the land-side. That fool-helmsman, his hand on the spokes, was lifting his knees high, stamping his feet, champing his mouth, like a reined-in horse. Confound him! And we were staggering within ten feet of the bank. I had to lean right out to swing the heavy shutter, and I saw a face amongst the leaves on the level with my own, looking at me very fierce and steady; and then suddenly, as though a veil had been removed from my eyes, I made out, deep in the tangled gloom, naked breasts, arms, legs, glaring eyes,—the bush was swarming with human limbs in movement, glistening, of bronze color. The twigs shook, swayed, and rustled, the arrows flew out of them, and then the shutter came to. 'Steer her straight,' I said to the helmsman. He held his head rigid, face forward; but his eyes rolled, he kept on lifting and setting down his feet gently, his mouth foamed a little. 'Keep quiet!' I said in a fury. I might just as well have ordered a tree not to sway in the wind. I darted out. Below me there was a great scuffle of feet on the iron deck; confused exclamations; a voice screamed, 'Can you turn back?' I caught sight of a V-shaped ripple on the water ahead. What? Another snag! A fusillade burst out under my feet. The pilgrims had opened with their Winchesters,[12] and were simply squirting lead into that bush. A deuce of a lot of smoke came up and drove slowly forward. I swore at it. Now I couldn't see the ripple or the snag either. I stood in the doorway, peering, and the arrows came in swarms. They might have been poisoned, but they looked as though they wouldn't kill a cat. The bush began to howl. Our wood-cutters raised a warlike whoop; the report of a rifle just at my back deafened me. I glanced over my shoulder, and the pilot-house was yet full of noise and smoke when I made a dash at the wheel. The fool-nigger had dropped everything, to throw the shutter open and let off that Martini-Henry. He stood before the wide opening, glaring, and I yelled at him to come back, while I straightened the sudden twist out of that steamboat. There was no room to turn even if I had wanted to, the snag was somewhere very near ahead in that confounded smoke, there was no time to lose, so I just crowded her into the bank—right into the bank, where I knew the water was deep.

"We tore slowly along the overhanging bushes

[11] British single-loading rifle.

[12] Early American breech-loading rifle.

in the whirl of broken twigs and flying leaves. The fusillade below stopped short, as I had foreseen it would when the squirts got empty. I threw my head back to a glinting whizz that traversed the pilot-house, in at one shutter-hole and out at the other. Looking past that mad helmsman, who was shaking the empty rifle and yelling at the shore, I saw vague forms of men running bent double, leaping, gliding, distinct, incomplete, evanescent. Something big appeared in the air before the shutter, the rifle went overboard, and the man stepped back swiftly, looked at me over his shoulder in an extraordinary, profound, familiar manner, and fell upon my feet. The side of his head hit the wheel twice, and the end of what appeared a long cane clattered round and knocked over a little camp-stool. It looked as though after wrenching that thing from somebody ashore he had lost his balance in the effort. The thin smoke had blown away, we were clear of the snag, and looking ahead I could see that in another hundred yards or so I would be free to sheer off, away from the bank; but my feet felt so very warm and wet that I had to look down. The man had rolled on his back and stared straight up at me; both hands clutched that cane. It was the shaft of a spear that, either thrown or lunged through the opening, had caught him in the side just below the ribs; the blade had gone in out of sight, after making a frightful gash; my shoes were full; a pool of blood lay very still, gleaming dark-red under the wheel; his eyes shone with an amazing luster. The fusillade burst out again. He looked at me anxiously, gripping the spear like something precious, with an air of being afraid I would try to take it away from him. I had to make an effort to free my eyes from his gaze and attend to steering. With one hand I felt above my head for the line of the steam whistle, and jerked out screech after screech hurriedly. The tumult of angry warlike yells was checked instantly, and then from the depths of the woods went out such a tremulous and prolonged wail of mournful fear and utter despair as may be imagined to follow the flight of the last hope from the earth. There was a great commotion in the bush; the shower of arrows stopped, a few dropping shots rang out sharply —then silence, in which the languid beat of the stern-wheel came plainly to my ears. I put the helm hard a-starboard at the moment when the pilgrim in pink pajamas, very hot and agitated, appeared in the doorway. 'The manager sends me—' he began in an official tone, and stopped short. 'Good God!' he said, glaring at the wounded man.

"We two whites stood over him, and his lustrous and inquiring glance enveloped us both. I declare it looked as though he would presently put to us some question in an understandable language; but he died without uttering a sound, without moving a limb, without twitching a muscle. Only in the very last moment, as though in response to some sign we could not see, to some whisper we could not hear, he frowned heavily, and that frown gave to his black death-mask an inconceivably somber, brooding, and menacing expression. The luster of inquiring glance faded swiftly into vacant glassiness. 'Can you steer?' I asked the agent eagerly. He looked very dubious; but I made a grab at his arm, and he understood at once I meant him to steer whether or no. To tell you the truth, I was morbidly anxious to change my shoes and socks. 'He is dead,' murmured the fellow, immensely impressed. 'No doubt about it,' said I, tugging like mad at the shoe-laces. 'And by the way, I suppose Mr. Kurtz is dead as well by this time.'

"For the moment that was the dominant thought. There was a sense of extreme disappointment, as though I had found out I had been striving after something altogether without a substance. I couldn't have been more disgusted if I had traveled all this way for the sole purpose of talking with Mr. Kurtz. Talking with . . . I flung one shoe overboard, and became aware that that was exactly what I had been looking forward to—a talk with Kurtz. I made the strange discovery that I had never imagined him as doing, you know, but as discoursing. I didn't say to myself, 'Now I will never see him,' or 'Now I will never shake him by the hand,' but, 'now I will never hear him.' The man presented himself as a voice. Not of course that I did not connect him with some sort of action. Hadn't I been told in all the tones of jealousy and admiration that he had collected, bartered, swindled, or stolen more ivory than all the other agents together? That was not the point. The point was in his being a gifted creature, and that of all his gifts the one that stood out preëminently, that carried with it a sense of real presence, was his ability to talk, his words—the gift of expression, the bewildering, the illuminating, the most exalted and the most contemptible, the pulsating stream of light, or the deceitful flow from the heart of an impenetrable darkness.

"The other shoe went flying unto the devil-god of that river. I thought, by Jove! it's all over. We are too late; he has vanished—the gift has vanished, by means of some spear, arrow, or club. I will never hear that chap speak after all, —and my sorrow had a startling extravagance of emotion, even such as I had noticed in the howling sorrow of these savages in the bush. I couldn't have felt more lonely desolation somehow, had I been robbed of a belief or had missed my destiny in life. . . . Why do you sigh in this beastly way, somebody? Absurd? Well absurd. Good Lord! mustn't a man ever—Here, give me some tobacco." . . .

There was a pause of profound stillness, then a match flared, and Marlow's lean face appeared, worn, hollow, with downward folds and drooped eyelids, with an aspect of concentrated attention; and as he took vigorous draws at his pipe, it seemed to retreat and advance out of the night in the regular flicker of the tiny flame. The match went out.

"Absurd!" he cried. "This is the worst of trying to tell. . . . Here you all are, each moored with two good addresses, like a hulk with two anchors, a butcher round one corner, a policeman round another, excellent appetites, and temperature normal—you hear—normal from year's end to year's end. And you say, Absurd! Absurd be—exploded! Absurd! My dear boys, what can you expect from a man who out of sheer nervousness had just flung overboard a pair of new shoes! Now I think of it, it is amazing I did not shed tears. I am, upon the whole, proud of my fortitude. I was cut to the quick at the idea of having lost the inestimable privilege of listening to the gifted Kurtz. Of course I was wrong. The privilege was waiting for me. Oh, yes, I heard more than enough. And I was right, too. A voice. He was very little more than a voice. And I heard—him—it—this voice—other voices—all of them were so little more than voices—and the memory of that time itself lingers around me, impalpable, like a dying vibration of one immense jabber, silly, atrocious, sordid, savage, or simply mean, without any kind of sense. Voices, voices—even the girl herself—now—"

He was silent for a long time.

"I laid the ghost of his gifts at last with a lie," he began, suddenly. "Girl! What? Did I mention a girl? Oh, she is out of it—completely. They —the women I mean—are out of it—should be out of it. We must help them to stay in that beautiful world of their own, lest ours gets worse. Oh, she had to be out of it. You should have heard the disinterred body of Mr. Kurtz saying, 'My Intended.' You would have perceived directly then how completely she was out of it. And the lofty frontal bone of Mr. Kurtz! They say the hair goes on growing sometimes, but this—ah—specimen, was impressively bald. The wilderness had patted him on the head and, behold, it was like a ball—an ivory ball; it had caressed him, and—lo!—he had withered; it had taken him, loved him, embraced him, got into his veins, consumed his flesh, and sealed his soul to its own by the inconceivable ceremonies of some devilish initiation. He was its spoiled and pampered favorite. Ivory? I should think so. Heaps of it, stacks of it. The old mud shanty was bursting with it. You would think there was not a single tusk left either above or below the ground in the whole country. 'Mostly fossil,' the manager had remarked, disparagingly. It was no more fossil than I am; but they call it fossil when it is dug up. It appears these niggers do bury the tusks sometimes—but evidently they couldn't bury this parcel deep enough to save the gifted Mr. Kurtz from his fate. We filled the steamboat with it, and had to pile a lot on the deck. Thus he could see and enjoy as long as he could see, because the appreciation of this favor had remained with him to the last. You should have heard him say, 'My ivory.' Oh, yes, I heard him. 'My Intended, my ivory, my station, my river, my—' everything belonged to him. It made me hold my breath in expectation of hearing the wilderness burst into a prodigious peal of laughter that would shake the fixed stars in their places. Everything belonged to him—but that was a trifle. The thing was to know what he belonged to, how many powers of darkness claimed him for their own. That was the reflection that made you creepy all over. It was impossible—it was not good for one either—trying to imagine. He had taken a high seat amongst the devils of the land—I mean literally. You can't understand. How could you?—with solid pavement under your feet, surrounded by kind neighbors ready to cheer you or to fall on you, stepping delicately between the butcher and the policeman, in the holy terror of scandal and gallows and lunatic asylums—how can you imagine what particular region of the first ages a man's untrammeled feet may take him into by the way of solitude—utter solitude without a policeman—by the way of silence—utter silence, where no warning voice of a kind neighbor can be heard whispering of public opinion? These little things make all the great difference. When they are gone you must fall back upon your own innate strength, upon your own capacity for faithfulness. Of course you may be too much of a fool to go wrong—too dull even to know you are being assaulted by the powers of darkness. I take it, no fool ever made a bargain for his soul with the devil: the fool is too much of a fool, or the devil too much of a devil—I don't know which. Or you may be such a thunderingly exalted creature as to be altogether deaf and blind to anything but heavenly sights and sounds. Then the earth for you is only a standing place—and whether to be like this is your loss or your gain I won't pretend to say. But most of us are neither one nor the other. The earth for us is a place to live in, where we must put up with sights, with sounds, with smells, too, by Jove!—breathe dead hippo, so to speak, and not be contaminated. And there, don't you see? your strength comes in, the faith in your ability for the digging of unostentatious holes to bury the stuff in—your power of devotion, not to yourself, but to an obscure, back-breaking business. And that's difficult enough. Mind, I am not trying to excuse or even explain—I am trying to account to myself for—for—Mr. Kurtz—for the shade of Mr. Kurtz. This initiated wraith from the back of Nowhere honored me with its amazing confidence before it vanished altogether. This was because it could speak English to me. The original Kurtz had been educated partly in England, and—as he was good enough to say himself—his sympathies were in the right place. His mother was half-English, his father was half-French. All Europe contributed to the making of Kurtz; and by and by I learned that, most appropriately, the International Society for the Suppression of Savage Customs had intrusted him with the making of a report, for its future guidance. And he had written it, too. I've seen it. I've read it. It was eloquent, vibrating with eloquence, but too high-strung, I think. Seventeen pages of close writing he had found time for! But this must have been before his—let us say—nerves, went wrong, and caused him to preside at certain midnight dances ending with unspeakable rites, which—as far as I reluctantly gathered from what I heard at various times—were offered up to him—do you understand?—to Mr. Kurtz himself. But it was a beautiful piece of writing. The opening paragraph, however, in the light of later information, strikes me now as ominous. He began with the argument that we whites, from the point of development we had arrived at, 'must necessarily appear to them [savages] in the nature of supernatural beings—we approach them with the might as of a deity,' and so on, and so on. 'By the simple exercise of our will we can exert a power for good practically unbounded,' etc. etc. From that point he soared and took me with him. The peroration was magnificent, though difficult to remember, you know. It gave me the notion of an exotic immensity ruled by an august Benevolence. It made me tingle with enthusiasm. This was the unbounded power of eloquence—of words—of burning noble words. There were no practical hints to interrupt the magic current of phrases, unless a kind of note at the foot of the last page, scrawled evidently much later, in an unsteady hand, may be regarded as the exposition of a method. It was very simple, and at the end of that moving appeal to every altruistic sentiment it blazed at you, luminous and terrifying, like a flash of lightning in a serene sky: 'Exterminate all the brutes!' The curious part was that he had apparently forgotten all about that valuable postscriptum, because, later on, when he in a sense came to himself, he repeatedly entreated me to take good care of 'my pamphlet' (he called it), as it was sure to have in the future a good influence upon his career. I had full information about all these things, and, besides, as it turned out, I was to have the care of his memory. I've done enough for it to give me the indisputable right to lay it, if I choose, for an everlasting rest in the dust-bin of progress, amongst all the sweepings and, figuratively speaking, all the dead cats of civilization. But then, you see, I can't choose. He won't be forgotten. Whatever he was, he was not common. He had the power to charm or frighten rudimentary souls into an aggravated witch-dance in his honor; he could also fill the small souls of the pilgrims with bitter misgiving: he had one devoted friend at least, and he had conquered one soul in the world that was neither rudimentary nor tainted with self-seeking. No; I can't forget him, though I am not prepared to affirm the fellow was exactly worth the life we lost in getting to him. I missed my late helmsman awfully,—I missed him even while his body was still lying in the pilot-house. Perhaps you will think it passing strange, this regret for a savage who was no more account than a grain of sand in a black Sahara. Well, don't you see, he had done something, he had steered; for months I had him at my back—a help—an instrument. It was a kind of partnership. He steered for me—I had to look after him, I worried about his deficiencies, and thus a subtle bond had been created, of which I only became aware when it was suddenly broken. And the intimate profundity of that look he gave me when he received his hurt remains to this day in my memory—like a claim of distant kinship affirmed in a supreme moment.

"Poor fool! If he had only left that shutter alone. He had no restraint, no restraint—just like Kurtz—a tree swayed by the wind. As soon as I had put on a dry pair of slippers, I dragged him out, after first jerking the spear out of his side, which operation I confess I performed with my eyes shut tight. His heels leaped together over the little door-step; his shoulders were pressed to my breast; I hugged him from behind desperately. Oh! he was heavy, heavy; heavier than any man on earth, I should imagine. Then without more ado I tipped him overboard. The current snatched him as though he had been a wisp of grass, and I saw the body roll over twice before I lost sight of it forever. All the pilgrims and the manager were then congregated on the awning-deck about the pilot-house, chattering at each other like a flock of excited magpies, and there was a scandalized murmur at my heartless promptitude. What they wanted to keep that body hanging about for I can't guess. Embalm it, maybe. But I had also heard another, and a very ominous, murmur on the deck below. My friends the wood-cutters were likewise scandalized, and with a better show of reason—though I admit that the reason itself was quite inadmissible. Oh! quite! I had made up my mind that if my late helmsman was to be eaten, the fishes alone should have him. He had been a very second-rate helmsman while alive, but now he was dead he might have become a first-class temptation, and possibly cause some startling trouble. Besides, I was anxious to take the wheel, the man in pink pajamas showing himself a hopeless duffer at the business.

"This I did directly the simple funeral was over. We were going half-speed, keeping right in the middle of the stream, and I listened to the talk about me. They had given up Kurtz, they had given up the station; Kurtz was dead, and the station had been burnt—and so on—and so on. The red-haired pilgrim was beside himself with the thought that at least this poor Kurtz had been properly avenged. 'Say! We must have made glorious slaughter of them in the bush. Eh? What do you think? Say?' He positively danced, the bloodthirsty little gingery beggar. And he had nearly fainted when he saw the wounded man! I could not help saying, 'You made a glorious lot of smoke, anyhow.' I had seen, from the way the tops of the bushes rustled and flew, that almost all the shots had gone too high. You can't hit anything unless you take aim and fire from the shoulder; but these chaps fired from the hip with their eyes shut. The retreat, I maintained—and I was right—was caused by the screeching of the steam-whistle. Upon this they forgot Kurtz, and began to howl at me with indignant protests.

"The manager stood by the wheel murmuring confidentially about the necessity of getting well away down the river before dark at all events, when I saw in the distance a clearing on the river-side and the outlines of some sort of building. 'What's this?' I asked. He clapped his hands in wonder. 'The station!' he cried. I edged in at once, still going half-speed.

"Through my glasses I saw the slope of a hill interspersed with rare trees and perfectly free from undergrowth. A long decaying building on the summit was half buried in the high grass; the large holes in the peaked roof gaped black from afar; the jungle and the woods made a background. There was no enclosure or fence of any kind; but there had been one apparently, for near the house half-a-dozen slim posts remained in a row, roughly trimmed, and with their upper ends ornamented with round carved balls. The rails, or whatever there had been between, had disappeared. Of course the forest surrounded all that. The river-bank was clear, and on the water-side I saw a white man under a hat like a cartwheel beckoning persistently with his whole arm. Examining the edge of the forest above and below, I was almost certain I could see movements—human forms gliding here and there. I steamed past prudently, then stopped the engines and let her drift down. The man on the shore began to shout, urging us to land. 'We have been attacked,' screamed the manager. 'I know—I know. It's all right,' yelled back the other, as cheerful as you please. 'Come along. It's all right. I am glad.'

"His aspect reminded me of something I had seen—something funny I had seen somewhere. As I maneuvered to get alongside, I was asking myself, 'What does this fellow look like?' Suddenly I got it. He looked like a harlequin. His clothes had been made of some stuff that was brown holland probably, but it was covered with patches all over, with bright patches, blue, red, and yellow,—patches on the back, patches on the front, patches on elbows, on knees; colored binding around his jacket, scarlet edging at the bottom of his trousers; and the sunshine made him look extremely gay and wonderfully neat withal, because you could see how beautifully all this patching had been done. A beardless, boyish face, very fair, no features to speak of, nose peeling, little blue eyes, smiles and frowns chasing each other over that open countenance like sunshine and shadow on a wind-swept plain. 'Look out, captain!' he cried: 'there's a snag lodged in here last night.' What! Another snag? I confess I swore shamefully. I had nearly holed my cripple, to finish off that charming trip. The harlequin on the bank turned his little pug-nose up to me. 'You English?' he asked, all smiles. 'Are you?' I shouted from the wheel. The smiles vanished, and he shook his head as if sorry for my disappointment. Then he brightened up. 'Never mind!' he cried, encouragingly. 'Are we in time?' I asked. 'He is up there,' he replied, with a toss of the head up the hill, and becoming gloomy all of a sudden. His face was like the autumn sky, overcast one moment and bright the next.

"When the manager, escorted by the pilgrims, all of them armed to the teeth, had gone to the house this chap came on board. 'I say, I don't like this. These natives are in the bush,' I said. He assured me earnestly it was all right. 'They are simple people,' he added; 'well, I am glad you came. It took me all my time to keep them off.' 'But you said it was all right,' I cried. 'Oh, they meant no harm,' he said; and as I stared he corrected himself, 'Not exactly.' Then vivaciously, 'My faith, your pilot-house wants a clean-up!' In the next breath he advised me to keep enough steam on the boiler to blow the whistle in case of any trouble. 'One good screech will do more for you than all your rifles. They are simple people,' he repeated. He rattled away at such a rate he quite overwhelmed me. He seemed to be trying to make up for lots of silence, and actually hinted, laughing, that such was the case. 'Don't you talk with Mr. Kurtz?' I said. 'You don't talk with that man—you listen to him,' he exclaimed with severe exaltation. 'But now—' He waved his arm, and in the twinkling of an eye was in the uttermost depths of despondency. In a moment he came up again with a jump, possessed himself of both my hands, shook them continuously, while he gabbled: 'Brother sailor . . . honor . . . pleasure . . . delight . . . introduce myself . . . Russian . . . son of an arch-priest . . . Government of Tambov. . . . What? Tobacco! English tobacco; the excellent English tobacco! Now, that's brotherly. Smoke? Where's a sailor that does not smoke?'

"The pipe soothed him, and gradually I made out he had run away from school, had gone to sea in a Russian ship; ran away again; served some time in English ships; was now reconciled with the arch-priest. He made a point of that. 'But when one is young one must see things, gather experience, ideas; enlarge the mind.' 'Here!' I interrupted. 'You can never tell! Here I met Mr. Kurtz,' he said, youthfully solemn and reproachful. I held my tongue after that. It appears he had persuaded a Dutch trading-house on the coast to fit him out with stores and goods, and had started for the interior with a light heart, and no more idea of what would happen to him than a baby. He had been wandering about that river for nearly two years alone, cut off from everybody and everything. 'I am not so young as I look. I am twenty-five,' he said. 'At first old Van Shuyten would tell me to go to the devil,' he narrated with keen enjoyment; 'but I stuck to him, and talked and talked, till at last he got afraid I would talk the hind-leg off his favorite dog, so he gave me some cheap things and a few guns, and told me he hoped he would never see my face again. Good old Dutchman, Van Shuyten. I've sent him one small lot of ivory a year ago, so that he can't call me a little thief when I get back. I hope he got it. And for the rest I don't care. I had some wood stacked for you. That was my old house. Did you see?'

"I gave him Towson's book. He made as though he would kiss me, but restrained himself. "The only book I had left, and I thought I had lost it,' he said, looking at it ecstatically. 'So many accidents happen to a man going about alone, you know. Canoes get upset sometimes—and sometimes you've got to clear out so quick when the people get angry.' He thumbed the pages. 'You made notes in Russian?' I asked. He nodded. 'I thought they were written in cipher,' I said. He laughed, then became serious. 'I had lots of trouble to keep these people off,' he said. 'Did they want to kill you?' I asked. 'Oh, no!' he cried, and checked himself. 'Why did they attack us?' I pursued. He hesitated, then said shamefacedly, 'They don't want him to go.' 'Don't they?' I said, curiously. He nodded a nod full of mystery and wisdom. 'I tell you,' he cried, 'this man has enlarged my mind.' He opened his arms wide, staring at me with his little blue eyes that were perfectly round."

III

"I looked at him, lost in astonishment. There he was before me, in motley, as though he had absconded from a troupe of mimes, enthusiastic, fabulous. His very existence was improbable, inexplicable, and altogether bewildering. He was an insoluble problem. It was inconceivable how he had existed, how he had succeeded in getting so far, how he had managed to remain—why he did not instantly disappear. 'I went a little farther,' he said, 'then still a little farther—till I had gone so far that I don't know how I'll ever get back. Never mind. Plenty time. I can manage. You take Kurtz away quick—quick—I tell you.' The glamour of youth enveloped his parti-colored rags, his destitution, his loneliness, the essential desolation of his futile wanderings. For months—for years—his life hadn't been worth a day's purchase; and there he was gallantly, thoughtlessly alive, to all appearance indestructible solely by the virtue of his few years and of his unreflecting audacity. I was seduced into something like admiration—like envy. Glamour urged him on, glamour kept him unscathed. He surely wanted nothing from the wilderness but space to breathe in and to push on through. His need was to exist, and to move onwards at the greatest possible risk, and with a maximum of privation. If the absolutely pure, uncalculating, unpractical spirit of adventure had ever ruled a human being, it ruled this be-patched youth. I almost envied him the possession of this modest and clear flame. It seemed to have consumed all thought of self so completely, that even while he was talking to you, you forgot that it was he—the man before your eyes—who had gone through these things. I did not envy him his devotion to Kurtz, though. He had not meditated over it. It came to him and he accepted it with a sort of eager fatalism. I must say that to me it appeared about the most dangerous thing in every way he had come upon so far.

"They had come together unavoidably, like two ships becalmed near each other, and lay rubbing sides at last. I suppose Kurtz wanted an audience, because on a certain occasion, when encamped in the forest, they had talked all night, or more probably Kurtz had talked. 'We talked of everything,' he said, quite transported at the recollection. 'I forgot there was such a thing as sleep. The night did not seem to last an hour. Everything! Everything! . . . Of love, too.' 'Ah, he talked to you of love!' I said, much amused. 'It isn't what you think,' he cried, almost passionately. 'It was in general. He made me see things—things.'

"He threw his arms up. We were on deck at the time, and the headman of my wood-cutters, lounging near by, turned upon him his heavy and glittering eyes. I looked around, and I don't know why, but I assure you that never, never before, did this land, this river, this jungle, the very arch of this blazing sky, appear to me so hopeless and so dark, so impenetrable to human thought, so pitiless to human weakness. 'And, ever since, you have been with him, of course?' I said.

"On the contrary. It appears their intercourse had been very much broken by various causes.

He had, as he informed me proudly, managed to nurse Kurtz through two illnesses (he alluded to it as you would to some risky feat), but as a rule Kurtz wandered alone far in the depths of the forest. 'Very often coming to this station, I had to wait days and days before he would turn up,' he said. 'Ah, it was worth waiting for! —sometimes.' 'What was he doing? exploring or what?' I asked. 'Oh, yes, of course'; he had discovered lots of villages, a lake, too—he did not know exactly in what direction; it was dangerous to inquire too much—but mostly his expeditions had been for ivory. 'But he had no goods to trade with by that time,' I objected. 'There's a good lot of cartridges left even yet,' he answered, looking away. 'To speak plainly, he raided the country,' I said. He nodded. 'Not alone, surely!' He muttered something about the villages round that lake. 'Kurtz got the tribe to follow him, did he?' I suggested. He fidgeted a little. 'They adored him,' he said. The tone of these words was so extraordinary that I looked at him searchingly. It was curious to see his mingled eagerness and reluctance to speak of Kurtz. The man filled his life, occupied his thoughts, swayed his emotions. 'What can you expect?' he burst out; 'he came to them with thunder and lightning, you know—and they had never seen anything like it—and very terrible. He could be very terrible. You can't judge Mr. Kurtz as you would an ordinary man. No, no, no! Now—just to give you an idea—I don't mind telling you, he wanted to shoot me, too, one day—but I don't judge him.' 'Shoot you!' I cried. 'What for?' 'Well, I had a small lot of ivory the chief of that village near my house gave me. You see I used to shoot game for them. Well, he wanted it, and wouldn't hear reason. He declared he would shoot me unless I gave him the ivory and then cleared out of the country, because he could do so, and had a fancy for it, and there was nothing on earth to prevent him killing whom he jolly well pleased. And it was true, too. I gave him the ivory. What did I care! But I didn't clear out. No, no. I couldn't leave him. I had to be careful, of course, till we got friendly again for a time. He had his second illness then. Afterwards I had to keep out of the way; but I didn't mind. He was living for the most part in those villages on the lake. When he came down to the river, sometimes he would take to me, and sometimes it was better for me to be careful. This man suffered too much. He hated all this, and somehow he couldn't get away. When I had a chance I begged him to try and leave while there was time; I offered to go back with him. And he would say yes, and then he would remain; go off on another ivory hunt; disappear for weeks; forget himself amongst these people—forget himself—you know.' 'Why! he's mad,' I said. He protested indignantly. Mr. Kurtz couldn't be mad. If I had heard him talk, only two days ago, I wouldn't dare hint at such a thing. . . . I had taken up my binoculars while we talked, and was looking at the shore, sweeping the limit of the forest at each side and at the back of the house. The consciousness of there being people in that bush, so silent, so quiet—as silent and quiet as the ruined house on the hill—made me uneasy. There was no sign on the face of nature of this amazing tale that was not so much told as suggested to me in desolate exclamations, completed by shrugs, in interrupted phrases, in hints ending in deep sighs. The woods were unmoved, like a mask—heavy, like the closed door of a prison—they looked with their air of hidden knowledge, of patient expectation, of unapproachable silence. The Russian was explaining to me that it was only lately that Mr. Kurtz had come down to the river, bringing along with him all the fighting men of that lake tribe. He had been absent for several months—getting himself adored, I suppose—and had come down unexpectedly, with the intention to all appearance of making a raid either across the river or down stream. Evidently the appetite for more ivory had got the better of the—what shall I say?—less material aspirations. However he had got much worse suddenly. 'I heard he was lying helpless, and so I came up—took my chance,' said the Russian. 'Oh, he is bad, very bad.' I directed my glass to the house. There were no signs of life, but there was the ruined roof, the long mud wall peeping above the grass, with three little square window-holes, no two of the same size; all this brought within reach of my hand, as it were. And then I made a brusque movement, and one of the remaining posts of that vanished fence leaped up in the field of my glass. You remember I told you I had been struck at the distance by certain attempts at ornamentation, rather remarkable in the ruinous aspect of the place. Now I had suddenly a nearer view, and its result was to make me throw my head back as if before a blow. Then I went carefully from post to post with my glass, and I saw my mistake. These round knobs were not ornamental but symbolic; they were expressive and puzzling, striking and disturbing—food for thought and also for vultures if there had been any looking down from the sky; but at all events for such ants as were industrious enough to ascend the pole. They would have been even more impressive, those heads on the stakes, if their faces had not been turned to the house. Only one, the first I had made out, was facing my way. I was not so shocked as you may think. The start back I had given was really nothing but a movement of surprise. I had expected to see a knob of wood there, you know. I returned deliberately to the first I had seen—and there it was, black, dried, sunken, with closed eyelids,—a head that seemed to sleep at the top of that pole, and with the shrunken dry lips showing a narrow white line of the teeth, was smiling, too, smiling continuously at some endless and jocose dream of that eternal slumber.

"I am not disclosing any trade secrets. In fact, the manager said afterwards that Mr. Kurtz's methods had ruined the district. I have no opinion on that point, but I want you clearly to understand that there was nothing exactly profitable in these heads being there. They only showed that Mr. Kurtz lacked restraint in the gratification of his various lusts, that there was something wanting in him—some small matter which, when the pressing need arose, could not be found under his magnificent eloquence. Whether he knew of this deficiency himself I can't say. I think the knowledge came to him at last—only at the very last. But the wilderness had found him out early, and had taken on him a terrible vengeance for the fantastic invasion. I think it had whispered to him things about himself which he did not know, things of which he had no conception till he took counsel with this great solitude—and the whisper had proved irresistibly fascinating. It echoed loudly within him because he was hollow at the core. . . . I put down the glass, and the head that had appeared near enough to be spoken to seemed at once to have leaped away from me into inaccessible distance.

"The admirer of Mr. Kurtz was a bit crestfallen. In a hurried indistinct voice he began to assure me he had not dared to take these—say, symbols—down. He was not afraid of the natives; they would not stir till Mr. Kurtz gave the word. His ascendancy was extraordinary. The camps of these people surrounded the place, and the chiefs came every day to see him. They would crawl. . . . 'I don't want to know anything of the ceremonies used when approaching Mr. Kurtz,' I shouted. Curious, this feeling that came over me that such details would be more intolerable than those heads drying on the stakes under Mr. Kurtz's windows. After all, that was only a savage sight, while I seemed at one bound to have been transported into some lightless region of subtle horrors, where pure, uncomplicated savagery was a positive relief, being something that had a right to exist—obviously—in the sunshine. The young man looked at me with surprise. I suppose it did not occur to him that Mr. Kurtz was no idol of mine. He forgot I hadn't heard any of these splendid monologues on, what was it? on love, justice, conduct of life—or what not. If it had come to crawling before Mr. Kurtz, he crawled as much as the veriest savage of them all. I had no idea of the conditions, he said: these heads were the heads of rebels. I shocked him excessively by laughing. Rebels! What would be the next definition I was to hear? There had been enemies, criminals, workers—and these were rebels. Those rebellious heads looked very subdued to me on their sticks. 'You don't know how such a life tries a man like Kurtz,' cried Kurtz's last disciple. 'Well, and you?' I said. 'I! I! I am a simple man. I have no great thoughts. I want nothing from anybody. How can you compare me to . . . ?' His feelings were too much for speech, and suddenly he broke down. 'I don't understand,' he groaned. 'I've been doing my best to keep him alive, and that's enough. I had no hand in all this. I have no abilities. There hasn't been a drop of medicine or a mouthful of invalid food for months here. He was shamefully abandoned. A man like this, with such ideas. Shamefully! Shamefully! I—I—haven't slept for the last ten nights . . . .'

"His voice lost itself in the calm of the evening. The long shadows of the forest had slipped down hill while we talked, had gone far beyond the ruined hovel, beyond the symbolic row of stakes. All this was in the gloom, while we down there were yet in the sunshine, and the stretch of the river abreast of the clearing glittered in a still and dazzling splendor, with a murky and overshadowed bend above and below. Not a living soul was seen on the shore. The bushes did not rustle.

"Suddenly round the corner of the house a group of men appeared, as though they had come up from the ground. They waded waist-deep in the grass, in a compact body, bearing an improvised stretcher in their midst. Instantly, in the emptiness of the landscape, a cry arose whose shrillness pierced the still air like a sharp arrow flying straight to the very heart of the land; and, as if by enchantment, streams of human beings—of naked human beings—with spears in their hands, with bows, with shields, with wild glances and savage movements, were poured into the clearing by the dark-faced and pensive forest. The bushes shook, the grass swayed for a time, and then everything stood still in attentive immobility.

" 'Now, if he does not say the right thing to them we are all done for,' said the Russian at my elbow. The knot of men with the stretcher had stopped, too, halfway to the steamer, as if petrified. I saw the man on the stretcher sit up, lank and with an uplifted arm, above the shoulders of the bearers. 'Let us hope that the man who can talk so well of love in general will find some particular reason to spare us this time,' I said. I resented bitterly the absurd danger of our situation, as if to be at the mercy of that atrocious phantom had been a dishonoring necessity. I could not hear a sound, but through my glasses I saw the thin arm extended commandingly, the lower jaw moving, the eyes of that apparition shining darkly far in its bony head that nodded with grotesque jerks. Kurtz—Kurtz—that means short in German—don't it? Well, the name was as true as everything else in his life—and death. He looked at least seven feet long. His covering had fallen off, and his body emerged from it pitiful and appalling as from a winding-sheet. I could see the cage of his ribs all astir, the bones of his arm waving. It was as though an animated image of death carved out of old ivory had been shaking its hand with menaces at a motionless crowd of men made of dark and glittering bronze. I saw him open his mouth wide—it gave him a weirdly voracious aspect, as though he had wanted to swallow all the air, all the earth, all the men before him. A deep voice reached me faintly. He must have been shouting. He fell back suddenly. The stretcher shook as the bearers staggered forward again, and almost at the same time I noticed that the crowd of savages was vanishing without any perceptible movement of retreat, as if the forest that had ejected these beings so suddenly had drawn them in again as the breath is drawn in a long aspiration.

"Some of the pilgrims behind the stretcher carried his arms—two shot-guns, a heavy rifle, and a light revolver-carbine—the thunderbolts of that pitiful Jupiter.[13] The manager bent over him murmuring as he walked beside his head. They laid him down in one of the little cabins—just a room for a bedplace and a camp-stool or two, you know. We had brought his belated correspondence, and a lot of torn envelopes and open letters littered his bed. His hand roamed feebly amongst these papers. I was struck by the fire of his eyes and the composed languor of his expression. It was not so much the exhaustion of disease. He did not seem in pain. This shadow looked satiated and calm, as though for the moment it had had its fill of all the emotions.

"He rustled one of the letters, and looking straight in my face said, 'I am glad.' Somebody had been writing to him about me. These special recommendations were turning up again. The volume of tone he emitted without effort, almost without the trouble of moving his lips, amazed me. A voice! a voice! It was grave, profound, vibrating, while the man did not seem capable of a whisper. However, he had enough strength in him—factitious no doubt—to very nearly make an end of us, as you shall hear directly.

"The manager appeared silently in the doorway; I stepped out at once and he drew the curtain after me. The Russian, eyed curiously by the pilgrims, was staring at the shore. I followed the direction of his glance.

"Dark human shapes could be made out in the distance, flitting indistinctly against the gloomy border of the forest, and near the river two bronze figures, leaning on tall spears, stood in the sunlight under fantastic head-dresses of spotted skins, warlike and still in statuesque repose. And from right to left along the lighted

[13] Chief Roman god, god of light, of the sky and weather, and of the state, its welfare, and its laws.

shore moved a wild and gorgeous apparition of a woman.

"She walked with measured steps, draped in striped and fringed cloths, treading the earth proudly, with a slight jingle and flash of barbarous ornaments. She carried her head high; her hair was done in the shape of a helmet; she had brass leggings to the knee, brass wire gauntlets to the elbow, a crimson spot on her tawny cheek, innumerable necklaces of glass beads on her neck; bizarre things, charms, gifts of witch-men, that hung about her, glittered and trembled at every step. She must have had the value of several elephant tusks upon her. She was savage and superb, wild-eyed and magnificent; there was something ominous and stately in her deliberate progress. And in the hush that had fallen suddenly upon the whole sorrowful land, the immense wilderness, the colossal body of the fecund and mysterious life seemed to look at her, pensive, as though it had been looking at the image of its own tenebrous and passionate soul.

"She came abreast of the steamer, stood still, and faced us. Her long shadow fell to the water's edge. Her face had a tragic and fierce aspect of wild sorrow and of dumb pain mingled with the fear of some struggling, half-shaped resolve. She stood looking at us without a stir, and like the wilderness itself, with an air of brooding over an inscrutable purpose. A whole minute passed, and then she made a step forward. There was a low jingle, a glint of yellow metal, a sway of fringed draperies, and she stopped as if her heart had failed her. The young fellow by my side growled. The pilgrims murmured at my back. She looked at us all as if her life had depended upon the unswerving steadiness of her glance. Suddenly she opened her bared arms and threw them up rigid above her head, as though in an uncontrollable desire to touch the sky, and at the same time the swift shadows darted out on the earth, swept around on the river, gathering the steamer into a shadowy embrace. A formidable silence hung over the scene.

"She turned away slowly, walked on, following the bank, and passed into the bushes to the left. Once only her eyes gleamed back at us in the dusk of the thickets before she disappeared.

"'If she had offered to come aboard I really think I would have tried to shoot her,' said the man of patches, nervously. 'I have been risking my life every day for the last fortnight to keep her out of the house. She got in one day and kicked up a row about those miserable rags I picked up in the storeroom to mend my clothes with. I wasn't decent. At least it must have been that, for she talked like a fury to Kurtz for an hour, pointing at me now and then. I don't understand the dialect of this tribe. Luckily for me, I fancy Kurtz felt too ill that day to care, or there would have been mischief. I don't understand. . . . No—it's too much for me. Ah, well, it's all over now.'

"At this moment I heard Kurtz's deep voice behind the curtain: 'Save me!—save the ivory, you mean. Don't tell me. Save *me!* Why, I've had to save you. You are interrupting my plans now. Sick! Sick! Not so sick as you would like to believe. Never mind. I'll carry my ideas out yet—I will return. I'll show you what can be done. You with your little peddling notions—you are interfering with me. I will return. I . . . .'

"The manager came out. He did me the honor to take me under the arm and lead me aside. 'He is very low, very low,' he said. He considered it necessary to sigh, but neglected to be consistently sorrowful. 'We have done all we could for him—haven't we? But there is no disguising the fact, Mr. Kurtz has done more harm than good to the Company. He did not see the time was not ripe for vigorous action. Cautiously, cautiously—that's my principle. We must be cautious yet. The district is closed to us for a time. Deplorable! Upon the whole, the trade will suffer. I don't deny there is a remarkable quantity of ivory—mostly fossil. We must save it, at all events—but look how precarious the position is—and why? Because the method is unsound.' 'Do you,' said I, looking at the shore, 'call it "unsound method"?' 'Without doubt,' he exclaimed, hotly. 'Don't you?' . . . 'No method at all,' I murmured after a while. 'Exactly,' he exulted. 'I anticipated this. Shows a complete want of judgment. It is my duty to point it out in the proper quarter.' 'Oh,' said I, 'that fellow —what's his name?—the brickmaker, will make a readable report for you.' He appeared confounded for a moment. It seemed to me I had never breathed an atmosphere so vile, and I turned mentally to Kurtz for relief—positively for relief. 'Nevertheless I think Mr. Kurtz is a remarkable man,' I said with emphasis. He started, dropped on me a cold heavy glance, said very quietly, 'he *was,*' and turned his back on me. My hour of favor was over: I found myself lumped along with Kurtz as a partisan of methods for which the time was not ripe: I was unsound! Ah! but it was something to have at least a choice of nightmares.

"I had turned to the wilderness really, not to Mr. Kurtz, who, I was ready to admit, was as good as buried. And for a moment it seemed to me as if I also were buried in a vast grave full of unspeakable secrets. I felt an intolerable weight oppressing my breast, the smell of the damp earth, the unseen presence of victorious corruption, the darkness of an impenetrable night. . . . The Russian tapped me on the shoulder. I heard him mumbling and stammering something about 'brother seaman—couldn't conceal—knowledge of matters that would affect Mr. Kurtz's reputation.' I waited. For him evidently Mr. Kurtz was not in his grave; I suspect that for him Mr. Kurtz was one of the immortals. 'Well!' said I at last, 'speak out. As it happens, I am Mr. Kurtz's friend—in a way.'

"He stated with a good deal of formality that had we not been 'of the same profession,' he would have kept the matter to himself without regard to consequences. 'He suspected there was an active ill will towards him on the part of these white men that—' 'You are right,' I said, remembering a certain conversation I had overheard. 'The manager thinks you ought to be hanged.' He showed a concern at this intelligence which amused me at first. 'I had better get out of the way quietly,' he said, earnestly. 'I can do no more for Kurtz now, and they would soon find some excuse. What's to stop them? There's a military post three hundred miles from here.' 'Well, upon my word,' said I, 'perhaps you had better go if you have any friends amongst the savages near by.' 'Plenty,' he said. 'They are simple people—and I want nothing, you know.' He stood biting his lip, then: 'I don't want any harm to happen to these whites here, but of course I was thinking of Mr. Kurtz's reputation—but you are a brother seaman and—' 'All right,' said I, after a time. 'Mr. Kurtz's reputation is safe with me.' I did not know how truly I spoke.

"He informed me, lowering his voice, that it was Kurtz who had ordered the attack to be made on the steamer. 'He hated sometimes the idea of being taken away—and then again. . . . But I don't understand these matters. I am a simple man. He thought it would scare you away—that you would give it up, thinking him dead. I could not stop him. Oh, I had an awful time of it this last month.' 'Very well,' I said. 'He is all right now.' 'Ye-e-es,' he muttered, not very convinced apparently. 'Thanks,' said I; 'I shall keep my eyes open.' 'But quiet—eh?' he urged, anxiously. 'It would be awful for his reputation if anybody here—' I promised a complete discretion with great gravity. 'I have a canoe and three black fellows waiting not very far. I am off. Could you give me a few Martini-Henry cartridges?' I could, and did, with proper secrecy. He helped himself, with a wink at me, to a handful of my tobacco. 'Between sailors—you know—good English tobacco.' At the door of the pilot-house he turned round—'I say, haven't you a pair of shoes you could spare?' He raised one leg. 'Look.' The soles were tied with knotted strings sandal-wise under his bare feet. I rooted out an old pair, at which he looked with admiration before tucking them under his left arm. One of his pockets (bright red) was bulging with cartridges, from the other (dark blue) peeped 'Towson's Inquiry,' etc., etc. He seemed to think himself excellently well equipped for a renewed encounter with the wilderness. 'Ah! I'll never, never meet such a man again. You ought to have heard him recite poetry—his own, too, it was, he told me. Poetry!' He rolled his eyes at the recollection of these delights. 'Oh, he enlarged my mind!' 'Good-by,' said I. He shook hands and vanished in the night. Sometimes I ask myself whether I had ever really seen him—whether it was possible to meet such a phenomenon! . . .

"When I woke up shortly after midnight his warning came to my mind with its hint of danger that seemed, in the starred darkness, real enough to make me get up for the purpose of having a look around. On the hill a big fire burned, illuminating fitfully a crooked corner of the station-house. One of the agents with a picket of a few of our blacks, armed for the purpose, was keeping guard over the ivory; but deep within the forest, red gleams that wavered, that seemed to sink and rise from the ground amongst confused columnar shapes of intense blackness, showed the exact position of the camp where Mr. Kurtz's adorers were keeping their uneasy vigil. The monotonous beating of a big drum filled the air with muffled shocks and a lingering vibration. A steady droning sound of many men chanting each to himself some weird incantation came out from the black, flat wall of the woods as the humming of bees comes out of a hive, and had a strange narcotic effect upon my half-awake senses. I believe I dozed off leaning over the rail, till an abrupt burst of yells, an overwhelming outbreak of a pent-up and mysterious frenzy, woke me up in a bewildered wonder. It was cut short all at once, and the low droning went on with an effect of audible and soothing silence. I glanced casually into the little cabin. A light was burning within, but Mr. Kurtz was not there.

"I think I would have raised an outcry if I had believed my eyes. But I didn't believe them at first—the thing seemed so impossible. The fact is I was completely unnerved by a sheer blank fright, pure abstract terror, unconnected with any distinct shape of physical danger. What made this emotion so overpowering was—how shall I define it?—the moral shock I received, as if something altogether monstrous, intolerable to thought and odious to the soul, had been thrust upon me unexpectedly. This lasted of course the merest fraction of a second, and then the usual sense of commonplace, deadly danger, the possibility of a sudden onslaught and massacre, or something of the kind, which I saw impending, was positively welcome and composing. It pacified me, in fact, so much, that I did not raise an alarm.

"There was an agent buttoned up inside an ulster and sleeping on a chair on deck within three feet of me. The yells had not awakened him; he snored very slightly; I left him to his slumbers and leaped ashore. I did not betray Mr. Kurtz—it was ordered I should never betray him—it was written I should be loyal to the nightmare of my choice. I was anxious to deal with this shadow by myself alone,—and to this day I don't know why I was so jealous of sharing with any one the peculiar blackness of that experience.

"As soon as I got on the bank I saw a trail—a broad trail through the grass. I remember the exultation with which I said to myself, 'He can't walk—he is crawling on all-fours—I've got him.' The grass was wet with dew. I strode rapidly with clenched fists. I fancy I had some vague notion of falling upon him and giving him a drubbing. I don't know. I had some imbecile thoughts. The knitting old woman with the cat obtruded herself upon my memory as a most improper person to be sitting at the other end of such an affair. I saw a row of pilgrims squirting lead in the air out of Winchesters held to the hip. I thought I would never get back to the steamer, and imagined myself living alone and unarmed in the woods to an advanced age. Such silly things—you know. And I remember I confounded the beat of the drum with the beating of my heart, and was pleased at its calm regularity.

"I kept to the track though—then stopped to listen. The night was very clear; a dark blue space, sparkling with dew and starlight, in which black things stood very still. I thought I could see a kind of motion ahead of me. I was strangely cocksure of everything that night. I actually left the track and ran in a wide semicircle (I verily believe chuckling to myself) so as to get in front of that stir, of that motion I had seen—if indeed I had seen anything. I was circumventing Kurtz as though it had been a boyish game.

"I came upon him, and, if he had not heard me coming, I would have fallen over him, too, but he got up in time. He rose, unsteady, long, pale, indistinct, like a vapor exhaled by the earth, and swayed slightly, misty and silent before me; while at my back the fires loomed between the trees, and the murmur of many voices issued from the forest. I had cut him off cleverly; but when actually confronting him I seemed to come to my senses, I saw the danger in its right proportion. It was by no means over yet. Suppose he began to shout? Though he could hardly stand, there was still plenty of vigor in his voice. 'Go away—hide yourself,' he said, in that profound tone. It was very awful. I glanced back. We were within thirty yards from the nearest fire. A black figure stood up, strode on long black legs, waving long black arms, across the glow. It had horns—antelope horns, I think—on its head. Some sorcerer, some witch-man, no doubt: it looked fiend-like enough. 'Do you know what you are doing?' I whispered. 'Perfectly,' he answered, raising his voice for that single word: it sounded to me far off and yet loud, like a hail through a speaking-trumpet. If he makes a row we are lost, I thought to myself. This clearly was not a case for fisticuffs, even apart from the very natural aversion I had to beat that Shadow—this wandering and tormented thing. 'You will be lost,' I said—'utterly lost.' One gets sometimes such a flash of inspiration, you know. I did say the right thing, though indeed he could not have been more irretrievably lost than he was at this very moment, when the foundations of our intimacy were being laid—to endure—to endure—even to the end—even beyond.

" 'I had immense plans,' he muttered irresolutely. 'Yes,' said I; 'but if you try to shout I'll smash your head with—' There was not a stick or a stone near. 'I will throttle you for good,' I corrected myself. 'I was on the threshold of great things,' he pleaded, in a voice of longing, with a wistfulness of tone that made my blood run cold. 'And now for this stupid scoundrel—' 'Your success in Europe is assured in any case,' I affirmed, steadily. I did not want to have the throttling of him, you understand—and indeed it would have been very little use for any practical purpose. I tried to break the spell—the heavy, mute spell of the wilderness—that seemed to draw him to its pitiless breast by the awakening of forgotten and brutal instincts, by the memory of gratified and monstrous passions. This alone, I was convinced, had driven him out to the edge of the forest, to the bush, towards the gleam of fires, the throb of drums, the drone of weird incantations; this alone had beguiled his unlawful soul beyond the bounds of permitted aspirations. And, don't you see, the terror of the position was not in being knocked on the head—though I had a very lively sense of that danger, too—but in this, that I had to deal with a being to whom I could not appeal in the name of anything high or low. I had, even like the niggers, to invoke him—himself—his own exalted and incredible degradation. There was nothing either above or below him, and I knew it. He had kicked himself loose of the earth. Confound the man! he had kicked the very earth to pieces. He was alone, and I before him did not know whether I stood on the ground or floated in the air. I've been telling you what we said—repeating the phrases we pronounced—but what's the good? They were common everyday words—the familiar vague sounds exchanged on every waking day of life. But what of that? They had behind them, to my mind, the terrific suggestiveness of words heard in dreams, of phrases spoken in nightmares. Soul! If anybody had ever struggled with a soul, I am the man. And I wasn't arguing with a lunatic either. Believe me or not, his intelligence was perfectly clear—concentrated, it is true, upon himself with horrible intensity, yet clear; and therein was my only chance—barring, of course, the killing him there and then, which wasn't so good, on account of unavoidable noise. But his soul was mad. Being alone in the wilderness, it had looked within itself, and, by heavens! I tell you, it had gone mad. I had—for my sins, I suppose—to go through the ordeal of looking into it myself. No eloquence could have been so withering to one's belief in mankind as his final burst of sincerity. He struggled with himself, too. I saw it,—I heard it. I saw the inconceivable mystery of a soul that knew no restraint, no faith, and no fear, yet struggling blindly with itself. I kept my head pretty well; but when I had him at last stretched on the couch, I wiped my forehead, while my legs shook under me as though I had carried half a ton on my back down that hill. And yet I had only supported him, his bony arm clasped around my neck—and he was not much heavier than a child.

"When next day we left at noon, the crowd, of whose presence behind the curtain of trees I had been acutely conscious all the time, flowed out of the woods again, filled the clearing, covered the slope with a mass of naked, breathing, quivering, bronze bodies. I steamed up a bit, then swung downstream, and two thousand eyes followed the evolutions of the splashing, thumping, fierce river-demon beating the water with its terrible tail and breathing black smoke into the air. In front of the first rank, along the river, three men, plastered with bright red earth from head to foot, strutted to and fro restlessly. When we came abreast again, they faced the river, stamped their feet, nodded their horned heads, swayed their scarlet bodies; they shook towards the fierce river-demon a bunch of black feathers, a mangy skin with a pendent tail—something that looked like a dried gourd; they shouted periodically together strings of amazing words that resembled no sounds of human language; and the deep murmurs of the crowd, interrupted suddenly, were like the responses of some satanic litany.

"We had carried Kurtz into the pilot-house: there was more air there. Lying on the couch, he stared through the open shutter. There was an eddy in the mass of human bodies, and the woman with helmeted head and tawny cheeks rushed out to the very brink of the stream. She put out her hands, shouted something, and all that wild mob took up the shout in a roaring chorus of articulated, rapid, breathless utterance.

" 'Do you understand this?' I asked.

"He kept on looking out past me with fiery, longing eyes, with a mingled expression of wistfulness and hate. He made no answer, but I saw a smile, a smile of indefinable meaning, appear on his colorless lips that a moment after twitched convulsively. 'Do I not?' he said slowly, gasping, as if the words had been torn out of him by a supernatural power.

"I pulled the string of the whistle, and I did this because I saw the pilgrims on deck getting out their rifles with an air of anticipating a jolly lark. At the sudden screech there was a movement of abject terror through that wedged mass of bodies. 'Don't! don't you frighten them away,' cried someone on deck disconsolately. I pulled the string time after time. They broke and ran, they leaped, they crouched, they swerved, they dodged the flying terror of the sound. The three red chaps had fallen flat, face down on the shore, as though they had been shot dead. Only the barbarous and superb woman did not so much as flinch, and stretched tragically her bare arms after us over the somber and glittering river.

"And then that imbecile crowd down on the deck started their little fun, and I could see nothing more for smoke.

"The brown current ran swiftly out of the heart of darkness, bearing us down towards the sea with twice the speed of our upward progress; and Kurtz's life was running swiftly, too, ebbing, ebbing out of his heart into the sea of inexorable time. The manager was very placid, he had no vital anxieties now, he took us both in with a comprehensive and satisfied glance: the 'affair' had come off as well as could be wished. I saw the time approaching when I would be left alone of the party of 'unsound method.' The pilgrims looked upon me with disfavor. I was, so to speak, numbered with the dead. It is strange how I accepted this unforeseen partnership, this choice of nightmares forced upon me in the tenebrous land invaded by these mean and greedy phantoms.

"Kurtz discoursed. A voice! a voice! It rang deep to the very last. It survived his strength to hide in the magnificent folds of eloquence the barren darkness of his heart. Oh, he struggled! he struggled! The wastes of his weary brain were haunted by shadowy images now—images of wealth and fame revolving obsequiously round his unextinguishable gift of noble and lofty expression. My Intended, my station, my career, my ideas—these were the subjects for the occasional utterances of elevated sentiments. The shade of the original Kurtz frequented the bedside of the hollow sham, whose fate it was to be buried presently in the mold of primeval earth. But both the diabolic love and the unearthly hate of the mysteries it had penetrated fought for the possession of that soul satiated with primitive emotions, avid of lying fame, of sham distinction, of all the appearances of success and power.

"Sometimes he was contemptibly childish. He desired to have kings meet him at railway stations on his return from some ghastly Nowhere, where he intended to accomplish great things. 'You show them you have in you something that is really profitable, and then there will be no limits to the recognition of your ability,' he would say. 'Of course you must take care of the motives—right motives—always.' The long reaches that were like one and the same reach, monotonous bends that were exactly alike, slipped past the steamer with their multitude of secular trees looking patiently after this grimy fragment of another world, the forerunner of change, of conquest, of trade, of massacres, of blessings. I looked ahead—piloting. 'Close the shutter,' said Kurtz suddenly one day; 'I can't bear to look at this.' I did so. There was a silence. 'Oh, but I will wring your heart yet!' he cried at the invisible wilderness.

"We broke down—as I had expected—and had to lie up for repairs at the head of an island. This delay was the first thing that shook Kurtz's confidence. One morning he gave me a packet of papers and a photograph—the lot tied together with a shoestring. 'Keep this for me,' he said. 'This noxious fool' (meaning the manager) 'is capable of prying into my boxes when I am not looking.' In the afternoon I saw him. He was lying on his back with closed eyes, and I withdrew quietly, but I heard him mutter, "Live rightly, die, die . . . .' I listened. There was nothing more. Was he rehearsing some speech in his sleep, or was it a fragment of a phrase from some newspaper article? He had been writing for the papers and meant to do so again, 'for the furthering of my ideas. It's a duty.'

"His was an impenetrable darkness. I looked at him as you peer down at a man who is lying at the bottom of a precipice where the sun never shines. But I had not much time to give him, because I was helping the engine-driver to take to pieces the leaky cylinders, to straighten a bent connecting-rod and in other such matters. I lived in an infernal mess of rust, filings, nuts, bolts, spanners, hammers, ratchet-drills—things I abominate, because I don't get on with them. I tended the little forge we fortunately had aboard; I toiled wearily in a wretched scrap-heap—unless I had the shakes too bad to stand.

"One evening coming in with a candle I was startled to hear him say a little tremulously, 'I am lying here in the dark waiting for death.' The light was within a foot of his eyes. I forced myself to murmur, 'Oh, nonsense!' and stood over him as if transfixed.

"Anything approaching the change that came over his features I have never seen before, and hope never to see again. Oh, I wasn't touched. I was fascinated. It was as though a veil had been rent. I saw on that ivory face the expression of somber pride, of ruthless power, of craven terror—of an intense and hopeless despair. Did he live his life again in every detail of desire, temptation, and surrender during that supreme moment of complete knowledge? He cried in a whisper at some image, at some vision—he cried out twice, a cry that was no more than a breath—

" 'The horror! The horror!'

"I blew the candle out and left the cabin. The pilgrims were dining in the mess-room, and I took my place opposite the manager, who lifted his eyes to give me a questioning glance, which I successfully ignored. He leaned back, serene, with that peculiar smile of his sealing the unexpressed depths of his meanness. A continuous shower of small flies streamed upon the lamp, upon the cloth, upon our hands and faces. Suddenly the manager's boy put his insolent black head in the doorway, and said in a tone of scathing contempt—

" 'Mistah Kurtz—he dead.'

"All the pilgrims rushed out to see. I remained, and went on with my dinner. I believe I was considered brutally callous. However, I did not eat much. There was a lamp in there—light, don't you know—and outside it was so beastly, beastly dark. I went no more near the remarkable man who had pronounced a judgment upon the adventures of his soul on this earth. The voice was gone. What else had been there? But I am of course aware that next day the pilgrims buried something in a muddy hole.

"And then they very nearly buried me.

"However, as you see, I did not go to join Kurtz there and then. I did not. I remained to dream the nightmare out to the end, and to show my loyalty to Kurtz once more. Destiny. My destiny! Droll thing life is—that mysterious arrangement of merciless logic for a futile purpose. The most you can hope from it is some knowledge of yourself—that comes too late—a crop of unextinguishable regrets. I have wrestled with death. It is the most unexciting contest you can imagine. It takes place in an impalpable grayness, with nothing underfoot, with nothing around, without spectators, without clamor, without glory, without the great desire of victory, without the great fear of defeat, in a sickly atmosphere of tepid skepticism, without much belief in your own right, and still less in that of your adversary. If such is the form of ultimate wisdom, then life is a greater riddle than some of us think it to be. I was within a hair's breadth of the last opportunity for pronouncement, and I found with humiliation that probably I would have nothing to say. This is the reason why I affirm that Kurtz was a remarkable man. He had something to say. He said it. Since I had peeped over the edge myself, I understood better the meaning of his stare, that could not see the flame of the candle, but was wide enough to embrace the whole universe, piercing enough to penetrate all the hearts that beat in the darkness. He had summed up—he had judged. 'The horror!' He was a remarkable man. After all, this was the expression of some sort of belief; it had candor, it had conviction, it had a vibrating note of revolt in its whisper, it had the appalling face of a glimpsed truth—the strange commingling of desire and hate. And it is not my own extremity I remember best—a vision of grayness without form filled with physical pain, and a careless contempt for the evanescence of all things—even of this pain itself. No! It is his extremity that I seem to have lived through. True, he had made that last stride, he had stepped over the edge, while I had been permitted to draw back my hesitating foot. And perhaps in this is the whole difference; perhaps all the wisdom, and all truth, and all sincerity, are just compressed into that inappreciable moment of time in which we step over the threshold of the invisible. Perhaps! I like to think my summing-up would not have been a word of careless contempt. Better his cry—much better. It was an affirmation, a moral victory paid for by innumerable defeats, by abominable terrors, by abominable satisfactions. But it was a victory! That is why I have remained loyal to Kurtz to the last, and even beyond, when a long time after I heard once more, not his own choice, but the echo of his magnificent eloquence thrown to me from a soul as translucently pure as a cliff of crystal.

"No, they did not bury me, though there is a period of time which I remember mistily, with a shuddering wonder, like a passage through some inconceivable world that had no hope in it and no desire. I found myself back in the sepulchral city resenting the sight of people hurrying through the streets to filch a little money from each other, to devour their infamous cookery, to gulp their unwholesome beer, to dream their insignificant and silly dreams. They trespassed upon my thoughts. They were intruders whose knowledge of life was to me an irritating pretense, because I felt so sure they could not possibly know the things I knew. Their bearing, which was simply the bearing of commonplace individuals going about their business in the assurance of perfect safety, was offensive to me like the outrageous flauntings of folly in the face of a danger it is unable to comprehend. I had no particular desire to enlighten them, but I had some difficulty in restraining myself from laughing in their faces, so full of stupid importance. I daresay I was not very well at that time. I tottered about the streets—there were various affairs to settle—grinning bitterly at perfectly respectable persons. I admit my behavior was inexcusable, but then my temperature was seldom normal in these days. My dear aunt's endeavors to 'nurse up my strength' seemed altogether beside the mark. It was not my strength that wanted nursing, it was my imagination that wanted soothing. I kept the bundle of papers given me by Kurtz, not knowing exactly what to do with it. His mother had died lately, watched over, as I was told, by his Intended. A clean-shaved man, with an official manner and wearing gold-rimmed spectacles, called on me one day and made inquiries, at first circuitous, afterwards suavely pressing, about what he was pleased to denominate certain 'documents.' I was not surprised, because I had had two rows with the manager on the subject out there. I had refused to give up the smallest scrap out of that package, and I took the same attitude with the spectacled man. He became darkly menacing at last, and with much heat argued that the Company had the right to every bit of information about its 'territories.' And said he, 'Mr. Kurtz's knowledge of unexplored regions must have been necessarily extensive and peculiar—owing to his great abilities and to the deplorable circumstances in which he had been placed: therefore—' I assured him Mr. Kurtz's knowledge, however extensive, did not bear upon the problems of commerce or administration. He invoked then the name of science. 'It would be an incalculable loss if,' etc., etc. I offered him the report on the 'Suppression of Savage Customs,' with the postscriptum torn off. He took it up eagerly, but ended by sniffing at it with an air of contempt. 'This is not what we had a right to expect,' he remarked. 'Expect nothing else,' I said. 'There are only private letters.' He withdrew upon some threat of legal proceedings, and I saw him no more; but another fellow, calling himself Kurtz's cousin, appeared two days later, and was anxious to hear all the details about his dear relative's last moments. Incidentally he gave me to understand that Kurtz had been essentially a great musician. "There was the making of an immense success,' said the man, who was an organist, I believe, with lank gray hair flowing over a greasy coat-collar. I had no reason to doubt his statement; and to this day I am unable to say what was Kurtz's profession, whether he ever had any—which was the greatest of his talents. I had taken him for a painter who wrote for the papers, or else for a journalist who could paint

—but even the cousin (who took snuff during the interview) could not tell me what he had been—exactly. He was a universal genius—on that point I agreed with the old chap, who thereupon blew his nose noisily into a large cotton handkerchief and withdrew in senile agitation, bearing off some family letters and memoranda without importance. Ultimately a journalist anxious to know something of the fate of his 'dear colleague' turned up. This visitor informed me Kurtz's proper sphere ought to have been politics 'on the popular side.' He had furry straight eyebrows, bristly hair cropped short, an eyeglass on a broad ribbon, and, becoming expansive, confessed his opinion that Kurtz really couldn't write a bit—'but heavens! how that man could talk. He electrified large meetings. He had faith—don't you see?—he had the faith. He could get himself to believe anything—anything. He would have been a splendid leader of an extreme party.' 'What party?' I asked. 'Any party,' answered the other. 'He was an—an—extremist.' Did I not think so? I assented. Did I know, he asked, with a sudden flash of curiosity, 'what it was that had induced him to go out there?' 'Yes,' said I, and forthwith handed him the famous Report for publication, if he thought fit. He glanced through it hurriedly, mumbling all the time, judged 'it would do,' and took himself off with this plunder.

"Thus I was left at last with a slim packet of letters and the girl's portrait. She struck me as beautiful—I mean she had a beautiful expression. I know that the sunlight can be made to lie, too, yet one felt that no manipulation of light and pose could have conveyed the delicate shade of truthfulness upon those features. She seemed ready to listen without mental reservation, without suspicion, without a thought for herself. I concluded I would go and give her back her portrait and those letters myself. Curiosity? Yes; and also some other feeling perhaps. All that had been Kurtz's had passed out of my hands: his soul, his body, his station, his plans, his ivory, his career. There remained only his memory and his Intended—and I wanted to give that up, too, to the past, in a way—to surrender personally all that remained of him with me to that oblivion which is the last word of our common fate. I don't defend myself. I had no clear perception of what it was I really wanted. Perhaps it was an impulse of unconscious loyalty, or the fulfillment of one of those ironic necessities that lurk in the facts of human existence. I don't know. I can't tell. But I went.

"I thought his memory was like the other memories of the dead that accumulate in every man's life—a vague impress on the brain of shadows that had fallen on it in their swift and final passage; but before the high and ponderous door, between the tall houses of a street as still and decorous as a well-kept alley in a cemetery, I had a vision of him on the stretcher, opening his mouth voraciously, as if to devour all the earth with all its mankind. He lived then before me; he lived as much as he had ever lived—a shadow insatiable of splendid appearances, of frightful realities; a shadow darker than the shadow of the night, and draped nobly in the folds of a gorgeous eloquence. The vision seemed to enter the house with me—the stretcher, the phantom-bearers, the wild crowd of obedient worshipers, the gloom of the forests, the glitter of the reach between the murky bends, the beat of the drum, regular and muffled like the beating of a heart—the heart of a conquering darkness. It was a moment of triumph for the wilderness, an invading and vengeful rush which, it seemed to me, I would have to keep back alone for the salvation of another soul. And the memory of what I had heard him say afar there, with the horned shapes stirring at my back, in the glow of fires, within the patient woods, those broken phrases came back to me, were heard again in their ominous and terrifying simplicity. I remembered his abject pleading, his abject threats, the colossal scale of his vile desires, the meanness, the torment, the tempestuous anguish of his soul. And later on I seemed to see his collected languid manner, when he said one day, 'This lot of ivory now is really mine. The Company did not pay for it. I collected it myself at a very great personal risk. I am afraid they will try to claim it as theirs though. H'm. It is a difficult case. What do you think I ought to do—resist? Eh? I want no more than justice.' . . . He wanted no more than justice—no more than justice. I rang the bell before a mahogany door on the first floor, and while I waited he seemed to stare at me out of the glassy panel—stare with that wide and immense stare embracing, condemning, loathing all the universe. I seemed to hear the whispered cry, 'The horror! The horror!'

"The dusk was falling. I had to wait in a lofty drawing-room with three long windows from floor to ceiling that were like three luminous and bedraped columns. The bent gilt legs and backs of the furniture shone in indistinct curves. The tall marble fireplace had a cold and monumental whiteness. A grand piano stood massively in a corner; with dark gleams on the flat surfaces like a somber and polished sarcophagus. A high door opened—closed. I rose.

"She came forward, all in black, with a pale head, floating towards me in the dusk. She was in mourning. It was more than a year since his death, more than a year since the news came; she seemed as though she would remember and mourn forever. She took both my hands in hers and murmured, 'I had heard you were coming.' I noticed she was not very young—I mean not girlish. She had a mature capacity for fidelity, for belief, for suffering. The room seemed to have grown darker, as if all the sad light of the cloudy evening had taken refuge on her forehead. This fair hair, this pale visage, this pure brow, seemed surrounded by an ashy halo from which the dark eyes looked out at me. Their glance was guileless, profound, confident, and trustful. She carried her sorrowful head as though she were proud of that sorrow, as though she would say, I—I alone know how to mourn him as he deserves. But while we were still shaking hands, such a look of awful desolation came upon her face that I perceived she was one of those creatures that are not the playthings of Time. For her he had died only yesterday. And, by Jove! the impression was so powerful that for me, too, he seemed to have died only yesterday—nay, this very minute. I saw her and him in the same instant of time—his death and her sorrow—I saw her sorrow in the very moment of his death. Do you understand? I saw them together—I heard them together. She had said, with a deep catch of the breath, 'I have survived' while my strained ears seemed to hear distinctly, mingled with her tone of despairing regret, the summing up whisper of his eternal condemnation. I asked myself what I was doing there, with a sensation of panic in my heart as though I had blundered into a place of cruel and absurd mysteries not fit for a human being to behold. She motioned me to a chair. We sat down. I laid the packet gently on the little table, and she put her hand over it. . . . 'You knew him well,' she murmured, after a moment of mourning silence.

" 'Intimacy grows quickly out there,' I said. 'I knew him as well as it is possible for one man to know another.'

" 'And you admired him,' she said. 'It was impossible to know him and not to admire him. Was it?'

" 'He was a remarkable man,' I said, unsteadily. Then before the appealing fixity of her gaze, that seemed to watch for more words on my lips, I went on, 'It was impossible not to—'

" 'Love him,' she finished eagerly, silencing me into an appalled dumbness. 'How true! how true! But when you think that no one knew him so well as I! I had all his noble confidence. I knew him best.'

" 'You knew him best,' I repeated. And perhaps she did. But with every word spoken the room was growing darker, and only her forehead, smooth and white, remained illumined by the unextinguishable light of belief and love.

" 'You were his friend,' she went on. 'His friend,' she repeated, a little louder. 'You must have been, if he had given you this, and sent you to me. I feel I can speak to you—and oh! I must speak. I want you—you have heard his last words—to know I have been worthy of him. . . . . It is not pride. . . . Yes! I am proud to know I understood him better than any one on earth—he told me so himself. And since his mother died I have had no one—no one—to—to—'

"I listened. The darkness deepened. I was not even sure he had given me the right bundle. I rather suspect he wanted me to take care of another batch of his papers which, after his death, I saw the manager examining under the lamp. And the girl talked, easing her pain in the certitude of my sympathy; she talked as thirsty men drink. I had heard that her engagement with Kurtz had been disapproved by her people. He wasn't rich enough or something. And indeed I don't know whether he had not been a pauper all his life. He had given me some reason to infer that it was his impatience of comparative poverty that drove him out there.

" '. . . Who was not his friend who had heard him speak once?' she was saying. 'He drew men towards him by what was best in them.' She looked at me with intensity. 'It is the gift of the great,' she went on, and the sound of her low voice seemed to have the accompaniment of all the other sounds, full of mystery, desolation, and sorrow, I had ever heard—the ripple of the river, the soughing of the trees swayed by the wind, the murmurs of the crowds, the faint ring of incomprehensible words cried from afar, the whisper of a voice speaking from beyond the threshold of an eternal darkness. 'But you have heard him! You know!' she cried.

" 'Yes I know,' I said with something like despair in my heart, but bowing my head before the faith that was in her, before that great and saving illusion that shone with an unearthly glow in the darkness, in the triumphant darkness from which I could not have defended her —from which I could not even defend myself.

" 'What a loss to me—to us!'— she corrected herself with beautiful generosity; then added in a murmur, 'To the world.' By the last gleams of twilight I could see the glitter of her eyes, full of tears—of tears that would not fall.

" 'I have been very happy—very fortunate— very proud,' she went on. 'Too fortunate. Too happy for a little while. And now I am unhappy for—for life.'

"She stood up; her fair hair seemed to catch all the remaining light in a glimmer of gold. I rose, too.

" 'And of all this,' she went on, mournfully, 'of all his promise, and of all his greatness, of his generous mind, of his noble heart, nothing remains—nothing but a memory. You and I—'

" 'We shall always remember him,' I said, hastily.

" 'No!' she cried. 'It is impossible that all this should be lost—that such a life should be sacrificed to leave nothing—but sorrow. You know what vast plans he had. I knew of them, too— I could not perhaps understand—but others knew of them. Something must remain. His words, at least, have not died.'

" 'His words will remain,' I said.

" 'And his example,' she whispered to herself. 'Men looked up to him—his goodness shone in every act. His example—'

" 'True,' I said; 'his example, too. Yes, his example. I forgot that.'

" 'But I do not. I cannot—I cannot believe— not yet. I cannot believe that I shall never see him again, that nobody will see him again, never, never, never.'

"She put out her arms as if after a retreating figure, stretching them black and with clasped pale hands across the fading and narrow sheen of the window. Never see him! I saw him clearly enough then. I shall see this eloquent phantom as long as I live, and I shall see her, too, a tragic and familiar Shade, resembling in this gesture another one, tragic also, and bedecked with powerless charms, stretching bare brown arms over the glitter of the infernal stream, the stream of darkness. She said suddenly very low, 'He died as he lived.'

" 'His end,' said I, with dull anger stirring in me, 'was in every way worthy of his life.'

" 'And I was not with him,' she murmured. My anger subsided before a feeling of infinite pity.

" 'Everything that could be done—' I mumbled.

" 'Ah, but I believed in him more than any one on earth—more than his own mother, more than—himself. He needed me! Me! I would have treasured every sigh, every word, every sign, every glance.'

"I felt like a chill grip on my chest. 'Don't,' I said, in a muffled voice.

" 'Forgive me. I—I—have mourned so long in silence—in silence. . . . You were with him —to the last? I think of his loneliness. Nobody near to understand him as I would have understood. Perhaps no one to hear. . . .'

" 'To the very end,' I said, shakily. 'I heard his very last words. . . .' I stopped in a fright.

" 'Repeat them,' she murmured in a heartbroken tone. 'I want—I want—something— something—to—live with.'

"I was on the point of crying at her, 'Don't you hear them?' The dusk was repeating them in a persistent whisper all around us, in a whisper that seemed to swell menacingly like the first whisper of a rising wind. 'The horror! The horror!'

" 'His last word—to live with,' she insisted. 'Don't you understand I loved him—I loved him —I loved him!'

"I pulled myself together and spoke slowly.

" 'The last word he pronounced was—your name.'

"I heard a light sigh and then my heart stood still, stopped dead short by an exulting and terrible cry, by the cry of inconceivable triumph and of unspeakable pain. 'I knew it— I was sure!' . . . She knew. She was sure. I heard her weeping; she had hidden her face in her hands. It seemed to me that the house would collapse before I could escape, that the heavens would fall upon my head. But nothing happened. The heavens do not fall for such a trifle. Would they have fallen, I wonder, if I had rendered Kurtz that justice which was his due? Hadn't he said he wanted only justice? But I couldn't. I could not tell her. It would have been too dark—too dark altogether. . . ."

Marlow ceased, and sat apart, indistinct and silent, in the pose of a meditating Buddha. Nobody moved for a time. "We have lost the first of the ebb," said the Director suddenly. I raised my head. The offing was barred by a black bank of clouds, and the tranquil waterway leading to the uttermost ends of the earth flowed somber under an overcast sky—seemed to lead into the heart of an immense darkness.

Comments and Questions

Some qualified readers believe "Heart of Darkness" to be the greatest story written in English. Even allowing for some exaggeration, the opinion is a tremendous tribute to a Pole (Joseph Theodor Konrad Nalecz Korzeniowski) who entered the marine service at seventeen years, began to learn English at twenty-one, and finished his first novel, *Almayer's Folly,* at thirty-seven. "Heart of Darkness" was written at the height of his literary power (1898): what is the nature of this achievement?

Whose story is it? Some readers give the story to Marlow, others to Kurtz. It has been argued that unless we understand the psychological transformation that takes place within Marlow, the meaning of the story is lost. On the other hand, unless we understand the cause of Marlow's transformation there is no story at all—and the cause is the story of Kurtz. The symbolic action of the story can be found by answering at least four questions: What kind of man was Kurtz before he left for Africa? Why did he go? What happened to him at the Inner Station? And, most important of all, why does Marlow call Kurtz's final "judgment," or "affirmation," ("The horror! The horror!") a "moral victory"?

Before we probe these questions, let us note that the story's basic integrating symbol—the symbol that fuses and makes meaningful all the facts—is the ivory. The ivory operates here as a beckoning crown operates in *Macbeth.* How else explain the ironic asides of Marlow (for example, "the jolly pioneers of progress") and the Faust theme? What is the slow process by which Kurtz gives his soul to evil (the Devil)?

Before Kurtz left for Africa he had been a talented man, "a universal genius" whose "impatience of comparative poverty . . . drove him" to Africa to make his fortune to overcome the objections of his Intended's family to their marriage. The ivory and also his talents, recognized by the Company, were to bring him happiness. Kurtz left as "an emissary of pity, and science, and progress . . . equipped with moral ideas of some sort," and yet when Marlow found him at the Inner Station, Kurtz had been accepted as a deity who "presided at certain midnight dances ending with unspeakable rites, which . . . were offered up to him. . . ." What had happened to Kurtz?

Kurtz had been confronted with two basic temptations: his desire to make a fortune through ivory, and his discovery of his latent kinship with the savages, as Marlow discovered in himself. Marlow tells us: The savages "howled and leaped, and spun, and made horrid faces; but what thrilled you was just the thought of their humanity—like yours—the . . . remote kinship with this wild and passionate uproar." Within Kurtz these two temptations coalesced, and he yielded to their combined power by using his authority as deity to help him steal "more ivory than all the other agents together." "The wilderness," Marlow tells us, "had patted him on the head, and, behold, it was like a ball—an ivory ball [the integrating symbol] . . . ; it had taken him, loved him, embraced him, got into his veins, consumed his flesh, and sealed his soul to its own by the inconceivable ceremonies of some devilish initiation. . . . [The] wilderness . . . seemed to draw him to its pitiless breast *by the awakening of forgotten and brutal instincts,* by the memory of gratified and monstrous passions." (Italics added.) "If," Marlow says, "anybody had ever struggled with a soul, I am the man."

These quoted passages, interpreted within

the context of the entire story, will help us to answer our final question, why does Marlow call Kurtz's final judgment a "moral victory"? When Marlow found Kurtz crawling through the grass back to the village, Marlow told him, "You will be lost—utterly lost," and Kurtz permitted himself (he could have roused the warriors against Marlow) to be carried back to the riverboat. This was the first basic decision by Kurtz, an affirmation that he had bargained with evil and had lost. When therefore, just before he died, he cried, "The horror! The horror!" he had, as Marlow tells us, "pronounced a judgment upon the adventures of his soul on this earth." The judgment was a moral victory because Kurtz had not only acknowledged the evil in himself, but his final vision "was wide enough to penetrate *all the hearts that beat in the darkness.*" (Italics added.) The judgment is a bitter warning to all men against the ever-latent evil in their hearts. Kurtz's discovery came too late; the implication for us is obvious.

The story, then, has at least three levels of meaning, all related to the title. Literally, the heart of darkness means, of course, the heart of Africa—the savage darkness outside civilization. Symbolically, it means the heart of Kurtz; but deepest of all it means the heart of mankind which was—shall we say?—at its birth given to evil, a condition man has fought against for centuries. Kurtz's judgment, "The horror!" seems to come as a result of this insight into the hearts of all men, and this revelation to Marlow appears to be the cause of Marlow's psychological transformation.

The theme of universal guilt, prominent in the history of letters, is presented also in Eliot's "The Hollow Men" (p. 345), but Eliot, unlike Conrad, does not only warn us of the consequences, he tells us we are no longer even sensitive to its presence. Eliot's epigraph, *"Mistah Kurtz—he dead,"* implies in the context of the poem that we, unlike Kurtz, will not cross "With direct eyes, to death's other Kingdom." Kurtz saw the horror of evil, affirmed the evil, and gained a "moral victory," while by contrast "We grope together / And avoid speech," neither living nor dying heroically.

Poetry

. . . is "news that stays news"
EZRA POUND

The verse is mine but friend, when you declaim it,
It seems like yours, so grievously you maim it.
MARTIAL

PRELIMINARIES

ROBERT FROST
1874–1963

Stopping by Woods on a Snowy Evening

Whose woods these are I think I know.
His house is in the village though;
He will not see me stopping here
To watch his woods fill up with snow.

My little horse must think it queer
To stop without a farmhouse near
Between the woods and frozen lake
The darkest evening of the year.

He gives his harness bells a shake
To ask if there is some mistake.
The only other sound's the sweep
Of easy wind and downy flake.

The woods are lovely, dark and deep.
But I have promises to keep,
And miles to go before I sleep,
And miles to go before I sleep.

The definitions of poetry, the hymns of praise, and the essays on the nature of poetry would cram the shelves of any modest public library and overflow onto the floors as well. Good talk about poetry is nevertheless rare, and even the best of it will rest lightly on fallow ground until we ourselves have learned how to penetrate the inner life of a few poems. We cannot be talked into enjoying the pleasures of poetry, but we can bring ourselves to such pleasures by learning to understand individual poems.

"General Preliminaries" (p. 1) implies that each type of literature has a structure of its own. If we wish to understand the structure of a poem, it seems sensible to begin by examining one. We shall learn much about poetry in general if we can discover exactly what Frost has done and how he has done it.

The Plain Sense of a Poem

As we read Frost's poem for the first time, a certain kind of sense comes through to us almost immediately. This sense we shall call the poem's plain sense, sometimes called literal sense or literal meaning. The plain sense gives us the literal facts of a poem, and with such facts all understanding of a poem begins, but does *not* end.

The plain sense of Frost's poem tells us that the speaker, returning home at dusk in his one-horse sleigh, stops to enjoy the peace and solitude of the occasion: the snow is falling softly, the woods are inviting, there is no other human being to break the silence. But the horse finds no reason for stopping: it is growing dark, there is no house in sight, and the miles stretch before them. Reflecting on his horse's impatience, the speaker concedes that he should move on to keep the commitments he has made.

But in drawing the plain sense from the poem we have raised many questions. Unless this poem means more than the paraphrase above includes, does the poem merit further consideration? Will another kind of approach to the poem reveal meanings not yet located? These and other questions we must answer if we are to understand the poem fully. Let us note before we proceed that paraphrasing the poem helped to raise the questions about the poem's fullest meaning. Unless the plain sense is clearly understood before further analysis of a poem begins, the reader is likely to misconstrue the total meaning of the poem.

Imagery

A little closer reading of the poem shows us that Frost is depending on our ability to see and hear imaginatively. When he uses such words as *woods* and *horse,* he depends on our ability to see the real woods and horse. When the horse "gives his harness bells a shake," and when we are told that

> The only other sound's the sweep
> Of easy wind and downy flake,

the poet depends on our ability to hear these sounds. Contrary to some popular opinion, there is no mystery in imagery. Its function in poetry is identical with its function in everyday speech: it presents to the reader his concrete world of things, and recalls the sight and sound and feel of them. With imagery the poet peoples and furnishes the world of his poem, and causes us to experience that world as directly and unmistakably as we experience life itself. Indeed, it is sometimes said that imagery is the very basis of poetry, and as we proceed we shall observe the force of this assertion. (For further exploration of imagery, see "Imagery," p. 218.)

Figurative Language

A still closer reading of Frost's poem shows that he has used some of his imagery in a special way. When we read that

> My little horse must think it queer
> To stop without a farmhouse near,

we suspect that this is no ordinary horse. And when we read further that

> He gives his harness bells a shake
> To ask if there is some mistake,

we know that this is a very special horse, one that asks questions. At this point in our attempt to understand the poem we are moving from the plain sense to the figurative sense of the poem. The speaker in the poem is not alone, as he seemed to be in the first stanza, and we sense a conflict of some sort between him and the horse. The horse, having been given some human characteristics, becomes in a sense a human being and challenges the speaker in some significant way. By comparing the horse with a human being, the poet has described him figuratively.

There are other figures in the poem, as in the lines,

> The only other sound's the *sweep*
> Of *easy* wind and *downy* flake,

in which both the wind and snow are described figuratively, not literally. The wind moves gracefully, easily, with the curving, hushed motion of an unseen broom; and the snowflakes are as soft as the down, or fluffy feathers, on a young bird.

It is customary at this point in most books on the nature of poetry to describe in abstract terms the reason for using figurative language. Suppose we forego this temptation and permit the poem itself to tell us. Perhaps the poem can answer the question most often asked by students and general readers alike: "Why doesn't the poet say what he *means?* If by downy flake he means soft flake, why doesn't he say so?" Such questions are usually asked impatiently, as if only poets resorted to figures of speech. But our everyday speech is peppered (!) with figures of speech. We "go on a lark," "lead a dog's life," "smell a rat," "stumble in our thinking," and "walk the straight and narrow path." Aren't we saying what we mean? We are saying exactly what we mean, and so is Frost. The word *soft* is too general: there is also soft steel and soft wood. How soft is soft? We know how soft Frost's flakes are: they are as soft as down—about as soft as soft can be.

The figure of speech not only says exactly what the poet means, *it also invites the reader to help to say it.* To understand what Frost means by "downy flake," we must transfer the relevant characteristics from the down of birds to the snowflakes. This is an imaginative act, not a passive acceptance. *The figure requires us to participate in the life of the poem.* (For further exploration of figures, see "Figure and Symbol," p. 266.)

Symbolism

We now return to Frost's little horse. The poet has described the horse figuratively by giving him certain characteristics of a person. The horse thinks it queer "to stop without a farmhouse near," and he therefore asks "if there is some mistake" about this stopping. He is challenging the "impractical" sense of the driver with his own horse sense. When the writer uses one thing to stand for another, we call it a symbol. The horse stands for horse sense, and operates as a symbol in the poem, as we shall observe later.

Not all figures of speech contain symbols, and not all symbols in a poem are embedded in figures of speech. (For further explanation of this distinction, see "Figure and Symbol," p. 266.) The horse is a figure and a symbol, but what about the "woods," the "promises," and the "miles"? These things are not figuratively described, but they could be symbols. And if they are, what do they stand for? Why is the driver of the horse tempted to interrupt his journey by watching the woods fill up with snow? Why does he regard them as "lovely, dark and deep"? To whom has he given "promises," and what kind of promises? And while we are bearing down on this seemingly innocent little poem, questioning every literal stroke of the poet's pen, let us ask what kind of "miles" are meant. And is the "sleep" only temporary or permanent?

Perhaps these questions have already suggested that many symbols in poetry have been made conventional through long use. Just as the handclasp in everyday life stands for friendliness, the word *dark* or *darkest* in poetry may stand for something unknown or forbidding or secretive, perhaps even tragic. The title of Arthur Koestler's novel *Darkness at Noon* is completely symbolic, and suggests that some tragedy throws its shadow over our century. Here a warning is appropriate: such words as *darkness, noon, light, black,* and *white* are not always used symbolically. How, then, do we know when they are so used? Symbols are identified and their meaning made clear by the full context of the poem. In fact, this principle determines the meaning of all the elements in every poem. It can be stated this way: *the whole poem helps to determine the meaning of its parts, and, in turn, each part helps to determine the meaning of the whole poem.*

The Meaning of a Poem: The Parts and the Whole

As the first step in understanding a poem, we have seen how helpful it is to make a paraphrase of its plain sense. We are now in a position to make a different kind of paraphrase, one that includes the figurative-symbolic meaning of the poem. We are seeing again the method used in all creative literature (as we saw in "General Preliminaries"), a method we have already seen operate in fiction. As we begin, we keep in mind imagery, figurative language, and symbolism. We should enjoy this detective work, determined to let nothing important escape us.

Frost's imagery gives us the life-texture of the situation and makes it credible, or believable. Within this context of reality we can think and feel as we do in real life: we can participate in the life of the poem. But in order to do so we must understand the relationships of the imagery, figures, and symbols: their relationships make the symbolic meaning of the poem.

Why is the driver tempted to interrupt his journey? Is it because nature has invited him to her communion? The solitude and peace of the woods softly filling with snow tempt him to leave off this moving from place to place—to what end is all this journeying? The woods, "lovely, dark and deep," invite him to leave the traffic of the world on "the darkest evening of the year," the time of his life when his personal burdens weigh most heavily upon him.* But the dramatic device of the horse shows us the conflict within the man: shall he yield to this temptation or move on to fulfill his promises? The noise of the harness bells breaks his reverie, and asks for his decision.

Having come so far in this symbolic interpretation of the poem, it is no longer possible to regard the "promises," the "miles," and the "sleep" as mere literal facts.

The last stanza,

The woods are lovely, dark and deep.
But I have promises to keep,
And miles to go before I sleep,
And miles to go before I sleep.

can therefore be paraphrased by saying that the driver consents to move on, to forego entering a world of his own, because he has promises and responsibilities to fulfill to humanity during the years before he dies. Interpreted figuratively, these lines reconcile the conflict within the driver. This conflict is a condition which exists in most, if not all, human beings, and for this reason we say that Frost's poem has universal value, or universality.

* Some readers have found a death wish in this poem. In a public lecture at the State University of Iowa, April 13, 1959, Frost stated explicitly that the poem "is not concerned with death." His statement, of course, does not settle the matter. Nevertheless the tension in the poem is surely between the horse and the driver, and they hardly represent life and death.

Rhythm and Rhyme

There are other elements, not yet mentioned, which Frost has used to fashion the total meaning of his poem. It is sometimes difficult for readers to believe that such matters as rhythm and rhyme are used to convey meaning. Popular opinion regards them as troublesome technical matters of interest to the specialist only, or at best as ornaments on the poetic Christmas tree. Once again let us forego the customary abstract definitions of such matters and let the poet's practice provide the instruction.

After all we have now discovered about Frost's compact, sensitive lyric, we can hardly suspect him of decorating his poem with the trinkets of rhythm and rhyme to exhibit his cleverness. Here, it should be made very clear that poetry should be spoken aloud: poetry is speech, and the voice, or tone, of the poet communicates his attitude toward the facts of the poem. Unless we *hear* Frost's lines being spoken aloud, all of our observations below will miss the mark.

A very old definition of poetry regards it as a fusion of sound and sense.* Note that word *fusion:* not a mechanical combination, but a fusion, a melting together of sound and sense. In our paraphrase of the figurative meaning of the poem above, we apparently discussed the sense while ignoring the sound. But—now the secret comes out—this was not so. Experienced readers of poetry know that the division is impossible because as one reads for sense, one is either consciously or unconsciously being influenced by the sound. Hence before our paraphrase of the poem had been started, the sound of the poem had already done its work, exerting its influence on the writer of the paraphrase. Now let us see just how skillful Frost has been.

As we read the poem aloud, we hear and feel the movement within each line. In a good poem the right sound is fused with the right sense, thus:

> Whose woods these are I think I know.
> His house is in the vil-lage though.

* As Pope put it, "The sound must seem an Echo to the sense" (p. 253). Frost speaks of "the sound of sense."

Now let us change the word order but not the words themselves:

> I think I know whose woods these are
> Though his house is in the village.

Here, the wrong sound has distorted the sense.

As we read Frost's arrangement aloud, we hear the four pulsations or beats in each line. Because there are four beats we call the line *tetrameter* (tetra = four), a line of four feet. We hear also that each foot contains two syllables, the first one unstressed and the second one stressed (whŏse wóóds), which foot we call *iambic*. The iambic foot is acknowledged to be the most natural rhythm in colloquial English, that is, in our familiar, everyday spoken language. Compare Frost's lines with these (read them aloud):

> 'Twas the night before Christ-mas, when all
> through the house,
> Not a crea-ture was stir-ring, not e-ven a
> mouse.

This anapestic rhythm is appropriate to give us the feel of galloping reindeer and the excitement of Christmas Eve, but it is hardly appropriate for the colloquial expression with which Frost speaks to us directly, simply, and naturally. It should be clear, then, that his rhythm is not a decoration, *but rather a basic element in the poem's structure and meaning.*

A brief examination of Frost's rhyme scheme will show how consciously and purposefully it must have been chosen. It runs:

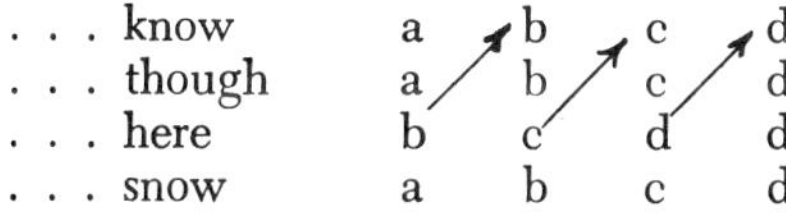

One of the purposes of rhyme is to tie the sense together with sound. Note, then, three important consequences of Frost's rhyme scheme. First, three of the four lines in each stanza (except the last stanza) rhyme; hence, these stanzas are very compact sound-and-sense units. Second, the *third* line in each stanza always rhymes with the *first* line in the following stanza; hence the sound helps to pass the sense from one stanza to the next. And third, in the last stanza all four lines rhyme; hence, the sound is brought to rest just as the reconciliation of the conflict within the driver is brought to rest, and as he will be brought to rest upon his arrival at home. And note particularly that the symbols involved in the rhyming words *deep, keep,* and *sleep* are the key symbols which finally reveal the full meaning of the poem. (For further explanation of the functions of rhythm and rhyme, see "Rhythm and Rhyme," p. 221.)

Are we ready to say that these matters are accidents or pretty decorations or troublesome technical matters outside the full meaning of Frost's poem? Hardly. Frost has demonstrated to us the truth of Stephen Spender's acute remark that "a poem *means* the sum of everything which it *is*. . . ." (See Spender's essay, "On Teaching Modern Poetry," p. 687.) The sum of everything which Frost's poem *is* contains more than we have already located, but we have located and discussed the poem's basic factors, the factors which must be understood in order to interpret the meaning of almost any poem.

What Have We Learned?

We have learned that a poem is a living organism which contains the necessary elements of its own life. If "a poem *means* the sum of everything which it *is*," we must not only understand everything in the poem: we must be aware of all its parts as they work together to make the total meaning of the poem. If the poem is a good one, and this is surely one test, every element in it contributes to its meaning.

We have learned further that a poem has at least two levels of meaning: the literal level and the figurative-symbolic level. We have seen that a poem suggests much more than it says literally: like lovers' conversation, a poem gives out hints of extensive meanings along the way. Students often refer to the figurative meaning as the hidden meaning, as if the poet had set out to hide his meaning in order to make the poem difficult. Ordinarily, poets have outgrown the game of hide-and-seek, but they do write figuratively for such reasons as Frost has already demonstrated.

And we have learned that a poem possesses a concentration and intensity which help to make it memorable. *The right word in the right place, the intimate fusion of sound and sense, and the economy of rich suggestion are virtues of the structure of most poetry.*

THE MISREADING OF POEMS

Most misreadings of poems come from the reader's failure to realize that there are many languages within the English language, such as the languages of science, history, journalism, and, of course, the language of poetry itself. By using *language* in this sense, we mean a unified pattern of words including certain specific devices to communicate a very specific meaning. Poetry has such a language of its own. For example, when Frost says,

> My little horse must think it queer
> To stop without a farmhouse near,

we immediately sense the language of poetry, not of science or history, because of the devices of rhythm (iambic tetrameter), rhyme (*queer-near*), figurative language (a horse that thinks), and symbol (a horse that stands for practical sense as against the impractical sense of the driver).

It is best, of course, to learn in a positive way what to look for in a poem, and what to do with what we find, but nevertheless we may save ourselves some difficulty if we first identify a few blind alleys to be avoided.

To illustrate some basic causes of misreading a poem, suppose we begin by examining a few student comments on the following poem.

HART CRANE
1899–1932

North Labrador

A land of leaning ice
Hugged by plaster-grey arches of sky,
Flings itself silently
Into eternity.

"Has no one come here to win you,
Or left you with the faintest blush
Upon your glittering breasts?
Have you no memories, O Darkly Bright?"

Cold-hushed, there is only the shifting of
moments

That journey toward no Spring—
No birth, no death, no time nor sun
In answer.

Failure on the Literal Level*

Incredible as it may seem, the failures on this level are legion. Few readers admit guilt, yet most of us are sinners. One reader of "North Labrador" read *Spring* (l. 10) as running water, and asked why the word had been capitalized. It is easy to smile at this error, but even practiced readers are victims of similar kinds of mistakes. We can avoid failure on the literal level by asking questions like these about every poem: *Who* is speaking to whom? *What* is the situation in the poem? *Where* are we geographically, and in time? Further, the literal level is determined by applying the same basic disciplines we use in reading prose: we should seek to understand the sentence structure—the very grammar—the vocabulary (how many failures here!), the pronouns (especially *its*), and even the punctuation. Elementary? Yes, and indispensable. True, the full meaning of a poem does not end with its literal sense, but neither will figurative meaning begin without it.

Failure to Rise to the Figurative Level

Having examined "North Labrador," three readers commented as follows. "I think this poem is rather stupid. It is quite evident that no one could survive on a sheet of ice. But the author does ask the question, 'why has no one settled here?' There seems to be little point to it." Despite that slight stirring in his third sentence, this reader is truly shackled, and even the second stanza, which compares North Labrador to a woman, does no more than to shake his prose chains. Another reader begins to worry about those chains: "I like the arrangement of this poem. It leaves one with thoughts about it, and I wonder just what is meant." Still another reader threatens to break loose and rise to the figurative level: "The words [images] in this one caught my attention first—they are quite descriptive and put me in a mood. I can see the cold desolation, the colorlessness, and can feel the moments plodding by with a pointless, 'toward no Spring,' sameness." This reader is on his way to poetic liberation. When he sees that the entire poem is literally about North Labrador but figuratively about the utter loneliness and emotional starvation of the human heart, he will have learned a basic lesson in the reading of poems.

To rise to the figurative level of a poem requires imagination, or the ability to perceive comparisons—to understand, for example, that Hart Crane is making a comment on humanity by talking about North Labrador. Crane had seen the dramatic comparison with his imagination, and he has therefore used certain aspects of North Labrador to comment on a tragic situation in the human heart.

Failure to Recognize Irony

Many readers, churning with good spirits and ready to accept their world at face value, are likely to accept irony at face value, too. The failure to recognize irony is closely related to the failure to rise to the figurative level because irony, like simile and metaphor, is a figure of speech. Yet it is a special kind of figure because it relies more on *contrast* than on comparison, and consequently the poet depends on the reader to bring a special knowledge to the ironical statement to understand the contrast. In extended pieces of literature, of course, the author himself may provide the necessary special knowledge.

When Burns writes,

My love is like a red red rose,

he is emphasizing the comparison, not the contrast, between the loved one and the beauties of the rose. But when Sandburg writes in *The People, Yes* (p. 295),

"The czar has eight million men with guns
    and bayonets.
"Nothing can happen to the czar.
"The czar is the voice of God and shall live
    forever.
"Turn and look at the forest of steel and
    cannon
"Where the czar is guarded by eight million
    soldiers.
"Nothing can happen to the czar."

* For a demonstration of the difference between the literal and figurative levels as found, for example, in Frost's "Stopping by Woods on a Snowy Evening," see "The Plain Sense of a Poem," p. 218, and compare "The Meaning of a Poem," p. 220.

he is emphasizing the contrast between the czar and the voice of God that shall live forever. With our knowledge of what did happen to the czar we understand Sandburg's irony in having the speaker naively believe that "nothing can happen to the czar" because he "is guarded by eight million soldiers." And the irony is further compounded by the suggestion that the voice of God will live forever because of the protection of guns and bayonets.

The title of Eliot's poem "The Love Song of J. Alfred Prufrock" (p. 390) is ironic for the reader if he catches the suggestion of a prude dressed in a frock coat (a Prince Albert) contemplating the act of love-making. "Love Song" is intended to recall the sensations of love songs long admired, and the reader may remember two famous lines from a Shakespearian sonnet (p. 262):

> Love alters not with his brief hours and weeks,
> But bears it out even to the edge of doom.

Prufrock's love song tells us why he hovers on the edge of doom, but hardly for the reasons offered by Shakespeare. By such a contrast Eliot exposes Prufrock's frustration: Eliot's use of the word *love* is ironic because Prufrock is capable only of self-love.

As a poetic device irony accomplishes some valuable effects for the poet. He can profess a restraint and detachment while often his emotions are intensely aroused. This posture plus the double meaning of the irony are likely to appeal to the sophisticated intelligence of readers who come to feel that they and the poet share recondite meanings obscure to less perceptive minds. Irony, indeed, has enjoyed a long philosophical career, and its enjoyment is a mark of the mature mind. It produces an unmistakable tone in a poem, and tone itself, we shall come to see later, becomes a figure of speech as it pervades an entire poem. (See "Figure and Symbol," p. 266.)

Preconceptions About the Nature of Poetry

One of the most persistent preconceptions holds that a poem must contain ideas, penetrating abstractions about the meaning of life—or, the reverse, a poem must be "pure" and never "soiled" with "thought."* Either position disqualifies a huge share of the world's distinguished poetry, and this act alone should alert us to the untenable dogmatism. *Must* we make a decision between Robley Wilson, Jr.'s "The Great Teachers" (p. 370) and Coleridge's "Kubla Khan" (p. 321)? The judgment of the years says no.

Another preconception can become a little militant at times against pessimism. One reader of Crane's "North Labrador" writes that "This one appears to be on the gloomy side of things and it didn't appeal to me at all." This statement is closely allied to another reader's comment, "I don't think I am a better person for having read it." These preconceptions, too, would disqualify another huge share of the world's poems. We shall come to see that the fine poets do not arbitrarily decree that either optimism or pessimism is superior, nor do they assume that the proper function of a poem is to offer morals in capsule form. "North Labrador," for example, is actually a religious poem in the deepest sense, but Crane includes no explicitly stated prescription for happiness here or for salvation later. His comment appears by indirection and inference: the isolated soul who "journeys toward no Spring" is a cold, tragic soul who has been cut off from the warmth of love and affection. But Crane feels no responsibility for spelling out the prescription by adding another stanza saying, "Don't be like that avoid it at all cost!" Beware of judging a poem by its optimism or pessimism. It is better to ask, is the poem true? Does it enlarge my understanding and sympathies?

Preconceptions in favor of or against one doctrine or another can produce curious results in the reading of poems. Some readers constantly search for the confirming doctrine; they are determined to find what they already believe. This attitude of mind used as an approach to poems can bring unfortunate consequences. It may violate the poem's meaning to make it conform to the reader's belief. It is comfortable to have a great poet on our side, and the temptation to

* For a defense of this latter position, see the Introduction by George Moore to his *An Anthology of Pure Poetry*. New York: Liveright Publishing Corporation, 1924.

stretch him into place is not always resisted, but the art of the poem may be undervalued if the poem fails to confirm the reader's belief. Milton's *Paradise Lost* suffered this fate when T. S. Eliot found Milton's theology unpalatable, although, to Eliot's credit, he later recanted. Or this attitude of mind may overpraise the art of the poem if the poem does confirm the reader's belief.

The last-mentioned preconception is perhaps the most difficult to correct because it is quite natural—but still wrong—to accept without critical examination a poem's art simply because we agree with the poem's point of view. Forty-nine college students still without instruction in poetry on the college level were asked to judge seven poems which ranged from very good to bad. Thirty students commented favorably on the poorest poem of the seven, titled "A Visit to Mom and Dad," and five students thought it to be the best of the lot. After six weeks of experience in analyzing and judging many poems, these readers changed their opinion radically concerning the value of "A Visit to Mom and Dad" because they had learned that no subject, however close to their hearts, necessarily makes a good poem. (See "The Language of Poetry," especially p. 253 , for a demonstration of this principle.)

These readers were victims of what is known as *stock response*. To facilitate everyday living most of us gather a pattern of attitudes and a hierarchy of values by which we make decisions, issue opinions, and guide our everyday behavior. We are likely to react quickly against certain ideas and key words and in favor of others, sometimes without examining the context of the idea or key word. Debaters, candidates for office, and advertisers make a conscious study of our stock responses, and play the human console accordingly. And so do some writers of verse. In his poem, "Edgar A. Guest Considers 'The Old Woman Who Lived in a Shoe' and the Good Old Verities at the Same Time" (p. 233), Untermeyer satirizes Guest's way of appealing to our stock responses (the "Good Old Verities" are our generalized notions about children, parents, the home, sacrifice).

But we should be very clear about the relationship of stock responses and poems. There is nothing inherently wrong with stock responses. The point is, *what has the poet done with them?* The good poet—the poet devoted to his art—tries to furnish within the poem itself the attitudes and reasons for our participating in his belief. The poor poet simply pushes buttons marked "God," "Country," "Mom," and "Dad," and gives us no fresh experience, no insights, no "temporary stay against confusion." The logical question is: if the poet has no more to offer than his rhyming of our stock responses, why should he write?

Other preconceptions which sidetrack readers have to do with the sound of a poem, its form, and even its length. "North Labrador" brought such comments as these: "It's choppy. I prefer things that read a little smoother." Another reader: "I don't care for this style of writing." Another: "It's awfully short." But still another reader disagrees: "This reads easily and sounds like poetry should." These contradictory comments emerge from a failure to understand one of the basic principles of all poems: the poet selects the means (the technical devices) to produce his desired end. The sound and sense of a good poem are a fusion, an organic whole, and we must first comprehend the whole before we judge the means, or the technical matters. We shall soon see that Frost's "Departmental" (p. 232) is choppy, and that Burns's "Sweet Afton" (p. 232) is smoother and more flowing. And we shall see, too, that if either poem had the other's rhythm, both poems would be quite meaningless, indeed a little silly.

The only serviceable cure for the preconceptions brought to the reading of poems is to refuse to accept or reject *any* part of a poem until after the poem's totality has been mastered. Briefly, we should not read *into* poems; we should read *out* of poems whatever the poets have put into them. Once we have completely surrounded a poem's meaning it is our privilege to use the poem for any purpose whatever: as a document in the history of sensibility, as a confirmation or denial of the value of some sensuous experience or idea—but *not* before we have surrounded the poem's meaning. There is simply no other way.*

* For a revealing study of the causes of the misreadings of poems see I. A. Richards, *Practical Criticism, a Study of Literary Judgment*. New York: Harcourt Brace Jovanovich, Inc., 1929 and 1952, especially pp. 13–17.

ROBERT BROWNING
1812–1889

My Last Duchess
Ferrara

Now that we have absorbed some initial instruction on the reading of poetry, including some pitfalls to be avoided, suppose we put our preliminary knowledge to work on a poem. Browning's influence on the new twentieth-century poetry is now well known; he is indeed very much a "modern." "My Last Duchess" is a concentrated little dramatic scene in which the Duke describes his own character through his words and actions. Although the poem is a dramatic monologue, we can easily supply the conversation that has taken place between the Duke and his listener, the Count's emissary.

That's my last Duchess painted on the wall
Looking as if she were alive. I call
That piece a wonder, now: Frà Pandolf's hands
Worked busily a day, and there she stands.
Will't please you sit and look at her? I said
"Frà Pandolf" by design, for never read
Strangers like you that pictured countenance,
The depth and passion of its earnest glance,
But to myself they turned (since none puts by
The curtain I have drawn for you, but I)
And seemed as they would ask me, if they durst,
How such a glance came there; so, not the first
Are you to turn and ask thus. Sir, 'twas not
Her husband's presence only, called that spot
Of joy into the Duchess' cheek: perhaps
Frà Pandolf chanced to say, "Her mantle laps
Over my lady's wrist too much," or "Paint
Must never hope to reproduce the faint
Half-flush that dies along her throat." Such stuff
Was courtesy, she thought, and cause enough
For calling up that spot of joy. She had
A heart—how shall I say?—too soon made glad,
Too easily impressed; she liked whate'er
She looked on, and her looks went everywhere.
Sir, 'twas all one! My favor at her breast,
The dropping of the daylight in the West,
The bough of cherries some officious fool
Broke in the orchard for her, the white mule
She rode with round the terrace—all and each
Would draw from her alike the approving speech,
Or blush, at least. She thanked men,—good! but thanked
Somehow—I know not how—as if she ranked
My gift of a nine-hundred-years-old name
With anybody's gift. Who'd stoop to blame
This sort of trifling? Even had you skill
In speech—(which I have not)—to make your will
Quite clear to such an one, and say, "Just this
Or that in you disgusts me; here you miss,
Or there exceed the mark"—and if she let
Herself be lessoned so, nor plainly set
Her wits to yours, forsooth, and made excuse,
—E'en then would be some stooping; and I choose
Never to stoop. Oh, sir, she smiled, no doubt,
Whene'er I passed her; but who passed without
Much the same smile? This grew; I gave commands;
Then all smiles stopped together. There she stands
As if alive. Will't please you rise? We'll meet
The company below then. I repeat,
The Count your master's known munificence
Is ample warrant that no just pretence
Of mine for dowry will be disallowed;
Though his fair daughter's self, as I avowed
At starting, is my object. Nay, we'll go
Together down, sir. Notice Neptune, though,
Taming a sea-horse, thought a rarity,
Which Claus of Innsbruck cast in bronze for me!

Analytical Dialogue on "My Last Duchess"

The following dialogue on "My Last Duchess" is one way of analyzing a poem, that is, accounting for all the important matters which make the poem meaningful. This conversation between a student and his professor actually contains about nineteen principles which when observed help us to read poems accurately. The first principle appears in the opening comment by A: he has stated, very briefly, the plain, or literal, sense of the poem. He knows what the poem is "about."

But Z refuses to allow the poem to rest there, and the analysis is under way. What other principles of accurate reading can be found?

Z: You have read the poem?

A: Yes, and I think I understand it fairly well. It's about a Duke who had his wife killed because she was too pleasant to everybody.

Z: If that's all there is to it, why do so many people enjoy—and remember—this poem?

A: It's sensational; I suppose that's why.

Z: Perhaps, but in essence the story is commonplace. Newspapers every day carry accounts of murders committed for the slightest reasons. "Husband Has Wife Killed Because She Smiled at Everybody"—such a headline and the story would get passing attention, but few people would paste the account into a scrapbook. There must be something else to make this bit of writing memorable. Shall we see if we can find out what it is?

A: All right. Where do we start?

Z: With the title. Anything worth noting about the title? What does "Last" mean? Does it mean final?

A: Certainly not. The Duke's going to have another duchess. Probably "Last" means former or latest.

Z: Latest? Would that meaning imply that the Duke might have had another duchess—or several other duchesses—before the last one?

A: I don't know.

Z: Well, neither do I, and since such an idea has no bearing on the poem as it is told, suppose we discard it.

A: I have no objection. Besides I want you to know that I looked up Ferrara: it's a place in Italy, northern Italy.

Z: Good. That gives us something to go on, doesn't it? Ferrara is a real place. The speaker is an Italian duke, and the subject of his remarks is his former wife. Now if we want to be orderly about our inquiry, we ought to know to whom the Duke is speaking.

A: I didn't find that out until near the end of the poem when the Duke mentioned a count as the master of the person the Duke is talking to. He evidently was visiting the Duke to make marriage arrangements for the Count's daughter. I felt sorry for her.

Z: You should. Actually the daughter of the Count is the real object of all the Duke's talk, isn't she?

A: How do you know?

Z: Because the Duke obviously is not talking at random; he's not revealing his arrogance and cruelty for the fun of hearing himself talk. He is issuing a sharp, clear warning: "This is precisely the way my former duchess conducted herself; I did not attempt to school her in proper behavior; I choose never to stoop; I do not intend to stoop to my next Duchess; but if you like, here is a warning to her." Since it is unlikely that the Count would resist a ducal connection for his daughter, one may hope that he and his daughter were given a verbatim report of the Duke's comments.

A: I read somewhere that the stop before the painting of the Duchess was simply part of an art tour with the pause before Neptune as another part of the tour.

Z: Does that interpretation fit the facts? What were the Duke and the Count's emissary doing immediately *before* the poem opens?

A: They were discussing the proposed wedding and how much dowry the Count would provide. The lines about the dowry come near the end of the poem—lines 48 to 53 beginning with the words, "I repeat."

Z: And where were they going after settling this question?

A: To "meet the company below."

Z: Do you think it likely that an art tour would be sandwiched between these two actions? Isn't it more likely that the deliberate pause before the portrait was planned by the Duke in advance as *part* of the negotiations for the hand of the Count's daughter?

A: Let me ask you a question: Why didn't the poem end as the Duke and the emissary descend the stairs? What's the significance of Neptune taming a sea horse?

Z: A much debated question. Some critics make a parallel between the Duke and Neptune: the Duke tamed a wife as Neptune tamed a sea horse. Is there any difficulty here?

A: Sounds plausible to me—but wait a minute: the Duke really didn't tame his wife, did he? He didn't make any effort to tame her; he simply removed her without warning. I would say the parallel breaks down.

Z: Agreed. Other critics say that the bronze

statue and the portrait were equally interesting as art forms. I think this interpretation is only partly true. The Duke must have realized that in talking of his last Duchess there had inevitably been "some stooping," some condescension, a curious sort of charitableness, a touch of magnanimity. He was relieved to be done with the warning. He could return to casualness and hope that the reference to the bronze would be linked to the portrait as simply another work of art. And it may be that having used the portrait to point a moral and adorn a tale, he himself could *now* classify the portrait as simply another of his art treasures. You look skeptical.

A: I feel skeptical. The poem doesn't say all that, does it?

Z: No.

A: Why doesn't it?

Z: Because you, along with millions of other readers, would not enjoy being told everything in a-b-c fashion. The poet could have made his lines as clear as

Thirty days hath September,
April, June, and November.

These are useful lines but not very absorbing.

A: Nevertheless, I don't like puzzles.

Z: Unless you can solve them?

A: Yes.

Z: A good poem is an open puzzle—all the parts are there, and some of the fun is in putting them firmly together. This poet, for example, wanted you and me to enter into the character of a cold, arrogant, devious, observing, suspicious, scheming, all-powerful husband. He had confidence that you could provide these adjectives even though he uses none of them himself. He wanted you to speculate about the Duchess, too. Do you know anything about women?

A: Not much.

Z: Do you think you would like the Duchess?

A: Yes, I think so. She was easygoing and popular, I imagine, with everybody except her husband.

Z: Any more adjectives for her?

A: You might call her charming, genial, and I imagine she was pretty. She was democratic. She could blush easily, which shows she was sensitive.

Z: Good. But did she have any fault, any blind spot?

A: She didn't pay enough attention to her husband?

Z: Why didn't she?

A: How should I know?

Z: Do you recall how close an observer the husband was? He knew when his wife smiled and why, and when she blushed; and he could repeat the phrases or describe the actions which would call forth these genial responses.

A: Maybe she didn't notice that he was watching her, or maybe she felt so innocent that she didn't notice. You mean her weakness was a blindness to her husband watching her? That isn't a weakness.

Z: Doubtless even if she had studied her husband's expression she would have seen little warning in its monotonous impassiveness. But what did she lack which women pride themselves on having?

A: A woman's intuition?

Z: Precisely. "All smiles stopped together"—that is, suddenly and finally. No hint of the Duke's displeasure ever reached the Duchess until it was too late. If she had had intuition, she . . .

A: Excuse me for interrupting, but didn't you say this was to be an orderly discussion? We began with the title, and that's as far as we went in orderliness.

Z: But haven't we been *essentially* well organized? We analyzed the title, then the speaker, then the person spoken of. We mentioned the person spoken to, and we set forth the real purpose of the Duke's remarks. We haven't said much about setting. How much do we know about that?

A: Much. The country is Italy, the city Ferrara, and the local address, the palace of the Duke. As I see it, the Duke and emissary have stopped at the head of a stairway, marble, I think, but the poet doesn't say so. There the Duke draws back curtains and reveals a portrait. He steps back and sits down with the emissary—on a bench of some sort. I suppose, possibly like those in museums. After the Duke finishes, they rise and go down the stairs together.

Z: Why together?

A: Because the Duke is feeling in good spirits;

everything is going well and he feels democratic.

Z: That's the chief reason. Another is that the emissary is entitled to be treated as his master, the Count, would have been treated. Are we ready for a straightforward statement of the poem's contents, including the action before the poem opened—the antecedent action?

A: We ought to be ready. Please proceed.

Z: The proud Duke of Ferrara, dissatisfied with the indiscriminate geniality of his wife, puts her away, and later decides to negotiate with a Count for the hand of his daughter. The emissary of the Count arrives at the ducal residence and goes into conference with the Duke over marriage terms. At the conclusion of a friendly talk, the Duke uses the portrait of his last Duchess as the pretext for warning his duchess-to-be of the conduct expected of her. The warning delivered, the conferees go to meet the Duke's guests, who perhaps were assembled to hear the news of the betrothal. Anything left out?

A: That is the story, all right. Do you suppose that was the form the story had when the poet sat down to write?

Z: An important and observant question. I think almost surely the poet worked from the straightforward story, his raw materials. Details and arrangement make the poem. We cannot say how much material he discarded, but all surplusage is gone. Give these same basic materials to any number of writers and the result will be any number of versions, some of which might be excellent, but none, one feels, superior to this poem.

A: I can see that. He might have told us more about Frà Pandolf—a smooth flatterer. Or the emissary might have been in love with the Count's daughter and—

Z: Hold on! You've jumped the fence, and that way lies Tristan and Isolde.

A: Who?

Z: Never mind. You might look them up sometime and see how many versions there are of *that* affair. Now, I want you to consider for a moment the problems our poet faced, and the artistic tact he used in solving them.

A: Do we have to do this?

Z: No, but you have entered very well into one level of enjoyment, and I thought you might like to try, briefly, another level—the level of technical artistry.

A: Sounds forbidding, but go ahead.

Z: For one thing, the poet deliberately imposed upon himself the limitations of the dramatic monologue.

A: Please define. I know your habits on examinations.

Z: The dramatic monologue is the name given to poems in which a single speaker talks aloud to one or more listeners. If there are no listeners, by the way, the speaker is indulging in dramatic soliloquy. There are enough ordinary difficulties in telling a story, but the difficulties of the dramatic monologue are extraordinary.

A: It doesn't look so terribly difficult. It flows so easily that at first I didn't even notice the rhymes. But I grant the difficulty. Why did the poet choose this form?

Z: The results of great art always look easy. As for your question, the poet must have decided that this was the one effective way *for him* to tell his story. Since we agree that he was successful, we are likely to agree that he chose the right form. Shall we list some of the "handicaps" which the poet imposed upon himself?

A: If you wish.

Z: Will you name the first and perhaps most obvious one?

A: I defer to you. You have my permission to name the whole list.

Z: I'll name the first, and you will then be able to name the second. One, the poet excluded himself from the poem—no comments, no moral. All dramatic writers do this, more or less. Two?

A: He doesn't say how to read the poem, is that it?

Z: Yes. He omits stage directions. Few dramatic writers do that. This means that within a short speech he must include the setting (time and place), the exposition, and the antecedent action, all in such a natural way that these elements are absorbed into the forward motion of the poem. Three, he had to watch the time element with special care. He could allow the Duke to be greatly skilled in speech—in spite of the Duke's protests to the contrary—but a long speech at the particular time would have been out of character. Four?

A: Four, if you please.

Z: This is most important. The Duke had to say things which would reveal his true (cruel) nature, and yet the reader must believe that this particular character would actually say such things. Here the motivation must be strong and convincing. As we have already seen, the motivation—a warning to the Count's daughter—is strong and convincing.

A: The poem is believable all right. Would you call this a great poem?

Z: One measure—not the only measure—of a poem's validity is its staunchness before searching questions. By this test the poem is great. An inferior poem would not fare so well.

So far we have been concerned to note how the figurative-symbolic level develops from the literal level of a poem. The first poem below is the Latin original; the second is a literal translation of it; and the third poem shows us what Jonson made of the original. It should not be assumed, of course, that Jonson was obligated to render the Latin poem into English in a slavish way; had he tried to do so the Latin rhythms and idiom would have defeated him poetically (artistically). To note the differences between the second and third poems teaches us much about the nature of poetry. What makes Jonson's poem poetry? If you read Latin readily, why not convert Catullus' poem to your own poetic version?

G. VALERIUS CATULLUS[1]
84 ?–54 B.C.

Carmen V, Ad Lesbiam

Vivamus, mea Lesbia, atque amemus,
Rumoresque senum seueriorum
Omnes unius aestimemus assis.
Soles occidere et redire possunt:
Nobis, cum semel occidit breuis lux,
Nox est perpetua una dormienda.
Da mi basia mille, deinde centum,
Dein mille altera, dein secunda centum,
Deinde usque altera mille, deinde centum:
Dein, cum milia multa fecerimus,
Conturbabimus illa, ne sciamus,
Aut ne quis malus inuidere possit,
Cum tantum sciat esse basiorum.

[1] One of the greatest of Roman lyric poets, and an epigrammatist. The Lesbia celebrated in his poems was probably Clodia, the notorious sister of Publius Clodius. He is the Sirmione in Tennyson's "Frater Ave Atque Vale."

To Lesbia[1]

Let us live, my Lesbia, and let us love,
And let us estimate all the gossip of prudish old men
As worth only a penny.
Suns can set and then rise again,
But as for us, when once our brief light sets,
There is only an everlasting night of sleep.
Give me a thousand kisses, then a hundred,
Then another thousand, then a second hundred,
Then still another thousand, then a hundred:
Then after we shall have run up many thousands,
We shall confuse the count, so that we do not know it,
And no wicked person may be able to put the evil eye on us,
When he knows that our kisses were just so many.

[1] We are indebted to Professor Albert Rapp of the University of Tennessee for this literal translation.

BEN JONSON
1572–1637

Come, My Celia

Come, my Celia, let us prove
While we may the sports of love;
Time will not be ours forever,
He at length our good will sever.
Spend not then his gifts in vain;
Suns that set may rise again,
But if once we lose this light,
'Tis with us perpetual night.
Why should we defer our joys?

Fame and rumor are but toys.
Cannot we delude the eyes
Of a few poor household spies?
Or his easier ears beguile,
So removëd by our wile?
'Tis no sin love's fruit to steal;
But the sweet theft to reveal,
To be taken, to be seen,
These have crimes accounted been.

ARCHIBALD MacLEISH
1892–

You Also, Gaius Valerius Catullus

Fat-kneed god! Feeder of mangy leopards![1]
You who brought me into that one's bed[2]
Whose breath is sweeter than a grass-fed
heifer—
If *you* had not willed it, *I* had not willed it—
You who dumped me like a sack of milt[3]
Limp in her eager taking arms as though
Her breast were no more than a bench to lie on,
Listen! Muncher of the pale-pipped apples!
Keeper of paunchy house-cats! Boozy god!
Dump me where you please, but not
hereafter
Where the dawn has that *particular* laughter.

TONE AND THE PLEASURES OF POETRY

One of the open secrets of this book lies in the belief that readers cannot be required or forced to enjoy poetry, much less to understand it. But we can be led into understanding by first reading good poems whose meaning and structure are quite immediately clear, especially if the poems give us a good-natured jolt or touch some universal feeling or attitude. Our immediate concern is to feel the delight of the fusion of *sound and sense.* The following poems have been chosen because the fusion can be immediately felt. No reader, however, is expected to enjoy every good poem he reads regardless of his skill in reading poems: our past experiences, backgrounds, and temperaments will help and hinder enjoyment of poems; so if you can find even two or three of these poems that come alive for you, you are on your way.

One more word about sound and sense. The poet has made the fusion, and we must read both sound and sense simultaneously. Read each poem *aloud,* and *let it have its way with you.* Will you be one-and-twenty, or have you been one-and-twenty? In either case Housman has a twinkling word for you.

A. E. HOUSMAN
1859–1936

When I Was One-and-Twenty

When I was one-and-twenty
  I heard a wise man say,
"Give crowns and pounds and guineas
  But not your heart away;
Give pearls away and rubies
  But keep your fancy free."
But I was one-and-twenty,
  No use to talk to me.

When I was one-and-twenty
  I heard him say again,
"The heart out of the bosom
  Was never given in vain;
'Tis paid with sighs a-plenty
  And sold for endless rue."
And I am two-and-twenty,
  And oh, 'tis true, 'tis true.

Housman's problem here was to make us *feel* the jaunty cocksureness of the young speaker in the poem who ignores the wise man's advice until the speaker's own experience confirms it. Housman could have told us he was jaunty and cocksure, but Housman has the speaker present

[1] Bacchus, the Roman god of wine, known as Dionysus to the Greeks, often pictured riding a chariot drawn by leopards. The Roman festival of Bacchus, known as the bacchanalian revels, was celebrated with dancing, song, and liberal merrymaking.
[2] The bed of Catullus's lover Clodia, known as Lesbia in his poems. See his poem "To Lesbia" above, with a literal translation.
[3] The male reproductive glands of fishes when filled with secretion; also the secretion itself.

himself to exhibit his jaunty cocksureness. How did Housman accomplish this? By having the sound—the rhythm, rhyme, and the clipped words—help to interpret the sense. Each line has only three feet (trimeter); each line's rhythm is well-nigh perfect (*sure*, like the young man); most words have only one syllable (clipped, jaunty); and the rhyme is repetitious—like the speaker until he grows into wisdom. The character of the speaker is clear because the sound has prepared us for a fuller sense of the poem.

Let us now hear a completely different fusion of sound and sense in Burns's poem.

ROBERT BURNS
1759–1796

Sweet Afton

Flow gently, sweet Afton! among thy green braes,[1]
Flow gently, I'll sing thee a song in thy praise;
My Mary's asleep by thy murmuring stream,
Flow gently, sweet Afton, disturb not her dream.

Thou stock-dove whose echo resounds through the glen,
Ye wild whistling blackbirds in yon thorny den,
Thou green-crested lapwing, thy screaming forbear,
I charge you, disturb not my slumbering fair.

How lofty, sweet Afton, thy neighboring hills,
Far marked with the courses of clear, winding rills;[2]
There daily I wander as noon rises high,
My flocks and my Mary's sweet cot[2] in my eye.[3]

How pleasant thy banks and green valleys below,
Where, wild in the woodlands, the primroses blow;
There oft, as mild ev'ning weeps over the lea,
The sweet-scented birk[4] shades my Mary and me.

Thy crystal stream, Afton, how lovely it glides,
And winds by the cot where my Mary resides;
How wanton thy waters her snowy feet lave,[5]
As, gathering sweet flowerets, she stems thy clear wave.

Flow gently, sweet Afton, among thy green braes,
Flow gently, sweet river, the theme of my lays;[6]
My Mary's asleep by thy murmuring stream,
Flow gently, sweet Afton, disturb not her dream.

[1] **Banks.** [2] Small brooks. [3] Cottage, small house. [4] Birch tree. [5] Bathe. [6] Songs.

Burns's problem here was to make us feel the mood of the speaker generated by his loved one, so the poet has employed the devices of his art—rhythm, rhyme, word sounds (onomatopoeia), and stanza form. With these devices he has accomplished a good deal. The sentiments of the speaker flow gently and tenderly as the river flows, and the tone of the poem is reminiscent of a tenderness muted and enriched by time. The flowing quality is produced by the four-footed line (tetrameter) with most feet having three syllables accented on the third syllable (anapestic foot), as in the first line:

Flow gent | ly sweet Af | ton among | thy green braes

Yet the couplets (*braes-praise; stream-dream*) present a series of disciplined sentiments which do not disappear in the strong force of the flowing rhythm. The poem's emotion is therefore measured, gentle, and yet strong as if it would match time in eternity.

Poems, we see, *do* speak for themselves *if we know how to listen*, but Frost's poem now speaks in a radically different manner.

ROBERT FROST
1874–1963

Departmental

An ant on the table cloth
Ran into a dormant moth
Of many times his size.
He showed not the least surprise.
His business wasn't with such.
He gave it scarcely a touch,

And was off on his duty run.
Yet if he encountered one
Of the hive's enquiry squad
Whose work is to find out God
And the nature of time and space,
He would put him onto the case.
Ants are a curious race;
One crossing with hurried tread
The body of one of their dead
Isn't given a moment's arrest—
Seems not even impressed.
But he no doubt reports to any
With whom he crosses antennae,
And they no doubt report
To the higher up at court.
Then word goes forth in Formic:
"Death's come to Jerry McCormic,
Our selfless forager Jerry.
Will the special Janizary[1]
Whose office it is to bury
The dead of the commissary
Go bring him home to his people.
Lay him in state on a sepal.
Wrap him for shroud in a petal.
Embalm him with ichor of nettle.
This is the word of your Queen."
And presently on the scene
Appears a solemn mortician;
And taking formal position,
With feelers calmly atwiddle,
Seizes the dead by the middle,
And heaving him high in air,
Carries him out of there.
No one stands round to stare.
It is nobody else's affair.

It couldn't be called ungentle.
But how thoroughly departmental.

This poem is a satire on our modern tendency to accept only individual responsibility in life instead of accepting some responsibility for the whole social structure. Literally Frost is talking about ants, but figuratively he is satirizing men. Satire is usually a light, sprightly form of ridicule, and Frost's *technical* problem was therefore to make us feel the force of his short jabs, needling, against our fragmentizing of life. By using the devices of the short, clipped line (trimeter) and the couplet form, and by ending many lines with abrupt stops (*report-court; Formic-McCormic; atwiddle-middle*), we see and feel these efficient little ants (men) scurrying to their single duties looking neither to the right nor left. And note that when Frost wants to rub the satire in, he rhymes three and even four successive lines (*space-case-race; air-there-stare-affair*). Perhaps we feel a little punch-drunk at the end of the poem.

If we are now alive to the various results of poets fusing sound and sense expertly, the following poems may provide us with a good deal of pleasure.

LOUIS UNTERMEYER
1885–

Edgar A. Guest Considers "The Old Woman Who Lived in a Shoe" and the Good Old Verities at the Same Time

---

Edgar A. Guest (1881–1959) wrote popular sentimental and moralistic verse, especially for the *Detroit Free Press,* which was syndicated throughout the United States. Untermeyer is satirizing the dead metaphors (see p. 268), the monotonous rhythms, and particularly the stock responses used by Guest to snare the uncritical reader. (For discussion of stock response see p. 225.)

It takes a heap o' children to make a home that's true,
And home can be a palace grand or just a plain old shoe;
But if it has a mother dear and a good old dad or two,
Why, that's the sort of good old home for good old me and you.

[1] A soldier of an elite corps.

Of all the institutions this side the Vale of Rest
Howe'er it be it seems to me a good old mother's best;
And fathers are a blessing, too, they give the place a tone;
In fact each child should try and have some parents of his own.

The food can be quite simple; just a sop of milk and bread
Are plenty when the kiddies know it's time to go to bed.
And every little sleepy-head will dream about the day
When he can go to work because a Man's Work is his Play.

And, oh, how sweet his life will seem, with nought to make him cross;
And he will never watch the clock and always mind the boss.
And when he thinks (as may occur), this thought will please him best:
That ninety million think the same—including

EDDIE GUEST

EMILY DICKINSON
1830–1886
The Pedigree of Honey

VERSION I

The pedigree of Honey
Does not concern the Bee,
Nor lineage of Ecstasy
Delay the Butterfly
On spangled journeys to the peak
Of some perceiveless thing—
The right of way to Tripoli
A more essential thing.

VERSION II

The Pedigree of Honey
Does not concern the Bee—
A Clover, any time, to him,
Is Aristocracy—

DOROTHY PARKER
1893–1967
Résumé

Razors pain you;
Rivers are damp;
Acids stain you;
And drugs cause cramp.
Guns aren't lawful;
Nooses give;
Gas smells awful;
You might as well live.

THE ENDURING BALLAD*
STORY BALLADS

ANONYMOUS
Barbra Allen

In London City where I once did dwell, there's where I got my learning,
I fell in love with a pretty young girl, her name was Barbra Allen.

* For more poems in the ballad tradition not included in this section see Burns, "Sweet Afton," p. 232; Moore, "Believe Me, If All Those Enduring Young Charms," p. 260; "O Western Wind, When Wilt Thou Blow," p. 313; "Jolly Good Ale and Old," p. 313; Housman, "The True Lover," p. 337; and Pound, "Ballad of the Goodly Fere," p. 342.

I courted her for seven long years, she said she would not have me;
Then straightaway home as I could go and liken to a dying.

I wrote her a letter on my death bed, I wrote it slow and moving;
"Go take this letter to my old true love and tell her I am dying."
She took the letter in her lily-white hand, she read it slow and moving;
"Go take this letter back to him, and tell him I am coming."

As she passed by his dying bed she saw his pale lips quivering;
"No better, no better I'll ever be until I get Barbra Allen."
As she passed by his dying bed; "You're very sick and almost dying,
No better, no better you will ever be, for you can't get Barbra Allen."

As she went down the long stair steps she heard the death bell toning,
And every bell appeared to say, "Hard-hearted Barbra Allen!"
As she went down the long piney walk she heard some small birds singing,
And every bird appeared to say, "Hard-hearted Barbra Allen!"

She looked to the East, she looked to the West, she saw the pale corpse coming,
"Go bring them pale corpse unto me, and let me gaze upon them.
Oh, mama, mama, go make my bed, go make it soft and narrow!
Sweet Willie died today for me, I'll die for him tomorrow!"

They buried Sweet Willie in the old church yard, they buried Miss Barbra beside him;
And out of his grave there sprang a red rose, and out of hers a briar.
They grew to the top of the old church tower, they could not grow any higher,
They hooked, they tied in a true love's knot, red rose around the briar.

ANONYMOUS

Sir Patrick Spens

The king sits in Dumferling toune,
  Drinking the blude-reid wine:
"Oh whar will I get guid sailor,
  To sail this schip of mine?"

Up and spak an eldern knicht,[1]
  Sat at the kings richt kne:
"Sir Patrick Spens is the best sailor
  That sails upon the se."

The king has written a braid [2] letter,
  And signd it wi his hand,
And sent it to Sir Patrick Spens,
Was walking on the sand.

The first line that Sir Patrick red,
  A loud lauch lauched he;
The next line that Sir Patrick red,
  The teir blinded his ee.

"O wha is this has don this deid,
  This ill deid don to me,
To send me out this time o' the yeir,
  To sail upon the se!

"Mak hast, mak haste, my mirry men all,
  Our guid schip sails the morne."
"O say na sae,[3] my master deir,
  For I feir a deadlie storme.

"Late, late yestreen I saw the new moone,
  Wi the auld moone in hir arme,
And I feir, I feir, my deir master,
  That we will cum to harme."

O our Scots nobles wer richt laith[4]
  To weet their cork-heild schoone,[5]

[1] Knight. [2] Stately.

[3] Not so. [4] Loath. [5] Cork-heeled shoes.

Bot lang owre[6] a' the play wer playd,
  Thair hats they swam aboone.[7]

O lang, lang may their ladies sit,
  Wi their fans into their hand,
Or eir[8] they se Sir Patrick Spens
  Cum sailing to the land.

O lang, lang may the ladies stand,
  Wi their gold kems[9] in their hair,
Waiting for their ain[10] deir lords,
  For they'll se thame na mair.

Haf owre, half owre[11] to Aberdour,
  It's fiftie fadom[12] deip,
And thair lies guid Sir Patrick Spens,
  Wi the Scots lords at his feit.

Comments and Questions

This poem, like "Barbra Allen," is an anonymous folk, or popular, ballad whose "final" shape includes the alterations which were made as the ballad passed from generation to generation. Like all literary forms, the ballad emerged to serve a purpose, and the purpose of the ballad seems to have been to celebrate, lament, or commemorate some dramatic incident which probably affected the community at the time.

1. Of the many versions of this old Scottish ballad, this one seems to have become the best established, perhaps because of its brevity, compression, and dramatic intensity. It is, in effect, a short story. What are the facts of the story?

2. This ballad has a surprising number of characteristics of the modern short story. Consider the narrator's point of view, panorama and scene, character portrayal, and dramatic elements. (For a discussion of these terms see "Fiction: Preliminaries," p. 10.) Note particularly the relative absence of author comment.

3. In what way does the tone of this ballad differ from that of "Barbra Allen"?

4. Note the metrical structure of "Sir Patrick Spens." It is written in conventional ballad stanza, the first and third lines having four feet (tetrameter), the second and fourth lines having three feet (trimeter), written mostly in iambic meter (thĕ kíng), and with a rhyme scheme of *abcb*. This form is sometimes called a classic structure and is quite different of course from the structure found in "Barbra Allen," which has roughly seven feet in each line, written in broken iambic meter. It is tempting to ask which ballad has the better technique, but it is sounder to ask, does each technique serve well the meaning of the poem? What is your opinion? Consider question 3 again before you conclude.

5. Compare "Sir Patrick Spens" with Pound's "Ballad of the Goodly Fere" (p. 342) and note the similar metrical effect.

[6] Before. [7] Above. [8] Before. [9] Combs. [10] Own. [11] Halfway over. [12] Fathom.

ANONYMOUS

The Daemon Lover

This old Scottish ballad and Bowen's story, "The Demon Lover" (p. 115), can be regarded as companion pieces. Although centuries separate them, the psychology involved in both ballad and story is strangely the same. Once more we recognize the universality (pp. 4–7) of imaginative literature.

"O where have you been, my long, long love,
  This long seven years and more?"—
"O I'm come to seek my former vows
  Ye granted me before."—

"O hold your tongue of your former vows,
  For they will breed sad strife;
O hold your tongue of your former vows,
  For I am become a wife."

He turn'd him right and round about,
  And the tear blinded his ee;[1]
"I wad never hae[2] trodden on Irish ground,
  If it had not been for thee.

[1] Eye. [2] Would never have.

"I might hae had a king's daughter,
Far, far beyond the sea;
I might have had a king's daughter,
Had it not been for love o' thee."—

"If ye might have had a king's daughter,
Yer sell[3] ye had to blame;
Ye might have taken the king's daughter,
For ye kend[4] that I was nane."—[5]

"O faulse are the vows of womankind,
But fair is their faulse bodie;
I never wad hae[6] trodden on Irish ground,
Had it not been for love o' thee."—

"If I was to leave my husband dear,
And my two babes also,
O what have you to take me to,
If with you I should go?"—

"I hae seven ships upon the sea,
The eighth brought me to land;
With four-and-twenty bold mariners,
And music on every hand."

She has taken up her two little babes,
Kiss'd them baith[7] cheek and chin;
"O fair ye weel, my ain[8] two babes,
For I'll never see you again."

She set her foot upon the ship,
No mariners could she behold;
But the sails were o' the taffetie,[9]
And the masts o' the beaten gold.

She had not sail'd a league, a league,
A league but barely three,
When dismal grew his countenance,
And drumlie[10] grew his ee.

The masts that were like the beaten gold,
Bent not on the heaving seas;
But the sails, that were o' the taffetie,
Fill'd not in the east land breeze.—

They had not sailed a league, a league,
A league but barely three,
Until she espied his cloven foot,
And she wept right bitterlie.

"O hold your tongue of your weeping," says he,
"Of your weeping now let me be;
I will show you how the lilies grow
On the banks of Italy."—

"O what hills are yon, yon pleasant hills,
That the sun shines sweetly on?"—
"O yon are the hills of heaven," he said,
"Where you will never win."—[11]

"O whaten[12] a mountain is yon," she said,
"All so dreary wi' frost and snow?"—
"O yon is the mountain of hell," he cried,
"Where you and I will go."

And aye when she turn'd her round about,
Aye taller he seem'd for to be;
Until that the tops o' that gallant ship
Nae[13] taller were than he.

The clouds grew dark, and the wind grew loud,
And the levin[14] fill'd her ee;
And waesome[15] wail'd the snaw-white sprites[16]
Upon the gurlie[17] sea.

He strack the tap-mast wi' his hand,
The fore-mast wi' his knee;
And he brake that gallant ship in twain,
And sank her in the sea.

[3] Yourself. [4] You knew. [5] None.
[6] I never would have. [7] Both. [8] Own.
[9] Taffeta, a lustrous fabric. [10] Gloomy, troubled.

[11] Attain; go to. [12] O what. [13] No.
[14] Lightning. [15] Sorrowful.
[16] Elves, fairies, or goblins. [17] Surly, stormy.

ANONYMOUS
Frankie and Johnny

Frankie and Johnny were lovers, great God how they could love!
Swore to be true to each other, true as the stars up above.
He was her man, but he done her wrong.

Frankie she was his woman, everybody knows.
She spent her forty dollars for Johnny a suit of clothes.
He was her man, but he done her wrong.

Frankie and Johnny went walking, Johnny in his brand new suit.
"O good Lawd," said Frankie, "but don't my Johnny look cute?"
He was her man, but he done her wrong.

Frankie went down to the corner, just for a bucket of beer.
Frankie said, "Mr. Bartender, has my loving Johnny been here?
He is my man, he wouldn't do me wrong."

"I don't want to tell you no story. I don't want to tell you no lie,
But your Johnny left here an hour ago with that lousy Nellie Blye.
He is your man, but he's doing you wrong."

Frankie went back to the hotel, she didn't go there for fun,
For under her red kimono she toted a forty-four gun.
He was her man, but he done her wrong.

Frankie went down to the hotel and looked in the window so high,
And there was her loving Johnny a-loving up Nellie Blye.
He was her man, but he was doing her wrong.

Frankie threw back her kimono, took out that old forty-four.
Root-a-toot-toot, three times she shot, right through the hardwood door.
He was her man, but he was doing her wrong.

Johnny grabbed off his Stetson, crying, "O Frankie don't shoot!"
Frankie pulled that forty-four, went root-a-toot-toot-toot-toot.
He was her man, but he done her wrong.

"Roll me over gently, roll me over slow,
Roll me on my right side, for my left side hurts me so,
I was her man, but I done her wrong."

With the first shot Johnny staggered, with the second shot he fell;
When the last bullet got him, there was a new man's face in hell.
He was her man, but he done her wrong.

"O, bring out your rubber-tired hearses, bring out your rubber-tired hacks;
Gonna take Johnny to the graveyard and ain't gonna bring him back.
He was my man, but he done me wrong."

"O, put me in that dungeon, put me in that cell,
Put me where the northeast wind blows from the southeast corner of hell.
I shot my man, cause he done me wrong!"

ANONYMOUS

The Wabash Cannon Ball

From the great Atlantic Ocean to the wide Pacific Shore,
From the ones we leave behind us to the ones we see once more,
She's mighty tall and handsome, and quite well known by all,
How we love the choo choo of the Wabash Cannon Ball.

Hear the bell and whistle calling,
Hear the wheels that go "clack clack,"
Hear the roaring of the engine,
As she rolls along the track.
The magic of the railroad wins hearts of one and all,
As we reach our destination on the Wabash Cannon Ball.

Listen to the rhythmic jingle and the rumble and the roar,
As she glides along the woodlands thro' the hills and by the shore.
You hear the mighty engine and pray that it won't stall,
While we safely travel on the Wabash Cannon Ball.

Hear the bell and whistle calling, etc.

She was coming from Atlanta on a cold December day,
As she rolled into the station, I could hear a woman say:
"He's mighty big and handsome, and sure did make me fall,
"He's a-coming tow'rd me on the Wabash Cannon Ball."

Hear the bell and whistle calling, etc.

ANONYMOUS

On Top of Old Smoky

On top of old Smoky, all covered with snow,
I lost my true lover for acourtin' too slow.
Now, courtin's a pleasure, but parting is grief,
And a false-hearted lover is worse than a thief;
For a thief will just rob you and take what you have,
But a false-hearted lover will lead you to the grave;
And the grave will decay you, and turn you to dust.
Not one boy in a hundred a poor girl can trust:
They'll hug you and kiss you, and tell you more lies
Than the crossties on a railroad, or stars in the skies.
So, come all you young maidens, and listen to me:
Never place your affections in a green willow tree;
For the leaves they will wither, and the roots they will die.
Your lover will forsake you, and you'll never know why.

JOHN CLARE
1793–1864

Meet Me in the Green Glen

This poem and the ones to follow are called literary ballads, or art ballads, conscious imitations of the popular, folk ballad. The ballads we have already read are primitive poems that survive probably because of their singing quality and their frank projection of elementary emotions; they have the charm of being understood immediately, of striking home without study. Now enters the professional poet.

Love, meet me in the green glen,
  Beside the tall elm-tree,
Where the sweetbrier smells so sweet agen;[1]
  There come with me,
    Meet me in the green glen.

Meet me at the sunset
  Down in the green glen,
Where we've often met
  By hawthorn-tree and foxes' den,
    Meet me in the green glen.

Meet me in the green glen,
  By sweetbrier bushes there;
Meet me by your own sen,[2]
  Where the wild thyme blossoms fair.
    Meet me in the green glen.

Meet me by the sweetbrier,
  By the mole-hill swelling there;
When the west glows like a fire
  God's crimson bed is there.
    Meet me in the green glen.

Comments

This lyric is helpful in interpreting Robert Penn Warren's novel *Meet Me in the Green Glen* (New York: Random House, Inc., 1971). The lyric's theme expresses the hope of the central character, Cassie Spottwood, who can be seen as a symbol of all mankind who would meet love in the green glen of happiness.

[1] Again. [2] Self.

JOHN KEATS
1795–1821

La Belle Dame sans Merci

Oh, what can ail thee, knight-at-arms,
Alone and palely loitering?
The sedge has withered from the lake,
And no birds sing.

Oh, what can ail thee, knight-at-arms,
So haggard and so woe-begone?
The squirrel's granary is full,
And the harvest's done.

I see a lily on thy brow,
With anguish moist and fever dew;
And on thy cheeks a fading rose
Fast withereth too.

"I met a lady in the meads,
Full beautiful—a faery's child;
Her hair was long, her foot was light,
And her eyes were wild.

"I made a garland for her head,
And bracelets too, and fragrant zone;[1]
She looked at me as she did love,
And made sweet moan.

"I set her on my pacing steed,
And nothing else saw all day long;
For sideways would she lean, and sing
A faery's song.

"She found me roots of relish sweet,
And honey wild, and manna-dew,
And sure in language strange she said,
'I love thee true.'

"She took me to her elfin grot,
And there she wept, and sighed full sore,
And there I shut her wild, wild eyes,
With kisses four.

"And there she lullèd me asleep,
And there I dreamed—ah! woe betide!—
The latest dream I ever dreamed
On the cold hill side.

"I saw pale kings and princes too,
Pale warriors, death-pale were they all,
They cried—'La Belle Dame sans Merci
Hath thee in thrall!'

"I saw their starved lips in the gloam,
With horrid warning gapèd wide;
And I awoke, and found me here
On the cold hill's side.

"And this is why I sojourn here
Alone and palely loitering,
Though the sedge is withered from the lake,
And no birds sing."

[1] Girdle, sash.

Comments and Questions

1. The title announces the ballad's general theme, the beautiful lady without pity. What is the specific theme? This is the most complex and self-conscious ballad we have yet read, and it includes more symbolism than we have yet encountered. What does the lady symbolize?

2. Who are the two speakers in the poem? How do lines 1–12 sustain or complement the remainder of the poem?

3. We note in passing that Keats's stanza form is similar to that in "Sir Patrick Spens" (p. 235). Can you hazard an explanation of why Keats's form differs in some respects from the other?

WILLIAM BUTLER YEATS
1865–1939

The Ballad of Father Gilligan

The old priest Peter Gilligan
Was weary night and day;
For half his flock were in their beds,
Or under green sods lay.

Once, while he nodded on a chair,
At the moth-hour of eve,
Another poor man sent for him,
And he began to grieve.

"I have no rest, nor joy, nor peace,
For people die and die";
And after cried he, "God forgive!
My body spake, not I!"

He knelt, and leaning on the chair
He prayed and fell asleep;
And the moth-hour went from the fields,
And stars began to peep.

They slowly into millions grew,
And leaves shook in the wind;
And God covered the world with shade,
And whispered to mankind.

Upon the time of sparrow-chirp
When the moths came once more,
The old priest Peter Gilligan
Stood upright on the floor.

"Mavrone, mavrone! the man has died
While I slept on the chair";
He roused his horse out of its sleep,
And rode with little care.

He rode now as he never rode,
By rocky lane and fen;
The sick man's wife opened the door:
"Father! you come again!"

"And is the poor man dead?" he cried.
"He died an hour ago."
The old priest Peter Gilligan
In grief swayed to and fro.

"When you were gone, he turned and died
As merry as a bird."
The old priest Peter Gilligan
He knelt him at that word.

"He Who hath made the night of stars
For souls who tire and bleed,
Sent one of His great angels down
To help me in my need.

"He Who is wrapped in purple robes,
With planets in His care,
Had pity on the least of things
Asleep upon a chair."

WILLIAM SHAKESPEARE
1564–1616

The Seven Ages of Man

All the world's a stage,
And all the men and women merely players.
They have their exits and their entrances,
And one man in his time plays many parts,
His acts being seven ages. At first the infant,
Mewling[1] and puking in the nurse's arms.
Then the whining schoolboy, with his satchel
And shining morning face, creeping like snail
Unwillingly to school. And then the lover,
Sighing like furnace, with a woeful ballad[2]
Made to his mistress' eyebrow. Then a soldier,
Full of strange oaths and bearded like the pard,[3]
Jealous in honor,[4] sudden and quick in quarrel,
Seeking the bubble reputation[5]
Even in the cannon's mouth. And then the
justice,
In fair round belly with good capon lined,[6]
With eyes severe and beard of formal cut,
Full of wise saws[7] and modern instances;[8]
And so he plays his part. The sixth age shifts
Into the lean and slippered Pantaloon,[9]
With spectacles on nose and pouch on side;
His youthful hose, well saved, a world too wide
For his shrunk shank, and his big manly voice,
Turning again toward childish treble, pipes
And whistles in his sound. Last scene of all,
That ends this strange eventful history,
Is second childishness and mere oblivion,
Sans[10] teeth, sans eyes, sans taste, sans every-
thing.

—*As You Like It,* II. vii. 139–166

OGDEN NASH
1902–1971

The Seven Spiritual Ages of Mrs. Marmaduke Moore

Mrs. Marmaduke Moore, at the age of ten
(Her name was Jemima Jevons then),
Was the quaintest of little country maids.

[1] Whimpering. [2] Poem. [3] Leopard. [4] Sensitive about honor. [5] As quickly burst as a bubble. [6] Magistrate bribed with a chicken. [7] Sayings. [8] Commonplace illustrations. [9] The foolish old man of Italian comedy. [10] Without.

Her pigtails slapped on her shoulderblades;
She fed the chickens, and told the truth
And could spit like a boy through a broken
tooth.
She could climb a tree to the topmost perch,
And she used to pray in the Methodist church.

At the age of twenty her heart was pure,
And she caught the fancy of Mr. Moore.
He broke his troth (to a girl named Alice),
And carried her off to his city palace,
Where she soon forgot her childhood piety
And joined in the orgies of high society.
Her voice grew English, or, say, Australian,
And she studied to be an Episcopalian.

At thirty our lives are still before us,
But Mr. Moore had a friend in the chorus.
Connubial bliss was overthrown
And Mrs. Moore now slumbered alone.
Hers was a nature that craved affection;
She gave herself up to introspection;
Then, finding theosophy rather dry,
Found peace in the sweet Bahai and Bahai.

Forty? and still an abandoned wife.
She felt old urges stirring to life.
She dipped her locks in a bowl of henna
And booked a passage through to Vienna.
She paid a professor a huge emolument
To demonstrate what his ponderous volume
meant.
Returning, she preached to the unemployed
The gospel according to St. Freud.

Fifty! she haunted museums and galleries,
And pleased young men by augmenting their
salaries.
Oh, it shouldn't occur, but it does occur,
That poets are made by fools like her.
Her salon was full of frangipani,
Roumanian, Russian and Hindustani,
And she conquered par as well as bogey
By reading a book and going Yogi.

Sixty! and time was on her hands—
Maybe remorse and maybe glands.
She felt a need for a free confession
To publish each youthful indiscretion,
And before she was gathered to her mothers,
To compare her sinlets with those of others,
Mrs. Moore gave a joyous whoop,
And immersed herself in the Oxford group.

That is the story of Mrs. Moore,
As far as it goes. But of this I'm sure—
When seventy stares her in the face
She'll have found some other state of grace.
Mohammed may be her Lord and master,
Or Zeus, or Mithros, or Zoroaster.
For when a lady is badly sexed
God knows what God is coming next.

GWENDOLYN BROOKS
1917–

the ballad of chocolate Mabbie

It was Mabbie without the grammar school
gates.
And Mabbie was all of seven.
And Mabbie was cut from a chocolate bar.
And Mabbie thought life was heaven.

The grammar school gates were the pearly
gates,
For Willie Boone went to school.
When she sat by him in history class
Was only her eyes were cool.

It was Mabbie without the grammar school gates
Waiting for Willie Boone.
Half hour after the closing bell!
He would surely be coming soon.

Oh, warm is the waiting for joys, my dears!
And it cannot be too long.
Oh, pity the little poor chocolate lips
That carry the bubble of song!

Out came the saucily bold Willie Boone.
It was woe for our Mabbie now.
He wore like a jewel a lemon-hued lynx
With sand-waves loving her brow.

It was Mabbie alone by the grammar school
gates.
Yet chocolate companions had she:
Mabbie on Mabbie with hush in the heart.
Mabbie on Mabbie to be.

MARGARET A. WALKER 1915–

Molly Means

Old Molly Means was a hag and a witch;
Chile of the devil, the dark, and sitch.
Her heavy hair hung thick in ropes
And her blazing eyes was black as pitch.
Imp at three and wench at 'leben
She counted her husbands to the number seben.
O Molly, Molly, Molly Means
There goes the ghost of Molly Means.

Some say she was born with a veil on her face
So she could look through unnatchal space
Through the future and through the past
And charm a body or an evil place
And every man could well despise
The evil look in her coal black eyes.
Old Molly, Molly, Molly Means
Dark is the ghost of Molly Means.

And when the tale begun to spread
Of evil and of holy dread:
Her black-hand arts and her evil powers
How she cast her spells and called the dead,
The younguns was afraid at night
And the farmers feared their crops would blight.
Old Molly, Molly, Molly Means
Cold is the ghost of Molly Means.

Then one dark day she put a spell
On a young gal-bride just come to dwell
In the lane just down from Molly's shack
And when her husband coming riding back
His wife was barking like a dog
And on all fours like a common hog.
O Molly, Molly, Molly Means
Where is the ghost of Molly Means?

The neighbors come and they went away
And said she'd die before break of day
But her husband held her in his arms
And swore he'd break the wicked charms,
He'd search all up and down the land
And turn the spell on Molly's hand.
O Molly, Molly, Molly Means
Sharp is the ghost of Molly Means.

So he rode all day and he rode all night
And at the dawn he come in sight
Of a man who said he could move the spell
And cause the awful thing to dwell
On Molly Means, to bark and bleed
Till she died at the hands of her evil deed.
Old Molly, Molly, Molly Means
This is the ghost of Molly Means.

Sometimes at night through the shadowy trees
She rides along on a winter breeze.
You can hear her holler and whine and cry.
Her voice is thin and her moan is high,
And her cackling laugh or her barking cold
Bring terror to the young and old.
O Molly, Molly, Molly Means
Lean is the ghost of Molly Means.

THE RETURN OF THE MINSTREL: NEW FOLK AND COUNTRY BALLADS

The return of the minstrel, formerly a musical entertainer or traveling poet of the later Middle Ages, has become a national and international phenomenon during the last two decades. Recordings of these minstrels' songs are bought by the millions, and the performers entertain huge audiences in concert halls and millions of enthusiasts every week by radio and television. The folk ballad has a long and persistent tradition, and its resurgence may be a symbol of something very important in contemporary life, something too important to be ignored by the official literati of the poetic world.

For an excellent examination and historical explanation of this movement see Barbara Farris Graves and Donald J. McBain's book, *Lyric Voices: Approaches to the Poetry of Contemporary Song* (New York: John Wiley and Sons, Inc., 1972). The book contains many of the best of these lyrics, and the serious reader would do well to make the book his own.

Another valuable book, one which investigates the evolution of the lyric, is C. Day Lewis's *The Lyric Impulse* (Cambridge: Harvard University Press, 1965); chapter 5, "Country Lyrics," is especially valuable.

KRIS KRISTOFFERSON
1936–

Sunday Mornin' Comin' Down

Well, I woke up Sunday mornin'
with no way to hold my head that didn't hurt;
And the beer I had for breakfast wasn't bad,
so I had one more for dessert;
Then I fumbled in my closet
through my clothes and found my cleanest dirty shirt;
Then I washed my face, and combed my hair,
and stumbled down the stairs to meet the day.

I'd smoked my mind the night before
with cigarettes and songs I'd been pickin';
But I lit my first and watched a small kid
playing with a can that he was kickin';
Then I walked across the empty street and caught
the Sunday smell of someone fryin' chicken;
And it took me back to somethin' that
I'd lost somewhere somehow along the way.

On the Sunday mornin' sidewalk, I'm wishin, Lord, that I was stoned,
'Cause there's something in a Sunday that makes a body feel alone;
And there's nothing short of dyin' that's half as lonesome as the sound
On the sleeping city sidewalk; and Sunday mornin' comin' down.

In the park I saw a daddy
with a laughing little girl that he was swingin';
And I stopped beside a Sunday school
and listened to the song they were singin';
Then I headed down the street,
and somewhere far away a lonely bell was ringin';
And it echoed thru the canyon
like a disappearing dream of yesterday.

On the Sunday mornin' sidewalk, I'm wishin', Lord, that I was stoned,
'Cause there's something in a Sunday that make a body feel alone;
And there's nothing short of dyin' that's half as lonesome as the sound
On the sleeping city sidewalk; and Sunday mornin' comin' down.

KRIS KRISTOFFERSON and FRED FOSTER
1936–
1931–

Me and Bobby McGee

Busted flat in Baton Rouge,
Headin' for the trains;
Feelin' nearly faded as my jeans,
Bobby thumbed a diesel down
Just before it rained;
Took us all the way to New Orleans.

I took my harpoon out
of my dirty, red bandana
And was blowin' sad,
while Bobby sang the blues;

With them windshield wipers slappin' time
and Bobby clappin' hands
We fin'ly sang up ev'ry song that driver
knew.

Freedom's just another word for nothin' left to
lose,
Nothin' ain't worth nothin',
but it's free;
Feelin good was easy, Lord,
When Bobby sang the blues;
And feelin' good was good enough for me,
Good enough for me and Bobby McGee.

From the coal mines of Kentucky
To the California sun,
Bobby shared the secrets of my soul;
Standin' right beside me, Lord,
Through everything I done,
And every night she kept me from the cold.

Then somewhere near Salinas,
Lord, I let her slip away
Lookin' for the home
I hope she'll find;
And I'd trade all of my tomorrows
for a single yesterday,
Holdin' Bobby's body next to mine.

Freedom's just another word for nothin' left to
lose,
Nothin' left is all she left for me;
Feeling good was easy, Lord,
When Bobby sang the blues;
Nothin' left is all she left for me;
And buddy that was good was good enough for
me,
Good enough for me and Bobby McGee.

LEONARD COHEN
1934–

Stories of the Street[1]

The stories of the street are mine
The Spanish voices laugh
The Cadillacs go creeping down
Through the night and the poison gas.
I lean from my window sill
In this old hotel I chose
One hand on my suicide
One hand on the rose.

I know you've heard it's over now
And war must surely come
The cities they are broke in half
And the middle men are gone.
But let me ask you one more time
O, children of the dust,
All these hunters who are shrieking now
Do they speak for us?

And where do all these highways go
Now that we are free?
Why are the armies marching still
That were coming home to me?
O, lady with your legs so fine
O, stranger at your wheel
You are locked into your suffering
And your pleasures are the seal.

The age of lust is giving birth
And both the parents ask
The nurse to tell them fairy tales
On both sides of the glass
Now the infant with his cord
Is hauled in likc a kite
And one eye filled with blueprints
One eye filled with night.

O, come with me my little one
And we will find that farm
And grow us grass and apples there
And keep all the animals warm.
And if by chance I wake at night
And I ask you who I am
O, take me to the slaughter house
I will wait there with the lamb.

With one hand on a hexagram
And one hand on a girl
I balance on a wishing well
That all men call the world.
We are so small between the stars
So large against the sky
And lost among the subway crowds
I try to catch your eye.

[1] Words and Music by Leonard Cohen. Copyright © 1967 Stranger Music, Inc. Used by permission.

LEONARD COHEN
1934–

Hey, That's No Way to Say Goodbye[1]

I loved you in the morning
Our kisses deep and warm,
Your head upon the pillow
Like a sleepy golden storm.
Yes, many loved before us
I know that we are not new,
In city and in forest
They smiled like me and you,
But now it's come to distances
And both of us must try,
Your eyes are soft with sorrow,
Hey, that's no way to say goodbye.

I'm not looking for another
As I wander in my time,
Walk me to the corner
Our steps will always rhyme,
You know my love goes with you
As your love stays with me,
It's just the way it changes
Like the shoreline and the sea,
But let's not talk of love or chains
And things we can't untie,
Your eyes are soft with sorrow,
Hey, that's no way to say goodbye.

I loved you in the morning
Our kisses deep and warm,
Your head upon the pillow
Like a sleepy golden storm.
Yes, many loved before us
I know that we are not new,
In city and in forest
They smiled like me and you,
But let's not talk of love or chains
And things we can't untie,
Your eyes are soft with sorrow,
Hey, that's no way to say goodbye.

[1] Words and music by Leonard Cohen. Copyright © 1967 Stranger Music, Inc. Used by permission. All rights reserved.

TOM PAXTON
1937–

I Give You the Morning[1]

Ever again the morning creeps
Across your shoulder.
Through the frosted window pane
The sun grows bolder.
Your hair flows down your pillow,
You're still dreaming,
  I think I'll wake you now and hold you,
  Tell you again the things I told you,
  Behold, I give you the morning,
  I give you the day.

Through the waving curtain wall
The sun is streaming.
Far behind your flickering eyelids
You're still dreaming.
You're dreaming of the good times,
And you're smiling.
  I think I'll wake you now and hold you,
  Tell you again the things I told you.
  Behold, I give you the morning,
  I give you the day.

Close beneath our window sill,
The earth is humming.
Like an eager Christmas child,
The day is coming.
Listen to the morning song
It's singing.
  I think I'll wake you now and hold you,
  Tell you again the things I told you.
  Behold, I give you the morning,
  I give you the day.

Like an antique ballroom fan,
Your eyelids flutter.
Sunlight streams across your eyes
Through open shutter.
Now I think you're ready for the journey.
  I think I'll wake you now and hold you,
  Tell you again the things I told you.
  Behold, I give you the morning,
  I give you the day.

[1] Copyright © 1969 by United Artists Music Co., Inc. New York, New York. Used by permission.

RICHARD FARIÑA
1937–1966
Celebration for a Grey Day

Be quiet now and still. Be unafraid:
That hiss and garden tinkle is the rain,
That face you saw breathe on the window pane
Was just a startled cat with eyes of jade—
Cats worry in the rain, you know, and are
afraid.
The nervous laugh that creeps into our room
Is throated in a voice beyond the door.
We hear it once and then no more,
A distant echo tumbling from its loom.
Our time is measured in another room.

We know days pass away because we're told.
We lie alone and sense the reeling earth.
(You whisper in my ear it had some worth)
And I learn to keep you from the cold.
There are so many things that must be told.
I speak of lost regimes and distant times,
And mooneyed children whirling in the womb,
And legless beggars prophesying doom,
And afternoons of rain spun into rhyme.
(The patter of the rainfall marks our time.)

As does the waning moon. Or muted sun.
As do the nodding gods who ride the sea.
For even now, alone and still with me,
You sense the bonds that cannot be undone:
Our pulse is in the rain and moon and sun,
We take our breaths together and are one.

PETE SEEGER
1919–
Where Have All the Flowers Gone?[1]

Where have all the flowers gone?
Long time passing
Where have all the flowers gone?
Long time ago
Where have all the flowers gone?
Young girls have picked them, every one.
Oh, when will they ever learn?
Oh, when will they ever learn?

Where have all the young girls gone?
Long time passing
Where have all the young girls gone?
Long time ago
Where have all the young girls gone?
They've taken husbands, every one.
Oh, when will they ever learn?
Oh, when will they ever learn?

Where have all the husbands gone?
Long time passing
Where have all the husbands gone?
Long time ago
Where have all the husbands gone?
Gone for soldiers, every one.
Oh, when will they ever learn?
Oh, when will they ever learn?

Where have all the soldiers gone?
Long time passing
Where have all the soldiers gone?
Long time ago
Where have all the soldiers gone?
Gone to graveyards, every one.
Oh, when will they ever learn?
Oh, when will they ever learn?

Where have all the graveyards gone?
Long time passing
Where have all the graveyards gone?
Long time ago
Where have all the graveyards gone?
They're covered with flowers, every one.
Oh, when will they ever learn?
Oh, when will they ever learn?

Where have all the flowers gone?
Long time passing
Where have all the flowers gone?
Long time ago
Where have all the flowers gone?
Young girls have picked them, every one.
Oh, when will they ever learn?
Oh, when will they ever learn?

PAUL SIMON
1942–

The Sound of Silence

Hello darkness my old friend,
I've come to talk with you again,
Because a vision softly creeping,
Left its seeds while I was sleeping
And the vision that was planted in my brain
Still remains within the sound of silence.

In restless dreams I walked alone,
Narrow streets of cobble stone
'Neath the halo of a street lamp,
I turned my collar to the cold and damp
When my eyes were stabbed by the flash of a neon light
That split the night, and touched the sound of silence.

And in the naked light I saw
Ten thousand people maybe more,
People talking without speaking,
People hearing without listening,
People writing songs that voices never share
And no one dares disturb the sound of silence.

"Fools!" said I, "You do not know
Silence like a cancer grows.
Hear my words that I might teach you
Take my arms that I might reach you."
But my words like silent raindrops fell
And echoed, in the wells of silence.

And the people bowed and prayed
To the neon God they made,
And the sign flashed out its warning
In the words that it was forming.
And the sign said:
"The words of the prophets are written
on the subway walls and tenement halls"
And whispered in the sound of silence.

DONOVAN LEITCH[1]
1946–

Hampstead Incident

Standing by the Everyman
Digging the rigging on my sails
Rain fell through sounds of harpsichords
Through the spell of fairy tales

The heath was hung in magic mists
And gentle dripping glades
I'll taste the tastes until my mind
Drifts from this scene and fades

In the nighttime

Crystals sparkle in the grass
I polish them with thought
On my lash there in my eye
A star of light is caught

Fortunes told in grains of sand
Here I am is all I know
Can be stuck in children's hair
Everywhere I go

In the nighttime
In the nighttime

Gypsy is the clown of love
I paint his face a smile
Anyone we ever make
We always make in style

Strange young girls with radar screens
And hands as quick as pain
I want just now later on maybe
And even then I'll wait

In the nighttime
In the nighttime

Standing by the Everyman
Digging the rigging on my sails
Rain fell through sounds of harpsichords
Through the spell of fairy tales

The heath was hung in magic mists
And gentle dripping glades
I'll taste the tastes until my mind
Drifts from this scene and fades

In the nighttime
In the nighttime

[1] Better known as Donovan.

DONOVAN LEITCH[1]
1946–

The Lullaby of Spring

rain has showered far her drip
splash and trickle running
plant has flowered in the sand
shell and pebble sunning

so begins another spring
green leaves and of berries
chiff-chaff eggs are painted by
motherbird eating cherries

in a misty tangled sky
fast a wind is blowing
in a newborn rabbit's heart
river life is flowing

so begins another spring
green leaves and of berries
chiff-chaff eggs are painted by
motherbird eating cherries

from the dark and whetted soil
petals are unfolding
from the stony village kirk[2]
easter bells of old ring

so begins another spring
green leaves and of berries
chiff-chaff eggs are painted by
motherbird eating cherries

PHIL OCHS[1]
1940–1976

Crucifixion

And the night comes again to the circle-studded sky
The stars settle slowly, in loneliness they lie
Till the universe explodes as a falling star is raised
The planets are paralyzed, the mountains are amazed
But they all glow brighter from the brilliance of the blaze
With the speed of insanity, then, he dies.

In the green fields of turning a baby is born
His cries crease the wind and mingle with the morn
An assault upon the order, the changing of the guard
Chosen for a challenge that's hopelessly hard
And the only single sign is the sighing of the stars
But to the silence of distance they're sworn.

So dance, dance, dance
Teach us to be true
Come dance, dance, dance
'Cause we love you.

Images of innocence charge him to go on
But the decadence of history is looking for a pawn
To a nightmare of knowledge he opens up the gate
A blinding revelation is served upon his plate
That beneath the greatest love is a hurricane of hate
And God help the critic of the dawn.

So he stands on the sea and he shouts to the shore
But the louder that he screams the longer he's ignored
For the wine of oblivion is drunk to the dregs
And the merchants of the masses almost have to be begged
Till the giant is aware that someone's pulling at his leg
And someone is tapping at the door.

So dance, dance, dance
Teach us to be true
Come dance, dance, dance
'Cause we love you.

Then his message gathers meaning and it spreads across the land
The rewarding of the fame is the following of the man
But ignorance is everywhere and people have their way
And success is an enemy to the losers of the day

[1] Better known as Donovan. [2] Church.

[1] For information on the career and tragic suicide of Phil Ochs and the sources of this song-lyric, see John Berendt, "Phil Ochs Ain't Marchin' Anymore," *Esquire,* October, 1976.

In the shadows of the churches who knows what they pray
And blood is the language of the band.

The Spanish bulls are beaten, the crowd is soon beguiled
The matador is beautiful, a symphony of style
Excitement is ecstatic, passion places bets
Gracefully he bows to ovations that he gets
But the hands that are applauding are slippery with sweat
And saliva is falling from their smiles.

So dance, dance, dance
Teach us to be true
Come dance, dance, dance
'Cause we love you.

Then this overflow of life is crushed into a liar
The gentle soul is ripped apart and tossed into the fire
It's the burial of beauty, it's the victory of night
Truth becomes a tragedy limping from the light
The heavens are horrified, they stagger from the sight
And the cross is trembling with desire.

They say they can't believe it, it's a sacrilegious shame
Now who would want to hurt such a hero of the game
But you know I predicted it, I knew he had to fall
How did it happen, I hope his suffering was small
Tell me every detail, I've got to know it all
And do you have a picture of the pain?

So dance, dance, dance
Teach us to be true
Come dance, dance, dance
'Cause we love you.

Time takes her toll and the memory fades
But his glory is growing in the magic that he made
Reality is ruined, there is nothing more to fear
The drama is distorted to what they want to hear
Swimming in their sorrow in the twisting of a tear
As they wait for the new thrill parade.

The eyes of the rebel have been branded by the blind
To the safety of sterility the threat has been refined
The child was created to the slaughter house he's led
So good to be alive when the eulogies are read
The climax of emotion, the worship of the dead
As the cycle of sacrifice unwinds.

So dance, dance, dance
Teach us to be true
Come dance, dance, dance
'Cause we love you.

And the night comes again to the circle-studded sky
The stars settle slowly, in loneliness they lie
Till the universe explodes as a falling star is raised
The planets are paralyzed, the mountains are amazed
But they all glow brighter from the brilliance of the blaze
With the speed of insanity, then, he dies.

PHIL OCHS
1940–1976

Nobody's Buying Flowers from the Flower Lady

Millionaires and paupers walk the lonely street
Rich and poor companions of the restless feet
Strangers in a foreign land strike a match with a tremblin' hand
Learned too much to ever understand
But nobody's buying flowers from the flower lady.

Lovers quarrel, snarl away their happiness
Kisses crumble in a web of loneliness
It's written by the poison pen, voices break before they bend
The door is slammed, it's over once again
But nobody's buying flowers from the flower lady.

Poets agonize, they cannot find the words
The stone stares at the sculptor, asks are you absurd

The painter paints his brushes black, through the canvas runs a crack
The portrait of the pain never answers back
But nobody's buying flowers from the flower lady.

Soldiers disillusioned come home from the war
Sarcastic students tell them not to fight no more
And they argue through the night, black is black and white is white
Walk away both knowing they are right
Still nobody's buying flowers from the flower lady.

Smoke dreams of escaping soul are drifting by
Dull the pain of living as they slowly die
Smiles change into a sneer, washed away by whiskey tears
In the quicksand of their minds they disappear
But nobody's buying flowers from the flower lady.

Feeble aged people almost to their knees
Complain about the present using memories
Never found their pot of gold, wrinkled hands pound weary holes
Each line screams out you're old, you're old, you're old
But nobody's buying flowers from the flower lady.

And the flower lady hobbles home without a sale
Tattered shreds of petals leave a fading trail
Not a pause to hold a rose, even she no longer knows
The lamp goes out, the evening now is closed
And nobody's buying flowers from the flower lady.

CARL OGLESBY
1935–

Black Panther

I warned you things were crumbling
You could feel the storm in the air
You just showed me your Japanese umbrella
So cool, so debonair

Icecubes tinkled
The conversation strayed
To cocktail observations
On the one who was trying to pray

I cried in the name of your Jesus
Beware the big-time brass
You just stood there with your lollipop eyes
Like stoned on a kilo of grass

Oh the panther with the burning wound
Has found your perfume trail
You sit there tolling your I Ching changes
And you won't even open your special-delivery mail

Oh the panther gonna get your mama
Oh the panther gonna love your lamb
Spaced out of your mind on your dime horoscope
You got the virgin going down on the ram

Don't you know your garden is weedy
Don't you know your vineyards are bare
Dry well, poison water,
And your stallion is eating your mare

Well footman, footman, better shut the gates
Make sure the windows are closed
I told you baby that was just not enough
You just sat in your swing sniffing your rose

Footman, footman, better bring his coach
Better bring round this young man's cape
Seems to me it's about time he should leave
He's had a bit much of that old vino veritas grape

But the footman, he just stands there
Just looks you cold up and down
So you tell him, Boy, don't get insolent
And you try not to notice his frown

Then you feel yourself growing weary
And you hear a strange breathing at your side
Well maybe you better hurry up baby
Better find yourself some place to hide

Then the trees, they turn into husbands
The roses turn into wives
The night comes down, it's black panther town
The children turn into knives

Well, I warned you in the morning
You would never make high noon

You just swiveled around like some satisfied woman
Crooning your personal tunes

But now that your fine lips are bleeding
And you burn from a thousand rapes
And your bare body is learning
The name of the game and the stakes

You'll remember the way back to human
You'll remember the way back to soul
You'll remember the way it all come down
You'll pick up your ruins and go down one more road

JACK BLANCHARD
1930–

Tennessee Bird Walk[1]

Take away the trees, and the birds all have to sit upon the ground, uum,
Take away their wings, and the birds will have to walk to get around.
And take away the bird baths and dirty birds will soon be everywhere,
Take away their feathers, and the birds will walk around in underwear,
Take away their chirp, and the birds will have to whisper when they sing,
And take away their common sense, and they'll be headed southward in the Spring.

Oh, remember me, my darling,
When Spring is in the air,
And the baldheaded birds are whispering everywhere,
You can see them walking southward in their dirty underwear,
That's Tennessee bird walk.

How about some trees, so the birds won't have to sit upon the ground, uum,
How about some wings, so the birds won't have to walk to get around.
And how about a bird bath or two, so the birds will all be clean,
How about some feathers, so their underwear no longer can be seen,
How about a chirp, so the birds won't have to whisper when they sing,
And how about some common sense, so they won't be blocking traffic in the Spring.

Oh, remember me, my darling,
When Spring is in the air,
And the baldheaded birds are whispering everywhere,
You can see them walking southward in their dirty underwear,
That's Tennessee bird walk.

JOHNNY HARTFORD
1937–

Gentle on My Mind[1]

It's knowing that your door is always open and your path is free to walk,
That makes me tend to leave my sleeping bag rolled up and stashed behind your couch,

[1] "Tennessee Bird Walk," copyright © Back Bay Music. All rights reserved. Used by permission of Mietus Copyright Management.

[1] "Gentle on my Mind" by John Hartford © 1967, 1968 Glaser Publications, Inc. Used by permission of the copyright owner, Ensign Music Corporation.

And it's knowing that I'm not shackled by forgotten words and bonds
And the ink stains that have dried upon some line,
That keeps you in the backroads by the rivers of my memory that keeps
you ever
Gentle on my mind.

It's not clinging to the rocks and ivy planted on their columns now that binds me
Or something that somebody said because they thought we fit together walkin',
It's just knowing that the world will not be cursing or forgiving when I walk along
Some railroad track and find
That you're moving on the backroads by the rivers of my memory and for hours
You're just gentle on my mind.

Though the wheat fields and the clothes lines and junkyards and the highways
Come between us
And some other woman crying to her mother 'cause she turned and I was gone.
I still run in silence, tears of joy might stain my face and summer sun might
Burn me 'til I'm blind
But not to where I cannot see you walkin' on the backroads by the rivers flowing
Gentle on my mind.

I dip my cup of soup from the gurglin' cracklin' caldron in some train yard
My beard a rough'ning coal pile and a dirty hat pulled low across my face.
Through cupped hands 'round a tin can I pretend I hold you to my breast and find
That you're waving from the backroads by the rivers of my memory ever smilin'
Ever gentle on my mind.

THE LANGUAGE OF POETRY

If we are to understand and enjoy all that good poems offer us, we should know what to look for. The person who says that "I don't know much about poetry, but I know what I like," should say rather that he likes only what he knows and understands, which is obviously too little. Self-defense may be human, but as a learning process it can be fatal.

We have already said there are many languages within the English language—the language of science, of journalism, of history, of philosophy (p. 222). True, all of these languages have some basic things in common which make them English instead of French or German, such as grammatical structure and vocabulary. If we read that "North Labrador is a land of ice covered by grey sky, a silence where time has no meaning," the description is clear to anyone schooled in the basic devices of the English language. But when Hart Crane says (p. 222) that North Labrador is

> A land of leaning ice
> Hugged by plaster-grey arches of sky [that]
> Flings itself silently
> Into eternity,

we know that special language devices are being used to create a special kind of comment on North Labrador. We have already been introduced to the basic devices in "Poetry: Preliminaries" (p. 218), but the time has now arrived to explore them more thoroughly to prepare us for some penetrating poems yet to come. In a very real sense we need the right keys to unlock the many corridors of poetic experience.

RHYTHM AND RHYME: THE PROPER FUSION OF SOUND AND SENSE

Pope saw clearly that

> True ease in writing comes from art, not chance,
> As those move easiest who have learn'd to dance.

'Tis not enough no harshness gives offense,
The sound must seem an Echo to the sense.
—"An Essay on Criticism," ll. 362–365

Rhythm and rhyme, the basis of sound, are used to convey *meaning* in poetry. Most readers readily acknowledge that they can produce delightful effects for their own sake, as they do for some readers in Poe's "The Bells," but it is not usually understood that rhythm and rhyme actually help in shaping the meaning of a poem. The popular myth runs: the *idea* must be put into some form or frame, of course, but the idea is really the important matter—as if the idea has been put into a fancy basket to be delivered to the reader in appropriate style. A brief demonstration of this erroneous approach to poems may be more substantial than a book of arguments.

GEORGE WASHINGTON DOANE 1799–1859

Evening

Softly now the light of day
Fades upon my sight away;
Free from care, from labor free,
Lord, I would commune with Thee:

Thou, whose all-pervading eye,
  Naught escapes, without, within,
Pardon each infirmity,
  Open fault and secret sin.

Soon, for me, the light of day
Shall forever pass away;
Then, from sin and sorrow free,
Take me, Lord, to dwell with Thee:

Thou, who, sinless, yet hast known
  All of man's infirmity;
Then from Thine eternal throne,
  Jesus, look with pitying eye.

This poem presents a perfectly sound religious idea, acceptable to thousands of readers regardless of their sectarian doctrine. The first stanza says roughly that with the fading of "the light of day" the poet "would commune" with God. The second stanza asks omniscient God to pardon the speaker's sins. The third stanza includes a nice touch by now using "the light of day" to mean life. When this light passes forever away, the speaker wishes to dwell with God, free from earthly sin and sorrow. The last stanza asks God, sinless though He is, to look with pity upon man's earthly infirmity.

The poem contains humility, and a distaste for all sins which bring sorrow—who would quarrel with such sentiments? Do such sentiments make a good *poem?* A brief examination of its rhythm and rhyme will help to answer the question.

Note the rhyme scheme:

aabb	*cdcd*	*aabb*	*ecec*
(couplets)		(couplets)	

Does there seem to be any reason why stanzas 1 and 3 only should be written in couplets? If we examine the *logic* of the poem, stanzas 3 and 4 should be reversed, permitting the poem to come to rest with the line,

Take me, Lord, to dwell with Thee.

With this structure, the exact repetition of the rhymes in stanzas 1 and 4 would have real point by bringing to rest the tone which opens the poem in stanza 1. We note further that most of the rhymes are hackneyed and trite: *day* calls for *away, free* calls for *Thee,* and so on. Instead of awakening our sensibilities and surprising us with the fresh word, the rhymes discourage our expectancy, and the sense of the poem slips through our lulled wits. Line 3 seems to be especially awkward, beginning and ending with the same word, *free,* which rhymes with *Thee* in line 4.

The entire poem, save the last line, is written in monotonous tetrameter. Hardly the slightest variation exists except in the last line, where it is the least appropriate if we assume that the function of the last line is to bring the action to rest. Further, the monotonous regularity of the accented beat sometimes accents unimportant words: *upon,* line 2; *would,* line 4. To summarize, the poem is not memorable, condensed, or rigidly organized; and the religious idea, *which could have been made a religious experience* for the reader, lies dormant and ineffective.

FRANCIS QUARLES
1592–1644

A Good-Night

Close now thine eyes and rest secure;
Thy soul is safe enough, thy body sure;
He that loves thee, he that keeps
And guards thee, never slumbers, never sleeps.
The smiling conscience in a sleeping breast
Has only peace, has only rest;
The music and the mirth of kings
Are all but very discords, when she sings;
Then close thine eyes and rest secure;
No sleep so sweet as thine, no rest so sure.

The idea in this religious poem can be simply stated: a free conscience brings the peace and security provided by God. It requires no subtle analysis, however, to discover the shaping influences of rhythm and rhyme which have helped to make the poem so superior to the paraphrase.

Although the lyric is written in five couplets which could have been monotonous, the poet has provided a good deal of variation in only ten lines. Note that the first line of each couplet is tetrameter, and the second line pentameter except the third couplet—the middle couplet—which is reversed to break the rhythmic regularity. Note further that although the poem uses an iambic foot, the accent in the first foot does not always come on the second syllable. To *read* the accent on the second syllable of lines 1, 3, 6, and 10 would certainly violate their meaning. Note the difference in lines 3 and 4:

He that loves thee, he that keeps
And guards thee, never slumbers, never sleeps.

In one respect at least the rhyme scheme is especially appropriate. The sense of the poem has to do with restful security, and the rhyme helps to produce such an effect in the reader by closing the poem with the same sound that opened it, *secure-sure*. That is, the sound actually helps to interpret the sense. If further proof is necessary, suppose we change the word order a bit in the first four lines:

Close thine eyes now and rest secure;
Thy body is sure, thy soul safe enough;
He that keeps, he that loves thee
And guards thee, never sleeps, never slumbers.

The sense is still there—or is it?

The Emergent Tone

We are not concerned with exhibiting the extreme subtleties in the fusion of sound and sense in poetry, nor are we encouraging anyone to underestimate their importance. We wish to make clear that rhythm and rhyme help to shape the exact meaning of a poem. They help to establish the tone, which is in effect the poet's attitude toward the sense, or facts, of the poem, and *the reader must allow the tone to help him interpret the poem.* (See comments on Burns's "Sweet Afton," p. 232.) He must read the poem aloud and listen for the poet's voice, his attitude, because that attitude has shaped the meaning of the entire poem. Some readers have misunderstood, for example, Donne's "Go and Catch a Falling Star," calling it bitter and cynical because they have ignored Donne's tone (see p. 282 for the poem and comments). Tone is less tangible than image and figure (indeed, we borrow a term from music to describe it), but no less real. We shall see when we consider figures of speech and symbols (p. 266) that tone can actually become a figure of speech when the *entire* poem is meaningful only on the figurative level.

The Shaping Mechanics of Verse

Because poetry is an art, many people are irritated with the phrase "the mechanics of verse." "What does it matter"—the objection runs—"whether the line is iambic or trochaic, tetrameter or pentameter? I don't want to write poetry; I just want to read it." The argument seems to make good sense until we press that word *read* a little. Whether or not we read a poem aloud, we must be able to "hear" and feel its rhythms as well as to understand its sense. In a good poem the fusion of rhythm and sense is there, and we must read the fusion, not rhythm *or* sense, to experience the whole poem. To emphasize the rhythm as we read produces singsong; to emphasize the sense loses the poet's tone and attitude. To read both rhythm and sense simultaneously requires an elementary knowledge of the *foot,* the *line,* and the *stanza.*

THE FOOT. The foot is the smallest unit of stressed and unstressed syllables found in verse.

An elementary knowledge includes four kinds of feet.

1. *Iamb:* One unstressed and one stressed syllable, as in *delight*. This line is composed of iambic feet:

How small | a part | of time | they share

2. *Anapest:* Two unstressed and one stressed syllable, as in *underneath*. This line is composed chiefly of anapestic feet:

It was man | y and man | y a year | ago

3. *Trochee:* One stressed and one unstressed syllable, as in *happen* and *trochee*. This line is composed of trochaic feet:

Should you | ask me | whence these |
stories

4. *Dactyl:* One stressed and two unstressed syllables, as in *Michigan* and *elephant*. This line is composed of dactylic feet:

Take her up | tenderly

THE LINE. The line, called also *a verse*, determines the basic rhythmical pattern of the poem, and provides a principle of order for the sense. Lines are named according to the number of feet they possess, as follows:

One foot—monometer
Two feet—dimeter
Three feet—trimeter
Four feet—tetrameter
Five feet—pentameter
Six feet—hexameter
Seven feet—heptameter
Eight feet—octameter

Lines are therefore described according to the *kind* and *number* of feet they possess. For example, the line used to illustrate iambic meter is called *iambic tetrameter:*

How small | a part | of time | they share
1 2 3 4

This line is *dactylic dimeter:*

Take her up | tenderly
1 2

Most poems, like most of those we have already read, have lines composed of from three to five feet because these units of verse best serve the sense communicated by most poets. Poe's "The Raven" is an exception with its octameter line because the poet is working for a special tone and is using internal rhyme (p. 257) to help achieve his tone. His octameter line can be seen actually as two tetrameter units which are sometimes rhymed:

Once up|on a | midnight | dreary, || while I
| pondered, | weak and | weary

Now that we have come so far in our brief analysis of the foot and the line, we see that few poems are written exclusively with the same line or even the same foot. To avoid monotony, to achieve special effects, and—most important—to fuse the sound and sense, poets employ many kinds of variations. Although we have scanned the line from "The Raven" as "regular" trochaic octameter verse, we do not read it that way because the resulting sound would violate the sense. We actually read the line something like this:

Once up|on a | midnight | dreary, | while I
| pondered, | weak and | weary

There are, then, actually two degrees of stress, called primary (′) and secondary (″), which are made necessary by the poem's sense.

Another kind of variation in the line is made by substituting one kind of foot for another. The substitution of the anapestic foot for the iambic foot is found in Bryant's "Green River":

When breez|es are soft | and skies | are fair,
I steal | an hour | from stud|y and care

Note another kind of substitution, dimeter for tetrameter, in Waller's "Song" (p. 277):

Go, love|ly Rose,
Tell her | that wastes | her time | and me,
That now | she knows
When I | resem|ble her | to thee
How sweet | and fair | she seems | to be.

Because everyone does not read poetry the same way—not even highly qualified readers—

we should be extremely reluctant to draw dogmatic generalizations about the scansion of any poem. Almost every serious poem has both metrical and rhetorical rhythm unless it is written in free verse (see p. 258). There is movement of sound and movement of sense in every poem, and generally some compromise between the two must be made if the total meaning of the poem is not to be violated. This statement is especially true of poems with rhyme, and even more true of poems with internal rhyme. The reading of poems, especially aloud, is an accomplished art, but it will not be accomplished unless the reader knows what goes on in the poem.

RHYME. Rhyme is perhaps the most obvious technical device in poetry, yet its effects can be most subtle. Like all other devices, it is used for a specific purpose in each poem, and to judge its usefulness we must understand that purpose. The limerick depends heavily on rhyme:

There once was a man from Nantucket
Who kept all his cash in a bucket;
    But his daughter, named Nan,
    Ran away with a man,
And as for the bucket, Nantucket.

Some limericks combine a substantial subject with humor as does this one that plays with Einstein's famous theory of relativity:

There was a young lady named Bright,
Whose speed was far faster than light;
    She set out one day
    In a relative way,
And returned home the previous night.

Rhyme is used here to produce a humorous effect by emphasizing the element of surprise. The use of rhyme in Blake's "The Tiger" (p. 278) is more subtle:

Tiger! Tiger! burning bright
In the forests of the night,
What immortal hand or eye
Could frame thy fearful symmetry?

The rhyme *bright-night* suggests a paradox (p. 268), an apparent contradiction that upon close examination proves to be true. The rhyme *eye-symmetry* is even more subtle in its suggestion that an immortal eye, really unknown to us and by suggestion part of the "night," frames this symmetry, fearful because, by suggestion, it, too, is part of the "night." To hit the rhymes in "The Tiger" as we are expected to do in the limerick would violate the poem's meaning. In fact, by alternating a perfect rhyme, *bright-night,* with an imperfect rhyme, *eye-symmetry,* Blake has discouraged us from over-emphasizing the rhymes in the stanza.

There are many kinds of rhymes, used to achieve different purposes. The principal rhymes are *perfect* and *imperfect,* subdivided as follows:

Masculine (perfect): final accented syllables rhyme.

lie-die; resist-consist

Feminine or Multiple (perfect): rhyming accented syllables are followed by identical unaccented syllables:

raven-craven; comparison-garrison

Sprung or near-rhyme (imperfect): similar but not identical vowels rhyme:

blood-good; strong-unstrung;
eye-symmetry

Rhyme is found in two positions:

End-rhyme: at the end of the lines, the usual position, as in "The Tiger."

Internal rhyme: within the line.

The splendor *falls* on castle *walls*

STANZA FORM. A stanza is a pattern of lines which usually presents a unit of poetic experience. If the poem is composed of two or more stanzas, the pattern is generally repeated. There are many variations, of course, in stanza form, but we shall note only the standard forms which appear most frequently in American and English poetry. An alert reader will, of course, examine the stanza in any poem to determine how and why it helps to shape the poem's meaning. As we become more experienced in reading poetry—and more conditioned by standard stanza forms—certain expectancies are established in us which help to interpret the various forms.

Heroic Couplet: two rhymed iambic pentameter lines; each couplet is usually a complete unit, as in Pope:

Hope springs eternal in the human breast;
Man never is, but always to be, blessed.
—"An Essay on Man"

The couplet is not confined to iambic pentameter lines; Jonson, for example, uses iambic tetrameter in "Come, My Celia" (p. 230):

Come, my Celia, let us prove
While we may the sports of love;
Time will not be ours forever,
He at length our good will sever.

Swinburne uses anapestic pentameter couplets in a chorus of "Atalanta in Calydon":

We have seen thee, O Love, thou art fair;
        thou art goodly, O Love;
Thy wings make light in the air as the wings
        of a dove.

Ballad Stanza: four-line iambic, alternately tetrameter and trimeter, rhyming *abcb,* as in "Sir Patrick Spens" (p. 235):

The king sits in Dumferling toune,
  Drinking the blude-reid wine:
"O whar will I get guid sailor,
  To sail this schip of mine?"

The Sonnet: fourteen iambic pentameter lines, grouped variously according to the purpose of the poet.

The *Italian,* sometimes called *Petrarchan* or *legitimate,* sonnet has two parts: an octet, or eight lines, rhyming *abbaabba;* and a sestet, or six lines, using new rhymes, rhyming *cdcdcd* or some other combination. Wordsworth's "Composed upon Westminster Bridge" (p. 279) and Milton's "On His Blindness" (p. 281) are sonnets in the Italian form.

The *English,* sometimes called the *Shakespearian,* sonnet has three four-line units, or quatrains, and a concluding couplet, rhyming, *ababcdcdefefgg.* Drayton's "Since There's No Help" (p. 281) and the sonnets by Shakespeare, of course, are examples of the English form.

Usually, but not necessarily, the octet of a sonnet presents a problem or conflict, and the sestet offers a resolution or simply a comment on the conflict. Frost observed with characteristic humor that after the eighth line a sonnet takes a turn for better or worse. (See pp. 279–282 for six sonnets and further commentary on the sonnet form.)

The Spenserian Stanza: devised by Edmund Spenser (1552–1599) and used in *The Faerie Queene,* contains nine lines, eight of iambic pentameter, and the last of iambic hexameter (an Alexandrine), rhyming *ababbcbcc.* Because of the excellent effects it can be made to produce, this stanza form seems to be forever fresh and useful.

Blank Verse: iambic pentameter verse free from rhyme, the metrical line which seems to fit best the natural rhythms of our language. Shakespeare used it in his plays (*Hamlet,* p. 428), Milton chose it for *Paradise Lost,* T. S. Eliot gave it to the present-day stage in *The Cocktail Party,* and Frost used it with extraordinary effectiveness in "A Masque of Reason" (p. 376).

Free Verse: Free verse—not to be confused with blank verse—is verse which does not adhere to any exact metrical pattern. Although much of the world's poetry is written in free verse, sometimes called *vers libre,* many handbooks and textbooks on poetry give it a wide berth as if the whole matter were of little importance or not quite respectable.

There are both good and bad metrical verse and free verse, but the sins of one are not the virtues of the other. Bad metrical verse is perfectly, monotonously, and mechanically regular; bad free verse is rhetorically undisciplined and formless. Writers of good metrical verse resort to many variations, as we have seen, and the more they use, the closer they come to free verse. Writers of good free verse use a firm rhetorical discipline which often approximates a metrical form, and the firmer the rhetorical discipline the closer it comes to metrical verse. Are the differences between the two following passages very marked?

To be, or not to be—that is the question:
Whether 'tis nobler in the mind to suffer
The slings and arrows of outrageous fortune
Or to take arms against a sea of troubles,
And by opposing end them. To die—to sleep—
No more; and by a sleep to say we end
The heartache, and the thousand natural
        shocks
That flesh is heir to. 'Tis a consummation
Devoutly to be wished. . . .
        —Shakespeare, *Hamlet,* III, i, 56–64

This, this is he; softly a while;
Let us not break in upon him.
O change beyond report, thought, or belief!
See how he lies at random, carelessly diffused,
With languished head unpropt,
As one past hope, abandoned,
And by himself given over,
In slavish habit, ill-fitted weeds

O'er-worn and soiled.
Or do my eyes misrepresent? Can this be he,
That heroic, that renowned,
Irresistible Samson? whom, unarmed,
No strength of man, or fiercest wild beast, could withstand;
Who tore the lion as the lion tears the kid;
Ran on embattled armies clad in iron,
And, weaponless himself,
Made arms ridiculous, useless the forgery
Of brazen shield and spear, the hammered cuirass,
Chalybean-tempered steel, and frock of mail
Adamantean proof. . . .

—Milton, *Samson Agonistes*

Both these passages are shaped by a firm rhetorical discipline. Shakespeare is using blank verse liberally varied to permit the sense to strike home. To attempt to read any line metrically simply violates the sense; for example:

˘ ´ ˘ ´ ˘ ´ ˘ ´ ˘
The heart-ache and the thousand natural
´
shocks

Rhetorically, it scans something like this:

˘ ´ ″ ´ ˘ ´ ˘ ´ ″
The heart-ache and the thousand natural
´
shocks

Although the passage from Milton is written in free verse, the metrical verse often shows itself (lines 5, 6, 8, 9, and so on), and the rhetorical discipline never falters. It seems quite pointless to ask, is metrical verse superior to free verse? It seems better to ask, does the verse form properly shape the meaning of the poem?

The rhythm of good free verse is the rhythm of thought. Much so-called poetic prose is actually free verse written in prose form. We all know "Psalm 23," King James Version, in its prose form; it is easily converted:

The Lord is my shepherd;
I shall not want.

He maketh me to lie down in green pastures:
He leadeth me beside the still waters.
He restoreth my soul:
He leadeth me in the paths of righteousness
For his name's sake.
Yea, though I walk
Through the valley of the shadow of death,
I will fear no evil:
For thou art with me;
Thy rod and thy staff
They comfort me.

Thou preparest a table before me
In the presence of mine enemies:
Thou anointest my head with oil;
My cup runneth over.

Surely goodness and mercy shall follow me
All the days of my life:
And I will dwell in the house of the Lord
For ever.

As we ask ourselves some questions about the poems to follow, perhaps we can observe the appropriate uses of metrical and free verse.

WILLIAM WORDSWORTH
1770–1850

My Heart Leaps Up

My heart leaps up when I behold
A rainbow in the sky:
So was it when my life began;
So is it now I am a man;
So be it when I shall grow old,
Or let me die!
The Child is father of the Man;
And I could wish my days to be
Bound each to each by natural piety.

Comments and Questions

1. Although Wordsworth uses metrical verse, the poem is, compared to a sonnet, quite irregular in form. All lines are written in iambic meter, but note that they vary from dimeter to pentameter. Note further that the rhyme scheme is somewhat unusual: *abccabcdd.* We do not ask, is it right for Wordsworth to depart from the more regular forms? The question is, does the poem's irregular form shape the poem's meaning? Does the sound help to interpret the sense? The poem's form is certainly no accident. Why is line 6 the shortest, and line 9 the longest? Why do the last two lines rhyme?

Why do lines 1 and 5 rhyme, and lines 2 and 6? The answers to these questions are related to the total experience provided by the poem.

2. How good a poem is it?

3. What do you think Freud might have said about the line "The Child is father of the Man"?

WALT WHITMAN
1819–1892

Poets to Come

Poets to come! orators, singers, musicians to come!
Not to-day is to justify me and answer what I am for,
But you, a new brood, native, athletic, continental, greater than before known,
Arouse! for you must justify me.

I myself but write one or two indicative words for the future,
I but advance a moment only to wheel and hurry back in the darkness.

I am a man who, sauntering along without fully stopping, turns a casual look upon you
and then averts his face,
Leaving it to you to prove and define it,
Expecting the main things from you.

Comments and Questions

1. We ask the same basic question of Whitman's poem that we asked of Wordsworth's: Does the poem's free-verse form help to interpret the sense? How do the lines of varying length help to communicate Whitman's attitude toward the facts of the poem? Why is line 7 the longest and most supple, and line 9 the shortest?

2. Do the lines move with the rhythm of thought in the poem? Support your opinion with evidence from the poem.

THOMAS MOORE
1779–1852

Believe Me, If All Those Endearing Young Charms

Believe me, if all those endearing young charms,
Which I gaze on so fondly today,
Were to change by tomorrow, and fleet in my arms,
Like fairy-gifts fading away,
Thou wouldst still be adored, as this moment thou art,
Let thy loveliness fade as it will,
And around the dear ruin each wish of my heart
Would entwine itself verdantly still.

It is not while beauty and youth are thine own,
And thy cheeks unprofaned by a tear,
That the fervor and faith of a soul can be known,
To which time will but make thee more dear;
No, the heart that has truly loved never forgets,
But as truly loves on to the close,
As the sun-flower turns on her god, when he sets,
The same look which she turned when he rose.

Comments and Questions

1. The regularity of Moore's lyric—a brief subjective and musical poem—is apparent:

the foot is anapestic, the lines alternate between tetrameter and trimeter, and the rhyme scheme has a definite pattern (*ababcdcd,* and so on). Compared with "My Heart Leaps Up" and "Poets to Come," is Moore's poem dull and monotonous, or does his form help shape the meaning of the poem?

2. The poem, we said, is a lyric. Does this fact help to account for its form?

3. How good a poem is it?

GEORGE HERBERT
1593–1633

Easter Wings

It is interesting to note a device used by a few seventeenth-century poets: the form of the poem below speaks for itself. Joseph Addison (1672–1719) called this sort of thing "false wit," which we may translate as false poetic form. What is your opinion? For a more subtle example of the use of typography as a means to an effect, see Cummings' "Among Crumbling People," p. 274.

Lord, who createdst man in wealth and store,
Though foolishly he lost the same,
Decaying more and more
Till he became
Most poor;
With thee
Oh, let me rise
As larks, harmoniously,
And sing this day thy victories;
Then shall the fall further the flight in me.

My tender age in sorrow did begin;
And still with sicknesses and shame
Thou didst so punish sin,
That I became
Most thin.
With thee
Let me combine,
And feel this day thy victory;
For if I imp my wing on thine,
Affliction shall advance the flight in me.

IMAGERY

There are in general two ways of speaking: abstractly and concretely. If we say "George is an honest, just man with a good deal of integrity," we have described him with abstract terms. If we say "As George was following the stranger, he saw the stranger's pocketbook slip to the sidewalk, he picked it up, quickened his step, and returned it to him"—we have described George with concrete terms. In the first statement we have spoken *about* George; in the second statement we have allowed George's *act to speak* for George himself. In the first statement we testify to his honesty; in the second statement the act testifies for him, and it may be the more convincing. The second statement illustrates the basic method of the creative writer, especially the poet.

In the second statement we "image" or—as we say—we imagine George's act. We see it all happen because of the concrete details involved: *stranger, pocketbook, sidewalk,* and *step.* Such words are called *imagery* in a poem because they bring real, concrete life into it; they represent the life that the poet wants the reader to experience. Except in poorly constructed, superficial poems, these images are not mere decorations—they are in great part a poet's *method* of thinking. This principle we must understand if we are to enter the inner life of a good poem, and not to enter it is to bypass the poem's higher level, the figurative level of meaning.

Some poems rely almost exclusively on imagery for their meaning, as we shall see when we later explore MacLeish's "You, Andrew Marvell" (p. 263). Poets can rely on images for meaning if the images are carefully *selected* (not the approximate image, but the *exact* image) and *arranged* because we think naturally in images as children constantly demonstrate. The third-grade child who wrote,

Six little pigs sitting on a fence,
Not one of them had any sense,

was thinking in images because it is our natural way. Note how our mind searches for meaning by grouping these images: *table, bottle, cabinet, glasses, alcohol, men*—and we see a barroom. Yet, note what happens when we add only two more images: *test tube, Bunsen burner.* The *regrouped* images become a laboratory because the last two images alter the *grouped* meaning of the first six.*

In that little demonstration of how we think in images there are many lessons for the readers of poems, but for our purposes here chiefly these: we must understand the poem as an organic whole—we must allow the meaning of each image to come clear in its natural setting with all the other images. And we must make sure that all the images are included in our interpretation of the poem's meaning. We are driven back to our basic principle ("Poetry: Preliminaries," p. 218): the whole poem helps to determine the meaning of its parts, and, in turn, each part helps to determine the meaning of the whole. When we interpret a poem's imagery, the observance of this principle is imperative.

We are now in a position to understand why imagery is the life of a good poem. With imagery the poet allows life to present itself, and we can hear, see, smell, feel, and touch experience. As we read the following poem, we are immediately involved with sense experience—concrete life itself.

EMILY DICKINSON
1830–1886

I Taste a Liquor Never Brewed

I taste a liquor never brewed—
From Tankards scooped in Pearl—
Not all the Vats upon the Rhine
Yield such an Alcohol!

Inebriate of Air—am I—
And Debauchee of Dew—
Reeling—thro endless summer days—
From inns of Molten Blue—

When "Landlords" turn the drunken Bee
Out of the Foxglove's door—
When Butterflies—renounce their "drams"—
I shall but drink the more!

Till Seraphs[1] swing their snowy Hats—
And Saints—to windows run—
To see the little Tippler
Leaning against the—Sun—

* For a psychological explanation of the creative process, see Norman R. F. Maier and H. Willard Reninger, *A Psychological Approach to Literary Criticism*. New York: Appleton-Century-Crofts, 1933, esp. chap. III.

[1] Six-winged angels standing in the presence of God.

Comments

Through images—many of which are also figures and symbols—this poem presents a theme which, as such, is never mentioned directly. The "liquor never brewed" is the exhilarating aspect of nature in which we participate by entering Emily Dickinson's sensuous world, and we participate fully because the images are fresh and unusual. "Scooped in Pearl," "inebriate of Air," and "reeling . . . from inns of Molten Blue" are not the worn counters of expression. They are sharp, concrete, arresting sense impressions which communicate meaning, quite unforgettably.

We see, then, that the purpose of imagery is to communicate meaning, not merely to serve as a graceful embellishment. If we understand this distinction before we investigate imagery further, our study can become a genuine pleasure instead of an academic chore. Many of the poems in this section use imagery in striking and original ways and, read carefully, they can help to cultivate our sensitivity to imagery as communication. For most poets, imagery actually becomes a way of thinking, or of translating abstractions into concrete experience. Indeed, imagery is the chief means the poet has of creating reality —*his* own sense of the reality of the inner and outer world and their relationships. Here are Shakespeare and Donne thinking in images.

WILLIAM SHAKESPEARE
1564–1616

Sonnet 116: Let Me Not to the Marriage of True Minds

Let me not to the marriage of true minds
Admit impediments. Love is not love
Which alters when it alteration finds,

Or bends with the remover to remove.
Oh, no! it is an ever-fixed mark
That looks on tempests and is never shaken;
It is the star to every wandering bark,
Whose worth's unknown, although his height be taken.
Love's not Time's fool, though rosy lips and cheeks
Within his bending sickle's compass come;
Love alters not with his brief hours and weeks,
But bears it out even to the edge of doom.
  If this be error and upon me proved,
  I never writ, nor no man ever loved.

powerfully suggestive Donne's images are, try to state the plain sense of the poem in literal language only. What are the basic images, and how does Donne relate them to define the sensation of love?

2. What is the tone of the poem? Is Donne serious about this idea of love or is there a trace of extravagance in the poem?

3. Donne is well known for his technical dexterity. Does it serve or override the sense in this poem? Is the poem merely technically admirable or does it also present a valuable experience?

JOHN DONNE
1572–1631

The Good-Morrow

I wonder, by my troth, what thou and I
Did, till we loved? Were we not weaned till then,
But sucked on country pleasures, childishly?
Or snorted we in the seven sleepers' den?
'Twas so; but this, all pleasures fancies be.
If ever any beauty I did see,
Which I desired, and got, 'twas but a dream of thee.

And now good morrow to our waking souls,
Which watch not one another out of fear;
For love all love of other sights controls,
And makes one little room an everywhere.
Let sea-discoverers to new worlds have gone,
Let maps to other, worlds on worlds have shown;
Let us possess one world, each hath one, and is one.

My face in thine eye, thine in mine appears,
And true plain hearts do in the faces rest;
Where can we find two better hemispheres
Without sharp north, without declining west?
Whatever dies was not mixed equally;
If our two loves be one, or thou and I
Love so alike that none do slacken, none can die.

Comments and Questions

1. Much like Shakespeare's "Sonnet 116," this poem is a definition of love presented in images and figures. To realize just how

SAMUEL TAYLOR COLERIDGE
1772–1834

On Donne's Poetry[1]

With Donne, whose muse on dromedary trots,
Wreathe iron pokers into true-love knots;
Rhyme's sturdy cripple, fancy's maze and clue,
Wit's forge and fire-blast, meaning's press and screw.

ARCHIBALD MacLEISH
1892–

You, Andrew Marvell

And here face down beneath the sun
And here upon earth's noonward height
To feel the always coming on
The always rising of the night:

To feel creep up the curving east
The earthy chill of dusk and slow
Upon those under lands the vast
And ever climbing shadow grow

And strange at Ectaban[1] the trees
Take leaf by leaf the evening strange

[1] In addition to Donne's "The Good-Morrow" above, see also his "Go and Catch a Falling Star," p. 282; "Holy Sonnet, VII," p. 309; "Woman's Constancy," p. 315, and "The Canonization," p. 315.

[1] The ancient capital of Media, presently a part of Iran.

The flooding dark about their knees
The mountains over Persia change

And now at Kermanshah[2] the gate
Dark empty and the withered grass
And through the twilight now the late
Few travelers in the westward pass

And Baghdad darken and the bridge
Across the silent river gone
And through Arabia the edge
Of evening widen and steal on

And deepen on Palmyra's[3] street
The wheel rut in the ruined stone
And Lebanon fade out and Crete
High through the clouds and overblown

And over Sicily the air
Still flashing with the landward gulls
And loom and slowly disappear
The sails above the shadowy hulls

And Spain go under and the shore
Of Africa the gilded sand
And evening vanish and no more
The low pale light across that land

Nor now the long light on the sea:

And here face downward in the sun
To feel how swift how secretly
The shadow of the night comes on . . .

Comments and Questions

Edwin Arlington Robinson called this poem "really a magical thing." It must be read aloud three or four times in a leisurely way to appreciate Robinson's comment. What produces the magic? Many poetic devices working together, of course, not the least of them the imagery. The title is undoubtedly a reference to Marvell's "To His Coy Mistress" (p. 285), particularly to such well-known lines as:

> But at my back I always hear
> Time's wingéd chariot hurrying near;
> And yonder all before us lie
> Deserts of vast eternity.

These lines and MacLeish's poem are concerned with the relentless movement of time —thieving time, as the Elizabethans called it. Note that the sound never diminishes until the last line, and the suspense is evenly distributed from beginning to end, helped along by the relentless stress of almost perfect (regular) iambic meter. The tone of the poem is one of restrained resignation and perhaps profound regret.

To get at the specific meaning of the poem —a meaning more specific than that of relentless time—we must account for the first and last stanzas, which are quite different from the others with their specific references to cities and countries. Where is the "here," the vantage point from which the poet speaks and feels this relentless time? Some readers have felt that "here" means MacLeish's native land, America, and the poet has confirmed it.* Working with this clue, can we read the poem as saying that young America will someday also experience the ravages of time as the older countries have? We may now return to the tremendous importance of the images, important because they seem to answer the question affirmatively. Note how the images move from "noonward height" in the first stanza to these images in the following stanzas: "the earthy chill," "the flooding dark," "the withered grass," "Spain go under," and "evening vanish." And finally, line 34 repeats the image in line 1, implying that America, too, will have its withered grass and its evening vanish. It is important to recognize that MacLeish has not offered his argument in some logical frame; he has depended upon his images to make us feel the force of his specific theme. This technique is quite characteristic of much modern poetry, depending as it does so heavily on imagery and unusual symbolism.

---

[2] City in Iran. [3] An ancient flourishing city in Syria, presently a poor Arab village.

* Norman C. Stageberg and Wallace L. Anderson, *Poetry as Experience*. New York: American Book Company, 1952, p. 465.

GERARD MANLEY HOPKINS
1844–1889

Spring and Fall: To a Young Child

Márgarét, are you gríeving
Over Goldengrove[1] unleaving?
Léaves, líke the things of man, you
With your fresh thoughts care for, can you?
Áh, ás the heart grows older
It will come to such sights colder
By and by, nor spare a sigh
Though worlds of wanwood leafmeal lie;
And yet you wíll weep and know why.
Now no matter, child, the name:
Sórrow's spríngs áre the same.
Nor mouth had, no nor mind, expressed
What heart heard of, ghost guessed:[2]
It ís the blight man was born for,
It is Margaret you mourn for.

Comments and Questions

1. This poem will not be understood or enjoyed through hurried reading, but the subtle fusion of sound and sense can be enjoyed if we first understand the poem's literal sense. The sense is actually not difficult, but it is highly concentrated: every word counts, and every line moves the sense along without interruption. Put the literal sense into writing, and account for every phrase in the poem. How did you interpret line 9? Note that the poet stresses *will,* not *weep.* The first word in lines 14 and 15 is very important, and line 15 summarizes the meaning of the poem.

2. Perhaps you have already discovered how thoroughly fused the sound and sense are. Note the rhyme in the first couplet: how does it contribute to meaning? What is the relationship of the first and last couplets? Note especially the rhyme *born for—mourn for.*

[1] Literally an estate in Wales, near Llansa in Flintshire; figuratively a color of vanishing youth.

[2] Ll. 12–13. *I Corinthians,* 2:9 and 13: "But as it is written, Eye hath not seen, nor ear heard, neither have entered into the heart of man, the things which God hath prepared for them that love him." "Which things also we speak, not in the words which man's wisdom teacheth, but which the Holy Ghost teacheth; comparing spiritual things with spiritual." Also *Isaiah,* 64:4:

> For since the beginning of the world *men* have not heard, nor perceived by the ear,
> Neither hath the eye seen, O God, besides thee, *What* he hath prepared for him that waiteth for him. . . .

ROBERT FROST
1874–1963

Neither Out Far nor In Deep

The people along the sand
All turn and look one way.
They turn their backs on the land.
They look at the sea all day.

As long as it takes to pass
A ship keeps raising its hull;
The wetter ground like glass
Reflects a standing gull.

The land may vary more;
But whatever the truth may be—
The water comes ashore,
And the people look at the sea.

They cannot look out far.
They cannot look in deep.
But when was that ever a bar
To any watch they keep?

Comments and Questions

In this poem the plain sense, the rhyme scheme, the rhythm, the images—in fact, everything seems to be simple. By this time, however, we have had enough experience with poems to suspect that Frost's little poem means something more than meets the eye, and we recall that our analysis of his "Stopping by Woods on a Snowy Evening" ("Poetry: Preliminaries," p. 218) found the something more in his figures and symbols. Like so many of Frost's poems, the one above is disarmingly simple, but let us arm ourselves just the same. The following subsection, "Figure and Symbol," will explore these matters: we use this poem to introduce the problems.

Frost's figures and symbols here are quite conventional, made so by repeated use and time. As usual, we come to figures and symbols through the images, and the central images here are "people," "land," "sea," and "watch." Practiced readers have developed the habit of asking questions of poems, whatever questions a poem seems to raise. Who are these "people"? Because they are completely unidentified, they must represent (see the symbol appear?) all of us, humanity. Why do "they turn their back on the land" and all "look at the sea"? The clue to the answer lies in line 10: they are looking for truth. Why do they look to the sea for it—is there no truth to be found on the land? The land gives us our bearings and represents the known, but the sea is limitless and mysterious to the eye and represents the unknown, exciting the imagination. We scrutinize the unknown, and little by little extract more meaning from it, but our progress toward the great, final answers is small ("they cannot look out far") because their subtleties are too great ("they cannot look in deep"). Nevertheless, the human race keeps the watch and continues to scrutinize the unknown, and there is hope ("the water comes ashore") that we shall know more and more about our destiny.

It is not entirely uncommon for some readers who really enjoy poems to protest at this point, asking in good faith, "*Must* we scatter the beauty of this little poem by all this analysis—is it really necessary to read all this *into* [note well, *into*] the poem?" The answer to this impatient question is not simple, and if the questioner is impatient enough, the answer is never adequate. A preliminary answer says it all depends on what is meant by "the beauty of this little poem." If a reader is satisfied with the sound and the harmony of the images, for him that is beauty enough. But there is no reason why this reader should legislate for other readers who find beauty, too, in the meaningful truth provided by the poem's figures and symbols. Such is the beginning of the answer to the impatient question; we hope a fuller answer will be found in the subsection to follow. (See Spender's "On Teaching Modern Poetry," p. 687, for commentary on this controversy.)

FIGURE AND SYMBOL

Now that we have seen how images bring concrete life (sensuous experience) into a poem, and how poets think naturally with them (as we all do), we are prepared to see how poets use these images in special ways, sometimes to say things which can be said in no other way.

Figures and symbols are images used in a particular way to explore the less known through the known. Joseph Conrad describes an old Chinese shipowner as having "a face like an ancient lemon." The images in this figure are the face and the lemon, the first unknown to us, the second well known. Our imagination is required to transfer the *revelant* characteristics of the ancient lemon to the face, and we "see" it as wrinkled, jaundiced, dried-up, oval-shaped, and toughened by time—but the irrelevant characteristic of the lemon we allow to drop away. That is, we must make the proper association between the face and the lemon, and when someone insists on transferring the complete lemon or no lemon at all to the face, we say he has no imagination. For such a person poetry is simply an empty art because he cannot interpret figurative meaning. (See p. 223 on "Failure to Rise to the Figurative Level.")

Conrad could have used the adjectives mentioned above (*wrinkled, jaundiced*) instead of the figure; he could have described the Chinese face with a paragraph, but he would have lost his economy of means and concentrated suggestiveness provided by the figure. But figures can be used even on a higher level to communicate experience which cannot be communicated in any other way. To communicate the subtleties of the love experience has always placed a tremendous burden on language and the poets, and we therefore find love poems rife with figures (and symbols—see below) of all kinds. On falling deeply in love how would you explain and describe the exact shades and depths of feeling to a person who had never experienced such love? With abstract terms? Try it, and despair. We are quickly forced into a series of figures to compare the love experiences with other experiences which are somewhat related to love:

> "Shall I compare thee to a summer's day?"
> (Shakespeare, p. 314)

> "My love is like a red red rose."
> (Burns, p. 320)

Figures were not concocted as decorations: poetic necessity was originally the mother of communicative invention.

Poetry, then, understood in its most basic sense does not mean merely a collection of rhymes, rhythms, and images: it is actually a way of thinking and feeling (E. E. Cummings would probably write *thinkfeeling* and he would be right) used to explore the unknown. Writers of prose as well as poets use this method, and here is Vernon Louis Parrington, scholar and master of figurative language, speaking of Herman Melville:

> The golden dreams of transcendental faith, that buoyed up Emerson and gave hope to Thoreau, turned to ashes in his mouth; the white gleams of mysticism that now and then lighted up his path died out and left him in darkness.

Like Melville, Macbeth saw his own dreams perish; when he saw his darkness coming, Shakespeare makes him say:

> Tomorrow, and tomorrow, and tomorrow,
> Creeps in this petty pace from day to day
> To the last syllable of recorded time;
> And all our yesterdays have lighted fools
> The way to dusty death. Out, out, brief candle!
> Life's but a walking shadow, a poor player
> That struts and frets his hour upon the stage
> And then is heard no more. It is a tale
> Told by an idiot, full of sound and fury,
> Signifying nothing.
>
> —*Macbeth,* V. v. 19–28

A full analysis and explanation of everything said by Shakespeare in these ten lines would require many prose pages. Why is this so?

The answer lies in the nature of Shakespeare's figurative language, especially in its economy and tremendous suggestiveness. Shakespeare could have had Macbeth tell us simply that life is meaningless—why did he use ten lines to tell us that? (Such a question is sometimes asked impatiently by the literal mind.) Because Shakespeare wants us to participate in Macbeth's tragic flash of insight by having us transfer the relevant characteristics of *petty pace, last syllable, dusty death, brief candle, a walking shadow, a player that struts and frets* to Macbeth's feeling about life at this moment. These images we understand, and when Shakespeare uses them as figures too, we understand Macbeth. This act of transferrence we call the *imaginative process:* in our mind, life for Macbeth is *as* meaningless as a shadow, a fretting player, an idiot's tale. Is it any wonder that Macbeth cries, "Out, out, brief candle!" when its flickering light signifies nothing to be lived for?

Kinds of Figures

We are so accustomed to figures of speech in our everyday reading and conversation that unpracticed readers of poems sometimes overlook some figures and read them literally. It is best therefore to have the kinds of figures in mind, and to add their names to our critical vocabulary. Figurative language is sometimes called metaphorical language, or simply metaphor because its Greek ancestor *metapherein* means to carry meaning beyond its literal meaning (*meta* = beyond + *pherein* = to bring—that is, to bring beyond). *Regardless, then, of the* kind *of figure we observe, its basic function is always to carry meaning from the literal to the figurative level.*

Simile: a stated comparison, introduced by *like* or *as.* For example, "My love is like a red red rose." "There is no frigate like a book."

Metaphor: an implied comparison, with *like* or *as* omitted. For example, "Life's but a walking shadow"—instead of saying "Life is *like* a walking shadow."

Personification: giving human characteristics to an object, animal, or an abstract idea. Personification is a metaphor, of course, in the sense that there is an implied comparison between a nonhuman thing and a human being. For example, "There Honor comes, a pilgrim gray"; "My little horse must think it queer / To stop without a farmhouse near."

Synecdoche: using a part for the whole. For example, "Fifty winters [years] passed him by." Or using the whole for the part: for example, "the halcyon year"—meaning summer.

Metonymy: describing one thing by using the term for another thing closely associated with it.

For example, "the crown" used for "the king."

Hyperbole: an exaggeration used for special effect. For example, "Drink to me only with thine eyes"; "Go and catch a falling star."

Irony: a statement whose real meaning is completely opposed to its professed, or surface meaning. (See p. 223.) For example, " 'The czar is the voice of God and shall live forever.' "

Paradox: a statement whose surface, obvious meaning seems to be illogical, even absurd, but which makes good sense upon closer examination. For example: speaking of humanity Somerset Maugham observed, "the normal is the rarest thing in the world." Another example, Christ "lives that death may die." One more, "He couldn't find it because he knew where it was." Donne is famous for his paradoxes; see "The Canonization" (p. 315) for his paradoxical proof that unholy lovers are saints. Irony, of course, is related to paradox because in each the surface meaning is never the real meaning, and hence both rely on an indirect method, a well-established device in poetry.

Dead Metaphor: a metaphor which has lost its figurative meaning through endless use. For example, "the back of the chair"; "the face of the clock."

Allusion: a reference to some well-known place, event, or person. Not a comparison in the exact sense, but a figure in the sense that it implies more than its narrow meaning. For example: "No! I am not Prince Hamlet, nor was meant to be"; "Miniver loved the Medici"; "There is a stubborn torch that flames from Marathon to Concord."

The Entire Poem as Figure: a poem which can be understood and enjoyed on the literal level, but when properly interpreted *as a whole* is completely figurative. There are many examples in this book: Frost's "Departmental" (p. 232), Herrick's "Delight in Disorder" (p. 316), and so on. It is not argued that such poems should be read literally only, but only that they can be, just as *Gulliver's Travels* and *Alice in Wonderland* can be read as stories without implications.

Tone: in some serious treatments of the relation of tone to meaning in poems, it is often implied that tone is actually an extended figure of speech. For example, more than an occasional reader misinterprets Donne's "Go and Catch a Falling Star" because he misreads Donne's tone and calls the poem bitter or cynical. (See p. 282 for the poem and relevant comments on this problem.)

Symbol

A symbol, defined most simply, is one thing used to stand for, to represent, another thing. A lion stands for strength and courage; a lamb stands for gentleness; a burning torch held aloft stands for liberty. The word's Greek ancestor is *symballein,* meaning to compare by throwing together. A symbol is therefore a figure of speech, although there is a technical difference between the two which should be understood in order to identify the *kinds* of symbol in poems.

If Shakespeare had written,

> Life's like a walking shadow,

he would have used a simile because the comparison is *stated.* He did write,

> Life's but a walking shadow,

and he therefore used a metaphor which *implies* the comparison without explicitly stating it, but note that both terms of the figure, *life* and *shadow,* are still present in the metaphor. If Shakespeare had dropped one term, *life,* and had used only *shadow* to stand for life, he would have used a symbol.

A symbol, however, is not necessarily related to metaphor. It can stand on its own feet by representing through continued use and common understanding a simple object or a complex pattern of associations or ideas. When we use the Cross to represent Christianity, we do not imply that the Cross is *like* Christianity; we simply say it stands for it, and the device works because the association is universally understood. When Frost says in "Birches,"

> I'd like to go [*toward* heaven] by climbing a
> birch tree.
> And climb black branches up a snow-white
> trunk,

almost any reader of poems should sense that Frost is up to something with those *"black branches"* and that *"snow-white* trunk." And of course he is. The "snow-white trunk" stands for the ideal which reaches toward heaven, and the black branches are life's dark realities we shall have to climb *over* and *with* to complete the climb to the top of the ideal. These are *conven-*

tional symbols, made so by use and time, recognized by practiced readers of poetry.

But some poets depart from conventional symbols to invent their own for their special purposes because, we assume, the conventional symbols will not properly communicate new sensations in a new age. Such symbols are called *arbitrary* or *personal* symbols, and must be understood in the poem's complete context, not by any previous mutual understanding between poet and reader. A good deal of "modern" poetry relies heavily on textual symbolism, and it accounts for some of the obscurity some readers find in modern poetry. When Eliot begins "The Love Song of J. Alfred Prufrock" (p. 390) with these lines,

> Let us go then, you and I,
> When the evening is spread out aginst the sky
> Like a patient etherised upon a table,

the explanation of his symbols must be found in the remainder of the poem, not in any conventional meaning of patients who are etherized upon tables.

Genuine understanding of metaphor and symbol will not be achieved, however, through theoretical explanations: let us examine them in action in the poems that follow.

EMILY DICKINSON
1830–1886

There Is No Frigate Like a Book

There is no Frigate like a Book
To take us Lands away
Nor any Coursers like a Page
Of prancing Poetry—
This Travel may the poorest take
Without offence of Toll—
How frugal is the Chariot
That bears the Human soul.

Comments

The reader unable to read figurative language would find this poem incomprehensible. Structurally and rhetorically the poem is simple, but unless we can visualize a book as a "ship" taking us to new intellectual and emotional "lands," and a page as a spirited "horse," no amount of abstract explanation will help us to understand the poem. Because the poem's structure is simple, the poem readily reveals the basic problem in reading poetry; but regardless of the complexity of a poem's structure and rhetoric, unless we can interpret the meaning of image, figure, and symbol, no amount of work on structure will make the poem clear. Even at the risk of laboring the obvious, this principle must be made absolutely clear: it is repeatedly overlooked even by practiced readers.

T. S. ELIOT
1888-1965

Morning at the Window

They are rattling breakfast plates in basement kitchens,
And along the trampled edges of the street
I am aware of the damp souls of housemaids
Sprouting despondently at area gates.

The brown waves of fog toss up to me
Twisted faces from the bottom of the street,
And tear from a passer-by with muddy skirts
An aimless smile that hovers in the air
And vanishes along the level of the roofs.

Comments and Questions

Except for a few images, Eliot's poem appears to be written in plain statement. The literal situation is simple: the speaker is perhaps looking from a second-floor window or balcony as he sees and hears the movements and noises appropriate to the neighborhood's morning activities. Breakfast plates rattle, housemaids appear at the gates, waves of fog rise to reveal faces in the street, faces with problems in them, and the fog vanishes over the roofs. But the unusual images press for meaning—they tell us this literal reading will not do. Why the "basement" kitchens? Why the "trampled edges" of the street? Why the "damp souls" and why do they "sprout" despondently? We go back to the title, suspecting we have been trapped by irony. Morning is a conventional symbol of hope and energy, but neither is in this poem. As we account for the brown (stained) waves of fog, the twisted (abnormal, perverted) faces, the aimless smile whose owner has lost his bearings, we see that Eliot finds humanity living in the slums—this, we understand, is our morning now whose hope and energy have vanished over the roofs of the world. We shall meet more of Eliot's theme —the degeneration of our time—in "The Love Song of J. Alfred Prufrock" (p. 390), and "The Hollow Men" (p. 345).

But note the sharp precision of the scene in the poem—no plain statement, no abstractions, no message wrapped up and labeled in the final line, no stale figures and symbols. What does Eliot depend on instead? The poem below will tell us—an acknowledged manifesto of modern poetry.

ARCHIBALD MacLEISH
1892–

Ars Poetica

A poem should be palpable and mute
As a globed fruit,

Dumb
As old medallions to the thumb,

Silent as the sleeve-worn stone
Of casement ledges where the moss has grown—

A poem should be wordless
As the flight of birds.

*

A poem should be motionless in time
As the moon climbs,

Leaving, as the moon releases
Twig by twig the night-entangled trees,

Leaving, as the moon behind the winter leaves,
Memory by memory the mind—

A poem should be motionless in time
As the moon climbs.

*

A poem should be equal to:
Not true.

For all the history of grief
An empty doorway and a maple leaf.

For love
The leaning grasses and two lights above the sea—

A poem should not mean
But be.

Comments and Questions

Ars poetica means the art of poetry, or, in this case, MacLeish's definition of a poem. We can assume that he is describing what he means by a good poem as contrasted, say, with a lecture or perhaps an essay.

In presenting his *ars poetica* as a poem MacLeish assumed a double responsibility: he must not only make the sense of the poem describe a poem, but he must also cause this poem to be an example of the kind of poem of which he approves.

The poem has stimulated a good deal of controversy, especially the final "couplet." What does the poem mean—what, according to MacLeish, is a good poem? The structure, a series of couplets (except lines 13–14 and 21–22), is not complicated; so the difficulty must be chiefly in the figures and symbols, especially in the paradoxes (see p. 268).

The poem has three principal divisions, lines 1–8, 9–16, and 17–end; each division presents a basic principle of a good poem. First, "a poem should be palpable and mute" (dumb, silent, wordless). Literally, this dictum is nonsense, but MacLeish is not speaking literally—and *no* poem, he is saying by implication, ever should. A poem should speak concretely (palpably) through images, by presenting things which speak silently for themselves. That is, the poet should not talk about things in some general abstract way; he should permit things to speak for themselves. The "globed fruit," the "old medallions," the "casement ledges," and the "flight of birds" will tell their own stories by their presence. The reader must find the meaning of the thing in the thing itself.

Second (lines 9–16), a poem should be timeless and universal in its attitudes, timeless as the moon is timeless and as memories are. An event is always timely, but the meaning of an event in human terms is timeless and universal.

The third division of the poem (lines 17–end) seems to give the most difficulty, although its meaning has already been partially explained in the previous lines. "A poem should be equal to" the experience presented *as experience* in the whole poem, and "not true" as a theory or a propositional truth is true—not merely abstractly true. A poem's truth should be self-evident as it emerges from the poem's images which represent experience, not a labored truth sustained by argument. "A poem should not mean" as an argument means, but should "be" its own witness for its own kind of truth. Commenting on the nature of art, without directly mentioning "Ars Poetica," MacLeish seems to put the poem's meaning into prose:

> Art is a method of dealing with our experience of this world, which makes that experience, *as* experience, recognizable to the spirit. . . . Art is not a technique for extracting truths. . . . Art is an organization of experience in terms of experience, the purpose of which is the recognition of experience. ["A poem should be equal to: / Not true."] It is an interpreter between ourselves and that which has happened to us, the purpose of which is to make legible what it is that has happened. . . . It is an organization of experience comprehensible not in terms of something else, but of itself; not in terms of significance, but of itself; not in terms of truth even, but of itself. ["A poem should not mean / But be."] The truth of a work of art is the truth of its organization. It has no other truth." *

When Stephen Spender says that "a poem *means* the sum of everything which it *is* . . . ," he is saying much the same thing. (See Spender's essay, "On Teaching Modern Poetry," p. 687.)

For our immediate purposes the value of MacLeish's poem lies in his explanation and use of a method used by many modern poets, including T. S. Eliot and others whom we shall read later. This method—to summarize briefly for the moment—relies chiefly on textual symbols, compound images, and communication by association, rather than on logical structure.

* *A Time to Speak.* Boston: Houghton Mifflin Company, 1940, pp. 84–85.

E. E. CUMMINGS
1894–1962
The Cambridge Ladies

As we have moved progressively through the poems by Moore, Dickinson, Eliot, and MacLeish, we have moved away from the older poetry with its conventional techniques and attitudes into the newer, modern poetry. We have learned that the language (the poetic devices of symbol, rhythm, and sound) of Dickinson is somewhat different from Moore's language; and that the language of Eliot is sharply different from the poetic language used by both Moore and Dickinson. We have, in short, been involved with a *reading* problem—which means a problem of *understanding.*

Many qualified readers believe that the most celebrated modern poetic innovator is E. E. Cummings. Although he has never achieved the almost universal popularity of a Frost, Cummings has appealed especially to young people. One Cummings biographer, Charles Norman, reports that "when Cummings went to Bennington College in Vermont to give a reading, the entire audience of girls rose as he mounted the platform and chanted . . . in unison his poem 'Buffalo Bill's.' "

On first meeting Cummings' poetry the reader is likely to assume that he is confronted with the whims of a dabbler who delights in linguistic pyrotechnics in order to confuse and astonish a public he does not deserve. But the young who are slow to accept the chains of conventional grammatical and rhetorical practice (as Hemingway, Dos Passos, and Faulkner refuse to do) are ready to consider Hemingway's argument that "there is a fourth and fifth dimension that can be gotten" in prose—and, implies Cummings, in poetry, too. In short, there is no reason to believe that conventionally accepted textbook language forms, regardless of how "liberal" and "descriptive," are adequate to communicate all personal, subjective experience, especially the intensely personal experience of a Cummings. The basic question for the creative writer is not, is this language pattern "acceptable"? The question is, how far may language be stretched and distorted to communicate my experience and still reach the sensibilities of the enlightened reader? Shakespeare took some chances, Eliot took them, and Cummings took even greater chances (of not being understood—there is no other criterion involved) and at times he was downright reckless. Actually, the only question for the *reader* confronted by language is, at what point am I lost? Under such circumstances it is obvious that Cummings has not written for the language-shackled reader, and only insofar as the reader is willing to explore experience not expressed in bread-and-butter forms can he be happy with Cummings' poems.*

Let us now examine three of Cummings' poems. The first poem is a sonnet which is somewhat unconventional; the second poem is more unconventional; and the third poem represents Cummings at his liberated best.

---

the Cambridge ladies who live in furnished souls
are unbeautiful and have comfortable minds
(also, with the church's protestant blessings
daughters, unscented shapeless spirited)
they believe in Christ and Longfellow, both dead,
are invariably interested in so many things—
at the present writing one still finds
delighted fingers knitting for the is it Poles?
perhaps. While permanent faces coyly bandy
scandal of Mrs. N and Professor D
. . . . the Cambridge ladies do not care, above
Cambridge if sometimes in its box of
sky lavender and cornerless, the
moon rattles like a fragment of angry candy

Comments and Questions

It is easy to become impatient with Cummings, and although some of his poems may deserve our impatience, his best ones teach us in the most extraordinary way the importance of the fusion of sound and sense, and the contribution technique (the devices of poetry working together) makes to meaning.

"The Cambridge Ladies" is one of his more conventional poems, but still an appropriate one to sharpen our wits on. Cummings calls the poem a sonnet, but when we compare it with Shakespeare's "Sonnet 18" (p. 314), the differences are apparent. True, Cummings' sonnet has fourteen lines, but the rhyme scheme in the octet is quite irregular for the form; the sestet is a little unusual; and the rhythm is only roughly iambic pentameter. Compared to Shakespeare's sonnet, Cummings' threatens to become shapeless with each succeeding beat, as if it would run off its track on the next curve. Is his sonnet therefore inferior? Not if we recall one of our basic principles: no device is good or bad in a poem except as its use makes it so. The tone (Cummings attitude toward his subject) of his sonnet is radically different from Shakespeare's, and Cummings' devices, working together, produce the tone he wants us to hear.

Are the Cambridge ladies local specimens only or do they finally symbolize certain traits in a type of woman? What do they believe in; what are their spiritual resources (always the concern of the artist)? Surely the tone is satiric, and it helps us to interpret the meaning of every image, figure, and symbol. Instead of having free souls to embrace spiritual values wherever found, their souls are dull ("unbeautiful") rooms already furnished (by family and religious inheritance) in which their minds can live "comfortably" without

* For a perceptive explanation of Cummings' technique see Ralph J. Mills, Jr., "The Poetry of Innocence: Notes on E. E. Cummings," *English Journal*, Nov. 1959, pp. 433–442.

fear of the new, original, or challenging. They believe in the *dead* Christ and Longfellow. Christ alive (T. S. Eliot's "tiger" in his poem "Gerontion") would indeed threaten the complacency of these Cambridge ladies; and Cummings' placing Longfellow—a symbol of Harvard's earlier Genteel Tradition—against a tremendous spiritual force like Christ throws into sharp relief the decadence of the ladies. They knit for—"is it Poles?" It does not matter for whom because knitting is socially fashionable at the moment (the war effort?). They fill their empty minds with scandal, an excitement used as a substitute for adventures they fear to touch themselves. What can we make of the last four lines? Cummings' satiric thrust against the ladies' superficiality helps us to find their lives lived in a neat little box scented with lavender, shielded from life's bruises by round corners. And if the moon—a conventional symbol of love, mystery, and adventures—has been reduced *within* their box to the ladies' size to be regarded by these children as candy, we should express no surprise to hear the moon's protest rattle in anger against its confinement.

Is the sonnet really shapeless compared to Shakespeare's? Not if each has a shape appropriate to fusing the poem's sound and sense. The even-flowing lines of Shakespeare are not appropriate for Cummings' satiric jabs, and our being jolted by the sound prepares us to *experience* the sense of the sonnet—we *feel* the sense as well as comprehend it intellectually.

E. E. CUMMINGS
1894–1962

Pity This Busy Monster, Manunkind

pity this busy monster,manunkind,

not. Progress is a comfortable disease:
your victim(death and life safely beyond)

plays with the bigness of his littleness
—electrons deify one razorblade
into a mountainrange;lenses extend

unwish through curving wherewhen till unwish
returns on its unself.
                                    A world of made
is not a world of born—pity poor flesh

and trees,poor stars and stones,but never this
fine specimen of hypermagical

ultraomnipotence. We doctors know

a hopeless case if—listen:there's a hell
of a good universe next door;let's go

Comments

This unconventional sonnet is a satire on humanity. The creature manunkind (mankind, humankind, and man unkind), surrounded by his world and universe, never gets beyond the image of himself as he rummages around in his little circle of materialism ("plays with the bigness of his littleness"). The heart of his tragedy,

> lenses extend
> unwish through curving wherewhen till unwish
> returns on its unself,

comes clear if we understand that "curving wherewhen" ("where" as space and "when" as time) refers to Einstein's concept of "space-time" as a single dimension. When in his "A Masque of Reason" (p. 376), ll. 159–161) Frost's character God says to Job,

> You got your age reversed
> When time was found to be a space dimension
> That could, like any space, be turned around in?

Frost is using the same Einstein concept. Man, then, says Cummings, looking out at the universe through his telescopes, only "returns on its unself" instead of extending the self beyond its "hypermagical ultraomnipotence."

E. E. CUMMINGS
1894–1962
Among Crumbling People

a
mong crum
bling people(a
long ruined streets
hither and)softly

thither between (tumb
ling)
houses(as
the kno

wing spirit prowls,its
nose winces
before a dissonance of

Rish and Foses)
until
(finding one's self
at some distance from the
crooked town)a

harbour fools the sea(
while
emanating the triple
starred

Hotel du Golf . . . that notable structure
or ideal edifice . . . situated or established
. . . far from the noise of waters
:)one's

eye perceives
(as the ego approaches)
painfully sterilized contours;
within

which
"ladies&gentlemen"
—under

glass—
are:
asking.

?each
oth?
er
rub,
!berq;
:uestions

Comments

We see at a glance that this is one of Cummings' less conventional poems. Either the strange form helps to interpret its meaning or we have been hoodwinked. The key to both its meaning and form lies in the first line: the people are crumbling, for reasons given in the poem, as the form itself crumbles away in the last ten lines. The plain, literal sense seems to be this: The knowing spirit prowls along ruined streets among crumbling people and their houses, wincing before the incompatible odors of fish and roses ("Rish and Foses") until the spirit finds in the Hotel du Golf an "ideal edifice" with "sterilized contours," inhabitants who live "under glass," asking each other ("rubber") questions without point or meaning.

But to find the poem's full meaning we must understand how the various devices help to interpret its figurative meaning. For example, note the combined effect of the irregular lines and the parentheses. Lines 1–3 are themselves dropping off, and the knowing spirit prowls around and among the parentheses. We read *outside* the parentheses that the spirit moves "among crumbling people . . . softly thither between . . . houses"; but we read *within* the parentheses that the spirit moves "along ruined streets hither and . . . tumbling. . . ." The purpose of such devices is apparently to cause us to *experience* this ruined topsy-turvy world that the knowing (critical, evaluating) spirit investigates and finds wanting. We find another device in Cummings' use of the slurred " 'ladies&gentlemen' " to show the lack of discrimination and taste in another kind of crumbling people, those who live "under glass" in "sterilized contours." These people are exhibited as dead specimens in showcases whose inner life has disintegrated.

The effect of the poem, then, is to cause us to experience through this unusual fusion of sound, sense, *and* the typographical form of the poem on the page two kinds of people: those who live among external ruins (streets, houses, incompatible odors), and those who live with their own internal ruins—their soulless lives.

THE COMMENT ON EXPERIENCE: FROM SENSUOUS EXPERIENCE TO DOMINANT ATTITUDE

Some wit has said that poetry is the art of saying something by saying something else just as good. He was thinking, of course, of the poet's use of figures of speech and symbolism. But the wit really missed the point by failing to see that poetry is the art of saying something that can hardly be said in any other way. Poetic language is not a substitute for some other language with which the poet could make things clearer were he less obstinate and aesthetic. Poetic language exists simply because no other language has been found to communicate our attitudes and feelings toward certain kinds of experience.

In this section we shall begin with poems that contain little or no comment—poems of sensuous experience—and pass along to poems with increasingly more comment. Our purpose is not merely to classify poems according to the degree of comment they possess. *We use this device to make us sensitive to whatever is happening within the poem, to make us aware of the kind of experience the poet has provided.* And, certainly not least, to demonstrate that one kind of poem is not superior to another because it happens to present a sensuous experience or an intellectual experience which appeals immediately to our temperament or prejudices. We should recognize such prejudices when we hear it said, "nature poetry is the best poetry," or "philosophical poetry is best because philosophy is the highest wisdom." A student of poetry may finally adopt such an attitude or other, but let us not begin with it. Let us begin with an attitude that focuses our attention on the *experience* and *quality of art* in each poem. Our prejudices will develop fast enough without encouragement; we require no course or book to point the way.

Some poets have presented their objects with little or no comment, as Emerson has done in "The Snow-Storm," while others have used some object as a basis for their comment, making the comment instead of the object the life of the poem, as Jonson has done in "Song, to Celia" (p. 230). Other poets have gone beyond to the object-comment combination by using a situation or animal as a symbol, as Blake has used an animal as a symbol of raw life force (interpreted by some readers as evil) in "The Tiger" (p. 278).

As we approach the middle of this section, the poems will include attitudes which are more prominently implied or stated than they are in the earlier poems. Some readers will say that the poems contain more ideas, and are therefore more valuable than poems of sensuous experience like Emerson's "The Snow-Storm."

It is easy to become dogmatic about the relation of poetry to ideas—to thought, philosophy, and the meaning of life. The greatest poetry, says one group, is philosophical poetry, and they produce as their proof such poems as Milton's *Paradise Lost,* Tennyson's "In Memoriam," and Jeffers' "Meditation on Saviors." The finest poetry, counters another group, is "pure poetry" by which they mean poetry of sensuous experience never "soiled" with "thought." Fortunately for those of us who would roam freely through the entire history of poetry, choosing as we go, no school of critics has ever successfully legislated for or against one kind of poetry. Every decade or so such legislation is attempted, of course, as, for example, at present John Donne and his fellow metaphysicals are brought forward as the heroes, while Shelley and his brother romantics are permitted to languish. Not even Shakespeare escapes the legislators, and we read with some astonishment that *Hamlet* is an "artistic failure." We should not frown upon the legislators because another group always takes their place, and the new agitation is stimulating while it lasts even though their wine making is at times only the production of new bottles with loose corks.

Perhaps we can avoid the confusions created by the dogmatic legislators of successive generations by reminding ourselves of two or three basic matters we have already examined a little. Through the centuries good poets have explored and commented upon almost every phase of experience regardless of the winds of critical doctrine which have howled around them. The winds blow away and the poems remain. The moral here is obvious: each one of us tries to understand—absorb, digest, assimilate—the experiences provided by hundreds of poems, and we call those experiences good which make some substantial contribution to our expanding personal sensibilities and to our awareness of the world around us. Further, we remind ourselves that the quality of a poem is first determined by its artistic qualities—that it should be first judged as a poem, not as an idea or argument. And further, in this poetic realm of subjective experience each one of us must become his own critic who finally establishes his own hierarchy of poems. If we permit someone else to make the hierarchy, we shall not know who we are, and to know who we are is the final lesson of the humanities, including poetry.

RALPH WALDO EMERSON
1803–1882

The Snow-Storm

Announced by all the trumpets of the sky,
Arrives the snow, and, driving o'er the fields,
Seems nowhere to alight: the whited air
Hides hills and woods, the river, and the heaven,
And veils the farm-house at the garden's end.
The sled and traveller stopped, the courier's feet
Delayed, all friends shut out, the housemates sit
Around the radiant fireplace, enclosed
In a tumultuous privacy of storm.

Come see the north wind's masonry,
Out of an unseen quarry evermore
Furnished with tile, the fierce artificer
Curves his white bastions with projected roof
Round every windward stake, or tree, or door.
Speeding, the myriad-handed, his wild work
So fanciful, so savage, nought cares he
For number or proportion. Mockingly,
On coop or kennel he hangs Parian wreaths;
A swan-like form invests the hidden thorn;
Fills up the farmer's lane from wall to wall,
Maugre the farmer's sighs; and at the gate
A tapering turret overtops the work.
And when his hours are numbered, and the world
Is all his own, retiring, as he were not,
Leaves, when the sun appears, astonished Art
To mimic in slow structures, stone by stone,
Built in an age, the mad wind's night-work,
The frolic architecture of the snow.

BEN JONSON
1572-1637

Song, to Celia

Drink to me only with thine eyes,
And I will pledge with mine;
Or leave a kiss but in the cup
And I'll not look for wine.
The thirst that from the soul doth rise
Doth ask a drink divine;
But might I of Jove's nectar sup,
I would not change for thine.

I sent thee late a rosy wreath,
Not so much honoring thee
As giving it a hope that there
It could not withered be;
But thou thereon didst only breathe,
And sent'st it back to me;
Since when it grows, and smells, I swear,
Not of itself but thee!

Comments and Questions

1. This poem has been set to music, and you may have known it first as a song. What qualities of the poem provide its *inherent* music?

2. Like Browning's "My Last Duchess" (p. 226) the poem is a dramatic lyric. What makes it dramatic?

3. Does the poem present sensuous experience exclusively, or has Jonson included some comment on experience? Confirm your opinion with evidence from the poem.

ROBERT HERRICK
1591–1674

To Daffodils

Fair daffodils, we weep to see
You haste away so soon;
As yet the early-rising sun

Has not attained his noon.
Stay, stay,
Until the hasting day
Has run
But to the even-song;
And having prayed together, we
Will go with you along.

We have short time to stay, as you;
We have as short a spring,
As quick a growth to meet decay,
As you, or anything.
We die
As your hours do, and dry
Away
Like to the summer's rain,
Or as the pearls of morning's dew,
Ne'er to be found again.

WALTER SAVAGE LANDOR
1775–1864
Rose Aylmer

Ah, what avails the sceptred race,
Ah, what the form divine!
What every virtue, every grace!
Rose Aylmer, all were thine.

Rose Aylmer, who these wakeful eyes
May weep, but never see,
A night of memories and of sighs
I consecrate to thee.

CONSTANTINE P. CAVAFY
(Konstantinos P. Kabaphēs)
1863–1933
Candles[1]

The days of our future stand before us
like a row of little lighted candles—
golden, warm, and lively little candles.

The days gone by remain behind us,
a mournful line of burnt-out candles;
the nearest ones are still smoking,
cold candles, melted and bent.

I do not want to look at them; their form saddens
me,
and it saddens me to recall their first light.
I look ahead at my lighted candles.

I do not want to turn back, lest I see and shudder—
how quickly the somber line lengthens,
how quickly the burnt-out candles multiply.

[1] Translated from the Greek by Rae Dalven.

EDMUND WALLER
1606–1687
Song

Go, lovely Rose,
Tell her that wastes her time and me,
That now she knows,
When I resemble her to thee,
How sweet and fair she seems to be.

Tell her that's young,
And shuns to have her graces spied,
That hadst thou sprung
In deserts where no men abide,
Thou must have uncommended died.

Small is the worth
Of beauty from the light retir'd:
Bid her come forth,
Suffer herself to be desir'd,
And not blush so to be admir'd.

Then die, that she
The common fate of all things rare
May read in thee,
How small a part of time they share,
That are so wondrous sweet and fair.

Comments

In some of the poems in this section we have found not only descriptions of natural objects and people but comments on them as well. Waller's poem goes even further by including an argument. The lover has observed the delicacy of the rose and the speed with which it fades. Looking for an argument to persuade the woman he loves, he uses the rose as an example of a natural object which exhibits its brief delicacy for the admiration of men. This is the lover's generalization, and with it he bids his lady to

> Suffer herself to be desir'd,
> And not blush so to be admir'd.

Perhaps we can locate the art in the poem by recognizing what makes the poem persuasive. The method is not the debater's—the appeal is hardly to the rational intellect. Waller relies chiefly on the emotional appeal generated by the sound—the music—which *moves* us to consider or accept the sense, or the abstract argument. The art of the poem requires us to participate in the lover's feelings, and in a sense we become the lover, moved by his urgency.

WILLIAM BLAKE
1757–1827

The Tiger

Tiger! Tiger! burning bright
In the forests of the night,
What immortal hand or eye
Could frame thy fearful symmetry?

In what distant deeps or skies
Burnt the fire of thine eyes?
On what wings dare he aspire?
What the hand dare seize the fire?

And what shoulder, and what art,
Could twist the sinews of thy heart?
And when thy heart began to beat,
What dread hand? and what dread feet?

What the hammer? what the chain?
In what furnace was thy brain?
What the anvil? What dread grasp
Dare its deadly terrors clasp?

When the stars threw down their spears,
And watered heaven with their tears,
Did he smile his work to see?
Did he who made the Lamb make thee?

Tiger! Tiger! burning bright
In the forests of the night,
What immortal hand or eye,
Dare frame thy fearful symmetry?

WILLIAM BLAKE
1757–1827

The Lamb

Little Lamb, who made thee?
Dost thou know who made thee?
Gave thee life, and bid thee feed,
By the stream and o'er the mead;
Gave thee clothing of delight,
Softest clothing, woolly, bright;
Gave thee such a tender voice,
Making all the vales rejoice?
Little Lamb, who made thee?
Dost thou know who made thee?

Little Lamb, I'll tell thee,
Little Lamb, I'll tell thee:
He is callèd by thy name,
For he calls himself a Lamb.
He is meek, and he is mild;
He became a little child.
I a child, and thou a lamb,
We are callèd by his name.
Little Lamb, God bless thee!
Little Lamb, God bless thee!

Comments and Questions

1. As line 20 of "The Tiger" indicates, Blake's two poems can be considered profitably as companion pieces. Both poems, of course, have a symbolic level of meaning. Describe the meaning of each symbol.

2. Considered together, how do the poems complement each other? In what way does Blake suggest that some thoughtful conclusion should emerge from his questioning?

WILLIAM CULLEN BRYANT
1794–1878

To a Waterfowl

Whither, midst falling dew,
While glow the heavens with the last steps of
day,

Far, through their rosy depths, dost thou pursue
Thy solitary way?

Vainly the fowler's eye
Might mark thy distant flight to do thee wrong,
As, darkly seen against the crimson sky,
Thy figure floats along.

Seek'st thou the plashy brink
Of weedy lake, or marge of river wide,
Or where the rocking billows rise and sink
On the chafed ocean-side?

There is a Power whose care
Teaches thy way along that pathless coast—
The desert and illimitable air—
Lone wandering, but not lost.

All day thy wings have fanned,
At that far height, the cold, thin atmosphere,
Yet stoop not, weary, to the welcome land,
Though the dark night is near.

And soon that toil shall end;
Soon shalt thou find a summer home, and rest,
And scream among thy fellows; reeds shall bend,
Soon, o'er thy sheltered nest.

Thou'rt gone, the abyss of heaven
Hath swallowed up thy form; yet, on my heart
Deeply has sunk the lesson thou hast given,
And shall not soon depart.

He who, from zone to zone,
Guides through the boundless sky thy certain flight,
In the long way that I must tread alone,
Will lead my steps aright.

Comments and Questions

1. Bryant has here used an old device of drawing a lesson from nature. If there is a Power that directs the waterfowl safely to home and rest, the same Power, concludes the speaker, "will lead my steps aright." Regardless of your agreement or disagreement with Bryant's theme, what do you think of his explicitly labeling his theme a "lesson"? Bryant wrote during a period when delivering explicit messages in poetic form was fashionable,* but if we can believe MacLeish's "Ars Poetica" (p. 270) and the practice of most modern poets, messages are to be perceived but not heard—implied but not stated—and certainly not labeled. What is your view of the matter?

2. Note the somewhat unusual metrical structure of the stanzas: the first and fourth lines contain three feet (trimeter), and the second and third lines contain five feet (pentameter). The rhyme scheme is *abab*. How does this structure of sound help to create the tone of the poem?

WILLIAM WORDSWORTH
1770–1850

Composed upon Westminster Bridge

We now examine six sonnets which provide us with various kinds of experiences. We remind ourselves that the sonnet generally, but not always, presents a situation in the octet, and disposes of it in one way or another in the sestet. The form is therefore quite appropriate for presenting some phase of sensuous experience in the octet, and for commenting on, or expressing ideas about, that experience in the sestet. (See p. 258 for sonnet forms.)

Earth has not anything to show more fair;
Dull would he be of soul who could pass by
A sight so touching in its majesty;
This city now doth, like a garment, wear
The beauty of the morning; silent, bare,
Ships, towers, domes, theatres, and temples lie
Open unto the fields, and to the sky;
All bright and glittering in the smokeless air.
Never did sun more beautifully steep
In his first splendor, valley, rock, or hill;
Ne'er saw I, never felt, a calm so deep!
The river glideth at his own sweet will:

* For another example see the final stanza of Longfellow's "The Village Blacksmith." Longfellow was a contemporary of Bryant.

Dear God! The very houses seem asleep;
And all that mighty heart is lying still!

Comments and Questions

This sonnet gives us an opportunity to consider some questions often asked by students and readers in general. The questions run like these: Must we always grasp a poem like an orange to squeeze every last drop of subtle meaning from it? Can't we just *enjoy* a poem? Must we drive all the fun out of poetry with this everlasting search for meaning?

These are fair questions; suppose we try to answer them with the help of Wordsworth's sonnet.

The sonnet provides us with many levels of appreciation, just as a rich experience in life does. Many readers have called the sonnet beautiful, undoubtedly because it provides a very satisfying sensuous experience: the liquid sound of rhythm and rhyme, the clear images of nature, the simple but dignified diction, and the structure on the literal level which is quite easily understood, all combine to give us a valuable experience. Once we have placed ourselves on the bridge and have absorbed this lovely picture of London lying still at full dawn, we can understand the natural resentment expressed by some readers against an analysis to find the sonnet's meaning. On this sensuous level the sonnet is quite clear and certainly of great value. But should these readers try to legislate against any further meaning the sonnet possesses any more than the philosophical readers should try to legislate against the sensuous readers? When students ask, can't we just enjoy the poem? the answer is a resounding yes—but we should ask further, how *many* ways can the poem be enjoyed? That, too, is a fair question. Perhaps we can help to find the answer by asking a few other questions.

1. We have already admitted that the poem provides a lovely experience; some readers have called it "charming," "enchanting." How would you describe your experience?

2. Wordsworth's images are undoubtedly partly responsible for our favorable sensuous reaction—lines 6–8, for example, are striking. A picture so packed with images would probably have little unity unless it had a central image. Does the sonnet have one?

3. Suppose we assume that the central image is in lines 4–5:

> This city now doth, like a garment, wear
> The beauty of the morning. . . .

Why has Wordsworth personified the city? Have you noted particularly line 14?

4. What is the nature of the garment? "The beauty of the morning," Wordsworth says, by which he means nature. Perhaps the garment is a symbol which stands for a special kind of Nature. Perhaps the "smokeless air," contrasted with the smoke and grime of normal city atmosphere, is a symbol of purity of spirit which pervades the entire scene. Does the tone of the poem seem to be religious?

5. Is there any reason why the sonnet cannot be enjoyed on more than one level of appreciation and understanding? Is there any reason why these levels should not be coordinated to arrive at the *full* meaning of the poem?

WILLIAM SHAKESPEARE
1564–1616

Sonnet 29: When in Disgrace with Fortune and Men's Eyes

When in disgrace with fortune and men's eyes,
I all alone beweep my outcast state
And trouble deaf heaven with my bootless[1] cries
And look upon myself and curse my fate,
Wishing me like to one more rich in hope,
Featured like him, like him with friends possessed,
Desiring this man's art[2] and that man's scope,[3]
With what I most enjoy contented least;
Yet in these thoughts myself almost despising,
Haply I think on thee, and then my state,
Like to the lark at break of day arising
From sullen earth, sings hymns at heaven's gate;
For thy sweet love remembered such wealth brings

[1] Futile. [2] Skill. [3] Range of opportunity.

That then I scorn to change my state with kings.

WILLIAM SHAKESPEARE
1564–1616

Sonnet 30: When to the Sessions of Sweet Silent Thought

When to the sessions of sweet silent thought[1]
I summon up remembrance of things past,
I sigh the lack of many a thing I sought,
And with old woes new wail my dear time's waste.
Then can I drown an eye, unused to flow,
For precious friends hid in death's dateless[2] night,
And weep afresh love's long-since canceled woe,
And moan the expense of many a vanished sight—[3]
Then can I grieve at grievances foregone,[4]
And heavily from woe to woe tell o'er
The sad account of fore-bemoaned moan,
Which I new pay as if not paid before.
But if the while I think on thee, dear friend,
All losses are restored and sorrows end.

MICHAEL DRAYTON
1563–1631

Since There's No Help

Since there's no help, come let us kiss and part—
Nay, I have done, you get no more of me;
And I am glad, yea, glad with all my heart,
That thus so cleanly I myself can free.
Shake hands for ever, cancel all our vows,
And when we meet at any time again,
Be it not seen in either of our brows
That we one jot of former love retain.
Now at the last gasp of Love's latest breath,
When, his pulse failing, Passion speechless lies,
When Faith is kneeling by his bed of death,
And Innocence is closing up his[1] eyes,
—Now if thou wouldst, when all have given him over,
From death to life thou might'st him yet recover.

JOHN MILTON
1608–1674

On His Blindness

When I consider how my light is spent
Ere half my days in this dark world and wide,
And that one talent which is death to hide
Lodged with me useless, though my soul more bent
To serve therewith my Maker, and present
My true account, lest he returning chide;
"Doth God exact day-labor, light denied?"
I fondly[1] ask. But Patience, to prevent
That murmur, soon replies, "God doth not need
Either man's work or his own gifts. Who best
Bear his mild yoke, they serve him best. His state
Is kingly: thousands at his bidding speed,
And post o'er land and ocean without rest;
They also serve who only stand and wait."

Comments and Questions

1. The five sonnets we have now read indicate that the poets have used the form to present personal matters, and to draw conclusions from their experiences. Milton's blindness was a tremendous blow to his poetic aspirations, and when total blindness came in 1652, *Paradise Lost* was still to be written. Can you find evidences of Milton's struggle within himself in the *rhetorical* and *metrical* structure of the sonnet? Compare his sonnet with Wordsworth's "Composed upon Westminster Bridge" above; how does the sound of each differ from the other?

2. The word *talent* in line 3 can be related to *Matthew,* 25: 14–30. What is your conclusion about Milton's meaning?

---

[1] L. 1: see Shakespeare's *Othello,* III. iii. 138 ff.
[2] Endless. [3] Lament the cost of lost objects.
[4] Past distresses.

[1] Love's.

[1] Foolishly.

PERCY BYSSHE SHELLEY
1792–1822

Ozymandias[1]

I met a traveler from an antique land
Who said: Two vast and trunkless legs of stone
Stand in the desert. Near them, on the sand,
Half sunk, a shattered visage lies, whose frown,
And wrinkled lip, and sneer of cold command,
Tell that its sculptor well those passions read
Which yet survive, stamped on these lifeless things,
The hand that mocked them, and the heart that fed:
And on the pedestal these words appear:
"My name is Ozymandias, King of Kings:
Look on my works, ye Mighty, and despair!"
Nothing beside remains. Round the decay
Of that colossal wreck, boundless and bare
The lone and level sands stretch far away.

Comments and Questions

1. It has been said that this sonnet "is an ironic poem on the vanity and futility of a tyrant's power." What is your opinion of the comment?
2. Does the sonnet express a universal truth? Confirm your opinion with evidence from the poem.

JOHN DONNE
1572–1631

Go and Catch a Falling Star

Go and catch a falling star,
Get with child a mandrake root,
Tell me where all past years are,
Or who cleft the devil's foot,
Teach me to hear mermaids singing,
Or to keep off envy's stinging,
And find
What wind
Serves to advance an honest mind.

If thou be'st born to strange sights,
Things invisible to see,
Ride ten thousand days and nights
Till age snow white hairs on thee,
Thou, when thou return'st, wilt tell me
All strange wonders that befell thee,
And swear
No where
Lives a woman true and fair.

If thou find'st one, let me know;
Such a pilgrimage were sweet.
Yet do not; I would not go,
Though at next door we might meet.
Though she were true when you met her,
And last till you write your letter,
Yet she
Will be
False, ere I come, to two or three.

Comments

With Donne's poem we are confronted with a fascinating example of poetic sophistication.

If his poem is to be interpreted rightly, we must be sensitive to its *tone*. Certainly if the tone is missed or violated by the reader, the poem will be badly misconstrued—and has been, repeatedly, by unpracticed readers. Donne wrote in the Elizabethan Age (the English Renaissance), a period when poetry was used to comment on almost everything from the most serious aspects of religion to inconsequential personal feuds. Elizabethan poets, being men first and poets afterwards (Heaven applaud!), debated endlessly the place and value of woman. Indeed, a courtier of the time, professional poet or not, was expected to have among his many accomplishments the ability to turn a few pretty verses in favor of his lady. In time, of course, many such poems became conventionalized as the ladies became idealized, and part of the convention consisted of placing the lady beyond reach while the lover languished in pain. Here is Sir Philip Sidney (1554–1586) languishing:

Loving in truth, and fain in verse my love to show,
That she, dear she, might take some pleasure of my pain,
Pleasure might cause her read, reading might make her know,

[1] Ramses II (1295–1225 B.C.), Pharaoh of Egypt, whose statue at Thebes bore the inscription: "I am Ozymandias, king of kings: if anyone wishes to know what I am and where I lie, let him surpass me in some of my exploits."

Knowledge might pity win, and pity grace obtain,—
I sought fit words to paint the blackest face of woe. . . .

Donne revolted against this tradition, and "Go and Catch a Falling Star" is part of the revolt (see also his "Woman's Constancy," p. 315). But to have shown his displeasure in some boorish heavy-handed way would have been no part of Donne's temperament, and he therefore uses a jaunty, bantering tone simply to redress the lack of balance in the convention of his time. Donne's friendly contemporary critics would praise the poem for its "wit," not meaning humor as we use the word, but meaning the "swift play and flash of mind" and the poetic skill to make the poet's theme sharp and memorable. We may disagree with Donne's theme, but what reader can ignore or forget the poem? To call it "bitter" or "cynical" is to miss the poem completely. Its tone is quite otherwise except for the reader who is the victim of his stock responses (see p. 225).

The entire poem is actually a figure of speech, in this case *hyperbole* (see p. 268), or an extravagant statement used for a particular effect. The poem is a tall tale rendered in superb images and sophisticated tone. To comprehend such a tone and place it in proper perspective is simply part of an educated person's equipment: in the adult world he will meet the attitude repeatedly.

WILLIAM SHAKESPEARE
1564–1616

Sonnet 130: My Mistress' Eyes Are Nothing Like the Sun

My mistress' eyes are nothing like the sun;
Coral is far more red than her lips' red:
If snow be white, why then her breasts are dun;
If hairs be wires, black wires grow on her head.
I have seen roses damask'd,[1] red and white,
But no such roses see I in her cheeks;
And in some perfumes is there more delight
Than in the breath that from my mistress reeks.
I love to hear her speak, yet well I know
That music hath a far more pleasing sound:
I grant I never saw a goddess go,—
My mistress, when she walks, treads on the ground.
And yet, by heaven, I think my love as rare
As any she[2] belied with false compare.

[1] Variegated.

[2] Woman.

Comments and Questions

We see that Shakespeare, too, had some comments to make on the poetic convention of idealizing women. Why does he purposely hack out some of these rough lines (l. 4 especially) and violate our ears with ugly stabs? Why does he resort to words like *dun* and *reeks?*

HUMAN VALUES AND THE CRITICISM OF EXPERIENCE: PHILOSOPHICAL POEMS*

Almost all poetry is in one sense or another a criticism, or an evaluation, of experience. In some poems the criticism is only implied, at times quite subtly; in others it is boldly stated.

If we stop to consider the nature and interests of the artist, regardless of his medium, it should surprise no one that he is usually critical of his age. By critical we mean that in exploring human experience he tries to sift the genuine and enduring from the shoddy and vulgar to erect a hierarchy of values. Above all, the artist is interested in *human values.* The phrase is often used but seldom defined.

The nature of these human values should be found in the poems, but perhaps we can prepare ourselves a little to recognize them as we come upon them later. There are two kinds of basic values, means values and end values. If we say that a house is worth $35,000, we are speaking of a means value because the house is a means to an end—the good life. All material things—

* See Archibald MacLeish's *The Continuing Journey* (Boston: Houghton Mifflin, 1967) for a good discussion of the human values in our time, including certain questionable values represented in some contemporary literature.

land, food, clothing, automobiles—possess means values, or, as they are more frequently called, material values.

The consequences which accrue from using these material things we call living, or life, which we label good, mediocre, or bad, according to our basis of judgment, or our philosophy of life. We ask, what is the good life? Suppose we say it is the consequence of the whole man, body and spirit, living successfully with one's self, with society, and with the universe. The values which emerge from such a life we call end values, or human values. They are the values most prized by the artist, including the poet. Think back, for a moment, over the poems we have already read: what have the poets been interested in, means values or end values? Have they explored food, clothing, automobiles, material property, riches? Not often, of course; but when they have, what was their *attitude* toward them? Think of Frost's "Neither Out Far nor In Deep" (p. 265) and Shelley's "Ozymandias" (p. 282). The burden of these poems is the *ends* in life; they ask the implied question, what shall we live *for*? Thoreau answered when he said, "the cost of a thing is the amount of what I will call life which is required to be exchanged for it. . . ." *

The artist—whether poet, painter, sculptor, or composer—does at least two things: he explores the inner world of personality, the essential man; and he records the consequences on the individual man of his having lived in any given civilization. Poems are the products of poets confronted by their environment, and the poems become value judgments on that environment. The poems of previous times therefore become documents or depositories where the human values of former ages are found.

We have implied above that man is confronted with three inescapable things: *himself*, *society*, and *the universe*. The poems to follow explore these relationships.

THE INDIVIDUAL: PSYCHOLOGICAL VALUES

These values emerge when the poet explores the nature and worth of the individual, and especially when the individual must struggle with conflicts within himself. The poet is immensely interested in the personal and spiritual resources of the individual, and many poets seem to find the world's most basic tragedy in our lack of them.

* *Walden*, ch. 1.

EDWIN ARLINGTON ROBINSON 1869–1935

Miniver Cheevy

Miniver Cheevy, child of scorn,
  Grew lean while he assailed the seasons;
He wept that he was ever born,
  And he had reasons.

Miniver loved the days of old
  When swords were bright and steeds were prancing;
The vision of a warrior bold
  Would set him dancing.

Miniver sighed for what was not,
  And dreamed, and rested from his labors;
He dreamed of Thebes and Camelot,
  And Priam's neighbors.

Miniver mourned the ripe renown
  That made so many a name so fragrant;
He mourned Romance, now on the town,
  And Art, a vagrant.

Miniver loved the Medici,
  Albeit he had never seen one;
He would have sinned incessantly
  Could he have been one.

Miniver cursed the commonplace
  And eyed a khaki suit with loathing;
He missed the medieval grace
  Of iron clothing.

Miniver scorned the gold he sought,
  But sore annoyed was he without it;

Miniver thought, and thought, and thought,
And thought about it.

Miniver Cheevy, born too late,
Scratched his head and kept on thinking;
Miniver coughed, and called it fate,
And kept on drinking.

Comments

Robinson, a failure in practical affairs for years, was unusually sensitive to personal failure and frustration. Miniver is used as a symbol of all the Minivers in the world who because of their psychological structure cannot reconcile themselves to the realities of their environment. Miniver is a romantic in the sense that for him the heroic world lies in the past. What is the poet's attitude toward Miniver? What are his assumptions and their consequences in the poem?

Two attitudes are apparent: the poet is sympathetic with Miniver, yet he smiles at the humor and irony, albeit tragic, of his predicament. Many practical people would condemn Miniver as a lazy vagrant without ambition. Robinson sees further: he is too wise psychologically to be trapped by making a complicated situation simple. He knows that the predicament of the Minivers in the world is not simple. Miniver's problem is not social or philosophical, but rather psychological in the sense that Robinson apparently believes that Miniver's temperament prevents him from reconciling himself to a modern, industrial society. Miniver was simply "born too late," his temperament is his "fate," and no amount of "thinking" finds a solution for him. What, then, is Miniver to do? He "kept on drinking" —not literally only, of course, but figuratively; he kept on escaping to a romantic world in which he could live.

Robinson's basic assumption is that men—men like Miniver at least—do what they must do, what they are temperamentally equipped to do. This interpretation of human character, begun as a psychological investigation, soon attaches itself to philosophical speculation and becomes a part of a long philosophical tradition summarized by the phrase, "Character is fate."

ANDREW MARVELL
1621–1678
To His Coy Mistress

The two poems to follow explore man's deepest and most crucial emotion, the love experience. Marvell's "To His Coy Mistress" reflects the survival of the Elizabethan notion of thieving time (see also MacLeish's "You, Andrew Marvell," p. 263) as it touches love; Browning's "A Toccata of Galuppi's" (p. 286) reflects a Victorian conflict in the love experience. Both of the poems finally go beyond the love experience as such to comment on basic human values which belong to no age or century alone. It is this universal meaning that we finally look for by reading the *totality* of each poem as a figure of speech—as a symbol.

Had we but world enough, and time,
This coyness, Lady, were no crime.
We would sit down and think which way
To walk and pass our long love's day.
Thou by the Indian Ganges' side
Shouldst rubies find: I by the tide
Of Humber would complain. I would
Love you ten years before the Flood,
And you should, if you please, refuse
Till the conversion of the Jews.
My vegetable love should grow
Vaster than empires, and more slow;
An hundred years should go to praise
Thine eyes and on thy forehead gaze;
Two hundred to adore each breast,
But thirty thousand to the rest;
An age at least to every part,
And the last age should show your heart.
For, Lady, you deserve this state,
Nor would I love at lower rate.
But at my back I always hear
Time's wingèd chariot hurrying near;
And yonder all before us lie
Deserts of vast eternity.
Thy beauty shall no more be found,
Nor, in thy marble vault, shall sound

My echoing song; then worms shall try
That long preserved virginity,
And your quaint honor turn to dust,
And into ashes all my lust:
The grave's a fine and private place,
But none, I think, do there embrace.
  Now therefore, while the youthful hue
Sits on thy skin like morning dew
And while thy willing soul transpires
At every pore with instant fires,
Now let us sport us while we may,
And now, like amorous birds of prey,
Rather at once our time devour
Than languish in his slow-chapt power.
Let us roll all our strength and all
Our sweetness up into one ball,
And tear our pleasures with rough strife
Thorough[1] the iron gates of life:
Thus, though we cannot make our sun
Stand still, yet we will make him run.

[1] Through.

Comments

The plain sense of this poem is clear enough, coming to us in three parts: Had we but time enough, says the lover to his desired, your coyness (prolonging the chase) would be appropriate and exciting—anticipation is greater than realization (ll. 1–20). But, argues the lover, time is against this leisurely approach to consummation (ll. 21–32), and therefore let us devour rather than languish (ll. 33–end). The poem, then, is an argument much like Waller's "Song" ("Go, lovely Rose," p. 277), and as such is impeccably logical, but in the realm of love logic is quite useless. The persuasion must come from the art of the poem, which moves us to accept the abstract argument. The basic devices are hyperbole (exaggeration), the impatience of the lover created by the crisp couplets in short lines, and the images of rich emotional content. We may agree with the lover's argument not merely because he is logical, but because we *participate* in his emotional need and urgency, which are common to us all.

ROBERT BROWNING
1812–1889

A Toccata of Galuppi's

I

Oh, Galuppi, Baldassaro, this is very sad to find!
I can hardly misconceive you; it would prove me deaf and blind;
But although I take your meaning, 'tis with such a heavy mind!

II

Here you come with your old music, and here's all the good it brings.
What, they lived once thus at Venice where the merchants were the kings,
Where St. Mark's is, where the Doges used to wed the sea with rings?

III

Ay, because the sea's the street there; and 'tis arched by . . . what you call
. . . Shylock's bridge with houses on it, where they kept the carnival:
I was never out of England—it's as if I saw it all!

IV

Did young people take their pleasure when the sea was warm in May?
Balls and masks begun at midnight, burning ever to mid-day
When they made up fresh adventures for the morrow, do you say?

V

Was a lady such a lady, cheeks so round and lips so red,—
On her neck the small face buoyant, like a bell-flower on its bed,
O'er the breast's superb abundance where a man might base his head?

VI

Well, and it was graceful of them they'd break talk off and afford
—She, to bite her mask's black velvet, he, to finger on his sword,
While you sat and played Toccatas, stately at the clavichord?

VII

What? Those lesser thirds so plaintive, sixths diminished, sigh on sigh,
Told them something? Those suspensions, those solutions—"Must we die?"
Those commiserating sevenths—"Life might last! we can but try!"

VIII

"Were you happy?"—"Yes."—"And are you still as happy?"—'Yes. And you?"
—"Then, more kisses!"—"Did *I* stop them, when a million seemed so few?"
Hark! the dominant's persistence, till it must be answered to!

IX

So an octave struck the answer. Oh, they praised you, I dare say!
"Brave Galuppi! that was music! good alike at grave and gay!
I can always leave off talking, when I hear a master play."

X

Then they left you for their pleasure: till in due time, one by one,
Some with lives that came to nothing, some with deeds as well undone,
Death came tacitly and took them where they never see the sun.

XI

But when I sit down to reason, think to take my stand nor swerve,
While I triumph o'er a secret wrung from nature's close reserve,
In you come with your cold music, till I creep thro' every nerve.

XII

Yes, you, like a ghostly cricket, creaking where a house was burned—
"Dust and ashes, dead and done with, Venice spent what Venice earned!
The soul, doubtless, is immortal—where a soul can be discerned.

XIII

"Yours for instance, you know physics, something of geology,
Mathematics are your pastime; souls shall rise in their degree;
Butterflies may dread extinction,—you'll not die, it cannot be!

XIV

"As for Venice and its people merely born to bloom and drop,
Here on earth they bore their fruitage, mirth and folly were the crop;
What of soul was left, I wonder, when the kissing had to stop?

XV

"Dust and ashes!" So you creak it, and I want the heart to scold.
Dear dead women, with such hair, too—what's become of all the gold
Used to hang and brush their bosoms? I feel chilly and grown old.

Comments and Questions

Few poems demonstrate so well as this one the contribution which sound makes to sense. Browning's musical education began early, and he remained devoted to music throughout his life, as his poetry testifies. Baldassare Galuppi (1706–1785) was a famous Venetian composer of light operas, church music, sonatas, and toccatas. If "A Toccata of Galuppi's" is read aloud with sympathy and understanding, the characteristics of the toccata are quite apparent. It is a composition written for the organ or clavichord (forerunner of the modern piano), characterized by brilliant full chords and running passages, free fantasia style, and quite unrestrained by any fixed form. The word *toccata* is the past participle of Italian *toccare,* to touch, meaning that the instrument is touched, not played, which produces the effect of a series of rapid tones touched but not held. Life is quickly conjured up and quickly fades away.

To enable us to see that Browning is actually using the toccata in more than one way, we should fix the facts of the poem clearly in mind. The scientific Englishman whose reliance on reason has caused him to look askance at love and the emotions is moved by Galuppi's toccata to reconsider his devotion to reason and science. Although he has never been out of England, the music paints pictures of old Venice in his mind, Venice the traditional harbor of love and romance—"It's as if I saw it all!" The questions he asks in stanzas IV–VI clearly indicate that his reliance on reason is shaken. The music causes him to hear the young couple discussing the meaning of the music to them (VII–IX): they are made to feel that although death will finally overtake them, they can try to pursue their love and frivolity—that the attempt will be at least a temporary reward. Knowing that the lovers did go to their death, he puts them away with soft, regretful words (X), but the music still persists to challenge his failure to rely on love and affection regardless of how fleeting they seem to be (XI–XIV): his rationalizing will not sustain him, and he feels "chilly and grown old." Briefly, he has missed the essence of life and knows it (XV).

1. As usual, a statement of the facts of a poem omits much of the essential poetic experience. How deeply is the Englishman really moved by the music? Explain the meaning of the music's comment in stanza XIII. What do the butterflies and mathematics symbolize?

2. The poem is, of course, actually a dramatic dialogue. Have you any idea how we can get at Browning's attitude toward the antagonists? The answer to this question lies partly in the tone of the poem, and its tone is greatly determined by Browning's use of the toccata's characteristics in his metrical structure. To put the question another way, to what extent does the sound help to interpret the sense? Confirm your opinion with specific evidence from the poem.

WILLIAM SHAKESPEARE
1564–1616

Sonnet 55: Not Marble, nor the Gilded Monuments

Not marble, nor the gilded monuments
Of princes, shall outlive this powerful rhyme;
But you shall shine more bright in these contents[1]
Than unswept stone,[2] besmeared with sluttish time.
When wasteful war shall statues overturn,
And broils[3] root out the work of masonry,
Nor Mars his sword nor war's quick fire shall burn
The living record of your memory.
'Gainst death and all-oblivious enmity
Shall you pace forth; your praise shall still find room
Even in the eyes of all posterity
That wear this world out to the ending doom.[4]
So, till the judgment[5] that yourself arise,
You live in this, and dwell in lovers' eyes.

[1] Verses. [2] Stone monument unswept by time. [3] Tumult. [4] Last Judgment. [5] Till Judgment Day.

Comments

Love poetry, always dominant in the history of literature, is of course an exploration of psychological values. Nothing is more personal than the love experience; nothing operates with greater impact on personality; nothing is so subtle in its influence on human character. In this sonnet Shakespeare's attitude toward love is highly complimentary. Let us compare his attitude with MacLeish's below.

ARCHIBALD MacLEISH
1892–
(for Adele)

"Not Marble nor the Gilded Monuments"

The praisers of women in their proud and beautiful poems,
Naming the grave mouth and the hair and the eyes,
Boasted those they love should be forever remembered:
These were lies.

The words sound but the face in the Istrian[1] sun is forgotten.
The poet speaks but to her dead ears no more.
The sleek throat is gone—and the breast that was troubled to listen:
Shadow from door.

Therefore I will not praise your knees nor your fine walking
Telling you men shall remember your name as long
As lips move or breath is spent or the iron of English
Rings from a tongue.

I shall say you were young, and your arms straight, and your mouth scarlet:
I shall say you will die and none will remember you:
Your arms change, and none remember the swish of your garments,
Nor the click of your shoe.

Not with my hand's strength, not with difficult labor
Springing the obstinate words to the bones of your breast
And the stubborn line to your young stride and the breath to your breathing
And the beat to your haste
Shall I prevail on the hearts of unborn men to remember.

(What is a dead girl but a shadowy ghost
Or a dead man's voice but a distant and vain affirmation
Like dream words most)

Therefore I will not speak of the undying glory of women.
I will say you were young and straight and your skin fair
And you stood in the door and the sun was a shadow of leaves on your shoulders
And a leaf on your hair—

I will not speak of the famous beauty of dead women:
I will say the shape of a leaf lay once on your hair.
Till the world ends and the eyes are out and the mouths broken
Look! It is there!

[1] Istria, a peninsula in northeast "Sunny Italy."

ANONYMOUS

There Is No Love

There is no love. We for a moment stand
And hold at bay inevitable pain,
Aghast and passionate, hand in eager hand
Before we face our loneliness again.

THE INDIVIDUAL AND SOCIETY: SOCIAL VALUES

Social values are likely to emerge from poetry whenever a poet explores the relationships of the individual and society, especially when the needs of the individual differ from the demands of society. Although social values have appeared in the poetry of every age, they have become more prominent since the convergence of modern democracy, industrial civilization, and modern science. In the older agrarian societies, personal and social morals tended to coalesce, but in our industrial civilization private and public morals seem to grow further apart, and the repercussions of this conflict find their way into imaginative literature.

The poems in this subsection are concerned chiefly with the theme of a democratic morality which always honors, of course, the dignity of the individual and the preservation of his social rights and responsibilities.

WILLIAM WORDSWORTH
1770–1850
Lines Written in Early Spring

I heard a thousand blended notes,
While in a grove I sate reclined,
In that sweet mood when pleasant thoughts
Bring sad thoughts to the mind.

To her fair works did Nature link
The human soul that through me ran;
And much it grieved my heart to think
What man has made of man.

Through primrose tufts, in that green bower,
The periwinkle trailed its wreaths;
And 'tis my faith that every flower
Enjoys the air it breathes.

The birds around me hopped and played,
Their thoughts I cannot measure:—
But the least motion which they made,
It seemed a thrill of pleasure.

The budding twigs spread out their fan,
To catch the breezy air;
And I must think, do all I can,
That there was pleasure there.

If this belief from heaven be sent,
If such be Nature's holy plan,
Have I not reason to lament
What man has made of man?

Wordsworth seems to have raised the right question. The poets to follow furnish a variety of comments on what man has made of man.

AMY LOWELL
1874–1925
The Dinner-Party

FISH

"So . . ." they said,
With their wine-glasses delicately poised,
Mocking at the thing they cannot understand.
"So . . . " they said again,
Amused and insolent.
The silver on the table glittered,
And the red wine in the glasses
Seemed the blood I had wasted
In a foolish cause.

GAME

The gentleman with the grey-and-black whiskers
Sneered languidly over his quail.
Then my heart flew up and labored,
Then I burst from my own holding
And hurled myself forward.
With straight blows I beat upon him,
Furiously, with red-hot anger, I thrust against him.
But my weapon slithered over his polished surface,
And I recoiled upon myself,
Panting.

DRAWING-ROOM

In a dress all softness and half-tones,
Indolent and half-reclined,
She lay upon a couch,
With the firelight reflected in her jewels.
But her eyes had no reflection,
They swam in a grey smoke,
The smoke of smoldering ashes,
The smoke of her cindered heart.

COFFEE

They sat in a circle with their coffee-cups.
One dropped in a lump of sugar,
One stirred with a spoon.
I saw them as a circle of ghosts
Sipping blackness out of beautiful china,
And mildly protesting against my coarseness
In being alive.

TALK

They took dead men's souls
And pinned them on their breasts for ornament;
Their cuff-links and tiaras
Were gems dug from a grave;
They were ghouls battening on exhumed thoughts;
And I took a green liqueur from a servant
So that he might come near me
And give me the comfort of a living thing.

ELEVEN O'CLOCK

The front door was hard and heavy,
It shut behind me on the house of ghosts.
I flattened my feet on the pavement
To feel it solid under me;
I ran my hand along the railings
And shook them,
And pressed their pointed bars
Into my palms.
The hurt of it reassured me,
And I did it again and again
Until they were bruised.
When I woke in the night
I laughed to find them aching,
For only living flesh can suffer.

Comments and Questions

The poet assumes that a democratic morality, discussed briefly above (p. 289), is a valuable code to live by. She assumes that social well-being, or the happiness of humanity, depends upon the sympathetic contact of all members of the community. The guests at the dinner party act upon no such assumption, and their violation of the democratic morality creates certain consequences exhibited in the poem. The guests' feeling of class superiority denies them not only sympathy for humanity, but—and more important—it perverts their own humanity as well. Their tragedy lies in their being unable to see that their attitude toward mankind corrupts themselves.

1. In what ways does the technique in this poem resemble that used in Eliot's "The Love Song of J. Alfred Prufrock" (p. 390)? Consider the use of image, symbol, and especially dramatic opposition.

2. What is the full meaning of the last line in the poem?

NANCY PRICE
1925–

Centennial of Shiloh[1]

Now Shiloh seems as old as Marathon;
each battle wears the other's somber face.
With names like watchfires: Waterloo, Verdun,
Troy, Hastings, Dunkirk, Crecy, Lexington,
the ancient slaughters keep an austere grace.

Naked as youths by Michelangelo
engraved on battlefields, or winged like birds,
or submarine as fish, men still would know
death when they saw him. Through the night at Shiloh
the dying sang; everyone knew the words.

For the kilomegaton voice, the bombsight eye
where are the words, the tune we can recall?
One hundred years from Shiloh cities die
under the faceless, detonated sky
where death spreads like a cloud, a drifting pall
that has no name, no human shape at all.

Comments and Questions

A perceptive critic writes about this poem:

> The point of the poem is that, until the present, battle's "somber face" has always had at least an "austere grace." Even in its brutality, war remained comprehensible and in

[1] Shiloh: The site in Tennessee of a famous battle of the United States Civil War, April 6–7, 1862.

a way personal. But now the voice of battle speaks with a kilomegaton of force, the eye is that of the bombsight, and the death-dealing radioactive cloud is ". . . a drifting pall/ that has no name, no human shape at all." Hardly anything could better suggest the dreadful apocalypse of a world whose values have depreciated to a point where an atomic war is possible. (Edwin J. Maurer, *Midwest, A Literary Review,* Spring 1964.)

1. On one level, then, we learn from the poem how the tragedy of war has been driven more deeply into the life of mankind. Is there another level of meaning in the poem?

2. The phrases, "the faceless, detonated sky" and "no human shape at all" are powerfully suggestive. Is war itself used as a symbol to suggest what is happening to modern man in peace as well as in war? Is *the* upsetting symbol "faceless"? We see again the penetration of the symbol in poetry.

KARL SHAPIRO
1913–

Movie Actress

I sit a queen, and am no widow, and shall see no sorrow

She is young and lies curved on the velvety floor of her fame
Like a prize-winning cat on a mirror of fire and oak,
And her dreams are as black as the Jew who uncovered her name;

She is folded in magic and hushed in the pride of her cloak
Which is woven of worship like silk for the hollows of eyes
That are raised in the dark to her image that shimmered and spoke;

And she speaks in her darkness alone and her emptiness cries
Till her voice is as shuddering tin in the wings of a stage,
And her beauty seems wrong as the wig of a perfect disguise;

She is sick with the shadow of shadow, diseased with the rage
Of the whiteness of light and the heat of interior sun,
And she faints like a pauper to carry the weight of her wage;

She is coarse with the honors of power, the duties of fun
And amazed at the regions of pleasure where skill is begun.

ROBINSON JEFFERS
1887–1962

Shine, Republic[1]

The quality of these trees, green height; of the sky, shining; of water, a clear flow; of
the rock, hardness

[1] This poem and the two poems to follow can be read as a trilogy, although Jeffers never announced them as such.

And reticence: each is noble in its quality. The love of freedom has been the quality of Western man.

There is a stubborn torch that flames from Marathon to Concord, its dangerous beauty binding three ages
Into one time; the waves of barbarism and civilization have eclipsed but have never quenched it.

For the Greeks the love of beauty, for Rome of ruling; for the present age the passionate love of discovery;
But in one noble passion we are one; and Washington, Luther, Tacitus, Aeschylus, one kind of man.

And you, America, that passion made you. You were not born to prosperity, you were born to love freedom.
You did not say "en masse," you said "independence." But we cannot have all the luxuries and freedom also.

Freedom is poor and laborious; that torch is not safe but hungry, and often requires blood for its fuel.
You will tame it against it burn too clearly, you will hood it like a kept hawk, you will perch it on the wrist of Caesar.

But keep the tradition, conserve the forms, the observances, keep the spot sore. Be great, carve deep your heel-marks.
The states of the next age will no doubt remember you, and edge their love of freedom with contempt of luxury.

Comments and Questions

1. It has been said that "the proper study of Americans is liberty." Roughly, Jeffers' poem says the same thing, but what *precisely* does the poem say?

2. Stanza 4 contains attitudes which Jeffers expresses in many poems. Is he right?

ROBINSON JEFFERS
1887–1962

Shine, Perishing Republic

While this America settles in the mould of its vulgarity, heavily thickening to empire,
And protest, only a bubble in the molten mass, pops and sighs out, and the mass hardens,

I sadly smiling remember that the flower fades to make fruit, the fruit rots to make earth.
Out of the mother; and through the spring exultances, ripeness and decadence; and home to the mother.

You making haste haste on decay; not blameworthy; life is good, be it stubbornly long or suddenly

A mortal splendor: meteors are not needed less than mountains: shine, perishing republic.

But for my children, I would have them keep their distance from the thickening center; corruption
Never has been compulsory, when the cities lie at the monster's feet there are left the mountains.

And boys, be in nothing so moderate as in love of man, a clever servant, insufferable master.
There is the trap that catches noblest spirits, that caught—they say—God, when he walked on earth.

Comments and Questions

The British writer W. Somerset Maugham (1874–1965) is reported to have said, "If a nation values anything more than freedom, it will lose its freedom; and if it is comfort or money that it values more, it will lose that, too." This statement can be used as a steppingstone from Jeffers' "Shine, Republic" to his poem above. In the latter poem Jeffers finds America on the way to empire because it has given up the "passion" for freedom that has made it. Students of Jeffers recognize his basic pattern of belief in this area as something like this: Civilizations have always risen and inevitably fallen, this cycle always moving from east to west. (See Oswald Spengler's *The Decline of the West*, 1918–1922, a book which is said to have influenced Jeffers.) Why do civilizations fall? Freedom and wealth are irreconcilable, according to Jeffers, because man is driven by desire (self-love) to achieve power over his fellow man, and he will sell his freedom to achieve it. Men and their nations therefore travel the cycle of freedom, desire, wealth, loss of freedom, and ruin. Men then travel westward—as the Pilgrims and others did in the early seventeenth century; they fight to regain their freedom, win it, and travel the cycle to ruin once more. The implication of the two poems above is clear: America is next.

1. Is agreement with Jeffers' point of view necessary to the enjoyment of his art?

2. What are the essential characteristics of his art as they differ from those of almost all other poems in this section? Jeffers has said that "a tidal recurrence is the one essential quality of the speech of poetry." How appropriate is Jeffers' free verse in the two poems above? If it illustrates his quoted statement, show how.

3. Note how Jeffers thinks in images, and how logically those images progress from line to line. Trace this progress of image-thinking through "Shine, Perishing Republic."

ROBINSON JEFFERS
1887–1962

Shine, Empire

Powerful and armed, neutral in the midst of madness, we might have held the whole world's balance and stood
Like a mountain in a wind. We were misled and took sides. We have chosen to share the crime and the punishment.

Perhaps justly, being part of Europe. Three thousand miles of ocean would hardly wash out the stains

Of all that mish-mash, blood, language, religion, snobbery. Three thousand miles in a ship would not make Americans.

I have often in weak moments thought of this people as something higher than the natural run of the earth.
I was quite wrong; we are lower. We are the people who hope to win wars with money as we win elections.

Hate no one. Roosevelt's intentions were good, and Hitler is a patriot. They have split the planet into two millstones
That will grind small and bloody; but still let us keep some dignity, these days are tragic, and fight without hating.

It is war, and no man can see an end of it. We must put freedom away and stiffen into bitter empire.
All Europe was hardly worth the precarious freedom of one of our states: what will her ashes fetch?

If I were hunting in the Ventana canyons again with my strong sons, and to sleep under stars,
I should be happy again. It is not time for happiness. Happy the blind, the witless, the dead.

Now, thoroughly compromised, we aim at world rule, like Assyria, Rome, Britain, Germany, to inherit those hordes
Of guilt and doom. I am American, what can I say but again, "Shine, perishing republic?" . . . Shine, empire.

CARL SANDBURG
1878–1967
From The People, Yes

The following passages have been taken from Carl Sandburg's long poem *The People, Yes.* Walt Whitman, who asked repeatedly for a poet to represent the common people, said that "Literature, strictly considered, has never recognized the People. . . . I know of nothing more rare, even in this country, than a fit scientific estimate and reverent appreciation of the People. . . ." Whitman would have welcomed Sandburg.

The People, Yes can be read, for the most part, as a soliloquy spoken by the people. Sandburg has presented in free-verse lines the attitudes, hopes, and in some instances the actual talk of common folk. We shall recognize many of our common proverbs although we may not have realized before the extent of their poetic quality.

Section 1

From the four corners of the earth,
from corners lashed in wind
and bitten with rain and fire,
from places where the winds begin
and fogs are born with mist children,

tall men from tall rocky slopes came
and sleepy men from sleepy valleys,
their women tall, their women sleepy,
with bundles and belongings,
with little ones babbling, "Where to now?
what next?"

The people of the earth, the family of man,
wanted to put up something proud to look at,
a tower from the flat land of earth
on up through the ceiling into the top of the sky.

And the big job got going,
the caissons and pilings sunk,
floors, walls and winding staircases
aimed at the stars high over,
aimed to go beyond the ladders of the moon.

And God Almighty could have struck them dead
or smitten them deaf and dumb.

And God was a whimsical fixer.
God was an understanding Boss
with another plan in mind,
And suddenly shuffled all the languages,
changed the tongues of men
so they all talked different
And the masons couldn't get what the hodcarriers said,
The helpers handed the carpenters the wrong tools,
Five hundred ways to say, "Who are you?"
Changed ways of asking, "Where do we go from here?"
Or of saying, "Being born is only the beginning,"
Or, "Would you just as soon sing as make that noise?"
Or, "What you don't know won't hurt you."
And the material-and-supply men started disputes
With the hauling gangs and the building trades
And the architects tore their hair over the blueprints
And the brickmakers and the mule skinners talked back
To the straw bosses who talked back to the superintendents
And the signals got mixed; the men who shovelled the bucket
Hooted the hoisting men—and the job was wrecked.

Some called it the Tower of Babel job[1]
And the people gave it many other names.
The wreck of it stood as a skull and a ghost,
a memorandum hardly begun,
swaying and sagging in tall hostile winds,
held up by slow friendly winds.

[1] See p. 364, footnote 2, for comment on the Tower of Babel.

From *Section 29*

The people, yes—
Born with bones and heart fused in deep and violent secrets
Mixed from a bowl of sky blue dreams and sea slime facts—
A seething of saints and sinners, toilers, loafers, oxen, apes
In a womb of superstition, faith, genius, crime, sacrifice—
The one and only source of armies, navies, work-gangs,
The living flowing breath of the history of nations,
Of the little Family of Man hugging the little ball of Earth,
And a long hall of mirrors, straight, convex and concave,
Moving and endless with scrolls of the living,
Shimmering with phantoms flung from the past,
Shot over with lights of babies to come, not yet here.

From *Section 30*

We'll see what we'll see.
Time is a great teacher.
Today me and tomorrow maybe you.
This old anvil laughs at many broken hammers.
What is bitter to stand against today may be sweet to remember tomorrow.
Fine words butter no parsnips. Moonlight dries no mittens.
Whether the stone bumps the jug or the jug bumps the stone it is bad for the jug.
One hand washes the other and both wash the face.
Better leave the child's nose dirty than wring it off.
We all belong to the same big family and have the same smell.
Handling honey, tar or dung some of it sticks to the fingers.
The liar comes to believe his own lies.
He who burns himself must sit on the blisters.
God alone understands fools.
The dumb mother understands the dumb child.
To work hard, to live hard, to die hard, and then to go to hell after all would be too damned hard.
You can fool all the people part of the time and part of the people all the time but you can't fool all the people all of the time.
It takes all kinds of people to make a world.

What is bred in the bone will tell.
Between the inbreds and the cross-breeds the argument goes on.
You can breed them up as easy as you can breed them down.
"I don't know who my ancestors were," said a mongrel, "but we've been descending for a long time."
"My ancestors," said the Cherokee-blooded Oklahoman, "didn't come over in the *Mayflower* but we was there to meet the boat."

From *Section 31*

"Your low birth puts you beneath me,"
said Harmodius, Iphicrates replying,
"The difference between us is this.
My family begins with me.
Yours ends with you."

From *Section 41*

"Why did the children
put beans in their ears
when the one thing we told the children
they must not do
was put beans in their ears?"

"Why did the children
pour molasses on the cat
when the one thing we told the children
they must not do
was pour molasses on the cat?"

From *Section 50*

"Isn't that an iceberg on the horizon, Captain?"
"Yes, Madam."
"What if we get in a collision with it?"
"The iceberg, Madam, will move right along as though nothing had happened."

From *Section 86*

The people, yes, the people,
Until the people are taken care of one way or another,
Until the people are solved somehow for the day and hour,
Until then one hears "Yes but the people what about the people?"
Sometimes as though the people is a child to be pleased or fed
Or again a hoodlum you have to be tough with
And seldom as though the people is a caldron and a reservoir
Of the human reserves that shape history. . . .

"The czar has eight million men with guns and bayonets.
"Nothing can happen to the czar.
"The czar is the voice of God and shall live forever.
"Turn and look at the forest of steel and cannon
"Where the czar is guarded by eight million soldiers.
"Nothing can happen to the czar."
They said that for years and in the summer of 1914
In the year of Our Lord Nineteen Hundred and Fourteen
As a portent and an assurance they said with owl faces:
"Nothing can happen to the czar."
Yet the czar and his bodyguard of eight million vanished
And the czar stood in a cellar before a little firing squad
And the command of fire was given
And the czar stepped into regions of mist and ice
The czar travelled into an ethereal uncharted siberia
While two kaisers also vanished from thrones
Ancient and established in blood and iron—
Two kaisers backed by ten million bayonets
Had their crowns in a gutter, their palaces mobbed.
In fire, chaos, shadows,
In hurricanes beyond foretelling of probabilities,

In the shove and whirl of unforeseen combustions
  The people, yes, the people,
Move eternally in the elements of surprise,
Changing from hammer to bayonet and back to hammer,
The hallelujah chorus forever shifting its star soloists.

From *Section 107*

  The people will live on.
The learning and blundering people will live on.
  They will be tricked and sold and again sold
And go back to the nourishing earth for rootholds,
  The people so peculiar in renewal and comeback,
  You can't laugh off their capacity to take it.
The mammoth rests between his cyclonic dramas. . . .

This old anvil laughs at many broken hammers.
  There are men who can't be bought.
  The fireborn are at home in fire.
  The stars make no noise.
  You can't hinder the wind from blowing.
  Time is a great teacher.
  Who can live without hope?
In the darkness with a great bundle of grief the people march.
In the night, and overhead a shovel of stars for keeps, the people march:
  "Where to? what next?"

ARCHIBALD MacLEISH
1892–
America Was Promises

In an introduction to this poem MacLeish comments on its theme:

> Like all promises, America was a promise which some believed would come true of itself. Like the promises in the fairy tales. This is the meaning of the title of the poem. And the meaning of the poem itself is that the promises do not come true of themselves—that they must be made to come true—that they must be made to come true, not by the idea of Man, the idea of the People, but by *people*, by *men*.

Who is the voyager in these leaves?
Who is the traveler in this journey
Deciphers the revolving night: receives
The signal from the light returning?

America was promises to whom?

East were the
Dead kings and the remembered sepulchres:
West was the grass.
The groves of the oaks were at evening.

Eastward are the nights where we have slept.

And we move on: we move down:
With the first light we push forward:
We descend from the past as a wandering people from mountains.
We cross into the day to be discovered.
The dead are left where they fall—at dark
At night late under the coverlets.
We mark the place with the shape of our teeth on our fingers.
The room is left as it was: the love

Who is the traveler in these leaves these
Annual waters and beside the doors
Jonquils: then the rose: the eaves
Heaping the thunder up: the mornings
Opening on like great valleys
Never till now approached: the familiar trees
Far off: distant with the future:
The hollyhocks beyond the afternoons:
The butterflies over the ripening fruit on the balconies:
And all beautiful
All before us

America was always promises.
From the first voyage and the first ship there were promises—
"the tropic bird which does not sleep at sea"
"the great mass of dark heavy clouds which is a sign"
"the drizzle of rain without wind which is a sure sign"
"the whale which is an indication"
"the stick appearing to be carved with iron"
"the stalk loaded with roseberries"
"and all these signs were from the west"
"and all night heard birds passing."[1]

Who is the voyager on these coasts?
Who is the traveler in these waters
Expects the future as a shore: foresees
Like Indies to the west the ending—he
The rumor of the surf intends?

[1] Passages taken from Columbus's journal: the evidences of the land he noted as he sailed west on an ocean that seemed to have no end.

America was promises—to whom?

Jefferson knew:[2]
Declared it before God and before history:
Declares it still in the remembering tomb.
The promises were Man's: the land was his—
Man endowed by his Creator:
Earnest in love: perfectible by reason:
Just and perceiving justice: his natural nature
Clear and sweet at the source as springs in trees are.
It was Man the promise contemplated.
The times had chosen Man: no other:
Bloom on his face of every future:
Brother of stars and of all travelers:
Brother of time and of all mysteries:
Brother of grass also: of fruit trees.
It was Man who had been promised: who should have.
Man was to ride from the Tidewater: over the Gap:
West and South with the water: taking the book with him:[3]
Taking the wheat seed: corn seed: pip of apple:
Building liberty a farmyard wide:
Breeding for useful labor: for good looks:
For husbandry: humanity: for pride—
Practising self-respect and common decency.

And Man turned into men in Philadelphia
Practising prudence on a long-term lease:
Building liberty to fit the parlor:
Bred for crystal on the frontroom shelves:
Just and perceiving justice by the dollar:
Patriotic with the bonds at par
(And their children's children brag of their deeds for the Colonies).
Man rode up from the Tidewater: over the Gap:
Turned into men: turned into two-day settlers:
Lawyers with the land-grants in their caps:
Coon-skin voters wanting theirs and getting it.

Turned the promises to capital: invested it.

[2] ll. 46–47: Thomas Jefferson (1743–1826), having served as John Adams's Vice President (1797–1801), succeeded him to become the third President of the U.S. (1801–1809). In all of Jefferson's writings there is probably no more cogent statement of his political philosophy than found in these words in The Declaration of Independence: "We hold these truths to be self-evident: that all men are created equal; that they are endowed by their Creator with certain inalienable rights; that among these are life, liberty, and the pursuit of happiness. That to secure these rights, governments are instituted among men, *deriving their just powers from the consent of the governed. . . .*" (italics added). He wanted not only a new kind of government, based on the will and wisdom of the people, but more importantly, a new specific kind of civilization as an example for the remainder of the world. For the serious student who looks for a brief, authentic statement of Jefferson's beliefs we recommend Gilbert Chinard's Introduction to his *Thomas Jefferson, the Apostle of Americanism,* Boston: Little, Brown and Co., 1929. [3] "The book" stands for books, learning. Jefferson's passion was for human liberty and learning: the sciences, the arts, music, and the human mind.

America was always promises:
"the wheel like a sun as big as a cart wheel
with many sorts of pictures on it
the whole of fine gold"

"twenty golden ducks
beautifully worked and very natural looking
and some like dogs of the kind they keep"[4]

And they waved us west from the dunes: they cried out
Colua! Colua!
Mexico! Mexico! . . . Colua!

America was promises to whom?

Old Man Adams knew.[5] He told us—
An aristocracy of compound interest
Hereditary through the common stock!
We'd have one sure before the mare was older.
"The first want of every man was his dinner:
The second his girl." Kings were by the pocket.
Wealth made blood made wealth made blood made wealthy.
Enlightened selfishness gave lasting light.
Winners bred grandsons: losers only bred!

And the Aristocracy of politic selfishness
Bought the land up: bought the towns: the sites:
The goods: the government: the people. Bled them.
Sold them. Kept the profit. Lost itself.

The Aristocracy of Wealth and Talents
Turned its talents into wealth and lost them.
Turned enlightened selfishness to wealth.

[4] These quotations have been taken from Bernal Díaz del Castillo, *The True History of the Conquest of New Spain* (3 vols., 1632; translated into English by Alfred Percival Maudsley, London, Printed for the Hakluyt Society, 1908–1916). Bernal Díaz (1496–1584) was one of the Spanish conquerors who came to Cuba in 1514, and served under Cortés in the conquest of Mexico. Montezuma sent ambassadors to Cortés with these gold gifts. [5] John Adams (1735–1826), second President of the U.S. (1797–1801). Although he and Jefferson signed The Declaration of Independence as written by Jefferson, they often differed widely on how the new nation was to be governed. Adams wanted a strong central government, and had less faith in the wisdom of the people to govern themselves; according to Jefferson, who was antagonistic to the Adams administration, Adams's *Discourses on Davila* (1791) leaned toward hereditary monarchy and aristocracy.

Turned self-interest into bankbooks: balanced them.
Bred out: bred to fools: to hostlers:
Card sharps: well dressed women: dancefloor doublers.
The Aristocracy of Wealth and Talents
Sold its talents: bought the public notice:
Drank in public: went to bed in public:
Patronized the arts in public, pal'd with
Public authors public beauties: posed in
Public postures for the public page.
The Aristocracy of Wealth and Talents
Withered of talent and ashamed of wealth
Bred to sonsinlaw: insane relations:
Girls with open secrets: sailors' Galahads:
Prurient virgins with the tales to tell:
Women with dead wombs and living wishes.

The Aristocracy of Wealth and Talents
Moved out: settled on the Continent:
Sat beside the water at Rapallo:[6]
Died in a rented house: unwept: unhonored.

*

And the child says I see the lightning on you.

The weed between the railroad tracks
Tasting of sweat: tasting of poverty:
The bitter and pure taste where the hawk hovers:
Native as the deer bone in the sand

O my America for whom?

For whom the promises? For whom the river
"It flows west! Look at the ripple of it!"
The grass "So that it was wonderful to see
And endless without end with wind wonderful!"
The Great Lakes: landless as oceans: their beaches
Coarse sand: clean gravel: pebbles:
Their bluffs smelling of sunflowers: smelling of surf:
Of fresh water: of wild sunflowers . . . wilderness.
For whom the evening mountains on the sky:
The night wind from the west: the moon descending?

[6] An Italian seaport and resort.

Tom Paine knew.[7]
Tom Paine knew the People.[8]
The promises were spoken to the People.
History was voyages toward the People.
Americas were landfalls of the People.
Stars and expectations were the signals of the People.

Whatever was truly built the People had built it.
Whatever was taken down they had taken down.
Whatever was worn they had worn—ax-handles: fiddle-bows:
Sills of doorways: names for children: for mountains.
Whatever was long forgotten they had forgotten—
Fame of the great: names of the rich and their mottos.
The People had the promises: they'd keep them.
They waited their time in the world: they had wise sayings.
They counted out their time by day to day.
They counted it out day after day into history.
They had time and to spare in the spill of their big fists.
They had all the time there was like a handful of wheat seed.
When the time came they would speak and the rest would listen.

And the time came and the People did not speak.

The time came: the time comes: the speakers
Come and these who speak are not the People.

These who speak with gunstocks at the doors:
These the coarse ambitious priest[9]
Leads by the bloody fingers forward:
These who reach with stiffened arm to touch

[7] Thomas Paine (1737–1809), notable for his *The American Crisis,* 1776–1783, sixteen pamphlets in support of the Revolutionary War; and *The Rights of Man,* 1791–1792, a defense of the French Revolution championed by Jefferson. [8] ll. 139–143: "the People" here are, of course, Tom Paine's. They contrast with "the people" (l. 211)—that is, the lower-case people, humanity itself—as they also contrast with Jefferson's "Man" and Adams's "Aristocracy of Wealth and Talents." In his review of Carl Sandburg's poem *The People, Yes* (p. 295) MacLeish makes this intention clear: "Out of the book comes the true smell and sound of humanity, the warm, endless, unending movement of man. . . . Out of the book comes for the first time in our literature the people of America. Whitman's men were Man. Sandburg's are men of this earth. It has taken our generation a long time to admit that we were not only a nation but a *people.* Now we are. The People. Yes." (MacLeish's *A Time to Speak,* Boston: Houghton Mifflin Co., 1940, p. 40.) MacLeish dedicated his poem "Frescoes for Mr. Rockefeller's City" to Sandburg. [9] A reference to Father Charles Edward Coughlin (b. 1891), Canadian-born American Catholic priest who delivered a series of Sunday afternoon radio sermons from his church, the Shrine of the Little Flower, in Royal Oak, Michigan (c. 1939–1940). He advocated the nationalization of natural resources and banking institutions, and attacked Wall Street, Communism, and the Jews. His newspaper *Social Justice* was devoted chiefly to anti-Semitism, and he was associated with the Christian Front, an anti-Semitic, pro-Fascist organization. James T. Farrell's short novel *Tommy Gallagher's Crusade* (1939) shows the consequences of the influence of Father Moylan, a radio priest, on Tommy who blames his own failure on the Jewish people. For further information see Sheldon Marcus, *Father Coughlin, the Tumultuous Life of the Priest of the Little Flower,* Boston: Little, Brown and Company, 1973.

What none who took dared touch before:
These who touch the truth are not the People.

These the savage fables of the time
Lick at the fingers as a bitch will waked at morning:
These who teach the lie are not the People.

The time came: the time comes

Comes and to whom? To these? Was it for these
The surf was secret on the new-found shore?
Was it for these the branch was on the water?—
These whom all the years were toward
The golden images the clouds the mountains?

Never before: never in any summer:
Never were days so generous: stars so mild:
Even in old men's talk or in books or remembering
Far back in a gone childhood
Or farther still to the light where Homer wanders—
The air all lucid with the solemn blue
That hills take at the distance beyond change. . . .
That time takes also at the distances.

Never were there promises as now:
Never was green deeper: earth warmer:
Light more beautiful to see: the sounds of
Water lovelier: the many forms of
Leaves: stones: clouds: beasts: shadows
Clearer more admirable or the faces
More like answering faces or the hands
Quicker: more brotherly:

the aching taste of
Time more salt upon the tongue: more human

Never in any summer: and to whom?

At dusk: by street lights: in the rooms we ask this.

We do not ask for Truth now from John Adams.
We do not ask for Tongues from Thomas Jefferson.
We do not ask for Justice from Tom Paine.
We ask for answers.

And there is an answer.

There is Spain Austria Poland China Bohemia.[10]
There are dead men in the pits in all those countries.
Their mouths are silent but they speak. They say
"The promises are theirs who take them."

Listen! Brothers! Generation!
Listen! You have heard these words. Believe it!
Believe the promises are theirs who take them!

Believe unless we take them for ourselves
Others will take them for the use of others!
Believe unless we take them for ourselves
All of us: one here: another there:
Men not Man: people not the People:
Hands: mouths: arms: eyes: not syllables—
Believe unless we take them for ourselves
Others will take them: not for us: for others!

Believe unless we take them for ourselves
Now: soon: by the clock: before tomorrow:
Others will take them: not for now: for longer!

Listen! Brothers! Generation!
Companions of leaves: of the sun: of the slow evenings:
Companions of the many days: of all of them:
Listen! Believe the speaking dead! Believe
The journey is our journey. O believe
The signals were to us: the signs: the birds by
Night: the breaking surf.

Believe
America is promises to
Take!
America is promises to
Us
To take them
Brutally
With love but
Take them.

O believe this!

[10] The countries where humanity had lost its inalienable rights through authoritarian brutality.

ROBERT FROST
1874–1963
The Gift Outright[1]

In his essay "An Extemporaneous Talk for Students," Frost says this poem "is my story of the revolutionary war. . . . The dream was to occupy the land with character—that's another way to put it—to occupy a new land with character."

The land was ours before we were the land's.
She was our land more than a hundred years
Before we were her people. She was ours
In Massachusetts, in Virginia,
But we were England's, still colonials,
Possessing what we still were unpossessed by,
Possessed by what we now no more possessed.
Something we were withholding made[2] us weak
Until we found out that it was ourselves
We were withholding from our land of living,
And forthwith found salvation in surrender.
Such as we were we gave ourselves outright
(The deed of gift was many deeds of war)
To the land vaguely realizing westward,
But still unstoried, artless, unenhanced,
Such as she was, such as she would become.

"THE TRIAL BY EXISTENCE": METAPHYSICAL VALUES

For many of our most fundamental and searching questions about life we have answers whose truth can be demonstrated beyond doubt. We no longer must *assume*, for example, that certain causes bring certain diseases; we *know* that such-and-such germs cause certain diseases. Science has provided the exact knowledge. But for other fundamental and searching questions we have no answers which can be verified beyond doubt. For example: Was the universe planned by a supreme being or was it an accident? Is death final or a passage to another life? What is the essential character of nature, and what can we learn from it?—is it something to follow, ignore, or repel? Are we the victims of forces over which we have no control, or do we have some measure of free will? To summarize: What is the meaning of life? Is there any more basic question?

Where do we go for answers? It is possible to go to a branch of philosophy called metaphysics: no need to shy from a word which is quite easily understood. The word is of Greek origin, *meta*—beyond and *physikos*—external nature. That is, when we ask questions whose answers are to be looked for beyond the demonstrable knowledge grounded in physical or natural causes, we go to metaphysics. Metaphysics is the source of our *assumptions* about life, and we all live by certain assumptions whether or not we realize it. In religion we call them articles of faith. For example, if we assume that our earthly sins are punishable after death, certain consequences in our behavior are likely to follow immediately. If we assume no freedom to direct our own actions (freedom of will), other consequences are likely to follow, and so on.

Are you tempted to argue that such matters hardly concern you, that you know very well what to live for, and that nature and the universe can take care of themselves? True, they will take care of themselves, and of you, too—but will you be satisfied with the results? Will you be prepared to meet and absorb those results gracefully? To help us do so is one of the values of tragic drama.

When verifiable scientific knowledge runs dry, we do not stop asking questions: in fact, some of the most important questions are still to be asked, and man has always insisted upon looking for answers. We shall see this insistence in the poets to follow. From its beginnings poetry has pursued metaphysical problems, and poets are often referred to as prophets. The Greek poets and dramatists dealt with the metaphysical and religious questions of their day; Milton's *Paradise Lost* is built on a pattern of metaphysical assumptions; and the poems below are nothing if not metaphysical in their implications.

[1] Read by Frost at the inauguration of John F. Kennedy as President of the United States, January 20, 1961. [2] Although *made* is used in *The Poetry of Robert Frost* (Holt, Rinehart and Winston, 1969, p. 348), Frost used *left* when he read the poem at President Kennedy's inauguration.

ROBERT FROST
1874–1963

The Secret Sits

We dance round in a ring and suppose,
But the Secret sits in the middle and knows.

JAMES HEARST
1900–

Truth

How the devil do I know
if there are rocks in your field,
plow it and find out.
If the plow strikes something
harder than earth, the point
shatters at a sudden blow
and the tractor jerks sidewise
and dumps you off the seat—
because the spring hitch
isn't set to trip quickly enough
and it never is—probably
you hit a rock. That means
the glacier emptied his pocket
in your field as well as mine,
but the connection with a thing
is the only truth that I know of,
so plow it.

EMILY DICKINSON
1830–1886

Because I Could Not Stop for Death

Because I could not stop for Death—
He kindly stopped for me—
The Carriage held but just Ourselves—
And Immortality.

We slowly drove—He knew no haste
And I had put away
My labor and my leisure too,
For His Civility—

We passed the School, where Children strove
At Recess—in the Ring—
We passed the Fields of Gazing Grain—
We passed the Setting Sun—

Or rather—He passed Us—
The Dews drew quivering and chill—
For only Gossamer, my Gown—
My Tippet[1]—only Tulle[2]—

We paused before a House that seemed
A Swelling of the Ground—
The Roof was scarcely visible—
The Cornice—in the Ground—

Since then—'tis Centuries—and yet
Feels shorter than the Day
I first surmised the Horses Heads
Were toward Eternity—

Comments

We are all compelled finally to take some attitude toward death, and poets, too, have pursued the theme relentlessly. The conventional attitude toward death is often somber, awed, and hushed, but Emily Dickinson's attitude is hardly conventional. Death is here represented as the driver of a carriage who courts the lady by taking her for a drive; they are alone except for the passenger Immortality—what company could be more appropriate? Is the poet equating death with love? It seems so, but note that this idea is not pushed to sentimentality. Instead of drawing a commonplace moral from the situation she has created, she simply presents the situation. She presents it, in fact, a little ironically: death, in his "Civility," "kindly" stops for his beloved who puts aside both her "labor" and her "leisure." Could the arrival of death be more natural, less awesome? Stanzas 3–5 give us the sensation of passing from life to eternity, and finally (stanza 6) the realization that we were headed for eternity from the beginning of our life. Can we say that the poet's attitude toward death is sane and normal? She makes the process of passing from life to death seem natural, inevitable, and appropriate to life as we know it. At least, this is her assumption about the nature of death, and we are left free to contemplate it. We are left also, let it be said, with a beautiful poetic experience, regardless of our attitude toward her assumption.

---

[1] Shoulder cape. [2] A sheer mesh fabric.

JOHN DONNE
1572–1631

Holy Sonnet, VII: At the Round Earth's Imagined Corners

At the round earth's imagined corners,[1] blow
Your trumpets, angels; and arise, arise
From death, you numberless infinities
Of souls, and to your scattered bodies go;
All whom the flood did, and fire shall o'erthrow,
All whom war, dearth, age, agues, tyrannies,
Despair, law, chance hath slain, and you whose eyes
Shall behold God and never taste death's woe.
But let them sleep, Lord, and me mourn a space,
For if above all these, my sins abound,
'Tis late to ask abundance of thy grace
When we are there; here on this lowly ground [2]
Teach me how to repent; for that's as good
As if thou'hadst sealed my pardon with thy blood.[3]

Comments and Questions

As usual, Donne has used a highly concentrated rhetorical structure which must be read carefully, including the syntax on the literal level. For his poetic purposes, Donne invokes the angels to blow their trumpets to summon the dead to Judgment Day. The "numberless infinities of souls" are expected to return to their "scattered bodies" to be judged: some shall be condemned to "fire" and others "shall behold God and never taste death's woe." The octet is Donne's method of projecting himself, imaginatively, into Judgment Day, and this imaginative act causes him to consider his own sins, and by implication the earthly sins of all of us. Shall we rely on God's grace on Judgment Day, or repent and dissolve our sins here on earth? The implication of the poem is that we should do the latter.

1. What are Donne's two basic metaphysical assumptions?

2. If you cannot accept the assumption of Judgment Day as a reality, is the poem valueless to you? This question admits of at least two answers. We can say, of course, that agreement with a poem's meaning is not necessary to the appreciation of the poem as a *poem.* Let us assume that the sonnet is a fine poem, good art. Now, if we disagree with Donne's metaphysical assumption of Judgment Day, can we agree with the poem's meaning on the psychological level? Is it necessary—to put our point into nontheological terms—to accept the image of Judgment Day to agree with Donne's second assumption that sins should be dissolved before death?

[1] The earth conceived of as having four corners.
[2] The earth. [3] Christ's crucifixion.

RALPH WALDO EMERSON
1803–1882

Brahma

If the red slayer think he slays,
  Or if the slain think he is slain,
They know not well the subtle ways
  I keep, and pass, and turn again.

Far or forgot to me is near;
  Shadow and sunlight are the same;
The vanished gods to me appear;
  And one to me are shame and fame.

They reckon ill who leave me out;
  When me they fly, I am the wings;
I am the doubter and the doubt,
  And I the hymn the Brahmin sings.

The strong gods pine for my abode,
  And pine in vain the sacred Seven;[1]
But thou, meek lover of the good!
  Find me, and turn thy back on heaven.

Comments and Questions

"Brahma" has troubled many Western readers for over a century, although the Asian Indian student seems to absorb it with little

[1] The highest saints in Brahminism, none of them Brahma.

difficulty.* The poem is one more attempt to understand the relationships among God, man (body *and* soul), and nature. It is one more attempt of the finite mind, which is limited by space and time, to place itself in infinity, which, of course, is not limited by space and time.

"Brahma" is a fusion of Hindu religion and Emerson's Transcendentalism. Its paradoxes (see p. 268) all come from the basic assumption of the unity of all existence: that God (Brahma), man, the soul, and nature are *one,* and if the reader of the poem will keep in mind the *image of the circle* to represent this unity, he is on his way. This unity, or circle, Emerson calls "the perfect whole," meaning as he says,

> Line in nature is not found;
> Unit and universe are round. . . .
> —"Uriel"

Emerson can therefore say about each one of us as he says of himself, "the currents of the Universal Being circulate through me; I am part and parcel of God." Hence, as the paradoxes of the poem indicate, there is no death, no distance, no time, no fragments of God, man, and nature. Instead there is harmony of all, no beginning, no end—the circle. Such things as distance and time have been invented by man to administer his daily life, but they must be laid aside to penetrate his nature and destiny.

1. All this is not to say that we can understand this poem through a trance or mystical osmosis. There are facts and concrete references to be understood. Who is Brahma?—simply to substitute your God may not be the answer. Who are the sacred Seven? And why seven? Why not eight?—is there something significant about the *number* seven? Why "*meek* lover of the good"? It is not necessary to guess the meaning of these references: we can *know.*

2. Why should Brahma advise us to turn our back on "heaven"? Is Brahma's heaven of a different kind? If the sacred Seven, each with a planet as a heaven for himself, pine for Brahma's abode, what do they pine for?

3. For help in answering that question we can go to the Hindu *Bhagavadgītā* (c. fifth century B.C.), a popular religious and philosophical poem: "He who does work for Me, he who looks upon Me as his goal, he who worships Me, free from attachment, he who is free from enmity to all creatures, he goes to me. . . ." (XI, 55). One interpreter, S. Radhakrishnan, observes: "This verse is the substance of the whole teaching of the *Gītā.* We must carry out our duties, directing the spirit to God and with detachment from all interest in the things of the world and free from enmity towards any living being." Could Brahma's abode be immortality, not merely personal immortality, but rather the continuity of all life? Confirm your answer with reference to the *entire* poem.

* The editors are indebted to S. P. Misra, Professor of English and Head of the Department of English and Modern European Languages, Gorakhpur University, India; and to Mrs. Mavis Ulrick, Senior Lecturer in English, Baikunthi Devi Kanya College, Agra, India, a visiting teacher of English at the University of Northern Iowa, 1963–1964, for help with this poem. "Brahma" is probably the best-known and most-analyzed American poem in the Indian universities today.

THOMAS HARDY
1840–1928

Hap[1]

If but some vengeful god would call to me
From up the sky, and laugh: "Thou suffering thing,
Know that thy sorrow is my ecstasy,
That thy love's loss is my hate's profiting!"
Then would I bear it, clench myself, and die,
Steeled by the sense of ire unmerited;
Half-eased in that a Powerfuller than I
Had willed and meted me the tears I shed.

But not so. How arrives it joy lies slain,
And why unblooms the best hope ever sown?
—Crass Casualty obstructs the sun and rain,
And dicing Time for gladness casts a moan. . . .
These purblind Doomsters had as readily strown
Blisses about my pilgrimage as pain.

[1] Chance, haphazard.

ROBERT FROST
1874–1963

The Trial by Existence[1]

[1]
Even the bravest that are slain
  Shall not dissemble their surprise
On waking to find valor reign,
  Even as on earth, in paradise;
And where they sought without the sword
  Wide fields of asphodel fore'er,
To find that the utmost reward
  Of daring should be still to dare.

[2]
The light of heaven falls whole and white
  And is not shattered into dyes,
The light for ever is morning light;
  The hills are verdured pasturewise;
The angel hosts with freshness go,
  And seek with laughter what to brave—
And binding all is the hushed snow
  Of the far-distant breaking wave.

[3]
And from a cliff top is proclaimed
  The gathering of the souls for birth,
The trial by existence named,
  The obscuration upon earth.
And the slant spirits trooping by
  In streams and cross- and counter-streams
Can but give ear to that sweet cry
  For its suggestion of what dreams!

[4]
And the more loitering are turned
  To view once more the sacrifice
Of those who for some good discerned
  Will gladly give up paradise.
And a white shimmering concourse rolls
  Toward the throne to witness there
The speeding of devoted souls
  Which God makes His especial care.

[5]
And none are taken but who will,
  Having first heard the life read out
That opens earthward, good and ill,
  Beyond the shadow of a doubt;
And very beautifully God limns,
  And tenderly, life's little dream,
But naught extenuates or dims,
  Setting the thing that is supreme.

[6]
Nor is there wanting in the press
  Some spirit to stand simply forth,
Heroic in its nakedness,
  Against the uttermost of earth.
The tale of earth's unhonored things
  Sounds nobler there than 'neath the sun;
And the mind whirls and the heart sings,
  And a shout greets the daring one.

[7]
But always God speaks at the end:
  "One thought in agony of strife
The bravest would have by for friend,
  The memory that he chose the life;
But the pure fate to which you go
  Admits no memory of choice,
Or the woe were not earthly woe
  To which you give the assenting voice."

[8]
And so the choice must be again,
  But the last choice is still the same;
And the awe passes wonder then,
  And a hush falls for all acclaim.
And God has taken a flower of gold
  And broken it, and used therefrom
The mystic link to bind and hold
  Spirit to matter till death come.

[9]
'Tis of the essence of life here,
  Though we choose greatly, still to lack
The lasting memory at all clear,
  That life has for us on the wrack
Nothing but what we somehow chose;
  Thus are we wholly stripped of pride
In the pain that has but one close,
  Bearing it crushed and mystified.

[1] See *John*, 3:13, 6:61 ff; and *Ephesians*, 4:1 ff.

Comments and Questions

We have seen above how Emerson and Hardy have met the question of the meaning of life. Emerson would have us find its meaning by finding God within ourselves; Hardy finds no meaning that a rational man can accept; and Frost rejects the metaphysics of both of them.

For Frost, as for many of us, the meaning of life is a big question mark. In a poem published years after the appearance of "The Trial by Existence," Frost could conclude that "the strong are saying nothing until they see."* We recall his couplet (p. 308):

> We dance round in a ring and suppose,
> But the Secret sits in the middle and knows.

Nevertheless, he keeps after the Secret to find at least "enough to go on." Regardless of our opinion of Hardy's conclusion in "Hap," he raises the dogging question,

> How arrives it joy lies slain,
> And why unblooms the best hope ever sown?

"The Trial by Existence" is one of Frost's ways of getting at the question.

In few poems has he been so direct, and without a trace of his customary light satiric smile. Observe the conventional line and stanza form, and the scarcity of the Frost idiom and bantering tone. Here he seems to feel the need of all the conventional stability he can muster to support a metaphysic which would not appeal to an audience brought up on Longfellow. In one respect the tone is characteristic: Is he saying that with this poem *he* will stand "against the uttermost of earth"? He always has, and this poem may be part of his early creed, never later altered.

Suppose we regard the poem as a parable, or perhaps better a fable—a fictitious story used to illustrate certain assumptions and conclusions. Stanzas 3–8 present a little drama in six scenes; the other stanzas present Frost's assumptions and conclusions. The point of departure in his thinking is pretty clear: he intends to examine our easy assumption which holds that although life on earth is very often tragic and baffling, paradise will be quite a different matter.

In stanza 1 he is quick to say that "even the bravest that are slain" on earth should not be surprised to find *even* in paradise that "the utmost reward / Of daring should be still to dare." Stanza 2 describes heaven, and, by contrast, the earth. In heaven it is possible to see clearly and to understand the nature of things—there the secret becomes clear; but on earth the "light" *is* "shattered into dyes," and the whites, grays, and blacks intermingle to veil the secret.

The little drama in stanzas 3–8 is designed by Frost as a parable to illustrate his assumption about life, found in stanza 9. In stanza 3 the souls gather for birth, which is a joyous occasion for those who have endured the "trial by existence" and have returned to heaven (ll. 21–24). Stanzas 4 and 5 underscore the circumstances of "birth." The souls exercise freedom of choice: "for some good discerned" they "will gladly give up paradise." That the trial and "sacrifice" are freely chosen (the doctrine of free will as opposed to fatalism or determinism) is a cardinal assumption in the poem. Stanza 5 makes clear that no warning by God about "life's little dream" can diminish the enthusiasm of those who have chosen the trial. There is always the eager one, says stanza 6, ready to stand "against the uttermost of earth." God warns the departing souls (stanza 7) that part of their "earthly woe" will be in their not remembering they have chosen the trial. Stanza 8 rounds off the dramatic action of the parable as God the creator furnishes the "mystic link"—the pulse of life—to fuse the daring spirit and the willing flesh until death comes on earth.

Having finished his parable, Frost draws his conclusions from it in stanza 9: We are "crushed and mystified" by the "pain" of the "trial by existence" because we forget, or ignore, that the gift of free will includes the responsibilities for our choices. No need, implies Frost, for Hardy to shout abuse at "some vengeful god": whatever "life has for us on the wrack" there is "nothing but what we somehow chose."

1. The poem has at least a score of implications, as a thoughtful poem usually does. What evidence is there that Frost is not merely rationalizing but is getting at something important?

2. In lines 27–28 Frost says that the souls "for some good discerned / Will gladly give up paradise." Has the word "paradise" more than one meaning here?

3. What would J. Alfred Prufrock think of the notion of standing "against the uttermost of earth"? (See p. 390.)

---

* See p. 341 for the poem.

WALTER SAVAGE LANDOR 1775–1864

Dying Speech of an Old Philosopher[1]

I strove with none, for none was worth my strife:
Nature I loved, and, next to Nature, Art:
I warm'd both hands before the fire of Life;
It sinks; and I am ready to depart.

THE DIMENSIONS OF POETIC EXPERIENCE

ANONYMOUS

O Western Wind, When Wilt Thou Blow[1]

O Western wind, when wilt thou blow
That the small rain down can rain?
Christ, that my love were in my arms
And I in my bed again!

ANONYMOUS

Jolly Good Ale and Old

I cannot eat but little meat,
My stomach is not good;
But sure I think that I can drink
With him that wears a hood.
Though I go bare, take ye no care,
I nothing am a-cold;
I stuff my skin so full within
Of jolly good ale and old,

Back and side go bare, go bare;
Both foot and hand go cold;
But, belly, God send thee good ale enough,
Whether it be new or old.

I love no roast but a nut-brown toast,
And a crab[1] laid in the fire;
A little bread shall do me stead;
Much bread I not desire.
No frost nor snow, no wind, I trow,
Can hurt me if I wold;
I am so wrapped and thoroughly lapped
Of jolly good ale and old.
Back and side go bare, go bare, etc.

And Tib, my wife, that as her life
Loveth well good ale to seek,
Full oft drinks she till ye may see
The tears run down her cheek:
Then doth she trowl to me the bowl
Even as a maltworm should,
And saith, "Sweetheart, I took my part
Of this jolly good ale and old."
Back and side go bare, go bare, etc.

Now let them drink till they nod and wink,
Even as good fellows should do;
They shall not miss to have the bliss
Good ale doth bring men to;
And all poor souls that have scoured bowls
Or have them lustily trolled,
God save the lives of them and their wives,
Whether they be young or old.
Back and side go bare, go bare;
Both foot and hand go cold;
But, belly, God send thee good ale enough,
Whether it be new or old.

THREE POEMS BY MICHELANGELO (TRANS. GEORGE SANTAYANA)

Michelangelo Buonarroti probably comes as near to being a universal artistic genius as the world is ever likely to know. As a sculptor he carved from a single block of marble the famous statue of David; his world-famous Pietà, carved from white Carrara marble, representing the Virgin Mary with the dead body of Christ held on her knees, is now near the entrance to St. Peter's in Rome, a cathedral he helped to plan and build. His paintings include those on the ceiling of the Sistine Chapel in Rome, and the great fresco of the

[1] Written on his seventy-fourth birthday, 1849.

[1] It is said that this is the oldest poem in English for which we have recorded music. The manuscript is in the Bodleian Library, Oxford University, England.

[1] Crab apple.

Last Judgment on the east wall of the Chapel. As a poet he left a number of remarkable sonnets and madrigals, including the three poems below.

A very readable life of Michelangelo is Irving Stone, *The Agony and the Ecstasy, A Novel of Michelangelo,* Garden City: Doubleday and Co., 1961. Standard biographies are plentiful, available in most libraries.

MICHELANGELO
1475–1564

I Know Not If from Uncreated Spheres

"Non so se s'è la desiata luce"[1]

I know not if from uncreated spheres
Some longed-for ray it be that warms my breast,
Or lesser light, in memory expressed,
Of some once lovely face, that reappears,
Or passing rumour ringing in my ears,
Or dreamy vision, once my bosom's guest,
That left behind I know not what unrest,
Haply the reason of these wayward tears.
But what I feel and seek, what leads me on,
Comes not of me; nor can I tell aright
Where shines the hidden star that sheds this light.
Since I beheld thee, sweet and bitter fight
Within me. Resolution have I none.
Can this be, Master, what thine eyes have done?

[1] "I know not if this be the longed-for light."

MICHELANGELO
1475–1564

The Haven and Last Refuge of My Pain

"Il mio refugio"[1]

The haven and last refuge of my pain
(A safe and strong defence)
Are tears and supplications, but in vain.
Love sets upon me banded with Disdain,
One armed with pity and one armed with death,
And as death smites me, pity lends me breath.
Else had my soul long since departed thence.
She pineth to remove
Whither her hopes of endless peace abide
And beauty dwelleth without beauty's pride,
There her last bliss to prove.
But still the living fountain of her tears
Wells in the heart when all thy truth appears,
Lest death should vanquish love.

[1] "My refuge."

MICHELANGELO
1475–1564

Ravished by All That to the Eyes Is Fair

"Gli occhi miei vaghi delle cose belle"[1]

Ravished by all that to the eyes is fair,
Yet hungry for the joys that truly bless,
My soul can find no stair
To mount to heaven, save earth's loveliness.
For from the stars above
Descends a glorious light
That lifts our longing to their highest height
And bears the name of love.
Nor is there aught can move
A gentle heart, or purge or make it wise,
But beauty and the starlight of her eyes.

[1] "My eyes eager for beautiful things."

WILLIAM SHAKESPEARE
1564–1616

Sonnet 18: Shall I Compare Thee to a Summer's Day?

Shall I compare thee to a summer's day?
Thou art more lovely and more temperate:
Rough winds do shake the darling buds of May,
And summer's lease hath all too short a date:
Sometime too hot the eye of heaven shines,
And often is his gold complexion dimmed;
And every fair from fair sometime declines,[1]
By chance or nature's changing course untrimmed;[2]
But thy eternal summer shall not fade
Nor lose possession of that fair thou owest;[3]

[1] Every beautiful thing finally loses its beauty.
[2] Stripped of gay apparel. [3] Ownest.

Nor shall Death brag thou wander'st in his shade,
When in eternal lines to time thou growest:
  So long as men can breathe, or eyes can see,
  So long lives this,[4] and this gives life to thee.

WILLIAM SHAKESPEARE
1564–1616

Sonnet 33: Full Many a Glorious Morning Have I Seen

Full many a glorious morning have I seen
Flatter the mountain-tops with sovereign eye,
Kissing with golden face the meadows green,
Gilding pale streams with heavenly alchemy;
Anon permit the basest clouds to ride
With ugly rack [1] on his celestial face,
And from the forlorn world his visage hide,
Stealing unseen to west with this disgrace:
Even so my sun[2] one early morn did shine
With all-triumphant splendour on my brow;
But out, alack! he was but one hour mine;
The region[3] cloud hath mask'd him from me now.
  Yet him for this my love no whit disdaineth;
  Suns of the world may stain[4] when heaven's sun staineth.

WILLIAM SHAKESPEARE
1564–1616

Sonnet 73: That Time of Year Thou Mayst in Me Behold

That time of year thou mayst in me behold
When yellow leaves, or none, or few, do hang
Upon those boughs which shake against the cold,
Bare ruined choirs, where late the sweet birds sang.
In me thou seest the twilight of such day
As after sunset fadeth in the west;
Which by and by black night doth take away,
Death's second self, that seals up all in rest.
In me thou seest the glowing of such fire,
That [1] on the ashes of his[2] youth doth lie,
As the death-bed whereon it must expire,
Consum'd with that which it was nourished by.
  This thou perceiv'st, which makes thy love more strong.
  To love that well which thou must leave ere long.

JOHN DONNE
1572–1631

Woman's Constancy

Now thou hast loved me one whole day,
To-morrow when thou leav'st, what wilt thou say?
Wilt thou then antedate some new-made vow?
  Or say that now
We are not just those persons which we were?
Or, that oaths made in reverential fear
Of love, and his wrath, any may forswear?
Or, as true deaths true marriages untie,
So lovers' contracts, images of those,
Bind but till sleep, death's image,[1] them unloose?
  Or, your own end to justify,
For having purposed change and falsehood, you
Can have no way but falsehood to be true? [2]
Vain lunatic, against these scapes I could
  Dispute and conquer, if I would;
  Which I abstain to do,
For by to-morrow, I may think so too.

JOHN DONNE
1572–1631

The Canonization

For God's sake hold your tongue, and let me love,
  Or chide my palsy, or my gout,
My five gray hairs, or ruined fortune flout,
  With wealth your state, your mind with arts improve,
    Take you a course, get you a place,[1]
    Observe his honor, or his grace,
Or the king's real, or his stampèd face.[2]

[4] This poem.

[1] Storm clouds. [2] My friend. [3] Upper air, not ground winds. [4] Be obscured; become dim or dull.

[1] As. [2] Its.

[1] Sleep which is an image of death. [2] Ll. 12–13: In your declaration of love, you must be false again to rid yourself of the false declaration. That is, one falsehood demands another.

[1] Office. [2] As on a coin.

Contemplate; what you will approve,
So you will let me love.

Alas, alas, who's injured by my love?
What merchant's ships have my sighs drowned?
Who says my tears have overflowed his ground?
When did my colds a forward spring remove?[3]
When did the heats which my veins fill
Add one more to the plaguey bill?[4]
Soldiers find wars, and lawyers find out still
Litigious men, which quarrels move,
Though she and I do love.

Call us what you will, we are made such by love;
Call her one, me another fly,
We are tapers[5] too, and at our own cost die,[6]
And we in us find the eagle and the dove.[7]
The phoenix[8] riddle hath more wit
By us; we two being one, are it.[9]
So to one neutral thing both sexes fit,
We die and rise the same, and prove
Mysterious by this love.

We can die by it, if not live by love,
And if unfit for tombs and hearse
Our legend[10] be, it will be fit for verse;
And if no piece or chronicle[11] we prove,
We'll build in sonnets pretty rooms;
As well a well-wrought urn becomes
The greatest ashes, as half-acre tombs,
And by these hymns, all shall approve
Us *canonized*[12] for love;

And thus invoke us; you whom reverend love
Made one another's hermitage;
You, to whom love was peace, that now is rage;
Who did the whole world's soul contract, and drove
Into the glasses of your eyes
(So made such mirrors, and such spies,
That they did all to you epitomize),
Countries, towns, courts: beg from above
A pattern[13] of your love!

[3] Delay. [4] Weekly list of plague victims. [5] Candles that burn out, die. [6] *Die* has the secondary meaning of achieving consummation in sexual intercourse, as in ll. 26 and 28 also. [7] *Eagle*, strength; *dove*, purity. [8] Fabulous bird of no sex that rose immortal from its own ashes. [9] We die to rise as one love-wedded being. [10] Story of a saint's life. [11] History. [12] Made saints. [13] Likeness, copy.

ROBERT HERRICK
1591–1674

Delight in Disorder

A sweet disorder in the dress
Kindles in clothes a wantonness;
A lawn[1] about the shoulders thrown
Into a fine distractïon,
An erring lace, which here and there
Enthralls the crimson stomacher,[2]
A cuff neglectful, and thereby
Ribands to flow confusedly,
A winning wave, deserving note,
In the tempestuous petticoat,
A careless shoe-string, in whose tie
I see a wild civility,
Do more bewitch me than when art[3]
Is too precise in every part.

[1] Fine linen, as a scarf. [2] Center front section of a waist or underwaist or an unusually heavily embroidered or jeweled separate piece for the center front of a bodice. [3] Conscious effort to achieve a desired effect.

JOHN MILTON
1608–1674

On Shakespeare

What needs my Shakespeare for his honor'd bones
The labor of an age in pilèd stones,
Or that his hallow'd relics should be hid
Under a star-ypointing[1] pyramid?
Dear son of memory, great heir of fame,
What need'st thou such weak witness of thy name?
Thou in our wonder and astonishment
Hast built thyself a livelong monument.
For whilst to th' shame of slow-endeavoring art
Thy easy numbers[2] flow, and that each heart
Hath from the leaves of thy unvalu'd[3] book
Those Delphic[4] lines with deep impression took,
Then thou, our fancy of itself bereaving,
Dost make us marble with too much conceiving,[5]
And so sepúlcher'd in such pomp does lie,
That kings for such a tomb would wish to die.

[1] Old English for star-pointing. [2] Verses. [3] Invaluable. [4] Inspired. [5] Imagining.

WILLIAM CARTWRIGHT
1611–1643

No Platonic Love[1]

Some readers would call this early seventeenth-century poem amazingly modern, although Chaucer (1340?–1400) would have absorbed it with ease. For a brief discussion of Cartwright's general point of view, see the comment on Donne's "Go and Catch a Falling Star," p. 282.

Tell me no more of minds embracing minds,
And hearts exchanged for hearts;
That spirits spirits meet, as winds do winds,
And mix their subtlest parts;
That two unbodied essences may kiss,
And then like angels, twist and feel one bliss.

I was that silly thing that once was wrought
To practise this thin love;
I climbed from sex to soul, from soul to thought;
But thinking there to move,
Headlong I rolled from thought to soul, and then
From soul I lighted at the sex again.

As some strict down-looked men pretend to fast
Who yet in closets eat,
So lovers who profess they spirits taste,
Feed yet on grosser meat;
I know they boast they souls to souls convey,
Howe'er they meet, the body is the way.

Come, I will undeceive thee: they that tread
Those vain aerial ways
Are like young heirs and alchemists, misled
To waste their wealth and days;
For searching thus to be forever rich,
They only find a med'cine for the itch.

[1] The Greek philosopher Plato (427?–347 B.C.) wrote *The Symposium*, a dialogue on ideal love. "Platonic love" became a popular term for spiritual love between the sexes without sexual complications. See J. V. Cunningham's poem "The Metaphysical Amorist," p. 355, which has a theme similar to Cartwright's.

RICHARD LOVELACE
1618–1658

To Lucasta, Going to the Wars

Tell me not, Sweet, I am unkind,
That from the nunnery
Of thy chaste breast and quiet mind
To war and arms I fly.

True, a new mistress now I chase,
The first foe in the field;
And with a stronger faith embrace
A sword, a horse, a shield.

Yet this inconstancy is such
As thou too shalt adore;
I could not love thee, Dear, so much,
Loved I not Honor more.

THOMAS GRAY
1716–1771

Elegy Written in a Country Churchyard

The Curfew tolls the knell of parting day,
The lowing herd wind slowly o'er the lea,
The plowman homeward plods his weary way,
And leaves the world to darkness and to me.

Now fades the glimmering landscape on the sight,
And all the air a solemn stillness holds,
Save where the beetle wheels his droning flight,
And drowsy tinklings lull the distant folds;

Save that from yonder ivy-mantled tower
The moping owl does to the moon complain
Of such, as wandering near her secret bower,
Molest her ancient solitary reign.

Beneath those rugged elms, that yew-tree's shade,
Where heaves the turf in many a mould'ring heap.
Each in his narrow cell for ever laid,
The rude Forefathers of the hamlet sleep.

The breezy call of incense-breathing Morn,
The swallow twitt'ring from the straw-built shed,
The cock's shrill clarion, or the echoing horn,[1]
No more shall rouse them from their lowly bed.

For them no more the blazing hearth shall burn,
Or busy housewife ply her evening care:
No children run to lisp their sire's return,
Or climb his knees the envied kiss to share.

Oft did the harvest to their sickle yield,
Their furrow oft the stubborn glebe has broke;
How jocund did they drive their team afield!
How bowed the woods beneath their sturdy stroke!

Let not Ambition mock their useful toil,
Their homely joys, and destiny obscure;
Nor Grandeur hear with a disdainful smile
The short and simple annals of the poor.

The boast of heraldry, the pomp of power,
And all that beauty, all that wealth e'er gave,
Awaits[2] alike th' inevitable hour.
The paths of glory lead but to the grave.

Nor you, ye Proud, impute to These the fault,
If Memory o'er their Tomb no Trophies raise,
Where through the long-drawn aisle and fretted vault
The pealing anthem swells the note of praise.

Can storied urn[3] or animated [4] bust
Back to its mansion call the fleeting breath?
Can Honor's voice provoke[5] the silent dust,
Or Flattery soothe the dull cold ear of Death?

Perhaps in this neglected spot is laid
Some heart once pregnant with celestial fire;
Hands, that the rod of empire might have swayed,
Or waked to ecstasy the living lyre.

But Knowledge to their eyes her ample page
Rich with the spoils of time did ne'er unroll:
Chill Penury repressed their noble rage,[6]
And froze the genial [7] current of the soul.

Full many a gem of purest ray serene,
The dark unfathomed caves of ocean bear:
Full many a flower is born to blush unseen,
And waste its sweetness on the desert air.

Some village-Hampden,[8] that with dauntless breast
The little Tyrant of his fields withstood;
Some mute inglorious Milton here may rest,
Some Cromwell guiltless of his country's blood.

Th' applause of list'ning senates to command,
The threats of pain and ruin to despise,
To scatter plenty o'er a smiling land,
And read their history in a nation's eyes,

Their lot forbade: not circumscribed alone
Their growing virtues, but their crimes confined;
Forbade to wade through slaughter to a throne,
And shut the gates of mercy on mankind,

The struggling pangs of conscious truth to hide
To quench the blushes of ingenuous shame,
Or heap the shrine of Luxury and Pride
With incense kindled at the Muse's flame.

Far from the madding crowd's ignoble strife,
Their sober wishes never learned to stray;
Along the cool sequestered vale of life
They kept the noiseless tenor of their way.

Yet ev'n these bones from insult to protect,
Some frail memorial still erected nigh,
With uncouth rhymes and shapeless sculpture decked,
Implores the passing tribute of a sigh.

Their name, their years, spelt by th' unlettered muse,
The place of fame and elegy supply;
And many a holy text around she strews,
That teach the rustic moralist to die.

[1] Of the hunt, early in the morning. [2] The subject of the verb *awaits* is *hour*. [3] Such as Keats describes in his "Ode on a Grecian Urn" (see p. 325). [4] Lifelike. [5] Call forth.

[6] Inspired mood. [7] Creative. [8] John Hampden (1594–1643), whose leadership in Parliament resisted the tyranny of Charles I.

For who to dumb Forgetfulness a prey,
This pleasing anxious being e'er resigned,
Left the warm precincts of the cheerful day,
Nor cast one longing ling'ring look behind?

On some fond breast the parting soul relies,
Some pious drops the closing eye requires;
Ev'n from the tomb the voice of Nature cries,
Ev'n in our Ashes live their wonted Fires.

For[9] thee, who mindful of th' unhonored Dead
Dost in these lines their artless tale relate,
If chance,[10] by lonely contemplation led,
Some kindred Spirit shall inquire thy fate,

Haply some hoary-headed Swain may say,
"Oft have we seen him at the peep of dawn
Brushing with hasty steps the dews away
To meet the sun upon the upland lawn.

"There at the foot of yonder nodding beech
That wreathes its old fantastic roots so high,
His listless length at noontide would he stretch,
And pore upon the brook that babbles by.

"Hard by yon wood, now smiling as in scorn,
Mutt'ring his wayward fancies he would rove,
Now drooping, woeful wan, like one forlorn,
Or crazed with care, or crossed in hopeless love.

"One morn I missed him on the customed hill,
Along the heath and near his favorite tree;
Another came; nor yet beside the rill,
Nor up the lawn, nor at the wood was he;

"The next with dirges due in sad array
Slow through the church-way path we saw him borne.
Approach and read (for thou cans't read) the lay,
Graved on the stone beneath yon agèd thorn."

THE EPITAPH

Here rests his head upon the lap of earth
A youth to fortune and to fame unknown.
Fair Science frowned not on his humble birth,
And Melancholy marked him for her own.

Large was his bounty, and his soul sincere,
Heaven did a recompense as largely send:
He gave to Misery all he had, a tear,
He gained from Heaven ('twas all he wished) a friend.

No further seek his merits to disclose,
Or draw his frailties from their dread abode,
(There they alike in trembling hope repose)
The bosom of his Father and his God.

[9] As for. [10] If it should chance.

WILLIAM BLAKE
1757–1827

The Little Black Boy

My mother bore me in the southern wild,
And I am black, but O! my soul is white;
White as an angel is the English child,
But I am black, as if bereav'd of light.

My mother taught me underneath a tree,
And sitting down before the heat of day,
She took me on her lap and kissed me,
And pointing to the east, began to say:

"Look on the rising sun: there God does live,
And gives his light, and gives his heat away;
And flowers and trees and beasts and men receive
Comfort in morning, joy in the noonday.

"And we are put on earth a little space,
That we may learn to bear the beams of love;
And these black bodies and this sunburnt face
Is but a cloud, and like a shady grove.

"For when our souls have learn'd the heat to bear,
The cloud will vanish; we shall hear his voice,
Saying: 'Come out from the grove, my love and care,
And round my golden tent like lambs rejoice.'"

Thus did my mother say, and kissed me;
And thus I say to little English boy:
When I from black and he from white cloud free,
And round the tent of God like lambs we joy,

I'll shade him from the heat, till he can bear
To lean in joy upon our father's knee;
And then I'll stand and stroke his silver hair,
And be like him, and he will then love me.

ROBERT BURNS
1759–1796

My Love Is Like a Red Red Rose

My love is like a red red rose
  That's newly sprung in June:
My love is like the melodie
  That's sweetly played in tune.

So fair art thou, my bonnie lass,
  So deep in love am I:
And I will love thee still, my dear,
  Till a' the seas gang dry.

Till a' the seas gang dry, my dear,
  And the rocks melt wi' the sun:
And I will love thee still, my dear,
  While the sands o' life shall run.

And fare thee weel, my only love,
  And fare thee weel awhile!
And I will come again, my love,
  Tho' it were ten thousand mile.

WILLIAM WORDSWORTH
1770–1850

I Wandered Lonely as a Cloud

I wandered lonely as a cloud
That floats on high o'er vales and hills,
When all at once I saw a crowd,
A host, of golden daffodils;
Beside the lake, beneath the trees,
Fluttering and dancing in the breeze.

Continuous as the stars that shine
And twinkle on the milky way,
They stretched in never-ending line
Along the margin of a bay:
Ten thousand saw I at a glance,
Tossing their heads in sprightly dance.
The waves beside them danced; but they
Out-did the sparkling waves in glee:
A poet could not but be gay,
In such a jocund company:
I gazed—and gazed—but little thought
What wealth the show to me had brought:

For oft, when on my couch I lie
In vacant or in pensive mood,
They flash upon that inward eye
Which is the bliss of solitude;
And then my heart with pleasure fills,
And dances with the daffodils.

WILLIAM WORDSWORTH
1770–1850

It Is a Beauteous Evening

It is a beauteous evening, calm and free;
The holy time is quiet as a nun
Breathless with adoration; the broad sun
Is sinking down in its tranquillity;
The gentleness of heaven broods o'er the sea:
Listen! the mighty Being is awake,
And doth with his eternal motion make
A sound like thunder—everlastingly.
Dear child! dear girl! that walkest with me here,
If thou appear untouched by solemn thought,
Thy nature is not therefore less divine:
Thou liest in Abraham's bosom all the year,
And worship'st at the Temple's inner shrine,
God being with thee when we know it not.

WILLIAM WORDSWORTH
1770–1850

The World Is Too Much with Us

The world is too much with us; late and soon,
Getting and spending, we lay waste our powers;
Little we see in Nature that is ours;
We have given our hearts away, a sordid boon!
This Sea that bares her bosom to the moon;
The winds that will be howling at all hours,
And are up-gathered now like sleeping flowers;
For this, for everything, we are out of tune;
It moves us not.—Great God! I'd rather be
A Pagan suckled in a creed outworn;
So might I, standing on this pleasant lea,

Have glimpses that would make me less forlorn:
Have sight of Proteus rising from the sea;
Or hear old Triton[1] blow his wreathèd [2] horn.

SAMUEL TAYLOR COLERIDGE
1772–1834

Kubla Khan: Or a Vision in a Dream[1]

In Xanadu did Kubla Khan[2]
A stately pleasure-dome decree;
Where Alph, the sacred river, ran
Through caverns measureless to man
Down to a sunless sea.

So twice five miles of fertile ground
With walls and towers were girdled round:

[1] Sea gods of classical mythology. Proteus could assume any shape. Triton, son of Neptune, could raise and calm the waves by blasts on his conch-shell trumpet. [2] Spiral.

[1] The poem was written in 1798, not 1797 as Coleridge erroneously states. A preface by the author explains the genesis and composition of the poem; "In the summer of the year of 1797 [1798], the Author, then in ill health, had retired to a lonely farm-house. . . . In consequence of a slight indisposition, an anodyne [it was opium] had been prescribed, from the effects of which he fell asleep in his chair at the moment that he was reading the following sentence, or words of the same substance, in 'Purchas's Pilgrimage': 'Here the Khan Kubla commanded a palace to be built, and a stately garden thereunto. And thus ten miles of fertile ground were enclosed with a wall.' The author continued for about three hours in a profound sleep, at least of the external senses, during which time he has the most vivid confidence, that he could not have composed less than from two to three hundred lines; if that indeed can be called composition in which all the images rose up before him as *things*, with a parallel production of the correspondent expressions, without any sensation or consciousness of effort. On awaking he appeared to himself to have a distinct recollection of the whole, and taking his pen, ink and paper, instantly and eagerly wrote down the lines that are here preserved. At this moment he was unfortunately called out by a person on business from Porlock, and detained by him above an hour, and on his return to his room, found, to his no small surprise and mortification, that though he still retained some vague and dim recollection of the general purport of the vision, yet, with the exception of some eight or ten scattered lines and images, all the rest had passed away like the images on the surface of a stream into which a stone has been cast, but, alas! without the after restoration of the latter!" [2] Founder of the Mongol dynasty in China.

And here were gardens bright with sinuous rills,
Where blossomed many an incense-bearing tree;
And here were forests ancient as the hills
Enfolding sunny spots of greenery.

But oh! that deep romantic chasm which slanted
Down the green hill athwart [3] a cedarn cover!
A savage place! as holy and enchanted
As e'er beneath a waning moon was haunted
By woman wailing for her demon-lover!
And from this chasm, with ceaseless turmoil seething,
As if this earth in fast thick pants were breathing
A mighty fountain momently[4] was forced:
Amid whose swift half-intermitted burst
Huge fragments vaulted like rebounding hail,
Or chaffy grain beneath the thresher's flail:
And 'mid these dancing rocks at once and ever
It flung up momently the sacred river.
Five miles meandering with a mazy motion
Through wood and dale the sacred river ran,
Then reached the caverns measureless to man,
And sank in tumult to a lifeless ocean:
And 'mid this tumult Kubla heard from far
Ancestral voices prophesying war!

The shadow of the dome of pleasure
Floated midway on the waves;
Where was heard the mingled measure
From the fountain and the caves.
It was a miracle of rare device,
A sunny pleasure-dome with caves of ice!

A damsel with a dulcimer[5]
In a vision once I saw:
It was an Abyssinian maid,
And on her dulcimer she played,
Singing of Mount Abora.
Could I revive with me
Her symphony and song,
To such a deep delight 'twould win me,
That with music loud and long,
I would build that dome in air,
That sunny dome! those caves of ice!
And all who heard should see them there,—
And all should cry, Beware! Beware!—
His flashing eyes, his floating hair!
Weave a circle round him thrice,
And close your eyes with holy dread,
For he on honey-dew hath fed,
And drunk the milk of Paradise.

[3] Across. [4] Continuously. [5] Wire-stringed instrument played with light hammers in the hand.

LEIGH HUNT
1784–1859

The Glove and the Lions

King Francis was a hearty king, and loved a royal sport,
And one day as his lions fought, sat looking on the court;
The nobles filled the benches, and the ladies in their pride,
And 'mongst them sat the Count de Lorge, with one for whom he sighed:
And truly 'twas a gallant thing to see that crowning show,
Valour and love, and a king above, and the royal beasts below.

Ramped and roared the lions, with horrid laughing jaws;
They bit, they glared, gave blows like beams, a wind went with their paws;
With wallowing might and stifled roar they rolled on one another,
Till all the pit with sand and mane was in a thunderous smother;
The bloody foam above the bars came whisking through the air;
Said Francis then, "Faith, gentlemen, we're better here than there."

De Lorge's love o'erheard the King, a beauteous lively dame
With smiling lips and sharp bright eyes, which always seemed the same;
She thought, the Count my lover is brave as brave can be;
He surely would do wondrous things to show his love of me;
King, ladies, lovers, all look on; the occasion is divine;
I'll drop my glove, to prove his love; great glory will be mine.

She dropped her glove, to prove his love, then looked at him and smiled;
He bowed, and in a moment leaped among the lions wild:
The leap was quick, return was quick, he has regained his place,
Then threw the glove, but not with love, right in the lady's face.
"By God!" said Francis, "rightly done!" and he rose from where he sat:
"No love," quoth he, "but vanity, sets love a task like that."

GEORGE GORDON, LORD BYRON
1788–1824

Prometheus[1]

1

Titan! to whose immortal eyes
  The sufferings of mortality,
  Seen in their sad reality,
Were not as things that gods despise;
What was thy pity's recompense?
A silent suffering, and intense;
The rock, the vulture, and the chain,
All that the proud can feel of pain,
The agony they do not show,
The suffocating sense of woe,
  Which speaks but in its loneliness,
And then is jealous lest the sky
Should have a listener, nor will sigh
  Until its voice is echoless.

---

[1] Prometheus (Greek, "forethought") was employed by Zeus to make men of mud and water, but pitying them Prometheus stole fire from heaven and gave it to them. Hence Prometheus (adj., Promethean) has come to mean a benefactor of mankind. He is celebrated by Aeschylus, Shelley, Bridges, and other writers. "Promethean heat," the divine spark, is used by Shakespeare in *Othello*, V. ii. 14, and "Promethean fire" in *Love's Labor's Lost*, IV. iii. 302–304:

2

Titan! to thee the strife was given
  Between the suffering and the will,
  Which torture where they cannot kill;
And the inexorable Heaven,
And the deaf tyranny of Fate,
The ruling principle of Hate,
Which for its pleasure doth create
The things it may annihilate,
Refused thee even the boon to die:
The wretched gift eternity
Was thine—and thou hast borne it well.
All that the Thunderer wrung from thee
Was but the menace which flung back
On him the torments of thy rack;
The fate thou didst so well foresee,
But would not to appease him tell;
And in thy Silence was his Sentence,
And in his Soul a vain repentance,
And evil dread so ill dissembled,
That in his hand the lightnings trembled.

3

Thy Godlike crime was to be kind,
  To render with thy precepts less
  The sum of human wretchedness,
And strengthen Man with his own mind;
But baffled as thou wert from high,
Still in thy patient energy,
In the endurance, and repulse
  Of thine impenetrable Spirit,
Which Earth and Heaven could not convulse,
  A mighty lesson we inherit:
Thou art a symbol and a sign
  To Mortals of their fate and force;
Like thee, Man is in part divine,
  A troubled stream from a pure source;
And Man in portions can foresee
His own funereal destiny;
His wretchedness, and his resistance,
And his sad unallied existence:
To which his Spirit may oppose
Itself—an equal to all woes,
  And a firm will, and a deep sense,
Which even in torture can descry
  Its own concenter'd recompense,
Triumphant where it dares defy,
And making Death a Victory.

From women's eyes this doctrine I derive:
They are the ground, the books, the academes,
From whence doth spring the true Promethean fire.

JOHN KEATS
1795–1821

On First Looking into Chapman's Homer

Much have I traveled in the realms of gold,[1]
And many goodly states and kingdoms seen;
Round many western islands[2] have I been
Which bards in fealty to Apollo[3] hold.
Oft of one wide expanse had I been told
That deep-browed Homer ruled as his demesne;
Yet did I never breathe its pure serene
Till I heard Chapman speak out loud and bold:
Then felt I like some watcher of the skies
When a new planet swims into his ken;
Or like stout Cortez[4] when with eagle eyes
He stared at the Pacific—and all his men
Looked at each other with a wild surmise—
Silent, upon a peak in Darien.[5]

[1] Great literature. [2] Modern European literature. [3] God of poetry. [4] Keats's error: it was Balboa. [5] Isthmus of Panama.

JOHN KEATS
1795–1821

Ode to a Nightingale

1

My heart aches, and a drowsy numbness pains
  My sense, as though of hemlock I had drunk,
Or emptied some dull opiate to the drains
  One minute past, and Lethe-wards had sunk:
'Tis not through envy of thy happy lot,
  But being too happy in thy happiness,—
    That thou, light-wingèd Dryad[1] of the trees,
      In some melodious plot
Of beechen green, and shadows numberless,
    Singest of summer in full-throated ease.

2

O, for a draught of vintage! that hath been
  Cooled a long age in the deep-delvèd earth,
Tasting of Flora[2] and the country-green,
  Dance, and Provençal[3] song, and sunburnt mirth!

[1] Tree nymph. [2] Goddess of flowers. [3] Provence, original home of the troubadours in southeastern France.

O for a beaker full of the warm South,
Full of the true, the blushful Hippocrene,[4]
With beaded bubbles winking at the brim,
And purple-stainèd mouth;
That I might drink, and leave the world unseen,
And with thee fade away into the forest dim:

3

Fade far away, dissolve, and quite forget
What thou among the leaves hast never known,
The weariness, the fever, and the fret
Here, where men sit and hear each other groan;
Where palsy shakes a few, sad, last gray hairs,
Where youth grows pale, and spectre-thin, and dies;
Where but to think is to be full of sorrow
And leaden-eyed despairs,
Where Beauty cannot keep her lustrous eyes
Or new Love pine at them beyond to-morrow.

4

Away! away! for I will fly to thee,
Not charioted by Bacchus and his pards,[5]
But on the viewless wings of Poesy,
Though the dull brain perplexes and retards:
Already with thee! tender is the night,
And haply the Queen-Moon is on her throne,
Clustered around by all her starry Fays;[6]
But here there is no light,
Save what from heaven is with the breezes blown
Through verdurous glooms and winding mossy ways.

5

I cannot see what flowers are at my feet,
Nor what soft incense hangs upon the boughs,
But, in embalmèd [7] darkness, guess each sweet
Wherewith the seasonable month endows
The grass, the thicket, and the fruit-tree wild;
White hawthorn, and the pastoral eglantine;
Fast-fading violets covered up in leaves;
And mid-May's eldest child,
The coming musk-rose, full of dewy wine,
The murmurous haunt of flies on summer eves.

6

Darkling I listen; and, for many a time
I have been half in love with easeful Death,
Called him soft names in many a musèd rhyme,
To take into the air my quiet breath;
Now more than ever seems it rich to die,
To cease upon the midnight with no pain,
While thou art pouring forth thy soul abroad
In such an ecstasy!
Still wouldst thou sing, and I have ears in vain—
To thy high requiem become a sod.

7

Thou wast not born for death, immortal Bird!
No hungry generations tread thee down;
The voice I hear this passing night was heard
In ancient days by emperor and clown:
Perhaps the self-same song that found a path
Through the sad heart of Ruth, when, sick for home,
She stood in tears amid the alien corn;[8]
The same that oft-times hath
Charmed magic casements, opening on the foam
Of perilous seas, in faery lands forlorn.

8

Forlorn! the very word is like a bell
To toll me back from thee to my sole self!
Adieu! the fancy cannot cheat so well
As she is famed to do, deceiving elf.
Adieu! adieu! thy plaintive anthem fades
Past the near meadows, over the still stream,
Up the hill-side; and now 'tis buried deep
In the next valley-glades:
Was it a vision, or a waking dream?
Fled is that music:—Do I wake or sleep?

[4] Drinking from this fountain supposedly induced poetic inspiration. [5] Leopards. [6] Fairies.
[7] Fragrant.

[8] Ll. 66–67: see *Ruth,* 2.

JOHN KEATS
1795–1821

Ode on a Grecian Urn

1

Thou still unravished bride of quietness,
Thou foster-child of silence and slow time,
Sylvan historian, who canst thus express
A flowery tale more sweetly than our rime:
What leaf-fringed legend haunts about thy shape
Of deities or mortals, or of both,
In Tempe[1] or the dales of Arcady? [2]
What men or gods are these? What maidens loth?
What mad pursuit? What struggles to escape?
What pipes and timbrels? [3] What wild ecstasy?

2

Heard melodies are sweet, but those unheard
Are sweeter; therefore, ye soft pipes, play on;
Not to the sensual[4] ear, but, more endeared,
Pipe to the spirit ditties of no tone:
Fair youth, beneath the trees, thou canst not leave
Thy song, nor ever can those trees be bare;
Bold Lover, never, never canst thou kiss,
Though winning near the goal—yet, do not grieve;
She cannot fade, though thou hast not thy bliss,
Forever wilt thou love, and she be fair!

3

Ah, happy, happy boughs! That cannot shed
Your leaves, nor ever bid the Spring adieu:
And, happy melodist, unwearièd,
Forever piping songs forever new;
More happy love! more happy, happy love!
Forever warm and still to be enjoy'd,
Forever panting, and forever young;
All breathing human passion far above,
That leaves a heart high-sorrowful and cloyed,
A burning forehead, and a parching tongue.

[1] Valley in Thessaly. [2] Central hill region in southern Greece, long associated in poetry with pastoral life. [3] Small drums or tambourines. [4] Sensuous, physical, actual.

4

Who are these coming to the sacrifice?
To what green altar, O mysterious priest,
Lead'st thou that heifer lowing at the skies,
And all her silken flanks with garlands drest?
What little town by river or sea shore,
Or mountain-built with peaceful citadel,
Is emptied of this folk, this pious morn?
And, little town, thy streets for evermore
Will silent be; and not a soul to tell
Why thou art desolate, can e'er return.

5

O Attic[5] shape! Fair Attitude! with brede[6]
Of marble men and maidens overwrought,
With forest branches and the trodden weed;
Thou, silent form, dost tease us out of thought
As doth eternity: Cold Pastoral! [7]
When old age shall this generation waste,
Thou shalt remain, in midst of other woe
Than ours, a friend to man, to whom thou sayst,
"Beauty is truth, truth beauty,"—that is all
Ye know on earth, and all ye need to know.

HENRY WADSWORTH
LONGFELLOW
1807–1882

Nature

As a fond mother, when the day is o'er,
Leads by the hand her little child to bed,
Half willing, half reluctant to be led,
And leave his broken playthings on the floor,
Still gazing at them through the open door,
Nor wholly reassured and comforted
By promises of others in their stead,
Which, though more splendid, may not please him more;
So Nature deals with us, and takes away
Our playthings one by one, and by the hand
Leads us to rest so gently, that we go
Scarce knowing if we wish to go or stay,
Being too full of sleep to understand
How far the unknown transcends the what we know.

[5] Of Attica, Athenian. [6] Embroidery, braid.
[7] Pastoral scene fired in cold marble or clay.

Comments

For another poet who relies on Nature for guidance see Bryant's "To a Waterfowl," p. 278. Longfellow and Bryant were contemporaries. For a poet who relies on a quite different, mystical nature see Whitman's "Song of Myself," p. 327.

ALFRED, LORD TENNYSON
1809–1892

Break, Break, Break

Break, break, break,
On thy cold gray stones, O Sea!
And I would that my tongue could utter
The thoughts that arise in me.

O well for the fisherman's boy,
That he shouts with his sister at play!
O well for the sailor lad,
That he sings in his boat on the bay!

And the stately ships go on
To their haven under the hill;
But O for the touch of a vanished hand,
And the sound of a voice that is still!

Break, break, break,
At the foot of thy crags, O Sea!
But the tender grace of a day that is dead
Will never come back to me.

ALFRED, LORD TENNYSON
1809–1892

Tears, Idle Tears

Tears, idle tears, I know not what they mean,
Tears from the depth of some divine despair
Rise in the heart, and gather to the eyes,
In looking on the happy Autumn-fields,
And thinking of the days that are no more.

Fresh as the first beam glittering on a sail,
That brings our friends up from the underworld,
Sad as the last which reddens over one
That sinks with all we love below the verge;
So sad, so fresh, the days that are no more.

Ah, sad and strange as in dark summer dawns
The earliest pipe of half-awakened birds
To dying ears, when unto dying eyes
The casement slowly grows a glimmering square;
So sad, so strange, the days that are no more.

Dear as remembered kisses after death,
And sweet as those by hopeless fancy feigned
On lips that are for others; deep as love,
Deep as first love, and wild with all regret;
O Death in Life, the days that are no more!

(From *The Princess*)

ALFRED, LORD TENNYSON
1809–1892

The Eagle

He clasps the crag with crooked hands;
Close to the sun in lonely lands,
Ringed with the azure world, he stands.

The wrinkled sea beneath him crawls;
He watches from his mountain walls,
And like a thunderbolt he falls.

ROBERT BROWNING
1812–1889

Porphyria's Lover

The rain set early in to-night,
The sullen wind was soon awake,
It tore the elm-tops down for spite,
And did its worst to vex the lake:
I listened with heart fit to break.
When glided in Porphyria; straight
She shut the cold out and the storm,
And kneeled and made the cheerless grate
Blaze up, and all the cottage warm;
Which done, she rose, and from her form
Withdrew the dripping cloak and shawl,
And laid her soiled gloves by, untied
Her hat and let the damp hair fall,
And, last, she sat down by my side
And called me. When no voice replied,
She put my arm about her waist,
And made her smooth white shoulder bare,

And all her yellow hair displaced,
  And, stopping, made my cheek lie there,
  And spread, o'er all, her yellow hair,
Murmuring how she loved me—she
  Too weak, for all her heart's endeavor,
To set its struggling passion free
  From pride, and vainer ties dissever,
  And give herself to me forever.
But passion sometimes would prevail,
  Nor could to-night's gay feast restrain
A sudden thought of one so pale
  For love of her, and all in vain:
  So, she was come through wind and rain.
Be sure I looked up at her eyes
  Happy and proud; at last I knew
Porphyria worshipped me; surprise
  Made my heart swell, and still it grew
  While I debated what to do.
That moment she was mine, mine, fair,
  Perfectly pure and good: I found
A thing to do, and all her hair
  In one long yellow string I wound
  Three times her little throat around,
And strangled her. No pain felt she;
  I am quite sure she felt no pain.
As a shut bud that holds a bee,
  I warily oped her lids: again
  Laughed the blue eyes without a stain.
And I untightened next the tress
  About her neck; her cheek once more
Blushed bright beneath my burning kiss:
  I propped her head up as before,
  Only, this time my shoulder bore
Her head, which droops upon it still:
  The smiling rosy little head,
So glad it has its utmost will,
  That all it scorned at once is fled,
  And I, its love, am gained instead!
Porphyria's love: she guessed not how
  Her darling one wish would be heard.
And thus we sit together now,
  And all night long we have not stirred,
  And yet God has not said a word!

WALT WHITMAN
1819–1892

One's-Self I Sing

One's-Self I sing, a simple separate person,
Yet utter the word Democratic, the word En-Masse.

Of physiology from top to toe I sing,
Not physiognomy alone nor brain alone is worthy for the Muse. I say the Form complete is worthier far,
The Female equally with the Male I sing.

Of Life immense in passion, pulse, and power,
Cheerful, for freest action form'd under the laws divine,
The Modern Man I sing.

WALT WHITMAN
1819–1892

From Song of Myself[1]

1

I celebrate myself, and sing myself,
And what I assume you shall assume,
For every atom belonging to me as good belongs to you.

I loafe and invite my soul,
I lean and loafe at my ease observing a spear of summer grass.

My tongue, every atom of my blood, form'd from this soil, this air,
Born here of parents born here from parents the same, and their parents the same,

[1] Whitman regards himself as the voice of the divine average in humanity as ll. 2–3 make clear. The phrase "O divine average!" is used in his poem "Starting from Paumanok."

I, now thirty-seven years old in perfect health begin,
Hoping to cease not till death.

Creeds and schools in abeyance,
Retiring back a while sufficed at what they are, but never forgotten,
I harbor for good or bad, I permit to speak at every hazard,
Nature without check with original energy.[2]

2

Houses and rooms are full of perfumes, the shelves are crowded with perfumes,
I breathe the fragrance myself and know it and like it,
The distillation would intoxicate me also, but I shall not let it.[3]

The atmosphere is not a perfume, it has no taste of the distillation, it is odorless,
It is for my mouth forever, I am in love with it,
I will go to the bank by the wood and become undisguised and naked,
I am mad for it to be in contact with me.
The smoke of my own breath,
Echoes, ripples, buzz'd whispers, love-root, silk-thread, crotch and vine,
My respiration and inspiration, the beating of my heart, the passing of blood and air through my lungs,
The sniff of green leaves and dry leaves, and of the shore and dark-color'd sea-rocks, and of hay in the barn,
The sound of the belch'd words of my voice loos'd to the eddies of the wind,
A few light kisses, a few embraces, a reaching around of arms,
The play of shine and shade on the trees as the supple boughs wag,
The delight alone or in the rush of the streets, or along the fields and hill-sides,
The feeling of health, the full-noon trill, the song of me rising from bed and meeting the sun.

Have you reckon'd a thousand acres much? Have you reckon'd the earth much?
Have you practis'd so long to learn to read?
Have you felt so proud to get at the meaning of poems?
Stop this day and night with me and you shall possess the origin of all poems,[4]
You shall possess the good of the earth and sun, (there are millions of suns left.)
You shall no longer take things at second or third hand, nor look through the eyes of the dead, nor feed on the spectres in books,
You shall not look through my eyes either, nor take things from me,
You shall listen to all sides and filter them from your self.

3

I have heard what the talkers were talking, the talk of the beginning and the end,
But I do not talk of the beginning or the end.

There was never any more inception than there is now,
Nor any more youth or age than there is now,

[2] Ll. 10–13 are cardinal in Whitman's thought. As John Burroughs (1837–1921), American naturalist, friend to Whitman, and author of *Whitman, A Study* (1896) was quick to see, these lines present his single theme: reliance on absolute nature. [3] Whitman rejects the artificial in order to embrace nature. See ll. 32–35. [4] Because he insists on reading nature, not men's interpretation of nature. There is, of course, a good deal of mysticism in Whitman's own interpretation of nature.

And will never be any more perfection than there is now,
Nor any more heaven or hell than there is now.

Urge and urge and urge,
Always the procreant urge of the world.
Out of the dimness opposite equals advance, always substance and increase, always sex,
Always a knit of identity, always distinction, always a breed of life.

To elaborate is no avail, learn'd and unlearn'd feel that it is so.

Sure as the most certain sure, plumb in the uprights, well entretied,[5] braced in the beams,
Stout as a horse, affectionate, haughty, electrical,
I and this mystery here we stand.

Clear and sweet is my soul, and clear and sweet is all that is not my soul.

Lack one lacks both, and the unseen is proved by the seen,
Till that becomes unseen and receives proof in its turn.

Showing the best and dividing it from the worst age vexes age,
Knowing the perfect fitness and equanimity of things, while they discuss I am silent, and go bathe and admire myself.

Welcome is every organ and attribute of me, and of any man hearty and clean,
Not an inch nor a particle of an inch is vile, and none shall be less familiar than the rest.

I am satisfied—I see, dance, laugh, sing;
As the hugging and loving bed-fellow sleeps at my side through the night, and withdraws at the peep of the day with stealthy tread,
Leaving the baskets cover'd with white towels swelling the house with their plenty,
Shall I postpone my acceptation and realization and scream at my eyes,
That they turn from gazing after and down the road,
And forthwith cipher and show me to a cent,
Exactly the value of one and exactly the value of two, and which is ahead?

WALT WHITMAN
1819–1892

Years of the Modern

This poem has been called Whitman's greatest vision, one that the United Nations hopes to make a reality.

Years of the modern! years of the unperform'd!
Your horizon rises, I see it parting away for more august dramas,

[5] A carpenter's vernacular meaning "crossed-braced" as between two joists or walls.

I see not America only, not only Liberty's nation but other nations preparing,
I see tremendous entrances and exists, new combinations, the solidarity of races,
I see that force advancing with irresistible power on the world's stage,
(Have the old forces, the old wars, played their parts? are the acts suitable to them closed?)
I see Freedom, completely arm'd and victorious and very haughty, with Law on one side and Peace on the other,
A stupendous trio all issuing forth against the idea of caste;
What historic denouements are these we so rapidly approach?
I see men marching and countermarching by swift millions,
I see the frontiers and boundaries of the old aristocracies broken,
I see the landmarks of European kings removed,
I see this day the People beginning their landmarks, (all others give way;)
Never were such sharp questions ask'd as this day,
Never was average man, his soul, more energetic, more like a God,
Lo, how he urges and urges, leaving the masses no rest!
His daring foot is on land and sea everywhere, he colonizes the Pacific, the archipelagoes,
With the steamship, the electric telegraph, the newspaper, the wholesale engines of war,
With these and the world-spreading factories he interlinks all geography, all lands;
What whispers are these O lands, running ahead of you, passing under the seas?
Are all nations communing? is there going to be but one heart to the globe?
Is humanity forming en-masse? for lo, tyrants tremble, crowns grow dim,
The earth, restive, confronts a new era, perhaps a general divine war,
No one knows what will happen next, such portents fill the days and nights;
Years prophetical! the space ahead as I walk, as I vainly try to pierce it, is full of phantoms,
Unborn deeds, things soon to be, project their shapes around me,
This incredible rush and heat, this strange ecstatic fever of dreams O years!
Your dreams O years, how they penetrate through me! (I know not whether I sleep or wake;)
The perform'd America and Europe grow dim, retiring in shadow behind me,
The unperform'd, more gigantic than ever, advance, advance upon me.

WALT WHITMAN
1819–1892

Native Moments

Native moments—when you come upon me—ah you are here now,
Give me now libidinous joys only,
Give me the drench of my passions, give me life coarse and rank,
To-day I go consort with Nature's darlings, to-night too,
I am for those who believe in loose delights, I share the midnight orgies of young men,
I dance with the dancers, and drink with the drinkers,
The echoes ring with our indecent calls, I pick out some low person for my dearest friend,
He shall be lawless, rude, illiterate, he shall be one condemn'd by others for deeds done,

I will play a part no longer, why should I exile myself from my companions?
O you shunn'd persons, I at least do not shun you,
I come forthwith in your midst, I will be your poet,
I will be more to you than to any of the rest.

EZRA POUND
1885–1972

A Pact

I make a pact with you, Walt Whitman—
I have detested you long enough.
I come to you as a grown child
Who has had a pig-headed father;
I am old enough now to make friends.
It was you that broke the new wood,
Now is a time for carving.
We have one sap and one root—
Let there be commerce between us.

MATTHEW ARNOLD
1822–1888

In Harmony with Nature
To a Preacher

"In harmony with Nature"? Restless fool,
Who with such heat dost preach what were to thee,
When true, the last impossibility—
To be like Nature strong, like Nature cool!
Know, man hath all which Nature hath, but more,
And in that *more* lie all his hopes of good.
Nature is cruel, man is sick of blood;
Nature is stubborn, man would fain adore;

Nature is fickle, man hath need of rest;
Nature forgives no debt, and fears no grave;
Man would be mild, and with safe conscience blest.

Man must begin, know this, where Nature ends;
Nature and man can never be fast friends.
Fool, if thou canst not pass her, rest her slave!

Comments

Arnold's poem is clearly part of the eternal controversy over man's relation to nature. Arnold's basic point of view, found in lines 5–8, has been widely quoted by the humanists against the naturalists. The controversy, as old as Greek thought, became especially virulent in England after the appearance of Darwin's *The Origin of Species* in 1859; and later (after World War I) the controversy became involved in the Neo-Humanist movement in the United States. For definitions of these points of view, see the *Encyclopaedia Britannica.*

MATTHEW ARNOLD
1822–1888

Dover Beach

The sea is calm tonight,
The tide is full, the moon lies fair
Upon the straits;—on the French coast, the light
Gleams and is gone; the cliffs of England stand,
Glimmering and vast, out in the tranquil bay.
Come to the window, sweet is the night air!
Only, from the long line of spray
Where the sea meets the moon-blanch'd land,
Listen! you hear the grating roar
Of pebbles which the waves draw back, and fling,
At their return, up the high strand,
Begin, and cease, and then again begin,
With tremulous cadence slow, and bring
The eternal note of sadness in.

Sophocles long ago
Heard it on the Aegean, and it brought
Into his mind the turbid ebb and flow
Of human misery; we
Find also in the sound a thought,
Hearing it by this distant northern sea.

The Sea of Faith
Was once, too, at the full, and round earth's shore
Lay like the folds of a bright girdle furl'd.

But now I only hear
Its melancholy, long, withdrawing roar,
Retreating, to the breath
Of the night-wind, down the vast edges drear
And naked shingles[1] of the world.

Ah, love, let us be true
To one another! for the world, which seems
To lie before us like a land of dreams,
So various, so beautiful, so new,
Hath really neither joy, nor love, nor light,
Nor certitude, nor peace, nor help for pain;
And we are here as on a darkling plain
Swept with confused alarms of struggle and flight,
Where ignorant armies clash by night.

[1] Pebbled beaches.

ANTHONY HECHT
1922–

The Dover Bitch
A Criticism of Life
(For Andrews Wanning)

So there stood Matthew Arnold and this girl
With the cliffs of England crumbling away behind them,
And he said to her, "Try to be true to me,
And I'll do the same for you, for things are bad
All over, etc., etc."
Well now, I knew this girl. It's true she had read
Sophocles in a fairly good translation
And caught that bitter allusion to the sea,
But all the time he was talking she had in mind
The notion of what his whiskers would feel like
On the back of her neck. She told me later on
That after a while she got to looking out
At the lights across the channel, and really felt sad,
Thinking of all the wine and enormous beds
And blandishments in French and the perfumes.
And then she got really angry. To have been brought
All the way down from London, and then be addressed
As a sort of mournful cosmic last resort
Is really tough on a girl, and she was pretty.
Anyway, she watched him pace the room
And finger his watch-chain and seem to sweat a bit,
And then she said one or two unprintable things.
But you mustn't judge her by that. What I mean to say is,
She's really all right. I still see her once in a while
And she always treats me right. We have a drink
And I give her a good time, and perhaps it's a year
Before I see her again, but there she is,
Running to fat, but dependable as they come.
And sometimes I bring her a bottle of *Nuit d'Amour*.[1]

[1] Night of Love, a perfume.

GEORGE MEREDITH
1828–1909

Tragic Memory

In our old shipwrecked days there was an hour,
When in the firelight steadily aglow,
Joined slackly, we beheld the red chasm grow
Among the clicking coals. Our library-bower
That eve was left to us: and hushed we sat
As lovers to whom Time is whispering.
From sudden-opened doors we heard them sing:
The nodding elders mixed good wine with chat.
Well knew we that Life's greatest treasure lay
With us, and of it was our talk. "Ah, yes!
Love dies!" I said: I never thought it less.
She yearned to me that sentence to unsay.
Then when the fire domed blackening, I found
Her cheek was salt against my kiss, and swift
Up the sharp scale of sobs her breast did lift:—
Now am I haunted by that taste! that sound!

EMILY DICKINSON
1830–1886

The Soul Selects Her Own Society

The Soul selects her own Society—
Then—shuts the Door—
To her divine Majority—
Present no more—

Unmoved—she notes the Chariots—
pausing—
At her low Gate—
Unmoved—an Emperor be kneeling
Upon her Mat—

I've known her—from an ample nation—
Choose One—
Then—close the Valves of her attention—
Like Stone—

EMILY DICKINSON
1830–1886

Some Keep the Sabbath Going to Church

Some keep the sabbath going to Church—
I keep it, staying at Home—
With a Bobolink for a Chorister—
And an Orchard, for a Dome—

Some keep the Sabbath in Surplice—
I just wear my Wings—
And instead of tolling the Bell, for Church,
Our little Sexton—sings.

God preaches, a noted Clergyman—
And the sermon is never long,
So instead of getting to Heaven, at last—
I'm going, all along.

EMILY DICKINSON
1830–1886

I Died for Beauty

I died for Beauty—but was scarce
Adjusted in the Tomb
When One who died for Truth, was lain
In an adjoining Room—

He questioned softly "Why I failed"?
"For Beauty", I replied—
"And I—for Truth—Themself are One—
We Bretheren, are", He said—

And so, as Kinsmen, met a Night—
We talked between the Rooms—
Until the Moss had reached our lips—
And covered up—our names—

EMILY DICKINSON
1830–1886

I Had Been Hungry, All the Years

I had been hungry, all the Years—
My Noon had Come—to dine—
I trembling drew the Table near—
And touched the Curious Wine—

'Twas this on Tables I had seen—
When turning, hungry, Home
I looked in Windows, for the Wealth
I could not hope—for Mine—

I did not know the ample Bread—
'Twas so unlike the Crumb
The Birds and I, had often shared
In Nature's—Dining Room—

The Plenty hurt me—'twas so new—
Myself felt ill—and odd—
As Berry—of a Mountain Bush—
Transplanted—to the Road—

Nor was I hungry—so I found
That Hunger—was a way
Of Persons outside Windows—
The Entering—takes away—

EMILY DICKINSON
1830–1886

He Preached upon "Breadth"

He preached upon "Breadth" till it argued him
narrow—
The Broad are too broad to define
And of "Truth" until it proclaimed him a Liar—
The Truth never flaunted a Sign—

Simplicity fled from his counterfeit presence
As Gold the Pyrites would shun—
What confusion would cover the innocent Jesus
To meet so enabled a Man!

EMILY DICKINSON
1830–1886

My Life Closed Twice Before Its Close

My life closed twice before its close;
It yet remains to see
If Immortality unveil
A third event to me,

So huge, so hopeless to conceive
As these that twice befel.
Parting is all we know of heaven,
And all we need of hell.

EMILY DICKINSON
1830–1886

Success Is Counted Sweetest

Success is counted sweetest
By those who ne'er succeed.
To comprehend a nectar
Requires sorest need.

Not one of all the purple Host
Who took the Flag today
Can tell the definition
So clear of Victory

As he defeated—dying—
On whose forbidden ear
The distant strains of triumph
Burst agonized and clear!

EMILY DICKINSON
1830–1886

These Are the Days When Birds Come Back

These are the days when Birds come back—
A very few—a Bird or two—
To take a backward look.

These are the days when skies resume
The old—old sophistries of June—
A blue and gold mistake.

Oh fraud that cannot cheat the Bee—
Almost thy plausibility
Induces my belief.

Till ranks of seeds their witness bear—
And softly thro' the altered air
Hurries a timid leaf.

Oh Sacrament of summer days,
Oh Last Communion in the Haze—
Permit a child to join.

Thy sacred emblems to partake—
Thy consecrated bread to take
And thine immortal wine!

EMILY DICKINSON
1830–1886

Much Madness Is Divinest Sense

Much Madness is divinest Sense—
To a discerning Eye—
Much Sense—the starkest Madness—
'Tis the Majority
In this, as All, prevail—
Assent—and you are sane—
Demur—you're straightway dangerous—
And handled with a Chain—

EMILY DICKINSON
1830–1886

This World Is Not Conclusion

This World is not Conclusion.
A Species stands beyond—
Invisible, as Music—
But positive, as Sound—
It beckons, and it baffles—
Philosophy—dont know—
And through a Riddle, at the last—
Sagacity, must go—
To guess it, puzzles scholars—
To gain it, Men have borne
Contempt of Generations

And Crucifixion, shown—
Faith slips—and laughs, and rallies—
Blushes, if any see—
Plucks at a twig of Evidence—
And asks a Vane, the way—
Much Gesture, from the Pulpit—
Strong Hallelujahs roll—
Narcotics cannot still the Tooth
That nibbles at the soul—

EMILY DICKINSON
1830–1886

I Could Not Prove the Years Had Feet

I could not prove the Years had feet—
Yet confident they run
Am I, from symptoms that are past
And Series that are done—

I find my feet have further Goals—
I smile upon the Aims
That felt so ample—Yesterday—
Today's—have vaster claims—

I do not doubt the self I was
Was competent to me—
But something awkward in the fit—
Proves that—outgrown—I see—

EMILY DICKINSON
1830–1886

This Is My Letter to the World

This is my letter to the World
That never wrote to Me—
The simple News that Nature told—
With tender Majesty

Her Message is committed
To Hands I cannot see—
For love of Her—Sweet—countrymen—
Judge tenderly—of Me

THOMAS HARDY
1840–1928

The Last Chrysanthemum

Why should this flower delay so long
To show its tremulous plumes?
Now is the time of plaintive robin-song,
When flowers are in their tombs.

Through the slow summer, when the sun
Called to each frond and whorl
That all he could for flowers was being done,
Why did it not uncurl?

It must have felt that fervid call
Although it took no heed,
Waking but now, when leaves like corpses fall,
And saps all retrocede.

Too late its beauty, lonely thing,
The season's shine is spent,
Nothing remains for it but shivering
In tempests turbulent.

Had it a reason for delay,
Dreaming in witlessness
That for a bloom so delicately gay
Winter would stay its stress?

—I talk as if the thing were born
With sense to work its mind;
Yet it is but one mask of many worn
By the Great Face behind.

THOMAS HARDY
1840–1928

The Man He Killed

"Had he and I but met
By some old ancient inn,
We should have sat us down to wet
Right many a nipperkin!

"But ranged as infantry,
And staring face to face,
I shot at him as he at me,
And killed him in his place.

"I shot him dead because—
Because he was my foe,
Just so: my foe of course he was;
That's clear enough; although

"He thought he'd 'list, perhaps,
Off-hand like—just as I—
Was out of work—had sold his traps—
No other reason why.

"Yes; quaint and curious war is!
You shoot a fellow down
You'd treat if met where any bar is,
Or help to half-a-crown."

GERARD MANLEY HOPKINS
1844–1889

The Windhover:[1]
To Christ Our Lord

Definitions of terms in the poem can be helpful, but the exact shade of meaning of each basic term depends more than usual on the complete, highly figurative context of the entire poem.

I caught this morning morning's minion,[2] king-
dom of daylight's dauphin,[3] dapple-dawn-drawn Falcon, in his riding
Of the rolling level underneath him steady air, and striding
High there, how he rung upon the rein of a wimpling[4] wing
In his ecstasy! then off, off forth on swing,
As a skate's heel sweeps smooth on a bow-bend: the hurl and gliding
Rebuffed the big wind. My heart in hiding
Stirred for a bird,—the achieve of, the mastery of the thing!

Brute beauty and valour and act, oh, air, pride, plume, here
Buckle![5] AND the fire that breaks from thee then, a billion
Times told lovelier, more dangerous, O my chevalier![6]

No wonder of it: shéer plód makes plough down sillion[7]
Shine, and blue-bleak embers, ah my dear,
Fall, gall themselves, and gash[8] gold-vermilion.

[1] A member of the falcon family popularly so named because of its habit of hovering in the air over one spot. Known in England as a kestrel; in the United States as a sparrow hawk. [2] One highly favored, a darling. [3] Literally heir to the throne; figuratively Christ, Son of God. [4] Turning or twisting on the wing. [5] Interpreted variously. Probably buckle together, to join together the heroic qualities in l. 9. [6] Literally knight; figuratively Christ. [7] A plough's furrow; the ridge between the furrows. [8] Probably Christ's blood.

OSCAR WILDE
1856–1900

The Harlot's House

We caught the tread of dancing feet,
We loitered down the moonlit street,
And stopped beneath the harlot's house.

Inside, above the din and fray,
We heard the loud musicians play
The "Treues Liebes Herz"[1] of Strauss.

Like strange mechanical grotesques,
Making fantastic arabesques,
The shadows raced across the blind.

[1] "Dear True Heart."

We watched the ghostly dancers spin
To sound of horn and violin,
Like black leaves wheeling in the wind.

Like wire-pulled automatons,
Slim silhouetted skeletons
Went sidling through the slow quadrille.

They took each other by the hand,
And danced a stately saraband;
Their laughter echoed thin and shrill.

Sometimes a clockwork puppet pressed
A phantom lover to her breast,
Sometimes they seemed to try to sing.

Sometimes a horrible marionette
Came out, and smoked its cigarette
Upon the steps like a live thing.

Then, turning to my love, I said,
"The dead are dancing with the dead,
The dust is whirling with the dust."

But she—she heard the violin,
And left my side and entered in:
Love passed into the house of lust.

Then suddenly the tune went false,
The dancers wearied of the waltz,
The shadows ceased to wheel and whirl.

And down the long and silent street,
The dawn, with silver-sandalled feet,
Crept like a frightened girl.

CLAUDE McKAY
1890–1948
Harlem Dancer

Applauding youths laughed with young prostitutes
And watched her perfect, half-clothed body sway;
Her voice was like the sound of blended flutes
Blown by black players on a picnic day.
She sang and danced on gracefully and calm,
The light gauze hanging loose about her form;
To me she seemed a proudly-swaying palm
Grown lovelier for passing through a storm.
Upon her swarthy neck black shiny curls
Luxuriant fell; and tossing coins in praise,
The wine-flushed, bold-eyed boys, and even the girls,
Devoured her shape with eager, passionate gaze;
But looking at her falsely-smiling face,
I knew her self was not in that strange place.

A. E. HOUSMAN
1859–1936
The True Lover

The lad came to the door at night,
When lovers crown their vows,
And whistled soft and out of sight
In shadow of the boughs.

"I shall not vex you with my face
Henceforth, my love, for aye;
So take me in your arms a space
Before the east is grey.

"When I from hence away am past
I shall not find a bride,
And you shall be the first and last
I ever lay beside."

She heard and went and knew not why;
Her heart to his she laid;
Light was the air beneath the sky
But dark under the shade.

"Oh do you breathe, lad, that your breast
Seems not to rise and fall,
And here upon my bosom prest
There beats no heart at all?"

"Oh loud, my girl, it once would knock,
You should have felt it then;
But since for you I stopped the clock
It never goes again."

"Oh lad, what is it, lad, that drips
Wet from your neck on mine?
What is it falling on my lips,
My lad, that tastes of brine?"

"Oh like enough 'tis blood, my dear,
For when the knife has slit
The throat across from ear to ear
'Twill bleed because of it."

Under the stars the air was light
But dark below the boughs,
The still air of the speechless night,
When lovers crown their vows.

GEORGE SANTAYANA[1]
1863–1952

The Poet's Testament

I give back to the earth what the earth gave,
All to the furrow, nothing to the grave,
The candle's out, the spirit's vigil spent;
Sight may not follow where the vision went.

I leave you but the sound of many a word
In mocking echoes haply overheard,
I sang to heaven. My exile made me free,
From world to world, from all worlds carried me.

Spared by the Furies, for the Fates were kind,
I paced the pillared cloisters of the mind;
All times my present, everywhere my place,
Nor fear, nor hope, nor envy saw my face.

Blow what winds would, the ancient truth was mine,
And friendship mellowed in the flush of wine,
And heavenly laughter, shaking from its wings
Atoms of light and tears for mortal things.

To trembling harmonies of field and cloud,
Of flesh and spirit was my worship vowed.
Let form, let music, let all-quickening air
Fulfil in beauty my imperfect prayer.

WILLIAM BUTLER YEATS
1865–1939

The Wild Swans at Coole

The trees in their autumn beauty,
The woodland paths are dry,
Under the October twilight the water
Mirrors a still sky;
Upon the brimming water among the stones
Are nine-and-fifty swans.

[1] See pp. 313–314 for three poems by Michelangelo translated into English by Santayana.

The nineteenth autumn has come upon me
Since I first made my count;
I saw, before I had well finished,
All suddenly mount
And scatter wheeling in great broken rings
Upon their clamorous wings.

I have looked upon those brilliant creatures,
And now my heart is sore.
All's changed since I, hearing at twilight,
The first time on this shore,
The bell-beat of their wings above my head,
Trod with a lighter tread.

Unwearied still, lover by lover,
They paddle in the cold
Companionable streams or climb the air;
Their hearts have not grown old;
Passion or conquest, wander where they will,
Attend upon them still.

But now they drift on the still water
Mysterious, beautiful;
Among what rushes will they build,
By what lake's edge or pool
Delight men's eyes when I awake some day
To find they have flown away?

WILLIAM BUTLER YEATS
1865–1939

The Second Coming

Turning and turning in the widening gyre[1]
The falcon cannot hear the falconer;
Things fall apart; the centre cannot hold;
Mere anarchy is loosed upon the world,
The blood-dimmed tide is loosed, and everywhere
The ceremony of innocence is drowned;
The best lack all conviction, while the worst
Are full of passionate intensity.

Surely some revelation is at hand;
Surely the Second Coming[2] is at hand.
The Second Coming! Hardly are those words out

[1] Circular or spiral movement. [2] Related to the second coming of Christ is Yeats's conviction that the approaching end of an historical cycle of 2000 years would bring a new age.

When a vast image out of *Spiritus Mundi*[3]
Troubles my sight: somewhere in sands of the desert
A shape with lion body and the head of a man,
A gaze blank and pitless as the sun,
Is moving its slow thighs, while all about it
Reel shadows of the indignant desert birds.
The darkness drops again; but now I know
That twenty centuries of stony sleep
Were vexed to nightmare by a rocking cradle,
And what rough beast, its hour come round at last,
Slouches towards Bethlehem to be born?

EDWIN ARLINGTON ROBINSON 1869–1935

Mr. Flood's Party

Old Eben Flood,[1] climbing alone one night
Over the hill between the town below
And the forsaken upland hermitage
That held as much as he should ever know
On earth again of home, paused warily.
The road was his with not a native near;
And Eben, having leisure, said aloud,
For no man else in Tilbury Town[2] to hear:
"Well, Mr. Flood, we have the harvest moon
Again, and we may not have many more;
The bird is on the wing, the poet says,
And you and I have said it here before.
Drink to the bird." He raised up to the light
The jug that he had gone so far to fill,
And answered huskily: "Well, Mr. Flood,
Since you propose it, I believe I will."

Alone, as if enduring to the end
A valiant armor of scarred hopes outworn,
He stood there in the middle of the road
Like Roland's ghost winding a silent horn.[3]

[3] Literally world spirit. For Yeats it means the "general mind," or our collective consciousness penetrating the future.

[1] Ebb and flood, the passing of time. [2] Though this happens to be Robinson's name for Gardiner, Maine where he was reared, the name is of no consequence. [3] Hero of the tales in the Charlemagne cycle; the defender of the Christians against the Saracens. The implication in ll. 19–20 is that Eben, like Roland, sounds his horn only to find his friends dead.

Below him, in the town among the trees,
Where friends of other days had honored him,
A phantom salutation of the dead
Rang thinly till old Eben's eyes were dim.

Then, as a mother lays her sleeping child
Down tenderly, fearing it may awake,
He set the jug down slowly at his feet
With trembling care, knowing that most things break;
And only when assured that on firm earth
It stood, as the uncertain lives of men
Assuredly did not, he paced away,
And with his hand extended paused again:

"Well, Mr. Flood, we have not met like this
In a long time; and many a change has come
To both of us, I fear, since last it was
We had a drop together. Welcome home!"
Convivially returning with himself,
Again he raised the jug up to the light;
And with an acquiescent quaver said:
"Well, Mr. Flood, if you insist, I might.

"Only a very little, Mr. Flood—
For auld lang syne. No more, sir; that will do."
So, for the time, apparently it did,
And Eben evidently thought so too;
For soon amid the silver loneliness
Of night he lifted up his voice and sang,
Secure, with only two moons listening
Until the whole harmonious landscape rang—

"For auld lang syne." The weary throat gave out,
The last word wavered, and the song was done.
He raised again the jug regretfully
And shook his head, and was again alone.
There was not much that was ahead of him,
And there was nothing in the town below—
Where strangers would have shut the many doors
That many friends had opened long ago.

Comments

Robinson has written a number of psychological portraits, including "Miniver Cheevy" (p. 284). For a perceptive analysis of "Mr. Flood's Party" see Wallace L. Anderson's essay (p. 695); for an excellent introduction to Robinson's poems see Anderson's *Edwin Arlington*

Robinson: A Critical Introduction, Boston: Houghton Mifflin Co., 1967, from which his essay has been taken.

RALPH HODGSON
1871–1962

Eve

Eve, with her basket, was
Deep in the bells and grass,
Wading in bells and grass
Up to the knees,
Picking a dish of sweet
Berries and plums to eat,
Down in the bells and grass
Under the trees.

Mute as a mouse in a
Corner the cobra lay,
Curled round a bough of the
Cinnamon tall. . . .
Now to get even and
Humble proud Heaven and
Now was the moment or
Never at all.

'Eva!' Each syllable
Light as a flower fell,
'Eva!' he whispered the
Wondering maid,
Soft as a bubble sung
Out of a linnet's lung,
Soft and most silverly
'Eva!' he said.

Picture that orchard sprite,
Eve, with her body white,
Supple and smooth to her
Slim finger tips,
Wondering, listening,
Listening, wondering,
Eve with a berry
Half-way to her lips.

Oh had our simple Eve
Seen through the make-believe!
Had she but known the
Pretender he was!
Out of the boughs he came,
Whispering still her name,
Tumbling in twenty rings
Into the grass.

Here was the strangest pair
In the world anywhere,
Eve in the bells and grass
Kneeling, and he
Telling his story low. . . .
Singing birds saw them go
Down the dark path to
The Blasphemous Tree.

Oh what a clatter when
Titmouse and Jenny Wren
Saw him successful and
Taking his leave!
How the birds rated him,
How they all hated him!
How they all pitied
Poor motherless Eve!

Picture her crying
Outside in the lane,
Eve, with no dish of sweet
Berries and plums to eat,
Haunting the gate of the
Orchard in vain. . . .
Picture the lewd delight
Under the hill to-night—
'Eva!' the toast goes round,
'Eva!' again.

TED HUGHES
1930–

Theology

No, the serpent did not
Seduce Eve to the apple.
All that's simply
Corruption of the facts.

Adam ate the apple.
Eve ate Adam.
The serpent ate Eve.
This is the dark intestine.

The serpent, meanwhile,
Sleeps his meal off in Paradise—
Smiling to hear
God's querulous calling.

ROBERT FROST
1874–1963

The Strong Are Saying Nothing

The soil now gets a rumpling soft and damp,
And small regard to the future of any weed.
The final flat of the hoe's approval stamp
Is reserved for the bed of a few selected seed.

There is seldom more than a man to a harrowed piece.
Men work alone, their lots plowed far apart,
One stringing a chain of seed in an open crease,
And another stumbling after a halting cart.

To the fresh and black of the squares of early mold
The leafless bloom of a plum is fresh and white;
Though there's more than a doubt if the weather is not too cold
For the bees to come and serve its beauty aright.

Wind goes from farm to farm in wave on wave,
But carries no cry of what is hoped to be.
There may be little or much beyond the grave,
But the strong are saying nothing until they see.

ROBERT FROST
1874–1963

Acquainted with the Night

I have been one acquainted with the night.
I have walked out in rain—and back in rain.
I have outwalked the furthest city light.

I have looked down the saddest city lane.
I have passed by the watchman on his beat
And dropped my eyes, unwilling to explain.

I have stood still and stopped the sound of feet
When far away an interrupted cry
Came over houses from another street,

But not to call me back or say good-by;
And further still at an unearthly height
One luminary clock against the sky

Proclaimed the time was neither wrong nor right.
I have been one acquainted with the night.

WALLACE STEVENS
1879–1955

Peter Quince[1] at the Clavier

I

Just as my fingers on these keys
Make music, so the selfsame sounds
On my spirit make a music, too.

Music is feeling, then, not sound;
And thus it is that what I feel,
Here in this room, desiring you,

Thinking of your blue-shadowed silk,
Is music. It is like the strain
Waked in the elders by Susanna.[2]

Of a green evening, clear and warm,
She bathed in her still garden, while
The red-eyed elders watching, felt

The basses of their beings throb
In witching chords, and their thin blood[3]
Pulse pizzicati[4] of Hosanna.

II

In the green water, clear and warm,
Susanna lay.
She searched
The touch of springs,
And found
Concealed imaginings.
She sighed,
For so much melody.

Upon the bank, she stood
In the cool
Of spent emotions.

[1] Carpenter and poet of sorts in Shakespeare's *A Midsummer Night's Dream.* [2] The story of Susanna and the Elders is conveniently found in *The Bible Designed to Be Read as Living Literature,* New York: Simon and Schuster (1936), pp. 858–862. As a part of the Apocrypha the story is rarely included in Protestant Bibles. [3] A reference to the advanced age of the Elders. [4] Creating sound by plucking instead of bowing the instrument.

She felt, among the leaves,
The dew
Of old devotions.

She walked upon the grass,
Still quivering.
The winds were like her maids,
On timid feet,
Fetching her woven scarves,
Yet wavering.

A breath upon her hand
Muted the night.
She turned—
A cymbal crashed,
And roaring horns.

III

Soon, with a noise like tambourines,
Came her attendant Byzantines.

They wondered why Susanna cried
Against the elders by her side;

And as they whispered, the refrain
Was like a willow swept by rain.

Anon, their lamps' uplifted flame
Revealed Susanna and her shame.

And then, the simpering Byzantines
Fled, with a noise like tambourines.

IV

Beauty is momentary in the mind—[5]
The fitful tracing of a portal;
But in the flesh it is immortal.
The body dies; the body's beauty lives.
So evenings die, in their green going,
A wave, interminably flowing.
So gardens die, their meek breath scenting
The cowl of winter, done repenting.
So maidens die, to the auroral
Celebration of a maiden's choral.
Susanna's music touched the bawdy strings
Of those white elders; but, escaping,
Left only Death's ironic scraping.
Now, in its immortality, it plays
On the clear viol of her memory,
And makes a constant sacrament of praise.

[5] Ll. 51–58: Stevens's theory of beauty. See his "Sunday Morning," l. 63: "Death is the mother of beauty" (p. 389).

D. H. LAWRENCE
1885–1930

Piano

Softly, in the dusk, a woman is singing to me;
Taking me back down the vista of years, till I see
A child sitting under the piano, in the boom of the tingling strings
And pressing the small, poised feet of a mother who smiles as she sings.

In spite of myself the insidious mastery of song
Betrays me back, till the heart of me weeps to belong
To the old Sunday evenings at home, with winter outside
And hymns in the cozy parlor, the tinkling piano our guide.

So now it is vain for the singer to burst into clamor
With the great black piano appassionato.[1] The glamor
Of childish days is upon me, my manhood is cast
Down in the flood of remembrance, I weep like a child for the past.

[1] Impassioned, deeply emotional.

EZRA POUND
1885–1972

Ballad of the Goodly Fere[1]

Simon Zelotes[2] speaketh it somewhile after the Crucifixion.

[1]

Ha' we lost the goodliest fere o' all
For the priests and the gallows tree?
Aye lover he was of brawny men,
O' ships and the open sea.

[1] *Fere:* literally a traveling comrade. [2] A disciple of Christ (not to be confused with Simon Peter; see *Acts,* 1:13) and one of the zealots (Zelotes) who bitterly opposed the Roman domination of Palestine. In having us see Christ through Simon's eyes, Pound provides a rather unconventional Christ who is nevertheless surprisingly supported by the scriptures.

[2]
When they came wi' a host to take Our Man
His smile was good to see;
"First let these go!" quo' our Goodly Fere,
"Or I'll see ye damned," says he.

[3]
Aye, he sent us out through the crossed high spears,
And the scorn of his laugh rang free;
"Why took ye not me when I walked about
Alone in the town?" says he.[3]

[4]
Oh, we drunk his "Hale" in the good red wine
When we last made company;
No capon priest was the Goodly Fere
But a man o' men was he.[4]

[5]
I ha' seen him drive a hundred men
Wi' a bundle o' cords swung free,
That they took the high and holy house
For their pawn and treasury.[5]

[6]
They'll no' get him a' in a book I think,
Though they write it cunningly;
No mouse of the scrolls[6] was the Goodly Fere
But aye loved the open sea.

[7]
If they think they ha' snared our Goodly Fere
They are fools to the last degree.
"I'll go to the feast," quo' our Goodly Fere,
"Though I go to the gallows tree." [7]

[8] [8]
"Ye ha' seen me heal the lame and blind,
And wake the dead," says he;
"Ye shall see one thing to master all:
'Tis how a brave man dies on the tree."

[9]
A son of God was the Goodly Fere
That bade us his brothers be.
I ha' seen him cow a thousand men.
I have seen him upon the tree.[9]

[10]
He cried no cry when they drave the nails
And the blood gushed hot and free;
The hounds of the crimson sky gave tongue
But never a cry cried he.[10]

[11]
I ha' seen him cow a thousand men
On the hills o' Galilee;
They whined as he walked out calm between,
Wi' his eyes like the grey o' the sea,

[12]
Like the sea that brooks no voyaging
With the winds unleashed and free,
Like the sea that he cowed at Genseret
Wi' twey words spoke' suddently.[11]

[13]
A master of men was the Goodly Fere,
A mate of the wind and sea;
If they think they ha' slain our Goodly Fere
They are fools eternally.

[14]
I ha' seen him eat o' the honey-comb[12]
Sin' they nailed him to the tree.

[3] Christ challenges and needles his captors; see *Matthew*, 26:55. [4] L. 16: see *Matthew*, 11:19 for confirmation. "No capon priest," rather, a full-blooded male. [5] The cleansing of the Temple: see *John*, 2:13–17. [6] No creeper through scriptures; instead a man who fought for his principles. [7] Christ was not tricked; he entered Jerusalem knowing what would happen. See *Matthew*, 16:21–23; 20:17–19. [8] A continuation of the prophecy in *Matthew* above. See also *Luke*, 18:35–43.

[9] Stanzas 9 and 11: reference to the Nazareth incident where Christ's fellow Galileans "filled with wrath . . . rose up, and thrust him out of the city, and led him unto the brow of the hill . . . that they might cast him down headlong. But he, passing through the midst of them, went his own way." *Luke*, 4:28–30. [10] See *Matthew*, 27:45, 51; *Luke*, 23:44–45. [11] Genseret (Gennesaret in *Luke*, 5:1), another name for Galilee. The words Christ spoke: "Peace, be still," as in *Mark*, 4:39. [12] Honey-comb: see *Luke*, 24:42–49 which begins: "And they gave him a piece of a broiled fish, and of a honeycomb."

EZRA POUND
1885–1972

Envoi (1919)

Go, dumb-born book,
Tell her that sang me once that song of Lawes;[1]
Hadst thou but song
As thou hast subjects known,
Then were there cause in thee that should condone
Even my faults that heavy upon me lie,
And build her glories their longevity.

Tell her that sheds
Such treasure in the air,
Recking[2] naught else but that her graces give
Life to the moment,
I would bid them live
As roses might, in magic amber laid,[3]
Red overwrought with orange and all made
One substance and one colour
Braving time.

Tell her that goes
With song upon her lips
But sings not out the song, nor knows
The maker of it, some other mouth,
May be as fair as hers,
Might, in new ages, gain her worshippers,
When our two dusts with Waller's[4] shall be laid,
Siftings on siftings in oblivion,
Till change hath broken down
All things save Beauty alone.

ROBINSON JEFFERS
1887–1962

Science[1]

Man, introverted man, having crossed
In passage and but a little with the nature of things this latter century
Has begot giants; but being taken up
Like a maniac with self-love and inward conflicts cannot manage his hybrids.
Being used to deal with edgeless dreams,
Now he's bred knives on nature turns them also inward: they have thirsty points though.
His mind forebodes his own destruction;
Actaeon[2] who saw the goddess naked among leaves and his hounds tore him.
A little knowledge, a pebble from the shingle,[3]
A drop from the oceans: who would have dreamed this infinitely little too much?[4]

ROBINSON JEFFERS
1887–1962

The Bloody Sire[1]

It is not bad. Let them play.
Let the guns bark and the bombing-plane
Speak his prodigious blasphemies.
It is not bad, it is high time,
Stark violence is still the sire of all the world's values.

What but the wolf's tooth whittled so fine
The fleet limbs of the antelope?
What but fear winged the birds, and hunger
Jeweled with such eyes the great goshawk's head?
Violence has been the sire of all the world's values.

Who would remember Helen's[2] face
Lacking the terrible halo of spears?

[1] Henry Lawes (1596–1662), composer who set to music Edmund Waller's "Song" (Go, lovely Rose"), p. 277, songs by Shakespeare, and Milton's *Comus*. [2] Caring for. [3] To withstand time. [4] See footnote 1.

[1] Published years before the hydrogen bomb existed, this poem can now be read as a tragic prophecy. [2] Having seen Diana bathing while he was hunting, Actaeon was changed by her into a stag and his hounds tore him. [3] Seashore. [4] A century earlier Hawthorne observed, ". . . and even heroism—so deadly a gripe is Science laying on our noble possibilities—will become a matter of very minor importance." ("Chiefly About War Matters," *The Writings of Nathaniel Hawthorne*, Boston and New York, 1898, Riverside Edition, XII, 336.)

[1] This poem, surely a contemporary comment on World War II, troubled Jeffers because he thinks poetry "is the worse for being timely"; but today, over thirty-five years later, the poem threatens to become timeless. For a later companion poem, see Price, "Centennial of Shiloh," p. 291. [2] Undoubtedly a reference to Helen of Troy, wife of Menelaus, whose elopement with Paris brought about the siege and destruction of Troy.

Who formed Christ but Herod[3] and Caesar,
The cruel and bloody victories of Caesar?
Violence, the bloody sire of all the world's values.

Never weep, let them play,
Old violence is not too old to beget new values.

T. S. ELIOT
1888–1965
The Hollow Men

Mistah Kurtz—he dead.[1]
A penny for the Old Guy[2]

I

We are the hollow men
We are the stuffed men
Leaning together
Headpiece filled with straw. Alas!
Our dried voices, when
We whisper together
Are quiet and meaningless
As wind in dry grass
Or rats' feet over broken glass
In our dry cellar

Shape without form, shade without colour,
Paralysed force, gesture without motion;

Those who have crossed
With direct eyes, to death's other Kingdom
Remember us—if at all—not as lost
Violent souls, but only
As the hollow men
The stuffed men.

II

Eyes I dare not meet in dreams
In death's dream kingdom
These do not appear:
There, the eyes are
Sunlight on a broken column
There, is a tree swinging
And voices are
In the wind's singing
More distant and more solemn
Than a fading star.

Let me be no nearer
In death's dream kingdom
Let me also wear
Such deliberate disguises
Rat's coat, crowskin, crossed staves
In a field
Behaving as the wind behaves
No nearer—

Not that final meeting
In the twilight kingdom

III

This is the dead land
This is cactus land
Here the stone images
Are raised, here they receive
The supplication of a dead man's hand
Under the twinkle of a fading star.

Is it like this
In death's other kingdom
Waking alone
At the hour when we are
Trembling with tenderness
Lips that would kiss
Form prayers to broken stone.

IV

The eyes are not here
There are no eyes here

[3] Herod the Great (73?–4 B.C.) who destroyed the babes of Bethlehem (*Matthew*, 2:16).

[1] The epigraph, taken from Joseph Conrad's novella "Heart of Darkness," p. 170, is an announcement of the death of the character Kurtz. He had gone into the Congo to gather ivory for his fortune, taking with him "moral ideas of some sort" to serve him as an "emissary of pity, and science, and progress." But in his eagerness to gather huge quantities of ivory, he allowed the natives to make a god of him and yielded also to other temptations including presiding "at certain midnight dances ending with unspeakable rites" that brought his degeneration and death. Before his death, however, Kurtz saw the "horror" of evil, affirmed it, and gained a "moral victory." The epigraph understood in the context of Eliot's poem suggests that we in our time, unlike Kurtz, will not cross "with direct eyes, to death's other Kingdom" because we hardly recognize the presence of the evil that engulfs us. [2] Guy Fawkes (1570–1606) was involved in the Gunpowder Plot to blow up the English Houses of Parliament, November 5, 1605; he was arrested, tried, and executed. November 5 is still celebrated in England by burning Fawkes in effigy while the children beg "a penny for the Old Guy."

In this valley of dying stars
In this hollow valley
This broken jaw of our lost kingdoms

In this last of meeting places
We grope together
And avoid speech
Gathered on this beach of the tumid river

Sightless, unless
The eyes reappear
As the perpetual star
Multifoliate rose
Of death's twilight kingdom
The hope only
Of empty men.

V

Here we go round the prickly pear
Prickly pear prickly pear
Here we go round the prickly pear
At five o'clock in the morning.

Between the idea
And the reality
Between the motion
And the act
Falls the Shadow
For Thine is the Kingdom

Between the conception
And the creation
Between the emotion
And the response
Falls the Shadow
Life is very long

Between the desire
And the spasm
Between the potency
And the existence
Between the essence
And the descent
Falls the Shadow
For Thine is the Kingdom

For Thine is
Life is
For Thine is the

This is the way the world ends
This is the way the world ends
This is the way the world ends
Not with a bang but a whimper.

T. S. ELIOT
1888–1965

The Cultivation of Christmas[1] Trees

This poem, published rather late in Eliot's life in 1954, thirty-seven years after "The Love Song of J. Alfred Prufrock" (p. 390) and twenty-five years after "The Hollow Men" (p. 345), states in a positive way Eliot's religious beliefs which are stated indirectly and ironically in the two earlier poems. The poem should be better known by those members of the younger generation who now search for spiritual stability to replace an ever-fleeting materialism.

There are several attitudes towards Christmas,
Some of which we may disregard:
The social, the torpid, the patently commercial,[2]
The rowdy (the pubs being open till midnight),
And the childish—which is not that of the child[3]
For whom the candle is a star, and the gilded angel
Spreading its wings at the summit of the tree
Is not only a decoration, but an angel.
The child wonders at the Christmas Tree:
Let him continue in the spirit of wonder
At the Feast[4] as an event not accepted as a pretext;
So that the glittering rapture, the amazement
Of the first-remembered Christmas Tree,

[1] Christmas: Christ's mass, a celebration of the Eucharist (Gr. grateful, and akin to Gr. *chairein,* to rejoice), a grateful rejoicing for the birth of Christ. Hence the title can be read as the cultivation (annual renewal) of the rejoicing within ourselves, the tree being a symbol of the event. [2] Patently commercial: Openly, unabashedly materialistic. In "A Masque of Reason" (p. 376, ll. 5–8) Frost uses the modern Christmas tree as a fraudulent symbol of the true, original Christmas season. [3] L. 5: "At the same time came the disciples unto Jesus, saying, Who is the greatest in the kingdom of heaven? And Jesus called a little child unto him, and set him in the midst of them. And said, Verily I say unto you, Except ye be converted, and become as little children, ye shall not enter into the kingdom of heaven." *Matthew,* 18:1–4. [4] Feast: festival of the nativity, i.e., Christmas.

So that the surprises, delight in new possessions
(Each one with its peculiar and exciting smell),
The expectation of the goose or turkey
And the expected awe on its appearance,
So that the reverence and the gaiety
May not be forgotten in later experience,
In the bored habituation, the fatigue, the tedium,
The awareness of death, the consciousness of failure,
Or in the piety of the convert
Which may be tainted with a self-conceit
Displeasing to God and disrespectful to the children
(And here I remember also with gratitude
St. Lucy,[5] her carol, and her crown of fire):[6]
So that before the end, the eightieth Christmas
(By "eightieth" meaning whichever is the last)
The accumulated memories of annual emotion
May be concentrated into a great joy
Which shall be also a great fear, as on the occasion
When fear came upon every soul:[7]
Because the beginning shall remind us of the end
And the first coming of the second coming.[8]

EDNA ST. VINCENT MILLAY
1892–1950
To Jesus on His Birthday

For this your mother sweated in the cold,
For this you bled upon the bitter tree:
A yard of tinsel ribbon bought and sold;
A paper wreath; a day at home for me.
The merry bells ring out, the people kneel;
Up goes the man of God before the crowd;
With voice of honey and with eyes of steel
He drones your humble gospel to the proud.
Nobody listens. Less than the wind that blows
Are all your words to us you died to save.
O Prince of Peace! O Sharon's dewy Rose!
How mute you lie within your vaulted grave.
The stone the angel rolled away with tears
Is back upon your mouth these thousand years.

[5] Swedish child Saint about thirteen years of age. [6] Each year Sweden installs a Queen of Lights who wears a crown of lighted candles. The "crown of fire" probably refers to the fire of purification. [7] Ll. 31–32. See *Luke,* 2:7–14 which says in part: And Mary "brought forth her firstborn son. . . . And there were in the same country shepherds abiding in the field. . . . and the glory of the Lord shone round about them; and they were sore afraid. And the angel said unto them, Fear not. . . . For unto you is born this day . . . a Saviour, which is Christ the Lord." [8] L. 34 can be read on at least two levels: "first coming," the birth of Christ and of us; "second coming," the resurrection of Christ and our being born again, on earth and in heaven.

Comments

As one of the great religious and historical figures of the world, Jesus has been interpreted in many ways. Compare the one above with these interpretations: Hughes, "On the Road," p. 112; Hopkins, "The Windhover: To Christ Our Lord," p. 336; and Pound, "Ballad of the Goodly Fere," p. 342.

E. B. WHITE
1899–
I Paint What I See[1]

A Ballad of Artistic Integrity, on the Occasion of the Removal of Some Rather Expensive Murals from the RCA Building.

"What do you paint, when you paint on a wall?"
Said John D.'s grandson Nelson.[2]
"Do you paint just anything there at all?
"Will there be any doves, or a tree in fall?
"Or a hunting scene, like an English hall?"

"I paint what I see," said Rivera.

"What are the colors you use when you paint?"
Said John D.'s grandson Nelson.
"Do you use any red in the beard of a saint?
"If you do, is it terribly red, or faint?
"Do you use any blue? Is it Prussian?"

"I paint what I paint," said Rivera.

[1] A commentary on the murals for Rockefeller Center in New York City painted by the Mexican artist Diego Rivera (1886–1957). [2] Nelson Rockefeller, the grandson of John D. Rockefeller, former Governor of New York and later the Vice President of the United States.

"Whose is that head that I see on my wall?"
  Said John D.'s grandson Nelson.
"Is it anyone's head whom we know, at all?
"A Rensselaer, or a Saltonstall?
"Is it Franklin D.? Is it Mordaunt Hall?
"Or is it the head of a Russian?"

"I paint what I think," said Rivera.

"I paint what I paint, I paint what I see,
  "I paint what I think," said Rivera,
"And the thing that is dearest in life to me
"In a bourgeois hall is Integrity;
  "However . . .
"I'll take out a couple of people drinkin'
"And put in a picture of Abraham Lincoln;
"I could even give you McCormick's reaper
"And still not make my art much cheaper.
"But the head of Lenin has got to stay
"Or my friends will give me the bird today,
  "The bird, the bird, forever."

"It's not good taste in a man like me,"
  Said John D.'s grandson Nelson,
"To question an artist's integrity
"Or mention a practical thing like a fee,
"But I know what I like to a large degree,
  "Though art I hate to hamper;
"For twenty-one thousand conservative bucks
"You painted a radical. I say shucks,
  "I never could rent the offices—
  "The capitalistic offices.
"For this, as you know, is a public hall
"And people want doves, or a tree in fall,
"And though your art I dislike to hamper,
"I owe a *little* to God and Gramper,
  "And after all,
  "It's *my* wall . . ."

"We'll see if it is," said Rivera.

HART CRANE
1899–1932

To Brooklyn Bridge

[1]
How many dawns, chill from his rippling rest
The seagull's wings shall dip and pivot him,
Shedding white rings of tumult, building high
Over the chained bay waters Liberty—

[2]
Then, with inviolate curve, forsake our eyes
As apparitional as sails that cross
Some page of figures to be filed away;
—Till elevators drop us from our day . . .

[3]
I think of cinemas, panoramic sleights
With multitudes bent toward some flashing scene
Never disclosed, but hastened to again,
Foretold to other eyes on the same screen;

[4]
And Thee, across the harbor, silver-paced
As though the sun took step of thee, yet left
Some motion ever unspent in thy stride,—
Implicitly thy freedom staying thee!

[5]
Out of some subway scuttle, cell or loft
A bedlamite speeds to thy parapets,
Tilting there momently, shrill shirt ballooning,
A jest falls from the speechless caravan.

[6]
Down Wall, from girder into street noon leaks,
A rip-tooth of the sky's acetylene;
All afternoon the cloud-flown derricks turn . . .
Thy cables breathe the North Atlantic still.

[7]
And obscure as that heaven of the Jews,
Thy guerdon . . . Accolade thou dost bestow
Of anonymity time cannot raise:
Vibrant reprieve and pardon thou dost show.

[8]
O harp and altar, of the fury fused,
(How could mere toil align thy choiring strings!)
Terrific threshold of the prophet's pledge,
Prayer of pariah, and the lover's cry,—

[9]
Again the traffic lights that skim thy swift
Unfractioned idiom, immaculate sigh of stars,
Beading thy path—condense eternity:
And we have seen night lifted in thine arms.

[10]
Under thy shadow by the piers I waited;
Only in darkness is thy shadow clear.
The City's fiery parcels all undone,
Already snow submerges an iron year . . .

[11]
O Sleepless as the river under thee,
Vaulting the sea, the prairies' dreaming sod,
Unto us lowliest sometime sweep, descend
And of the curveship lend a myth to God.

Comments

This poem is used by Crane as a "Proem," or preface, to his long poem, "The Bridge," the major effort of his brief career.

Crane has said that in the entire poem, "The Bridge," he was attempting to recreate the "Myth of America." He was much concerned about the future of America because, as he said, "I feel persuaded that here are destined to be discovered certain as yet undefined spiritual quantities. . . ." Brooklyn Bridge he made the symbol of America, the "threshold" of these spiritual quantities. The "Proem: To Brooklyn Bridge" is an invocation to and a eulogy of his basic symbol, Brooklyn Bridge.

JAMES HEARST
1900–

Landmark

The road wound back among the hills of mind
Rutted and worn, in a wagon with my father
Who wore a horsehide coat and knew the way
Toward home, I saw him and the tree together.

For me now fields are whirling in a wheel
And the spokes are many paths in all directions,
Each day I come to crossroads after dark,
No place to stay, no aunts, no close connections.

Calendars shed their leaves, mark down a time
When chrome danced brightly. The roadside tree is rotten,
I told a circling hawk, widen the gate
For the new machine, a landmark's soon forgotten.

You say the word, he mocked, I'm used to exile.
But the furrow's tongue never tells the harvest true,
When my engine saw had redesigned the landscape
For a tractor's path, the stump bled what I knew.

Comments

Having owned and cultivated a fertile Iowa farm most of his life, James Hearst is one of the few authentic rural poetic voices in American literature. For another poem of his that emerges from such authenticity, see "Truth," p. 308.

1. In "Landmark" the symbols that represent the conflict between the older and newer values are, of course, the tree and the machine. What values are in conflict?

2. Why does the "furrow never tell the harvest true"? What harvest does the poet value?

ARNA BONTEMPS
1902–1973

Southern Mansion

Poplars are standing there still as death
And ghosts of dead men
Meet their ladies walking
Two by two beneath the shade
And standing on the marble steps.

There is a sound of music echoing
Through the open door
And in the field there is
Another sound tinkling in the cotton:
Chains of bondmen dragging on the ground.

The years go back with an iron clank,
A hand is on the gate,
A dry leaf trembles on the wall.
Ghosts are walking.
They have broken roses down
And poplars stand there still as death.

COUNTEE CULLEN
1903–1946

For John Keats,[1] Apostle of Beauty

Not writ in water,[2] nor in mist,
Sweet lyric throat, thy name;
Thy singing lips that cold death kissed[3]
Have seared his own with flame.

COUNTEE CULLEN
1903–1946

Yet Do I Marvel

I doubt not God is good, well-meaning, kind,
And did He stoop to quibble could tell why
The little buried mole continues blind,
Why flesh that mirrors Him must some day die,
Make plain the reason tortured Tantalus[1]
Is baited by the fickle fruit, declare
If merely brute caprice dooms Sisyphus[2]
To struggle up a never-ending stair.
Inscrutable His ways are, and immune
To catechism by a mind too strewn
With petty cares to slightly understand
What awful brain compels His awful hand.
Yet do I marvel at this curious thing:
To make a poet black, and bid him sing!

PHYLLIS McGINLEY
1905–

The Day After Sunday

Always on Monday, God's in the morning papers,
His Name is a headline, His Works are rumored abroad.
Having been praised by men who are movers and shapers,
From prominent Sunday pulpits, newsworthy is God.

On page 27, just opposite Fashion Trends,
One reads at a glance how He scolded the Baptists a little,
Was firm with the Catholics, practical with the Friends,
To Unitarians pleasantly noncommittal.

In print are His numerous aspects, too: God smiling,
God vexed, God thunderous, God whose mansions are pearl,
Political God, God frugal, God reconciling
Himself with science, God guiding the Camp Fire Girl.

Always on Monday morning the press reports
God as revealed to His vicars in various guises—
Benevolent, stormy, patient, or out of sorts.
God knows which God is the God God recognizes.

[1] Keats's poems are found on pp. 240, 323, and 325. [2] Keats wrote for his own epitaph, "Here lies one whose name was writ in water." [3] Keats (1795–1821) suffered an untimely death.

[1] Tantalus. In Greek mythology, the son of Zeus and a Lydian king who divulged the secrets of the gods to mortals and was punished by being submerged up to the chin in a river of Hades with a tree of fruit above his head. Whenever he tried to eat the fruit or drink the water they moved just beyond his reach causing him agonizing thirst and hunger. The nature of his punishment gave us the word *tantalize.*
[2] Sisyphus. A legendary king of Corinth whose work in the world of shades is to roll a huge stone to the top of a hill where it constantly rolls back. Hence "a labor of Sisyphus" is endless and exhausting.

FRANK MARSHALL DAVIS
1905–

Roosevelt Smith

You ask what happened to Roosevelt Smith

Well . . .

Conscience and the critics got him

Roosevelt Smith was the only dusky child born and bred in the village of Pine City, Nebraska

At college they worshipped the novelty of a black poet and predicted fame

At twenty-three he published his first book . . . the critics said he imitated Carl Sandburg, Edgar Lee Masters and Vachel Lindsay . . . they raved about a wealth of racial material and the charm of darky dialect

So for two years Roosevelt worked and observed in Dixie

At twenty-five a second book . . . Negroes complained about plantation scenes and said he dragged Aframerica's good name in the mire for gold . . . "Europe," they said, "honors Dunbar for his 'Ships That Pass in the Night' [1] and not for his dialect which they don't understand"

For another two years Roosevelt strove for a different medium of expression

At twenty-seven a third book . . . The critics said the density of Gertrude Stein or T. S. Eliot hardly fitted the simple material to which a Negro had access

For another two years Roosevelt worked

At twenty-nine his fourth book . . . the critics said a Negro had no business initiating the classic forms of Keats, Browning and Shakespeare . . . "Roosevelt Smith," they announced, "has nothing original and is merely a blackface white. His African heritage is a rich source should he use it"

So for another two years Roosevelt went into the interior of Africa

At thirty-one his fifth book . . . interesting enough, the critics said, but since it followed nothing done by any white poet it was probably just a new kind of prose

Day after the reviews came out Roosevelt traded conscience and critics for the leather pouch and bunions of a mail carrier and read in the papers until his death how little the American Negro had contributed to his nation's literature . . .[2]

[1] A short romantic poem by Paul Laurence Dunbar (1872–1906) which, implies Davis, is honored in Europe because it has little or nothing to reflect the realities of Negro life as they are reflected in such poems by Dunbar as "A Death Song" and "When Malindy Sings." Further, Davis implies, the English would be impressed by Dunbar's title "Ships That Pass in the Night" because an English romantic novel with the same title (1893) written by Bearice Harraden had sold over a million copies.

[2] See Dudley Randall's "Black Poet, White Critic," p. 357.

SAMUEL BECKETT
1906–

Que Ferais-Je sans Ce Monde sans Visage sans Questions

que ferais-je sans ce monde sans visage sans questions
où être ne dure qu'un instant où chaque instant
verse dans le vide dans l'oubli d'avoir été
sans cette onde où à la fin
corps et ombre ensemble s'engloutissent
que ferais-je sans ce silence gouffre des murmures
haletant furieux vers le secours vers l'amour
sans ce ciel qui s'élève
sur la poussière de ses lests

que ferais-je je ferais comme hier comme
aujourd'hui
regardant par mon hublot si je ne suis pas seul
à errer et à virer loin de toute vie
dans un espace pantin
sans voix parmi les voix
enfermées avec moi

SAMUEL BECKETT
1906–

What Would I Do Without This World Faceless Incurious[1]

what would I do without this world faceless
incurious
where to be lasts but an instant where every
instant
spills in the void the ignorance of having been
without this wave where in the end
body and shadow together are engulfed
what would I do without this silence where the
murmurs die
the pantings the frenzies towards succour towards love
without this sky that soars
above its ballast dust

what would I do what I did yesterday and the
day before
peering out of my deadlight looking for another
wandering like me eddying far from all the living
in a convulsive space
among the voices voiceless
that throng my hiddenness

Comments

This short poem presents in a condensed way Beckett's interpretation of the universe as a chaotic disorganization that leaves us wandering and rootless. The imagery and structure of his poem help to convey the confusion he finds in life. This is not to say that the poem itself is confused: a careful and persistent reading finds the world's confusion described in an unusual way reminiscent of some of Eliot's poems. If upon a *first* reading the reader is confused, perhaps such is Beckett's very strategy, as it may be in his notable play *Waiting for Godot* in which humanity desperately waits for help from the Universal Being (Godot) who never arrives.

[1] Translated from the French by the author.

W. H. AUDEN
1907–1973

Lullaby[1]

Lay your sleeping head, my love,
Human on my faithless arm;
Time and fevers burn away
Individual beauty from
Thoughtful children, and the grave
Proves the child ephemeral:
But in my arms till break of day
Let the living creature lie,
Mortal, guilty, but to me
The entirely beautiful.

Soul and body have no bounds:
To lovers as they lie upon
Her tolerant enchanted slope
In their ordinary swoon,
Grave the vision Venus sends
Of supernatural sympathy,
Universal love and hope;
While an abstract insight wakes
Among the glaciers and the rocks
The hermit's carnal ecstasy.

Certainty, fidelity
On the stroke of midnight pass
Like vibrations of a bell
And fashionable madmen raise
Their pedantic boring cry:
Every farthing of the cost,
All the dreaded cards foretell,
Shall be paid, but from this night
Not a whisper, not a thought,
Not a kiss nor look be lost.

[1] Editors have previously used "Lay Your Sleeping Head" as the title; Auden has now supplied one. He has made four word changes: l. 20, *carnal* for *sensual;* l. 34, *welcome* for *sweetness;* l. 36, *our* for *the;* l. 37, *find* for *see.* Any sensitive, critical reader of poetry would probably ask himself why Auden made the changes.

Beauty, midnight, vision dies:
Let the winds of dawn that blow
Softly round your dreaming head
Such a day of welcome show
Eye and knocking heart may bless,
Find our mortal world enough;
Noons of dryness find you fed
By the involuntary powers,
Nights of insult let you pass
Watched by every human love.

W. H. AUDEN
1907–1973
Musée des Beaux Arts[1]

About suffering they were never wrong,
The Old Masters: how well they understood
Its human position; how it takes place
While someone else is eating or opening a window or just walking dully along;
How, when the aged are reverently, passionately waiting
For the miraculous birth, there always must be
Children who did not specially want it to happen, skating
On a pond at the edge of the wood:
They never forgot
That even the dreadful martyrdom must run its course
Anyhow in a corner, some untidy spot
Where the dogs go on with their doggy life and the torturer's horse
Scratches its innocent behind on a tree.
In Brueghel's *Icarus,*[2] for instance: how everything turns away
Quite leisurely from the disaster; the ploughman may
Have heard the splash, the forsaken cry,
But for him it was not an important failure; the sun shone
As it had to on the white legs disappearing into the green
Water; and the expensive delicate ship that must have seen
Something amazing, a boy falling out of the sky,
Had somewhere to get to and sailed calmly on.

[1] Museum of Fine Arts. [2] A painting by the Flemish Pieter Brueghel (1525–1569) in the Royal Museum in Brussels. Icarus, flying with his father Daedalus, flew too close to the sun which melted the wax holding on his wings, and pitched him into the sea. The adjective *Icarian* has come to mean soaring too high for safety.

W. H. AUDEN
1907–1973
The Unknown Citizen

To JS/07/M/378
This Marble Monument
Is Erected by the State

He was found by the Bureau of Statistics to be
One against whom there was no official complaint,
And all the reports on his conduct agree
That, in the modern sense of an old-fashioned word, he was a saint,
For in everything he did he served the Greater Community.
Except for the War till the day he retired
He worked in a factory and never got fired,
But satisfied his employers, Fudge Motors Inc.
Yet he wasn't a scab[1] or odd in his views,
For his Union reports that he paid his dues,
(Our report on his Union shows it was sound)
And our Social Psychology workers found
That he was popular with his mates and liked a drink.
The Press are convinced that he bought a paper every day
And that his reactions to advertisements were normal in every way.
Policies taken out in his name prove that he was fully insured,
And his Health-card shows he was once in hospital but left it cured.
Both Producers Research and High-Grade Living declare
He was fully sensible to the advantages of the Instalment Plan
And had everything necessary to the Modern Man,
A phonograph, a radio, a car and a frigidaire.
Our researchers into Public Opinion are content

[1] A union member or nonmember disloyal to the union during a strike.

That he held the proper opinions for the time of year;
When there was peace, he was for peace; when there was war, he went.
He was married and added five children to the population,
Which our Eugenist[2] says was the right number for a parent of his generation,
And our teachers report that he never interfered with their education.
Was he free? Was he happy? The question is absurd:
Had anything been wrong, we should certainly have heard.

STEPHEN SPENDER
1909–

I Think Continually of Those Who Were Truly Great

I think continually of those who were truly great.
Who, from the womb, remembered the soul's history
Through corridors of light where the hours are suns,
Endless and singing. Whose lovely ambition
Was that their lips, still touched with fire,
Should tell of the Spirit, clothed from head to foot in song.
And who hoarded from the Spring branches
The desires falling across their bodies like blossoms.

What is precious, is never to forget
The essential delight of the blood drawn from ageless springs
Breaking through rocks in worlds before our earth.
Never to deny its pleasure in the morning simple light
Nor its grave evening demand for love.
Never to allow gradually the traffic to smother
With noise and fog, the flowering of the Spirit.

Near the snow, near the sun, in the highest fields,
See how these names are fêted by the waving grass
And by the streamers of white cloud
And whispers of wind in the listening sky.
The names of those who in their lives fought for life,
Who wore at their hearts the fire's centre.
Born of the sun, they travelled a short while toward the sun,
And left the vivid air signed with their honour.

[2] One versed in eugenics, the science which aims at improving the human race by controlling the hereditary qualities through proper mating.

Comments

Spender's essay "On Teaching Modern Poetry" (p. 687) includes a good deal of comment on the nature of modern poetry, and the kinds of value to be found in it. The reader may find it profitable to consider Spender's poem in the light of his critical opinions.

STEPHEN SPENDER
1909–

An Elementary School Classroom in a Slum

Far far from gusty waves these children's faces.
Like rootless weeds, the hair torn round their pallor.
The tall girl with her weighed-down head. The paper-
seeming boy, with rat's eyes. The stunted, unlucky heir
Of twisted bones, reciting a father's gnarled disease,
His lesson from his desk. At back of the dim class
One unnoted, sweet and young. His eyes live in a dream
Of squirrel's game, in tree room, other than this.

On sour cream walls, donations. Shakespeare's head,
Cloudless at dawn, civilized dome riding all cities.
Belled, flowery, Tyrolese valley. Open-handed map
Awarding the world its world. And yet, for these
Children, these windows, not this world, are world,
Where all their future's painted with a fog,
A narrow street sealed in with a lead sky,
Far far from rivers, capes, and stars of words.

Surely, Shakespeare is wicked, the map a bad example
With ships and sun and love tempting them to steal—
For lives that slyly turn in their cramped holes
From fog to endless night? On their slag heap, these children
Wear skins peeped through by bones and spectacles of steel
With mended glass, like bottle bits on stones.
All of their time and space are foggy slum.
So blot their maps with slums as big as doom.

Unless, governor, teacher, inspector, visitor,
This map becomes their window and these windows
That shut upon their lives like catacombs,
Break O break open till they break the town
And show the children to green fields, and make their world
Run azure on gold sands, and let their tongues
Run naked into books, the white and green leaves open
History theirs whose language is the sun.

J. V. CUNNINGHAM
1911–
The Metaphysical Amorist

You are the problem I propose,
My dear, the text my musings glose:[1]
I call you for convenience love.
By definition you're a cause
Inferred by necessary laws—
You are so to the saints above.
But in this shadowy lower life
I sleep with a terrestrial wife
And earthy children I beget.
Love is a fiction I must use,
A privilege I can abuse,
And sometimes something I forget.

Now, in the heavenly other place
Love is in the eternal mind
The luminous form whose shade she is,
A ghost discarnate,[2] thought defined.
She was so to my early bliss,
She is so while I comprehend
The forms my senses apprehend,
And in the end she will be so.

Her whom my hands embrace I kiss,
Her whom my mind infers I know.
The one exists in time and space
And as she was she will not be;
The other is in her own grace
And is *She is* eternally.

Plato![3] you shall not plague my life.
I married a terrestrial wife.
And Hume![4] she is not mere sensation
In sequence of observed relation.
She has two forms—ah, thank you, Duns!—,[5]
I know her in both ways at once.
I knew her, yes, before I knew her,
And by both means I must construe her,
And none among you shall undo her.

[1] Archaic form of *gloze,* to make glozes or glosses upon; to discuss, expound, interpret.

[2] Having no physical body; incorporeal. [3] Plato (427?–347 B.C.), Greek philosopher, wrote *The Symposium* on ideal love. "Platonic love" has become a popular term for spiritual love between the sexes without sexual implications. See William Cartwright's poem "No Platonic Love" (p. 317), which has a theme similar to Cunningham's. [4] David Hume (1711–1776), Scottish philosopher, restricted human knowledge to the experience of ideas, impressions, and sensations. The speaker in the poem therefore rebukes him in ll. 29–30. [5] John Duns Scotus (1265?–1308), Scottish scholastic theologian, was an extreme realist in philosophy (non-Platonic), so the speaker embraces him.

DELMORE SCHWARTZ 1913–1966

In the Naked Bed, in Plato's Cave[1]

In the naked bed, in Plato's cave,
Reflected headlights slowly slid the wall,
Carpenters hammered under the shaded window,
Wind troubled the window curtains all night long,
A fleet of trucks strained uphill, grinding,
Their freights covered, as usual.
The ceiling lightened again, the slanting diagram
Slid slowly forth.
Hearing the milkman's chop,
His striving up the stair, the bottle's chink,
I rose from bed, lit a cigarette,
And walked to the window. The stony street
Displayed the stillness in which buildings stand,
The street-lamp's vigil and the horse's patience.
The winter sky's pure capital
Turned me back to bed with exhausted eyes.

Strangeness grew in the motionless air. The loose
Film grayed. Shaking wagons, hooves' waterfalls,
Sounded far off, increasing, louder and nearer.
A car coughed, starting. Morning, softly
Melting the air, lifted the half-covered chair
From underseas, kindled the looking-glass,
Distinguished the dresser and the white wall.
The bird called tentatively, whistled, called,
Bubbled and whistled, so! Perplexed, still wet
With sleep, affectionate, hungry and cold. So, so,
O son of man,[2] the ignorant night, the travail
Of early morning, the mystery of beginning
Again and again,
while History is unforgiven.

[1] Plato's (Greek philosopher, 427?–347 B.C.) famous simile, or allegory, "according to which those who are destitute of philosophy may be compared to prisoners in a cave, who are only able to look in one direction because they are bound, and who have a fire behind them and a wall in front. Between them and the wall there is nothing; all that they see are shadows of themselves, and of objects behind them, cast on the wall by the light of the fire. Inevitably they regard these shadows as real, and have no notion of the objects to which they are due. At last some man succeeds in escaping from the cave to the light of the sun; for the first time he sees real things, and becomes aware that he had hitherto been deceived by shadows." (Bertrand Russell, *A History of Western Philosophy*, New York: Simon and Schuster, Inc., 1945, p. 125.) [2] God's statement to the prophet Ezekiel in the valley of dry bones; the bones arise, take on flesh, and live. See *Ezekiel*, 37:3–10 for the entire situation.

ROBERT E. HAYDEN 1913–

Frederick Douglass[1]

When it is finally ours, this freedom, this liberty, this beautiful
and terrible thing, needful to man as air,
usable as earth; when it belongs at last to all,
when it is truly instinct, brain matter, diastole, systole,
reflex action; when it is finally won; when it is more
than the gaudy mumbo jumbo of politicians:
this man, this Douglass, this former slave, this Negro
beaten to his knees, exiled, visioning a world
where none is lonely, more hunted, alien,
this man, superb in love and logic, this man
shall be remembered. Oh, not with statues' rhetoric,
not with legends and poems and wreaths of bronze alone,
but with the lives grown out of his life, the lives
fleshing his dream of the beautiful, needful thing.

[1] Frederick Douglass (1817–1895), an early, powerful champion of emancipation and enfranchisement for Negroes, born a slave in Maryland, escaped (1838) to New York, and legally won his freedom in 1846. He became a poet, a distinguished anti-slavery orator and autobiographer, worked with William Lloyd Garrison on *The Liberator,* broke with Garrison in 1847, and launched his own weekly, *The North Star,* and later his *Frederick Douglass' Paper* and *Douglass' Monthly*. In a letter to his former master, Thomas Arnold, Douglass stated his position during the Civil War: "We are fighting for unity of idea, unity of sentiment, unity of object, unity of institutions, in which there will be no North, no South, no East, no West, no black, no white, but a solidarity of the nation, making every slave free, and every free man a voter."

For further information on Douglass consult Philip S. Foner, *Frederick Douglass,* New York: Citadel Press, 1961; or see Douglass's autobiography, *The Life and Times of Frederick Douglass,* revised 1892.

DUDLEY RANDALL
1914–

Black Poet, White Critic[1]

A critic advises
not to write on controversial subjects
like freedom or murder,
but to treat universal themes
and timeless symbols
like the white unicorn.

A white unicorn?

DUDLEY RANDALL
1914–

Booker T. and W.E.B.[1]

"It seems to me," said Booker T.,
"It shows a mighty lot of cheek
To study chemistry and Greek
When Mister Charlie needs a hand
To hoe the cotton on his land,
And when Miss Ann looks for a cook,
Why stick your nose inside a book?"

"I don't agree," said W.E.B.,
"If I should have the drive to seek
Knowledge of chemistry or Greek,
I'll do it. Charles and Miss can look
Another place for hand or cook.
Some men rejoice in skill of hand,
And some in cultivating land,
But there are others who maintain
The right to cultivate the brain."

"It seems to me," said Booker T.,
"That all you folks have missed the boat
Who shout about the right to vote,
And spend vain days and sleepless nights
In uproar over civil rights.
Just keep your mouths shut, do not grouse,
But work, and save, and buy a house."

"I don't agree," said W.E.B.,
"For what can property avail
If dignity and justice fail.
Unless you help to make the laws,
They'll steal your house with trumped-up clause.
A rope's as tight, a fire as hot,
No matter how much cash you've got.
Speak soft, and try your little plan,
But as for me, I'll be a man."

"It seems to me," said Booker T.—

"I don't agree,"
Said W.E.B.

[1] See Davis's "Roosevelt Smith" p. 350.

[1] Booker T. Washington (1856–1915) and Dr. William Edward Burghardt Du Bois (1868–1963)—Author's note. Du Bois preferred the initials W. E. B.

This poem suggests (as good poems usually do) more than it explicitly says. A basic disagreement between Washington and Du Bois, who was twelve years younger than Washington, appeared when the Negroes began to settle in white Harlem about 1905, a result of the rise of black economic nationalism. Washington's National Negro Business League, founded in 1900 and identified with the Afro-American Realty Company, was a powerful influence on the Negro move into Harlem. Washington and his Negro business allies had become aggressive in economics but remained conservative in civil rights politics. Du Bois, disagreeing with this conservatism, believed that unless the Negro fought for and won his civil rights there was no guarantee that his new economic status would remain safe. Stanzas 2 and 3 in the poem present the opposing points of view, and line 32 tells us where the poet stands. For a full account of this disagreement consult Harold Cruse, *The Crisis of the Negro Intellectual*, New York: William Morrow and Co., 1967, especially pp. 11–63.

RANDALL JARRELL
1914–1965

The Emancipators[1]

When you[2] ground the lenses[3] and the moons[4]
swam free
From that great wanderer; when the apple[5]
shone

[1] Jarrell observes: "Galileo, Newton, and Bruno are the great emancipators addressed in the first stanza. . . ." *Selected Poems*, 1955, p. xiii. [2] Galileo Galilei (1564–1642), Italian astronomer and physicist who supported Copernicus's (1473–1543) contention that the earth and planets revolve around the sun; regarded as heresy at the time. [3] The telescope he made. [4] Jupiter's satellites which he discovered (1610). [5] Sir Isaac Newton (1642–1727); seeing an apple fall led him to the law of gravitation. Byron wrote:

> When Newton saw an apple fall, he found,
> In that slight startle from his contemplation. . . .
> A mode of proving that the earth turned round,
> In a most natural whirl called gravitation.
>
> *Don Juan*, X. I.

Like a sea-shell through your prism, voyager;[6]
When, dancing in pure flame, the Roman mercy,[7]
Your doctrines blew like ashes from your bones;[8]

Did you think, for an instant, past the numerals
Jellied in Latin[9] like bacteria in broth,
Snatched for by holy Europe like a sign?
Past sombre tables[10] inched out with the lives
Forgotten or clapped for by the wigged Societies?[11]

You guessed this? The earth's face altering with iron,
The smoke ranged like a wall against the day?
—The equations metamorphose into use: the free
Drag their slight bones from tenements to vote
To die with their children in your factories.

Man is born in chains,[12] and everywhere we see him dead.
On your earth they sell nothing but our lives.
You knew that what you died for was our deaths?
You learned, those years, that what men wish is Trade?
It was you who understood; it is we who change.[13]

[6] Voyager through the realms of thought. Wordsworth's lines are found on Newton's statue in Trinity College, Cambridge:

> The marble index of a mind for ever
> Voyaging through strange seas of Thought alone.
> "The Prelude"

[7] Roman Catholic Church took Bruno's life before his soul was completely damned. [8] Ll. 4–5: Giordano Bruno (*c.* 1548–1600), Italian philosopher, critic of Christianity, and supporter of the Copernican system (see footnote 2); burned at the stake for heresy. [9] Probably scientific terms (numerals). [10] Scientific formulas or charts. [11] Royal Societies. [12] "Man is born free, and everywhere he is in chains."—Rousseau (1712–1778), *The Social Contract,* 1762. [13] Final stanza: implies that the freedom man thought he had achieved is an illusion.

RANDALL JARRELL
1914–1965

Second Air Force[1]

Far off, above the plain the summer dries,
The great loops of the hangars sway like hills.
Buses and weariness and loss, the nodding soldiers
Are wire, the bare frame building, and a pass
To what was hers; her head hides his square patch
And she thinks heavily: My son is grown.
She sees a world: sand roads, tar-paper barracks,
The bubbling asphalt of the runways, sage,
The dunes rising to the interminable ranges,
The dim flights moving over clouds like clouds.
The armorers[2] in their patched faded green,
Sweat-stiffened, banded with brass cartridges,
Walk to the line; their Fortresses, all tail,
Stand wrong and flimsy on their skinny legs,
And the crews climb to them clumsily as bears.
The head withdraws into its hatch (a boy's),
The engines rise to their blind laboring roar,
And the green, made beasts run home to air.
Now in each aspect death is pure.
(At twilight they wink over men like stars
And hour by hour, through the night, some see
The great lights floating in—from Mars, from Mars.)
How emptily the watchers see them gone.

They go, there is silence; the woman and her son
Stand in the forest of the shadows, and the light
Washes them like water. In the long-sunken city
Of evening, the sunlight stills like sleep
The faint wonder of the drowned; in the evening,
In the last dreaming light, so fresh, so old,
The soldiers pass like beasts, unquestioning,
And the watcher for an instant understands

[1] Jarrell's note: "In 'Second Air Force' the woman visiting her son remembers what she has read on the front page of her newspaper the week before, a conversation between a bomber, in flames over Germany, and one of the fighters protecting it: 'Then I heard the bomber call me in: "Little Friend, Little Friend, I got two engines on fire. Can you see me, Little Friend?" I said, "I'm crossing right over you. Let's go home."' " *Selected Poems,* 1955, p. xvi.
[2] Fliers.

What there is then no need to understand;
But she wakes from her knowledge, and her stare,
A shadow now, moves emptily among
The shadows learning in their shadowy fields
The empty missions.
Remembering,
She hears the bomber calling, *Little Friend!*
To the fighter hanging in the hostile sky,
And sees the ragged flame eat, rib by rib,
Along the metal of the wing into her heart:
The lives stream out, blossom, and float steadily
To the flames of the earth, the flames
That burn like stars above the lands of men.

She saves from the twilight that takes everything
A squadron shipping, in its last parade—
Its dogs run by it, barking at the band—
A gunner walking to his barracks, half-asleep,
Starting at something, stumbling (above, invisible,
The crews in the steady winter of the sky
Tremble in their wired fur); and feels for them
The love of life for life. The hopeful cells
Heavy with someone else's death, cold carriers
Of someone else's victory, grope past their lives
Into her own bewilderment: The years meant *this?*

But for them the bombers answer everything.

DYLAN THOMAS
1914–1953
The Force That Through the Green Fuse Drives the Flower

The force that through the green fuse drives the flower
Drives my green age; that blasts the roots of trees
Is my destroyer.
And I am dumb to tell the crooked rose
My youth is bent by the same wintry fever.

The force that drives the water through the rocks
Drives my red blood; that dries the mouthing streams
Turns mine to wax.
And I am dumb to mouth unto my veins
How at the mountain spring the same mouth sucks.

The hand that whirls the water in the pool
Stirs the quicksand; that ropes the blowing wind
Hauls my shroud sail.
And I am dumb to tell the hanging man
How of my clay is made the hangman's lime.

The lips of time leech to the fountain head;
Love drips and gathers, but the fallen blood
Shall calm her sores.
And I am dumb to tell a weather's wind
How time has ticked a heaven round the stars.

And I am dumb to tell the lover's tomb
How at my sheet goes the same crooked worm.

DYLAN THOMAS
1914–1953
Do Not Go Gentle into That Good Night

Do not go gentle into that good night,
Old age should burn and rave at close of day;
Rage, rage against the dying of the light.

Though wise men at their end know dark is right,
Because their words had forked no lightning they
Do not go gentle into that good night.

Good men, the last wave by, crying how bright
Their frail deeds might have danced in a green bay,
Rage, rage against the dying of the light.

Wild men who caught and sang the sun in flight,
And learn, too late, they grieved it on its way,
Do not go gentle into that good night.

Grave men, near death, who see with blinding sight
Blind eyes could blaze like meteors and be gay,

Rage, rage against the dying of the light.

And you, my father, there on the sad height,
Curse, bless, me now with your fierce tears, I pray.
Do not go gentle into that good night.
Rage, rage against the dying of the light.

OWEN DODSON
1914–

Sorrow Is the Only Faithful One

Sorrow is the only faithful one:
The lone companion clinging like a season
To its original skin no matter what the variations.

If all the mountains paraded
Eating the valleys as they went
And the sun were a coiffure on the highest peak,

Sorrow would be there between
The sparkling and the giant laughter
Of the enemy when the clouds come down to swim.

But I am less, unmagic, black,
Sorrow clings to me more than to doomsday mountains
Or erosion scars on a palisade.

Sorrow has a song like a leech
Crying because the sand's blood is dry
And the stars reflected in the lake

Are water for all their twinkling
And bloodless for all their charm.
I have blood, and a song.

Sorrow is the only faithful one.

WILLIAM STAFFORD
1914–

Travelling Through the Dark

Travelling through the dark I found a deer
dead on the edge of the Wilson River road.
It is usually best to roll them into the canyon:
that road is narrow; to swerve might make more dead.

By glow of the tail-light I stumbled back of the car
and stood by the heap, a doe, a recent killing;
she had stiffened already, almost cold.
I dragged her off; she was large in the belly.

My fingers touching her side brought me the reason—
her side was warm; her fawn lay there waiting,
alive, still, never to be born.
Beside that mountain road I hesitated.

The car aimed ahead its lowered parking lights;
under the hood purred the steady engine.
I stood in the glare of the warm exhaust turning red;
around our group I could hear the wilderness listen.

I thought hard for us all—my only swerving—
then pushed her over the edge into the river.

MARGARET A. WALKER
1915–

For Malcolm X[1]

All you violated ones with gentle hearts;
You violent dreamers whose cries shout heart-break;
Whose voices echo clamors of our cool capers,
And whose black faces have hollowed pits for eyes.
All you gambling sons and hooked children and bowery bums
Hating white devils and black bourgeoisie,
Thumbing your noses at your burning red suns,
Gather round this coffin and mourn your dying swan.

Snow-white moslem head-dress around a dead black face!
Beautiful were your sand-papering words against our skins!
Our blood and water pour from your flowing wounds.
You have cut open our breasts and dug scalpels in our brains.

[1] See Imamu Amiri Baraka, "A Poem for Black Hearts," p. 371, for another poem on Malcolm X. See also *The Autobiography of Malcolm X*, New York: Grove Press, Inc., 1964, especially ch. 19. Malcolm X was assassinated in Harlem on Feb. 21, 1965.

When and Where will another come to take your holy place?
Old man mumbling in his dotage, or crying child, unborn?

GWENDOLYN BROOKS
1917–

From The Children of the Poor

1

People who have no children can be hard:
Attain a mail of ice and insolence:
Need not pause in the fire, and in no sense
Hesitate in the hurricane to guard.
And when wide world is bitten and bewarred
They perish purely, waving their spirits hence
Without a trace of grace or of offense
To laugh or fail, diffident, wonder-starred.
While through a throttling dark we others hear
The little lifting helplessness, the queer
Whimper-whine; whose unridiculous
Lost softness softly makes a trap for us.
And makes a curse. And makes a sugar of
The malocclusions, the inconditions of love.

LAWRENCE FERLINGHETTI
1919–

In Goya's Greatest Scenes

In Goya's greatest scenes[1] we seem to see
the people of the world
exactly at the moment when
they first attained the title of
'suffering humanity'
They writhe upon the page
in a veritable rage
of adversity
Heaped up
groaning with babies and bayonets
under cement skies
in an abstract landscape of blasted trees
bent statues bats wings and beaks
slippery gibbets
cadavers and carnivorous cocks
and all the final hollering monsters
of the
'imagination of disaster'
they are so bloody real
it is as if they really still existed

And they do

[1] Francisco José de Goya y Lucientes (1746–1828), Spanish master painter, etcher, and lithographer, and chief painter to the Spanish King; widely known for his unrestrained realistic portrayal of contemporary life in Spain, and of "suffering humanity" as his famous painting "The Execution" testifies. It is said that "he loathed the horrors of organized killings, and when asked why he painted such things, he answered curtly, 'To have the pleasure of saying eternally to men that they stop being barbarians.' " In the first twenty lines of his poem Ferlinghetti is obviously referring to "The Execution," and in the remaining lines he asks, have such matters changed in our time? For a popular contemporary account of Goya see Richard Schiekel and the Editors of Time-Life Books, *The World of Goya, 1746–1828,* New York: Time-Life Books, 1968.

Only the landscape is changed

They still are ranged along the roads
plagued by legionaires
false windmills and demented roosters

They are the same people
only further from home

on freeways fifty lanes wide
on a concrete continent
spaced with bland billboards
illustrating imbecile illusions of happiness

The scene shows fewer tumbrils[2]
but more maimed citizens
in painted cars
and they have strange license plates
and engines
that devour America

[2] A vehicle carrying condemned prisoners (such as political prisoners during the French Revolution) to a place of execution.

JAMES A. EMANUEL
1921–

Emmett Till[1]

I hear a whistling
Through the water.
Little Emmett
Won't be still.
He keeps floating
Round the darkness,
Edging through
The silent chill.

Tell me, please,
That bedtime story
Of the fairy
River Boy
Who swims forever,
Deep in treasures,
Necklaced in
A coral toy.

[1] Emmett Till was a fourteen-year-old black boy from Chicago who, when visiting relatives in Mississippi in 1955, was murdered and thrown into the Tallahatchie River for allegedly whistling at a white woman. The poet says about this poem, "I intended . . . to help make Emmett Till's name legendary in our nation's history, to make him 'swim forever' in the darkness of the American dream."

LOUIS SIMPSON
1923–

To the Western World[1]

This poem and Mooney's "Assassination at Memphis" (p. 363) can be read as companion pieces in the sense that they contrast the founding of the new American civilization by successive generations working and dying to "civilize the ground," and the slow erosion of American civilization by the fear of change which has inevitably brought hatred, violence, and death. Has America forgotten the wisdom of the ancient doctrine that the only permanent thing is change? Or as the Greek philosopher Heraclitus has put it, "the sun is

[1] Within his book of poems, *A Dream of Governors*, 1959, Simpson significantly places this poem in the section titled "My America."

new each day." Or as Emerson told his countrymen when he urged them in 1836 to break their chains with the past and to "enjoy an original relation to the universe," "the sun shines today also."

A siren sang, and Europe turned away
From the high castle and the shepherd's crook.
Three caravels[2] went sailing to Cathay[3]
On the strange ocean, and the captains shook
Their banners out across the Mexique Bay.

And in our early days we did the same.
Remembering our fathers in their wreck
We crossed the sea from Palos[4] where they came
And saw, enormous to the little deck,
A shore in silence waiting for a name.

The treasures of Cathay were never found.
In this America, this wilderness
Where the axe echoes with a lonely sound,
The generations labor to possess
And grave by grave we civilize the ground.

STEPHEN MOONEY
1915–1971

Assassination at Memphis

And grave by grave we civilize the ground.[1]
—LOUIS SIMPSON

Although the occasion of this poem was the assassination of Martin Luther King, Jr., April 4, 1968, the poem suggests, especially lines 25–29, that something precious beyond Dr. King was destroyed. We see once more how the poet in all civilizations has used the timely event to explore what may finally become a timeless universal of history.

On tables not far from here
there is no salt.
Axes struck into the wood
as in a chopping-block.
And there are beds with no sheets,
mattresses with slits
showing cotton that oozes blood.
The drops are filled with axes.[2]
Who can be hungry?
The tables, the beds shrink to the size of toys,
thrown away, but the Salvation Army has vanished.
And who can lie down to sleep?
This is the year of the axe
and the mattress.
The bodies
have crawled to the floor and
out the window, and floated
to the river and down
to the artificial lakes.
They are all gone under the dams
and down into quicksand.
The trucks are silent
under other people's carports, the sun
drawn by magnets toward night and secrecy.
Strangers and enemies are watching
shows on television, dying for interruptions
that will explain who is guilty.

What has happened is the silence
of hearts moved only by death.

STEPHEN MOONEY
1915–1971

The Garden

There is no evidence. But here was a marriage
In which the husband killed the wife—sometimes

---

[2] Sailing ship, especially a small fifteenth- and sixteenth-century ship with broad bows, high narrow poop, and lateen sails. [3] The name given to a country in eastern Asia, approximating northern China, by Marco Polo (1254?–1324), a Venetian traveler and adventurer. He is the hero of Donn Byrne's novel *Messer Marco Polo,* 1921. [4] Former seaport in southwest Spain on the Tinto River southeast of Huelva. Columbus sailed from there August 3, 1492.

[1] The final line of "To the Western World" above.

[2] L. 8: the sharp, tragic imagery in this line may be a prophecy as we consider what *The Commercial Appeal* of Memphis said the morning after the assassination: "To many millions of American Negroes, Dr. Martin Luther King, Jr., was the prophet of their crusade for racial equality. He was their voice of anguish, their eloquence in humiliation, their battle cry for human dignity. He forged for them the weapons of nonviolence that withstood and blunted the ferocity of segregation." Note the contrasting use of "axe" in this line and in l. 13 of Simpson's poem.

It goes the other way. It took him several years
Industriously pushing her ankle-deep
Into the greensward of the formal garden
While she, resisting statuesquely, grew genteel
Under the neighbors' eyes. "In fact, it's not
Unpleasant here," she sighed, and the ground rose up
Two inches higher on her legs.
Nobody could dispute
That she was courteously cared for. Day after day
The clocks chimed on the landings of three flights
Of stairs, each waiting until the last one finished
To let the masculine bass bells sound one by one
Through open windows, clearly. Nourishing meals
Were brought to her on time.
Naturally
She was bathed at night, after the moon went down.
Sometimes, faintly, someone passing
On the other side of the hedge would think he saw
The husband making love to her, and pause
To watch their shadows wrestle darkly, forming
A kind of fire that gives no light. The leaves
Would rustle, and the stranger would steal on,
Moved by faint expectations.
One night she sank
Into the ground well past her knees; and now
She could touch the grass without bending over,
Feeling it under her fanned-out palms
Like close-cropped human hair. From this time on
She liked her situation better: As she learned
To hope for nothing, to remember nothing,
As she learned at last to wait, the trip down
Went faster. At once the legless torso
—Her husband's hands faithfully at her shoulders—
Became a bust, a head, a frontal bone,
A lost curl of hair. The final push
Happened in full day, when the lawn-sprinklers
Were making showers of wet light. Three birds
Flew through the spray, and rapid rainbows
Whirled all the light away.
Far off, the cockatoos
Cried in the warning jungle. Fish
Nibbled algae in the fragile ponds;
And carelessly among remote Gibraltars
Submerged in the Atlantic, a school
Of eels swam through an open door
Under a steep escarpment, out of mind.

ROBERT LOWELL
1917–1977

As a Plane Tree by the Water[1]

Darkness has called to darkness, and disgrace
Elbows about our windows in this planned
Babel of Boston[2] where our money talks
And multiplies the darkness of a land
Of preparation[3] where the Virgin[4] walks
And roses spiral her enamelled face
Or fall to splinters on unwatered streets.
Our Lady of Babylon,[5] go by, go by,
I was once the apple of your eye;
Flies, flies[6] are on the plane tree, on the streets.

The flies, the flies, the flies of Babylon
Buzz in my ear-drums while the devil's long
Dirge of the people detonates the hour
For floating cities where his golden tongue
Enchants the masons of the Babel Tower

[1] "Blessed *is* the man that walketh not in the counsel of the ungodly . . .
But his delight *is* in the law of the LORD . . .
And he shall be like a tree planted by the rivers of water. . . ."
Psalm 1.

The Douai version of the Bible adds *plane* before *tree* in the final line, meaning broad-leaved. [2] A reference to the Tower of Babel, or Babylon, which was the Old Testament man's supreme expression of self-will and pride in trying to build a tower that would reach heaven and so place man on a level with God. Noting this pride, God confounded the builders' language to halt the building and scattered men "upon the face of all the earth." (*Genesis*, 11:1–9.) Likewise Boston, a "planned Babel" where money multiplies the darkness. [3] A land of preparation for the next world; see *Hebrews*, 11:13–16. [4] The Virgin Mary; apparently an image of her is being carried (walks) in an Easter procession. [5] Used in contrast to the Virgin; the great whore of Babylon (*Revelation*, 17:1–6, 18). Boston, the new Babylon. [6] Symbol of the plagues; see *Exodus*, 8:20–24; 9:3, 6.

To raise tomorrow's city to the sun
That never sets upon these hell-fire streets
Of Boston, where the sunlight is a sword
Striking at the withholder of the Lord:
Flies, flies are on the plane tree, on the streets.

Flies strike the miraculous waters of the iced
Atlantic and the eyes of Bernadette
Who saw Our Lady standing in the cave
At Massabielle, saw her so squarely that
Her vision put out reason's eyes.[7] The grave
Is open-mouthed and swallowed up in Christ.[8]
O walls of Jericho! And all the streets
To our Atlantic wall are singing: "Sing,
Sing for the resurrection of the King." [9]
Flies, flies are on the plane tree, on the streets.

[7] Ll. 21–25: A reference to St. Bernadette (Soubirous) who in 1859, at the age of fourteen, claimed to have seen the Blessed Virgin in a cave in the Massabielle rocks in the Pyrenees near Lourdes, France. The cave contains a spring whose waters have become "miraculous waters" of healing, a shrine. The image of Bernadette is apparently being carried in the Easter procession. [8] Ll. 25–26: The grave is open at this Eastertime, as witnessed by the processional, and death is "swallowed up" by Christ's victorious resurrection. [9] The impregnable, the walls of Jericho, has been taken; death has been assailed and conquered by Christ. But not so in Boston (l. 30).

ROBERT LOWELL
1917–1977
The Dead in Europe

After the planes unloaded, we fell down
Buried together, unmarried men and women;
Not crown of thorns,[1] not iron, not Lombard crown,[2]
Not grilled and spindle spires pointing to heaven
Could save us. Raise us, Mother,[3] we fell down
Here hugger-mugger in the jellied fire:[4]
Our sacred earth in our day was our curse.

Our Mother, shall we rise on Mary's day
In Maryland, wherever corpses married
Under the rubble, bundled together? Pray
For us whom the blockbusters married and buried;
When Satan scatters us on Rising-day,[5]
O Mother, snatch our bodies from the fire:
Our sacred earth in our day was our curse.

Mother, my bones are trembling and I hear
The earth's reverberations and the trumpet[6]
Bleating into my shambles. Shall I bear,
(O Mary!) unmarried man and powder-puppet,
Witness to the Devil! Mary, hear,
O Mary, marry earth, sea, air and fire;
Our sacred earth in our day is our curse.

[1] The crown of thorns of Christ. [2] Apparently an ironic reference to the bankers and money lenders of Lombardy, established in Lombard Street, London. The Lombard crown is a reference to the Teutons who invaded Italy in 568 to establish a kingdom. Lowell's reference is probably purposely ambiguous. [3] The Virgin Mary, mother of Christ. [4] Jumbled in the bomb fire. [5] The Last Judgment (Judgment Day). "And I saw the dead, small and great, stand before God; and the books were opened: and another book was opened, which is *the book* of life: and the dead were judged out of those things which were written in the books, according to their works. And the sea gave up the dead which were in it; and death and hell delivered up the dead which were in them: and they were judged every man according to their works." *Revelation,* 20:12–13. [6] Trumpets that wake the dead for the Last Judgment. See Donne's "Holy Sonnet, VII," p. 309.

MONA VAN DUYN
1921–
An Annual and Perennial Problem

"Among annuals and perennials, there are not many that can properly be classed among these Heavy *and frankly seductive odors. No gardener should plant these in quantities near the house, or porch, or patio without realizing that many of them, in spite of exquisite fragrance, have a past steeped in sin."*

Taylor's Garden Guide[1]

[1] Norman Taylor, *Taylor's Garden Guide,* New York: D. Van Nostrand and Co., 1957.

One should have known, I suppose, that you can't even trust
the lily-of-the-valley, for all it seems so chaste.

The whole lily family, in fact, is "brooding and sultry."
It's a good thing there's a Garden Guide, nothing paltry

about *their* past. Why, some are so "stinking" one expert cried,
" 'May dogs devour its hateful bulbs!' " Enough said.

We'd better not try to imagine . . . But it's hard to endure
the thought of them sitting brazenly in churches, looking pure.

The tuberose fragrance "is enhanced by dusk and becomes"
(remember, they're taken right into some people's homes,

perhaps with teen-age children around in that air!)
"intoxicating with darkness." Well, there you are.

You hear it said sometimes that in a few cases
the past can be lived down. There's no basis

for that belief—these flowers have had plenty of time.
Sinners just try to make decent folks do the same.

What we've always suspected is true. We're not safe anywhere.
Dark patios, of course—But even at our own back door

from half a block off the jasmine may try to pollute us,
and Heaven protect us all from the trailing arbutus!

JAMES DICKEY
1923–

Adultery

We have all been in rooms
We cannot die in, and they are odd places, and sad.
Often Indians are standing eagle-armed on hills

In the sunrise   open wide to the Great Spirit
Or gliding in canoes   or cattle are browsing on the walls
Far away   gazing down with the eyes of our children

Not far away   or there are men driving
The last railspike, which has turned
Gold in their hands. Gigantic forepleasure lives

Among such scenes, and we are alone with it
At last. There is always some weeping
Between us   and someone is always checking

A wrist watch by the bed to see how much
Longer we have left. Nothing can come
Of this   nothing can come

Of us: of me with my grim techniques
Or you who have sealed your womb
With a ring of convulsive rubber:

Although we come together,
Nothing will come of us. But we would not give
It up, for death is beaten

By praying Indians   by distant cows   historical

Hammers by hazardous meetings that bridge
A continent. One could never die here

Never die never die
While crying. My lover, my dear one
I will see you next week

When I'm in town. I will call you
If I can. Please get hold of please don't
Oh God, Please don't any more I can't bear . . .
Listen:

We have done it again we are
Still living. Sit up and smile,
God bless you. Guilt is magical.

DONALD JUSTICE
1925–

Counting the Mad

This one was put in a jacket,
This one was sent home,
This one was given bread and meat
But would eat none,
And this one cried No No No No
All day long.

This one looked at the window
As though it were a wall,
This one saw things that were not there,
This one things that were,
And this one cried No No No No
All day long.

This one thought himself a bird,
This one a dog
And this one thought himself a man,
An ordinary man,
And cried and cried No No No No
All day long.

ALLEN GINSBERG
1926–

Last Night in Calcutta

Still night. The old clock Ticks,
half past two. A ringing of crickets
awake in the ceiling. The gate is locked
on the street outside—sleepers, mustaches,
nakedness, but no desire. A few mosquitos
waken the itch, the fan turns slowly—
a car thunders along the black asphalt,
a bull snorts, something is expected—
Time sits solid in the four yellow walls.
No one is here, emptiness filled with train
whistles & dog barks, answered a block away.
Pushkin[1] sits on the bookshelf, Shakespeare's
complete works as well as Blake's unread—
O Spirit of Poetry, no use calling on you
babbling in this emptiness furnished with
beds
under the bright oval mirror—perfect
night for sleepers to dissolve in tranquil
blackness, and rest there eight hours
—Waking to stained fingers, bitter mouth
and lung gripped by cigarette hunger,
what to do with this big toe, this arm
this eye in the starving skeleton-filled
sore horse tramcar-heated Calcutta in
Eternity—sweating and teeth rotted away—
Rilke[2] at least could dream about lovers,
the old breast excitement and trembling belly,
is that it? And the vast starry space—
If the brain changes matter breathes
fearfully back on man—But now
the great crash of buildings and planets
breaks thru the walls of language and drowns
me under its Ganges[3] heaviness forever.
No escape but thru Bangkok and New York
death.
Skin is sufficient to be skin, that's all
it ever could be, tho screams of pain in the
kidney
make it sick of itself, a wavy dream
dying to finish its all too famous misery
—Leave immortality for another to suffer like
a fool,
not get stuck in the corner of the universe
sticking morphine in the arm and eating meat.

[1] Alexander Pushkin (1799–1837), famous Russian poet. [2] The German poet Rainer Maria Rilke (1875–1926), whose *Duino Elegies* celebrates angels and lovers of immortal power. [3] The sacred river of India.

W. D. SNODGRASS
1926–

What We Said

Stunned in that first estrangement,
We went through the turning woods
Where inflamed leaves sick as words
Spun, wondering what the change meant.

Half gone, our road led onwards
By barbed wire, past the ravine
Where a lost couch, snarled in vines,
Spilled its soiled, gray innards

Into a garbage mound.
We came, then, to a yard
Where tarpaper, bottles and charred
Boards lay on the trampled ground.

This had been someone's lawn.
And, closing up like a wound,
The cluttered hole in the ground
A life had been built upon.

In the high grass, cars had been.
On the leafless branches, rags
And condoms fluttered like the flags
Of new orders moving in.

We talked of the last war, when
Houses, cathedral towns, shacks—
Whole continents went into wreckage.
What fools could do that again?

Ruin on every side—
We would set our loves in order,
Surely, we told each other.
Surely. That's what we said.

JAMES WRIGHT
1927–

The Blessing

Just off the highway to Rochester, Minnesota,
Twilight bounds softly forth on the grass.
And the eyes of those two Indian ponies
Darken with kindness.
They have come gladly out of the willows
To welcome my friend and me.
We step over the barbed wire into the pasture
Where they have been grazing all day, alone.
They ripple tensely, they can hardly contain
their happiness
That we have come.
They bow shyly as wet swans. They love each
other.
There is no loneliness like theirs.
At home once more,
They begin munching the young tufts of spring
in the darkness.
I would like to hold the slenderer one in my
arms,
For she has walked over to me
And nuzzled my left hand.
She is black and white,
Her mane falls wild on her forehead,
And the light breeze moves me to caress her
long ear
That is delicate as the skin over a girl's wrist.
Suddenly I realize
That if I stepped out of my body I would break
Into blossom.

ANNE SEXTON
1928–1974

The Kiss

My mouth blooms like a cut.
I've been wronged all year, tedious
nights, nothing but rough elbows in them
and delicate boxes of Kleenex calling *crybaby*
crybaby, you fool!

Before today my body was useless.
Now it's tearing at its square corners.
It's tearing old Mary's garments off, knot by knot
and see—Now it's shot full of these electric bolts.
Zing! A resurrection!

Once it was a boat, quite wooden
and with no business, no salt water under it
and in need of some paint. It was no more
than a group of boards. But you hoisted her,
rigged her.
She's been elected.

My nerves are turned on. I hear them like
musical instruments. Where there was silence
the drums, the strings are incurably playing. You
did this.
Pure genius at work. Darling, the composer has
stepped into fire.

DONALD HALL
1928–

Self-Portrait As a Bear

Here is a fat animal, a bear
that is partly a dodo.
Ridiculous wings hang at his shoulders
while he plods in the brickyards
at the edge of the city, smiling
and eating flowers. He eats them
because he loves them
because they are beautiful
because they love him.
It is eating flowers which makes him fat.
He carries his huge stomach
over the gutters of damp leaves
in the parking lots in October,
but inside that paunch
he knows there are fields of lupine
and meadows of mustard and poppy.
He encloses sunshine.
Winds bend the flowers
in combers across the valley,
birds hang on the stiff wind,
at night there are showers, and the sun
lifts through a haze every morning
of the summer in the stomach.

ADRIENNE RICH
1929–

Living in Sin

She had thought the studio would keep itself;
no dust upon the furniture of love.
Half heresy, to wish the taps less vocal,
the panes relieved of grime. A plate of pears,
a piano with a Persian shawl, a cat
stalking the picturesque amusing mouse
had risen at his urging.
Not that at five each separate stair would writhe
under the milkman's tramp; that morning light
so coldly would delineate the scraps
of last night's cheese and three sepulchral bottles;
that on the kitchen shelf among the saucers
a pair of beetle-eyes would fix her own—
envoy from some black village in the mouldings . . .
Meanwhile, he, with a yawn,
sounded a dozen notes upon the keyboard,
declared it out of tune, shrugged at the mirror,
rubbed at his beard, went out for cigarettes;
while she, jeered by the minor demons,
pulled back the sheets and made the bed and found
a towel to dust the table-top,
and let the coffee-pot boil over on the stove,
By evening she was back in love again,
though not so wholly but throughout the night
she woke sometimes to feel the daylight coming
like a relentless milkman up the stairs.

GARY SNYDER
1930–

A Walk

Sunday the only day we don't work:
Mules farting around the meadow,
                    Murphy fishing,
The tent flaps in the warm
Early sun: I've eaten breakfast and I'll
                    take a walk
To Benson Lake. Packed a lunch,
Goodbye. Hopping on creekbed boulders
Up the rock throat three miles
                    Piute Creek—
In steep gorge glacier-slick rattlesnake country
Jump, land by a pool, trout skitter,
The clear sky. Deer tracks.
Bad places by a falls, boulders big as houses,
Lunch tied to belt,
I stemmed up a crack and almost fell
But rolled out safe on a ledge
                    and ambled on.
Quail chicks freeze underfoot, color of stone
Then run cheep! away, hen quail fussing.
Craggy west end of Benson Lake—after edging
Past dark creek pools on a long white slope—
Lookt down in the ice-black lake
                    lined with cliff
From far above: deep shimmering trout.
A lone duck in a gunsightpass
                    steep side hill
Through slide-aspen and talus, to the east end,
Down to grass, wading a wide smooth stream
Into camp. At last.
                    By the rusty three-year-
Ago left-behind cookstove
Of the old trail crew,
Stoppt and swam and ate my lunch.

ROBLEY WILSON, JR.
1930–

The Great Teachers[1]

Love is not love
Which alters when it alteration finds.

It never bothered Socrates,
Who clustered close about him
His own images, ghostly togas
Milk-pure, frozen in flowing out.
The naive boys with crossed ankles
Rocked on their doubled fists,
The alert rows of them mirror
To the equanimities of love.

It never bothered Aristotle.
Thought was a sun his pupils
Tethered to like cavalries
Making a shambles of the past.
They brought him precious spoils
For the apartments of his mind;
Heavy with plunder, he divined
The blinded temperance of love.

It never bothered the Saviour
On the populous mountainsides,
Where the confusion of bared heads
Made like trees an orderly bowing.
If gospel truth sits oddly in
The mind, His vision meets
Upon some special confidence
The humble intersects of love.

It never bothers great teachers.
We learn them best when they are men
Poised on the sills of life, and see
How they lean out from it
To touch truth. We presume to teach
But grow old and hang back from risk.
We ask our children: *What is love?*
And are, too, endlessly betrayed.

[1] The poem was first published in *The Reporter*, Sept. 22, 1966. The epigraph, taken from Shakespeare's "Sonnet 116" (p. 262), was added later.

ROBLEY WILSON, JR.
1930–

War

Sometimes I have wanted to go to war.
The stories are always good—Thermopylae
Was good, the Gallic campaigns were as good
As you could get against barbarians,
The Crusades were outright inspirational.

Everyone ought to go off to a war
Before he is too old to have the good
Of it. The people we call pacifist
Forget (or never learned) the power of it,
The sense of godliness killing provides.

Who would not want to be the angel, high
Over the enemy's cities with wings
Broad as the foreshadow of death? What boy
Cannot recall from his pitiless dreams
That carnage laid about him in his bed

Of adults and girls? War is for the young
And keeps them young; war is to make a man
Immortal; war is to subvert boredom
And the indiscriminacy of states.
Who favors war knows what liberty is.

Think about us. War would spare us the vice
Of guilt, the curse of inadequate love,
The remorse of aimlessness. War transforms;
It is a place to start from, props up pride,
Writes history. Out of war, art makes itself.

Sometimes I have wanted to go to war,
To turn flame in anyone's heart. Old names
Dazzle me: Alexander, Genghis Khan,
Caesar, Napoleon—will any man
Shrink from riding such splendor to his grave?

Are you the one gone soft now over peace?
Nonsense. Woman has always profited
From men at war. Since time began, if you
Camp-followed any conqueror, you, too,
Could count a hundred lovers on the sand.

SYLVIA PLATH[1]
1932–1963

Two Views of a Cadaver Room

1

The day she visited the dissecting room
They had four men laid out, black as burnt turkey,
Already half unstrung. A vinegary fume
Of the death vats clung to them;
The white-smocked boys started working.
The head of his cadaver had caved in,
And she could scarcely make out anything
In that rubble of skull plates and old leather.
A sallow piece of string held it together.

In their jars the snail-nosed babies moon and glow.
He hands her the cut-out heart like a cracked heirloom.

2

In Brueghel's panorama of smoke and slaughter
Two people only are blind to the carrion army:
He, afloat in the sea of her blue satin
Skirts, sings in the direction
Of her bare shoulder, while she bends,
Fingering a leaflet of music, over him,
Both of them deaf to the fiddle in the hands
Of the death's-head shadowing their song.
These Flemish lovers flourish; not for long.

Yet desolation, stalled in paint, spares the little country
Foolish, delicate, in the lower right-hand corner.

SYLVIA PLATH[1]
1932–1963

Suicide off Egg Rock

Behind him the hotdogs split and drizzled
On the public grills, and the ochreous salt flats,
Gas tanks, factory stacks—that landscape
Of imperfections his bowels were part of—
Rippled and pulsed in the glassy updraft.
Sun struck the water like a damnation.
No pit of shadow to crawl into,
And his blood beating the old tattoo
I am, I am, I am. Children
Were squealing where combers broke and the spindrift
Raveled wind-ripped from the crest of the wave.
A mongrel working his legs to a gallop
Hustled a gull flock to flap off the sandspit.

He smoldered, as if stone-deaf, blindfold,
His body beached with the sea's garbage,
A machine to breathe and beat forever.
Flies filing in through a dead skate's eyehole
Buzzed and assailed the vaulted brainchamber.
The words in his book wormed off the pages.
Everything glittered like blank paper.

Everything shrank in the sun's corrosive
Ray but Egg Rock on the blue wastage.
He heard when he walked into the water

The forgetful surf creaming on those ledges.

[1] *The Bell Jar* (New York: Harper & Row, 1971) is a fictionalized autobiography by Sylvia Plath.

IMAMU AMIRI BARAKA[1]
1934–

A Poem for Black Hearts[2]

For Malcolm's eyes, when they broke
the face of some dumb white man. For
Malcolm's hands raised to bless us
all black and strong in his image
of ourselves, for Malcolm's words
fire darts, the victor's tireless
thrusts, words hung above the world
change as it may, he said it, and
for this he was killed, for saying,
and feeling, and being/change, all
collected hot in his heart, For Malcolm's
heart, raising us above our filthy cities,
for his stride, and his beat, and his address
to the grey monsters of the world, For Malcolm's
pleas for your dignity, black men, for your life,

[1] Earlier known as LeRoi Jones.
[2] See Margaret A. Walker's poem, "For Malcom X," p. 360, and the footnote to the poem.

black men, for the filling of your minds
with righteousness, For all of him dead and
gone and vanished from us, and all of him which
clings to our speech-black god of our time.
For all of him, and all of yourself, look up,
black man, quit stuttering and shuffling, look up,
black man, quit whining and stooping, for all of him,
For Great Malcolm a prince of the earth, let nothing in us rest
until we avenge ourselves for his death, stupid animals
that killed him, let us never breathe a pure breath if
we fail, and white men call us faggots till the end of
the earth.

IMAMU AMIRI BARAKA[1]
1934–

Preface to a Twenty Volume Suicide Note

Lately, I've become accustomed to the way
The ground opens up and envelops me
Each time I go out to walk the dog.
Or the broad edged silly music the wind
Makes when I run for a bus—

Things have come to that.

And now, each night I count the stars,
And each night I get the same number.
And when they will not come to be counted
I count the holes they leave.

Nobody sings anymore.

And then last night, I tiptoed up
To my daughter's room and heard her
Talking to someone, and when I opened
The door, there was no one there . . .
Only she on her knees,
Peeking into her own clasped hands.

[1] Earlier known as LeRoi Jones.

MARK STRAND
1934–

From a Litany

There is an open field I lie down in a hole I once dug and I praise the sky.
I praise the clouds that are like lungs of light.
I praise the owl that wants to inhabit me and the hawk that does not.
I praise the mouse's fury, the wolf's consideration.
I praise the dog that lives in the household of people and shall never be one of them.
I praise the whale that lives under the cold blankets of salt.
I praise the formations of squid, the domes of meandra.
I praise the secrecy of doors, the openness of windows.
I praise the depth of closets.
I praise the wind, the rising generations of air.
I praise the trees on whose branches shall sit the Cock of Portugal and the Polish Cock.
I praise the palm trees of Rio and those that shall grow in London.
I praise the gardeners, the worms and the small plants that praise each other.
I praise the sweet berries of Georgetown, Maine and the song of the white-throated sparrow.
I praise the poets of Waverly Place and Eleventh Street, and the one whose bones turn to dark emeralds when he stands upright in the wind.
I praise the clocks for which I grow old in a day and young in a day.
I praise all manner of shade, that which I see and that which I do not.
I praise all roofs from the watery roof of the pond to the slate roof of the customs house.

I praise those who have made of their bodies final embassies of flesh.
I praise the failure of those with ambition, the authors of leaflets and notebooks of
nothing.
I praise the moon for suffering men.
I praise the sun its tributes.
I praise the pain of revival and the bliss of decline.
I praise all for nothing because there is no price.
I praise myself for the way I have with a shovel and I praise the shovel.
I praise the motive of praise by which I shall be reborn.
I praise the morning whose sun is upon me.
I praise the evening whose son I am.

RICHARD RACKSTRAW
1936–1974

The Word

You are walking the track, counting
the ties, perhaps, as a hunter
whose pockets are empty, whose rage
steadies him. The gun you carry is open.

You have hunted for years. Thin animals
are your familiars. You have loved
the hollows of their eyes, the tensile
marrow of their wills in such silence.

Now bruised from the sun, your eyes
darken like roses. It is almost night.
You are walking into a distance
the late-autumn Monarch[1] flies.

Deep in your thought was a word
the sound of dry flesh pawing at
the door of a cabin. You opened the door
and the word, the word came in.

DIANE WAKOSKI
1937–

You, Letting the Trees Stand As My Betrayer

You replaced the Douglas firs
that reached
like mechanics' hands
outside my windows

trying to understand the glass
with furry, needle-tipped noses

You,
who understood me
in the rain

or at least
accepted me.

The trees never left
my windows
even when they put on gloves
for age;
they had married the glass
with the thud of falling cones.
They remembered my name
on windy nights.

But you
are my betrayer
who tried to frighten me with trees one night.
Then chopped them down
outside my windows
the next day

You ride a motorcycle
past wintry trees
and summer trees
and never once
think of me.
But my friends are
the falling branches
that will tilt you
and snap your neck one day.
I dream of your thick body
uprooted

[1] A large migratory American butterfly of unusual size and beauty. When this poem was written, their winter home was a mystery; hence the author is using their flight as a symbol related to "walking into a distance." Very recently the monarchs' winter home was found to be in Mexico, a literal fact unrelated to the poem.

and torn by a storm
on a motorcycle track.

You chopped down my trees—
they were my legs—
and unlike George Washington you did tell
many lies.
You are my betrayer,
you woodsman,
the man who stomps into the heart of this
forest.

ERICA JONG
1942–

How You Get Born

One night, your mother is listening to the walls.
The clock whirrs like insect wings.
The ticking says lonely lonely lonely.

In the living room, the black couch swallows her.
She trusts it more than men,
but no one will ever love her
enough.

She doesn't yet know you
so how can she love you?
She loves you like God or Shakespeare.
She loves you like Mozart.

You are trembling in the walls like music.
You cross the ceiling in a phantom car of light.

Meanwhile unborn,
you wait in a heavy rainsoaked cloud
for your father's thunderbolt.
Your mother lies in the living room dreaming
your hands.
Your mother lies in the living room dreaming
your eyes.

She awakens & a shudder shakes her teeth.
The world is beginning again after the flood.

She slides into bed beside that gray-faced man,
your father.
She opens her legs to your coming.

NIKKI GIOVANNI
1943–

Kidnap Poem

ever been kidnapped
by a poet
if i were a poet
i'd kidnap you
put you in my phrases and meter
you to jones beach
or maybe coney island
or maybe just to my house
lyric you in lilacs
dash you in the rain
blend into the beach
to complement my see
play the lyre for you
ode you with my love song
anything to win you
wrap you in the red Black green
show you off to mama
yeah if i were a poet i'd kid
nap you

JAMES TATE
1943–

The Lost Pilot

for my father, 1922-1944

Your face did not rot
like the others—the co-pilot,
for example, I saw him

yesterday. His face is corn-
mush: his wife and daughter,
the poor ignorant people, stare

as if he will compose soon.
He was more wronged than Job.
But your face did not rot

like the others—it grew dark,
and hard like ebony;
the features progressed in their

distinction. If I could cajole
you to come back for an evening,
down from your compulsive

orbiting, I would touch you,
read your face as Dallas,
your hoodlum gunner, now,

with the blistered eyes, reads
his braille editions. I would
touch your face as a disinterested

scholar touches an original page.
However frightening, I would
discover you, and I would not

turn you in; I would not make
you face your wife, or Dallas,
or the co-pilot, Jim. You

could return to your crazy
orbiting, and I would not try
to fully understand what

it means to you. All I know
is this: when I see you,
as I have seen you at least

once every year of my life,
spin across the wilds of the sky
like a tiny, African god,

I feel dead. I feel as if I were
the residue of a stranger's life,
that I should pursue you.

My head cocked toward the sky,
I cannot get off the ground,
and, you, passing over again,

fast, perfect, and unwilling
to tell me that you are doing
well, or that it was mistake

that placed you in that world,
and me in this; or that misfortune
placed these worlds in us.

FOUR MODERN CLASSICS

WILLIAM BUTLER YEATS
1865–1939

Among School Children

I

I walk through the long schoolroom questioning;[1]
A kind old nun in a white hood replies;
The children learn to cipher and to sing,
To study reading-books and history,
To cut and sew, be neat in everything
In the best modern way—the children's eyes
In momentary wonder stare upon
A sixty-year-old smiling public man.

II

I dream of a Ledaean body,[2] bent
Above a sinking fire, a tale that she
Told of a harsh reproof, or trivial event
That changed some childish day to tragedy—
Told, and it seemed that our two natures blent
Into a sphere from youthful sympathy,
Or else, to alter Plato's parable,[3]
Into the yolk and white of the one shell.

III

And thinking of that fit of grief or rage
I look upon one child or t'other there
And wonder if she stood so at that age—
For even daughters of the swan can share
Something of every paddler's heritage—
And had that colour upon cheek or hair,
And thereupon my heart is driven wild:
She stands before me as a living child.

IV

Her present image floats into the mind—
Did Quattrocento[4] finger fashion it
Hollow of cheek as though it drank the wind
And took a mess of shadows for its meat?
And I though never of Ladaean kind
Had pretty plumage once—enough of that,
Better to smile on all that smile, and show
There is a comfortable kind of old scarecrow.

[1] Yeats was an Irish Senator (1922–1928) interested in reforming the educational system.

[2] As beautiful as Leda and Helen of Troy, her daughter (see l. 20) whose father, Zeus, in the form of a swan had possessed Leda. Yeats's poem "Leda and the Swan" celebrates the event. [3] Plato's *Symposium* tells us that Zeus "cut men in two . . . as you might divide an egg with a hair," and hence "each of us when separated is but the indenture of a man, having one side only like a flat fish, and he is always looking for his other half." [4] An Italian term used by the art historians to describe schools and styles of fifteenth-century painting as, for example, Botticelli's female figures.

V

What youthful mother, a shape upon her lap
Honey of generation[5] had betrayed,
And that must sleep, shriek, struggle to escape
As recollection or the drug decide,
Would think her son, did she but see that shape
With sixty or more winters on its head,
A compensation for the pang of his birth,
Or the uncertainty of his setting forth?

VI

Plato thought nature but a spume that plays
Upon a ghostly paradigm of things;[6]
Soldier Aristotle played the taws
Upon the bottom of a king of kings;[7]
World-famous golden-thighed Pythagoras[8]
Fingered upon a fiddle-stick or strings
What a star sang and careless Muses heard:
Old clothes upon old sticks to scare a bird.[9]

VII

Both nuns and mothers worship images,
But those the candles light are not as those
That animate a mother's reveries,
But keep a marble or a bronze repose.
And yet they too break hearts—O Presences
That passion, piety or affection knows,
And that all heavenly glory symbolise—
O self-born mockers of man's enterprise;

VIII

Labour is blossoming or dancing where
The body is not bruised to pleasure soul,
Nor beauty born out of its own despair,
Nor blear-eyed wisdom out of midnight oil.
O chestnut-tree, great-rooted blossomer,
Are you the leaf, the blossom or the bole?
O body swayed to music, O brightening glance,
How can we know the dancer from the dance?

[5] Yeats's note: "I have taken the 'honey of generation' from Porphyry's essay on 'The Cave of the Nymphs,' but find no warrant in Porphyry for considering it the 'drug' that destroys the 'recollection' of pre-natal freedom. He blamed a cup of oblivion given in the zodiacal sign of Cancer." Porphyry's original name was Malchus (232?–304?), Greek scholar and neoplatonic philosopher. [6] Plato regarded physical reality as an imperfect representation of ideal reality (Plato's philosophy of idealism). [7] The pupil of Plato, Aristotle nevertheless taught that our world does possess reality.

[8] Greek philosopher (fl. *c.* 530 B.C.) whose later followers thought him a god with a golden thigh, taught the transmigration of souls (reincarnation); and that reality is found in the mathematical relationships which govern its order and harmony. Such mysticism intrigued Yeats. [9] See l. 32.

ROBERT FROST
1874–1963

A Masque of Reason

"The Trial by Existence" (p. 311) and "A Masque of Reason" are companion pieces through which Frost explores some of his basic metaphysical assumptions. Both poems are concerned with the trial of man on the earth, and our failure to find ultimate answers to the meaning of that trial which leaves us "bearing it crushed and mystified." True to Frost's belief that "everything written is as good as it is dramatic," both poems are little verse plays, especially "A Masque of Reason" with its four characters—and the warning is clear: its meaning emerges from the interaction of the characters' points of view, not from the assumptions of any single character regardless of his importance.

Frost thinks of "A Masque of Reason" as being a forty-third chapter (see the final line) for *The Book of Job,* which implies either that he answers the question, "Why do the innocent suffer?" or that he pursues the question further with commentary of his own. In any event, knowing the basic events in *Job* will increase our understanding of Frost's poem, although a fresh and intimate reading of *Job* is urgently recommended.*

The "Prologue" to *Job* (chaps. 1–2) makes it clear that Satan has taunted God by arguing that the "perfect and upright" Job "fears God and eschews evil" only because "his substance is increased in the land." God accepts the challenge and permits Satan to test Job with afflictions. Reduced to abject poverty and with his children dead, Job suffers intensely from boils while his wife advises him to "curse God, and die." Later, three friends counsel and finally warn him to confess his sins. Job stoutly maintains his innocence, challenges God's justice, and yearns to meet God face to face to ask why an innocent man should suffer. God appears "out of the whirlwind," and Job, awed by God's presence and knowledge, repents of his belligerent challenge to God ("What is the Almighty, that we should serve him?" 21:15)—but not of the crimes falsely alleged by his friends—and is returned to prosperity. "A Masque of Reason" begins with Job still wondering what he had done "to deserve such pain" and waiting to "come to rest in an official verdict."

A fair oasis in the purest desert.
A man sits leaning back against a palm.
His wife lies by him looking at the sky.

Man You're not asleep?
Wife No, I can hear you. Why?
Man I said the incense tree's on fire again.
Wife You mean the Burning Bush?[1]
Man The Christmas Tree.
Wife I shouldn't be surprised.
Man The strangest light!
Wife There's a strange light on everything today.
Man The myrrh tree gives it. Smell the rosin burning?
The ornaments the Greek artificers
Made for the Emperor Alexius,[2]
The Star of Bethlehem, the pomegranates,
The birds, seem all on fire with Paradise.
And hark, the gold enameled nightingales
Are singing. Yes, and look, the Tree is troubled.
Someone's caught in the branches.
Wife So there is.
Man He can't get out.
Wife He's loose! He's out!
It's God.
I'd know Him by Blake's picture[3] anywhere.
Now what's He doing?

* The serious student of *Job* will be rewarded by consulting *The Interpreter's Bible,* Nashville: Abingdon Press, vol. III (1954), pp. 877–1198, including the Text, Exegesis, and Exposition. For a briefer but excellent commentary, see *The Westminster Study Edition of the Holy Bible,* Philadelphia: The Westminster Press, 1948, pp. 638–690.

1 *Exodus,* 3:2. The Angel of the Lord appeared to Moses "in a flame of fire out of the midst of a bush . . . and the bush was not consumed." 2 Alexius Comnenus (1048–1118), first of the Comneni dynasty of Byzantine emperors. 3 A reference to William Blake's (1757–1827) engravings for the Bible, especially to one titled, "Then the Lord Answered Job out of the Whirlwind." Blake furnished engravings for many of his own books of poetry.

Man Pitching throne, I guess,
Here by our atoll.
Wife Something Byzantine.[4]

(The throne's a plywood flat, prefabricated,
That God pulls lightly upright on its hinges
And stands beside, supporting it in place.)

Perhaps for an Olympic Tournament,
Or Court of Love.
Man More likely Royal Court—
Or Court of Law, and this is Judgment Day.
I trust it is. Here's where I lay aside
My varying opinion of myself
And come to rest in an official verdict.
Suffer yourself to be admired, my love,
As Waller says.[5]
Wife Or not admired. Go over
And speak to Him before the others come.
Tell Him He may remember you: you're Job.
God Oh, I remember well: you're Job, my Patient.
How are you now? I trust you're quite recovered,
And feel no ill effects from what I gave you.
Job [6] Gave me in truth: I like the frank admission.
I am a name for being put upon.
But, yes, I'm fine, except for now and then
A reminiscent twinge of rheumatism.
The letup's heavenly. You perhaps will tell us
If that is all there is to be of Heaven,
Escape from so great pains of life on earth
It gives a sense of letup calculated
To last a fellow to Eternity.
God Yes, by and by. But first a larger matter.
I've had you on my mind a thousand years
To thank you someday for the way you helped me
Establish once for all the principle
There's no connection man can reason out
Between his just deserts and what he gets.
Virtue may fail and wickedness succeed.
'Twas a great demonstration we put on.
I should have spoken sooner had I found
The word I wanted. You would have supposed
One who in the beginning *was* the Word [7]
Would be in a position to command it.
I have to wait for words like anyone.
Too long I've owed you this apology
For the apparently unmeaning sorrow
You were afflicted with in those old days.

[4] From Byzantium, the ancient name of Constantinople. A reference to the ornate Byzantine architecture notable for such features as the circle, dome, and round arch. St. Sophia at Constantinople and St. Mark at Venice are examples of Byzantine architecture. [5] "Song" ("Go, lovely rose"), p. 277. [6] By referring to Job first as "Man," Frost is, of course, using Job as a symbol of mankind, a symbol frequently used in connection with *The Book of Job.* [7] *John,* 1:1. "In the beginning was the Word, and the Word was with God, and the Word was God."

But it was of the essence of the trial
You shouldn't understand it at the time.
It had to seem unmeaning to have meaning.
And it came out all right. I have no doubt
You realize by now the part you played
To stultify the Deuteronomist[8]
And change the tenor of religious thought.
My thanks are to you for releasing me
From moral bondage to the human race.
The only free will there at first was man's,
Who could do good or evil as he chose.
I had no choice but I must follow him
With forfeits and rewards he understood—
Unless I liked to suffer loss of worship.
I had to prosper good and punish evil.
You changed all that. You set me free to reign.
You are the Emancipator of your God,
And as such I promote you to a saint.[9]

Job You hear Him, Thyatira:[10] we're a saint.
Salvation in our case is retroactive.
We're saved, we're saved, whatever else it means.

Jobs' Wife Well, after all these years!

Job This is my wife.

Job's Wife If You're the deity I assume You are
(I'd know You by Blake's picture anywhere)—

God The best, I'm told, I ever have had taken.

Job's Wife —I have a protest I would lodge with You.
I want to ask You if it stands to reason
That women prophets should be burned as witches,
Whereas men prophets are received with honor.

Job Except in their own country, Thyatira.

God You're not a witch?

Job's Wife No.

God Have you ever been one?

Job Sometimes she thinks she has and gets herself
Worked up about it. But she really hasn't—
Not in the sense of having to my knowledge
Predicted anything that came to pass.

Job's Wife The Witch of Endor[11] was a friend of mine.

God You wouldn't say she fared so very badly.
I noticed when she called up Samuel
His spirit had to come. Apparently
A witch was stronger than a prophet there.

[8] The name given to the unknown writer of the six books of history following *Deuteronomy* who interprets the history of the Hebrew nation with the so-called "Deuteronomic formula" which holds that obedience to God's laws will bring prosperity while disobedience will bring material disaster to the nation. The formula was later used in the Wisdom books (*Job, Proverbs,* and *Ecclesiastes*) as the Wisdom formula," but now applied to the individual instead of the nation. Frost states the result of the formula in l. 76. [9] Job had demonstrated his own integrity, but, more important to God, by proving that not all men "serve for pay" (l. 353), Job had vindicated God against Satan. [10] Frost's name for Job's wife; she is given no name in the Bible. [11] *I Samuel,* 28:3–25.

Job's Wife But she was burned for witchcraft.
God That is not
Of record in my Note Book.[12]
Job's Wife Well, she was.
And I should like to know the reason why.[13]
God There you go asking for the very thing
We've just agreed I didn't have to give.

(*The throne collapses. But He picks it up*
And this time locks it up and leaves it.)

Where has she been the last half hour or so?
She wants to know why there is still injustice.
I answer flatly: That's the way it is,
And bid my will avouch it like Macbeth.[14]
We may as well go back to the beginning
And look for justice in the case of Segub.[15]
Job Oh, Lord, Let's not go *back* to anything.
God Because your wife's past won't bear looking into?
In our great moment what did you do, Madam?
What did you try to make your husband say? [16]
Job's Wife No, let's not live things over. I don't care.
I stood by Job. I may have turned on You.
Job scratched his boils[17] and tried to think what he
Had done or not done to or for the poor.
The test is always how we treat the poor.
It's time the poor were treated by the state
In some ways not so penal as the poorhouse.
That's one thing more to put on Your agenda.
Job hadn't done a thing, poor innocent.[18]
I told him not to scratch: it made it worse.
If I said once I said a thousand times,
Don't scratch! And when, as rotten as his skin,
His tents blew all to pieces, I picked up
Enough to build him every night a pup tent
Around him so it wouldn't touch and hurt him.
I did my wifely duty. I should tremble!
All You can seem to do is lose Your temper
When reason-hungry mortals ask for reasons.[19]
Of course, in the abstract high singular
There isn't any universal reason;
And no one but a man would think there was.
You don't catch women trying to be Plato.
Still there must be lots of unsystematic
Stray scraps of palliative reason
It wouldn't hurt You to vouchsafe the faithful.

[12] Her death is not recorded in the Bible (God's "Note Book"). [13] See footnote 26 for l. 241. [14] See *Macbeth*, III. i. 118–120. [15] *I Kings*, 16:34. Frost's line implies that the sacrifice of Segub's life by his father, Hiel, cannot be defended. See also *Joshua*, 6:26. [16] "Then said his wife unto him, Dost thou still retain thine integrity? Curse God, and die." *Job*, 2:9. [17] The Biblical term implies a terrible disease, perhaps elephantiasis, which disfigured Job's face and bred worms or maggots in his sores. [18] As Job stoutly maintains throughout his afflictions. Why, he asks, should the innocent suffer? [19] Thyatira believes that instead of giving Job reasons for his pain, God challenged him with questions to induce awe and reverence in him. See footnote 21 for l. 172.

You thought it was agreed You needn't give them.
You thought to suit Yourself. I've not agreed
To anything with anyone.
Job There, there,
You go to sleep. God must await events
As well as words.
Job's Wife I'm serious. God's had
Aeons of time and still it's mostly women
Get burned for prophecy, men almost never.
Job God needs time just as much as you or I
To get things done. Reformers fail to see that.
She'll go to sleep. Nothing keeps her awake
But physical activity I find.
Try to read to her and she drops right off.
God She's beautiful.
Job Yes, she was just remarking
She now felt younger by a thousand years
Than the day she was born.
God That's about right,
I should have said. You got your age reversed
When time was found to be a space dimension[20]
That could, like any space, be turned around in?
Job Yes, both of us: we saw to that at once.
But, God, I have a question too to raise.
(My wife gets in ahead of me with hers.)
I need some help about this reason problem
Before I am too late to be got right
As to what reasons I agree to waive.
I'm apt to string along with Thyatira.
God knows—or rather, You know (God forgive me)
I waived the reason for my ordeal—but—
I have a question even there to ask—
In confidence.[21] There's no one here but her,
And she's a woman: she's not interested
In general ideas and principles.
God What are her interests, Job?
Job Witch-women's rights.
Humor her there or she will be confirmed
In her suspicion You're no feminist.
You have it in for women, she believes.
Kipling invokes You as Lord God of Hosts.[22]
She'd like to know how You would take a prayer
That started off Lord God of Hostesses.
God I'm charmed with her.
Job Yes, I could see You were.
But to my question. I am much impressed

[20] An oblique reference to Einstein's concept of "space-time" as a single dimension. [21] Job is saying that when God "answered" him "out of the whirlwind" (38:1 to 41:34) Job was given no reasons for his ordeal. Nothing had been more urgent to Job than to meet God face to face (19:25–27; 23:3–5), and according to Frost, Job's (man's) urgency still exists. [22] Rudyard Kipling's (1865–1936) poem, "Recessional."

With what You say we have established,[23]
Between us, You and I.

God I make you see?
It would be too bad if Columbus-like
You failed to see the worth of your achievement.

Job You call it mine.

God We groped it out together.
Any originality it showed
I give you credit for. My forte is truth,
Or metaphysics, long the world's reproach
For standing still in one place true forever;
While science goes self-superseding on.
Look at how far we've left the current science
Of Genesis behind. The wisdom there, though,
Is just as good as when I uttered it.
Still, novelty has doubtless an attraction.

Job So it's important who first thinks of things?

God I'm a great stickler for the author's name.
By proper names I find I do my thinking.

Job's Wife God, who invented earth?

Job What, still awake?

God Any originality it showed
Was of the Devil. He invented Hell,
False premises that are the original
Of all originality, the sin
That felled the angels, Wolsey should have said.[24]
As for the earth, we groped that out together,
Much as your husband, Job, and I together
Found out the discipline man needed most
Was to learn his submission to unreason;
And that for man's own sake as well as mine,
So he won't find it hard to take his orders
From his inferiors in intelligence
In peace and war—especially in war.

Job So he won't find it hard to take his war.

God You have the idea. There's not much I can tell you.

Job All very splendid. I am flattered proud
To have been in on anything with You.
'Twas a great demonstration if You say so.
Though incidentally I sometimes wonder
Why it had had to be at my expense.

God It had to be at somebody's expense.
Society can never think things out:
It has to see them acted out by actors,
Devoted actors at a sacrifice—
The ablest actors I can lay my hands on.[25]
Is that your answer?

[23] See ll. 47–79. The point of view expressed in them does not appear in *Job*. [24] See Shakespeare, *Henry VIII*, III. ii. 440–441. [25] Ll. 222–226 do not constitute a random remark by Frost merely to interject a theory of his (although the remark *does* represent a factor in his poetic theory); some Bible commentators regard *Job* as a play whose function is as Frost describes it.

Job No, for I have yet
To ask my question. We disparage reason.
But all the time it's what we're most concerned with.
There's will as motor and there's will as brakes.
Reason is, I suppose, the steering gear.
The will as brakes can't stop the will as motor
For very long. We're plainly made to go.
We're going anyway and may as well
Have some say as to where we're headed for;
Just as we will be talking anyway
And may as well throw in a little sense.
Let's do so now. Because I let You off
From telling me Your reason, don't assume
I thought You had none. Somewhere back
I knew You had one.[26] But this isn't it
You're giving me. You say we groped this out.
But if You will forgive me the irreverence,
It sounds to me as if You thought it out,
And took Your time to it. It seems to me
An afterthought, a long-long-after-thought.
I'd give more for one least beforehand reason
Than all the justifying ex-post-facto
Excuses trumped up by You for theologists.
The front of being answerable to no one
I'm with You in maintaining to the public.
But, Lord, we showed them what. The audience
Has all gone home to bed. The play's played out.
Come, after all these years—to satisfy me.
I'm curious. And I'm a grown-up man:
I'm not a child for You to put me off
And tantalize me with another "Oh, because."
You'd be the last to want me to believe
All Your effects were merely lucky blunders.
That would be unbelief and atheism.
The artist in me cries out for design.
Such devilish ingenuity of torture
Did seem unlike You, and I tried to think
The reason might have been some other person's.
But there is nothing You are not behind.
I did not ask then, but it seems as if
Now after all these years You might indulge me.
Why did You hurt me so? I am reduced
To ask flatly for a reason—outright.

God I'd tell you, Job—

Job All right, don't tell me, then,
If you don't want to. I don't want to know.
But what is all this secrecy about?
I fail to see what fun, what satisfaction
A God can find in laughing at how badly
Men fumble at the possibilities

[26] Man's inevitable insistence on finding ordered sense in life and especially the reasons for things understandable to man.

When left to guess forever for themselves.
The chances are when there's so much pretense
Of metaphysical profundity
The obscurity's a fraud to cover nothing.
I've come to think no so-called hidden value's
Worth going after. Get down into things,
It will be found there's no more given there
Than on the surface. If there ever was,
The crypt was long since rifled by the Greeks.
We don't know where we are, or who we are.
We don't know one another; don't know You;
Don't know what time it is. We don't know, don't we?
Who says we don't? Who got up these misgivings?
Oh, we know well enough to go ahead with.
I mean we seem to know enough to act on.
It comes down to a doubt about the wisdom
Of having children—after having had them,
So there is nothing we can do about it
But warn the children they perhaps should have none.
You could end this by simply coming out
And saying plainly and unequivocally
Whether there's any part of man immortal.
Yet You don't speak. Let fools bemuse themselves
By being baffled for the sake of being.
I'm sick of the whole artificial puzzle.[27]

Job's Wife You won't get any answers out of God.

God My kingdom, what an outbreak!

Job's Wife Job is right.
Your kingdom, yes, Your kingdom come on earth.
Pray tell me what does that mean? Anything?
Perhaps that earth is going to crack someday
Like a big egg and hatch a heaven out
Of all the dead and buried from their graves.
One simple little statement from the throne
Would put an end to such fantastic nonsense;[28]
And, too, take care of twenty of the four
And twenty freedoms on the party docket.
Or is it only four?[29] My extra twenty
Are freedoms from the need of asking questions.
(I hope You know the game called twenty questions.)
For instance, is there such a thing as Progress?
Job says there's no such thing as Earth's becoming
An easier place for man to save his soul in.
Except as a hard place to save his soul in,
A trial ground where he can try himself[30]
And find out whether he is any good,

[27] See *Job,* 10:1 and 15. [28] See *Revelation,* 20–21. [29] Apparently a reference to the Four Freedoms proposed by President Franklin D. Roosevelt in his message to Congress (January 6, 1941): (1) freedom of speech and expression, (2) freedom of every person to worship God in his own way, (3) freedom from want, and (4) freedom from fear. [30] See "The Trial by Existence," p. 311.

It would be meaningless. It might as well
Be Heaven at once and have it over with.

God Two pitching on like this tend to confuse me.
One at a time, please. I will answer Job first.
I'm going to tell Job why I tortured him,
And trust it won't be adding to the torture.
I was just showing off to the Devil, Job,
As is set forth in Chapters One and Two.
(*Job takes a few steps pacing.*) Do you mind?
(*God eyes him anxiously.*)

Job No. No, I mustn't.
'Twas human of You. I expected more
Than I could understand and what I get
Is almost less than I can understand.
But I don't mind. Let's leave it as it stood.
The point was it was none of my concern.
I stick to that. But talk about confusion!—
How is that for a mix-up, Thyatira?—
Yet I suppose what seems to us confusion
Is not confusion, but the form of forms,
The serpent's tail stuck down the serpent's throat,
Which is the symbol of eternity
And also of the way all things come round,
Or of how rays return upon themselves,
To quote the greatest Western poem yet.[31]
Though I hold rays deteriorate to nothing:
First white, then red, then ultrared, then out.[32]

God Job, you must understand my provocation.
The tempter comes to me and I am tempted.[33]
I'd had about enough of his derision
Of what I valued most in human nature.
He thinks he's smart. He thinks he can convince me
It is no different with my followers
From what it is with his. Both serve for pay.
Disinterestedness never did exist,
And if it did, it wouldn't be a virtue.
Neither would fairness. You have heard the doctrine.
It's on the increase. He could count on no one:
That was his lookout. I could count on you.
I wanted him forced to acknowledge so much.
I gave you over to him, but with safeguards.
I took care of you. And before you died
I trust I made it clear I took your side
Against your comforters in their contention
You must be wicked to deserve such pain.

[31] In conversation with one of the editors of this book (Nov. 19, 1960) Frost identified this poem as Emerson's "Uriel," especially ll. 21–24 which read: "'Line in nature is not found; / Unit and universe are round; / In vain produced, all rays return; / Evil will bless, and ice will burn.'" [32] This line might be read in this way: First a clear light (knowledge or reason), then the heat of argument with less light, then argument in anger, then neither—nothing. [33] Satan had said to God, "Thou hast blessed the work of his [Job's] hands, and his substance is increased in the land. But put forth thy hand now, and touch all that he hath, and he will curse thee to thy face." *Job*, 1:10–11.

That's Browning and sheer Chapel Non-conformism.[34]
Job God, please, enough for now. I'm in no mood
For more excuses.
God What I mean to say:
Your comforters were wrong.[35]
Job Oh, that committee!
God I saw you had no fondness for committees.
Next time you find yourself pressed onto one
For the revision of the Book of Prayer
Put that in if it isn't in already:
Deliver us from committees. 'Twill remind me.
I would do anything for you in reason.
Job Yes, yes.
God You don't seem satisfied.
Job I am.
God You're pensive.
Job Oh, I'm thinking of the Devil.
You must remember he was in on this.
We can't leave him out.
God No. No, we don't need to.
We're too well off.
Job Someday we three should have
A good old get-together celebration.
God Why not right now?
Job We can't without the Devil.
God The Devil's never very far away.
He too is pretty circumambient.
He has but to appear. He'll come for me,
Precipitated from the desert air.—
Show yourself, son.—I'll get back on my throne
For this I think. I find it always best
To be upon my dignity with him.

(*The Devil enters like a sapphire wasp*
That flickers mica wings. He lifts a hand
To brush away a disrespectful smile.
Job's wife sits up.)

Job's Wife Well, if we aren't all here,
Including me, the only Dramatis
Personae needed to enact the problem.
Job We've waked her up.
Job's Wife I haven't been asleep.

[34] "Chapel Non-conformism" is a reference to certain Protestant sects (called also Dissenters and Non-cons) who refused the Church of England's Act of Uniformity ("unfeigned assent to all and everything contained in The Book of Common Prayer"). According to Frost's God the Nonconformists believe that pain is used to punish the wicked. L. 364, except for the first word, is an exact quotation from Browning's poem, "'Childe Roland to the Dark Tower Came,'"—"He must be wicked to deserve such pain" (l. 84), a comment on a horribly ugly horse. Frost's God, then, is using Browning's line as a credo of the Nonconformists with whom, of course, Frost's God disagrees. [35] Eliphaz, Bildad, and Zophar, whom Job calls "miserable comforters" (16:2), are rebuked by God for falsely accusing Job of crimes (42:7–8). They are used here by Frost to symbolize traditional habits of thought which neither Frost's God nor *Job's* God subscribes to. For the "comforters'" speeches, see *Job,* chaps. 4–31.

I've heard what you were saying—every word.

Job What did we say?

Job's Wife You said the Devil's in it.

Job She always claims she hasn't been asleep.—
And what else did we say?

Job's Wife Well, what led up—
Something about—(*The three men laugh.*)
—The Devil's being God's best inspiration.

Job Good, pretty good.

Job's Wife Wait till I get my Kodak.—
Would you two please draw in a little closer?
No—no, that's not a smile there. That's a grin.
Satan, what ails you? Where's the famous tongue,
Thou onetime Prince of Conversationists?
This is polite society you're in,
Where good and bad are mingled every which way,
And ears are lent to any sophistry
Just as if nothing mattered but our manners.
You look as if you either hoped or feared
You were more guilty of mischief than you are.
Nothing has been brought out that for my part
I'm not prepared for or that Job himself
Won't find a formula for taking care of.

Satan Like the one Milton found to fool himself
About his blindness.[36]

Job's Wife Oh, he speaks! He *can* speak!
That strain again! Give me excess of it![37]
As dulcet as a pagan temple gong!
He's twitting us.—Oh, by the way, you haven't
By any chance a Lady Apple on you?
I saw a boxful in the Christmas market.
How I should prize one personally from you.

God Don't *you* twit. He's unhappy. Church neglect
And figurative use have pretty well
Reduced him to a shadow of himself.

Job's Wife *That* explains why he's so diaphanous
And easy to see through. But where's he off to?
I thought there were to be festivities
Of some kind. We could have charades.

God He has his business he must be about.
Job mentioned him and so I brought him in,
More to give his reality its due
Than anything.

Job's Wife He's very real to me
And always will be.—Please don't go. Stay, stay
But to the evensong, and having played
Together we will go with you along.[38]
There are who won't have had enough of you
If you go now.—Look how he takes no steps!

[36] See "On His Blindness," p. 281. Satan is equating the tragic blow of blindness which struck Milton in mid-career with Job's afflictions. [37] Shakespeare, *Twelfth Night,* I. 1–4. [38] See Herrick's poem, "To Daffodils," p. 276, ll. 8–10, for the source of ll. 435–437 above.

He isn't really going, yet he's leaving.
Job (*Who has been standing dazed with new ideas*)
He's on that tendency that like the Gulf Stream,
Only of sand, not water, runs through here.
It has a rate distinctly different
From the surrounding desert; just today
I stumbled over it and got tripped up.
Job's Wife Oh, yes, that tendency!—Oh, do come off it.
Don't let it carry you away. I hate
A tendency. The minute you get on one
It seems to start right off accelerating.
Here, take my hand.

(*He takes it and alights*
In three quick steps as off an escalator.
The tendency, a long, long narrow strip
Of middle-aisle church carpet, sisal hemp,
Is worked by hands invisible offstage.)

I want you in my group beside the throne—
Must have you. There, that's just the right arrangement.
Now someone can light up the Burning Bush
And turn the gold enameled artificial birds on.
I recognize them. Greek artificers
Devised them for Alexius Comnenus.
That won't show in the picture. That's too bad.
Neither will I show. That's too bad moreover.
Now if you three have settled anything
You'd as well smile as frown on the occasion.[39]

(*Here endeth Chapter Forty-three of Job.*)

[39] Reminiscent of Voltaire's saying, "It is better to laugh than to hang oneself."

Comments

Frost's poem was first published in a separate volume in 1945, supposedly to help celebrate his seventieth birthday. Somewhat later his birth year was found to be 1874 rather than 1875, which hardly diminished the brilliance of the celebration. When the editors of this book were deciding which of the two companion poems, "A Masque of Reason" and "A Masque of Mercy" (1947), to include in their Second Edition (1960), the two poems were laid in front of Frost for his opinion. Without hesitation he put his hand on "A Masque of Reason" without comment. For an enlightening commentary on the poem see Peter J. Stanlis, "Robert Frost's 'A Masque of Reason': An Analysis," p. 696.

WALLACE STEVENS*
1879–1955

Sunday Morning[1]

I

Complacencies of the peignoir,[2] and late
Coffee and oranges in a sunny chair,
And the green freedom of a cockatoo
Upon a rug mingle to dissipate
The holy hush of ancient sacrifice.

* Stevens's attitudes in this poem have been somewhat controversial. For two other controversial poems on the nature of paradise see Frost's "The Trial by Existence" (p. 311) and Emerson's "Brahma" (p. 309).
[1] Double meaning: religious Sunday, and sun day as in ll. 2, 19–21, 91–97, 110. Stevens's basic question: where is the true paradise? The answer is found in the replies to the woman's troubled questionings. [2] Negligee.

She dreams a little, and she feels the dark
Encroachment of that old catastrophe,[3]
As a calm darkens among water-lights.
The pungent oranges and bright, green wings
Seem things in some procession of the dead,
Winding across wide water,[4] without sound.
The day is like wide water, without sound,
Stilled for the passing of her dreaming feet
Over the seas, to silent Palestine,
Dominion of the blood and sepulchre.[5]

II

Why should she give her bounty to the dead?
What is divinity if it can come
Only in silent shadows and in dreams?
Shall she not find in comforts of the sun,
In pungent fruit and bright, green wings, or else
In any balm or beauty of the earth,
Things to be cherished like the thought of heaven?
Divinity must live within herself:
Passions of rain, or moods in falling snow;
Grievings in loneliness, or unsubdued
Elations when the forest blooms; gusty
Emotions on wet roads on autumn nights;
All pleasures and all pains, remembering
The bough of summer and the winter branch.
These are the measures destined for her soul.

III

Jove[6] in the clouds had his inhuman birth.
No mother suckled him, no sweet land gave
Large-mannered motions to his mythy mind.
He moved among us, as a muttering king,
Magnificent, would move among his hinds,
Until our blood, commingling, virginal,
With heaven, brought such requital to desire
The very hinds discerned it, in a star.
Shall our blood fail? Or shall it come to be
The blood of paradise? And shall the earth
Seem all of paradise that we shall know?

[3] The crucifixion or possibly death in general.
[4] "And he showed me a pure river of water of life, clear as crystal, proceeding out of the throne of God and of the Lamb." *Revelation*, 22:1. ". . . . And whosoever will, let him take of the water of life freely." *Revelation*, 22:17.
[5] Ll. 14–15: Palestine, the Christian Holy Land, the scene of Christ's crucifixion (blood) and the tomb (sepulchre).
[6] God of the sky and king of gods and men (Latin—Jupiter, Greek—Zeus). Milton in *Paradise Lost* makes Jove one of the fallen angels (i. 512).

The sky will be much friendlier then than now,
A part of labor and a part of pain,
And next in glory to enduring love,
Not this dividing and indifferent blue.

IV

She says, "I am content when wakened birds,
Before they fly, test the reality
Of misty fields, by their sweet questionings;
But when the birds are gone, and their warm fields
Return no more, where, then, is paradise?"
There is not any haunt of prophecy,
Nor any old chimera of the grave,
Neither the golden underground, nor isle
Melodious, where spirits gat[7] them home,
Nor visionary south, nor cloudy palm
Remote on heaven's hill, that has endured
As April's green endures; or will endure
Like her remembrance of awakened birds,
Or her desire for June and evening, tipped
By the consummation of the swallow's wings.

V

She says, "But in contentment I still feel
The need of some imperishable bliss."
Death is the mother of beauty;[8] hence from her,
Alone, shall come fulfilment to our dreams
And our desires. Although she strews the leaves
Of sure obliteration on our paths,
The path sick sorrow took, the many paths
Where triumph rang its brassy phrase, or love
Whispered a little out of tenderness,
She makes the willow shiver in the sun
For maidens who were wont to sit and gaze
Upon the grass, relinquished to their feet.
She causes boys to pile new plums and pears
On disregarded plate. The maidens taste
And stray impassioned in the littering leaves.

VI

Is there no change of death in paradise?
Does ripe fruit never fall? Or do the boughs
Hang always heavy in that perfect sky,
Unchanging, yet so like our perishing earth,
With rivers like our own that seek for seas
They never find, the same receding shores
That never touch with inarticulate pang?
Why set the pear upon those river-banks

[7] Got.
[8] A basic paradox of Stevens's.

Or spice the shores with odors of the plum?
Alas, that they should wear our colors there,
The silken weavings of our afternoons,
And pick the strings of our insipid lutes!
Death is the mother of beauty, mystical,
Within whose burning bosom we devise
Our earthly mothers waiting, sleeplessly.

VII

Supple and turbulent, a ring of men
Shall chant in orgy on a summer morn
Their boisterous devotion to the sun,
Not as a god, but as a god might be,
Naked among them, like a savage source.[9]
Their chant shall be a chant of paradise,
Out of their blood, returning to the sky;
And in their chant shall enter, voice by voice,
The windy lake wherein their lord delights,
The trees, like serafin,[10] and echoing hills,
That choir among themselves long afterward.
They shall know well the heavenly fellowship
Of men that perish and of summer morn.
And whence they came and whither they shall go
The dew upon their feet shall manifest.

VIII

She hears, upon that water[11] without sound,
A voice that cries, "The tomb in Palestine[12]
Is not the porch of spirits lingering.
It is the grave of Jesus, where he lay."
We live in an old chaos of the sun,
Or old dependency of day and night,
Or island solitude, unsponsored, free,
Of that wide water, inescapable.
Deer walk upon our mountains, and the quail
Whistle about us their spontaneous cries;
Sweet berries ripen in the wilderness;
And, in the isolation of the sky,
At evening, casual flocks of pigeons make
Ambiguous undulations as they sink,
Downward to darkness, on extended wings.

[9] Untamed, primitive (savage) source of energy? [10] Seraphim (pl.), highest order of angels at God's throne. See Dickinson's "I Taste a Liquor Never Brewed," final stanza (p. 262). [11] Again, the ebb and flow of generations as in l. 11. [12] Ll. 107–112: the passage seems to mean that Jesus was but a man who like us was "unsponsored, free." Compare the interpretation of Jesus found in Pound's poem "Ballad of the Goodly Fere," p. 342.

T. S. ELIOT
1888–1965

The Love Song of J. Alfred Prufrock

S'io credessi che mia risposta fosse
a persona che mai tornasse al mondo,
questa fiamma staria senza più scosse.
Ma per ciò che giammai di questo fondo
non tornò vivo alcun, s'i'odo il vero,
senza tema d'infamia ti rispondo.[1]

Let us go then, you and I,[2]
When the evening is spread out against the sky
Like a patient etherised upon a table;
Let us go, through certain half-deserted streets,
The muttering retreats
Of restless nights in one-night cheap hotels
And sawdust restaurants with oyster-shells:
Streets that follow like a tedious argument
Of insidious intent
To lead you to an overwhelming question . . .
Oh, do not ask 'What is it?'
Let us go and make our visit.

In the room the women come and go
Talking of Michelangelo.

The yellow fog that rubs its back upon the window-panes,
The yellow smoke that rubs its muzzle on the window-panes,
Licked its tongue into the corners of the evening,
Lingered upon the pools that stand in drains,
Let fall upon its back the soot that falls from chimneys,
Slipped by the terrace, made a sudden leap,
And seeing that it was a soft October night,
Curled once about the house, and fell asleep.

[1] If I believed that my answer might belong
To anyone who ever returned to the world,
This flame would leap no more.
But since, however, from these depths
No one ever returns alive, if I know the truth,
Then without fear of infamy I answer you.
Dante, *Inferno*, xxvii, 61–66.

[2] Probably Prufrock's divided self; the entire poem seems to support this interpretation.

And indeed there will be time
For the yellow smoke that slides along the street
Rubbing its back upon the window-panes;
There will be time, there will be time
To prepare a face to meet the faces that you meet;
There will be time to murder and create,
And time for all the works and days of hands[3]
That lift and drop a question on your plate;
Time for you and time for me,
And time yet for a hundred indecisions,
And for a hundred visions and revisions,
Before the taking of a toast and tea.

In the room the women come and go
Talking of Michelangelo.

And indeed there will be time
To wonder, 'Do I dare?' and, 'Do I dare?'
Time to turn back and descend the stair,
With a bald spot in the middle of my hair—
(They will say: 'How his hair is growing thin!')
My morning coat, my collar mounting firmly to the chin,
My necktie rich and modest, but asserted by a simple pin—
(They will say: 'But how his arms and legs are thin!')
Do I dare
Disturb the universe?
In a minute there is time
For decisions and revisions which a minute will reverse.

For I have known them all already, known them all—
Have known the evenings, mornings, afternoons,
I have measured out my life with coffee spoons;
I know the voices dying with a dying fall
Beneath the music from a farther room.
So how should I presume?

And I have known the eyes already, known them all—
The eyes that fix you in a formulated phrase,
And when I am formulated, sprawling on a pin,
When I am pinned and wriggling on the wall,
Then how should I begin
To spit out all the butt-ends of my days and ways?
And how should I presume?

And I have known the arms already, known them all—
Arms that are braceleted and white and bare
(But in the lamplight, downed with light brown hair!)
Is it perfume from a dress
That makes me so digress?
Arms that lie along a table, or wrap about a shawl.
And should I then presume?
And how should I begin?

. . . . .

Shall I say, I have gone at dusk through narrow streets
And watched the smoke that rises from the pipes
Of lonely men in shirt-sleeves, leaning out of windows? . . .

I should have been a pair of ragged claws
Scuttling across the floors of silent seas.

. . . . .

And the afternoon, the evening, sleeps so peacefully!
Smoothed by long fingers,
Asleep . . . tired . . . or it malingers,
Stretched on the floor, here beside you and me.
Should I, after tea and cakes and ices,
Have the strength to force the moment to its crisis?
But though I have wept and fasted, wept and prayed,
Though I have seen my head (grown slightly bald) brought in upon a platter,[4]
I am no prophet—and here's no great matter;
I have seen the moment of my greatness flicker,

[3] An allusion to the Greek poet (8th century B.C.) Hesiod's *Works and Days*, a poem celebrating hard work in the fields.

[4] Like the head of John the Baptist. At the request of Salome who had pleased Herod with her dancing at his birthday feast, Herod executed John the Baptist who was in prison, and had his head brought in on a platter. See *Matthew*, 14:3–11.

And I have seen the eternal Footman[5] hold my coat, and snicker,
And in short, I was afraid.

And would it have been worth it, after all,
After the cups, the marmalade, the tea,
Among the porcelain, among some talk of you and me,
Would it have been worth while,
To have bitten off the matter with a smile,
To have squeezed the universe into a ball[6]
To roll it towards some overwhelming question,
To say: 'I am Lazarus,[7] come from the dead,
Come back to tell you all, I shall tell you all'—
If one, settling a pillow by her head,
  Should say: 'That is not what I meant at all.
  That is not it, at all.'

And would it have been worth it, after all,
Would it have been worth while,
After the sunsets and the dooryards and the sprinkled streets,
After the novels, after the teacups, after the skirts that trail along the floor—
And this, and so much more?—
It is impossible to say just what I mean!
But as if a magic lantern threw the nerves in patterns on a screen:
Would it have been worth while
If one, settling a pillow or throwing off a shawl,
And turning toward the window, should say:
  'That is not it at all,
  That is not what I meant, at all.'

. . . . .

No! I am not Prince Hamlet, nor was meant to be;
Am an attendant lord, one that will do
To swell a progress,[8] start a scene or two,

[5] Probably Death and his waiting carriage. Compare Dickinson's concept of death in "Because I Could Not Stop for Death," p. 308. [6] See Marvell's "To His Coy Mistress," ll. 41–42, p. 285. [7] Lazarus, the brother of Mary and Martha, who was raised from death by Christ. See *John,* 11:1–44; and *Luke,* 16:19–26. [8] A progress in Elizabethan times was a journey, usually led by the Queen, attended by her court, into her kingdom. Ll. 111–119 refer to Shakespeare's *Hamlet* (see p. 428) including Prince Hamlet, Polonius the advisor to the King, and Osric "the Fool."

Advise the prince; no doubt, an easy tool,
Deferential, glad to be of use,
Politic, cautious, and meticulous;
Full of high sentence, but a bit obtuse;
At times, indeed, almost ridiculous—
Almost, at times, the Fool.

I grow old . . I grow old . . .
I shall wear the bottoms of my trousers rolled.[9]

Shall I part my hair behind? Do I dare to eat a peach?
I shall wear white flannel trousers, and walk upon the beach.
I have heard the mermaids singing, each to each.

I do not think that they will sing to me.

I have seen them riding seaward on the waves
Combing the white hair of the waves blown back
When the wind blows the water white and black.

We[10] have lingered in the chambers of the sea
By sea-girls wreathed with seaweed red and brown
Till human voices wake us, and we drown.

Comments

What we learned about modern poetry from reading MacLeish's "Ars Poetica" (p. 270) will help us to read Eliot's poem. Four mat-

[9] Ll. 121–123 have troubled editors, critics, and general readers alike. Why should Prufrock roll the bottom of his white flannel trousers when he walks upon the beach? When the poem was first published in *Poetry,* 1915, the summer uniform for men was a combination of a dark blue coat and white flannel trousers with cuffs. Dry cleaning at the time was not the proficient process it is today, so the older men especially rolled their white trousers whenever dirt threatened to soil them. But most young men, more impressed with their manly style and romantic presence than with threatening dirt, refused to roll their trousers and regarded any man who did so as a sissy. That Prufrock rolled his trousers even as a young man, despite his protest that he "grows old," is one more way for Eliot to dramatize Prufrock's fear of love and life. [10] It is significant that the "I" in the poem abruptly changes to "We." Are we in our time all Prufrocks till *human* voices wake us, and we drown? As we read Eliot's "The Hollow Men," p. 345, it would seem so; consider the epigraph of the poem, and the footnote regarding it.

ters are very important. First, most of Eliot's symbols are textual (personal). They are not conventional symbols whose meanings are immediately apparent; they must be understood in the complete context of the poem. Second, Eliot does not provide transitions between the scenes of his story; whatever logical sequence exists is implied, not stated. Note the absence of any conventional transition, for example, between lines 12 and 13. The transitions are implicit in the meaning of the poem. Third, Eliot uses the method of dramatic opposition, and this method, once understood, will help us to make the transitions between apparently unrelated scenes. Prufrock is opposed to Michelangelo, John the Baptist, Lazarus, Shakespeare, in order to contrast sharply the great values of the past with those represented by Prufrock. And fourth, Eliot uses a method he calls the "objective correlative" by which he dramatizes sensations, emotions, and feelings through "a set of objects, a situation, a chain of events. . . ." For example, instead of having Prufrock tell us directly that he has wasted his life in frivolous activity, Eliot has him say, "I have measured out my life with coffee spoons," and we participate in Prufrock's emotion of frustration. By correlating Prufrock's frustration with the objective act of measuring out his life in useless activity, Eliot dramatizes Prufrock's sensations.

Two facts about the poem should help us get started: it is a soliloquy, and the title is ironic. The action takes place in Prufrock's mind where Eliot objectifies Prufrock's neurotic self. The love song is a far cry from those we have read by Shakespeare, Herrick, Marvell, Landor, and others. The poem is in effect a psychological self-analysis of a man who is incapable of love, physically and spiritually, who cannot "force the moment to its crisis," who is "in short . . . afraid." He is a man divided, like Hamlet, but unlike Hamlet he never welds himself together for any heroic action; he does not "Have the strength to force the moment to its crisis." One of the most thoughtful interpretations of the poem is found in Grover Smith's "A Critique of 'The Love Song of J. Alfred Prufrock,' " p. 703.

Drama

In tragic life, God wot,
No villain need be! Passions spin the plot:
We are betrayed by what is false within.
GEORGE MEREDITH

PRELIMINARIES

A backward glance at the sections on fiction and poetry may recall to us many dramatic moments. We may have observed that the conversation of Mrs. Ansley and Mrs. Slade in "Roman Fever" was like a scene from a play, or that "My Last Duchess" is drama of a special sort. When we say *dramatic,* we may have in mind *intense.* If so, we have the right notion of the nature of drama, for although all forms of literature are concentrations or distillations of human experience, drama has its own peculiar intensity and rightly lends its name to other forms when they become especially vivid. We are not, then, unfamiliar with what is dramatic when we approach drama itself.

We know, too, that drama is simply one way of telling a story. All the terms which we have applied to fiction—plot, characters, setting, exposition, antecedent action, crisis, and others—apply equally well to drama. How drama tells a story may be seen most clearly in a representative specimen, a conventional one-act play by one of America's great dramatists. While reading, keep tab on your first impressions.

EUGENE O'NEILL
1888–1953

Ile

CHARACTERS

BEN, *the cabin boy*
THE STEWARD
CAPTAIN KEENEY
SLOCUM, *second mate*
MRS. KEENEY
JOE, *a harpooner*
Members of the crew of the steam whaler Atlantic Queen

SCENE: CAPTAIN KEENEY'S *cabin on board the steam whaling ship* Atlantic Queen—*a small, square compartment about eight feet high with a skylight in the center looking out on the poop deck. On the left [the stern of the ship] a long bench with rough cushions is built in against the wall. In front of the bench, a table. Over the bench, several curtained portholes.*

In the rear, left, a door leading to the CAPTAIN'S *sleeping quarters. To the right of the door a small organ, looking as if it were brand-new, is placed against the wall.*

On the right, to the rear, a marble-topped sideboard. On the sideboard, a woman's sewing basket. Farther forward, a doorway leading to the companionway, and past the officers' quarters to the main deck.

In the center of the room, a stove. From the middle of the ceiling a hanging lamp is suspended. The walls of the cabin are painted white.

There is no rolling of the ship, and the light which comes through the skylight is sickly and faint, indicating one of those gray days of calm when ocean and sky are alike dead. The silence is unbroken except for the measured tread of someone walking up and down on the poop deck overhead.

It is nearing two bells—one o'clock—in the afternoon of a day in the year 1895.

At the rise of the curtain there is a moment of intense silence. Then THE STEWARD *enters and commences to clear the table of the few dishes which still remain on it after the* CAPTAIN'S *dinner. He is an old, grizzled man dressed in dungaree pants, a sweater, and a woolen cap with earflaps. His manner is sullen and angry. He stops stacking up the plates and casts a quick glance upward at the skylight; then tiptoes over to the closed door in rear and listens with his ear pressed to the crack. What he hears makes his face darken and he mutters a furious curse. There is a noise from the doorway on the right and he darts back to the table.*

BEN *enters. He is an overgrown, gawky boy with a long, pinched face. He is dressed in sweater, fur cap, etc. His teeth are chattering with the cold and he hurries to the stove, where he stands for a moment shivering, blowing on his hands, slapping them against his sides, on the verge of crying.*

THE STEWARD [*In relieved tones—seeing who it is.*] Oh, 'tis you, is it? What're ye shiverin' 'bout? Stay by the stove where ye belong and ye'll find no need of chatterin'.

BEN It's c-c-cold. [*Trying to control his chattering teeth—derisively.*] Who d'ye think it were—the Old Man?

THE STEWARD [*Makes a threatening move—* BEN *shrinks away.*] None o' your lip, young un, or I'll learn ye. [*More kindly.*] Where was it ye've been all o' the time—the fo'c's'tle?

BEN Yes.

THE STEWARD Let the Old Man see ye up for'ard monkeyshinin' with the hands and ye'll get a hidin' ye'll not forget in a hurry.

BEN Aw, he don't see nothin'. [*A trace of awe in his tones—he glances upward.*] He just walks up and down like he didn't notice nobody—and stares at the ice to the no'th'ard.

THE STEWARD [*The same tone of awe creeping into his voice.*] He's always starin' at the ice. [*In a sudden rage, shaking his fist at the skylight.*] Ice, ice, ice! Damn him and damn the ice! Holdin' us in for nigh on a year—nothin' to see but ice—stuck in it like a fly in molasses!

BEN [*Apprehensively.*] Ssshh! He'll hear ye.

THE STEWARD [*Raging.*] Aye, damn him, and damn the Arctic seas, and damn this stinkin' whalin' ship of his, and damn me for a fool to ever ship on it! [*Subsiding as if realizing the uselessness of this outburst—shaking his head—slowly, with deep conviction.*] He's a hard man—as hard a man as ever sailed the seas.

BEN [*Solemnly.*] Aye.

THE STEWARD The two years we all signed up for are done this day. Blessed Christ! Two years o' this dog's life, and no luck in the fishin', and the hands half starved with the food runnin' low, rotten as it is; and not a sign of him turnin' back for home! [*Bitterly.*] Home! I begin to doubt if ever I'll set foot on land again. [*Excitedly.*] What is it he thinks he's goin' to do? Keep us all up here after our time is worked out till the last man of us is starved to death or frozen? We've grub enough hardly to last out the voyage back if we started now. What are the men goin' to do 'bout it? Did ye hear any talk in the fo'c's'tle?

BEN [*Going over to him—in a half-whisper.*] They said if he don't put back south for home today they're goin' to mutiny.

THE STEWARD [*With grim satisfaction.*] Mutiny? Aye, 'tis the only thing they can do; and serve him right after the manner he's treated them—'s if they weren't no better nor dogs.

BEN The ice is all broke up to s'uth'ard. They's clear water 's far 's you can see. He ain't got no excuse for not turnin' back for home, the men says.

THE STEWARD [*Bitterly.*] He won't look nowheres but no'th'ard where they's only the ice to see. He don't want to see no clear water. All he thinks on is gittin' the ile—'s if it was our fault he ain't had good luck with the whales. [*Shaking his head.*] *I* think the man's mighty nigh losin' his senses.

BEN [*Awed.*] D'you really think he's crazy?

THE STEWARD Aye, it's the punishment o' God on him. Did ye ever hear of a man who wasn't crazy do the things he does? [*Pointing to the door in rear.*] Who but a man that's mad would take his woman—and as sweet a woman as ever was—on a stinkin' whalin' ship to the Arctic seas to be locked in by the rotten ice for nigh on a year, and maybe lose her senses forever—for it's sure she'll never be the same again.

BEN [*Sadly.*] She useter be awful nice to me before—[*His eyes grow wide and frightened.*] she got—like she is.

THE STEWARD Aye, she was good to all of us. 'Twould have been hell on board without her; for he's a hard man—a hard, hard man—a driver if there ever were one. [*With a grim laugh.*] I hope he's satisfied now—drivin' her on till she's near lost her mind. And who could blame her? 'Tis a God's wonder we're not a ship full of crazed people—with the damned ice all the time, and the quiet so thick you're afraid to hear your own voice.

BEN [*With a frightened glance toward the door on right.*] She don't never speak to me no more—jest looks at me 's if she didn't know me.

THE STEWARD She don't know no one—but him. She talks to him—when she does talk—right enough.

BEN She does nothin' all day long now but sit and sew—and then she cries to herself without makin' no noise. I've seen her.

THE STEWARD Aye, I could hear her through the door a while back.

BEN [*Tiptoes over to the door and listens.*] She's cryin' now.

THE STEWARD [*Furiously—shaking his fist.*] God send his soul to hell for the devil he is! [*There is the noise of someone coming slowly down the companionway stairs.* THE STEWARD *hurries to his stacked-up dishes. He is so nervous from fright that he knocks off the top one, which falls and breaks on the floor. He stands aghast, trembling with dread.* BEN *is violently rubbing off the organ with a piece of cloth which he has snatched from his pocket.* CAPTAIN KEENEY *appears in the doorway on right and comes into the cabin, removing his fur cap as he does so. He is a man of about forty, around five-ten in height but looking much shorter on account of the enormous proportions of his shoulders and chest. His face is massive and deeply lined, with gray-blue eyes of a bleak hardness, and a tightly clenched, thin-lipped mouth. His thick hair is long and gray. He is dressed in a heavy blue jacket and blue pants stuffed into his sea-boots.*

He is followed into the cabin by the SECOND MATE, *a rangy six-footer with a lean weather-beaten face. The* MATE *is dressed about the same as the* CAPTAIN. *He is a man of thirty or so.*]

KEENEY [*Comes toward* THE STEWARD*—with a stern look on his face.* THE STEWARD *is visibly frightened and the stack of dishes rattle in his trembling hands.* KEENEY *draws back his fist and* THE STEWARD *shrinks away. The fist is gradually lowered and* KEENEY *speaks slowly.*] 'Twould be like hitting a worm. It is nigh on two bells, Mr. Steward, and this truck not cleared yet.

THE STEWARD [*Stammering.*] Y-y-yes, sir.

KEENEY Instead of doin' your rightful work ye've been below here gossipin' old woman's talk with that boy. [*To* BEN, *fiercely.*] Get out o' this, you! Clean up the chart room. [BEN *darts past the* MATE *to the open doorway.*] Pick up that dish, Mr. Steward!

THE STEWARD [*Doing so with difficulty.*] Yes, sir.

KEENEY The next dish you break, Mr. Steward, you take a bath in the Bering Sea at the end of a rope.

THE STEWARD [*Tremblingly.*] Yes, sir. [*He hurries out. The* SECOND MATE *walks slowly over to the* CAPTAIN.]

MATE I warn't 'specially anxious the man at the wheel should catch what I wanted to say to you, sir. That's why I asked you to come below.

KEENEY [*Impatiently.*] Speak your say, Mr. Slocum.

MATE [*Unconsciously lowering his voice.*] I'm afeard there'll be trouble with the hands by the look o' things. They'll likely turn ugly, every blessed one o' them, if you don't put back. The two years they signed up for is up today.

KEENEY And d'you think you're tellin' me somethin' new, Mr. Slocum? I've felt it in the air this long time past. D'you think I've not seen their ugly looks and the grudgin' way they worked? [*The door in rear is opened and* MRS. KEENEY *stands in the doorway. She is a slight, sweet-faced little woman primly dressed in black. Her eyes are red from weeping and her face drawn and pale. She takes in the cabin with a frightened glance and stands as if fixed to the spot by some nameless dread, clasping and unclasping her hands nervously. The two men turn and look at her.*]

KEENEY [*With rough tenderness.*] Well, Annie?

MRS. KEENEY [*As if awakening from a dream.*] David, I— [*She is silent. The* MATE *starts for the doorway.*]

KEENEY [*Turning to him—sharply.*] Wait!

MATE Yes, sir.

KEENEY D'you want anything, Annie?

MRS. KEENEY [*After a pause, during which she*

seems to be endeavoring to collect her thoughts.] I thought maybe—I'd go up on deck, David, to get a breath of fresh air. [*She stands humbly awaiting his permission. He and the* MATE *exchange a significant glance.*]

KEENEY It's too cold, Annie. You'd best stay below today. There's nothing to look at on deck—but ice.

MRS. KEENEY [*Monotonously.*] I know—ice, ice, ice! But there's nothing to see down here but these walls. [*She makes a gesture of loathing.*]

KEENEY You can play the organ, Annie.

MRS. KEENEY [*Dully.*] I hate the organ. It puts me in mind of home.

KEENEY [*A touch of resentment in his voice.*] I got it jest for you.

MRS. KEENEY [*Dully.*] I know. [*She turns away from them and walks slowly to the bench on left. She lifts up one of the curtains and looks through a porthole; then utters an exclamation of joy.*] Ah, water! Clear water! As far as I can see! How good it looks after all these months of ice! [*She turns around to them, her face transfigured with joy.*] Ah, now I must go up on the deck and look at it, David.

KEENEY [*Frowning.*] Best not today, Annie. Best wait for a day when the sun shines.

MRS. KEENEY [*Desperately.*] But the sun never shines in this terrible place.

KEENEY [*A tone of command in his voice.*] Best not today, Annie.

MRS. KEENEY [*Crumbling before this command—abjectly.*] Very well, David. [*She stands there staring straight before her as if in a daze. The two men look at her uneasily.*]

KEENEY [*Sharply.*] Annie!

MRS. KEENEY [*Dully.*] Yes, David.

KEENEY Me and Mr. Slocum has business to talk about—ship's business.

MRS KEENEY Very well, David. [*She goes slowly out, rear, and leaves the door three-quarters shut behind her.*]

KEENEY Best not have her on deck if they's goin' to be any trouble.

MATE Yes, sir.

KEENEY And trouble they's goin' to be. I feel it in my bones. [*Takes a revolver from the pocket of his coat and examines it.*] Got your'n?

MATE Yes, sir.

KEENEY Not that we'll have to use 'em—not if I know their breed of dog—just to frighten 'em up a bit. [*Grimly.*] I ain't never been forced to use one yit; and trouble I've had by land and by sea 's long as I kin remember, and will have till my dyin' day, I reckon.

MATE [*Hesitatingly.*] Then you ain't goin'—to turn back?

KEENEY Turn back! Mr. Slocum, did you ever hear o' me pointin' s'uth for home with only a measly four hundred barrel of ile in the hold?

MATE [*Hastily.*] No, sir—but the grub's gittin' low.

KEENEY They's enough to last a long time yit, if they're careful with it; and they's plenty o' water.

MATE They say it's not fit to eat—what's left; and the two years they signed on fur is up today. They might make trouble for you in the courts when we git home.

KEENEY To hell with 'em! Let them make what law trouble they kin. I don't give a damn 'bout the money. I've got to git the ile! [*Glancing sharply at the* MATE.] You ain't turnin' no damned sea-lawyer, be you, Mr. Slocum?

MATE [*Flushing.*] Not by a hell of a sight, sir.

KEENEY What do the fools want to go home fur now? Their share o' the four hundred barrel wouldn't keep 'em in chewin' terbacco.

MATE [*Slowly.*] They wants to git back to their folks an' things, I s'pose.

KEENEY [*Looking at him searchingly.*] 'N you want to turn back, too. [*The* MATE *looks down confusedly before his sharp gaze.*] Don't lie, Mr. Slocum. It's writ down plain in your eyes. [*With grim sarcasm.*] I hope, Mr. Slocum, you ain't agoin' to jine the men agin me.

MATE [*Indignantly.*] That ain't fair, sir, to say sich things.

KEENEY [*With satisfaction.*] I warn't much afeard o' that, Tom. You been with me nigh on ten year and I've learned ye whalin'. No man kin say I ain't a good master, if I be a hard one.

MATE I warn't thinkin' of myself, sir—'bout turnin' home, I mean. [*Desperately.*] But Mrs. Keeney, sir—seems like she ain't jest satisfied up here, ailin' like—what with the cold an' bad luck an' the ice an' all.

KEENEY [*His face clouding—rebukingly but not severely.*] That's my business, Mr. Slocum. I'll thank you to steer a clear course o' that. [*A pause.*] The ice'll break up soon to no'th'ard. I could see it startin' today. And when it goes and we git some sun Annie'll perk up. [*Another pause—then he bursts forth.*] It ain't the damned money what's keepin' me up in the Northern seas, Tom. But I can't go back to Homeport with a measly four hundred barrel of ile. I'd die fust. I ain't never come back home in all my days without a full ship. Ain't that truth?

MATE Yes, sir; but this voyage you been ice-bound, an'—

KEENEY [*Scornfully.*] And d'you s'pose any of 'em would believe that—any o' them skippers I've beaten voyage after voyage? Can't you hear 'em laughin' and sneerin'—Tibbots 'n' Harris 'n' Simms and the rest—and all o' Homeport makin' fun o' me? "Dave Keeney what boasts he's the best whalin' skipper out o' Homeport comin' back with a measly four hundred barrel of ile?" [*The thought of this drives him into a frenzy, and he smashes his fist down on the marble top of the sideboard.*] Hell! I got to git the ile, I tell you. How could I figger on this ice? It's never been so bad before in the thirty year I been acomin' here. And now it's breakin' up. In a couple o' days it'll be all gone. And they's whale here, plenty of 'em. I know they is and I ain't never gone wrong yit. I got to git the ile! I got to git it in spite of all hell, and by God, I ain't agoin' home till I do git it! [*There is the sound of subdued sobbing from the door in rear. The two men stand silent for a moment, listening. Then* KEENEY *goes over to the door and looks in. He hesitates for a moment as if he were going to enter—then closes the door softly.* JOE, *the harpooner, an enormous six-footer with a battered, ugly face, enters from right and stands waiting for the* CAPTAIN *to notice him.*]

KEENEY [*Turning and seeing him.*] Don't be standin' there like a gawk, Harpooner. Speak up!

JOE [*Confusedly.*] We want—the men, sir—they wants to send a depitation aft to have a word with you.

KEENEY [*Furiously.*] Tell 'em to go to—[*Checks himself and continues grimly.*] Tell 'em to come. I'll see 'em.

JOE Aye, aye, sir. [*He goes out.*]

KEENEY [*With a grim smile.*] Here it comes, the trouble you spoke of, Mr. Slocum, and we'll make short shift of it. It's better to crush such things at the start than let them make headway.

MATE [*Worriedly.*] Shall I wake up the First and Fourth, sir? We might need their help.

KEENEY No, let them sleep. I'm well able to handle this alone, Mr. Slocum. [*There is the shuffling of footsteps from outside and five of the crew crowd into the cabin, led by* JOE. *All are dressed alike—sweaters, sea-boots, etc. They glance uneasily at the* CAPTAIN, *twirling their fur caps in their hands.*]

KEENEY [*After a pause.*] Well? Who's to speak fur ye?

JOE [*Stepping forward with an air of bravado.*] I be.

KEENEY [*Eyeing him up and down coldly.*] So you be. Then speak your say and be quick about it.

JOE [*Trying not to wilt before the* CAPTAIN'*s glance and avoiding his eyes.*] The time we signed up for is done today.

KEENEY [*Icily.*] You're tellin' me nothin' I don't know.

JOE You ain't pintin' fur home yit, far 's we kin see.

KEENEY No, and I ain't agoin' to till this ship is full of ile.

JOE You can't go no further no'th with the ice afore ye.

KEENEY The ice is breaking up.

JOE [*After a slight pause during which the others mumble angrily to one another.*] The grub we're gittin' now is rotten.

KEENEY It's good enough fur ye. Better men than ye are have eaten worse. [*There is a chorus of angry exclamations from the crowd.*]

JOE [*Encouraged by this support.*] We ain't agoin' to work no more less you puts back for home.

KEENEY [*Fiercely.*] You ain't, ain't you?

JOE No; and the law courts'll say we was right.

KEENEY To hell with your law courts! We're at sea now and I'm the law on this ship. [*Edging up toward the* HARPOONER.] And every mother's son of you what don't obey orders goes in irons. [*There are more angry exclamations from the crew.* MRS. KEENEY *appears in the doorway in rear and looks on with startled eyes. None of the men notice her.*]

JOE [*With bravado.*] Then we're agoin' to mutiny and take the old hooker home ourselves. Ain't we, boys? [*As he turns his head to look *at the others,* KEENEY'S *fist shoots out to the side of his jaw.* JOE *goes down in a heap and lies there.* MRS. KEENEY *gives a shriek and hides her face in her hands. The men pull out their sheath knives and start a rush, but stop when they find themselves confronted by the revolvers of* KEENEY *and the* MATE.]

KEENEY [*His eyes and voice snapping.*] Hold still! [*The men stand huddled together in a sullen silence.* KEENEY'S *voice is full of mockery.*] You've found out it ain't safe to mutiny on this ship, ain't you? And now git for'ard where ye belong, and—[*He gives* JOE'S *body a contemptuous kick.*] drag him with you. And remember the first man of ye I see shirkin' I'll shoot dead as sure as there's a sea under us, and you can tell the rest the same. Git for'ard now! Quick! [*The men leave in cowed silence, carrying* JOE *with them.* KEENEY *turns to the* MATE *with a short laugh and puts his revolver back in his pocket.*] Best get up on deck, Mr. Slocum, and see to it they don't try none of their skulkin' tricks. We'll have to keep an eye peeled from now on. I know 'em.

MATE Yes, sir. [*He goes out, right.* KEENEY *hears his wife's hysterical weeping and turns around in surprise—then walks slowly to her side.*]

KEENEY [*Putting an arm around her shoulder—with gruff tenderness.*] There, there, Annie. Don't be afeard. It's all past and gone.

MRS. KEENEY [*Shrinking away from him.*] Oh, I can't bear it! I can't bear it any longer!

KEENEY [*Gently.*] Can't bear what, Annie?

MRS. KEENEY [*Hysterically.*] All this horrible brutality, and these brutes of men, and this terrible ship, and this prison cell of a room, and the ice all around, and the silence. [*After this outburst she calms down and wipes her eyes with her handkerchief.*]

KEENEY [*After a pause during which he looks down at her with a puzzled frown.*] Remember, I warn't hankerin' to have you come on this voyage, Annie.

MRS. KEENEY I wanted to be with you, David, don't you see? I didn't want to wait back there in the house all alone as I've been doing these last six years since we were married—waiting, and watching, and fearing—with nothing to keep my mind occupied—not able to go back teaching school on account of being Dave Keeney's wife. I used to dream of sailing on the great, wide, glorious ocean. I wanted to be by your side in the danger and vigorous life of it all. I wanted to see you the hero they make you out to be in Homeport. And instead— [*Her voice grows tremulous.*] all I find is ice and cold—and brutality! [*Her voice breaks.*]

KEENEY I warned you what it'd be, Annie. "Whalin' ain't no ladies' tea-party," I says to you, and "you better stay to home where you've got all your woman's comforts." [*Shaking his head.*] But you was so set on it.

MRS. KEENEY [*Wearily.*] Oh, I know it isn't your fault, David. You see, I didn't believe you. I guess I was dreaming about the old Vikings in the story books and I thought you were one of them.

KEENEY [*Protestingly.*] I done my best to make it as cozy and comfortable as could be. [MRS. KEENEY *looks around her in wild scorn.*] I even sent to the city for that organ for ye, thinkin' it might be soothin' to ye to be playin' it times when they was calms and things was dull like.

MRS. KEENEY [*Wearily.*] Yes, you were very kind, David. I know that. [*She goes to left and lifts the curtains from the porthole and looks out—then suddenly bursts forth:*] I won't stand it—I can't stand it—pent up by these walls like a prisoner. [*She runs over to him and throws her arms around him, weeping. He puts his arm protectingly over her shoulders.*] Take me away from here, David! If I don't get away from here, out of this terrible ship, I'll go mad! Take me home, David! I can't think any more. I feel as if the cold and the silence were crushing down on my brain. I'm afraid. Take me home!

KEENEY [*Holds her at arm's length and looks at her face anxiously.*] Best go to bed, Annie. You ain't yourself. You got fever. Your eyes look so strange like. I ain't never seen you look this way before.

MRS. KEENEY [*Laughing hysterically.*] It's the ice and the cold and the silence—they'd make any one look strange.

KEENEY [*Soothingly.*] In a month or two, with good luck, three at the most, I'll have her filled with ile and then we'll give her everything she'll stand and pint for home.

MRS. KEENEY But we can't wait for that—I

can't wait. I want to get home. And the men won't wait. They want to get home. It's cruel, it's brutal for you to keep them. You must sail back. You've got no excuse. There's clear water to the south now. If you've a heart at all you've got to turn back.

KEENEY [*Harshly.*] I can't, Annie.

MRS. KEENEY Why can't you?

KEENEY A woman couldn't rightly understand my reason.

MRS. KEENEY [*Wildly.*] Because it's a stupid, stubborn reason. Oh, I heard you talking with the Second Mate. You're afraid the other captains will sneer at you because you didn't come back with a full ship. You want to live up to your silly reputation even if you do have to beat and starve men and drive me mad to do it.

KEENEY [*His jaw set stubbornly.*] It ain't that, Annie. Them skippers would never dare sneer to my face. It ain't so much what any one'd say—but— [*He hesitates, struggling to express his meaning.*] you see—I've always done it—since my first voyage as skipper. I always come back—with a full ship—and—it don't seem right not to—somehow. I been always first whalin' skipper out o' Homeport, and—Don't you see my meanin', Annie? [*He glances at her. She is not looking at him but staring dully in front of her, not hearing a word he is saying.*] Annie! [*She comes to herself with a start.*] Best turn in, Annie, there's a good woman. You ain't well.

MRS. KEENEY [*Resisting his attempts to guide her to the door in rear.*] David! Won't you please turn back?

KEENEY [*Gently.*] I can't, Annie—not yet awhile. You don't see my meanin'. I got to git the ile.

MRS. KEENEY It'd be different if you needed the money, but you don't. You've got more than plenty.

KEENEY [*Impatiently.*] It ain't the money I'm thinkin' of. D'you think I'm as mean as that?

MRS. KEENEY [*Dully.*] No—I don't know—I can't understand— [*Intensely.*] Oh, I want to be home in the old house once more and see my own kitchen again, and hear a woman's voice talking to me and be able to talk to her. Two years! It seems so long ago—as if I'd been dead and could never go back.

KEENEY [*Worried by her strange tone and the far-away look in her eyes.*] Best to go to bed, Annie. You ain't well.

MRS. KEENEY [*Not appearing to hear him.*] I used to be lonely when you were away. I used to think Homeport was a stupid, monotonous place. Then I used to go down on the beach, especially when it was windy and the breakers were rolling in, and I'd dream of the fine free life you must be leading. [*She gives a laugh which is half a sob.*] I used to love the sea then. [*She pauses; then continues with slow intensity:*] But now—I don't ever want to see the sea again.

KEENEY [*Thinking to humor her.*] 'Tis no fit place for a woman, that's sure. I was a fool to bring ye.

MRS. KEENEY [*After a pause—passing her hand over her eyes with a gesture of pathetic weariness.*] How long would it take us to reach home—if we started now?

KEENEY [*Frowning.*] 'Bout two months, I reckon, Annie, with fair luck.

MRS. KEENEY [*Counts on her fingers—then murmurs with a rapt smile.*] That would be August, the latter part of August, wouldn't it? It was on the twenty-fifth of August we were married, David, wasn't it?

KEENEY [*Trying to conceal the fact that her memories have moved him—gruffly.*] Don't *you* remember?

MRS. KEENEY [*Vaguely—again passes her hand over her eyes.*] My memory is leaving me—up here in the ice. It was so long ago. [*A pause—then she smiles dreamily.*] It's June now. The lilacs will be all in bloom in the front yard—and the climbing roses on the trellis to the side of the house—they're budding. [*She suddenly covers her face with her hands and commences to sob.*]

KEENEY [*Disturbed.*] Go in and rest, Annie. You're all wore out cryin' over what can't be helped.

MRS. KEENEY [*Suddenly throwing her arms around his neck and clinging to him.*] You love me, don't you, David?

KEENEY [*In amazed embarrassment at this outburst.*] Love you? Why d'you ask me such a question, Annie?

MRS. KEENEY [*Shaking him—fiercely.*] But you do, don't you, David? Tell me!

KEENEY I'm your husband, Annie, and you're my wife. Could there be aught but love between us after all these years?

MRS. KEENEY [*Shaking him again—still more fiercely.*] Then you do love me. Say it!

KEENEY [*Simply.*] I do, Annie.

MRS. KEENEY [*Shaking him again—her hands drop to her sides.* KEENEY *regards her anxiously. She passes her hand across her eyes and murmurs half to herself:*] I sometimes think if we could only have had a child. [KEENEY *turns away from her, deeply moved. She grabs his arm and turns him around to face her—intensely.*] And I've always been a good wife to you, haven't I, David?

KEENEY [*His voice betraying his emotion.*] No man has ever had a better, Annie.

MRS. KEENEY And I've never asked for much from you, have I, David? Have I?

KEENEY You know you could have all I got the power to give ye, Annie.

MRS. KEENEY [*Wildly.*] Then do this this once for my sake, for God's sake—take me home! It's killing me, this life—the brutality and cold and horror of it. I'm going mad. I can feel the threat in the air. I can hear the silence threatening me—day after gray day and every day the same. I can't bear it. [*Sobbing.*] I'll go mad, I know I will. Take me home, David, if you love me as you say. I'm afraid. For the love of God, take me home! [*She throws her arms around him, weeping against his shoulder. His face betrays the tremendous struggle going on within him. He holds her out at arm's length, his expression softening. For a moment his shoulders sag, he becomes old, his iron spirit weakens as he looks at her tear-stained face.*]

KEENEY [*Dragging out the words with an effort.*] I'll do it, Annie—for your sake—if you say it's needful for ye.

MRS. KEENEY [*Wild with joy—kissing him.*] God bless you for that, David! [*He turns away from her silently and walks toward the companionway. Just at that moment there is a clatter of footsteps on the stairs and the* SECOND MATE *enters the cabin.*]

MATE [*Excitedly.*] The ice is breakin' up to no'th'ard, sir. There's a clear passage through the floe, and clear water beyond, the lookout says. [KEENEY *straightens himself like a man coming out of a trance.* MRS. KEENEY *looks at the* MATE *with terrified eyes.*]

KEENEY [*Dazedly—trying to collect his thoughts.*] A clear passage? To no'th'ard?

MATE Yes, sir.

KEENEY [*His voice suddenly grim with determination.*] Then get her ready and we'll drive her through.

MATE Aye, aye, sir.

MRS. KEENEY [*Appealingly.*] David!

KEENEY [*Not heeding her.*] Will the men turn to willin' or must we drag 'em out?

MATE They'll turn to willin' enough. You put the fear o' God into 'em, sir. They're meek as lambs.

KEENEY Then drive 'em—both watches. [*With grim determination.*] They's whale t'other side o' this floe and we're going to git 'em.

MATE Aye, aye, sir. [*He goes out hurriedly. A moment later there is the sound of scuffling feet from the deck outside and the* MATE'*s voice shouting orders.*]

KEENEY [*Speaking aloud to himself—derisively.*] And I was agoin' home like a yaller dog!

MRS. KEENEY [*Imploringly.*] David!

KEENEY [*Sternly.*] Woman, you ain't adoin' right when you meddle in men's business and weaken 'em. You can't know my feelin's. I got to prove a man to be a good husband for ye to take pride in. I got to git the ile, I tell ye.

MRS. KEENEY [*Supplicatingly.*] David! Aren't you going home?

KENNEY [*Ignoring this question—commandingly.*] You ain't well. Go and lay down a mite. [*He starts for the door.*] I got to git on deck. [*He goes out. She cries after him in anguish:*] David! [*A pause. She passes her hand across her eyes—then commences to laugh hysterically and goes to the organ. She sits down and starts to play wildly an old hymn.* KEENEY *reënters from the doorway to the deck and stands looking at her angrily. He comes over and grabs her roughly by the shoulder.*]

KEENEY Woman, what foolish mockin' is this? [*She laughs wildly and he starts back from her in alarm.*] Annie! What is it? [*She doesn't answer him.* KEENEY'*s voice trembles.*] Don't you know me, Annie? [*He puts both hands on her shoulders and turns her around so that he *can look into her eyes. She stares up at him with a stupid expression, a vague smile on her lips. He stumbles away from her, and she commences softly to play the organ again.*]

KEENEY [*Swallowing hard—in a hoarse whisper, as if he had difficulty in speaking.*] You said—you was agoin' mad—God! [*A long wail is heard from the deck above.*] Ah bl-o-o-o-ow! [*A moment later the* MATE'S *face appears through the skylight. He cannot see* MRS. KEENEY.]

MATE [*In great excitement.*] Whales, sir—a whole school of 'em—off the star'b'd quarter 'bout five miles away—big ones!

KEENEY [*Galvanized into action.*] Are you lowerin' the boats?

MATE Yes, sir.

KEENEY [*With grim decision.*] I'm acomin' with ye.

MATE Aye, aye, sir. [*Jubilantly.*] You'll git the ile now right enough, sir. [*His head is withdrawn and he can be heard shouting orders.*]

KEENEY [*Turning to his wife.*] Annie! Did you hear him? I'll get the ile. [*She doesn't answer or seem to know he is there. He gives a hard laugh, which is almost a groan.*] I know you're foolin' me, Annie. You ain't out of your mind —[*Anxiously.*] be you? I'll git the ile now right enough—jest a little while longer, Annie —then we'll turn hom'ard. I can't turn back now, you see that, don't ye? I've got to git the ile. [*In sudden terror.*] Answer me! You ain't mad, be you? [*She keeps on playing the organ, but makes no reply. The* MATE'S *face appears again through the skylight.*]

MATE All ready, sir. [KEENEY *turns his back on his wife and strides to the doorway, where he stands for a moment and looks back at her in anguish, fighting to control his feelings.*]

MATE Comin', sir?

KEENEY [*His face suddenly grown hard with determination.*] Aye. [*He turns abruptly and goes out.* MRS. KEENEY *does not appear to notice his departure. Her whole attention seems centered in the organ. She sits with half-closed eyes, her body swaying a little from side to side to the rhythm of the hymn. Her fingers move faster and faster and she is playing wildly and discordantly as*

[*The Curtain Falls.*]

FIRST IMPRESSIONS

All that a play is at the moment we read it and all that we are during the reading interact to produce our first impressions. (Compare "Fiction: Preliminaries," p. 10.) When we move away from what may be called *natural response* into conscious analysis of what we have read, two things are likely to happen: (1) the play changes; (2) we change. A new interaction takes place in which we act upon the play and the play acts upon us. The moment that we ask questions and attempt to answer them, we modify natural response and start analysis.

Natural response and conscious analysis are not completely separate processes. How separate they are depends greatly upon the reader. An untrained reader will passively allow what he is reading to act upon him; analysis for him is a separate process. The trained reader, even during the first reading, will begin applying analytical method which will modify his natural response. The point here, however, is that for the untrained and the trained reader analysis alone will yield the more complex meaning—and therefore the full pleasure—of a serious literary work.

Our natural response to *Ile* doubtless involves our attitude toward Captain Keeney. Do we like him? Probably not. Do we like Annie? Perhaps we do. The important question, however, is this one: Is our liking or disliking a character more, or less, significant than the credibility of the character? (Compare "Fiction: Preliminaries," p. 10.) Some of the best-drawn characters in literature are villains: Claudius, for example, in *Hamlet.* We may dislike them on a moral level but like them as fully realized persons. In short, we need to warn ourselves that sympathy for Annie should not make us think of her as an artistically finer character than Captain Keeney, whom we may despise. Analysis will make this conclusion clear.

We should bear in mind that the analysis of *Ile* represents one approach, always with modifications, to the understanding of any play. *Miss Julie* (p. 533), also a one-act play, differs in many ways from *Ile* but will respond to the same sort of analysis applied to *Ile.* The nine full-length plays are, of course, more complicated in structure than the one-act plays, but the same method of analysis will apply to them, too.

THE FACTS OF THE PLAY

We should first of all have before us the literal facts with which the play was built. These materials are not the play, but without a sure knowledge of them we cannot reach what is essential in the play.

> In 1889 Annie, a schoolteacher with romantic notions of the sea, married Captain Keeney, the most successful whaling-boat skipper of Homeport. Childless after four years and imagining her husband's life at sea as free and venturesome compared to the monotonous life of Homeport, Annie won reluctant permission to accompany her husband on a voyage which began in June 1893. Before the voyage, Captain Keeney installed an organ in his cabin so that Annie might have the comfort of music during the long days ahead. Meager luck during the first year at sea played out completely when the *Atlantic Queen* became ice-locked in the Arctic Ocean and remained immovable until the exact day arrived ending the two-year contracts signed by the crew.
>
> On this day, with the ice barrier broken to the south, the crew through a deputation demands on threat of mutiny that the ship be sailed homeward. Captain Keeney, with no intention of failing to get "ile" at whatever cost, knocks down the crew's spokesman and, with weapons, holds control of the ship. Annie, cured of all romantic notions of the sea and verging on madness, uses all her resources to force her husband to start for home. The final appeal to his love for her wins momentarily, but a report from the Second Mate that the ice to the north is broken and whales sighted returns Captain Keeney to his purpose of getting the "ile." Annie's mind gives way, and the play ends with Captain Keeney off after the whales and his wife wildly playing hymns on the organ.

Here are the materials. What does O'Neill make of this story? What do we make of it?

EXPOSITION AND ANTECEDENT ACTION

Exposition explains. It sets forth the information we need in order to understand the present action. If we look back at our summary of the play, we see that the first paragraph is straight exposition, an explanation of what has gone on before the play opened. Everything which occurred before the play opened is called *antecedent action* and is a part of the exposition. The playwright has the task of giving us as much of the exposition as possible through the medium of dialogue, dialogue which must be carefully motivated to appear casual and natural.

We need some information before the dialogue begins. The direct statements of the author are used chiefly to set the stage, to describe the characters, to indicate "stage business," and to direct the correct reading of the lines. He also gives us the key to what is antecedent action:

> *it is nearing two bells—one o'clock—in the afternoon of a day in the year 1895.*

Here is our starting point. Everything which occurred before the moment indicated is antecedent action.

Before a word is spoken tension is established through a bit of stage business. (Stage business is action without dialogue.) The Steward—

> . . . *tiptoes over to the closed door in rear and listens with his ear pressed to the crack. What he hears makes his face darken and he mutters a furious curse.*

What, we ask, is the significance of this action? We know that we have our first hint of the kind of play this is to be. Eavesdropping can be amusing, even farcical. The muttered curse, the tiptoeing give us warning of the play's tone. (Tone represents the author's attitude toward the facts of the play and determines how the play should be regarded by the reader.) Even before this, we as readers have taken heed of the author's serious intent in the words describing the atmosphere of the setting:

> . . . *the light which comes through the skylight is sickly and faint, indicating one of those gray days of calm when ocean and sky are alike dead.*

The tread of "someone walking up and down the poop deck" brings the monotony of sight and sound into unison. We are ready for a serious play, for perhaps a tragic play, before the first word is spoken.

Two minor characters, the Steward and Ben, appear first and talk naturally, yet economically, for our benefit. With their appearance the present action begins, even though the chief ingredient of their talk involves past action. In other words, exposition, antecedent action, and present action blend into one action. The cruel cold is made real by Ben's chattering speech. It is a fact of here and now. It is also a fact of the past and a portent of things to come. Ice and cold are prime factors. The Old Man (Captain Keeney) is "always starin' at the ice," says the Steward in awed tones. (Is it Ice versus Captain Keeney? we ask.) Then the Steward rages: "Ice, ice, ice! Damn him and damn the ice!" The past year of hardships is equally chargeable to the unyielding ice and to the unyielding Captain. Nothing can be done about the ice. What about the Captain? "What are the men goin' to do 'bout it?" asks the Steward. Ben replies: "They said if he don't put back south for home today they're goin' to mutiny." If this were to be a simple struggle between Captain and crew, we are now ready to meet the central character, "a hard man—as hard a man as ever sailed the seas."

The hardness of Captain Keeney, however, is to be given emphasis through his treatment of his wife, Annie. We must know what manner of woman she was and is. Ben attests: "She useter be awful nice to me before—[*His eyes grow wide and frightened.*] she got—like she is." The Steward adds: "'Twould have been hell on board without her." When Ben tiptoes to the door and hears Annie crying, we recall the Steward's action as the play opens. We have learned that Annie is a sweet, amiable person, in every way a contrast to her husband. We are now ready to meet Captain Keeney and later his wife.

Exposition, including references to antecedent action, does not stop of course with the introduction of the main characters. From the dialogue between Captain Keeney and the Second Mate, and between the Captain and his wife, we learn still more details as the present action moves forward. What we learn has already been summarized under "The Facts of the Play."

SETTING

Setting tells us where and when the action takes place and is correlated with the exposition. Setting is the *environment* of the play. (A similar term, *panorama,* is used in connection with short stories. See "Fiction: Preliminaries.") If we were in a theater to see *Ile*, the program would inform us that the action takes place in "Captain Keeney's cabin aboard the steam whaling vessel *Atlantic Queen*" and would add: "Time: afternoon of a day in the year 1895." That much information would be sufficient, since the remainder of the description serves as directions for staging which would be visible as soon as the curtain went up. *As readers we must set our own stage.*

We are accustomed to this demand from a writer, for in reading fiction we were constantly aware of the background of the action. We note differences, however, in that the dramatist must attend first of all to the setting of each scene, whereas the writer of short stories—or novels, or narrative poems—may intersperse descriptive passages as appropriate. We note, too, that the dramatist is crisp and precise in his description and confines himself for the most part to utilitarian prose. (George Bernard Shaw is an exception to this rule and frequently wrote novelistic plays. Even some of O'Neill's stage directions go beyond pure usefulness.) He is writing, not for a reader who might savor his style, but for a stage manager who will be expected to build the semblance of *"a small, square compartment about eight feet high with a skylight in the center looking out on the poop deck."*

Here, perhaps, we should ask: What difference does the setting make? Our answer, at first, is that the setting is important, and we cite the author's care in emphasizing the relation of the ice-bound ship to the characters. We are to be given a view of a microcosm, a little world, far removed and long removed from the larger world. We feel that we must understand the characters in relation to their restricted and unfavorable environment. In one sense, then, the setting, including the ice fields which have held the ship immovable, controls the characters and through them the action. We realize at once, however, that this answer may not be fully satisfactory. Would time and place have had the same effect on any other group of characters? Possibly not. We suspect that the setting of *Ile* simply tests characters which are already formed. We begin to suspect that setting represents something beyond itself, that it is in reality an *opposing force,* a symbol of challenge to man. Accepting the challenge, a man (or woman) may win or lose.

We see only the *"small, square compartment,"* but we know what is outside. The remainder of the ship is there with water to the south and ice to the north. To the north also are whales, the immediate goal. But do these things complete the setting? Are we looking at a true microcosm? Does the larger world have nothing to do with this smaller world? Clearly it does have much to do with it. In a sense the *Atlantic Queen* has invisible but powerful lines connecting it to Homeport. Homeport is part of the setting, a reality in the minds of every character. The men are desperate to complete the voyage and return even though to return without oil means a dead loss to them. Annie is frantic to "be home in the old house once more," to see her kitchen, to talk to women and to hear them talk. Yet, it is Homeport's ties with Captain Keeney that are strongest of all—he dares not go back unsuccessful, to occupy a position less exalted than "first whalin' skipper out o' Homeport." Part of the setting, then, is a place seen only in the mind's eyes of the characters and of the readers or observers of this play.

PLOT

The action in *Ile* is simple and straightforward. If in the beginning of our analysis it was useful to assemble a fairly detailed summary of the facts, it is equally necessary at this point to look at the essence of the action. Stripped of details, it is the story of a ship's captain who, in pursuit of whale oil, ignores hardships, subdues a mutinous crew, nearly succumbs to his wife's pleas, but reasserts himself in time to drive his wife mad and, apparently, in the end to win through to his goal. Except when the Captain knocks down the spokesman for the crew, the external action is limited to nothing more exciting than the dropping of a dish. Yet tension steadily mounts as we await the answer to the question: What course will Captain Keeney take?

Let us note first the dropping of the dish by the Steward. The agitation of the Steward at the approach of the Captain causes the accident. More important, after the Captain appears we no longer have to depend on hearsay about his hardness and cruelty, we see cruelty in action:

> [KEENEY *draws back his fist and* THE STEWARD *shrinks away. The fist is gradually lowered and* KEENEY *speaks slowly.*] 'Twould be like hitting a worm.

A moment later he adds:

> The next dish you break, Mr. Steward, you take a bath in the Bering Sea at the end of a rope.

Here, then, is the hard man made real. We know now what to expect of him.

Before we proceed let us look at a diagram of the action. This diagram represents an "action line." Three separate interdependent conflicts are involved: Captain Keeney against natural forces (the Ice); Captain Keeney against the rights of men (the Crew); Captain Keeney against the claims of home and love (Annie).

Let us suppose that Captain Keeney upon being petitioned by his men had agreed to return home. Or suppose, on the other hand, everybody had agreed that getting the "ile" was the thing to do. Would either situation have made a play? Why not? Is it that we naturally dislike to see and hear people agree with each other? Is it that we prefer to witness a clash? We do enjoy a contest, and doubtless this is one good reason for emphasizing conflict. We must look further, however, for a basic answer to our reason for enjoying conflict. Agreement is an end, a result. Disagreement is a means to an end, an active process. Agreement is static; disagreement is dynamic. When agreement is reached, the struggle is over. Our first interest, then, must be centered in the struggle, which will be resolved into some sort of agreement.

Action Line of *Ile*

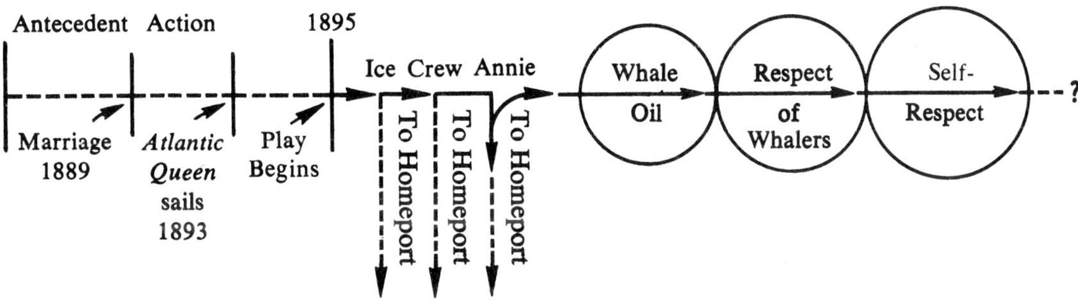

Ile clearly depends upon disagreement or conflict. So many plays depend upon a clash of interests or personalities—clashes which may be expressed in talk or a blow, or may be waged within a character—that conflict is said to be the essence of drama. In reading *Ile* we are spectators of a combat in which the central figure, Captain Keeney, stands against all comers—the capricious Bering Sea, the crew, his wife. Will he win, and if he does, at what cost?

We have mentioned the word *crisis,* a useful term to describe a turning point. A play consists of one or more minor crises and one major crisis. The major crisis is the climax of the play. (Compare "Fiction: Preliminaries.") In *Ile* a minor crisis occurs when the crew through its deputation challenges Captain Keeney. Before the challenge we do not know the answers to such questions as these: Will Captain Keeney yield to a reasonable appeal? Will he yield to threats? Will he be forced to yield? As our diagram indicates, the Captain did not waver from his determined course; the men are vanquished and that question is settled. This settling of a question (or questions) constitutes a *minor resolution.* Agreement of a sort is reached.

No sooner is this minor crisis resolved than the action leading to the major crisis begins. Annie is more powerful than the men; Captain Keeney cannot settle this issue by a blow. He is apparently beaten:

> KEENEY—[*Dragging out the words with an effort.*] I'll do it, Annie—for your sake—if you say it's needful for ye.

For a brief moment disaster seems averted. We have hardly time to frame the question, Will Captain Keeney make good his promise? before we have the answer, an answer which clearly settles the major issue. The ice has broken, leaving a clear passage northward.

> KEENEY—[*His voice suddenly grim with determination.*] Then get her ready and we'll drive her through.

With this speech the issue is settled and the major resolution begins.

CHARACTERS

Our interest in how the play will come out is legitimate, but once we know the answer, other and more important questions confront us. Can the pursuit of whale oil, whether successful or not, be very important? Do we really care whether Captain Keeney wins or loses? Why should we care what happens to him or to Annie or to the crew of an obscure whaling ship? We have admiration for courage, of course, and pity for weakness. Are these emotions of admiration and pity stirred sufficiently to account for our concern? Perhaps. If the characters are credible, we see in them characteristics which we may call *universal qualities,* for we have seen these qualities in other people and detect them in ourselves.

Without Captain Keeney there would be no play, for he helps to create the forces that oppose him. The ice is a dread and a menace because he refuses to be beaten by it. The crew is mutinous because he makes them so. Annie becomes mad because in a real sense he wills that she shall go mad. We begin to see that the action, the plot, of this play is relatively unimportant. *Given these particular characters under these particular circumstances we realize that what happened must inevitably have happened.*

Is this, then, a character play? Certainly Captain Keeney is a man of strong will and single purpose, cruel, somber, destructive of anybody and anything which seeks to oppose him. Accustomed to winning through his ruthlessness, he has developed a contempt for lesser men and a determination never to hear "laughin' and sneerin'" at his expense. In direct conflict with his men he wins easily. "I know 'em," he says. Next he faces his distraught wife and bends to her appeal. We see a hint of softness, but it is the softness born of bewilderment and loss of words to explain his actions. He knows that he scorns the "ile" itself and the money it will bring. Why then, Annie wants to know, not turn homeward? Is he afraid of words from other whaling captains? Note the reply:

> It ain't so much what any one'd say—but—[*He hesitates, struggling to express his meaning.*] you see—I've always done it—since my first voyage as skipper. I always come back with a full ship—and—it don't seem right not to—somehow. I been always first whalin' skipper out o' Homeport, and—Don't you see my meanin', Annie?

Perhaps Annie did see his meaning, but to her it was invalid. With this speech and others of like import, the play, we realize, takes on a significance beyond its literal meaning. Captain Keeney, Annie, the men, the ice wastes, Homeport fall into a pattern of universal significance. We have been reading a play in which each character is a symbol, each object something beyond itself. Older plays of this sort personified such abstractions as Vice, Virtue, Everyman. The personifications in *Ile* are not so clearcut, but we can identify them.

SYMBOLIC MEANING

Although Captain Keeney does not represent Everyman, he does stand for every man's deepest desire to excel. He is the fanatic who drives straight for his goal without swerving and with a ruthless disregard for those with tentative goals or those with insufficient will to draw a straight line. His force requires the submission of others: first, by a physical blow and the threat of a weapon, he wins his easiest victory; next, in a more difficult struggle, he bends to the power of human love but quickly regains his control and renounces his "weakness." The men who momentarily oppose him do not seek victory at any cost, though surely they would have won if they had so willed. They are the usual men, accustomed to go so far and no farther. One notes, however, that some will go farther than others. Mr. Slocum, the Second Mate, may someday become a Captain of Keeney's stamp. Joe the Harpooner, spokesman for the crew, has doubtless won his place by successfully asserting himself. All members of the "depitation" are chosen men. Always a man of some will can find submissiveness in men of feebler will.

Annie perhaps is the Usual Woman, kind, loving, appalled by cruelty. Her husband does not say, "*You* couldn't rightly understand my reason"; he does say, "*A woman* couldn't rightly understand my reason." Annie replies, "Because it's a stupid, stubborn reason." Yet, such stupid, stubborn reasons lie at the base of Captain Keeney's success, a success which had attracted Annie: "I wanted to see you the hero they make you out to be in Homeport." Does Captain Keeney suspect, perhaps know, that even his wife would not think him a hero if he turned back? Apparently so, for he says, "I got to prove a man to be a good husband for ye to take pride in. I got to get the ile, I tell ye."

Homeport means what its name implies. For the men it represents release. For Annie it stands for sanity, for the normal, the warm, the safe things in life. For Captain Keeney it is a tribunal, a place of judgment to which at intervals he must return for the verdict. There must be no chance for an adverse decision. No excuses will do. He would not excuse another skipper; he does not expect, nor want, to be excused himself. The question will be: "Is your ship filled with oil?" The oil itself must be the answer.

In opposition to Homeport are the ice wastes of the Arctic seas. Droughts, floods, typhoons, earthquakes—there can be no malice in these, but when they touch man to his harm, he may shake his fist or go down on his knees. Captain Keeney could not strike down nor argue with nature. He could wait. The Usual Men and the Usual Women could wait, too, but not so long. The Ice Wastes won victory after victory down to the last man. Then, just as victory over the fanatic was about to go elsewhere, a cry rang out: "The ice is breakin' up to no'th'ard, sir." And in a moment: "Whales, sir—a whole school of 'em."

Has nature at last relented? Is this to be taken as an instance of reward for the persevering? Is this a happy ending? Hardly. If the ice had broken up a month before, all might have been well. If the ice had held fast a day longer, all might have been well. It is as though the Ice Wastes had played a closely calculated game with the end in view of mocking the fanatic. (Compare Creon's belated decision in *Antigone*, which begins on p. 411.) He will get his "ile." He will return to Homeport with a full ship and a mad wife. These things we know. Beyond these things we may speculate. Would the sort of price paid be too high even for a man like Captain Keeney? Would his pride remain in being "first whalin' skipper out o' Homeport"? We cannot be sure of the answers to these questions, but we can suspect that the struck target, in this instance, shattered into rubble.

APPLYING OUR OBSERVATIONS TO OTHER PLAYS

What we have observed about how a story is told in *Ile* may be applied, always with modifications, to other plays. It may be well to review our procedure by listing, point by point, the steps which we have taken.

1. We began with *first impressions.* As soon as you have completed a first reading of a play, take the time to examine what you think and feel about what you have read. Do you like the play? Before rereading the play, can you say *why* you liked it or did not like it? Were you amused, excited, depressed, apathetic as you read? Were you chiefly interested in the outcome? Or did the outcome matter less than the credibility of the persons involved? Did you find yourself thinking: "I know people like these characters"? On the other hand, did you say to yourself: "These characters are outside the range of my experience"? Such questions as these will help you to realize your first impressions.

2. The next step is to record the *facts of the play.* As we have seen in our analysis of *Ile,* the first event with any bearing on the present action of the play occurred six years before the play opened when Captain Keeney married Annie. We did not pick up this fact until late in the play. Your task, then, in assembling the facts is to look first of all for the chronological starting point and then to piece together a straightforward narrative. At the end of this process, you may be surprised to find how many significant facts, all bearing on a right interpretation, you overlooked during the first reading.

3. We have chosen to consider *exposition and antecedent* action next, but it would be just as convenient to consider setting at this point. Through gathering the facts, you have had to settle the matter of antecedent action. The exposition, partly through direct statement of the author and partly through dialogue, reveals the tone of the play. Is the tone serious, light, whimsical? How does the author intend that we shall regard his play? In what way does he let us know what our attitude should be? Do the stage directions establish the *atmosphere* and thereby prepare us for what may legitimately happen in such an atmosphere? Is the dialogue in keeping with the atmosphere? Is the action credible in relation to the characters and the atmosphere?

4. Next we have considered the *setting.* Playwrights normally must give careful attention to *time* and *place,* the two elements of setting. In *Ile* setting is of major significance, though time, but not timing, is of much less importance than place. The invisible setting, we have noted, plays a strong part in the drama. The Greek convention of the unities of time and place (the action to occur in one place and within a day) reduces the significance of setting in *Antigone.* The characters in *Hamlet* respond to place—the mist-shrouded battlements of Elsinore in Act I, for example—and readers (but especially audiences) know at once that a tragedy will unfold. Historical time, too, is of the essence in details and in a larger sense, for morality in *Hamlet* is the morality of a primitive, revenge-approving society only vaguely aware of Christian ethics. In *The Physician in Spite of Himself,* Molière uses settings as mere backdrops against which the romping action can take place. The gloom that saturates Ibsen's *Ghosts* is emphasized by the pervading "rain and mist" that, ironically, dissolve before the sun as darkness settles over the mind of the protagonist. Strindberg's *Miss Julie* observes the unities of time and place. Both the place (a manor house kitchen) and the time (Midsummer Eve, a festive occasion for servants) vitally affect the play's three characters and their actions. Although *The Playboy of the Western World* has universal appeal, its setting is highly localized: it is pure Irish. The characters are a product of Celtic genes and a distinctive environment. Place and time, consequently, are a pervasive influence. In *The Visit,* Duerrenmatt virtually makes a character of "the shabby and ruined" central European town. Its desolation reflects a degradation that the composite citizenry wishes to escape at any cost. Historic time, and therefore place, are important in Camus' *Caligula.* Place in *The Sunshine Boys* summarizes what has happened to an over-the-hill comedian. Time is pinned down by the many references to living persons.

Key questions are these: Is the setting what it is simply because the characters are what they are? Or are the characters at least partly what they are because the setting is what it is? The function of the setting in relation to characters and plot can be determined by answering these questions.

5. The where and when of the play settled, we turn now to what happens, the *plot.* Here we note that the playwright—even the Absurdist who appears to eschew action—must be severely selective. In traditional plays every action must advance the play toward a minor crisis and point all minor crises toward the major crisis. A dish dropped, as in *Ile,* must have its signif-

icance. We may ask, then, what is the function of each act in relation to the crises? Next, is there a cause-and-effect relationship linking one action with the next? In *Ile,* Captain Keeney's conflict with the crew does not bring about the conflict with Annie. In other words, the second conflict does not grow out of the first. On the other hand, each action in *Antigone* grows out of a preceding action. Another question is this one: Is the action inevitable? To put it another way, does the action happen because the characters are what they are? If it does, the play is essentially a character play. The actions of Captain Keeney grow inevitably out of his character. What about the actions of Antigone? of Creon? of Hamlet? of Claudius? of Miss Julie? of Caligula? of Willie?

In examining the plot it is useful to construct an action line. Record on the line, with spaced dashes, the antecedent action; then at spaced intervals on an unbroken line indicate the minor crises which lead to the major crisis; end the line with the resolution of the final crisis, the *denouement.*

6. When we examine the *characters* of a play, we find use for our total knowledge of human nature. Are the characters believable when tested by what we know of ourselves added to what we know about other human beings? Believability is relative, of course, and some characters come close to absolute believability, while others remain more or less distant. One probably does not doubt the reality of Captain Keeney. What of Haemon, Gertrude, Sganarelle, Mrs. Alving, Jean, Pegeen, Claire Zachanassian, Caesonia, Al—to name only one character from each of the other plays in this collection? Each character presents a fresh problem in credibility. An example of such a problem is Antigone. What she does and what she is are to be explained in part by reference to a whole system of mythology. Do we have to believe in the system of mythology in order to believe in Antigone? We face a different problem with Caligula, who seems a madman, but whose madness clearly has method in it.

For any play, we may ask: How *consistent* are the characters? What we are asking is, if a character has done this, would he also do that? Such a question is tricky. An element of inconsistency may be the most revealing trait in a character. Miss Julie becomes more credible, not less, when she wavers. Dramatists, however, are wary of glaring inconsistencies, for the limits of time make it difficult to justify them.

7. Our last step is a *summing up.* What do all the parts mean? If the play has a general meaning, then it is certain that we have been involved with symbols. Do the characters stand simply for themselves or do they represent something beyond themselves? Does the play emphasize a theme, an idea, a way of life? If there is a theme, can you state it in a single sentence and then support that sentence with evidence from the play?

The foregoing suggestions for play analysis are by no means exhaustive. Little has been said, for example, about staging and the use of stage properties—*props*—those items which are referred to in the dialogue and which may be essential to the working out of the action. Of one thing every student can be certain: as authority over a play increases, pleasure also increases, even if in the end it turns into the negative fun of damning the play!

A NOTE ON SEEING PLAYS

Although there are closet dramas (plays to be read and not staged, such as Frost's "A Masque of Reason," p. 376), the vast majority of plays are written to be presented before an audience. In a very real sense, therefore, a play is not a complete work of art until it is acted out before an audience. An imaginative reader can do much toward staging the play in his own mind and, perhaps, even acting out the various parts. This sort of multiple role for the reader calls for a great deal of intellectual, even emotional, energy, but the rewards, though differing from those experienced in seeing a play, are great.

SOPHOCLES
496–406 B.C.
Antigone*

Antigone was written some twenty-four hundred years ago. Today it is still being per-

* The translation based upon the text of Sir Richard C. Jebb has been somewhat modified by the editors and carefully checked and further modified by Professor Albert Rapp. We are deeply indebted to Professor Rapp for his assistance.

formed, not simply as a curiosity but as a vital drama with ample modern significance.

If we follow our outline for reviewing a play, we shall see that *Antigone* requires only slightly different treatment from that accorded a modern play. Our *first impressions,* however, may be affected by a few technical details. It is best, therefore, to anticipate some of the questions which one would naturally ask upon first contact with Greek drama.

The first question involves the interrelationships of the characters. We need to know what Sophocles expected his audience to know about the family relationships of the royal house of Thebes. We may begin with Labdacus, the father of Laius. Laius married Jocasta and by her had a son, Oedipus, part of whose story is told in Sophocles' *Oedipus Rex.* Oedipus, under a curse of the gods, murdered his father without knowing that his victim was his father and then married Jocasta in ignorance that she was his mother. Oedipus and Jocasta had four children: two boys, Eteocles and Polynices; and two girls, Antigone and Ismene. Eteocles succeeded Oedipus as king of Thebes but was killed by his brother, Polynices, who, with six other champions, had come to Thebes to take the throne. In the duel Polynices also was killed. The throne passed then to Creon, who was the brother of Jocasta and, therefore, the uncle of Jocasta's and Oedipus' four children. Creon's wife was Eurydice and their children were Megareus and Haemon.

These relationships may be summarized in two diagrams:

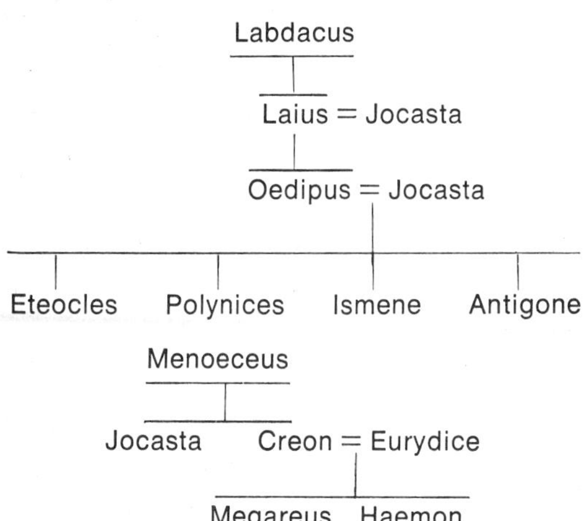

The second question involves the Chorus, a technique infrequently used in modern plays (but compare *The Visit,* 586, and *Caligula,* p. 619). You will see what functions are actually performed by the Chorus in *Antigone.* You will see that it does these things: (1) it provides as needed poetic interludes which suggest the passage of time; (2) it acts as spokesman for public opinion; (3) it occasionally is expository; (4) it helps to set the mood and to point up the universal significance of what is happening. You will note that it can be wise, and it can be stupid; that it vacillates and yet can make up its mind. In many ways it has all the virtues and vices of a general public.

With this much information available for reference, you should now be prepared to read this surprisingly modern play. Pronunciations of proper names used in the play are indicated in a listing on p. 427.

CHARACTERS

ANTIGONE } *daughters of Oedipus, former*
ISMENE } *king of Thebes*
CREON, *present king of Thebes*
EURYDICE, *wife of Creon*
HAEMON, *son of Creon and betrothed of Antigone*
TIRESIAS, *blind soothsayer*
GUARD, *assigned to watch unburied corpse of Polynices*
FIRST MESSENGER
SECOND MESSENGER
CHORUS OF THEBAN ELDERS

SCENE: *All dialogue is spoken before the Royal Palace at Thebes.* ISMENE *enters first, followed by* ANTIGONE.

ANTIGONE Ismene, sister, my own dear sister, do you know any evil, bequeathed to us by Oedipus, which Zeus will not fulfill while we live? Nothing painful is there, nothing ruinous, no shame, no dishonor, that I have not seen in your woes and mine. And now what of this new edict the King has just proclaimed to all Thebes? Do you know of it? Have you heard? Or has it been hidden from you that our friends are threatened with the doom of our enemies?

ISMENE No word of friends, Antigone, glad or painful, has come to me, since we two sisters lost two brothers, killed in one day by a twofold blow. I know the Argive host withdrew last night; but more, good or bad, I know not.

ANTIGONE So I thought and therefore arranged to see you where you alone may hear.

ISMENE What is it? It is plain that you have dark news.

ANTIGONE Has not Creon destined our brothers, the one to honored burial, the other to unburied shame? Eteocles, they say, with due observance of right and custom, he has buried properly for joining honorably the dead below. But the body of Polynices—Creon has published to Thebes that none shall bury him, or mourn, but leave unwept, without a tomb, a welcome feast for birds. Such, I have heard, is the edict the good Creon has set forth for you and me—yes, for *me*—and is coming here to proclaim it clearly to those who have not heard, for it's a heavy matter, since whoever disobeys, his punishment is death by public stoning. [*Pause.*] You know it now, and you will soon show whether you are nobly bred or unworthy of a noble family.

ISMENE Poor sister—if all this is true, what could I do or undo?

ANTIGONE Will you help me do what must be done?

ISMENE What must be done? What do you mean?

ANTIGONE Will you help me lift the body?

ISMENE You would bury him?—when it is forbidden?

ANTIGONE I will do my part—and yours too, if you will not—for a brother. To him I will not be false.

ISMENE Would you dare when Creon has forbidden it?

ANTIGONE He has no right to keep me from my own.

ISMENE Antigone! Remember how our father perished, amid hate and scorn, when sins, self-revealed, moved him to strike out his eyes with his own hands; then the mother-wife, two names in one, with a twisted noose ended her life; and last, our two brothers—each killed by the other's hand. Now is it our turn? We two left all alone—think how we shall die more miserably than all the rest if we defy a king's decree or his powers. No, we must remember, first that we were born women and should not strive with men; next, that we are ruled by the stronger and must obey in these things and even in worse ones. May the dead forgive me, but I must obey our ruler. It is foolish to do otherwise.

ANTIGONE I will not beg you. No, even if you offered now to help, you would not be welcome as my helper. Go your way. I will bury him and count it gain to die in doing that. I shall join a loved one, sinless my crime. I owe more allegiance to the dead than to the living, for with the dead I shall abide forever. But *you*—live on and disobey the laws of the gods.

ISMENE I intend no dishonor to the gods—but to defy the State—I am too weak for that.

ANTIGONE Such be your excuse. I go to heap earth on the brother whom I love.

ISMENE How I fear for you, Antigone!

ANTIGONE You need not. Be fearful for yourself.

ISMENE At least be careful. Tell no one your plan and neither will I.

ANTIGONE Announce it to all Thebes. I shall hate you even more if you don't.

ISMENE You have hot courage for a chilling act!

ANTIGONE My act will please where it counts most to please.

ISMENE Perhaps, but you are attempting what you cannot do.

ANTIGONE If my strength is not enough, at least I will have tried.

ISMENE A hopeless task should not be tried.

ANTIGONE If you continue talking in this way, I shall hate you and so will the dead! Leave me alone to suffer this dread thing. For I shall be suffering nothing as dreadful as a dishonorable death.

ISMENE Go, then, if you must, but remember no matter how foolish your deed, those who love you will love you still. [*Exit* ANTIGONE *left.* ISMENE *enters the Palace through one of the two side-doors.*]

[*Enter* CHORUS *of Theban elders.*]

CHORUS Beam of the sun, fairest light that ever dawned on Thebes of the seven gates, you have shone forth at last, eye of the golden day, arisen above Dirce's stream! The warrior of the white shield, who came from Argos in battle array, has been stirred by you to headlong flight.

He advanced against our land by reason of the vexed claims of Polynices; and, like a shrill-screaming eagle, he flew over our country, sheathed in snow-white wings, with an armed multitude and with plumage of helmets.

He paused above our homes; he ravened around our seven portals with spears athirst for blood; but he fled, before his jaws were glutted with gore or his fire had consumed our towers. Fierce was the noise of battle raised behind him as he wrestled with, but could not conquer, his dragon foe.

For Zeus utterly abhors the boast of a proud tongue; and when he beheld the Argives coming on in a great stream, their golden harness clanging, he smote with brandished fire one who was at that moment about to shout "Victory" from atop our ramparts.

Down to the earth with a crash fell the invader, torch in hand, he who but a moment before, in the frenzy of the mad attack, was blowing against us the blasts of his hot hate. But his threats fared not as he had hoped; and to our other foes the Wargod also dealt havoc, a mighty helper at our need.

For, seven invaders at seven gates, matched against seven, left a tribute of their bronze for Zeus who turned the battle; except for the two brothers, who crossed spears with each other and are sharers in a common death.

But since victory has come to us, let joy be ours in Thebes, city of the many chariots; let us enjoy forgetfulness after the recent wars, and let us visit all the temples of the gods with night-long dance and song; and may Bacchus be our leader, Bacchus whose dancing shakes the land of Thebes.

But behold, the king of the land comes, Creon, son of Menoeceus, our new ruler by the new fortunes that the gods have given; what matter is he pondering, that he has summoned this conference of elders to hear?

[*Enter* CREON, *from the central door of the Palace. Dressed as a king, he has with him two* ATTENDANTS.]

CREON Sirs, the vessel of our State, after being tossed on wild waves, has once more been safely steadied by the gods: and you, of all the people, have been called here because I knew, first of all, how true and constant was your reverence for the royal power of Laius; and again, how, when Oedipus was ruler and then perished, you were still loyal to his children. Since then, his sons have fallen, each felled by the other, each stained with a brother's blood;—and now I possess the throne and all its powers, by right of near kinship to the dead.

No man can be fully known, in soul and spirit and mind, until he has been schooled in rule and law-giving. If the supreme ruler of a State does not seek the best counsel, I hold and have ever held such a person to be base. If one holds a friend of more worth to him than his fatherland, that person has no place in my regard. For I—Zeus, who sees everything, is my witness—I would not be silent if I saw ruin, instead of safety, coming to the citizens; the country's foes would never be friends of mine, for our country is the ship that bears us safe and we cannot have any friends unless the ship of state prospers in its voyage.

Such are the rules by which I guard the greatness of Thebes. In accord with these rules, I have published an edict to the citizens concerning the sons of Oedipus: that Eteocles, who fell fighting for our city, fighting with great courage, shall be entombed and favored with every rite that follows the noblest dead to their rest. But for his brother, Polynices, who came back from exile and sought to consume with fire the city of his fathers and the shrines of his father's gods, who sought to taste of kinsmen's blood and to lead the rest into slavery—touching this man, it has been proclaimed to our people that no one shall bury him or lament his death, but leave him unburied, a corpse for birds and dogs to eat, a ghastly, shameful sight.

Never, by deed of mine, shall the wicked stand in honor before the just, but whoever has good will towards Thebes, he shall be honored of me in both his life and death.

CHORUS Such is your pleasure, Creon, son of Menoeceus, touching this city's foe and its friend. And you have the power to make good your order both for the dead and the living.

CREON See, then, that my mandate is enforced.

CHORUS Give this task to some younger man.

CREON I don't mean that. Watchers of the corpse are at their posts.

CHORUS What further then, do you have in mind?

CREON That you do not side with breakers of these commands.

CHORUS No man is foolish enough to be in love with death.

CREON That would be the penalty. But always someone can be tempted to his ruin through love of gain.

[*Enter* GUARD.]

GUARD O King, I will not say that I come breathless from speed, or that I have plied a nimble foot, for often my thoughts made me stop, and I would wheel around and start back. My mind was holding large discourse with me: "Fool, why hurry to your certain doom?" "Wretch, loitering again? And if Creon hears the story from someone else, will you not pay for it?" So debating, I went on my way without eagerness, and thus a short road was made long. At last, however, I have come hither—to you; and though what I will say may amount to little, I will say it, for I come holding tight to one hope: that I can suffer nothing but what is my fate.

CREON And what makes you so fearful?

GUARD First let me tell you about myself—I did not do the deed—I did not see the doer—it is not right that I should come to any harm.

CREON You shrewdly build a fence around yourself. Clearly you must have strange news.

GUARD Yes, truly. Dread news makes one pause.

CREON Then tell it, will you, and so get you gone?

GUARD Well, this is it—the corpse—someone has just given it burial and gone away—after sprinkling dry dust on the flesh, with other pious rites.

CREON What do you say? What living man has dared do this?

GUARD I know not. No mark of a pickaxe was seen there, no earth thrown up by mattock. The ground was hard and dry, unbroken, without track of wheels. Whoever did it left no trace. And when the first day-watchman showed it to us, dread wonder fell on all. The dead man was veiled from us—not really buried but strewn with dust, as by the hand of one who feared a curse. There was no evidence that any beast of prey or dog had come near him or torn him.

Then everyone began accusing everyone else and, without anyone to stop it, a fight nearly broke out. Every man was the accused, and no one was convicted but all denied any knowledge of the act. And we were ready to take red-hot iron in our hands—to walk through fire—to swear by the gods that we had not done the deed—that we knew nothing of the planning or the doing.

At last, when we had got nowhere with our searching, someone spoke who made all of us bow our heads in fright, for we could neither deny him nor escape misfortune if we obeyed. He said this deed must not be hidden but must be reported to you. And this seemed best; and the lot fell to me. So here I am—as unwelcome as unwilling, I know, for no man likes a bearer of bad news.

CHORUS O King, think you by chance this deed might be the work of gods?

CREON Stop, before your words fill me completely with anger and you be found not only old but foolish. You say what is not to be believed, that the gods are concerned with this corpse. Was it for high reward of trusty service that they hid his nakedness, the nakedness of one who came to burn their columned shrines and sacred treasures, to burn their land, and scatter its laws to the wind? Or do you imagine the gods honoring the wicked? It cannot be. No! From the first there were certain ones in this city that muttered against me, chafing at this edict, wagging their heads in secret; and kept not their necks bowed to the yoke like men contented with my rule.

It is by them, I am certain, that these have been lured and bribed to do the deed. No evil surpasses the power of money. Money lays cities low, drives men from their homes, misguides and warps honest souls till they do shameful things, and still teaches folks to practice villainies and to know every godless deed.

But the men who did this thing for hire have made it certain they shall pay the price. Now, as Zeus is my god, know this—I swear it: If you do not find the one who buried the corpse and bring him before me, death alone shall not be enough for you; before death, you will be tortured until you clear up this outrage. Your lesson will be to steal with sure knowledge of how bribes are won and how it is not good to accept gain from every source. You will find more loss in evil than profit.

GUARD May I speak? Or shall I just turn and go?

CREON Know you not that even your voice is now an offense in my ears?

GUARD In your ears or in your soul?

CREON And would you define the location of my pain?

GUARD I may offend your ears but the doer offends your soul.

CREON You are a born babbler, that's clear.

GUARD Maybe, but never the doer of the deed.

CREON Yes, and more than that—the seller of your life for silver.

GUARD Ah, me! It is sad, certainly, that a judge should misjudge.

CREON Let your fancy play with the word "judgment" if you wish;—but, if you fail to catch the doers of these things, you shall swear that evil gains bring sorrows. [*Exit into Palace.*]

GUARD Well, heaven send that he be found! But whether he is caught or not—fortune will decide that—you will not see me here again. Saved once, beyond my best hope, I owe the gods great thanks. [*Exit.*]

CHORUS Wonders are many, and none is more wonderful than man: he has power to cross the white sea, driven by the stormy south-wind, plunging under surges that threaten to engulf him; and Earth, eldest of the gods, immortal, unwearied, does he master, turning the soil as the ploughs go to and fro year after year.

And the soaring race of birds, the tribes of savage beasts, and the brood of the sea, he traps in the meshes of his snares, man excellent in cunning. And he masters by his arts the beast whose den is in the wilderness, who roams the hills; he breaks the horse of shaggy mane and puts the yoke upon his neck; he tames the tireless mountain bull.

And speech, and lightning thought, and all the interweavings that shape a state has he taught himself; how to be sheltered from arrowy frost and the rushing rain. Yes, nothing is beyond his power; from baffling diseases he has devised escapes and only against Death shall he call for help in vain.

Cunning beyond fancy's dream is the fertile skill which now brings him to evil, now to good. When he honors the laws of the land and the justice which he has sworn by the gods to uphold, his city stands proud, but no city has he who, for his foolishness, lives with sin. Never may such a one share my hearth, or share my thoughts.

[*Enter the* GUARD *from the left, leading in* ANTIGONE.]

CHORUS What sight is this? My soul stands amazed. I know her. It is Antigone. O, unhappy child and child of an unhappy father—Oedipus! What does this mean? *You* brought a prisoner? *You,* disloyal to the King's laws, and arrested for your folly?

GUARD Here she is. She did it. We caught her burying him. But where is Creon?

CHORUS He comes forth again from the Palace, at the right time.

CREON What is it? What has happened that makes my coming timely?

GUARD O King, men should be careful of their words, for second-thoughts may correct the first intention. I could have sworn that I should not soon be here again—scared by the threats by which you blasted me. But there is no pleasure like one unexpected, and I have returned, in spite of my oath, bringing this girl —who was taken doing grace to the dead. This time, be sure, there was no casting of lots, for this piece of luck belongs to me and to no one else. And now, Sire, take her yourself, question her, examine her as you will, but I hope I have gained the right to be free and completely rid of this trouble.

CREON And your prisoner here—how and where did you take her?

GUARD She was burying the man, as I said.

CREON Do you mean what you say? Do you?

GUARD I saw her burying the corpse that you had forbidden to bury. Is that plain and clear?

CREON And how was she seen? how taken in the act?

GUARD It happened this way. When we had come to the place—with your dreadful threats ringing in our ears—we swept away all the dust from the corpse and bared the dank body; and sat us down on the brow of the hill, to the windward to avoid the smell of him. Every man was wide awake and kept his neighbors awake with torrents of threats against anyone who shirked his task.

So it went, until the sun was straight overhead, and the heat began to burn: and then suddenly a whirlwind lifted a storm of dust, which filled the plain, covered the leaves of the trees, and choked the air. We closed our eyes and bore this plague of the gods.

And then, after a long time, the dust storm passed and the girl was seen. Like a bird bitter at finding its nest stripped of nestlings, she cried aloud when she saw the bare corpse. She wailed aloud and called down curses on the doers of the deed. Without hesitation she brought dust in her hands; and then from a bronze pitcher, three times she poured a drink-offering upon the corpse.

We rushed forward when we saw it and closed in on our quarry, who stood there undismayed. Then we charged her with her past and present doings and she denied nothing—a joy and a pain to me at the same time. To have escaped from one's own troubles is a great joy, but it is painful to bring troubles to others. However that may be, all such things mean less to me than my own safety.

CREON You—whose head is bowed—do you admit or do you deny the deed?

ANTIGONE I admit it; I make no denial.

CREON [*To the* GUARD.] You may go now, free and clear of a serious charge. [*Exit* GUARD.] [*To* ANTIGONE.] Now, tell me—in few words—did you know than an edict had forbidden this?

ANTIGONE I knew it—why shouldn't I? It was public.

CREON And you dared to transgress that law?

ANTIGONE Yes, for it was not Zeus that had issued that edict; nor was it a law given to men by Justice which lives with the gods below; nor did I consider your decrees so powerful as to override the unwritten and unfailing laws of heaven. For heaven's laws are eternal and no man knows when they were first put forth.

Not from dread of any human pride could I answer to the gods for breaking *these*. Die I must—I knew that well (how should I not know it?)—even without your edict. But if I am to die before my time, I count that gain, for when one lives, as I do, boxed in by evils, can one count death as anything but gain?

Therefore for me to meet this doom is a trifling grief, but if I had allowed my mother's son to remain unburied, that would have grieved me; for death, I am not grieved. And if my deeds are foolhardy in your sight, perhaps a foolish judge condemns my folly.

CHORUS She shows herself the passionate child of a passionate father and does not know how to bend before trouble.

CREON Yet I would have you know that stubbornness is most often humbled. It is the hardest iron, baked to brittleness in the fire, that you shall oftenest see snapped and shivered; and I have known wild horses brought tame by a little curbing; there is no room for pride among slaves.—This girl became versed in violence when she broke the laws that have been set forth; and, that done, behold a second insult as she boasts of this and exults in her defiance.

Now, truly I am no man—she is the man—if victory in this rests with her and brings no penalty. No! be she sister's child, or even nearer to me in blood than any that worship Zeus at the altar of the house, she and her kinfolk shall not avoid direct punishment, for I charge also her sister with a full share in plotting this burial.

Summon Ismene—for I saw her within just now—raving as if out of her mind. So often, before the deed, the mind convicts itself in its treason while plotting dark evil. But this, too, is truly hateful, when one has been caught in a crime and makes that crime a glory.

ANTIGONE Would you do more than kill me?

CREON Nothing more, no. That done, I am satisfied.

ANTIGONE Why, then, do you delay? In all your talk there is nothing pleasing to me—may there never be!—and my words, I suppose, are unpleasant to you. And yet, for glory—how could I have won greater glory than by giving burial to my own brother? All here would agree to this were they not afraid to say so. But royalty—blessed in so many ways—has the power to do and say what it will.

CREON You are in error. No citizens of Thebes agree with you.

ANTIGONE Yes they do. But fear of you seals their mouths.

CREON And are not you ashamed to be so different?

ANTIGONE No, for there is nothing shameful in honoring a brother.

CREON Was it not a brother, too, who died in the opposite cause?

ANTIGONE Brother by the same mother and the same father.

CREON Why then do you do honor which is impious in the sight of Eteocles?

ANTIGONE Eteocles would not think my act impious.

CREON He would think so, if you make him but equal in honor with the wicked.

ANTIGONE It was his brother—not his slave—that perished.

CREON Laying waste this land, while *he* fell defending it.

ANTIGONE No matter. Duty must be paid the dead.

CREON But good deserves more than evil.

ANTIGONE Who can know such things? In the land of the dead that may not be the law.

CREON A foe is never a friend—not even in death.

ANTIGONE It is not my nature to hate but to love.

CREON Join the dead, then, and love them. While I live, no woman shall rule me.

[*Enter* ISMENE, *led in by two* ATTENDANTS.]

CHORUS Ismene comes, shedding the tears of a loving sister; her darkened brow casts a shadow over her cheeks as tears break in rain over her fair face.

CREON And you, who, lurking like a viper in my house, were secretly sucking my life-blood, while I knew not I was nurturing two traitors to rise against my throne—come, tell me, will you confess your part in this burial, or will you deny knowledge of it?

ISMENE I have done the deed—if my sister allows my claim—and share the guilt with her.

ANTIGONE No. Justice will not allow that. You did not consent to the deed and neither did I allow you a part in it.

ISMENE But, now that you are in it, I am not ashamed to take my place by your side.

ANTIGONE Whose was the deed, Hades and the dead know. A friend in words has not my love.

ISMENE But, Antigone, do not reject me. Let me die with you and thereby honor the dead.

ANTIGONE You shall not die with me, nor claim a deed you had no part in. My death is enough.

ISMENE If I lose you, what will life mean to me?

ANTIGONE Ask Creon; you care only for him.

ISMENE Why do you mock me to no purpose?

ANTIGONE If, indeed, I mock you, it is with pain that I do so.

ISMENE Tell me—how can I help you, even now?

ANTIGONE Save yourself. I shall not mind.

ISMENE Have pity, Antigone. May I not die with you?

ANTIGONE Your choice was to live; mine, to die.

ISMENE At least your choice was made over my protest.

ANTIGONE One world approved your choice; another approved mine.

ISMENE Yes, the offense is the same for both of us.

ANTIGONE Be reconciled. Live . . . My life has long been given to death so that I might serve the dead.

CREON One of these creatures, it appears, is newly mad; the other has been mad from the beginning.

ISMENE Yes, O King, for the mind of the unfortunate often goes astray.

CREON Yours did when you joined your sister.

ISMENE How could I endure life without her?

CREON She lives no more. Speak not as though she did.

ISMENE But will you put to death the betrothed of your son?

CREON Never mind that. There are other fields for him to plough.

ISMENE But not such a love as bound him to her.

CREON I will not countenance an evil wife for a son of mine.

ANTIGONE Haemon, dearest. How your father wrongs you!

CREON Enough and too much of you and your marriage!

CHORUS Would you indeed take this girl from your son?

CREON Not I, but Death.

CHORUS It is determined that she shall die?

CREON Determined, yes. [*To the* ATTENDANTS.] No more delay. Take them inside, the proper place for women, for even the bold seek to escape when life stands face to face with Death. [*Exit* ATTENDANTS, *guarding* ANTIGONE *and* ISMENE.]

CHORUS Blessed are they whose days have never tasted of evil. When a house has once been shaken from heaven, the curse passes from generation to generation of the race; even as, when the surge is driven from the deep by the fierce breath of Thracian gales, it roils the black sands from the depths, and there is a sullen roar from wind-vexed headlands that front the blows of the storm.

In the house of Labdacus[1] sorrows are heaped upon the sorrows of the dead, and generation is not freed by generation, but some god strikes them down, and the race has no deliverance.

For now that hope, the light of which had spread above the last root of the house of Oedipus—that hope, now, is brought low in blood-stained dust by the infernal gods, by folly in speech, and frenzy of heart.

Your power, O Zeus, what human trespass can limit? That power which is unquelled by sleep or the long march of months, as you dwell in dazzling splendor on Olympus, ageless but not aged.

And so, through the future, near or far, as through the past, shall this law stand: Nothing that is great comes into the life of man without a curse.

But hope is to many men a comfort, and to many a false lure of foolish desires; and man loses his awareness until suddenly his foot is burned against the hot fire. It is a wise and famous saying that evil comes to seem good to him whose mind the gods draw to mischief, and thus man fares not long free of suffering.

But Haemon comes, the last of your sons. Does he come to lament the doom of his promised bride, Antigone, and bitter over the loss of his marriage hopes?

[*Enter* HAEMON.]

CREON We shall know soon, better than prophets could tell us. My son, hearing the unalterable doom of your betrothed, are you come in anger against your father? Or do I still hold your love in spite of my action?

HAEMON Father, I am your son, and you in your wisdom trace rules for me that I shall follow. I cannot regard marriage as a greater gain than your good guidance.

CREON Yes, my son, your heart's fixed law should be to obey your father. Men pray to have loyal sons who will deal evil to their enemies and honor to their friends. But he who is father to unprofitable children has sown trouble for himself and comfort to his enemies. Therefore, my son, do not seize impulsively the pleasures offered by a woman, for know this: that joys grow cold if an evil woman shares your bed and home. For what wound could strike deeper than a false love? Loathe this girl as if she were your enemy and let her find a husband in Hades. For I have apprehended her, alone of all the city, in open disobedience. I will not make myself a liar to my people—I will put her to death.

Let her appeal as she will to the claims of kinship.[2] If I tolerate crime in my own kindred, I must bear the crimes of strangers. He who does his duty in his own household will be found righteous in matters of State too. But if anyone breaks the law and thinks to dictate to his rulers, such a one can win no praise from me. No, the one whom the State appoints must be obeyed, in little things and great, in just things and unjust. I am certain that that one who thus obeys would be a good ruler no less than a good subject, and in any battle would stand his ground where he was set, loyal and brave at his comrade's side.

But disobedience is the worst of evils. It ruins cities, desolates homes, and causes the defeat of armies; whereas unquestioning obedience saves the lives of multitudes. Consequently, we must support the cause of order and not allow a mere woman to worst us. If we must fall from power, it is better to fall before a man than to be called weaker than a woman.

CHORUS To us, unless the years have stolen our wits, you seem to say wisely what you say.

HAEMON Father, the gods implant reason in men, the highest of all things we have. I have not the skill nor the desire to prove you wrong; yet, what I have to say may be of some use. At least, as your son, I may report, for your good, all that men say or do, or find to blame. The dread of your displeasure forbids the citizens to speak up with words offensive to you; but I can hear the murmurs in the dark, the lamentings of the city for this

[1] Labdacus was the father of Laius, who was the father of Oedipus. See chart on p. 412.

[2] Antigone was Creon's niece. See chart on p. 412.

maiden. The people say, "No woman ever merited her doom less—none ever was to die shamefully for such glorious deeds; who when her own brother had fallen in bloody battle, would not leave him unburied to be eaten by dogs and birds. Does not *she* deserve golden reward?"

Such is the whispered rumor that spreads in secret. For me, father, no treasure is so precious as your welfare. What fairer exchange is there than a son's pride in his father and a father's pride in his son? Do not, therefore, keep to a single line of thought as though it were the only path. For if any man thinks that he alone is wise, that in speech and thought he has no equal, such a man when laid open to view will be found empty.

No, though a man be wise, it is not shameful for him to learn and to give way if need be. As you have seen, trees survive that bend to winter's torrents, while the unbending perish root and branch. So also, he who keeps the sheet of his sail taut and never slackens it before a gale, upsets the boat.

Father, forego your wrath. Permit yourself to change. For, if as young as I am I may say so, the next best thing to natural wisdom is wisdom acquired through accepting advice.

CHORUS Sire, it would seem that Haemon has spoken wisely just as you also have spoken wisely. There seems much to be said on both sides.

CREON Elders of Thebes—are we at our age to be schooled by this young fellow?

HAEMON In nothing that is not right, but even if I am young, you should consider what I have said, not my years.

CREON Is it right to be disobedient?

HAEMON No one should respect evil-doers.

CREON Is not your lady tainted with that malady?

HAEMON The people of Thebes say no.

CREON Shall the people of Thebes prescribe how I shall rule?

HAEMON Surely that is a childish question.

CREON Am I to rule this land by judgment other than my own?

HAEMON No city belongs to one man.

CREON Is not the city held to be the ruler's?

HAEMON You would make a good ruler over a desert.

CREON This boy, it appears, is the woman's champion.

HAEMON Not at all—unless you are a woman. My concern is for you.

CREON You show this by open feud with your father!

HAEMON Only because you are offending against Justice.

CREON Do I offend by respecting my own authority?

HAEMON You show no respect by trampling on the rights of the gods.

CREON What a coward—to give way to a woman!

HAEMON You will not find me in league with baseness.

CREON All your words, at least, plead for that girl.

HAEMON And for you, and for me, and for the gods of the dead.

CREON You will never marry her this side of the grave.

HAEMON Then she must die, but she will not die alone.

CREON Your boldness now runs to open threats?

HAEMON What threat is it to argue against error?

CREON You will regret this foolish effort to teach me wisdom.

HAEMON If you were not my father, I should have said that you are not very wise.

CREON Slave to this woman, don't go on chattering so!

HAEMON Would you alone speak and hear no answer?

CREON Do you say that? By the heaven above us—be sure of this: you shall suffer for taunting me in this outrageous way. Drag forth that hated thing that she may die now, in his presence—before his eyes—at his side!

HAEMON No, not at my side—never shall that be; nor shall you ever set eyes again upon my face. Rave as you will to such followers as can endure you. [*Exit* HAEMON.]

CHORUS He is gone, O King, in angry haste; a youthful mind, when stung, is dangerous.

CREON Let him rave to the top of his bent and good speed to him, but he shall not save these two girls from their doom.

CHORUS Indeed? Do you intend to slay them both?

CREON No—you are right—not her who had no part in the matter.

CHORUS And how will you slay the other?

CREON I will take her where the path is loneliest and wall her up alive in a rocky cave, with food enough so we may not be responsible for her blood. There, let her pray to Hades, the only god she loves; perhaps she will obtain from him protection against death; or else she will learn, if a little late, how useless is reverence for the dead. [*Exit* CREON.]

CHORUS Love, the unconquered, master of wealth, who keep your vigil on the soft cheeks of a maiden, you roam over the sea and among the dwellers of the wilds; no one escapes you, be he god or mortal man; and he who receives you is like a thing possessed.

The just themselves have their minds warped by you, to their ruin. You it is who have stirred the present strife of kinsmen. The light you kindled in the eyes of the fair bride is victorious; it is a power enthroned beside the eternal laws, and Aphrodite works her unconquerable will.

[ANTIGONE *enters, between* GUARDS.]

But now I am carried beyond the bounds of loyalty to my king, and I cannot keep back the streaming tears, as I see Antigone make her way to the bridal chamber of eternal sleep.

ANTIGONE Look upon me, my countrymen, setting forth on my last way, gazing for the last time on the light of the sun, which for me shall be no more. For Hades, who offers sleep to all, is leading me, while yet alive, to the shore of Acheron. No wedding-chant will there be for me, no bridal day; but I am betrothed of the Lord of the Dark Lake.

CHORUS But glory and praise will go with you to that deep place of the dead. Wasting sickness has not stricken you, nor were you taken away by the sword; but alive, mistress of your fate, you pass to Hades as has no other mortal.

ANTIGONE I have heard that, long ago, Niobe,[3] daughter of Tantalus, was doomed to die a piteous death on the heights of Sipylus. There, rigid rocks encompassed her like ivy, and she was beaten upon by snow and rain, which even now—they say—mingle with her tears. Most like hers is the fate which brings me to my rest.

CHORUS Yes, but she was a goddess, born of gods. We are mortal. Yet it is great renown for a woman to share the doom of a goddess both in her life and after death.

ANTIGONE Oh, you are mocking me! In the name of our father's gods, cannot you wait till I am gone, but must taunt me to my face? You, at least, O fount of Dirce and many-charioted Thebes, will bear witness by what laws I pass to the rock-sealed tomb—unhappy me, unwept of friends, who have no home on earth nor in the shades, no home among the living or the dead!

CHORUS But you stepped forth to the utmost limits of daring, my child; and you are now paying for that before the throne of Law. Yet I also think you are paying for your father's sins.

ANTIGONE You have touched my bitterest thought, awakening the ever-new lament for my father and for the terrible doom visited on the house of Labdacus. Horrible thoughts!—the marriage of mother and son—a mother slumbering at the side of her son—my father! From what manner of parents did I take my miserable being! Now to them I go, accursed, unwed, to share their home! And, Polynices, ill-starred in marriage,[4] in death you have undone my life!

CHORUS An act of reverence is worthy of some praise, but a challenge against authority will bring retribution. Your self-will has brought ruin upon you.

ANTIGONE Unwept, without friends, without marriage-songs, I am led on a journey which

---

[3] Niobe, an earlier queen of Thebes, had reared seven fine sons and seven lovely daughters. Pride in this accomplishment made Niobe consider herself above the gods, until one day she insulted Leto, the mother of Apollo and Diana. In punishment, all fourteen children were destroyed by the arrows of Apollo and Diana; and Niobe was turned into a stone on the side of Mount Sipylus. In summer, tears could be seen issuing from the stone.

[4] Polynices had married an Argive princess. The marriage opened the way to Argive backing for an assault on Thebes, during which Polynices lost his life and thereby brought on Antigone's defiance of Creon.

cannot longer be delayed. I shall never see again the holy light of the sun, and for my fate no tear is shed, no friend laments.

[*Enter* CREON.]

CREON Know you not that songs and wailings before death would never cease if it profited to utter them? Away with her! And when you have placed her, according to my order, in her vaulted grave, leave her there, alone; either to die, or to go on living in her tomb. In any case, our hands are clean. This, however, is certain: she shall henceforth be deprived of the light of day.

ANTIGONE Tomb, bridal-chamber, eternal prison in the cave rock, there I must go to join my own—those many who have perished and dwell now with Persephone. Last of all, most miserable of all, before my time, I join the others. But I have good hope my coming will be welcome to my father and pleasant to my mother and more than welcome to you, my brothers, for when you died, with my own hands I washed and dressed you and poured libations at your graves. It is for tending your corpse, Polynices, that I have won this reward.

And yet I honored you rightly, the wise will say. [But I would not have taken this task upon me had I had a mother, or if a husband had been left unburied. What reason for this, you ask? The husband lost, another might have been found and another child might have replaced the first one; but with both my father and my mother dead, I could never have another brother. This is why I held you, Polynices, first in honor, but Creon held me guilty of a sin and outrage. And now I go alive to the vaults of death.][5]

What law of heaven have I transgressed? Unfortunate that I am, why should I look to the gods any more—where is any ally for me—when by piety I have earned the name of impious? If my punishment is sanctioned by the gods, I shall soon know, but if the sin is with my judges, I could wish them no fuller measure of evil than they have heaped upon me.

CHORUS Still the same tempest of the soul vexes this maiden with the same fierce gusts.

CREON All the more reason for her guards to act at once!

ANTIGONE Ah, that word has the sound of death.

CREON Your doom will be fulfilled.

ANTIGONE O city of my fathers, O eldest gods of our race, they lead me away—now, now—they linger no longer! Look upon me, princes of Thebes, the last daughter of the house of your kings—see what has come upon me—and from whom, because I feared to cast away the fear of Heaven! [ANTIGONE *is led away by the* GUARDS.]

CHORUS Even thus suffered Danaë, in her beauty exchanging the light of day for brass-bound walls; and in that dungeon, secret as the grave, she was held close prisoner. She, too, was of proud lineage, O Antigone, and she received into her in a golden shower the seed of Zeus. But dread is the mysterious power of fate. There is no deliverance from it by wealth or by war, by walled city, or dark sea-beaten ships.[6]

So suffered Lycurgus, too, when shackles tamed him, the son of Dryas, that King of the Edonians, so quick to anger. He paid for his frenzied taunts at the hands of Dionysus; for he too was shut away in a rocky prison. There the fierce exuberance of his madness slowly passed. He learned to know the power of the god whom in his frenzy he had mocked, when he angered the Muses by trying to quench the Bacchanalian fire of the Maenads.[7]

And by the waters of the Dark Rocks, the waters of the twofold sea, are the shores of Bosporus and Thracian Salmydessus. Here Ares, hard by the city, saw the blinding wounds inflicted by Idothea, fierce wife of Phineus, upon his two children. With weaving-needle she, bloody-handed, put out the light of their eyes, which craved for vengeance. They too were then entombed, as you; and

[5] This bracketed passage has been challenged as illogical and perhaps spurious—though all manuscripts contain it. Can it be defended?

[6] Danaë's father, Acrisius, locked his daughter in a bronze tower to keep a prophecy from coming to pass, to wit, that Danaë would give birth to a son who would kill Acrisius. Zeus, however, descended in a golden shower through the roof and impregnated Danaë. She gave birth to Perseus who, later, at an athletic festival accidentally killed Acrisius with a discus.

[7] Lycurgus, opposed to Dionysus (Roman Bacchus), tried to stop revelry in the god's honor. For this he was shut up in a rocky prison. Soon afterward he went blind and died.

deep in misery, they cried out against their cruel doom, those sons of a mother cursed by her marriage. Yet she was of Erechtheid blood, nursed amid her father's storms, a true child of Boreas, swift as wind, a daughter of the gods brought low by the gray Fates.[8] So it was, Antigone.

[*Enter from the right* TIRESIAS, *a blind seer, led by a* BOY.]

TIRESIAS Princes of Thebes, we have come with linked steps, both served by the eyes of one, for in this way the blind may walk.

CREON And what word do you bring, old man?

TIRESIAS I will tell you and you must take heed.

CREON Indeed, Tiresias, it has not been my custom to ignore your counsel.

TIRESIAS Thereby you have thus far steered well the city's course.

CREON I freely grant how much I owe to you.

TIRESIAS Hear this then: once more you stand on fate's fine edge.

CREON What mean you? Your words send a shudder through me.

TIRESIAS You will learn—you will learn when you hear my foretelling. As I sat in my accustomed place to read the voices of the birds, I heard a strange thing: they were screaming in feverish rage and their language was lost in jabber. And I knew from the whirr of their wings they were tearing murderously at each other.

In fear at what I had heard, I prepared a burnt-sacrifice, but the Fire-god offered no fire; a dank moisture oozed from the flesh and trickled upon the embers which smoked and sputtered. The gall of the sacrifice vanished into the air and the fat-larded thighs were bared of the fat. My boy assured me that no signs came, and my offering was a failure.

And who should be blamed for this failure? It is your evil counsel which has brought this sickness upon the city. The altars of Thebes have been tainted—all of them—by birds and dogs which have torn at the corpse of Oedipus' son; and therefore the gods no longer accept prayers and sacrifices at our hands or the flame of meat-offerings; nor does any bird give a clear sign by his shrill cry, for they have tasted a slain man's blood.

Take heed of these things, my son. All men may sin, but when a sin has been committed, the sinner is not forever lost if he will but heal the mischief he has done and not stubbornly cling to his error.

Self-will is folly. Give honor to the dead, for what courage is needed to slay the slain again? It is your good that I have sought, and for that reason you should accept what I have said.

CREON Old man, you join the others in the sport of shooting at me—a fair target for everyone's arrows. The tribe of seers has long made a business of me. Gain your gains, drive your trade, if you like, in the gold-mines of Sardis or India, but try not for advantage of me. You shall not hide that man in the grave —no, though the eagles of Zeus should carry morsels from the body to their Master's throne —no, not even for dread of such defilement will I allow his burial, for I know well enough no mortal can defile the gods. But you, aged Tiresias, how shameful the fall of wisdom when it dresses shameful thoughts in fair words—all for the sake of gain!

TIRESIAS Ah, does any man know, does any man consider . . . ?

CREON Go ahead. What sage comment do you have for us now?

TIRESIAS How precious, above all riches, is good counsel.

CREON True; as evil counsel is the worst of crimes.

TIRESIAS And you are tainted with that sickness.

CREON I would not answer the seer with a taunt.

TIRESIAS But you do by saying that I prophesy lies.

CREON Well, the tribe of prophets has always had an eye for money.

TIRESIAS And the race of tyrants loves base gain.

CREON Do you know you are speaking to your King?

TIRESIAS I know it. It was through me that you saved Thebes.

CREON You are a wise prophet, but not necessarily honest.

[8] Idothea was the second wife of the prophet Phineus. (She is called in other accounts Idaea, Dia, or Erytia.) Some versions have Phineus himself blinding his two children by a former marriage, because of charges made against them by their stepmother.

TIRESIAS You will taunt me into revealing a dread secret.

CREON Out with it!—only expect no profit for your words.

TIRESIAS As far as you're concerned, they'll bring no profit.

CREON You will not shake my determination.

TIRESIAS Then know this—and know it well—that the sun's swift chariot will not run many more courses before you shall have given a son of yours to death, a corpse in payment for corpses; because you have ruthlessly consigned a living soul to the tomb, and because you have kept from the tomb one who belongs there, and leave his corpse unburied, unhonored, unhallowed. These things are not for you to do, nor even for the gods. These are your crimes; and because of them avenging destroyers lie in wait for you; the Furies of Hell pursue you that you may suffer the ills you have brought to others.

Judge now if I speak these things as a hireling. Soon in your house shall rise the wailing of men and of women. And a tumult of hatred against you shall echo from all the cities nearby because some of their sons had their only burial-rites from dogs, or from wild beasts, or from carrion birds—a pollution to the hearths and altars of each city.

You have provoked me to launch these arrows at your heart, sure arrows from which you cannot escape.

Come boy, lead me home. Let him spend his rage on younger men or learn to control his tongue and sweeten his mind if he can. [*Exit* TIRESIAS.]

CHORUS He has gone, O King, and left behind his dread prophecies. In all the time it has taken to change my hair from dark to white, I have never known him to prophesy falsely.

CREON I, too, know it well and am troubled in soul. It is bad to give way, but it may be worse to stand firm.

CHORUS It would be well, son of Menoeceus, to accept advice.

CREON What advice? What should I do? Speak, and I will obey.

CHORUS Free Antigone from her rocky vault. And make a tomb for the unburied Polynices.

CREON And this is your advice? You would have me yield?

CHORUS Yes, Creon, and speedily. The gods strike swiftly and cut short the follies of men.

CREON It is hard to give way, but I do so. I obey. One must not wage a vain war against destiny.

CHORUS Do these things yourself. Do not leave them to others.

CREON I will go at once. Slaves! Take tools for digging and hurry to yonder hill. Since my mind is made up, I will myself unbind Antigone even as I myself bound her. But my mind is dark with foreboding. It had been best to keep the established laws, even to life's end. [*Exit* CREON *with* SERVANTS.]

CHORUS O god of many names, glory of the Cadmean bride, offspring of loud-thundering Zeus! You who watch over famed Italia and reign over the hospitable valley of Eleusis! O Bacchus, dweller in Thebes, mother-city of the Bacchantes, by the soft-gliding stream of Ismenus, on the soil where the fierce dragon's teeth were sown!

You have seen where torch-flames glare through smoke, and rise above the twin peaks, where dance the Corycian nymphs, your votaries, hard by Castalia's stream.

You come from the ivy-mantled slopes of Nysa's hills, from the green shore with many-clustered vines; and you hear your name in the streets of Thebes lifted up by immortal voices.

Thebes, of all cities, you hold first in honor, you, and also your mother whom the lightning struck. Now, when all our people bow before a violent plague, come with healing feet over the Parnassian height, over the moaning sea!

O you with whom the stars rejoice as they move, the stars whose breath is fire; O master of the voices of the night; son begotten of Zeus; come to us, O King, with your attendant Bacchantes, who in night-long frenzy dance before you, the Giver of Good Gifts, Bacchus!

[*Enter* MESSENGER *from the left of the stage.*]

MESSENGER Citizens of Thebes, the mortal life of man is never assured. Fortune raises and Fortune humbles the lucky or the unlucky from day to day, and no one can foretell what will be from what is. For Creon once was blessed, as I count bliss. He had saved Thebes from its enemies. He was clothed with sole authority in the land; he reigned, the glorious father of princely children. And now—all has been lost. For when a man has had life's pleasures taken from him, I count him as good as dead, a breathing corpse. Heap up riches, if you will, live like a king, but if there is no joy, I would not give the shadow of a shadow for such a life.

CHORUS What new sorrow has come to our princes?

MESSENGER Death. And the guilt is on those that live.

CHORUS Who is the slayer and who the slain? Speak!

MESSENGER Haemon is dead, his blood spilled by no stranger.

CHORUS By his father's hand or by his own?

MESSENGER By his own, in anger with his father for the murder.

CHORUS O prophet, how true, then, have proved your words!

MESSENGER So much you have heard. You must decide what to do.

CHORUS Ah, Eurydice, Creon's unfortunate wife, approaches. Perhaps she comes by chance, or perhaps she has heard the news of her son.

[*Enter* EURYDICE.]

EURYDICE People of Thebes, I heard what you were saying as I was going forth to salute with prayers the goddess Athena. Just as I was opening the gate, the messages of woe struck my ears. Filled with terror, I sank back into the arms of my handmaids, my senses numbed. Now, say again what you have already said. I shall hear it as one who is no stranger to sorrow.

MESSENGER Dear lady, I will tell what I saw and leave no word of the truth untold. Why, indeed, should I soothe you with words which would soon be proved false? Truth is always best.

I attended your lord as his guide to the farthest part of the plain, where the body of Polynices, torn by dogs, still lay unhonored. We prayed to Hecate and to Pluto,[9] in mercy to restrain their anger. We washed the body with holy washing and with freshly broken boughs we solemnly burned such relics as there were. Then we raised a high mound of native earth. After that we turned away to enter the maiden's wedding chamber with its rocky couch, the caverned mansion of the bride of Death. From far off, one of us heard loud wailing at the bride's unblessed bower, and came to tell our master Creon.

As the King drew nearer, uncertain sounds of bitter crying floated about him. He groaned. In anguish he muttered: "Wretched that I am, can my foreboding be true? Am I going on the saddest way that I ever went? My son's voice greets me. Go, my servants—hasten, and when you have reached the tomb, passed through the opening where the stones have been wrenched away to the cave's very mouth and look—see if it is Haemon's voice that I know—or if my ear is fooled by the gods."

This search, ordered by our despairing master, we went to make, and in the innermost part of the vault we saw Antigone hanging by the neck. The halter was fashioned from the fine linen thread of her dress. Haemon held his arms about her waist—crying out over the death of his bride, and his father's cruelty, and his own ill-starred love.

But his father, when he saw his son, raised a dreadful cry, and went in and called to him with the voice of despair: "O unhappy son, what have you done? What thoughts possess you? What kind of mischance has made you mad? Come away, my boy! I pray you—I implore!" But the boy glared at him with fierce eyes, spat in his face, and without a word of answer, drew forth his cross-fitted sword. His father fled, and the sword missed. Then, insane with anger, Haemon leaned with all his weight against the blade and drove it half its length into his side. While consciousness was fading, he clasped Antigone to his weak embrace and, gasping, spilled his blood on her pale cheek.

Corpse embracing corpse he lies. He has won his wedding rites, poor youth—not here, but in the halls of Death. He has shown to man that of all curses that plague mankind, ill counsel is the sovereign curse. [EURYDICE *retires into the Palace.*]

CHORUS What do you make of this? She has left without a word.

MESSENGER I, too, am startled; yet I feed on the hope that she simply wishes not to vent in public her grief over such sorrowful news.

[9] Hecate was a goddess of the underworld and Pluto its ruler.

She will perhaps set her handmaids to mourn in privacy. She has had many lessons in woe and may do nothing rash.

CHORUS I do not know. But to me, at any rate, too much silence seems to bode evil, no less than loud lamenting.

MESSENGER Well, I will go in, and learn whether in truth she is hiding some rash purpose in the depths of her passionate heart. Yes, you say true: too much silence may have a dangerous meaning. [*Exit* MESSENGER.]

[*Enter* CREON *from the left, with* ATTENDANTS, *carrying in a shroud the body of* HAEMON.]

CHORUS See, yonder the King himself draws near, bearing that which tells too clear a tale—the work (if one may say so) not of a stranger's madness but of his own misdeeds.

CREON Woe for the sins of a darkened soul, stubborn sins, shadowed by Death. Look on us—the father who has slain—the son who has perished! Darkest sorrow is mine for the wretched blindness of my stubborn will! Oh, my poor son, you have died in your youth, victim of an ill-timed doom—woe to me! Fled is your spirit, not by your folly but because of mine.

CHORUS Ah, too late you seem to see the right.

CREON I have learned the bitter lesson. But then, oh then, some god—I think—struck me from above with heavy weight, and hurled me into the ways of cruelty—overthrowing and trampling on my joy. Bitter woe comes to the labors of man.

[*Enter* MESSENGER *from the Palace.*]

MESSENGER Sire, you come bearing sorrow; you are soon to look upon more within your Palace.

CREON What more? What pain is yet to be added?

MESSENGER Your queen has died, true mother of that corpse. Unhappy lady, her blows are newly dealt.

CREON O Death, is there no end to your greed? Have you no mercy? You bearer of these evil, bitter words, what do you say? Already I was dead, yet you have struck me anew! What said you, my son? What is this new message—of my wife's death—of slaughter heaped on slaughter! [*The central door of the Palace is opened revealing the corpse of* EURYDICE.]

CHORUS You can see for yourself—for now nothing is hidden.

CREON Still another horror! What fate, ah what, can yet await me? I have just lifted my son in my arms, and now another corpse lies before me. Unhappy mother! Unhappy son!

MESSENGER There at the altar she lay, stabbed with the sharp knife, and as her eyes grew dim she wailed for the noble sacrifice of Megareus, and then for the fate of Haemon who lies there. With her last breath, she invoked a curse upon you, the slayer of your sons.

CREON O terror! I shake with dread! Is there no one to strike me to the heart with two-edged sword? Miserable, miserable, overwhelmed by anguish!

MESSENGER Yes, both deaths—your son's, your wife's—are charged to you by her whose corpse you see.

CREON Her last act—how—how did she it?

MESSENGER When she had learned the fate of her son, with her own hand she drove the sharp knife home to her heart.

CREON No man can be found guilty of this but I. Wretched that I am, I own the crime—it was I who murdered you. Take me away, my servants. My life is as death. Lead me away with all speed.

CHORUS This were best, if best can be found in evil. Swiftness is best when only trouble is before us.

CREON Let it come, I say. Let it appear, that fairest of fates for me that brings my last day. Yes! best fate of all. Let it come, that never may I look on tomorrow's light.

CHORUS These things are for the future which is not known. Present tasks claim our care.

CREON These, at any rate, are my fervent prayers.

CHORUS Pray no more, for mortals have no escape from what will be.

CREON Lead me away, I beg you, a rash, foolish man who has unwittingly murdered a son and a wife. I know not where to cast my eyes or where to seek support, for all has gone amiss with everything I have touched, and upon my head a crushing fate has fallen. [*Exit* CREON.]

CHORUS Wisdom is the crown of happiness and reverence for the gods must be inviolate. The great words of prideful men are punished with great blows, which, in old age, teach the chastened to be wise.

Pronunciation of Proper Names in
Antigone

Antigone	Ān-ti′-gō-nē
Ares	Ā′-rēz
Bacchantes	Băc-căn′-tēz
Corycian	Cŏr-ĭsh′-yăn
Creon	Crē′-ŏn
Danaë	Dăn′-ā-ē
Dirce	Dŭr′-sē
Eleusis	Ĕl-yū′-sis
Eteocles	Ē-tē′-ō-klēz
Eurydice	Yū-rĭ′-dĭ-sē
Haemon	Hē′-mŏn
Hecate	Hĕ-că-tē
Ismene	Ī̆z-mē′-nē
Ismenus	Ī̆z-mē′-nŭs
Labdacus	Lăb′-dă-cŭs
Laius	Lāy′-ŭs
Lycurgus	Lȳ-cŭr′-gŭs
Megareus	Mĕ-gă′-rē-ŭs
Menoeceus	Men-ē′-sē-us
Niobe	Nī′-ō-bé
Nysa	Nĭ′-suh
Oedipus	Ē′-dĭ-pŭs
Phineus	Fĭn′-ē-us
Polynices	Pōlē-nĭ-sēz
Salmydessus	Săl-mĭ-dĕs′-sus
Thebes	Thēb′z
Tiresias	Tĭ-rē′-sē-ăs

Comments and Questions

1. FIRST IMPRESSIONS. Was the play difficult to understand? Did you like it? If so, why? If not, why not? Is the action credible? Here first impressions may be misleading, and you may wish to answer two other questions: credible for twenty-four hundred years ago? credible for our time? Hasty answers to these last two questions are likely to be wrong. Answer them anyway and then, after analyzing the play more thoroughly, see whether or not you wish to modify your answers.

2. THE FACTS OF THE PLAY. The facts are simple enough, but you should record them as completely as possible. The problem here is to find the precise event which has any bearing on the present action. Does one need to go back farther than the duel between Eteocles and Polynices which resulted in the deaths of these two brothers of Antigone?

3. EXPOSITION AND ANTECEDENT ACTION. Sophocles, as we have said, depended upon the fact that his audience knew the history of the Theban royal house. He, therefore, allows Ismene to say to Antigone:

> Remember how our father perished, amid hate and scorn, when sins, self-revealed, moved him to strike out his eyes with his own hands.

The Greek audience knew that "our father" was Oedipus and that his "awful sin" had been the murder of his father and marriage to his mother. This allusion and the ones which follow in Ismene's speech were simple reminders to the Greeks and did not tell them what they did not already know. The point of course is that the problem of exposition was simplified for the Greek dramatist.

4. SETTING. Greek drama, for the most part, preserved what Aristotle and Renaissance writers on drama identified as the three unities; that is, the unities of time, place, and action. Unity of time required that all the action should be completed in one day; unity of place that the action should occur in one place. *Antigone,* of course, observes these unities. Of how much importance, then, is setting to this play? Discuss. In what sense does time become of the essence? Consider Creon's actions after he capitulates to the gods. (Compare O'Neill's treatment of time in *Ile.* See Action Line, p. 407.)

5. PLOT. List the sequence of actions which make up the plot. In what way does the plot represent unity of action? What is the essential conflict? Do all actions rise out of this conflict? At what point is the conflict resolved? When, in other words, does Creon realize the terrible implications of his defiance of the gods? What happens after Creon decides to reverse his decrees concerning Polynices and Antigone? Why does Creon bury Polynices before attempting to save Antigone? Explain carefully.

6. CHARACTER. In spite of the title of this play, is Antigone the chief character? Discuss. Although you may find the comparison a curious one, consider the likenesses and

differences between Captain Keeney (*Ile*) and Creon. (You may look forward to comparing Creon and Madame Zachanassian in *The Visit,* p. 586.) What are Creon's strengths and weaknesses? Antigone's? Ismene's? Haemon's? Eurydice's? What sort of character does the Chorus have? Consider its wisdom, its doubts, its waverings, its decisions. Can a case be made for identifying the chorus with public opinion?

7. THE SUMMING PROCESS. What does your analysis add up to? What is the meaning of the play? Is the play concerned only with the question of whether or not Polynices should be buried? Or is it concerned with a conflict between the claims of the State and the claims of the gods? Or does it go beyond even this large issue to an even larger one—man's fate?

How does one get at such questions? Perhaps by asking a few others. Would every man have acted as Creon did? every woman as Antigone? A king other than Creon might have refused burial to both Eteocles and Polynices on the grounds that both were guilty of fratricide. Still someone else in Creon's place might have refused burial to Eteocles and granted it to Polynices on the grounds that Polynices through ridding Thebes of Eteocles had made way for a better man to mount the throne. And what of Antigone? Another daughter might have seen the justice in Creon's action or, like Ismene, might have bent to his will. We are forced to see that because Creon and Antigone acted as they did and not in some other way, they are *individuals responsible for what happened to them.*

Perhaps this conclusion is clear enough, but what of Ismene, Haemon, and Eurydice? What is their guilt? Ismene seems cautious. Is that her weakness or her strength? Haemon is dragged into conflict and destroyed by it. Could he have avoided destruction? Think carefully before you answer. Eurydice seems the most innocent of the bystanders. If she is without fault, how is her suicide to be explained?

If we pull things together now, we may glimpse a vastly disturbing conclusion about man's fate. (Compare with Frost's "A Masque of Reason," p. 376.) Creon is guilty of a murderous drive to have his own way. He is crushed. Antigone is stubborn but ranges herself on the side of the gods. She is crushed. Haemon speaks with the voice of reason, stands for principles, but fails. He is crushed. Eurydice, without any part in the struggle, is overwhelmed by it. She is crushed. Ismene, timid and willing to accept what she assumes cannot be changed, survives, but survives without any of the persons she loves.

What is the pattern for this wholesale laying-low of the mighty and the near-mighty? Consider the last lines of the play:

> Wisdom is the crown of happiness and reverence for the gods must be inviolate. The great words of prideful men are punished with great blows, which, in old age, teach the chastened to be wise.

Do these statements account for what has happened to each of the characters?

Many other approaches to this play are possible, but whatever the approach, full meaning is to be realized only after each part of the play has been related to all the other parts.

WILLIAM SHAKESPEARE
1564–1616

The Tragedy of Hamlet, Prince of Denmark

A critical essay on *Hamlet* appears on pp. 706 716. The play should be read first, then Charlton's comments, then the play should be reviewed. It is also suggested that a first reading of the play be uninterrupted by references to the many footnotes. The gist will be clear. Since, however, Elizabethan English differs from modern English just enough to require some "translation," it will prove useful to check all annotations during the second reading.

DRAMATIS PERSONAE

CLAUDIUS, *King of Denmark*

HAMLET, *son to former King, nephew to Claudius*

POLONIUS, *Lord Chamberlain*
HORATIO, *friend to Hamlet*
LAERTES, *son to Polonius*
Courtiers: VOLTEMAND, CORNELIUS, ROSENCRANTZ, GUILDENSTERN, OSRIC, A GENTLEMAN
A PRIEST
Officers: MARCELLUS, BERNARDO
FRANCISCO, *a soldier*
REYNALDO, *servant to Polonius*
PLAYERS
TWO CLOWNS, *gravediggers*
FORTINBRAS, *Prince of Norway*
A NORWEGIAN CAPTAIN
ENGLISH AMBASSADORS
GERTRUDE, *Queen of Denmark, Hamlet's mother*
OPHELIA, *daughter to Polonius*
GHOST OF HAMLET'S FATHER
LORDS, LADIES, OFFICERS, SOLDIERS, MESSENGERS, ATTENDANTS

ACT I

Scene I [*Elsinore. A platform before the Castle.*]

[*Enter two* SENTINELS—*first,* FRANCISCO, *who paces up and down at his post; then* BERNARDO, *who approaches him.*]

BERNARDO Who's there?
FRANCISCO Nay, answer me. Stand and unfold yourself.
BERNARDO Long live the King!
FRANCISCO Bernardo?
BERNARDO He.
FRANCISCO You come most carefully upon your hour.
BERNARDO 'Tis now struck twelve. Get thee to bed, Francisco.
FRANCISCO For this relief much thanks. 'Tis bitter cold,
And I am sick at heart.
BERNARDO Have you had quiet guard?
FRANCISCO Not a mouse stirring.
BERNARDO Well, good night.
If you do meet Horatio and Marcellus,
The rivals of my watch, bid them make haste.
[*Enter* HORATIO *and* MARCELLUS.]
FRANCISCO I think I hear them. Stand, ho! Who is there?
HORATIO Friends to this ground.
MARCELLUS And liegemen to the Dane.
FRANCISCO Give you good night.
MARCELLUS O, farewell, honest soldier.
Who hath reliev'd you?
FRANCISCO Bernardo hath my place.
Give you good night. [*Exit.*]
MARCELLUS Holla, Bernardo!
BERNARDO Say—
What, is Horatio there?
HORATIO A piece of him.
BERNARDO Welcome, Horatio. Welcome, good Marcellus.
MARCELLUS What, has this thing appear'd again to-night?
BERNARDO I have seen nothing.
MARCELLUS Horatio says 'tis but our fantasy,
And will not let belief take hold of him
Touching this dreaded sight, twice seen of us.
Therefore I have entreated him along,
With us to watch the minutes of this night,
That, if again this apparition come,
He may approve our eyes and speak to it.
HORATIO Tush, tush, 'twill not appear.
BERNARDO Sit down awhile,
And let us once again assail your ears,
That are so fortified against our story,
What we two nights have seen.
HORATIO Well, sit we down,
And let us hear Bernardo speak of this.
BERNARDO Last night of all,
When yond same star that's westward from the pole
Had made his course t' illume that part of heaven
Where now it burns, Marcellus and myself,

Scene i, set in darkness, after midnight.
3 *Long live the king!* (possibly the watchword. Francisco cannot yet see Bernardo clearly.)
6 *carefully,* punctually.
9 *sick at heart,* depressed (unaccountably).
13 *rivals,* partners.
14 *ground,* Denmark.
15 *the Dane,* newly crowned Claudius.
19 *A piece of him* (a bit of mild humor, denoting Horatio's lack of enthusiasm for this cold midnight watch.)
23 *fantasy,* imagination.
25 *of us,* by us.
29 *approve our eyes,* agree that we have indeed seen what we have told him we have seen. *speak to it,* accost the "dreaded sight" (something Marcellus and Bernardo had not dared to do).

The bell then beating one—

[*Enter* GHOST.]

MARCELLUS Peace! break thee off! Look where it comes again!

BERNARDO In the same figure, like the King that's dead.

MARCELLUS Thou art a scholar; speak to it, Horatio.

BERNARDO Looks it not like the King? Mark it, Horatio.

HORATIO Most like. It harrows me with fear and wonder.

BERNARDO It would be spoke to.

MARCELLUS Question it, Horatio.

HORATIO What art thou that usurp'st this time of night
Together with that fair and warlike form
In which the majesty of buried Denmark
Did sometimes march? By heaven I charge thee speak!

MARCELLUS It is offended.

BERNARDO See, it stalks away!

HORATIO Stay! Speak, speak! I charge thee speak!

[*Exit* GHOST.]

MARCELLUS 'Tis gone and will not answer.

BERNARDO How now, Horatio? You tremble and look pale.
Is not this something more than fantasy?
What think you on't?

HORATIO Before my God, I might not this believe
Without the sensible and true avouch
Of mine own eyes.

MARCELLUS Is it not like the King?

HORATIO As thou art to thyself.
Such was the very armour he had on
When he th' ambitious Norway combated.
So frown'd he once when, in an angry parle,
He smote the sledded Polacks on the ice.
'Tis strange.

MARCELLUS Thus twice before, and jump at this dead hour,
With martial stalk hath he gone by our watch.

HORATIO In what particular thought to work I know not;
But, in the gross and scope of my opinion,
This bodes some strange eruptions to our state.

MARCELLUS Good now, sit down, and tell me he that knows,
Why this same strict and most observant watch
So nightly toils the subject of the land,
And why such daily cast of brazen cannon
And foreign mart for implements of war;
Why such impress of shipwrights, whose sore task
Does not divide the Sunday from the week.
What might be toward, that this sweaty haste
Doth make the night joint-labourer with the day?
Who is't that can inform me?

HORATIO That can I.
At least, the whisper goes so. Our last king,
Whose image even but now appear'd to us,
Was, as you know, by Fortinbras of Norway,
Thereto prick'd on by a most emulate pride,
Dar'd to the combat; in which our valiant Hamlet
(For so this side of our known world esteem'd him)
Did slay this Fortinbras; who, by a seal'd compact,
Well ratified by law and heraldry,
Did forfeit, with his life, all those his lands
Which he stood seiz'd of, to the conqueror;
Against the which a moiety competent
Was gaged by our king; which had return'd
To the inheritance of Fortinbras,
Had he been vanquisher, as, by the same comart
And carriage of the article design'd,
His fell to Hamlet. Now, sir, young Fortinbras,
Of unimproved mettle hot and full,
Hath in the skirts of Norway, here and there,

42 *Thou art a scholar,* you are a schooled young man (so you will know how to address this spirit in the proper form).
44 *harrows,* distresses.
49 *sometimes,* formerly.
62 *angry parle,* loud negotiations (which resulted in a battle between the King of Denmark, Hamlet's father, and "the sledded Polacks").
65 *jump,* exactly.
68 *gross and scope* (my) general view (imprecise and intuitive).
70–79 (Marcellus picks up Horatio's vague suggestion and mentions evidences that something of great moment—preparations for imminent war, perhaps—is going on in Denmark.)
75 *impress,* conscription.
77 *might be toward,* might be about to happen.
90 *moiety competent,* a sufficient portion.
91 *gaged,* pledged.
93 *comart,* bargain agreed upon.

Shark'd up a list of lawless resolutes,
For food and diet, to some enterprise
That hath a stomach in't; which is no other,
As it doth well appear unto our state,
But to recover of us, by strong hand
And terms compulsatory, those foresaid lands
So by his father lost; and this, I take it,
Is the main motive of our preparations,
The source of this our watch, and the chief head
Of this post-haste and romage in the land.

BERNARDO I think it be no other but e'en so.
Well may it sort that this portentous figure
Comes armed through our watch, so like the King
That was and is the question of these wars.

HORATIO A mote it is to trouble the mind's eye.
In the most high and palmy state of Rome,
A little ere the mightiest Julius fell,
The graves stood tenantless, and the sheeted dead
Did squeak and gibber in the Roman streets;
As stars with trains of fire, and dews of blood,
Disasters in the sun; and the moist star
Upon whose influence Neptune's empire stands
Was sick almost to doomsday with eclipse.
And even the like precurse of fierce events,
As harbingers preceding still the fates
And prologue to the omen coming on,
Have heaven and earth together demonstrated
Unto our climature and countrymen.
[*Enter* GHOST *again.*]
But soft! behold! Lo, where it comes again!
I'll cross it, though it blast me.—Stay, illusion!
[*Spreads his arms.*]
If thou hast any sound, or use of voice,
Speak to me.
If there be any good thing to be done,
That may to thee do ease, and grace to me,
Speak to me.
If thou art privy to thy country's fate,
Which happily foreknowing may avoid,
O, speak!
Or if thou hast uphoarded in thy life
Extorted treasure in the womb of earth
(For which, they say, you spirits oft walk in death),
[*The cock crows.*]
Speak of it! Stay, and speak!—Stop it, Marcellus!

MARCELLUS Shall I strike at it with my partisan?

HORATIO Do, if it will not stand.

BERNARDO 'Tis here!

HORATIO 'Tis here!

MARCELLUS 'Tis gone!
[*Exit* GHOST.]
We do it wrong, being so majestical,
To offer it the show of violence;
For it is as the air, invulnerable,
And our vain blows malicious mockery.

BERNARDO It was about to speak, when the cock crew.

HORATIO And then it started, like a guilty thing
Upon a fearful summons. I have heard
The cock, that is the trumpet to the morn,
Doth with his lofty and shrill-sounding throat
Awake the god of day; and at his warning,
Whether in sea or fire, in earth or air,
Th' extravagant and erring spirit hies
To his confine; and of the truth herein
This present object made probation.

MARCELLUS It faded on the crowing of the cock.
Some say that ever, 'gainst that season comes
Wherein our Saviour's birth is celebrated,

98 *Shark'd up,* took any war-willing, desperate men, as allegedly sharks indiscriminately gather their prey.
100 *a stomach,* valor.
106 *head,* motive.
107 *romage,* feverish activity.
112-125 (Horatio calls the appearance of the Ghost a portent similar to the horrendous natural events that preceded the murder of Julius Caesar.)
117 (Some scholars assume that a line before this line has been lost. Why?)
118 *moist star,* the moon.
119 (The moon controls Neptune's empire, the oceans.)
122 *harbingers,* officers who precede the king to make arrangements for his care; here forerunners of disaster.
123 *omen,* terrible happening.
126 *soft!,* hush!
127 *blast,* destroy.
131 *to thee do ease, and grace to me,* bring the ghost relief without disgracing Horatio. (Note the repetition of the imperative, "Speak to me." The implication is that Horatio, if told what to do, will do it—provided the deed be honorable.)
138 *the cock crows,* (a conventional signal to ghosts that they must retire.)
140 *partisan,* a shafted weapon wih a broad blade.
143-146 (Marcellus makes the sensible observation that it is a mere "mockery" to try to harm a ghost.)
154 *extravagant and erring,* wandering out-of-bounds.
156 *made probation,* offered proof.
158 *'gainst,* immediately preceding.

The bird of dawning singeth all night long;
And then, they say, no spirit dare stir abroad,
The nights are wholesome, then no planets strike,
No fairy takes, nor witch hath power to charm,
So hallow'd and so gracious is the time.

HORATIO So have I heard and do in part believe it.
But look, the morn, in russet mantle clad,
Walks o'er the dew of yon high eastward hill.
Break we our watch up; and by my advice
Let us impart what we have seen to-night
Unto young Hamlet; for, upon my life,
This spirit, dumb to us, will speak to him.
Do you consent we shall acquaint him with it,
As needful in our loves, fitting our duty?

MARCELLUS Let's do't, I pray; and I this morning know
Where we shall find him most conveniently.
[*Exeunt.*]

Scene II [*Elsinore. A room of state in the Castle.*]

[*Flourish. Enter* CLAUDIUS, *King of Denmark,* GERTRUDE *the Queen,* HAMLET, POLONIUS, LAERTES, *and his sister* OPHELIA, (VOLTEMAND, CORNELIUS,) *Lords Attendant.*]

KING Though yet of Hamlet our dear brother's death
The memory be green, and that it us befitted
To bear our hearts in grief, and our whole kingdom
To be contracted in one brow of woe,
Yet so far hath discretion fought with nature
That we with wisest sorrow think on him
Together with remembrance of ourselves.
Therefore our sometime sister, now our queen,
Th' imperial jointress to this warlike state,
Have we, as 'twere with a defeated joy,
With an auspicious, and a dropping eye,
With mirth in funeral, and with dirge in marriage,
In equal scale weighing delight and dole,
Taken to wife; nor have we herein barr'd
Your better wisdoms, which have freely gone
With this affair along. For all, our thanks.
Now follows, that you know, young Fortinbras,
Holding a weak supposal of our worth,
Or thinking by our late dear brother's death
Our state to be disjoint and out of frame,
Colleagued with this dream of his advantage,
He hath not fail'd to pester us with message
Importing the surrender of those lands
Lost by his father, with all bands of law,
To our most valiant brother. So much for him.
Now for ourself and for this time of meeting.
Thus much the business is: we have here writ
To Norway, uncle of young Fortinbras,
Who, impotent and bedrid, scarcely hears
Of this his nephew's purpose, to suppress
His further gait herein, in that the levies,
The lists, and full proportions are all made
Out of his subject; and we here dispatch
You, good Cornelius, and you, Voltemand,
For bearers of this greeting to old Norway,
Giving to you no further personal power
To business with the King, more than the scope
Of these dilated articles allow. [*Gives a paper.*]
Farewell, and let your haste commend your duty.

CORNELIUS, VOLTEMAND In that, and all things, will we show our duty.

KING We doubt it nothing. Heartily farewell.

162 *wholesome,* healthful in every respect.
163 *takes,* puts under a spell.
165 *in part believe it,* some (of their lore) I believe. (Later on Hamlet also in part believes but is firmly convinced only by the evidence provided, not by the Ghost, but by the effect of the mousetrap play. See III, ii.)
Scene ii, morning of the same day.
2 *us,* all Danes.
5 *discretion,* moderation (there can be too much of a noble sentiment, even grief.)
6 *wisest sorrow,* sorrow held in check (so that affairs of state can go forward).
9 *jointress,* co-inheritor (of the Danish throne).
10–16 (Claudius is here attempting to justify his quick marriage, a marriage of joy against a backdrop of sorrow over the death of Hamlet's father. He reminds his Council that it had tacitly approved the action.)
18 *a weak supposal of our worth,* an underestimate of my ability to rule.
21 *Colleagued . . . advantage,* produced a (foolish) dream of superiority.
24 *bands,* sanctions.
38 *dilated,* fully expressed.
40 *will we show our duty,* we will do what we are ordered to do. (The subservience of Cornelius and Voltemand shows that Claudius has indeed taken over as a respected king.)

[*Exeunt* VOLTEMAND *and* CORNELIUS.]
And now, Laertes, what's the news with you?
You told us of some suit. What is't, Laertes?
You cannot speak of reason to the Dane
And lose your voice. What wouldst thou beg, Laertes,
That shall not be my offer, not thy asking?
The head is not more native to the heart,
The hand more instrumental to the mouth,
Than is the throne of Denmark to thy father.
What wouldst thou have, Laertes?

LAERTES My dread lord,
Your leave and favour to return to France;
From whence though willingly I came to Denmark
To show my duty in your coronation,
Yet now I must confess, that duty done,
My thoughts and wishes bend again toward France
And bow them to your gracious leave and pardon.

KING Have you your father's leave? What says Polonius?

POLONIUS He hath, my lord, wrung from me my slow leave
By laboursome petition, and at last
Upon his will I seal'd my hard consent.
I do beseech you give him leave to go.

KING Take thy fair hour, Laertes. Time be thine,
And thy best graces spend it at thy will!
But now, my cousin Hamlet, and my son—

HAMLET [*Aside.*] A little more than kin, and less than kind!

KING How is it that the clouds still hang on you?

HAMLET Not so, my lord. I am too much i' th' sun.

QUEEN Good Hamlet, cast thy nighted colour off,
And let thine eye look like a friend on Denmark.
Do not for ever with thy vailed lids
Seek for thy noble father in the dust.
Thou know'st 'tis common. All that lives must die,
Passing through nature to eternity.

HAMLET Ay, madam, it is common.

QUEEN If it be,
Why seems it so particular with thee?

HAMLET Seems, madam? Nay, it is. I know not "seems."
'Tis not alone my inky cloak, good mother,
Nor customary suits of solemn black,
Nor windy suspiration of forc'd breath,
No, nor the fruitful river in the eye,
Nor the dejected haviour of the visage,
Together with all forms, moods, shapes of grief,
That can denote me truly. These indeed seem,
For they are actions that a man might play;
But I have that within which passeth show—
These but the trappings and the suits of woe.

KING 'Tis sweet and commendable in your nature, Hamlet,
To give these mourning duties to your father;
But you must know, your father lost a father;
That father lost, lost his, and the survivor bound
In filial obligation for some term
To do obsequious sorrow. But to persever
In obstinate condolement is a course
Of impious stubbornness. 'Tis unmanly grief;
It shows a will most incorrect to heaven,
A heart unfortified, a mind impatient,
An understanding simple and unschool'd;
For what we know must be, and is as common
As any the most vulgar thing to sense,
Why should we in our peevish opposition
Take it to heart? Fie! 'tis a fault to heaven,
A fault against the dead, a fault to nature,
To reason most absurd, whose common theme
Is death of fathers, and who still hath cried,
From the first corse till he that died to-day,

42-63 (Laertes further supports with complete deference the new king, who probably has been helped to the throne by Polonius, Laertes' father.)
51 *leave and favour,* generous permission.
56 *leave and pardon,* permission to go back (to France).
62 *fair hour,* youth (and make best use of it).
63 *graces,* qualities (of character).
64 *cousin,* kinsman.
65 (Hamlet's first words indicate an intuitive bitterness. He is doubly kin to Claudius—son and nephew—but has no kindly feeling toward his father's successor.)
67 *too much i' th' sun,* in the unwanted forefront of affairs.
69 *Denmark,* the King of Denmark.
70-73 (Gertrude, a simple soul, counsels with the cliché that "all that lives must die.")
76-86 (Hamlet's outward appearance is but a weak representation of his inward sorrow.)

"This must be so." We pray you throw to earth
This unprevailing woe, and think of us
As of a father; for let the world take note
You are the most immediate to our throne,
And with no less nobility of love
Than that which dearest father bears his son
Do I impart toward you. For your intent
In going back to school in Wittenberg,
It is most retrograde to our desire;
And we beseech you, bend you to remain
Here in the cheer and comfort of our eye,
Our chiefest courtier, cousin, and our son.

QUEEN Let not thy mother lose her prayers, Hamlet.
I pray thee stay with us, go not to Wittenberg.

HAMLET I shall in all my best obey you, madam.

KING Why, 'tis a loving and a fair reply.
Be as ourself in Denmark. Madam, come.
This gentle and unforc'd accord of Hamlet
Sits smiling to my heart; in grace whereof,
No jocund health that Denmark drinks to-day
But the great cannon to the clouds shall tell,
And the King's rouse the heaven shall bruit again,
Respeaking earthly thunder. Come away.
[*Flourish. Exeunt all but* HAMLET.]

HAMLET O that this too too solid flesh would melt,
Thaw, and resolve itself into a dew!
Or that the Everlasting had not fix'd
His canon 'gainst self-slaughter! O God! God!
How weary, stale, flat, and unprofitable
Seem to me all the uses of this world!
Fie on't! ah, fie! 'Tis an unweeded garden
That grows to seed; things rank and gross in nature
Possess it merely. That it should come to this!
But two months dead! Nay, not so much, not two.
So excellent a king, that was to this
Hyperion to a satyr; so loving to my mother
That he might not beteem the winds of heaven
Visit her face too roughly. Heaven and earth!
Must I remember? Why, she would hang on him
As if increase of appetite had grown
By what it fed on; and yet, within a month—
Let me not think on't! Frailty, thy name is woman!—
A little month, or ere those shoes were old
With which she followed my poor father's body
Like Niobe, all tears—why she, even she
(O God! a beast that wants discourse of reason
Would have mourn'd longer) married with my uncle;
My father's brother, but no more like my father
Than I to Hercules. Within a month,
Ere yet the salt of most unrighteous tears
Had left the flushing in her galled eyes,
She married. O, most wicked speed, to post
With such dexterity to incestuous sheets!
It is not, nor it cannot come to good.
But break, my heart, for I must hold my tongue!
[*Enter* HORATIO, MARCELLUS, *and* BERNARDO.]

HORATIO Hail to your lordship!

HAMLET I am glad to see you well.
Horatio!—or I do forget myself.

HORATIO The same, my lord, and your poor servant ever.

HAMLET Sir, my good friend—I'll change that name with you.
And what make you from Wittenberg, Horatio?
Marcellus?

MARCELLUS My good lord!

HAMLET I am very glad to see you.—[*To* BERNARDO.] Good even, sir.—
But what, in faith, make you from Wittenberg?

HORATIO A truant disposition, good my lord.

HAMLET I would not hear your enemy say so,
Nor shall you do my ear that violence
To make it truster of your own report
Against yourself. I know you are no truant.
But what is your affair in Elsinore?
We'll teach you to drink deep ere you depart.

HORATIO My lord, I came to see your father's funeral.

HAMLET I prithee do not mock me, fellow student.
I think it was my mother's wedding.

HORATIO Indeed, my lord, it followed hard upon.

140 *Hyperion to a satyr,* the sun god to a creature half human and half goat.
141 *beteem,* allow.

155 *galled,* irritated (by salty tears).
175 *to drink deep,* to exchange many toasts.

HAMLET Thrift, thrift, Horatio! The funeral bak'd meats
Did coldly furnish forth the marriage tables.
Would I had met my dearest foe in heaven
Or ever I had seen that day, Horatio!
My father—methinks I see my father.
HORATIO O, where, my lord?
HAMLET In my mind's eye, Horatio.
HORATIO I saw him once. He was a goodly king.
HAMLET He was a man, take him for all in all.
I shall not look upon his like again.
HORATIO My lord, I think I saw him yester-night.
HAMLET Saw? who?
HORATIO My lord, the King your father.
HAMLET The King my father?
HORATIO Season your admiration for a while
With an attent ear, till I may deliver,
Upon the witness of these gentlemen,
This marvel to you.
HAMLET For God's love let me hear!
HORATIO Two nights together had these gentlemen
(Marcellus and Bernardo) on their watch
In the dead vast and middle of the night
Been thus encount'red. A figure like your father,
Armed at point exactly, cap-a-pe,
Appears before them and with solemn march
Goes slow and stately by them. Thrice he walk'd
By their oppress'd and fear-surprised eyes,
Within his truncheon's length; whilst they distill'd
Almost to jelly with the act of fear,
Stand dumb and speak not to him. This to me
In dreadful secrecy impart they did,
And I with them the third night kept the watch;
Where, as they had deliver'd, both in time,
Form of the thing, each word made true and good,
The apparition comes. I knew your father.
These hands are not more like.
HAMLET But where was this?
MARCELLUS My lord, upon the platform where we watch'd.
HAMLET Did you not speak to it?
HORATIO My lord, I did;
But answer made it none. Yet once methought
It lifted up it head and did address
Itself to motion, like as it would speak;
But even then the morning cock crew loud,
And at the sound it shrunk in haste away
And vanish'd from our sight.
HAMLET 'Tis very strange.
HORATIO As I do live, my honour'd lord, 'tis true;
And we did think it writ down in our duty
To let you know of it.
HAMLET Indeed, indeed, sirs. But this troubles me.
Hold you the watch to-night?
BOTH [MARCELLUS *and* BERNARDO.] We do, my lord.
HAMLET Arm'd, say you?
BOTH Arm'd, my lord.
HAMLET From top to toe?
BOTH My lord, from head to foot.
HAMLET Then saw you not his face?
HORATIO O, yes, my lord! He wore his beaver up.
HAMLET What, look'd he frowningly?
HORATIO A countenance more in sorrow than in anger.
HAMLET Pale or red?
HORATIO Nay, very pale.
HAMLET And fix'd his eyes upon you?
HORATIO Most constantly.
HAMLET I would I had been there.
HORATIO It would have much amaz'd you.
HAMLET Very like, very like. Stay'd it long?
HORATIO While one with moderate haste might tell a hundred.
BOTH Longer, longer.
HORATIO Not when I saw't.
HAMLET His beard was grizzled—no?
HORATIO It was, as I have seen it in his life,
A sable silver'd.
HAMLET I will watch to-night.
Perchance 'twill walk again.
HORATIO I warr'nt it will.

182 *dearest foe,* worst enemy.
186 *goodly,* good-looking or handsome.
192 *Season your admiration,* control your wonderment.
198 *the dead vast,* unlimited darkness.
200 *at point . . . cap-a-pe,* completely, from head to foot.
204 *truncheon's length,* the distance represented by a short baton.
216 *it head,* its head.
230 *beaver,* visor.
238 *tell,* count.

HAMLET If it assume my noble father's person,
I'll speak to it, though hell itself should gape
And bid me hold my peace. I pray you all,
If you have hitherto conceal'd this sight,
Let it be tenable in your silence still;
And whatsoever else shall hap to-night,
Give it an understanding but no tongue.
I will requite your loves. So, fare you well.
Upon the platform, 'twixt eleven and twelve,
I'll visit you.

ALL Our duty to your honour.

HAMLET Your loves, as mine to you. Farewell.
[*Exeunt* (*all but* HAMLET).]
My father's spirit—in arms? All is not well.
I doubt some foul play. Would the night were come!
Till then sit still, my soul. Foul deeds will rise,
Though all the earth o'erwhelm them, to men's eyes. [*Exit.*]

Scene III [*Elsinore. A room in the house of* POLONIUS.]

[*Enter* LAERTES *and* OPHELIA.]

LAERTES My necessaries are embark'd. Farewell.
And, sister, as the winds give benefit
And convoy is assistant, do not sleep,
But let me hear from you.

OPHELIA Do you doubt that?

LAERTES For Hamlet, and the trifling of his favour,
Hold it a fashion, and a toy in blood;
A violet in the youth of primy nature,
Forward, not permanent—sweet, not lasting,
The perfume and suppliance of a minute;
No more.

OPHELIA No more but so?

LAERTES Think it no more.
For nature crescent does not grow alone
In thews and bulk; but as this temple waxes
The inward service of the mind and soul
Grows wide withal. Perhaps he loves you now,
And now no soil nor cautel doth besmirch
The virtue of his will; but you must fear,
His greatness weigh'd, his will is not his own;
For he himself is subject to his birth.
He may not, as unvalued persons do,
Carve for himself, for on his choice depends
The safety and health of this whole state,
And therefore must his choice be circumscrib'd
Unto the voice and yielding of that body
Whereof he is the head. Then if he says he loves you,
It fits your wisdom so far to believe it
As he in his particular act and place
May give his saying deed; which is no further
Than the main voice of Denmark goes withal.
Then weigh what loss your honour may sustain
If with too credent ear you list his songs,
Or lose your heart, or your chaste treasure open
To his unmast'red importunity.
Fear it, Ophelia, fear it, my dear sister,
And keep you in the rear of your affection,
Out of the shot and danger of desire.
The chariest maid is prodigal enough
If she unmask her beauty to the moon.
Virtue itself scapes not calumnious strokes.
The canker galls the infants of the spring
Too oft before their buttons be disclos'd,
And in the morn and liquid dew of youth
Contagious blastments are most imminent.
Be wary then; best safety lies in fear.
Youth to itself rebels, though none else near.

OPHELIA I shall th' effect of this good lesson keep
As watchman to my heart. But, good my brother,
Do not as some ungracious pastors do,
Show me the steep and thorny way to heaven,
Whiles, like a puff'd and reckless libertine,
Himself the primrose path of dalliance treads
And recks not his own rede.

244 *assume,* put on (Hamlet has yet no way to be sure the figure is really the ghost of his father).
256 *I doubt some foul play,* I suspect some sort of crime has been committed.
Scene iii, afternoon of the same day.
3 *convoy,* mail service.
5–10 (Laertes warns his sister not to take seriously Hamlet's courting, for it is simply the fashion of young princes to flirt. Obviously Ophelia does not think much of this advice.)
9 *perfume and suppliance of a minute,* fragrance pleasant now but soon gone.
11 *nature crescent,* nature moving towards dominance.
15 *cautel,* deceit.
23 *voice and yielding,* assent (of Denmark).
30 *credent,* easily believing.
36 *chariest,* most modest, most careful.
37 *to the moon,* to the man in the moon?
39 *infants of the spring,* early flowers.
45–51 (Ophelia makes light, effective fun of her brother and punctures his pompous balloon.)

LAERTES O, fear me not!

[*Enter* POLONIUS.]

I stay too long. But here my father comes.
A double blessing is a double grace;
Occasion smiles upon a second leave.

POLONIUS Yet here, Laertes? Aboard, aboard, for shame!
The wind sits in the shoulder of your sail,
And you are stay'd for. There—my blessing with thee!
And these few precepts in thy memory
Look thou character. Give thy thoughts no tongue,
Nor any unproportion'd thought his act.
Be thou familiar, but by no means vulgar:
Those friends thou hast, and their adoption tried,
Grapple them unto thy soul with hoops of steel;
But do not dull thy palm with entertainment
Of each new-hatch'd, unfledg'd comrade. Beware
Of entrance to a quarrel; but being in,
Bear't that th' opposed may beware of thee.
Give every man thine ear, but few thy voice;
Take each man's censure, but reserve thy judgment.
Costly thy habit as thy purse can buy,
But not express'd in fancy; rich, not gaudy;
For the apparel oft proclaims the man,
And they in France of the best rank and station
Are most select and generous, chief in that.
Neither a borrower nor a lender be;
For loan oft loses both itself and friend,
And borrowing dulls the edge of husbandry.
This above all—to thine own self be true,
And it must follow, as the night the day,
Thou canst not then be false to any man.
Farewell. My blessing season this in thee!

LAERTES Most humbly do I take my leave, my lord.

POLONIUS The time invites you. Go, your servants tend.

LAERTES Farewell, Ophelia, and remember well
What I have said to you.

OPHELIA 'Tis in my memory lock'd,
And you yourself shall keep the key of it.

LAERTES Farewell. [*Exit.*]

POLONIUS What is't, Ophelia, he hath said to you?

OPHELIA So please you, something touching the Lord Hamlet.

POLONIUS Marry, well bethought!
'Tis told me he hath very oft of late
Given private time to you, and you yourself
Have of your audience been most free and bounteous.
If it be so—as so 'tis put on me,
And that in way of caution—I must tell you
You do not understand yourself so clearly
As it behooves my daughter and your honour.
What is between you? Give me up the truth.

OPHELIA He hath, my lord, of late made many tenders
Of his affection to me.

POLONIUS Affection? Pooh! You speak like a green girl,
Unsifted in such perilous circumstance.
Do you believe his tenders, as you call them?

OPHELIA I do not know, my lord, what I should think.

POLONIUS Marry, I will teach you! Think yourself a baby
That you have ta'en these tenders for true pay,
Which are not sterling. Tender yourself more dearly,
Or (not to crack the wind of the poor phrase,
Running it thus) you'll tender me a fool.

OPHELIA My lord, he hath importun'd me with love
In honourable fashion.

POLONIUS Ay, fashion you may call it. Go to, go to!

OPHELIA And hath given countenance to his speech, my lord,
With almost all the holy vows of heaven.

POLONIUS Ay, springes to catch woodcocks! I do know.
When the blood burns, how prodigal the soul
Lends the tongue vows. These blazes, daughter,
Giving more light than heat, extinct in both
Even in their promise, as it is a-making,
You must not take for fire. From this time

55-81 (Polonius offers what is, no doubt, sound advice, but is he merely mouthing a series of clichés?)

99 *tenders,* assurances.
108 *crack the wind of a poor phrase,* overdo or ride to wheezing a bad pun.
109 *you'll tender me a fool,* you'll present me with an illegitimate grandchild (and thereby make a fool of me?)
115 *springes,* traps.

Be something scanter of your maiden presence.
Set your entreatments at a higher rate
Than a command to parley. For Lord Hamlet,
Believe so much in him, that he is young,
And with a larger tether may he walk
Than may be given you. In few, Ophelia,
Do not believe his vows; for they are brokers,
Not of that dye which their investments show,
But mere implorators of unholy suits,
Breathing like sanctified and pious bawds,
The better to beguile. This is for all:
I would not, in plain terms, from this time forth
Have you so slander any moment leisure
As to give words or talk with the Lord Hamlet.
Look to't, I charge you. Come your ways.

OPHELIA I shall obey, my lord. [*Exeunt.*]

Scene IV [*Elsinore. The platform before the Castle.*]

[*Enter* HAMLET, HORATIO, *and* MARCELLUS.]

HAMLET The air bites shrewdly; it is very cold.
HORATIO It is a nipping and an eager air.
HAMLET What hour now?
HORATIO I think it lacks of twelve.
MARCELLUS No, it is struck.
HORATIO Indeed! I heard it not. It then draws near the season
Wherein the spirit held his wont to walk.
[*A flourish of trumpets, and two pieces go off.*]
What does this mean, my lord?
HAMLET The King doth wake to-night and takes his rouse,
Keeps wassail, and the swagg'ring upspring reels,
And, as he drains his draughts of Rhenish down,
The kettledrum and trumpet thus bray out
The triumph of his pledge.
HORATIO Is it a custom?
HAMLET Ay, marry, is't;
But to my mind, though I am native here
And to the manner born, it is a custom
More honour'd in the breach than the observance.
This heavy-headed revel east and west
Makes us traduc'd and tax'd of other nations;
They clip us drunkards and with swinish phrase
Soil our addition; and indeed it takes
From our achievements, though perform'd at height,
The pith and marrow of our attribute.
So oft it chances in particular men
That, for some vicious mole of nature in them,
As in their birth,—wherein they are not guilty,
Since nature cannot choose his origin,—
By the o'ergrowth of some complexion,
Oft breaking down the pales and forts of reason,
Or by some habit that too much o'erleavens
The form of plausive manners, that these men
Carrying, I say, the stamp of one defect,
Being nature's livery, or fortune's star,
Their virtues else—be they as pure as grace,
As infinite as man may undergo—
Shall in the general censure take corruption
From that particular fault. The dram of e'il
Doth all the noble substance often dout
To his own scandal.

[*Enter* GHOST.]

HORATIO Look, my lord, it comes!
HAMLET Angels and ministers of grace defend us!
Be thou a spirit of health or goblin damn'd,
Bring with thee airs from heaven or blasts from hell,
By thy intents wicked or charitable,
Thou com'st in such a questionable shape
That I will speak to thee. I'll call thee Hamlet,
King, father, royal Dane. O, answer me!
Let me not burst in ignorance, but tell
Why thy canoniz'd bones, hearsed in death,

125 *larger tether,* more leeway to make love (for he is a man, a prince, and as such may take advantage of the double standard.)
127 *brokers,* cheaters (offering false promises to gain a "sale").
Scene iv, after midnight, about 24 hours later than Scene i.
6 *spirit* (Horatio is careful not to say "the ghost of your father.")
9 *swagg'ring upspring,* a lively dance.
12 *the triumph of his pledge,* the lusty feat of swigging down at one gulp liquor drunk as a toast.
19 *clip,* name.
20 *Soil our addition,* blemish our reputation.
23-38 (These lines advance the notion that a man or a nation—no matter how virtuous otherwise—may be disgraced by one fault, in this case the reputation for carousing.)
43 *questionable shape,* in a shape (like that of the dead king) to be questioned.
47 *canoniz'd,* given church-approved burial service. *hearsed,* entombed.

Have burst their cerements; why the sepulchre
Wherein we saw thee quietly inurn'd,
Hath op'd his ponderous and marble jaws
To cast thee up again. What may this mean
That thou, dead corse, again in complete steel,
Revisits thus the glimpses of the moon,
Making night hideous, and we fools of nature
So horridly to shake our disposition
With thoughts beyond the reaches of our souls?
Say, why is this? wherefore? What should we do?

[GHOST *beckons* HAMLET.]

HORATIO It beckons you to go away with it,
As if it some impartment did desire
To you alone.

MARCELLUS Look with what courteous action
It waves you to a more removed ground.
But do not go with it!

HORATIO No, by no means!

HAMLET It will not speak. Then will I follow it.

HORATIO Do not, my lord!

HAMLET Why, what should be the fear?
I do not set my life at a pin's fee;
And for my soul, what can it do to that,
Being a thing immortal as itself?
It waves me forth again. I'll follow it.

HORATIO What if it tempt you toward the flood, my lord,
Or to the dreadful summit of the cliff
That beetles o'er his base into the sea,
And there assume some other, horrible form
Which might deprive your sovereignty of reason
And draw you into madness? Think of it.
The very place puts toys of desperation,
Without more motive, into every brain
That looks so many fadoms to the sea
And hears it roar beneath.

HAMLET It waves me still.
Go on. I'll follow thee.

MARCELLUS You shall not go, my lord.

HAMLET Hold off your hands!

HORATIO Be rul'd. You shall not go.

HAMLET My fate cries out
And makes each petty artire in this body
As hardy as the Nemean lion's nerve.

[GHOST *beckons.*]

Still am I call'd. Unhand me, gentlemen.
By heaven, I'll make a ghost of him that lets me!—
I say, away!—Go on. I'll follow thee.

[*Exeunt* GHOST *and* HAMLET.]

HORATIO He waxes desperate with imagination.

MARCELLUS Let's follow. 'Tis not fit thus to obey him.

HORATIO Have after. To what issue will this come?

MARCELLUS Something is rotten in the state of Denmark.

HORATIO Heaven will direct it.

MARCELLUS Nay, let's follow him. [*Exeunt.*]

Scene V [*Elsinore. The Castle. Another part of the fortifications.*]

[*Enter* GHOST *and* HAMLET.]

HAMLET Whither wilt thou lead me? Speak! I'll go no further.

GHOST Mark me.

HAMLET I will.

GHOST My hour is almost come,
When I to sulph'rous and tormenting flames
Must render up myself.

HAMLET Alas, poor ghost!

GHOST Pity me not, but lend thy serious hearing
To what I shall unfold.

HAMLET Speak. I am bound to hear.

GHOST So art thou to revenge, when thou shalt hear.

HAMLET What?

GHOST I am thy father's spirit,
Doom'd for a certain term to walk the night,
And for the day confin'd to fast in fires,

53 *glimpses,* short views (because of scudding clouds).
54 *fools of nature,* (made to act like fools by a nature which denies us access to the supernatural).
59 *impartment,* communication.
65 *a pin's fee,* the value of a pin.
75–78 (Elsinore is perched on a crag below which is a rough-water channel which separates Denmark from Sweden. Horatio warns that, once Hamlet is lured to the brink of the crag, the Ghost, which may be a demon, will simply allow the hypnotic effect of height and the roaring sea to cause the Prince to pitch forward to his destruction.)

81 *My fate cries out,* my destiny is calling.
83 *Nemean lion's nerve,* sinews of the lion of Nemea (the killing of which was one of the twelve labors of Hercules).
85 *lets me,* tries to stop me.
1 *I'll go no further* (Hamlet does not yet know whether he is being tricked by a demon.)
3 *flames* (of purgatory).
6 *bound,* eager.

Till the foul crimes done in my days of nature
Are burnt and purg'd away. But that I am forbid
To tell the secrets of my prison house,
I could a tale unfold whose lightest word
Would harrow up thy soul, freeze thy young blood,
Make thy two eyes, like stars, start from their spheres,
Thy knotted and combined locks to part,
And each particular hair to stand an end
Like quills upon the fretful porpentine.
But this eternal blazon must not be
To ears of flesh and blood. List, list, O, list!
If thou didst ever thy dear father love—

HAMLET O God!

GHOST Revenge his foul and most unnatural murther.

HAMLET Murther?

GHOST Murther most foul, as in the best it is;
But this most foul, strange, and unnatural.

HAMLET Haste me to know't, that I, with wings as swift
As meditation or the thoughts of love,
May sweep to my revenge.

GHOST I find thee apt;
And duller shouldst thou be than the fat weed
That rots itself in ease on Lethe wharf,
Wouldst thou not stir in this. Now, Hamlet, hear.
'Tis given out that, sleeping in my orchard,
A serpent stung me. So the whole ear of Denmark
Is by a forged process of my death
Rankly abus'd. But know, thou noble youth,
The serpent that did sting thy father's life
Now wears his crown.

HAMLET O my prophetic soul!
My uncle?

GHOST Ay, that incestuous, that adulterate beast,
With witchcraft of his wit, with traitorous gifts—
O wicked wit and gifts, that have the power
So to seduce!—won to his shameful lust
The will of my most seeming-virtuous queen.
O Hamlet, what a falling-off was there,
From me, whose love was of that dignity
That it went hand in hand even with the vow
I made to her in marriage, and to decline
Upon a wretch whose natural gifts were poor
To those of mine!
But virtue, as it never will be mov'd,
Though lewdness court it in a shape of heaven,
So lust, though to a radiant angel link'd,
Will sate itself in a celestial bed
And prey on garbage.
But soft! methinks I scent the morning air.
Brief let me be. Sleeping within my orchard,
My custom always of the afternoon,
Upon my secure hour thy uncle stole,
With juice of cursed hebona in a vial,
And in the porches of my ears did pour
The leperous distilment; whose effect
Holds such an enmity with blood of man
That swift as quicksilver it courses through
The natural gates and alleys of the body,
And with a sudden vigour it doth posset
And curd, like eager droppings into milk,
The thin and wholesome blood. So did it mine;
And a most instant tetter bark'd about,
Most lazar-like, with vile and loathsome crust
All my smooth body.
Thus was I, sleeping, by a brother's hand
Of life, of crown, of queen, at once dispatch'd;
Cut off even in the blossoms of my sin,
Unhous'led, disappointed, unanel'd,
No reck'ning made, but sent to my account
With all my imperfections on my head.

HAMLET O, horrible! O, horrible! most horrible!

GHOST If thou hast nature in thee, bear it not.
Let not the royal bed of Denmark be

12 *foul crimes* (The elder Hamlet has committed only the "crime" of living but must expiate just the same his common human failings.)
13-22 (No mortal could bear to be told what purgatory—*prison house*, 14—is like.)
33 *Lethe*, river of oblivion in Hades.
35 *orchard*, garden area (of the Palace).
40 *O my prophetic soul!*, O how right my intuitions! (that some evil caused my father's death).
42 *adulterate* (suggests that Gertrude had been untrue, but perhaps the Ghost regarded the quick marriage as adultery).
62 *hebona*, sap of the ebony tree (apparently as poisonous as hemlock).
68 *posset*, coagulate.
71 *tetter bark'd about*, eczema made the skin resemble the rough bark of a tree.
76 *sin*, sinfulness (see footnote to 12, above).
77 *Unhous'led, disappointed, unanel'd*, unconfessed, unready, not having received extreme unction.

A couch for luxury and damned incest.
But, howsoever thou pursuest this act,
Taint not thy mind, nor let thy soul contrive
Against thy mother aught. Leave her to heaven,
And to those thorns that in her bosom lodge
To prick and sting her. Fare thee well at once.
The glowworm shows the matin to be near
And gins to pale his uneffectual fire.
Adieu, adieu, adieu! Remember me. [*Exit.*]

HAMLET O all you host of heaven! O earth! What else?
And shall I couple hell? Hold, hold, my heart!
And you, my sinews, grow not instant old,
But bear me stiffly up. Remember thee?
Ay, thou poor ghost, while memory holds a seat
In this distracted globe. Remember thee?
Yea, from the table of my memory
I'll wipe away all trivial fond records,
All saws of books, all forms, all pressures past
That youth and observation copied there,
And thy commandment all alone shall live
Within the book and volume of my brain,
Unmix'd with baser matter. Yes, by heaven!
O most pernicious woman!
O villain, villain, smiling, damned villain!
My tables! Meet it is I set it down
That one may smile, and smile, and be a villain;
At least I am sure it may be so in Denmark.
[*Writes.*]
So, uncle, there you are. Now to my word:
It is 'Adieu, adieu! Remember me.'
I have sworn't.

HORATIO [*Within.*] My lord, my lord!

[*Enter* HORATIO *and* MARCELLUS.]

MARCELLUS Lord Hamlet!

HORATIO Heaven secure him!

HAMLET So be it!

MARCELLUS Illo, ho, ho, my lord!

HAMLET Hillo, ho, ho, boy! Come, bird, come.

MARCELLUS How is't, my noble lord?

HORATIO What news, my lord?

HAMLET O, wonderful!

HORATIO Good my lord, tell it.

HAMLET No, you will reveal it.

HORATIO Not I, my lord, by heaven!

MARCELLUS Nor I, my lord.

HAMLET How say you then? Would heart of man once think it?
But you'll be secret?

BOTH Ay, by heaven, my lord.

HAMLET There's ne'er a villain dwelling in all Denmark
But he's an arrant knave.

HORATIO There needs no ghost, my lord, come from the grave
To tell us this.

HAMLET Why, right! You are in the right!
And so, without more circumstance at all,
I hold it fit that we shake hands and part;
You, as your business and desire shall point you,
For every man hath business and desire,
Such as it is; and for my own poor part,
Look you, I'll go pray.

HORATIO These are but wild and whirling words, my lord.

HAMLET I am sorry they offend you, heartily;
Yes, faith, heartily.

HORATIO There's no offence, my lord.

HAMLET Yes, by Saint Patrick, but there is, Horatio,
And much offence too. Touching this vision here,
It is an honest ghost, that let me tell you.
For your desire to know what is between us,
O'ermaster't as you may. And now, good friends,
As you are friends, scholars, and soldiers,
Give me one poor request.

HORATIO What is't, my lord? We will.

HAMLET Never make known what you have seen to-night.

BOTH My lord, we will not.

HAMLET Nay, but swear't.

HORATIO In faith,
My lord, not I.

MARCELLUS Nor I, my lord—in faith.

HAMLET Upon my sword.

MARCELLUS We have sworn, my lord, already.

83 *luxury,* lechery.
93 *shall I couple hell?,* shall I conspire with hell? (if necessary to gain my revenge).
97 *distracted globe* (Hamlet's) confused head.
100 *saws,* wise sayings.
107 *My tables!,* my notebooks.
115-116 (Hamlet is reminded by the cry of Marcellus of the falconer's sound in calling back a hawk.)

127 *circumstance,* ceremony.
138 *an honest ghost,* above-board, nondemonic ghost.
147 *Upon my sword* (the blade and the hilt form a cross, so that an oath taken on a sword would be like swearing on a holy instrument.)

HAMLET Indeed, upon my sword, indeed.
[GHOST *cries under the stage.*]
GHOST Swear.
HAMLET Aha boy, say'st thou so? Art thou there, truepenny?
Come on! You hear this fellow in the cellarage.
Consent to swear.
HORATIO Propose the oath, my lord.
HAMLET Never to speak of this that you have seen.
Swear by my sword.
GHOST [*Beneath.*] Swear.
HAMLET Hic et ubique? Then we'll shift our ground.
Come hither, gentlemen,
And lay your hands again upon my sword.
Never to speak of this that you have heard:
Swear by my sword.
GHOST [*Beneath.*] Swear by his sword.
HAMLET Well said, old mole! Canst work i' th' earth so fast?
A worthy pioner! Once more remove, good friends.
HORATIO O day and night, but this is wondrous strange!
HAMLET And therefore as a stranger give it welcome.
There are more things in heaven and earth, Horatio,
Than are dreamt of in your philosophy.
But come!
Here, as before, never, so help you mercy,
How strange or odd soe'er I bear myself
(As I perchance hereafter shall think meet
To put an antic disposition on),
That you, at such times seeing me, never shall,
With arms encumb'red thus, or this head-shake,
Or by pronouncing of some doubtful phrase,
As "Well, well, we know," or "We could, an if we would,"
Or "If we list to speak," or "There be, an if they might,"
Or such ambiguous giving out, to note
That you know aught of me—this not to do,
So grace and mercy at your most need help you,
Swear.
GHOST [*Beneath.*] Swear.
[*They swear.*]
HAMLET Rest, rest, perturbed spirit! So, gentlemen,
With all my love I do commend me to you;
And what so poor a man as Hamlet is
May do t' express his love and friending to you,
God willing, shall not lack. Let us go in together;
And still your fingers on your lips, I pray.
The time is out of joint. O cursed spite
That ever I was born to set it right!
Nay, come, let's go together. [*Exeunt.*]

ACT II

Scene I [*Elsinore. A room in the house of* POLONIUS.]

[*Enter* POLONIUS *and* REYNALDO.]
POLONIUS Give him this money and these notes, Reynaldo.
REYNALDO I will, my lord.
POLONIUS You shall do marvell's wisely, good Reynaldo,
Before you visit him, to make inquire
Of his behaviour.
REYNALDO My lord, I did intend it.
POLONIUS Marry, well said, very well said. Look you, sir,
Enquire me first what Danskers are in Paris;
And how, and who, what means, and where they keep,
What company, at what expense; and finding
By this encompassment and drift of question
That they do know my son, come you more nearer
Than your particular demands will touch it.
Take you, as 'twere, some distant knowledge of him;

150 *truepenny,* good old boy (a slangy term, implying the easy relationship Hamlet—temporarily—has established with the Ghost).
156 *Hic et ubique?,* here and everywhere.
163 *pioner,* a digger in the earth.
167 *philosophy,* scientific attitude (which does not acknowledge the possibility of ghosts).
172 *antic,* whimsical, feigning madness.
174 *encumb'red,* folded (in a knowing but not telling manner).
177 *list,* chose.
189 *spite,* imposition (the implication is that unjust powers have saddled Hamlet with a highly unwelcome duty).
Scene i, Scholars estimate that six to eight weeks elapse between I, v and II, i.
3 *marvell's,* extraordinarily.

As thus, "I know his father and his friends,
And in part him." Do you mark this, Reynaldo?

REYNALDO Ay, very well, my lord.

POLONIUS "And in part him, but," you may say, "not well.
But if't be he I mean, he's very wild
Addicted so and so"; and there put on him
What forgeries you please; marry, none so rank
As may dishonour him—take heed of that;
But, sir, such wanton, wild, and usual slips
As are companions noted and most known
To youth and liberty.

REYNALDO As gaming, my lord.

POLONIUS Ay, or drinking, fencing, swearing, quarrelling,
Drabbing. You may go so far.

REYNALDO My lord, that would dishonour him.

POLONIUS Faith, no, as you may season it in the charge.
You must not put another scandal on him,
That he is open to incontinency.
That's not my meaning. But breathe his faults so quaintly
That they may seem the taints of liberty,
The flash and outbreak of a fiery mind,
A savageness in unreclaimed blood,
Of general assault.

REYNALDO But, my good lord—

POLONIUS Wherefore should you do this?

REYNALDO Ay, my lord,
I would know that.

POLONIUS Marry, sir, here's my drift,
And I believe it is a fetch of warrant.
You laying these slight sullies on my son
As 'twere a thing a little soil'd i' th' working,
Mark you,
Your party in converse, him you would sound,
Having ever seen in the prenominate crimes
The youth you breathe of guilty, be assur'd
He closes with you in this consequence:
"Good sir," or so, or "friend," or "gentleman"—
According to the phrase or the addition
Of man and country—

REYNALDO Very good, my lord.

POLONIUS And then, sir, does 'a this—'a does—
What was I about to say? By the mass, I was
about to say something! Where did I leave?

REYNALDO At "closes in the consequence," at
"friend or so," and "gentleman."

POLONIUS At "closes in the consequence"—Ay, marry!
He closes thus: "I know the gentleman.
I saw him yesterday, or t'other day,
Or then, or then, with such or such; and, as you say,
There was 'a gaming; there o'ertook in's rouse;
There falling out at tennis"; or perchance,
"I saw him enter such a house of sale,"
Videlicet, a brothel, or so forth.
See you now—
Your bait of falsehood takes this carp of truth;
And thus do we of wisdom and of reach,
With windlasses and with assays of bias
By indirections find directions out.
So, by my former lecture and advice,
Shall you my son. You have me, have you not?

REYNALDO My lord, I have.

POLONIUS God b' wi' ye, fare ye well!

REYNALDO Good my lord! [*Going.*]

POLONIUS Observe his inclination in yourself.

REYNALDO I shall, my lord.

POLONIUS And let him ply his music.

REYNALDO Well, my lord.

POLONIUS Farewell! [*Exit* REYNALDO.]

[*Enter* OPHELIA.]

How now, Ophelia? What's the matter?

OPHELIA O my lord, my lord, I have been so affrighted!

POLONIUS With what, i' th' name of God?

OPHELIA My lord, as I was sewing in my closet,
Lord Hamlet, with his doublet all unbrac'd,
No hat upon his head, his stockings foul'd,
Ungart'red, and down-gyved to his ankle;
Pale as his shirt, his knees knocking each other,
And with a look so piteous in purport

20 *forgeries,* false accusations.
26 *Drabbing,* whoring.
35 *Of general assault,* of common occurrence (in young men).
38 *a fetch of warrant,* fully justified.
43 *prenominate,* aforementioned.
45 *closes with,* goes along with.
58 *o'ertook in's rouse,* done in by overdrinking.
61 *Videlicet,* that is, or namely.
65 *windlasses . . . assays of bias,* indirect ways . . . attempts by curved means, as with a bowling ball.
68 *you have me,* you understand me.
78 *unbrac'd,* unlaced.
80 *down-gyved,* drooping.

As if he had been loosed out of hell
To speak of horrors—he comes before me.

POLONIUS Mad for thy love?

OPHELIA My lord, I do not know,
But truly I do fear it.

POLONIUS What said he?

OPHELIA He took me by the wrist and held me hard;
Then goes he to the length of all his arm,
And, with his other hand thus o'er his brow,
He falls to such perusal of my face
As he would draw it. Long stay'd he so.
At last, a little shaking of mine arm,
And thrice his head thus waving up and down,
He rais'd a sigh so piteous and profound
As it did seem to shatter all his bulk
And end his being. That done, he lets me go.
And with his head over his shoulder turn'd
He seem'd to find his way without his eyes,
For out o' doors he went without their help
And to the last bended their light on me.

POLONIUS Come, go with me. I will go seek the King.
This is the very ecstasy of love,
Whose violent property fordoes itself
And leads the will to desperate undertakings
As oft as any passion under heaven
That does afflict our natures. I am sorry.
What, have you given him any hard words of late?

OPHELIA No, my good lord; but, as you did command,
I did repel his letters and denied
His access to me.

POLONIUS That hath made him mad.
I am sorry that with better heed and judgment
I had not quoted him. I fear'd he did but trifle
And meant to wrack thee; but beshrew my jealousy!
By heaven, it is as proper to our age
To cast beyond ourselves in our opinions
As it is common for the younger sort
To lack discretion. Come, go we to the King.
This must be known; which, being kept close, might move
More grief to hide than hate to utter love.
Come. [*Exeunt.*]

[85] *Mad,* insane.
[102] *ecstasy,* excess (to the point of madness).
[112] *quoted,* credited.
[113] *wrack,* ruin. *beshrew,* curse.
[118] *close,* concealed.

Scene II [*Elsinore. A room in the Castle.*]

[*Flourish. Enter* KING *and* QUEEN, ROSENCRANTZ, *and* GUILDENSTERN, *cum aliis.*]

KING Welcome, dear Rosencrantz and Guildenstern.
Moreover that we much did long to see you,
The need we have to use you did provoke
Our hasty sending. Something have you heard
Of Hamlet's transformation. So I call it,
Sith nor th' exterior nor the inward man
Resembles that it was. What it should be,
More than his father's death, that thus hath put him
So much from th' understanding of himself,
I cannot dream of. I entreat you both
That, being of so young days brought up with him,
And since so neighbour'd to his youth and haviour,
That you vouchsafe your rest here in our court
Some little time; so by your companies
To draw him on to pleasures, and to gather
So much as from occasion you may glean,
Whether aught to us unknown afflicts him thus
That, open'd, lies within our remedy.

QUEEN Good gentlemen, he hath much talk'd of you,
And sure I am two men there are not living
To whom he more adheres. If it will please you
To show us so much gentry and good will
As to expend your time with us awhile
For the supply and profit of our hope,
Your visitation shall receive such thanks
As fits a king's remembrance.

ROSENCRANTZ Both your Majesties
Might, by the sovereign power you have of us,
Put your dread pleasures more into command
Than to entreaty.

GUILDENSTERN But we both obey,
And here give up ourselves, in the full bent,
To lay our service at your feet,
To be commanded.

KING Thanks, Rosencrantz and gentle Guildenstern.

QUEEN Thanks, Guildenstern and gentle Rosencrantz.

[13] *vouchsafe your rest,* agree to stay.
[22] *gentry,* gentle manliness.
[24] *supply and profit,* realization and advancement (accomplishing).

And I beseech you instantly to visit
My too much changed son.—Go, some of you,
And bring these gentlemen where Hamlet is.

GUILDENSTERN Heavens make our presence and our practices
Pleasant and helpful to him!

QUEEN Ay, amen!

[*Exeunt* ROSENCRANTZ *and* GUILDENSTERN (*with some Attendants*).]

[*Enter* POLONIUS.]

POLONIUS Th' ambassadors from Norway, my good lord,
Are joyfully return'd.

KING Thou still hast been the father of good news.

POLONIUS Have I, my lord? Assure you, my good liege,
I hold my duty as I hold my soul,
Both to my God and to my gracious king;
And I do think—or else this brain of mine
Hunts not the trail of policy so sure
As it hath us'd to do—that I have found
The very cause of Hamlet's lunacy.

KING O, speak of that! That do I long to hear.

POLONIUS Give first admittance to th' ambassadors.
My news shall be the fruit to that great feast.

KING Thyself do grace to them, and bring them in.

[*Exit* POLONIUS.]

He tells me, my dear Gertrude, he hath found
The head and source of all your son's distemper.

QUEEN I doubt it is no other but the main,
His father's death and our o'erhasty marriage.

KING Well, we shall sift him.

[*Enter* POLONIUS, VOLTEMAND, *and* CORNELIUS.]

Welcome, my good friends.
Say, Voltemand, what from our brother Norway?

VOLTEMAND Most fair return of greetings and desires.
Upon our first, he sent out to suppress
His nephew's levies; which to him appear'd
To be a preparation 'gainst the Polack,
But better look'd into, he truly found
It was against your Highness; whereat griev'd,
That so his sickness, age, and impotence
Was falsely borne in hand, sends out arrests
On Fortinbras; which he, in brief, obeys,
Receives rebuke from Norway, and, in fine,
Makes vow before his uncle never more
To give th' assay of arms against your Majesty.
Whereon old Norway, overcome with joy,
Gives him three thousand crowns in annual fee
And his commission to employ those soldiers,
So levied as before, against the Polack;
With an entreaty, herein further shown,

[*Gives a paper.*]

That it might please you to give quiet pass
Through your dominions for this enterprise,
On such regards of safety and allowance
As therein are set down.

KING It likes us well;
And at our more consider'd time we'll read,
Answer, and think upon this business.
Meantime we thank you for your well-took labour.
Go to your rest; at night we'll feast together.
Most welcome home! [*Exeunt Ambassadors.*]

POLONIUS This business is well ended.
My liege, and madam, to expostulate
What majesty should be, what duty is,
Why day is day, night night, and time is time,
Were nothing but to waste night, day, and time.
Therefore, since brevity is the soul of wit,
And tediousness the limbs and outward flourishes,
I will be brief. Your noble son is mad.
Mad call I it; for, to define true madness,
What is't but to be nothing else but mad?
But let that go.

QUEEN More matter, with less art.

POLONIUS Madam, I swear I use no art at all.
That he is mad, 'tis true: 'tis true 'tis pity;
And pity 'tis 'tis true. A foolish figure!
But farewell it, for I will use no art.
Mad let us grant him then. And now remains
That we find out the cause of this effect—
Or rather say, the cause of this defect,
For this effect defective comes by cause.
Thus it remains, and the remainder thus.
Perpend.
I have a daughter (have while she is mine),
Who in her duty and obedience, mark,
Hath given me this. Now gather, and surmise.

[(*Reads*) *the letter.*]

47 *policy,* statecraft (as Polonius understands it).
56 *doubt,* suspect.
67 *borne in hand,* acted upon.

86 *expostulate,* describe.
90 *wit,* wisdom.
105 *Perpend,* listen carefully.

"To the celestial, and my soul's idol, the most beautified Ophelia."—
That's an ill phrase, a vile phrase; "beautified" is a vile phrase. But you shall hear. Thus:
[*Reads.*]
"In her excellent white bosom, these, &c."

QUEEN Came this from Hamlet to her?

POLONIUS Good madam, stay awhile. I will be faithful.
[*Reads.*]
"Doubt thou the stars are fire;
Doubt that the sun doth move;
Doubt truth to be a liar;
But never doubt I love.
"O dear Ophelia, I am ill at these numbers;
I have not art to reckon my groans; but that I love thee best, O most best, believe it. Adieu.
"Thine evermore, most dear lady, whilst this machine is to him, HAMLET."
This, in obedience, hath my daughter shown me;
And more above, hath his solicitings,
As they fell out by time, by means, and place,
All given to mine ear.

KING But how hath she
Receiv'd his love?

POLONIUS What do you think of me?

KING As of a man faithful and honourable.

POLONIUS I would fain prove so. But what might you think,
When I had seen this hot love on the wing
(As I perceiv'd it, I must tell you that,
Before my daughter told me), what might you,
Or my dear Majesty your queen here, think,
If I had play'd the desk or table book,
Or given my heart a winking, mute and dumb,
Or look'd upon this love with idle sight?
What might you think? No, I went round to work
And my young mistress thus I did bespeak:
"Lord Hamlet is a prince, out of thy star.
This must not be." And then I prescripts gave her,
That she should lock herself from his resort,
Admit no messengers, receive no tokens.
Which done, she took the fruits of my advice,
And he, repulsed, a short tale to make,
Fell into a sadness, then into a fast,
Thence to a watch, thence into a weakness,
Thence to a lightness, and, by this declension,
Into the madness wherein now he raves,
And all we mourn for.

KING Do you think 'tis this?

QUEEN It may be, very like.

POLONIUS Hath there been such a time—I would fain know that—
That I have positively said " 'Tis so,"
When it prov'd otherwise?

KING Not that I know.

POLONIUS [*Points to his head and shoulder.*]
Take this from this, if this be otherwise.
If circumstances lead me, I will find
Where truth is hid, though it were hid indeed
Within the centre.

KING How may we try it further?

POLONIUS You know sometimes he walks four hours together
Here in the lobby.

QUEEN So he does indeed.

POLONIUS At such a time I'll loose my daughter to him.
Be you and I behind an arras then.
Mark the encounter. If he love her not,
And be not from his reason fall'n thereon,
Let me be no assistant for a state,
But keep a farm and carters.

KING We will try it.

[*Enter* HAMLET, *reading on a book.*]

QUEEN But look where sadly the poor wretch comes reading.

POLONIUS Away, I do beseech you, both away!
I'll board him presently. O, give me leave.
[*Exeunt* KING *and* QUEEN, (*with Attendants*).]
How does my good Lord Hamlet?

HAMLET Well, God-a-mercy.

POLONIUS Do you know me, my lord?

HAMLET Excellent well. You are a fishmonger.

POLONIUS Not I, my lord.

HAMLET Then I would you were so honest a man.

POLONIUS Honest, my lord?

HAMLET Ay, sir. To be honest, as this world goes, is to be one man pick'd out of ten thousand.

POLONIUS That's very true, my lord.

124 *machine,* body.
126 *above,* besides.
136 *play'd the desk or table book,* filed the matter away (stored information and did not act on it).
141 *out of thy star,* not included in your destiny.
148 *watch,* wakefulness.
170 *board,* accost.

HAMLET For if the sun breed maggots in a dead dog, being a god kissing carrion—Have you a daughter?

POLONIUS I have, my lord.

HAMLET Let her not walk i' th' sun. Conception is a blessing, but not as your daughter may conceive. Friend, look to't.

POLONIUS [*Aside.*] How say you by that? Still harping on my daughter. Yet he knew me not at first. He said I was a fishmonger. He is far gone, far gone! And truly in my youth I suff'red much extremity for love—very near this. I'll speak to him again.—What do you read, my lord?

HAMLET Words, words, words.

POLONIUS What is the matter, my lord?

HAMLET Between who?

POLONIUS I mean, the matter that you read, my lord.

HAMLET Slanders, sir; for the satirical rogue says here that old men have grey beards; that their faces are wrinkled; their eyes purging thick amber and plum-tree gum; and that they have a plentiful lack of wit, together with most weak hams. All which, sir, though I most powerfully and potently believe, yet I hold it not honesty to have it thus set down; for you yourself, sir, should be old as I am if, like a crab, you could go backward.

POLONIUS [*Aside.*] Though this be madness, yet there is method in't.—Will you walk out of the air, my lord?

HAMLET Into my grave?

POLONIUS Indeed, that is out o' th' air. [*Aside.*] How pregnant sometimes his replies are! a happiness that often madness hits on, which reason and sanity could not so prosperously be delivered of. I will leave him and suddenly contrive the means of meeting between him and my daughter.—My honourable lord, I will most humbly take my leave of you.

HAMLET You cannot, sir, take from me anything that I will more willingly part withal—except my life, except my life, except my life.

[*Enter* ROSENCRANTZ *and* GUILDENSTERN.]

POLONIUS Fare you well, my lord.

HAMLET These tedious old fools!

POLONIUS You go to seek the Lord Hamlet. There he is.

ROSENCRANTZ [*To* POLONIUS.] God save you sir!

[*Exit* (POLONIUS).]

GUILDENSTERN My honour'd lord!

ROSENCRANTZ My most dear lord!

HAMLET My excellent good friends! How dost thou, Guildenstern? Ah, Rosencrantz! Good lads, how do ye both?

ROSENCRANTZ As the indifferent children of the earth.

GUILDENSTERN Happy in that we are not overhappy. On Fortune's cap we are not the very button.

HAMLET Nor the soles of her shoe?

ROSENCRANTZ Neither, my lord.

HAMLET Then you live about her waist, or in the middle of her favours?

GUILDENSTERN Faith, her privates we.

HAMLET In the secret parts of Fortune? O, most true! she is a strumpet. What news?

ROSENCRANTZ None, my lord, but that the world's grown honest.

HAMLET Then is doomsday near! But your news is not true. Let me question more in particular. What have you, my good friends, deserved at the hands of Fortune that she sends you to prison hither?

GUILDENSTERN Prison, my lord?

HAMLET Denmark's a prison.

ROSENCRANTZ Then is the world one.

HAMLET A goodly one; in which there are many confines, wards, and dungeons, Denmark being one o' th' worst.

ROSENCRANTZ We think not so, my lord.

HAMLET Why, then 'tis none to you; for there is nothing either good or bad but thinking makes it so. To me it is a prison.

ROSENCRANTZ Why, then your ambition makes it one. 'Tis too narrow for your mind.

HAMLET O God, I could be bounded in a nutshell and count myself a king of infinite space, were it not that I have bad dreams.

GUILDENSTERN Which dreams indeed are ambition; for the very substance of the ambitious is merely the shadow of a dream.

HAMLET A dream itself is but a shadow.

ROSENCRANTZ Truly, and I hold ambition of so airy and light a quality that it is but a shadow's shadow.

HAMLET Then are our beggars bodies, and our monarchs and outstretch'd heroes the beggars' shadows. Shall we to th' court? for, by my fay, I cannot reason.

190 *How say you by that?*, What did I tell you!

236 *indifferent children*, ordinary persons.

BOTH We'll wait upon you.

HAMLET No such matter! I will not sort you with the rest of my servants; for, to speak to you like an honest man, I am most dreadfully attended. But in the beaten way of friendship, what make you at Elsinore?

ROSENCRANTZ To visit you, my lord; no other occasion.

HAMLET Beggar that I am, I am even poor in thanks; but I thank you; and sure, dear friends, my thanks are too dear a halfpenny. Were you not sent for? Is it your own inclining? Is it a free visitation? Come, deal justly with me. Come, come! Nay, speak.

GUILDENSTERN What should we say, my lord?

HAMLET Why, anything—but to th' purpose. You were sent for; and there is a kind of confession in your looks, which your modesties have not craft enough to colour. I know the good King and Queen have sent for you.

ROSENCRANTZ To what end, my lord?

HAMLET That you must teach me. But let me conjure you by the rights of our fellowship, by the consonancy of our youth, by the obligation of our ever-preserved love, and by what more dear a better proposer could charge you withal, be even and direct with me, whether you were sent for or no.

ROSENCRANTZ [*Aside to* GUILDENSTERN.] What say you?

HAMLET [*Aside.*] Nay then, I have an eye of you.—If you love me, hold not off.

GUILDENSTERN My lord, we were sent for.

HAMLET I will tell you why. So shall my anticipation prevent your discovery, and your secrecy to the King and Queen moult no feather. I have of late—but wherefore I know not—lost all my mirth, forgone all custom of exercises; and indeed, it goes so heavily with my disposition that this goodly frame, the earth, seems to me a sterile promontory; this most excellent canopy, the air, look you, this brave o'erhanging firmament, this majestical roof fretted with golden fire—why, it appeareth no other thing to me than a foul and pestilent congregation of vapours. What a piece of work is a man! how noble in reason! how infinite in faculties! in form and moving how express and admirable! in action how like an angel! in apprehension how like a god! the beauty of the world, the paragon of animals! And yet to me what is this quintessence of dust? Man delights not me—no, nor woman neither, though by your smiling you seem to say so.

ROSENCRANTZ My lord, there was no such stuff in my thoughts.

HAMLET Why did you laugh then, when I said "Man delights not me"?

ROSENCRANTZ To think, my lord, if you delight not in man, what lenten entertainment the players shall receive from you. We coted them on the way, and hither are they coming to offer you service.

HAMLET He that plays the king shall be welcome—his Majesty shall have tribute of me; the adventurous knight shall use his foil and target; the lover shall not sigh gratis; the humorous man shall end his part in peace; the clown shall make those laugh whose lungs are tickle o' th' sere; and the lady shall say her mind freely, or the blank verse shall halt for't. What players are they?

ROSENCRANTZ Even those you were wont to take such delight in, the tragedians of the city.

HAMLET How chances it they travel? Their residence, both in reputation and profit, was better both ways.

ROSENCRANTZ I think their inhibition comes by the means of the late innovation.

HAMLET Do they hold the same estimation they did when I was in the city? Are they so follow'd?

ROSENCRANTZ No indeed are they not.

HAMLET How comes it? Do they grow rusty?

ROSENCRANTZ Nay, their endeavour keeps in the wonted pace; but there is, sir, an eyrie of children, little eyases, that cry out on the top of question and are most tyrannically clapp'd for't. These are now the fashion, and so berattle the common stages (so they call them)

291 *too dear a halfpenny,* not worth a halfpenny.
315 *prevent,* forestall. *discovery,* disclosure.
322 *brave,* magnificent.

341 *lenten,* spare.
342 *coted,* passed.
351 *tickle o' th' sere,* easily amused.
359–360 *inhibition . . . innovation* (decision to leave) . . . new fashion (in play-acting).
367–368 *eyrie . . . eyases,* covey . . . baby hawks.
369 *tyrannically,* loudly.
370–371 *berattle the common stages,* berate (make fun of) adult actors.

that many wearing rapiers are afraid of goose-quills and dare scarce come thither.

HAMLET What, are they children? Who maintains 'em? How are they escoted? Will they pursue the quality no longer than they can sing? Will they not say afterwards, if they should grow themselves to common players (as it is most like, if their means are no better), their writers do them wrong to make them exclaim against their own succession.

ROSENCRANTZ Faith, there has been much to do on both sides; and the nation holds it no sin to tarre them to controversy. There was, for a while, no money bid for argument unless the poet and the player went to cuffs in the question.

HAMLET Is't possible?

GUILDENSTERN O, there has been much throwing about of brains.

HAMLET Do the boys carry it away?

ROSENCRANTZ Ay, that they do, my lord—Hercules and his load too.

HAMLET It is not very strange; for my uncle is King of Denmark, and those that would make mows at him while my father lived give twenty, forty, fifty, a hundred ducats apiece for his picture in little. 'Sblood, there is something in this more than natural, if philosophy could find it out.

[*Flourish for the Players.*]

GUILDENSTERN There are the players.

HAMLET Gentlemen, you are welcome to Elsinore. Your hands, come! Th' appurtenance of welcome is fashion and ceremony. Let me comply with you in this garb, lest my extent to the players (which I tell you must show fairly outwards) should more appear like entertainment than yours. You are welcome. But my uncle-father and aunt-mother are deceiv'd.

GUILDENSTERN In what, my dear lord?

HAMLET I am but mad north-north-west. When the wind is southerly I know a hawk from a handsaw.

[*Enter* POLONIUS.]

POLONIUS Well be with you, gentlemen!

HAMLET Hark you, Guildenstern—and you too—at each ear a hearer! That great baby you see there is not yet out of his swaddling clouts.

ROSENCRANTZ Happily he's the second time come to them; for they say an old man is twice a child.

HAMLET I will prophesy he comes to tell me of the players. Mark it.—You say right, sir; a Monday morning; 'twas so indeed.

POLONIUS My lord, I have news to tell you.

HAMLET My lord, I have news to tell you. When Roscius was an actor in Rome—

POLONIUS The actors are come hither, my lord.

HAMLET Buzz, buzz!

POLONIUS Upon my honour—

HAMLET Then came each actor on his ass—

POLONIUS The best actors in the world, either for tragedy, comedy, history, pastoral, pastoral-comical, historical-pastoral, tragical-historical, tragical-comical-historical-pastoral; scene individable, or poem unlimited. Seneca cannot be too heavy, nor Plautus too light. For the law of writ and the liberty, these are the only men.

HAMLET O Jephthah, judge of Israel, what a treasure hadst thou!

POLONIUS What treasure had he, my lord?

HAMLET Why,

"One fair daughter, and no more,
The which he loved passing well."

POLONIUS [*Aside.*] Still on my daughter.

HAMLET Am I not i' th' right, old Jephthah?

POLONIUS If you call me Jephthah, my lord, I have a daughter that I love passing well.

HAMLET Nay, that follows not.

POLONIUS What follows then, my lord?

HAMLET Why,

"As by lot, Got wot,"

and then, you know,

"It came to pass, as most like it was."

372–373 *many wearing rapiers . . . goosequills,* armed adults . . . pens (used to make fun of "common stages" and those who attended them).
375 *escoted,* financed.
376–377 *pursue the quality . . . sing?,* continue to act until their voices change?
384 *tarre,* egg on.
396 *make mows,* make faces.

436–437 *law of writ and the liberty,* the three unities (time, place, and action) and freedom from them.
439 *Jephthah* (subject of a popular song from which Hamlet quotes below).

The first row of the pious chanson will show you more; for look where my abridgment comes.

[*Enter four or five* PLAYERS.]

You are welcome, masters; welcome, all.—I am glad to see thee well.—Welcome, good friends.—O, my old friend? Why, thy face is valanc'd since I saw thee last. Com'st thou to beard me in Denmark?—What, my young lady and mistress? By'r Lady, your ladyship is nearer to heaven than when I saw you last by the altitude of a chopine. Pray God your voice, like a piece of uncurrent gold, be not crack'd within the ring.—Masters, you are all welcome. We'll e'en to't like French falconers, fly at anything we see. We'll have a speech straight. Come, give us a taste of your quality. Come, a passionate speech.

1. PLAYER What speech, my good lord?

HAMLET I heard thee speak me a speech once, but it was never acted; or if it was, not above once; for the play, I remember, pleas'd not the million, 'twas caviar to the general; but it was (as I receiv'd it, and others, whose judgments in such matters cried in the top of mine) an excellent play, well digested in the scenes, set down with as much modesty as cunning. I remember one said there were no sallets in the lines to make the matter savoury, nor no matter in the phrase that might indict the author of affectation; but call'd it an honest method, as wholesome as sweet, and by very much more handsome than fine. One speech in't I chiefly lov'd. 'Twas Æneas' tale to Dido, and thereabout of it especially where he speaks of Priam's slaughter. If it live in your memory, begin at this line—let me see, let me see:

"The rugged Pyrrhus, like th' Hyrcanian
beast—"

'Tis not so; it begins with Pyrrhus:

"The rugged Pyrrhus, he whose sable arms,
Black as his purpose, did the night resemble
When he lay couched in the ominous horse,
Hath now this dread and black complexion
smear'd
With heraldry more dismal. Head to foot
Now is he total gules, horridly trick'd
With blood of fathers, mothers, daughters,
sons,
Bak'd and impasted with the parching streets,
That lend a tyrannous and a damned light
To their lord's murther. Roasted in wrath and
fire,
And thus o'ersized with coagulate gore,
With eyes like carbuncles, the hellish Pyrrhus
Old grandsire Priam seeks."

So, proceed you.

POLONIUS Fore God, my lord, well spoken, with good accent and good discretion.

1. PLAYER "Anon he finds him,
Striking too short at Greeks. His antique
sword,
Rebellious to his arm, lies where it falls,
Repugnant to command. Unequal match'd,
Pyrrhus at Priam drives, in rage strikes wide;
But with the whiff and wind of his fell sword
Th' unnerved father falls. Then senseless
Ilium,
Seeming to feel this blow, with flaming top
Stoops to his base, and with a hideous crash
Takes prisoner Pyrrhus' ear. For lo! his sword,
Which was declining on the milky head
Of reverend Priam, seem'd i' th' air to stick.
So, as a painted tyrant, Pyrrhus stood,
And, like a neutral to his will and matter,
Did nothing.
But, as we often see, against some storm,
A silence in the heavens, the rack stand still,

455 *row . . . chanson,* stanza . . . song.
456 *abridgment,* interruption.
460 *valanc'd,* bearded.
461–462 *young lady* (boy who acted young women's parts).
464 *chopine,* short stilt.
465–466 *not crack'd within the ring,* not made worthless as a cracked coin (a pun: Hamlet hopes the boy's voice has not cracked).
475 *caviar to the general,* sturgeon eggs (not pleasing) to most people.
477–478 *cried in the top of mine,* outshouted my voice.
479–480 *modesty . . . cunning,* artistic control . . . skill.
481 *sallets,* salads (presumably spicy).
484 *honest,* unaffected.
487 *Dido,* mythological Queen of Carthage.
488 *Priam's slaughter,* Trojan king's death (described in Virgil's *Aeneid*).
491 *Hyrcanian beast* (Hyrcania was a province of the Persian empire.)
495 *ominous horse* (the wooden horse, a gift to the Trojans, in which the Greek warriors hid and thereby gained entrance to Troy.)
498 *gules . . . trick'd,* red . . . adorned.
503 *o'ersized,* glazed.
512 *repugnant,* refusing (Priam's order to obey).
514 *the whiff and wind* (the weak old man is blown down by the swish of Pyrrhus' sword.)

The bold winds speechless, and the orb below
As hush as death—anon the dreadful thunder
Doth rend the region; so, after Pyrrhus' pause,
Aroused vengeance sets him new awork;
And never did the Cyclops' hammers fall
On Mars's armour, forg'd for proof eterne,
With less remorse than Pyrrhus' bleeding sword
Now falls on Priam.
Out, out, thou strumpet Fortune! All you Gods,
In general synod take away her power;
Break all the spokes and fellies from her wheel,
And bowl the round nave down the hill of heaven,
As low as to the fiends!"

POLONIUS This is too long.

HAMLET It shall to the barber's, with your beard.—Prithee say on. He's for a jig or a tale of bawdry, or he sleeps. Say on; come to Hecuba.

1. PLAYER "But who, O who, had seen the mobled queen—"

HAMLET "The mobled queen"?

POLONIUS That's good! "Mobled queen" is good.

1. PLAYER "Run barefoot up and down, threat'ning the flames
With bisson rheum; a clout upon that head
Where late the diadem stood, and for a robe,
About her lank and all o'erteemed loins,
A blanket, in the alarm of fear caught up—
Who this had seen, with tongue in venom steep'd
'Gainst Fortune's state would treason have pronounc'd.
But if the gods themselves did see her then,
When she saw Pyrrhus make malicious sport
In mincing with his sword her husband's limbs,
The instant burst of clamour that she made
(Unless things mortal move them not at all)
Would have made milch the burning eyes of heaven
And passion in the gods."

POLONIUS Look, whe'r he has not turn'd his colour, and has tears in's eyes. Prithee no more!

HAMLET 'Tis well. I'll have thee speak out the rest of this soon.—Good my lord, will you see the players well bestow'd? Do you hear? Let them be well us'd; for they are the abstract and brief chronicles of the time. After your death you were better have a bad epitaph than their ill report while you live.

POLONIUS My lord, I will use them according to their desert.

HAMLET God's bodykins, man, much better! Use every man after his desert, and who should scape whipping? Use them after your own honour and dignity. The less they deserve, the more merit is in your bounty. Take them in.

POLONIUS Come, sirs.

HAMLET Follow him, friends. We'll hear a play to-morrow.

[*Exeunt* POLONIUS *and* PLAYERS (*except the* FIRST).]

Dost thou hear me, old friend? Can you play "The Murther of Gonzago"?

1. PLAYER Ay, my lord.

HAMLET We'll ha't to-morrow night. You could, for a need, study a speech of some dozen or sixteen lines which I would set down and insert in't, could you not?

1. PLAYER Ay, my lord.

HAMLET Very well. Follow that lord—and look you mock him not.

[*Exit* FIRST PLAYER.]

My good friends, I'll leave you till night. You are welcome to Elsinore.

ROSENCRANTZ Good my lord!

HAMLET Ay, so, God b' wi' ye!

[*Exeunt* (ROSENCRANTZ *and* GUILDENSTERN).]

Now I am alone.
O, what a rogue and peasant slave am I!
Is it not monstrous that this player here,
But in a fiction, in a dream of passion,
Could force his soul so to his own conceit
That, from her working, all his visage wann'd,
Tears in his eyes, distraction in's aspect,
A broken voice, and his whole function suiting
With forms to his conceit? And all for nothing!
For Hecuba!

530 *Cyclops* (one-eyed giant, workman for Vulcan, god of armor-making.)
535–538 (A request to the gods to destroy the wheel of fickle Fortune.)
541 *jig,* short, comic exchange (acted-out jokes).
545 *mobled,* muffled.
548 *bisson rheum . . . clout,* blinding tears . . . a cloth.
550 *o'erteemed loins,* loins worn out by excessive child-bearing.

What's Hecuba to him, or he to Hecuba,
That he should weep for her? What would he do,
Had he the motive and the cue for passion
That I have? He would drown the stage with tears
And cleave the general ear with horrid speech;
Make mad the guilty and appal the free,
Confound the ignorant, and amaze indeed
The very faculties of eyes and ears.
Yet I,
A dull and muddy-mettled rascal, peak
Like John-a-dreams, unpregnant of my cause,
And can say nothing! No, not for a king,
Upon whose property and most dear life
A damn'd defeat was made. Am I a coward?
Who calls me villain? breaks my pate across?
Plucks off my beard and blows it in my face?
Tweaks me by th' nose? gives me the lie i' th' throat
As deep as to the lungs? Who does me this, ha?
'Swounds, I should take it! for it cannot be
But I am pigeon-liver'd and lack gall
To make oppression bitter, or ere this
I should have fatted all the region kites,
With this slave's offal. Bloody, bawdy villain!
Remorseless, treacherous, lecherous, kindless villain!
O, vengeance!
Why, what an ass am I! This is most brave,
That I, the son of a dear father murther'd,
Prompted to my revenge by heaven and hell,
Must (like a whore) unpack my heart with words
And fall a-cursing like a very drab,
A scullion!
Fie upon't! foh! About, my brain! Hum, I have heard
That guilty creatures, sitting at a play,
Have by the very cunning of the scene
Been struck so to the soul that presently
They have proclaim'd their malefactions;
For murther, though it have no tongue, will speak
With most miraculous organ. I'll have these players
Play something like the murther of my father
Before mine uncle. I'll observe his looks;
I'll tent him to the quick. If he but blench,
I know my course. The spirit that I have seen
May be a devil; and the devil hath power
T' assume a pleasing shape; yea, and perhaps
Out of my weakness and my melancholy,
As he is very potent with such spirits,
Abuses me to damn me. I'll have grounds
More relative than this. The play's the thing
Wherein I'll catch the conscience of the King.
[*Exit.*]

ACT III

Scene I [*Elsinore. A room in the Castle.*]

[*Enter* KING, QUEEN, POLONIUS, OPHELIA, ROSENCRANTZ, GUILDENSTERN, *and* LORDS.]

KING And can you by no drift of circumstance
Get from him why he puts on this confusion,
Grating so harshly all his days of quiet
With turbulent and dangerous lunacy?

ROSENCRANTZ He does confess he feels himself distracted,
But from what cause he will by no means speak.

GUILDENSTERN Nor do we find him forward to be sounded,
But with a crafty madness keeps aloof
When we would bring him on to some confession
Of his true state.

QUEEN Did he receive you well?

ROSENCRANTZ Most like a gentleman.

GUILDENSTERN But with much forcing of his disposition.

ROSENCRANTZ Niggard of question, but of our demands
Most free in his reply.

QUEEN Did you assay him

605 *Hecuba,* Priam's wife.
613 *by heaven and hell* (Heaven asks vengeance because Claudius deserves punishment; hell eggs on by stirring hatred in Hamlet.)
636 *about,* get to work.
638 *cunning,* skill (in the acting).
645 *tent,* watch intently.
1 *by no drift of circumstance,* by no trick of questioning.
2 *puts on this confusion,* dresses (himself) in madness.
13 *demands,* questions.

To any pastime?

ROSENCRANTZ Madam, it so fell out that certain players
We o'erraught on the way. Of these we told him,
And there did seem in him a kind of joy
To hear of it. They are here about the court,
And, as I think, they have already order
This night to play before him.

POLONIUS 'Tis most true;
And he beseech'd me to entreat your Majesties
To hear and see the matter.

KING With all my heart, and it doth much content me
To hear him so inclin'd.
Good gentlemen, give him a further edge
And drive his purpose on to these delights.

ROSENCRANTZ We shall, my lord.

[*Exeunt* ROSENCRANTZ *and* GUILDENSTERN.]

KING Sweet Gertrude, leave us too;
For we have closely sent for Hamlet hither,
That he, as 'twere by accident, may here
Affront Ophelia.
Her father and myself (lawful espials)
Will so bestow ourselves that, seeing unseen,
We may of their encounter frankly judge
And gather by him, as he is behav'd,
If't be th' affliction of his love, or no,
That thus he suffers for.

QUEEN I shall obey you;
And for your part, Ophelia, I do wish
That your good beauties be the happy cause
Of Hamlet's wildness. So shall I hope your virtues
Will bring him to his wonted way again,
To both your honours.

OPHELIA Madam, I wish it may.

[*Exit* QUEEN.]

POLONIUS Ophelia, walk you here.—Gracious, so please you,
We will bestow ourselves.—[*To* OPHELIA] Read on this book,
That show of such an exercise may colour
Your loneliness.—We are oft to blame in this,
'Tis too much prov'd, that with devotion's visage
And pious action we do sugar o'er
The devil himself.

KING [*Aside.*] O, 'tis too true!
How smart a lash that speech doth give my conscience!
The harlot's cheek, beautied with plast'ring art,
Is not more ugly to the thing that helps it
Than is my deed to my most painted word.
O heavy burthen!

POLONIUS I hear him coming. Let's withdraw, my lord.

[*Exeunt* (KING *and* POLONIUS).]

[*Enter* HAMLET.]

HAMLET To be, or not to be—that is the question:
Whether 'tis nobler in the mind to suffer
The slings and arrows of outrageous fortune
Or to take arms against a sea of troubles,
And by opposing end them. To die—to sleep—
No more; and by a sleep to say we end
The heartache, and the thousand natural shocks
That flesh is heir to. 'Tis a consummation
Devoutly to be wish'd. To die—to sleep.
To sleep—perchance to dream: ay, there's the rub!
For in that sleep of death what dreams may come
When we have shuffled off this mortal coil,
Must give us pause. There's the respect
That makes calamity of so long life.
For who would bear the whips and scorns of time,
Th' oppressor's wrong, the proud man's contumely,
The pangs of despis'd love, the law's delay,
The insolence of office, and the spurns
That patient merit of th' unworthy takes,
When he himself might his quietus make
With a bare bodkin? Who would these fardels bear,
To grunt and sweat under a weary life,
But that the dread of something after death—
The undiscover'd country, from whose bourn
No traveller returns—puzzles the will,
And makes us rather bear those ills we have
Than fly to others that we know not of?

17 *o'erraught,* overtook.
29 *closely,* privately.
31 *affront,* meet (face to face).
32 *espials,* eavesdroppers.

76 *bodkin,* needle—or perhaps dagger. *fardels,* burdens.
79 *bourn,* borders.

Thus conscience does make cowards of us all,
And thus the native hue of resolution
Is sicklied o'er with the pale cast of thought,
And enterprises of great pith and moment
With this regard their currents turn awry
And lose the name of action.—Soft you now.
The fair Ophelia!—Nymph, in thy orisons
Be all my sins rememb'red.

OPHELIA Good my lord,
How does your honour for this many a day?

HAMLET I humbly thank you; well, well, well.

OPHELIA My lord, I have remembrances of yours
That I have longed long to re-deliver.
I pray you, now receive them.

HAMLET No, not I!
I never gave you aught.

OPHELIA My honour'd lord, you know right well you did,
And with them words of so sweet breath compos'd
As made the things more rich. Their perfume lost,
Take these again; for to the noble mind
Rich gifts wax poor when givers prove unkind.
There, my lord.

HAMLET Ha, ha! Are you honest?

OPHELIA My lord?

HAMLET Are you fair?

OPHELIA What means your lordship?

HAMLET That if you be honest and fair, your honesty should admit no discourse to your beauty.

OPHELIA Could beauty, my lord, have better commerce than with honesty?

HAMLET Ay, truly; for the power of beauty will sooner transform honesty from what it is to a bawd than the force of honesty can translate beauty into his likeness. This was sometime a paradox, but now the time gives it proof. I did love you once.

OPHELIA Indeed, my lord, you made me believe so.

HAMLET You should not have believ'd me; for virtue cannot so inoculate our old stock but we shall relish of it. I loved you not.

OPHELIA I was the more deceived.

HAMLET Get thee to a nunnery! Why wouldst thou be a breeder of sinners? I am myself indifferent honest, but yet I could accuse me of such things that it were better my mother had not borne me. I am very proud, revengeful, ambitious; with more offences at my beck than I have thoughts to put them in, imagination to give them shape, or time to act them in. What should such fellows as I do, crawling between earth and heaven? We are arrant knaves all; believe none of us. Go thy ways to a nunnery. Where's your father?

OPHELIA At home, my lord.

HAMLET Let the doors be shut upon him, that he may play the fool nowhere but in's own house. Farewell.

OPHELIA O, help him, you sweet heavens!

HAMLET If thou dost marry, I'll give thee this plague for thy dowry: be thou as chaste as ice, as pure as snow, thou shalt not escape calumny. Get thee to a nunnery. Go, farewell. Or if thou wilt needs marry, marry a fool; for wise men know well enough what monsters you make of them. To a nunnery, go; and quickly too. Farewell.

OPHELIA O heavenly powers, restore him!

HAMLET I have heard of your paintings too, well enough. God hath given you one face, and you make yourselves another. You jig, you amble, and you lisp; you nickname God's creatures and make your wantonness your ignorance. Go to, I'll no more on't! it hath made me mad. I say, we will have no moe marriages. Those that are married already—all but one—shall live; the rest shall keep as they are. To a nunnery, go. [*Exit*]

OPHELIA O, what a noble mind is here o'erthrown!
The courtier's, scholar's, soldier's, eye, tongue, sword,
Th' expectancy and rose of the fair state,
The glass of fashion and the mould of form,
Th' observ'd of all observers—quite, quite down!
And I, of ladies most deject and wretched,
That suck'd the honey of his music vows,
Now see that noble and most sovereign reason,
Like sweet bells jangled, out of tune and harsh;

89 *orisons,* prayers.
103 *honest,* virginal.
121 *inoculate our old stock,* produce a change in our store (of original sinfulness).
142 *plague,* black reputation.
146 *monsters,* cuckolds.
150 *paintings,* rougings.
154–155 *make your wantonness your ignorance,* blame your licentiousness on innocence.

That unmatch'd form and feature of blown youth
Blasted with ecstasy. O, woe is me
T' have seen what I have seen, see what I see!

[*Enter* KING *and* POLONIUS.]

KING Love? his affections do not that way tend;
Nor what he spake, though it lack'd form a little,
Was not like madness. There's something in his soul
O'er which his melancholy sits on brood;
And I do doubt the hatch and the disclose
Will be some danger; which for to prevent,
I have in quick determination
Thus set it down: he shall with speed to England
For the demand of our neglected tribute.
Haply the seas, and countries different,
With variable objects, shall expel
This something-settled matter in his heart,
Whereon his brains still beating puts him thus
From fashion of himself. What think you on't?

POLONIUS It shall do well. But yet do I believe
The origin and commencement of his grief
Sprung from neglected love.—How now, Ophelia?
You need not tell us what Lord Hamlet said.
We heard it all.—My lord, do as you please;
But if you hold it fit, after the play
Let his queen mother all alone entreat him
To show his grief. Let her be round with him;
And I'll be plac'd, so please you, in the ear
Of all their conference. If she find him not,
To England send him; or confine him where
Your wisdom best shall think.

KING It shall be so.
Madness in great ones must not unwatch'd go.

[*Exeunt.*]

Scene II [*Elsinore. A hall in the Castle.*]

[*Enter* HAMLET *and three of the* PLAYERS.]

HAMLET Speak the speech, I pray you, as I pronounc'd it to you, trippingly on the tongue. But if you mouth it, as many of our players do, I had as live the town crier spoke my lines. Nor do not saw the air too much with your hand, thus, but use all gently; for in the very torrent, tempest, and (as I may say) whirlwind of your passion, you must acquire and beget a temperance that may give it smoothness. O, it offends me to the soul to hear a robustious periwig-pated fellow tear a passion to tatters, to very rags, to split the ears of the groundlings, who (for the most part) are capable of nothing but inexplicable dumb shows and noise. I would have such a fellow whipp'd for o'erdoing Termagant. It out-herods Herod. Pray you avoid it.

PLAYER I warrant your honour.

HAMLET Be not too tame neither; but let your own discretion be your tutor. Suit the action to the word, the word to the action; with this special observance, that you o'erstep not the modesty of nature: for anything so overdone is from the purpose of playing, whose end, both at the first and now, was and is, to hold, as 'twere, the mirror up to nature; to show virtue her own feature, scorn her own image, and the very age and body of the time his form and pressure. Now this overdone, or come tardy off, though it make the unskilful laugh, cannot but make the judicious grieve; the censure of the which one must in your allowance o'erweigh a whole theatre of others. O, there be players that I have seen play, and heard others praise, and that highly (not to speak it profanely), that, neither having the accent of Christians, nor the gait of Christian, pagan, nor man, have so strutted and bellowed that I have thought some of Nature's journeymen had made men, and not made them well, they imitated humanity so abominably.

PLAYER I hope we have reform'd that indifferently with us, sir.

HAMLET O, reform it altogether! And let those that play your clowns speak no more than is set down for them. For there be of them that will themselves laugh, to set on some quantity

169 *blown,* full-blown.
170 *ecstasy,* insanity.
176 *doubt,* fear.
180 *our neglected tribute,* their unpaid debt.

4 *live,* lief.
29 *pressure,* impression.
30 *unskilful,* those lacking taste.
32 *the censure of the which one,* the judgment of one (judicious person).
43–44 ***indifferently,*** passably.

of barren spectators to laugh too, though in the mean time some necessary question of the play be then to be considered. That's villanous and shows a most pitiful ambition in the fool that uses it. Go make you ready.

[*Exeunt* PLAYERS.]

[*Enter* POLONIUS, ROSENCRANTZ, *and* GUILDENSTERN.]

How now, my lord? Will the King hear this piece of work?

POLONIUS And the Queen too, and that presently.

HAMLET Bid the players make haste. [*Exit* POLONIUS.] Will you two help to hasten them?

BOTH We will, my lord.

[*Exeunt they two.*]

HAMLET What, ho, Horatio!

[*Enter* HORATIO.]

HORATIO Here, sweet lord, at your service.

HAMLET Horatio, thou art e'en as just a man
As e'er my conversation cop'd withal.

HORATIO O, my dear lord!

HAMLET Nay, do not think I flatter;
For what advancement may I hope from thee,
That no revenue hast but thy good spirits
To feed and clothe thee? Why should the poor be flatter'd?
No, let the candied tongue lick absurd pomp,
And crook the pregnant hinges of the knee
Where thrift may follow fawning. Dost thou hear?
Since my dear soul was mistress of her choice
And could of men distinguish, her election
Hath seal'd thee for herself. For thou hast been
As one, in suff'ring all, that suffers nothing;
A man that Fortune's buffets and rewards
Hast ta'en with equal thanks; and blest are those
Whose blood and judgment are so well commingled
That they are not a pipe for Fortune's finger
To sound what stop she please. Give me that man
That is not passion's slave, and I will wear him
In my heart's core, ay, in my heart of heart,
As I do thee. Something too much of this!
There is a play to-night before the King.
One scene of it comes near the circumstance,
Which I have told thee, of my father's death.
I prithee, when thou seest that act afoot,
Even with the very comment of thy soul
Observe my uncle. If his occulted guilt
Do not itself unkennel in one speech,
It is a damned ghost that we have seen,
And my imaginations are as foul
As Vulcan's stithy. Give him heedful note;
For I mine eyes will rivet to his face,
And after we will both our judgments join
In censure of his seeming.

HORATIO Well, my lord.
If he steal aught the whilst this play is playing,
And scape detecting, I will pay the theft.

[*Sound a flourish. Enter Trumpets and Kettle-drums. Danish march. Enter* KING, QUEEN, POLONIUS, OPHELIA, ROSENCRANTZ, GUILDENSTERN, *and other* LORDS *attendant, with the* GUARD *carrying torches.*]

HAMLET They are coming to the play. I must be idle.
Get you a place.

KING How fares our cousin Hamlet?

HAMLET Excellent, i' faith; of the chameleon's dish. I eat the air, promise-cramm'd. You cannot feed capons so.

KING I have nothing with this answer, Hamlet. These words are not mine.

HAMLET No, nor mine now. [*To* POLONIUS.] My lord, you play'd once i' th' university, you say?

POLONIUS That did I, my lord, and was accounted a good actor.

HAMLET What did you enact?

POLONIUS I did enact Julius Cæsar; I was kill'd i' th' Capitol; Brutus kill'd me.

HAMLET It was a brute part of him to kill so capital a calf there. Be the players ready?

ROSENCRANTZ Ay, my lord. They stay upon your patience.

QUEEN Come hither, my dear Hamlet, sit by me.

HAMLET No, good mother. Here's metal more attractive.

POLONIUS [*To the* KING.] O, ho! do you mark that?

56–57 *presently,* immediately.
63 *just,* well-balanced.
64 *cop'd withal,* had to do with.
71 *thrift,* reward.

99 *idle,* mad.
102–103 ***chameleon's dish,*** air.

HAMLET Lady, shall I lie in your lap?

[*Sits down at* OPHELIA'*s feet.*]

OPHELIA No, my lord.

HAMLET I mean, my head upon your lap?

OPHELIA Ay, my lord.

HAMLET Do you think I meant country matters?

OPHELIA I think nothing, my lord.

HAMLET That's a fair thought to lie between maids' legs.

OPHELIA What is, my lord?

HAMLET Nothing.

OPHELIA You are merry, my lord.

HAMLET Who, I?

OPHELIA Ay, my lord.

HAMLET O God, your only jig-maker! What should a man do but be merry? For look you how cheerfully my mother looks, and my father died within 's two hours.

OPHELIA Nay, 'tis twice two months, my lord.

HAMLET So long? Nay then, let the devil wear black, for I'll have a suit of sables. O heavens! die two months ago, and not forgotten yet? Then there's hope a great man's memory may outlive his life half a year. But, by'r Lady, he must build churches then; or else shall he suffer not thinking on, with the hobby-horse, whose epitaph is "For O, for O, the hobby-horse is forgot!"

[*Hautboys play. The dumb show enters.*]

Enter a KING and a QUEEN very lovingly; the QUEEN embracing him, and he her. She kneels, and makes show of protestation unto him. He takes her up, and declines his head upon her neck. He lays him down upon a bank of flowers. She, seeing him asleep, leaves him. Anon comes in a fellow, takes off his crown, kisses it, pours poison in the sleeper's ears, and leaves him. The QUEEN returns, finds the KING dead, and makes passionate action. The POISONER with some three or four MUTES, come in again, seem to condole with her. The dead body is carried away. The POISONER wooes the QUEEN with gifts; she seems harsh and unwilling awhile, but in the end accepts his love.

[*Exeunt.*]

OPHELIA What means this, my lord?

HAMLET Marry, this is miching malhecho; it means mischief.

OPHELIA Belike this show imports the argument of the play.

[*Enter* PROLOGUE.]

HAMLET We shall know by this fellow. The players cannot keep counsel; they'll tell all.

OPHELIA Will he tell us what this show meant?

HAMLET Ay, or any show that you'll show him. Be not you asham'd to show, he'll not shame to tell you what it means.

OPHELIA You are naught, you are naught! I'll mark the play.

PROLOGUE For us, and for our tragedy,
Here stooping to your clemency,
We beg your hearing patiently.

[*Exit.*]

HAMLET Is this a prologue, or the posy of a ring?

OPHELIA 'Tis brief, my lord.

HAMLET As woman's love.

[*Enter (two* PLAYERS *as)* KING *and* QUEEN.]

KING Full thirty times hath Phœbus' cart gone round
Neptune's salt wash and Tellus' orbed ground,
And thirty dozen moons with borrowed sheen
About the world have times twelve thirties been,
Since love our hearts, and Hymen did our hands,
Unite comutual in most sacred bands.

QUEEN So many journeys may the sun and moon
Make us again count o'er ere love be done!
But woe is me! you are so sick of late,
So far from cheer and from your former state,
That I distrust you. Yet, though I distrust,
Discomfort you, my lord, it nothing must;
For women's fear and love holds quantity,
In neither aught, or in extremity.
Now what my love is, proof hath made you know;
And as my love is siz'd, my fear is so.

139 *jig-maker,* comic song writer.
149–150 *suffer not thinking on,* risk not being remembered.
154 *miching malhecho,* underhanded crime.
159 *keep counsel,* keep a secret.
164 *naught,* naughty.
173 *Phoebus' cart,* the sun's chariot.
174 *Neptune's salt wash,* the ocean. *Tellus' orbed ground,* the earth.
177 *Hymen,* god of marriage.
183 *distrust you,* am concerned about you.

Where love is great, the littlest doubts are fear;
Where little fears grow great, great love grows there.

KING Faith, I must leave thee, love, and shortly too;
My operant powers their functions leave to do.
And thou shalt live in this fair world behind,
Honour'd, belov'd, and haply one as kind
For husband shalt thou—

QUEEN O, confound the rest!
Such love must needs be treason in my breast.
In second husband let me be accurst!
None wed the second but who kill'd the first.

HAMLET [*Aside.*] Wormwood, wormwood!

QUEEN The instances that second marriage move
Are base respects of thrift, but none of love.
A second time I kill my husband dead
When second husband kisses me in bed.

KING I do believe you think what now you speak;
But what we do determine oft we break.
Purpose is but the slave to memory,
Of violent birth, but poor validity;
Which now, like fruit unripe, sticks on the tree,
But fall unshaken when they mellow be.
Most necessary 'tis that we forget
To pay ourselves what to ourselves is debt.
What to ourselves in passion we propose,
The passion ending, doth the purpose lose.
The violence of either grief or joy
Their own enactures with themselves destroy.
Where joy most revels, grief doth most lament;
Grief joys, joy grieves, on slender accident.
This world is not for aye, nor 'tis not strange
That even our loves should with our fortunes change;
For 'tis a question left us yet to prove,
Whether love lead fortune, or else fortune love.
The great man down, you mark his favourite flies,
The poor advanc'd makes friends of enemies;
And hitherto doth love on fortune tend,
For who not needs shall never lack a friend,
And who in want a hollow friend doth try,
Directly seasons him his enemy.
But, orderly to end where I begun,
Our wills and fates do so contrary run
That our devices still are overthrown;
Our thoughts are ours, their ends none of our own.
So think thou wilt no second husband wed;
But die thy thoughts when thy first lord is dead.

QUEEN Nor earth to me give food, nor heaven light,
Sport and repose lock from me day and night,
To desperation turn my trust and hope,
An anchor's cheer in prison be my scope,
Each opposite that blanks the face of joy
Meet what I would have well, and it destroy,
Both here and hence pursue me lasting strife,
If, once a widow, ever I be wife!

HAMLET If she should break it now!

KING 'Tis deeply sworn. Sweet, leave me here awhile.
My spirits grow dull, and fain I would beguile
The tedious day with sleep.

QUEEN Sleep rock thy brain,

[(*He*) *sleeps.*]

And never come mischance between us twain!

[*Exit.*]

HAMLET Madam, how like you this play?

QUEEN The lady doth protest too much, methinks.

HAMLET O, but she'll keep her word.

KING Have you heard the argument? Is there no offence in't?

HAMLET No, no! They do but jest, poison in jest; no offence i' th' world.

KING What do you call the play?

HAMLET "The Mousetrap." Marry, how? Tropically. This play is the image of a murther done in Vienna. Gonzago is the duke's name; his wife, Baptista. You shall see anon. 'Tis a knavish piece of work; but what o' that? Your Majesty, and we that have free souls, it touches us not. Let the gall'd jade winch; our withers are unwrung.

[*Enter* LUCIANUS.]

This is one Lucianus, nephew to the King.

OPHELIA You are as good as a chorus, my lord.

HAMLET I could interpret between you and your love, if I could see the puppets dallying.

192 *operant powers,* vital force.
195 *O, confound the rest!* (Don't mention the possibility of another husband for me!)

256–257 *Tropically,* figuratively.
262–263 *gall'd jade winch; our withers are unwrung,* the sore horse may wince, but this (horse's) neck is not rubbed raw.
267 *puppets,* (Ophelia and her imagined lover.)

OPHELIA You are keen, my lord, you are keen.

HAMLET It would cost you a groaning to take off my edge.

OPHELIA Still better, and worse.

HAMLET So you must take your husbands.—Begin, murtherer. Pox, leave thy damnable faces, and begin! Come, the croaking raven doth bellow for revenge.

LUCIANUS Thoughts black, hands apt, drugs fit, and time agreeing;
Confederate season, else no creature seeing;
Thou mixture rank, of midnight weeds collected,
With Hecate's ban thrice blasted, thrice infected,
Thy natural magic and dire property
On wholesome life usurp immediately.
[*Pours the poison in his ears.*]

HAMLET He poisons him i' th' garden for's estate. His name's Gonzago. The story is extant, and written in very choice Italian. You shall see anon how the murtherer gets the love of Gonzago's wife.

OPHELIA The King rises.

HAMLET What, frighted with false fire?

QUEEN How fares my lord?

POLONIUS Give o'er the play.

KING Give me some light! Away!

ALL Lights, lights, lights!

[*Exeunt all but* HAMLET *and* HORATIO.]

HAMLET Why, let the strucken deer go weep,
The hart ungalled play;
For some must watch, while some must sleep:
Thus runs the world away.

Would not this, sir, and a forest of feathers—if the rest of my fortunes turn Turk with me—with two Provincial roses on my raz'd shoes, get me a fellowship in a cry of players, sir?

HORATIO Half a share

HAMLET A whole one I!
For thou dost know, O Damon dear,
This realm dismantled was
Of Jove himself; and now reigns here
A very, very—pajock.

HORATIO You might have rhym'd.

HAMLET O good Horatio, I'll take the ghost's word for a thousand pound! Didst perceive?

HORATIO Very well, my lord.

HAMLET Upon the talk of the poisoning?

HORATIO I did very well note him.

HAMLET Aha! Come, some music! Come, the recorders!
For if the King like not the comedy,
Why then, belike he likes it not, perdy.
Come, some music!

[*Enter* ROSENCRANTZ *and* GUILDENSTERN.]

GUILDENSTERN Good my lord, vouchsafe me a word with you.

HAMLET Sir, a whole history.

GUILDENSTERN The King, sir—

HAMLET Ay, sir, what of him?

GUILDENSTERN Is in his retirement, marvellous distemper'd.

HAMLET With drink, sir?

GUILDENSTERN No, my lord; rather with choler.

HAMLET Your wisdom should show itself more richer to signify this to the doctor; for for me to put him to his purgation would perhaps plunge him into far more choler.

GUILDENSTERN Good my lord, put your discourse into some frame, and start not so wildly from my affair.

HAMLET I am tame, sir; pronounce.

GUILDENSTERN The Queen, your mother, in most great affliction of spirit hath sent me to you.

HAMLET You are welcome.

GUILDENSTERN Nay, good my lord, this courtesy is not of the right breed. If it shall please you to make me a wholesome answer, I will do your mother's commandment; if not, your pardon and my return shall be the end of my business.

HAMLET Sir, I cannot.

GUILDENSTERN What, my lord?

HAMLET Make you a wholesome answer; my wit's diseas'd. But, sir, such answer as I can make, you shall command; or rather, as you say, my mother. Therefore no more, but to the matter! My mother, you say—

277 *Confederate season,* right moment.
279 *ban,* curse.
288 *false fire* (only gunpowder, no bullet).
294 *hart,* male deer.
297 *this . . . forest of feathers,* (the way the foregoing lines were spoken) . . . player's extravagant costume.
298 *turn Turk,* play false.
306 *pajock,* peacock.
314 *recorders,* musical instruments.
326 *choler,* bile (a bilious attack).

ROSENCRANTZ Then thus she says: your behaviour hath struck her into amazement and admiration.

HAMLET O wonderful son, that can so stonish a mother! But is there no sequel at the heels of this mother's admiration? Impart.

ROSENCRANTZ She desires to speak with you in her closet ere you go to bed.

HAMLET We shall obey, were she ten times our mother. Have you any further trade with us?

ROSENCRANTZ My lord, you once did love me.

HAMLET And do still, by these pickers and stealers!

ROSENCRANTZ Good my lord, what is your cause of distemper? You do surely bar the door upon your own liberty, if you deny your griefs to your friend.

HAMLET Sir, I lack advancement.

ROSENCRANTZ How can that be, when you have the voice of the King himself for your succession in Denmark?

HAMLET Ay, sir, but "while the grass grows"—the proverb is something musty.

[*Enter the* PLAYERS *with recorders.*]

O, the recorders! Let me see one. To withdraw with you—why do you go about to recover the wind of me, as if you would drive me into a toil?

GUILDENSTERN O my lord, if my duty be too bold, my love is too unmannerly.

HAMLET I do not well understand that. Will you play upon this pipe?

GUILDENSTERN My lord, I cannot.

HAMLET I pray you.

GUILDENSTERN Believe me, I cannot.

HAMLET I do beseech you.

GUILDENSTERN I know no touch of it, my lord.

HAMLET It is as easy as lying. Govern these ventages with your fingers and thumbs, give it breath with your mouth, and it will discourse most eloquent music. Look you, these are the stops.

GUILDENSTERN But these cannot I command to any utt'rance of harmony. I have not the skill.

HAMLET Why, look you now, how unworthy a thing you make of me! You would play upon me; you would seem to know my stops; you would pluck out the heart of my mystery; you would sound me from my lowest note to the top of my compass; and there is much music, excellent voice, in this little organ, yet cannot you make it speak. 'Sblood, do you think I am easier to be play'd on than a pipe? Call me what instrument you will, though you can fret me, you cannot play upon me.

[*Enter* POLONIUS.]

God bless you, sir!

POLONIUS My lord, the Queen would speak with you, and presently.

HAMLET Do you see yonder cloud that's almost in shape of a camel?

POLONIUS By th' mass, and 'tis like a camel indeed.

HAMLET Methinks it is like a weasel.

POLONIUS It is back'd like a weasel.

HAMLET Or like a whale.

POLONIUS Very like a whale.

HAMLET Then will I come to my mother by-and-by.—They fool me to the top of my bent.—I will come by-and-by.

POLONIUS I will say so. [*Exit.*]

HAMLET "By-and-by" is easily said.—Leave me, friends.

[*Exeunt all but* HAMLET.]

'Tis now the very witching time of night,
When churchyards yawn, and hell itself breathes out
Contagion to this world. Now could I drink hot blood
And do such bitter business as the day
Would quake to look on. Soft! now to my mother!
O heart, lose not thy nature; let not ever
The soul of Nero enter this firm bosom.
Let me be cruel, not unnatural;
I will speak daggers to her, but use none.
My tongue and soul in this be hypocrites—

353–354 *amazement and admiration,* bewilderment and wonder.
359 *closet,* bedroom.
363–364 *pickers and stealers,* two hands.
367 *liberty,* freedom of action.
373 *"while the grass grows"* (the old saw which ends, "the horse starves").
374 *musty,* lacking in frankness.
376–377 *go about to recover the wind of me,* try to discover my purposes.
378 *toil,* trap.
389 *ventages,* holes, or stops, in the instrument.

405 *fret,* bar of wire or wood to guide fingering (also, a pun?).
418–419 *by-and-by,* at once.
430 *Nero* (Roman emperor who murdered his mother).

How in my words somever she be shent,
To give them seals never, my soul, consent!

Scene III [*A room in the Castle.*]

[*Enter* KING, ROSENCRANTZ, *and* GUILDENSTERN.]

KING I like him not, nor stands it safe with us
To let his madness range. Therefore prepare you;
I your commission will forthwith dispatch,
And he to England shall along with you.
The terms of our estate may not endure
Hazard so near us as doth hourly grow
Out of his lunacies.

GUILDENSTERN We will ourselves provide.
Most holy and religious fear it is
To keep those many many bodies safe
That live and feed upon your Majesty.

ROSENCRANTZ The single and peculiar life is bound
With all the strength and armour of the mind
To keep itself from noyance; but much more
That spirit upon whose weal depends and rests
The lives of many. The cesse of majesty
Dies not alone, but like a gulf doth draw
What's near it with it. It is a massy wheel,
Fix'd on the summit of the highest mount,
To whose huge spokes ten thousand lesser things
Are mortis'd and adjoin'd; which when it falls,
Each small annexment, petty consequence,
Attends the boist'rous ruin. Never alone
Did the king sigh, but with a general groan.

KING Arm you, I pray you, to this speedy voyage;
For we will fetters put upon this fear,
Which now goes too free-footed.

BOTH We will haste us.

[*Exeunt* GENTLEMEN.]

[*Enter* POLONIUS.]

POLONIUS My lord, he's going to his mother's closet.
Behind the arras I'll convey myself
To hear the process. I'll warrant she'll tax him home;
And, as you said, and wisely was it said,
'Tis meet that some more audience than a mother,
Since nature makes them partial, should o'erhear
The speech, of vantage. Fare you well, my liege.
I'll call upon you ere you go to bed
And tell you what I know.

KING Thanks, dear my lord.

[*Exit* (POLONIUS).]

O, my offence is rank, it smells to heaven;
It hath the primal eldest curse upon't,
A brother's murther! Pray can I not,
Though inclination be as sharp as will.
My stronger guilt defeats my strong intent,
And, like a man to double business bound,
I stand in pause where I shall first begin,
And both neglect. What if this cursed hand
Were thicker than itself with brother's blood.
Is there not rain enough in the sweet heavens
To wash it white as snow? Whereto serves mercy
But to confront the visage of offence?
And what's in prayer but this twofold force,
To be forestalled ere we come to fall,
Or pardon'd being down? Then I'll look up;
My fault is past. But, O, what form of prayer
Can serve my turn? "Forgive me my foul murther"?
That cannot be; since I am still possess'd
Of those effects for which I did the murther—
My crown, mine own ambition, and my queen.
May one be pardon'd and retain th' offence?
In the corrupted currents of this world
Offence's gilded hand may shove by justice,
And oft 'tis seen the wicked prize itself
Buys out the law; but 'tis not so above.
There is no shuffling; there the action lies
In his true nature, and we ourselves compell'd,
Even to the teeth and forehead of our faults,
To give in evidence. What then? What rests?
Try what repentance can. What can it not?
Yet what can it when one cannot repent?
O wretched state! O bosom black as death!
O limed soul, that, struggling to be free,

434 *shent,* castigated.
3 *dispatch,* prepare.
11 *peculiar,* individual.
13 *noyance,* harm.
15 *cesse,* demise.
24 *arm you,* make ready.

29 *tax him home,* scold him thoroughly.
37 *primal eldest curse* (curse upon Cain for murdering his brother Abel.)

Art more engag'd! Help, angels! Make assay.
Bow, stubborn knees; and heart with strings of steel,
Be soft as sinews of the new-born babe!
All may be well. [*He kneels.*]

[*Enter* HAMLET.]

HAMLET Now might I do it pat, now he is praying;
And now I'll do't. And so he goes to heaven,
And so am I reveng'd. That would be scann'd.
A villain kills my father; and for that,
I, his sole son, do this same villain send
To heaven.
Why, this is hire and salary, not revenge!
He took my father grossly, full of bread,
With all his crimes broad blown, as flush as May;
And how his audit stands, who knows save heaven?
But in our circumstances and course of thought,
'Tis heavy with him; and am I then reveng'd,
To take him in the purging of his soul,
When he is fit and season'd for his passage?
No.
Up, sword, and know thou a more horrid hent.
When he is drunk asleep; or in his rage;
Or in th' incestuous pleasure of his bed;
At gaming, swearing, or about some act
That has no relish of salvation in't—
Then trip him, that his heels may kick at heaven,
And that his soul may be as damn'd and black
As hell, whereto it goes. My mother stays
This physic but prolongs thy sickly days.

[*Exit.*]

KING [*Rises.*] My words fly up, my thoughts remain below.
Words without thoughts never to heaven go.

[*Exit.*]

Scene IV [*The* QUEEN'S *closet.*]

[*Enter* QUEEN *and* POLONIUS.]

POLONIUS He will come straight. Look you lay home to him.

[73] *pat,* easily.
[75] *scann'd,* examined (thought about).
[80] *full of bread,* filled with earthly satisfactions.
[82] *his audit,* judgment of him.
[83] *our circumstance,* our restricted, human point of view.
[88] *hent,* moment.
[96] *physic,* purgation (temporary getting rid of the decision to kill Claudius).

Tell him his pranks have been too broad to bear with,
And that your Grace hath screen'd and stood between
Much heat and him. I'll silence me even here.
Pray you be round with him.

HAMLET [*Within.*] Mother, mother, mother!

QUEEN I'll warrant you; fear me not. Withdraw; I hear him coming.

[POLONIUS *hides behind the arras.*]

[*Enter* HAMLET.]

HAMLET Now, mother, what's the matter?

QUEEN Hamlet, thou hast thy father much offended.

HAMLET Mother, you have my father much offended.

QUEEN Come, come, you answer with an idle tongue.

HAMLET Go, go, you question with a wicked tongue.

QUEEN Why, how now, Hamlet?

HAMLET What's the matter now?

QUEEN Have you forgot me?

HAMLET No, by the rood, not so!
You are the Queen, your husband's brother's wife,
And (would it were not so!) you are my mother.

QUEEN Nay, then I'll set those to you that can speak.

HAMLET Come, come, and sit you down. You shall not budge!
You go not till I set you up a glass
Where you may see the inmost part of you.

QUEEN What wilt thou do? Thou wilt not murther me?
Help, help, ho!

POLONIUS [*Behind.*] What, ho! help, help, help!

HAMLET [*Draws.*] How now? a rat? Dead for a ducat, dead!

[(*Makes a pass through the arras and*) *kills* POLONIUS.]

POLONIUS [*Behind.*] O, I am slain!

QUEEN O me, what hast thou done?

HAMLET Nay, I know not. Is it the King?

QUEEN O, what a rash and bloody deed is this!

HAMLET A bloody deed—almost as bad, good mother,

[2] *broad,* free-wheeling.
[17] *those* (a threat stating that if Hamlet will not listen to his mother, others with greater power will handle him.)

As kill a king, and marry with his brother.
QUEEN As kill a king?
HAMLET Ay, lady, it was my word.
[*Lifts up the arras and sees* POLONIUS.]
Thou wretched, rash, intruding fool, farewell!
I took thee for thy better. Take thy fortune.
Thou find'st to be too busy is some danger.
Leave wringing of your hands. Peace! sit you down
And let me wring your heart; for so I shall
If it be made of penetrable stuff;
If damned custom have not braz'd it so
That it is proof and bulwark against sense.
QUEEN What have I done that thou dar'st wag thy tongue
In noise so rude against me?
HAMLET Such an act
That blurs the grace and blush of modesty;
Calls virtue hypocrite; takes off the rose
From the fair forehead of an innocent love,
And sets a blister there; makes marriage vows
As false as dicers' oaths. O, such a deed
As from the body of contraction plucks
The very soul, and sweet religion makes
A rhapsody of words! Heaven's face doth glow;
Yea, this solidity and compound mass,
With tristful visage, as against the doom,
Is thought-sick at the act.
QUEEN Ay me, what act,
That roars so loud and thunders in the index?
HAMLET Look here upon this picture, and on this,
The counterfeit presentment of two brothers.
See what a grace was seated on this brow;
Hyperion's curls; the front of Jove himself;
An eye like Mars, to threaten and command;
A station like the herald Mercury
New lighted on a heaven-kissing hill:
A combination and a form indeed
Where every god did seem to set his seal
To give the world assurance of a man.
This was your husband. Look you now what follows.
Here is your husband, like a mildew'd ear
Blasting his wholesome brother. Have you eyes?
Could you on this fair mountain leave to feed,
And batten on this moor? Ha! have you eyes?
You cannot call it love; for at your age
The heydey in the blood is tame, it's humble,
And waits upon the judgment; and what judgment
Would step from this to this? Sense sure you have,
Else could you not have motion; but sure that sense
Is apoplex'd; for madness would not err,
Nor sense to ecstasy was ne'er so thrall'd
But it reserv'd some quantity of choice
To serve in such a difference. What devil was't
That thus hath cozen'd you at hoodman-blind?
Eyes without feeling, feeling without sight,
Ears without hands or eyes, smelling sans all,
Or but a sickly part of one true sense
Could not so mope.
O shame! where is thy blush? Rebellious hell,
If thou canst mutine in a matron's bones,
To flaming youth let virtue be as wax
And melt in her own fire. Proclaim no shame
When the compulsive ardour gives the charge,
Since frost itself as actively doth burn,
And reason panders will.
QUEEN O Hamlet, speak no more!
Thou turn'st mine eyes into my very soul,
And there I see such black and grained spots
As will not leave their tinct.
HAMLET Nay, but to live
In the rank sweat of an enseamed bed,
Stew'd in corruption, honeying and making love
Over the nasty sty!
QUEEN O, speak to me no more!
These words like daggers enter in mine ears.
No more, sweet Hamlet!
HAMLET A murtherer and a villain!
A slave that is not twentieth part the tithe
Of your precedent lord; a vice of kings;
A cutpurse of the empire and the rule,

33 *too busy,* too much a busybody.
40 *Such an act,* hasty marriage (Some scholars say the act is adultery, but it is doubtful that the Ghost would be protective of Gertrude if he thought she had had an affair with Claudius.)
44 *blister,* brand.
46 *contraction,* marriage vows.
48 *glow,* blush with shame.
52 *index,* table of contents.
58 *station,* posture.
67 *batten,* gorge.
74 *ecstasy,* madness.
77 *cozen'd,* fooled.
79 *sans,* without.
81 *so mope,* be so insensitive.
88 *reason panders will,* reason becomes a slave to ardor.
92 *enseamed,* greasy.

That from a shelf the precious diadem stole
And put it in his pocket!

QUEEN No more!

[*Enter the* GHOST *in his nightgown.*]

HAMLET A king of shreds and patches!—
Save me and hover o'er me with your wings,
You heavenly guards! What would your gracious figure?

QUEEN Alas, he's mad!

HAMLET Do you not come your tardy son to chide,
That, laps'd in time and passion, lets go by
Th' important acting of your dread command?
O, say!

GHOST Do not forget. This visitation
Is but to whet thy almost blunted purpose.
But look, amazement on thy mother sits.
O, step between her and her fighting soul!
Conceit in weakest bodies strongest works.
Speak to her, Hamlet.

HAMLET How is it with you, lady?

QUEEN Alas, how is't with you,
That you do bend your eye on vacancy,
And with th' incorporal air do hold discourse?
Forth at your eyes your spirits wildly peep;
And, as the sleeping soldiers in th' alarm,
Your bedded hairs, like life in excrements,
Start up and stand on end. O gentle son,
Upon the heat and flame of thy distemper
Sprinkle cool patience! Whereon do you look?

HAMLET On him, on him! Look you how pale he glares!
His form and cause conjoin'd, preaching to stones,
Would make them capable.—Do not look upon me,
Lest with this piteous action you convert
My stern effects. Then what I have to do
Will want true colour—tears perchance for blood.

QUEEN To whom do you speak this?

HAMLET Do you see nothing there?

QUEEN Nothing at all; yet all that is I see.

HAMLET Nor did you nothing hear?

QUEEN No, nothing but ourselves.

HAMLET Why, look you there! Look how it steals away!
My father, in his habit as he liv'd!
Look where he goes even now out at the portal!

[*Exit* GHOST.]

QUEEN This is the very coinage of your brain.
This bodiless creation ecstasy
Is very cunning in.

HAMLET Ecstasy?
My pulse as yours doth temperately keep time
And makes as healthful music. It is not madness
That I have utt'red. Bring me to the test,
And I the matter will reword; which madness
Would gambol from. Mother, for love of grace,
Lay not that flattering unction to your soul,
That not your trespass but my madness speaks.
It will but skin and film the ulcerous place,
Whiles rank corruption, mining all within,
Infects unseen. Confess yourself to heaven;
Repent what's past; avoid what is to come;
And do not spread the compost on the weeds
To make them ranker. Forgive me this my virtue;
For in the fatness of these pursy times
Virtue itself of vice must pardon beg—
Yea, curb and woo for leave to do him good.

QUEEN O Hamlet, thou hast cleft my heart in twain.

HAMLET O, throw away the worser part of it,
And live the purer with the other half.
Good night—but go not to my uncle's bed.
Assume a virtue, if you have it not.
That monster, custom, who all sense doth eat
Of habits evil, is angel yet in this,
That to the use of actions fair and good
He likewise gives a frock or livery,
That aptly is put on. Refrain to-night,
And that shall lend a kind of easiness
To the next abstinence; the next more easy;
For use almost can change the stamp of nature,
And either [master] the devil, or throw him out
With wondrous potency. Once more, good night;
And when you are desirous to be blest,
I'll blessing beg of you.—For this same lord,
I do repent; but heaven hath pleas'd it so,
To punish me with this, and this with me,

102 *shreds and patches,* disreputable appearance (figurative).
121 *bedded,* groomed. *excrements,* outgrowths.
144 *gambol from,* skip away from.
153 *pursy,* over-fat.
172 *this same lord,* Polonius.

That I must be their scourge and minister.
I will bestow him, and will answer well
The death I gave him. So again, good night.
I must be cruel, only to be kind;
Thus bad begins, and worse remains behind.
One word more, good lady.

QUEEN What shall I do?

HAMLET Not this, by no means, that I bid you do:
Let the bloat King tempt you again to bed;
Pinch wanton on your cheek; call you his mouse;
And let him, for a pair of reechy kisses,
Or paddling in your neck with his damn'd fingers,
Make you to ravel all this matter out,
That I essentially am not in madness,
But mad in craft. 'Twere good you let him know;
For who that's but a queen, fair, sober, wise,
Would from a paddock, from a bat, a gib,
Such dear concernings hide? Who would do so?
No, in despite of sense and secrecy,
Unpeg the basket on the house's top,
Let the birds fly, and like the famous ape,
To try conclusions, in the basket creep
And break your own neck down.

QUEEN Be thou assur'd, if words be made of breath,
And breath of life, I have no life to breathe
What thou hast said to me.

HAMLET I must to England; you know that?

QUEEN Alack,
I had forgot! 'Tis so concluded on.

HAMLET There's letters seal'd; and my two schoolfellows,
Whom I will trust as I will adders fang'd,
They bear the mandate; they must sweep my way
And marshal me to knavery. Let it work;
For 'tis the sport to have the enginer
Hoist with his own petar; and 't shall go hard
But I will delve one yard below their mines
And blow them at the moon. O, 'tis most sweet
When in one line two crafts directly meet.
This man shall set me packing.
I'll lug the guts into the neighbour room.—
Mother, good night.—Indeed, this counsellor
Is now most still, most secret, and most grave,
Who was in life a foolish prating knave.
Come, sir, to draw toward an end with you.
Good night, mother.

[(*Exit the* QUEEN. *Then*) *exit* HAMLET, *tugging in* POLONIUS.]

ACT IV

Scene I [*Elsinore. A room in the Castle.*]

[*Enter* KING *and* QUEEN, *with* ROSENCRANTZ *and* GUILDENSTERN.]

KING There's matter in these sighs. These profound heaves
You must translate; 'tis fit we understand them.
Where is your son?

QUEEN Bestow this place on us a little while.

[*Exeunt* ROSENCRANTZ *and* GUILDENSTERN.]

Ah, mine own lord, what have I seen tonight!

KING What, Gertrude? How does Hamlet?

QUEEN Mad as the sea and wind when both contend
Which is the mightier. In his lawless fit,
Behind the arras hearing something stir,
Whips out his rapier, cries "A rat, a rat!"
And in this brainish apprehension kills
The unseen good old man.

KING O heavy deed!
It had been so with us, had we been there.
His liberty is full of threats to all—
To you yourself, to us, to every one.
Alas, how shall this bloody deed be answer'd?
It will be laid to us, whose providence
Should have kept short, restrain'd, and out of haunt
This mad young man. But so much was our love
We would not understand what was most fit,
But, like the owner of a foul disease,
To keep it from divulging, let it feed
Even on the pith of life. Where is he gone?

179 *worse remains behind* (murder of Claudius is yet to come.)
182 *bloat,* swollen with drink.
184 *reechy,* slobbery.
207 *Hoist with his own petar,* Blown up with his own bomb.

11 *brainish apprehension,* demented notion.
18 *out of haunt,* away from others.

QUEEN To draw apart the body he hath kill'd;
O'er whom his very madness, like some ore
Among a mineral of metals base,
Shows itself pure. He weeps for what is done.

KING O Gertrude, come away!
The sun no sooner shall the mountains touch
But we will ship him hence; and this vile deed
We must with all our majesty and skill
Both countenance and excuse. Ho, Guildenstern!

[*Enter* ROSENCRANTZ *and* GUILDENSTERN.]

Friends both, go join you with some further aid.
Hamlet in madness hath Polonius slain,
And from his mother's closet hath he dragg'd him.
Go seek him out; speak fair, and bring the body
Into the chapel. I pray you haste in this.

[*Exeunt* (ROSENCRANTZ *and* GUILDENSTERN).]

Come, Gertrude, we'll call up our wisest friends
And let them know both what we mean to do
And what's untimely done. [So haply slander—]
Whose whisper o'er the world's diameter,
As level as the cannon to his blank,
Transports his pois'ned shot—may miss our name
And hit the woundless air.—O, come away!
My soul is full of discord and dismay.

[*Exeunt.*]

Scene II [*Elsinore. A passage in the Castle.*]

[*Enter* HAMLET.]

HAMLET Safely stow'd.

GENTLEMEN [*Within.*] Hamlet! Lord Hamlet!

HAMLET But soft! What noise? Who calls on Hamlet? O, here they come.

[*Enter* ROSENCRANTZ *and* GUILDENSTERN.]

ROSENCRANTZ What have you done, my lord, with the dead body?

HAMLET Compounded it with dust, whereto 'tis kin.

ROSENCRANTZ Tell us where 'tis, that we may take it thence
And bear it to the chapel.

HAMLET Do not believe it.

ROSENCRANTZ Believe what?

HAMLET That I can keep your counsel, and not mine own. Besides, to be demanded of a sponge, what replication should be made by the son of a king?

ROSENCRANTZ Take you me for a sponge, my lord?

HAMLET Ay, sir; that soaks up the King's countenance, his rewards, his authorities. But such officers do the King best service in the end. He keeps them, like an ape, in the corner of his jaw; first mouth'd, to be last swallowed. When he needs what you have glean'd, it is but squeezing you and, sponge, you shall be dry again.

ROSENCRANTZ I understand you not, my lord.

HAMLET I am glad of it. A knavish speech sleeps in a foolish ear.

ROSENCRANTZ My lord, you must tell us where the body is and go with us to the King.

HAMLET The body is with the King, but the King is not with the body. The King is a thing—

GUILDENSTERN A thing, my lord?

HAMLET Of nothing. Bring me to him. Hide fox, and all after.

[*Exeunt.*]

Scene III [*Elsinore. A room in the Castle.*]

[*Enter* KING.]

KING I have sent to seek him and to find the body.
How dangerous is it that this man goes loose!
Yet must not we put the strong law on him.
He's lov'd of the distracted multitude,
Who like not in their judgment, but their eyes;
And where 'tis so, th' offender's scourge is weigh'd,
But never the offence. To bear all smooth and even,

25 *ore,* precious metal.
42 *level,* accurate aim. *blank,* target.

11 *counsel,* secrets.
13 *replication,* formal reply.
34–35 *Hide fox* (reference to the child's game, hounds and the fox, with Hamlet pretending to be the fox.)
4 *distracted,* fooled.
7 *bear,* manage.

This sudden sending him away must seem
Deliberate pause. Diseases desperate grown
By desperate appliance are reliev'd,
Or not at all.

[*Enter* ROSENCRANTZ.]

How now? What hath befall'n?

ROSENCRANTZ Where the dead body is bestow'd, my lord,
We cannot get from him.

KING But where is he?

ROSENCRANTZ Without, my lord; guarded, to know your pleasure.

KING Bring him before us.

ROSENCRANTZ Ho, Guildenstern! Bring in my lord.

[*Enter* HAMLET *and* GUILDENSTERN (*with* ATTENDANTS).]

KING Now, Hamlet, where's Polonius?

HAMLET At supper.

KING At supper? Where?

HAMLET Not where he eats, but where he is eaten. A certain convocation of politic worms are e'en at him. Your worm is your only emperor for diet. We fat all creatures else to fat us, and we fat ourselves for maggots. Your fat king and your lean beggar is but variable service—two dishes, but to one table. That's the end.

KING Alas, alas!

HAMLET A man may fish with the worm that hath eat of a king, and eat of the fish that hath fed of that worm.

KING What dost thou mean by this?

HAMLET Nothing but to show you how a king may go a progress through the guts of a beggar.

KING Where is Polonius?

HAMLET In heaven. Send thither to see. If your messenger find him not there, seek him i' th' other place yourself. But indeed, if you find him not within this month, you shall nose him as you go up the stairs into the lobby.

KING Go seek him there. [*To* ATTENDANTS.]

HAMLET He will stay till you come.

[*Exeunt* ATTENDANTS.]

KING Hamlet, this deed, for thine especial safety,—
Which we do tender as we dearly grieve
For that which thou hast done,—must send thee hence
With fiery quickness. Therefore prepare thyself.
The bark is ready and the wind at help,
Th' associates tend, and everything is bent
For England.

HAMLET For England?

KING Ay, Hamlet.

HAMLET Good.

KING So is it, if thou knew'st our purposes.

HAMLET I see a cherub that sees them. But come, for England! Farewell, dear mother.

KING Thy loving father, Hamlet.

HAMLET My mother! Father and mother is man and wife; man and wife is one flesh; and so, my mother. Come, for England! [*Exit.*]

KING Follow him at foot; tempt him with speed aboard.
Delay it not; I'll have him hence to-night.
Away! for everything is seal'd and done
That else leans on th' affair. Pray you make haste.

[*Exeunt* ROSENCRANTZ *and* GUILDENSTERN.]

And, England, if my love thou hold'st at aught,—
As my great power thereof may give thee sense,
Since yet thy cicatrice looks raw and red
After the Danish sword, and thy free awe
Pays homage to us,—thou mayst not coldly set
Our sovereign process, which imports at full,
By letters congruing to that effect,
The present death of Hamlet. Do it, England;
For like the hectic in my blood he rages,
And thou must cure me. Till I know 'tis done,
Howe'er my haps, my joys were ne'er begun.

[*Exit.*]

Scene IV [*Near Elsinore.*]

[*Enter* FORTINBRAS *with his* ARMY *over the stage.*]

9 *deliberate pause,* the result of thoughtful deliberation.

34 *a progress,* royal visits to estates of noblemen.

51 *I see a cherub,* I see as a cherub (everything).

57 *tempt him,* coax him.

60 *leans on,* pertains to.

65 *coldly set,* be indifferent to.

67 *congruing,* informing.

69 *the hectic,* constant fever.

71 *haps,* fortune (what happens to me).

FORTINBRAS Go, Captain, from me greet the Danish king.
Tell him that by his license Fortinbras
Craves the conveyance of a promis'd march
Over his kingdom. You know the rendezvous.
If that his Majesty would aught with us,
We shall express our duty in his eye;
And let him know so.

CAPTAIN I will do't, my lord.

FORTINBRAS Go softly on.

[*Exeunt (all but the* CAPTAIN).]

[*Enter* HAMLET, ROSENCRANTZ, (GUILDENSTERN,) *and others.*]

HAMLET Good sir, whose powers are these?

CAPTAIN They are of Norway, sir.

HAMLET How purpos'd, sir, I pray you?

CAPTAIN Against some part of Poland.

HAMLET Who commands them, sir?

CAPTAIN The nephew to old Norway, Fortinbras.

HAMLET Goes it against the main of Poland, sir,
Or for some frontier?

CAPTAIN Truly to speak, and with no addition,
We go to gain a little patch of ground
That hath in it no profit but the name.
To pay five ducats, five, I would not farm it;
Nor will it yield to Norway or the Pole
A ranker rate, should it be sold in fee.

HAMLET Why, then the Polack never will defend it.

CAPTAIN Yes, it is already garrison'd.

HAMLET Two thousand souls and twenty thousand ducats
Will not debate the question of this straw.
This is th' imposthume of much wealth and peace,
That inward breaks, and shows no cause without
Why the man dies.—I humbly thank you, sir.

CAPTAIN God b' wi' you, sir. [*Exit.*]

ROSENCRANTZ Will't please you go, my lord?

HAMLET I'll be with you straight. Go a little before.

[*Exeunt all but* HAMLET.]

How all occasions do inform against me
And spur my dull revenge! What is a man,
If his chief good and market of his time
Be but to sleep and feed? A beast, no more.
Sure he that made us with such large discourse,
Looking before and after, gave us not
That capability and godlike reason
To fust in us unus'd. Now, whether it be
Bestial oblivion, or some craven scruple
Of thinking too precisely on th' event,—
A thought which, quarter'd, hath but one part wisdom
And ever three parts coward,—I do not know
Why yet I live to say "This thing's to do,"
Sith I have cause, and will, and strength, and means
To do't. Examples gross as earth exhort me.
Witness this army of such mass and charge,
Led by a delicate and tender prince,
Whose spirit, with divine ambition puff'd,
Makes mouths at the invisible event,
Exposing what is mortal and unsure
To all that fortune, death, and danger dare,
Even for an eggshell. Rightly to be great
Is not to stir without great argument,
But greatly to find quarrel in a straw
When honour's at the stake. How stand I then,
That have a father kill'd, a mother stain'd,
Excitements of my reason and my blood,
And let all sleep, while to my shame I see
The imminent death of twenty thousand men
That for a fantasy and trick of fame
Go to their graves like beds, fight for a plot
Whereon the numbers cannot try the cause,
Which is not tomb enough and continent
To hide the slain? O, from this time forth,
My thoughts be bloody, or be nothing worth!

[*Exit.*]

Scene V [*Elsinore. A room in the Castle.*]

[*Enter* HORATIO, QUEEN, *and a* GENTLEMAN.]

QUEEN I will not speak with her.

GENTLEMAN She is importunate, indeed distract.
Her mood will needs be pitied.

QUEEN What would she have?

3 *conveyance,* escort.
8 *softly,* quietly.
22 *a ranker rate,* a higher return.
27 *imposthume,* ulcer (hidden within but damaging).
34 *market of his time,* wager for his time.
39 *fust,* become moldy.
61 *a fantasy,* fanciful imagining.
64 *continent,* able to contain.

GENTLEMAN She speaks much of her father; says she hears
There's tricks i' th' world, and hems, and beats her heart;
Spurns enviously at straws; speaks things in doubt,
That carry but half sense. Her speech is nothing,
Yet the unshaped use of it doth move
The hearers to collection; they aim at it,
And botch the words up fit to their own thoughts;
Which, as her winks and nods and gestures yield them,
Indeed would make one think there might be thought,
Though nothing sure, yet much unhappily.

HORATIO 'Twere good she were spoken with; for she may strew
Dangerous conjectures in ill-breeding minds.

QUEEN Let her come in.
[*Exit* GENTLEMAN.]
[*Aside.*] To my sick soul (as sin's true nature is)
Each toy seems prologue to some great amiss.
So full of artless jealousy is guilt
It spills itself in fearing to be spilt.

[*Enter* OPHELIA *distracted.*]

OPHELIA Where is the beauteous Majesty of Denmark?

QUEEN How now, Ophelia?

OPHELIA [*Sings.*] How should I your true-love know
From another one?
By his cockle hat and staff
And his sandal shoon.

QUEEN Alas, sweet lady, what imports this song?

OPHELIA Say you? Nay, pray you mark.
[*Sings.*] He is dead and gone, lady,
He is dead and gone;
At his head a grass-green turf,
At his heels a stone.
O, ho!

QUEEN Nay, but Ophelia—

OPHELIA Pray you mark.
[*Sings.*] White his shroud as the mountain snow—

[*Enter* KING.]

QUEEN Alas, look here, my lord!

OPHELIA [*Sings.*] Larded all with sweet flowers;
Which bewept to the grave did not go
With true-love showers.

KING How do you, pretty lady?

OPHELIA Well, God dild you! They say the owl was a baker's daughter. Lord, we know what we are, but know not what we may be. God be at your table!

KING Conceit upon her father.

OPHELIA Pray let's have no words of this; but when they ask you what it means, say you this:
[*Sings.*] To-morrow is Saint Valentine's day
All in the morning betime,
And I a maid at your window,
To be your Valentine.
Then up he rose and donn'd his clo'es
And dupp'd the chamber door,
Let in the maid, that out a maid
Never departed more.

KING Pretty Ophelia!

OPHELIA Indeed, la, without an oath, I'll make an end on't!
[*Sings.*] By Gis and by Saint Charity,
Alack, and fie for shame!
Young men will do't if they come to't.
By Cock, they are to blame.
Quoth she, "Before you tumbled me,
You promis'd me to wed."
He answers:
"So would I 'a' done, by yonder sun,
An thou hadst not come to my bed."

KING How long hath she been thus?

OPHELIA I hope all will be well. We must be patient; but I cannot choose but weep to think they would lay him i' th' cold ground. My brother shall know of it; and so I thank you for your good counsel. Come, my coach! Good night, ladies. Good night, sweet ladies. Good night, good night. [*Exit.*]

6 *spurns enviously at straws,* takes offense over small things.
9 *collection,* combined interpretations (of Ophelia's ravings).
15 *ill-breeding,* evilly imagining.
42 *God dild you,* God be good to you.
46 *Conceit upon,* suggested by thoughts of her father.
55 *dupp'd,* opened.
60 *By Gis,* by Jesus.
63 *by Cock,* by God.
64 *tumbled,* had intercourse with.

KING Follow her close; give her good watch, I pray you.
[*Exit* HORATIO.]
O, this is the poison of deep grief; it springs
All from her father's death. O Gertrude, Gertrude,
When sorrows come, they come not single spies,
But in battalions! First, her father slain;
Next, your son gone, and he most violent author
Of his own just remove; the people muddied,
Thick and unwholesome in their thoughts and whispers
For good Polonius' death, and we have done but greenly
In hugger-mugger to inter him; poor Ophelia
Divided from herself and her fair judgment,
Without the which we are pictures or mere beasts;
Last, and as much containing as all these,
Her brother is in secret come from France;
Feeds on his wonder, keeps himself in clouds,
And wants not buzzers to infect his ear
With pestilent speeches of his father's death,
Wherein necessity, of matter beggar'd,
Will nothing stick our person to arraign
In ear and ear. O my dear Gertrude, this,
Like to a murd'ring piece, in many places
Gives me superfluous death.
[*A noise within.*]
QUEEN Alack, what noise is this?
KING Where are my Switzers? Let them guard the door.
[*Enter a* MESSENGER.]
What is the matter?
MESSENGER Save yourself, my lord:
The ocean, overpeering of his list,
Eats not the flats with more impetuous haste
Than young Laertes, in a riotous head,
O'erbears your officers. The rabble call him lord;
And, as the world were now but to begin,
Antiquity forgot, custom not known,
The ratifiers and props of every word,
They cry "Choose we! Laertes shall be king!"
Caps, hands, and tongues applaud it to the clouds,
"Laertes shall be king! Laertes king!"
[*A noise within.*]
QUEEN How cheerfully on the false trail they cry!
O, this is counter, you false Danish dogs!
KING The doors are broke.
[*Enter* LAERTES *with others.*]
LAERTES Where is this king?—Sirs, stand you all without.
ALL No, let's come in!
LAERTES I pray you give me leave.
ALL We will, we will!
LAERTES I thank you. Keep the door. [*Exeunt his Followers.*] O thou vile king,
Give me my father!
QUEEN Calmly, good Laertes.
LAERTES That drop of blood that's calm proclaims me bastard;
Cries cuckold to my father; brands the harlot
Even here between the chaste unsmirched brows
Of my true mother.
KING What is the cause, Laertes,
That thy rebellion looks so giantlike?
Let him go, Gertrude. Do not fear our person.
There's such divinity doth hedge a king
That treason can but peep to what it would,
Acts little of his will. Tell me, Laertes,
Why thou art thus incens'd. Let him go, Gertrude.
Speak, man.
LAERTES Where is my father?
KING Dead.
QUEEN But not by him!
KING Let him demand his fill.
LAERTES How came he dead? I'll not be juggled with:
To hell, allegiance! vows, to the blackest devil!
Conscience and grace, to the profoundest pit!
I dare damnation. To this point I stand,
That both the worlds I give to negligence,

83 *muddied,* muddled.
85 *greenly,* too innocently.
86 *in hugger-mugger,* without respectful (proper) ceremony.
91 *wonder,* speculation (without action).
92 *buzzers,* irresponsible gossipers.
95 *stick,* hesitate.
99 *Switzers,* Swiss guards.
101 *overpeering of his list,* surging over its high-water mark.
107 *the ratifiers and props* (antiquity and custom should determine who should be king, but the rabble ignore old customs.)
112 *counter,* opposite (to the true scent).
126 *peep to,* look from afar.

Let come what comes; only I'll be reveng'd
Most throughly for my father.

KING Who shall stay you?

LAERTES My will, not all the world!
And for my means, I'll husband them so well
They shall go far with little.

KING Good Laertes,
If you desire to know the certainty
Of your dear father's death, is't writ in your revenge
That swoopstake you will draw both friend and foe,
Winner and loser?

LAERTES None but his enemies.

KING Will you know them then?

LAERTES To his good friends thus wide I'll ope my arms
And, like the kind life-rend'ring pelican,
Repast them with my blood.

KING Why, now you speak
Like a good child and a true gentleman.
That I am guiltless of your father's death,
And am most sensibly in grief for it,
It shall as level to your judgment pierce
As day does to your eye.

[*A noise within.*] "Let her come in."

LAERTES How, now? What noise is that?

[*Enter* OPHELIA.]

O heat, dry up my brains! Tears seven times salt
Burn out the sense and virtue of mine eye!
By heaven, thy madness shall be paid by weight
Till our scale turn the beam. O rose of May!
Dear maid, kind sister, sweet Ophelia!
O heavens! is't possible a young maid's wits
Should be as mortal as an old man's life?
Nature is fine in love, and where 'tis fine,
It sends some precious instance of itself
After the thing it loves.

OPHELIA [*Sings.*]

They bore him barefac'd on the bier
(Hey non nony, nony, hey nony)
And in his grave rain'd many a tear.

Fare you well, my dove!

LAERTES Hadst thou thy wits, and didst persuade revenge
It could not move thus.

OPHELIA You must sing "A-down a-down, and you call him a-down-a." O, how the wheel becomes it! It is the false steward, that stole his master's daughter.

LAERTES This nothing's more than matter.

OPHELIA There's rosemary, that's for remembrance. Pray you, love, remember. And there is pansies, that's for thoughts.

LAERTES A document in madness! Thoughts and remembrance fitted.

OPHELIA There's fennel for you, and columbines. There's rue for you, and here's some for me. We may call it herb of grace o' Sundays. O, you must wear your rue with a difference! There's a daisy. I would give you some violets, but they wither'd all when my father died. They say he made a good end.

[*Sings.*] For bonny sweet Robin is all my joy.

LAERTES Thought and affliction, passion, hell itself,
She turns to favour and to prettiness.

OPHELIA [*Sings.*]

And will he not come again?
And will he not come again?
No, no, he is dead;
Go to thy deathbed;
He never will come again.

His beard was as white as snow,
All flaxen was his poll.
He is gone, he is gone,
And we cast away moan.
God 'a' mercy on his soul!

And of all Christian souls, I pray God. God b' wi' you. [*Exit.*]

LAERTES Do you see this, O God?

KING Laertes, I must commune with your grief,
Or you deny me right. Go but apart,
Make choice of whom your wisest friends you will,
And they shall hear and judge 'twixt you and me.
If by direct or by collateral hand

144 *swoopstake,* in one fell swoop.
153 *as level to your judgment pierce,* aim so accurately as to convince without question.

174 *wheel,* spinning wheel (rhythmic in accompanying the singing of ballads).
177 *this nothing's more than matter,* this meaninglessness carries more effect than sane speech would.
183 *fennel* (represents deceit).
184 *rue* (represents sadness, or ruefulness).

They find us touch'd, we will our kingdom give,
Our crown, our life, and all that we call ours,
To you in satisfaction; but if not,
Be you content to lend your patience to us,
And we shall jointly labour with your soul
To give it due content.

LAERTES Let this be so.
His means of death, his obscure funeral—
No trophy, sword, nor hatchment o'er his bones,
No noble rite nor formal ostentation,—
Cry to be heard, as 'twere from heaven to earth,
That I must call't in question.

KING So you shall;
And where th' offence is let the great axe fall.
I pray you go with me.
[*Exeunt.*]

Scene VI [*Elsinore. Another room in the Castle.*]

[*Enter* HORATIO *and an Attendant.*]

HORATIO What are they that would speak with me?

SERVANT Seafaring men, sir. They say they have letters for you.

HORATIO Let them come in.
[*Exit Attendant.*]
I do not know from what part of the world
I should be greeted, if not from Lord Hamlet.

[*Enter* SAILORS.]

SAILOR God bless you, sir.

HORATIO Let him bless thee too.

SAILOR 'A shall, sir, an't please him. There's a letter for you, sir,—it comes from th' ambassador that was bound for England—if your name be Horatio, as I am let to know it is.

HORATIO [*Reads the letter.*] "Horatio, when thou shalt have overlook'd this, give these fellows some means to the King. They have letters for him. Ere we were two days old at sea, a pirate of very warlike appointment gave us chase. Finding ourselves too slow of sail, we put on a compelled valour, and in the grapple I boarded them. On the instant they got clear of our ship; so I alone became their prisoner. They have dealt with me like thieves of mercy; but they knew what they did: I am to do a good turn for them. Let the King have the letters I have sent, and repair thou to me with as much speed as thou wouldest fly death. I have words to speak in thine ear will make thee dumb; yet are they much too light for the bore of the matter. These good fellows will bring thee where I am. Rosencrantz and Guildenstern hold their course for England. Of them I have much to tell thee. Farewell.
"He that thou knowest thine, HAMLET."

Come, I will give you way for these your letters,
And do't the speedier that you may direct me
To him from whom you brought them.
[*Exeunt.*]

Scene VII [*Elsinore. Another room in the Castle.*]

[*Enter* KING *and* LAERTES.]

KING Now must your conscience my acquittance seal,
And you must put me in your heart for friend,
Sith you have heard, and with a knowing ear,
That he which hath your noble father slain
Pursued my life.

LAERTES It well appears. But tell me
Why you proceeded not against these feats
So crimeful and so capital in nature,
As by your safety, wisdom, all things else,
You mainly were stirr'd up.

KING O, for two special reasons,
Which may to you, perhaps, seem much unsinew'd,
But yet to me they are strong. The Queen his mother
Lives almost by his looks; and for myself,—
My virtue or my plague, be it either which,—
She's so conjunctive to my life and soul
That, as the star moves not but in his sphere,
I could not but by her. The other motive
Why to a public count I might not go
Is the great love the general gender bear him,
Who, dipping all his faults in their affection,
Would, like the spring that turneth wood to stone,
Convert his gyves to graces; so that my arrows,

217 *hatchment,* gravestone.
221 *the great axe,* vengeance.

10 *much unsinew'd,* without strength.
18 *general gender,* ordinary citizens.
21 *gyves,* fetters.

Too slightly timber'd for so loud a wind,
Would have reverted to my bow again,
And not where I had aim'd them.

LAERTES And so have I a noble father lost;
A sister driven into desp'rate terms,
Whose worth, if praises may go back again,
Stood challenger on mount of all the age
For her perfections. But my revenge will come.

KING Break not your sleeps for that. You must not think
That we are made of stuff so flat and dull
That we can let our beard be shook with danger,
And think it pastime. You shortly shall hear more.
I lov'd your father, and we love ourself,
And that, I hope, will teach you to imagine—

[*Enter a* MESSENGER *with letters.*]

How now? What news?

MESSENGER Letters, my lord, from Hamlet:
This to your Majesty; this to the Queen.

KING From Hamlet? Who brought them?

MESSENGER Sailors, my lord, they say; I saw them not.
They were given me by Claudio; he receiv'd them
Of him that brought them.

KING Laertes, you shall hear them.
Leave us.

[*Exit* MESSENGER.]

[*Reads.*] "High and Mighty,—You shall know I am set naked on your kingdom. To-morrow shall I beg leave to see your kingly eyes; when I shall (first asking your pardon thereunto) recount the occasion of my sudden and more strange return.

"HAMLET."

What should this mean? Are all the rest come back?
Or is it some abuse, and no such thing?

LAERTES Know you the hand?

KING 'Tis Hamlet's character, "Naked!"
And in a postscript here, he says "alone."
Can you advise me?

LAERTES I am lost in it, my lord. But let him come!
It warms the very sickness in my heart
That I shall live and tell him to his teeth,
"Thus didest thou."

KING If it be so, Laertes
(As how should it be so? how otherwise?),
Will you be rul'd by me?

LAERTES Ay, my lord,
So you will not o'errule me to a peace.

KING To thine own peace. If he be now return'd,
As checking at his voyage, and that he means
No more to undertake it, I will work him
To an exploit now ripe in my device,
Under the which he shall not choose but fall;
And for his death no wind of blame shall breathe,
But even his mother shall uncharge the practice
And call it accident.

LAERTES My lord, I will be rul'd;
The rather, if you could devise it so
That I might be the organ.

KING It falls right.
You have been talk'd of since your travel much,
And that in Hamlet's hearing, for a quality
Wherein they say you shine. Your sum of parts
Did not together pluck such envy from him
As did that one; and that, in my regard,
Of the unworthiest siege.

LAERTES What part is that, my lord?

KING A very riband in the cap of youth—
Yet needful too; for youth no less becomes
The light and careless livery that it wears
Than settled age his sables and his weeds,
Importing health and graveness. Two months since
Here was a gentleman of Normandy.
I have seen myself, and serv'd against, the French,
And they can well on horseback; but this gallant
Had witchcraft in't. He grew unto his seat,
And to such wondrous doing brought his horse
As had he been incorps'd and demi-natur'd
With the brave beast. So far he topp'd my thought

51 *abuse*, trick.

68 *uncharge the practice*, accept what happens.
77 *siege*, rank.
88 *incorps'd and demi-natur'd*, a part of the horse and thus a kind of half-man, half-horse.

That I, in forgery of shapes and tricks,
Come short of what he did.

LAERTES A Norman was't?

KING A Norman.

LAERTES Upon my life, Lamound.

KING The very same.

LAERTES I know him well. He is the brooch indeed
And gem of all the nation.

KING He made confession of you;
And gave you such a masterly report
For art and exercise in your defence,
And for your rapier most especially,
That he cried out 'twould be a sight indeed
If one could match you. The scrimers of their nation
He swore had neither motion, guard, nor eye,
If you oppos'd them. Sir, this report of his
Did Hamlet so envenom with his envy
That he could nothing do but wish and beg
Your sudden coming o'er to play with you.
Now, out of this—

LAERTES What out of this, my lord?

KING Laertes, was your father dear to you?
Or are you like the painting of a sorrow,
A face without a heart?

LAERTES Why ask you this?

KING Not that I think you did not love your father;
But that I know love is begun by time,
And that I see, in passages of proof,
Time qualifies the spark and fire of it.
There lives within the very flame of love
A kind of wick or snuff that will abate it;
And nothing is at a like goodness still;
For goodness, growing to a plurisy,
Dies in his own too-much. That we would do,
We should do when we would; for this "would" changes,
And hath abatements and delays as many
As there are tongues, are hands, are accidents;
And then this "should" is like a spendthrift sigh,
That hurts by easing. But to the quick o' th' ulcer!
Hamlet comes back. What would you undertake
To show yourself your father's son in deed
More than in words?

LAERTES To cut his throat i' th' church!

KING No place indeed should murther sanctuarize;
Revenge should have no bounds. But, good Laertes,
Will you do this? Keep close within your chamber.
Hamlet return'd shall know you are come home.
We'll put on those shall praise your excellence
And set a double varnish on the fame
The Frenchman gave you; bring you in fine together
And wager on your heads. He, being remiss
Most generous, and free from all contriving,
Will not peruse the foils; so that with ease,
Or with a little shuffling, you may choose
A sword unbated, and, in a pass of practice,
Requite him for your father.

LAERTES I will do't!
And for that purpose I'll anoint my sword.
I bought an unction of a mountebank,
So mortal that, but dip a knife in it,
Where it draws blood no cataplasm so rare,
Collected from all simples that have virtue
Under the moon, can save the thing from death
This is but scratch'd withal. I'll touch my point
With this contagion, that, if I gall him slightly,
It may be death.

KING Let's further think of this,
Weigh what convenience both of time and means
May fit us to our shape. If this should fail,
And that our drift look through our bad performance,
'Twere better not assay'd. Therefore this project
Should have a back or second, that might hold
If this did blast in proof. Soft! let me see.
We'll make a solemn wager on your cunnings—
I ha't!
When in your motion you are hot and dry—

101 *scrimers,* fencers.
118 *plurisy,* overabundance.

135 *remiss,* easygoing.
138 *shuffling,* trickery.
142 *mountebank,* medicine man.
144 *cataplasm,* poultice.
148 *gall,* break the skin.
155 *blast in proof,* blow up when tested.

As make your bouts more violent to that end—
And that he calls for drink, I'll have prepar'd him
A chalice for the nonce; whereon but sipping,
If he by chance escape your venom'd stuck,
Our purpose may hold there.—But stay, what noise?

[*Enter* QUEEN.]

How now, sweet queen?

QUEEN One woe doth tread upon another's heel,
So fast they follow. Your sister's drown'd, Laertes.

LAERTES Drown'd! O, where?

QUEEN There is a willow grows aslant a brook,
That shows his hoar leaves in the glassy stream.
There with fantastic garlands did she come
Of crowflowers, nettles, daisies, and long purples
That liberal shepherds give a grosser name,
But our cold maids do dead men's fingers call them.
There on the pendent boughs her coronet weeds
Clamb'ring to hang, an envious sliver broke,
When down her weedy trophies and herself
Fell in the weeping brook. Her clothes spread wide
And, mermaid-like, awhile they bore her up;
Which time she chaunted snatches of old tunes,
As one incapable of her own distress,
Or like a creature native and indued
Unto that element; but long it could not be
Till that her garments, heavy with their drink,
Pull'd the poor wretch from her melodious lay
To muddy death.

LAERTES Alas, then she is drown'd?

QUEEN Drown'd, drown'd.

LAERTES Too much of water hast thou, poor Ophelia,
And therefore I forbid my tears; but yet
It is our trick; nature her custom holds,
Let shame say what it will. When these are gone,
The woman will be out. Adieu, my lord.
I have a speech of fire, that fain would blaze
But that this folly douts it. [*Exit.*]

KING Let's follow, Gertrude.
How much I had to do to calm his rage!
Now fear I this will give it start again;
Therefore let's follow.

[*Exeunt.*]

ACT V

Scene I

[*Elsinore. A churchyard.*]

[*Enter two* CLOWNS (*with spades and pickaxes*).]

CLOWN Is she to be buried in Christian burial when she wilfully seeks her own salvation?

OTHER I tell thee she is; therefore make her grave straight. The crowner hath sate on her, and finds it Christian burial.

CLOWN How can that be, unless she drown'd herself in her own defence?

OTHER Why, 'tis found so.

CLOWN It must be *se offendendo*; it cannot be else. For here lies the point: if I drown myself wittingly, it argues an act; and an act hath three branches—it is to act, to do, and to perform; argal, she drown'd herself wittingly.

OTHER Nay, but hear you, Goodman Delver!

CLOWN Give me leave. Here lies the water; good. Here stands the man; good. If the man go to this water and drown himself, it is, will he nill he, he goes—mark you that. But if the water come to him and drown him, he drowns not himself. Argal, he that is not guilty of his own death shortens not his own life.

OTHER But is this law?

CLOWN Ay, marry, is't—crowner's quest law.

OTHER Will you ha' the truth an't? If this had not been a gentlewoman, she should have been buried out o' Christian burial.

CLOWN Why, there thou say'st! And the more

161 *for the nonce,* for the occasion.
162 *stuck,* thrust.
171 *long purples,* orchids.
172 *liberal,* licentious.
175 *envious,* malicious.
180 *incapable,* unwitting.

191 *woman,* coward.
193 *folly douts,* weeping douses.
Clowns, rustics (gravediggers).
4 *crowner,* coroner.
9 *se offendendo,* self-offense (a mistake for *se defendendo,* self-defense).
13 *argal,* therefore (for *ergo*).
17–18 *will he nill he,* willy-nilly.
23 *quest,* inquest.

pity that great folk should have count'nance in this world to drown or hang themselves more than their even-Christen. Come, my spade! There is no ancient gentlemen but gar-d'ners, ditchers, and grave-makers. They hold up Adam's profession.

OTHER Was he a gentleman? 34

CLOWN 'A was the first that ever bore arms.

OTHER Why, he had none.

CLOWN What, art a heathen? How dost thou understand the Scripture? The Scripture says Adam digg'd. Could he dig without arms? I'll put another question to thee. If thou answerest me not to the purpose, confess thyself—

OTHER Go to! 42

CLOWN What is he that builds stronger than either the mason, the shipwright, or the carpenter?

OTHER The gallows-maker; for that frame outlives a thousand tenants. 47

CLOWN I like thy wit well, in good faith. The gallows does well. But how does it well? It does well to those that do ill. Now, thou dost ill to say the gallows is built stronger than the church. Argal, the gallows may do well to thee. To't again, come!

OTHER Who builds stronger than a mason, a shipwright, or a carpenter? 55

CLOWN Ay, tell me that, and unyoke.

OTHER Marry, now I can tell!

CLOWN To't.

OTHER Mass, I cannot tell. 59

[*Enter* HAMLET *and* HORATIO *afar off.*]

CLOWN Cudgel thy brains no more about it, for your dull ass will not mend his pace with beating; and when you are ask'd this question next, say "a grave-maker." The houses he makes lasts till doomsday. Go, get thee to Yaughan; fetch me a stoup of liquor. 66

[*Exit* SECOND CLOWN.]

[(CLOWN *digs and*) *sings.*]

In youth when I did love, did love
Methought it was very sweet;
To contract—O—the time for—a—my behove,
O, methought there—a—was nothing—a—meet. 70

HAMLET Has this fellow no feeling of his business, that he sings at grave-making?

HORATIO Custom hath made it in him a property of easiness.

HAMLET 'Tis e'en so. The hand of little employment hath the daintier sense. 76

CLOWN [*Sings.*]

But age with his stealing steps
Hath clawed me in his clutch,
And hath shipped me intil the land,
As if I had never been such. 80

[*Throws up a skull.*]

HAMLET That skull had a tongue in it, and could sing once. How the knave jowls it to the ground, as if 'twere Cain's jawbone, that did the first murther! This might be the pate of a politician, which this ass now o'erreaches; one that would circumvent God, might it not? 86

HORATIO It might, my lord.

HAMLET Or of a courtier, which could say "Good morrow, sweet lord! How dost thou, good lord?" This might be my Lord Such-a-one, that prais'd my Lord Such-a-one's horse when he meant to beg it—might it not?

HORATIO Ay, my lord. 93

HAMLET Why, e'en so! and now my Lady Worm's, chapless, and knock'd about the mazzard with a sexton's spade. Here's fine revolution, an we had the trick to see't. Did these bones cost no more the breeding but to play at loggets with 'em? Mine ache to think o't.

CLOWN [*Sings.*]

A pickaxe and a spade, a spade, 100
For and a shrouding sheet;
O, a pit of clay for to be made
For such a guest is meet.

[*Throws up* (*another skull*).]

30 *even-Christen,* fellow Christians.
56 *unyoke,* unharness (call it a day).
66 *Yaughan,* John. *stoup,* large mug.
69 *contract . . . behove,* to shorten time to my benefit.
74 *Custom . . . easiness* (long practice in grave digging leaves him with an untroubled mind.)
78 *clawed,* grabbed.
79 *intil,* into.
82 *jowls,* tosses.
85 *o'erreaches,* acts superior to.
95 *chapless,* without a lower jaw.
95–96 *mazzard,* head.
99 *loggets,* a game played with small pieces of wood.

HAMLET There's another. Why may not that be the skull of a lawyer? Where be his quiddits now, his quillets, his cases, his tenures, and his tricks? Why does he suffer this rude knave now to knock him about the sconce with a dirty shovel, and will not tell him of his action of battery? Hum! This fellow might be in's time a great buyer of land, with his statutes, his recognizances, his fines, his double vouchers, his recoveries. Is this the fine of his fines, and the recovery of his recoveries, to have his fine pate full of fine dirt? Will his vouchers vouch him no more of his purchases, and double ones too, than the length and breadth of a pair of indentures? The very conveyances of his lands will scarcely lie in this box; and must th' inheritor himself have no more, ha?

HORATIO Not a jot more, my lord.

HAMLET Is not parchment made of sheepskins?

HORATIO Ay, my lord, and of calveskins too.

HAMLET They are sheep and calves which seek out assurance in that. I will speak to this fellow. Whose grave's this, sirrah?

CLOWN Mine, sir.

[*Sings.*] O, a pit of clay for to be made
For such a guest is meet.

HAMLET I think it be thine indeed for thou liest in't.

CLOWN You lie out on't, sir, and therefore 'tis not yours. For my part, I do not lie in't, yet it is mine.

HAMLET Thou dost lie in't, to be in't and say it is thine. 'Tis for the dead, not for the quick; therefore thou liest.

CLOWN 'Tis a quick lie, sir; 'twill away again from me to you.

HAMLET What man dost thou dig it for?

CLOWN For no man, sir.

HAMLET What woman then?

CLOWN For none neither.

HAMLET Who is to be buried in't?

CLOWN One that was a woman, sir; but, rest her soul, she's dead.

HAMLET How absolute the knave is! We must speak by the card, or equivocation will undo us. By the Lord, Horatio, this three years I have taken note of it, the age is grown so picked that the toe of the peasant comes so near the heel of the courtier he galls his kibe. —How long hast thou been a grave-maker?

CLOWN Of all the days i' th' year, I came to't that day that our last king Hamlet overcame Fortinbras.

HAMLET How long is that since?

CLOWN Cannot you tell that? Every fool can tell that. It was the very day that young Hamlet was born—he that is mad, and sent into England.

HAMLET Ay, marry, why was he sent into England?

CLOWN Why, because 'a was mad. 'A shall recover his wits there; or, if 'a do not, 'tis no great matter there.

HAMLET Why?

CLOWN 'Twill not be seen in him there. There the men are as mad as he.

HAMLET How came he mad?

CLOWN Very strangely, they say.

HAMLET How strangely?

CLOWN Faith, e'en with losing his wits.

HAMLET Upon what ground?

CLOWN Why, here in Denmark. I have been sexton here, man and boy, thirty years.

HAMLET How long will a man lie i' th' earth ere he rot?

CLOWN Faith, if 'a be not rotten before 'a die (as we have many pocky corses now-a-days that will scarce hold the laying in), 'a will last you some eight year or nine year. A tanner will last you nine year.

HAMLET Why he more than another?

CLOWN Why, sir, his hide is so tann'd with his trade that 'a will keep out water a great while; and your water is a sore decayer of your whoreson dead body. Here's a skull now. This skull hath lien you i' th' earth three-and-twenty years.

HAMLET Whose was it?

CLOWN A whoreson mad fellow's it was. Whose do you think it was?

HAMLET Nay, I know not.

CLOWN A pestilence on him for a mad rogue! 'A pour'd a flagon of Rhenish on my head

105–106 *quiddits . . . quillets,* tricky definitions . . . quibbles.
108 *sconce,* pate.
113 *fine,* end, result.
118 *indentures,* contracts.
137 *quick,* alive.
149 *by the card,* accurately.
152 *so picked,* so refined.
153 ***galls his kibe,*** rubs raw the chilblains on his heel.

once. This same skull, sir, was Yorick's skull, the King's jester.

HAMLET This?

CLOWN E'en that.

HAMLET Let me see. [*Takes the skull.*] Alas, poor Yorick! I knew him, Horatio. A fellow of infinite jest, of most excellent fancy. He hath borne me on his back a thousand times. And now how abhorred in my imagination it is! My gorge rises at it. Here hung those lips that I have kiss'd I know not how oft. Where be your gibes now? your gambols? your songs? your flashes of merriment that were wont to set the table on a roar? Not one now, to mock your own grinning? Quite chapfall'n? Now get you to my lady's chamber, and tell her, let her paint an inch thick, to this favour she must come. Make her laugh at that. Prithee, Horatio, tell me one thing.

HORATIO What's that, my lord?

HAMLET Dost thou think Alexander look'd o' this fashion i' th' earth?

HORATIO E'en so.

HAMLET And smelt so? Pah!

[*Puts down the skull.*]

HORATIO E'en so, my lord.

HAMLET To what base uses we may return, Horatio! Why may not imagination trace the noble dust of Alexander till he find it stopping a bunghole?

HORATIO 'Twere to consider too curiously, to consider so.

HAMLET No, faith, not a jot; but to follow him thither with modesty enough, and likelihood to lead it; as thus: Alexander died, Alexander was buried, Alexander returneth into dust; the dust is earth; of earth we make loam; and why of that loam (whereto he was converted) might they not stop a beer barrel?
Imperious Cæsar, dead and turn'd to clay,
Might stop a hole to keep the wind away.
O, that that earth which kept the world in awe
Should patch a wall t' expel the winter's flaw!
But soft! but soft! aside! Here comes the King—

[*Enter* (PRIESTS *with*) *a coffin* (*in funeral procession*), KING, QUEEN, LAERTES, *with* LORDS *attendant.*]

The Queen, the courtiers. Who is this they follow?
And with such maimed rites? This doth betoken
The corse they follow did with desp'rate hand
Fordo it own life. 'Twas of some estate.
Couch we awhile, and mark.

[*Retires with* HORATIO.]

LAERTES What ceremony else?

HAMLET That is Laertes,
A very noble youth. Mark.

LAERTES What ceremony else?

PRIEST Her obsequies have been as far enlarg'd
As we have warranty. Her death was doubtful;
And, but that great command o'ersways the order,
She should in ground unsanctified have lodg'd
Till the last trumpet. For charitable prayers,
Shards, flints, and pebbles should be thrown on her.
Yet here she is allow'd her virgin crants,
Her maiden strewments, and the bringing home
Of bell and burial.

LAERTES Must there no more be done?

PRIEST No more be done.
We should profane the service of the dead
To sing a requiem and such rest to her
As to peace-parted souls.

LAERTES Lay her i' th' earth;
And from her fair and unpolluted flesh
May violets spring! I tell thee, churlish priest,
A minist'ring angel shall my sister be
When thou liest howling.

HAMLET What, the fair Ophelia?

QUEEN Sweets to the sweet! Farewell.

[*Scatters flowers.*]

I hop'd thou shouldst have been my Hamlet's wife;
I thought thy bride-bed to have deck'd, sweet maid,
And not have strew'd thy grave.

LAERTES O, treble woe
Fall ten times treble on that cursed head
Whose wicked deed thy most ingenious sense
Depriv'd thee of! Hold off the earth awhile,
Till I have caught her once more in mine arms.

242 *maimed,* incomplete.
254 *shards,* pieces of broken pottery.
255 *crants,* garland.
271 *ingenious sense,* keen intellect.

[*Leaps in the grave.*]
Now pile your dust upon the quick and dead
Till of this flat mountain you have made
T' o'ertop old Pelion or the skyish head
Of blue Olympus.

HAMLET [*Comes forward.*] What is he whose grief
Bears such an emphasis? whose phrase of sorrow
Conjures the wand'ring stars, and makes them stand
Like wonder-wounded hearers? This is I,
Hamlet the Dane. [*Leaps in after Laertes.*]

LAERTES The devil take thy soul!
[*Grapples with him.*]

HAMLET Thou pray'st not well.
I prithee take thy fingers from my throat;
For, though I am not splenitive and rash,
Yet have I in me something dangerous,
Which let thy wisdom fear. Hold off thy hand!

KING Pluck them asunder.

QUEEN Hamlet, Hamlet!

ALL Gentlemen!

HORATIO Good my lord, be quiet.

[*The* ATTENDANTS *part them, and they come out of the grave.*]

HAMLET Why, I will fight with him upon this theme
Until my eyelids will no longer wag.

QUEEN O my son, what theme?

HAMLET I lov'd Ophelia. Forty thousand brothers
Could not (with all their quantity of love)
Make up my sum. What wilt thou do for her?

KING O, he is mad, Laertes.

QUEEN For love of God, forbear him!

HAMLET 'Swounds, show me what thou't do.
Woo't weep? woo't fight? woo't fast? woo't tear thyself?
Woo't drink up esill? eat a crocodile?
I'll do't. Dost thou come here to whine?
To outface me with leaping in her grave?
Be buried quick with her, and so will I.
And if thou prate of mountains, let them throw
Millions of acres on us, till our ground,
Singeing his pate against the burning zone,
Make Ossa like a wart! Nay, an thou'lt mouth,
I'll rant as well as thou.

QUEEN This is mere madness;
And thus a while the fit will work on him.
Anon, as patient as the female dove
When that her golden couplets are dis-clos'd,
His silence will sit drooping.

HAMLET Hear you, sir!
What is the reason that you use me thus?
I lov'd you ever. But it is no matter.
Let Hercules himself do what he may,
The cat will mew, and dog will have his day.
[*Exit.*]

KING I pray thee, good Horatio, wait upon him.
[*Exit* HORATIO.]
[*To* LAERTES.] Strengthen your patience in our last night's speech.
We'll put the matter to the present push.—
Good Gertrude, set some watch over your son.—
This grave shall have a living monument.
An hour of quiet shortly shall we see;
Till then in patience our proceeding be.
[*Exeunt.*]

Scene II [*Elsinore. A hall in the Castle.*]

[*Enter* HAMLET *and* HORATIO.]

HAMLET So much for this, sir; now shall you see the other.
You do remember all the circumstance?

HORATIO Remember it, my lord!

HAMLET Sir, in my heart there was a kind of fighting
That would not let me sleep. Methought I lay
Worse than the mutines in the bilboes. Rashly—
And prais'd be rashness for it; let us know,
Our indiscretion sometime serves us well

276 *Pelion,* a high mountain (on which giants piled Mt. Ossa).
279 *conjures,* affects.
284 *splenitive,* easily angered.
299 *esill,* vinegar.
305 *burning zone,* celestial area bounded by the Tropics of Cancer and Capricorn.
318 *to the present push,* into immediate action.
6 *mutines,* mutineers. *bilboes,* irons (stocks).
7 *rashness,* unreasoned action.

When our deep plots do pall; and that should learn us
There's a divinity that shapes our ends,
Rough-hew them how we will—

HORATIO That is most certain.

HAMLET Up from my cabin,
My sea-gown scarf'd about me, in the dark
Grop'd I to find out them; had my desire,
Finger'd their packet, and in fine withdrew
To mine own room again; making so bold
(My fears forgetting manners) to unseal
Their grand commission; where I found, Horatio
(O royal knavery!), an exact command,
Larded with many several sorts of reasons,
Importing Denmark's health, and England's too,
With, hoo! such bugs and goblins in my life—
That, on the supervise, no leisure bated,
No, not to stay the grinding of the axe,
My head should be struck off.

HORATIO Is't possible?

HAMLET Here's the commission; read it at more leisure.
But wilt thou hear me how I did proceed?

HORATIO I beseech you.

HAMLET Being thus benetted round with villanies,
Or I could make a prologue to my brains,
They had begun the play. I sat me down;
Devis'd a new commission; wrote it fair.
I once did hold it, as our statists do,
A baseness to write fair, and labour'd much
How to forget that learning; but, sir, now
It did me yeoman's service. Wilt thou know
Th' effect of what I wrote?

HORATIO Ay, good my lord.

HAMLET An earnest conjuration from the King,
As England was his faithful tributary,
As love between them like the palm might flourish,
As peace should still her wheaten garland wear
And stand a comma 'tween their amities,
And many such-like as's of great charge,
That, on the view and knowing of these contents,
Without debatement further, more or less,
He should the bearers put to sudden death,
Not shriving time allow'd.

HORATIO How was this seal'd?

HAMLET Why, even in that was heaven ordinant.
I had my father's signet in my purse,
Which was the model of that Danish seal;
Folded the writ up in the form of th' other,
Subscrib'd it, gave't th' impression, plac'd it safely,
The changeling never known. Now, the next day
Was our sea-fight; and what to this was sequent
Thou know'st already.

HORATIO So Guildenstern and Rosencrantz go to't.

HAMLET Why, man, they did make love to this employment!
They are not near my conscience; their defeat
Does by their own insinuation grow.
'Tis dangerous when the baser nature comes
Between the pass and fell incensed points
Of mighty opposites.

HORATIO Why, what a king is this!

HAMLET Does it not, thinks't thee, stand me now upon
He that hath kill'd my king, and whor'd my mother;
Popp'd in between th' election and my hopes;
Thrown out his angle for my proper life,
And with such coz'nage—is't not perfect conscience
To quit him with this arm? And is't not to be damn'd
To let this canker of our nature come
In further evil?

HORATIO It must be shortly known to him from England
What is the issue of the business there.

HAMLET It will be short; the interim is mine,
And a man's life's no more than to say "one."
But I am very sorry, good Horatio,
That to Laertes I forgot myself;
For by the image of my cause I see
The portraiture of his. I'll court his favours.

[9] *deep plots,* carefully planned actions.
[15] *finger'd,* stole.
[22] *bugs,* bugbears.
[23] *on the supervise,* on the reading of the document.
[30] *or,* ere (before).
[47] *shriving time,* time for confession and absolution.
[48] *ordinant,* helpful.
[58] *defeat,* destruction.
[59] *their own insinuation,* their own efforts to become involved in the plot.

But sure the bravery of his grief did put me
Into a tow'ring passion.

HORATIO Peace! Who comes here?

[*Enter young* OSRIC, *a courtier.*]

OSRIC Your lordship is right welcome back to Denmark.

HAMLET I humbly thank you, sir. [*Aside to* HORATIO.] Dost know this waterfly?

HORATIO [*Aside to* HAMLET.] No, my good lord.

HAMLET [*Aside to* HORATIO.] Thy state is the more gracious; for 'tis a vice to know him. He hath much land, and fertile. Let a beast be lord of beasts, and his crib shall stand at the king's mess. 'Tis a chough; but, as I say, spacious in the possession of dirt.

OSRIC Sweet lord, if your lordship were at leisure, I should impart a thing to you from his Majesty.

HAMLET I will receive it, sir, with all diligence of spirit. Put your bonnet to his right use. 'Tis for the head.

OSRIC I thank your lordship, it is very hot.

HAMLET No, believe me, 'tis very cold; the wind is northerly.

OSRIC It is indifferent cold, my lord, indeed.

HAMLET But yet methinks it is very sultry and hot for my complexion.

OSRIC Exceedingly, my lord; it is very sultry, as 'twere—I cannot tell how. But, my lord, his Majesty bade me signify to you that he has laid a great wager on your head. Sir, this is the matter—

HAMLET I beseech you remember.

[HAMLET *moves him to put on his hat.*]

OSRIC Nay, good my lord; for mine ease, in good faith. Sir, here is newly come to court Laertes; believe me, an absolute gentleman, full of most excellent differences, of very soft society and great showing. Indeed, to speak feelingly of him, he is the card or calendar of gentry; for you shall find in him the continent of what part a gentleman would see.

HAMLET Sir, his definement suffers no perdition in you; though, I know, to divide him inventorially would dozy th' arithmetic of memory, and yet but yaw neither in respect of his quick sail. But, in the verity of extolment, I take him to be a soul of great article, and his infusion of such dearth and rareness as, to make true diction of him, his semblable is his mirror, and who else would trace him, his umbrage, nothing more.

OSRIC Your lordship speaks most infallibly of him.

HAMLET The concernancy, sir? Why do we wrap the gentleman in our more rawer breath?

OSRIC Sir?

HORATIO [*Aside to* HAMLET.] Is't not possible to understand in another tongue? You will do't, sir, really.

HAMLET What imports the nomination of this gentleman?

OSRIC Of Laertes?

HORATIO [*Aside.*] His purse is empty already. All's golden words are spent.

HAMLET Of him, sir.

OSRIC I know you are ignorant—

HAMLET I would you did, sir; yet, in faith, if you did, it would not much approve me. Well, sir?

OSRIC You are ignorant of what excellence Laertes is—

HAMLET I dare not confess that, lest I should compare with him in excellence; but to know a man well were to know himself.

OSRIC I mean, sir, for his weapon; but in the imputation laid on him by them, in his meed he's unfellowed.

HAMLET What's his weapon?

OSRIC Rapier and dagger.

HAMLET That's two of his weapons—but well.

OSRIC The King, sir, hath wager'd with him six Barbary horses; against the which he has impon'd, as I take it, six French rapiers and poniards, with their assigns, as girdle, hangers, and so. Three of the carriages, in faith, are very dear to fancy, very responsive to the hilts, most delicate carriages, and of very liberal conceit.

HAMLET What call you the carriages?

HORATIO [*Aside to* HAMLET.] I knew you must

84 *waterfly,* gorgeous, flitty creature.
90 *chough,* jackdaw (chatterer).
113 *differences,* superiorities (that set him apart).
120 *dozy,* confuse.
121 *yaw,* steer badly (and drop behind).
124 *his infusion,* his natural quality.
125 *semblable,* seeming.
127 *umbrage,* shadow.
152–153 *meed,* competence. *unfellowed,* nobody can equal.
159 *impon'd,* put up.
163–164 *liberal conceit,* handsomely designed.

be edified by the margent ere you had done.

OSRIC The carriages, sir, are the hangers.

HAMLET The phrase would be more germane to the matter if we could carry cannon by our sides. I would it might be hangers till then. But on! Six Barbary horses against six French swords, their assigns, and three liberal-conceited carriages: that's the French bet against the Danish. Why is this all impon'd, as you call it?

OSRIC The King, sir, hath laid that, in a dozen passes between yourself and him, he shall not exceed you three hits; he hath laid on twelve for nine, and it would come to immediate trial if your lordship would vouchsafe the answer.

HAMLET How if I answer no?

OSRIC I mean, my lord, the opposition of your person in trial.

HAMLET Sir, I will walk here in the hall. If it please his Majesty, it is the breathing time of day with me. Let the foils be brought, the gentleman willing, and the King hold his purpose, I will win for him if I can; if not, I will gain nothing but my shame and the odd hits.

OSRIC Shall I redeliver you e'en so?

HAMLET To this effect, sir, after what flourish your nature will.

OSRIC I commend my duty to your lordship.

HAMLET Yours, yours. [*Exit* OSRIC.] He does well to commend it himself; there are no tongues else for's turn.

HORATIO This lapwing runs away with the shell on his head.

HAMLET He did comply with his dug before he suck'd it. Thus has he, and many more of the same bevy that I know the drossy age dotes on, only got the tune of the time and outward habit of encounter—a kind of yesty collection, which carries them through and through the most fann'd and winnowed opinions; and do but blow them to their trial—the bubbles are out.

[*Enter a* LORD.]

LORD My lord, his Majesty commended him to you by young Osric, who brings back to him, that you attend him in the hall. He sends to know if your pleasure hold to play with Laertes, or that you will take longer time.

HAMLET I am constant to my purposes; they follow the King's pleasure. If his fitness speaks, mine is ready; now or whensoever, provided I be so able as now.

LORD The King and Queen and all are coming down.

HAMLET In happy time.

LORD The Queen desires you to use some gentle entertainment to Laertes before you fall to play.

HAMLET She well instructs me.

[*Exit* LORD.]

HORATIO You will lose this wager, my lord.

HAMLET I do not think so. Since he went into France I have been in continual practice. I shall win at the odds. But thou wouldst not think how ill all's here about my heart. But it is no matter.

HORATIO Nay, good my lord—

HAMLET It is but foolery; but it is such a kind of gaingiving as would perhaps trouble a woman.

HORATIO If your mind dislike anything, obey it. I will forestall their repair hither and say you are not fit.

HAMLET Not a whit, we defy augury; there's a special providence in the fall of a sparrow. If it be now, 'tis not to come; if it be not to come, it will be now; if it be not now, yet it will come: the readiness is all. Since no man knows aught of what he leaves, what is't to leave betimes? Let be.

[*Enter* KING, QUEEN, LAERTES, (OSRIC), *and* LORDS, *with other* ATTENDANTS *with foils and gauntlets. A Table and flagons of wine on it.*]

KING Come, Hamlet, come, and take this hand from me.

[*The* KING *puts* LAERTES' *hand into* HAMLET'S.]

HAMLET Give me your pardon, sir. I have done you wrong;
But pardon't, as you are a gentleman.

167 *edified by the margent,* impressed by the marginal note.
172–176 (The terms of the wager are made deliberately intricate so that Hamlet will think the duel is regarded by Claudius simply as a sporting event.)
186 *breathing time,* time for physical exercise.
198–199 *lapwing . . . shell,* this (precocious) bird . . . (gets going before it has lost part of the) shell.
202 *drossy,* degenerate.
204 *yesty,* frothy.
206 *fann'd and winnowed,* sophisticated to the point of absurdity.

222 *entertainment,* cordiality. *fall to play,* start the fencing.
232 *gaingiving,* portent or omen.

This presence knows,
And you must needs have heard, how I am punish'd
With sore distraction. What I have done
That might your nature, honour, and exception
Roughly awake, I here proclaim was madness.
Was't Hamlet wrong'd Laertes? Never Hamlet.
If Hamlet from himself be ta'en away,
And when he's not himself does wrong Laertes,
Then Hamlet does it not, Hamlet denies it.
Who does it, then? His madness. If't be so,
Hamlet is of the faction that is wrong'd;
His madness is poor Hamlet's enemy.
Sir, in this audience,
Let my disclaiming from a purpos'd evil
Free me so far in your most generous thoughts
That I have shot my arrow o'er the house
And hurt my brother.

LAERTES I am satisfied in nature,
Whose motive in this case should stir me most
To my revenge. But in my terms of honour
I stand aloof, and will no reconcilement
Till by some elder masters of known honour
I have a voice and precedent of peace
To keep my name ungor'd. But till that time
I do receive your offer'd love like love,
And will not wrong it.

HAMLET I embrace it freely,
And will this brother's wager frankly play.
Give us the foils. Come on.

LAERTES Come, one for me.

HAMLET I'll be your foil, Laertes. In mine ignorance
Your skill shall, like a star i' th' darkest night
Stick fiery off indeed.

LAERTES You mock me, sir.

HAMLET No, by this hand.

KING Give them the foils, young Osric. Cousin Hamlet,
You know the wager?

HAMLET Very well, my lord.
Your Grace has laid the odds o' th' weaker side.

KING I do not fear it, I have seen you both;
But since he is better'd, we have therefore odds.

LAERTES This is too heavy; let me see another.

HAMLET This likes me well. These foils have all a length? [*Prepare to play.*]

OSRIC Ay, my good lord.

KING Set me the stoups of wine upon that table.
If Hamlet give the first or second hit,
Or quit in answer of the third exchange,
Let all the battlements their ordnance fire;
The King shall drink to Hamlet's better breath,
And in the cup an union shall he throw
Richer than that which four successive kings
In Denmark's crown have worn. Give me the cups;
And let the kettle to the trumpet speak,
The trumpet to the cannoneer without,
The cannons to the heavens, the heaven to earth,
"Now the King drinks to Hamlet." Come, begin.
And you the judges, bear a wary eye.

HAMLET Come on, sir.

LAERTES Come, my lord. [*They play.*]

HAMLET One.

LAERTES No.

HAMLET Judgment!

OSRIC A hit, a very palpable hit.

LAERTES Well, again!

KING Stay, give me drink. Hamlet, this pearl is thine;
Here's to thy health.

[*Drum; trumpets sound; a piece goes off* (*within*).]

Give him the cup.

HAMLET I'll play this bout first; set it by awhile.
Come. [*They play.*] Another hit. What say you?

LAERTES A touch, a touch; I do confess't.

KING Our son shall win.

QUEEN He's fat, and scant of breath.
Here, Hamlet, take my napkin, rub thy brows.
The Queen carouses to thy fortune, Hamlet.

247 *this presence,* the King and Queen.
250 *exception,* resentment.
267 *elder masters,* authorities (on what constitutes a proper defense of one's honor).
291 *stoups,* large mugs.
296 *an union,* a large, perfect pearl.
299 *kettle,* kettledrum.
311 *fat,* soft.

HAMLET Good madam!
KING Gertrude, do not drink.
QUEEN I will, my lord; I pray you pardon me. [*Drinks.*]
KING [*Aside.*] It is the poison'd cup; it is too late.
HAMLET I dare not drink yet, madam; by-and-by.
QUEEN Come, let me wipe thy face.
LAERTES My lord, I'll hit him now.
KING I do not think't.
LAERTES [*Aside.*] And yet it is almost against my conscience.
HAMLET Come for the third, Laertes! You but dally.
I pray you pass with your best violence;
I am afeard you make a wanton of me.
LAERTES Say you so? Come on. [*Play.*]
OSRIC Nothing neither way.
LAERTES Have at you now!
[(LAERTES *wounds* HAMLET; *then,*) *in scuffling, they change rapiers* (*and* HAMLET *wounds* LAERTES).]
KING Part them! They are incens'd.
HAMLET Nay come! again! [*The* QUEEN *falls.*]
OSRIC Look to the Queen there, ho!
HORATIO They bleed on both sides. How is it, my lord?
OSRIC How is't, Laertes?
LAERTES Why, as a woodcock to mine own springe, Osric.
I am justly kill'd with mine own treachery.
HAMLET How does the Queen?
KING She sounds to see them bleed.
QUEEN No, no! the drink, the drink! O my dear Hamlet!
The drink, the drink! I am poison'd. [*Dies.*]
HAMLET O villany! Ho! let the door be lock'd.
Treachery! Seek it out.
[LAERTES *falls.*]
LAERTES It is here, Hamlet. Hamlet, thou art slain;
No med'cine in the world can do thee good.
In thee there is not half an hour of life.
The treacherous instrument is in thy hand,
Unbated and envenom'd. The foul practice
Hath turn'd itself on me. Lo, here I lie,
Never to rise again. Thy mother's poison'd.
I can no more. The King, the King's to blame.
HAMLET The point envenom'd too?
Then, venom, to thy work. [*Hurts the* KING.]
ALL Treason! treason!
KING O, yet defend me, friends! I am but hurt.
HAMLET Here, thou incestuous, murd'rous, damned Dane,
Drink off this potion! Is thy union here?
Follow my mother. [KING *dies.*]
LAERTES He is justly serv'd.
It is a poison temper'd by himself.
Exchange forgiveness with me, noble Hamlet.
Mine and my father's death come not upon thee,
Nor thine on me! [*Dies.*]
HAMLET Heaven make thee free of it! I follow thee.
I am dead, Horatio. Wretched queen, adieu!
You that look pale and tremble at this chance,
That are but mutes or audience to this act,
Had I but time (as this fell sergeant, Death,
Is strict in his arrest) O, I could tell you—
But let it be. Horatio, I am dead;
Thou liv'st; report me and my cause aright
To the unsatisfied.
HORATIO Never believe it.
I am more an antique Roman than a Dane.
Here's yet some liquor left.
HAMLET As th'art a man,
Give me the cup. Let go! By heaven, I'll ha't.
O good Horatio, what a wounded name
(Things standing thus unknown) shall live behind me!
If thou didst ever hold me in thy heart,
Absent thee from felicity awhile,
And in this harsh world draw thy breath in pain,
To tell my story.
[*March afar off, and shot within.*]
What warlike noise is this?
OSRIC Young Fortinbras, with conquest come from Poland,
To the ambassadors of England gives
This warlike volley.
HAMLET O, I die, Horatio!
The potent poison quite o'ercrows my spirit.
I cannot live to hear the news from England,
But I do prophesy th' election lights
On Fortinbras. He has my dying voice.
So tell him, with th' occurrents, more and less,
Which have solicited—the rest is silence.
[*Dies.*]

323 *make a wanton of me,* treat me too carelessly.
332 *sounds,* swoons.
363 *the unsatisfied,* the uninformed.

HORATIO Now cracks a noble heart. Good night, sweet prince,
And flights of angels sing thee to thy rest!
[*March within.*]
Why does the drum come hither?
[*Enter* FORTINBRAS *and* ENGLISH AMBASSADORS, *with* DRUM, COLOURS, *and* ATTENDANTS.]
FORTINBRAS Where is this sight?
HORATIO What is it you would see?
If aught of woe or wonder, cease your search.
FORTINBRAS This quarry cries on havoc. O proud Death,
What feast is toward in thine eternal cell
That thou so many princes at a shot
So bloodily hast struck?
AMBASSADOR The sight is dismal;
And our affairs from England come too late.
The ears are senseless that should give us hearing
To tell him his commandment is fulfill'd,
That Rosencrantz and Guildenstern are dead.
Where should we have our thanks?
HORATIO Not from his mouth,
Had it th' ability of life to thank you.
He never gave commandment for their death.
But since, so jump upon this bloody question,
You from the Polack wars, and you from England,
Are here arriv'd, give order that these bodies
High on a stage be placed to the view;
And let me speak to th' yet unknowing world
How these things came about. So shall you hear
Of carnal, bloody, and unnatural acts;
Of accidental judgments, casual slaughters;
Of deaths put on by cunning and forc'd cause;
And, in this upshot, purposes mistook
Fall'n on th' inventors' heads. All this can I
Truly deliver.
FORTINBRAS Let us haste to hear it,
And call the noblest to the audience.
For me, with sorrow I embrace my fortune.
I have some rights of memory in this kingdom,
Which now to claim my vantage doth invite me.
HORATIO Of that I shall have also cause to speak,
And from his mouth whose voice will draw on more.

387 *havoc*, massacre.
398 *so jump*, so opportunely.

But let this same be presently perform'd,
Even while men's minds are wild, lest more mischance
On plots and errors happen.
FORTINBRAS Let four captains
Bear Hamlet like a soldier to the stage;
For he was likely, had he been put on,
To have prov'd most royally; and for his passage
The soldiers' music and the rites of war
Speak loudly for him.
Take up the bodies. Such a sight as this
Becomes the field, but here shows much amiss.
Go, bid the soldiers shoot.
[*Exeunt marching, after the which a peal of ordinance are shot off.*]

Comments and Questions

T. S. Eliot has observed that in Shakespeare's plays there are "several levels of significance. For the simplest auditors there is the plot, for the more thoughtful the characters and conflict of characters, for the more literary the words and phrasing, for the more musically sensitive the rhythm, and for auditors of greater sensitivity and understanding a meaning which reveals itself gradually." He adds that this classification is not clear cut and that "the sensitiveness of every auditor is acted upon by all these elements at once, though in different degrees of consciousness." (*The Use of Poetry and the Use of Criticism,* Cambridge, Mass.: Harvard University Press, 1933.) The chief point here is that by digging deep into a Shakespearian play one may discover how virtually inexhaustible are the treasures. Explorations into *Hamlet,* one of the richest of plays, will reveal all the layers of interest observed by T. S. Eliot. One may start by looking next at H. B. Charlton's essay on *Hamlet,* p. 706. After reading Charlton's analysis, one may profitably use the outline for play dissection set forth on pp. 410–411.

If one allows *Hamlet* simply to flow over one's receptive sensibilities, the effect is overwhelmingly powerful. It is tempting to suggest that the reader follow this course, for close, sharp questioning will surely reveal some disturbing flaws in the play. Charlton, in his analysis of the play, interprets without attempting to justify everything Shakespeare has done.

1. The working out of the action in *Hamlet* is intricate, but the central problem is simple indeed, as Charlton puts it: "A son is called upon to kill his father's murderer" (p. 706). What, then, is the central problem, the problem that allowed Shakespeare to create an absorbing, five-act play?

2. All drama rests upon conflict. In this play, the overt conflict involves which two characters? Hamlet is immobilized by an inner conflict. What about Claudius? Is he also immobilized?

3. Is Claudius all evil, Hamlet all virtue? Consider Hamlet's words after he killed Polonius, his treatment of Ophelia, his desire not only to kill Claudius but to send his soul to hell. Does Claudius have any saving grace?

4. Shakespeare rarely neglected his minor characters. What sort of individuals are Polonius, Laertes, and even such lesser persons as Rosencrantz, Guildenstern, and Osric? Gertrude has been described as a "sheep in the sun." What does that phrase suggest?

5. Does one have the feeling that inevitable doom hangs over Hamlet as it did over Antigone? Discuss the differences.

6. In Act V, scene ii, ll. 81–195, Hamlet indulges in word-sparring with a dandified courtier, Osric. The exchange is amusing, but is it dramatically justified?

7. Ophelia, pure and innocent, in her madness sings some bawdy verses. Comment.

8. Virtually every critic of Shakespeare has attempted to "pluck out the heart" of Hamlet's mystery. Do you think there is a mystery? If so, what do you think it is?

MOLIÈRE (JEAN-BAPTISTE POQUELIN)
1622–1673

The Physician in Spite of Himself

CHARACTERS (in order of appearance)

SGANARELLE, *Martine's husband*
MARTINE, *Sganarelle's wife*
M. ROBERT, *Sganarelle's neighbour*
VALÈRE, *Géronte's servant*
LUCAS, *Jacqueline's husband*
GÉRONTE, *Lucinde's father*
JACQUELINE, *Lucas's wife*
LÉANDRE, *Lucinde's lover*
THIBAUT, *peasant*
PERRIN, *Thibaut's son*
LUCINDE, *Géronte's daughter, in love with Léandre*

ACT I [*A Forest.*]

Scene I [SGANARELLE, MARTINE *appearing on the stage, quarrelling*]

SGANARELLE No; I tell you that I will do nothing of the kind. It is for me to speak, and to be master.

MARTINE And I tell you that I will have you live as I like, and that I am not married to you to put up with your freaks.

SGANARELLE Oh! what a nuisance it is to have a wife! Aristotle is perfectly right in saying that a woman is worse than a devil.

MARTINE Look at the clever man with his silly Aristotle!

SGANARELLE Yes, clever indeed. Find me another faggot-binder who can argue upon things as I can, who has served a famous physician for six years, and who, when only a boy, knew his grammar by heart!

MARTINE Plague on the arrant fool.

SGANARELLE Plague on the slut!

MARTINE Cursed be the hour and the day when I took it into my head to say yes.

SGANARELLE Cursed be the cuckold of a notary that made me sign my own ruination.

MARTINE Certainly it well becomes you to complain on that score. Ought you not rather to thank Heaven every minute of the day that you have me for a wife? Did you deserve to marry a woman like me?

SGANARELLE It is true you did me too much honour, and I had great occasion to be satisfied with my wedding-night. Zounds! do not make me open my mouth too wide: I might say certain things . . .

MARTINE Well! What could you say?

SGANARELLE Enough; let us drop the subject. It is enough that we know what we know, and that you were very lucky to meet with me.

MARTINE What do you call very lucky to meet with you? A fellow who will drive me to the hospital—a debauched, deceitful wretch, who gobbles up every farthing I have got!

SGANARELLE That is a lie: I drink part of it.

MARTINE Who sells piecemeal every stick of furniture in the house!

SGANARELLE That is living upon one's means.

MARTINE Who has taken the very bed from under me!

SGANARELLE You will get up all the earlier.

MARTINE In short, who does not leave me a stick in the whole house.

SGANARELLE There will be less trouble in moving.

MARTINE And who from morning to night does nothing but gamble and guzzle.

SGANARELLE That is done in order not to get in the dumps.

MARTINE And what am I to do all the while with my family?

SGANARELLE Whatever you like.

MARTINE I have got four poor children on my hands.

SGANARELLE Put them down.

MARTINE Who keep asking me every moment for bread.

SGANARELLE Whip them. When I have had enough to eat and to drink, every one in the house ought to be satisfied.

MARTINE And do you mean to tell me, you sot, that things can always go on so?

SGANARELLE Wife, let us proceed gently, if you please.

MARTINE That I am to bear forever with your insolence and your debauchery?

SGANARELLE Do not let us get into a passion, wife.

MARTINE And that I do not know the way to bring you back to your duty?

SGANARELLE Wife, you know that I am not very patient, and that my arm is somewhat heavy.

MARTINE I laugh at your threats.

SGANARELLE My sweet wife, my pet, your skin is itching as usual.

MARTINE I will let you see that I am not afraid of you.

SGANARELLE My dearest rib, you have set your heart upon a thrashing.

MARTINE Do you think that I am frightened at your talk?

SGANARELLE Sweet object of my affections, I shall box your ears for you.

MARTINE Drunkard!

SGANARELLE I shall thrash you.

MARTINE Wine-cask!

SGANARELLE I shall pummel you.

MARTINE Infamous wretch!

SGANARELLE I shall curry your skin for you.

MARTINE Wretch! villain! deceiver! cur! scoundrel! gallows-bird! churl! rogue! scamp! thief! . . .

SGANARELLE You will have it, will you? [*Takes a stick and beats her.*]

MARTINE [*Shrieking.*] Help! help! help! help!

SGANARELLE That is the best way of quieting you.

Scene II [M. ROBERT, SGANARELLE, MARTINE.]

M. ROBERT Hulloa, hulloa, hulloa! Fie! What is this? What a disgraceful thing! Plague take the scamp to beat his wife so.

MARTINE [*Her arms akimbo, speaks to* M. ROBERT, *and makes him draw back; at last she gives him a slap on the face.*] I like him to beat me, I do.

M. ROBERT If that is the case, I consent with all my heart.

MARTINE What are you interfering with?

M. ROBERT I am wrong.

MARTINE Is it any of your business?

M. ROBERT You are right.

MARTINE Just look at this impertinent fellow, who wishes to hinder husbands from beating their wives!

M. ROBERT I apologize.

MARTINE What have you got to say to it?

M. ROBERT Nothing.

MARTINE Is it for you to poke your nose into it?

M. ROBERT No.

MARTINE Mind your own business.

M. ROBERT I shall not say another word.

MARTINE It pleases me to be beaten.

M. ROBERT Agreed.

MARTINE It does not hurt you.

M. ROBERT That is true.

MARTINE And you are a fool to interfere with what does not concern you.

M. ROBERT Neighbour, I ask your pardon with all my heart. Go on, thrash and beat your wife as much as you like; I shall help you, if you wish it. [*He goes towards* SGANARELLE, *who also speaks to him, makes him draw back, and beats him with the stick he has been using.*]

SGANARELLE I do not wish it.

M. ROBERT Ah! that is a different thing.

SGANARELLE I will beat her if I like; and I will not beat her if I do not like.

M. ROBERT Very good.

SGANARELLE She is my wife, and not yours.

M. ROBERT Undoubtedly.

SGANARELLE It is not for you to order me about.

M. ROBERT Just so.

SGANARELLE I do not want your help.

M. ROBERT Exactly so.

SGANARELLE And it is like your impertinence to meddle with other people's business. Remember that Cicero says that between the tree and the finger you should not put the bark. [*He drives him away, then comes back to his wife, and says to her, squeezing her hand:*]

Scene III [SGANARELLE, MARTINE.]

SGANARELLE Come, let us make it up. Shake hands.

MARTINE Yes, after having beaten me thus!

SGANARELLE Never mind that. Shake hands.

MARTINE I will not.

SGANARELLE Eh?

MARTINE No.

SGANARELLE Come, wife!

MARTINE I shall not.

SGANARELLE Come, I tell you.

MARTINE I will do nothing of the kind.

SGANARELLE Come, come, come.

MARTINE No; I will be angry.

SGANARELLE Bah! it is a trifle. Do.

MARTINE Leave me alone.

SGANARELLE Shake hands, I tell you.

MARTINE You have treated me too ill.

SGANARELLE Well! I beg your pardon; put your hand there.

MARTINE I forgive you [*Aside, softly.*]; but I shall make you pay for it.

SGANARELLE You are silly to take notice of it; these are trifles that are necessary now and then to keep up good feeling; and five or six strokes of a cudgel between people who love each other, only brighten the affections. There now! I am going to the wood, and I promise you that you shall have more than a hundred faggots to-day.

Scene IV [MARTINE, *alone.*]

Go, my lad, whatever look I may put on, I shall not forget to pay you out; and I am dying to hit upon something to punish you for the blows you gave me. I know well enough that a wife has always the means of being avenged upon her husband; but that is too delicate a punishment for my hangdog; I want a revenge that shall strike home a little more, or it will not pay me for the insult which I have received.

Scene V [VALÈRE, LUCAS, MARTINE.]

LUCAS [*To* VALÈRE, *without seeing* MARTINE.] I'll be blowed but we have undertaken a curious errand; and I do not know, for my part, what we shall get by it.

VALÈRE [*To* LUCAS, *without seeing* MARTINE.] What is the use of grumbling, good foster-father? We are bound to do as our master tells us; and, besides, we have both of us some interest in the health of his daughter, our mistress; for her marriage, which is put off through her illness, will no doubt bring us in something. Horace, who is generous, is the most likely to succeed among her suitors; and although she has shown some inclination for a certain Léandre, you know well enough that her father would never consent to receive him for his son-in-law.

MARTINE [*Musing on one side, thinking herself alone.*] Can I not find out some way of avenging myself?

LUCAS [*To* VALÈRE.] But what an idea has he taken into his head, since the doctors are quite at a loss.

VALÈRE [*To* LUCAS.] You may sometimes find by dint of seeking, what cannot be found at once; and often in the most unlikely spots you may . . .

MARTINE [*Still thinking herself alone.*] Yes; I must pay him out, no matter at what cost. Those cudgel blows lie heavy on my stomach; I cannot digest them; and . . . [*She is saying all this musingly, and as she moves, she comes in contact with the two men.*] Ah, gentlemen, I beg your pardon, I did not notice you, and was puzzling my brain about something that perplexes me.

VALÈRE Every one has his troubles in this world, and we also are looking for something that we should be very glad to find.

MARTINE Is it something in which I can assist you?

VALÈRE Perhaps. We are endeavouring to meet with some clever man, some special physician, who could give some relief to our master's daughter, seized with an illness which has at once deprived her of the use of her tongue. Several physicians have already exhausted all their knowledge on her behalf; but sometimes one may find people with wonderful secrets, and certain peculiar remedies, who very often succeed where others have failed; and that is the sort of man we are looking for.

MARTINE [*Softly and aside.*] Ah! This is an inspiration from Heaven to revenge myself on my rascal. [*Aloud.*] You could never have addressed yourselves to any one more able to find what you want; and we have a man here, the most wonderful fellow in the world for desperate maladies.

VALÈRE Ah! for mercy's sake, where can we meet with him?

MARTINE You will find him just now in that little spot yonder, where he is amusing himself in cutting wood.

LUCAS A doctor who cuts wood!

VALÈRE Who is amusing himself in gathering some simples, you mean to say?

MARTINE No; he is a strange fellow who takes delight in this; a fantastic, eccentric, whimsical man, whom you would never take to be what he really is. He goes about dressed in a most extraordinary fashion, pretends sometimes to be very ignorant, keeps his knowledge to himself, and dislikes nothing so much every day as using the marvellous talents which God has given him for the healing art.

VALÈRE It is a wonderful thing that all these great men have always some whim, some slight grain of madness mixed with their learning.

MARTINE The madness of this man is greater than can be imagined, for sometimes he has to be beaten before he will own his ability; and I warn you beforehand that you will not succeed, that he will never own that he is a physician, unless you take each a stick, and compel him, by dint of blows, to admit at last what he will conceal at first. It is thus that we act when we have need of him.

VALÈRE What a strange delusion!

MARTINE That is true; but, after that, you shall see that he works wonders.

VALÈRE What is his name?

MARTINE His name is Sganarelle. But it is very easy to recognise him. He is a man with a large black beard, and wears a ruff, and a yellow and green coat.

LUCAS A yellow and green coat! He is then a parrot-doctor?

VALÈRE But is it really true that he is as clever as you say?

MARTINE As clever. He is a man who works miracles. About six months ago, a woman was given up by all the other physicians; she was considered dead at least six hours, and they were going to bury her, when they dragged by force the man we are speaking of to her bedside. Having seen her, he poured a small drop of something into her mouth; and at that very instant she rose from her bed, and began immediately to walk in her room as if nothing had happened.

LUCAS Ah!

VALÈRE It must have been a drop of liquid gold.

MARTINE Possibly so. Not more than three weeks ago, a young child, twelve years old, fell from the top of the belfry, and smashed his head, arms, and legs on the stones. No sooner took they our man to it, than he rubbed the whole body with a certain ointment, which he knows how to prepare; and the child immediately rose on its legs, and ran away to play at chuck-farthing.

LUCAS Hah!

VALÈRE This man must have the universal cure-all.

MARTINE Who doubts it?

LUCAS Odds-bobs! that is the very man we want. Let us go quickly and fetch him.

VALÈRE We thank you for the service you have rendered us.

MARTINE But do not fail to remember the warning I have given you.

LUCAS Hey! Zooks! leave it to us. If he wants nothing but a thrashing, we will gain our point.

VALÈRE [*To* LUCAS.] We are very glad to have met with this woman; and I conceive the best hopes in the world from it.

Scene VI [SGANARELLE, VALÈRE, LUCAS.]

SGANARELLE [*Singing behind the Scene.*] La, la, la . . .

VALÈRE I hear someone singing and cutting wood.

SGANARELLE [*Coming on, with a bottle in his hand, without perceiving* VALÈRE *or* LUCAS.] La, la, la. . . . Really I have done enough to deserve a drink. Let us take a little breath. [*He drinks.*] This wood is as salt as the very devil. [*Sings.*]

What pleasure's so sweet as the bottle can give,
What music's so good as thy little gull-gull!
My fate might be envied by all on the earth
Were my dear jolly flask but constantly full.
Say why, my sweet bottle, I pray thee, say why
Since, full you're delightful, you ever are dry?

Come! Zounds! we must take care not to get the blues.

VALÈRE [*Softly to* LUCAS.] This is the very man.

LUCAS [*Softly to* VALÈRE.] I think you are right, and that we have just hit upon him.

VALÈRE Let us look a little closer.

SGANARELLE [*Hugging the bottle.*] Ah! you little rogue! I love you, my pretty dear! [*He sings; but perceiving* LUCAS *and* VALÈRE, *who are examining him, he lowers his voice.*] *My fate . . . might be envied . . . by all . . . on the earth.* [*Seeing that they examine him more closely.*] Whom the deuce do these people want?

VALÈRE [*To* LUCAS.] It is surely he.

LUCAS [*To* VALÈRE.] There he is, exactly as he has been described to us.

SGANARELLE [*Aside. At this point he puts down his bottle; and when* VALÈRE *stoops down to bow to him, he thinks that it is in order to snatch it away, and puts it on the other side. As* LUCAS *is doing the same thing as* VALÈRE, SGANARELLE *takes it up again, and hugs it to his breast, with various grimaces which make a great deal of by-play.*] They are consulting each other, while looking at me. What can be their intentions!

VALÈRE Sir, is not your name Sganarelle?

SGANARELLE Hey! What!

VALÈRE I ask you if your name is not Sganarelle.

SGANARELLE [*Turning first to* VALÈRE, *then to* LUCAS.] Yes, and no. It depends on what you want with him.

VALÈRE We want nothing with him, but to offer him our utmost civilities.

SGANARELLE In that case my name is Sganarelle.

VALÈRE We are delighted to see you, Sir. We have been recommended to you for what we are in search of; and we have come to implore your help, of which we are in want.

SGANARELLE If it be anything, gentlemen, that belongs to my little trade, I am quite ready to oblige you.

VALÈRE You are too kind to us, Sir. But put your hat on, Sir, if you please; the sun might hurt you.

LUCAS Pray, Sir, put it on.

SGANARELLE [*Aside.*] What a deal of ceremony these people use. [*He puts his hat on.*]

VALÈRE You must not think it strange, Sir, that we have addressed ourselves to you. Clever people are always much sought after, and we have been informed of your capacity.

SGANARELLE It is true, gentlemen, that I am the best hand in the world at making faggots.

VALÈRE Oh! Sir . . .

SGANARELLE I spare no pains, and make them in a fashion that leaves nothing to be desired.

VALÈRE That is not the question we have come about, Sir.

SGANARELLE But I charge a hundred and ten sous the hundred.

VALÈRE Let us not speak about that, if you please.

SGANARELLE I pledge you my word that I could not sell them for less.

VALÈRE We know what is what, Sir.

SGANARELLE If you know what is what, you know that I charge that price.

VALÈRE This is a joke, Sir, but . . .

SGANARELLE It is no joke at all, I cannot bate a farthing.

VALÈRE Let us talk differently, please.

SGANARELLE You may find some elsewhere for less; there be faggots and faggots; but for those which I make . . .

VALÈRE Let us change the conversation, pray, Sir.

SGANARELLE I take my oath that you shall not have them for less, not a fraction.

VALÈRE Fie! Fie!

SGANARELLE No, upon my word, you shall have to pay that price. I am speaking frankly, and I am not the man to overcharge.

VALÈRE Ought a gentleman like you, Sir, to amuse himself with those clumsy pretences, to lower himself to talk thus? Ought so learned a man, such a famous physician as you are, wish to disguise himself in the eyes of the world and keep buried his great talents?

SGANARELLE [*Aside.*] He is mad.

VALÈRE Pray, Sir, do not dissemble with us.

SGANARELLE What do you mean?

LUCAS All this beating about the bush is useless. We know what we know.

SGANARELLE What do you know? What do you want with me? For whom do you take me?

VALÈRE For what you are, a great physician.

SGANARELLE Physician yourself; I am not one, and I have never been one.

VALÈRE [*Aside.*] Now the fit is on him. [*Aloud.*] Sir, do not deny things any longer, and do not, if you please, make us have recourse to unpleasant extremities.

SGANARELLE Have recourse to what?

VALÈRE To certain things that we should be sorry for.

SGANARELLE Zounds! Have recourse to whatever you like. I am not a physician, and do not understand what you mean.

VALÈRE [*Aside.*] Well, I perceive that we shall have to apply the remedy. [*Aloud.*] Once more, Sir, I pray you to confess what you are.

LUCAS Odds-bobs, do not talk any more nonsense; and confess plainly that you are a physician.

SGANARELLE [*Aside.*] I am getting in a rage.

VALÈRE What is the good of denying what all the world knows?

LUCAS Why all these funny falsehoods? What is the good of it?

SGANARELLE One word is as good as a thousand, gentlemen. I tell you that I am not a physician.

VALÈRE You are not a physician?

SGANARELLE No.

LUCAS You are not a physician?

SGANARELLE No, I tell you.

VALÈRE Since you will have it so, we must make up our minds to do it. [*They each take a stick, and thrash him.*]

SGANARELLE Hold! hold! hold, gentlemen! I will be anything you like.

VALÈRE Why, Sir, do you oblige us to use this violence?

LUCAS Why do you make us take the trouble of giving you a beating?

VALÈRE I assure you that I regret it with all my heart.

LUCAS Upon my word I am sorry for it, too.

SGANARELLE What the devil does it all mean, gentlemen? For pity's sake, is it a joke, or are you both gone out of your minds, to wish to make me out a physician?

VALÈRE What! you do not give in yet, and you still deny being a physician?

SGANARELLE The devil take me if I am one!

LUCAS Are you not a physician?

SGANARELLE No, plague choke me! [*They begin to thrash him again.*] Hold! hold! Well, gentlemen, yes, since you will have it so, I am a physician, I am a physician—an apothecary into the bargain, if you like. I prefer saying yes to everything to being knocked about so.

VALÈRE Ah! that is right, Sir; I am delighted to see you so reasonable.

LUCAS It does my heart good to hear you speak in this way.

VALÈRE I beg your pardon with all my heart.

LUCAS I hope you will forgive me for the liberty I have taken.

SGANARELLE [*Aside.*] Bless my soul! Am I perhaps myself mistaken, and have I become a physician without being aware of it?

VALÈRE You shall not regret, Sir, having shown us what you are; and you shall certainly be satisfied.

SGANARELLE But, tell me, gentlemen, may you not be yourselves mistaken? Is it quite certain that I am a physician?

LUCAS Yes, upon my word!

SGANARELLE Really and truly?

VALÈRE Undoubtedly.

SGANARELLE The devil take me if I knew it!

VALÈRE Nonsense! You are the cleverest physician in the world.

SGANARELLE Ha, ha!

LUCAS A physician who has cured I do not know how many complaints.

SGANARELLE The dickens I have!

VALÈRE A woman was thought dead for six hours; she was ready to be buried when you, with a drop of something, brought her to again, and made her walk at once about the room.

SGANARELLE The deuce I did!

LUCAS A child of twelve fell from the top of the belfry, by which he had his head, his legs, and his arms smashed; and you, with I do not know what ointment, made him immediately get up on his feet, and off he ran to play chuck-farthing.

SGANARELLE The deuce I did!

VALÈRE In short, Sir, you will be satisfied with us, and you shall earn whatever you like, if you allow us to take you where we intend.

SGANARELLE I shall earn whatever I like?

VALÈRE Yes.

SGANARELLE In that case I am a physician: there is no doubt of it. I had forgotten it; but I recollect it now. What is the matter? Where am I to go?

VALÈRE We will conduct you. The matter is to see a girl who has lost her speech.

SGANARELLE Indeed! I have not found it.

VALÈRE [*Softly to* LUCAS.] How he loves his joke! [*To* SGANARELLE.] Come along, Sir!

SGANARELLE Without a physician's gown!

VALÈRE We will get one.

SGANARELLE [*Presenting his bottle to* VALÈRE.] You carry this. I put my juleps in there. [*Turning round to* LUCAS *and spitting on the ground.*] And you, stamp on this, by order of the physician.

LUCAS Odds sniggers! this is a physician I like. I think he will do, for he is a comical fellow.

ACT II [*A room in* GÉRONTE'*s house.*]

Scene I [GÉRONTE, VALÈRE, LUCAS, JACQUELINE.]

VALERE Yes, Sir, I think you will be satisfied; we have brought the greatest physician in the world with us.

LUCAS Oh! Zooks! this one beats everything; all the others are not worthy to hold the candle to him.

VALÈRE He is a man who has performed some marvellous cures.

LUCAS Who has put dead people on their legs again.

VALÈRE He is somewhat whimsical, as I have told you; and at times there are moments when his senses wander, and he does not seem what he really is.

LUCAS Yes, he loves a joke, and one would say sometimes that he has got a screw loose somewhere.

VALÈRE But in reality he is quite scientific; and very often he says things quite beyond anyone's comprehension.

LUCAS When he sets about it, he talks as finely as if he were reading a book.

VALÈRE He has already a great reputation hereabout, and everybody comes to consult him.

GÉRONTE I am very anxious to see him; send him to me quickly.

VALÈRE I am going to fetch him.

Scene II [GÉRONTE, JACQUELINE, LUCAS.]

JACQUELINE Upon my word, Sir, this one will do just the same as all the rest. I think it will be six of the one and half-a-dozen of the others; and the best medicine to give to your daughter would, in my opinion, be a handsome strapping husband, for whom she could have some love.

GÉRONTE Lord bless my soul, nurse dear, you are meddling with many things.

LUCAS Hold your tongue, mother Jacqueline; it is not for you to poke your nose there.

JACQUELINE I tell you, and a dozen more of you, that all these physicians do her no good; that your daughter wants something else than rhubarb and senna, and that a husband is a plaster which cures all girls' complaints.

GÉRONTE Would any one have her in her present state, with that affliction on her? and when I intended her to marry, has she not opposed my wishes?

JACQUELINE No wonder. You wished to give her a man whom she does not like. Why did you not give her to Monsieur Léandre, who takes her fancy? She would have been very obedient, and I vouch for it that he will take her as she is, if you but give her to him.

GÉRONTE Léandre is not the man we want; he has not got a fortune like the other.

JACQUELINE He has got an uncle who is so rich, and he is the heir.

GÉRONTE All these expectations seem to me but moonshine. Brag is a good dog, but Holdfast is a better; and we run a great risk in waiting for dead men's shoes. Death is not always at the beck and call of gentlemen heirs; and while the grass grows, the cow starves.

JACQUELINE That is all well and good, but I have always heard that in marriage, as in everything else, happiness excels riches. Fathers and mothers have this cursed habit of asking always, "How much has he got?" and "How much has she got?" And gaffer Peter has married his Simonette to that lout Thomas, because he has got a few more vineyards than young Robin, for whom the girl had a fancy; and now the poor creature is as yellow as a guinea, and has not looked like herself ever since. That is a good example for you, Sir. After all, folks have but their pleasure in this world; and I would sooner give my daughter a husband whom she likes than have all the riches in the country.

GÉRONTE Bless, me, nurse, how you chatter! Hold your tongue, let me beg of you; you take too much upon yourself, and you will spoil your milk.

LUCAS [*Slapping* GÉRONTE'S *shoulder at every word.*] Indeed, be silent; you are too saucy. The master does not want your speeches, and he knows what he is about. All you have got to do is to suckle your baby, without arguing so much. Our master is the girl's father, and he is good and clever enough to know what she wants.

GÉRONTE Gently, gently.

LUCAS [*Still slapping* GÉRONTE'S *shoulder.*] I wish to show her her place, and teach her the respect due to you, Sir.

GÉRONTE Very well. But it does not need all this gesticulating.

Scene III [VALÈRE, SGANARELLE, GÉRONTE, LUCAS, JACQUELINE.]

VALÈRE Look out, Sir, here is our physician coming.

GÉRONTE [*To* SGANARELLE.] I am delighted to see you, Sir, at my house, and we have very great need of you.

SGANARELLE [*In a physician's gown with a very pointed cap.*] Hippocrates says . . . that we should both put our hats on.

GÉRONTE Hippocrates says that?

SGANARELLE Yes.

GÉRONTE In which chapter, if you please?

SGANARELLE In his chapter . . . on hats.

GÉRONTE Since Hippocrates says so, we must obey.

SGANARELLE Doctor, having heard of the marvellous things . . .

GÉRONTE To whom are you speaking, pray?

SGANARELLE To you.

GÉRONTE I am not a physician.

SGANARELLE You are not a physician?

GÉRONTE Indeed I am not.

SGANARELLE Really?

GÉRONTE *Really.* [SGANARELLE *takes a stick and thrashes* GÉRONTE.] Oh! Oh! Oh!

SGANARELLE Now you are a physician, I have never taken any other degree.

GÉRONTE [*To* VALÈRE.] What a devil of a fellow you have brought me here!

VALÈRE Did I tell you that he was a funny sort of a physician?

GÉRONTE Yes; but I shall send him about his business with his fun.

LUCAS Do not take any notice of it, Sir. It is only his joking.

GÉRONTE The joking does not suit me.

SGANARELLE Sir, I beg your pardon for the liberty I have taken.

GÉRONTE I am your humble servant, Sir.

SGANARELLE I am sorry . . .

GÉRONTE It is nothing.

SGANARELLE For the cudgelling I . . .

GÉRONTE There is no harm done.

SGANARELLE Which I have had the honour to give you.

GÉRONTE Do not say any more about it, Sir. I have a daughter who is suffering from a strange complaint.

SGANARELLE I am delighted, Sir, that your daughter has need of my skill; and I wish, with all my heart, that you stood in the same need of it, you and all your family, in order to show you my wish to serve you.

GÉRONTE I am obliged to you for these kind feelings.

SGANARELLE I assure you that I am speaking from my very heart.

GÉRONTE You really do me too much honour.

SGANARELLE What is your daughter's name?

GÉRONTE Lucinde.

SGANARELLE Lucinde! Ah! a pretty name to physic! Lucinde!

GÉRONTE I will just see what she is doing.

SGANARELLE Who is that tall woman?

GÉRONTE She is my baby's nurse.

Scene IV [SGANARELLE, JACQUELINE, LUCAS.]

SGANARELLE [*Aside.*] The deuce! that is a fine piece of household furniture. [*Aloud.*] Ah, nurse! Charming nurse! my physic is the very humble slave of your nurseship, and I should like to be the fortunate little nursling to suck the milk of your good graces. [*He puts his hand on her bosom.*] All my nostrums, all my skill, all my cleverness, is at your service; and . . .

LUCAS By your leave, M. Doctor; leave my wife alone, I pray you.

SGANARELLE What! is she your wife?

LUCAS Yes.

SGANARELLE Oh! indeed! I did not know that, but I am very glad of it for the love of both. [*He pretends to embrace* LUCAS, *but embraces the nurse.*]

LUCAS [*Pulling* SGANARELLE *away, and placing himself between him and his wife.*] Gently, if you please.

SGANARELLE I assure you that I am delighted that you should be united together. I congratulate her upon having such a husband as you; and I congratulate you upon having a wife so handsome, so discreet, and so well shaped as she is. [*He pretends once more to embrace* LUCAS, *who holds out his arms, he slips under them and embraces the nurse.*]

LUCAS [*Pulling him away again.*] Do not pay so many compliments, I beg of you.

SGANARELLE Shall I not rejoice with you about such a lovely harmony?

LUCAS With me as much as you like; but a truce to compliments with my wife.

SGANARELLE I have both your happiness equally at heart; and if I embrace you to show my delight in you, I embrace her to show my delight in her. [*Same by-play.*]

LUCAS [*Pulling him away for the third time.*] Odds boddikins, Doctor, what capers you cut!

Scene V [GÉRONTE, SGANARELLE, LUCAS, JACQUELINE.]

GÉRONTE My daughter will be here directly, Sir.

SGANARELLE I am awaiting her, Sir, with all my physic.

GÉRONTE Where is it?

SGANARELLE [*Touching his forehead.*] In there.

GÉRONTE That is good.

SGANARELLE But as I feel much interested in your family, I should like to test the milk of your nurse, and examine her breasts. [*He draws close to* JACQUELINE.]

LUCAS [*Pulling him away, and swinging him round.*] Nothing of the sort, nothing of the sort. I do not wish it.

SGANARELLE It is the physician's duty to see the breasts of the nurse.

LUCAS Duty or no duty, I will not have it.

SGANARELLE Have you the audacity to contradict a physician? Out with you.

LUCAS I do not care a straw about a physician.

SGANARELLE [*Looking askance at him.*] I will give you a fever.

JACQUELINE [*Taking* LUCAS *by the arm, and swinging him around also.*] Get out of the way. Am I not big enough to take my own part, if he does anything to me which he ought not to do?

LUCAS I will not have him touch you, I will not.

SGANARELLE For shame you rascal, to be jealous of your wife.

GÉRONTE Here comes my daughter.

Scene VI [LUCINDE, GÉRONTE, SGANARELLE, VALÈRE, LUCAS, JACQUELINE.]

SGANARELLE Is this the patient?

GÉRONTE Yes, I have but one daughter; and I would never get over it if she were to die.

SGANARELLE Do not let her do anything of the kind. She must not die without a prescription of the physician.

GÉRONTE A chair here!

SGANARELLE [*Seated between* GÉRONTE *and*

LUCINDE.] This is not at all an unpleasant patient, and I am of the opinion that she would not be at all amiss for a man in very good health.

GÉRONTE You have made her laugh, Sir.

SGANARELLE So much the better. It is the best sign in the world when a physician makes the patient laugh. [*To* LUCINDE.] Well, what is the matter? What ails you? What is it you feel?

LUCINDE [*Replies by motions, by putting her hands to her mouth, her head, and under her chin.*] Ha, hi, ho, ha!

SGANARELLE What do you say?

LUCINDE [*Continues the same motions.*] Ha, hi, ho, ha, ha, hi, ho!

SGANARELLE What is that?

LUCINDE Ha, hi, ho!

SGANARELLE [*Imitating her.*] Ha, hi, ho, ha, ha! I do not understand you. What sort of language do you call that?

GÉRONTE That is just where her complaint lies, Sir. She has become dumb, without our having been able till now to discover the cause. This accident has obliged us to postpone her marriage.

SGANARELLE And why so?

GÉRONTE He whom she is going to marry wishes to wait for her recovery to conclude the marriage.

SGANARELLE And who is this fool that does not want his wife to be dumb? Would to Heaven that mine had that complaint! I should take particular care not to have her cured.

GÉRONTE To the point, Sir. We beseech you to use all your skill to cure her of this affliction.

SGANARELLE Do not make yourself uneasy. But tell me, does this pain oppress her much?

GÉRONTE Yes, Sir.

SGANARELLE So much the better. Is the suffering very acute?

GÉRONTE Very acute.

SGANARELLE That is right. Does she go to . . . you know where?

GÉRONTE Yes.

SGANARELLE Freely?

GÉRONTE That I know nothing about.

SGANARELLE Is the matter healthy?

GÉRONTE I do not understand these things.

SGANARELLE [*Turning to the patient.*] Give me your hand. [*To* GÉRONTE.] The pulse tells me that your daughter is dumb.

GÉRONTE Sir, that is what is the matter with her; ah! yes, you have found it out at the first touch.

SGANARELLE Of course!

JACQUELINE See how he has guessed her complaint.

SGANARELLE We great physicians, we know matters at once. An ignoramus would have been nonplussed, and would have told you: it is this, that, or the other; but I hit the nail on the head from the very first, and I tell you that your daughter is dumb.

GÉRONTE Yes; but I should like you to tell me whence it arises.

SGANARELLE Nothing is easier; it arises from loss of speech.

GÉRONTE Very good. But the reason of her having lost her speech, pray?

SGANARELLE Our best authorities will tell you that it is because there is an impediment in the action of her tongue.

GÉRONTE But, once more, your opinion upon this impediment in the action of her tongue.

SGANARELLE Aristotle on this subject says . . . a great many clever things.

GÉRONTE I dare say.

SGANARELLE Ah! He was a great man!

GÉRONTE No doubt.

SGANARELLE Yes, a very great man. [*Holding out his arm, and putting a finger of the other hand in the bend.*] A man who was, by this, much greater than I. But to come back to our argument: I hold that this impediment in the action of her tongue is caused by certain humours, which among us learned men, we call peccant humours; peccant—that is to say . . . peccant humours; inasmuch as the vapours formed by the exhalations of the influences which rise in the very region of diseases, coming, . . . as we may say to. . . . Do you understand Latin?

GÉRONTE Not in the least.

SGANARELLE [*Suddenly rising.*] You do not understand Latin?

GÉRONTE No.

SGANARELLE [*Assuming various comic attitudes.*] *Cabricias arci thuram, catalamus, singulariter, nominativo, hœc musa,* the muse, *bonus, bona, bonum. Deus sanctus, estne oratio latinas? Etiam.* Yes. *Quare?* Why? *Quia substantivo et adjectivum, concordat in generi, numerum, et casus.*

GÉRONTE Ah! Why did I not study?

JACQUELINE What a clever man!

LUCAS Yes, it is so beautiful that I do not understand a word of it.

SGANARELLE Thus these vapours which I speak of, passing from the left side, where the liver is, to the right side, where we find the heart, it so happens that the lungs, which in Latin we call *armyan,* having communication with the brain, which in Greek we style *nasmus,* by means of *vena cava,* which in Hebrew, is termed *cubile,* meet in their course the said vapours, which fill the ventricles of the omoplata; and because the said vapours . . . now understand well this argument, pray . . . and because these said vapours are endowed with a certain malignity . . . listen well to this, I beseech you.

GÉRONTE Yes.

SGANARELLE Are endowed with a certain malignity which is caused . . . pay attention here, if you please.

GÉRONTE I do.

SGANARELLE Which is caused by the acridity of these humours engendered in the concavity of the diaphragm, it happens that these vapours. . . . *Ossabandus, nequeis, nequer, potarinum, puipsa milus.* That is exactly the reason that your daughter is dumb.

JACQUELINE Ah! How well this gentleman explains all this.

LUCAS Why does not my tongue wag as well as his?

GÉRONTE It is undoubtedly impossible to argue better. There is but one thing that I cannot exactly make out: that is the whereabouts of the liver and the heart. It appears to me that you place them differently from where they are; that the heart is on the left side, and the liver on the right.

SGANARELLE Yes; this was formerly; but we have changed all that, and we now-a-days practice the medical art on an entirely new system.

GÉRONTE I did not know that, and I pray you pardon my ignorance.

SGANARELLE There is no harm done; and you are not obliged to be so clever as we are.

GÉRONTE Certainly not. But what think you, Sir, ought to be done for this complaint?

SGANARELLE What do I think ought to be done?

GÉRONTE Yes.

SGANARELLE My advice is to put her to bed again, and make her, as a remedy, take plenty of bread soaked in wine.

GÉRONTE Why so, sir?

SGANARELLE Because there is in bread and wine mixed together a sympathetic virtue which produces speech. Do you not see that they give nothing else to parrots, and that, by eating it, they learn to speak?

GÉRONTE That is true. Oh! the great man! Quick, plenty of bread and wine.

SGANARELLE I shall come back to-night to see how the patient is getting on.

Scene VII [GÉRONTE, SGANARELLE, JACQUELINE.]

SGANARELLE [*To* JACQUELINE.] Stop a little, you. [*To* GÉRONTE.] Sir, I must give some medicine to your nurse.

JACQUELINE To me, Sir? I am as well as can be.

SGANARELLE So much the worse, nurse, so much the worse. This excess of health is dangerous, and it would not be amiss to bleed you a little gently, and to administer some little soothing injection.

GÉRONTE But, my dear Sir, that is a method which I cannot understand. Why bleed folks when they are not ill?

SGANARELLE It does not matter, the method is salutary; and as we drink for the thirst to come, so must we bleed for the disease to come.

JACQUELINE [*Going.*] I do not care a fig for all this, and I will not have my body made an apothecary's shop.

SGANARELLE You object to my remedies; but we shall know how to bring you to reason.

Scene VIII [GÉRONTE, SGANARELLE.]

SGANARELLE I wish you good day.

GÉRONTE Stay a moment, if you please.

SGANARELLE What are you going to do?

GÉRONTE Give you your fee, Sir.

SGANARELLE [*Putting his hands behind him, from under his gown, while* GÉRONTE *opens his purse.*] I shall not accept it, Sir.

GÉRONTE Sir.

SGANARELLE Not at all.

GÉRONTE One moment.

SGANARELLE On one consideration.

GÉRONTE Pray!

SGANARELLE You are jesting.

GÉRONTE That is settled.

SGANARELLE I shall do nothing of the kind.

GÉRONTE What!

SGANARELLE I do not practise for money's sake.

GÉRONTE I am convinced of that.

SGANARELLE [*After having taken the money.*] Are they good weight?

GÉRONTE Yes, Sir.

SGANARELLE I am not a mercenary physician.

GÉRONTE I am well aware of it.

SGANARELLE I am not actuated by interest.

GÉRONTE I do not for a moment think so.

SGANARELLE [*Alone, looking at the money he has received.*] Upon my word, this does not promise badly; and provided . . .

Scene IX [LÉANDRE, SGANARELLE.]

LÉANDRE I have been waiting some time for you, Sir, and I have come to beg your assistance.

SGANARELLE [*Feeling his pulse.*] That is a very bad pulse.

LÉANDRE I am not ill, Sir; and it is not for that I am come to you.

SGANARELLE If you are not ill, why the devil do you not tell me so?

LÉANDRE No. To tell you the matter in a few words, my name is Léandre. I am in love with Lucinde to whom you have just paid a visit; and as all access to her is denied to me, through the ill-temper of her father, I venture to beseech you to serve me in my love affair, and to assist me in a stratagem that I have invented, so as to say a few words to her, on which my whole life and happiness absolutely depend.

SGANARELLE [*In apparent anger.*] Whom do you take me for? How dare you address yourself to me to assist you in your love affair, and to wish me to lower the dignity of a physician by an affair of that kind!

LÉANDRE Do not make a noise, Sir!

SGANARELLE [*Driving him back.*] I will make a noise. You are an impertinent fellow.

LÉANDRE Ah! gently, Sir.

SGANARELLE An ill-mannered jackanapes.

LÉANDRE Pray!

SGANARELLE I will teach you that I am not the kind of man you take me for, and that it is the greatest insolence . . .

LÉANDRE [*Taking out a purse.*] Sir . . .

SGANARELLE To wish to employ me . . . [*Taking the purse.*] I am not speaking about you, for you are a gentleman; and I should be delighted to be of any use to you; but there are certain impertinent people in this world who take folks for what they are not; and I tell you candidly that this puts me in a passion.

LÉANDRE I ask your pardon, Sir, for the liberty I have . . .

SGANARELLE You are jesting. What is the affair in question?

LÉANDRE You must know then, Sir, that this disease which you wish to cure is a feigned complaint. The physicians have argued about it, as they ought to do, and they have not failed to give it as their opinion—this one, that it arose from the brain; that one, from the intestines; another, from the spleen; another, again, from the liver; but the fact is that love is its real cause, and that Lucinde has only invented this illness in order to free herself from a marriage with which she has been harassed. But for fear that we may be seen together, let us retire; and I will tell you as we go along, what I wish you to do.

SGANARELLE Come along, then, Sir. You have inspired me with an inconceivable interest in your love; and if all my medical science does not fail me, the patient shall either die or be yours.

ACT III [A *place near* GÉRONTE'S *house.*]

Scene I [LÉANDRE, SGANARELLE.]

LÉANDRE I think that I am not at all badly got up for an apothecary; and as her father has scarcely ever seen me, this change of dress and wig is likely enough, I think, to disguise me.

SGANARELLE There is no doubt of it.

LÉANDRE Only I should like to know five or six big medical words to leaven my conversation with, and to give me the air of a learned man.

SGANARELLE Go along, go along; it is not at all

necessary. The dress is sufficient; and I know no more about it than you do.

LÉANDRE How is that!

SGANARELLE The devil take me if I understand anything about medicine! You are a gentleman, and I do not mind confiding in you, as you have confided in me.

LÉANDRE What! Then you are not really . . .

SGANARELLE No, I tell you. They have made me a physician in the teeth of my protests. I have never attempted to be so learned as that; and all my studies did not go farther than the lowest class at school. I do not know how the idea has come to them; but when I saw that in spite of everything they would have it that I was a physician, I made up my mind to be so at somebody's expense. You would not believe, however, how this error has spread, and how everyone is possessed, and believes me to be a learned man. They come seeking me on all sides; and if things go on in this way, I am resolved to stick to the profession all my life. I find that it is the best trade of all; for, whether we manage well or ill, we are paid just the same. Bad workmanship never recoils on us; and we cut the material we have to work with pretty much as we like. A shoemaker, in making a pair of shoes, cannot spoil a scrap of leather without having to bear the loss; but in our business we may spoil a man without its costing us a farthing. The blunders are never put down to us, and it is always the fault of the fellow who dies. The best of this profession is, that there is the greatest honesty and discretion among the dead; for you never find them complain of the physician who has killed them.

LÉANDRE It is true that the dead are very honourable in that respect.

SGANARELLE [*Seeing some people advancing towards him.*] There come some people, who seem anxious to consult me. [*To* LÉANDRE.] Go and wait for me near the house of your ladylove.

Scene II [THIBAUT, PERRIN, SGANARELLE.]

THIBAUT Sir, we come to look for you, my son Perrin and myself.

SGANARELLE What is the matter?

THIBAUT His poor mother, whose name is Perrette, has been on a bed of sickness for the last six months.

SGANARELLE [*Holding out his hand as if to receive money.*] What would you have me do to her?

THIBAUT I would like you to give me some little doctor's stuff to cure her.

SGANARELLE We must first see what is the matter with her.

THIBAUT She is ill with the hypocrisy, Sir.

SGANARELLE With the hypocrisy?

THIBAUT Yes; I mean she is swollen everywhere. They say that there is a lot of seriosities in her inside, and that her liver, her belly, or her spleen, as you would call it, instead of making blood makes nothing but water. She has, every other day, the quotiguian fever, with lassitude and pains in the muscles of her legs. We can hear in her throat phlegms that are ready to choke her, and she is often taken with syncoles and conversions, so that we think she is going off the hooks. We have got in our village an apothecary—with respect be it said—who has given her, I do not know how much stuff; and it has cost me more than a dozen good crowns in clysters, saving your presence, in apostumes which he has made her swallow, in infections of hyacinth, and in cordial potions. But all this, as people say, was nothing but an ointment of fiddle-faddle. He wanted to give her a certain drug called ametile wine; but I was downright afeard that this would send her to the other world altogether; because they tell me that those big physicians kill, I do not know how many, with that new-fangled potion.

SGANARELLE [*Still holding out his hand, and moving it about to show that he wants money.*] Let us come to the point, friend, let us come to the point.

THIBAUT The point is, Sir, that we have come to beg of you to tell us what we must do.

SGANARELLE I do not understand you at all.

PERRIN My mother is ill, Sir, and here are two crowns which we have brought you to give us some stuff.

SGANARELLE Ah! you I do understand. There is a lad who speaks clearly, and explains himself as he should. You say that your mother is ill with the dropsy; that she is swollen all over her body; that she has a fever, with pains in the legs; that she sometimes is taken with syncopes and convulsions, that is to say with fainting fits.

PERRIN Indeed, Sir! that is just it.

SGANARELLE I understand you at once. Your father does not know what he says. And now you ask me for a remedy?

PERRIN Yes sir.

SGANARELLE A remedy to cure her?

PERRIN That is just what I mean.

SGANARELLE Take this then. It is a piece of cheese which you must make her take.

PERRIN A piece of cheese, Sir?

SGANARELLE Yes; it is a kind of prepared cheese, in which there is gold, coral, and pearls, and a great many other precious things.

PERRIN I am very much obliged to you, Sir, and I shall go and make her take it directly.

SGANARELLE Go, and if she dies, do not fail to bury her in the best style you can.

Scene III

[*The scene changes, and represents, as in the Second Act, a room in* GÉRONTE'S *house.* JACQUELINE, SGANARELLE, LUCAS, *at the far end of the stage.*]

SGANARELLE Here is the pretty nurse. Ah! you darling nurse, I am delighted at this meeting; and the sight of you is like rhubarb, cassia, and senna to me, which purges all melancholy from my mind.

JACQUELINE Upon my word, M. Physician, it is no good talking to me in that style, and I do not understand your Latin at all.

SGANARELLE Get ill, nurse, I beg of you; get ill for my sake. I shall have all the pleasure in the world of curing you.

JACQUELINE I am your humble servant; I would much rather not be cured.

SGANARELLE How I grieve for you, beautiful nurse, in having such a jealous and troublesome husband.

JACQUELINE What am I to do, Sir? It is as a penance for my sins; and where the goat is tied down she must browse.

SGANARELLE What! Such a clod-hopper as that! a fellow who is always watching you, and will let no one speak to you!

JACQUELINE Alas! you have seen nothing yet; and that is only a small sample of his bad temper.

SGANARELLE Is it possible? and can a man have so mean a spirit as to ill-use a woman like you? Ah! I know some, sweet nurse, and who are not very far off, who would only be too glad to kiss your little feet! Why should such a handsome woman have fallen into such hands! and a mere animal, a brute, a stupid, a fool. . . . Excuse me, nurse, for speaking in that way of your husband.

JACQUELINE Oh! Sir, I know full well that he deserves all these names.

SGANARELLE Undoubtedly, nurse, he deserves them; and he also deserves that you should plant something on his head to punish him for his suspicions.

JACQUELINE It is true enough that if I had not his interest so much at heart, he would drive me to do some strange things.

SGANARELLE Indeed it would just serve him right if you were to revenge yourself upon him with some one. The fellow richly deserves it all, I tell you, and if I were fortunate enough, fair nurse, to be chosen by you . . . [*While* SGANARELLE *is holding out his arms to embrace* JACQUELINE, LUCAS *passes his head under them, and comes between the two.* SGANARELLE *and* JACQUELINE *stare at* LUCAS, *and depart on opposite sides, but the doctor does so in a very comic manner.*]

Scene IV

[GÉRONTE, LUCAS.]

GÉRONTE I say, Lucas, have not you seen our physician here?

LUCAS Indeed I have seen him, by all the devils, and my wife, too.

GÉRONTE Where can he be?

LUCAS I do not know; but I wish he were with the devil.

GÉRONTE Just go and see what my daughter is doing.

Scene V

[SGANARELLE, LÉANDRE, GERONTE.]

GÉRONTE I was just inquiring after you, Sir.

SGANARELLE I have just been amusing myself in your court with expelling the superfluity of drink. How is the patient?

GÉRONTE Somewhat worse since your remedy.

SGANARELLE So much the better; it shows that it takes effect.

GÉRONTE Yes; but while it is taking effect, I am afraid it will choke her.

SGANARELLE Do not make yourself uneasy; I have some remedies that will make it all right! and I will wait until she is at death's door.

GÉRONTE [*Pointing to* LÉANDRE.] Who is this man that is with you?

SGANARELLE [*Intimates by motions of his hands that it is an apothecary.*] It is . . .

GÉRONTE What?

SGANARELLE He who . . .

GÉRONTE Oh!

SGANARELLE Who . . .

GÉRONTE I understand.

SGANARELLE Your daughter will want him.

Scene VI [LUCINDE, GÉRONTE, LÉANDRE, JACQUELINE, SGANARELLE.]

JACQUELINE Here is your daughter, Sir, who wishes to stretch her limbs a little.

SGANARELLE That will do her good. Go to her, M. Apothecary, and feel her pulse, so that I may consult with you presently about her complaint. [*At this point he draws* GÉRONTE *to one end of the stage, and putting one arm upon his shoulder, he places his hand under his chin, with which he makes him turn towards him, each time that* GÉRONTE *wants to look at what is passing between his daughter and the apothecary, while he holds the following discourse with him.*] Sir, it is a great and subtle question among physicians to know whether women or men are more easily cured. I pray you to listen to this, if you please. Some say "no," others say "yes": I say both "yes" and "no"; inasmuch as the incongruity of the opaque humours, which are found in the natural temperament of women, causes the brutal part to struggle for the mastery over the sensitive, we find that the conflict of their opinion depends on the oblique motion of the circle of the moon; and as the sun, which darts its beams on the concavity of the earth, meets . . .

LUCINDE [*To* LÉANDRE.] No; I am not at all likely to change my feelings.

GÉRONTE Hark! my daughter speaks! O great virtue of the remedy! O excellent physician! How deeply am I obliged to you, Sir, for this marvellous cure! And what can I do for you after such a service?

SGANARELLE [*Strutting about the stage, fanning himself with his hat.*] This case has given me some trouble.

LUCINDE Yes, father, I have recovered my speech; but I have recovered it to tell you that I will never have any other husband than Léandre, and that it is in vain for you to wish to give me to Horace.

GÉRONTE But . . .

LUCINDE Nothing will shake the resolution I have taken.

GÉRONTE What . . .

LUCINDE All your fine arguments will be in vain.

GÉRONTE If . . .

LUCINDE All your talking will be of no use.

GÉRONTE I . . .

LUCINDE I have made up my mind about the matter.

GÉRONTE But . . .

LUCINDE No paternal authority can compel me to marry against my will.

GÉRONTE I have . . .

LUCINDE You may try as much as you like.

GÉRONTE It . . .

LUCINDE My heart cannot submit to this tyranny.

GÉRONTE The . . .

LUCINDE And I will sooner go into a convent than marry a man I do not love.

GÉRONTE But . . .

LUCINDE [*In a loud voice.*] No. By no means. It is of no use. You waste your time. I shall do nothing of the kind. I am fully determined.

GÉRONTE Ah! what a torrent of words! One cannot hold out against it. [*To* SGANARELLE.] I beseech you, Sir, to make her dumb again.

SGANARELLE That is impossible. All that I can do in your behalf is to make you deaf, if you like.

GÉRONTE I thank you. [*To* LUCINDE.] Do you think . . .

LUCINDE No; all your reasoning will not have the slightest effect upon me.

GÉRONTE You shall marry Horace this very evening.

LUCINDE I would sooner marry death itself.

SGANARELLE [*To* GÉRONTE.] Stop, for Heaven's sake! stop. Let me doctor this matter; it is a disease that has got hold of her, and I know the remedy to apply to it.

GÉRONTE Is it possible, indeed, Sir, that you can cure this disease of the mind also?

SGANARELLE Yes; let me manage it. I have remedies for everything; and our apothecary will serve us capitally for this cure. [*To* LÉANDRE.] A word with you. You perceive that the passion she has for this Léandre is altogether against the wishes of the father; that there is no time to lose; that the humours are very acrimonious; and that it becomes necessary to find speedily a remedy for this complaint, which may get worse by delay. As for myself, I see but one, which is a dose of purgative flight, mixed, as it should be, with two drachms of matrimonium, made up into pills. She may, perhaps, make some difficulty about taking this remedy; but as you are a clever man in your profession, you must induce her to consent to it, and make her swallow the thing as best you can. Go and take a little turn in the garden with her to prepare the humours, while I converse here with her father; but, above all, lose not a moment. Apply the remedy quick! apply the specific!

Scene VII [GÉRONTE, SGANARELLE.]

GÉRONTE What drugs are those you have just mentioned, Sir? It seems to me that I never heard of them before.

SGANARELLE They are drugs which are used only in urgent cases.

GÉRONTE Did you ever see such insolence as hers?

SGANARELLE Daughters are a little headstrong at times.

GÉRONTE You would not believe how she is infatuated with this Léandre.

SGANARELLE The heat of the blood produces those things in young people.

GÉRONTE As for me, the moment I discovered the violence of this passion, I took care to keep my daughter under lock and key.

SGANARELLE You have acted wisely.

GÉRONTE And I have prevented the slightest communication between them.

SGANARELLE Just so.

GÉRONTE They would have committed some folly, if they had been permitted to see each other.

SGANARELLE Undoubtedly.

GÉRONTE And I think she would have been the girl to run away with him.

SGANARELLE You have argued very prudently.

GÉRONTE I was informed that he tried every means to get speech of her.

SGANARELLE The rascal!

GÉRONTE But he will waste his time.

SGANARELLE Aye! Aye!

GÉRONTE And I will effectually prevent him from seeing her.

SGANARELLE He has no fool to deal with, and you know some tricks of which he is ignorant. One must get up very early to catch you asleep.

Scene VIII [LUCAS, GÉRONTE, SGANARELLE.]

LUCAS Odds-bobs, Sir, here is a pretty to do. Your daughter has fled with her Léandre. It was he that played the apothecary, and this is the physician who has performed this nice operation.

GÉRONTE What! to murder me in this manner! Quick, fetch a magistrate, and take care that he does not get away. Ah villain! I will have you punished by the law.

LUCAS I am afraid, Master Doctor, that you will be hanged. Do not stir a step, I tell you.

Scene IX [MARTINE, SGANARELLE, LUCAS.]

MARTINE [*To* LUCAS.] Good gracious! what a difficulty I have had to find this place! Just tell me what has become of the physician I recommended to you?

LUCAS Here he is; just going to be hanged.

MARTINE What! my husband hanged! Alas, and for what?

LUCAS He has helped some one to run away with master's daughter.

MARTINE Alas, my dear husband, is it true that you are going to be hanged?

SGANARELLE Judge for yourself. Ah!

MARTINE And must you be made an end of in the presence of such a crowd.

SGANARELLE What am I to do?

MARTINE If you had only finished cutting our wood, I should be somewhat consoled.

SGANARELLE Leave me, you break my heart.

MARTINE No, I will remain to encourage you to die; and I will not leave you until I have seen you hanged.

SGANARELLE Ah!

Scene X [GÉRONTE, SGANARELLE, MARTINE.]

GÉRONTE [*To* SGANARELLE.] The magistrate will be here directly, and we shall put you in a place of safety where they will be answerable for you.

SGANARELLE [*On his knees, hat in hand.*] Alas! will not a few strokes with a cudgel do instead?

GÉRONTE No; no; the law shall decide. But what do I see?

Scene XI [GÉRONTE, LÉANDRE, LUCINDE, SGANARELLE, LUCAS, MARTINE.]

LÉANDRE Sir, I appear before you as Léandre, and am come to restore Lucinde to your authority. We intended to run away, and get married; but this design has given away to a more honourable proceeding. I will not presume to steal away your daughter, and it is from your hands alone that I will obtain her. I must at the same time acquaint you, that I have just now received some letters informing me of the death of my uncle, and that he has left me heir to all his property.

GÉRONTE Really, Sir, your virtue is worthy of my utmost consideration, and I give you my daughter with the greatest pleasure in the world.

SGANARELLE [*Aside.*] The physician has had a narrow escape!

MARTINE Since you are not going to be hanged, you may thank me for being a physician, for I have procured you this honour.

SGANARELLE Yes, it is you who procured me, I do not know how many thwacks with a cudgel.

LÉANDRE [*To* SGANARELLE.] The result has proved too happy to harbour any resentment.

SGANARELLE Be it so. [*To* MARTINE.] I forgive you the blows on account of the dignity to which you have elevated me; but prepare yourself henceforth to behave with great respect towards a man of my consequence; and consider that the anger of a physician is more to be dreaded than people imagine.

Comments and Questions

This play, along with many others by Molière, represents the laughing theater at its best. It is all sunlight and no shadows. For this reason, serious analysis may seem out of place. The greatness of the art, however, has challenged critics for three hundred years, and serious analysis does help one to enter more fully into the pure fun; to laugh again at what he has laughed at before.

1. You may have been mildly puzzled by the many scenes. What occurs when a new scene is indicated? How does Molière's practice in this respect differ from modern practice? Compare, for example, the scenes in *Ghosts*, next.

2. The facts of the play are preposterous. What are the literal facts? How does each bit of action grow out of the preceding action?

3. How does the plot involving Sganarelle and Martine encompass the plot involving Léandre, Lucinde and Géronte? Outline both plots.

4. Discuss the by-play, that is, the action that the author indicates for the actors through stage directions. How much of the play's effect must depend upon the ability and agility of the actors? Compare *The Sunshine Boys*, p. 647. Consider particularly the scene in which Sganarelle makes advances to Jacqueline in the presence of Lucas, her husband (see II, iv).

5. Point out the passages in which Molière satirizes practitioners of medicine. Is the satire directed as much at the gullibility of people as at physicians? Is any of the satire still applicable today? Discuss.

HENRIK IBSEN
1828–1906

Ghosts

CHARACTERS

MRS. ALVING (HELEN), *widow of Captain Alving, late Chamberlain to the King*

OSWALD ALVING, *her son, a painter*

PASTOR MANDERS

JACOB ENGSTRAND, *a carpenter*

REGINA ENGSTRAND, *Mrs. Alving's maid*

The action takes place at Mrs. Alving's country house, beside one of the large fiords in western Norway.

ACT I

A spacious garden-room, with one door to the left, and two doors to the right. In the middle of the room a round table, with chairs about it. On the table lie books, periodicals, and newspapers. In the foreground to the left a window, and by it a small sofa, with a work-table in front of it. In the background, the room is continued into a somewhat narrower conservatory, which is shut in by glass walls with large panes. In the right-hand wall of the conservatory is a door leading down into the garden. Through the glass wall one catches a glimpse of a gloomy fjord-landscape, veiled by steady rain.

ENGSTRAND, *the carpenter, stands by the garden door. His left leg is somewhat bent; he has a clump of wood under the sole of his boot.* REGINA, *with an empty garden syringe in her hand, hinders him from advancing.*

REGINA [*In a low voice.*] What do you want? Stop where you are. You're positively dripping.

ENGSTRAND It's the Lord's own rain, my girl.

REGINA It's the devil's rain, *I* say.

ENGSTRAND Lord! how you talk, Regina. [*Limps a few steps forward into the room.*] What I wanted to say was this—

REGINA Don't clatter so with that foot of yours, I tell you! The young master's asleep upstairs.

ENGSTRAND Asleep? In the middle of the day?

REGINA It's no business of yours.

ENGSTRAND I was out on the loose last night—

REGINA I can quite believe that.

ENGSTRAND Yes, we're weak vessels, we poor mortals, my girl—

REGINA So it seems.

ENGSTRAND —and temptations are manifold in this world, you see; but all the same, I was hard at work, God knows, at half-past five this morning.

REGINA Very well; only be off now. I won't stop here and have *rendezvous*[1] with you.

ENGSTRAND What is it you won't have?

REGINA I won't have any one find you here; so just you go about your business.

ENGSTRAND [*Advances a step or two.*] Blest if I go before I've had a talk with you. This afternoon I shall have finished my work at the school-house, and then I shall take to-night's boat and be off home to the town.

REGINA [*Mutters.*] A pleasant journey to you.

ENGSTRAND Thank you, my child. To-morrow the Asylum's to be opened, and then there'll be fine doings, no doubt, and plenty of intoxicating drink going, you know. And nobody shall say of Jacob Engstrand that he can't keep out of temptation's way.

REGINA Oh!

ENGSTRAND You see, there are to be any number of swells here to-morrow. Pastor Manders is expected from town, too.

REGINA He's coming to-day.

ENGSTRAND There, you see! And I should be cursedly sorry if he found out anything to my disadvantage, don't you understand?

REGINA Oh! is that your game?

ENGSTRAND Is what my game?

REGINA [*Looking hard at him.*] What trick are you going to play on Pastor Manders?

ENGSTRAND Hush! hush! Are you crazy? Do *I* want to play any trick on Pastor Manders? Oh no! Pastor Manders has been far too kind to me for that. But I just wanted to say, you know—that I mean to set off home again to-night.

REGINA The sooner the better, say I.

ENGSTRAND Yes, but I want to take you with me, Regina.

REGINA [*Open-mouthed.*] You want me—? What are you talking about?

ENGSTRAND I want to take you home, I say.

REGINA [*Scornfully.*] Never in this world shall you get me home with you.

ENGSTRAND We'll see about that.

REGINA Yes, you may be sure we'll see about it! I, who have been brought up by a lady like Mrs. Alving! I, who am treated almost as a daughter here! Is it me you want to go home with you?—to a house like yours? For shame!

ENGSTRAND What the devil do you mean? Do you set yourself up against your father, girl?

REGINA [*Mutters without looking at him.*] You've said often enough I was no child of yours.

ENGSTRAND Stuff! Why should you trouble about that?

REGINA Haven't you many a time sworn at me and called me a—? *Fi donc!*

1 This and other French words used by Regina are in that language in the original.

ENGSTRAND Curse me, now, if ever I used such an ugly word.

REGINA Oh! I know quite well what word you used.

ENGSTRAND Well, but that was only when I was a bit on, don't you know? Hm! Temptations are manifold in this world, Regina.

REGINA Ugh!

ENGSTRAND And besides, it was when your mother rode her high horse. I had to find something to twit her with, my child. She was always setting up for a fine lady. [*Mimics.*] "Let me go, Engstrand; let me be. Remember I've been three years in Chamberlain Alving's family at Rosenvold." [*Laughs.*] Mercy on us! She could never forget that the Captain was made a Chamberlain while she was in service here.

REGINA Poor mother! you very soon worried her into her grave.

ENGSTRAND [*Turns on his heel.*] Oh, of course! I'm to be blamed for everything.

REGINA [*Turns away; half aloud.*] Ugh! And that leg too!

ENGSTRAND What do you say, girl?

REGINA *Pied de mouton.*

ENGSTRAND Is that English, eh?

REGINA Yes.

ENGSTRAND Oh, ah; you've picked up some learning out here; and that may come in useful now, Regina.

REGINA [*After a short silence.*] What do you want with me in town?

ENGSTRAND Can you ask what a father wants with his only child? Am I not a lonely and forsaken widower?

REGINA Oh! don't try on any nonsense like that! Why do you want me?

ENGSTRAND Well, let me tell you, I've been thinking of starting a new line of business.

REGINA [*Contemptuously.*] You've tried that often enough, and never done any good.

ENGSTRAND Yes, but this time you shall see, Regina! Devil take me—

REGINA [*Stamps.*] Don't swear!

ENGTRAND Hush, hush; you're right enough there, my girl. What I wanted to say was just this—I've laid by a very tidy pile from this Orphanage job.

REGINA Have you? That's a good thing for you.

ENGSTRAND What can a man spend his ha'pence on here in the country?

REGINA Well, what then?

ENGSTRAND Why, you see, I thought of putting the money into some paying speculation. I thought of a sort of sailors' tavern—

REGINA Horrid!

ENGSTRAND A regular high-class affair, of course; not a mere pigstye for common sailors. No! damn it! it would be for captains and mates, and—and—all those swells, you know.

REGINA And I was to—?

ENGSTRAND You were to help, to be sure. Only for appearance' sake, you understand. Devil a bit of hard work shall you have, my girl. You shall do exactly what you like.

REGINA Oh, indeed!

ENGSTRAND But there must be a petticoat in the house; that's as clear as daylight. For I want to have it a little lively in the evenings, with singing and dancing, and so forth. You must remember they're weary wanderers on the ocean of life. [*Nearer.*] Now don't be stupid and stand in your own light, Regina. What can become of you out here? Your mistress has given you a lot of learning; but what good is it to you? You're to look after the children at the new Orphanage, I hear. Is that the sort of thing for you, eh? Are you so desperately bent upon wearing yourself out for the sake of the dirty brats?

REGINA No; if things go as I want them to, then—well, there's no saying—there's no saying.

ENGSTRAND What do you mean by "there's no saying"?

REGINA Never you mind. How much money have you saved up here?

ENGSTRAND What with one thing and another, a matter of seven or eight hundred crowns.[2]

REGINA That's not so bad.

ENGSTRAND It's enough to make a start with, my girl.

REGINA Aren't you thinking of giving me any?

ENGSTRAND No, I'm damned if I am!

REGINA Not even of sending me a scrap of stuff for a new dress?

ENGSTRAND If you'll come to town with me, you can get dresses enough.

REGINA Pooh! I can do that on my own account if I want to.

[2] A "krone" was equal to approximately twenty-seven cents.

ENGSTRAND No, a father's guiding hand is what you want, Regina. Now, I've my eye on a capital house in Little Harbour Street. It won't need much ready-money, and it could be a sort of sailors' home, you know.

REGINA But I will *not* live with you. I have nothing whatever to do with you. Be off!

ENGSTRAND You wouldn't remain long with me, my girl. No such luck! If you knew how to play your cards, such a fine girl as you've grown in the last year or two—

REGINA Well?

ENGSTRAND You'd soon get hold of some mate —or perhaps even a captain—

REGINA I won't marry any one of that sort. Sailors have no *savoir vivre*.

ENGSTRAND What haven't they got?

REGINA I know what sailors are, I tell you. They're not the sort of people to marry.

ENGSTRAND Then never mind about marrying them. You can make it pay all the same. [*More confidentially.*] He—the Englishman—the man with the yacht—he gave three hundred dollars, he did; and she wasn't a bit handsomer than you.

REGINA [*Going towards him.*] Out you go!

ENGSTRAND [*Falling back.*] Come, come! You're not going to strike me, I hope.

REGINA Yes, if you begin to talk about mother I shall strike you. Get away with you, I say. [*Drives him back towards the garden door.*] And don't bang the doors. Young Mr. Alving—

ENGSTRAND He's asleep; I know. It's curious how you're taken up about young Mr. Alving —[*More softly.*] Oho! it surely can't be he that—?

REGINA Be off at once! You're crazy, I tell you! No, not that way. There comes Pastor Manders. Down the kitchen stairs with you.

ENGSTRAND [*Towards the right.*] Yes, yes, I'm going. But just you talk to him that's coming there. He's the man to tell you what a child owes its father. For I am your father all the same, you know. I can prove it from the church-register.

[*He goes out through the second door to the right, which* REGINA *has opened, and fastens again after him.* REGINA *glances hastily at herself in the mirror, dusts herself with her pocket handkerchief, and settles her collar; then she busies herself with the flowers.* PASTOR MANDERS, *in an overcoat, with an umbrella, and with a small travelling-bag on a strap over his shoulder, comes through the garden door into the conservatory.*]

MANDERS Good morning, Miss Engstrand.

REGINA [*Turning round, surprised and pleased.*] No, really! Good morning, Pastor Manders. Is the steamer in already?

MANDERS It's just in. [*Enters the sitting-room.*] Terrible weather we've been having lately.

REGINA [*Follows him.*] It's such blessed weather for the country, sir.

MANDERS Yes, you're quite right. We townspeople think too little about that. [*He begins to take off his overcoat.*]

REGINA Oh, mayn't I help you? There! Why, how wet it is! I'll just hang it up in the hall. And your umbrella, too—I'll open it and let it dry.

[*She goes out with the things through the second door on the right.* PASTOR MANDERS *takes off his travelling-bag and lays it and his hat on a chair. Meanwhile* REGINA *comes in again.*]

MANDERS Ah! it's a comfort to get safe under cover. Everything going on well here?

REGINA Yes, thank you, sir.

MANDERS You have your hands full, I suppose, in preparation for to-morrow?

REGINA Yes, there's plenty to do, of course.

MANDERS And Mrs. Alving is at home, I trust?

REGINA Oh dear, yes. She's just upstairs looking after the young master's chocolate.

MANDERS Yes, by-the-bye—I heard down at the pier that Oswald had arrived.

REGINA Yes, he came the day before yesterday. We didn't expect him before to-day.

MANDERS Quite strong and well, I hope?

REGINA Yes, thank you, quite; but dreadfully tired with the journey. He has made one rush all the way from Paris. I believe he came the whole way in one train. He's sleeping a little now, I think; so perhaps we'd better talk a little quietly.

MANDERS Hush!—as quietly as you please.

REGINA [*Arranging an arm-chair beside the table.*] Now, do sit down, Pastor Manders, and make yourself comfortable. [*He sits down; she puts a footstool under his feet.*] There! are you comfortable now, sir?

MANDERS Thanks, thanks, I'm most comfortable. [*Looks at her.*] Do you know, Miss

Engstrand, I positively believe you've grown since I last saw you.

REGINA Do you think so, sir? Mrs. Alving says my figure has developed too.

MANDERS Developed? Well, perhaps a little; just enough. [*Short pause.*]

REGINA Shall I tell Mrs. Alving you are here?

MANDERS Thanks, thanks, there's no hurry, my dear child. By-the-bye, Regina, my good girl, just tell me: how is your father getting on out here?

REGINA Oh, thank you, he's getting on well enough.

MANDERS He called upon me last time he was in town.

REGINA Did he, indeed? He's always so glad of a chance of talking to you, sir.

MANDERS And you often look in upon him at his work, I daresay?

REGINA I? Oh, of course, when I have time, I—

MANDERS Your father is not a man of strong character, Miss Engstrand. He stands terribly in need of a guiding hand.

REGINA Oh, yes; I daresay he does.

MANDERS He needs to have some one near him whom he cares for, and whose judgment he respects. He frankly admitted that when he last came to see me.

REGINA Yes, he mentioned something of the sort to me. But I don't know whether Mrs. Alving can spare me; especially now that we've got the new Orphanage to attend to. And then I should be so sorry to leave Mrs. Alving; she has always been so kind to me.

MANDERS But a daughter's duty, my good girl —Of course we must first get your mistress' consent.

REGINA But I don't know whether it would be quite proper for me, at my age, to keep house for a single man.

MANDERS What! My dear Miss Engstrand! When the man is your own father!

REGINA Yes, that may be; but all the same— Now if it were in a thoroughly respectable house, and with a real gentleman—

MANDERS But, my dear Regina—

REGINA —one I could love and respect, and be a daughter to—

MANDERS Yes, but my dear, good child—

REGINA Then I should be glad to go to town. It's very lonely out here; you know yourself, sir, what it is to be alone in the world. And I can assure you I'm both quick and willing. Don't you know of any such place for me, sir?

MANDERS I? No, certainly not.

REGINA But, dear, dear sir, do remember me if—

MANDERS [*Rising.*] Yes, yes, certainly, Miss Engstrand.

REGINA For if I—

MANDERS Will you be so good as to fetch your mistress?

REGINA I will, at once, sir. [*She goes out to the left.*]

MANDERS [*Paces the room two or three times, stands a moment in the background with his hands behind his back, and looks out over the garden. Then he returns to the table, takes up a book, and looks at the title-page; starts, and looks at several.*] Hm—indeed!

[MRS. ALVING *enters by the door on the left; she is followed by* REGINA, *who immediately goes out by the first door on the right.*]

MRS. ALVING [*Holds out her hand.*] Welcome, my dear Pastor.

MANDERS How do you do, Mrs. Alving? Here I am as I promised.

MRS. ALVING Always punctual to the minute.

MANDERS You may believe it wasn't so easy for me to get away. With all the Boards and Committees I belong to—

MRS. ALVING That makes it all the kinder of you to come so early. Now we can get through our business before dinner. But where's your luggage?

MANDERS [*Quickly.*] I left it down at the inn. I shall sleep there to-night.

MRS. ALVING [*Suppressing a smile.*] Are you really not to be persuaded, even now, to pass the night under my roof?

MANDERS No, no, Mrs. Alving; many thanks. I shall stay down there as usual. It's so convenient for starting again.

MRS. ALVING Well, you must have your own way. But I really should have thought we two old people—

MANDERS Now you're making fun of me. Ah! you're naturally in great spirits to-day—what between to-morrow's festival and Oswald's return.

MRS. ALVING Yes; you can think what a delight it is to me! It's more than two years since he was home last. And now he has promised to stay with me all winter.

MANDERS Has he really? That's very nice and dutiful of him. For I can well believe that life in Rome and Paris has far more attractions.

MRS. ALVING True. But here he has his mother, you see. My own darling boy, he hasn't forgotten his old mother!

MANDERS It would be grievous indeed, if absence and absorption in art and that sort of thing were to blunt his natural feelings.

MRS. ALVING Yes, you may well say so. But there's nothing of that sort to fear in him. I'm quite curious to see whether you'll know him again. He'll be down presently; he's upstairs just now, resting a little on the sofa. But do sit down, my dear Pastor.

MANDERS Thank you. Are you quite at liberty—?

MRS. ALVING Certainly. [*She sits by the table.*]

MANDERS Very well. Then you shall see—[*He goes to the chair where his travelling-bag lies, takes out a packet of papers, sits down on the opposite side of the table, and tries to find a clear space for the papers.*] Now, to begin with, here is—[*Breaking off.*]—Tell me, Mrs. Alving, how do these books come here?

MRS. ALVING These books? They are books I am reading.

MANDERS Do you read this sort of literature?

MRS. ALVING Certainly I do.

MANDERS Do you feel better or happier for reading of this kind?

MRS. ALVING I feel, so to speak, more secure.

MANDERS That's strange. How do you mean?

MRS. ALVING Well, I seem to find explanation and confirmation of all sorts of things I myself have been thinking. For that's the wonderful part of it, Pastor Manders, there's really nothing new in those books, nothing but what most people think and believe. Only most people either don't formulate it to themselves, or else keep quiet about it.

MANDERS Great heavens! Do you really believe that most people—?

MRS. ALVING I do, indeed.

MANDERS But surely not in this country? Not here, among us?

MRS. ALVING Yes, certainly, among us too.

MANDERS Well, I really must say—!

MRS. ALVING For the rest, what do you object to in these books?

MANDERS Object to in them? You surely don't suppose that I have nothing to do but study such productions as these?

MRS. ALVING That is to say, you know nothing of what you are condemning.

MANDERS I have read enough *about* these writings to disapprove of them.

MRS. ALVING Yes; but your own opinion—

MANDERS My dear Mrs. Alving, there are many occasions in life when one must rely upon others. Things are so ordered in this world; and it's well that they are. How could society get on otherwise?

MRS. ALVING Well, I daresay you're right there.

MANDERS Besides, I of course don't deny that there may be much that is interesting in such books. Nor can I blame you for wishing to keep up with the intellectual movements that are said to be going on in the great world, where you have let your son pass so much of his life. But—

MRS. ALVING But?

MANDERS [*Lowering his voice.*] But one shouldn't talk about it, Mrs. Alving. One is certainly not bound to account to everybody for what one reads and thinks within one's own four walls.

MRS. ALVING Of course not; I quite think so.

MANDERS Only think, now, how you are bound to consider the interests of this Orphanage which you decided on founding at a time when you thought very differently on spiritual matters—so far as I can judge.

MRS. ALVING Oh yes; I quite admit that. But it was about the Orphanage—

MANDERS It was about the Orphanage we were to speak; yes. All I say is: prudence, my dear lady! And now we'll get to business. [*Opens the packet, and takes out a number of papers.*] Do you see these?

MRS. ALVING The documents?

MANDERS All—and in perfect order. I can tell you it was hard work to get them in time. I had put on strong pressure. The authorities are almost painfully scrupulous when you want them to come to the point. But here they are at last. [*Looks through the bundle.*] See! here is the formal deed of gift of the parcel of ground known as Solvik in the

Manor of Rosenvold, with all the newly-constructed buildings, schoolrooms, master's house, and chapel. And here is the legal fiat for the endowment and for the Regulations of the Institution. Will you look at them? [*Reads.*] "Regulation for the Children's Home to be known as 'Captain Alving's Foundation.' "

MRS. ALVING [*Looks long at the paper.*] So there it is.

MANDERS I have chosen the designation "Captain" rather than "Chamberlain." "Captain" looks less pretentious.

MRS. ALVING Oh, yes; just as you think best.

MANDERS And here you have the Bank Account of the capital lying at interest to cover the current expenses of the Orphanage.

MRS. ALVING Thank you; but please keep it—it will be more convenient.

MANDERS With pleasure. I think we will leave the money in the Bank for the present. The interest is certainly not what we could wish—four per cent, and six months' notice of withdrawal. If a good mortgage could be found later on—of course it must be a first mortgage and an undoubted security—then we could consider the matter.

MRS. ALVING Certainly, my dear Pastor Manders. You are the best judge in these things.

MANDERS I will keep my eyes open at any rate. But now there's one thing more which I have several times been intending to ask you.

MRS. ALVING And what's that?

MANDERS Shall the Orphanage buildings be insured or not?

MRS. ALVING Of course they must be insured.

MANDERS Well, stop a minute, Mrs. Alving. Let us look into the matter a little more closely.

MRS. ALVING I have everything insured; buildings and movables and stock and crops.

MANDERS Of course you have—on your own estate. And so have I—of course. But here, you see, it's quite another matter. The Orphanage is to be consecrated, as it were, to a higher purpose.

MRS. ALVING Yes, but that's no reason—

MANDERS For my own part, I should not see the smallest impropriety in guarding against all contingencies—

MRS. ALVING No, I should think not.

MANDERS But what is the general feeling in the neighbourhood? You, of course, know better than I.

MRS. ALVING Hm—the general feeling—

MANDERS Is there any considerable number of people—really responsible people—who might be scandalised?

MRS. ALVING What do you mean by "really responsible people"?

MANDERS Well, I mean people in such independent and influential positions that one cannot help allowing some weight to their opinions.

MRS. ALVING There are several people of that sort here, who would very likely be shocked if—

MANDERS There, you see! In town we have many such people. Think of all my colleague's adherents! People would be only too ready to interpret our action as a sign that neither you nor I had the right faith in a Higher Providence.

MRS. ALVING But for your own part, my dear Pastor, you can at least tell yourself that—

MANDERS Yes, I know—I know; my conscience would be quite easy, that is true enough. But nevertheless we should not escape grave misinterpretation; and that might very likely react unfavourably upon the Orphanage.

MRS. ALVING Well, in that case, then—

MANDERS Nor can I lose sight of the difficult—I may even say painful—position *I* might perhaps get into. In the leading circles of the town people are much taken up about this Orphanage. It is, of course, founded partly for the benefit of the town, as well; and it is to be hoped it will, to a considerable extent, result in lightening our Poor Rates. Now, as I have been your adviser, and have had the business matters in my hands, I cannot but fear that I may have to bear the brunt of fanaticism.

MRS. ALVING Oh, you mustn't run the risk of that.

MANDERS To say nothing of the attacks that would assuredly be made upon me in certain papers and periodicals, which—

MRS. ALVING Enough, my dear Pastor Manders. That consideration is quite decisive.

MANDERS Then you do not wish the Orphanage insured?

MRS. ALVING No. We'll let it alone.

MANDERS [*Leaning back in his chair.*] But if a disaster were to happen?—one can never tell. Would you be able to make good the damage?

MRS. ALVING No; I tell you plainly I should do nothing of the kind.

MANDERS Then I must tell you, Mrs. Alving, we are taking no small responsibility upon ourselves.

MRS. ALVING Do you think we can do otherwise?

MANDERS No, that's just the thing; we really cannot do otherwise. We must not expose ourselves to misinterpretation; and we have no right whatever to give offence to our neighbours.

MRS. ALVING You, as a clergyman, certainly should not.

MANDERS I really think, too, we may trust that such an institution has fortune on its side; in fact, that it stands under a Special Providence.

MRS. ALVING Let us hope so, Pastor Manders.

MANDERS Then we'll let the matter alone.

MRS. ALVING Yes, certainly.

MANDERS Very well. Just as you think best. [*Makes a note.*] Then—no insurance.

MRS. ALVING It's rather curious that you should just happen to mention the matter to-day.

MANDERS I have often thought of asking you about it—

MRS. ALVING —for we very nearly had a fire down there yesterday.

MANDERS You don't say so!

MRS. ALVING Oh, it was of no importance. A heap of shavings had caught fire in the carpenter's workshop.

MANDERS Where Engstrand works?

MRS. ALVING Yes. They say he's often very careless with matches.

MANDERS He has so many things in his head, that man—so many temptations. Thank God, he's now striving to lead a decent life, I hear.

MRS. ALVING Indeed! Who says so?

MANDERS He himself assures me of it. And he's certainly a capital workman.

MRS. ALVING Oh, yes; so long as he's sober.

MANDERS Yes, that's a sad weakness. But he's often driven to it by his bad leg, he says. Last time he was in town I was really touched by him. He came and thanked me so warmly for having got him work here, so that he might be near Regina.

MRS. ALVING He doesn't see much of *her*.

MANDERS Oh, yes; he has a talk with her every day. He told me so himself.

MRS. ALVING Well, it may be so.

MANDERS He feels so acutely that he needs some one to hold him back when temptation comes. That's what I can't help liking about Jacob Engstrand; he comes to you helplessly, accusing himself and confessing his own weakness. The last time he was talking to me—Believe me, Mrs. Alving, supposing it were a real necessity for him to have Regina home again—

MRS. ALVING [*Rising hastily.*] Regina!

MANDERS —you must not set yourself against it.

MRS. ALVING Indeed I shall set myself against it! And besides—Regina is to have a position in the Orphanage.

MANDERS But, after all, remember he's her father—

MRS. ALVING Oh! I know best what sort of a father he has been to her. No! she shall never go to him with my goodwill.

MANDERS [*Rising.*] My dear lady, don't take the matter so warmly. You misjudge Engstrand sadly. You seem to be quite terrified—

MRS. ALVING [*More quietly.*] It makes no difference. I have taken Regina into my house, and there she shall stay. [*Listens.*] Hush, my dear Mr. Manders; don't say any more about it. [*Her face lights up with gladness.*] Listen! there's Oswald coming downstairs. Now we'll think of no one but him.

[OSWALD ALVING, *in a light overcoat, hat in hand and smoking a large meerschaum, enters through the door on the left; he stops in the doorway.*]

OSWALD Oh! I beg your pardon; I thought you were in the study. [*Comes forward.*] Good-morning, Pastor Manders.

MANDERS [*Staring.*] Ah—! How strange—!

MRS. ALVING Well now, what do you think of him, Mr. Manders?

MANDERS I—I—can it really be—?

OSWALD Yes, it's really the Prodigal Son, sir.

MANDERS [*Protesting.*] My dear young friend—!

OSWALD Well, then, the Reclaimed Son.

MRS. ALVING Oswald remembers how much you were opposed to his becoming a painter.

MANDERS To our human eyes many a step seems dubious which afterwards proves—[*Wrings his hand.*] Anyhow, welcome, welcome home. Why, my dear Oswald—I suppose I may call you by your Christian name?

OSWALD What else should you call me?

MANDERS Very good. What I wanted to say was this, my dear Oswald—you mustn't believe that I utterly condemn the artist's calling. I have no doubt there are many who can keep their inner self unharmed in that profession, as in any other.

OSWALD Let us hope so.

MRS. ALVING [*Beaming with delight.*] I know one who has kept both his inner and outer self unharmed. Just look at him, Mr. Manders.

OSWALD [*Moves restlessly about the room.*] Yes, yes, my dear mother; let's say no more about it.

MANDERS Why, certainly—that's undeniable. And you have begun to make a name for yourself already. The newspapers have often spoken of you, most favourably. By-the-bye, just lately they haven't mentioned you so often, I fancy.

OSWALD [*Up in the conservatory.*] I haven't been able to paint so much lately.

MRS. ALVING Even a painter needs a little rest now and then.

MANDERS I can quite believe it. And meanwhile he can be gathering his forces for some great work.

OSWALD Yes—Mother, will dinner soon be ready?

MRS. ALVING In less than half-an-hour. He has a capital appetite, thank God.

MANDERS And a taste for tobacco, too.

OSWALD I found my father's pipe in my room, and so—

MANDERS Aha! then that accounts for it.

MRS. ALVING For what?

MANDERS When Oswald stood there, in the doorway, with the pipe in his mouth, I could have sworn I saw his father, large as life.

OSWALD No, really?

MRS. ALVING Oh! how can you say so? Oswald takes after me.

MANDERS Yes, but there's an expression about the corners of the mouth—something about the lips that remind one exactly of Alving; at any rate, now that he's smoking.

MRS. ALVING Not in the least. Oswald has rather a clerical curve about his mouth, I think.

MANDERS Yes, yes; some of my colleagues have much the same expression.

MRS. ALVING But put your pipe away, my dear boy; I won't have smoking in here.

OSWALD [*Does so.*] By all means. I only wanted to try it; for I once smoked it when I was a child.

MRS. ALVING You?

OSWALD Yes. I was quite small at the time. I recollect I came up to father's room one evening when he was in great spirits.

MRS. ALVING Oh, you can't recollect anything of these times.

OSWALD Yes, I recollect distinctly. He took me up on his knees, and gave me the pipe. "Smoke, boy," he said; "smoke away, boy." And I smoked as hard as I could, until I felt I was growing quite pale, and the perspiration stood in great drops on my forehead. Then he burst out laughing heartily—

MANDERS That was most extraordinary.

MRS. ALVING My dear friend, it's only something Oswald has dreamt.

OSWALD No, mother, I assure you I didn't dream it. For—don't you remember *this?*—you came and carried me out into the nursery. Then I was sick, and I saw you were crying. —Did father often play such pranks?

MANDERS In his youth he overflowed with the joy of life—[3]

OSWALD And yet he managed to do so much in the world; so much that was good and useful; and he died so young, too.

MANDERS Yes, you have inherited the name of an active and worthy man, my dear Oswald Alving. No doubt it will be an incentive to you—

OSWALD It ought to, indeed.

MANDERS It was good of you to come home for the ceremony in his honour.

OSWALD I could do no less for my father.

MRS. ALVING And I am to keep him so long! That's the best of all.

MANDERS You're going to pass the winter at home, I hear.

OSWALD My stay is indefinite, sir. But, oh! how delightful it is to be at home again!

MRS. ALVING [*Beaming.*] Yes, isn't it?

MANDERS [*Looking sympathetically at him.*]

[3] "Var en særdeles livsglad mand"—literally, "was a man who took the greatest pleasure in life," *la joie de vivre*—an expression which frequently recurs in this play.

You went out into the world early, my dear Oswald.

OSWALD I did. I sometimes wonder whether it wasn't *too* early.

MRS. ALVING Oh, not at all. A healthy lad is all the better for it; especially when he's an only child. He oughtn't to hang on at home with his mother and father and get spoilt.

MANDERS It's a very difficult question, Mrs. Alving. A child's proper place is, and must be, the home of his fathers.

OSWALD There I quite agree with you, Pastor Manders.

MANDERS Only look at your own son—there's no reason why we shouldn't say it in his presence—what has the consequence been for him? He's six or seven and twenty, and has never had the opportunity of learning what home life really is.

OSWALD I beg your pardon, Pastor; there you're quite mistaken.

MANDERS Indeed? I thought you had lived almost exclusively in artistic circles.

OSWALD So I have.

MANDERS And chiefly among the younger artists.

OSWALD Yes, certainly.

MANDERS But I thought few of these young fellows could afford to set up house and support a family.

OSWALD There are many who can't afford to marry, sir.

MANDERS Yes, that's just what I say.

OSWALD But they can have a home for all that. And several of them have, as a matter of fact; and very pleasant, comfortable homes they are, too.

[MRS. ALVING *follows with breathless interest; nods, but says nothing.*]

MANDERS But I am not talking of bachelors' quarters. By a "home" I understand the home of a family, where a man lives with his wife and children.

OSWALD Yes; or with his children and his children's mother.

MANDERS [*Starts; clasps his hands.*] But, good heavens—!

OSWALD Well?

MANDERS Lives with—his children's mother!

OSWALD Yes. Would you have him turn his children's mother out of doors?

MANDERS Then it's illicit relations you are talking of! Irregular marriages, as people call them!

OSWALD I have never noticed anything particularly irregular about the life these people lead.

MANDERS But how is it possible that a—a young man or young woman with any decent principles can endure to live in that way?—in the eyes of all the world!

OSWALD What are they to do? A poor young artist—a poor girl—it costs a lot to get married. What are they to do?

MANDERS What are they to do? Let me tell you, Mr. Alving, what they ought to do. They ought to exercise self-restraint from the first; that's what they ought to do.

OSWALD Such talk won't go far with warm-blooded young people, over head and ears in love.

MRS. ALVING No, it wouldn't go far.

MANDERS [*Continuing.*] How can the authorities tolerate such things? Allow them to go on in the light of day? [*To* MRS. ALVING.] Had I not cause to be deeply concerned about your son? In circles where open immorality prevails, and has even a sort of prestige—!

OSWALD Let me tell you, sir, that I have been a constant Sunday-guest in one or two such irregular homes—

MANDERS On Sunday of all days!

OSWALD Isn't that the day to enjoy oneself? Well, never have I heard an offensive word, and still less have I witnessed anything that could be called immoral. No; do you not know when and where I have come across immorality in artistic circles?

MANDERS No, thank heaven, I don't!

OSWALD Well, then, allow me to inform you. I have met with it when one or other of our pattern husbands and fathers has come to Paris to have a look around on his own account, and has done the artists the honour of visiting their humble haunts. *They* knew what was what. These gentlemen could tell us all about places and things we had never dreamt of.

MANDERS What! Do you mean to say that respectable men from home here would—?

OSWALD Have you never heard these respectable men, when they got home again, talking about the way in which immorality was running rampant abroad?

MANDERS Yes, of course.

MRS. ALVING I have too.

OSWALD Well, you may take their word for it. They know what they're talking about! [*Presses his hands to his head.*] Oh! that that great, free, glorious life out there should be defiled in such a way!

MRS. ALVING You mustn't get excited, Oswald. You will do yourself harm.

OSWALD Yes; you're quite right, mother. It's not good for me. You see, I'm wretchedly worn out. I'll go for a little turn before dinner. Excuse me, Pastor; I know you can't take my point of view; but I couldn't help speaking out.

[*He goes out through the second door to the right.*]

MRS. ALVING My poor boy!

MANDERS You may well say so. Then that's what he has come to!

[MRS. ALVING *looks at him silently.*]

MANDERS [*Walking up and down.*] He called himself the Prodigal Son—alas! alas!

[MRS. ALVING *continues looking at him.*]

MANDERS And what do you say to all this?

MRS. ALVING I say that Oswald was right in every word.

MANDERS [*Stands still.*] Right! Right! In such principles?

MRS. ALVING Here, in my loneliness, I have come to the same way of thinking, Pastor Manders. But I've never dared to say anything. Well! now my boy shall speak for me.

MANDERS You are much to be pitied, Mrs. Alving. But now I must speak seriously to you. And now it is no longer your business manager and adviser, your own and your late husband's early friend, who stands before you. It is the priest—the priest who stood before you in the moment of your life when you had gone most astray.

MRS. ALVING And what has the priest to say to me?

MANDERS I will first stir up your memory a little. The time is well chosen. To-morrow will be the tenth anniversary of your husband's death. To-morrow the memorial in his honour will be unveiled. To-morrow I shall have to speak to the whole assembled multitude. But to-day I will speak to you alone.

MRS. ALVING Very well, Pastor Manders. Speak.

MANDERS Do you remember that after less than a year of married life you stood on the verge of an abyss? That you forsook your house and home? That you fled from your husband? Yes, Mrs. Alving—fled, fled, and refused to return to him, however much he begged and prayed you?

MRS. ALVING Have you forgotten how infinitely miserable I was in that first year?

MANDER It is only the spirit of rebellion that craves for happiness in this life. What right have we human beings to happiness? No, we have to do our duty! And your duty was to hold firmly to the man you had once chosen and to whom you were bound by a holy tie.

MRS. ALVING You know very well what sort of life Alving was leading—what excesses he was guilty of.

MANDERS I know very well what rumours there were about him, and I am the last to approve the life he led in his young days, if report did not wrong him. But a wife is not to be her husband's judge. It was your duty to bear with humility the cross which a Higher Power had, for your own good, laid upon you. But instead of that you rebelliously throw away the cross, desert the backslider whom you should have supported, go and risk your good name and reputation and—nearly succeed in ruining other people's reputation into the bargain.

MRS. ALVING Other people's? One other person's, you mean.

MANDERS It was incredibly reckless of you to seek refuge with me.

MRS. ALVING With our clergyman? With our intimate friend?

MANDERS Just on that account. Yes, you may thank God that I possessed the necessary firmness; that I dissuaded you from your wild designs; and that it was vouchsafed me to lead you back to the path of duty, and home to your lawful husband.

MRS. ALVING Yes, Pastor Manders, it was certainly your work.

MANDERS I was but a poor instrument in a Higher Hand. And what a blessing has it not been to you, all the days of your life, that I got you to resume the yoke of duty and obedience! Did not everything happen as I foretold? Did not Alving turn his back on his errors, as a man should? Did he not live with you from that time, lovingly and blamelessly, all his days? Did he not become a benefactor to the whole district? And did he not raise you up to him so that you little by little became his assistant in all his undertakings? And a capital assistant, too—Oh! I know, Mrs. Alving, that praise is due to you. But now I come to the next great error in your life.

MRS. ALVING What do you mean?

MANDERS Just as you once disowned a wife's duty, so you have since disowned a mother's.

MRS. ALVING Ah!

MANDERS You have been all your life under the dominion of a pestilent spirit of self-will. All your efforts have been bent towards emancipation and lawlessness. You have never known how to endure any bond. Everything that has weighed upon you in life you have cast away without care or conscience, like a burden you could throw off at will. It did not please you to be a wife any longer, and you left your husband. You found it troublesome to be a mother, and you sent your child forth among strangers.

MRS. ALVING Yes. That is true. I did so.

MANDERS And thus you have become a stranger to him.

MRS. ALVING No! No! I am not.

MANDERS Yes, you are; and must be. And how have you got him back again? Bethink yourself well, Mrs. Alving. You have sinned greatly against your husband;—that you recognise by raising yonder memorial to him. Recognise now, also, how you have sinned against your son. There may be time to lead him back from the paths of error. Turn back yourself, and save what may yet be saved in him. For [*With uplifted forefinger.*] verily, Mrs. Alving, you are a guilt-laden mother!—This I have thought it my duty to say to you. [*Silence.*]

MRS. ALVING [*Slowly and with self-control.*] You have now spoken out, Pastor Manders; and to-morrow you are to speak publicly in memory of my husband. I shall not speak to-morrow. But I will speak frankly to you, as you have spoken to me.

MANDERS To be sure; you will plead excuses for your conduct—

MRS. ALVING No. I will only narrate.

MANDERS Well?

MRS. ALVING All that you have just said about me and my husband and our life after you had brought me back to the path of duty—as you called it—about all that you know nothing from personal observation. From that moment you, who had been our intimate friend, never set foot in our house again.

MANDERS You and your husband left the town immediately after.

MRS. ALVING Yes; and in my husband's lifetime you never came to see us. It was business that forced you to visit me when you undertook the affairs of the Orphanage.

MANDERS [*Softly and uncertainly.*] Helen—if that is meant as a reproach, I would beg you to bear in mind—

MRS. ALVING —the regard you owed to your position, yes; and that I was a runaway wife. One can never be too careful with such unprincipled creatures.

MANDERS My dear—Mrs. Alving, you know that is an absurd exaggeration—

MRS. ALVING Well well, suppose it is. My point is that your judgment as to my married life is founded upon nothing but current gossip.

MANDERS Well, I admit that. What then?

MRS. ALVING Well, then, Mr. Manders—I will tell you the truth. I have sworn to myself that one day you should know it—you alone!

MANDERS What is the truth, then?

MRS. ALVING The truth is that my husband died just as dissolute as he had lived all his days.

MANDERS [*Feeling after a chair.*] What do you say?

MRS. ALVING After nineteen years of marriage, as dissolute—in his desires at any rate—as he was before you married us.

MANDERS And those—those wild oats, those irregularities, those excesses, if you like, you call "a dissolute life"?

MRS. ALVING Our doctor used the expression.

MANDERS I don't understand you.

MRS. ALVING You need not.

MANDERS It almost makes me dizzy. Your whole married life, the seeming union of all these years, was nothing more than a hidden abyss!

MRS. ALVING Nothing more. Now you know it.

MANDERS This is—it will take me long to accustom myself to the thought. I can't grasp it! I can't realise it! But how was it possible to—? How could such a state of things be kept dark?

MRS. ALVING That has been my ceaseless struggle, day after day. After Oswald's birth, I thought Alving seemed to be a little better. But it didn't last long. And then I had to struggle twice as hard, fighting for life or death, so that nobody should know what sort of a man my child's father was. And you know what power Alving had of winning people's hearts. Nobody seemed able to believe anything but good of him. He was one of those people whose life does not bite upon their reputation. But at last, Mr. Manders—for you must know the whole story—the most repulsive thing of all happened.

MANDERS More repulsive than the rest?

MRS. ALVING I had gone on bearing with him, although I knew very well the secrets of his life out of doors. But when he brought the scandal within our own walls—

MANDERS Impossible! Here!

MRS. ALVING Yes; here in our own house. It was there [*Pointing towards the first door on the right.*] in the dining-room, that I first got to know of it. I was busy with something in there, and the door was standing ajar. I heard our house-maid come up from the garden, with water for those flowers.

MANDERS Well—?

MRS. ALVING Soon after I heard Alving come too. I heard him say something softly to her. And then I heard—[*With a short laugh.*]—oh! it still sounds in my ears, so hateful and yet so ludicrous—I heard my own servant-maid whisper, "Let me go, Mr. Alving! Let me be."

MANDERS What unseemly levity on his part! But it cannot have been more than levity, Mrs. Alving; believe me, it cannot.

MRS. ALVING I soon knew what to believe. Mr. Alving had his way with the girl; and that connection had consequences, Mr. Manders.

MANDERS [*As though petrified.*] Such things in this house! in this house!

MRS. ALVING I had borne a great deal in this house. To keep him at home in the evenings—and at night—I had to make myself his boon companion in his secret orgies up in his room. There I have had to sit alone with him, to clink glasses and drink with him, and to listen to his ribald, silly talk. I have had to fight with him to get him dragged to bed—

MANDERS [*Moved.*] And you were able to bear all that?

MRS. ALVING I had to bear it for my little boy's sake. But when the last insult was added; when my own servant-maid—Then I swore to myself: This shall come to an end. And so I took the reins into my own hand—the whole control over him and everything else. For now I had a weapon against him, you see; he dared not oppose me. It was then I sent Oswald from home. He was in his seventh year, and was beginning to observe and ask questions, as children do. That I could not bear. It seemed to me the child must be poisoned by merely breathing the air of this polluted house. That was why I sent him away. And now you can see, too, why he was never allowed to set foot inside his home so long as his father lived. No one knows what it has cost me.

MANDERS You have indeed had a life of trial.

MRS. ALVING I could never have borne it if I hadn't had my work. For I may truly say that I have worked! All those additions to the estate—all the improvements—all the useful appliances, that won Alving such general praise—do you suppose *he* had energy for anything of the sort?—he who lay all day on the sofa and read an old court guide! No; this I will tell you too: it was I who urged him on when he had his better intervals; it was I who had to drag the whole load when he relapsed into his evil ways, or sank into querulous wretchedness.

MANDERS And to that man you raise a memorial?

MRS. ALVING There you see the power of an evil conscience.

MANDERS Evil—? What do you mean?

MRS. ALVING It always seemed to me impossible but that the truth must come out and be believed. So the Asylum was to deaden all rumours and banish doubt.

MANDERS In that you have certainly not missed your aim, Mrs. Alving.

MRS. ALVING And besides, I had one other reason. I did not wish that Oswald, my own boy, should inherit anything whatever from his father.

MANDERS Then it is Alving's fortune that—?

MRS. ALVING Yes. The sums I have spent upon the Orphanage, year by year, make up the amount—I have reckoned it up precisely—the amount which made Lieutenant Alving a good match in his day.

MANDERS I don't quite understand—

MRS. ALVING It was my purchase-money. I do not choose that that money should pass into Oswald's hands. My son shall have everything from me—everything. [OSWALD ALVING *enters through the second door to the right; he has taken off his hat and overcoat in the hall.* MRS. ALVING *goes towards him.*] Are you back again already? my dear, dear boy!

OSWALD Yes. What can a fellow do out of doors in this eternal rain? But I hear dinner's ready. That's capital!

REGINA [*With a parcel, from the dining-room.*] A parcel has come for you, Mrs. Alving. [*Hands it to her.*]

MRS. ALVING [*With a glance at* MR. MANDERS.] No doubt copies of the ode for to-morrow's ceremony.

MANDERS Hm—

REGINA And dinner is ready.

MRS. ALVING Very well. We'll come directly. I'll just— [*Begins to open the parcel.*]

REGINA [*To* OSWALD.] Would Mr. Alving like red or white wine?

OSWALD Both, if you please.

REGINA *Bien.* Very well, sir. [*She goes into the dining-room.*]

OSWALD I may as well help to uncork it. [*He also goes into the dining-room, the door of which swings half open behind him.*]

MRS. ALVING [*Who has opened the parcel.*] Yes, as I thought. Here is the Ceremonial Ode, Pastor Manders.

MANDERS [*With folded hands.*] With what countenance I'm to deliver my discourse to-morrow—!

MRS. ALVING Oh! you'll get through it somehow.

MANDERS [*Softly, so as not to be heard in the dining-room.*] Yes; it would not do to provoke scandal.

MRS. ALVING [*Under her breath, but firmly.*] No. But then this long, hateful comedy will be ended. From the day after to-morrow it shall be for me as though he who is dead had never lived in this house. No one shall be here but my boy and his mother. [*From within the dining-room comes the noise of a chair overturned, and at the same moment is heard.*]

REGINA [*Sharply, but whispering.*] Oswald! take care! are you mad? Let me go!

MRS. ALVING [*Starts in terror.*] Ah!

[*She stares wildly towards the half-opened door.* OSWALD *is heard coughing and humming. A bottle is uncorked.*]

MANDERS [*Excited.*] What in the world is the matter? What is it, Mrs. Alving?

MRS. ALVING [*Hoarsely.*] Ghosts! The couple from the conservatory—risen again!

MANDERS What! Is it possible! Regina—? Is she—?

MRS. ALVING Yes. Come. Not another word!

[*She seizes* MR. MANDERS *by the arm, and walks unsteadily towards the dining-room.*]

ACT II

[*The same room. The mist still lies heavy over the landscape.* MANDERS *and* MRS. ALVING *enter from the dining-room.*]

MRS. ALVING [*Still in the doorway.*] Hearty appetite, Mr. Manders. [*Turns back towards the dining-room.*] Aren't you coming too, Oswald?

OSWALD [*From within.*] No, thank you. I think I shall go out a little.

MRS. ALVING Yes, do. The weather seems brighter now. [*She shuts the dining-room door, goes to the hall door, and calls.*] Regina!

REGINA [*Outside.*] Yes, Mrs. Alving.

MRS. ALVING Go down to the laundry, and help with the garlands.

REGINA I'll go directly, Mrs. Alving.

[MRS. ALVING *assures herself that* REGINA *goes; then shuts the door.*]

MANDERS I suppose he can't overhear us in there?

MRS. ALVING Not when the door is shut. Besides, he's just going out.

MANDERS I'm still quite upset. I can't think how I could get down a morsel of dinner.

MRS. ALVING [*Controlling her nervousness, walks up and down.*] No more can I. But what's to be done now?

MANDERS Yes; what's to be done? Upon my honour, I don't know. I'm so utterly without experience in matters of this sort.

MRS. ALVING I'm quite convinced that, so far, no mischief has been done.

MANDERS No; heaven forbid! But it's an unseemly state of things, nevertheless.

MRS. ALVING The whole thing is an idle fancy of Oswald's; you may be sure of that.

MANDERS Well, as I say, I'm not accustomed to affairs of the kind. But I should certainly think—

MRS. ALVING Out of the house she must go, and that immediately. That's as clear as daylight.

MANDERS Yes, of course she must.

MRS. ALVING But where to? It would not be right to—

MANDERS Where to? Home to her father, of course.

MRS. ALVING To whom did you say?

MANDERS To her— But then Engstrand is not —? Good God, Mrs. Alving, it's impossible! You must be mistaken after all.

MRS. ALVING Alas! I'm mistaken in nothing. Johanna confessed all to me, and Alving could not deny it. So there was nothing to be done but to get the matter hushed up.

MANDERS No, you could do nothing else.

MRS. ALVING The girl left our service at once, and got a good sum of money to hold her tongue for the time. The rest she managed for herself when she got into the town. She renewed her old acquaintance with Engstrand, no doubt gave him to understand how much money she had received, and told him some tale about a foreigner who put in here with a yacht that summer. So she and Engstrand got married in hot haste. Why, you married them yourself.

MANDERS But then how to account for—? I recollect distinctly Engstrand coming to give notice of the marriage. He was broken down with contrition, and reproached himself so bitterly for the misbehaviour he and his sweetheart had been guilty of.

MRS. ALVING Yes; of course he had to take the blame upon himself.

MANDERS But such a piece of duplicity on his part! And towards me too! I never could have believed it of Jacob Engstrand. I shan't fail to give him a serious talking to; he may be sure of that. And then the immorality of such a connection! For money! How much did the girl receive?

MRS. ALVING Three hundred dollars.

MANDERS There! think of that! for a miserable three hundred dollars to go and marry a fallen woman!

MRS. ALVING Then what have you to say of me? I went and married a fallen man.

MANDERS But—good heavens!—what are you talking about? A fallen man?

MRS. ALVING Do you think Alving was any purer when I went with him to the altar than Johanna was when Engstrand married her?

MANDERS Well, but there's a world of difference between the two cases—

MRS. ALVING Not so much difference after all, except in the price—a wretched three hundred dollars and a whole fortune.

MANDERS How can you compare the two cases? You had taken counsel with your own heart and with your friends.

MRS. ALVING [*Without looking at him.*] I thought you understood where what you call my heart had strayed to at the time.

MANDERS [*Distantly.*] Had I understood anything of the kind, I should not have continued a daily guest in your husband's house.

MRS. ALVING Well, the fact remains that with myself I took no counsel whatever.

MANDERS Well then, with your nearest relatives—as your duty bade you—with your mother and both your aunts.

MRS. ALVING Yes, that's true. Those three cast up the account for me. Oh! it's marvellous how clearly they made out that it would be downright madness to refuse such an offer. If mother could only see me now, and know what all that grandeur has come to!

MANDERS Nobody can be held responsible for the result. This, at least, remains clear; your marriage was in accordance with law and order.

MRS. ALVING [*At the window.*] Oh! that perpetual law and order! I often think that's what does all the mischief here in the world.

MANDERS Mrs. Alving, that is a sinful way of talking.

MRS. ALVING Well, I can't help it; I can endure all this constraint and cowardice no longer. It's too much for me. I must work my way out to freedom.

MANDERS What do you mean by that?

MRS. ALVING [*Drumming on the window-sill.*] I ought never to have concealed the facts of

Alving's life. But at that time I was afraid to do anything else—afraid on my own account. I was such a coward.

MANDERS A coward?

MRS. ALVING If people had come to know anything, they would have said—"Poor man! with a runaway wife, no wonder he kicks over the traces."

MANDERS Such remarks might have been made with a certain show of right.

MRS. ALVING [*Looking steadily at him.*] If I were what I ought to be, I should go to Oswald and say, "Listen, my boy; your father was self-indulgent and vicious—"

MANDERS Merciful heavens—!

MRS. ALVING —and then I should tell him all I have told you—every word of it.

MANDERS The idea is shocking, Mrs. Alving.

MRS. ALVING Yes; I know that. I know that very well. I'm shocked at it myself. [*Goes away from the window.*] I'm such a coward.

MANDERS You call it "cowardice" to do your plain duty? Have you forgotten that a son should love and honour his father and mother?

MRS. ALVING Don't let us talk in such general terms. Let us ask: should Oswald love and honour Chamberlain Alving?

MANDERS Is there no voice in your mother's heart that forbids you to destroy your son's ideals?

MRS. ALVING But what about the truth?

MANDERS But what about the ideals?

MRS. ALVING Oh! Ideals! Ideals! If only I weren't such a coward!

MANDERS Do not despise ideals, Mrs. Alving; they will avenge themselves cruelly. Take Oswald's case; he, unfortunately, seems to have few enough ideals as it is; but I can see that his father stands before him as an ideal.

MRS. ALVING You're right there.

MANDERS And this habit of mind you have yourself implanted and fostered by your letters.

MRS. ALVING Yes; in my superstitious awe for Duty and Decency I lied to my boy, year after year. Oh! what a coward, what a coward I've been!

MANDERS You have established a happy illusion in your son's heart, Mrs. Alving, and assuredly you ought not to undervalue it.

MRS. ALVING Hm; who knows whether it's so happy after all—? But, at any rate, I won't have any goings-on with Regina. He shan't go and ruin the poor girl.

MANDERS No; good God! that would be dreadful!

MRS. ALVING If I knew he was in earnest, and that it would be for his happiness—

MANDERS What? What then?

MRS. ALVING But it couldn't be; for I'm sorry to say Regina is not a girl to make him happy.

MANDERS Well, what then? What do you mean?

MRS. ALVING If I weren't such a pitiful coward I would say to him, "Marry her, or make what arrangement you please, only let us have nothing underhand about it."

MANDERS Good heavens, would you let them *marry!* Anything so dreadful—! so unheard of—!

MRS. ALVING Do you really mean "unheard of"? Frankly, Pastor Manders, do you suppose that throughout the country there aren't plenty of married couples as closely akin as they?

MANDERS I don't in the least understand you.

MRS. ALVING Oh yes, indeed you do.

MANDERS Ah, you are thinking of the possibility that—Yes, alas! family life is certainly not always so pure as it ought to be. But in such a case as you point to, one can never know—at least with any certainty. Here, on the other hand—that you, a mother, can think of letting your son—!

MRS. ALVING But I can't—I wouldn't for anything in the world; that's precisely what I am saying.

MANDERS No, because you are a "coward," as you put it. But if you were not a "coward," then—? Good God! a connection so shocking.

MRS. ALVING So far as that goes, they say we're all sprung from connections of that sort. And who is it that arranged the world so, Pastor Manders?

MANDERS Questions of that kind I must decline to discuss with you, Mrs. Alving; you are far from being in the right frame of mind for them. But that you dare to call your scruples "cowardly"—!

MRS. ALVING Let me tell you what I mean. I am timid and half-hearted because I cannot get rid of the Ghosts that haunt me.

MANDERS What do you say haunts you?

MRS. ALVING Ghosts! When I heard Regina and Oswald in there, I seemed to see Ghosts before me. I almost think we're all of us Ghosts, Pastor Manders. It's not only what we have inherited from our father and mother that "walks" in us. It's all sorts of dead ideas, and lifeless old beliefs, and so forth. They have no vitality, but they cling to us all the same, and we can't get rid of them. Whenever I take up a newspaper, I seem to see Ghosts gliding between the lines. There must be Ghosts all the country over, as thick as the sand of the sea. And then we are, one and all, so pitifully afraid of the light.

MANDERS Ah! here we have the fruits of your reading! And pretty fruits they are, upon my word! Oh! those horrible, revolutionary, freethinking books!

MRS. ALVING You are mistaken, my dear Pastor. It was you yourself who set me thinking; and I thank you for it with all my heart.

MANDERS I?

MRS. ALVING Yes—when you forced me under the yoke you called Duty and Obligation; when you praised as right and proper what my whole soul rebelled against as something loathsome. It was then that I began to look into the seams of your doctrine. I wanted only to pick at a single knot; but when I had got that undone, the whole thing ravelled out. And then I understood that it was all machine-sewn.

MANDERS [*Softly, with emotion.*] And was that the upshot of my life's hardest battle?

MRS. ALVING Call it rather your most pitiful defeat.

MANDERS It was my greatest victory, Helen—the victory over myself.

MRS. ALVING It was a crime against us both.

MANDERS When you went astray, and came to me crying, "Here I am; take me!" I commanded you, saying, "Woman, go home to your lawful husband." Was that a crime?

MRS. ALVING Yes, I think so.

MANDERS We two do not understand each other.

MRS. ALVING Not now, at any rate.

MANDERS Never—never in my most secret thoughts have I regarded you otherwise than as another's wife.

MRS. ALVING Oh!—indeed?

MANDERS Helen—!

MRS. ALVING People so easily forget their past selves.

MANDERS I do not. I am what I always was.

MRS. ALVING [*Changing the subject.*] Well, well, well; don't let us talk of old times any longer. You are now over head and ears in Commissions and Boards of Direction, and I am fighting my battle with Ghosts both within me and without.

MANDERS Those without I shall help you to lay. After all the shocking things I've heard from you today, I cannot in conscience permit an unprotected girl to remain in your house.

MRS. ALVING Don't you think the best plan would be to get her provided for?—I mean, by a good marriage.

MANDERS No doubt. I think it would be desirable for her in every respect. Regina is now at the age when— Of course I don't know much about these things, but—

MRS. ALVING Regina matured very early.

MANDERS Yes, did she not? I have an impression that she was remarkably well developed, physically, when I prepared her for confirmation. But in the meantime, she must go home, under her father's eye.—Ah! but Engstrand is not— That he—that *he*—could so hide the truth from me!

[*A knock at the door into the hall.*]

MRS. ALVING Who can that be? Come in!

ENGSTRAND [*In his Sunday clothes, in the doorway.*] I beg your pardon humbly, but—

MANDERS Ah! Hm—

MRS. ALVING Is that you, Engstrand?

ENGSTRAND —there was none of the servants about, so I took the great liberty of just knocking.

MRS. ALVING Oh! very well. Come in. Do you want to speak to me?

ENGSTRAND [*Comes in.*] No, I'm greatly obliged to you; it was with his Reverence I wanted to have a word or two.

MANDERS [*Walking up and down the room.*] Hm—indeed! You want to speak to me, do you?

ENGSTRAND Yes, I should like so much to—

MANDERS [*Stops in front of him.*] Well; may I ask what you want?

ENGSTRAND Well, it was just this, your Reverence; we've been paid off down yonder—my grateful thanks to you, ma'am,—and now everything's finished. I've been thinking it would be but right and proper if we, that have been working so honestly together all this time—well, I was thinking we ought to end up with a little prayer-meeting tonight.

MANDERS A prayer-meeting? Down at the Orphanage?

ENGSTRAND Oh, if your Reverence doesn't think it proper—

MANDERS Oh yes! I do; but—hm—

ENGSTRAND I've been in the habit of offering up a little prayer in the evenings, myself.

MRS. ALVING Have you?

ENGSTRAND Yes, every now and then—just a little exercise, you might call it. But I'm a poor, common man, and have little enough gift, God help me! and so I thought, as the Reverend Mr. Manders happened to be here, I'd—

MANDERS Well, you see, Engstrand, I must first ask you a question. Are you in the right frame of mind for such a meeting? Do you feel your conscience clear and at ease?

ENGSTRAND Oh! God help us, your Reverence! we'd better not talk about conscience.

MANDERS Yes, that's just what we must talk about. What have you to answer?

ENGSTRAND Why—one's conscience—it can be bad enough now and then.

MANDERS Ah, you admit that. Then will you make a clean breast of it, and tell the truth about Regina?

MRS. ALVING [*Quickly.*] Mr. Manders!

MANDERS [*Reassuringly.*] Just let me—

ENGSTRAND About Regina! Lord! how you frighten me! [*Looks at* MRS. ALVING.] There's nothing wrong about Regina, is there?

MANDERS We'll hope not. But I mean, what is the truth about you and Regina? You pass for her father, eh!

ENGSTRAND [*Uncertain.*] Well—hm—your Reverence knows all about me and poor Johanna.

MANDERS Come, no more prevarication! Your wife told Mrs. Alving the whole story before quitting her service.

ENGSTRAND Well, then, may—! Now, did she really?

MANDERS So you're found out, Engstrand.

ENGSTRAND And she swore and took her Bible oath—

MANDERS Did she take her Bible oath?

ENGSTRAND No; she only swore; but she did it so earnestly.

MANDERS And you have hidden the truth from me all these years? Hidden it from me! from me, who have trusted you without reserve, in everything.

ENGSTRAND Well, I can't deny it.

MANDERS Have I deserved this of you, Engstrand? Haven't I always been ready to help you in word and deed, so far as it stood in my power? Answer me. Have I not?

ENGSTRAND It would have been a poor look-out for me many a time but for the Reverend Mr. Manders.

MANDERS And you reward me thus! You cause me to enter falsehoods in the Church Register, and you withhold from me, year after year, the explanations you owed alike to me and to truth. Your conduct has been wholly inexcusable, Engstrand; and from this time forward all is over between us.

ENGSTRAND [*With a sigh.*] Yes! I suppose it must be.

MANDERS How can you possibly justify yourself?

ENGSTRAND How could I think she'd gone and made bad worse by talking about it? Will your Reverence just fancy yourself in the same trouble as poor Johanna—

MANDERS I!

ENGSTRAND Lord bless you! I don't mean just exactly the same. But I mean, if your Reverence had anything to be ashamed of in the eyes of the world, as the saying is— We men oughtn't to judge a poor woman too hardly, your Reverence.

MANDERS I am not doing so. It's you I am reproaching.

ENGSTRAND Might I make so bold as to ask your Reverence a bit of a question?

MANDERS Yes, ask away.

ENGSTRAND Isn't it right and proper for a man to raise up the fallen?

MANDERS Most certainly it is.

ENGSTRAND And isn't a man bound to keep his sacred word?

MANDERS Why, of course he is; but—

ENGSTRAND When Johanna had got into trouble through that Englishman—or it might have been an American or a Russian, as they call them—well, you see, she came down into the town. Poor thing! she'd sent me about my business once or twice before: for she couldn't bear the sight of anything but what was handsome; and I'd got this damaged leg. Your Reverence recollects how I ventured up into a dancing-saloon, where seafaring people carried on with drink and devilry, as the saying goes. And then, when I was for giving them a bit of an admonition to lead a new life—

MRS. ALVING [*At the window.*] Hm—

MANDERS I know all about that, Engstrand; the ruffians threw you downstairs. You've told me of the affair already.

ENGSTRAND I'm not puffed up about it, your Reverence. But what I wanted to say was, that then she came and confessed all to me, with weeping and gnashing of teeth. I can tell your Reverence I was sore at heart to hear it.

MANDERS Were you indeed, Engstrand? Well, go on.

ENGSTRAND So I said to her, "The American, he's sailing about on the boundless sea. And as for you, Johanna," said I, "you've committed a grievous sin and you're a fallen creature. But Jacob Engstrand," said I, "he's got two good legs to stand upon, *he* has—" You know, your Reverence, I was speaking figurative-like.

MANDERS I understand quite well. Go on.

ENGSTRAND Well, that was how I raised her up and made an honest woman of her, so that folks shouldn't get to know how she'd gone astray with foreigners.

MANDERS All that was very good of you. Only I can't approve of your stooping to take money—

ENGSTRAND Money? I? Not a farthing!

MANDERS [*Inquiringly to* MRS. ALVING.] But—

ENGSTRAND Oh, wait a minute!—now I recollect. Johanna had a trifle of money. But I would have nothing to do with it. "No," said I, "that's mammon; that's the wages of sin. This dirty gold—or notes, or whatever it was —we'll just fling that back to the American," said I. But he was gone and away, over the stormy sea, your Reverence.

MANDERS Was he really, my good fellow?

ENGSTRAND Ay, sir. So Johanna and I, we agreed that the money should go to the child's education; and so it did, and I can account for every blessed farthing of it.

MANDERS Why, this alters the case considerably.

ENGSTRAND That's just how it stands, your Reverence. And I make so bold as to say I've been an honest father to Regina, so far as my poor strength went; for I'm but a poor creature, worse luck!

MANDERS Well, well, my good fellow—

ENGSTRAND But I may make bold to say that I've brought up the child, and lived kindly with poor Johanna, and ruled over my own house, as the Scripture has it. But I could never think of going up to your Reverence and puffing myself up and boasting because I too had done some good in the world. No, sir; when anything of that sort happens to Jacob Engstrand, he holds his tongue about it. It doesn't happen so very often, I daresay. And when I do come to see your Reverence, I find a mortal deal to say about what's wicked and weak. For I do say—as I was saying just now—one's conscience isn't always as clean as it might be.

MANDERS Give me your hand, Jacob Engstrand.

ENGSTRAND Oh, Lord! your Reverence—

MANDERS Come, no nonsense. [*Wrings his hand.*] There we are!

ENGSTRAND And if I might humbly beg your Reverence's pardon—

MANDERS You? On the contrary, it's I who ought to beg your pardon—

ENGSTRAND Lord, no, sir!

MANDERS Yes, certainly. And I do it with all my heart. Forgive me for misunderstanding you. And I wish I could give you some proof of my hearty regret, and of my good-will towards you—

ENGSTRAND Would your Reverence?

MANDERS With the greatest pleasure.

ENGSTRAND Well then, there's the very opportunity now. With the money I've saved here, I was thinking I might set up a Sailors' Home down in the town.

MRS. ALVING *You?*

ENGSTRAND Yes; it too might be a sort of Orphanage, in a manner of speaking. There are many temptations for seafaring folk ashore. But in this Home of mine, a man might feel as under a father's eye, I was thinking.

MANDERS What do you say to this, Mrs. Alving?

ENGSTRAND It isn't much I've got to start with, the Lord help me! But if I could only find a helping hand, why—

MANDERS Yes, yes; we'll look into the matter. I entirely approve of your plan. But now, go before me and make everything ready, and get the candles lighted, so as to give the place an air of festivity. And then we'll pass an edifying hour together, my good fellow; for now I quite believe you're in the right frame of mind.

ENGSTRAND Yes, I trust I am. And so I'll say good-bye, ma'am, and thank you kindly; and take good care of Regina for me—[*Wipes a tear from his eye.*]—poor Johanna's child; hm, it's an odd thing, now; but it's just as if she'd grown into the very apple of my eye. It is indeed.

[*He bows and goes out through the hall.*]

MANDERS Well, what do you say of that man now, Mrs. Alving? That threw a totally different light on matters, didn't it?

MRS. ALVING Yes, it certainly did.

MANDERS It only shows how excessively careful one must be in judging one's fellow-creatures. But it's a great joy to ascertain that one has been mistaken. Don't you think so?

MRS. ALVING I think you are, and will always be, a great baby, Manders.

MANDERS I?

MRS. ALVING [*Laying her two hands upon his shoulders.*] And I say that I've half a mind to put my arms round your neck, and kiss you.

MANDERS [*Stepping hastily back.*] No, no! God bless me! What an idea!

MRS. ALVING [*With a smile.*] Oh! you needn't be afraid of me.

MANDERS [*By the table.*] You have sometimes such an exaggerated way of expressing yourself. Now, I'll just collect all the documents, and put them in my bag. [*He does so.*] There, now. And now, good-bye for the present. Keep your eyes open when Oswald comes back. I shall look in again later.

[*He takes his hat and goes out through the hall door.*]

MRS. ALVING [*Sighs, looks for a moment out of the window, sets the room in order a little, and is about to go into the dining-room, but stops at the door with a half-suppressed cry.*] Oswald, are you still at table?

OSWALD [*In the dining-room.*] I'm only finishing my cigar.

MRS. ALVING I thought you'd gone for a little walk.

OSWALD In such weather as this? [*A glass clinks.* MRS. ALVING *leaves the door open, and sits down with her knitting on the sofa by the window.*] Wasn't that Pastor Manders that went out just now?

MRS. ALVING Yes; he went down to the Orphanage.

OSWALD Hm. [*The glass and decanter clink again.*]

MRS. ALVING [*With a troubled glance.*] Dear Oswald, you should take care of that liqueur. It's strong.

OSWALD It keeps out the damp.

MRS. ALVING Wouldn't you rather come in to me?

OSWALD I mayn't smoke in there.

MRS. ALVING You know quite well you may smoke cigars.

OSWALD Oh! all right then; I'll come in. Just a tiny drop more first! There! [*He comes into the room with his cigar, and shuts the door after him. A short silence.*] Where's Manders gone to?

MRS. ALVING I've just told you; he went down to the Orphanage.

OSWALD Oh, ah; so you did.

MRS. ALVING You shouldn't sit so long at table after dinner, Oswald.

OSWALD [*Holding his cigar behind him.*] But I find it so pleasant, mother. [*Strokes and pets her.*] Just think what it is for me to come home and sit at mother's own table, in mother's room, and eat mother's delicious dinners.

MRS. ALVING My dear, dear boy!

OSWALD [*Somewhat impatiently walks about and smokes.*] And what else can I do with myself here? I can't set to work at anything.

MRS. ALVING Why can't you?

OSWALD In such weather as this? Without a single ray of sunlight the whole day? [*Walks up the room.*] Oh! not to be able to work!

MRS. ALVING Perhaps it was not quite wise of you to come home?

OSWALD Oh, yes, mother; I had to.

MRS. ALVING Why? I would ten times rather forego the joy of having you here than—

OSWALD [*Stops beside the table.*] Now just tell me, mother; does it really make you so very happy to have me home again?

MRS. ALVING *Does* it make me happy!

OSWALD [*Crumpling up a newspaper.*] I should have thought it must be pretty much the same to you whether I was in existence or not.

MRS. ALVING Have you the heart to say that to your mother, Oswald?

OSWALD But you've got on very well without me all this time.

MRS. ALVING Yes; I've got on without you. That's true.

[*A silence. Twilight gradually falls.* OSWALD *walks to and fro across the room. He has laid his cigar down.*]

OSWALD [*Stops beside* MRS. ALVING.] Mother, may I sit on the sofa beside you?

MRS. ALVING [*Makes room for him.*] Yes do, my dear boy.

OSWALD [*Sits down.*] Now I'm going to tell you something, mother.

MRS. ALVING [*Anxiously.*] Well?

OSWALD [*Looks fixedly before him.*] For I can't go on hiding it any longer.

MRS. ALVING Hiding what? What is it?

OSWALD [*As before.*] I could never bring myself to write to you about it; and since I've come home—

MRS. ALVING [*Seizes him by the arm.*] Oswald, what *is* the matter?

OSWALD [*As before.*] Both yesterday and to-day I've tried to put the thoughts away from me—to get free from them; but it won't do.

MRS. ALVING [*Rising.*] Now you must speak out, Oswald.

OSWALD [*Draws her down to the sofa again.*] Sit still; and then I'll try to tell you. I complained of fatigue after my journey—

MRS. ALVING Well, what then?

OSWALD But it isn't that that's the matter with me; it isn't any ordinary fatigue—

MRS. ALVING [*Tries to jump up.*] You're not ill, Oswald?

OSWALD [*Draws her down again.*] Do sit still, mother. Only take it quietly. I'm not downright ill, either; not what's commonly called "ill." [*Clasps his hands above his head.*] Mother, my mind is broken down—ruined—I shall never be able to work again. [*With his hands before his face, he buries his head in her lap, and breaks into bitter sobbing.*]

MRS. ALVING [*White and trembling.*] Oswald! Look at me! No, no; it isn't true.

OSWALD [*Looks up with despair in his eyes.*] Never to be able to work again! Never! never! It will be like living death! Mother, can you imagine anything so horrible?

MRS. ALVING My poor boy! How has this horrible thing come over you?

OSWALD [*Sits upright.*] That's just what I can't possibly grasp or understand. I've never led a dissipated life—never, in any respect. You mustn't believe that of me, mother. I've never done that.

MRS. ALVING I'm sure you haven't, Oswald.

OSWALD And yet this has come over me just the same—this awful misfortune!

MRS. ALVING Oh, but it will pass away, my dear, blessed boy. It's nothing but over-work. Trust me, I am right.

OSWALD [*Sadly.*] I thought so too at first; but it isn't so.

MRS. ALVING Tell me the whole story from beginning to end.

OSWALD Well, I will.

MRS. ALVING When did you first notice it?

OSWALD It was directly after I had been home last time, and had got back to Paris again. I began to feel the most violent pains in my head—chiefly in the back of my head, I thought. It was as though a tight iron ring was being screwed round my neck and upwards.

MRS. ALVING Well, and then?

OSWALD At first I thought it was nothing but the ordinary headache I had been so plagued with when I was growing up—

MRS. ALVING Yes, yes—

OSWALD But it wasn't that. I soon found that out. I couldn't work. I wanted to begin upon a big new picture, but my powers seemed to fail me; all my strength was crippled; I couldn't form any definite images; everything swam before me—whirling round and round. Oh! it was an awful state! At last I sent for a doctor, and from him I learned the truth.

MRS. ALVING How do you mean?

OSWALD He was one of the first doctors in Paris. I told him my symptoms, and then he set to work asking me a heap of questions which I thought had nothing to do with the matter. I couldn't imagine what the man was after—

MRS. ALVING Well?

OSWALD At last he said: "You have been worm-eaten from your birth." He used that very word—*vermoulu.*

MRS. ALVING [*Breathlessly.*] What did he mean by that?

OSWALD I didn't understand either, and begged him to explain himself more clearly. And then the old cynic said—[*Clenching his fist.*] Oh—!

MRS. ALVING What did he say?

OSWALD He said, "The sins of the fathers are visited upon the children."

MRS. ALVING [*Rising slowly.*] The sins of the fathers—!

OSWALD I very nearly struck him in the face—

MRS. ALVING [*Walks away across the floor.*] The sins of the fathers—

OSWALD [*Smiles sadly.*] Yes; what do you think of that? Of course I assured him that such a thing was out of the question. But do you think he gave in? No, he stuck to it; and it was only when I produced your letters and translated the passages relating to father—

MRS. ALVING But then?

OSWALD Then of course he was bound to admit that he was on the wrong track; and so I got to know the truth—the incomprehensible truth! I ought to have held aloof from my bright and happy life among my comrades. It had been too much for my strength. So I had brought it upon myself!

MRS. ALVING Oswald! Oh no, don't believe it!

OSWALD No other explanation was possible, he said. That's the awful part of it. Incurably ruined for life—by my own heedlessness! All that I meant to have done in the world—I never dare think of again—I'm not *able* to think of it. Oh! if I could but live over again, and undo all I've done! [*He buries his face in the sofa.* MRS. ALVING *wrings her hands and walks, in silent struggle, backwards and forwards.* OSWALD, *after a while, looks up and remains resting upon his elbow.*] If it had only been something inherited, something one wasn't responsible for! But this! To have thrown away so shamefully, thoughtlessly, recklessly, one's own happiness, one's own health, everything in the world—one's future, one's very life!

MRS. ALVING No, no, my dear, darling boy! It's impossible. [*Bends over him.*] Things are not so desperate as you think.

OSWALD Oh! you don't know— [*Springs up.*] And then, mother, to cause you all this sorrow! Many a time I've almost wished and hoped that at bottom you didn't care so very much about me.

MRS. ALVING I, Oswald? My only boy! You are all I have in the world! The only thing I care about!

OSWALD [*Seizes both her hands and kisses them.*] Yes, mother dear, I see it well enough. When I'm at home, I see it, of course; and that's the hardest part for me. But now you know the whole story, and now we won't talk any more about it to-day. I daren't think of it for long together. [*Goes up the room.*] Get me something to drink, mother.

MRS. ALVING Drink? What do you want to drink now?

OSWALD Oh! anything you like. You have some cold punch in the house.

MRS. ALVING Yes, but my dear Oswald—

OSWALD Don't refuse me, mother. Do be nice, now! I must have something to wash down all these gnawing thoughts. [*Goes into the conservatory.*] And then—it's so dark here! [MRS. ALVING *pulls a bell-rope on the right.*] And this ceaseless rain! It may go on week after week for months together. Never to get a glimpse of the sun! I can't recollect ever having seen the sun shine all the times I've been at home.

MRS. ALVING Oswald, you're thinking of going away from me.

OSWALD Hm—[*Drawing a deep breath.*]—I'm not thinking of anything. I can't think of anything. [*In a low voice.*] I let thinking alone.

REGINA [*From the dining-room.*] Did you ring, ma'am?

MRS. ALVING Yes; let us have the lamp in.

REGINA I will, directly. It's ready lighted. [*Goes out.*]

MRS. ALVING [*Goes across to* OSWALD.] Oswald, be frank with me.

OSWALD Well, so I am, mother. [*Goes to the table.*] I think I've told you enough.

[REGINA *brings the lamp and sets it upon the table.*]

MRS. ALVING Regina, you might fetch us a half-bottle of champagne.

OSWALD [*Puts his arm round* MRS. ALVING'S *neck.*] That's just what I wanted. I knew mother wouldn't let her boy be thirsty.

MRS. ALVING My own, poor, darling Oswald, how could I deny you anything now?

OSWALD [*Eagerly.*] Is that true, mother? Do you mean it?

MRS. ALVING How? What?

OSWALD That you couldn't deny me anything.

MRS. ALVING My dear Oswald—

OSWALD Hush!

REGINA [*Brings a tray with a half-bottle of*

champagne and two glasses, which she sets on the table.] Shall I open it?

OSWALD No, thanks. I'll do it myself.

[REGINA *goes out again.*]

MRS. ALVING [*Sits down by the table.*] What was it you meant, I mustn't deny you?

OSWALD [*Busy opening the bottle.*] First let's have a glass—or two.

[*The cork pops; he pours wine into one glass, and is about to pour it into the other.*]

MRS. ALVING [*Holding her hand over it.*] Thanks; not for me.

OSWALD Oh! won't you? Then I will!

[*He empties the glass, fills, and empties it again; then he sits down by the table.*]

MRS. ALVING [*In expectation.*] Well?

OSWALD [*Without looking at her.*] Tell me—I thought you and Pastor Manders seemed so odd—so quiet—at dinner to-day.

MRS. ALVING Did you notice it?

OSWALD Yes. Hm— [*After a short silence.*] Tell me: what do you think of Regina?

MRS. ALVING What I think?

OSWALD Yes; isn't she splendid?

MRS. ALVING My dear Oswald, you don't know her as I do—

OSWALD Well?

MRS. ALVING Regina, unfortunately, was allowed to stay at home too long. I ought to have taken her earlier in my house.

OSWALD Yes, but isn't she splendid to look at, mother?

[*He fills his glass.*]

MRS. ALVING Regina has many serious faults.

OSWALD Oh, what does it matter?

[*He drinks again.*]

MRS. ALVING But I'm fond of her, nevertheless, and I'm responsible for her. I wouldn't for all the world have any harm happen to her.

OSWALD [*Springs up.*] Mother! Regina is my only salvation.

MRS. ALVING [*Rising.*] What do you mean by that?

OSWALD I can't go on bearing all this anguish of mind alone.

MRS. ALVING Haven't you got your mother to share it with you?

OSWALD Yes, that's what I thought; and so I came home to you. But that won't do. I see it won't do. I can't endure my life here.

MRS. ALVING Oswald!

OSWALD I must live differently, mother. That's why I must leave you. I won't have you looking on at it.

MRS. ALVING My unhappy boy! But, Oswald, while you're so ill as this—

OSWALD If it were only the illness, I should stay with you, mother, you may be sure; for you are the best friend I have in the world.

MRS. ALVING Yes, indeed I am, Oswald; am I not?

OSWALD [*Wanders restlessly about.*] But it's all the torment, the remorse; and besides that, the great, killing dread. Oh! that awful dread!

MRS. ALVING [*Walking after him.*] Dread? What dread? What do you mean?

OSWALD Oh, you mustn't ask me any more! I don't know. I can't describe it. [MRS. ALVING *goes over to the right and pulls the bell.*] What is it you want?

MRS. ALVING I want my boy to be happy—that's what I want. He shan't go on racking his brains. [*To* REGINA, *who comes in at the door.*] More champagne—a whole bottle. [REGINA *goes.*]

OSWALD Mother!

MRS. ALVING Do you think we don't know how to live here at home?

OSWALD Isn't she splendid to look at? How beautifully she's built! And so thoroughly healthy!

MRS. ALVING [*Sits by the table.*] Sit down, Oswald; let us talk quietly together.

OSWALD [*Sits.*] I daresay you don't know, mother, that I owe Regina some reparation.

MRS. ALVING You?

OSWALD For a bit of thoughtlessness, or whatever you like to call it—very innocent, anyhow. When I was home last time—

MRS. ALVING Well?

OSWALD She used often to ask me about Paris, and I used to tell her one thing and another. Then I recollect I happened to say to her one day, "Wouldn't you like to go there yourself?"

MRS. ALVING Well?

OSWALD I saw her face flush, and then she said, "Yes, I should like it of all things." "Ah, well," I replied, "it might perhaps be managed"—or something like that.

MRS. ALVING And then?

OSWALD Of course I'd forgotten the whole

thing; but the day before yesterday I happened to ask her whether she was glad I was to stay at home so long—

MRS. ALVING Yes?

OSWALD And then she looked so strangely at me and asked, "But what's to become of my trip to Paris?"

MRS. ALVING Her trip!

OSWALD And so I got out of her that she had taken the thing seriously; that she had been thinking of me the whole time, and had set to work to learn French—

MRS. ALVING So that was why she did it!

OSWALD Mother! when I saw that fresh, lovely, splendid girl standing there before me—till then I had hardly noticed her—but when she stood there as though with open arms ready to receive me—

MRS. ALVING Oswald!

OSWALD —then it flashed upon me that my salvation lay in her; for I saw that she was full of the joy of life.[4]

MRS. ALVING [*Starts.*] The joy of life? Can there be salvation in that?

REGINA [*From the dining-room, with a bottle of champagne.*] I'm sorry to have been so long, but I had to go to the cellar. [*Puts the bottle on the table.*]

OSWALD And now fetch another glass.

REGINA [*Looks at him in surprise.*] There is Mrs. Alving's glass, Mr. Alving.

OSWALD Yes, fetch one for yourself, Regina. [REGINA *starts and gives a lightning-like side glance at* MRS. ALVING.] Why do you wait?

REGINA [*Softly and hesitatingly.*] Is it Mrs. Alving's wish?

MRS. ALVING Fetch the glass, Regina.

[REGINA *goes out into the dining-room.*]

OSWALD [*Follows her with his eyes.*] Have you noticed how she walks?—so firmly and lightly!

MRS. ALVING It can never be, Oswald!

OSWALD It's a settled thing. Can't you see that? It's no use saying anything against it. [REGINA *enters with an empty glass, which she keeps in her hand.*] Sit down, Regina.

[REGINA *looks inquiringly at* MRS. ALVING.]

MRS. ALVING Sit down. [REGINA *sits on a chair by the dining-room door, still holding the empty glass in her hand.*] Oswald, what were you saying about the joy of life?

OSWALD Ah! the joy of life, mother—that's a thing you don't know much about in these parts. I've never felt it here.

MRS. ALVING Not when you're with me?

OSWALD Not when I'm at home. But you don't understand that.

MRS. ALVING Yes, yes; I think I almost understand it—now.

OSWALD And then, too, the joy of work! At bottom, it's the same thing. But that, too, you know nothing about.

MRS. ALVING Perhaps you're right, Oswald; tell me more about it.

OSWALD Well, I only mean that here people are brought up to believe that work is a curse and a punishment for sin, and that life is something miserable, something we want to be done with, the sooner the better.

MRS. ALVING "A vale of tears," yes; and we take care to make it one.

OSWALD But in the great world people won't hear of such things. There, nobody really believes such doctrines any longer. There, you feel it bliss and ecstasy merely to draw the breath of life. Mother, have you noticed that everything I've painted has turned upon the joy of life?—always, always upon the joy of life?—light and sunshine and glorious air and faces radiant with happiness. That's why I'm afraid of remaining at home with you.

MRS. ALVING Afraid? What are you afraid of here, with me?

OSWALD I'm afraid lest all my instincts should be warped into ugliness.

MRS. ALVING [*Looks steadily at him.*] Do you think that would be the way of it?

OSWALD I know it. You may live the same life here as there, and yet it won't be the same life.

MRS. ALVING [*Who has been listening eagerly, rises, her eyes big with thought, and says.*] Now I see the connection.

OSWALD What is it you see?

MRS. ALVING I see it now for the first time. And now I can speak.

OSWALD [*Rising.*] Mother, I don't understand you.

REGINA [*Who has also risen.*] Perhaps I ought to go?

[4] Livsglæde—"la joie de vivre."

MRS. ALVING No. Stay here. Now I can speak. Now, my boy, you shall know the whole truth. And then you can choose. Oswald! Regina!

OSWALD Hush! Here's Manders—

MANDERS [*Comes in by the hall door.*] There! We've had a most edifying time down there.

OSWALD So have we.

MANDERS We must stand by Engstrand and his Sailors' Home. Regina must go to him and help him—

REGINA No thank you, sir.

MANDERS [*Noticing her for the first time.*] What? You here? and with a glass in your hand!

REGINA [*Hastily putting the glass down.*] *Pardon!*

OSWALD Regina is going with me, Mr. Manders.

MANDERS Going with you!

OSWALD Yes; as my wife—if she wishes it.

MANDERS But, good God—

REGINA I can't help it, sir.

OSWALD Or she'll stay here, if I stay.

REGINA [*Involuntarily.*] Here!

MANDERS I am thunderstruck at your conduct, Mrs. Alving.

MRS. ALVING They will do neither one thing nor the other; for now I can speak out plainly.

MANDERS You surely won't do that. No, no, no!

MRS. ALVING Yes, I can speak and I will. And no ideal shall suffer after all.

OSWALD Mother! What on earth are you hiding from me?

REGINA [*Listening.*] Oh, ma'am! listen! Don't you hear shouts outside?

[*She goes into the conservatory and looks out.*]

OSWALD [*At the window on the left.*] What's going on? Where does that light come from?

REGINA [*Cries out.*] The Orphanage is on fire!

MRS. ALVING [*Rushing to the window.*] On fire?

MANDERS On fire! Impossible! I've just come from there.

OSWALD Where's my hat? Oh, never mind it—Father's Orphanage!

[*He rushes out through the garden door.*]

MRS. ALVING My shawl, Regina! It's blazing!

MANDERS Terrible! Mrs. Alving, it's a judgment upon this abode of sin.

MRS. ALVING Yes, of course. Come, Regina.

[*She and* REGINA *hasten out through the hall.*]

MANDERS [*Clasps his hands together.*] And uninsured, too.

[*He goes out the same way.*]

ACT III

[*The room as before. All the doors stand open. The lamp is still burning on the table. It is dark out of doors; there is just a faint glow from the conflagration in the background at the left.*]

MRS. ALVING, *with a shawl over her head, stands in conservatory and looks out.* REGINA, *also with a shawl on, stands a little behind her.*]

MRS. ALVING All burnt!—burnt to the ground!

REGINA The basement is still burning.

MRS. ALVING How is it Oswald doesn't come home? There's nothing to be saved.

REGINA Would you like me to take down his hat to him?

MRS. ALVING Hasn't he even got his hat on?

REGINA [*Pointing to the hall.*] No; there it hangs.

MRS. ALVING Let it be. He must come up now. I'll go and look for him myself.

[*She goes out through the garden door.*]

MANDERS [*Comes in from the hall.*] Isn't Mrs. Alving here?

REGINA She's just gone down the garden.

MANDERS This is the most terrible night I ever went through.

REGINA Yes; isn't it a dreadful misfortune, sir?

MANDERS Oh, don't talk about it! I can hardly bear to think of it.

REGINA How *can* it have happened?

MANDERS Don't ask me, Regina! How should *I* know? Do *you*, too—? Isn't it enough that your father—?

REGINA What about him?

MANDERS Oh! he has driven me clean out of my mind—

ENGSTRAND [*Comes through the hall.*] Your Reverence!

MANDERS [*Turns round in terror.*] Are you after me here, too?

ENGSTRAND Yes, strike me dead, but I must—Oh, Lord! what am I saying? It's an awfully ugly business, your Reverence.

MANDERS [*Walks to and fro.*] Alas! alas!

REGINA What's the matter?

ENGSTRAND Why, it all came of that prayer-meeting, you see. [*Softly.*] The bird's limed, my girl. [*Aloud.*] And to think that it's my fault that it's his Reverence's fault!

MANDERS But I assure you, Engstrand—

ENGSTRAND There wasn't another soul except

your Reverence that ever touched the candles down there.

MANDERS [*Stops.*] Ah! so you declare. But I certainly can't recollect that I ever had a candle in my hand.

ENGSTRAND And I saw as clear as daylight how your Reverence took the candle and snuffed it with your fingers, and threw away the snuff among the shavings.

MANDERS And you stood and looked on?

ENGSTRAND Yes; I saw it as plain as a pikestaff.

MANDERS It's quite beyond my comprehension. Besides, it's never been my habit to snuff candles with my fingers.

ENGSTRAND And very risky it looked, that it did! But is there so much harm done after all, your Reverence?

MANDERS [*Walks restlessly to and fro.*] Oh, don't ask me!

ENGSTRAND [*Walks with him.*] And your Reverence hadn't insured it, neither?

MANDERS [*Continuing to walk up and down.*] No, no, no; you've heard that already.

ENGSTRAND [*Following him.*] Not insured! And then to go right down and set light to the whole thing. Lord! Lord! what a misfortune!

MANDERS [*Wipes the sweat from his forehead.*] Ay, you may well say that, Engstrand.

ENGSTRAND And to think that such a thing should happen to a benevolent Institution, that was to have been a blessing both to town and country, as the saying is! The newspapers won't handle your Reverence very gently, I expect.

MANDERS No; that's just what I'm thinking of. That's almost the worst of it. All the malignant attacks and accusations—! Oh! it's terrible only to imagine it.

MRS. ALVING [*Comes in from the garden.*] He can't be got away from the fire.

MANDERS Ah! there you are, Mrs. Alving!

MRS. ALVING So you've escaped your Inaugural Address, Pastor Manders.

MANDERS Oh! I should so gladly—

MRS. ALVING [*In an undertone.*] It's all for the best. That Orphanage would have done no good to anybody.

MANDERS Do you think not?

MRS. ALVING Do you think it would?

MANDERS It's a terrible misfortune, all the same.

MRS. ALVING Let us speak plainly of it, as a piece of business. Are you waiting for Mr. Manders, Engstrand?

ENGSTRAND [*At the hall door.*] Ay, ma'am; indeed I am.

MRS. ALVING Then sit down meanwhile.

ENGSTRAND Thank you, ma'am; I'd rather stand.

MRS. ALVING [*To* MANDERS.] I suppose you're going by the steamer?

MANDERS Yes; it starts in an hour.

MRS. ALVING Be so good as to take all the papers with you. I won't hear another word about this affair. I have other things to think about.

MANDERS Mrs. Alving—

MRS. ALVING Later on I shall send you a Power of Attorney to settle everything as you please.

MANDERS That I shall very readily undertake. The original destination of the endowment must now be completely changed, alas!

MRS. ALVING Of course it must.

MANDERS I think, first of all, I shall arrange that the Solvik property shall pass to the parish. The land is by no means without value. It can always be turned to account for some purpose or other. And the interest of the money in the Bank I could, perhaps, best apply for the benefit of some undertaking that has proved itself a blessing to the town.

MRS. ALVING Do just as you please. The whole matter is now completely indifferent to me.

ENGSTRAND Give a thought to my Sailors' Home, your Reverence.

MANDERS Yes, that's not a bad suggestion. That must be considered.

ENGSTRAND Oh, devil take considering—I beg your pardon!

MANDERS [*With a sigh.*] And I'm sorry to say I don't know how long I shall be able to retain control of these things—whether public opinion may not compel me to retire. It entirely depends upon the result of the official inquiry into the fire—

MRS. ALVING What are you talking about?

MANDERS And the result can by no means be foretold.

ENGSTRAND [*Comes close to him.*] Ay, but it can though. For here stands Jacob Engstrand.

MANDERS Well, well, but—?

ENGSTRAND [*More softly.*] And Jacob Engstrand isn't the man to desert a noble benefactor in the hour of need, as the saying is.

MANDERS Yes, but my good fellow—how—?

ENGSTRAND Jacob Engstrand may be likened to a guardian angel, he may, your Reverence.

MANDERS No, no; I can't accept that.

ENGSTRAND Oh! you will though, all the same. I know a man that's taken others' sins upon himself before now, I do.

MANDERS Jacob! [*Wrings his hand.*] You are a rare character. Well, you shall be helped with your Sailors' Home. That you may rely upon. [ENGSTRAND *tries to thank him, but cannot for emotion.* MR. MANDERS *hangs his travelling-bag over his shoulder.*] And now let's be off. We two go together.

ENGSTRAND [*At the dining-room door, softly to* REGINA.] You come along too, girl. You shall live as snug as the yolk in an egg.

REGINA [*Tosses her head.*] *Merci!*

[*She goes out into the hall and fetches* MANDERS's *overcoat.*]

MANDERS Good-bye, Mrs. Alving! and may the spirit of Law and Order descend upon this house, and that quickly.

MRS. ALVING Good-bye, Manders.

[*She goes up towards the conservatory, as she sees* OSWALD *coming in through the garden door.*]

ENGSTRAND [*While he and* REGINA *help* MANDERS *to get his coat on.*] Good-bye, my child. And if any trouble should come to you, you know where Jacob Engstrand is to be found. [*Softly.*] Little Harbour Street, hm—! [*To* MRS. ALVING *and* OSWALD.] And the refuge for wandering mariners shall be called "Captain Alving's Home," that it shall! And if I'm spared to carry on that house in my own way, I venture to promise that it shall be worthy of his memory.

MANDERS [*In the doorway.*] Hm-hm!—Now come, my dear Engstrand. Good-bye! Good-bye!

[*He and* ENGSTRAND *go out through the hall.*]

OSWALD [*Goes towards the table.*] What house was he talking about?

MRS. ALVING Oh, a kind of Home that he and Manders want to set up.

OSWALD It will burn down like the other.

MRS. ALVING What makes you think so?

OSWALD Everything will burn. All that recalls father's memory is doomed. Here am I, too, burning down.

[REGINA *starts and looks at him.*]

MRS. ALVING Oswald! you oughtn't to have remained so long down there, my poor boy!

OSWALD [*Sits down by the table.*] I almost think you're right.

MRS. ALVING Let me dry your face, Oswald; you're quite wet.

[*She dries his face with her pocket-handkerchief.*]

OSWALD [*Stares indifferently in front of him.*] Thanks, mother.

MRS. ALVING Aren't you tired, Oswald? Would you like to sleep?

OSWALD [*Nervously.*] No, no—I can't sleep. I never sleep. I only pretend to. [*Sadly.*] That will come soon enough.

MRS. ALVING [*Looking sorrowfully at him.*] Yes, you really are ill, my blessed boy.

REGINA [*Eagerly.*] Is Mr. Alving ill?

OSWALD [*Impatiently.*] Oh, do shut all the doors! This killing dread—

MRS. ALVING Shut the doors, Regina.

[REGINA *shuts them and remains standing by the hall door.* MRS. ALVING *takes her shawl off.* REGINA *does the same.* MRS. ALVING *draws a chair across to* OSWALD's, *and sits by him.*]

MRS. ALVING There now! I'm going to sit beside you—

OSWALD Ah! do. And Regina shall stay here, too. Regina shall be with me always. You'll come to the rescue, Regina, won't you?

REGINA I don't understand—

MRS. ALVING To the rescue?

OSWALD Yes—in the hour of need.

MRS. ALVING Oswald, have you not your mother to come to the rescue?

OSWALD You? [*Smiles.*] No, mother; *that* rescue you will never bring me. [*Laughs sadly.*] You! ha ha! [*Looks earnestly at her.*] Though, after all, it lies nearest to you. [*Impetuously.*] Why don't you say "thou"[1] to me Regina? Why don't you call me "Oswald"?

REGINA [*Softly.*] I don't think Mrs. Alving would like it.

MRS. ALVING You shall soon have leave to do it. And sit over here beside us, won't you?

[REGINA *sits down quietly and hesitatingly at the other side of the table.*]

MRS. ALVING And now, my poor suffering boy, I'm going to take the burden off your mind—

OSWALD You, mother?

MRS. ALVING —all the gnawing remorse and self-reproach you speak of.

OSWALD And you think you can do that?

[1] "Sige du" = Fr. *tutoyer.*

MRS. ALVING Yes, now I can, Oswald. You spoke of the joy of life; and at that word a new light burst for me over my life and all it has contained.

OSWALD [*Shakes his head.*] I don't understand you.

MRS. ALVING You ought to have known your father when he was a young lieutenant. He was brimming over with the joy of life!

OSWALD Yes, I know he was.

MRS. ALVING It was like a breezy day only to look at him. And what exuberant strength and vitality there was in him!

OSWALD Well—?

MRS. ALVING Well then, child of joy as he was —for he *was* like a child at that time—he had to live here at home in a half-grown town, which had no joys to offer him—only dissipations. He had no object in life—only an official position. He had no work into which he could throw himself heart and soul; he had only business. He had not a single comrade that knew what the joy of life meant—only loungers and boon-companions—

OSWALD Mother!

MRS. ALVING So the inevitable happened.

OSWALD The inevitable?

MRS. ALVING You said yourself, this evening, what would happen to you if you stayed at home.

OSWALD Do you mean to say that father—?

MRS. ALVING Your poor father found no outlet for the overpowering joy of life that was in him. And I brought no brightness into his home.

OSWALD Not even you?

MRS. ALVING They had taught me a lot about duties and so on, which I had taken to be true. Everything was marked out into duties —into my duties, and his duties, and—I'm afraid I made home intolerable for your poor father, Oswald.

OSWALD Why did you never write me anything about all this?

MRS. ALVING I have never before seen it in such a light that I could speak of it to you, his son.

OSWALD In what light did you see it then?

MRS. ALVING [*Slowly.*] I saw only this one thing, that your father was a broken-down man before you were born.

OSWALD [*Softly.*] Ah!

[*He rises and walks away to the window.*]

MRS. ALVING And then, day after day, I dwelt on the one thought that by rights Regina should be at home in this house—just like my own boy.

OSWALD [*Turning round quickly.*] Regina!

REGINA [*Springs up and asks, with bated breath.*] I?

MRS. ALVING Yes, now you know it, both of you.

OSWALD Regina!

REGINA [*To herself.*] So mother was that kind of woman, after all.

MRS. ALVING Your mother had many good qualities, Regina.

REGINA Yes, but she was one of that sort, all the same. Oh! I've often suspected it; but— And now, if you please, ma'am, may I be allowed to go away at once?

MRS. ALVING Do you really wish it, Regina?

REGINA Yes, indeed I do.

MRS. ALVING Of course you can do as you like; but—

OSWALD [*Goes toward* REGINA.] Go away now? Isn't this your home?

REGINA *Merci*, Mr. Alving!—or now, I suppose, I may say Oswald. But I can tell you this wasn't what I expected.

MRS. ALVING Regina, I have not been frank with you—

REGINA No, that you haven't, indeed. If I'd known that Oswald was ill, why— And now, too, that it can never come to anything serious between us— I really can't stop out here in the country and wear myself out nursing sick people.

OSWALD Not even one who is so near to you?

REGINA No, that I can't. A poor girl must make the best of her young days, or she'll be left out in the cold before she knows where she is. And I, too, have the joy of life in me, Mrs. Alving.

MRS. ALVING Yes, I see you have. But don't throw yourself away, Regina.

REGINA Oh! what must be, must be. If Oswald takes after his father, I take after my mother, I daresay. May I ask, ma'am, if Mr. Manders knows all this about me?

MRS. ALVING Mr. Manders knows all about it.

REGINA [*Puts on her shawl hastily.*] Well then, I'd better make haste and get away by this steamer. Pastor Manders is so nice to deal with; and I certainly think I've as much right to a little of that money as he has—that brute of a carpenter.

MRS. ALVING You're heartily welcome to it, Regina.

REGINA [*Looks hard at her.*] I think you might have brought me up as a gentleman's daughter, ma'am; it would have suited me better. [*Tosses her head.*] But it's done now—it doesn't matter! [*With a bitter side glance at the corked bottle.*] All the same, I may come to drink champagne with gentlefolks yet.

MRS. ALVING And if you ever need a home, Regina, come to me.

REGINA No, thank you, ma'am. Mr. Manders will look after me, I know. And if the worst comes to the worst, I know of one house where I've every right to a place.

MRS. ALVING Where is that?

REGINA "Captain Alving's Home."

MRS. ALVING Regina—now I see it—you're going to your ruin.

REGINA Oh, stuff! Good-bye.

[*She nods and goes out through the hall.*]

OSWALD [*Stands at the window and looks out.*] Is she gone?

MRS. ALVING Yes.

OSWALD [*Murmuring aside to himself.*] I think it's a great mistake, all this.

MRS. ALVING [*Goes behind him and lays her hands on his shoulders.*] Oswald, my dear boy; has it shaken you very much?

OSWALD [*Turn his face towards her.*] All that about father, do you mean?

MRS. ALVING Yes, about your unhappy father. I'm so afraid it may have been too much for you.

OSWALD Why should you fancy that? Of course it came upon me as a great surprise; but, after all, it can't matter much to me.

MRS. ALVING [*Draws her hands away.*] Can't matter! That your father was so infinitely miserable!

OSWALD Of course I can pity him as I would anybody else; but—

MRS. ALVING Nothing more? Your own father!

OSWALD [*Impatiently.*] Oh, there! "father," "father"! I never knew anything of father. I don't remember anything about him except that he once made me sick.

MRS. ALVING That's a terrible way to speak! Should a son not love his father, all the same?

OSWALD When a son has nothing to thank his father for? has never known him? Do you really cling to that old superstition?—you who are so enlightened in other ways?

MRS. ALVING Is it only a superstition—?

OSWALD Yes; can't you see it, mother? It's one of those notions that are current in the world, and so—

MRS. ALVING [*Deeply moved.*] Ghosts!

OSWALD [*Crossing the room.*] Yes; you may well call them Ghosts.

MRS. ALVING [*Wildly.*] Oswald!—then you don't love me, either!

OSWALD You I know, at any rate.

MRS. ALVING Yes, you know me; but is that all?

OSWALD And of course I know how fond you are of me, and I can't but be grateful to you. And you can be so very useful to me, now that I'm ill.

MRS. ALVING Yes, can't I, Oswald? Oh! I could almost bless the illness that has driven you home to me. For I can see very plainly you are not mine; I have to win you.

OSWALD [*Impatiently.*] Yes, yes, yes; all these are just so many phrases. You must recollect I'm a sick man, mother. I can't be much taken up with other people; I have enough to do thinking about myself.

MRS. ALVING [*In a low voice.*] I shall be patient and easily satisfied.

OSWALD And cheerful too, mother.

MRS. ALVING Yes, my dear boy, you're quite right. [*Goes towards him.*] Have I relieved you of all remorse and self-reproach now?

OSWALD Yes, you have. But who's to relieve me of the dread?

MRS. ALVING The dread?

OSWALD [*Walks across the room.*] Regina could have been got to do it.

MRS. ALVING I don't understand you. What is all this about dread—and Regina?

OSWALD Is it very late, mother?

MRS. ALVING It's early morning. [*She looks out through the conservatory.*] The day is dawning over the hills; and the weather is fine, Oswald. In a little while you shall see the sun.

OSWALD I'm glad of that. Oh! I may still have much to rejoice in and live for—

MRS. ALVING Yes, much—much, indeed!

OSWALD Even if I can't work—

MRS. ALVING Oh! you'll soon be able to work again, my dear boy, now that you haven't got all those gnawing and depressing thoughts to brood over any longer.

OSWALD Yes, I'm glad you were able to rid me of all those fancies; and when I've got one thing more arranged— [*Sits on the sofa.*] Now we'll have a little talk, mother.

MRS. ALVING Yes, let us.

[*She pushes an arm-chair towards the sofa, and sits down close to him.*]

OSWALD And meantime the sun will be rising. And then you'll know all. And then I shan't have that dread any longer.

MRS. ALVING What am I to know?

OSWALD [*Not listening to her.*] Mother, didn't you say, a little while ago, that there was nothing in the world you wouldn't do for me, if I asked you?

MRS. ALVING Yes, to be sure I said it.

OSWALD And you'll stick to it, mother?

MRS. ALVING You may rely on that, my dear and only boy! I have nothing in the world to live for but you alone.

OSWALD All right, then; now you shall hear. Mother, you have a strong, steadfast mind, I know. Now you're to sit quite still when you hear it.

MRS. ALVING What dreadful thing can it be—?

OSWALD You're not to scream out. Do you hear? Do you promise me that? We'll sit and talk about it quite quietly. Promise me, mother?

MRS. ALVING Yes, yes; I promise. Only speak.

OSWALD Well, you must know that all this fatigue, and my inability to think of work—all that is not the illness itself—

MRS. ALVING Then what is the illness itself?

OSWALD The disease I have as my birthright [*He points to his forehead and adds very softly.*]—is seated here.

MRS. ALVING [*Almost voiceless.*] Oswald! No, no!

OSWALD Don't scream. I can't bear it. Yes, it's seated here—waiting. And it may break out any day—at any moment.

MRS. ALVING Oh! what horror!

OSWALD Now, do be quiet. That's how it stands with me—

MRS. ALVING [*Jumps up.*] It's not true, Oswald. It's impossible. It can't be so.

OSWALD I have had one attack down there already. It was soon over. But when I got to know what had been the matter with me, then the dread came upon me raging and tearing; and so I set off home to you as fast as I could.

MRS. ALVING Then this is the dread—?

OSWALD Yes, for it's so indescribably loathsome, you know. Oh! if it had only been an ordinary mortal disease—! For I'm not so afraid of death—though I should like to live as long as I can.

MRS. ALVING Yes, yes, Oswald, you must!

OSWALD But this is so unutterably loathsome! To become a little baby again. To have to be fed! To have to— Oh, it's not to be spoken of!

MRS. ALVING The child has his mother to nurse him.

OSWALD [*Jumps up.*] No, never; that's just what I won't have. I can't endure to think that perhaps I should lie in that state for many years—get old and grey. And in the meantime you might die and leave me. [*Sits in* MRS. ALVING'S *chair.*] For the doctor said it wouldn't necessarily prove fatal at once. He called it a sort of softening of the brain—or something of the kind. [*Smiles sadly.*] I think that expression sounds so nice. It always sets me thinking of cherry-coloured velvet—something soft and delicate to stroke.

MRS. ALVING [*Screams.*] Oswald!

OSWALD [*Springs up and paces the room.*] And now you have taken Regina from me. If I'd only had her! She would come to the rescue, I know.

MRS. ALVING [*Goes to him.*] What do you mean by that, my darling boy? Is there any help in the world that I wouldn't give you?

OSWALD When I got over my attack in Paris, the doctor told me that when it came again—and it will come again—there would be no more hope.

MRS. ALVING He was heartless enough to—

OSWALD I demanded it of him. I told him I had preparations to make. [*He smiles cunningly.*] And so I had. [*He takes a little box from his inner breast pocket and opens it.*] Mother, do you see this?

MRS. ALVING What is that?

OSWALD Morphia.

MRS. ALVING [*Looks horrified at him.*] Oswald—my boy!

OSWALD I've scraped together twelve pilules—

MRS. ALVING [*Snatches at it.*] Give me the box, Oswald.

OSWALD Not yet, mother.

[*He hides the box again in his pocket.*]

MRS. ALVING I shall never survive this!

OSWALD It must be survived. Now if I'd had Regina here, I should have told her how things stood with me, and begged her to come to the rescue at the last. She would have done it. I'm certain she would.

MRS. ALVING Never!

OSWALD When the horror had come me, and she saw me lying there helpless, like a little new-born baby, impotent, lost, hopeless, past all saving—

MRS. ALVING Never in all the world would Regina have done this.

OSWALD Regina would have done it. Regina was so splendidly light-hearted. And she would soon have wearied of nursing an invalid like me—

MRS. ALVING Then heaven be praised that Regina is not here.

OSWALD Well then, it's you that must come to the rescue, mother.

MRS. ALVING [*Screams aloud.*] I!

OSWALD Who is nearer to it than you?

MRS. ALVING I! your mother!

OSWALD For that very reason.

MRS. ALVING I, who gave you life!

OSWALD I never asked you for life. And what sort of a life have you given me? I won't have it. You shall take it back again.

MRS. ALVING Help! Help!

[*She runs out into the hall.*]

OSWALD [*Going after her.*] Don't leave me. Where are you going?

MRS. ALVING [*In the hall.*] To fetch the doctor, Oswald. Let me go.

OSWALD [*Also outside.*] You shall not go. And no one shall come in. [*The locking of a door is heard.*]

MRS. ALVING [*Comes in again.*] Oswald—Oswald!—my child!

OSWALD [*Follows her.*] Have you a mother's heart for me, and yet can see me suffer from this unutterable dread?

MRS. ALVING [*After a moment's silence, commands herself, and says.*] Here's my hand upon it.

OSWALD Will you—?

MRS. ALVING If it's ever necessary. But it will never be necessary. No, no; it's impossible.

OSWALD Well, let us hope so, and let us live together as long as we can. Thank you, mother.

[*He seats himself in the arm-chair which* MRS. ALVING *has moved to the sofa. Day is breaking. The lamp is still burning on the table.*]

MRS. ALVING [*Drawing near cautiously.*] Do you feel calm now?

OSWALD Yes.

MRS. ALVING [*Bending over him.*] It has been a dreadful fancy of yours, Oswald—nothing but a fancy. All this excitement has been too much for you. But now you shall have a long rest; at home with your mother, my own blessed boy. Everything you point to you shall have, just as when you were a little child. There now. That crisis is over now. You see how easily it passed. Oh! I was sure it would— And do you see, Oswald, what a lovely day we're going to have? Brilliant sunshine! Now you'll really be able to see your home.

[*She goes to the table and puts the lamp out. Sunrise. The glacier and the snow-peaks in the background glow in the morning light.*]

OSWALD [*Sits in the arm-chair with his back towards the landscape, without moving. Suddenly he says.*] Mother, give me the sun.

MRS. ALVING [*By the table, starts and looks at him.*] What do you say?

OSWALD [*Repeats, in a dull, toneless voice.*] The sun. The sun.

MRS. ALVING [*Goes to him.*] Oswald, what's the matter with you? (OSWALD *seems to shrink together in the chair; all his muscles relax; his face is expressionless, his eyes have a glassy stare.* MRS. ALVING *is quivering with terror.*] What is this? [*Shrieks.*] Oswald, what's the matter with you? [*Falls on her knees beside him and shakes him.*] Oswald, Oswald! look at me! Don't you know me?

OSWALD [*Tonelessly as before.*] The sun. The sun.

MRS. ALVING [*Springs up in despair, entwines her hands in her hair and shrieks.*] I can't bear it! [*Whispers, as though petrified.*] I can't bear it! Never! [*Suddenly.*] Where has he got them? [*Fumbles hastily in his breast.*] Here! [*Shrinks back a few steps and screams.*] No; no; no! Yes!—No; no!

[*She stands a few steps from him with her hands twisted in her hair, and stares at him in speechless terror.*]

OSWALD [*Sits motionless as before and says.*] The sun. The sun.

Comments and Questions

Ibsen is regarded as the father of realistic drama. *Ghosts* qualifies as realistic on one level, but perhaps not on another. The characters are surely ordinary people who talk ordinary prose, not poetry, and who do nothing to shake the world. No Hamlet here, no Antigone. What happens no doubt became the subject of gossip in a small Norwegian community. Yet the play itself did disturb Europe vastly, did, along with Ibsen's other plays, open a new way to write drama.

Is the realism complete? All the action takes place in "a spacious garden-room." The play begins at mid-morning of one day and ends, less than twenty-four hours later, at sunrise of the next day. During that short time, everything comes to a head, a series of climaxes in the lives of *all* the characters. In observing the Greek unities of time, place, and action, Ibsen puts something of a strain on one's willing suspension of disbelief, particularly since the one new event of the play—the burning of the Orphanage—also occurs on this fateful night. "Fateful" is the word, for by adhering to the unities, the playwright called attention to a destiny not decreed by the gods but just as inexorably by genetics.

1. Realism requires that there be no heroes, no villains. Is there a villain in this play? Is there a hero?

2. A writer of rare thrift, Ibsen makes each speech count and yet manages to maintain the casualness of offhand conversation. Because of the economy and naturalness of the dialogue, it is necessary to make an especially careful summary of the plain facts before attempting to assess the meaning of the whole play. Revelations come thick and fast, all designed to set straight misinterpretations of past events and misconceptions of the sort of man Captain Alving was. Is the Captain, though long dead, a key character?

3. Is there a single thesis to this play? If so, what is it? Are there subordinate theses? What about the role of Mrs. Alving as a woman who submitted to a male's dominance and, then, too late, rebelled?

4. This is a play of reversals. Describe the reversals that occur in each of the characters. A reversal happens when two individuals radically change positions. Consider these relationships: Pastor Manders—Jacob Engstrand; Mrs. Alving—Regina; Oswald—Regina; Pastor Manders—Mrs. Alving.

5. Pastor Manders professes to be shocked by what Mrs. Alving has been reading. We are not told the specific titles of the offending books. We may, however, deduce the nature of the material. What was the subject matter? Would it bother anyone today? Note that Manders admits that he has not read the books; he has only heard about them and read what others have said about them. Does this admission invalidate the Pastor's opinions? Discuss.

6. Joseph Wood Krutch in *The Modern Temper* (New York: Harcourt Brace Jovanovich, 1929) compares *Hamlet* and *Ghosts* in this fashion: "We can believe in Oswald but we cannot believe in Hamlet, and a light has gone out in the universe." Why does Krutch rule out the possibility of believing both in Hamlet and in Oswald?

7. Aristotle contended that great tragedy produces in viewers a sense of elation, not of depression. For example, we do not despair when Hamlet dies. We are uplifted. We do despair when Oswald sinks into imbecility, for what happens to him, observes Krutch, "is trivial and meaningless." Do you think that Krutch is right? Discuss.

AUGUST STRINDBERG
1849–1912

Miss Julie[1]
A Naturalistic Tragedy

(Translated by Elizabeth Sprigge)

AUTHOR'S FOREWORD

Theatre has long seemed to me—in common with much other art—a *Biblia Pauperum*, a Bible in pictures for those who cannot read what is written or printed; and I see the playwright as a lay preacher peddling the ideas of his time in popular form, popular enough for the middle-classes, mainstay of theatre audiences, to

[1] See A. Alvarez's essay on "August Strindberg," p. 716.

grasp the gist of the matter without troubling their brains too much. For this reason theatre has always been an elementary school for the young, the semi-educated, and for women who still have a primitive capacity for deceiving themselves and letting themselves be deceived —who, that is to say, are susceptible to illusion and to suggestion from the author. I have therefore thought it not unlikely that in these days, when that rudimentary and immature thought-process operating through fantasy appears to be developing into reflection, research and analysis, that theatre, like religion, might be discarded as an outworn form for whose appreciation we lack the necessary conditions. This opinion is confirmed by the major crisis still prevailing in the theatres of Europe, and still more by the fact that in those countries of culture, producing the greatest thinkers of the age, namely England and Germany, drama—like other fine arts—is dead.

Some countries, it is true, have attempted to create a new drama by using the old forms with up-to-date contents, but not only has there been insufficient time for these new ideas to be popularized, so that the audience can grasp them, but also people have been so wrought up by the taking of sides that pure, disinterested appreciation has become impossible. One's deepest impressions are upset when an applauding or a hissing majority dominates as forcefully and openly as it can in the theatre. Moreover, as no new form has been devised for these new contents, the new wine has burst the old bottles.

In this play I have not tried to do anything new, for this cannot be done, but only to modernize the form to meet the demands which may, I think, be made on this art today. To this end I chose—or surrendered myself to—a theme which claims to be outside the controversial issues of today, since questions of social climbing or falling, of higher or lower, better or worse, of man and woman, are, have been, and will be of lasting interest. When I took this theme from a true story told me some years ago, which made a deep impression, I saw it as a subject for tragedy, for as yet it is tragic to see one favored by fortune go under, and still more to see a family heritage die out, although a time may come when we have grown so developed and enlightened that we shall view with indifference life's spectacle, now seeming so brutal, cynical, and heartless. Then we shall have dispensed with those inferior, unreliable instruments of thought called feelings, which become harmful and superfluous as reasoning develops.

The fact that my heroine rouses pity is solely due to weakness; we cannot resist fear of the same fate overtaking us. The hyper-sensitive spectator may, it is true, go beyond this kind of pity, while the man with belief in the future may actually demand some suggestion for remedying the evil—in other words some kind of policy. But, to begin with, there is no such thing as absolute evil; the downfall of one family is the good fortune of another, which thereby gets a chance to rise, and, fortune being only comparative, the alternation of rising and falling is one of life's principal charms. Also, to the man of policy, who wants to remedy the painful fact that the bird of prey devours the dove, and lice the bird of prey, I should like to put the question: why should it be remedied? Life is not so mathematically idiotic as only to permit the big to eat the small; it happens just as often that the bee kills the lion or at least drives it mad.

That my tragedy depresses many people is their own fault. When we have grown strong as the pioneers of the French revolution, we shall be happy and relieved to see the national parks cleared of ancient rotting trees which have stood too long in the way of others equally entitled to a period of growth—as relieved as we are when an uncurable invalid dies.

My tragedy "The Father" was recently criticized for being too sad—as if one wants cheerful tragedies! Everybody is clamoring for this supposed "joy of life," and theatre managers demand farces, as if the joy of life consisted in being ridiculous and portraying all human beings as suffering from St. Vitus's dance or total idiocy. I myself find the joy of life in its strong and cruel struggles, and my pleasure in learning, in adding to my knowledge. For this reason I have chosen for this play an unusual situation, but an instructive one—an exception, that is to say, but a great exception, one proving the rule, which will no doubt annoy all lovers of the commonplace. What will offend simple minds is that my plot is not simple, nor its point of view single. In real life an action—this, by the way, is a somewhat new discovery—is generally caused by a whole series of motives, more or less fundamental, but as a rule the spectator chooses just one of these—the one which his mind can most easily grasp or that does most credit to his intelligence. A suicide is committed. Business troubles, says the man of affairs. Unrequited love, say the women. Sickness, says the invalid. Despair, says the down-and-out. But it is possible that the motive lay in all or none of these directions, or that the dead man concealed his actual motive by revealing quite another, likely to reflect more to his glory.

I see Miss Julie's tragic fate to be the result of many circumstances: the mother's character, the father's mistaken upbringing of the girl, her own nature, and the influence of her fiancé on a weak, degenerate mind. Also, more directly, the festive mood of Midsummer Eve, her father's absence, her monthly indisposition, her preoccupation with animals, the excitement of dancing, the magic of dusk, the strongly aphrodisiac influence of flowers, and finally the chance that drives the couple into a room alone—to which must be added the urgency of the excited man.

My treatment of the theme, moreover, is neither exclusively physiological nor psychological. I have not put the blame wholly on the inheritance from her mother, nor on her physical condition at the time, nor on immorality. I have not even preached a moral sermon; in the absence of a priest I leave this to the cook.

I congratulate myself on this multiplicity of motives as being up-to-date, and if others have done the same thing before me, then I congratulate myself on not being alone in my "paradoxes," as all innovations are called.

In regard to the drawing of the characters, I have made my people somewhat "characterless" for the following reasons. In the course of time the word character has assumed manifold meanings. It must have originally signified the dominating trait of the soul-complex, and this was confused with temperament. Later it became the middle-class term for the automaton, one whose nature had become fixed or who had adapted himself to a particular rôle in life. In fact a person who had ceased to grow was called a character, while one continuing to develop—the skillful navigator of life's river, sailing not with sheets set fast, but veering before the wind to luff again—was called characterless, in a derogatory sense, of course, because he was so hard to catch, classify, and keep track of. This middle-class conception of the immobility of the soul was transferred to the stage where the middle-class has always ruled. A character came to signify a man fixed and finished: one who invariably appeared either drunk or jocular or melancholy, and characterization required nothing more than a physical defect such as a club-foot, a wooden leg, a red nose; or the fellow might be made to repeat some such phrase as: "That's capital!" or: "Barkis is willin'!" This simple way of regarding human beings still survives in the great Molière. Harpagon is nothing but a miser, although Harpagon might have been not only a miser, but also a first-rate financier, an excellent father, and a good citizen. Worse still, his "failing" is a distinct advantage to his son-in-law and his daughter, who are his heirs, and who therefore cannot criticize him, even if they have to wait a while to get to bed. I do not believe, therefore, in simple stage characters; and the summary judgments of authors—this man is stupid, that one brutal, this jealous, that stingy, and so forth—should be challenged by the Naturalists who know the richness of the soul-complex and realize that vice has a reverse side very much like virtue.

Because they are modern characters, living in a period of transition more feverishly hysterical than its predecessor at least, I have drawn my figures vacillating, disintegrated, a blend of old and new. Nor does it seem to me unlikely that, through newspapers and conversations, modern ideas may have filtered down to the level of the domestic servant.

My souls (characters) are conglomerations of past and present stages of civilization, bits from books and newspapers, scraps of humanity, rags and tatters of fine clothing, patched together as is the human soul. And I have added a little evolutionary history by making the weaker steal and repeat the words of the stronger, and by making the characters borrow ideas or "suggestions" from one another.

Miss Julie is a modern character, not that the half-woman, the man-hater, has not existed always, but because now that she has been discovered she has stepped to the front and begun to make a noise. The half-woman is a type who thrusts herself forward, selling herself nowadays for power, decorations, distinctions, diplomas, as formerly for money. The type implies degeneration; it is not a good type and it does not endure; but it can unfortunately transmit its misery, and degenerate men seem instinctively to choose their mates from among such women, and so they breed, producing offspring of indeterminate sex to whom life is torture. But fortunately they perish, either because they cannot come to terms with reality, or because their repressed instincts break out uncontrollably, or again because their hopes of catching up with men are shattered. The type is tragic, revealing a desperate fight against nature, tragic too in its Romantic inheritance now dissipated by Naturalism, which wants nothing but happiness—and for happiness strong and sound species are required.

But Miss Julie is also a relic of the old warrior nobility now giving way to the new nobility of nerve and brain. She is a victim of the discord which a mother's "crime" has produced in a family, a victim too of the day's complaisance, of circumstances, of her own defective constitution, all of which are equivalent to the Fate or Universal Law of former days. The Naturalist has abolished guilt with God, but the consequences of the action—punishment, imprisonment or the fear of it—he cannot abolish, for the simple reason that they remain whether he is acquitted or not. An injured fellow-being is not so complacent as outsiders, who have not been injured, can afford to be. Even if the father had felt impelled to take no vengeance, the daughter would have taken vengeance on herself, as she does here, from that innate or acquired sense of honor which the upper-classes inherit—whether from Barbarism or Aryan forebears, or from the chivalry of the Middle Ages, who knows? It is a very beautiful thing, but it has become a danger nowadays to the preservation of the race. It is the nobleman's *hara-kiri,* the Japanese law of inner conscience which compels him to cut his own stomach open at the insult of another, and which survives in modified form in the duel, a privilege of the nobility. And so the valet Jean lives on, but Miss Julie cannot live without honor. This is the thrall's advantage over the nobleman, that he lacks this fatal preoccupation with honor. And in all of us Aryans there is something of the nobleman, or the Don Quixote, which makes us sympathize with the man who commits suicide because he has done something ignoble and lost his honor. And we are noblemen enough to suffer at the sight of fallen greatness littering the earth like a corpse—yes, even if the fallen rise again and make restitution by honorable deeds. Jean, the valet, is a race-builder, a man of marked characteristics. He was a laborer's son who has educated himself towards becoming a gentleman. He has learnt easily, through his well-developed senses (smell, taste, vision)—and he also has a sense of beauty. He has already bettered himself, and is thick-skinned enough to have no scruples about using other people's services. He is already foreign to his associates, despising them as part of the life he has turned his back on, yet also fearing and fleeing from them because they know his secrets, pry into his plans, watch his rise with envy, and look forward with pleasure to his fall. Hence his dual, indeterminate character, vacillating between love of the heights and hatred of those who have already achieved them. He is, he says himself, an aristocrat; he has learned the secrets of good society. He is polished, but vulgar within; he already wears his tails with taste, but there is no guarantee of his personal cleanliness.

He has some respect for his young lady, but he is frightened of Kristin, who knows his dangerous secrets, and he is sufficiently callous not to allow the night's events to wreck his plans for the future. Having both the slave's brutality and the master's lack of squeamishness, he can see blood without fainting and take disaster by the horns. Consequently he emerges from the battle unscathed, and probably ends his days as a hotel-keeper. And even if *he* does not become a Rumanian Count, his son will doubtless go to the university and perhaps become a county attorney.

The light which Jean sheds on a lower-class conception of life, life seen from below, is on the whole illuminating—when he speaks the truth, which is not often, for he says what is favorable to himself rather than what is true. When Miss Julie suggests that the lower-classes must be oppressed by the attitude of their superiors, Jean naturally agrees, as his object is to gain her sympathy; but when he perceives the advantage of separating himself from the common herd, he at once takes back his words.

It is not because Jean is now rising that he has the upper hand of Miss Julie, but because he is a man. Sexually he is the aristocrat because of his virility, his keener senses, and his capacity for taking the initiative. His inferiority is mainly due to the social environment in which he lives, and he can probably shed it with his valet's livery.

The slave mentality expresses itself in his worship of the Count (the boots), and his religious superstition; but he worships the Count chiefly because he holds that higher position for which Jean himself is striving. And this worship remains even when he has won the daughter of the house and seen how empty is that lovely shell.

I do not believe that a love relationship in the "higher" sense could exist between two individuals of such different quality, but I have made Miss Julie imagine that she is in love, so as to lessen her sense of guilt, and I let Jean suppose that if his social position were altered he would truly love her. I think love is like the hyacinth which has to strike roots in darkness *before* it can produce a vigorous flower. In this case it shoots up quickly, blossoms and goes to seed all at the same time, which is why the plant dies so soon.

As for Kristin, she is a female slave, full of servility and sluggishness acquired in front of the kitchen fire, and stuffed full of morality and religion, which are her cloak and scapegoat. She goes to church as a quick and easy way of unloading her household thefts on to Jesus and taking on a fresh cargo of guiltlessness. For the rest she is a minor character, and I have therefore sketched her in the same manner as the Pastor and the Doctor in "The Father," where I wanted ordinary human beings, as are most country pastors and provincial doctors. If these minor characters seem abstract to some people this is due to the fact that ordinary people are to a certain extent abstract in pursuit of their work; that is to say, they are without individuality, showing, while working, only one side of themselves. And as long as the spectator does not feel a need to see them from other sides, there is nothing wrong with my abstract presentation.

In regard to the dialogue, I have departed somewhat from tradition by not making my characters catechists who ask stupid questions in order to elicit a smart reply. I have avoided the symmetrical, mathematical construction of French dialogue, and let people's minds work irregularly, as they do in real life where, during a conversation, no topic is drained to the dregs, and one mind finds in another a chance cog to engage in. So too the dialogue wanders, gathering in the opening scenes material which is later picked up, worked over, repeated, expounded and developed like the theme in a musical composition.

The plot speaks for itself, and as it really only concerns two people, I have concentrated on these, introducing only one minor character, the cook, and keeping the unhappy spirit of the father above and behind the action. I have done this because it seems to me that the psychological process is what interests people most today. Our inquisitive souls are no longer satisfied with seeing a thing happen; we must also know how it happens. We want to see the wires themselves, to watch the machinery, to examine the box with the false bottom, to take hold of the magic ring in order to find the join, and look at the cards to see how they are marked.

In this connection I have had in view the documentary novels of the Goncourt brothers, which appeal to me more than any other modern literature.

As far as the technical side of the work is concerned I have made the experiment of abolishing the division into acts. This is because I have come to the conclusion that our capacity for illusion is disturbed by the intervals, during which the audience has time to reflect and escape from the suggestive influence of the author-hypnotist. My play will probably take an hour and a half, and as one can listen to a lecture, a sermon, or a parliamentary debate for as long as that or longer, I do not think a theatrical performance will be fatiguing in the same length of time. As early as 1872, in one of my first dramatic attempts, "The Outlaw," I tried this concentrated form, although with scant success. The play was written in five acts, and only when finished did I become aware of the restless, disjointed effect that it produced. The script was burnt and from the ashes rose a single well-knit act—fifty pages of print, playable in one hour. The form of the present play is, therefore, not new, but it appears to be my own, and changing tastes may make it timely. My hope is one day to have an audience educated enough to sit through a whole evening's entertainment in one act, but one would have to try this out to see. Meanwhile, in order to provide respite for the audience and the players, without allowing the audience to escape from the illusion, I have introduced three art forms: monologue, mime, and ballet. These are all part of drama, having their origins in classic tragedy, monody having become monologue and the chorus, ballet.

Monologue is now condemned by our realists as unnatural, but if one provides motives for it one makes it natural, and then can use it to advantage. It is, surely, natural for a public speaker to walk up and down the room practicing his speech, natural for an actor to read his part aloud, for a servant girl to talk to her cat, a mother to prattle to her child, an old maid to chatter to her parrot, and a sleeper to talk in his sleep. And in order that the actor may have a chance, for once, of working independently, free from the author's direction, it is better that the monologue should not be written, but only indicated. For since it is of small importance what is said in one's sleep or to the parrot or to the cat—none of it influences the action—a talented actor, identifying himself with the atmosphere and the situation, may improvise better than the author, who cannot calculate ahead how much may be said or how long taken without waking the audience from the illusion.

Some Italian theatres have, as we know, returned to improvisation, thereby producing actors who are creative, although within the bounds set by the author. This may well be a step forward, or even the beginning of a new art-form worthy to be called *productive*.

In places where monologue would be unnatural I have used mime, leaving here an even wider scope for the actor's imagination, and more chance for him to win independent laurels. But so as not to try the audience beyond endurance, I have introduced music—fully justified by the Midsummer Eve dance—to exercise its powers of persuasion during the dumb show. But I beg the musical director to consider carefully his choice of compositions, so that conflicting moods are not induced by selections from the current operetta or dance show, or by folk-tunes of too local a character.

The ballet I have introduced cannot be replaced by the usual kind of "crowd-scene," for such scenes are too badly played—a lot of grinning idiots seizing the opportunity to show off and thus destroying the illusion. And as peasants cannot improvise their taunts, but use ready-made phrases with a double meaning, I have not composed their lampoon, but taken a little-known song and dance which I myself noted down in the Stockholm district. The words are not quite to the point, but this too is intentional, for the cunning, i.e. weakness, of the slave prevents him from direct attack. Nor can there be clowning in a serious action, or coarse joking in a situation which nails the lid on a family coffin.

As regards the scenery, I have borrowed from impressionist painting its asymmetry and its economy; thus, I think, strengthening the illusion. For the fact that one does not see the whole room and all the furniture leaves scope for conjecture—that is to say imagination is roused and complements what is seen. I have succeeded too in getting rid of those tiresome exits through doors, since scenery doors are made of canvas, and rock at the slightest touch. They cannot even express the wrath of an irate head of the family who, after a bad dinner, goes out slamming the door behind him, "so that the whole house shakes." On the stage it rocks. I have also kept to a single set, both in order to let the characters develop in their métier and to break away from overdecoration. When one has only one set, one may expect it to be realistic; but as a matter of fact nothing is harder than to get a stage room that looks something like a room, however easily the scene painter can produce flaming volcanoes and water-falls. Presumably the walls must be of canvas; but it seems about time to dispense with painted shelves and cooking utensils. We are asked to accept so many stage conventions that we might at least be spared the pain of painted pots and pans.

I have set the back wall and the table diagonally so that the actors may play full-face and in half-profile when they are sitting opposite one another at the table. In the opera *Aïda* I saw a diagonal background, which led the eye to unfamiliar perspectives and did not look like mere reaction against boring straight lines.

Another much needed innovation is the abolition of foot-lights. This lighting from below is said to have the purpose of making the actors' faces fatter. But why, I ask, should all actors have fat faces? Does not this under-lighting flatten out all the subtlety of the lower part of the face, specially the jaw, falsify the shape of the nose and throw shadows up over the eyes? Even if this were not so, one thing is certain: that the lights hurt the performers' eyes, so that the full play of their expression is lost. The footlights strike part of the retina usually protected —except in sailors who have to watch sunlight on water—and therefore one seldom sees anything other than a crude rolling of the eyes, either sideways or up towards the gallery, showing their whites. Perhaps this too causes that tiresome blinking of the eyelashes, especially by actresses. And when anyone on the stage wants to speak with his eyes, the only thing he can do is to look straight at the audience, with whom he or she then gets into direct communication, outside the framework of the set—a habit called, rightly or wrongly, "greeting one's friends."

Would not sufficiently strong side-lighting, with some kind of reflectors, add to the actor's powers of expression by allowing him to use the face's greatest asset:—the play of the eyes?

I have few illusions about getting the actors to play *to* the audience instead of *with* it, although this is what I want. That I shall see an actor's back throughout a critical scence is beyond my dreams, but I do wish crucial scenes could be played, not in front of the prompter's box, like duets expecting applause, but in the place required by the action. So, no revolutions, but just some small modifications, for to make the stage into a real room with the fourth wall missing would be too upsetting altogether.

I dare not hope that the actresses will listen to what I have to say about make-up, for they would rather be beautiful than life-like, but the actor might consider whether it is to his advantage to create an abstract character with grease-paints, and cover his face with it like a mask. Take the case of a man who draws a choleric charcoal line between his eyes and then, in this fixed state of wrath, has to smile at some repartee. What a frightful grimace the result is! And equally, how is that false forehead, smooth as a billiard ball, to wrinkle when the old man loses his temper?

In a modern psychological drama, where the subtlest reactions of a character need to be mirrored in the face rather than expressed by sound and gesture, it would be worth while experimenting with powerful side-lighting on a small stage and a cast without make-up, or at least with the minimum.

If, in addition, we could abolish the visible orchestra, with its distracting lamps and its faces turned toward the audience; if we could have the stalls raised so that the spectators' eyes were higher than the players' knees; if we could get rid of the boxes (the center of my target), with their tittering diners and supper-parties, and have total darkness in the auditorium during the performance; and if, first and foremost, we could have a *small* stage and a *small* house, then perhaps a new dramatic art might arise, and theatre once more become a place of entertainment for educated people. While waiting for such a theatre we may as well go on writing so as to stock that repertory of the future.

I have made an attempt! If it has failed, there is time enough to try again!

CHARACTERS

MISS JULIE, *aged 25*
JEAN, *the valet, aged 30*
KRISTIN, *the cook, aged 35*

SCENE: *The large kitchen of a Swedish manor house in a country district in the 1880's.*

Midsummer Eve.

The kitchen has three doors, two small ones into JEAN'S *and* KRISTIN'S *bedrooms, and a large, glass-fronted double one, opening on to a courtyard. This is the only way to the rest of the house.*

Through these glass doors can be seen part of a fountain with a cupid, lilac bushes in flower and the tops of some Lombardy poplars. On one wall are shelves edged with scalloped paper on which are kitchen utensils of copper, iron and tin.

To the left is the corner of a large tiled range and part of its chimney-hood, to the right the end of the servants' dinner table with chairs beside it.

The stove is decorated with birch boughs, the floor strewn with twigs of juniper. On the end of the table is a large Japanese spice jar full of lilac.

There are also an ice-box, a scullery table and a sink.

Above the double door hangs a big old-fashioned bell; near it is a speaking-tube.

A fiddle can be heard from the dance in the barn near-by.

KRISTIN *is standing at the stove, frying something in a pan. She wears a light-colored cotton dress and a big apron.*

JEAN *enters, wearing livery and carry a pair of large riding-boots with spurs, which he puts in a conspicuous place.*

JEAN Miss Julie's crazy again to-night, absolutely crazy.

KRISTIN Oh, so you're back, are you?

JEAN When I'd taken the Count to the station, I came back and dropped in at the Barn for a dance. And who did I see there but our young lady leading off with the gamekeeper. But the moment she sets eyes on me, up she rushes and invites me to waltz with her. And how she waltzed—I've never seen anything like it! She's crazy.

KRISTIN Always has been, but never so bad as this last fortnight since the engagement was broken off.

JEAN Yes, that was a pretty business, to be sure. He's a decent enough chap, too, even if he isn't rich. Oh, but they're choosy! [*Sits down at the end of the table.*] In any case, it's a bit odd that our young—er—lady would rather stay at home with yokels than go with her father to visit her relations.

KRISTIN Perhaps she feels a bit awkward, after that bust-up with her fiancé.

JEAN Maybe. That chap had some guts, though. Do you know the sort of thing that was going on, Kristin? I saw it with my own eyes, though I didn't let on I had.

KRISTIN You saw them . . . ?

JEAN Didn't I just! Came across the pair of them one evening in the stable-yard. Miss Julie was doing what she called "training" him. Know what that was? Making him jump over her riding-whip—the way you teach a dog. He did it twice and got a cut each time for his pains, but when it came to the third go, he snatched the whip out of her hand and broke it into smithereens. And then he cleared off.

KRISTIN What goings on! I never did!

JEAN Well, that's how it was with that little affair . . . Now, what have you got for me, Kristin? Something tasty?

KRISTIN [*Serving from the pan to his plate.*] Well, it's just a little bit of kidney I cut off their joint.

JEAN [*Smelling it.*] Fine! That's my special delice. [*Feels the plate.*] But you might have warmed the plate.

KRISTIN When you choose to be finicky you're worse than the Count himself. [*Pulls his hair affectionately.*]

JEAN [*Crossly.*] Stop pulling my hair. You know how sensitive I am.

KRISTIN There, there! It's only love, you know. [JEAN *eats.* KRISTIN *brings a bottle of beer.*]

JEAN Beer on Midsummer Eve? No thanks! I've got something better than that. [*From a drawer in the table brings out a bottle of red wine with a yellow seal.*] Yellow seal, see! Now get me a glass. You use a glass with a stem of course when you're drinking it straight.

KRISTIN [*Giving him a wine-glass.*] Lord help the woman who gets you for a husband, you old fusser! [*She puts the beer in the ice-box and sets a small saucepan on the stove.*]

JEAN Nonsense! You'll be glad enough to get a fellow as smart as me. And I don't think it's done you any harm, people calling me your fiancé. [*Tastes the wine.*] Good. Very good indeed. But not quite warmed enough. [*Warms the glass in his hand.*] We bought this in Dijon. Four francs the liter without the bottle, and duty on top of that. What are you cooking now? It stinks.

KRISTIN Some bloody muck Miss Julie wants for Diana.

JEAN You should be more refined in your speech, Kristin. But why should you spend a holiday cooking for that bitch? Is she sick or what?

KRISTIN Yes, she's sick. She sneaked out with the pug at the lodge and got in the usual mess. And that, you know, Miss Julie won't have.

JEAN Miss Julie's too high-and-mighty in some respects, and not enough in others, just like her mother before her. The Countess was more at home in the kitchen and cowsheds than anywhere else, but would she ever go driving with only one horse? She went round with her cuffs filthy, but she had to have the coronet on the cuff-links. Our young lady—to come back to her—hasn't any proper respect for herself or her position. I mean she isn't refined. In the Barn just now she dragged the gamekeeper away from Anna and made him dance with her—no waiting to be asked. We wouldn't do a thing like that. But that's what happens when the gentry try to behave like the common people—they become common . . . Still she's a fine girl. Smashing! What shoulders! And what—er—etcetera!

KRISTIN Oh come off it! I know what Clara says, and she dresses her.

JEAN Clara? Pooh, you're all jealous! But I've been out riding with her . . . and as for her dancing!

KRISTIN Listen, Jean. You will dance with me, won't you, as soon as I'm through.

JEAN Of course I will.

KRISTIN Promise?

JEAN Promise? When I say I'll do a thing I do it. Well, thanks for the supper. It was a real treat. [*Corks the bottle.*]

[JULIE *appears in the doorway, speaking to someone outside.*]

JULIE I'll be back in a moment. Don't wait.

[JEAN *slips the bottle into the drawer and rises respectfully.* JULIE *enters and joins* KRISTIN *at the stove.*]

Well, have you made it? [KRISTIN *signs that* JEAN *is near them.*]

JEAN [*Gallantly.*] Have you ladies got some secret?

JULIE [*Flipping his face with her handkerchief.*] You're very inquisitive.

JEAN What a delicious smell! Violets.

JULIE [*Coquettishly.*] Impertinence! Are you an expert of scent too? I must say you know how to dance. Now don't look. Go away. [*The music of a schottische begins.*]

JEAN [*With impudent politeness.*] Is it some witches' brew you're cooking on Midsummer Eve? Something to tell your stars by, so you can see your future?

JULIE [*Sharply.*] If you could see that you'd have good eyes. [*To* KRISTIN.] Put it in a bottle and cork it tight. Come and dance this schottische with me, Jean.

JEAN [*Hesitating.*] I don't want to be rude, but I've promised to dance this one with Kristin.

JULIE Well, she can have another, can't you, Kristin? You'll lend me Jean, won't you?

KRISTIN [*Bottling.*] It's nothing to do with me. When you're so condescending, Miss, it's not his place to say no. Go on, Jean, and thank Miss Julie for the honor.

JEAN Frankly speaking, Miss, and no offense meant, I wonder if it's wise for you to dance twice running with the same partner, specially as those people are so ready to jump to conclusions.

JULIE [*Flaring up.*] What did you say? What sort of conclusions? What do you mean?

JEAN [*Meekly.*] As you choose not to understand, Miss Julie, I'll have to speak more plainly. It looks bad to show a preference for one of your retainers when they're all hoping for the same unusual favor.

JULIE Show a preference! The very idea! I'm surprised at you. I'm doing the people an honor by attending their ball when I'm mistress of the house, but if I'm really going to dance, I mean to have a partner who can lead and doesn't make me look ridiculous.

JEAN If those are your orders, Miss, I'm at your service.

JULIE [*Gently.*] Don't take it as an order. Tonight we're all just people enjoying a party. There's no question of class. So now give me your arm. Don't worry, Kristin. I shan't steal your sweetheart.

[JEAN *gives* JULIE *his arm and leads her out.*]

[*Left alone,* KRISTIN *plays her scene in an unhurried, natural way, humming to the tune of the schottische, played on a distant violin. She clears* JEAN*'s place, washes up and puts things away, then takes off her apron, brings out a small mirror from a drawer, props it against the jar of lilac, lights a candle, warms a small pair of tongs and curls her fringe. She goes to the door and listens, then turning back to the table finds* MISS JULIE*'s handkerchief. She smells it, then meditatively smooths it out and folds it.*]

[*Enter* JEAN.]

JEAN She really *is* crazy. What a way to dance! With people standing grinning at her too from behind the doors. What's got into her, Kristin?

KRISTIN Oh, it's just her time coming on. She's always queer then. Are you going to dance with me now?

JEAN Then you're not wild with me for cutting that one.

KRISTIN You know I'm not—for a little thing like that. Besides, I know my place.

JEAN [*Putting his arm round her waist.*] You're a sensible girl, Kristin, and you'll make a very good wife . . .

[*Enter* JULIE, *unpleasantly surprised.*]

JULIE [*With forced gaiety.*] You're a fine beau—running away from your partner.

JEAN Not away, Miss Julie, but as you see back to the one I deserted.

JULIE [*Changing her tone.*] You really can dance, you know. But why are you wearing your livery on a holiday. Take it off at once.

JEAN Then I must ask you to go away for a moment, Miss. My black coat's here. [*Indicates it hanging on the door to his room.*]

JULIE Are you so shy of me—just over changing a coat? Go into your room then—or stay here and I'll turn my back.

JEAN Excuse me then, Miss. [*He goes to his room and is partly visible as he changes his coat.*]

JULIE Tell me, Kristin, is Jean your fiancé? You seem very intimate.

KRISTIN My fiancé? Yes, if you like. We call it that.

JULIE Call it?

KRISTIN Well, you've had a fiancé yourself, Miss, and . . .

JULIE But we really were engaged.

KRISTIN All the same it didn't come to anything.

[JEAN *returns in his black coat.*]

JULIE *Très gentil, Monsieur Jean. Très gentil.*[1]

JEAN *Vous voulez plaisanter, Madame.*

JULIE *Et vous voulez parler français.* Where did you learn it?

JEAN In Switzerland, when I was steward at one of the biggest hotels in Lucerne.

JULIE You look quite the gentleman in that get-up. Charming. [*Sits at the table.*]

JEAN Oh, you're just flattering me!

JULIE [*Annoyed.*] Flattering you?

JEAN I'm too modest to believe you would pay real compliments to a man like me, so I must take it you are exaggerating—that this is what's known as flattery.

JULIE Where on earth did you learn to make speeches like that? Perhaps you've been to the theater a lot.

JEAN That's right. And traveled a lot too.

JULIE But you come from this neighborhood, don't you?

JEAN Yes, my father was a laborer on the next estate—the District Attorney's place. I often used to see you, Miss Julie, when you were little, though you never noticed me.

JULIE Did you really?

JEAN Yes. One time specially I remember . . . but I can't tell you about that.

JULIE Oh do! Why not? This is just the time.

JEAN No, I really can't now. Another time perhaps.

JULIE Another time means never. What harm in now?

JEAN No harm, but I'd rather not. [*Points to* KRISTIN, *now fast asleep.*] Look at her.

JULIE She'll make a charming wife, won't she? I wonder if she snores.

JEAN No, she doesn't, but she talks in her sleep.

JULIE [*Cynically.*] How do you know she talks in her sleep?

JEAN [*Brazenly.*] I've heard her. [*Pause. They look at one another.*]

JULIE Why don't you sit down?

JEAN I can't take such a liberty in your presence.

JULIE Supposing I order you to.

JEAN I'll obey.

JULIE Then sit down. No, wait a minute. Will you get me a drink first?

JEAN I don't know what's in the ice-box. Only beer, I expect.

JULIE There's no only about it. My taste is so simple I prefer it to wine.

[JEAN *takes a bottle from the ice-box, fetches a glass and plate and serves the beer.*]

JEAN At your service.

JULIE Thank you. Won't you have some yourself?

JEAN I'm not really a beer-drinker, but if it's an order . . .

JULIE Order? I should have thought it was ordinary manners to keep your partner company.

JEAN That's a good way of putting it. [*He opens another bottle and fetches a glass.*]

JULIE Now drink my health. [*He hesitates.*] I believe the man really is shy.

[JEAN *kneels and raises his glass with mock ceremony.*]

JEAN To the health of my lady!

JULIE Bravo! Now kiss my shoe and everything will be perfect. [*He hesitates, then boldly takes hold of her foot and lightly kisses it.*] Splendid. You ought to have been an actor.

JEAN [*Rising.*] We can't go on like this, Miss Julie. Someone might come in and see us.

[1] JULIE Very nice, Monsieur Jean, very nice.
JEAN You like to joke, Madame.
JULIE And you want to speak French.

JULIE Why would that matter?

JEAN For the simple reason that they'd talk. And if you knew the way their tongues were wagging out there just now, you . . .

JULIE What were they saying? Tell me. Sit down.

JEAN [*Sitting.*] No offense meant, Miss, but . . . well, their language wasn't nice, and they were hinting . . . oh, you know quite well what. You're not a child, and if a lady's seen drinking alone at night with a man—and a servant at that—then . . .

JULIE Then what? Besides, we're not alone. Kristin's here.

JEAN Yes, asleep.

JULIE I'll wake her up. [*Rises.*] Kristin, are you asleep? [KRISTIN *mumbles in her sleep.*] Kristin! Goodness, how she sleeps!

KRISTIN [*In her sleep.*] The Count's boots are cleaned—put the coffee on—yes, yes, at once . . . [*Mumbles incoherently.*]

JULIE [*Tweaking her nose.*] Wake up, can't you!

JEAN [*Sharply.*] Let her sleep.

JULIE What?

JEAN When you've been standing at the stove all day you're likely to be tired at night. And sleep should be respected.

JULIE [*Changing her tone.*] What a nice idea. It does you credit. Thank you for it. [*Holds out her hand to him.*] Now come out and pick some lilac for me. [*During the following* KRISTIN *goes sleepily in to her bedroom.*]

JEAN Out with you, Miss Julie?

JULIE Yes.

JEAN It wouldn't do. It really wouldn't.

JULIE I don't know what you mean. You can't possibly imagine that . . .

JEAN I don't, but others do.

JULIE What? That I'm in love with the valet?

JEAN I'm not a conceited man, but such a thing's been known to happen, and to these rustics nothing's sacred.

JULIE You, I take it, are an aristocrat.

JEAN Yes, I am.

JULIE And I am coming down in the world.

JEAN Don't come down, Miss Julie. Take my advice. No one will believe you came down of your own accord. They'll all say you fell.

JULIE I have a higher opinion of our people than you. Come and put it to the test. Come on. [*Gazes into his eyes.*]

JEAN You're very strange, you know.

JULIE Perhaps I am, but so are you. For that matter everything is strange. Life, human beings, everything, just scum drifting about on the water until it sinks—down and down. That reminds me of a dream I sometimes have, in which I'm on top of a pillar and can't see any way of getting down. When I look down I'm dizzy; I have to get down but I haven't the courage to jump. I can't stay there and I long to fall, but I don't fall. There's no respite. There can't be any peace at all for me until I'm down, right down on the ground. And if I did get to the ground I'd want to be under the ground . . . Have you ever felt like that?

JEAN No. In my dream I'm lying under a great tree in a dark wood. I want to get up, up to the top of it, and look out over the bright landscape where the sun is shining and rob that high nest of its golden eggs. And I climb and climb, but the trunk is so thick and smooth and it's so far to the first branch. But I know if I can once reach that first branch I'll go to the top just as if I'm on a ladder. I haven't reached it yet, but I shall get there, even if only in my dreams.

JULIE Here I am chattering about dreams with you. Come on. Only into the park. [*She takes his arm and they go toward the door.*]

JEAN We must sleep on nine midsummer flowers tonight; then our dreams will come true, Miss Julie. [*They turn at the door. He has a hand to his eye.*]

JULIE Have you got something in your eye? Let me see.

JEAN Oh, it's nothing. Just a speck of dust. It'll be gone in a minute.

JULIE My sleeve must have rubbed against you. Sit down and let me see to it. [*Takes him by the arm and makes him sit down, bends his head back and tries to get the speck out with the corner of her handkerchief.*] Keep still now, quite still. [*Slaps his hand.*] Do as I tell you. Why, I believe you're trembling, big, strong man though you are! [*Feels his biceps.*] What muscles!

JEAN [*Warning.*] Miss Julie!

JULIE Yes, Monsieur Jean?

JEAN *Attention. Je ne suis qu'un homme.*[2]

[2] Careful. I'm only a man.

JULIE Will you stay still! There now. It's out. Kiss my hand and say thank you.

JEAN [*Rising.*] Miss Julie, listen. Kristin's gone to bed now. Will you listen?

JULIE Kiss my hand first.

JEAN Very well, but you'll have only yourself to blame.

JULIE For what?

JEAN For what! Are you still a child at twenty-five? Don't you know it's dangerous to play with fire?

JULIE Not for me. I'm insured.

JEAN [*Bluntly.*] No, you're not. And even if you are, there's still stuff here to kindle a flame.

JULIE Meaning yourself?

JEAN Yes. Not because I'm me, but because I'm a man and young and . . .

JULIE And good-looking? What incredible conceit! A Don Juan perhaps? Or a Joseph? Good Lord, I do believe you are a Joseph!

JEAN Do you?

JULIE I'm rather afraid so.

[JEAN *goes boldly up and tries to put his arms round her and kiss her. She boxes his ears.*] How dare you!

JEAN Was that in earnest or a joke?

JULIE In earnest.

JEAN Then what went before was in earnest too. You take your games too seriously and that's dangerous. Anyhow I'm tired of playing now and beg leave to return to my work. The Count will want his boots first thing and it's past midnight now.

JULIE Put those boots down.

JEAN No. This is my work, which it's my duty to do. But I never undertook to be your playfellow and I never will be. I consider myself too good for that.

JULIE You're proud.

JEAN In some ways—not all.

JULIE Have you ever been in love?

JEAN We don't put it that way, but I've been gone on quite a few girls. And once I went sick because I couldn't have the one I wanted. Sick, I mean, like those princes in the Arabian Nights who couldn't eat or drink for love.

JULIE Who was she? [*No answer.*] Who was she?

JEAN You can't force me to tell you that.

JULIE If I ask as an equal, ask as a—friend? Who was she?

JEAN You.

JULIE [*Sitting.*] How absurd!

JEAN Yes, ludicrous if you like. That's the story I wouldn't tell you before, see, but now I will . . . Do you know what the world looks like from below? No, you don't. No more than the hawks and falcons do whose backs one hardly ever sees because they're always soaring up aloft. I lived in a laborer's hovel with seven other children and a pig, out in the gray fields where there isn't a single tree. But from the window I could see the wall round the Count's park with apple-trees above it. That was the Garden of Eden, guarded by many terrible angels with flaming swords. All the same I and the other boys managed to get to the tree of life. Does all this make you despise me?

JULIE Goodness, all boys steal apples!

JEAN You say that now, but all the same you do despise me. However, one time I went into the Garden of Eden with my mother to weed the onion beds. Close to the kitchen garden there was a Turkish pavilion hung all over with jasmine and honeysuckle. I hadn't any idea what it was used for, but I'd never seen such a beautiful building. People used to go in and then come out again, and one day the door was left open. I crept up and saw the walls covered with pictures of kings and emperors, and the windows had red curtains with fringes—you know now what the place was, don't you? I . . . [*Breaks off a piece of lilac and holds it for* JULIE *to smell. As he talks, she takes it from him.*] I had never been inside the manor, never seen anything but the church, and this was more beautiful. No matter where my thoughts went, they always came back—to that place. The longing went on growing in me to enjoy it fully, just once. *Enfin,*[3] I sneaked in, gazed and admired. Then I heard someone coming. There was only one way out for the gentry, but for me there was another and I had no choice but to take it. [JULIE *drops the lilac on the table.*] Then I took to my heels, plunged through the raspberry canes, dashed across the strawberry beds and found myself on the rose terrace. There I saw a pink dress and a pair of white stockings—it was you. I crawled into

[3] Well.

a weed pile and lay there right under it among prickly thistles and damp rank earth. I watched you walking among the roses and said to myself: "If it's true that a thief can get to heaven and be with the angels, it's pretty strange that a laborer's child here on God's earth mayn't come in the park and play with the Count's daughter."

JULIE [*Sentimentally.*] Do you think all poor children feel the way you did?

JEAN [*Taken aback, then rallying.*] *All* poor children? . . . Yes, of course they do. Of course.

JULIE It must be terrible to be poor.

JEAN [*With exaggerated distress.*] Oh yes, Miss Julie, yes. A dog may lie on the Countess's sofa, a horse may have his nose stroked by a young lady, but a servant . . . [*Change of tone.*] well, yes, now and then you meet one with guts enough to rise in the world, but how often? Anyhow, do you know what I did? Jumped in the millstream with my clothes on, was pulled out and got a hiding. But the next Sunday, when Father and all the rest went to Granny's, I managed to get left behind. Then I washed with soap and hot water, put my best clothes on and went to church so as to see you. I did see you and went home determined to die. But I wanted to die beautifully and peacefully, without any pain. Then I remembered it was dangerous to sleep under an elder bush. We had a big one in full bloom, so I stripped it and climbed into the oats-bin with the flowers. Have you ever noticed how smooth oats are? Soft to touch as human skin . . . Well, I closed the lid and shut my eyes, fell asleep, and when they woke me I was very ill. But I didn't die, as you see. What I meant by all that I don't know. There was no hope of winning you—you were simply a symbol of the hopelessness of ever getting out of the class I was born in.

JULIE You put things very well, you know. Did you go to school?

JEAN For a while. But I've read a lot of novels and been to the theater. Besides, I've heard educated folk talking—that's what's taught me most.

JULIE Do you stand round listening to what we're saying?

JEAN Yes, of course. And I've heard quite a bit too! On the carriage box or rowing the boat. Once I heard you, Miss Julie, and one of your young lady friends . . .

JULIE Oh! Whatever did you hear?

JEAN Well, it wouldn't be nice to repeat it. And I must say I was pretty startled. I couldn't think where you had learnt such words. Perhaps, at bottom, there isn't as much difference between people as one's led to believe.

JULIE How dare you! We don't behave as you do when we're engaged.

JEAN [*Looking hard at her.*] Are you sure? It's no use making out so innocent to me.

JULIE The man I gave my love to was a scoundrel.

JEAN That's what you always say—afterward.

JULIE Always?

JEAN I think it must be always. I've heard the expression several times in similar circumstances.

JULIE What circumstances?

JEAN Like those in question. The last time . . .

JULIE [*Rising.*] Stop. I don't want to hear any more.

JEAN Nor did *she*—curiously enough. May I go to bed now please?

JULIE [*Gently.*] Go to bed on Midsummer Eve?

JEAN Yes. Dancing with that crowd doesn't really amuse me.

JULIE Get the key of the boathouse and row me out on the lake. I want to see the sun rise.

JEAN Would that be wise?

JULIE You sound as though you're frightened for your reputation.

JEAN Why not? I don't want to be made a fool of, nor to be sent packing without references when I'm trying to better myself. Besides, I have Kristin to consider.

JULIE So now it's Kristin.

JEAN Yes, but it's you I'm thinking about too. Take my advice and go to bed.

JULIE Am I to take orders from you?

JEAN Just this once, for your own sake. Please. It's very late and sleepiness goes to one's head and makes one rash. Go to bed. What's more, if my ears don't deceive me, I hear people coming this way. They'll be looking for me, and if they find us here, you're done for.

[*The* CHORUS *approaches, singing. During the following dialogue the song is heard in snatches, and in full when the peasants enter.*]

Out of the wood two women came,
Tridiri-ralla, tridiri-ra.
The feet of one were bare and cold,
Tridiri-ralla-la.

The other talked of bags of gold,
Tridiri-ralla, tridiri-ra.
But neither had a sou to her name,
Tridiri-ralla-la.

The bridal wreath I give to you,
Tridiri-ralla, tridiri-ra.
But to another I'll be true,
Tridiri-ralla-la.

JULIE I know our people and I love them, just as they do me. Let them come. You'll see.

JEAN No, Miss Julie, they don't love you. They take your food, then spit at it. You must believe me. Listen to them, just listen to what they're singing . . . No, don't listen.

JULIE [*Listening.*] What are they singing?

JEAN They're mocking—you and me.

JULIE Oh no! How horrible! What cowards!

JEAN A pack like that's always cowardly. But against such odds there's nothing we can do but run away.

JULIE Run away? Where to? We can't get out and we can't go into Kristin's room.

JEAN Into mine then. Necessity knows no rules. And you can trust me. I really am your true and devoted friend.

JULIE But supposing . . . supposing they were to look for you in there?

JEAN I'll bolt the door, and if they try to break in I'll shoot. Come on. [*Pleading.*] Please come.

JULIE [*Tensely.*] Do you promise . . . ?

JEAN I swear!

[JULIE *goes quickly into his room and he excitedly follows her.*

Led by the fiddler, the peasants enter in festive attire with flowers in their hats. They put a barrel of beer and a keg of spirits, garlanded with leaves, on the table, fetch glasses and begin to carouse. The scene becomes a ballet. They form a ring and dance and sing and mime: "Out of the wood two women came." *Finally they go out, still singing.* JULIE *comes in alone. She looks at the havoc in the kitchen, wrings her hands, then takes out her powder puff and powders her face.*

JEAN *enters in high spirits.*]

JEAN Now you see! And you heard, didn't you? Do you still think it's possible for us to stay here?

JULIE No, I don't. But what can we do?

JEAN Run away. Far away. Take a journey.

JULIE Journey? But where to?

JEAN Switzerland. The Italian lakes. Ever been there?

JULIE No. Is it nice?

JEAN Ah! Eternal summer, oranges, evergreens . . . ah!

JULIE But what would we do there?

JEAN I'll start a hotel. First-class accommodation and first-class customers.

JULIE Hotel?

JEAN There's life for you. New faces all the time, new languages—no time for nerves or worries, no need to look for something to do—work rolling up of its own accord. Bells ringing night and day, trains whistling, buses coming and going, and all the time gold pieces rolling on to the counter. There's life for you!

JULIE For *you*. And I?

JEAN Mistress of the house, ornament of the firm. With your looks, and your style . . . oh, it's bound to be a success! Terrific! You'll sit like a queen in the office and set your slaves in motion by pressing an electric button. The guests will file past your throne and nervously lay their treasure on your table. You've no idea the way people tremble when they get their bills. I'll salt the bills and you'll sugar them with your sweetest smiles. Ah, let's get away from here! [*Produces a timetable.*] At once, by the next train. We shall be at Malmö at six-thirty, Hamburg eight-forty next morning, Frankfurt-Basle the following day, and Como by the St. Gotthard Pass in—let's see—three days. Three days!

JULIE That's all very well. But Jean, you must give me courage. Tell me you love me. Come and take me in your arms.

JEAN [*Reluctantly.*] I'd like to, but I daren't. Not again in this house. I love you—that goes without saying. You can't doubt that, Miss Julie, can you?

JULIE [*Shyly, very feminine.*] Miss? Call me Julie. There aren't any barriers between us now. Call me Julie.

JEAN [*Uneasily.*] I can't. As long as we're in

this house, there *are* barriers between us. There's the past and there's the Count. I've never been so servile to anyone as I am to him. I've only got to see his gloves on a chair to feel small. I've only to hear his bell and I shy like a horse. Even now, when I look at his boots, standing there so proud and stiff, I feel my back beginning to bend. [*Kicks the boots.*] It's those old, narrow-minded notions drummed into us as children . . . but they can soon be forgotten. You've only got to get to another country, a republic, and people will bend themselves double before my porter's livery. Yes, double they'll bend themselves, but I shan't. I wasn't born to bend. I've got guts, I've got character, and once I reach that first branch, you'll watch me climb. Today I'm valet, next year I'll be proprietor, in ten years I'll have made a fortune, and then I'll go to Rumania, get myself decorated and I may, I only say *may*, mind you, end up as a Count.

JULIE [*Sadly.*] That would be very nice.

JEAN You see in Rumania one can buy a title, and then you'll be a Countess after all. My Countess.

JULIE What do I care about all that? I'm putting those things behind me. Tell me you love me, because if you don't . . . if you don't, what am I?

JEAN I'll tell you a thousand times over—later. But not here. No sentimentality now or everything will be lost. We must consider this thing calmly like reasonable people. [*Takes a cigar, cuts and lights it.*] You sit down there and I'll sit here and we'll talk as if nothing has happened.

JULIE My God, have you no feelings at all?

JEAN Nobody has more. But I know how to control them.

JULIE A short time ago you were kissing my shoe. And now . . .

JEAN [*Harshly.*] Yes, that was then. Now we have something else to think about.

JULIE Don't speak to me so brutally.

JEAN I'm not. Just sensibly. One folly's been committed, don't let's have more. The Count will be back at any moment and we've got to settle our future before that. Now, what do you think of my plans? Do you approve?

JULIE It seems a very good idea—but just one thing. Such a big undertaking would need a lot of capital. Have you got any?

JEAN [*Chewing his cigar.*] I certainly have. I've got my professional skill, my wide experience, and my knowledge of foreign languages. That's capital worth having, it seems to me.

JULIE But it won't buy even one railway ticket.

JEAN Quite true. That's why I need a backer to advance some ready cash.

JULIE How could you get that at a moment's notice?

JEAN You must get it, if you want to be my partner.

JULIE I can't. I haven't any money of my own. [*Pause.*]

JEAN Then the whole thing's off.

JULIE And . . . ?

JEAN We go on as we are.

JULIE Do you think I'm going to stay under this roof as your mistress? With everyone pointing at me. Do you think I can face my father after this? No. Take me away from here, away from this shame, this humiliation. Oh my God, what have I done? My God, my God! [*Weeps.*]

JEAN So that's the tune now, is it? What have you done? Same as many before you.

JULIE [*Hysterically.*] And now you despise me. I'm falling, I'm falling.

JEAN Fall as far as me and I'll lift you up again.

JULIE Why was I so terribly attracted to you? The weak to the strong, the falling to the rising? Or was it love? Is that love? Do you know what love is?

JEAN Do I? You bet I do. Do you think I never had a girl before?

JULIE The things you say, the things you think!

JEAN That's what life's taught me, and that's what I am. It's no good getting hysterical or giving yourself airs. We're both in the same boat now. Here, my dear girl, let me give you a glass of something special. [*Opens the drawer, takes out the bottle of wine and fills two used glasses.*]

JULIE Where did you get that wine?

JEAN From the cellar.

JULIE My father's burgundy.

JEAN Why not, for his son-in-law?

JULIE And I drink beer.

JEAN That only shows your taste's not so good as mine.

JULIE Thief!

JEAN Are you going to tell on me?

JULIE Oh God! The accomplice of a petty thief! Was I blind drunk? Have I dreamt this whole night? Midsummer Eve, the night for innocent merrymaking.

JEAN Innocent, eh?

JULIE Is anyone on earth as wretched as I am now?

JEAN Why should *you* be? After such a conquest. What about Kristin in there? Don't you think she has any feelings?

JULIE I did think so, but I don't any longer. No. A menial is a menial . . .

JEAN And a whore is a whore.

JULIE [*Falling to her knees, her hands clasped.*] O God in heaven, put an end to my miserable life! Lift me out of his filth in which I'm sinking. Save me! Save me!

JEAN I must admit I'm sorry for you. When I was in the onion bed and saw you up there among the roses, I . . . yes, I'll tell you now . . . I had the same dirty thoughts as all boys.

JULIE You, who wanted to die because of me?

JEAN In the oats-bin? That was just talk.

JULIE Lies, you mean.

JEAN [*Getting sleepy.*] More or less. I think I read a story in some paper about a chimney-sweep who shut himself up in a chest full of lilac because he'd been summonsed for not supporting some brat . . .

JULIE So this is what you're like.

JEAN I had to think up something. It's always the fancy stuff that catches the women.

JULIE Beast!

JEAN *Merde!*

JULIE Now you have seen the falcon's back.

JEAN Not exactly its *back*.

JULIE I was to be the first branch.

JEAN But the branch was rotten.

JULIE I was to be a hotel sign.

JEAN And I the hotel.

JULIE Sit at your counter, attract your clients and cook their accounts.

JEAN I'd have done that myself.

JULIE That any human being can be so steeped in filth!

JEAN Clean it up then.

JULIE Menial! Lackey! Stand up when I speak to you.

JEAN Menial's whore, lackey's harlot, shut your mouth and get out of here! Are you the one to lecture me for being coarse? Nobody of my kind would ever be as coarse as you were tonight. Do you think any servant girl would throw herself at a man that way? Have you ever seen a girl of my class asking for it like that? I haven't. Only animals and prostitutes.

JULIE [*Broken.*] Go on. Hit me, trample on me—it's all I deserve. I'm rotten. But help me! If there's any way out at all, help me.

JEAN [*More gently.*] I'm not denying myself a share in the honor of seducing you, but do you think anybody in my place would have dared look in your direction if you yourself hadn't asked for it? I'm still amazed . . .

JULIE And proud.

JEAN Why not? Though I must admit the victory was too easy to make me lose my head.

JULIE Go on hitting me.

JEAN [*Rising.*] No. On the contrary I apologize for what I've said. I don't hit a person who's down—least of all a woman. I can't deny there's a certain satisfaction in finding that what dazzled one below was just moonshine, that that falcon's back is gray after all, that there's powder on the lovely cheek, that polished nails can have black tips, that the handkerchief is dirty although it smells of scent. On the other hand it hurts to find that what I was struggling to reach wasn't high and isn't real. It hurts to see you fallen so low you're far lower than your own cook. Hurts like when you see the last flowers of summer lashed to pieces by rain and turned to mud.

JULIE You're talking as if you're already my superior.

JEAN I am. I might make you a Countess, but you could never make me a Count, you know.

JULIE But I am the child of a Count, and you could never be that.

JEAN True, but I might be the father of Counts if . . .

JULIE You're a thief. I'm not.

JEAN There are worse things than being a thief —much lower. Besides, when I'm in a place I regard myself as a member of the family to some extent, as one of the children. You don't call it stealing when children pinch a berry from overladen bushes. [*His passion is roused again.*] Miss Julie, you're a glorious woman, far too good for a man like me. You were carried away by some kind of madness, and now you're trying to cover up your mistake by persuading yourself you're in love with me. You're not, although you may find me physically attractive, which means your love's no better than mine. But I wouldn't be satisfied with being nothing but an animal for you, and I could never make you love me.

JULIE Are you sure?

JEAN You think there's a chance? Of my loving you, yes, of course. You're beautiful, refined [*Takes her hand.*], educated, and you can be nice when you want to be. The fire you kindle in a man isn't likely to go out. [*Puts his arm round her.*] You're like mulled wine, full of spices, and your kisses . . . [*He tries to pull her to him, but she breaks away.*]

JULIE Let go of me! You won't win me that way.

JEAN Not that way, how then? Not by kisses and fine speeches, not by planning the future and saving you from shame? How then?

JULIE How? How? I don't know. There isn't any way. I loathe you—loathe you as I loathe rats, but I can't escape from you.

JEAN Escape with me.

JULIE [*Pulling herself together.*] Escape? Yes, we must escape. But I'm so tired. Give me a glass of wine. [*He pours it out. She looks at her watch.*] First we must talk. We still have a little time. [*Empties the glass and holds it out for more.*]

JEAN Don't drink like that. You'll get tipsy.

JULIE What's that matter?

JEAN What's it matter? It's vulgar to get drunk. Well, what have you got to say?

JULIE We've got to run away, but we must talk first—or rather, I must, for so far you've done all the talking. You've told me about your life, now I want to tell you about mine, so that we really know each other before we begin this journey together.

JEAN Wait. Excuse my saying so, but don't you think you may be sorry afterward if you give away your secrets to me?

JULIE Aren't you my friend?

JEAN On the whole. But don't rely on me.

JULIE You can't mean that. But anyway everyone knows my secrets. Listen. My mother wasn't well-born; she came of quite humble people, and was brought up with all those new ideas of sex-equality and women's rights and so on. She thought marriage was quite wrong. So when my father proposed to her, she said she would never become his *wife* . . . but in the end she did. I came into the world, as far as I can make out, against my mother's will, and I was left to run wild, but I had to do all the things a boy does—to prove women are as good as men. I had to wear boys' clothes; I was taught to handle horses—and I wasn't allowed in the dairy. She made me groom and harness and go out hunting; I even had to try to plough. All the men on the estate were given the women's jobs, and the women the men's, until the whole place went to rack and ruin and we were the laughing-stock of the neighborhood. At last my father seemed to have come to his senses and rebelled. He changed everything and ran the place his own way. My mother got ill—I don't know what was the matter with her, but she used to have strange attacks and hide herself in the attic or the garden. Sometimes she stayed out all night. Then came the great fire which you have heard people talking about. The house and the stables and the barns—the whole place burnt to the ground. In very suspicious circumstances. Because the accident happened the very day the insurance had to be renewed, and my father had sent the new premium, but through some carelessness of the messenger it arrived too late. [*Refills her glass and drinks.*]

JEAN Don't drink any more.

JULIE Oh, what does it matter? We were destitute and had to sleep in the carriages. My father didn't know how to get money to rebuild, and then my mother suggested he should borrow from an old friend of hers, a local brick manufacturer. My father got the loan and, to his surprise, without having to pay interest. So the place was rebuilt. [*Drinks.*] Do you know who set fire to it?

JEAN Your lady mother.

JULIE Do you know who the brick manufacturer was?

JEAN Your mother's lover?

JULIE Do you know whose the money was?

JEAN Wait . . . no, I don't know that.

JULIE It was my mother's.

JEAN In other words the Count's, unless there was a settlement.

JULIE There wasn't any settlement. My mother had a little money of her own which she didn't want my father to control, so she invested it with her—friend.

JEAN Who grabbed it.

JULIE Exactly. He appropriated it. My father came to know all this. He couldn't bring an action, couldn't pay his wife's lover, nor prove it was his wife's money. That was my mother's revenge because he made himself master in his own house. He nearly shot himself then—at least there's a rumor he tried and didn't bring it off. So he went on living, and my mother had to pay dearly for what she'd done. Imagine what those five years were like for me. My natural sympathies were with my father, yet I took my mother's side, because I didn't know the facts. I'd learnt from her to hate and distrust men—you know how she loathed the whole male sex. And I swore to her I'd never become the slave of any man.

JEAN And so you got engaged to that attorney.

JULIE So that he should be my slave.

JEAN But he wouldn't be.

JULIE Oh yes, he wanted to be, but he didn't have the chance. I got bored with him.

JEAN Is that what I saw—in the stable-yard?

JULIE What did you see?

JEAN What I saw was him breaking off the engagement.

JULIE That's a lie. It was I who broke it off. Did he say it was him? The cad.

JEAN He's not a cad. Do you hate men, Miss Julie?

JULIE Yes . . . most of the time. But when that weakness comes, oh . . . the shame!

JEAN Then do you hate me?

JULIE Beyond words. I'd gladly have you killed like an animal.

JEAN Quick as you'd shoot a mad dog, eh?

JULIE Yes.

JEAN But there's nothing here to shoot with—and there isn't a dog. So what do we do now?

JULIE Go abroad.

JEAN To make each other miserable for the rest of our lives?

JULIE No, to enjoy ourselves for a day or two, for a week, for as long as enjoyment lasts, and then—to die . . .

JEAN Die? How silly! I think I would be far better to start a hotel.

JULIE [*Without listening.*] . . . die on the shores of Lake Como, where the sun always shines and at Christmas time there are green trees and glowing oranges.

JEAN Lake Como's a rainy hole and I didn't see any oranges outside the shops. But it's a good place for tourists. Plenty of villas to be rented by—er—honeymoon couples. Profitable business that. Know why? Because they all sign a lease for six months and all leave after three weeks.

JULIE [*Naïvely.*] After three weeks? Why?

JEAN They quarrel, of couse. But the rent has to be paid just the same. And then it's let again. So it goes on and on, for there's plenty of love although it doesn't last long.

JULIE You don't want to die with me?

JEAN I don't want to die at all. For one thing I like living and for another I consider suicide's a sin against the Creator who gave us life.

JULIE You believe in God—*you?*

JEAN Yes, of course. And I go to church every Sunday. Look here, I'm tired of all this. I'm going to bed.

JULIE Indeed! And do you think I'm going to leave things like this? Don't you know what you owe the woman you've ruined?

JEAN [*Taking out his purse and throwing a silver coin on the table.*] There you are. I don't want to be in anybody's debt.

JULIE [*Pretending not to notice the insult.*] Don't you know what the law is?

JEAN There's no law unfortunately that punishes a woman for seducing a man.

JULIE But can you see anything for it but to go abroad, get married and then divorce?

JEAN What if I refuse this misalliance?

JULIE Misalliance?

JEAN Yes, for me. I'm better bred than you, see! Nobody in my family committed arson.

JULIE How do you know?

JEAN Well, you can't prove otherwise, because we haven't any family records outside the Registrar's office. But I've seen your family tree in that book on the drawing-room table. Do you know who the founder of your family was? A miller who let his wife sleep with the King one night during the Danish war. I haven't any ancestors like that. I haven't any ancestors at all, but I might become one.

JULIE This is what I get for confiding in someone so low, for sacrificing my family honor . . .

JEAN Dishonor! Well, I told you so. One shouldn't drink, because then one talks. And one shouldn't talk.

JULIE Oh, how ashamed I am, how bitterly ashamed! If at least you loved me!

JEAN Look here—for the last time—what do you want? Am I to burst into tears? Am I to jump over your riding whip? Shall I kiss you and carry you off to Lake Como for three weeks, after which . . . What am I to do? What do you want? This is getting unbearable, but that's what comes of playing around with women. Miss Julie, I can see how miserable you are; I know you're going through hell, but I don't understand you. We don't have scenes like this; we don't go in for hating each other. We make love for fun in our spare time, but we haven't all day and all night for it like you. I think you must be ill. I'm sure you're ill.

JULIE Then you must be kind to me. You sound almost human now.

JEAN Well, be human yourself. You spit at me, then won't let me wipe it off—on you.

JULIE Help me, help me! Tell me what to do, where to go.

JEAN Jesus, as if I knew!

JULIE I've been mad, raving mad, but there must be a way out.

JEAN Stay here and keep quiet. Nobody knows anything.

JULIE I can't. People do know. Kristin knows.

JEAN They don't know and they wouldn't believe such a thing.

JULIE [*Hesitating.*] But—it might happen again.

JEAN That's true.

JULIE And there might be—consequences.

JEAN [*In panic.*] Consequences! Fool that I am I never thought of that. Yes, there's nothing for it but to go. At once. I can't come with you. That would be a complete give-away. You must go alone—abroad—anywhere.

JULIE Alone? Where to? I can't.

JEAN You must. And before the Count gets back. If you stay, we know what will happen. Once you've sinned you feel you might as well go on, as the harm's done. Then you get more and more reckless and in the end you're found out. No. You must go abroad. Then write to the Count and tell him everything, except that it was me. He'll never guess that —and I don't think he'll want to.

JULIE I'll go if you come with me.

JEAN Are you crazy, woman? "Miss Julie elopes with valet." Next day it would be in the headlines, and the Count would never live it down.

JULIE I can't go. I can't stay. I'm so tired, so completely worn out. Give me orders. Set me going. I can't think any more, can't act . . .

JEAN You see what weaklings you are. Why do you give yourselves airs and turn up your noses as if you're the lords of creation? Very well, I'll give you your orders. Go upstairs and dress. Get money for the journey and come down here again.

JULIE [*Softly.*] Come up with me.

JEAN To your room? Now you've gone crazy again. [*Hesitates a moment.*] No! Go along at once. [*Takes her hand and pulls her to the door.*]

JULIE [*As she goes.*] Speak kindly to me, Jean.

JEAN Orders always sound unkind. Now you know. Now you know.

[*Left alone,* JEAN *sighs with relief, sits down at the table, takes out a note-book and pencil and adds up figures, now and then aloud. Dawn begins to break.* KRISTIN *enters dressed for church, carrying his white dickey and tie.*]

KRISTIN Lord Jesus, look at the state the place is in! What have you been up to? [*Turns out the lamp.*]

JEAN Oh, Miss Julie invited the crowd in. Did you sleep through it? Didn't you hear anything?

KRISTIN I slept like a log.

JEAN And dressed for church already.

KRISTIN Yes, you promised to come to Communion with me today.

JEAN Why, so I did. And you've got my bib and tucker, I see. Come on then. [*Sits.* KRISTIN *begins to put his things on. Pause. Sleepily.*] What's the lesson today?

KRISTIN It's about the beheading of John the Baptist, I think.

JEAN That's sure to be horribly long. Hi,

you're choking me! Oh Lord, I'm so sleepy, so sleepy!

KRISTIN Yes, what have you been doing up all night? You look absolutely green.

JEAN Just sitting here talking with Miss Julie.

KRISTIN She doesn't know what's proper, that one. [*Pause.*]

JEAN I say, Kristin.

KRISTIN What?

JEAN It's queer really, isn't it, when you come to think of it? Her.

KRISTIN What's queer?

JEAN The whole thing. [*Pause.*]

KRISTIN [*Looking at the half-filled glasses on the table.*] Have you been drinking together too?

JEAN Yes.

KRISTIN More shame you. Look me straight in the face.

JEAN Yes.

KRISTIN Is it possible? Is it possible?

JEAN [*After a moment.*] Yes, it is.

KRISTIN Oh! This I would never have believed. How low!

JEAN You're not jealous of her, surely?

KRISTIN No, I'm not. If it had been Clara or Sophie I'd have scratched your eyes out. But not of her. I don't know why; that's how it is though. But it's disgusting.

JEAN You're angry with her then.

KRISTIN No. With you. It was wicked of you, very very wicked. Poor girl. And, mark my words, I won't stay here any longer now—in a place where one can't respect one's employers.

JEAN Why should one respect them?

KRISTIN You should know since you're so smart. But you don't want to stay in the service of people who aren't respectable, do you? I wouldn't demean myself.

JEAN But it's rather a comfort to find out they're no better than us.

KRISTIN I don't think so. If they're no better there's nothing for us to live up to. Oh and think of the Count! Think of him. He's been through so much already. No, I won't stay in the place any longer. A fellow like you too! If it had been that attorney now or somebody of her own class . . .

JEAN Why, what's wrong with . . .

KRISTIN Oh, you're all right in your own way, but when all's said and done there is a difference between one class and another. No, this is something I'll never be able to stomach. That our young lady who was so proud and so down on men you'd never believe she'd let one come near her should go and give herself to one like you. She who wanted to have poor Diana shot for running after the lodge-keeper's pug. No. I must say . . . ! Well, I won't stay here any longer. On the twenty-fourth of October I quit.

JEAN And then?

KRISTIN Well, since you mention it, it's about time you began to look around, if we're ever going to get married.

JEAN But what am I to look for? I shan't get a place like this when I'm married.

KRISTIN I know you won't. But you might get a job as porter or caretaker in some public institution. Government rations are small but sure, and there's a pension for the widow and children.

JEAN That's all very fine, but it's not in my line to start thinking at once about dying for my wife and children. I must say I had rather bigger ideas.

KRISTIN You and your ideas! You've got obligations too, and you'd better start thinking about them.

JEAN Don't *you* start pestering me about obligations. I've had enough of that. [*Listens to a sound upstairs.*] Anyway we've plenty of time to work things out. Go and get ready now and we'll be off to church.

KRISTIN Who's that walking about upstairs?

KRISTIN [*Going.*] You don't think the Count could have come back without our hearing him?

JEAN [*Scared.*] The Count? No, he can't have. He'd have rung for me.

KRISTIN God help us! I've never known such goings on. [*Exit.*]

[*The sun has now risen and is shining on the tree-tops. The light gradually changes until it slants in through the windows.* JEAN *goes to the door and beckons.* JULIE *enters in traveling clothes, carrying a small bird-cage covered with a cloth which she puts on a chair.*]

JULIE I'm ready.

JEAN Hush! Kristin's up.

JULIE [*In a very nervous state.*] Does she suspect anything?

JEAN Not a thing. But, my God, what a sight you are!

JULIE Sight? What do you mean?

JEAN You're white as a corpse and—pardon me—your face is dirty.

JULIE Let me wash then. [*Goes to the sink and washes her face and hands.*] There. Give me a towel. Oh! The sun is rising!

JEAN And that breaks the spell.

JULIE Yes. The spell of Midsummer Eve . . . But listen, Jean. Come with me. I've got the money.

JEAN [*Skeptically.*] Enough?

JULIE Enough to start with. Come with me. I can't travel alone today. It's Midsummer Day, remember. I'd be packed into a suffocating train among crowds of people who'd all stare at me. And it would stop at every station while I yearned for wings. No, I can't do that, I simply can't. There will be memories too; memories of Midsummer Days when I was little. The leafy church—birch and lilac—the gaily spread dinner table, relatives, friends—evening in the park—dancing and music and flowers and fun. Oh, however far you run away—there'll always be memories in the baggage car—and remose and guilt.

JEAN I will come with you, but quickly now then, before it's too late. At once.

JULIE Put on your things. [*Picks up the cage.*]

JEAN No luggage, mind. That would give us away.

JULIE No, only what we can take with us in the carriage.

JEAN [*Fetching his hat.*] What on earth have you got there? What is it?

JULIE Only my greenfinch. I don't want to leave it behind.

JEAN Well, I'll be damned! We're to take a bird-cage along, are we? You're crazy. Put that cage down.

JULIE It's the only thing I'm taking from my home. The only living creature who cares for me since Diana went off like that. Don't be cruel. Let me take it.

JEAN Put that cage down, I tell you—and don't talk so loud. Kristin will hear.

JULIE No, I won't leave it in strange hands. I'd rather you killed it.

JEAN Give the little beast here then and I'll wring its neck.

JULIE But don't hurt it, don't . . . no, I can't.

JEAN Give it here. I *can*.

JULIE [*Taking the bird out of the cage and kissing it.*] Dear little Serena, must you die and leave your mistress?

JEAN Please don't make a scene. It's *your* life and future we're worrying about. Come on, quick now!

[*He snatches the bird from her, puts it on a board and picks up a chopper.* JULIE *turns away.*]

You should have learnt how to kill chickens instead of target-shooting. Then you wouldn't faint at a drop of blood.

JULIE [*Screaming.*] Kill me too! Kill me! You who can butcher an innocent creature without a quiver. Oh, how I hate you, how I loathe you! There is blood between us now. I curse the hour I first saw you. I curse the hour I was conceived in my mother's womb.

JEAN What's the use of cursing. Let's go.

JULIE [*Going to the chopping-block as if drawn against her will.*] No, I won't go yet. I can't . . . I must look. Listen! There's a carriage. [*Listens without taking her eyes off the board and chopper.*] You don't think I can bear the sight of blood. You think I'm so weak. Oh, how I should like to see your blood and your brains on a chopping-block! I'd like to see the whole of your sex swimming like that in a sea of blood. I think I could drink out of your skull, bathe my feet in your broken breast and eat your heart roasted whole. You think I'm weak. You think I love you, that my womb yearned for your seed and I want to carry your offspring under my heart and nourish it with my blood. You think I want to bear your child and take your name. By the way, what is your name? I've never heard your surname. I don't suppose you've got one. I should be "Mrs. Hovel" or "Madam Dunghill." You dog wearing my collar, you lackey with my crest on your buttons! I share you with my cook; I'm my own servant's rival! Oh! Oh! Oh! . . . You think I'm a coward and will run away. No, now I'm going to stay—and let the storm break. My father will come back . . . find his desk broken open . . . his money gone. Then he'll ring that bell—twice for the valet—and then he'll send for the police . . . and I shall tell everything. Everything. Oh how wonderful to make an end of it all—a real end! He has a stroke and dies and that's the end of all of us. Just peace and quietness . . . eternal rest. The coat of arms broken on the coffin and the Count's line extinct . . . But the valet's line goes on in an orphanage, wins laurels in the gutter and ends in jail.

JEAN There speaks the noble blood! Bravo, Miss Julie. But now, don't let the cat out of the bag.

[KRISTIN *enters dressed for church, carrying a prayer-book.* JULIE *rushes to her and flings herself into her arms for protection.*]

JULIE Help me, Kristin! Protect me from this man!

KRISTIN [*Unmoved and cold.*] What goings-on for a feast day morning! [*Sees the board.*] And what a filthy mess. What's it all about? Why are you screaming and carrying on so?

JULIE Kristin, you're a woman and my friend. Beware of that scoundrel!

JEAN [*Embarrassed.*] While you ladies are talking things over, I'll go and shave. [*Slips into his room.*]

JULIE You must understand. You must listen to me.

KRISTIN I certainly don't understand such loose ways. Where are you off to in those traveling clothes? And he had his hat on, didn't he, eh?

JULIE Listen, Kristin. Listen, I'll tell you everything.

KRISTIN I don't want to know anything.

JULIE You must listen.

KRISTIN What to? Your nonsense with Jean? I don't care a rap about that; it's nothing to do with me. But if you're thinking of getting him to run off with you, we'll soon put a stop to that.

JULIE [*Very nervously.*] Please try to be calm, Kristin, and listen. I can't stay here, nor can Jean—so we must go abroad.

KRISTIN Hm, hm!

JULIE [*Brightening.*] But you see, I've had an idea. Supposing we all three go—abroad—to Switzerland and start a hotel together . . . I've got some money, you see . . . and Jean and I could run the whole thing—and I thought you would take charge of the kitchen. Wouldn't that be splendid? Say yes, do. If you come with us everything will be fine. Oh do say yes! [*Puts her arms round* KRISTIN.]

KRISTIN [*Coolly thinking.*] Hm, hm.

JULIE [*Presto tempo.*] You've never traveled, Kristin. You should go abroad and see the world. You've no idea how nice it is traveling by train—new faces all the time and new countries. On our way through Hamburg we'll go to the zoo—you'll love that—and we'll go to the theater and the opera too . . . and when we get to Munich there'll be the museums, dear, and pictures by Rubens and Raphael—the great painters, you know . . . You've heard of Munich, haven't you? Where King Ludwig lived—you know, the king who went mad. . . . We'll see his castles—some of his castles are still just like in fairy-tales . . . and from there it's not far to Switzerland—and the Alps. Think of the Alps, Kristin dear, covered with snow in the middle of summer . . . and there are oranges there and trees that are green the whole year round . . .

[JEAN *is seen in the door of his room, sharpening his razor on a strop which he holds with his teeth and his left hand. He listens to the talk with satisfaction and now and then nods approval.* JULIE *continues, tempo prestissimo.*]

And then we'll get a hotel . . . and I'll sit at the desk, while Jean receives the guests and goes out marketing and writes letters . . . There's life for you! Trains whistling, buses driving up, bells ringing upstairs and downstairs . . . and I shall make out the bills—and I shall cook them too . . . you've no idea how nervous travelers are when it comes to paying their bills. And you—you'll sit like a queen in the kitchen . . . of course there won't be any standing at the stove for you. You'll always have to be nicely dressed and ready to be seen, and with your looks—no, I'm not flattering you—one fine day you'll catch yourself a husband . . . some rich Englishman, I shouldn't wonder—they're the ones who are easy [*Slowing down.*] to catch . . . and then we'll get rich and build ourselves a villa on Lake Como . . . of course it rains there a little now and then—but [*Dully.*] the sun must shine there too sometimes—even though it seems gloomy—and if not—then we can come home again—come back—[*Pause.*]—here—or somewhere else . . .

KRISTIN Look here, Miss Julie, do you believe all that yourself?

JULIE [*Exhausted.*] Do I believe it?

KRISTIN Yes.

JULIE [*Wearily.*] I don't know. I don't believe anything any more. [*Sinks down on the bench; her head in her arms on the table.*] Nothing. Nothing at all.

KRISTIN [*Turning to* JEAN.] So you meant to beat it, did you?

JEAN [*Disconcerted, putting the razor on the table.*] Beat it? What are you talking about? You've heard Miss Julie's plan, and though she's tired now with being up all night, it's a perfectly sound plan.

KRISTIN Oh, is it? If you thought I'd work for that . . .

JEAN [*Interrupting.*] Kindly use decent language in front of your mistress. Do you hear?

KRISTIN Mistress?

JEAN Yes.

KRISTIN Well, well, just listen to that!

JEAN Yes, it would be a good thing if you did listen and talked less. Miss Julie is your mistress and what's made you lose your respect for her now ought to make you feel the same about yourself.

KRISTIN I've always had enough self-respect——

JEAN To despise other people.

KRISTIN —not to go below my own station. Has the Count's cook ever gone with the groom or the swine-herd? Tell me that.

JEAN No, you were lucky enough to have a high-class chap for your beau.

KRISTIN High-class all right—selling the oats out of the Count's stable.

JEAN You're a fine one to talk—taking a commission on the groceries and bribes from the butcher.

KRISTIN What the devil . . . ?

JEAN And now you can't feel any respect for your employers. You, you!

KRISTIN Are you coming to church with me? I should think you need a good sermon after your fine deeds.

JEAN No, I'm not going to church today. You can go alone and confess your own sins.

KRISTIN Yes, I'll do that and bring back enough forgiveness to cover yours too. The Saviour suffered and died on the cross for all our sins, and if we go to Him with faith and a penitent heart, He takes all our sins upon Himself.

JEAN Even grocery thefts?

JULIE Do you believe that, Kristin?

KRISTIN That is my living faith, as sure as I stand here. The faith I learnt as a child and have kept ever since, Miss Julie. "But where sin abounded, grace did much more abound."

JULIE Oh, if I had your faith! Oh, if . . .

KRISTIN But you see you can't have it without God's special grace, and it's not given to all to have that.

JULIE Who is it given to then?

KRISTIN That's the great secret of the workings of grace, Miss Julie. God is no respecter of persons, and with Him the last shall be first . . .

JULIE Then I suppose He does respect the last.

KRISTIN [*Continuing.*] . . . and it is easier for a camel to go through the eye of a needle than for a rich man to enter into the kingdom of God. That's how it is, Miss Julie. Now I'm going—alone, and on my way I shall tell the groom not to let any of the horses out, in case anyone should want to leave before the Count gets back. Good-by.

[*Exit.*]

JEAN What a devil! And all on account of a greenfinch.

JULIE [*Wearily.*] Never mind the greenfinch. Do you see any way out of this, any end to it?

JEAN [*Pondering.*] No.

JULIE If you were in my place, what would you do?

JEAN In your place? Wait a bit. If I was a woman—a lady of rank who had—fallen. I don't know. Yes, I do know now.

JULIE [*Picking up the razor and making a gesture.*] This?

JEAN Yes. But *I* wouldn't do it, you know. There's a difference between us.

JULIE Because you're a man and I'm a woman? What is the difference?

JEAN The usual difference—between man and woman.

JULIE [*Holding the razor.*] I'd like to. But I can't. My father couldn't either, that time he wanted to.

JEAN No, he didn't want to. He had to be revenged first.

JULIE And now my mother is revenged again, through me.

JEAN Didn't you ever love your father, Miss Julie?

JULIE Deeply, but I must have hated him too —unconsciously. And he let me be brought up to despise my own sex, to be half woman, half man. Whose fault is what's happened? My father's, my mother's, or my own? My own? I haven't anything that's my own. I haven't one single thought that I didn't get from my father, one emotion that didn't come from my mother, and as for this last idea—about all people being equal—I got that from him, my fiancé—that's why I call him a cad. How can it be my fault? Push the responsibility on to Jesus, like Kristin does? No, I'm too proud and—thanks to my father's teaching—too intelligent. As for all that about a rich person not being able to get into heaven, it's just a lie, but Kristin, who has money in the savings-bank, will certainly not get in. Whose fault is it? What does it matter whose fault it is? In any case I must take the blame and bear the consequences.

JEAN Yes, but . . . [*There are two sharp rings on the bell.* JULIE *jumps to her feet.* JEAN *changes into his livery.*] The Count is back. Supposing Kristin . . . [*Goes to the speaking-tube, presses it and listens.*]

JULIE Has he been to his desk yet?

JEAN This is Jean, sir. [*Listens.*] Yes, sir. [*Listens.*] Yes, sir, very good, sir. [*Listens.*] At once, sir? [*Listens.*] Very good, sir. In half an hour.

JULIE [*In panic.*] What did he say? My God, what did he say?

JEAN He ordered his boots and his coffee in half an hour.

JULIE Then there's half an hour . . . Oh, I'm so tired! I can't do anything. Can't be sorry, can't run away, can't stay, can't live—can't die. Help me. Order me, and I'll obey like a dog. Do me this last service—save my honor, save his name. You know what I ought to do, but haven't the strength to do. Use your strength and order me to do it.

JEAN I don't know why—I can't now—I don't understand . . . It's just as if this coat made me—I can't give you orders—and now that the Count has spoken to me—I can't quite explain, but . . . well, that devil of a lackey is bending my back again. I believe if the Count came down now and ordered me to cut my throat, I'd do it on the spot.

JULIE Then pretend you're him and I'm you. You did some fine acting before, when you knelt to me and played the aristocrat. Or . . . Have you ever seen a hypnotist at the theater? [*He nods.*] He says to the person "Take the broom," and he takes it. He says "Sweep," and he sweeps . . .

JEAN But the person has to be asleep.

JULIE [*As if in a trance.*] I am asleep already . . . the whole room has turned to smoke—and you look like a stove—a stove like a man in black with a tall hat—your eyes are glowing like coals when the fire is low—and your face is a white patch like ashes. [*The sunlight has now reached the floor and lights up* JEAN.] How nice and warm it is! [*She holds out her hands as though warming them at a fire.*] And so light—and so peaceful.

JEAN [*Putting the razor in her hand.*] Here is the broom. Go now while it's light—out to the barn—and . . . [*Whispers in her ear.*]

JULIE [*Waking.*] Thank you. I am going now—to rest. But just tell me that even the first can receive the gift of grace.

JEAN The first? No, I can't tell you that. But wait . . . Miss Julie, I've got it! You aren't one of the first any longer. You're one of the last.

JULIE That's true. I'm one of the very last. I *am* the last. Oh! . . . But now I can't go. Tell me again to go.

JEAN No, I can't now either. I can't.

JULIE And the first shall be last.

JEAN Don't think, don't think. You're taking my strength away too and making me a coward. What's that? I thought I saw the bell move . . . To be so frightened of a bell! Yes, but it's not just a bell. There's somebody behind it—a hand moving it—and something else moving the hand—and if you stop your ears—if you stop your ears—yes, then it rings louder than ever. Rings and rings until you answer—and then it's too late. Then the police come and . . . and . . . [*The bell rings twice loudly.* JEAN *flinches, then straightens himself up.*] It's horrible. But there's no other way to end it . . . Go!

[JULIE *walks firmly out through the door.*]

[*Curtain.*]

Comments and Questions

Modern drama got its start in Scandinavia more than one hundred years ago. Ibsen is its acknowledged father, Strindberg a notable disciple who carried on and added to Ibsen's dramatic innovations. Both writers embraced what they themselves labeled Naturalism, a term closely akin to Realism. Characters were to represent ordinary human beings influenced by heredity and environment, inescapably selfish, and to be analyzed with scientific precision.

Strindberg's carefully thought-out Foreword to *Miss Julie* sets forth what a realistic drama should do. Perhaps one should read the play first, then the Foreword to see how the author's convictions have been translated into art.

1. Strindberg calls *Miss Julie* a "Naturalistic Tragedy." This description suggests a departure from classical tragedy. Many differences will be apparent if one compares Strindberg's play with *Antigone* or with *Hamlet.* What are the major differences?
2. Strindberg gained a reputation as a misogynist, a hater of women. Does this attitude show itself in *Miss Julie*? If so, how? If so, does the play suffer? Discuss.
3. What is the central conflict? Does this conflict contain more than one element?
4. List the innovations in staging that the author calls for in the Foreword. Which ones have become routine in today's theaters? Are sets, for example, still flimsy? What has happened to theater lighting?
5. Strindberg says that Jean, the valet, seldom speaks the truth. Can you identify the speeches that probably represent what he really feels and believes?
6. Why does the author place the main action downstairs in the kitchen rather than, say, upstairs in the drawing-room?
7. Are there symbols in the play? Consider, for example, Kristin's stove and the Count's riding-boots.
8. Compare in detail *Ghosts* and *Miss Julie.*

JOHN MILLINGTON SYNGE
1871–1909

The Playboy of the Western World

PREFACE

In writing *The Playboy of the Western World,* as in my other plays, I have used one or two words only that I have not heard among the country people of Ireland, or spoken in my own nursery before I could read the newspapers. A certain number of the phrases I employ I have heard also from herds and fishermen along the coast from Kerry to Mayo, or from beggar-women and ballad-singers nearer Dublin; and I am glad to acknowledge how much I owe to the folk-imagination of these fine people. Any-one who has lived in real intimacy with the Irish peasantry will know that the wildest sayings and ideas in this play are tame indeed, compared with the fancies one may hear in any little hill-side cabin in Geesala, or Carraroe, or Dingle Bay. All art is a collaboration; and there is little doubt that in the happy ages of literature, striking and beautiful phrases were as ready to the story-teller's or the playwright's hand, as the rich cloaks and dresses of his time. It is probable that when the Elizabethan dramatist took his ink-horn and sat down to his work he used many phrases that he had just heard, as he sat at dinner, from his mother or his children. In Ireland, those of us who know the people have the same privilege. When I was writing *The Shadow of the Glen,* some years ago, I got more aid than any learning could have given me from a chink in the floor of the old Wicklow house where I was staying, that let me hear what was being said by the servant girls in the kitchen. This matter, I think, is of importance, for in countries where the imagination of the people, and the language they use, is rich and living, it is possible for a writer to be rich and copious in his words, and at the same time to give the reality, which is the root of all poetry, in a comprehensive and natural form. In the modern literature of towns, however, richness is found only in sonnets, or prose poems, or in one or two elaborate books that are far away from the profound and common interests of life. One has, on one side, Mallarmé and Huysmans producing this literature; and on the other, Ibsen and Zola dealing with the reality of life in joyless and pallid words. On the stage one must have reality, and one must have joy; and that is why the intellectual modern drama has failed, and people have grown sick of the false joy of the musical comedy, that has been given them in place of the rich joy found only in what is superb and wild in reality. In a good play every speech should be as fully flavoured as a nut or apple, and such speeches cannot be written by anyone who works among people who have shut their lips on poetry. In Ireland, for a few years more, we have a popular imagination that is fiery and magnificent, and tender; so that those of us who wish to write start with a chance that is not given to writers in places where the springtime of the local life has been forgotten, and the harvest is a memory only, and the straw has been turned into bricks.

J. M. S.

January 21, 1907

CHARACTERS

CHRISTOPHER MAHON

OLD MAHON, *his father, a squatter*

MICHAEL JAMES FLAHERTY, called MICHAEL JAMES, *a publican*

MARGARET FLAHERTY, called PEGEEN MIKE, *his daughter*

SHAWN KEOGH, *her cousin, a young farmer*

WIDOW QUIN, *a woman of about thirty*

PHILLY CULLEN and JIMMY FARRELL, *small farmers*

SARA TANSEY, SUSAN BRADY, HONOR BLAKE, *and* NELLY, *village girls*

A BELLMAN *or Town Crier*

SOME PEASANTS

The action takes place near a village, on a wild coast of Mayo.[1] *The first Act passes on an evening of autumn, the other two Acts on the following day.*

ACT I

SCENE: *Country public-house or shebeen, very rough and untidy. There is a sort of counter on the right with shelves, holding many bottles and jugs, just seen above it. Empty barrels stand near the counter. At back, a little to left of counter, there is a door into the open air, then, more to the left, there is a settle with shelves above it, with more jugs, and a table beneath a window. At the left there is a large open fire place, with turf fire, and a small door into inner room.* PEGEEN, *a wild-looking but fine girl of about twenty, is writing at table. She is dressed in the usual peasant dress.*

PEGEEN [*Slowly as she writes.*] Six yards of stuff for to make a yellow gown. A pair of lace boots with lengthy heels on them and brassy eyes. A hat is suited for a wedding-day. A fine tooth comb. To be sent with three barrels of porter in Jimmy Farrell's creel cart on the evening of the coming Fair to Mister Michael James Flaherty. With the best compliments of this season. Margaret Flaherty.

SHAWN KEOGH [*A fat and fair young man comes in as she signs, looks round awkwardly, when he sees she is alone.*] Where's himself?

PEGEEN [*Without looking at him.*] He's coming. [*She directs the letter.*] To Master Shea-

[1] The county of Mayo is located in the northwest of Ireland, exposed to the Atlantic Ocean. Most of the communities and areas mentioned throughout the play can be located on a standard map of Ireland.

mus Mulroy, Wine and Spirit Dealer, Castlebar.

SHAWN [*Uneasily.*] I didn't see him on the road.

PEGEEN How would you see him [*Licks stamp and puts it on letter.*] and it dark night this half hour gone by?

SHAWN [*Turning toward the door again.*] I stood a while outside wondering would I have a right to pass on or to walk in and see you, Pegeen Mike, [*Comes to fire.*] and I could hear the cows breathing, and sighing in the stillness of the air, and not a step moving any place from this gate to the bridge.

PEGEEN [*Putting letter in envelope.*] It's above at the cross-roads he is, meeting Philly Cullen; and a couple more are going along with him to Kate Cassidy's wake.

SHAWN [*Looking at her blankly.*] And he's going that length in the dark night?

PEGEEN [*Impatiently.*] He is surely, and leaving me lonesome on the scruff of the hill. [*She gets up and puts envelope on dresser, then winds clock.*] Isn't it long the nights are now, Shawn Keogh, to be leaving a poor girl with her own self counting the hours to the dawn of day?

SHAWN [*With awkward humour.*] If it is, when we're wedded in a short while you'll have no call to complain, for I've little will to be walking off to wakes or weddings in the darkness of the night.

PEGEEN [*With rather scornful good humour.*] You're making mighty certain, Shaneen, that I'll wed you now.

SHAWN Aren't we after making a good bargain, the way we're only waiting these days on Father Reilly's dispensation[2] from the bishops, or the Court of Rome?

PEGEEN [*Looking at him teasingly, washing up at dresser.*] It's a wonder, Shaneen, the Holy Father'd be taking notice of the likes of you; for if I was him I wouldn't bother with this place where you'll meet none but Red Linahan, has a squint in his eye, and Patcheen is lame in his heel, or the mad Mulrannies were driven from California and they lost in their wits. We're a queer lot these times to go troubling the Holy Father on his sacred seat.

SHAWN [*Scandalized.*] If we are, we're as good this place as another, maybe, and as good these times as we were for ever.

PEGEEN [*With scorn.*] As good, is it? Where now will you meet the like of Daneen Sullivan knocked the eye from a peeler,[3] or Marcus Quin, God rest him, got six months for maiming ewes, and he a great warrant to tell stories of holy Ireland till he'd have the old women shedding down tears about their feet. Where will you find the like of them, I'm saying?

SHAWN [*Timidly.*] If you don't, it's a good job, maybe; for [*With peculiar emphasis on the words.*] Father Reilly has small conceit to have that kind walking around and talking to the girls.

PEGEEN [*Impatiently, throwing water from basin out of the door.*] Stop tormenting me with Father Reilly [*Imitating his voice.*] when I'm asking only what way I'll pass these twelve hours of dark, and not take my death with the fear. [*Looking out of door.*]

SHAWN [*Timidly.*] Would I fetch you the Widow Quin, maybe?

PEGEEN Is it the like of that murderer? You'll not, surely.

SHAWN [*Going to her, soothingly.*] Then I'm thinking himself will stop along with you when he sees you taking on, for it'll be a long night-time with great darkness, and I'm after feeling a kind of fellow above in the furzy ditch, groaning wicked like a maddening dog, the way it's good cause you have, maybe, to be fearing now.

PEGEEN [*Turning on him sharply.*] What's that? Is it a man you seen?

SHAWN [*Retreating.*] I couldn't see him at all; but I heard him groaning out, and breaking his heart. It should have been a young man from his words speaking.

PEGEEN [*Going after him.*] And you never went near to see was he hurted or what ailed him at all?

SHAWN I did not, Pegeen Mike. It was a dark, lonesome place to be hearing the like of him.

PEGEEN Well, you're a daring fellow, and if they find his corpse stretched above in the dews of dawn, what'll you say then to the peelers, or the Justice of the Peace?

[2] A papal dispensation was required to permit marriage between cousins.

[3] A policeman.

SHAWN [*Thunderstruck.*] I wasn't thinking of that. For the love of God, Pegeen Mike, don't let on I was speaking of him. Don't tell your father and the men is coming above; for if they heard that story, they'd have great blabbing this night at the wake.

PEGEEN I'll maybe tell them, and I'll maybe not.

SHAWN They are coming at the door. Will you whisht, I'm saying?

PEGEEN Whisht yourself. [*She goes behind counter.* MICHAEL JAMES, *fat jovial publican, comes in followed by* PHILLY CULLEN, *who is thin and mistrusting, and* JIMMY FARRELL, *who is fat and amorous, about forty-five.*]

MEN [*Together.*] God bless you. The blessing of God on this place.

PEGEEN God bless you kindly.

MICHAEL [*To men who go to the counter.*] Sit down now, and take your rest. [*Crosses to* SHAWN *at the fire.*] And how is it you are, Shawn Keogh? Are you coming over the sands to Kate Cassidy's wake?

SHAWN I am not, Michael James. I'm going home the short cut to my bed.

PEGEEN [*Speaking across the counter.*] He's right too, and have you no shame, Michael James, to be quitting off for the whole night, and leaving myself lonesome in the shop?

MICHAEL [*Good-humouredly.*] Isn't it the same whether I go for the whole night or a part only? and I'm thinking it's a queer daughter you are if you'd have me crossing backward through the Stooks[4] of the Dead Women, with a drop taken.

PEGEEN If I am a queer daughter, it's a queer father'd be leaving me lonesome these twelve hours of dark, and I piling the turf with the dogs barking, and the calves mooing, and my own teeth rattling with the fear.

JIMMY [*Flatteringly.*] What is there to hurt you, and you a fine, hardy girl would knock the head of any two men in the place?

PEGEEN [*Working herself up.*] Isn't there the harvest boys with their tongues red for drink, and the ten tinkers is camped in the east glen, and the thousand militia—bad cess to them!—walking idle through the land. There's lots surely to hurt me, and I won't stop alone in it, let himself do what he will.

MICHAEL If you're that afeard, let Shawn Keogh stop along with you. It's the will of God, I'm thinking, himself should be seeing to you now.

[*They all turn on* SHAWN.]

SHAWN [*In horrified confusion.*] I would and welcome, Michael James, but I'm afeard of Father Reilly; and what at all would the Holy Father and the Cardinals of Rome be saying if they heard I did the like of that?

MICHAEL [*With contempt.*] God help you! Can't you sit in by the hearth with the light lit and herself beyond in the room? You'll do that surely, for I've heard tell there's a queer fellow above, going mad or getting his death, maybe, in the gripe of the ditch, so she'd be safer this night with a person here.

SHAWN [*With plaintive despair.*] I'm afeard of Father Reilly, I'm saying. Let you not be tempting me, and we near married itself.

PHILLY [*With cold contempt.*] Lock him in the west room. He'll stay then and have no sin to be telling to the priest.

MICHAEL [*To* SHAWN, *getting between him and the door.*] Go up now.

SHAWN [*At the top of his voice.*] Don't stop me, Michael James. Let me out of the door, I'm saying, for the love of the Almighty God. Let me out. [*Trying to dodge past him.*] Let me out of it, and may God grant you His indulgence in the hour of need.

MICHAEL [*Loudly.*] Stop your noising, and sit down by the hearth. [*Gives him a push and goes to counter laughing.*]

SHAWN [*Turning back, wringing his hands.*] Oh, Father Reilly and the saints of God, where will I hide myself today? Oh, St. Joseph, and St. Patrick, and St. Brigid, and St. James, have mercy on me now! [SHAWN *turns round, sees door clear, and makes a rush for it.*]

MICHAEL [*Catching him by the coat-tail.*] You'd be going, is it?

SHAWN [*Screaming.*] Leave me go, Michael James, leave me go, you old Pagan, leave me go, or I'll get the curse of the priests on you, and of the scarlet-coated bishops of the courts of Rome. [*With a sudden movement he pulls himself out of his coat, and disappears out of the door, leaving his coat in* MICHAEL'*s hands.*]

[4] Stacked sheaves of wheat; apparently superstition was attached to a field where grain was stacked.

MICHAEL [*Turning round, and holding up coat.*] Well, there's the coat of a Christian man. Oh, there's sainted glory this day in the lonesome west; and by the will of God I've got you a decent man, Pegeen, you'll have no call to be spying after if you've a score of young girls, maybe, weeding in your fields.

PEGEEN [*Taking up the defence of her property.*] What right have you to be making game of a poor fellow for minding the priest, when it's your own the fault is, not paying a penny pot-boy to stand along with me and give me courage in the doing of my work? [*She snaps the coat away from him, and goes behind counter with it.*]

MICHAEL [*Taken aback.*] Where would I get a pot-boy? Would you have me send the bellman screaming in the streets of Castlebar?

SHAWN [*Opening the door a chink and putting in his head, in a small voice.*] Michael James!

MICHAEL [*Imitating him.*] What ails you?

SHAWN The queer dying fellow's beyond looking over the ditch. He's come up, I'm thinking, stealing your hens. [*Looks over his shoulder.*] God help me, he's following me now, [*He runs into room.*] and if he's heard what I said, he'll be having my life, and I going home lonesome in the darkness of the night.

[*For a perceptible moment they watch the door with curiosity. Someone coughs outside. Then* CHRISTY MAHON, *a slight young man, comes in very tired and frightened and dirty.*]

CHRISTY [*In a small voice.*] God save all here!

MEN God save you kindly.

CHRISTY [*Going to the counter.*] I'd trouble you for a glass of porter, woman of the house. [*He puts down coin.*]

PEGEEN [*Serving him.*] You're one of the tinkers, young fellow, is beyond camped in the glen?

CHRISTY I am not; but I'm destroyed walking.

MICHAEL [*Patronizingly.*] Let you come up then to the fire. You're looking famished with the cold.

CHRISTY God reward you. [*He takes up his glass and goes a little way across to the left, then stops and looks about him.*] Is it often the polis do be coming into this place, master of the house?

MICHAEL If you'd come in better hours, you'd have seen "Licensed for the sale of Beer and Spirits, to be consumed on the premises," written in white letters above the door, and what would the polis want spying on me, and not a decent house within four miles, the way every living Christian is a bona fide,[5] saving one widow alone?

CHRISTY [*With relief.*] It's a safe house, so. [*He goes over to the fire, sighing and moaning. Then he sits down, putting his glass beside him and begins gnawing a turnip, too miserable to feel the others staring at him with curiosity.*]

MICHAEL [*Going after him.*] Is it yourself is fearing the polis? You're wanting, maybe?

CHRISTY There's many wanting.

MICHAEL Many surely, with the broken harvest and the ended wars. [*He picks up some stockings, etc., that are near the fire, and carries them away furtively.*] It should be larceny, I'm thinking.

CHRISTY [*Dolefully.*] I had it in my mind it was a different word and a bigger.

PEGEEN There's a queer lad. Were you never slapped in school, young fellow, that you don't know the name of your deed?

CHRISTY [*Bashfully.*] I'm slow at learning, a middling scholar only.

MICHAEL If you're a dunce itself, you'd have a right to know that larceny's robbing and stealing. Is it for the like of that you're wanting?

CHRISTY [*With a flash of family pride.*] And I the son of a strong farmer [*With a sudden qualm.*], God rest his soul, could have bought up the whole of your old house awhile since, from the butt of his tail-pocket, and not have missed the weight of it gone.

MICHAEL [*Impressed.*] If it's not stealing, it's maybe something big.

CHRISTY [*Flattered.*] Aye; it's maybe something big.

JIMMY He's a wicked-looking young fellow. Maybe he followed after a young woman on a lonesome night.

CHRISTY [*Shocked.*] Oh, the saints forbid, mister; I was all times a decent lad.

PHILLY [*Turning on* JIMMY.] You're a silly man, Jimmy Farrell. He said his father was a farmer a while since, and there's himself now

5 A person could be served drinks outside regular tavern hours if he had slept over three miles away on the previous night.

in a poor state. Maybe the land was grabbed from him, and he did what any decent man would do.

MICHAEL [*To* CHRISTY, *mysteriously.*] Was it bailiffs?

CHRISTY The divil a one.[6]

MICHAEL Agents?

CHRISTY The divil a one.

MICHAEL Landlords?

CHRISTY [*Peevishly.*] Ah, not at all, I'm saying. You'd see the like of them stories on any little paper of a Munster town. But I'm not calling to mind any person, gentle, simple, judge or jury, did the like of me.

[*They all draw nearer with delighted curiosity.*]

PHILLY Well, that lad's a puzzle-the-world.

JIMMY He'd beat Dan Davies' circus, or the holy missioners making sermons on the villainy of man. Try him again, Philly.

PHILLY Did you strike golden guineas out of solder, young fellow, or shilling coins itself?

CHRISTY I did not, mister, not sixpence nor a farthing coin.

JIMMY Did you marry three wives maybe? I'm told there's a sprinkling have done that among the holy Luthers of the preaching north.

CHRISTY [*Shyly.*] I never married with one, let alone with a couple or three.

PHILLY Maybe he went fighting for the Boers, the like of the man beyond, was judged to be hanged, quartered and drawn. Were you off east, young fellow, fighting bloody wars for Kruger and the freedom of the Boers?

CHRISTY I never left my own parish till Tuesday was a week.

PEGEEN [*Coming from counter.*] He's done nothing, so. [*To* CHRISTY.] If you didn't commit murder or a bad, nasty thing, or false coining, or robbery, or butchery, or the like of them, there isn't anything that would be worth your troubling for to run from now. You did nothing at all.

CHRISTY [*His feelings hurt.*] That's an unkindly thing to be saying to a poor orphaned traveller, has a prison behind him, and hanging before, and hell's gap gaping below.

PEGEEN [*With a sign to the men to be quiet.*] You're only saying it. You did nothing at all. A soft lad the like of you wouldn't slit the windpipe of a screeching sow.

[6] Not a one.

CHRISTY [*Offended.*] You're not speaking the truth.

PEGEEN [*In mock rage.*] Not speaking the truth, is it? Would you have me knock the head off you with the butt of the broom?

CHRISTY [*Twisting round on her with a sharp cry of horror.*] Don't strike me. I killed my poor father, Tuesday was a week, for doing the like of that.

PEGEEN [*With blank amazement.*] Is it killed your father?

CHRISTY [*Subsiding.*] With the help of God I did surely, and that the Holy Immaculate Mother may intercede for his soul.

PHILLY [*Retreating with* JIMMY.] There's a daring fellow.

JIMMY Oh, glory be to God!

MICHAEL [*With great respect.*] That was a hanging crime, mister honey. You should have had good reason for doing the like of that.

CHRISTY [*In a very reasonable tone.*] He was a dirty man, God forgive him, and he getting old and crusty, the way I couldn't put up with him at all.

PEGEEN And you shot him dead?

CHRISTY [*Shaking his head.*] I never used weapons. I've no license, and I'm a law-fearing man.

MICHAEL It was with a hilted knife maybe? I'm told, in the big world it's bloody knives they use.

CHRISTY [*Loudly, scandalized.*] Do you take me for a slaughter-boy?

PEGEEN You never hanged him, the way Jimmy Farrell hanged his dog from the license,[7] and had it screeching and wriggling three hours at the butt of a string, and himself swearing it was a dead dog, and the peelers swearing it had life?

CHRISTY I did not then. I just riz the loy[8] and let fall the edge of it on the ridge of his skull, and he went down at my feet like an empty sack, and never let a grunt or groan from him at all.

MICHAEL [*Making a sign to* PEGEEN *to fill* CHRISTY's *glass.*] And what way weren't you hanged, mister? Did you bury him then?

CHRISTY [*Considering.*] Aye. I buried him then. Wasn't I digging spuds in the field?

[7] Because he had no license for the dog.

[8] A narrow spade widely used in Ireland for digging peat.

MICHAEL And the peelers never followed after you the eleven days that you're out?

CHRISTY [*Shaking his head.*] Never a one of them, and I walking forward facing hog, dog, or divil on the highway of the road.

PHILLY [*Nodding wisely.*] It's only with a common week-day kind of a murderer them lads would be trusting their carcase, and that man should be a great terror when his temper's roused.

MICHAEL He should then. [*To* CHRISTY.] And where was it, mister honey, that you did the deed?

CHRISTY [*Looking at him with suspicion.*] Oh, a distant place, master of the house, a windy corner of high, distant hills.

PHILLY [*Nodding with approval.*] He's a close man, and he's right, surely.

PEGEEN That's be a lad with the sense of Solomon to have for a pot-boy, Michael James, if it's the truth you're seeking one at all.

PHILLY The peelers is fearing him, and if you'd that lad in the house there isn't one of them would come smelling around if the dogs itself were lapping poteen[9] from the dung-pit of the yard.

JIMMY Bravery's a treasure in a lonesome place, and a lad would kill his father, I'm thinking, would face a foxy divil with a pitchpike on the flags of hell.

PEGEEN It's the truth they're saying, and if I'd that lad in the house, I wouldn't be fearing the looséd kharki cut-throats,[10] or the walking dead.

CHRISTY [*Swelling with surprise and triumph.*] Well, glory be to God!

MICHAEL [*With deference.*] Would you think well to stop here and be pot-boy, mister honey, if we gave you good wages, and didn't destroy you with the weight of work?

SHAWN [*Coming forward uneasily.*] That'd be a queer kind to bring into a decent quiet household with the like of Pegeen Mike.

PEGEEN [*Very sharply.*] Will you whisht? Who's speaking to you?

SHAWN [*Retreating.*] A bloody-handed murderer the like of . . .

PEGEEN [*Snapping at him.*] Whisht I am saying; we'll take no fooling from your like at all. [*To* CHRISTY *with a honeyed voice.*] And you, young fellow, you'd have a right to stop, I'm thinking, for we'd do our all and utmost to content your needs.

CHRISTY [*Overcome with wonder.*] And I'd be safe in this place from the searching law?

MICHAEL You would, surely. If they're not fearing you, itself, the peelers in this place is decent droughty poor fellows, wouldn't touch a cur dog and not give warning in the dead of night.

PEGEEN [*Very kindly and persuasively.*] Let you stop a short while anyhow. Aren't you destroyed walking with your feet in bleeding blisters, and your whole skin needing washing like a Wicklow sheep?

CHRISTY [*Looking round with satisfaction.*] It's a nice room, and if it's not humbugging me you are, I'm thinking that I'll surely stay.

JIMMY [*Jumps up.*] Now, by the grace of God, herself will be safe this night, with a man killed his father holding danger from the door, and let you come on, Michael James, or they'll have the best stuff drunk at the wake.

MICHAEL [*Going to the door with men.*] And begging your pardon, mister, what name will we call you, for we'd like to know?

CHRISTY Christopher Mahon.

MICHAEL Well, God bless you, Christy, and a good rest till we meet again when the sun'll be rising to the noon of day.

CHRISTY God bless you all.

MEN God bless you.

[*They go out except* SHAWN, *who lingers at door.*]

SHAWN [*To* PEGEEN.] Are you wanting me to stop along with you and keep you from harm?

PEGEEN [*Gruffly.*] Didn't you say you were fearing Father Reilly?

SHAWN There'd be no harm staying now, I'm thinking, and himself in it too.

PEGEEN You wouldn't stay when there was need for you, and let you step off nimble this time when there's none.

SHAWN Didn't I say it was Father Reilly . . .

PEGEEN Go on, then, to Father Reilly [*In a jeering tone.*], and let him put you in the holy brotherhoods, and leave that lad to me.

SHAWN If I meet the Widow Quin . . .

PEGEEN Go on, I'm saying, and don't be waking this place with your noise. [*She hustles*

[9] It was illegal to distill or sell this strong whiskey.
[10] British soldiers.

him out and bolts the door.] That lad would wear the spirits from the saints of peace. [*Bustles about, then takes off her apron and pins it up in the window as a blind.* CHRISTY *watching her timidly. Then she comes to him and speaks with bland good-humour.*] Let you stretch out now by the fire, young fellow. You should be destroyed travelling.

CHRISTY [*Shyly again, drawing off his boots.*] I'm tired, surely, walking wild eleven days, and waking fearful in the night. [*He holds up one of his feet, feeling his blisters, and looking at them with compassion.*]

PEGEEN [*Standing beside him, watching him with delight.*] You should have had great people in your family, I'm thinking, with the little, small feet you have, and you with a kind of a quality name, the like of what you'd find on the great powers and potentates of France and Spain.

CHRISTY [*With pride.*] We were great surely, with wide and windy acres of rich Munster land.

PEGEEN Wasn't I telling you, and you a fine, handsome young fellow with a noble brow?

CHRISTY [*With a flash of delighted surprise.*] Is it me?

PEGEEN Aye. Did you never hear that from the young girls where you come from in the west or south?

CHRISTY [*With venom.*] I did not then. Oh, they're bloody liars in the naked parish where I grew a man.

PEGEEN If they are itself, you've heard it these days, I'm thinking, and you walking the world telling out your story to young girls or old.

CHRISTY I've told my story no place till this night, Pegeen Mike, and it's foolish I was here, maybe, to be talking free, but you're decent people, I'm thinking, and yourself a kindly woman, the way I wasn't fearing you at all.

PEGEEN [*Filling a sack with straw.*] You've said the like of that, maybe, in every cot and cabin where you've met a young girl on your way.

CHRISTY [*Going over to her, gradually raising his voice.*] I've said it nowhere till this night, I'm telling you, for I've seen none the like of you the eleven long days I am walking the world, looking over a low ditch or a high ditch on my north or my south, into stony scattered fields, or scribes[11] of bog, where you'd see young, limber girls, and fine prancing women making laughter with the men.

PEGEEN If you weren't destroyed travelling, you'd have as much talk and streeleen,[12] I'm thinking, as Owen Roe O'Sullivan[13] or the poets of the Dingle Bay, and I've heard all times it's the poets are your like, fine fiery fellows with great rages when their temper's roused.

CHRISTY [*Drawing a little nearer to her.*] You're a power of rings, God bless you, and would there be any offence if I was asking are you single now?

PEGEEN What would I want wedding so young?

CHRISTY [*With relief.*] We're alike, so.

PEGEEN [*She puts sack on settle and beats it up.*] I never killed my father. I'd be afeard to do that, except I was the like of yourself with blind rages tearing me within, for I'm thinking you should have had great tussling when the end was come.

CHRISTY [*Expanding with delight at the first confidential talk he has ever had with a woman.*] We had not then. It was a hard woman was come over the hill, and if he was always a crusty kind when he'd a hard woman setting him on, not the divil himself or his four fathers could put up with him at all.

PEGEEN [*With curiosity.*] And isn't it a great wonder that one wasn't fearing you?

CHRISTY [*Very confidentially.*] Up to the day I killed my father, there wasn't a person in Ireland knew the kind I was, and I there drinking, waking, eating, sleeping, a quiet, simple, poor fellow with no man giving me heed.

PEGEEN [*Getting a quilt out of the cupboard and putting it on the sack.*] It was the girls were giving you heed maybe, and I'm thinking it's most conceit[14] you'd have to be gaming with their like.

CHRISTY [*Shaking his head, with simplicity.*] Not the girls itself, and I won't tell you a lie.

[11] Wide expanses.

[12] Charmingly irresponsible, swaggering chatter; palaver.

[13] O'Sullivan (d. 1784) and other Jacobite poets from Munster in southern Ireland were strolling poets whose songs and deeds would excite Pegeen's imagination.

[14] Desire, inclination.

There wasn't anyone heeding me in that place saving only the dumb beasts of the field. [*He sits down at fire.*]

PEGEEN [*With disappointment.*] And I thinking you should have been living the like of a king of Norway or the Eastern world. [*She comes and sits besides him after placing bread and mug of milk on the table.*]

CHRISTY [*Laughing piteously.*] The like of a king, is it? And I after toiling, moiling, digging, dodging from the dawn till dusk with never a sight of joy or sport saving only when I'd be abroad in the dark night poaching rabbits on hills, for I was a divil to poach, God forgive me, [*Very naïvely.*] and I near got six months for going with a dung fork and stabbing a fish.

PEGEEN And it's that you'd call sport, is it, to be abroad in the darkness with yourself alone?

CHRISTY I did, God help me, and there I'd be as happy as the sunshine of St. Martin's Day, watching the light passing the north or the patches of fog, till I'd hear a rabbit starting to screech and I'd go running in the furze. Then when I'd my full share I'd come walking down where you'd see the ducks and geese stretched sleeping on the highway of the road, and before I'd pass the dunghill, I'd hear himself snoring out, a loud lonesome snore he'd be making all times, the while he was sleeping, and he a man'd be raging all times, the while he was waking, like a gaudy officer you'd hear cursing and damning and swearing oaths.

PEGEEN Providence and Mercy, spare us all!

CHRISTY It's that you'd say surely if you seen him and he after drinking for weeks, rising up in the red dawn, or before it maybe, and going out into the yard as naked as an ash tree in the moon of May, and shying clods against the visage of the stars till he'd put the fear of death into the banbhs[15] and the screeching sows.

PEGEEN I'd be well-nigh afeard of that lad myself, I'm thinking. And there was no one in it but the two of you alone?

CHRISTY The divil a one, though he'd sons and daughters walking all great states and territories of the world, and not a one of them, to this day, but would say their seven curses on him, and they rousing up to let a cough or sneeze, maybe, in the deadness of the night.

PEGEEN [*Nodding her head.*] Well, you should have been a queer lot. I never cursed my father the like of that, though I'm twenty and more years of age.

CHRISTY Then you'd have cursed mine, I'm telling you, and he a man never gave peace to any, saving when he'd get two months or three, or be locked in the asylums for battering peelers or assaulting men [*With depression.*] the way it was a bitter life he led me till I did up a Tuesday and halve his skull.

PEGEEN [*Putting her hand on his shoulder.*] Well, you'll have peace in this place, Christy Mahon, and none to trouble you, and it's near time a fine lad like you should have your good share of the earth.

CHRISTY It's time surely, and I a seemly fellow with great strength in me and bravery of . . .

[*Someone knocks.*]

CHRISTY [*Clinging to* PEGEEN.] Oh, glory! it's late for knocking, and this last while I'm in terror of the peelers, and the walking dead.

[*Knocking again.*]

PEGEEN Who's there?

VOICE [*Outside.*] Me.

PEGEEN Who's me?

VOICE The Widow Quin.

PEGEEN [*Jumping up and giving him the bread and milk.*] Go on now with your supper, and let on to be sleepy, for if she found you were such a warrant to talk, she's be stringing gabble till the dawn of day. [*He takes bread and sits shyly with his back to the door.*]

PEGEEN [*Opening door, with temper.*] What ails you, or what is it you're wanting at this hour of the night?

WIDOW QUIN [*Coming in a step and peering at* CHRISTY.] I'm after meeting Shawn Keogh and Father Reilly below, who told me of your curiosity man, and they fearing by this time he was maybe roaring, romping on your hands with drink.

PEGEEN [*Pointing to* CHRISTY.] Look now is he roaring and he stretched away drowsy with his supper and his mug of milk. Walk down and tell that to Father Reilly and to Shaneen Keogh.

WIDOW QUIN [*Coming forward.*] I'll not see them again, for I've their word to lead that lad forward for to lodge with me.

15 Young pigs; sucklings.

PEGEEN [*In blank amazement.*] This night, is it?

WIDOW QUIN [*Going over.*] This night. "It isn't fitting," says the priesteen, "to have his likeness lodging with an orphaned girl." [*To* CHRISTY.] God save you, mister!

CHRISTY [*Shyly.*] God save you kindly.

WIDOW QUIN [*Looking at him with half-amazed curiosity.*] Well, aren't you a little smiling fellow? It should have been great and bitter torments did rouse your spirits to a deed of blood.

CHRISTY [*Doubtfully.*] It should, maybe.

WIDOW QUIN It's more than "maybe" I'm saying, and it'd soften my heart to see you sitting so simple with your cup and cake, and you fitter to be saying your catechism than slaying your da.

PEGEEN [*At counter, washing glasses.*] There's talking when any'd see he's fit to be holding his head high with the wonders of the world. Walk on from this, for I'll not have him tormented and he destroyed travelling since Tuesday was a week.

WIDOW QUIN [*Peaceably.*] We'll be walking surely when his supper's done, and you'll find we're great company, young fellow, when it's of the like of you and me you'd hear the penny poets singing in an August Fair.

CHRISTY [*Innocently.*] Did you kill your father?

PEGEEN [*Contemptuously.*] She did not. She hit himself[16] with a worm pick, and the rusted poison did corrode his blood the way he never overed it, and died after. That was a sneaky kind of murder did win small glory with the boys itself. [*She crosses to* CHRISTY'*s left.*]

WIDOW QUIN [*With good-humour.*] If it didn't, maybe all knows a widow woman has buried her children and destroyed her man is a wiser comrade for a young lad than a girl, the like of you, who'd go helter-skeltering after any man would let you a wink upon the road.

PEGEEN [*Breaking out into wild rage.*] And you'll say that, Widow Quin, and you gasping with the rage you had racing the hill beyond to look on his face.

WIDOW QUIN [*Laughing derisively.*] Me, is it? Well, Father Reilly has cuteness to divide you now. [*She pulls* CHRISTY *up.*] There's great temptation in a man did slay his da, and we'd best be going, young fellow; so rise up and come with me.

PEGEEN [*Seizing his arm.*] He'll not stir. He's pot-boy in this place, and I'll not have him stolen off and kidnabbed while himself's abroad.

WIDOW QUIN It'd be a crazy pot-boy'd lodge him in the shebeen where he works by day, so you'd have a right to come on, young fellow, till you see my little houseen, a perch[17] off on the rising hill.

PEGEEN Wait till morning, Christy Mahon. Wait till you lay eyes on her leaky thatch is growing more pasture for her buck goat than her square of fields, and she without a tramp itself to keep in order her place at all.

WIDOW QUIN When you see me contriving in my little gardens, Christy Mahon, you'll swear the Lord God formed me to be living lone, and that there isn't my match in Mayo for thatching, or mowing, or shearing sheep.

PEGEEN [*With noisy scorn.*] It's true the Lord God formed you to contrive indeed. Doesn't the world know you reared a black lamb at your own breast, so that the Lord Bishop of Connaught felt the elements of a Christian, and he eating it after in a kidney stew? Doesn't the world know you've been seen shaving the foxy skipper from France for a threepenny bit, and a sop of grass tobacco would wring the liver from a mountain goat you'd meet leaping the hills?

WIDOW QUIN [*With amusement.*] Do you hear her now, young fellow? Do you hear the way she'll be rating at your own self when a week is by?

PEGEEN [*To* CHRISTY.] Don't heed her. Tell her to go into her pigsty and not plague us here.

WIDOW QUIN I'm going; but he'll come with me.

PEGEEN [*Shaking him.*] Are you dumb, young fellow?

CHRISTY [*Timidly, to* WIDOW QUIN.] God increase you; but I'm pot-boy in this place, and it's here I'd liefer stay.

PEGEEN [*Triumphantly.*] Now you have heard him, and go on from this.

WIDOW QUIN [*Looking round the room.*] It's lonesome this hour crossing the hill, and if he won't come along with me, I'd have a right

[16] Her husband.

[17] Short distance.

maybe to stop this night with yourselves. Let me stretch out on the settle, Pegeen Mike; and himself can lie by the hearth.

PEGEEN [*Short and fiercely.*] Faith, I won't. Quit off or I will send you now.

WIDOW QUIN [*Gathering her shawl up.*] Well, it's a terror to be aged a score.[18] [*To* CHRISTY.] God bless you now, young fellow, and let you be wary, or there's right torment will await you here if you go romancing with her like, and she waiting only, as they bade me say, on a sheepskin parchment to be wed with Shawn Keogh of Killakeen.

CHRISTY [*Going to* PEGEEN *as she bolts the door.*] What's that she's after saying?

PEGEEN Lies and blather, you've no call to mind. Well, isn't Shawn Keogh an impudent fellow to send up spying on me? Wait till I lay hands on him. Let him wait, I'm saying.

CHRISTY And you're not wedding him at all?

PEGEEN I wouldn't wed him if a bishop came walking for to join us here.

CHRISTY That God in glory may be thanked for that.

PEGEEN There's your bed now. I've put a quilt upon you I'm after quilting a while since with my own two hands, and you'd best stretch out now for your sleep, and may God give you a good rest till I call you in the morning when the cocks will crow.

CHRISTY [*As she goes to inner room.*] May God and Mary and St. Patrick bless you and reward you, for your kindly talk. [*She shuts the door behind her. He settles his bed slowly, feeling the quilt with immense satisfaction.*] Well, it's a clean bed and soft with it, and it's great luck and company I've won me in the end of time—two fine women fighting for the likes of me—till I'm thinking this night wasn't I a foolish fellow not to kill my father in the years gone by.

[*Curtain.*]

ACT II

SCENE: *As before. Brilliant morning light.* CHRISTY, *looking bright and cheerful, is cleaning a girl's boots.*

CHRISTY [*To himself, counting jugs on dresser.*] Half a hundred beyond. Ten there. A score that's above. Eighty jugs. Six cups and a broken one. Two plates. A power of glasses. Bottles, a school-master'd be hard set to count, and enough in them, I'm thinking, to drunken all the wealth and wisdom of the County Clare. [*He puts down the boot carefully.*] There's her boots now, nice and decent for her evening use, and isn't it grand brushes she has? [*He puts them down and goes by degrees to the looking-glass.*] Well, this'd be a fine place to be my whole life talking out with swearing Christians, in place of my old dogs and cat, and I stalking around, smoking my pipe and drinking my fill, and never a day's work but drawing a cork an odd time, or wiping a glass, or rinsing out a shiny tumbler for a decent man. [*He takes the looking-glass from the wall and puts it on the back of a chair; then sits down in front of it and begins washing his face.*] Didn't I know rightly I was handsome, though it was the divil's own mirror we had beyond, would twist a squint across an angel's brow; and I'll be growing fine from this day, the way I'll have a soft lovely skin on me and won't be the like of the clumsy young fellows do be ploughing all times in the earth and dung. [*He starts.*] Is she coming again? [*He looks out.*] Stranger girls. God help me, where'll I hide myself away and my long neck naked to the world? [*He looks out.*] I'd best go to the room maybe till I'm dressed again. [*He gathers up his coat and the looking-glass, and runs into the inner room. The door is pushed open, and* SUSAN BRADY *looks in, and knocks on door.*]

SUSAN There's nobody in it. [*Knocks again.*]

NELLY [*Pushing her in and following her, with* HONOR BLAKE *and* SARA TANSEY.] It'd be early for them both to be out walking the hill.

SUSAN I'm thinking Shawn Keogh was making game of us and there's no such man in it at all.

HONOR [*Pointing to straw and quilt.*] Look at that. He's been sleeping there in the night. Well, it'll be a hard case[1] if he's gone off now, the way we'll never set our eyes on a man killed his father, and we after rising early and

[18] She's a terror for a 20-year-old girl!

[1] Bad luck for us.

destroying ourselves running fast on the hill.

NELLY Are you thinking them's his boots?

SARA [*Taking them up.*] If they are, there should be his father's track on them. Did you never read in the papers the way murdered men do bleed and drip?

SUSAN Is that blood there, Sara Tansey?

SARA [*Smelling it.*] That's bog water, I'm thinking, but it's his own they are surely, for I never seen the like of them for whity mud, and red mud, and turf on them, and the fine sands of the sea. That man's been walking, I'm telling you. [*She goes down right, putting on one of his boots.*]

SUSAN [*Going to window.*] Maybe he's stolen off to Belmullet with the boots of Michael James, and you'd have a right so to follow after him, Sara Tansey, and you the one yoked the ass cart and drove ten miles to set your eyes on the man bit the yellow lady's nostril on the northern shore. [*She looks out.*]

SARA [*Running to window with one boot on.*] Don't be talking, and we fooled today. [*Putting on other boot.*] There's a pair do fit me well, and I'll be keeping them for walking to the priest, when you'd be ashamed this place, going up winter and summer with nothing worth while to confess at all.

HONOR [*Who has been listening at the door.*] Whisht! there's someone inside the room. [*She pushes door a chink open.*] It's a man.

[SARA *kicks off boots and puts them where they were. They all stand in a line looking through chink.*]

SARA I'll call him. Mister! Mister! [*He puts in his head.*] Is Pegeen within?

CHRISTY [*Coming in as meek as a mouse, with the looking-glass held behind his back.*] She's above on the cnuceen,[2] seeking the nanny goats, the way she'd have a sup of goat's milk for to colour my tea.

SARA And asking your pardon, is it you's the man killed his father?

CHRISTY [*Sidling toward the nail where the glass was hanging.*] I am, God help me!

SARA [*Taking eggs she has brought.*] Then my thousand welcomes to you, and I've run up with a brace of duck's eggs for your food today. Pegeen's ducks is no use, but these are the real rich sort. Hold out your hand and you'll see it's no lie I'm telling you.

CHRISTY [*Coming forward shyly, and holding out his left hand.*] They're a great and weighty size.

SUSAN And I run up with a pat of butter, for it'd be a poor thing to have you eating your spuds dry, and you after running a great way since you did destroy your da.

CHRISTY Thank you kindly.

HONOR And I brought you a little cut of cake, for you should have a thin stomach on you, and you that length walking the world.

NELLY And I brought you a little laying pullet—boiled and all she is—was crushed at the fall of night by the curate's car. Feel the fat of that breast, mister.

CHRISTY It's bursting, surely. [*He feels it with the back of his hand, in which he holds the presents.*]

SARA Will you pinch it? Is your right hand too sacred for to use at all? [*She slips round behind him.*] It's a glass he has. Well, I never seen to this day a man with a looking-glass held to his back. Them that kills their fathers is a vain lot surely.

[*Girls giggle.*]

CHRISTY [*Smiling innocently and piling presents on glass.*] I'm very thankful to you all today . . .

WIDOW QUIN [*Coming in quickly, at door.*] Sara Tansey, Susan Brady, Honor Blake! What in glory has you here at this hour of day?

GIRLS [*Giggling.*] That's the man killed his father.

WIDOW QUIN [*Coming to them.*] I know well it's the man; and I'm after putting him down in the sports below for racing, leaping, pitching, and the Lord knows what.

SARA [*Exuberantly.*] That's right, Widow Quin. I'll bet my dowry that he'll lick the world.

WIDOW QUIN If you will, you'd have a right to have him fresh and nourished in place of nursing a feast.[3] [*Taking presents.*] Are you fasting or fed, young fellow?

CHRISTY Fasting, if you please.

WIDOW QUIN [*Loudly.*] Well, you're the lot. Stir up now and give him his breakfast. [*To*

[2] Small hill.

[3] Needing to be fed.

CHRISTY.] Come here to me [*She puts him on bench beside her while the girls make tea and get his breakfast.*] and let you tell us your story before Pegeen will come, in place of grinning your ears off like the moon of May.

CHRISTY [*Beginning to be pleased.*] It's a long story; you'd be destroyed listening.

WIDOW QUIN Don't be letting on to be shy, a fine, gamey, treacherous lad the like of you. Was it in your house beyond you cracked his skull?

CHRISTY [*Shy but flattered.*] It was not. We were digging spuds in his cold, sloping, stony, divil's patch of a field.

WIDOW QUIN And you went asking money of him, or making talk of getting a wife would drive him from his farm?

CHRISTY I did not, then; but there I was, digging and digging, and "You squinting idiot," says he, "let you walk down now and tell the priest you'll wed the Widow Casey in a score of days."

WIDOW QUIN And what kind was she?

CHRISTY [*With horror.*] A walking terror from beyond the hills, and she two score and five years, and two hundredweights and five pounds in the weighing scales, with a limping leg on her, and a blinded eye, and she a woman of noted misbehavior with the old and young.

GIRLS [*Clustering round him, serving him.*] Glory be.

WIDOW QUIN And what did he want driving you to wed with her? [*She takes a bit of the chicken.*]

CHRISTY [*Eating with growing satisfaction.*] He was letting on I was wanting a protector from the harshness of the world, and he without a thought the whole while but how he'd have her hut to live in and her gold to drink.

WIDOW QUIN There's maybe worse than a dry hearth and a widow woman and your glass at night. So you hit him then?

CHRISTY [*Getting almost excited.*] I did not. "I won't wed her," says I, "when all know she did suckle me for six weeks when I came into the world, and she a hag this day with a tongue on her has the crows and seabirds scattered, the way they wouldn't cast a shadow on her garden with the dread of her curse."

WIDOW QUIN [*Teasingly.*] That one should be right company.

SARA [*Eagerly.*] Don't mind her. Did you kill him then?

CHRISTY "She's too good for the like of you," says he, "and go on now or I'll flatten you out like a crawling beast has passed under a dray." "You will not if I can help it," says I. "Go on," says he, "or I'll have the divil making garters of your limbs tonight." "You will not if I can help it," says I. [*He sits up, brandishing his mug.*]

SARA You were right surely.

CHRISTY [*Impressively.*] With that the sun came out between the cloud and the hill, and it shining green in my face. "God have mercy on your soul," says he, lifting a scythe; "or on your own," says I, raising the loy.

SUSAN That's a grand story.

HONOR He tells it lovely.

CHRISTY [*Flattered and confident, waving bone.*] He gave a drive with the scythe, and I gave a lep to the east. Then I turned around with my back to the north, and I hit a blow on the ridge of his skull, laid him stretched out, and he split to the knob of his gullet. [*He raises the chicken bone to his Adam's apple.*]

GIRLS [*Together.*] Well, you're a marvel! Oh, God bless you! You're the lad surely!

SUSAN I'm thinking the Lord God sent him this road to make a second husband to the Widow Quin, and she with a great yearning to be wedded, though all dread her here. Lift him on her knee, Sara Tansey.

WIDOW QUIN Don't tease him.

SARA [*Going over to dresser and counter very quickly, and getting two glasses and porter.*] You're heroes surely, and let you drink a supeen with your arms linked like the outlandish lovers in the sailor's song. [*She links their arms and gives them the glasses.*] There now. Drink a health to the wonders of the western world, the pirates, preachers, poteen-makers, with the jobbing jockies;[4] parching peelers, and the juries fill their stomachs selling judgments of the English law. [*Brandishing the bottle.*]

[4] Petty crooks or poteen-peddlers.

WIDOW QUIN That's a right toast, Sara Tansey. Now, Christy.

[*They drink with their arms linked, he drinking with his left hand, she with her right. As they are drinking,* PEGEEN MIKE *comes in with a milk can and stands aghast. They all spring away from* CHRISTY. *He goes down left.* WIDOW QUIN *remains seated.*]

PEGEEN [*Angrily, to* SARA.] What is it you're wanting?

SARA [*Twisting her apron.*] An ounce of tobacco.

PEGEEN Have you tuppence?

SARA I've forgotten my purse.

PEGEEN Then you'd best be getting it and not fooling us here. [*To the* WIDOW QUIN, *with more elaborate scorn.*] And what is it you're wanting, Widow Quin?

WIDOW QUIN [*Insolently.*] A penn'orth of starch.

PEGEEN [*Breaking out.*] And you without a white shift or a shirt in your whole family since the drying of the flood. I've no starch for the like of you, and let you walk on now to Killamuck.

WIDOW QUIN [*Turning to* CHRISTY, *as she goes out with the girls.*] Well, you're mighty huffy this day, Pegeen Mike, and, you young fellow, let you not forget the sports and racing when the noon is by.

[*They go out.*]

PEGEEN [*Imperiously.*] Fling out that rubbish and put them cups away. [CHRISTY *tidies away in great haste.*] Shove in the bench by the wall. [*He does so.*] And hang that glass on the nail. What disturbed it at all?

CHRISTY [*Very meekly.*] I was making myself decent only, and this a fine country for young lovely girls.

PEGEEN [*Sharply.*] Whisht your talking of girls. [*Goes to counter, right.*]

CHRISTY Wouldn't any wish to be decent in a place . . .

PEGEEN Whisht I'm saying.

CHRISTY [*Looks at her face for a moment with great misgivings, then as a last effort, takes up a loy, and goes toward her, with feigned assurance.*] It was with a loy the like of that I killed my father.

PEGEEN [*Still sharply.*] You've told me that story six times since the dawn of day.

CHRISTY [*Reproachfully.*] It's a queer thing you wouldn't care to be hearing it and them girls after walking four miles to be listening to me now.

PEGEEN [*Turning around astonished.*] Four miles!

CHRISTY [*Apologetically.*] Didn't himself say there were only four bona fides living in the place?

PEGEEN It's bona fides by the road they are, but that lot came over the river lepping the stones. It's not three perches when you go like that, and I was down this morning looking on the papers the post-boy does have in his bag. [*With meaning and emphasis.*] For there was great news this day, Christopher Mahon. [*She goes into room left.*]

CHRISTY [*Suspiciously.*] Is it news of my murder?

PEGEEN [*Inside.*] Murder, indeed.

CHRISTY [*Loudly.*] A murdered da?

PEGEEN [*Coming in again and crossing right.*] There was not, but a story filled half a page of the hanging of a man. Ah, that should be a fearful end, young fellow, and it worst of all for a man who destroyed his da, for the like of him would get small mercies, and when it's dead he is, they'd put him in a narrow grave, with cheap sacking wrapping him round, and pour down quicklime on his head, the way you'd see a woman pouring any frish-frash[5] from a cup.

CHRISTY [*Very miserably.*] Oh, God help me. Are you thinking I'm safe? You were saying at the fall of night, I was shut of jeopardy and I here with yourselves.

PEGEEN [*Severely.*] You'll be shut of jeopardy in no place if you go talking with a pack of wild girls the like of them do be walking abroad with the peelers, talking whispers at the fall of night.

CHRISTY [*With terror.*] And you're thinking they'd tell?

PEGEEN [*With mock sympathy.*] Who knows, God help you.

CHRISTY [*Loudly.*] What joy would they have to bring hanging to the likes of me?

PEGEEN It's queer joys they have, and who knows the thing they'd do, if it'd make the green stones cry itself to think of you swaying and swiggling at the butt of a rope, and you with a fine, stout neck, God bless you! the

[5] Slops, dregs.

way you'd be a half an hour, in great anguish, getting your death.

CHRISTY [*Getting his boots and putting them on.*] If there's that terror of them, it'd be best, maybe, I went on wandering like Esau or Cain and Abel on the sides of Neifin or the Erris plain.

PEGEEN [*Beginning to play with him.*] It would, maybe, for I've heard the Circuit Judges this place is a heartless crew.

CHRISTY [*Bitterly.*] It's more than Judges this place is a heartless crew. [*Looking up at her.*] And isn't it a poor thing to be starting again and I a lonesome fellow will be looking out on women and girls the way the needy fallen spirits do be looking on the Lord?

PEGEEN What call have you to be that lonesome when there's poor girls walking Mayo in their thousands now?

CHRISTY [*Grimly.*] It's well you know what call I have. It's well you know it's a lonesome thing to be passing small towns with the lights shining sideways when the night is down, or going in strange places with a dog noising before you and a dog noising behind, or drawn to the cities where you'd hear a voice kissing and talking deep love in every shadow of the ditch, and you passing on with an empty, hungry stomach failing from your heart.

PEGEEN I'm thinking you're an odd man, Christy Mahon. The oddest walking fellow I ever set my eyes on to this hour today.

CHRISTY What would any be but odd men and they living lonesome in the world?

PEGEEN I'm not odd, and I'm my whole life with my father only.

CHRISTY [*With infinite admiration.*] How would a lovely handsome woman the like of you be lonesome when all men should be thronging around to hear the sweetness of your voice, and the little infant children should be pestering your steps I'm thinking, and you walking the roads.

PEGEEN I'm hard set to know what way a coaxing fellow the like of yourself should be lonesome either.

CHRISTY Coaxing?

PEGEEN Would you have me think a man never talked with the girls would have the words you've spoken today? It's only letting on you are to be lonesome, the way you'd get around me now.

CHRISTY I wish to God I was letting on; but I was lonesome all times, and born lonesome, I'm thinking, as the moon of dawn. [*Going to door.*]

PEGEEN [*Puzzled by his talk.*] Well, it's a story I'm not understanding at all why you'd be worse than another, Christy Mahon, and you a fine lad with the great savagery to destroy your da.

CHRISTY It's little I'm understanding myself, saving only that my heart's scalded this day, and I am going off stretching out the earth between us, the way I'll not be waking near you another dawn of the year till the two of us do arise to hope or judgment with the saints of God, and now I'd best be going with my wattle in my hand, for hanging is a poor thing [*Turning to go.*], and it's little welcome only is left me in this house today.

PEGEEN [*Sharply.*] Christy! [*He turns round.*] Come here to me. [*He goes toward her.*] Lay down that switch and throw some sods on the fire. You're pot-boy in this place, and I'll not have you mitch[6] off from us now.

CHRISTY You were saying I'd be hanged if I stay.

PEGEEN [*Quite kindly at last.*] I'm after going down and reading the fearful crimes of Ireland for two weeks or three, and there wasn't a word of your murder. [*Getting up and going over to the counter.*] They've likely not found the body. You're safe so with ourselves.

CHRISTY [*Astonished, slowly.*] It's making game of me you were, [*Following her with fearful joy.*] and I can stay so, working at your side, and I not lonesome from this mortal day.

PEGEEN What's to hinder you from staying, except the widow woman or the young girls would inveigle you off?

CHRISTY [*With rapture.*] And I'll have your words from this day filling my ears, and that look is come upon you meeting my two eyes, and I watching you loafing around in the warm sun, or rinsing your ankles when the night is come.

PEGEEN [*Kindly, but a little embarrassed.*] I'm thinking you'll be a loyal young lad to have working around, and if you vexed me a while since with your leaguing with the girls, I

[6] Sneak.

wouldn't give a thraneen[7] for a lad hadn't a mighty spirit in him and a gamey heart.

[SHAWN KEOGH *runs in carrying a cleeve*[8] *on his back, followed by the* WIDOW QUIN.]

SHAWN [*To* PEGEEN.] I was passing below, and I seen your mountainy sheep eating cabbages in Jimmy's field. Run up or they'll be bursting surely.

PEGEEN Oh, God mend them! [*She puts a shawl over her head and runs out.*]

CHRISTY [*Looking from one to the other. Still in high spirit.*] I'd best go to her aid maybe. I'm handy with ewes.

WIDOW QUIN [*Closing the door.*] She can do that much, and there is Shaneen has long speeches for to tell you now. [*She sits down with an amused smile.*]

SHAWN [*Taking something from his pocket and offering it to* CHRISTY.] Do you see that, mister?

CHRISTY [*Looking at it.*] The half of a ticket to the Western States![9]

SHAWN [*Trembling with anxiety.*] I'll give it to you and my new hat [*Pulling it out of hamper.*]; and my breeches with the double seat [*Pulling it off.*]; and my new coat is woven from the blackest shearings for three miles around [*Giving him the coat.*]; I'll give you the whole of them, and my blessing, and the blessing of Father Reilly itself, maybe, if you'll quit from this and leave us in the peace we had till last night at the fall of dark.

CHRISTY [*With a new arrogance.*] And for what is it you're wanting to get shut of me?

SHAWN [*Looking to the* WIDOW *for help.*] I'm a poor scholar with middling faculties to coin a lie, so I'll tell you the truth, Christy Mahon. I'm wedding with Pegeen beyond, and I don't think well of having a clever fearless man the like of you dwelling in her house.

CHRISTY [*Almost pugnaciously.*] And you'd be using bribery for to banish me?

SHAWN [*In an imploring voice.*] Let you not take it badly, mister honey, isn't beyond the best place for you where you'll have golden chains and shiny coats and you riding upon hunters with the ladies of the land. [*He makes an eager sign to the* WIDOW QUIN *to come to help him.*]

WIDOW QUIN [*Coming over.*] It's true for him, and you'd best quit off and not have that poor girl setting her mind on you, for there's Shaneen thinks she wouldn't suit you though all is saying that she'll wed you now.

[CHRISTY *beams with delight.*]

SHAWN [*In terrified earnest.*] She wouldn't suit you, and she with the divil's own temper the way you'd be strangling one another in a score of days. [*He makes the movement of strangling with his hands.*] It's the like of me only that she's fit for, a quiet simple fellow wouldn't raise a hand upon her if she scratched itself.

WIDOW QUIN [*Putting* SHAWN'S *hat on* CHRISTY.] Fit them clothes on you anyhow, young fellow, and he'd maybe loan them to you for the sports. [*Pushing him toward inner door.*] Fit them on and you can give your answer when you have them tried.

CHRISTY [*Beaming, delighted with the clothes.*] I will then. I'd like herself to see me in them tweeds and hat. [*He goes into room and shuts the door.*]

SHAWN [*In great anxiety.*] He'd like herself to see them. He'll not leave us, Widow Quin. He's a score of divils in him the way it's well nigh certain he will wed Pegeen.

WIDOW QUIN [*Jeeringly.*] It's true all girls are fond of courage and do hate the like of you.

SHAWN [*Walking about in desperation.*] Oh, Widow Quin, what'll I be doing now? I'd inform again him, but he'd burst from Kilmainham[10] and he'd be sure and certain to destroy me. If I wasn't so God-fearing, I'd near have courage to come behind him and run a pike into his side. Oh, it's a hard case to be an orphan and not to have your father that you're used to, and you'd easy kill and make yourself a hero in the sight of all. [*Coming up to her.*] Oh, Widow Quin, will you find me some contrivance when I've promised you a ewe?

WIDOW QUIN A ewe's a small thing, but what would you give me if I did wed him and did save you so?

SHAWN [*With astonishment.*] You?

WIDOW QUIN Aye. Would you give me the red cow you have and the mountainy ram, and

[7] Worthless token.
[8] Basket.
[9] The United States.
[10] Penitentiary in Dublin.

the right of way across your rye path, and a load of dung at Michaelmas, and turbary[11] upon the western hill?

SHAWN [*Radiant with hope.*] I would surely, and I'd give you the wedding-ring I have, and the loan of a new suit, the way you'd have him decent on the wedding-day. I'd give you two kids for your dinner, and a gallon of poteen, and I'd call the piper on the long car to your wedding from Crossmolina or from Ballina. I'd give you . . .

WIDOW QUIN That'll do so, and let you whisht, for he's coming now again.

[CHRISTY *comes in very natty in the new clothes.* WIDOW QUIN *goes to him admiringly.*]

WIDOW QUIN If you seen yourself now, I'm thinking you'd be too proud to speak to us at all, and it'd be a pity surely to have your like sailing from Mayo to the Western World.

CHRISTY [*As proud as a peacock.*] I'm not going. If this is a poor place itself, I'll make myself contented to be lodging here.

[WIDOW QUIN *makes a sign to* SHAWN *to leave them.*]

SHAWN Well, I'm going measuring the racecourse while the tide is low, so I'll leave you the garments and my blessing for the sports today. God bless you! [*He wriggles out.*]

WIDOW QUIN [*Admiring* CHRISTY.] Well, you're mighty spruce, young fellow. Sit down now while you're quiet till you talk with me.

CHRISTY [*Swaggering.*] I'm going abroad on the hillside for to seek Pegeen.

WIDOW QUIN You'll have time and plenty for to seek Pegeen, and you heard me saying at the fall of night the two of us should be great company.

CHRISTY From this out I'll have no want of company when all sorts is bringing me their food and clothing, [*He swaggers to the door, tightening his belt.*] the way they'd set their eyes upon a gallant orphan cleft his father with one blow to the breeches belt. [*He opens door, then staggers back.*] Saints of glory! Holy angels from the throne of light!

WIDOW QUIN [*Going over.*] What ails you?

CHRISTY It's the walking spirit of my murdered da!

WIDOW QUIN [*Looking out.*] Is it that tramper?

CHRISTY [*Wildly.*] Where'll I hide my poor body from that ghost of hell?

[*The door is pushed open, and old* MAHON *appears on threshold.* CHRISTY *darts in behind door.*]

WIDOW QUIN [*In great amusement.*] God save you, my poor man.

MAHON [*Gruffly.*] Did you see a young lad passing this way in the early morning or the fall of night?

WIDOW QUIN You're a queer kind to walk in not saluting at all.

MAHON Did you see the young lad?

WIDOW QUIN [*Stiffly.*] What kind was he?

MAHON An ugly young streeler[12] with a murderous gob[13] on him, and a little switch in his hand. I met a tramper seen him coming this way at the fall of night.

WIDOW QUIN There's harvest hundreds do be passing these days for the Sligo boat. For what is it you're wanting him, my poor man?

MAHON I want to destroy him for breaking the head on me with the clout of a loy. [*He takes off a big hat, and shows his head in a mass of bandages and plaster, with some pride.*] It was he did that, and amn't I a great wonder to think I've traced him ten days with that rent in my crown?

WIDOW QUIN [*Taking his head in both hands and examining it with extreme delight.*] That was a great blow. And who hit you? A robber maybe?

MAHON It was my own son hit me, and he the divil a robber, or anything else, but a dirty, stuttering lout.

WIDOW QUIN [*Letting go his skull and wiping her hands in her apron.*] You'd best be wary of a mortified[14] scalp, I think they call it, lepping around with that wound in the splendour of the sun. It was a bad blow surely, and you should have vexed him fearful to make him strike that gash in his da.

MAHON Is it me?

WIDOW QUIN [*Amusing herself.*] Aye. And isn't it a great shame when the old and hardened do torment the young?

[11] The right to dig turf or peat on another's land, or the piece of land itself. Widow Quin seems most interested in the right.

[12] Stroller, vagrant.

[13] Face.

[14] Poisoned, perhaps gangrenous; dying.

MAHON [*Raging.*] Torment him, is it? And I after holding out with the patience of a martyred saint till there's nothing but destruction on, and I'm driven out in my old age with none to aid me.

WIDOW QUIN [*Greatly amused.*] It's a sacred wonder the way that wickedness will spoil a man.

MAHON My wickedness, is it? Amn't I after saying it is himself has me destroyed, and he a lier on walls, a talker of folly, a man you'd see stretched the half of the day in the brown ferns with his belly to the sun.

WIDOW QUIN Not working at all?

MAHON The divil a work, or if he did itself, you'd see him raising up a haystack like the stalk of a rush, or driving our last cow till he broke her leg at the hip, and when he wasn't at that he'd be fooling over little birds he had—finches and felts[15]—or making mugs at his own self in the bit of a glass we had hung on the wall.

WIDOW QUIN [*Looking at* CHRISTY.] What way was he so foolish? It was running wild after the girls maybe?

MAHON [*With a shout of derision.*] Running wild, is it? If he seen a red petticoat coming swinging over the hill, he'd be off to hide in the sticks, and you'd see him shooting out his sheep's eyes between the little twigs and the leaves, and his two ears rising like a hare looking out through a gap. Girls, indeed!

WIDOW QUIN It was drink maybe?

MAHON And he a poor fellow would get drunk on the smell of a pint. He'd a queer rotten stomach, I'm telling you, and when I gave him three pulls from my pipe a while since, he was taken with contortions till I had to send him in the ass cart to the females' nurse.

WIDOW QUIN [*Clasping her hands.*] Well, I never till this day heard tell of a man the like of that!

MAHON I'd take a mighty oath you didn't surely, and wasn't he the laughing joke of every female woman where four baronies meet, the way the girls would stop their weeding if they seen him coming the road to let a roar at him, and call him the looney of Mahon's.

WIDOW QUIN I'd give the world and all to see the like of him. What kind was he?

MAHON A small low fellow.

WIDOW QUIN And dark?

MAHON Dark and dirty.

WIDOW QUIN [*Considering.*] I'm thinking I seen him.

MAHON [*Eagerly.*] An ugly young blackguard.

WIDOW QUIN A hideous, fearful villain, and the spit of you.

MAHON What way is he fled?

WIDOW QUIN Gone over the hills to catch a coasting steamer to the north or south.

MAHON Could I pull up on him now?

WIDOW QUIN If you'll cross the sands below where the tide is out, you'll be in it as soon as himself, for he had to go round ten miles by the top of the bay. [*She points to the door.*] Strike down by the head beyond and then follow on the roadway to the north and east.

[MAHON *goes abruptly.*]

WIDOW QUIN [*Shouting after him.*] Let you give him a good vengeance when you come up with him, but don't put yourself in the power of the law, for it'd be a poor thing to see a judge in his black cap reading out his sentence on a civil warrior the like of you. [*She swings the door to and looks at* CHRISTY, *who is cowering in terror, for a moment, then she bursts into a laugh.*] Well, you're the walking Playboy[16] of the Western World, and that's the poor man you had divided to his breeches belt.

CHRISTY [*Looking out: then, to her.*] What'll Pegeen say when she hears that story? What'll she be saying to me now?

WIDOW QUIN She'll knock the head of you, I'm thinking, and drive you from the door. God help her to be taking you for a wonder, and you a little schemer making up the story you destroyed your da.

CHRISTY [*Turning to the door, nearly speechless with rage, half to himself.*] To be letting on he was dead, and coming back to his life, and following after me like an old weasel tracing a rat, and coming in here laying desolation between my own self and the fine women of Ireland, and he a kind of carcase that you'd fling upon the sea . . .

[15] Thrushes.

[16] Here used in the sense of *hoaxer* or *big talker*.

WIDOW QUIN [*More soberly.*] There's talking for a man's one only son.

CHRISTY [*Breaking out.*] His one son, is it? May I meet him with one tooth and it aching, and one eye to be seeing seven and seventy divils in the twists of the road, and one old timber leg on him to limp into the scalding grave. [*Looking out.*] There he is now crossing the strands, and that the Lord God would send a high wave to wash him from the world.

WIDOW QUIN [*Scandalized.*] Have you no shame? [*Putting her hand on his shoulder and turning him round.*] What ails you? Near crying, is it?

CHRISTY [*In despair and grief.*] Amn't I after seeing the lovelight of the star of knowledge shining from her brow, and hearing words would put you thinking on the holy Brigid speaking to the infant saints, and now she'll be turning again, and speaking hard words to me, like an old woman with a spavindy[17] ass she'd have, urging on a hill.

WIDOW QUIN There's poetry talk for a girl you'd see itching and scratching, and she with a stale stink of poteen on her from selling in the shop.

CHRISTY [*Impatiently.*] It's her like is fitted to be handling merchandise in the heavens above, and what'll I be doing now, I ask you, and I a kind of wonder was jilted by the heavens when a day was by.

[*There is a distant noise of girls' voices.* WIDOW QUIN *looks from window and comes to him, hurriedly.*]

WIDOW QUIN You'll be doing like myself, I'm thinking, when I did destroy my man, for I'm above many's the day, odd times in great spirits, abroad in the sunshine, darning a stocking or stitching a shift; and odd times again looking out on the schooners, hookers, trawlers is sailing the sea, and I thinking on the gallant hairy fellows are drifting beyond, and myself long years living alone.

CHRISTY [*Interested.*] You're like me, so.

WIDOW QUIN I am your like, and it's for that I'm taking a fancy to you, and I with my little houseen above where there'd be myself to tend you, and none to ask were you a murderer or what at all.

[17] Lame.

CHRISTY And what would I be doing if I left Pegeen?

WIDOW QUIN I've nice jobs you could be doing, gathering shells to make a whitewash for our hut within, building up a little goose-house, or stretching a new skin on an old curragh I have, and if my hut is far from all sides, it's there you'll meet the wisest old men, I tell you, at the corner of my wheel, and it's there yourself and me will have great times whispering and hugging. . . .

VOICES [*Outside, calling far away.*] Christy! Christy Mahon! Christy!

CHRISTY Is it Pegeen Mike?

WIDOW QUIN It's the young girls, I'm thinking, coming to bring you to the sports below, and what is it you'll have me to tell them now?

CHRISTY Aid me for to win Pegeen. It's herself only that I'm seeking now. [WIDOW QUIN *gets up and goes to window.*] Aid me for to win her, and I'll be asking God to stretch a hand to you in the hour of death, and lead you short cuts through the Meadows of Ease, and up the floor of Heaven to the Footstool of the Virgin's Son.

WIDOW QUIN There's praying.

VOICES [*Nearer.*] Christy! Christy Mahon!

CHRISTY [*With agitation.*] They're coming. Will you swear to aid and save me for the love of Christ?

WIDOW QUIN [*Looks at him for a moment.*] If I aid you, will you swear to give me a right of way I want, and a mountainy ram, and a load of dung at Michaelmas, the time that you'll be master here?

CHRISTY I will, by the elements and stars of night.

WIDOW QUIN Then we'll not say a word of the old fellow, the way Pegeen won't know your story till the end of time.

CHRISTY And if he chances to return again?

WIDOW QUIN We'll swear he's a maniac and not your da. I could take an oath I seen him raving on the sands today.

[*Girls run in.*]

SUSAN Come on to the sports below. Pegeen says you're to come.

SARA TANSEY The lepping's beginning, and we've a jockey's suit to fit upon you for the mule race on the sands below.

HONOR Come on, will you?

CHRISTY I will then if Pegeen's beyond.

SARA TANSEY She's in the boreen[18] making game of Shaneen Keogh.

CHRISTY Then I'll be going to her now. [*He runs out followed by the girls.*]

WIDOW QUIN Well, if the worst comes in the end of all, it'll be great game to see there's none to pity him but a widow woman, the like of me, has buried her children and destroyed her man. [*She goes out.*]

[*Curtain.*]

ACT III

SCENE: *As before. Later in the day.* JIMMY *comes in, slightly drunk.*

JIMMY [*Calls.*] Pegeen! [*Crosses to inner door.*] Pegeen Mike! [*Comes back again into the room.*] Pegeen! [PHILLY *comes in in the same state.*] [*To* PHILLY.] Did you see herself?

PHILLY I did not; but I sent Shawn Keogh with the ass cart for to bear him home. [*Trying cupboards which are locked.*] Well, isn't he a nasty man to get into such staggers at a morning wake? and isn't herself the divil's daughter for locking,[1] and she so fussy after that young gaffer, you might take your death with drought and none to heed you?

JIMMY It's little wonder she'd be fussy, and he after bringing bankrupt ruin on the roulette man, and the trick-o'-the-loop man, and breaking the nose of the cockshot-man, and winning all in the sports below, racing, lepping, dancing, and the Lord knows what! He's right luck, I'm telling you.

PHILLY If he has, he'll be rightly hobbled yet, and he not able to say ten words without making a brag of the way he killed his father, and the great blow he hit with the loy.

JIMMY A man can't hang by his own informing, and his father should be rotten by now.

[*Old* MAHON *passes window slowly.*]

PHILLY Supposing a man's digging spuds in that field with a long spade, and supposing he flings up the two halves of that skull, what'll be said then in the papers and the courts of law?

[18] Lane, country road.

[1] The Devil can't even keep track of her.

JIMMY They'd say it was an old Dane, maybe, was drowned in the flood. [*Old* MAHON *comes in and sits down near door listening.*] Did you never hear tell of the skulls they have in the city of Dublin, ranged out like blue jugs in a cabin of Connaught?

PHILLY And you believe that?

JIMMY [*Pugnaciously.*] Didn't a lad see them and he after coming from harvesting in the Liverpool boat? "They have them there," says he, "making a show of the great people there was one time walking the world. White skulls and black skulls and yellow skulls, and some with full teeth, and some haven't only but one."

PHILLY It was no lie, maybe, for when I was a young lad there was a graveyard beyond the house with the remnants of a man who had thighs as long as your arm. He was a horrid man, I'm telling you, and there was many a fine Sunday I'd put him together for fun, and he with shiny bones, you wouldn't meet the like of these days in the cities of the world.

MAHON [*Getting up.*] You wouldn't, is it? Lay your eyes on that skull, and tell me where and when there was another the like of it, is splintered only from the blow of a loy.

PHILLY Glory be to God! And who hit you at all?

MAHON [*Triumphantly.*] It was my own son hit me. Would you believe that?

JIMMY Well, there's wonders hidden in the heart of man!

PHILLY [*Suspiciously.*] And what way was it done?

MAHON [*Wandering about the room.*] I'm after walking hundreds and long scores of miles, winning clean beds and the fill of my belly four times in the day, and I doing nothing but telling stories of that naked truth. [*He comes to them a little aggressively.*] Give me a supeen and I'll tell you now.

[WIDOW QUIN *comes in and stands aghast behind him. He is facing* JIMMY *and* PHILLY, *who are on the left.*]

JIMMY Ask herself beyond. She's the stuff hidden in her shawl.

WIDOW QUIN [*Coming to* MAHON *quickly.*] You here, is it? You didn't go far at all?

MAHON I seen the coasting steamer passing, and I got a drought upon me and a cramping leg, so I said, "The divil go along with him," and turned again. [*Looking under her shawl.*] And let you give me a supeen, for I'm destroyed travelling since Tuesday was a week.

WIDOW QUIN [*Getting a glass, in a cajoling tone.*] Sit down then by the fire and take your ease for a space. You've a right to be destroyed indeed, with your walking, and fighting, and facing the sun. [*Giving him poteen from a stone jar she has brought in.*] There now is a drink for you, and may it be to your happiness and length of life.

MAHON [*Taking glass greedily and sitting down by fire.*] God increase you!

WIDOW QUIN [*Taking men to the right stealthily.*] Do you know what? That man's raving from his wound today, for I met him a while since telling a rambling tale of a tinker had him destroyed. Then he heard of Christy's deed, and he up and says it was his son had cracked his skull. O, isn't madness a fright, for he'll go killing someone yet, and he thinking it's the man has struck him so?

JIMMY [*Entirely convinced.*] It's a fright, surely. I knew a party was kicked in the head by a red mare, and he went killing horses a great while, till he eat the insides of a clock and died after.

PHILLY [*With suspicion.*] Did he see Christy?

WIDOW QUIN He didn't. [*With a warning gesture.*] Let you not be putting him in mind of him, or you'll be likely summoned if there's murder done. [*Looking round at* MAHON.] Whisht! He's listening. Wait now till you hear me taking him easy and unravelling all. [*She goes to* MAHON.] And what way are you feeling, mister? Are you in contentment now?

MAHON [*Slightly emotional from his drink.*] I'm poorly only, for it's a hard story the way I'm left today, when it was I did tend him from his hour of birth, and he a dunce never reached his second book, the way he'd come from school, many's the day, with his legs lamed under him, and he blackened with his beatings like a tinker's ass. It's a hard story, I'm saying, the way some do have their next and nighest raising up a hand of murder on them, and some is lonesome getting their death with lamentation in the dead of night.

WIDOW QUIN [*Not knowing what to say.*] To hear you talking so quiet, who'd know you were the same fellow we seen pass today?

MAHON I'm the same surely. The wrack and ruin of three score years; and it's a terror to live that length, I tell you, and to have your sons going to the dogs against you, and you wore out scolding them, and skelping them, and God knows what.

PHILLY [*To* JIMMY.] He's not raving. [*To* WIDOW QUIN.] Will you ask him what kind was his son?

WIDOW QUIN [*To* MAHON, *with a peculiar look.*] Was your son that hit you a lad of one year and a score maybe, a great hand at racing and lepping and licking the world?

MAHON [*Turning on her with a roar of rage.*] Didn't you hear me say he was the fool of men, the way from this out he'll know the orphan's lot with old and young making game of him and they swearing, raging, kicking at him like a mangy cur.

[*A great burst of cheering outside, some way off.*]

MAHON [*Putting his hands to his ears.*] What in the name of God do they want roaring below?

WIDOW QUIN [*With the shade of a smile.*] They're cheering a young lad, the champion Playboy of the Western World.

[*More cheering.*]

MAHON [*Going to window.*] It'd split my heart to hear them, and I with pulses in my brain-pan for a week gone by. Is it racing they are?

JIMMY [*Looking from door.*] It is then. They are mounting him for the mule race will be run upon the sands. That's the playboy on the winkered mule.

MAHON [*Puzzled.*] That lad, is it? If you said it was a fool he was, I'd have laid a mighty oath he was the likeness of my wandering son [*Uneasily, putting his hand to his head.*] Faith, I'm thinking I'll go walking for to view the race.

WIDOW QUIN [*Stopping him, sharply.*] You will not. You'd best take the road to Belmullet, and not be dilly-dallying in this place where there isn't a spot you could sleep.

PHILLY [*Coming forward.*] Don't mind her. Mount there on the bench and you'll have a view of the whole. They're hurrying before the tide will rise, and it'd be near over if you went down the pathway through the crags below.

MAHON [*Mounts on bench,* WIDOW QUIN *beside*

him.] That's a right view again the edge of the sea. They're coming now from the point. He's leading. Who is he at all?

WIDOW QUIN He's the champion of the world, I tell you, and there isn't a hop'orth isn't falling lucky to his hands today.

PHILLY [*Looking out, interested in the race.*] Look at that. They're pressing him now.

JIMMY He'll win it yet.

PHILLY Take your time, Jimmy Farrell. It's too soon to say.

WIDOW QUIN [*Shouting.*] Watch him taking the gate. There's riding.

JIMMY [*Cheering.*] More power to the young lad!

MAHON He's passing the third.

JIMMY He'll lick them yet!

WIDOW QUIN He'd lick them if he was running races with a score itself.

MAHON Look at the mule he has, kicking the stars.

WIDOW QUIN There was a lep! [*Catching hold of* MAHON *in her excitement.*] He's fallen! He's mounted again! Faith, he's passing them all!

JIMMY Look at him skelping her!

PHILLY And the mountain girls hooshing him on!

JIMMY It's the last turn! The post's cleared for them now!

MAHON Look at the narrow place. He'll be into the bogs! [*With a yell.*] Good rider! He's through it again!

JIMMY He's neck and neck!

MAHON Good boy to him! Flames, but he's in!

[*Great cheering, in which all join.*]

MAHON [*With hesitation.*] What's that? They're raising him up. They're coming this way. [*With a roar of rage and astonishment.*] It's Christy! by the stars of God! I'd know his way of spitting and he astride the moon.

[*He jumps down and makes for the door, but* WIDOW QUIN *catches him and pulls him back.*]

WIDOW QUIN Stay quiet, will you. That's not your son. [*To* JIMMY.] Stop him, or you'll get a month for the abetting of manslaughter and be fined as well.

JIMMY I'll hold him.

MAHON [*Struggling.*] Let me out! Let me out, the lot of you! till I have my vengeance on his head today.

WIDOW QUIN [*Shaking him, vehemently.*] That's not your son. That's a man is going to make a marriage with the daughter of this house, a place with fine trade, with a license, and with poteen too.

MAHON [*Amazed.*] That man marrying a decent and a moneyed girl! Is it mad yous are? Is it in a crazy-house for females that I'm landed now?

WIDOW QUIN It's mad yourself is with the blow upon your head. That lad is the wonder of the Western World.

MAHON I seen it's my son.

WIDOW QUIN You seen that you're mad. [*Cheering outside.*] Do you hear them cheering him in the zig-zags of the road? Aren't you after saying that your son's a fool, and how would they be cheering a true idiot born?

MAHON [*Getting distressed.*] It's maybe out of reason that that man's himself. [*Cheering again.*] There's none surely will go cheering him. Oh, I'm raving with a madness that would fright the world! [*He sits down with his hand to his head.*] There was one time I seen ten scarlet divils letting on they'd cork my spirit in a gallon can; and one time I seen rats as big as badgers sucking the life blood from the butt of my lug;[2] but I never till this day confused that dribbling idiot with a likely man. I'm destroyed surely.

WIDOW QUIN And who'd wonder when it's your brain-pan that is gaping now?

MAHON Then the blight of the sacred drought upon myself and him, for I never went mad to this day, and I not three weeks with the Limerick girls drinking myself silly, and parlatic[3] from the dusk to dawn. [*To* WIDOW QUIN, *suddenly.*] Is my visage astray?

WIDOW QUIN It is then. You're a sniggering maniac, a child could see.

MAHON [*Getting up more cheerfully.*] Then I'd best be going to the union[4] beyond, and there'll be a welcome before me, I tell you [*With great pride.*], and I a terrible and fearful case, the way that there I was one time, screeching in a straitened waistcoat, with seven doctors writing out my sayings a printed book. Would you believe that?

WIDOW QUIN If you're a wonder itself, you'd best be hasty, for them lads caught a maniac

[2] Lobe of my ear.
[3] Paralyzed; Mahon's version of *paralytic.*
[4] A workhouse and hospital for the unemployed.

one time and pelted the poor creature till he ran out, raving and foaming, and was drowned in the sea.

MAHON [*With philosophy.*] It's true mankind is the divil when your head's astray. Let me out now and I'll slip down the boreen, and not see them so.

WIDOW QUIN [*Showing him out.*] That's it. Run to the right, and not a one will see.

[*He runs off.*]

PHILLY [*Wisely.*] You're at some gaming, Widow Quin; but I'll walk after him and give him his dinner and a time to rest, and I'll see then if he's raving or as sane as you.

WIDOW QUIN [*Annoyed.*] If you go near that lad, let you be wary of your head, I'm saying. Didn't you hear him telling he was crazed at times?

PHILLY I heard him telling a power; and I'm thinking we'll have right sport, before night will fall. [*He goes out.*]

JIMMY Well, Philly's a conceited and foolish man. How could that madman have his senses and his brain-pan slit? I'll go after them and see him turn on Philly now.

[*He goes;* WIDOW QUIN *hides poteen behind counter. Then hubbub outside.*]

VOICES There you are! Good jumper! Grand lepper! Darlint boy! He's the racer! Bear him on, will you!

[CHRISTY *comes in, in jockey's dress, with* PEGEEN MIKE, SARA, *and other girls, and men.*]

PEGEEN [*To crowd.*] Go on now and don't destroy him and he drenching with sweat. Go along, I'm saying, and have your tug-of-warring till he's dried his skin.

CROWD Here's his prizes! A bagpipes! A fiddle was played by a poet in the years gone by! A flat and three-thorned blackthorn would lick the scholars out of Dublin town!

CHRISTY [*Taking prizes from the men.*] Thank you kindly, the lot of you. But you'd say it was little only I did this day if you'd seen me a while since striking my one single blow.

TOWN CRIER [*Outside, ringing a bell.*] Take notice, last event of this day! Tug-of-warring on the green below! Come on, the lot of you! Great achievements for all Mayo men!

PEGEEN Go on, and leave him for to rest and dry. Go on, I tell you, for he'll do no more. [*She hustles crowd out;* WIDOW QUIN *following them.*]

MEN [*Going.*] Come on, then. Good luck for the while!

PEGEEN [*Radiantly, wiping his face with her shawl.*] Well, you're the lad, and you'll have great times from this out when you could win that wealth of prizes, and you sweating in the heat of noon!

CHRISTY [*Looking at her with delight.*] I'll have great times if I win the crowning prize I'm seeking now, and that's your promise that you'll wed me in a fortnight, when our banns is called.

PEGEEN [*Backing away from him.*] You're right daring to go ask me that, when all knows you'll be starting to some girl in your own townland, when your father's rotten in four months, or five.

CHRISTY [*Indignantly.*] Starting from you, is it? [*He follows her.*] I will not, then, and when the airs is warming in four months, or five, it's then yourself and me should be pacing Neifin in the dews of night, the times sweet smells do be rising, and you'd see a little shiny new moon, maybe, sinking on the hills.

PEGEEN [*Looking at him playfully.*] And it's that kind of a poacher's love you'd make, Christy Mahon, on the sides of Neifin, when the night is down?

CHRISTY It's little you'll think if my love's a poacher's, or an earl's itself, when you'll feel my two hands stretched around you, and I squeezing kisses on your puckered lips, till I'd feel a kind of pity for the Lord God in all ages sitting lonesome in his golden chair.

PEGEEN That'll be right fun, Christy Mahon, and any girl would walk her heart out before she'd meet a young man was your like for eloquence, or talk, at all.

CHRISTY [*Encouraged.*] Let you wait, to hear me talking, till we're astray in Erris, when Good Friday's by, drinking a sup from a well, and making mighty kisses with our wetted mouths, or gaming in a gap of sunshine, with yourself stretched back unto your necklace, in the flowers of the earth.

PEGEEN [*In a lower voice, moved by his tone.*] I'd be nice so, is it?

CHRISTY [*With rapture.*] If the mitred bishops seen you that time, they'd be the like of the holy prophets, I'm thinking, do be straining the bars of Paradise to lay eyes on the Lady Helen of Troy, and she abroad, pacing back and forward, with a nosegay in her golden shawl.

PEGEEN [*With real tenderness.*] And what is it I have, Christy Mahon, to make me fitting entertainment for the like of you, that has such poet's talking, and such bravery of heart?

CHRISTY [*In a low voice.*] Isn't there the light of seven heavens in your heart alone, the way you'll be an angel's lamp to me from this out, and I abroad in the darkness, spearing salmons in the Owen, or the Carrowmore?

PEGEEN If I was your wife, I'd be along with you those nights, Christy Mahon, the way you'd see I was a great hand at coaxing bailiffs, or coining funny nicknames for the stars of night.

CHRISTY You, is it? Taking your death in the hailstones, or in the fogs of dawn.

PEGEEN Yourself and me would shelter easy in a narrow bush, [*With a qualm of dread.*] but we're only talking, maybe, for this would be a poor, thatched place to hold a fine lad is the like of you.

CHRISTY [*Putting his arm around her.*] If I wasn't a good Christian, it's on my naked knees I'd be saying my prayers and paters to every jackstraw you have roofing your head, and every stony pebble is paving the laneway to your door.

PEGEEN [*Radiantly.*] If that's the truth, I'll be burning candles from this out to the miracles of God that have brought you from the south today, and I, with my gowns bought ready, the way that I can wed you, and not wait at all.

CHRISTY It's miracles, and that's the truth. Me there toiling a long while, and walking a long while, not knowing at all I was drawing all times nearer to this holy day.

PEGEEN And myself, a girl, was tempted often to go sailing the seas till I'd marry a Jew-man, with ten kegs of gold, and I not knowing at all there was the like of you drawing nearer, like the stars of God.

CHRISTY And to think I'm long years hearing women talking that talk, to all bloody fools, and this the first time I've heard the like of your voice talking sweetly for my own delight.

PEGEEN And to think it's me is talking sweetly, Christy Mahon, and I the fright of seven townlands for my biting tongue. Well, the heart's a wonder; and, I'm thinking, there won't be our like in Mayo, for gallant lovers, from this hour, today. [*Drunken singing is heard outside.*] There's my father coming from the wake, and when he's had his sleep we'll tell him, for he's peaceful then. [*They separate.*]

MICHAEL [*Singing outside.*]

The jailor and the turnkey
  They quickly ran us down,
And brought us back as prisoners
  Once more to Cavan town.

[*He comes in supported by* SHAWN.]

There we lay bewailing
  All in a prison bound. . . .

[*He sees* CHRISTY. *Goes and shakes him drunkenly by the hand, while* PEGEEN *and* SHAWN *talk on the left.*]

MICHAEL [*To* CHRISTY.] The blessing of God and the holy angels on your head, young fellow. I hear tell you're after winning all in the sports below; and wasn't it a shame I didn't bear you along with me to Kate Cassidy's wake, a fine, stout lad, the like of you, for you'd never see the match of it for flows of drink, the way when we sunk her bones at noonday in her narrow grave, there were five men, aye, and six men, stretched out retching speechless on the holy stones.

CHRISTY [*Uneasily, watching* PEGEEN.] Is that the truth?

MICHAEL It is then, and aren't you a louty schemer to go burying your poor father unbeknownst when you'd a right to throw him on the crupper of a Kerry mule and drive him westwards, like holy Joseph in the days gone by, the way we could have given him a decent burial, and not have him rotting beyond, and not a Christian drinking a smart drop to the glory of his soul?

CHRISTY [*Gruffly.*] It's well enough he's lying, for the likes of him.

MICHAEL [*Slapping him on the back.*] Well, aren't you a hardened slayer? It'll be a poor thing for the household man where you go sniffing for a female wife; and [*Pointing to* SHAWN.] look beyond at that shy and decent

Christian I have chosen for my daughter's hand, and I after getting the gilded dispensation this day for to wed them now.

CHRISTY And you'll be wedding them this day, is it?

MICHAEL [*Drawing himself up.*] Aye, Are you thinking, if I'm drunk itself, I'd leave my daughter living single with a little frisky rascal is the like of you?

PEGEEN [*Breaking away from* SHAWN.] Is it the truth the dispensation's come?

MICHAEL [*Triumphantly.*] Father Reilly's after reading it in gallous[5] Latin, and "It's come in the nick of time," says he; "so I'll wed them in a hurry, dreading that young gaffer who'd capsize the stars."

PEGEEN [*Fiercely.*] He's missed his nick of time, for it's that lad, Christy Mahon, that I'm wedding now.

MICHAEL [*Loudly with horror.*] You'd be making him a son to me, and he wet and crusted with his father's blood?

PEGEEN Aye. Wouldn't it be a bitter thing for a girl to go marrying the like of Shaneen, and he a middling kind of a scarecrow, with no savagery or fine words in him at all?

MICHAEL [*Gasping and sinking on a chair.*] Oh, aren't you a heathen daughter to go shaking the fat of my heart, and I swamped and drownded with the weight of drink? Would you have them turning on me the way that I'd be roaring to the dawn of day with the wind upon my heart? Have you not a word to aid me, Shaneen? Are you not jealous at all?

SHAWN [*In great misery.*] I'd be afeard to be jealous of a man did slay his da.

PEGEEN Well, it'd be a poor thing to go marrying your like. I'm seeing there's a world of peril for an orphan girl, and isn't it a great blessing I didn't wed you, before himself came walking from the west or south?

SHAWN It's a queer story you'd go picking a dirty tramp up from the highways of the world.

PEGEEN [*Playfully.*] And you think you're a likely beau to go straying along with, the shiny Sundays of the opening year, when it's sooner on a bullock's liver you'd put a poor girl thinking than on the lily or the rose?

SHAWN And have you no mind of my weight of passion, and the holy dispensation, and the drift of heifers I am giving, and the golden ring?

PEGEEN I'm thinking you're too fine for the like of me, Shawn Keogh of Killakeen, and let you go off till you'd find a radiant lady with droves of bullocks on the plains of Meath, and herself bedizened in the diamond jewelries of Pharaoh's ma. That'd be your match, Shaneen. So God save you now! [*She retreats behind* CHRISTY.]

SHAWN Won't you hear me telling you . . . ?

CHRISTY [*With ferocity.*] Take yourself from this, young fellow, or I'll maybe add a murder to my deeds today.

MICHAEL [*Springing up with a shriek.*] Murder is it? Is it mad yous are? Would you go making murder in this place, and it piled with poteen for our drink tonight? Go on to the foreshore if it's fighting you want, where the rising tide will wash all traces from the memory of man. [*Pushing* SHAWN *toward* CHRISTY.]

SHAWN [*Shaking himself free, and getting behind* MICHAEL.] I'll not fight him, Michael James. I'd liefer live a bachelor, simmering in passions to the end of time, than face a lepping savage the like of him has descended from the Lord knows where. Strike him yourself, Michael James, or you'll lose my drift of heifers and my blue bull from Sneem.

MICHAEL Is it me fight him, when it's father-slaying he's bred to now? [*Pushing* SHAWN.] Go on, you fool, and fight him now.

SHAWN [*Coming forward a little.*] Will I strike him with my hand?

MICHAEL Take the loy is on your western side.

SHAWN I'd be afeard of the gallows if I struck him with that.

CHRISTY [*Taking up the loy.*] Then I'll make you face the gallows or quit off from this.

[SHAWN *flies out of the door.*]

CHRISTY Well, fine weather be after him [*Going to* MICHAEL, *coaxingly.*] and I'm thinking you wouldn't wish to have that quaking blackguard in your house at all. Let you give us your blessing and hear her swear her faith to me, for I'm mounted on the springtide of the stars of luck, the way it'll be good for any to have me in the house.

PEGEEN [*At the other side of* MICHAEL.] Bless us now, for I swear to God I'll wed him, and I'll not renege.

[5] Fine-sounding, over-acted.

MICHAEL [*Standing up in the centre, holding on to both of them.*] It's the will of God, I'm thinking, that all should win an easy or a cruel end, and it's the will of God that all should rear up lengthy families for the nurture of the earth. What's a single man, I ask you, eating a bit in one house and drinking a sup in another, and he with no place of his own, like an old braying jackass strayed upon the rocks? [*To* CHRISTY.] It's many would be in dread to bring your like into their house for to end them, maybe, with a sudden end; but I'm a decent man of Ireland, and I liefer face the grave untimely and I seeing a score of grandsons growing up little gallant swearers by the name of God, than go peopling my bedside with puny weeds the like of what you'd breed, I'm thinking, out of Shaneen Keogh. [*He joins their hands.*] A daring fellow is the jewel of the world, and a man did split his father's middle with a single clout, should have the bravery of ten, so may God and Mary and St. Patrick bless you, and increase you from this mortal day.

CHRISTY AND PEGEEN Amen, O Lord!

[*Hubbub outside.*]

[*Old* MAHON *rushes in, followed by all the crowd, and* WIDOW QUIN. *He makes a rush at* CHRISTY, *knocks him down, and begins to beat him.*]

PEGEEN [*Dragging back his arm.*] Stop that, will you? Who are you at all?

MAHON His father, God forgive me!

PEGEEN [*Drawing back.*] Is it rose from the dead?

MAHON Do you think I look so easy quenched with the tap of a loy? [*Beats* CHRISTY *again.*]

PEGEEN [*Glaring at* CHRISTY.] And it's lies you told, letting on you had him slitted, and you nothing at all.

CHRISTY [*Catching* MAHON's *stick.*] He's not my father. He's a raving maniac would scare the world. [*Pointing to* WIDOW QUIN.] Herself knows it is true.

CROWD You're fooling Pegeen! The Widow Quin seen him this day, and you likely knew! You're a liar!

CHRISTY [*Dumbfounded.*] It's himself was a liar, lying stretched out with an open head on him, letting on he was dead.

MAHON Weren't you off racing the hills before I got my breath with the start I had seeing you turn on me at all?

PEGEEN And to think of the coaxing glory we had given him, and he after doing nothing but hitting a soft blow and chasing northward in a sweat of fear. Quit off from this.

CHRISTY [*Piteously.*] You've seen my doings this day, and let you save me from the old man; for why would you be in such a scorch of haste to spur me to destruction now?

PEGEEN It's there your treachery is spurring me, till I'm hard set to think you're the one I'm after lacing in my heart-strings half-an-hour gone by. [*To* MAHON.] Take him on from this, for I think bad the world should see me raging for a Munster liar, and the fool of men.

MAHON Rise up now to retribution, and come on with me.

CROWD [*Jeeringly.*] There's the playboy! There's the lad thought he'd rule the roost in Mayo. Slate[6] him now, mister.

CHRISTY [*Getting up in shy terror.*] What is it drives you to torment me here, when I'd asked the thunders of the might of God to blast me if I ever did hurt to any saving only that one single blow.

MAHON [*Loudly.*] If you didn't, you're a poor good-for-nothing, and isn't it by the like of you the sins of the whole world are committed?

CHRISTY [*Raising his hands.*] In the name of the Almighty God. . . .

MAHON Leave troubling the Lord God. Would you have him sending down droughts, and fevers, and the old hen and the cholera morbus?

CHRISTY [*To* WIDOW QUIN.] Will you come between us and protect me now?

WIDOW QUIN I've tried a lot, God help me, and my share is done.

CHRISTY [*Looking round in desperation.*] And I must go back into my torment is it, or run off like a vagabond straying through the unions[7] with the dusts of August making mudstains in the gullet of my throat, or the winds of March blowing on me till I'd take an oath I felt them making whistles of my ribs within?

SARA Ask Pegeen to aid you. Her like does often change.

CHRISTY I will not then, for there's torment in the splendour of her like, and she a girl any moon of midnight would take pride to meet,

[6] Let him have it; give him a good scolding.

[7] Wandering from one parish workhouse to another.

facing southwards on the heaths of Keel. But what did I want crawling forward to scorch my understanding at her flaming brow?

PEGEEN [*To* MAHON, *vehemently, fearing she will break into tears.*] Take him on from this or I'll set the young lads to destroy him here.

MAHON [*Going to him, shaking his stick.*] Come on now if you wouldn't have the company to see you skelped.

PEGEEN [*Half laughing, through her tears.*] That's it, now the world will see him pandied,[8] and he an ugly liar was playing off the hero, and the fright of men.

CHRISTY [*To* MAHON, *very sharply.*] Leave me go!

CROWD That's it. Now, Christy. If them two set fighting, it will lick the world.

MAHON [*Making a grab at* CHRISTY.] Come here to me.

CHRISTY [*More threateningly.*] Leave me go, I'm saying.

MAHON I will maybe, when your legs is limping, and your back is blue.

CROWD Keep it up, the two of you. I'll back the old one. Now the playboy.

CHRISTY [*In low and intense voice.*] Shut your yelling, for if you're after making a mighty man of me this day by the power of a lie, you're setting me now to think if it's a poor thing to be lonesome, it's worse maybe to go mixing with the fools of earth.

[MAHON *makes a movement toward him.*]

CHRISTY [*Almost shouting.*] Keep off . . . lest I do show a blow unto the lot of you would set the guardian angels winking in the clouds above. [*He swings round with a sudden rapid movement and picks up a loy.*]

CROWD [*Half frightened, half amused.*] He's going mad! Mind yourselves! Run from the idiot!

CHRISTY If I am an idiot, I'm after hearing my voice this day saying words would raise the topknot on a poet in a merchant's town. I've won your racing, your lepping, and . . .

MAHON Shut your gullet and come on with me.

CHRISTY I'm going, but I'll stretch you first.

[*He runs at old* MAHON *with the loy, chases him out of the door, followed by crowd and* WIDOW QUIN. *There is a great noise outside, then a yell, and dead silence for a moment.*

[8] Beaten and exposed.

CHRISTY *comes in, half dazed, and goes to fire.*]

WIDOW QUIN [*Coming in, hurriedly, and going to him.*] They're turning again you. Come on, or you'll be hanged, indeed.

CHRISTY I'm thinking, from this out, Pegeen'll be giving me praises the same as in the hours gone by.

WIDOW QUIN [*Impatiently.*] Come by the back-door. I'd think bad to have you stifled on the gallows tree.

CHRISTY [*Indignantly.*] I will not, then. What good'd be my life-time, if I left Pegeen?

WIDOW QUIN Come on, and you'll be no worse than you were last night; and you with a double murder this time to be telling to the girls.

CHRISTY I'll not leave Pegeen Mike.

WIDOW QUIN [*Impatiently.*] Isn't there the match of her in every parish public, from Binghamstown unto the plain of Meath? Come on, I tell you, and I'll find you finer sweethearts at each waning moon.

CHRISTY It's Pegeen I'm seeking only, and what'd I care if you brought me a drift of chosen females, standing in their shifts itself, maybe, from this place to the Eastern World?

SARA [*Runs in, pulling off one of her petticoats.*] They're going to hang him. [*Holding out petticoat and shawl.*] Fit these upon him, and let him run off to the east.

WIDOW QUIN He's raving now; but we'll fit them on him, and I'll take him, in the ferry, to the Achill boat.

CHRISTY [*Struggling feebly.*] Leave me go, will you? When I'm thinking of my luck today, for she will wed me surely, and I a proven hero in the end of all.

[*They try to fasten petticoat round him.*]

WIDOW QUIN Take his left hand, and we'll pull him now. Come on, young fellow.

CHRISTY [*Suddenly starting up.*] You'll be taking me from her? You're jealous, is it, of her wedding me? Go on from this. [*He snatches up a stool, and threatens them with it.*]

WIDOW QUIN [*Going.*] It's in the mad-house they should put him, not in jail, at all. We'll go by the back-door, to call the doctor, and we'll save him so.

[*She goes out, with* SARA, *through inner room. Men crowd in the doorway.* CHRISTY *sits down again by the fire.*]

MICHAEL [*In a terrified whisper.*] Is the old lad killed surely?

PHILLY I'm after feeling the last gasps quitting his heart.

[*They peer in at* CHRISTY.]

MICHAEL [*With a rope.*] Look at the way he is. Twist a hangman's knot on it, and slip it over his head, while he's not minding at all.

PHILLY Let you take it, Shaneen. You're the soberest of all that's here.

SHAWN Is it me to go near him, and he the wickedest and worst with me? Let you take it, Pegeen Mike.

PEGEEN Come on, so.

[*She goes forward with the others, and they drop the double hitch over his head.*]

CHRISTY What ails you?

SHAWN [*Triumphantly, as they pull the rope tight on his arms.*] Come on to the peelers, till they stretch you now.

CHRISTY Me!

MICHAEL If we took pity on you, the Lord God would, maybe, bring us ruin from the law today, so you'd best come easy, for hanging is an easy and a speedy end.

CHRISTY I'll not stir. [*To* PEGEEN.] And what is it you'll say to me, and I after doing it this time in the face of all?

PEGEEN I'll say, a strange man is a marvel, with his mighty talk; but what's a squabble in your backyard, and the blow of a loy, have taught me that there's a great gap between a gallous story and a dirty deed. [*To* MEN.] Take him on from this, or the lot of us will be likely put on trial for his deed today.

CHRISTY [*With horror in his voice.*] And it's yourself will send me off, to have a horny-fingered hangman hitching his bloody slip-knots at the butt of my ear.

MEN [*Pulling rope.*] Come on, will you?

[*He is pulled down on the floor.*]

CHRISTY [*Twisting his legs round the table.*] Cut the rope, Pegeen, and I'll quit the lot of you, and live from this out, like the madmen of Keel, eating muck and green weeds, on the faces of the cliffs.

PEGEEN And leave us to hang, is it, for a saucy liar, the like of you? [*To* MEN.] Take him on, out from this.

SHAWN Pull a twist on his neck, and squeeze him so.

PHILLY Twist yourself. Sure he cannot hurt you, if you keep your distance from his teeth alone.

SHAWN I'm afeard of him. [*To* PEGEEN.] Lift a lighted sod, will you, and scorch his leg.

PEGEEN [*Blowing the fire, with a bellows.*] Leave go now, young fellow, or I'll scorch your shins.

CHRISTY You're blowing for to torture me. [*His voice rising and growing stronger.*] That's your kind, is it? Then let the lot of you be wary, for, if I've to face the gallows, I'll have a gay march down, I tell you, and shed the blood of some of you before I die.

SHAWN [*In terror.*] Keep a good hold, Philly. Be wary, for the love of God. For I'm thinking he would liefest wreak his pains on me.

CHRISTY [*Almost gaily.*] If I do lay my hands on you, it's the way you'll be at the fall of night, hanging as a scarecrow for the fowls of hell. Ah, you'll have a gallous jaunt I'm saying, coaching out through Limbo with my father's ghost.

SHAWN [*To* PEGEEN.] Make haste, will you? Oh, isn't he a holy terror, and isn't it true for Father Reilly, that all drink's a curse that has the lot of you so shaky and uncertain now?

CHRISTY If I can wring a neck among you, I'll have a royal judgment looking on the trembling jury in the courts of law. And won't there be crying out in Mayo the day I'm stretched upon the rope with ladies in their silks and satins snivelling in their lacy kerchiefs, and they rhyming songs and ballads on the terror of my fate? [*He squirms round on the floor and bites* SHAWN's *leg.*]

SHAWN [*Shrieking.*] My leg's bit on me. He's the like of a mad dog, I'm thinking, the way that I will surely die.

CHRISTY [*Delighted with himself.*] You will then, the way you can shake out hell's flags of welcome for my coming in two weeks or three, for I'm thinking Satan hasn't many have killed their da in Kerry, and in Mayo too.

[*Old* MAHON *comes in behind on all fours and looks on unnoticed.*]

MEN [*To* PEGEEN.] Bring the sod, will you?

PEGEEN [*Coming over.*] God help him so. [*Burns his leg.*]

CHRISTY [*Kicking and screaming.*] O, glory be to God!

[*He kicks loose from the table, and they all drag him toward the door.*]

JIMMY [*Seeing old* MAHON.] Will you look what's come in?

[*They all drop* CHRISTY *and run left.*]

CHRISTY [*Scrambling on his knees face to face with old* MAHON.] Are you coming to be killed a third time, or what ails you now?

MAHON For what is it they have you tied?

CHRISTY They're taking me to the peelers to have me hanged for slaying you.

MICHAEL [*Apologetically.*] It is the will of God that all should guard their little cabins from the treachery of law, and what would my daughter be doing if I was ruined or was hanged itself?

MAHON [*Grimly, loosening* CHRISTY.] It's little I care if you put a bag on her back, and went picking cockles till the hour of death; but my son and myself will be going our own way, and we'll have great times from this out telling stories of the villainy of Mayo, and the fools is here. [*To* CHRISTY, *who is freed.*] Come on now.

CHRISTY Go with you, is it? I will then, like a gallant captain with his heathen slave. Go on now and I'll see you from this day stewing my oatmeal and washing my spuds, for I'm master of all fights from now. [*Pushing* MAHON.] Go on, I'm saying.

MAHON Is it me?

CHRISTY Not a word out of you. Go on from this.

MAHON [*Walking out and looking back at* CHRISTY *over his shoulder.*] Glory be to God! [*With a broad smile.*] I am crazy again! [*Goes.*]

CHRISTY Ten thousand blessings upon all that's here, for you've turned me a likely gaffer in the end of all, the way I'll go romancing through a romping lifetime from this hour to the dawning of the judgment day. [*He goes out.*]

MICHAEL By the will of God, we'll have peace now for our drinks. Will you draw the porter, Pegeen?

SHAWN [*Going up to her.*] It's a miracle Father Reilly can wed us in the end of all, and we'll have none to trouble us when his vicious bite is healed.

PEGEEN [*Hitting him a box on the ear.*] Quit my sight. [*Putting her shawl over her head and breaking out into wild lamentations.*] Oh, my grief, I've lost him surely. I've lost the only Playboy of the Western World.

[*Curtain.*]

Comments and Questions

Synge's play presents a view of Ireland, a close look at a paradoxical people whose everyday speech has the lilt of poetry and whose everyday actions show a fondness for violence. The playwright in his Preface emphasizes the importance of "striking and beautiful phrases" but does not try to explain the hero-worship accorded a supposed murderer.

1. "All art is a collaboration," Synge observes. What does he mean? He goes on to speculate that in Elizabethan times a dramatist could draw on the speech of the common people for his effective lines. Does *Hamlet* (p. 428) contain such lines? Consider Act V, Scene i.

2. Synge disapproves of Ibsen who, he says, deals "with the reality of life in joyless and pallid words." Does the dialogue in *Ghosts* (p. 502) bear out this criticism? Is there a possible contradiction in the Irish dramatist's dictum that "on the stage one must have reality and one must have joy"? Discuss.

3. Pegeen rejects her suitor, Shawn, because he has "no savagery or fine words in him at all." Are these two elements basic to male appeal? Or is Pegeen expressing only a personal bias?

4. "The playboy of the western world"—what does this expansive epithet denote and connote? Recall where the play takes place. The play is filled with hyperboles. Cite some examples.

5. Christy's character changes once, again, and still one more time. Do we see him as he really is at the end of the play? Have events modified him in a significant way? Discuss.

6. *The Playboy of the Western World* had its first performance in Dublin on January 26, 1907. All went well for two acts, then suddenly the audience began to hiss, yell, and

catcall. Bedlam continued until the curtain was drawn, ending the play before it was over. The reason for the outburst? A line spoken by Christy: "a drift of chosen females, standing in their shifts itself." That line was a shocker in 1907 Ireland. Comment.

FRIEDRICH DUERRENMATT
1921–

The Visit

(Adapted by Maurice Valency)

CHARACTERS (*In order of appearance*)

HOFBAUER, *first man*
HELMESBERGER, *second man*
WECHSLER, *third man*
VOGEL, *fourth man*
PAINTER
STATION MASTER
BURGOMASTER
TEACHER
PASTOR
ANTON SCHILL
CLAIRE ZACHANASSIAN
CONDUCTOR
PEDRO CABRAL
BOBBY
POLICEMAN
FIRST GRANDCHILD
SECOND GRANDCHILD
MIKE
MAX
FIRST BLIND MAN
SECOND BLIND MAN
ATHLETE
FRAU BURGOMASTER
FRAU SCHILL
DAUGHTER
SON
DOCTOR NÜSSLIN
FRAU BLOCK, *first woman*
TRUCK DRIVER
REPORTER
TOWNSMAN

The action of the play takes place in and around the little town of Güllen, somewhere in Europe.

There are three acts.

ACT I

A railway-crossing bell starts ringing. Then is heard the distant sound of a locomotive whistle. The curtain rises.

The scene represents, in the simplest possible manner, a little town somewhere in Central Europe. The time is the present. The town is shabby and ruined, as if the plague had passed there. Its name, Güllen, is inscribed on the shabby signboard which adorns the façade of the railway station. This edifice is summarily indicated by a length of rusty iron paling, a platform parallel to the proscenium, beyond which one imagines the rails to be, and a baggage truck standing by a wall on which a torn timetable, marked "Fahrplan," *is affixed by three nails. In the station wall is a door with a sign:* "Eintritt Verboten."[1] *This leads to the* STATION MASTER'S *office.*

Left of the station is a little house of gray stucco, formerly whitewashed. It has a tile roof, badly in need of repair. Some shreds of travel posters still adhere to the windowless walls. A shingle hanging over the entrance, left, reads: "Männer."[2] *On the other side of the shingle reads:* "Damen."[3] *Along the wall of the little house there is a wooden bench, backless, on which four men are lounging cheerlessly, shabbily dressed, with cracked shoes. A fifth man is busied with paintpot and brush. He is kneeling on the ground, painting a strip of canvas with the words:* "Welcome, Clara."

The warning signal rings uninterruptedly. The sound of the approaching train comes closer and closer. The STATION MASTER *issues from his office, advances to the center of the platform and salutes.*

The train is heard thundering past in a direction parallel to the footlights, and is lost in the

[1] No Entrance. [2] Men. [3] Ladies.

distance. The men on the bench follow its passing with a slow movement of their heads, from left to right.

FIRST MAN The "Emperor." Hamburg-Naples.

SECOND MAN Then comes the "Diplomat."

THIRD MAN Then the "Banker."

FOURTH MAN And at eleven twenty-seven the "Flying Dutchman." Venice-Stockholm.

FIRST MAN Our only pleasure—watching trains.

[*The station bell rings again. The* STATION MASTER *comes out of his office and salutes another train. The men follow its course, right to left.*]

FOURTH MAN Once upon a time the "Emperor" and the "Flying Dutchman" used to stop here in Güllen. So did the "Diplomat," the "Banker," and the "Silver Comet."

SECOND MAN Now it's only the local from Kaffigen and the twelve-forty from Kalberstadt.

THIRD MAN The fact is, we're ruined.

FIRST MAN What with the Wagonworks shut down . . .

SECOND MAN The Foundry finished . . .

FOURTH MAN The Golden Eagle Pencil Factory all washed up . . .

FIRST MAN It's life on the dole.

SECOND MAN Did you say life?

THIRD MAN We're rotting.

FIRST MAN Starving.

SECOND MAN Crumbling.

FOURTH MAN The whole damn town.

[*The station bell rings.*]

THIRD MAN Once we were a center of industry.

PAINTER A cradle of culture.

FOURTH MAN One of the best little towns in the country.

FIRST MAN In the world.

SECOND MAN Here Goethe slept.

FOURTH MAN Brahms composed a quartet.

THIRD MAN Here Berthold Schwarz invented gunpowder.[4]

PAINTER And I once got first prize at the Dresden Exhibition of Contemporary Art. What am I doing now? Painting signs.

[*The station bell rings. The* STATION MASTER *comes out. He throws away a cigarette butt. The men scramble for it.*]

FIRST MAN Well, anyway, Madame Zachanassian will help us.

FOURTH MAN If she comes . . .

THIRD MAN If she comes.

SECOND MAN Last week she was in France. She gave them a hospital.

FIRST MAN In Rome she founded a free public nursery.

THIRD MAN In Leuthenaw, a bird sanctuary.

PAINTER They say she got Picasso to design her car.

FIRST MAN Where does she get all that money?

SECOND MAN An oil company, a shipping line, three banks and five railways—

FOURTH MAN And the biggest string of geisha houses in Japan.

[*From the direction of the town come the* BURGOMASTER, *the* PASTOR, *the* TEACHER *and* ANTON SCHILL. *The* BURGOMASTER, *the* TEACHER *and* SCHILL *are men in their fifties. The* PASTOR *is ten years younger. All four are dressed shabbily and are sad-looking. The* BURGOMASTER *looks official.* SCHILL *is tall and handsome, but graying and worn; nevertheless a man of considerable charm and presence. He walks directly to the little house and disappears into it.*]

PAINTER Any news, Burgomaster? Is she coming?

ALL Yes, is she coming?

BURGOMASTER She's coming. The telegram has been confirmed. Our distinguished guest will arrive on the twelve-forty from Kalberstadt. Everyone must be ready.

TEACHER The mixed choir is ready. So is the children's chorus.

BURGOMASTER And the church bell, Pastor?

PASTOR The church bell will ring. As soon as the new bell ropes are fitted. The man is working on them now.

BURGOMASTER The town band will be drawn up in the market place and the Athletic Association will form a human pyramid in her honor—the top man will hold the wreath with her initials. Then lunch at the Golden Apostle. I shall say a few words.

TEACHER Of course.

BURGOMASTER I had thought of illuminating the town hall and the cathedral, but we can't afford the lamps.

PAINTER Burgomaster—what do you think of this?

[*He shows the banner.*]

[4] Berthold Schwarz was a German monk who lived in the fourteenth century. The invention of gunpowder has been attributed to him and to many others.

BURGOMASTER [*Calls.*] Schill! Schill!

TEACHER Schill!

[SCHILL *comes out of the little house.*]

SCHILL Yes, right away. Right away.

BURGOMASTER This is more in your line. What do you think of this?

SCHILL [Looks at the sign.] No, no, no. That certainly won't do, Burgomaster. It's much too intimate. It shouldn't read: "Welcome, Clara." It should read: "Welcome Madame . . ."

TEACHER Zachanassian.

BURGOMASTER Zachanassian.

SCHILL Zachanassian.

PAINTER But she's Clara to us.

FIRST MAN Clara Wäscher.

SECOND MAN Born here.

THIRD MAN Her father was a carpenter. He built this.

[*All turn and stare at the little house.*]

SCHILL All the same . . .

PAINTER If I . . .

BURGOMASTER No, no, no. He's right. You'll have to change it.

PAINTER Oh, well, I'll tell you what I'll do. I'll leave this and I'll put "Welcome, Madame Zachanassian" on the other side. Then if things go well, we can always turn it around.

BURGOMASTER Good idea. [*To* SCHILL.] Yes?

SCHILL Well, anyway, it's safer. Everything depends on the first impression.

[*The train bell is heard. Two clangs. The* PAINTER *turns the banner over and goes to work.*]

FIRST MAN Hear that? The "Flying Dutchman" has just passed through Leuthenau.

FOURTH MAN Eleven twenty.

BURGOMASTER Gentlemen, you know that the millionairess is our only hope.

PASTOR Under God.

BURGOMASTER Under God. Naturally. Schill, we depend entirely on you.

SCHILL Yes, I know. You keep telling me.

BURGOMASTER After all, you're the only one who really knew her.

SCHILL Yes, I knew her.

PASTOR You were really quite close to one another, I hear, in those days.

SCHILL Close? Yes, we were close, there's no denying it. We were in love. I was young—good-looking, so they said—and Clara—you know, I can still see her in the great barn coming toward me—like a light out of the darkness. And in the Konradsweil Forest she'd come running to meet me—barefooted—her beautiful red hair streaming behind her. Like a witch. I was in love with her, all right. But you know how it is when you're twenty.

PASTOR What happened?

SCHILL [*Shrugs.*] Life came between us.

BURGOMASTER You must give me some points about her for my speech.

[*He takes out his notebook.*]

SCHILL I think I can help you there.

TEACHER Well, I've gone through the school records. And the young lady's marks were, I'm afraid to say, absolutely dreadful. Even in deportment. The only subject in which she was even remotely passable was natural history.

BURGOMASTER Good in natural history. That's fine. Give me a pencil.

[*He makes a note.*]

SCHILL She was an outdoor girl. Wild. Once, I remember, they arrested a tramp, and she threw stones at the policeman. She hated injustice passionately.

BURGOMASTER Strong sense of justice. Excellent.

SCHILL And generous . . .

ALL Generous?

SCHILL Generous to a fault. Whatever little she had, she shared—so good-heartedly. I remember once she stole a bag of potatoes to give to a poor widow.

BURGOMASTER [*Writing in notebook.*] Wonderful generosity—

TEACHER Generosity.

BURGOMASTER That, gentlemen, is something I must not fail to make a point of.

SCHILL And such a sense of humor. I remember once when the oldest man in town fell and broke his leg, she said, "Oh, dear, now they'll have to shoot him."

BURGOMASTER Well, I've got enough. The rest, my friend, is up to you.

[*He puts the notebook away.*]

SCHILL Yes, I know, but it's not so easy. After all, to part a woman like that from her millions—

BURGOMASTER Exactly. Millions. We have to think in big terms here.

TEACHER If she's thinking of buying us off with a nursery school—

ALL Nursery school!

PASTOR Don't accept.

TEACHER Hold out.

SCHILL I'm not so sure that I can do it. You know, she may have forgotten me completely.

BURGOMASTER [*He exchanges a look with the* TEACHER *and the* PASTOR.] Schill, for many years you have been our most popular citizen. The most respected and the best loved.

SCHILL Why, thank you . . .

BURGOMASTER And therefore I must tell you—last week I sounded out the political opposition, and they agreed. In the spring you will be elected to succeed me as Burgomaster. By unanimous vote.

[*The others clap their hands in approval.*]

SCHILL But, my dear Burgomaster—!

BURGOMASTER It's true.

TEACHER I'm a witness. I was at the meeting.

SCHILL This is—naturally, I'm terribly flattered—It's a completely unexpected honor.

BURGOMASTER You deserve it.

SCHILL Burgomaster! Well, well—! [*Briskly.*] Gentlemen, to business. The first chance I get, of course, I shall discuss our miserable position with Clara.

TEACHER But tactfully, tactfully—

SCHILL What do you take me for? We must feel our way. Everything must be correct. Psychologically correct. For example, here at the railway station, a single blunder, one false note, could be disastrous.

BURGOMASTER He's absolutely right. The first impression colors all the rest. Madame Zachanassian sets foot on her native soil for the first time in many years. She sees our love and she sees our misery. She remembers her youth, her friends. The tears well up into her eyes. Her childhood companions throng about her. I will naturally not present myself like this, but in my black coat with my top hat. Next to me, my wife. Before me, my two grandchildren all in white, with roses. My God, if it only comes off as I see it! If only it comes off. [*The station bell begins ringing.*] Oh, my God! Quick! We must get dressed.

FIRST MAN It's not her train. It's only the "Flying Dutchman."

PASTOR [*Calmly.*] We have still two hours before she arrives.

SCHILL For God's sake, don't let's lose our heads. We still have a full two hours.

BURGOMASTER Who's losing their heads? [*To* FIRST *and* SECOND MAN.] When her train comes, you two, Helmesberger and Vogel, will hold up the banner with "Welcome Madame Zachanassian." The rest will applaud.

THIRD MAN Bravo!

[*He applauds.*]

BURGOMASTER But, please, one thing—no wild cheering like last year with the government relief committee. It made no impression at all and we still haven't received any loan. What we need is a feeling of genuine sincerity. That's how we greet with full hearts our beloved sister who has been away from us so long. Be sincerely moved, my friends, that's the secret; be sincere. Remember you're not dealing with a child. Next a few brief words from me. Then the church bell will start pealing—

PASTOR If he can fix the ropes in time.

[*The station bell rings.*]

BURGOMASTER —Then the mixed choir moves in. And then—

TEACHER We'll form a line down here.

BURGOMASTER Then the rest of us will form in two lines leading from the station—

[*He is interrupted by the thunder of the approaching train. The men crane their heads to see it pass. The* STATION MASTER *advances to the platform and salutes. There is a sudden shriek of air brakes. The train screams to a stop. The four men jump up in consternation.*]

PAINTER But the "Flying Dutchman" never stops!

FIRST MAN It's stopping.

SECOND MAN In Güllen!

THIRD MAN In the poorest—

FIRST MAN The dreariest—

SECOND MAN The lousiest—

FOURTH MAN The most God-forsaken hole between Venice and Stockholm.

STATION MASTER It cannot stop!

[*The train noises stop. There is only the panting of the engine.*]

PAINTER It's stopped!

[*The* STATION MASTER *runs out.*]

OFFSTAGE VOICES What's happened? Is there an accident?

[*A hubbub of offstage voices, as if the passengers on the invisible train were alighting.*]

CLAIRE [*Offstage.*] Is this Güllen?

CONDUCTOR [*Offstage.*] Here, here, what's going on?

CLAIRE [*Offstage.*] Who the hell are you?

CONDUCTOR [*Offstage.*] But you pulled the emergency cord, madame!

CLAIRE [*Offstage.*] I always pull the emergency cord.

STATION MASTER [*Offstage.*] I must ask you what's going on here.

CLAIRE [*Offstage.*] And who the hell are you?

STATION MASTER [*Offstage.*] I'm the Station Master, madame, and I must ask you—

CLAIRE [*Enters.*] No!

[*From the right* CLAIRE ZACHANASSIAN *appears. She is an extraordinary woman. She is in her fifties, red-haired, remarkably dressed, with a face as impassive as that of an ancient idol, beautiful still, and with a singular grace of movement and manner. She is simple and unaffected, yet she has the haughtiness of a world power. The entire effect is striking to the point of the unbelievable. Behind her comes her fiancé,* PEDRO CABRAL, *tall, young, very handsome, and completely equipped for fishing, with creel and net, and with a rod case in his hand. An excited* CONDUCTOR *follows.*]

CONDUCTOR But, madame, I must insist! You have stopped the "Flying Dutchman." I must have an explanation.

CLAIRE Nonsense. Pedro.

PEDRO Yes, my love?

CLAIRE This is Güllen. Nothing has changed. I recognize it all. There's the forest of Konradsweil. There's a brook in it full of trout, where you can fish. And there's the roof of the great barn. Ha! God! What a miserable blot on the map.

[*She crosses the stage and goes off with* PEDRO.]

SCHILL My God! Clara!

TEACHER Claire Zachanassian!

ALL Claire Zachanassian!

BURGOMASTER And the town band? The town band! Where is it?

TEACHER The mixed choir! The mixed choir!

PASTOR The church bell! The church bell!

BURGOMASTER [*To the* FIRST MAN.] Quick! My dress coat. My top hat. My grandchildren. Run! Run! [FIRST MAN *runs off. The* BURGOMASTER *shouts after him.*] And don't forget my wife!

[*General panic. The* THIRD MAN *and* FOURTH MAN *hold up the banner, on which only part of the name has been painted: "Welcome Mad—"* CLAIRE *and* PEDRO *reenter, right.*]

CONDUCTOR [*Mastering himself with an effort.*] Madame. The train is waiting. The entire international railway schedule has been disrupted. I await your explanation.

CLAIRE You're a very foolish man. I wish to visit this town. Did you expect me to jump off a moving train?

CONDUCTOR [*Stupefied.*] You stopped the "Flying Dutchman" because you wished to visit the town?

CLAIRE Naturally.

CONDUCTOR [*Inarticulate.*] Madame!

STATION MASTER Madame, if you wished to visit the town, the twelve forty from Kalberstadt was entirely at your service. Arrival in Güllen, one seventeen.

CLAIRE The local that stops at Loken, Beisenbach, and Leuthenau? Do you expect me to waste three-quarters of an hour chugging dismally through this wilderness?

CONDUCTOR Madame, you shall pay for this!

CLAIRE Bobby, give him a thousand marks.

[BOBBY, *her butler, a man in his seventies, wearing dark glasses, opens his wallet. The townspeople gasp.*]

CONDUCTOR [*Taking the money in amazement.*] But, madame!

CLAIRE And three thousand for the Railway Widows' Relief Fund.

CONDUCTOR [*With the money in his hands.*] But we have no such fund, madame.

CLAIRE Now you have.

[*The* BURGOMASTER *pushes his way forward.*]

BURGOMASTER [*He whispers to the* CONDUCTOR *and* TEACHER.] The lady is Madame Claire Zachanassian!

CONDUCTOR Claire Zachanassian? Oh, my God! But that's naturally quite different. Needless to say, we would have stopped the train if we'd had the slightest idea. [*He hands the money back to* BOBBY.] Here, please. I couldn't dream of it. Four thousand. My God!

CLAIRE Keep it. Don't fuss.

CONDUCTOR Would you like the train to wait, madame, while you visit the town? The administration will be delighted. The cathedral porch. The town hall—

CLAIRE You may take the train away. I don't need it any more.

STATION MASTER All aboard!

[*He puts his whistle to his lips.* PEDRO *stops him.*]

PEDRO But the press, my angel. They don't

know anything about this. They're still in the dining car.

CLAIRE Let them stay there. I don't want the press in Güllen at the moment. Later they will come by themselves. [*To* STATION MASTER.] And now what are you waiting for?

STATION MASTER All aboard!

[*The* STATION MASTER *blows a long blast on his whistle. The train leaves. Meanwhile, the* FIRST MAN *has brought the* BURGOMASTER'S *dress coat and top hat. The* BURGOMASTER *puts on the coat, then advances slowly and solemnly.*]

CONDUCTOR I trust madame will not speak of this to the administration. It was a pure misunderstanding.

[*He salutes and runs for the train as it starts moving.*]

BURGOMASTER [*Bows.*] Gracious lady, as Burgomaster of the town of Güllen, I have the honor—

[*The rest of the speech is lost in the roar of the departing train. He continues speaking and gesturing, and at last bows amid applause as the train noises end.*]

CLAIRE Thank you, Mr. Burgomaster.

[*She glances at the beaming faces, and lastly at* SCHILL, *whom she does not recognize. She turns upstage.*]

SCHILL Clara!

CLAIRE [*Turns and stares.*] Anton?

SCHILL Yes. It's good that you've come back.

CLAIRE Yes. I've waited for this moment. All my life. Ever since I left Güllen.

SCHILL [*A little embarrassed.*] That is very kind of you to say, Clara.

CLAIRE And have you thought about me?

SCHILL Naturally. Always. You know that.

CLAIRE Those were happy times we spent together.

SCHILL Unforgettable.

[*He smiles reassuringly at the* BURGOMASTER.]

CLAIRE Call me by the name you used to call me.

SCHILL [*Whispers.*] My kitten.

CLAIRE What?

SCHILL [*Louder.*] My kitten.

CLAIRE And what else?

SCHILL Little witch.

CLAIRE I used to call you my black panther. You're gray now, and soft.

SCHILL But you are still the same, little witch.

CLAIRE I am the same? [*She laughs.*] Oh, no, my black panther, I am not at all the same.

SCHILL [*Gallantly.*] In my eyes you are. I see no difference.

CLAIRE Would you like to meet my fiancé? Pedro Cabral. He owns an enormous plantation in Brazil.

SCHILL A pleasure.

CLAIRE We're to be married soon.

SCHILL Congratulations.

CLAIRE He will be my eighth husband. [PEDRO *stands by himself downstage, right.*] Pedro, come here and show your face. Come along, darling—come here! Don't sulk. Say hello.

PEDRO Hello.

CLAIRE A man of few words! Isn't he charming? A diplomat. He's interested only in fishing. Isn't he handsome, in his Latin way? You'd swear he was a Brazilian. But he's not—he's a Greek. His father was a White Russian. We were betrothed by a Bulgarian priest. We plan to be married in a few days here in the cathedral.

BURGOMASTER Here in the cathedral? What an honor for us!

CLAIRE No. It was my dream, when I was seventeen, to be married in Güllen cathedral. The dreams of youth are sacred, don't you think so, Anton?

SCHILL Yes, of course.

CLAIRE Yes, of course. I think so, too. Now I would like to look at the town. [*The mixed choir arrives, breathless, wearing ordinary clothes with green sashes.*] What's all this? Go away. [*She laughs.*] Ha! Ha! Ha!

TEACHER Dear lady—[*He steps forward, having put on a sash also.*] Dear lady, as Rector of the high school and a devotee of that noble muse, Music, I take pleasure in presenting the Güllen mixed choir.

CLAIRE How do you do?

TEACHER Who will sing for you an ancient folk song of the region, with specially amended words—if you will deign to listen.

CLAIRE Very well. Fire away.

[*The* TEACHER *blows a pitch pipe. The mixed choir begins to sing the ancient folk song with the amended words. Just then the station bell starts ringing. The song is drowned in the roar of the passing express. The* STATION MASTER *salutes. When the train has passed, there is applause.*]

BURGOMASTER The church bell! The church bell! Where's the church bell?

[*The* PASTOR *shrugs helplessly.*]

CLAIRE Thank you, Professor. They sang beautifully. The big little blond bass—no, not that one—the one with the big Adam's apple—was most impressive. [*The* TEACHER *bows. The* POLICEMAN *pushes his way professionally through the mixed choir and comes to attention in front of* CLAIRE ZACHANASSIAN.] Now, who are you?

POLICEMAN [*Clicks heels.*] Police Chief Schultz. At your service.

CLAIRE [*She looks him up and down.*] I have no need of you at the moment. But I think there will be work for you by and by. Tell me, do you know how to close an eye from time to time?

POLICEMAN How else could I get along in my profession?

CLAIRE You might practice closing both.

SCHILL [*Laughs.*] What a sense of humor, eh?

BURGOMASTER [*Puts on the top hat.*] Permit me to present my grandchildren, gracious lady. Hermine and Adolphine. There's only my wife still to come.

[*He wipes the perspiration from his brow, and replaces the hat. The little girls present the roses with elaborate curtsies.*]

CLAIRE Thank you, my dears. Congratulations, Burgomaster. Extraordinary children.

[*She plants the roses in* PEDRO'S *arms. The* BURGOMASTER *secretly passes his top hat to the* PASTOR, *who puts it on.*]

BURGOMASTER Our pastor, madame.

[*The* PASTOR *takes off the hat and bows.*]

CLAIRE Ah. The pastor. How do you do? Do you give consolation to the dying?

PASTOR [*A bit puzzled.*] That is part of my ministry, yes.

CLAIRE And to those who are condemned to death?

PASTOR Capital punishment has been abolished in this country, madame.

CLAIRE I see. Well, it could be restored, I suppose.

[*The* PASTOR *hands back the hat. He shrugs his shoulders in confusion.*]

SCHILL [*Laughs.*] What an original sense of humor!

[*All laugh, a little blankly.*]

CLAIRE Well, I can't sit here all day—I should like to see the town.

[*The* BURGOMASTER *offers his arm.*]

BURGOMASTER May I have the honor, gracious lady?

CLAIRE Thank you, but these legs are not what they were. This one was broken in five places.

SCHILL [*Full of concern.*] My kitten!

CLAIRE When my airplane bumped into a mountain in Afghanistan. All the others were killed. Even the pilot. But as you see, I survived. I don't fly any more.

SCHILL But you're as strong as ever now.

CLAIRE Stronger.

BURGOMASTER Never fear, gracious lady. The town doctor has a car.

CLAIRE I never ride in motors.

BURGOMASTER You never ride in motors?

CLAIRE Not since my Ferrari crashed in Hong Kong.

SCHILL But how do you travel, then, little witch? On a broom?

CLAIRE Mike—Max! [*She claps her hands. Two huge bodyguards come in, left, carrying a sedan chair. She sits in it.*] I travel this way—a bit antiquated, of course. But perfectly safe. Ha! Ha! Aren't they magnificent? Mike and Max. I bought them in America. They were in jail, condemned to the chair. I had them pardoned. Now they're condemned to my chair. I paid fifty thousand dollars apiece for them. You couldn't get them now for twice the sum. The sedan chair comes from the Louvre. I fancied it so much that the President of France gave it to me. The French are so impulsive, don't you think so, Anton? Go!

[MIKE *and* MAX *start to carry her off.*]

BURGOMASTER You wish to visit the cathedral? And the old town hall?

CLAIRE No. The great barn. And the forest of Konradsweil. I wish to go with Anton and visit our old haunts once again.

THE PASTOR Very touching.

CLAIRE [*To the butler.*] Will you send my luggage and the coffin to the Golden Apostle?

BURGOMASTER The coffin?

CLAIRE Yes. I brought one with me. Go!

TEACHER Hip-hip—

ALL Hurrah! Hip-hip, hurrah! Hurrah!

[*They bear off in the direction of the town. The* TOWNSPEOPLE *burst into cheers. The church bell rings.*]

BURGOMASTER Ah, thank God—the bell at last.

[*The* POLICEMAN *is about to follow the*

others, when the two BLIND MEN *appear. They are not young, yet they seem childish—a strange effect. Though they are of different height and features, they are dressed exactly alike, and so create the effect of being twins. They walk slowly, feeling their way. Their voices, when they speak, are curiously high and flutelike, and they have a curious trick of repetition of phrases.*]

FIRST BLIND MAN We're in—

BOTH BLIND MEN Güllen.

FIRST BLIND MAN We breathe—

SECOND BLIND MAN We breathe—

BOTH BLIND MEN We breathe the air, the air of Güllen.

POLICEMAN [*Startled.*] Who are you?

FIRST BLIND MAN We belong to the lady.

SECOND BLIND MAN We belong to the lady. She calls us—

FIRST BLIND MAN Kobby.

SECOND BLIND MAN And Lobby.

POLICEMAN Madame Zachanassian is staying at the Golden Apostle.

FIRST BLIND MAN We're blind.

SECOND BLIND MAN We're blind.

POLICEMAN Blind? Come along with me, then. I'll take you there.

FIRST BLIND MAN Thank you, Mr. Policeman.

SECOND BLIND MAN Thanks very much.

POLICEMAN Hey! How do you know I'm a policeman, if you're blind?

BOTH BLIND MEN By your voice. By your voice.

FIRST BLIND MAN All policemen sound the same.

POLICEMAN You've had a lot to do with the police, have you, little men?

FIRST BLIND MAN Men he calls us!

BOTH BLIND MEN Men!

POLICEMAN What are you then?

BOTH BLIND MEN You'll see. You'll see.

[*The* POLICEMAN *claps his hands suddenly. The* BLIND MEN *turn sharply toward the sound. The* POLICEMAN *is convinced they are blind.*]

POLICEMAN What's your trade?

BOTH BLIND MEN We have no trade.

SECOND BLIND MAN We play music.

FIRST BLIND MAN We sing.

SECOND BLIND MAN We amuse the lady.

FIRST BLIND MAN We look after the beast.

SECOND BLIND MAN We feed it.

FIRST BLIND MAN We stroke it.

SECOND BLIND MAN We take it for walks.

POLICEMAN What beast?

BOTH BLIND MEN You'll see—you'll see.

SECOND BLIND MAN We give it raw meat.

FIRST BLIND MAN And she gives us chicken and wine.

SECOND BLIND MAN Every day—

BOTH BLIND MEN Every day.

POLICEMAN Rich people have strange tastes.

BOTH BLIND MEN Strange tastes—strange tastes.

[*The* POLICEMAN *puts on his helmet.*]

POLICEMAN Come along, I'll take you to the lady.

[*The two* BLIND MEN *turn and walk off.*]

BOTH BLIND MEN We know the way—we know the way.

[*The station and the little house vanish. A sign representing the Golden Apostle descends. The scene dissolves into the interior of the inn. The Golden Apostle is seen to be in the last stages of decay. The walls are cracked and moldering, and the plaster is falling from the ancient lath. A table represents the café of the inn. The* BURGOMASTER *and the* TEACHER *sit at this table, drinking a glass together. A procession of townspeople, carrying many pieces of luggage, passes. Then comes a coffin, and, last, a large box covered with a canvas. They cross the stage from right to left.*]

BURGOMASTER Trunks. Suitcases. Boxes. [*He looks up apprehensively at the ceiling.*] The floor will never bear the weight. [*As the large covered box is carried in, he peers under the canvas, then draws back.*] Good God!

TEACHER Why, what's in it?

BURGOMASTER A live panther. [*They laugh. The* BURGOMASTER *lifts his glass solemnly.*] Your health, Professor. Let's hope she puts the Foundry back on its feet.

TEACHER [*Lifts his glass.*] And the Wagonworks.

BURGOMASTER And the Golden Eagle Pencil Factory. Once that starts moving, everything else will go. *Prosit.*[5]

[*They touch glasses and drink.*]

TEACHER What does she need a panther for?

BURGOMASTER Don't ask me. The whole thing is too much for me. The Pastor had to go home and lie down.

TEACHER [*Sets down his glass.*] If you want to know the truth, she frightens me.

[5] Your health.

BURGOMASTER [*Nods gravely.*] She's a strange one.

TEACHER You understand, Burgomaster, a man who for twenty-two years has been correcting the Latin compositions of the students of Güllen is not unaccustomed to surprises. I have seen things to make one's hair stand on end. But when this woman suddenly appeared on the platform, a shudder tore through me. It was as though out of the clear sky all at once a fury descended upon us, beating its black wings—

[*The* POLICEMAN *comes in. He mops his face.*]

POLICEMAN Ah! Now the old place is livening up a bit!

BURGOMASTER Ah, Schultz, come and join us.

POLICEMAN Thank you. [*He calls.*] Beer!

BURGOMASTER Well, what's the news from the front?

POLICEMAN I'm just back from Schiller's barn. My God! What a scene! She had us all tiptoeing around in the straw as if we were in church. Nobody dared to speak above a whisper. And the way she carried on! I was so embarrassed I let them go to the forest by themselves.

BURGOMASTER Does the fiancé go with them?

POLICEMAN With his fishing rod and his landing net. In full marching order. [*He calls again.*] Beer!

BURGOMASTER That will be her seventh husband.

TEACHER Her eighth.

BURGOMASTER But what does she expect to find in the Konradsweil forest?

POLICEMAN The same thing she expected to find in the old barn, I suppose. The—the—

TEACHER The ashes of her youthful love.

POLICEMAN Exactly.

TEACHER It's poetry.

POLICEMAN Poetry.

TEACHER Sheer poetry! It makes one think of Shakespeare, of Wagner. Of Romeo and Juliet.

[*The* SECOND MAN *comes in as a waiter. The* POLICEMAN *is served his beer.*]

BURGOMASTER Yes, you're right. [*Solemnly.*] Gentlemen, I would like to propose a toast. To our great and good friend, Anton Schill, who is even now working on our behalf.

POLICEMAN Yes! He's really working.

BURGOMASTER Gentlemen, to the best-loved citizen of this town. My successor, Anton Schill!

[*They raise their glasses. At this point an unearthly scream is heard. It is the black panther howling offstage. The sign of the Golden Apostle rises out of sight. The lights go down. The inn vanishes. Only the wooden bench, on which the four men were lounging in the opening scene, is left on the stage, downstage right. The procession comes on upstage. The two bodyguards carry in* CLAIRE'*s sedan chair. Next to it walks* SCHILL. PEDRO *walks behind, with his fishing rod. Last come the two* BLIND MEN *and the butler.* CLAIRE *alights.*]

CLAIRE Stop! Take my chair off somewhere else. I'm tired of looking at you. [*The bodyguards and the sedan chair go off.*] Pedro darling, your brook is just a little further along down that path. Listen. You can hear it from here. Bobby, take him and show him where it is.

BOTH BLIND MEN We'll show him the way—we'll show him the way.

[*They go off, left.* PEDRO *follows.* BOBBY *walks off, right.*]

CLAIRE Look, Anton. Our tree. There's the heart you carved in the bark long ago.

SCHILL Yes. It's still there.

CLAIRE How it has grown! The trunk is black and wrinkled. Why, its limbs are twice what they were. Some of them have died.

SCHILL It's aged. But it's there.

CLAIRE Like everything else. [*She crosses, examining other trees.*] Oh, how tall they are. How long it is since I walked here, barefoot over the pine needles and the damp leaves! Look, Anton. A fawn.

SCHILL Yes, a fawn. It's the season.

CLAIRE I thought everything would be changed. But it's all just as we left it. This is the seat we sat on years ago. Under these branches you kissed me. And over there under the hawthorn, where the moss is soft and green, we would lie in each other's arms. It is all as it used to be. Only we have changed.

SCHILL Not so much, little witch. I remember the first night we spent together, you ran away and I chased you till I was quite breathless—

CLAIRE Yes.

SCHILL Then I was angry and I was going home, when suddenly I heard you call and I looked up, and there you were sitting in a tree, laughing down at me.

CLAIRE No. It was in the great barn. I was in the hayloft.

SCHILL Were you?

CLAIRE Yes. What else do you remember?

SCHILL I remember the morning we went swimming by the waterfall, and afterwards we were lying together on the big rock in the sun, when suddenly we heard footsteps and we just had time to snatch up our clothes and run behind the bushes when the old pastor appeared and scolded you for not being in school.

CLAIRE No. It was the schoolmaster who found us. It was Sunday and I was supposed to be in church.

SCHILL Really?

CLAIRE Yes. Tell me more.

SCHILL I remember the time your father beat you, and you showed me the cuts on your back, and I swore I'd kill him. And the next day I dropped a tile from a roof top and split his head open.

CLAIRE You missed him.

SCHILL No!

CLAIRE You hit old Mr. Reiner.

SCHILL Did I?

CLAIRE Yes. I was seventeen. And you were not yet twenty. You were so handsome. You were the best-looking boy in town.

[*The two* BLIND MEN *begin playing mandolin music offstage, very softly.*]

SCHILL And you were the prettiest girl.

CLAIRE We were made for each other.

SCHILL So we were.

CLAIRE But you married Mathilde Blumhard and her store, and I married old Zachanassian and his oil wells. He found me in a whorehouse in Hamburg. It was my hair that entangled him, the old golden beetle.

SCHILL Clara!

CLAIRE [*She claps her hands.*] Bobby! A cigar.

[BOBBY *appears with a leather case. He selects a cigar, puts it in a holder, lights it, and presents it to* CLAIRE.]

SCHILL My kitten smokes cigars!

CLAIRE Yes. I adore them. Would you care for one?

SCHILL Yes, please. I've never smoked one of those.

CLAIRE It's a taste I acquired from old Zachanassian. Among other things. He was a real connoisseur.

SCHILL We used to sit on this bench once, you and I, and smoke cigarettes. Do you remember?

CLAIRE Yes. I remember.

SCHILL The cigarettes I bought from Mathilde.

CLAIRE No. She gave them to you for nothing.

SCHILL Clara—don't be angry with me for marrying Mathilde.

CLAIRE She had money.

SCHILL But what a lucky thing for you that I did!

CLAIRE Oh?

SCHILL You were so young, so beautiful. You deserved a far better fate than to settle in this wretched town without any future.

CLAIRE Yes?

SCHILL If you had stayed in Güllen and married me, your life would have been wasted, like mine.

CLAIRE Oh?

SCHILL Look at me. A wretched shopkeeper in a bankrupt town!

CLAIRE But you have your family.

SCHILL My family! Never for a moment do they let me forget my failure, my poverty.

CLAIRE Mathilde has not made you happy?

SCHILL [*Shrugs.*] What does it matter?

CLAIRE And the children?

SCHILL [*Shakes his head.*] They're so completely materialistic. You know, they have no interest whatever in higher things.

CLAIRE How sad for you.

[*A moment's pause, during which only the faint tinkling of the music is heard.*]

SCHILL Yes. You know, since you went away my life has passed by like a stupid dream. I've hardly once been out of this town. A trip to a lake years ago. It rained all the time. And once five days in Berlin. That's all.

CLAIRE The world is much the same everywhere.

SCHILL At least you've seen it.

CLAIRE Yes. I've seen it.

SCHILL You've lived in it.

CLAIRE I've lived in it. The world and I have been on very intimate terms.

SCHILL Now that you've come back, perhaps things will change.

CLAIRE Naturally. I certainly won't leave my native town in this condition.

SCHILL It will take millions to put us on our feet again.

CLAIRE I have millions.

SCHILL One, two, three.

CLAIRE Why not?

SCHILL You mean—you will help us?

CLAIRE Yes.

[*A woodpecker is heard in the distance.*]

SCHILL I knew it—I knew it. I told them you were generous. I told them you were good. Oh, my kitten, my kitten.

[*He takes her hand. She turns her head away and listens.*]

CLAIRE Listen! A woodpecker.

SCHILL It's all just the way it was in the days when we were young and full of courage. The sun high above the pines. White clouds, piling up on one another. And the cry of the cuckoo in the distance. And the wind rustling the leaves, like the sound of surf on a beach. Just as it was years ago. If only we could roll back time and be together always.

CLAIRE Is that your wish?

SCHILL Yes. You left me, but you never left my heart. [*He raises her hand to his lips.*] The same soft little hand.

CLAIRE No, not quite the same. It was crushed in the plane accident. But they mended it. They mend everything nowadays.

SCHILL Crushed? You wouldn't know it. See, another fawn.

CLAIRE The old wood is alive with memories.

[PEDRO *appears, right, with a fish in his hand.*]

PEDRO See what I've caught, darling. See? A pike. Over two kilos.

[*The* BLIND MEN *appear onstage.*]

BOTH BLIND MEN [*Clapping their hands.*] A pike! A pike! Hurrah! Hurrah!

[*As the* BLIND MEN *clap their hands,* CLAIRE *and* SCHILL *exit, and the scene dissolves. The clapping of hands is taken up on all sides. The townspeople wheel in the walls of the café. A brass band strikes up a march tune. The door of the Golden Apostle descends. The townspeople bring in tables and set them with ragged tablecloths, cracked china, and glassware. There is a table in the center, upstage, flanked by two tables perpendicular to it, right and left. The* PASTOR *and the* BURGOMASTER *come in.* SCHILL *enters. Other townspeople filter in, left and right. One, the* ATHLETE, *is in gymnastic costume. The applause continues.*]

BURGOMASTER She's coming! [CLAIRE *enters upstage, center, followed by* BOBBY.] The applause is meant for you, gracious lady.

CLAIRE The band deserves it more than I. They blow from the heart. And the human pyramid was beautiful. You, show me your muscles. [*The* ATHLETE *kneels before her.*] Superb. Wonderful arms, powerful hands. Have you ever strangled a man with them?

ATHLETE Strangled?

CLAIRE Yes. It's perfectly simple. A little pressure in the proper place, and the rest goes by itself. As in politics.

[*The* BURGOMASTER'S *wife comes up, simpering.*]

BURGOMASTER [*Presents her.*] Permit me to present my wife, Madame Zachanassian.

CLAIRE Annette Dummermuth. The head of our class.

BURGOMASTER [*He presents another sour-looking woman.*] Frau Schill.

CLAIRE Mathilde Blumhard. I remember the way you used to follow Anton with your eyes, from behind the shop door. You've grown a little thin and dry, my poor Mathilde.

SCHILL My daughter, Ottilie.

CLAIRE Your daughter . . .

SCHILL My son, Karl.

CLAIRE Your son. Two of them!

[*The town* DOCTOR *comes in, right. He is a man of fifty, strong and stocky, with bristly black hair, a mustache, and a saber cut on his cheek. He is wearing an old cutaway.*]

DOCTOR Well, well, my old Mercedes got me here in time after all!

BURGOMASTER Dr. Nüsslin, the town physician. Madame Zachanassian.

DOCTOR Deeply honored, madame.

[*He kisses her hand.* CLAIRE *studies him.*]

CLAIRE It is you who signs the death certificates?

DOCTOR Death certificates?

CLAIRE When someone dies.

DOCTOR Why certainly. That is one of my duties.

CLAIRE And when the heart dies, what do you put down? Heart failure?

SCHILL [*Laughing.*] What a golden sense of humor!

DOCTOR Bit grim, wouldn't you say?

SCHILL [*Whispers.*] Not at all, not at all. She's promised us a million.

BURGOMASTER [*Turns his head.*] What?

SCHILL A million!

ALL [*Whisper.*] A million!

[CLAIRE *turns toward them.*]

CLAIRE Burgomaster.

BURGOMASTER Yes?

CLAIRE I'm hungry. [*The girls and the waiter fill glasses and bring food. There is a general stir. All take their places at the tables.*] Are you going to make a speech?

[*The* BURGOMASTER *bows,* CLAIRE *sits next to the* BURGOMASTER. *The* BURGOMASTER *rises, tapping his knife on his glass. He is radiant with good will. All applaud.*]

BURGOMASTER Gracious lady and friends. Gracious lady, it is now many years since you first left your native town of Güllen, which was founded by the Elector Hasso and which nestles in the green slope between the forest of Konradsweil and the beautiful valley of Pückenried. Much has taken place in this time, much that is evil.

TEACHER That's true.

BURGOMASTER The world is not what it was; it has become harsh and bitter, and we too have had our share of harshness and bitterness. But in all this time, dear lady, we have never forgotten our little Clara. [*Applause.*] Many years ago you brightened the town with your pretty face as a child, and now once again you brighten it with your presence. [*Polite applause.*] We haven't forgotten you, and we haven't forgotten your family. Your mother, beautiful and robust even in her old age—[*He looks for his notes on the table.*] —although unfortunately taken from us in the bloom of her youth by an infirmity of the lungs. Your respected father, Siegfried Wäscher, the builder, an example whose work next to our railway station is often visited—[SCHILL *covers his face.*]—that is to say, admired—a lasting monument of local design and local workmanship. And you, gracious lady, whom we remember as a golden-haired—[*He looks at her.*]—little red-headed sprite romping about our peaceful streets—on your way to school—which of us does not treasure your memory? [*He pokes nervously at his notebook.*] We will remember your scholarly attainments—

TEACHER Yes.

BURGOMASTER Natural history . . . Extraordinary sense of justice . . . And, above all, your supreme generosity. [*Great applause.*] We shall never forget how you once spent the whole of your little savings to buy a sack of potatoes for a poor starving widow who was in need of food. Gracious lady, ladies and gentlemen, today our little Clara has become the world-famous Claire Zachanassian who has founded hospitals, soup kitchens, charitable institutes, art projects, libraries, nurseries, and schools, and now that she has at last once more returned to the town of her birth, sadly fallen as it is, I say in the name of all her loving friends who have sorely missed her: Long live our Clara!

ALL Long live our Clara!

[*Cheers. Music. Fanfare. Applause.* CLAIRE *rises.*]

CLAIRE Mr. Burgomaster. Fellow townsmen. I am greatly moved by the nature of your welcome and the disinterested joy which you have manifested on the occasion of my visit to my native town. I was not quite the child the Burgomaster described in his gracious address . . .

BURGOMASTER Too modest, madame.

CLAIRE In school I was beaten—

TEACHER Not by me.

CLAIRE And the sack of potatoes which I presented to Widow Boll, I stole with the help of Anton Schill, not to save the old trull from starvation, but so that for once I might sleep with Anton in a real bed instead of under the trees of the forest. [*The townspeople look grave, embarrassed.*] Nevertheless, I shall try to deserve your good opinion. In memory of the seventeen years I spent among you, I am prepared to hand over as a gift to the town of Güllen the sum of one billion marks. Five hundred million to the town, and five hundred million to be divided per capita among the citizens.

[*There is a moment of dead silence.*]

BURGOMASTER A billion marks?

CLAIRE On one condition.

[*Suddenly a movement of uncontrollable joy breaks out. People jump on chairs, dance about, yell excitedly. The* ATHLETE *turns handsprings in front of the speaker's table.*]

SCHILL Oh, Clara, you astonishing, incredible, magnificent woman! What a heart! What a gesture! Oh—my little witch!

[*He kisses her hand.*]

BURGOMASTER [*Holds up his arms for order.*] Quiet! Quiet, please! On one condition, the gracious lady said. Now, madame, may we know what that condition is?

CLAIRE I will tell you. In exchange for my billion marks, I want justice.

[*Silence.*]

BURGOMASTER Justice, madam?

CLAIRE I wish to buy justice.

BURGOMASTER But justice cannot be bought, madame.

CLAIRE Everything can be bought.

BURGOMASTER I don't understand at all.

CLAIRE Bobby, step forward.

[*The butler goes to the center of the stage. He takes off his dark glasses and turns his face with a solemn air.*]

BOBBY Does anyone here present recognize me?

FRAU SCHILL Hofer! Hofer!

ALL Who? What's that?

TEACHER Not Chief Magistrate Hofer?

BOBBY Exactly. Chief Magistrate Hofer. When Madame Zachanassian was a girl, I was presiding judge at the criminal court of Güllen. I served there until twenty-five years ago, when Madame Zachanassian offered me the opportunity of entering her service as butler. I accepted. You may consider it a strange employment for a member of the magistracy, but the salary—

[CLAIRE *bangs the mallet on the table.*]

CLAIRE Come to the point.

BOBBY You have heard Madame Zachanassian's offer. She will give you a billion marks—when you have undone the injustice that she suffered at your hands here in Güllen as a girl.

[*All murmur.*]

BURGOMASTER Injustice at our hands? Impossible!

BOBBY Anton Schill . . .

SCHILL Yes?

BOBBY Kindly stand.

[SCHILL *rises. He smiles, as if puzzled. He shrugs.*]

SCHILL Yes?

BOBBY In those days, a bastardy case was tried before me. Madame Claire Zachanassian, at that time called Clara Wäscher, charged you with being the father of her illegitimate child. [*Silence.*] You denied the charge. And produced two witnesses in your support.

SCHILL That's ancient history. An absurd business. We were children. Who remembers?

CLAIRE Where are the blind men?

BOTH BLIND MEN Here we are. Here we are.

[MIKE *and* MAX *push them forward.*]

BOBBY You recognize these men, Anton Schill?

SCHILL I never saw them before in my life. What are they?

BOTH BLIND MEN We've changed. We've changed.

BOBBY What were your names in your former life?

FIRST BLIND MAN I was Jacob Hueblein. Jacob Hueblein.

SECOND BLIND MAN I was Ludwig Sparr. Ludwig Sparr.

BOBBY [*To* SCHILL.] Well?

SCHILL These names mean nothing to me.

BOBBY Jacob Hueblein and Ludwig Sparr, do you recognize the defendant?

FIRST BLIND MAN We're blind.

SECOND BLIND MAN We're blind.

SCHILL Ha-ha-ha!

BOBBY By his voice?

BOTH BLIND MEN By his voice. By his voice.

BOBBY At that trial, I was the judge. And you?

BOTH BLIND MEN We were the witnesses.

BOBBY And what did you testify on that occasion?

FIRST BLIND MAN That we had slept with Clara Wäscher.

SECOND BLIND MAN Both of us. Many times.

BOBBY And was it true?

FIRST BLIND MAN No.

SECOND BLIND MAN We swore falsely.

FIRST BLIND MAN Anton Schill bribed us.

SECOND BLIND MAN He bribed us.

BOBBY With what?

BOTH BLIND MEN With a bottle of schnapps.

BOBBY And now tell the people what happened to you. [*They hesitate and whimper.*] Speak!

FIRST BLIND MAN [*In a low voice.*] She tracked us down.

BOBBY Madame Zachanassian tracked them down. Jacob Hueblein was found in Canada. Ludwig Sparr in Australia. And when she found you, what did she do to you?

SECOND BLIND MAN She handed us over to Mike and Max.

BOBBY And what did Mike and Max do to you?

FIRST BLIND MAN They made us what you see.

[*The* BLIND MEN *cover their faces.* MIKE *and* MAX *push them off.*]

BOBBY And there you have it. We are all present in Güllen once again. The plaintiff. The defendant. The two false witnesses. The judge. Many years have passed. Does the plaintiff have anything further to add?

CLAIRE There is nothing to add.

BOBBY And the defendant?

SCHILL Why are you doing this? It was all dead and buried.

BOBBY What happened to the child that was born?

CLAIRE [*In a low voice.*] It lived a year.

BOBBY And what happened to you?

CLAIRE I became a whore.

BOBBY Why?

CLAIRE The judgment of the court left me no alternative. No one would trust me. No one would give me work.

BOBBY So. And now, what is the nature of the reparation you demand?

CLAIRE I want the life of Anton Schill.

[FRAU SCHILL *springs to Anton's side. She puts her arms around him. The children rush to him. He breaks away.*]

FRAU SCHILL Anton! No! No!

SCHILL No— No— She's joking. That happened long ago. That's all forgotten.

CLAIRE Nothing is forgotten. Neither the mornings in the forest, nor the nights in the great barn, nor the bedroom in the cottage, nor your treachery at the end. You said this morning that you wished that time might be rolled back. Very well—I have rolled it back. And now it is I who will buy justice. You bought it with a bottle of schnapps. I am willing to pay one billion marks.

[*The* BURGOMASTER *stands up, very pale and dignified.*]

BURGOMASTER Madame Zachanassian, we are not in the jungle. We are in Europe. We may be poor, but we are not heathens. In the name of the town of Güllen, I decline your offer. In the name of humanity. We shall never accept.

[*All applaud wildly. The applause turns into a sinister rhythmic beat. As* CLAIRE *rises, it dies away. She looks at the crowd, then at the* BURGOMASTER.]

CLAIRE Thank you, Burgomaster. [*She stares at him a long moment.*] I can wait.

[*She turns and walks off.*]

[*Curtain.*]

ACT II

The façade of the Golden Apostle, with a balcony on which chairs and a table are set out. To the right of the inn is a sign which reads: "ANTON SCHILL, HANDLUNG."[1] *Under the sign the shop is represented by a broken counter. Behind the counter are some shelves with tobacco, cigarettes, and liquor bottles. There are two milk cans. The shop door is imaginary, but each entrance is indicated by a doorbell with a tinny sound.*

It is early morning.

SCHILL *is sweeping the shop. The son has a pan and brush and also sweeps. The* DAUGHTER *is dusting. They are singing "The Happy Wanderer."*

SCHILL Karl—

[KARL *crosses with a dustpan.* SCHILL *sweeps dust into the pan. The doorbell rings.* THE THIRD MAN *appears, carrying a crate of eggs.*]

THIRD MAN 'Morning.

SCHILL Ah, good morning, Wechsler.

THIRD MAN Twelve dozen eggs, medium brown. Right?

SCHILL Take them, Karl. [*The* SON *puts the crate in a corner.*] Did they deliver the milk yet?

SON Before you came down.

THIRD MAN Eggs are going up again, Herr Schill. First of the month.

[*He gives* SCHILL *a slip to sign.*]

SCHILL What? Again? And who's going to buy them?

THIRD MAN Fifty pfennig a dozen.

SCHILL I'll have to cancel my order, that's all.

THIRD MAN That's up to you, Herr Schill.

[SCHILL *signs the slip.*]

[1] "Anton Schill, Merchandise."

SCHILL There's nothing else to do. [*He hands back the slip.*] And how's the family?

THIRD MAN Oh, scraping along. Maybe now things will get better.

SCHILL Maybe.

THIRD MAN [*Going.*] 'Morning.

SCHILL Close the door. Don't let the flies in. [*The children resume their singing.*] Now, listen to me, children. I have a little piece of good news for you. I didn't mean to speak of it yet awhile, but well, why not? Who do you suppose is going to be the next Burgomaster? Eh? [*They look up at him.*] Yes, in spite of everything. It's settled. It's official. What an honor for the family, eh? Especially at a time like this. To say nothing of the salary and the rest of it.

SON Burgomaster!

SCHILL Burgomaster. [*The* SON *shakes him warmly by the hand. The* DAUGHTER *kisses him.*] You see, you don't have to be entirely ashamed of your father. [*Silence.*] Is your mother coming down to breakfast soon?

DAUGHTER Mother's tired. She's going to stay upstairs.

SCHILL You have a good mother, at least. There you are lucky. Oh, well, if she wants to rest, let her rest. We'll have breakfast together, the three of us. I'll fry some eggs and open a tin of the American ham. This morning we're going to breakfast like kings.

SON I'd like to, only—I can't.

SCHILL You've got to eat, you know.

SON I've got to run down to the station. One of the laborers is sick. They said they could use me.

SCHILL You want to work on the rails in all this heat? That's no work for a son of mine.

SON Look, Father, we can use the money.

SCHILL Well, if you feel you have to.

[*The* SON *goes to the door. The* DAUGHTER *moves toward* SCHILL.]

DAUGHTER I'm sorry, Father. I have to go too.

SCHILL You too? And where is the young lady going, if I may be so bold?

DAUGHTER There may be something for me at the employment agency.

SCHILL Employment agency?

DAUGHTER It's important to get there early.

SCHILL All right. I'll have something nice for you when you get home.

SON *and* DAUGHTER [*Salute.*] Good day, Burgomaster.

[*The* SON *and* DAUGHTER *go out. The* FIRST MAN *comes into* SCHILL'*s shop. Mandolin and guitar music are heard offstage.*]

SCHILL Good morning, Hofbauer.

FIRST MAN Cigarettes. [SCHILL *takes a pack from the shelf.*] Not those. I'll have the green today.

SCHILL They cost more.

FIRST MAN Put it in the book.

SCHILL What?

FIRST MAN Charge it.

SCHILL Well, all right, I'll make an exception this time—seeing it's you, Hofbauer.

[SCHILL *writes in his cash book.*]

FIRST MAN [*Opening the pack of cigarettes.*] Who's that playing out there?

SCHILL The two blind men.

FIRST MAN They play well.

SCHILL To hell with them.

FIRST MAN They make you nervous? [SCHILL *shrugs. The* FIRST MAN *lights a cigarette.*] She's getting ready for the wedding, I hear.

SCHILL Yes. So they say.

[*Enter the* FIRST *and* SECOND WOMAN. *They cross to the counter.*]

FIRST WOMAN Good morning, good morning.

SECOND WOMAN Good morning.

FIRST MAN Good morning.

SCHILL Good morning, ladies.

FIRST WOMAN Good morning, Herr Schill.

SECOND WOMAN Good morning.

FIRST WOMAN Milk please, Herr Schill.

SCHILL Milk.

SECOND WOMAN And milk for me too.

SCHILL A liter of milk each. Right away.

FIRST WOMAN Whole milk, please, Herr Schill.

SCHILL Whole milk?

SECOND WOMAN Yes. Whole milk, please.

SCHILL Whole milk, I can only give you half a liter each of whole milk.

FIRST WOMAN All right.

SCHILL Half a liter of whole milk here, and half a liter of whole milk here. There you are.

FIRST WOMAN And butter please, a quarter kilo.

SCHILL Butter, I haven't any butter. I can give you some very nice lard?

FIRST WOMAN No. Butter.

SCHILL Goose fat? [*The* FIRST WOMAN *shakes her head.*] Chicken fat?

FIRST WOMAN Butter.

SCHILL Butter. Now, wait a minute, though. I have a tin of imported butter here somewhere. Ah. There you are. No, sorry, she asked first, but I can order some for you from Kalkerstadt tomorrow.

SECOND WOMAN And white bread.

SCHILL White bread.

[*He takes a loaf and a knife.*]

SECOND WOMAN The whole loaf.

SCHILL But a whole loaf would cost . . .

SECOND WOMAN Charge it.

SCHILL Charge it?

FIRST WOMAN And a package of milk chocolate.

SCHILL Package of milk chocolate—right away.

SECOND WOMAN One for me, too, Herr Schill.

SCHILL And a package of milk chocolate for you, too.

FIRST WOMAN We'll eat it here, if you don't mind.

SCHILL Yes, please do.

SECOND WOMAN It's so cool at the back of the shop.

SCHILL Charge it?

WOMEN Of course.

SCHILL All for one, one for all.

[*The* SECOND MAN *enters.*]

SECOND MAN Good morning.

THE TWO WOMEN Good morning.

SCHILL Good morning, Helmesberger.

SECOND MAN It's going to be a hot day.

SCHILL Phew!

SECOND MAN How's business?

SCHILL Fabulous. For a while no one came, and now all of a sudden I'm running a luxury trade.

SECOND MAN Good!

SCHILL Oh, I'll never forget the way you all stood by me at the Golden Apostle in spite of your need, in spite of everything. That was the finest hour of my life.

FIRST MAN We're not heathens, you know.

SECOND MAN We're behind you, my boy; the whole town's behind you.

FIRST MAN As firm as a rock.

FIRST WOMAN [*Munching her chocolate.*] As firm as a rock, Herr Schill.

BOTH WOMEN As firm as a rock.

SECOND MAN There's no denying it—you're the most popular man in town.

FIRST MAN The most important.

SECOND MAN And in the spring, God willing, you will be our Burgomaster.

FIRST MAN Sure as a gun.

ALL Sure as a gun.

[*Enter* PEDRO *with fishing equipment and a fish in his landing net.*]

PEDRO Would you please weigh my fish for me?

SCHILL [*Weighs it.*] Two kilos.

PEDRO Is that all?

SCHILL Two kilos exactly.

PEDRO Two kilos!

[*He gives* SCHILL *a tip and exits.*]

SECOND WOMAN The fiancé.

FIRST WOMAN They're to be married this week. It will be a tremendous wedding.

SECOND WOMAN I saw his picture in the paper.

FIRST WOMAN [*Sighs.*] Ah, what a man!

SECOND MAN Give me a bottle of schnapps.

SCHILL The usual?

SECOND MAN No, cognac.

SCHILL Cognac? But cognac costs twenty-two marks fifty.

SECOND MAN We all have to splurge a little now and again—

SCHILL Here you are. Three Star.

SECOND MAN And a package of pipe tobacco.

SCHILL Black or blond?

SECOND MAN English.

SCHILL English! But that makes twenty-three marks eighty.

SECOND MAN Chalk it up.

SCHILL Now, look. I'll make an exception this week. Only, you will have to pay me the moment your unemployment check comes in. I don't want to be kept waiting. [*Suddenly.*] Helmesberger, are those new shoes you're wearing?

SECOND MAN Yes, what about it?

SCHILL You too. Hofbauer. Yellow shoes! Brand new!

FIRST MAN So?

SCHILL [*To the women.*] And you. You all have new shoes! New shoes!

FIRST WOMAN A person can't walk around forever in the same old shoes.

SECOND WOMAN Shoes wear out.

SCHILL And the money. Where does the money come from?

FIRST WOMAN We got them on credit, Herr Schill.

SECOND WOMAN On credit.

SCHILL On credit? And where all of a sudden do you get credit?

SECOND MAN Everybody gives credit now.

FIRST WOMAN You gave us credit yourself.

SCHILL And what are you going to pay with? Eh? [*They are all silent.* SCHILL *advances upon them threateningly.*] With what? Eh? With what? With what?

[*Suddenly he understands. He takes his apron off quickly, flings it on the counter, gets his jacket, and walks off with an air of determination. Now the shop sign vanishes. The shelves are pushed off. The lights go up on the balcony of the Golden Apostle, and the balcony unit itself moves forward into the optical center.* CLAIRE *and* BOBBY *step out on the balcony.* CLAIRE *sits down.* BOBBY *serves coffee.*]

CLAIRE A lovely autumn morning. A silver haze on the streets and a violet sky above. Count Holk would have liked this. Remember him, Bobby? My third husband?

BOBBY Yes, madame.

CLAIRE Horrible man!

BOBBY Yes, madame.

CLAIRE Where is Monsieur Pedro? Is he up yet?

BOBBY Yes, madame. He's fishing.

CLAIRE Already? What a singular passion!

[PEDRO *comes in with the fish.*]

PEDRO Good morning, my love.

CLAIRE Pedro! There you are.

PEDRO Look, my darling. Four kilos!

CLAIRE A jewel! I'll have it grilled for your lunch. Give it to Bobby.

PEDRO Ah—it is so wonderful here! I like your little town.

CLAIRE Oh, do you?

PEDRO Yes. These people, they are all so—what is the word?

CLAIRE Simple, honest, hard-working, decent.

PEDRO But, my angel, you are a mind reader. That's just what I was going to say—however did you guess?

CLAIRE I know them.

PEDRO Yet when we arrived it was all so dirty, so—what is the word?

CLAIRE Shabby.

PEDRO Exactly. But now everywhere you go, you see them busy as bees, cleaning their streets—

CLAIRE Repairing their houses, sweeping—dusting—hanging new curtains in the windows—singing as they work.

PEDRO But you astonishing, wonderful woman! You can't see all that from here.

CLAIRE I know them. And in their gardens—I am sure that in their gardens they are manuring the soil for the spring.

PEDRO My angel, you know everything. This morning on my way fishing I said to myself, look at them all manuring their gardens. It is extraordinary—and it's all because of you. Your return has given them a new—what is the word?

CLAIRE Lease on life?

PEDRO Precisely.

CLAIRE The town was dying, it's true. But a town doesn't have to die. I think they realize that now. People die, not towns. Bobby! [BOBBY *appears.*] A cigar.

[*The lights fade on the balcony, which moves back upstage. Somewhat to the right, a sign descends. It reads:* "Polizei." *The* POLICEMAN *pushes a desk under it. This, with the bench, becomes the police station. He places a bottle of beer and a glass on the desk, and goes to hang up his coat offstage. The telephone rings.*]

POLICEMAN Schultz speaking. Yes, we have a couple of rooms for the night. No, not for rent. This is not the hotel. This is the Güllen police station.

[*He laughs and hangs up.* SCHILL *comes in. He is evidently nervous.*]

SCHILL Schultz.

POLICEMAN Hello, Schill. Come in. Sit down. Beer?

SCHILL Please.

[*He drinks thirstily.*]

POLICEMAN What can I do for you?

SCHILL I want you to arrest Madame Zachanassian.

POLICEMAN Eh?

SCHILL I said I want you to arrest Madame Zachanassian.

POLICEMAN What the hell are you talking about?

SCHILL I ask you to arrest this woman at once.

POLICEMAN What offense has the lady committed?

SCHILL You know perfectly well. She offered a billion marks—

POLICEMAN And you want her arrested for that?

[*He pours beer into his glass.*]

SCHILL Schultz! It's your duty.

POLICEMAN Extraordinary! Extraordinary idea!

[*He drinks his beer.*]

SCHILL I'm speaking to you as your next Burgomaster.

POLICEMAN Schill, that's true. The lady offered us a billion marks. But that doesn't entitle us to take police action against her.

SCHILL Why not?

POLICEMAN In order to be arrested, a person must first commit a crime.

SCHILL Incitement to murder.

POLICEMAN Incitement to murder is a crime. I agree.

SCHILL Well?

POLICEMAN And such a proposal—if serious—constitutes an assault.

SCHILL That's what I mean.

POLICEMAN But her offer can't be serious.

SCHILL Why?

POLICEMAN The price is too high. In a case like yours, one pays a thousand marks, at the most two thousand. But not a billion! That's ridiculous. And even if she meant it, that would only prove she was out of her mind. And that's not a matter for the police.

SCHILL Whether she's out of her mind or not, the danger to me is the same. That's obvious.

POLICEMAN Look, Schill, you show us where anyone threatens your life in any way—say, for instance, a man points a gun at you—and we'll be there in a flash.

SCHILL [*Gets up.*] So I'm to wait till someone points a gun at me?

POLICEMAN Pull yourself together, Schill. We're all for you in this town.

SCHILL I wish I could believe it.

POLICEMAN You don't believe it?

SCHILL No. No, I don't. All of a sudden my customers are buying white bread, whole milk, butter, imported tobacco. What does it mean?

POLICEMAN It means business is picking up.

SCHILL Helmesberger lives on the dole; he hasn't earned anything in five years. Today he bought French cognac.

POLICEMAN I'll have to try your cognac one of these days.

SCHILL And shoes. They all have new shoes.

POLICEMAN And what have you got against new shoes? I'm wearing a new pair myself.

[*He holds out his foot.*]

SCHILL You too?

POLICEMAN Why not?

[*He pours out the rest of his beer.*]

SCHILL Is that Pilsen you're drinking now?

POLICEMAN It's the only thing.

SCHILL You used to drink the local beer.

POLICEMAN Hogwash.

[*Radio music is heard offstage.*]

SCHILL Listen. You hear?

POLICEMAN "The Merry Widow." Yes.

SCHILL No. It's a radio.

POLICEMAN That's Bergholzer's radio.

SCHILL Bergholzer!

POLICEMAN You're right. He should close his window when he plays it. I'll make a note to speak to him.

[*He makes a note in his notebook.*]

SCHILL And how can Bergholzer pay for a radio?

POLICEMAN That's his business.

SCHILL And you, Schultz, with your new shoes and your imported beer—how are you going to pay for them?

POLICEMAN That's my business. [*His telephone rings. He picks it up.*] Police Station, Güllen. What? What? Where? Where? How? Right, we'll deal with it.

[*He hangs up.*]

SCHILL [*He speaks during the* POLICEMAN'S *telephone conversation.*] Schultz, listen. No. Schultz, please—listen to me. Don't you see they're all . . . Listen, please. Look, Schultz. They're all running up debts. And out of these debts comes this sudden prosperity. And out of this prosperity comes the absolute need to kill me.

POLICEMAN [*Putting on his jacket.*] You're imagining things.

SCHILL All she has to do is to sit on her balcony and wait.

POLICEMAN Don't be a child.

SCHILL You're all waiting.

POLICEMAN [*Snaps a loaded clip into the magazine of a rifle.*] Look, Schill, you can relax.

The police are here for your protection. They know their job. Let anyone, any time, make the slightest threat to your life, and all you have to do is let us know. We'll do the rest . . . Now, don't worry.

SCHILL No, I won't.

POLICEMAN And don't upset yourself. All right?

SCHILL Yes. I won't. [*Then suddenly, in a low tone.*] You have a new gold tooth in your mouth!

POLICEMAN What are you talking about?

SCHILL [*Taking the* POLICEMAN's *head in his hands, and forcing his lips open.*] A brand new, shining gold tooth.

POLICEMAN [*Breaks away and involuntarily levels the gun at* SCHILL.] Are you crazy? Look, I've no time to waste. Madame Zachanassian's panther's broken loose.

SCHILL Panther?

POLICEMAN Yes, it's at large. I've got to hunt it down.

SCHILL You're not hunting a panther and you know it. It's me you're hunting!

[*The* POLICEMAN *clicks on the safety and lowers the gun.*]

POLICEMAN Schill! Take my advice. Go home. Lock the door. Keep out of everyone's way. That way you'll be safe. Cheer up! Good times are just around the corner!

[*The lights dim in this area and light up on the balcony.* PEDRO *is lounging in a chair.* CLAIRE *is smoking.*]

PEDRO Oh, this little town oppresses me.

CLAIRE Oh, does it? So you've changed your mind?

PEDRO It is true, I find it charming, delightful—

CLAIRE Picturesque.

PEDRO Yes. After all, it's the place where you were born. But it is too quiet for me. Too provincial. Too much like all small towns everywhere. These people—look at them. They fear nothing, they desire nothing, they strive for nothing. They have everything they want. They are asleep.

CLAIRE Perhaps one day they will come to life again.

PEDRO My God—do I have to wait for that?

CLAIRE Yes, you do. Why don't you go back to your fishing?

PEDRO I think I will.

[PEDRO *turns to go.*]

CLAIRE Pedro.

PEDRO Yes, my love?

CLAIRE Telephone the president of Hambro's Bank.[2] Ask him to transfer a billion marks to my current account.

PEDRO A billion? Yes, my love.

[*He goes. The lights fade on the balcony. A sign is flown in. It reads:* "Rathaus."[3] *The* THIRD MAN *crosses the stage, right to left, wheeling a new television set on a hand truck. The counter of* SCHILL's *shop is transformed into the* BURGOMASTER's *office. The* BURGOMASTER *comes in. He takes a revolver from his pocket, examines it and sets it down on the desk. He sits down and starts writing.* SCHILL *knocks.*]

BURGOMASTER Come in.

SCHILL I must have a word with you, Burgomaster.

BURGOMASTER Ah, Schill. Sit down, my friend.

SCHILL Man to man. As your successor.

BURGOMASTER But of course. Naturally.

[SCHILL *remains standing. He looks at the revolver.*]

SCHILL Is that a gun?

BURGOMASTER Madame Zachanassian's black panther's broken loose. It's been seen near the cathedral. It's as well to be prepared.

SCHILL Oh, yes. Of course.

BURGOMASTER I've sent out a call for all able-bodied men with firearms. The streets have been cleared. The children have been kept in school. We don't want any accidents.

SCHILL [*Suspiciously.*] You're making quite a thing of it.

BURGOMASTER [*Shrugs.*] Naturally. A panther is a dangerous beast. Well? What's on your mind? Speak out. We're old friends.

SCHILL That's a good cigar you're smoking, Burgomaster.

BURGOMASTER Yes. Havana.

SCHILL You used to smoke something else.

BURGOMASTER Fortuna.

SCHILL Cheaper.

BURGOMASTER Too strong.

SCHILL A new tie? Silk?

BURGOMASTER Yes. Do you like it?

SCHILL And have you also bought new shoes?

BURGOMASTER [*Brings his feet out from under the desk.*] Why, yes. I ordered a new pair

[2] One of the principal banks of England. [3] "City Hall."

from Kalberstadt. Extraordinary! However did you guess?

SCHILL That's why I'm here.

[*The* THIRD MAN *knocks.*]

BURGOMASTER Come in.

THIRD MAN The new typewriter, sir.

BURGOMASTER Put it on the table. [*The* THIRD MAN *sets it down and goes.*] What's the matter with you? My dear fellow, aren't you well?

SCHILL It's you who don't seem well, Burgomaster.

BURGOMASTER What do you mean?

SCHILL You look pale.

BURGOMASTER I?

SCHILL Your hands are trembling. [*The* BURGOMASTER *involuntarily hides his hands.*] Are you frightened?

BURGOMASTER What have I to be afraid of?

SCHILL Perhaps this sudden prosperity alarms you.

BURGOMASTER Is prosperity a crime?

SCHILL That depends on how you pay for it.

BURGOMASTER You'll have to forgive me, Schill, but I really haven't the slightest idea what you're talking about. Am I supposed to feel like a criminal every time I order a new typewriter?

SCHILL Do you?

BURGOMASTER Well, I hope you haven't come here to talk about a new typewriter. Now, what was it you wanted?

SCHILL I have come to claim the protection of the authorities.

BURGOMASTER Ei! Against whom?

SCHILL You know against whom.

BURGOMASTER You don't trust us?

SCHILL That woman has put a price on my head.

BURGOMASTER If you don't feel safe, why don't you go to the police?

SCHILL I have just come from the police.

BURGOMASTER And?

SCHILL The chief has a new gold tooth in his mouth.

BURGOMASTER A new—? Oh, Schill, really! You're forgetting. This is Güllen, the town of humane traditions. Goethe slept here. Brahms composed a quartet. You must have faith in us. This is a law-abiding community.

SCHILL Then arrest this woman who wants to have me killed.

BURGOMASTER Look here, Schill. God knows the lady has every right to be angry with you. What you did there wasn't very pretty. You forced two decent lads to perjure themselves and had a young girl thrown out on the streets.

SCHILL That young girl owns half the world.

[*A moment's silence.*]

BURGOMASTER Very well, then, we'll speak frankly.

SCHILL That's why I'm here.

BURGOMASTER Man to man, just as you said. [*He clears his throat.*] Now—after what you did, you have no moral right to say a word against this lady. And I advise you not to try. Also—I regret to have to tell you this—there is no longer any question of your being elected Burgomaster.

SCHILL Is that official?

BURGOMASTER Official.

SCHILL I see.

BURGOMASTER The man who is chosen to exercise the high post of Burgomaster must have, obviously, certain moral qualifications. Qualifications which, unhappily, you no longer possess. Naturally, you may count on the esteem and friendship of the town, just as before. That goes without saying. The best thing will be to spread the mantle of silence over the whole miserable business.

SCHILL So I'm to remain silent while they arrange my murder?

[*The* BURGOMASTER *gets up.*]

BURGOMASTER [*Suddenly noble.*] Now, who is arranging your murder? Give me the names and I will investigate the case at once. Unrelentingly. Well? The names?

SCHILL You.

BURGOMASTER I resent this. Do you think we want to kill you for money?

SCHILL No. You don't want to kill me. But you want to have me killed.

[*The lights go down. The stage is filled with men prowling about with rifles, as if they were stalking a quarry. In the interval the* POLICEMAN'S *bench and the* BURGOMASTER'S *desk are shifted somewhat, so that they will compose the setting for the sacristy. The stage empties. The lights come up on the balcony.* CLAIRE *appears.*]

CLAIRE Bobby, what's going on here? What are all these men doing with guns? Whom are they hunting?

BOBBY The black panther has escaped, madame.

CLAIRE Who let him out?

BOBBY Kobby and Lobby, madame.

CLAIRE How excited they are! There may be shooting?

BOBBY It is possible, madame.

[*The lights fade on the balcony. The sacristan comes in. He arranges the set, and puts the altar cloth on the altar. Then* SCHILL *comes on. He is looking for the* PASTOR. *The* PASTOR *enters, left. He is wearing his gown and carrying a rifle.*]

SCHILL Sorry to disturb you, Pastor.

PASTOR God's house is open to all. [*He sees that* SCHILL *is staring at the gun.*] Oh, the gun? That's because of the panther. It's best to be prepared.

SCHILL Pastor, help me.

PASTOR Of course. Sit down. [*He puts the rifle on the bench.*] What's the trouble?

SCHILL [*Sits on the bench.*] I'm frightened.

PASTOR Frightened? Of what?

SCHILL Of everyone. They're hunting me down like a beast.

PASTOR Have no fear of man, Schill. Fear God. Fear not the death of the body. Fear the death of the soul. Zip up my gown behind, Sacristan.

SCHILL I'm afraid, Pastor.

PASTOR Put your trust in heaven, my friend.

SCHILL You see, I'm not well. I shake. I have such pains around the heart. I sweat.

PASTOR I know. You're passing through a profound psychic experience.

SCHILL I'm going through hell.

PASTOR The hell you are going through exists only within yourself. Many years ago you betrayed a girl shamefully, for money. Now you think that we shall sell you just as you sold her. No, my friend, you are projecting your guilt upon others. It's quite natural. But remember, the root of our torment lies always within ourselves, in our hearts, in our sins. When you have understood this, you can conquer the fears that oppress you; you have weapons with which to destroy them.

SCHILL Siemethofer has bought a new washing machine.

PASTOR Don't worry about the washing machine. Worry about your immortal soul.

SCHILL Stockers has a television set.

PASTOR There is also great comfort in prayer. Sacristan, the bands. [SCHILL *crosses to the altar and kneels. The sacristan ties on the* PASTOR's *bands.*] Examine your conscience, Schill. Repent. Otherwise your fears will consume you. Believe me, this is the only way. We have no other. [*The church bell begins to peal.* SCHILL *seems relieved.*] Now I must leave you. I have a baptism. You may stay as long as you like. Sacristan, the Bible, Liturgy, and Psalter. The child is beginning to cry. I can hear it from here. It is frightened. Let us make haste to give it the only security which this world affords.

SCHILL A new bell?

PASTOR Yes. It's tone is marvelous, don't you think? Full. Sonorous.

SCHILL [*Steps back in horror.*] A new bell! You too, Pastor? You too?

[*The* PASTOR *clasps his hands in horror. Then he takes* SCHILL *into his arms.*]

PASTOR Oh, God, God forgive me. We are poor, weak things, all of us. Do not tempt us further into the hell in which you are burning. Go Schill, my friend, go my brother, go while there is time.

[*The* PASTOR *goes.* SCHILL *picks up the rifle with a gesture of desperation. He goes out with it. As the lights fade, men appear with guns. Two shots are fired in the darkness. The lights come up on the balcony, which moves forward.*]

CLAIRE Bobby! What was that shooting? Have they caught the panther?

BOBBY He is dead, madame.

CLAIRE There were two shots.

BOBBY The panther is dead, madame.

CLAIRE I loved him. [*Waves* BOBBY *away.*] I shall miss him.

[*The* TEACHER *comes in with two little girls, singing. They stop under the balcony.*]

TEACHER Gracious lady, be so good as to accept our heartfelt condolences. Your beautiful panther is no more. Believe me, we are deeply pained that so tragic an event should mar your visit here. But what could we do? The panther was savage, a beast. To him our human laws could not apply. There was no other way—[SCHILL *appears with the gun. He looks dangerous. The girls run off, frightened. The* TEACHER *follows the girls.*] Children—children—children!

CLAIRE Anton, why are you frightening the children?

[*He works the bolt, loading the chamber, and raises the gun slowly.*]

SCHILL Go away, Claire—I warn you. Go away.

CLAIRE How strange it is, Anton! How clearly it comes back to me! The day we saw one another for the first time, do you remember? I was on a balcony then. It was a day like today, a day in autumn without a breath of wind, warm as it is now—only lately I am always cold. You stood down there and stared at me without moving. I was embarrassed. I didn't know what to do. I wanted to go back into the darkness of the room, where it was safe, but I couldn't. You stared up at me darkly, almost angrily, as if you wished to hurt me, but your eyes were full of passion. [SCHILL *begins to lower the rifle involuntarily.*] Then, I don't know why, I left the balcony and I came down and stood in the street beside you. You didn't greet me, you didn't say a word, but you took my hand and we walked together out of the town into the fields, and behind us came Kobby and Lobby, like two dogs, sniveling and giggling and snarling. Suddenly you picked up a stone and hurled it at them, and they ran yelping back into the town, and we were alone. [SCHILL *has lowered the rifle completely. He moves forward toward her, as close as he can come.*] That was the beginning, and everything else had to follow. There is no escape.

[*She goes in and closes the shutters.* SCHILL *stands immobile. The* TEACHER *tiptoes in. He stares at* SCHILL, *who doesn't see him. Then he beckons to the children.*]

TEACHER Come, children, sing. Sing.

[*They begin singing. He creeps behind* SCHILL *and snatches away the rifle.* SCHILL *turns sharply. The* PASTOR *comes in.*]

PASTOR Go, Schill—go!

[SCHILL *goes out. The children continue singing, moving across the stage and off. The Golden Apostle vanishes. The crossing bell is heard. The scene dissolves into the railway-station setting, as in Act One. But there are certain changes. The timetable marked* "Fahrplan" *is now new, the frame freshly painted. There is a new travel poster on the station wall. It has a yellow sun and the words:* "Reist in den Süden."[4] *On the other side of the Fahrplan is another poster with the words:* "Die Passionsspiele Oberammergau."[5] *The sound of passing trains covers the scene change.* SCHILL *appears with an old valise in his hand, dressed in a shabby trench coat, his hat on his head. He looks about with a furtive air, walking slowly to the platform. Slowly, as if by chance, the townspeople enter, from all sides.* SCHILL *hesitates, stops.*]

BURGOMASTER [*From upstage, center.*] Good evening, Schill.

SCHILL Good evening.

POLICEMAN Good evening.

SCHILL Good evening.

PAINTER [*Enters.*] Good evening.

SCHILL Good evening.

DOCTOR Good evening.

SCHILL Good evening.

BURGOMASTER So you're taking a little trip?

SCHILL Yes. A little trip.

POLICEMAN May one ask where to?

SCHILL I don't know.

PAINTER Don't know?

SCHILL To Kalberstadt.

BURGOMASTER [*With disbelief, pointing to the valise.*] Kalberstadt?

SCHILL After that—somewhere else.

PAINTER Ah. After that somewhere else.

[*The* FOURTH MAN *walks in.*]

SCHILL I thought maybe Australia.

BURGOMASTER Australia!

ALL Australia!

SCHILL I'll raise the money somehow.

BURGOMASTER But why Australia?

POLICEMAN What would you be doing in Australia?

SCHILL One can't always live in the same town, year in, year out.

PAINTER But Australia—

DOCTOR It's a risky trip for a man of your age.

BURGOMASTER One of the lady's little men ran off to Australia . . .

ALL Yes.

POLICEMAN You'll be much safer here.

PAINTER Much!

4 "Travel in the South."

5 "The Oberammergau Passion Play," portraying the suffering and death of Jesus, is performed in the south German village every ten years.

[SCHILL *looks about him in anguish, like a beast at bay.*]

SCHILL [*Low voice.*] I wrote a letter to the administration at Kaffigen.

BURGOMASTER Yes? And?

[*They are all intent on the answer.*]

SCHILL They didn't answer.

[*All laugh.*]

DOCTOR Do you mean to say you don't trust old friends? That's not very flattering, you know.

BURGOMASTER No one's going to do you any harm here.

DOCTOR No harm here.

SCHILL They didn't answer because our postmaster held up my letter.

PAINTER Our postmaster? What an idea.

BURGOMASTER The postmaster is a member of the town council.

POLICEMAN A man of the utmost integrity.

DOCTOR He doesn't hold up letters. What an idea!

STATION MASTER [*Announcers.*] Local to Kalberstadt!

[*The townspeople all cross down to see the train arrive. Then they turn, with their backs to the audience, in a line across the stage.* SCHILL *cannot get through to reach the train.*]

SCHILL [*In a low voice.*] What are you all doing here? What do you want of me?

BURGOMASTER We don't like to see you go.

DOCTOR We've come to see you off.

[*The sound of the approaching train grows louder.*]

SCHILL I didn't ask you to come.

POLICEMAN But we have come.

DOCTOR As old friends.

ALL As old friends.

[*The* STATION MASTER *holds up his paddle. The train stops with a screech of brakes. We hear the engine panting offstage.*]

VOICE [*Offstage.*] Güllen!

BURGOMASTER A pleasant journey.

DOCTOR And long life!

PAINTER And good luck in Australia!

ALL Yes, good luck in Australia.

[*They press around him jovially. He stands motionless and pale.*]

SCHILL Why are you crowding me?

POLICEMAN What's the matter now?

[*The* STATION MASTER *blows a long blast on his whistle.*]

SCHILL Give me room.

DOCTOR But you have plenty of room.

[*They all move away from him.*]

POLICEMAN Better get aboard, Schill.

SCHILL I see. I see. One of you is going to push me under the wheels.

POLICEMAN Oh, nonsense. Go on, get aboard.

SCHILL Get away from me, all of you.

BURGOMASTER I don't know what you want. Just get on the train.

SCHILL No. One of you will push me under.

DOCTOR You're being ridiculous. Now, go on, get on the train.

SCHILL Why are you all so near me?

DOCTOR The man's gone mad.

STATION MASTER 'Board!

[*He blows his whistle. The engine bell clangs. The train starts.*]

BURGOMASTER Get aboard, man. Quick.

[*The following speeches are spoken all together until the train noises fade away.*]

DOCTOR The train's starting.

ALL Get aboard, man. Get aboard. The train's starting.

SCHILL If I try to get aboard, one of you will hold me back.

ALL No, no.

BURGOMASTER Get on the train.

SCHILL [*In terror, crouches against the wall of the* STATION MASTER'S *office.*] No—no—no. No. [*He falls on his knees. The others crowd around him. He cowers on the ground, abjectly. The train sounds fade away.*] Oh, no—no—don't push me, don't push me!

POLICEMAN There. It's gone off without you.

[*Slowly they leave him. He raises himself up to a sitting position, still trembling. A* TRUCK DRIVER *enters with an empty can.*]

TRUCK DRIVER Do you know where I can get some water? My truck's boiling over. [SCHILL *points to the station office.*] Thanks. [*He enters the office, gets the water and comes out. By this time,* SCHILL *is erect.*] Missed your train?

SCHILL Yes.

TRUCK DRIVER To Kalberstadt?

SCHILL Yes.

TRUCK DRIVER Well, come with me. I'm going that way.

SCHILL This is my town. This is my home. [*With strange new dignity.*] No, thank you. I've changed my mind. I'm staying.

TRUCK DRIVER [*Shrugs.*] All right.

[*He goes out.* SCHILL *picks up his bag, looks right and left, and slowly walks off.*]

[*Curtain.*]

ACT III

Music is heard. Then the curtain rises on the interior of the old barn, a dim, cavernous structure. Bars of light fall across the shadowy forms, shafts of sunlight from the holes and cracks in the walls and roof. Overhead hang old rags, decaying sacks, great cobwebs. Extreme left is a ladder leading to the loft. Near it, an old haycart. Left, CLAIRE ZACHANASSIAN *is sitting in her gilded sedan chair, motionless, in her magnificent bridal gown and veil. Near the chair stands an old keg.*

BOBBY [*Comes in, treading carefully.*] The doctor and the teacher from the high school to see you, madame.

CLAIRE [*Impassive.*] Show them in.

[BOBBY *ushers them in as if they were entering a hall of state. The two grope their way through the litter. At last they find the lady, and bow. They are both well dressed in new clothes, but are very dusty.*]

BOBBY Dr. Nüsslin and Professor Müller.

DOCTOR Madame.

CLAIRE You look dusty, gentlemen.

DOCTOR [*Dusts himself off vigorously.*] Oh, forgive us. We had to climb over an old carriage.

TEACHER Our respects.

DOCTOR A fabulous wedding.

TEACHER Beautiful occasion.

CLAIRE It's stifling here. But I love this old barn. The smell of hay and old straw and axle grease—it is the scent of my youth. Sit down. All this rubbish—the haycart, the old carriage, the cask, even the pitchfork—it was all here when I was a girl.

TEACHER Remarkable place.

[*He mops his brow.*]

CLAIRE I thought the pastor's text was very appropriate. The lesson a trifle long.

TEACHER I Corinthians 13.[1]

[1] See I *Corinthians* 13:13: "But now abideth faith, hope, love, these three; and the greatest of these is love."

CLAIRE Your choristers sang beautifully, Professor.

TEACHER Bach. From the *St. Matthew Passion.*

DOCTOR Güllen has never seen such magnificence! The flowers! The jewels! And the people.

TEACHER The theatrical world, the world of finance, the world of art, the world of science . . .

CLAIRE All these worlds are now back in their Cadillacs, speeding toward the capital for the wedding reception. But I'm sure you didn't come here to talk about them.

DOCTOR Dear lady, we should not intrude on your valuable time. Your husband must be waiting impatiently.

CLAIRE No, no, I've packed him off to Brazil.

DOCTOR To Brazil, madame?

CLAIRE Yes. For his honeymoon.

TEACHER *and* DOCTOR Oh! But your wedding guests?

CLAIRE I've planned a delightful dinner for them. They'll never miss me. Now what was it you wished to talk about?

TEACHER About Anton Schill, madame.

CLAIRE Is he dead?

TEACHER Madame, we may be poor. But we have our principles.

CLAIRE I see. Then what do you want?

TEACHER [*He mops his brow again.*] The fact is, madame, in anticipation of your well-known munificence, that is, feeling that you would give the town some sort of gift, we have all been buying things. Necessities . . .

DOCTOR With money we don't have.

[*The* TEACHER *blows his nose.*]

CLAIRE You've run into debt?

DOCTOR Up to here.

CLAIRE In spite of your principles?

TEACHER We're human, madame.

CLAIRE I see.

TEACHER We have been poor for a long time. A long, long time.

DOCTOR [*He rises.*] The question is, how are we going to pay?

CLAIRE You already know.

TEACHER [*Courageously.*] I beg you, Madame Zachanassian, put yourself in our position for a moment. For twenty-two years I've been cudgeling my brains to plant a few seeds of knowledge in this wilderness. And all this time, my gallant colleague, Dr. Nüsslin, has been rattling around in his ancient Mercedes, from patient to patient, trying to keep these wretches alive. Why? Why have we spent our lives in this miserable hole? For money? Hardly. The pay is ridiculous.

DOCTOR And yet, the professor here has declined an offer to head the high school in Kalberstadt.

TEACHER And Dr. Nüsslin has refused an important post at the University of Erlangen. Madame, the simple fact is, we love our town. We were born here. It is our life.

DOCTOR That's true.

TEACHER What has kept us going all these years is the hope that one day the community will prosper again as it did in the days when we were young.

CLAIRE Good.

TEACHER Madame, there is no reason for our poverty. We suffer here from a mysterious blight. We have factories. They stand idle. There is oil in the valley of Pückenried.

DOCTOR There is copper under the Konradsweil Forest. There is power in our streams, in our waterfalls.

TEACHER We are not poor, madame. If we had credit, if we had confidence, the factories would open, orders and commissions would pour in. And our economy would bloom together with our cultural life. We would become once again like the towns around us, healthy and prosperous.

DOCTOR If the Wagonworks were put on its feet again—

TEACHER The Foundry.

DOCTOR The Golden Eagle Pencil Factory.

TEACHER Buy these plants, madame. Put them in operation once more, and I swear to you, Güllen will flourish and it will bless you. We don't need a billion marks. Ten million, properly invested, would give us back our life, and incidentally return to the investor an excellent dividend. Save us, madame. Save us, and we will not only bless you, we will make money for you.

CLAIRE I don't need money.

DOCTOR Madame, we are not asking for charity. This is business.

CLAIRE It's a good idea . . .

DOCTOR Dear lady! I knew you wouldn't let us down.

CLAIRE But it's out of the question. I cannot buy the Wagonworks. I already own them.

DOCTOR The Wagonworks?

TEACHER And the Foundry?

CLAIRE And the Foundry.

DOCTOR And the Golden Eagle Pencil Factory?

CLAIRE Everything. The valley of Pückenried with its oil, the forest of Konradsweil with its ore, the barn, the town, the streets, the houses, the shops, everything. I had my agents buy up this rubbish over the years, bit by bit, piece by piece, until I had it all. Your hopes were an illusion, your vision empty, your self-sacrifice a stupidity, your whole life completely senseless.

TEACHER Then the mysterious blight—

CLAIRE The mysterious blight was I.

DOCTOR But this is monstrous!

CLAIRE Monstrous. I was seventeen when I left this town. It was winter. I was dressed in a sailor suit and my red braids hung down my back. I was in my seventh month. As I walked down the street to the station, the boys whistled after me, and someone threw something. I sat freezing in my seat in the Hamburg Express. But before the roof of the great barn was lost behind the trees, I had made up my mind that one day I would come back . . .

TEACHER But, madame—

CLAIRE [*She smiles.*] And now I have. [*She claps her hands.*] Mike. Max. Take me back to the Golden Apostle. I've been here long enough.

[MIKE *and* MAX *start to pick up the sedan chair. The* TEACHER *pushes* MIKE *away.*]

TEACHER Madame. One moment. Please. I see it all now. I had thought of you as an avenging fury, a Medea, a Clytemnestra—but I was wrong. You are a warm-hearted woman who has suffered a terrible injustice, and now you have returned and taught us an unforgettable lesson. You have stripped us bare. But now that we stand before you naked, I know you will set aside these thoughts of vengeance. If we made you suffer, you too have put us through the fire. Have mercy, madame.

CLAIRE When I have had justice. Mike!

[*She signals to* MIKE *and* MAX *to pick up the sedan chair. They cross the stage. The* TEACHER *bars the way.*]

TEACHER But, madame, one injustice cannot

cure another. What good will it do to force us into crime? Horror succeeds horror, shame is piled on shame. It settles nothing.

CLAIRE It settles everything.

[*They move upstage toward the exit. The* TEACHER *follows.*]

TEACHER Madame, this lesson you have taught us will never be forgotten. We will hand it down from father to son. It will be a monument more lasting than any vengeance. Whatever we have been, in the future we shall be better because of you. You have pushed us to the extreme. Now forgive us. Show us the way to a better life. Have pity, madame—pity. That is the highest justice.

[*The sedan chair stops.*]

CLAIRE The highest justice has no pity. It is bright and pure and clear. The world made me into a whore; now I make the world into a brothel. Those who wish to go down, may go down. Those who wish to dance with me, may dance with me. [*To her porters.*] Go.

[*She is carried off. The lights black out. Downstage, right, appears* SCHILL'S *shop. It has a new sign, a new counter. The doorbell, when it rings, has an impressive sound.* FRAU SCHILL *stands behind the counter in a new dress. The* FIRST MAN *enters, left. He is dressed as a prosperous butcher, a few bloodstains on his snowy apron, a gold watch chain across his open vest.*]

FIRST MAN What a wedding! I'll swear the whole town was there. Cigarettes.

FRAU SCHILL Clara is entitled to a little happiness after all. I'm happy for her. Green or white?

FIRST MAN Turkish. The bridesmaids! Dancers and opera singers. And the dresses! Down to here.

FRAU SCHILL It's the fashion nowadays.

FIRST MAN Reporters! Photographers! From all over the world! [*In a low voice.*] They will be here any minute.

FRAU SCHILL What have reporters to do with us? We are simple people, Herr Hofbauer. There is nothing for them here.

FIRST MAN They're questioning everybody. They're asking everything. [*The* FIRST MAN *lights a cigarette. He looks up at the ceiling.*] Footsteps.

FRAU SCHILL He's pacing the room. Up and down. Day and night.

FIRST MAN Haven't seen him all week.

FRAU SCHILL He never goes out.

FIRST MAN It's his conscience. That was pretty mean, the way he treated poor Madame Zachanassian.

FRAU SCHILL That's true. I feel very badly about it myself.

FIRST MAN To ruin a young girl like that— God doesn't forgive it. [FRAU SCHILL *nods solemnly with pursed lips. The butcher gives her a level glance.*] Look, I hope he'll have sense enough to keep his mouth shut in front of the reporters.

FRAU SCHILL I certainly hope so.

FIRST MAN You know his character.

FRAU SCHILL Only too well, Herr Hofbauer.

FIRST MAN If he tries to throw dirt at our Clara and tell a lot of lies, how she tried to get us to kill him, which anyway she never meant—

FRAU SCHILL Of course not.

FIRST MAN —Then we'll really have to do something! And not because of the money— [*He spits.*] But out of ordinary human decency. God knows Madame Zachanassian has suffered enough through him already.

FRAU SCHILL She has indeed.

[*The* TEACHER *comes in. He is not quite sober.*]

TEACHER [*Looks about the shop.*] Has the press been here yet?

FIRST MAN No.

TEACHER It's not my custom, as you know, Frau Schill—but I wonder if I could have a strong alcoholic drink?

FRAU SCHILL It's an honor to serve you, Herr Professor. I have a good Steinhäger.[2] Would you like to try a glass?

TEACHER A very small glass.

[FRAU SCHILL *serves bottle and glass. The* TEACHER *tosses off a glass.*]

FRAU SCHILL Your hand is shaking, Herr Professor.

TEACHER To tell the truth, I have been drinking a little already.

FRAU SCHILL Have another glass. It will do you good.

[*He accepts another glass.*]

[2] A kind of gin.

TEACHER Is that he up there, walking?

FRAU SCHILL Up and down. Up and down.

FIRST MAN It's God punishing him.

[*The* PAINTER *comes in with the* SON *and the* DAUGHTER.]

PAINTER Careful! A reporter just asked us the way to this shop.

FIRST MAN I hope you didn't tell him.

PAINTER I told him we were strangers here.

[*They all laugh. The door opens. The* SECOND MAN *darts into the shop.*]

SECOND MAN Look out, everybody! The press! They are across the street in your shop, Hofbauer.

FIRST MAN My boy will know how to deal with them.

SECOND MAN Make sure Schill doesn't come down, Hofbauer.

FIRST MAN Leave that to me.

[*They group themselves about the shop.*]

TEACHER Listen to me, all of you. When the reporters come I'm going to speak to them. I'm going to make a statement. A statement to the world on behalf of myself as Rector of Güllen High School and on behalf of you all, for all your sakes.

PAINTER What are you going to say?

TEACHER I shall tell the truth about Claire Zachanassian.

FRAU SCHILL You're drunk, Herr Professor; you should be ashamed of yourself.

TEACHER I should be ashamed? You should all be ashamed!

SON Shut your trap. You're drunk.

DAUGHTER Please, Professor—

TEACHER Girl, you disappoint me. It is your place to speak. But you are silent and you force your old teacher to raise his voice. I am going to speak the truth. It is my duty and I am not afraid. The world may not wish to listen, but no one can silence me. I'm not going to wait—I'm going over to Hofbauer's shop now.

ALL No, you're not. Stop him. Stop him.

[*They all spring at the* TEACHER. *He defends himself. At this moment,* SCHILL *appears through the door upstage. In contrast to the others, he is dressed shabbily in an old black jacket, his best.*]

SCHILL What's going on in my shop? [*The townsmen let go of the* TEACHER *and turn to stare at* SCHILL.] What's the trouble, Professor?

TEACHER Schill, I am speaking out at last! I am going to tell the press everything.

SCHILL Be quiet, Professor.

TEACHER What did you say?

SCHILL Be quiet.

TEACHER You want me to be quiet?

SCHILL Please.

TEACHER But, Schill, if I keep quiet, if you miss this opportunity—they're over in Hofbauer's shop now . . .

SCHILL Please.

TEACHER As you wish. If you too are on their side, I have no more to say.

[*The doorbell jingles. A* REPORTER *comes in.*]

REPORTER Herr Schill.

SCHILL Er—no. Herr Schill's gone to Kalberstadt for the day.

REPORTER Oh, thank you. Good day.

[*He goes out.*]

PAINTER [*Mops his brow.*] Whew! Close shave.

[*He follows the* REPORTER *out.*]

SECOND MAN [*Walking up to* SCHILL.] That was pretty smart of you to keep your mouth shut. You know what to expect if you don't.

[*He goes.*]

FIRST MAN Give me a Havana. [SCHILL *serves him.*] Charge it. You bastard!

[*He goes.* SCHILL *opens his account book.*]

FRAU SCHILL Come along, children—

[FRAU SCHILL, *the* SON *and the* DAUGHTER *go off, upstage.*]

TEACHER They're going to kill you. I've known it all along, and you too, you must have known it. The need is too strong, the temptation too great. And now perhaps I too will join against you. I belong to them and, like them, I can feel myself hardening into something that is not human—not beautiful.

SCHILL It can't be helped.

TEACHER Pull yourself together, man. Speak to the reporters; you've no time to lose.

[SCHILL *looks up from his account book.*]

SCHILL No. I'm not going to fight any more.

TEACHER Are you so frightened that you don't dare open your mouth?

SCHILL I made Claire what she is, I made myself what I am. What should I do? Should I pretend that I'm innocent?

TEACHER No, you can't. You are as guilty as hell.

SCHILL Yes.

TEACHER You are a bastard.

SCHILL Yes.

TEACHER But that does not justify your murder. [SCHILL *looks at him.*] I wish I could believe that for what they're doing—for what they're going to do—they will suffer for the rest of their lives. But it's not true. In a little while they will have justified everything and forgotten everything.

SCHILL Of course.

TEACHER Your name will never again be mentioned in this town. That's how it will be.

SCHILL I don't hold it against you.

TEACHER But I do. I will hold it against myself all my life. That's why—

[*The doorbell jingles. The* BURGOMASTER *comes in. The* TEACHER *stares at him, then goes out without another word.*]

BURGOMASTER Good afternoon, Schill. Don't let me disturb you. I've just dropped in for a moment.

SCHILL I'm just finishing my accounts for the week.

[*A moment's pause.*]

BURGOMASTER The town council meets tonight. At the Golden Apostle. In the auditorium.

SCHILL I'll be there.

BURGOMASTER The whole town will be there. Your case will be discussed and final action taken. You've put us in a pretty tight spot, you know.

SCHILL Yes. I'm sorry.

BURGOMASTER The lady's offer will be rejected.

SCHILL Possibly.

BURGOMASTER Of course I may be wrong.

SCHILL Of course.

BURGOMASTER In that case—are you prepared to accept the judgment of the town? The meeting will be covered by the press, you know.

SCHILL By the press?

BURGOMASTER Yes, and the radio and the newsreel. It's a very ticklish situation. Not only for you—believe me, it's even worse for us. What with the wedding, and all the publicity, we've become famous. All of a sudden our ancient democratic institutions have become of interest to the world.

SCHILL Are you going to make the lady's condition public?

BURGOMASTER No, no, of course not. Not directly. We will have to put the matter to a vote—that is unavoidable. But only those involved will understand.

SCHILL I see.

BURGOMASTER As far as the press is concerned, you are simply the intermediary between us and Madame Zachanassian. I have whitewashed you completely.

SCHILL That is very generous of you.

BURGOMASTER Frankly, it's not for your sake, but for the sake of your family. They are honest and decent people.

SCHILL Oh—

BURGOMASTER So far we've all played fair. You've kept your mouth shut and so have we. Now can we continue to depend on you? Because if you have any idea of opening your mouth at tonight's meeting, there won't be any meeting.

SCHILL I'm glad to hear an open threat at last.

BURGOMASTER We are not threatening you. You are threatening us. If you speak, you force us to act—in advance.

SCHILL That won't be necessary.

BURGOMASTER So if the town decides against you?

SCHILL I will accept their decision.

BURGOMASTER Good. [*A moment's pause.*] I'm delighted to see there is still a spark of decency left in you. But—wouldn't it be better if we didn't have to call a meeting at all? [*He pauses. He takes a gun from his pocket and puts it on the counter.*] I've brought you this.

SCHILL Thank you.

BURGOMASTER It's loaded.

SCHILL I don't need a gun.

BURGOMASTER [*He clears his throat.*] You see? We could tell the lady that we had condemned you in secret session and you had anticipated our decision. I've lost a lot of sleep getting to this point, believe me.

SCHILL I believe you.

BURGOMASTER Frankly, in your place, I myself would prefer to take the path of honor. Get it over with, once and for all. Don't you agree? For the sake of your friends! For the sake of our children, your own children—you have a daughter, a son—Schill, you know our need, our misery.

SCHILL You've put me through hell, you and your town. You were my friends, you smiled and reassured me. But day by day I saw you change—your shoes, your ties, your suits—your hearts. If you had been honest with me then, perhaps I would feel differently toward you now. I might even use that gun you brought me. For the sake of my friends. But now I have conquered my fear. Alone. It was hard, but it's done. And now you will have to judge me. And I will accept your judgment. For me that will be justice. How it will be for you, I don't know. [*He turns away.*] You may kill me if you like. I won't complain, I won't protest, I won't defend myself. But I won't do your job for you either.

BURGOMASTER [*Takes up his gun.*] There it is. You've had your chance and you won't take it. Too bad. [*He takes out a cigarette.*] I suppose it's more than we can expect of a man like you. [SCHILL *lights the* BURGOMASTER'S *cigarette.*] Good day.

SCHILL Good day. [*The* BURGOMASTER *goes.* FRAU SCHILL *comes in, dressed in a fur coat. The* DAUGHTER *is in a new red dress. The* SON *has a new sports jacket.*] What a beautiful coat, Mathilde!

FRAU SCHILL Real fur. You like it?

SCHILL Should I? What a lovely dress, Ottilie!

DAUGHTER *C'est très chic, n'est-ce pas?* [3]

SCHILL What?

FRAU SCHILL Ottilie is taking a course in French.

SCHILL Very useful. Karl—whose automobile is that out there at the curb?

SON Oh, it's only an Opel. They're not expensive.

SCHILL You bought yourself a car?

SON On credit. Easiest thing in the world.

FRAU SCHILL Everyone's buying on credit now, Anton. These fears of yours are ridiculous. You'll see. Clara has a good heart. She only means to teach you a lesson.

DAUGHTER She means to teach you a lesson, that's all.

SON It's high time you got the point, Father.

SCHILL I get the point. [*The church bells start ringing.*] Listen. The bells of Güllen. Do you hear?

SON Yes, we have four bells now. It sounds quite good.

DAUGHTER Just like Gray's Elegy.

SCHILL What?

FRAU SCHILL Ottilie is taking a course in English literature.

SCHILL Congratulations! It's Sunday. I should very much like to take a ride in your car. Our car.

SON You want to ride in the car?

SCHILL Why not? I want to ride through the Konradsweil Forest. I want to see the town where I've lived all my life.

FRAU SCHILL I don't think that will look very nice for any of us.

SCHILL No—perhaps not. Well, I'll go for a walk by myself.

FRAU SCHILL Then take us to Kalberstadt, Karl, and we'll go to a cinema.

SCHILL A cinema? It's a good idea.

FRAU SCHILL See you soon, Anton.

SCHILL Good-bye, Ottilie. Good-bye, Karl. Good-bye, Mathilde.

FAMILY Good-bye.

[*They go out.*]

SCHILL Good-bye. [*The shop sign flies off. The lights black out. They come up at once on the forest scene.*] Autumn. Even the forest has turned to gold.

[SCHILL *wanders down to the bench in the forest. He sits.* CLAIRE'S *voice is heard.*]

CLAIRE [*Offstage.*] Stop. Wait here. [CLAIRE *comes in. She gazes slowly up at the trees, kicks at some leaves. Then she walks slowly down center. She stops before a tree, glances up the trunk.*] Bark-borers. The old tree is dying.

[*She catches sight of* SCHILL.]

SCHILL Clara.

CLAIRE How pleasant to see you here. I was visiting my forest. May I sit by you?

SCHILL Oh, yes. Please do. [*She sits next to him.*] I've just been saying good-bye to my family. They've gone to the cinema. Karl has bought himself a car.

CLAIRE How nice.

SCHILL Ottilie is taking French lessons. And a course in English literature.

[3] It's very smart, isn't it?

CLAIRE You see? They're beginning to take an interest in higher things.

SCHILL Listen. A finch. You hear?

CLAIRE Yes. It's a finch. And a cuckoo in the distance. Would you like some music?

SCHILL Oh, yes. That would be very nice.

CLAIRE Anything special?

SCHILL "Deep in the Forest."

CLAIRE Your favorite song. They know it.

[*She raises her hand. Offstage, the mandolin and guitar play the tune softly.*]

SCHILL We had a child?

CLAIRE Yes.

SCHILL Boy or girl?

CLAIRE Girl.

SCHILL What name did you give her?

CLAIRE I called her Genevieve.

SCHILL That's a very pretty name.

CLAIRE Yes.

SCHILL What was she like?

CLAIRE I saw her only once. When she was born. Then they took her away from me.

SCHILL Her eyes?

CLAIRE They weren't open yet.

SCHILL And her hair?

CLAIRE Black, I think. It's usually black at first.

SCHILL Yes, of course. Where did she die, Clara?

CLAIRE In some family. I've forgotten their name. Meningitis, they said. The officials wrote me a letter.

SCHILL Oh, I'm so very sorry, Clara.

CLAIRE I've told you about our child. Now tell me about myself.

SCHILL About yourself?

CLAIRE Yes. How I was when I was seventeen in the days when you loved me.

SCHILL I remember one day you waited for me in the great barn. I had to look all over the place for you. At last I found you lying in the haycart with nothing on and a long straw between your lips . . .

CLAIRE Yes. I was pretty in those days.

SCHILL You were beautiful, Clara.

CLAIRE You were strong. The time you fought with those two railwaymen who were following me, I wiped the blood from your face with my red petticoat. [*The music ends.*] They've stopped.

SCHILL Tell them to play "Thoughts of Home."

CLAIRE They know that too.

[*The music plays.*]

SCHILL Here we are, Clara, sitting together in our forest for the last time. The town council meets tonight. They will condemn me to death, and one of them will kill me. I don't know who and I don't know where. Clara, I only know that in a little while a useless life will come to an end.

[*He bows his head on her bosom. She takes him in her arms.*]

CLAIRE [*Tenderly.*] I shall take you in your coffin to Capri. You will have your tomb in the park of my villa, where I can see you from my bedroom window. White marble and onyx in a grove of green cypress. With a beautiful view of the Mediterranean.

SCHILL I've always wanted to see it.

CLAIRE Your love for me died years ago, Anton. But my love for you would not die. It turned into something strong, like the hidden roots of the forest; something evil, like white mushrooms that grow unseen in the darkness. And slowly it reached out for your life. Now I have you. You are mine. Alone. At last, and forever, a peaceful ghost in a silent house.

[*The music ends.*]

SCHILL The song is over.

CLAIRE Adieu, Anton.

[CLAIRE *kisses* ANTON, *a long kiss. Then she rises.*]

SCHILL Adieu.

[*She goes.* SCHILL *remains sitting on the bench. A row of lamps descends from the flies. The townsmen come in from both sides, each bearing his chair. A table and chairs are set upstage, center. On both sides sit the townspeople. The* POLICEMAN, *in a new uniform, sits on the bench behind* SCHILL. *All the townsmen are in new Sunday clothes. Around them are technicians of all sorts, with lights, cameras, and other equipment. The townswomen are absent. They do not vote. The* BURGOMASTER *takes his place at the table, center. The* DOCTOR *and the* PASTOR *sit at the same table, at his right, and the* TEACHER *in his academic gown, at his left.*]

BURGOMASTER [*At a sign from the radio technician, he pounds the floor with his wand of office.*] Fellow citizens of Güllen, I call this meeting to order. The agenda: there is only one matter before us. I have the honor to announce officially that Madame Claire Zachanassian, daughter of our beloved citizen, the famous architect Siegfried Wäscher, has decided to make a gift to the town of one billion marks. Five hundred million to the town, five hundred million to be divided per capita among the citizens. After certain necessary preliminaries, a vote will be taken, and you, as citizens of Güllen, will signify your will by a show of hands. Has anyone any objection to this mode of procedure? The pastor? [*Silence.*] The police? [*Silence.*] The town health official? [*Silence.*] The Rector of Güllen High School? [*Silence.*] The political opposition? [*Silence.*] I shall then proceed to the vote—[*The* TEACHER *rises. The* BURGOMASTER *turns in surprise and irritation.*] You wish to speak?

TEACHER Yes.

BURGOMASTER Very well.

[*He takes his seat. The* TEACHER *advances. The movie camera starts running.*]

TEACHER Fellow townsmen. [*The photographer flashes a bulb in his face.*] Fellow townsmen. We all know that by means of this gift, Madame Claire Zachanassian intends to attain a certain object. What is this object? To enrich the town of her youth, yes. But more than that, she desires by means of this gift to reestablish justice among us. This desire expressed by our benefactress raises an all-important question. Is it true that our community harbors in its soul such a burden of guilt?

BURGOMASTER Yes! True!

SECOND MAN Crimes are concealed among us.

THIRD MAN [*He jumps up.*] Sins!

FOURTH MAN [*He jumps up also.*] Perjuries!

PAINTER Justice!

TOWNSMEN Justice! Justice!

TEACHER Citizens of Güllen, this, then, is the simple fact of the case. We have participated in an injustice. I thoroughly recognize the material advantages which this gift opens to us—I do not overlook the fact that it is poverty which is the root of all this bitterness and evil. Nevertheless, there is no question here of money.

TOWNSMEN No! no!

TEACHER Here there is no question of our prosperity as a community, or our well-being as individuals—The question is—must be—whether or not we wish to live according to the principles of justice, those principles for which our forefathers lived and fought and for which they died, those principles which form the soul of our Western culture.

TOWNSMEN Hear! Hear!

[*Applause.*]

TEACHER [*Desperately, realizing that he is fighting a losing battle, and on the verge of hysteria.*] Wealth has meaning only when benevolence comes of it, but only he who hungers for grace will receive grace. Do you feel this hunger, my fellow citizens, this hunger of the spirit, or do you feel only that other profane hunger, the hunger of the body? That is the question which I, as Rector of your high school, now propound to you. Only if you can no longer tolerate the presence of evil among you, only if you can in no circumstances endure a world in which injustice exists, are you worthy to receive Madame Zachanassian's billion and fulfill the condition bound up with this gift. If not—[*Wild applause. He gestures desperately for silence.*] If not, then God have mercy on us!

[*The townsmen crowd around him, ambiguously, in a mood somewhat between threat and congratulation. He takes his seat, utterly crushed, exhausted by his effort. The* BURGOMASTER *advances and takes charge once again. Order is restored.*]

BURGOMASTER Anton Schill—[*The* POLICEMAN *gives* SCHILL *a shove.* SCHILL *gets up.*] Anton Schill, it is through you that this gift is offered to the town. Are you willing that this offer should be accepted?

[SCHILL *mumbles something.*]

RADIO REPORTER [*Steps to his side.*] You'll have to speak up a little, Herr Schill.

SCHILL Yes.

BURGOMASTER Will you respect our decision in the matter before us?

SCHILL I will respect your decision.

BURGOMASTER Then I proceed to the vote. All those who are in accord with the terms on which this gift is offered will signify the same by raising their right hands. [*After a moment, the* POLICEMAN *raises his hand. Then one by one the others. Last of all, very slowly, the* TEACHER.] All against? The offer is accepted.

I now solemnly call upon you, fellow townsmen, to declare in the face of all the world that you take this action, not out of love for worldly gain . . .

TOWNSMEN [*In chorus.*] Not out of love for worldly gain . . .

BURGOMASTER But out of love for the right.

TOWNSMEN But out of love for the right.

BURGOMASTER [*Holds up his hand, as if taking an oath.*] We join together, now, as brothers . . .

TOWNSMEN [*Hold up their hands.*] We join together, now, as brothers . . .

BURGOMASTER To purify our town of guilt . . .

TOWNSMEN To purify our town of guilt . . .

BURGOMASTER And to reaffirm our faith . . .

TOWNSMEN And to reaffirm our faith . . .

BURGOMASTER In the eternal power of justice.

TOWNSMEN In the eternal power of justice.

[*The lights go off suddenly.*]

SCHILL [*A scream.*] Oh, God!

VOICE I'm sorry, Herr Burgomaster. We seem to have blown a fuse. [*The lights go on.*] Ah—there we are. Would you mind doing that last bit again?

BURGOMASTER Again?

THE CAMERAMAN [*Walks forward.*] Yes, for the newsreel.

BURGOMASTER Oh, the newsreel. Certainly.

THE CAMERAMAN Ready now? Right.

BURGOMASTER And to reaffirm our faith . . .

TOWNSMEN And to reaffirm our faith . . .

BURGOMASTER In the eternal power of justice.

TOWNSMEN In the eternal power of justice.

THE CAMERAMAN [*To his assistant.*] It was better before, when he screamed "Oh, God."

[*The assistant shrugs.*]

BURGOMASTER Fellow citizens of Güllen, I declare this meeting adjourned. The ladies and gentlemen of the press will find refreshments served downstairs, with the compliments of the town council. The exits lead directly to the restaurant.

THE CAMERAMAN Thank you.

[*The newsmen go off with alacrity. The townsmen remain on the stage.* SCHILL *gets up.*]

POLICEMAN [*Pushes* SCHILL *down.*] Sit down.

SCHILL Is it to be now?

POLICEMAN Naturally, now.

SCHILL I thought it might be best to have it at my house.

POLICEMAN It will be here.

BURGOMASTER Lower the lights. [*The lights dim.*] Are they all gone?

VOICE All gone.

BURGOMASTER The gallery?

SECOND VOICE Empty.

BURGOMASTER Lock the doors.

THE VOICE Locked here.

SECOND VOICE Locked here.

BURGOMASTER Form a lane. [*The men form a lane. At the end stands the* ATHLETE *in elegant white slacks, a red scarf around his singlet.*] Pastor. Will you be so good?

[*The* PASTOR *walks slowly to* SCHILL.]

PASTOR Anton Schill, your heavy hour has come.

SCHILL May I have a cigarette?

PASTOR Cigarette, Burgomaster.

BURGOMASTER Of course. With pleasure. And a good one.

[*He gives his case to the* PASTOR, *who offers it to* SCHILL. *The* POLICEMAN *lights the cigarette. The* PASTOR *returns the case.*]

PASTOR In the words of the prophet Amos—

SCHILL Please—

[*He shakes his head.*]

PASTOR You're no longer afraid?

SCHILL No. I'm not afraid.

PASTOR I will pray for you.

SCHILL Pray for us all.

[*The* PASTOR *bows his head.*]

BURGOMASTER Anton Schill, stand up!

[SCHILL *hesitates.*]

POLICEMAN Stand up, you swine!

BURGOMASTER Schultz, please.

POLICEMAN I'm sorry. I was carried away.

[SCHILL *gives the cigarette to the* POLICEMAN. *Then he walks slowly to the center of the stage and turns his back on the audience.*] Enter the lane.

[SCHILL *hesitates a moment. He goes slowly into the lane of silent men. The* ATHLETE *stares at him from the opposite end.* SCHILL *looks in turn at the hard faces of those who surround him, and sinks slowly to his knees. The lane contracts silently into a knot as the men close in and crouch over. Complete silence. The knot of men pulls back slowly, coming downstage. Then it opens. Only the* DOCTOR *is left in the center of the stage, kneeling by the corpse, over which the* TEACHER'S *gown has been spread. The* DOCTOR *rises and takes off his stethoscope.*]

PASTOR Is it all over?

DOCTOR Heart failure.

BURGOMASTER Died of joy.

ALL Died of joy.

[*The townsmen turn their backs on the corpse and at once light cigarettes. A cloud of smoke rises over them. From the left comes* CLAIRE ZACHANASSIAN, *dressed in black, followed by* BOBBY. *She sees the corpse. Then she walks slowly to center stage and looks down at the body of* SCHILL.]

CLAIRE Uncover him. [BOBBY *uncovers* SCHILL'S *face. She stares at it a long moment. She sighs.*] Cover his face.

[BOBBY *covers it.* CLAIRE *goes out, up center.* BOBBY *takes the check from his wallet, holds it out peremptorily to the* BURGOMASTER, *who walks over from the knot of silent men. He holds out his hand for the check. The lights fade. At once the warning bell is heard, and the scene dissolves into the setting of the railway station. The gradual transformation of the shabby town into a thing of elegance and beauty is now accomplished. The railway station glitters with neon lights and is surrounded with garlands, bright posters, and flags. The townsfolk, men and women, now in brand new clothes, form themselves into a group in front of the station. The sound of the approaching train grows louder. The train stops.*]

STATION MASTER Güllen-Rome Express. All aboard, please. [*The church bells start pealing. Men appear with trunks and boxes, a procession which duplicates that of the lady's arrival, but in inverse order. Then come the* TWO BLIND MEN, *then* BOBBY, *and* MIKE *and* MAX *carrying the coffin. Lastly* CLAIRE. *She is dressed in modish black. Her head is high, her face as impassive as that of an ancient idol. The procession crosses the stage and goes off. The people bow in silence as the coffin passes. When* CLAIRE *and her retinue have boarded the train, the* STATION MASTER *blows a long blast.*] 'Bo—ard!

[*He holds up his paddle. The train starts and moves off slowly, picking up speed. The crowd turns slowly, gazing after the departing train in complete silence. The train sounds fade.*]

[*The curtain falls slowly.*]

Comments and Questions

Duerrenmatt has said that "Claire Zachanassian represents neither justice nor the Marshall Plan nor even the Apocalypse; let her be only what she is: the richest woman in the world, whose fortune has put her in a position to act like the heroine of a Greek tragedy: absolute, cruel, something like Medea." It is possible, of course, to read this play as straight melodrama, as a kind of dark fairy tale with an unacceptable ending. The most literal-minded person, however, would feel uneasy in accepting Claire and the other characters in this play as individuals without allegorical significance.

1. What evidence may be adduced to identify Claire with justice? In what ways does this identification break down? An even weaker case may be made for equating Claire's actions with actions taken by the United States under the Marshall Plan, but a case of sorts can be made. What is it? Can Claire be equated with the Apocalypse? In what way does this suggested identification break down almost at once? Since none of these identifications fits perfectly, one may be tempted to try others—Nemesis, for example.

2. What about Anton Schill? Is the play as much his as it is Claire's, or is it more? Explain. Can a case be made for his being the only *individual* in the play? Consider the villagers. Consider Claire's entourage. What may one conclude about these groups? Also, what is the dramatic purpose of Claire's wedding? Why does the author have the world's great flock to Güllen for this affair?

3. Claire's entourage is a human menagerie plus a black panther. The whole village of Güllen is slowly disciplined, tamed, and corrupted. How does this view of human frailties fit the tenets of Existentialism? See the discussion and the readings suggested in the footnote to "The Wall," p. 130.

4. Camus' *Caligula,* the next play, presents a ruler with absolute power. Compare Caligula and Claire Zachanassian. The statement that power corrupts and absolute power corrupts absolutely may be applied to the inordinately rich woman in *The Visit* and to the Roman Emperor. Is there a difference, however, in the way these two protagonists exert their authority? Is Claire corrupted by what she does? Or is she chiefly a corrupter? The same questions may be asked about Caligula. What motivates Claire? Caligula?

5. Compare the use of symbols in *The Visit* with their use in *Miss Julie.*

6. Captain Keeney in *Ile* is, within his tiny sphere, master. Compare what happened to him with what happens to Claire and Caligula.

ALBERT CAMUS
1913–1960
Caligula

(Translated by Stuart Gilbert)

Caligula (Gaius Caesar) was born twelve years after the birth of Christ and assassinated twenty-nine years later. As a child he was the darling of the Roman legionnaires, by whom he was given the name Caligula, which means Little Boots. At age twenty-five he succeeded Tiberius as Emperor with absolute power. Almost at once he began what has been called a reign of terror without parallel in history. His favorite banquet entertainments took the form of bloody executions, sometimes of criminals, frequently of innocent, respectable citizens. His was government by whim. Once when he could not find the enemy army (Germans), he dressed half his own men as the enemy and pursued them with the other half. He built an ivory stable with a golden manger for his favorite horse and made the animal a Consul.

Camus's play interprets this historical character in Absurdist terms. (See Martin Esslin's *The Theatre of the Absurd,* New York: Doubleday & Company, 1969, for an excellent discussion.) It has been said that insanity is in general suspect as a fictional device. Does Camus regard the actions of his Caligula as those of a madman?

CHARACTERS

CALIGULA
CÆSONIA
HELICON
SCIPIO
CHEREA
THE OLD PATRICIAN
METELLUS
LEPIDUS
INTENDANT
MEREIA
MUCIUS
MUCIUS' WIFE
PATRICIANS, KNIGHTS, POETS, GUARDS, SERVANTS

ACT I

A number of patricians, one a very old man, are gathered in a state room of the imperial palace. They are showing signs of nervousness.

FIRST PATRICIAN Still no news.

THE OLD PATRICIAN None last night, none this morning.

SECOND PATRICIAN Three days without news. Strange indeed!

THE OLD PATRICIAN Our messengers go out, our messengers return. And always they shake their heads and say: "Nothing."

SECOND PATRICIAN They've combed the whole countryside. What more can be done?

FIRST PATRICIAN We can only wait. It's no use meeting trouble halfway. Perhaps he'll return as abruptly as he left us.

THE OLD PATRICIAN When I saw him leaving the palace, I noticed a queer look in his eyes.

FIRST PATRICIAN Yes, so did I. In fact I asked him what was amiss.

SECOND PATRICIAN Did he answer?

FIRST PATRICIAN One word: "Nothing."

[*A short silence.* HELICON *enters. He is munching onions.*]

SECOND PATRICIAN [*In the same nervous tone.*] It's all very perturbing.

FIRST PATRICIAN Oh, come now! All young fellows are like that.

THE OLD PATRICIAN You're right there. They take things hard. But time smooths everything out.

SECOND PATRICIAN Do you really think so?

THE OLD PATRICIAN Of course. For one girl dead, a dozen living ones.

HELICON Ah? So you think that there's a girl behind it?

FIRST PATRICIAN What else should there be? Anyhow—thank goodness!—grief never lasts forever. Is any one of us here capable of mourning a loss for more than a year on end?

SECOND PATRICIAN Not I, anyhow.

FIRST PATRICIAN No one can do that.

THE OLD PATRICIAN Life would be intolerable if one could.

FIRST PATRICIAN Quite so. Take my case. I lost my wife last year. I shed many tears, and then I forgot. Even now I feel a pang of grief at times. But, happily, it doesn't amount to much.

THE OLD PATRICIAN Yes, Nature's a great healer.

[CHEREA *enters.*]

FIRST PATRICIAN Well . . . ?

CHEREA Still nothing.

HELICON Come, gentlemen! There's no need for consternation.

FIRST PATRICIAN I agree.

HELICON Worrying won't mend matters—and it's lunchtime.

THE OLD PATRICIAN That's so. We mustn't drop the prey for the shadow.

CHEREA I don't like the look of things. But all was going too smoothly. As an emperor, he was perfection's self.

SECOND PATRICIAN Yes, exactly the emperor we wanted; conscientious and inexperienced.

FIRST PATRICIAN But what's come over you? There's no reason for all these lamentations. We've no ground for assuming he will change. Let's say he loved Drusilla. Only natural; she was his sister. Or say his love for her was something more than brotherly; shocking enough, I grant you. But it's really going too far, setting all Rome in a turmoil because the girl has died.

CHEREA Maybe. But, as I said, I don't like the look of things; this escapade alarms me.

THE OLD PATRICIAN Yes, there's never smoke without fire.

FIRST PATRICIAN In any case, the interests of the State should prevent his making a public tragedy of . . . of, let's say, a regrettable attachment. No doubt such things happen; but the less said the better.

HELICON How can you be sure Drusilla is the cause of all this trouble?

SECOND PATRICIAN Who else should it be?

HELICON Nobody at all, quite likely. When there's a host of explanations to choose from, why pick on the stupidest, most obvious one?

[*Young* SCIPIO *enters.* CHEREA *goes toward him.*]

CHEREA Well?

SCIPIO Still nothing. Except that some peasants think they saw him last night not far from Rome, rushing through the storm.

[CHEREA *comes back to the patricians,* SCIPIO *following him.*]

CHEREA That makes three days, Scipio, doesn't it?

SCIPIO Yes . . . I was there, following him as I usually do. He went up to Drusilla's body. He stroked it with two fingers, and seemed lost in thought for a long while. Then he swung round and walked out, calmly enough. . . . And ever since we've been hunting for him—in vain.

CHEREA [*Shaking his head.*] That young man was too fond of literature.

SECOND PATRICIAN Oh, at his age, you know . . .

CHEREA At his age, perhaps; but not in his position. An artistic emperor is an anomaly. I grant you we've had one or two; misfits happen in the best of empires. But the others had the good taste to remember they were public servants.

FIRST PATRICIAN It made things run more smoothly.

THE OLD PATRICIAN One man, one job—that's how it should be.

SCIPIO What can we do, Cherea?

CHEREA Nothing.

SECOND PATRICIAN We can only wait. If he doesn't return, a successor will have to be found. Between ourselves—there's no shortage of candidates.

FIRST PATRICIAN No, but there's a shortage of the right sort.

CHEREA Suppose he comes back in an ugly mood?

FIRST PATRICIAN Oh, he's a mere boy; we'll make him see reason.

CHEREA And what if he declines to see it?

FIRST PATRICIAN [*Laughing.*] In that case, my friend, don't forget I once wrote a manual of revolutions. You'll find all the rules there.

CHEREA I'll look it up—if things come to that. But I'd rather be left to my books.

SCIPIO If you'll excuse me. . . .

[*Goes out.*]

CHEREA He's offended.

THE OLD PATRICIAN Scipio is young, and young people always hang together.

HELICON Scipio doesn't count, anyhow.

[*Enter a member of the imperial bodyguard.*]

THE GUARDMAN Caligula has been seen in the palace gardens.

[*All leave the room. The stage is empty for some moments. Then* CALIGULA *enters stealthily from the left. His legs are caked with mud, his garments dirty; his hair is wet, his look distraught. He brings his hand to his mouth several times. Then he approaches a mirror, stopping abruptly when he catches sight of his reflected self. After muttering some unintelligible words, he sits down on the right, letting his arms hang limp between his knees.* HELICON *enters, left. On seeing* CALIGULA, *he stops at the far end of the stage and contemplates him in silence.* CALIGULA *turns and sees him. A short silence.*]

HELICON [*Across the stage.*] Good morning, Caius.

CALIGULA [*In quite an ordinary tone.*] Good morning, Helicon.

[*A short silence.*]

HELICON You're looking tired.

CALIGULA I've walked a lot.

HELICON Yes, you've been away for quite a while.

[*Another short silence.*]

CALIGULA It was hard to find.

HELICON What was hard to find?

CALIGULA What I was after.

HELICON Meaning?

CALIGULA [*In the same matter-of-fact tone.*] The moon.

HELICON What?

CALIGULA Yes, I wanted the moon.

HELICON Ah. . . . [*Another silence.* HELICON *approaches* CALIGULA.] And why did you want it?

CALIGULA Well . . . it's one of the things I haven't got.

HELICON I see. And now—have you fixed it up to your satisfaction?

CALIGULA No. I couldn't get it.

HELICON Too bad!

CALIGULA Yes, and that's why I'm tired. [*Pauses. Then.*] Helicon!

HELICON Yes, Caius?

CALIGULA No doubt, you think I'm crazy.

HELICON As you know well, I never think.

CALIGULA Ah, yes. . . . Now, listen! I'm not mad; in fact I've never felt so lucid. What happened to me is quite simple; I suddenly felt a desire for the impossible. That's all. [*Pauses.*] Things as they are, in my opinion, are far from satisfactory.

HELICON Many people share your opinion.

CALIGULA That is so. But in the past I didn't realize it. *Now* I know. [*Still in the same matter-of-fact tone.*] Really, this world of ours, the scheme of things as they call it, is quite intolerable. That's why I want the moon, or happiness, or eternal life—something, in fact, that may sound crazy, but which isn't of this world.

HELICON That's sound enough in theory. Only, in practice one can't carry it through to its conclusion.

CALIGULA [*Rising to his feet, but still with perfect calmness.*] You're wrong there. It's just because no one *dares* to follow up his ideas to the end that nothing is achieved. All that's needed, I should say, is to be logical right through, at all costs. [*He studies* HELICON'S *face.*] I can see, too, what you're thinking. What a fuss over a woman's death! But that's not it. True enough, I seem to remember that a woman died some days ago; a woman whom I loved. But love, what is it? A side issue. And I swear to you her death is not the point; it's no more than the symbol of a truth that makes the moon essential to me. A childishly simple, obvious, almost silly truth, but one that's hard to come by and heavy to endure.

HELICON May I know what it is, this truth that you've discovered?

CALIGULA [*His eyes averted, in a toneless voice.*] Men die; and they are not happy.

HELICON [*After a short pause.*] Anyhow, Caligula, it's a truth with which one comes to terms, without much trouble. Only look at the people over there. This truth of yours doesn't prevent them from enjoying their meal.

CALIGULA [*With sudden violence.*] All it proves is that I'm surrounded by lies and self-deception. But I've had enough of that; I wish men to live by the light of truth. And I've the power to make them do so. For I know what they need and haven't got. They're without understanding and they need a teacher; someone who knows what he's talking about.

HELICON Don't take offense, Caius, if I give you a word of advice. . . . But that can wait. First, you should have some rest.

CALIGULA [*Sitting down. His voice is gentle again.*] That's not possible, Helicon. I shall never rest again.

HELICON But—why?

CALIGULA If I sleep, who'll give me the moon?

HELICON [*After a short silence.*] That's true.

CALIGULA [*Rising to his feet again, with an effort.*] Listen, Helicon . . . I hear footsteps, voices. Say nothing—and forget you've seen me.

HELICON I understand.

CALIGULA [*Looking back, as he moves toward the door.*] And please help me, from now on.

HELICON I've no reason not to do so, Caius. But I know very few things, and few things interest me. In what way can I help you?

CALIGULA In the way of . . . the impossible.

HELICON I'll do my best.

[CALIGULA *goes out.* SCIPIO *and* CÆSONIA *enter hurriedly.*]

SCIPIO No one! Haven't you seen him?

HELICON No.

CÆSONIA Tell me, Helicon. Are you quite sure he didn't say anything to you before he went away?

HELICON I'm not a sharer of his secrets, I'm his public. A mere onlooker. It's more prudent.

CÆSONIA Please don't talk like that.

HELICON My dear Cæsonia, Caius is an idealist as we all know. He follows his bent, and no one can foresee where it will take him. . . . But, if you'll excuse me, I'll go to lunch.

[*Exit* HELICON.]

CÆSONIA [*Sinking wearily onto a divan.*] One of the palace guards saw him go by. But all Rome sees Caligula everywhere. And Caligula, of course, sees nothing but his own idea.

SCIPIO What idea?

CÆSONIA How can I tell, Scipio?

SCIPIO Are you thinking of Drusilla?

CÆSONIA Perhaps. One thing is sure; he loved her. And it's a cruel thing to have someone die today whom only yesterday you were holding in your arms.

SCIPIO [*Timidly.*] And you . . . ?

CÆSONIA Oh, I'm the old, trusted mistress. That's my role.

SCIPIO Cæsonia, we must save him.

CÆSONIA So you, too, love him?

SCIPIO Yes. He's been very good to me. He encouraged me; I shall never forget some of the things he said. He told me life isn't easy, but it has consolations: religion, art, and the love one inspires in others. He often told me that the only mistake one makes in life is to cause others suffering. He tried to be a just man.

CÆSONIA [*Rising.*] He's only a child. [*She goes to the glass and scans herself.*] The only god I've ever had is my body, and now I shall pray this god of mine to give Caius back to me.

[CALIGULA *enters. On seeing* CÆSONIA *and* SCIPIO *he hesitates, and takes a backward step. At the same moment several men enter from the opposite side of the room: patricians and the* INTENDANT *of the palace. They stop short when they see* CALIGULA. CÆSONIA *turns. She and* SCIPIO *hurry toward* CALIGULA, *who checks them with a gesture.*]

INTENDANT [*In a rather quavering voice.*] We

. . . we've been looking for you, Cæsar, high and low.

CALIGULA [*In a changed, harsh tone.*] So I see.

INTENDANT We . . . I mean . . .

CALIGULA [*Roughly.*] What do you want?

INTENDANT We were feeling anxious, Cæsar.

CALIGULA [*Going toward him.*] What business had you to feel anxious?

INTENDANT Well . . . er . . . [*He has an inspiration.*] Well, as you know, there are points to be settled in connection with the Treasury.

CALIGULA [*Bursting into laughter.*] Ah, yes. The Treasury! That's so. The Treasury's of prime importance.

INTENDANT Yes, indeed.

CALIGULA [*Still laughing, to* CÆSONIA.] Don't you agree, my dear? The Treasury is all-important.

CÆSONIA No, Caligula. It's a secondary matter.

CALIGULA That only shows your ignorance. We are extremely interested in our Treasury. Everything's important: our fiscal system, public morals, foreign policy, army equipment, and agrarian laws. Everything's of cardinal importance, I assure you. And everything's on an equal footing: the grandeur of Rome and your attacks of arthritis. . . . Well, well, I'm going to apply my mind to all that. And, to begin with . . . Now listen well, Intendant.

INTENDANT We are listening, sir.

[*The patricians come forward.*]

CALIGULA You're our loyal subjects, are you not?

INTENDANT [*In a reproachful tone.*] Oh, Cæsar . . . !

CALIGULA Well, I've something to propose to you. We're going to make a complete change in our economic system. In two moves. Drastic and abrupt. I'll explain, Intendant . . . when the patricians have left. [*The patricians go out.* CALIGULA *seats himself beside* CÆSONIA, *with his arm around her waist.*] Now mark my words. The first move's this. Every patrician, everyone in the Empire who has any capital—small or large, it's all the same thing—is ordered to disinherit his children and make a new will leaving his money to the State.

INTENDANT But Cæsar . . .

CALIGULA I've not yet given you leave to speak. As the need arises, we shall have these people die; a list will be drawn up by us fixing the order of their deaths. When the fancy takes us, we may modify that order. And, of course, we shall step into their money.

CÆSONIA [*Freeing herself.*] But—what's come over you?

CALIGULA [*Imperturbably.*] Obviously the order of their going has no importance. Or, rather, all these executions have an equal importance—from which it follows that none has any. Really all those fellows are on a par, one's as guilty as another. [*To the* INTENDANT, *peremptorily.*] You are to promulgate this edict without a moment's delay and see it's carried out forthwith. The wills are to be signed by residents in Rome this evening; within a month at the latest by persons in the provinces. Send out your messengers.

INTENDANT Cæsar, I wonder if you realize . . .

CALIGULA Do I realize . . . ? Now, listen well, you fool! If the Treasury has paramount importance, human life has none. That should be obvious to you. People who think like you are bound to admit the logic of my edict, and since money is the only thing that counts, should set no value on their lives or anyone else's. I have resolved to be logical, and I have the power to enforce my will. Presently you'll see what logic's going to cost you! I shall eliminate contradictions and contradictors. If necessary, I'll begin with you.

INTENDANT Cæsar, my good will can be relied on, that I swear.

CALIGULA And mine, too; that I guarantee. Just see how ready I am to adopt your point of view, and give the Treasury the first place in my program. Really you should be grateful to me; I'm playing into your hand, and with your own cards. [*He pauses, before continuing in a flat, unemotional tone.*] In any case there is a touch of genius in the simplicity of my plan—which clinches the matter. I give you three seconds in which to remove yourself. One . . .

[*The* INTENDANT *hurries out.*]

CÆSONIA I can't believe it's you! But it was just a joke, wasn't it?—all you said to him.

CALIGULA Not quite that, Cæsonia. Let's say, a lesson in statesmanship.

SCIPIO But, Caius, it's . . . it's impossible!

CALIGULA That's the whole point.

SCIPIO I don't follow.

CALIGULA I repeat—that is my point. I'm exploiting the impossible. Or, more accurately, It's a question of making the impossible possible.

SCIPIO But that game may lead to—to anything! It's a lunatic's pastime.

CALIGULA No, Scipio. An emperor's vocation. [*He lets himself sink back wearily among the cushions.*] Ah, my dears, at last I've come to see the uses of supremacy. It gives impossibilities a run. From this day on, so long as life is mine, my freedom has no frontier.

CÆSONIA [*Sadly.*] I doubt if this discovery of yours will make us any happier.

CALIGULA So do I. But, I suppose, we'll have to live it through.

[CHEREA *enters.*]

CHEREA I have just heard of your return. I trust your health is all it should be.

CALIGULA My health is duly grateful. [*A pause. Then, abruptly.*] Leave us, Cherea. I don't want to see you.

CHEREA Really, Caius, I'm amazed . . .

CALIGULA There's nothing to be amazed at. I don't like literary men, and I can't bear lies.

CHEREA If we lie, it's often without knowing it. I plead Not Guilty.

CALIGULA Lies are never guiltless. And yours attribute importance to people and to things. That's what I cannot forgive you.

CHEREA And yet—since this world is the only one we have, why not plead its cause?

CALIGULA Your pleading comes too late, the verdict's given. . . . This world has no importance; once a man realizes that, he wins his freedom. [*He has risen to his feet.*] And that is why I hate you, you and your kind; because you are not free. You see in me the one free man in the whole Roman Empire. You should be glad to have at last among you an emperor who points the way to freedom. Leave me, Cherea; and you, too, Scipio, go—for what is friendship? Go, both of you, and spread the news in Rome that freedom has been given her at last, and with the gift begins a great probation.

[*They go out.* CALIGULA *has turned away, hiding his eyes.*]

CÆSONIA Crying?

CALIGULA Yes, Cæsonia.

CÆSONIA But, after all, what's changed in your life? You may have loved Drusilla, but you loved many others—myself included—at the same time. Surely that wasn't enough to set you roaming the countryside for three days and nights and bring you back with this . . . this cruel look on your face?

CALIGULA [*Swinging round on her.*] What nonsense is this? Why drag in Drusilla? Do you imagine love's the only thing that can make a man shed tears?

CÆSONIA I'm sorry, Caius. Only I was trying to understand.

CALIGULA Men weep because . . . the world's all wrong. [*She comes toward him.*] No, Cæsonia. [*She draws back.*] But stay beside me.

CÆSONIA I'll do whatever you wish. [*Sits down.*] At my age one knows that life's a sad business. But why deliberately set out to make it worse?

CALIGULA No, it's no good; you can't understand. But what matter? Perhaps I'll find a way out. Only, I feel a curious stirring within me, as if undreamed of things were forcing their way up into the light—and I'm helpless against them. [*He moves closer to her.*] Oh, Cæsonia, I knew that men felt anguish, but I didn't know what that word anguish meant. Like everyone else I fancied it was a sickness of the mind—no more. But no, it's my body that's in pain. Pain everywhere, in my chest, in my legs and arms. Even my skin is raw, my head is buzzing, I feel like vomiting. But worst of all is this queer taste in my mouth. Not blood, or death, or fever, but a mixture of all three. I've only to stir my tongue, and the world goes black, and everyone looks . . . horrible. How hard, how cruel it is, this process of becoming a man!

CÆSONIA What you need, my dear, is a good, long sleep. Let yourself relax, and above all stop thinking. I'll stay by you while you sleep. And when you wake, you'll find the world's got back its savor. Then you must use your power to good effect—for loving better what you still find lovable. For the possible, too, deserves to be given a chance.

CALIGULA Ah but for that I'd need to sleep, to let myself go—and that's impossible.

CÆSONIA So one always thinks when one is overtired. A time comes when one's hand is firm again.

CALIGULA But one must know where to place

it. And what's the use to me of a firm hand, what use is the amazing power that's mine, if I can't have the sun set in the east, if I can't reduce the sum of suffering and make an end of death? No, Cæsonia, it's all one whether I sleep or keep awake, if I've no power to tamper with the scheme of things.

CÆSONIA But that's madness, sheer madness. It's wanting to be a god on earth.

CALIGULA So you, too, think I'm mad. And yet —what is a god that I should wish to be his equal? No, it's something higher, far above the gods, that I'm aiming at, longing for with all my heart and soul. I am taking over a kingdom where the impossible is king.

CÆSONIA You can't prevent the sky from being the sky, or a fresh young face from aging, or a man's heart from growing cold.

CALIGULA [*With rising excitement.*] I want . . . I want to drown the sky in the sea, to infuse ugliness with beauty, to wring a laugh from pain.

CÆSONIA [*Facing him with an imploring gesture.*] There's good and bad, high and low, justice and injustice. And I swear to you these will never change.

CALIGULA [*In the same tone.*] And I'm resolved to change them . . . I shall make this age of ours a kingly gift—the gift of equality. And when all is leveled out, when the impossible has come to earth and the moon is in my hands—then, perhaps, I shall be transfigured and the world renewed; then men will die no more and at last be happy.

CÆSONIA [*With a little cry.*] And love? Surely you won't go back on love!

CALIGULA [*In a wild burst of anger.*] Love, Cæsonia! [*He grips her shoulders and shakes her.*] I've learned the truth about love; it's nothing, nothing! That fellow was quite right —you heard what he said, didn't you?—it's only the Treasury that counts. The fountainhead of all. Ah, now at last I'm going to live, really *live*. And living, my dear, is the opposite of loving. I know what I'm talking about —and I invite you to the most gorgeous of shows, a sight for gods to gloat on, a whole world called to judgment. But for that I must have a crowd—spectators, victims, criminals, hundreds and thousands of them. [*He rushes to the gong and begins hammering on it, faster and faster.*] Let the accused come forward. I want my criminals, and they all are criminals. [*Still striking the gong.*] Bring in the condemned men. I must have my public. Judges, witnesses, accused—all sentenced to death without a hearing. Yes, Cæsonia, I'll show them something they have never seen before, the one free man in the Roman Empire. [*To the clangor of the gong the palace has been gradually filling with noises; the clash of arms, voices, footsteps slow or hurried, coming nearer, growing louder. Some soldiers enter, and leave hastily.*] And you, Cæsonia, shall obey me. You must stand by me to the end. It will be marvelous, you'll see. Swear to stand by me, Cæsonia.

CÆSONIA [*Wildly, between two gong strokes.*] I needn't swear. You know I love you.

CALIGULA [*In the same tone.*] You'll do all I tell you.

CÆSONIA All, all, Caligula—but do, please stop. . . .

CALIGULA [*Still striking the gong.*] You will be cruel.

CÆSONIA [*Sobbing.*] Cruel.

CALIGULA [*Still beating the gong.*] Cold and ruthless.

CÆSONIA Ruthless.

CALIGULA And you will suffer, too.

CÆSONIA Yes, yes—oh, no, please . . . I'm—I'm going mad, I think! [*Some patricians enter, followed by members of the palace staff. All look bewildered and perturbed.* CALIGULA *bangs the gong for the last time, raises his mallet, swings round and summons them in a shrill, half-crazy voice.*]

CALIGULA Come here. All of you. Nearer. Nearer still. [*He is quivering with impatience.*] Your Emperor commands you to come nearer. [*They come forward, pale with terror.*] Quickly. And you, Cæsonia, come beside me. [*He takes her hand, leads her to the mirror, and with a wild sweep of his mallet effaces a reflection on its surface. Then gives a sudden laugh.*] All gone. You see, my dear? An end of memories; no more masks. Nothing, nobody left. Nobody? No, that's not true. Look, Cæsonia. Come here, all of you, and *look* . . .

[*He plants himself in front of the mirror in a grotesque attitude.*]

CÆSONIA [*Staring, horrified, at the mirror.*] Caligula! [CALIGULA *lays a finger on the glass.*

His gaze steadies abruptly and when he speaks his voice has a new, proud ardor.]

CALIGULA Yes . . . Caligula.

[*Curtain.*]

ACT II

Three years later.

A room in CHEREA'S *house, where the patricians met in secret.*

FIRST PATRICIAN It's outrageous, the way he's treating us.

THE OLD PATRICIAN He calls me "darling"! In public, mind you—just to make a laughing-stock of me. Death's too good for him.

FIRST PATRICIAN And fancy making us run beside his litter when he goes into the country.

SECOND PATRICIAN He says the exercise will do us good.

THE OLD PATRICIAN Conduct like that is quite inexcusable.

THIRD PATRICIAN You're right. That's precisely the sort of thing one can't forgive.

FIRST PATRICIAN He confiscated your property, Patricius. He killed your father, Scipio. He's taken your wife from you, Octavius, and forced her to work in his public brothel. He has killed your son, Lepidus. I ask you, gentlemen, can you endure this? I, anyhow, have made up my mind. I know the risks, but I also know this life of abject fear is quite unbearable. Worse than death, in fact. Yes, as I said, my mind's made up.

SCIPIO He made my mind up for me when he had my father put to death.

FIRST PATRICIAN Well? Can you still hesitate?

A KNIGHT No. We're with you. He's transferred our stalls at the Circus to the public, and egged us on to fight with the rabble—just to have a pretext for punishing us, of course.

THE OLD PATRICIAN He's a coward.

SECOND PATRICIAN A bully.

THIRD PATRICIAN A buffoon.

THE OLD PATRICIAN He's impotent—that's his trouble, I should say.

[*A scene of wild confusion follows, weapons are brandished, a table is overturned, and there is a general rush toward the door. Just at this moment* CHEREA *strolls in, composed as usual, and checks their onrush.*]

CHEREA What's all this about? Where are you going?

A PATRICIAN To the palace.

CHEREA Ah, yes. And I can guess why. But do you think you'll be allowed to enter?

THE PATRICIAN There's no question of asking leave.

CHEREA Lepidus, would you kindly shut that door? [*The door is shut.* CHEREA *goes to the overturned table and seats himself on a corner of it. The others turn toward him.*] It's not so simple as you think, my friends. You're afraid, but fear can't take the place of courage and deliberation. In short, you're acting too hastily.

A KNIGHT If you're not with us, go. But keep your mouth shut.

CHEREA I suspect I'm with you. But make no mistake. Not for the same reasons.

A VOICE That's enough idle talk.

CHEREA [*Standing up.*] I agree. Let's get down to facts. But, first, let me make myself clear. Though I am *with* you, I'm not *for* you. That, indeed, is why I think you're going about it the wrong way. You haven't taken your enemy's measure; that's obvious, since you attribute petty motives to him. But there's nothing petty about Caligula, and you're riding for a fall. You'd be better placed to fight him if you would try to see him as he really is.

A VOICE We see him as he is—a crazy tyrant.

CHEREA No. We've had experience of mad emperors. But this one isn't mad enough. And what I loathe in him is this: that he knows what he wants.

FIRST PATRICIAN And we, too, know it; he wants to murder us all.

CHEREA You're wrong. Our deaths are only a side issue. He's putting his power at the service of a loftier, deadlier passion; and it imperils everything we hold most sacred. True, it's not the first time Rome has seen a man wielding unlimited power; but it's the first time he sets no limit to his use of it, and counts mankind, and the world we know, for nothing. That's what appalls me in Caligula; that's what I want to fight. To lose one's life is no great matter; when the time comes I'll have the courage to lose mine. But what's intolerable is to see one's life being drained of meaning, to be told there's no reason for existing. A man can't live without some reason for living.

FIRST PATRICIAN Revenge is a good reason.

CHEREA Yes, and I propose to share it with you. But I'd have you know that it's not on your account, or to help you to avenge your petty humiliations. No, if I join forces with you, it's to combat a big idea—an ideal, if you like—whose triumph would mean the end of everything. I can endure your being made a mock of, but I cannot endure Caligula's carrying out his theories to the end. He is converting his philosophy into corpses and—unfortunately for us—it's a philosophy that's logical from start to finish. And where one can't refute, one strikes.

A VOICE Yes. We must *act*.

CHEREA We must take action, I agree. But a frontal attack's quite useless when one is fighting an imperial madman in the full flush of his power. You can take arms against a vulgar tyrant, but cunning is needed to fight down disinterested malice. You can only urge it on to follow its bent, and bide your time until its logic founders in sheer lunacy. As you see, I prefer to be quite frank, and I warn you I'll be with you only for a time. Afterward, I shall do nothing to advance your interests; all I wish is to regain some peace of mind in a world that has regained a meaning. What spurs me on is not ambition but fear, my very reasonable fear of that inhuman vision in which my life means no more than a speck of dust.

FIRST PATRICIAN [*Approaching him.*] I have an inkling of what you mean, Cherea. Anyhow, the great thing is that you, too, feel that the whole fabric of society is threatened. You, gentlemen, agree with me, I take it, that our ruling motive is of a moral order. Family life is breaking down, men are losing their respect for honest work, a wave of immorality is sweeping the country. Who of us can be deaf to the appeal of our ancestral piety in its hour of danger? Fellow conspirators, will you tolerate a state of things in which patricians are forced to run, like slaves, beside the Emperor's litter?

THE OLD PATRICIAN Will you allow them to be addressed as "darling"?

A VOICE And have their wives snatched from them?

ANOTHER VOICE And their money?

ALL TOGETHER No!

FIRST PATRICIAN Cherea, your advice is good, and you did well to calm our passion. The time is not yet ripe for action; the masses would still be against us. Will you join us in watching for the best moment to strike—and strike hard?

CHEREA Yes—and meanwhile let Caligula follow his dream. Or, rather, let's actively encourage him to carry out his wildest plans. Let's put method into his madness. And then, at last, a day will come when he's alone, a lonely man in an empire of the dead and kinsmen of the dead.

[*A general uproar. Trumpet calls outside. Then silence, but for whispers of a name:* "CALIGULA!" CALIGULA *enters with* CÆSONIA, *followed by* HELICON *and some soldiers. Pantomine.* CALIGULA *halts and gazes at the conspirators. Without a word he moves from one to the other, straightens a buckle on one man's shoulder, steps back to contemplate another, sweeps them with his gaze, then draws his hand over his eyes and walks out, still without a word.*]

CÆSONIA [*Ironically, pointing to the disorder of the room.*] Were you having a fight?

CHEREA Yes, we were fighting.

CÆSONIA [*In the same tone.*] Really? Might I know what you were fighting about?

CHEREA About . . . nothing in particular.

CÆSONIA Ah? Then it isn't true.

CHEREA What isn't true?

CÆSONIA You were *not* fighting.

CHEREA Have it your own way. We weren't fighting.

CÆSONIA [*Smiling.*] Perhaps you'd do better to tidy up the place. Caligula hates untidiness.

HELICON [*To the* OLD PATRICIAN.] You'll end by making him do something out of character.

THE OLD PATRICIAN Pardon . . . I don't follow. What have we done to him?

HELICON Nothing. Just nothing. It's fantastic being futile to that point; enough to get on anybody's nerves. Try to put yourselves in Caligula's place. [*A short pause.*] I see; doing a bit of plotting, weren't you now?

THE OLD PATRICIAN Really, that's too absurd. I hope Caligula doesn't imagine . . .

HELICON He doesn't imagine. He *knows*. But, I suppose, at bottom, he rather wants it. . . . Well, we'd better set to tidying up.

[*All get busy.* CALIGULA *enters and watches them.*]

CALIGULA [*To the* OLD PATRICIAN.] Good day, darling. [*To the others.*] Gentlemen, I'm on my way to an execution. But I thought I'd drop in at your place, Cherea, for a light meal. I've given orders to have food brought here for all of us. But send for your wives first. [*A short silence.*] Rufius should thank his stars that I've been seized with hunger. [*Confidentially.*] Rufius, I may tell you, is the knight who's going to be executed. [*Another short silence.*] What's this? None of you asks me why I've sentenced him to death? [*No one speaks. Meanwhile slaves lay the table and bring food.*] Good for you! I see you're growing quite intelligent. [*He nibbles an olive.*] It has dawned on you that a man needn't have done anything for him to die. [*He stops eating and gazes at his guests with a twinkle in his eye.*] Soldiers, I am proud of you. [*Three or four women enter.*] Good! Let's take our places. Anyhow. No order of precedence today. [*All are seated.*] There's no denying it, that fellow Rufius is in luck. But I wonder if he appreciates this short reprieve. A few hours gained on death, why, they're worth their weight in gold! [*He begins eating; the others follow suit. It becomes clear that* CALIGULA's *table manners are deplorable. There is no need for him to flick his olive stones onto his neighbors' plates, or to spit out bits of gristle over the dish, to to pick his teeth with his nails, or to scratch his head furiously. However, he indulges in these practices throughout the meal, without the least compunction. At one moment he stops eating, stares at* LEPIDUS, *one of the guests, and says roughly.*] You're looking grumpy, Lepidus. I wonder, can it be because I had your son killed?

LEPIDUS [*Thickly.*] Certainly not, Caius. Quite the contrary.

CALIGULA [*Beaming at him.*] "Quite the contrary!" It's always nice to see a face that hides the secrets of the heart. Your face is sad. But what about your heart? Quite the contrary—isn't that so, Lepidus?

LEPIDUS [*Doggedly.*] Quite the contrary, Cæsar.

CALIGULA [*More and more enjoying the situation.*] Really, Lepidus, there's no one I like better than you. Now let's have a laugh together, my dear friend. Tell me a funny story.

LEPIDUS [*Who has overrated his endurance.*] Please . . .

CALIGULA Good! Very good! Then it's I who'll tell the story. But you'll laugh, won't you, Lepidus? [*With a glint of malice.*] If only for the sake of your other son. [*Smiling again.*] In any case, as you've just told us, you're not in a bad humor. [*He takes a drink, then says in the tone of a teacher prompting a pupil.*] Quite . . . quite the . . .

LEPIDUS [*Wearily.*] Quite the contrary, Cæsar.

CALIGULA Splendid! [*Drinks again.*] Now listen. [*In a gentle, faraway tone.*] Once upon a time there was a poor young emperor whom nobody loved. He loved Lepidus, and to root out of his heart his love for Lepidus, he had his youngest son killed. [*In a brisker tone.*] Needless to say, there's not a word of truth in it. Still it's a funny story, eh? But you're not laughing. Nobody's laughing. Now listen! [*In a burst of anger.*] I insist on everybody's laughing. You, Lepidus, shall lead the chorus. Stand up, every one of you, and laugh. [*He thumps the table.*] Do you hear what I say? I wish to see you laughing, all of you. [*All rise to their feet. During this scene all the players,* CALIGULA *and* CÆSONIA *excepted, behave like marionettes in a puppet play.* CALIGULA *sinks back on his couch, beaming with delight, and bursts into a fit of laughter.*] Oh, Cæsonia! Just look at them! The game is up; honor, respectability, the wisdom of the nations, gone with the wind! The wind of fear has blown them all away. Fear, Cæsonia—don't you agree?—is a noble emotion, pure and simple, self-sufficient, like no other; it draws its patent of nobility straight from the guts. [*He strikes his forehead and drinks again. In a friendly tone.*] Well, well, let's change the subject. What have you to say, Cherea? You've been very silent.

CHEREA I'm quite ready to speak, Caius. When you give me leave.

CALIGULA Excellent. Then—keep silent. I'd rather have a word from our friend Mucius.

MUCIUS [*Reluctantly.*] As you will, Caius.

CALIGULA Then tell us something about your wife. And begin by sending her to this place, on my right. [MUCIUS' WIFE *seats herself beside* CALIGULA.] Well, Mucius? We're waiting.

MUCIUS [*Hardly knowing what he says.*] My wife . . . but . . . I'm very fond of her.

[*General laughter.*]

CALIGULA Why, of course, my friend, of course. But how ordinary of you! So unoriginal! [*He is leaning toward her, tickling her shoulder playfully with his tongue.*] By the way, when I came in just now, you were hatching a plot, weren't you? A nice bloody little plot?

OLD PATRICIAN Oh, Caius, how can you . . . ?

CALIGULA It doesn't matter in the least, my pet. Old age will be served. I won't take it seriously. Not one of you has the spunk for a heroic act. . . . Ah, it's just come to my mind, I have some affairs of state to settle. But, first, let the imperious desires that nature creates in us have their way.

[*He rises and leads* MUCIUS' WIFE *into an adjoining room.* MUCIUS *starts up from his seat.*]

CÆSONIA [*Amiably.*] Please, Mucius. Will you pour me out another glass of this excellent wine. [MUCIUS *complies; his movement of revolt is quelled. Everyone looks embarrassed. Chairs creak noisily. The ensuing conversation is in a strained tone.* CÆSONIA *turns to* CHEREA.] Now, Cherea, suppose you tell me why you people were fighting just now?

CHEREA [*Coolly.*] With pleasure, my dear Cæsonia. Our quarrel arose from a discussion whether poetry should be bloodthirsty or not.

CÆSONIA An interesting problem. Somewhat beyond my feminine comprehension, of course. Still it surprises me that your passion for art should make you come to blows.

CHEREA [*In the same rather stilted tone.*] That I can well understand. But I remember Caligula's telling me the other day that all true passion has a spice of cruelty.

CÆSONIA [*Helping herself from the dish in front of her.*] There's truth in that. Don't you agree, gentlemen?

THE OLD PATRICIAN Ah, yes. Caligula has a rare insight into the secret places of the heart.

FIRST PATRICIAN And how eloquently he spoke just now of courage!

SECOND PATRICIAN Really, he should put his ideas into writing. They would be most instructive.

CHEREA And, what's more, it would keep him busy. It's obvious he needs something to occupy his leisure.

CÆSONIA [*Still eating.*] You'll be pleased to hear that Caligula shares your views; he's working on a book. Quite a big one, I believe.

[CALIGULA *enters, accompanied by* MUCIUS' WIFE.]

CALIGULA Mucius, I return your wife, with many thanks. But excuse me, I've some orders to give.

[*He hurries out.* MUCIUS *has gone pale and risen to his feet.*]

CÆSONIA [*To* MUCIUS, *who is standing.*] This book of his will certainly rank among our Latin Classics. Are you listening, Mucius?

MUCIUS [*His eyes still fixed on the door by which* CALIGULA *went out.*] Yes. And what's the book about, Cæsonia?

CÆSONIA [*Indifferently.*] Oh, it's above my head, you know.

CHEREA May we assume it deals with the murderous power of poetry?

CÆSONIA Yes, something of that sort, I understand.

THE OLD PATRICIAN [*Cheerfully.*] Well anyhow, as our friend Cherea said, it will keep him busy.

CÆSONIA Yes, my love. But I'm afraid there's one thing you won't like quite so much about this book, and that's its title.

CHEREA What is it?

CÆSONIA *Cold Steel.*

[CALIGULA *hurries in.*]

CALIGULA Excuse me, but I've some urgent public work in hand. [*To the* INTENDANT.] Intendant, you are to close the public granaries. I have signed a decree to that effect; you will find it in my study.

INTENDANT But, sire . . .

CALIGULA Famine begins tomorrow.

INTENDANT But . . . but heaven knows what may happen—perhaps a revolution.

CALIGULA [*Firmly and deliberately.*] I repeat; famine begins tomorrow. We all know what famine means—a national catastrophe. Well, tomorrow there will be a catastrophe, and I shall end it when I choose. After all, I haven't so many ways of proving I am free. One is always free at someone else's expense. Absurd perhaps, but so it is. [*With a keen glance at* MUCIUS.] Apply this principle to your jealousy—and you'll understand better. [*In a meditative tone.*] Still, what an ugly thing is jealousy! A disease of vanity and the imagination. One pictures one's wife . . . [MUCIUS *clenches his fists and opens his mouth to speak. Before he can get a word out,* CALIGULA *cuts in.*] Now, gentlemen, let's go on with our meal. . . . Do you know, we've been doing quite a lot of work, with Helicon's assistance? Putting the final touches to a little monograph on execution—about which you will have much to say.

HELICON Assuming we ask your opinion.

CALIGULA Why not be generous, Helicon, and let them into our little secrets? Come now, give them a sample. Section Three, first paragraph.

HELICON [*Standing, declaims in a droning voice.*] "Execution relieves and liberates. It is universal, tonic, just in precept and in practice. A man dies because he is guilty. A man is guilty because he is one of Caligula's subjects. Now all men are Caligula's subjects. *Ergo,* all men are guilty and shall die. It is only a matter of time and patience."

CALIGULA [*Laughing.*] There's logic for you, don't you agree? That bit about patience was rather neat, wasn't it? Allow me to tell you, that's the quality I most admire in you . . . your patience. Now, gentlemen, you can disperse. Cherea doesn't need your presence any longer. Cæsonia, I wish you to stay. You too, Lepidus. Also our old friend Mereia. I want to have a little talk with you about our National Brothel. It's not functioning too well; in fact, I'm quite concerned about it.

[*The others file out slowly.* CALIGULA *follows* MUCIUS *with his eyes.*]

CHEREA At your orders, Caius. But what's the trouble? Is the staff unsatisfactory?

CALIGULA No, but the takings are falling off.

MEREIA Then you should raise the entrance fee.

CALIGULA There, Mereia, you missed a golden opportunity of keeping your mouth shut. You're too old to be interested in the subject, and I don't want your opinion.

MEREIA Then why ask me to stay?

CALIGULA Because, presently, I may require some cool, dispassionate advice.

[MEREIA *moves away.*]

CHEREA If you wish to hear my views on the subject, Caius, I'd say, neither coolly nor dispassionately, that it would be a blunder to raise the scale of charges.

CALIGULA Obviously. What's needed is a bigger turnover. I've explained my plan of campaign to Cæsonia, and she will tell you all about it. As for me, I've had too much wine, I'm feeling sleepy.

[*He lies down and closes his eyes.*]

CÆSONIA It's very simple. Caligula is creating a new order of merit.

CHEREA Sorry, I don't see the connection.

CÆSONIA No? But there is one. It will be called the Badge of Civic Merit and awarded to those who have patronized Caligula's National Brothel most assiduously.

CHEREA A brilliant idea!

CÆSONIA I agree. Oh, I forgot to mention that the badge will be conferred each month, after checking the admission tickets. Any citizen who has not obtained the badge within twelve months will be exiled, or executed.

CHEREA Why "or executed"?

CÆSONIA Because Caligula says it doesn't matter which—but it's important he should have the right of choosing.

CHEREA Bravo! The Public Treasury will wipe out its deficit in no time.

[CALIGULA *has half opened his eyes and is watching old* MEREIA *who, standing in a corner, has produced a small flask and is sipping its contents.*]

CALIGULA [*Still lying on the couch.*] What's that you're drinking, Mereia?

MEREIA It's for my asthma, Caius.

CALIGULA [*Rises, and thrusting the others aside, goes up to* MEREIA *and sniffs his mouth.*] No, it's an antidote.

MEREIA What an idea, Caius! You must be joking. I have choking fits at night and I've been in the doctor's hands for months.

CALIGULA So you're afraid of being poisoned?

MEREIA My asthma . . .

CALIGULA No. Why beat about the bush? You're afraid I'll poison you. You suspect me. You're keeping an eye on me.

MEREIA Good heavens, no!

CALIGULA You suspect me. I'm not to be trusted, eh?

MEREIA Caius!

CALIGULA [*Roughly.*] Answer! [*In a cool, judicial tone.*] If you take an antidote, it follows that you credit me with the intention of poisoning you. Q.E.D.

MEREIA Yes . . . I mean . . . no!

CALIGULA And thinking I intend to poison you, you take steps to frustrate my plan. [*He falls silent. Meanwhile* CÆSONIA *and* CHEREA *have moved away, backstage.* LEPIDUS *is watching the speakers with an air of consternation.*] That makes two crimes, Mereia, and a dilemma from which you can't escape. *Either* I have no wish to cause your death; in which case you are unjustly suspecting me, your emperor. *Or else* I desire your death; in which case, vermin that you are, you're trying to thwart my will. [*Another silence.* CALIGULA *contemplates the old man gloatingly.*] Well, Mereia, what have you to say to my logic?

MEREIA It . . . it's sound enough. Caius. Only it doesn't apply to the case.

CALIGULA A third crime. You take me for a fool. Now sit down and listen carefully. [*To* LEPIDUS.] Let everyone sit down. [*To* MEREIA.] Of these three crimes only one does you honor; the second one—because by crediting me with a certain wish and presuming to oppose it you are deliberately defying me. You are a rebel, a leader of revolt. And that needs courage. [*Sadly.*] I've a great liking for you, Mereia. And that is why you'll be condemned for crime number two, and not for either of the others. You shall die nobly, a rebel's death. [*While he talks* MEREIA *is shrinking together on his chair.*] Don't thank me. It's quite natural. Here. [*Holds out a phial. His tone is amiable.*] Drink this poison. [MEREIA *shakes his head. He is sobbing violently.* CALIGULA *shows signs of impatience.*] Don't waste time. Take it. [MEREIA *makes a feeble attempt to escape. But* CALIGULA *with a wild leap is on him, catches him in the center of the stage and after a brief struggle pins him down on a low couch. He forces the phial between his lips and smashes it with a blow of his fist. After some convulsive movements* MEREIA *dies. His face is streaming with blood and tears.* CALIGULA *rises, wipes his hands absent-mindedly, then hands* MEREIA'*s flask to* CÆSONIA.] What was it? An antidote?

CÆSONIA [*Calmly.*] No, Caligula. A remedy for asthma.

[*A short silence.*]

CALIGULA [*Gazing down at* MEREIA.] No matter. It all comes to the same thing in the end. A little sooner, a little later. . . .

[*He goes out hurriedly, still wiping his hands.*]

LEPIDUS [*In a horrified tone.*] What . . . what shall we do?

CÆSONIA [*Coolly.*] Remove that body to begin with, I should say. It's rather a beastly sight.

[CHEREA *and* LEPIDUS *drag the body into the wings.*]

LEPIDUS [*To* CHEREA.] We must act quickly.

CHEREA We'll need to be two hundred.

[*Young* SCIPIO *enters. Seeing* CÆSONIA, *he makes as if to leave.*]

CÆSONIA Come.

SCIPIO What do you want?

CÆSONIA Come nearer. [*She pushes up his chin and looks him in the eyes. A short silence. Then, in a calm, unemotional voice.*] He killed your father, didn't he?

SCIPIO Yes.

CÆSONIA Do you hate him?

SCIPIO Yes.

CÆSONIA And you'd like to kill him?

SCIPIO Yes.

CÆSONIA [*Withdrawing her hand.*] But—why tell me this?

SCIPIO Because I fear nobody. Killing him or being killed—either way out will do. And anyhow you won't betray me.

CÆSONIA That's so. I won't betray you. But I want to tell you something—or, rather, I'd like to speak to what is best in you.

SCIPIO What's best in me is—my hatred.

CÆSONIA Please listen carefully to what I'm going to say. It may sound hard to grasp, but it's as clear as daylight, really. And it's something that would bring about the one real revolution in this world of ours, if people would only take it in.

SCIPIO Yes? What is it?

CÆSONIA Wait! Try to call up a picture of your father's death, of the agony on his face as they were tearing out his tongue. Think of the blood streaming from his mouth, and recall his screams, like a tortured animal's.

SCIPIO Yes.

CÆSONIA And now think of Caligula.

SCIPIO [*His voice rough with hatred.*] Yes.

CÆSONIA Now listen. *Try to understand him.*

[*She goes out, leaving* SCIPIO *gaping after her in bewilderment.* HELICON *enters.*]

HELICON Caligula will be here in a moment. Suppose you go for your meal, young poet?

SCIPIO Helicon, help me.

HELICON Too dangerous, my lamb. And poetry means nothing to me.

SCIPIO You can help me. You know . . . so many things.

HELICON I know that the days go by—and growing boys should have their meals on time . . . I know, too, that you could kill Caligula . . . and he wouldn't greatly mind it.

[HELICON *goes out.* CALIGULA *enters.*]

CALIGULA Ah, it's you, Scipio. [*He pauses. One has the impression that he is somewhat embarrassed.*] It's quite a long time since I saw you last. [*Slowly approaches* SCIPIO.] What have you been up to? Writing more poems, I suppose. Might I see your latest composition?

SCIPIO [*Likewise ill at ease, torn between hatred and some less defined emotion.*] Yes, Cæsar, I've written some more poems.

CALIGULA On what subject?

SCIPIO Oh, on nothing in particular. Well, on Nature in a way.

CALIGULA A fine theme. And a vast one. And what has Nature done for you?

SCIPIO [*Pulling himself together, in a somewhat truculent tone.*] It consoles me for not being Cæsar.

CALIGULA Really? And do you think Nature could console me for being Cæsar?

SCIPIO [*In the same tone.*] Why not? Nature has healed worse wounds than that.

CALIGULA [*In a curiously young, unaffected voice.*] Wounds, you said? There was anger in your voice. Because I put your father to death? . . . That word you used—if you only knew how apt it is! My wounds! [*In a different tone.*] Well, well, there's nothing like hatred for developing the intelligence.

SCIPIO [*Stiffly.*] I answered your question about Nature.

[CALIGULA *sits down, gazes at* SCIPIO, *then brusquely grips his wrists and forces him to stand up. He takes the young man's face between his hands.*]

CALIGULA Recite your poem to me, please.

SCIPIO No, please, don't ask me that.

CALIGULA Why not?

SCIPIO I haven't got it on me.

CALIGULA Can't you remember it?

SCIPIO No.

CALIGULA Anyhow you can tell me what it's about.

SCIPIO [*Still hostile; reluctantly.*] I spoke of a . . . a certain harmony . . .

CALIGULA [*Breaking in; in a pensive voice.*] . . . between one's feet and the earth.

SCIPIO [*Looking surprised.*] Yes, it's almost that . . . and it tells of the wavy outline of the Roman hills and the sudden thrill of peace that twilight brings to them . . .

CALIGULA And the cries of swifts winding through the green dusk.

SCIPIO [*Yielding more and more to his emotion.*] Yes, yes! And that fantastic moment when the sky all flushed with red and gold swings round and shows its other side, spangled with stars.

CALIGULA And the faint smell of smoke and trees and streams that mingles with the rising mist.

SCIPIO [*In a sort of ecstasy.*] Yes, and the chirr of crickets, the coolness veining the warm air, the rumble of carts and the farmers' shouts, dogs barking . . .

CALIGULA And the roads drowned in shadow winding through the olive groves . . .

SCIPIO Yes, yes. That's it, exactly. . . . But how did you know?

CALIGULA [*Drawing* SCIPIO *to his breast.*] I wonder! Perhaps because the same eternal truths appeal to us both.

SCIPIO [*Quivering with excitement, burying his head on* CALIGULA's *breast.*] Anyhow, what does it matter! All I know is that everything I feel or think of turns to love.

CALIGULA [*Stroking his hair.*] That, Scipio, is a privilege of noble hearts—and how I wish I could share your . . . your limpidity! But my appetite for life's too keen; Nature can never sate it. You belong to quite another world, and you can't understand. You are single-minded for good; and I am single-minded—for evil.

SCIPIO I *do* understand.

CALIGULA No. There's something deep down in me—an abyss of silence, a pool of stagnant water, rotting weeds. [*With an abrupt change of manner.*] Your poem sounds very good indeed, but, if you really want my opinion. . . .

SCIPIO [*His head on* CALIGULA's *breast, murmurs.*] Yes?

CALIGULA All that's a bit . . . anemic.

SCIPIO [*Recoiling abruptly, as if stung by a serpent, and gazing, horrified, at* CALIGULA, *he cries hoarsely.*] Oh, you brute! You loathsome brute! You've fooled me again. I know! You were playing a trick on me, weren't you? And now you're gloating over your success.

CALIGULA [*With a hint of sadness.*] There's truth in what you say. I *was* playing a part.

SCIPIO [*In the same indignant tone.*] What a foul, black heart you have! And how all that wickedness and hatred must make you suffer!

CALIGULA [*Gently.*] That's enough.

SCIPIO How I loathe you! And how I pity you!

CALIGULA [*Angrily.*] Enough, I tell you.

SCIPIO And how horrible a loneliness like yours must be!

CALIGULA [*In a rush of anger, gripping the boy by the collar, and shaking him.*] Loneliness! What do *you* know of it? Only the loneliness of poets and weaklings. You prate of loneliness, but you don't realize that one is *never* alone. Always we are attended by the same load of the future and the past. Those we have killed are always with us. But *they* are no great trouble. It's those we have loved, those who loved us and whom we did not love; regrets, desires, bitterness and sweetness, whores and gods, the celestial gang! Always, always with us! [*He releases* SCIPIO *and moves back to his former place.*] Alone! Ah, if only in this loneliness, this ghoul-haunted wilderness of mine, I could know, but for a moment, real solitude, real silence, the throbbing stillness of a tree! [*Sitting down, in an access of fatigue.*] Solitude? No, Scipio, mine is full of gnashings of teeth, hideous with jarring sounds and voices. And when I am with the women I make mine and darkness falls on us and I think, now my body's had its fill, that I can feel myself my own at last, poised between death and life—ah, then my solitude is fouled by the stale smell of pleasure from the woman sprawling at my side.

[*A long silence.* CALIGULA *seems weary and despondent.* SCIPIO *moves behind him and approaches hesitantly. He slowly stretches out a hand toward him, from behind, and lays it on his shoulder. Without looking round,* CALIGULA *places his hand on* SCIPIO*'s.*]

SCIPIO All men have a secret solace. It helps them to endure, and they turn to it when life has wearied them beyond enduring.

CALIGULA Yes, Scipio.

SCIPIO Have you nothing of the kind in your life, no refuge, no mood that makes the tears well up, no consolation?

CALIGULA Yes, I have something of the kind.

SCIPIO What is it?

CALIGULA [*Very quietly.*] Scorn.

[*Curtain.*]

ACT III

A room in the imperial palace.

Before the curtain rises a rhythmic clash of cymbals and the thudding of a drum have been coming from the stage, and when it goes up we see a curtained-off booth, with a small proscenium in front, such as strolling players use at country fairs. On the little stage are CÆSONIA *and* HELICON, *flanked by cymbal players. Seated on benches, with their backs to the audience, are some patricians and young* SCIPIO.

HELICON [*In the tone of a showman at a fair.*] Walk up! Walk up! [*A clash of cymbals.*] Once more the gods have come to earth. They have assumed the human form of our heaven-born emperor, known to men as Caligula. Draw near, mortals of common clay; a holy miracle is taking place before your eyes. By a divine dispensation peculiar to Caligula's hallowed reign, the secrets of the gods will be revealed to you. [*Cymbals.*]

CÆSONIA Come, gentlemen. Come and adore him—and don't forget to give your alms. Today heaven and its mysteries are on show, at a price to suit every pocket.

HELICON For all to see, the secrets of Olympus, revelations in high places, featuring gods in undress, their little plots and pranks. Step this way! The whole truth about your gods! [*Cymbals.*]

CÆSONIA Adore him, and give your alms. Come near, gentlemen. The show's beginning.

[*Cymbals. Slaves are placing various objects on the platform.*]

HELICON An epoch-making reproduction of the life celestial, warranted authentic in every detail. For the first time the pomp and splendor of the gods are presented to the Roman public. You will relish our novel, breathtaking effects: flashes of lightning [*Slaves light Greek fires.*], peals of thunder [*They roll a barrel filled with stones.*], the divine event on its triumphal way. Now watch with all your eyes.

[*He draws aside the curtain. Grotesquely attired as Venus,* CALIGULA *beams down on them from a pedestal.*]

CALIGULA [*Amiably.*] I'm Venus today.

CÆSONIA Now for the adoration. Bow down. [*All but* SCIPIO *bend their heads.*] And repeat after me the litany of Venus called Caligula. "Our Lady of pangs and pleasures . . ."

THE PATRICIANS "Our Lady of pangs and pleasures . . ."

CÆSONIA "Born of the waves, bitter and bright with seafoam . . ."

THE PATRICIANS "Born of the waves, bitter and bright with seafoam . . ."

CÆSONIA "O Queen whose gifts are laughter and regrets . . ."

THE PATRICIANS "O Queen whose gifts are laughter and regrets . . ."

CÆSONIA "Rancors and raptures . . ."

THE PATRICIANS "Rancors and raptures . . ."

CÆSONIA "Teach us the indifference that kindles love anew . . ."

THE PATRICIANS "Teach us the indifference that kindles love anew . . ."

CÆSONIA "Make known to us the truth about this world—which is that it has none . . ."

THE PATRICIANS "Make known to us the truth about this world—which is that it has none . . ."

CÆSONIA "And grant us strength to live up to this verity of verities."

THE PATRICIANS "And grant us strength to live up to this verity of verities."

CÆSONIA Now, pause.

THE PATRICIANS Now, pause.

CÆSONIA [*After a short silence.*] "Bestow your gifts on us, and shed on our faces the light of your impartial cruelty, your wanton hatred; unfold above our eyes your arms laden with flowers and murders . . ."

THE PATRICIANS ". . . your arms laden with flowers and murders."

CÆSONIA "Welcome your wandering children home, to the bleak sanctuary of your heartless, thankless love. Give us your passions without object, your griefs devoid of reason, your raptures that lead nowhere . . ."

THE PATRICIANS ". . . your raptures that lead nowhere . . ."

CÆSONIA [*Raising her voice.*] "O Queen, so empty yet so ardent, inhuman yet so earthly, make us drunk with the wine of your equivalence, and surfeit us forever in the brackish darkness of your heart."

THE PATRICIANS "Make us drunk with the wine of your equivalence, and surfeit us forever in the brackish darkness of your heart." [*When the patricians have said the last response,* CALIGULA, *who until now has been quite motionless, snorts and rises.*]

CALIGULA [*In a stentorian voice.*] Granted, my children. Your prayer is heard. [*He squats cross-legged on the pedestal. One by one the patricians makes obeisance, deposit their alms, and line up on the right. The last, in his flurry, forgets to make an offering.* CALIGULA *bounds to his feet.*] Steady! Steady on! Come here, my lad. Worship's very well, but alms-giving is better. Thank you. We are appeased. Ah, if the gods had no wealth other than the love you mortals give them, they'd be as poor as poor Caligula. Now, gentlemen, you may go, and spread abroad the glad tidings of the miracle you've been allowed to witness. You have seen Venus, seen her godhead with your fleshly eyes, and Venus herself has spoken to you. Go, most favored gentlemen. [*The patricians begin to move away.*] Just a moment. When you leave, mind you take the exit on your left. I have posted sentries in the others, with orders to kill you.

[*The patricians file out hastily, in some disorder. The slaves and musicians leave the stage.*]

HELICON [*Pointing a threatening finger at* SCIPIO.] Naughty boy, you've been playing the anarchist again.

SCIPIO [*To* CALIGULA.] You spoke blasphemy, Caius.

CALIGULA Blasphemy? What's that?

SCIPIO You're befouling heaven, after bloodying the earth.

HELICON How this youngster loves big words!

[*He stretches himself on a couch.*]

CÆSONIA [*Composedly.*] You should watch your tongue, my lad. At this moment men are dying in Rome for saying much less.

SCIPIO Maybe—but I've resolved to tell Caligula the truth.

CÆSONIA Listen to him, Caligula! That was the

one thing missing in your Empire—a bold young moralist.

CALIGULA [*Giving* SCIPIO *a curious glance.*] Do you really believe in the gods, Scipio?

SCIPIO No.

CALIGULA Then I fail to follow. If you don't believe, why be so keen to scent out blasphemy?

SCIPIO One may deny something without feeling called on to besmirch it, or deprive others of the right of believing in it.

CALIGULA But that's humility, the real thing, unless I'm much mistaken. Ah, my dear Scipio, how glad I am on your behalf—and a trifle envious, too. Humility's the one emotion I may never feel.

SCIPIO It's not I you're envious of; it's the gods.

CALIGULA If you don't mind, that will remain our secret—the great enigma of our reign. Really, you know, there's only one thing for which I might be blamed today—and that's this small advance I've made upon the path of freedom. For someone who loves power the rivalry of the gods is rather irksome. Well, I've proved to these imaginary gods that any man, without previous training, if he applies his mind to it, can play their absurd parts to perfection.

SCIPIO That, Caius, is what I meant by blasphemy.

CALIGULA No, Scipio, it's clear-sightedness. I've merely realized that there's only one way of getting even with the gods. All that's needed is to be as cruel as they.

SCIPIO All that's needed is to play the tyrant.

CALIGULA Tell me, my young friend. What exactly *is* a tyrant?

SCIPIO A blind soul.

CALIGULA That's a moot point. I should say the real tyrant is a man who sacrifices a whole nation to his ideal or his ambition. But I have no ideal, and there's nothing left for me to covet by way of power or glory. If I use this power of mine, it's to compensate.

SCIPIO For what?

CALIGULA For the hatred and stupidity of the gods.

SCIPIO Hatred does not compensate for hatred. Power is no solution. Personally I know only one way of countering the hostility of the world we live in.

CALIGULA Yes? And what is it?

SCIPIO Poverty.

CALIGULA [*Bending over his feet and scrutinizing his toes.*] I must try that, too.

SCIPIO Meanwhile many men round you are dying.

CALIGULA Oh, come! Not so many as all that. Do you know how many wars I've refused to embark on?

SCIPIO No.

CALIGULA Three. And do you know why I refused?

SCIPIO Because the grandeur of Rome means nothing to you.

CALIGULA No. Because I respect human life.

SCIPIO You're joking, Caius.

CALIGULA Or, anyhow, I respect it more than I respect military triumphs. But it's a fact that I don't respect it more than I respect my own life. And if I find killing easy, it's because dying isn't hard for me. No, the more I think about it, the surer I feel that I'm no tyrant.

SCIPIO What does it matter, if it costs us quite as dear as if you were one?

CALIGULA [*With a hint of petulance.*] If you had the least head for figures you'd know that the smallest war a tyrant—however levelheaded he might be—indulged in would cost you a thousand times more than all my vagaries (shall we call them?) put together.

SCIPIO Possibly. But at least there'd be *some* sense behind a war; it would be understandable—and to understand makes up for much.

CALIGULA There's no understanding fate; therefore I choose to play the part of fate. I wear the foolish, unintelligible face of a professional god. And that is what the men who were here with you have learned to adore.

SCIPIO That, too, Caius, is blasphemy.

CALIGULA No, Scipio, it's dramatic art. The great mistake you people make is not to take the drama seriously enough. If you did, you'd know that any man can play lead in the divine comedy and become a god. All he needs do is to harden his heart.

SCIPIO You may be right, Caius. But I rather think you've done everything that was needed to rouse up against you a legion of human gods, ruthless as yourself, who will drown in blood your godhead of a day.

CÆSONIA Really, Scipio!

CALIGULA [*Peremptorily.*] No, don't stop him, Cæsonia. Yes, Scipio, you spoke truer than you knew; I've done everything needed to that end. I find it hard to picture the event you speak of—but I sometimes dream it. And in all those faces surging up out of the angry darkness, convulsed with fear and hatred, I see, and I rejoice to see, the only god I've worshipped on this earth; foul and craven as the human heart. [*Irritably.*] Now go. I've had enough of you, more than enough. [*In a different tone.*] I really must attend to my toenails; they're not nearly red enough, and I've no time to waste. [*All go, with the exception of* HELICON. *He hovers round* CALIGULA, *who is busy examining his toes.*] Helicon!

HELICON Yes?

CALIGULA Getting on with your task?

HELICON What task?

CALIGULA You know . . . the moon.

HELICON Ah yes, the moon. . . . It's a matter of time and patience. But I'd like to have a word with you.

CALIGULA I might have patience; only I have not much time. So you must make haste.

HELICON I said I'd do my utmost. But, first, I have something to tell you. Very serious news.

CALIGULA [*As if he has not heard.*] Mind you, I've had her already.

HELICON Whom?

CALIGULA The moon.

HELICON Yes, yes. . . . Now listen, please. Do you know there's a plot being hatched against your life?

CALIGULA What's more, I had her thoroughly. Only two or three times, to be sure. Still, I had her all right.

HELICON For the last hour I've been trying to tell you about it, only—

CALIGULA It was last summer. I'd been gazing at her so long, and stroking her so often on the marble pillars in the gardens that evidently she'd come to understand.

HELICON Please stop trifling, Caius. Even if you refuse to listen, it's my duty to tell you this. And if you shut your ears, it can't be helped.

CALIGULA [*Applying red polish to his toenails.*] This varnish is no good at all. But, to come back to the moon—it was a cloudless August night. [HELICON *looks sulkily away, and keeps silence.*] She was coy, to begin with. I'd gone to bed. First she was blood-red, low on the horizon. Then she began rising, quicker and quicker, growing brighter and brighter all the while. And the higher she climbed, the paler she grew, till she was like a milky pool in a dark wood rustling with stars. Slowly, shyly she approached, through the warm night air, soft, light as gossamer, naked in beauty. She crossed the threshold of my room, glided to my bed, poured herself into it, and flooded me with her smiles and sheen. . . . No, really this new varnish is a failure. . . . So you see, Helicon, I can say, without boasting, that I've had her.

HELICON Now will you listen, and learn the danger that's threatening you?

CALIGULA [*Ceasing to fiddle with his toes, and gazing at him fixedly.*] All I want, Helicon, is—the moon. For the rest, I've always known what will kill me. I haven't yet exhausted all that is to keep me living. That's why I want the moon. And you must not return till you have secured her for me.

HELICON Very well. . . . Now I'll do my duty and tell you what I've learned. There's a plot against you. Cherea is the ringleader. I came across this tablet which tells you all you need to know. See, I put it here.

[*He places the tablet on one of the seats and moves away.*]

CALIGULA Where are you off to, Helicon?

HELICON [*From the threshold.*] To get the moon for you.

[*There is a mouselike scratching at the opposite door.* CALIGULA *swings round and sees the* OLD PATRICIAN.]

THE OLD PATRICIAN [*Timidly.*] May I, Caius . . .

CALIGULA [*Impatiently.*] Come in! Come in! [*Gazes at him.*] So, my pet, you've returned to have another look at Venus.

THE OLD PATRICIAN Well . . . no. It's not quite that. Ssh! Oh, sorry, Caius! I only wanted to say . . . You know I'm very, very devoted to you—and my one desire is to end my days in peace.

CALIGULA Be quick, man. Get it out!

THE OLD PATRICIAN Well, it's . . . it's like this. [*Hurriedly.*] It's terribly serious, that's what I meant to say.

CALIGULA No, it isn't serious.

THE OLD PATRICIAN But—I don't follow. *What* isn't serious?

CALIGULA But what are we talking about, my love?

THE OLD PATRICIAN [*Glancing nervously round the room.*] I mean to say . . . [*Wriggles, shuffles, then bursts out with it.*] There's a plot afoot, against you.

CALIGULA There! You see. Just as I said; it isn't serious.

THE OLD PATRICIAN But, Caius, they mean to kill you.

CALIGULA [*Approaching him and grasping his shoulders.*] Do you know why I can't believe you?

THE OLD PATRICIAN [*Raising an arm, as if to take an oath.*] The gods bear witness, Caius, that . . .

CALIGULA [*Gently but firmly pressing him back toward the door.*] Don't swear. I particularly ask you not to swear. Listen, instead. Suppose it were true, what you are telling me—I'd have to assume you were betraying your friends, isn't that so?

THE OLD PATRICIAN [*Flustered.*] Well, Caius, considering the deep affection I have for you . . .

CALIGULA [*In the same tone as before.*] And I cannot assume *that.* I've always loathed baseness of that sort so profoundly that I could never restrain myself from having a betrayer put to death. But I know the man you are, my worthy friend. And I'm convinced you neither wish to play the traitor nor to die.

THE OLD PATRICIAN Certainly not, Caius. Most certainly not.

CALIGULA So you see I was right in refusing to believe you. You wouldn't stoop to baseness, would you?

THE OLD PATRICIAN Oh, no, indeed!

CALIGULA Nor betray your friends?

THE OLD PATRICIAN I need hardly tell you that, Caius.

CALIGULA Therefore it follows that there isn't any plot. It was just a joke—between ourselves, rather a silly joke—what you've just been telling me, eh?

THE OLD PATRICIAN [*Feebly.*] Yes, yes. A joke, merely a joke.

CALIGULA Good. So now we know where we are. Nobody wants to kill me.

THE OLD PATRICIAN Nobody. That's it. Nobody at all.

CALIGULA [*Drawing a deep breath; in measured tones.*] Then—leave me, sweetheart. A man of honor is an animal so rare in the present-day world that I couldn't bear the sight of one too long. I must be left alone to relish this unique experience. [*For some moments he gazes, without moving, at the tablet. He picks it up and reads it. Then, again, draws a deep breath. Then summons a palace guard.*]

CALIGULA Bring Cherea to me. [*The man starts to leave.*] Wait! [*The man halts.*] Treat him politely. [*The man goes out.* CALIGULA *falls to pacing the room. After a while he approaches the mirror.*] You decided to be logical, didn't you, poor simpleton? Logic for ever! The question now is: Where will that take you? [*Ironically.*] Suppose the moon were brought here, everything would be different. That was the idea, wasn't it? Then the impossible would become possible, in a flash the Great Change come, and all things be transfigured. After all, why shouldn't Helicon bring it off? One night, perhaps, he'll catch her sleeping in a lake, and carry her here, trapped in a glistening net, all slimy with weeds and water, like a pale bloated fish drawn from the depths. Why not, Caligula? Why not, indeed? [*He casts a glance round the room.*] Fewer and fewer people round me; I wonder why. [*Addressing the mirror, in a muffled voice.*] Too many dead, too many dead—that makes an emptiness. . . . No, even if the moon were mine, I could not retrace my way. Even were those dead men thrilling again under the sun's caress, the murders wouldn't go back underground for that. [*Angrily.*] Logic, Caligula; follow where logic leads. Power to the uttermost; willfulness without end. Ah, I'm the only man on earth to know the secret—that power can never be complete without a total self-surrender to the dark impulse of one's destiny. No, there's no return. I must go on and on, until the consummation.

[CHEREA *enters.* CALIGULA *is slumped in his chair, the cloak drawn tightly round him.*]

CHEREA You sent for me, Caius?

CALIGULA [*Languidly.*] Yes, Cherea.

[*A short silence.*]

CHEREA Have you anything particular to tell me?

CALIGULA No, Cherea.

[*Another silence.*]

CHEREA [*With a hint of petulance.*] Are you sure you really need my presence?

CALIGULA Absolutely sure, Cherea. [*Another silence. Then, as if suddenly recollecting himself.*] I'm sorry for seeming so inhospitable. I was following up my thoughts, and— Now do sit down, we'll have a friendly little chat. I'm in a mood for some intelligent conversation. [CHEREA *sits down. For the first time since the play began,* CALIGULA *gives the impression of being his natural self.*] Do you think, Cherea, that it's possible for two men of much the same temperament and equal pride to talk to each other with complete frankness—if only once in their lives? Can they strip themselves naked, so to speak, and shed their prejudices, their private interests, the lies by which they live?

CHEREA Yes, Caius, I think it possible. But I don't think you'd be capable of it.

CALIGULA You're right. I only wished to know if you agreed with me. So let's wear our masks, and muster up our lies. And we'll talk as fencers fight, padded on all the vital parts. Tell me, Cherea, why don't you like me?

CHEREA Because there's nothing likable about you, Caius. Because such feelings can't be had to order. And because I understand you far too well. One cannot like an aspect of oneself which one always tries to keep concealed.

CALIGULA But why is it you hate me?

CHEREA There, Caius, you're mistaken. I do not hate you. I regard you as noxious and cruel, vain and selfish. But I cannot hate you, because I don't think you are happy. And I cannot scorn you, because I know you are no coward.

CALIGULA Then why wish to kill me?

CHEREA I've told you why; because I regard you as noxious, a constant menace. I like, and need, to feel secure. So do most men. They resent living in a world where the most preposterous fancy may at any moment become a reality, and the absurd transfix their lives, like a dagger in the heart. I feel as they do; I refuse to live in a topsy-turvy world. I want to know where I stand, and to stand secure.

CALIGULA Security and logic don't go together.

CHEREA Quite true. My plan of life may not be logical, but at least it's sound.

CALIGULA Go on.

CHEREA There's no more to say. I'll be no party to your logic. I've a very different notion of my duties as a man. And I know that the majority of your subjects share my view. You outrage their deepest feelings. It's only natural that you should . . . disappear.

CALIGULA I see your point, and it's legitimate enough. For most men, I grant you, it's obvious. But *you,* I should have thought, would have known better. You're an intelligent man, and given intelligence, one has a choice; either to pay its price or to disown it. Why do you shirk the issue and neither disown it nor consent to pay its price?

CHEREA Because what I want is to live, and to be happy. Neither, to my mind, is possible if one pushes the absurd to its logical conclusions. As you see, I'm quite an ordinary sort of man. True, there are moments when, to feel free of them, I desire the death of those I love, or I hanker after women from whom the ties of family or friendship debar me. Were logic everything, I'd kill or fornicate on such occasions. But I consider that these passing fancies have no great importance. If everyone set to gratifying them, the world would be impossible to live in, and happiness, too, would go by the board. And these, I repeat, are the things that count, for me.

CALIGULA So, I take it, you believe in some higher principle?

CHEREA Certainly I believe that some actions are—shall I say?—more praiseworthy than others.

CALIGULA And *I* believe that all are on an equal footing.

CHEREA I know it, Caius, and that's why I don't hate you. I understand, and, to a point, agree with you. But you're pernicious, and you've got to go.

CALIGULA True enough. But why risk your life by telling me this?

CHEREA Because others will take my place, and because I don't like lying.

[*A short silence.*]

CALIGULA Cherea!

CHEREA Yes, Caius?

CALIGULA Do you think that two men of similar temperament and equal pride can, if only once in their lives, open their hearts to each other?

CHEREA That, I believe, is what we've just been doing.

CALIGULA Yes, Cherea. But you thought I was incapable of it.

CHEREA I was wrong, Caius. I admit it, and I thank you. Now I await your sentence.

CALIGULA My sentence? Ah, I see. [*Producing the tablet from under his cloak.*] You know what this is, Cherea?

CHEREA I knew you had it.

CALIGULA [*Passionately.*] You knew I had it! So your frankness was all a piece of play acting. The two friends did *not* open their hearts to each other. Well, well! It's no great matter. Now we can stop playing at sincerity, and resume life on the old footing. But first I'll ask you to make just one more effort; to bear with my caprices and my tactlessness a little longer. Listen well, Cherea. This tablet is the one and only piece of evidence against you.

CHEREA Caius, I'd rather go. I'm sick and tired of all these antics. I know them only too well, and I've had enough. Let me go, please.

CALIGULA [*In the same tense, passionate voice.*] No, stay. This tablet is the only evidence. Is that clear?

CHEREA Evidence? I never knew you needed evidence to send a man to his death.

CALIGULA That's true. Still, for once I wish to contradict myself. Nobody can object to that. It's so pleasant to contradict oneself occasionally; so restful. And I need rest, Cherea.

CHEREA I don't follow . . . and, frankly, I've no taste for these subtleties.

CALIGULA I know, Cherea, I know. You're not like me; you're an ordinary man, sound in mind and body. And naturally you've no desire for the extraordinary. [*With a burst of laughter.*] You want to live and to be happy. That's all!

CHEREA I think, Caius, we'd better leave it at that. . . . Can I go?

CALIGULA Not yet. A little patience, if you don't mind—I shall not keep you long. You see this thing—this piece of evidence? I choose to assume that I can't sentence you to death without it. That's my idea . . . and my repose. Well! See what becomes of evidence in an emperor's hands. [*He holds the tablet to a torch.* CHEREA *approaches. The torch is between them. The tablet begins to melt.*] You see, conspirator! The tablet's melting, and as it melts a look of innocence is dawning on your face. What a handsome forehead you have, Cherea! An how rare, how beautiful a sight is an innocent man! Admire my power. Even the gods cannot restore innocence without first punishing the culprit. But your emperor needs only a torch flame to absolve you and give you a new lease of hope. So carry on, Cherea; follow out the noble precepts we've been hearing, wherever they may take you. Meanwhile your emperor awaits his repose. It's his way of living and being happy.

[CHEREA *stares, dumfounded, at* CALIGULA. *He makes a vague gesture, seems to understand, opens his mouth to speak—and walks abruptly away. Smiling, holding the tablet to the flame,* CALIGULA *follows the receding figure with his gaze.*]

[*Curtain.*]

ACT IV

A room in the imperial palace.

The stage is in semidarkness. CHEREA *and* SCIPIO *enter.* CHEREA *crosses to the right, then comes back left to* SCIPIO.

SCIPIO [*Sulkily.*] What do you want of me?

CHEREA There's no time to lose. And we must know our minds, we must be resolute.

SCIPIO Who says I'm not resolute?

CHEREA You didn't attend our meeting yesterday.

SCIPIO [*Looking away.*] That's so, Cherea.

CHEREA Scipio, I am older than you, and I'm not in the habit of asking others' help. But, I won't deny it, I need you now. This murder needs honorable men to sponsor it. Among all these wounded vanities and sordid fears, our motives only, yours and mine, are disinterested. Of course I know that, if you leave us, we can count on your silence. But that is not the point. What I want is—for you to stay with us.

SCIPIO I understand. But I can't, oh, no, I *cannot* do as you wish.

CHEREA So you are with him?

SCIPIO No. But I cannot be against him. [*Pauses; then in muffled voice.*] Even if I killed him, my heart would still be with him.

CHEREA And yet—he killed your father!

SCIPIO Yes—and that's how it all began. But that, too, is how it ends.

CHEREA He denies what you believe in. He tramples on all that you hold sacred.

SCIPIO I know, Cherea. And yet something inside me is akin to him. The same fire burns in both our hearts.

CHEREA There are times when a man must make his choice. As for me, I have silenced in my heart all that might be akin to him.

SCIPIO But—*I*—I cannot make a choice. I have my own sorrow, but I suffer with him, too; I share his pain. I understand all—that is my trouble.

CHEREA So that's it. You have chosen to take his side.

SCIPIO [*Passionately.*] No, Cherea. I beg you, don't think that. I can never, never again take anybody's side.

CHEREA [*Affectionately; approaching* SCIPIO.] Do you know, I hate him even more for having made of you—what he has made.

SCIPIO Yes, he has taught me to expect everything of life.

CHEREA No, he has taught you despair. And to have instilled despair into a young heart is fouler than the foulest of the crimes he has committed up to now. I assure you, *that* alone would justify me in killing him out of hand.

[*He goes toward the door.* HELICON *enters.*]

HELICON I've been hunting for you high and low, Cherea. Caligula's giving a little party here, for his personal friends only. Naturally he expects you to attend it. [*To* SCIPIO.] You, my boy, aren't wanted. Off you go!

SCIPIO [*Looking back at* CHEREA *as he goes out.*] Cherea.

CHEREA [*Gently.*] Yes, Scipio?

SCIPIO Try to understand.

CHEREA [*In the same gentle tone.*] No, Scipio.

[SCIPIO *and* HELICON *go out. A clash of arms in the wings. Two soldiers enter at right, escorting the* OLD PATRICIAN *and the* FIRST PATRICIAN, *who show signs of alarm.*]

FIRST PATRICIAN [*To one of the soldiers, in a tone which he vainly tries to steady.*] But . . . but what *can* he want with us at this hour of the night?

SOLDIER Sit there. [*Points to the chairs on the right.*]

FIRST PATRICIAN If it's only to have us killed—like so many others—why all these preliminaries?

SOLDIER Sit down, you old mule.

THE OLD PATRICIAN Better do as he says. It's clear he doesn't know anything.

SOLDIER Yes, darling, quite clear. [*Goes out.*]

FIRST PATRICIAN We should have acted sooner; I always said so. Now we're in for the torture chamber.

[*The* SOLDIER *comes back with* CHEREA, *then goes out.*]

CHEREA [*Seating himself. He shows no sign of apprehension.*] Any idea what's happening?

FIRST PATRICIAN AND THE OLD PATRICIAN [*Speaking together.*] He's found out about the conspiracy.

CHEREA Yes? And then?

THE OLD PATRICIAN [*Shuddering.*] The torture chamber for us all.

CHEREA [*Still unperturbed.*] I remember that Caligula once gave eighty-one thousand sesterces to a slave who, though he was tortured nearly to death, wouldn't confess to a theft he had committed.

FIRST PATRICIAN A lot of consolation that is—for us!

CHEREA Anyhow, it shows that he appreciates courage. You ought to keep that in mind. [*To the* OLD PATRICIAN.] Would you very much mind not chattering with your teeth? It's a noise I particularly dislike.

THE OLD PATRICIAN I'm sorry, but—

FIRST PATRICIAN Enough trifling! Our lives are at stake.

CHEREA [*Coolly.*] Do you know Caligula's favorite remark?

THE OLD PATRICIAN [*On the verge of tears.*] Yes. He says to the executioner: "Kill him slowly, so that he feels what dying's like!"

CHEREA No, there's a better one. After an execution he yawns, and says quite seriously: "What I admire most is my imperturbability."

FIRST PATRICIAN Do you hear . . . ?

[*A clanking of weapons is heard off stage.*]

CHEREA That remark betrays a weakness in his make-up.

THE OLD PATRICIAN Would you be kind enough to stop philosophizing? It's something I particularly dislike.

[*A slave enters and deposits a sheaf of knives on a seat.*]

CHEREA [*Who has not noticed him.*] Still,

there's no denying it's remarkable, the effect this man has on all with whom he comes in contact. He forces one to think. There's nothing like insecurity for stimulating the brain. That, of course, is why he's so much hated.

THE OLD PATRICIAN [*Pointing a trembling finger.*] Look!

CHEREA [*Noticing the knives, in a slightly altered tone.*] Perhaps you were right.

FIRST PATRICIAN Yes, waiting was a mistake. We should have acted at once.

CHEREA I agree. Wisdom's come too late.

THE OLD PATRICIAN But it's . . . it's crazy. I don't want to die.

[*He rises and begins to edge away. Two soldiers appear, and, after slapping his face, force him back onto his seat. The* FIRST PATRICIAN *squirms in his chair.* CHEREA *utters some inaudible words. Suddenly a queer music begins behind the curtain at the back of the stage; a thrumming and tinkling of zithers and cymbals. The patricians gaze at each other in silence. Outlined on the illuminated curtain, in shadow play,* CALIGULA *appears, makes some grotesque dance movements, and retreats from view. He is wearing ballet dancer's skirts and his head is garlanded with flowers. A moment later a* SOLDIER *announces gravely:* "Gentlemen, the performance is over." *Meanwhile* CÆSONIA *has entered soundlessly behind the watching patricians. She speaks in an ordinary voice, but none the less they give a start on hearing it.*]

CÆSONIA Caligula has instructed me to tell you that, whereas in the past he always summoned you for affairs of state, today he invited you to share with him an artistic emotion. [*A short pause. Then she continues in the same tone.*] He added, I may say, that anyone who has not shared in it will be beheaded. [*They keep silent.*] I apologize for insisting, but I must ask you if you found that dance beautiful.

FIRST PATRICIAN [*After a brief hesitation.*] Yes, Cæsonia. It was beautiful.

THE OLD PATRICIAN [*Effusively.*] Lovely! Lovely!

CÆSONIA And you, Cherea?

CHEREA [*Icily.*] It was . . . very high art.

CÆSONIA Good. Now I can describe your artistic emotions to Caligula.

[CÆSONIA *goes out.*]

CHEREA And now we must act quickly. You two stay here. Before the night is out there'll be a hundred of us.

[*He goes out.*]

THE OLD PATRICIAN No, no. *You* stay. Let me go, instead. [*Sniffs the air.*] It smells of death here.

FIRST PATRICIAN And of lies. [*Sadly.*] I said that dance was beautiful!

THE OLD PATRICIAN [*Conciliatingly.*] And so it was, in a way. Most original.

[*Some patricians and knights enter hurriedly.*]

SECOND PATRICIAN What's afoot? Do you know anything? The Emperor's summoned us here.

THE OLD PATRICIAN [*Absent-mindedly.*] For the dance, maybe.

SECOND PATRICIAN What dance?

THE OLD PATRICIAN Well, I mean . . . er . . . the artistic emotion.

THIRD PATRICIAN I've been told Caligula's very ill.

FIRST PATRICIAN He's a sick man, yes . . .

THIRD PATRICIAN What's he suffering from? [*In a joyful tone.*] By God, is he going to die?

FIRST PATRICIAN I doubt it. His disease is fatal —to others only.

THE OLD PATRICIAN That's one way of putting it.

SECOND PATRICIAN Quite so. But hasn't he some other disease less serious, and more to our advantage?

FIRST PATRICIAN No. That malady of his excludes all others.

[*He goes out.* CÆSONIA *enters. A short silence.*]

CÆSONIA [*In a casual tone.*] If you want to know, Caligula has stomach trouble. Just now he vomited blood.

[*The patricians crowd round her.*]

SECOND PATRICIAN O mighty gods, I vow, if he recovers, to pay the Treasury two hundred thousand sesterces as a token of my joy.

THIRD PATRICIAN [*With exaggerated eagerness.*] O Jupiter, take my life in place of his!

[CALIGULA *has entered, and is listening.*]

CALIGULA [*Going up to the* SECOND PATRICIAN.] I accept your offer, Lucius. And I thank you. My Treasurer will call on you tomorrow. [*Goes to the* THIRD PATRICIAN *and embraces him.*] You can't imagine how touched I am. [*A short silence. Then, tenderly.*] So you love me, Cassius, as much as that?

THIRD PATRICIAN [*Emotionally.*] Oh, Cæsar, there's nothing, nothing I wouldn't sacrifice for your sake.

CALIGULA [*Embracing him again.*] Ah, Cassius, this is really too much; I don't deserve all this love. [CASSIUS *makes a protesting gesture.*] No, no, really I don't! I'm not worthy of it. [*He beckons to two soldiers.*] Take him away. [*Gently, to* CASSIUS.] Go, dear friend, and remember that Caligula has lost his heart to you.

THIRD PATRICIAN [*Vaguely uneasy.*] But—where are they taking me?

CALIGULA Why, to your death, of course. Your generous offer was accepted, and I feel better already. Even that nasty taste of blood in my mouth has gone. You've cured me, Cassius. It's been miraculous, and how proud you must feel of having worked the miracle by laying your life down for your friend—especially when that friend's none other than Caligula! So now you see me quite myself again, and ready for a festive night.

THIRD PATRICIAN [*Shrieking, as he is dragged away.*] No! No! I don't want to die. You can't be serious!

CALIGULA [*In a thoughtful voice, between the shrieks.*] Soon the sea roads will be golden with mimosas. The women will wear their lightest dresses. And the sky! Ah, Cassius, what a blaze of clean, swift sunshine! The smiles of life. [CASSIUS *is near the door.* CALIGULA *gives him a gentle push. Suddenly his tone grows serious.*] Life, my friend, is something to be cherished. Had you cherished it enough, you wouldn't have gambled it away so rashly. [CASSIUS *is led off.* CALIGULA *returns to the table.*] The loser must pay. There's no alternative. [*A short silence.*] Come, Cæsonia. [*He turns to the others.*] By the way, an idea has just waylaid me, and it's such an apt one that I want to share it with you. Until now my reign has been too happy. There's been no world-wide plague, no religious persecution, not even a rebellion—nothing in fact to make us memorable. And that, I'd have you know, is why I try to remedy the stinginess of fate. I mean—I don't know if you've followed me—that, well [*He gives a little laugh.*], it's I who replace the epidemics that we've missed. [*In a different tone.*] That's enough. I see Cherea's coming. Your turn, Cæsonia. [CALIGULA *goes out.* CHEREA *and the* FIRST PATRICIAN *enter.* CÆSONIA *hurries toward* CHEREA.]

CÆSONIA Caligula is dead.

[*She turns her head, as if to hide her tears; her eyes are fixed on the others, who keep silence. Everyone looks horrified, but for different reasons.*]

FIRST PATRICIAN You . . . you're *sure* this dreadful thing has happened? It seems incredible. Only a short while ago he was dancing.

CÆSONIA Quite so—and the effort was too much for him. [CHEREA *moves hastily from one man to the other. No one speaks.*] You've nothing to say, Cherea?

CHEREA [*In a low voice.*] It's a great misfortune for us all, Cæsonia.

[CALIGULA *bursts in violently and goes up to* CHEREA.]

CALIGULA Well played, Cherea. [*He spins round and stares at the others. Petulantly.*] Too bad! It didn't come off. [*To* CÆSONIA.] Don't forget what I told you.

[CALIGULA *goes out.* CÆSONIA *stares after him without speaking.*]

THE OLD PATRICIAN [*Hoping against hope.*] Is he ill, Cæsonia?

CÆSONIA [*With a hostile look.*] No, my pet. But what you don't know is that the man never has more than two hours' sleep and spends the best part of the night roaming about the corridors in his palace. Another thing you don't know—and you've never given a thought to—is what may pass in this man's mind in those deadly hours between midnight and sunrise. Is he ill? No, not ill—unless you invent a name and medicine for the black ulcers that fester in his soul.

CHEREA [*Seemingly affected by her words.*] You're right, Cæsonia. We all know that Caius . . .

CÆSONIA [*Breaking in emotionally.*] Yes, you know it—in your fashion. But, like all those who have none, you can't abide anyone who has too much soul. Healthy people loathe invalids. Happy people hate the sad. Too much soul! That's what bites you, isn't it? You prefer to label it a disease; that way all the dolts are justified and pleased. [*In a changed tone.*] Tell me, Cherea. Has love ever meant anything to you?

CHEREA [*Himself again.*] I'm afraid we're too old now, Cæsonia, to learn the art of love-making. And anyhow it's highly doubtful if Caligula will give us time to do so.

CÆSONIA [*Who has recovered her composure.*] True enough. [*She sits down.*] Oh, I was forgetting. . . . Caligula asked me to impart some news to you. You know, perhaps, that it's a red-letter day today, consecrated to art.

THE OLD PATRICIAN According to the calendar?

CÆSONIA No, according to Caligula. He's convoked some poets. He will ask them to improvise a poem on a set theme. And he particularly wants those of you who are poets to take part in the competition. He specially mentioned young Scipio and Metellus.

METELLUS But we're not ready.

CÆSONIA [*In a level tone, as if she has not heard him.*] Needless to say there are prizes. There will be penalties, too. [*Looks of consternation.*] Between ourselves, the penalties won't be so very terrible.

[CALIGULA *enters, looking gloomier than ever.*]

CALIGULA All ready?

CÆSONIA Yes. [*To a soldier.*] Bring in the poets.

[*Enter, two by two, a dozen poets, keeping step; they line up on the right of the stage.*]

CALIGULA And the others?

CÆSONIA Metellus! Scipio!

[*They cross the stage and take their stand beside the poets.* CALIGULA *seats himself, backstage on the left, with* CÆSONIA *and the patricians. A short silence.*]

CALIGULA Subject: death. Time limit: one minute.

[*The poets scribble feverishly on their tablets.*]

THE OLD PATRICIAN Who will compose the jury?

CALIGULA I. Isn't that enough?

THE OLD PATRICIAN Oh, yes, indeed. Quite enough.

CHEREA Won't you take part in the competition, Caius?

CALIGULA Unnecessary. I made my poem on that theme long ago.

THE OLD PATRICIAN [*Eagerly.*] Where can one get a copy of it?

CALIGULA No need to get a copy. I recite it every day, after my fashion. [CÆSONIA *eyes him nervously.* CALIGULA *rounds on her almost savagely.*] Is there anything in my appearance that displeases you?

CÆSONIA [*Gently.*] I'm sorry. . . .

CALIGULA No meekness, please. For heaven's sake, no meekness. You're exasperating enough as it is, but if you start being humble . . . [CÆSONIA *slowly moves away.* CALIGULA *turns to* CHEREA.] I continue. It's the only poem I have made. And it's proof that I'm the only true artist Rome has known—the only one, believe me—to match his inspiration with his deeds.

CHEREA That's only a matter of having the power.

CALIGULA Quite true. Other artists create to compensate for their lack of power. I don't need to make a work of art; I *live* it. [*Roughly.*] Well, poets, are you ready?

METELLUS I think so.

THE OTHERS Yes.

CALIGULA Good. Now listen carefully. You are to fall out of line and come forward one by one. I'll whistle. Number One will start reading his poem. When I whistle, he must stop, and the next begin. And so on. The winner, naturally, will be the one whose poem hasn't been cut short by the whistle. Get ready. [*Turning to* CHEREA, *he whispers.*] You see, organization's needed for everything, even for art.

[*Blows his whistle.*]

FIRST POET Death, when beyond thy darkling shore . . .

[*A blast of the whistle. The poet steps briskly to the left. The others will follow the same procedure. These movements should be made with mechanical precision.*]

SECOND POET In their dim cave, the Fatal Sisters Three . . .

[*Whistle.*]

THIRD POET Come to me death, beloved . . .

[*A shrill blast of the whistle. The* FOURTH POET *steps forward and strikes a dramatic posture. The whistle goes before he has opened his mouth.*]

FIFTH POET When I was in my happy infancy . . .

CALIGULA [*Yelling.*] Stop that! What earthly connection has a blockhead's happy infancy with the theme I set? The connection! Tell me the connection!

FIFTH POET But, Caius, I've only just begun, and . . .

[*Shrill blast.*]

SIXTH POET [*In a high-pitched voice.*] Ruthless, he goes his hidden ways . . .

[*Whistle.*]

SEVENTH POET [*Mysteriously.*] Oh, long, abstruse orison . . .

[*Whistle, broken off as* SCIPIO *comes forward without a tablet.*]

CALIGULA You haven't a tablet?

SCIPIO I do not need one.

CALIGULA Well, let's hear you. [*He chews at his whistle.*]

SCIPIO [*Standing very near* CALIGULA, *he recites listlessly, without looking at him.*]

Pursuit of happiness that purifies the heart,
Skies rippling with light,
O wild, sweet, festal joys, frenzy without
  hope!

CALIGULA [*Gently.*] Stop, please. The others needn't compete. [*To* SCIPIO.] You're very young to understand so well the lessons we can learn from death.

SCIPIO [*Gazing straight at* CALIGULA.] I was very young to lose my father.

CALIGULA [*Turning hastily.*] Fall in, the rest of you. No, really a sham poet is too dreadful an infliction. Until now I'd thought of enrolling you as my allies; I sometimes pictured a gallant band of poets defending me in the last ditch. Another illusion gone! I shall have to relegate you to my enemies. So now the poets are against me—and that looks much like the end of all. March out in good order. As you go past you are to lick your tablets so as to efface the atrocities you scrawled on them. Attention! Forward! [*He blows his whistle in short rhythmic jerks. Keeping step, the poets file out by the right, tonguing their immortal tablets.* CALIGULA *adds in a lower tone.*] Now leave me, everyone.

[*In the doorway, as they are going out,* CHEREA *touches the* FIRST PATRICIAN'S *shoulder, and speaks in his ear.*]

CHEREA Now's our opportunity.

[SCIPIO, *who has overheard, halts on the threshold and walks back to* CALIGULA.]

CALIGULA [*Acidly.*] Can't you leave me in peace—as your father's doing?

SCIPIO No, Caius, all that serves no purpose now. For now I know, I *know* that you have made your choice.

CALIGULA Won't you leave me in peace!

SCIPIO Yes, you shall have your wish; I am going to leave you, for I think I've come to understand you. There's no way out left to us, neither to you nor to me—who am like you in so many ways. I shall go away, far away, and try to discover the meaning of it all. [*He gazes at* CALIGULA *for some moments. Then, with a rush of emotion.*] Good-by, dear Caius. When all is ended, remember that I loved you. [*He goes out.* CALIGULA *makes a vague gesture. Then, almost savagely, he pulls himself together and takes some steps toward* CÆSONIA.]

CÆSONIA What did he say?

CALIGULA Nothing you'd understand.

CÆSONIA What are you thinking about?

CALIGULA About him. And about you, too. But it amounts to the same thing.

CÆSONIA What is the matter?

CALIGULA [*Staring at her.*] Scipio has gone. I am through with his friendship. But you, I wonder why you are still here. . . .

CÆSONIA Why, because you're fond of me.

CALIGULA No. But I think I'd understand—if I had you killed.

CÆSONIA Yes, that would be a solution. Do so, then. . . . But why, oh, why can't you relax, if only for a moment, and live freely, without constraint?

CALIGULA I have been doing that for several years; in fact I've made a practice of it.

CÆSONIA I don't mean that sort of freedom. I mean—Oh, don't you realize what it can be to live and love quite simply, naturally, in . . . in purity of heart?

CALIGULA This purity of heart you talk of—every man acquires it, in his own way. Mine has been to follow the essential to the end. . . . Still all that needn't prevent me from putting you to death. [*Laughs.*] It would round off my career so well, the perfect climax. [*He rises and swings the mirror round toward himself. Then he walks in a circle, letting his arms hang limp, almost without gestures; there is something feral in his gait as he continues speaking.*] How strange! When

I don't kill, I feel alone. The living don't suffice to people my world and dispel my boredom. I have an impression of an enormous void when you and the others are here, and my eyes see nothing but empty air. No, I'm at ease only in the company of my dead. [*He takes his stand facing the audience, leaning a little forward. He has forgotten* CÆSONIA'*s presence.*] Only the dead are real. They are of my kind. I see them waiting for me, straining toward me. And I have long talks with this man or that, who screamed to me for mercy and whose tongue I had cut out.

CÆSONIA Come. Lie down beside me. Put your head on my knees. [CALIGULA *does so.*] That's better, isn't it? Now rest. How quiet it is here!

CALIGULA Quiet? You exaggerate, my dear. Listen! [*Distant metallic tinklings, as of swords or armor.*] Do you hear those thousands of small sounds all around us, hatred stalking its prey? [*Murmuring voices, footsteps.*]

CÆSONIA Nobody would dare. . . .

CALIGULA Yes, stupidity.

CÆSONIA Stupidity doesn't kill. It makes men slow to act.

CALIGULA It can be murderous, Cæsonia. A fool stops at nothing when he thinks his dignity offended. No, it's not the men whose sons or fathers I have killed who'll murder me. *They*, anyhow, have understood. They're with me, they have the same taste in their mouths. But the others—those I made a laughingstock of—I've no defense against their wounded vanity.

CÆSONIA [*Passionately.*] *We* will defend you. There are many of us left who love you.

CALIGULA Fewer every day. It's not surprising. I've done all that was needed to that end. And then—let's be fair—it's not only stupidity that's against me. There's the courage and the simple faith of men who ask to be happy.

CÆSONIA [*In the same tone.*] No, *they* will not kill you. Or, if they tried, fire would come down from heaven and blast them, before they laid a hand on you.

CALIGULA From heaven! There is no heaven, my poor dear woman! [*He sits down.*] But why this sudden access of devotion? It wasn't provided for in our agreement, if I remember rightly.

CÆSONIA [*Who has risen from the couch and is pacing the room.*] Don't you understand? Hasn't it been enough to see you killing others, without my also knowing you'll be killed as well? Isn't it enough to feel you hard and cruel, seething with bitterness, when I hold you in my arms; to breathe a reek of murder when you lie on me? Day after day I see all that's human in you dying out, little by little. [*She turns toward him.*] Oh, I know. I know I'm getting old, my beauty on the wane. But it's you only I'm concerned for now; so much so that I've ceased troubling whether you love me. I only want you to get well, quite well again. You're still a boy, really; you've a whole life ahead of you. And, tell me, what greater thing can you want than a whole life?

CALIGULA [*Rising, looks at her fixedly.*] You've been with me a long time now, a very long time.

CÆSONIA Yes. . . . But you'll keep me, won't you?

CALIGULA I don't know. I only know that, if you're with me still, it's because of all those nights we've had together, nights of fierce, joyless pleasure; it's because you alone know me as I am. [*He takes her in his arms, bending her head back a little with his right hand.*] I'm twenty-nine. Not a great age really. But today when none the less my life seems so long, so crowded with scraps and shreds of my past selves, so complete in fact, you remain the last witness. And I can't avoid a sort of shameful tenderness for the old woman that you soon will be.

CÆSONIA Tell me that you mean to keep me with you.

CALIGULA I don't know. All I know—and it's the most terrible thing of all—is that this shameful tenderness is the one sincere emotion that my life has given up to now. [CÆSONIA *frees herself from his arms.* CALIGULA *follows her. She presses her back to his chest and he puts his arms round her.*] Wouldn't it be better that the last witness should disappear?

CÆSONIA That has no importance. All I know is: I'm happy. What you've just said has made me very happy. But why can't I share my happiness with you?

CALIGULA Who says I'm unhappy?

CÆSONIA Happiness is kind. It doesn't thrive on bloodshed.

CALIGULA Then there must be two kinds of

happiness, and I've chosen the murderous kind. For I *am* happy. There was a time when I thought I'd reached the extremity of pain. But, no, one can go farther yet. Beyond the frontier of pain lies a splendid, sterile happiness. Look at me. [*She turns toward him.*] It makes me laugh, Cæsonia, when I think how for years and years all Rome carefully avoided uttering Drusilla's name. Well, all Rome was mistaken. Love isn't enough for me; I realized it then. And I realize it again today, when I look at you. To love someone means that one's willing to grow old beside that person. That sort of love is right outside my range. Drusilla old would have been far worse than Drusilla dead. Most people imagine that a man suffers because out of the blue death snatches away the woman he loves. But his real suffering is less futile; it comes from the discovery that grief, too, cannot last. Even grief is vanity.

You see, I had no excuses, not the shadow of a real love, neither bitterness nor profound regret. Nothing to plead in my defense! But today—you see me still freer than I have been for years; freed as I am from memories and illusion. [*He laughs bitterly.*] I know now that nothing, *nothing* lasts. Think what that knowledge means! There have been just two or three of us in history who really achieved this freedom, this crazy happiness. Well, Cæsonia, you have seen out a most unusual drama. It's time the curtain fell, for you.

[*He stands behind her again, linking his forearm round* CÆSONIA's *neck.*]

CÆSONIA [*Terrified.*] No, it's impossible! How can you call it happiness, this terrifying freedom?

CALIGULA [*Gradually tightening his grip on* CÆSONIA's *throat.*] Happiness it is, Cæsonia; I know what I'm saying. But for this freedom I'd have been a contented man. Thanks to it, I have won the godlike enlightenment of the solitary. [*His exaltation grows as little by little he strangles* CÆSONIA, *who puts up no resistance, but holds her hands half opened, like a suppliant's, before her. Bending his head, he goes on speaking, into her ear.*] I live, I kill, I exercise the rapturous power of a destroyer, compared with which the power of a creator is merest child's play. And this, *this* is happiness; this and nothing else—this intolerable release, devastating scorn, blood, hatred all around me; the glorious isolation of a man who all his life long nurses and gloats over the ineffable joy of the unpunished murderer; the ruthless logic that crushes out human lives [*He laughs.*], that's crushing yours out, Cæsonia, so as to perfect at last the utter loneliness that is my heart's desire.

CÆSONIA [*Struggling feebly.*] Oh, Caius . . .

CALIGULA [*More and more excitedly.*] No. No sentiment. I must have done with it, for the time is short. My time is very short, dear Cæsonia. [CÆSONIA *is gasping, dying.* CALIGULA *drags her to the bed and lets her fall on it. He stares wildly at her; his voice grows harsh and grating.*] You, too, were guilty. But killing is not the solution. [*He spins round and gazes crazily at the mirror.*] Caligula! You, too; you, too, are guilty. Then what of it—a little more, a little less? Yet who can condemn me in this world where there is no judge, where nobody is innocent? [*He brings his eyes close to his reflected face. He sounds genuinely distressed.*] You see, my poor friend. Helicon has failed you. I won't have the moon. Never, never, never! But how bitter it is to know all, and to have to go through to the consummation! Listen! That was a sound of weapons. Innocence arming for the fray—and innocence will triumph. Why am I not in their place, among them? And I'm afraid. That's cruelest of all, after despising others, to find oneself as cowardly as they. Still, no matter. Fear, too, has an end. Soon I shall attain that emptiness beyond all understanding, in which the heart has rest. [*He steps back a few paces, then returns to the mirror. He seems calmer. When he speaks again his voice is steadier, less shrill.*]

Yet, really, it's quite simple. If I'd had the moon, if love were enough, all might have been different. But where could I quench this thirst? What human heart, what god, would have for me the depth of a great lake? [*Kneeling, weeping.*] There's nothing in this world, or in the other, made to my stature. And yet I know, and you, too, know [*Still weeping, he stretches out his arms toward the mirror.*] that all I need is for the impossible to be. The impossible! I've searched for it at the confines of the world, in the secret places of my heart. I've stretched out my hands [*His voice rises to a scream.*]; see, I stretch you my hands, but it's always you I find, you only, confronting me, and I've come to hate you. I have chosen a wrong path, a path that leads to nothing. My freedom isn't the right one. . . . Nothing, nothing yet. Oh, how oppressive is this darkness! Helicon has not come; we shall be forever guilty. The air tonight is heavy as the sum of human sorrows. [*A clash of arms and whisperings are heard in the wings.* CALIGULA *rises, picks up a stool, and returns to the mirror, breathing heavily. He contemplates himself, makes a slight leap forward, and, watching the symmetrical movement of his reflected self, hurls the stool at it, screaming.*] To history, Caligula! Go down to history! [*The mirror breaks and at the same moment armed conspirators rush in.* CALIGULA *swings round to face them with a mad laugh.* SCIPIO *and* CHEREA, *who are in front, fling themselves at him and stab his face with their daggers.* CALIGULA'S *laughter turns to gasps. All strike him, hurriedly, confusedly. In a last gasp, laughing and choking,* CALIGULA *shrieks.*] I'm still alive!

[*Curtain.*]

Comments and Questions

See Comments and Questions for *The Visit,* p. 618.

The basic tenet of Absurdism is that life is meaningless. In his book *The Modern Temper,* Joseph Wood Krutch contends that if indeed life has no meaning, there can be no tragedy, certainly none in the make-believe world of plays. Camus shows us a character intent upon finding substance in his life, a character free to do this completely on his own terms. Has Camus ruled out tragedy by having his protagonist find that life is nothing? Others may be boxed in by conventional morality, by fears and scruples, by hopes and aspirations, by a thousand and one pushing and pulling influences, but not Caligula. He was free—or was he?

1. "Freedom's just another word for nothin' left to lose," so sings the Me of "Me and Bobby McGee," p. 244. How would Caligula restate that observation? Consider Caligula's words to Cherea: "This world has no importance; once a man realizes that, he wins his freedom."
2. Although Caligula acts on whim, is there a pattern to his actions? If so, what is it?
3. Some say that Camus' play is simply a vehicle for examining ideas, that it is nothing more than a dramatized philosophical essay. Others regard the play as a chronicle of a human being agonizing in the inner recesses of his disturbed mind. Is Caligula a puppet on Camus' strings or a character as, say, Hamlet is a character?
4. Interpret Caligula's last words: "I'm still alive!"
5. Are any of the minor characters of consequence in the working out of the plot? If so, which ones, and in what way?

NEIL SIMON
1927–

The Sunshine Boys

CHARACTERS

WILLIE CLARK
BEN SILVERMAN
AL LEWIS
PATIENT
EDDIE
NURSE
REGISTERED NURSE

The action takes place in New York City.

ACT I *Scene I: A small apartment in an old hotel on upper Broadway in the mid-Eighties. It is an early afternoon in midwinter.*

Scene II: The following Monday, late morning.

ACT II *Scene I: A Manhattan television studio. Scene II: The same as* ACT I. *It is two weeks later, late afternoon.*

ACT I

Scene I

The scene is a two-room apartment in an old hotel on upper Broadway, in the mid-Eighties. It's rather a depressing place. There is a bed, a bureau, a small dining table with two chairs, an old leather chair that faces a TV set on a cheap, metal stand. There is a small kitchen to one side—partitioned off from the living room by a curtain—a small bathroom on the other. A window looks out over Broadway. It is early afternoon, midwinter.

At rise, the TV is on, and the banal dialogue of a soap opera drones on. In the leather chair sits WILLIE CLARK, *in slippers, pajamas and an old bathrobe.* WILLIE *is in his seventies. He watches the program but is constantly dozing off, then catching himself and watching for a few more minutes at a time. The set drones on and* WILLIE *dozes off. The tea kettle on the stove in the kitchen comes to a boil and whistles.* WILLIE*'s head perks up at the sound; he reaches over and picks up the telephone.*

WILLIE [*Into the phone.*] Hello? . . . Who's this?

[*The whistle continues from the kettle, and* WILLIE *looks over in that direction. He hangs up the phone and does not seem embarrassed or even aware of his own absentmindedness. He simply crosses into the kitchen and turns off the flame under the kettle.*]

VOICE FROM TV We'll be back with *Storm Warning* after this brief message from Lipton Tea.

WILLIE Don't worry, I'm not going anywhere.

[*He puts a tea ball into a mug and pours the boiling water in. Then he goes over to the dining table in the living room, takes a spoon, dips into a jar of honey, and pours it into his tea. He glances over at the TV set, which has just played the Lipton Tea commercial.*]

VOICE FROM TV And now for Part Three of today's *Storm Warning* . . .

WILLIE What happened to Part Two? I missed Part Two? [*He drinks his tea as Part Three continues and the banal dialogue drones on.* WILLIE *listens as he shuffles toward his chair. The TV set, which is away from the wall, has an electric plug running from it, along the ground and into the wall.* WILLIE, *who never seems to look where he's going, comes up against the cord with his foot, inadvertently pulling the cord out of its socket in the wall. The TV set immediately dies.* WILLIE *sits, then looks at the set. Obviously, no picture. He gets up and fiddles with the dials. How could his best friend desert him at a time like this? He hits the set on the top with his hand.*] What's the matter with you? [*He hits the set again and twists the knobs futilely, never thinking for a moment it might be something as simple as the plug. He slaps the picture tube.*] Come on, for Pete's sakes, what are you doing there? [*He stares at it in disbelief. He kicks the stand on which it rests. Then he crosses to the phone, and picks it up.*] Hello? . . . Sandy? . . . Let me have Sandy . . . Sandy? . . . My television's dead . . . My television . . . Is this Sandy? . . . My television died . . . No, not Willie. Mr. Clark to you, please . . . Never mind the jokes, wise guy, it's not funny . . . Send up somebody to fix my dead television . . . I didn't touch nothing . . . Nothing. I'm telling you . . . It's a crappy set . . . You live in a crappy hotel, you get a crappy television . . . The what? . . . The plug? . . . What plug? . . . Wait a minute. [*He lays the phone down, crosses to behind the set, bends down, picks up the plug and looks at it. He goes back to the telephone. Into the phone.*] Hello? . . . It's not the plug. It's something else. I'll fix it myself. [*He hangs up, goes over to the wall plug and plugs it in. The set goes back on.*] He tells me the plug . . . When he calls me Mr. Clark then I'll tell him it was the plug. [*He sits and picks up his cup of tea.*] The hell with all of 'em. [*There is a knock on the door.* WILLIE *looks at the wall on the opposite side of the room.*] Bang all you want, I'm not turning it off. I'm lucky it works.

[*There is a pause; then a knock on the front door again, this time accompanied by a male voice.*]

BEN'S VOICE Uncle Willie? It's me. Ben.

[WILLIE *turns and looks at the front door, not acknowledging that he was mistaken about the knocking on the other wall.*]

WILLIE Who's that?

BEN'S VOICE Ben.

WILLIE Ben? Is that you?

BEN'S VOICE Yes, Uncle Willie, it's Ben. Open the door.

WILLIE Wait a minute. [*He rises, crosses to the door, tripping over the TV cord again, disconnecting the set. He starts to unlatch the door, but has trouble manipulating it. His fingers are not too manipulative.*] Wait a minute . . . [*He is having great difficulty with it.*] . . . Wait a minute.

BEN'S VOICE Is anything wrong?

WILLIE [*Still trying.*] Wait a minute.

[*He tries forcing it.*]

BEN'S VOICE What's the matter?

WILLIE I'm locked in. The lock is broken, I'm locked in. Go down and tell the boy, Sandy. Tell Sandy that Mr. Clark is locked in.

BEN'S VOICE What is it, the latch?

WILLIE It's the latch. It's broken, I'm locked in. Go tell the boy Sandy, they'll get somebody.

BEN'S VOICE That happened last week. Don't try to force it. Just slide it out. [WILLIE *stares at the latch.*] Uncle Willie, do you hear me? Don't force it. Slide it out.

WILLIE [*Fiddling with the latch.*] Wait a minute. [*Carefully, he slides it open.*] It's open. Never mind, I did it myself.

[*He opens the door.* BEN SILVERMAN, *a well dressed man in his early thirties, enters. He is wearing a topcoat and carrying a shopping bag from Bloomingdale's, filled to the brim with assorted foodstuffs and a copy of the weekly* Variety.]

BEN You probably have to oil it.

WILLIE I don't have to oil nothing. The hell with 'em.

[BEN *hangs up his coat in the closet.*]

BEN [*Crosses to the table with the shopping bag.*] You feeling all right?

WILLIE What is this, Wednesday?

BEN [*Puzzled.*] Certainly. Don't I always come on Wednesdays?

WILLIE But this is Wednesday today?

BEN [*Puts his bag down.*] Yes, of course. Haven't you been out?

WILLIE When?

BEN Today. Yesterday. This week. You haven't been out all week?

WILLIE [*Crossing to him.*] Sunday. I was out Sunday. I went to the park Sunday.

[BEN *hands* WILLIE *the* Variety. WILLIE *tucks it under his arm and starts to look through the shopping bag.*]

BEN What are you looking for?

WILLIE [*Going through the bag.*] My *Variety.*

BEN I just gave it to you. It's under your arm.

WILLIE [*Looks under his arm.*] Why do you put it there? He puts it under my arm.

BEN [*Starts taking items out of the bag.*] Have you been eating properly? No corned beef sandwiches, I hope.

WILLIE [*Opens to the back section.*] Is this today's?

BEN Certainly it's today's. *Variety* comes out on Wednesday, doesn't it? And today is Wednesday.

WILLIE I'm just asking, don't get so excited. [BEN *shakes his head in consternation.*] . . . Because I already read last Wednesday's.

BEN [*Takes more items out.*] I got you six different kinds of soups. All low-sodium, salt-free. All very good for you . . . Are you listening?

WILLIE [*His head in the paper.*] I'm listening. You got six lousy-tasting soups . . . Did you see this?

BEN What?

WILLIE What I'm looking at. Did you see this?

BEN How do I know what you're looking at?

WILLIE Two new musicals went into rehearsals today and I didn't even get an audition. Why didn't I get an audition?

BEN Because there were no parts for you. One of them is a young rock musical and the other show is all black.

WILLIE What's the matter, I can't do black? I did black in 1928. And when I did black, you understood the words, not like today.

BEN I'm sorry, you're not the kind of black they're looking for. [*He shivers.*] Geez, it's cold in here. You know it's freezing in here? Don't they ever send up any heat?

WILLIE [*Has turned a page.*] How do you like that? Sol Burton died.

BEN Who?

WILLIE Sol Burton. The songwriter. Eighty-nine years old, went like that, from nothing.

BEN Why didn't you put on a sweater?

WILLIE I knew him very well . . . A terrible person. Mean, mean. He should rest in peace, but he was a mean person. His best friends didn't like him.

BEN [*Goes to the bureau for a sweater.*] Why is it so cold in here?

WILLIE You know what kind of songs he wrote? . . . The worst. The worst songs ever written were written by Sol Burton. [*He sings.*] "Lady, Lady, be my baby . . ." Did you ever hear anything so rotten? Baby he rhymes with lady . . . No wonder he's dead.

[*He turns the page.*]

BEN This radiator is ice-cold. Look, Uncle Willie, I'm not going to let you live here any more. You've got to let me find you another place . . . I've been asking you for seven years now. You're going to get sick.

WILLIE [*Still looking at* Variety.] Tom Jones is gonna get a hundred thousand dollars a week in Las Vegas. When Lewis and I were headlining at the Palace, the *Palace* didn't cost a hundred thousand dollars.

BEN That was forty years ago. And forty years ago this hotel was twenty years old. They should tear it down. They take advantage of all you people in here because they know you don't want to move.

[WILLIE *crosses to the table and looks into the shopping bag.*]

WILLIE No cigars?

BEN [*Making notes on his memo pad.*] You're not supposed to have cigars.

WILLIE Where's the cigars?

BEN You know the doctor told you you're not supposed to smoke cigars any more. I didn't bring any.

WILLIE Gimme the cigars.

BEN What cigars? I just said I don't have them. Will you forget the cigars?

WILLIE Where are they, in the bag?

BEN On the bottom. I just brought three. It's the last time I'm doing it.

WILLIE [*Takes out a bag with three cigars.*] How's your family? The children all right?

[*He removes one cigar.*]

BEN Suddenly you're interested in my family? It's not going to work, Uncle Willie. I'm not bringing you any more cigars.

WIILIE I just want to know how the children are.

BEN The children are fine. They're wonderful, thank you.

WILLIE Good. Next time bring the big cigars.

[*He puts two cigars in the breast pocket of his bathrobe and the other one in his mouth. He crosses into the kitchen looking for a light.*]

BEN You don't even know their names. What are the names of my children?

WILLIE Millie and Sidney.

BEN Amanda and Michael.

WILLIE What's the matter, you didn't like Millie and Sidney?

BEN I was *never* going to name them Millie and Sidney. You forgot, so you made something up. You forget everything. I'll bet you didn't drink the milk from last week. I'll bet it's still in the refrigerator. [*Crosses quickly, and opens the refrigerator and looks in.*] There's the milk from last week.

WILLIE [*Comes out of the kitchen, still looking for a light.*] Do they know who I am?

BEN [*Looking through the refrigerator.*] Who?

WILLIE Amanda and Sidney.

BEN Amanda and Michael. That you were a big star in vaudeville? They're three years old, Uncle Willie, you think they remember vaudeville? *I* never saw vaudeville . . . This refrigerator won't last another two days.

WILLIE Did you tell them six times on *The Ed Sullivan Show?*

[*He sits, tries a cigarette lighter. It's broken.*]

BEN They never heard of Ed Sullivan. Uncle Willie, they're three years old. They don't follow show business. [*Comes back into the living room and sees* WILLIE *with the cigar in his mouth.*] What are you doing? You're not going to smoke that now. You promised me you'd only smoke one after dinner.

WILLIE Am I smoking it? Do you see smoke coming from the cigar?

BEN But you've got it in your mouth.

WILLIE I'm rehearsing . . . After dinner I'll do the show.

BEN [*Crossing back into the kitchen.*] I'm in the most aggravating business in the whole world and I never get aggravated until I come here.

[*He opens the cupboards and looks in.*]

WILLIE [*Looking around.*] So don't come. I got Social Security.

BEN You think that's funny? I don't think that's funny, Uncle Willie.

WILLIE [*Thumbing through* Variety.] If you had a sense of humor, you'd think it was funny.

BEN [*Angrily, through gritted teeth.*] I have a *terrific* sense of humor.

WILLIE Like your father—he laughed once in 1932.

BEN I can't talk to you.

WILLIE Why, they're funny today? Tell me who you think is funny today, and I'll show you where he's not funny.

BEN Let's not get into that, huh? I've got to get back to the office. Just promise me you'll have a decent lunch today.

WILLIE If I were to tell a joke and got a laugh from you, I'd throw it out.

BEN How can I laugh when I see you like this, Uncle Willie? You sit in your pajamas all day in a freezing apartment watching soap operas on a thirty-five-dollar television set that doesn't have a horizontal hold. The picture just keeps rolling from top to bottom—pretty soon your eyes are gonna roll around your head . . . You never eat anything. You never go out because you don't know how to work the lock on the door. Remember when you locked yourself in the bathroom overnight? It's a lucky thing you keep bread in there, you would have starved . . . And you wonder why I worry.

WILLIE Calvin Coolidge, that's your kind of humor.

BEN Look, Uncle Willie, promise me you'll eat decently.

WILLIE I'll eat decently. I'll wear a blue suit, a white shirt and black shoes.

BEN And if you're waiting for a laugh, you're not going to get one from me.

WILLIE Who could live that long? Get me a job instead of a laugh.

BEN [*Sighs, exasperatedly.*] You know I've been trying, Uncle Willie. It's not easy. There's not much in town. Most of the work is commercials and . . . well, you know, we've had a little trouble in that area.

WILLIE The potato chips? The potato chips wasn't my fault.

BEN Forget the potato chips.

WILLIE What about the Shick Injector? Didn't I audition funny on the Shick Injector?

BEN You were very funny but your hand was shaking. And you can't show a man shaving with a shaky hand.

WILLIE Why couldn't you get me on the Alka-Seltzer? That's my kind of comedy. I got a terrific face for an upset stomach.

BEN I've submitted you twenty times.

WILLIE What's the matter with twenty-one?

BEN Because the word is out in the business that you can't remember the lines, and they're simply not interested.

WILLIE [*That hurt.*] I couldn't remember the lines? I COULDN'T REMEMBER THE LINES? I don't remember that.

BEN For the Frito-Lays potato chips. I sent you over to the studio, you couldn't even remember the address.

WILLIE Don't tell me I didn't remember the lines. The lines I remembered beautifully. The name of the potato chip I couldn't remember . . . What was it?

BEN Frito-Lays.

WIILIE Say it again.

BEN Frito-Lays.

WILLIE I still can't remember it—because it's not funny. If it's funny, I remember it. Alka-Seltzer is funny. You say "Alka-Seltzer," you get a laugh. The other word is not funny. What is it?

BEN Frito-Lays.

WILLIE Maybe in *Mexico* that's funny, not here. Fifty-seven years I'm in this business, you learn a few things. You know what makes an audience laugh. Do you know which words are funny and which words are *not* funny?

BEN You told me a hundred times, Uncle Willie. Words with a "K" in it are funny.

WILLIE Words with a "K" in it are funny. You didn't know that, did you? If it doesn't have a "K," it's not funny. I'll tell you which words always get a laugh.

[*He is about to count on his fingers.*]

BEN Chicken.

WILLIE Chicken is funny.

BEN Pickle.

WILLIE Pickle is funny.

BEN Cupcake.

WILLIE Cupcake is funny . . . Tomato is *not* funny. Roast beef is *not* funny.

BEN But cookie is funny.

WILLIE But cookie is funny.

BEN Uncle Willie, you've explained that to me ever since I was a little boy.

WILLIE Cucumber is funny.

BEN [*Falling in again.*] Car keys.

WILLIE Car keys is funny.

BEN Cleveland.

WILLIE Cleveland is funny . . . Maryland is *not* funny.

BEN Listen, I have to get back to the office, Uncle Willie, but there's something I'd like to talk to you about first. I got a call yesterday from C.B.S.

WILLIE Casey Stengel, that's a funny name; Robert Taylor is not funny.

BEN [*Sighs exasperatedly.*] Why don't you listen to me?

WILLIE I heard. You got a call from N.B.C.

BEN C.B.S.

WILLIE Whatever.

BEN C.B.S. is doing a big special next month. An hour and a half variety show. They're going to have some of the biggest names in the history of show business. They're trying to get Flip Wilson to host the show.

WILLIE Him I like. He gives me a laugh. With the dress and the little giggle and the red wig. That's a funny boy . . . What's the boy's name again?

BEN Flip Wilson. And it doesn't have a K.

WILLIE But he's *black,* with a "K." You see what I mean?

BEN [*Looks to heaven for help. It doesn't come.*] I do, I do. The theme of this variety show—

WILLIE What's the theme of the show?

BEN *The theme of the show* is the history of comedy dating from the early Greek times, through the days of vaudeville, right up to today's stars.

WILLIE Why couldn't you get me on this show?

BEN I *got* you on the show.

WILLIE Alone?

BEN With Lewis.

WILLIE [*Turns away.*] You ain't got me on the show.

BEN Let me finish.

WILLIE You're finished. It's no.

BEN Can't you wait until I'm through before you say "no"? Can't we discuss it for a minute?

WILLIE I'm busy.

BEN Doing what?

WILLIE Saying "no."

BEN You can have the courtesy of hearing me out. They begged me at C.B.S. *Begged* me.

WILLIE Talk faster, because you're coming up to another "no."

BEN They said to me the history of comedy in the United States would not be complete unless they included one of the greatest teams ever to come out of vaudeville, Lewis and Clark, The Sunshine Boys. The vice-president of C.B.S. said this to me on the phone.

WILLIE The vice-president said this?

BEN Yes. He is the greatest Lewis and Clark fan in this country. He knows by heart every one of your old routines.

WILLIE Then let *him* go on with that bastard.

BEN It's one shot. You would just have to do it one night, one of the old sketches. They'll pay ten thousand dollars for the team. That's top money for these shows, I promise you. Five thousand dollars apiece. And that's more money than you've earned in two years.

WILLIE I don't need money. I live alone. I got two nice suits, I don't have a pussycat, I'm very happy.

BEN You're *not* happy. You're miserable.

WILLIE *I'm happy!* I just *look* miserable!

BEN You're dying to go to work again. You call me six times a day in the office. I can't see over my desk for all your messages.

WILLIE Call me back sometime, you won't get so many messages.

BEN I call you every day of the week. I'm up here every Wednesday, rain or shine, winter or summer, flu or dipththeria.

WILLIE What are you, a mailman? You're a nephew. I don't ask you to come. You're my brother's son, you've been very nice to me. I appreciate it, but I've never asked you for anything . . . except for a job. You're a good boy but a stinking agent.

BEN I'M A GOOD AGENT? Damn it, don't say that to me, Uncle Willie, I'm a *goddamn good agent!*

WILLIE What are you screaming for? What is it, such a wonderful thing to be a good agent?

BEN [*Holds his chest.*] I'm getting chest pains. You give me chest pains, Uncle Willie.

WILLIE It's *my* fault you get excited?

BEN Yes, it's *your* fault! I only get chest pains on Wednesdays.

WILLIE So come on Tuesdays.

BEN [*Starts for the door.*] I'm going. I don't even want to discuss this with you any more. You're impossible to talk to. FORGET THE VARIETY SHOW!

[*He starts for the door.*]

WILLIE I forgot it.

BEN [*Stops.*] I'm not coming back any more. I'm not bringing you your *Variety* or your cigars or your low-sodium soups—do you understand, Uncle Willie? I'm not bringing you anything any more.

WILLIE Good. Take care of yourself. Say hello to Millie and Phyllis.

BEN [*Breathing heavily.*] Why won't you do this for me? I'm not asking you to be partners again. If you two don't get along, all right. But this is just for one night. One last show. Once you get an exposure like that, Alka-Seltzer will come begging to *me* to sign you up. Jesus, how is it going to look if I go back to the office and tell them I couldn't make a deal with my own uncle?

WILLIE My personal opinion? Lousy!

BEN [*Falls into a chair, exhausted.*] Do you really hate Al Lewis that much?

WILLIE [*Looks away.*] I don't discuss Al Lewis any more.

BEN [*Gets up.*] We *have* to discuss him, because C.B.S. is waiting for an answer today, and if we turn them down, I want to have a pretty good reason why. You haven't seen him in—what? ten years now.

WILLIE [*Takes a long time before answering.*] Eleven years!

BEN [*Amazed.*] You mean to tell me you haven't spoken to him in eleven years?

WILLIE I haven't *seen* him in eleven years. I haven't *spoken* to him in twelve years.

BEN You mean you saw him for a whole year that you didn't speak to him?

WILLIE It wasn't easy. I had to sneak around backstage a lot.

BEN But you spoke to him onstage.

WILLIE Not to *him*. If he played a gypsy, I spoke to the gypsy. If he played a lunatic, I spoke to the lunatic. But that bastard I didn't speak to.

BEN I can't believe that.

WILLIE You don't believe it? I can show you witnesses who *saw* me never speaking to him.

BEN It's been eleven years, Uncle Willie. Hasn't time changed anything for you?

WILLIE Yes. I hate him eleven years more.

BEN Why?

WILLIE Why? . . . You never met him?

BEN Sure I met him. I was fifteen years old. I met him once at that benefit at Madison Square Garden and once backstage at some television show. He seemed nice enough to me.

WILLIE That's only twice. You had to meet him three times to hate him.

BEN Uncle Willie, could I make a suggestion?

WILLIE He used to give me the finger.

BEN The what?

WILLIE The finger! The finger! He would poke me in the chest with the finger. [*He crosses to* BEN *and demonstrates on him by poking a finger in* BEN'S *chest every time he makes a point.*] He would say, "*Listen,* Doctor." [*Pokes finger.*] "I'm *telling* you, Doctor." [*Pokes finger.*] "You know what I *mean*, Doctor." [*Pokes finger.* BEN *rubs his chest in pain.*] Hurts, doesn't it? How'd you like it for forty-three years? I got a black and blue hole in my chest. My wife to her dying day thought it was a tattoo. I haven't worked with him in eleven years, it's just beginning to fade away . . . The man had the sharpest finger in show business.

BEN If you work with him again, I promise you I'll buy you a thick padded undershirt.

WILLIE You think I never did that? One night I put a steel plate under my shirt. He gave me the finger, he had it in a splint for a month.

BEN Something else must have happened you're not telling me about. You don't work with a person for forty-three years without some bond of affection remaining.

WILLIE You wanna hear other things? He used to spit in my face. Onstage *the man would spit in my face!*

BEN Not on purpose.

WILLIE [*Turns away.*] He tells me "not on purpose" . . . If there was some way I could have saved the spit, I would show it to you.

BEN You mean he would just stand there and spit in your face?

WILLIE What do you think, he's stupid? He

worked it into the act. He would stand with his nose on top of my nose and purposely only say words that began with a "T." [*As he demonstrates, he spits.*] "Tootsie Roll." [*Spit.*] "Tinker Toy." [*Spit.*] "Typing on the typewriter." [*Spits.* BEN *wipes his face.*] Some nights I thought I would drown! I don't know where he got it all from . . . I think he would drink all day and save it up for the night.

BEN I'll put it in the contract. If he spits at you, he won't get paid.

WILLIE If he can get another chance to spit at me, he wouldn't *want* to get paid.

BEN Then will you answer me one question? If it was all that bad, why did you stick together for forty-three years?

WILLIE [*Turns; looks at him.*] Because he was terrific. There'll never be another one like him . . . Nobody could time a joke the way he could time a joke. Nobody could say a line the way he said it. I knew what he was thinking, he knew what I was thinking. One person, that's what we were . . . No, no. Al Lewis was the best. The *best!* You understand?

BEN I understand.

WILLIE As an actor, no one could touch him. As a human being, no one *wanted* to touch him.

BEN [*Sighs.*] So what do I tell C.B.S.? No deal because Al Lewis spits?

WILLIE You know when the last time was we worked together?

BEN Eleven years ago on *The Ed Sullivan Show.*

WILLIE Eleven years ago on *The Ed Sullivan Show.* July twenty-seventh. He wouldn't put us on in the winter when people were watching, but never mind. We did The Doctor and the Tax Examination. You never saw that, did you?

BEN No, but I heard it's wonderful.

WILLIE What about a "classic"? A *classic!* A *dead* person watching that sketch would laugh. We did it maybe eight thousand times, it never missed . . . *That* night it missed. Something was wrong with him, he was rushing, his timing was off, his mind was someplace else. I thought he was sick. Still, we got terrific applause. Five times Ed Sullivan said, "How about that?" We got back into the dressing room, he took off his make-up, put on his clothes, and said to me, "Willie, if it's all the same to you, I'm retiring." I said, "What do you mean, retiring? It's not even nine o'clock. Let's have something to eat." He said, "I'm not retiring for the night. I'm retiring for what's left of my life." And he puts on his hat, walks out of the theater, becomes a stockbroker and I'm left with an act where I ask questions and there's no one there to answer. Never saw the man again to this day. Oh, he called me, I wouldn't answer. He wrote me, I tore it up. He sent me telegrams, they're probably still under the door.

BEN Well, Uncle Willie, with all due respect, you really weren't getting that much work any more. Maybe he was getting tired of doing the same thing for forty-three years. I mean a man has a right to retire when he wants, doesn't he?

WILLIE Not him. Don't forget, when he retired himself, he retired me too. And goddamn it, I wasn't ready yet. Now suddenly maybe he needs five thousand dollars, and he wants to come crawling back, the hell with him. I'm a single now . . .

BEN I spoke to Al Lewis on the phone last night. He doesn't even care about the money. He just wants to do the show for old times' sake. For his grandchildren who never saw him.

WILLIE Sure. He probably retired broke from the stock market. I guarantee you *those* high-class people never got a spit in the face once.

BEN Did you know his wife died two years ago? He's living with his daughter now, somewhere in New Jersey. He doesn't do anything any more. He's got very bad arthritis, he's got asthma, he's got poor blood circulation—

WILLIE I'll send him a pump. He'll outlive *you,* believe me.

BEN He wants very much to do this show, Willie.

WILLIE With arthritis? Forget it. Instead of a finger, he'll poke me with a cane.

BEN C.B.S. wants you to do the doctor sketch. Lewis told me he could get on a stage tonight and do that sketch letter perfect. He doesn't even have to rehearse it.

WILLIE I don't even want to discuss it . . . And in the second place, I would definitely not do it without a rehearsal.

BEN All right, then will you agree to this? Just

rehearse with him one day. If it doesn't work out, we'll call it off.

WILLIE I don't trust him. I think he's been planning this for eleven years. We rehearse all week and then he walks out on me just before the show.

BEN Let me call him on the phone. [*Going over to the phone.*] Let me set up a rehearsal time for Monday.

WILLIE WAIT A MINUTE! I got to think about this.

BEN We don't have that much time. C.B.S. is waiting to hear.

WILLIE What's their rush? What are they, going out of business?

BEN [*Picks up the phone.*] I'm dialing. I'm dialing him, Uncle Willie, okay?

WILLIE Sixty-forty—I get six thousand, he gets four thousand . . . What the hell can he buy in New Jersey anyway?

BEN [*Holding the phone.*] I can't do that, Uncle Willie . . . God, I hope this works out.

WILLIE Tell him I'm against it. I want him to know. I'll do it with an "against it."

BEN It's ringing.

WILLIE And he's got to come here. I'm not going there, you understand?

BEN He's got to be home. I told him I would call about one.

WILLIE Sure. You know what he's doing? He's practicing spitting.

BEN [*Into the phone.*] Hello? . . . Mr. Lewis? . . . Ben Silverman . . . Yes, fine, thanks . . . I'm here with him now.

WILLIE Willie Clark. The one he left on *The Ed Sullivan Show*. Ask him if he remembers.

BEN It's okay, Mr. Lewis . . . Uncle Willie said yes.

WILLIE With an "against it." Don't forget the "against it."

BEN No, he's very anxious to do it.

WILLIE [*Jumping up in anger.*] WHO'S ANXIOUS? I'M AGAINST IT! TELL HIM, you lousy nephew.

BEN Can you come here for rehearsal on Monday? . . . Oh, that'll be swell . . . In the morning. [*To* WILLIE.] About eleven o'clock? How long is the drive. About two hours?

WILLIE Make it nine o'clock.

BEN Be reasonable, Willie. [*Into the phone.*] Eleven o'clock is fine, Mr. Lewis . . . Can you give me your address, please, so I can send you the contracts? [*He takes a pen out of his pocket and writes in his notebook.*] One-one-nine, South Pleasant Drive . . .

WILLIE Tell him if he starts with the spitting or poking, I'm taking him to court. I'll have a man on the show watching. Tell him.

BEN West Davenport, New Jersey . . . Oh-nine-seven-seven-oh-four . . .

WILLIE I don't want any—[*Spitting.*]—"*T*oy *t*elephones *t*apping on *t*in *t*urtles." Tell him. Tell him.

[*Curtain.*]

Scene II

It is the following Monday, a few minutes before eleven in the morning.

The stage is empty. Suddenly the bathroom door opens and WILLIE *emerges. He is still wearing his slippers and the same pajamas, but instead of his bathrobe, he has made a concession to the occasion. He is wearing a double-breasted blue suit-jacket, buttoned, and he is putting a handkerchief in his pocket. He looks in the mirror, and brushes back his hair. He shuffles over to the window and looks out.*

There is a knock on the door. WILLIE *turns and stares at it. He doesn't move. There is another knock, and then we hear* BEN'S *voice.*

BEN'S VOICE Uncle Willie. It's Ben.

WILLIE Ben? Is that you?

BEN'S VOICE Yes. Open up. [WILLIE *starts toward the door, then stops.*]

WILLIE You're alone or he's with you?

BEN'S VOICE I'm alone.

WILLIE [*Nods.*] Wait a minute. [*The latch is locked again, and again he has trouble getting it open.*] Wait a minute.

BEN'S VOICE Slide it, don't push it.

WILLIE Wait a minute. I'll push it.

BEN'S VOICE *DON'T* PUSH IT! SLIDE IT!

WILLIE Wait a minute. [*He gets the lock open and opens the door.* BEN *walks in.*] You're supposed to slide it.

BEN I rushed like crazy. I didn't want him getting here before me. Did he call or anything?

WILLIE Where's the *Variety*?

BEN [*Taking off his coat.*] It's Monday, not Wednesday. Didn't you know it was Monday?

WILLIE I remembered, but I forgot.

BEN What are you wearing? What is that? You look half-dressed.

WILLIE Why, for him I should get *all* dressed?

BEN Are you all right? Are you nervous or anything?

WILLIE Why should *I* be nervous? *He* should be nervous. I don't get nervous.

BEN Good.

WILLIE Listen, I changed my mind. I'm not doing it.

BEN *What?*

WILLIE Don't get so upset. Everything is the same as before, except I'm not doing it.

BEN When did you decide this?

WILLIE I decided it when you asked me.

BEN No, you didn't. You told me you *would* do it.

WILLIE Well, it was a bad decision. This time I made a good one.

BEN Well, I'm sorry, you have to do it. I've already told C.B.S. that you would be rehearsing this week and, more important, that man is on his way over here now and I'm not going to tell him that you called it off.

WILLIE We'll leave him a note outside the door.

BEN We're not leaving any notes. That's why I came here this morning, I was afraid you would try something like this. I'm going to stay until I think you're both acting like civilized human beings, and then when you're ready to rehearse, I'm going to leave you alone. Is that understood?

WILLIE I'm sick. I woke up sick today.

BEN No, you're not.

WILLIE What are you, a doctor? You're an agent. I'm telling you I'm sick.

BEN What's wrong?

WILLIE I think I got hepatitis.

BEN You don't even know what hepatitis is.

WILLIE If you got it, what's the difference?

BEN There's nothing wrong with you except a good case of the nerves. You're not backing out, Willie. I don't care what kind of excuse you make, you're going to go through with this. You promised me you would give it at least one day.

WILLIE I'll pick another day.

BEN TODAY! You're going to-meet with him and rehearse with him TODAY. Now *stop* and just behave yourself.

WILLIE What do you mean, "behave yourself"? Who do you think you're talking to, Susan and Jackie?

BEN *Amanda* and Jackie!—Michael! I wish I were. I can reason with them. And now I'm getting chest pains on Monday.

WILLIE Anyway, he's late. He's purposely coming late to aggravate me.

BEN [*Looking out the window.*] He's not late. It's two minutes after eleven.

WILLIE So what is he, early? He's *late!*

BEN You're *looking* to start trouble, I can tell.

WILLIE I was up and dressed at eight o'clock, don't tell me.

BEN Why didn't you shave?

WILLIE Get me the Shick commercial, I'll shave. [*He looks in the mirror.*] I really think I got hepatitis. Look how green I look.

BEN You don't get green from hepatitis. You get yellow.

WILLIE Maybe I got a very bad case.

BEN [*Looks at his watch.*] Now you got me nervous. I wonder if I should call him? Maybe he's sick.

WILLIE [*Glares at him.*] You believe *he's* sick, but me you won't believe . . . Why don't you become *his* nephew?

[*Suddenly there is a knock on the door.* WILLIE *freezes and stares at it.*]

BEN That's him. You want me to get it—

WILLIE Get what? I didn't hear anything.

BEN [*Starts toward the door.*] All right, now take it easy. Please just behave yourself and give this a chance. Promise me you'll give it a chance.

WILLIE [*Starts for the kitchen.*] I'll give it every possible chance in the world . . . But it's not gonna work.

BEN Where are you going?

WILLIE To make tea. I feel like some hot tea.

[*He crosses into the kitchen and closes the curtain. Starts to fill up the kettle with water.*]

BEN [*Panicky.*] NOW? NOW? [BEN *looks at him, exasperated; a knock on the door again and* BEN *crosses to it and opens it.* AL LEWIS *stands there. He is also about seventy years old and is dressed in his best blue suit, hat, scarf, and carries a walking stick. He was probably quite a gay blade in his day, but time has slowed him down somewhat. Our first impression is that he is soft-spoken and pleasant—and a little nervous.*] Mr. Lewis, how do you do? I'm Ben Silverman.

[BEN, *nervous, extends his hand.*]

AL How are you? Hello. It's nice to see you. [*His eyes dart around looking for* WILLIE. *He doesn't see him yet.*] How do you do? . . . Hello . . . Hello . . . How are you?

BEN We met before, a long time ago. My father took me backstage, I forget the theater. It must have been fifteen, twenty years ago.

AL I remember . . . Certainly . . . It was backstage . . . Maybe fifteen, twenty years ago . . . I forget the theater.

BEN That's right.

AL Sure, I remember.

[*He has walked into the room and shoots a glance toward the kitchen.* WILLIE *doesn't look up from his tea-making.*]

BEN Please sit down. Uncle Willie's making some tea.

AL Thank you very much.

[*He sits on the edge of the table.*]

BEN [*Trying hard to make conversation.*] Er . . . Did you have any trouble getting in from Jersey?

AL My daughter drove me in. She has a car.

BEN Oh, that's nice.

AL A 1972 Chrysler . . . black . . .

BEN Yes, the Chrysler's a wonderful car.

AL The big one . . . the Imperial.

BEN I know. I drove it.

AL My daughter's car?

BEN No, the big Chrysler Imperial. I rented one in California.

AL [*Nods.*] No, she owns.

BEN I understand . . . Do you come into New York often?

AL Today's the first time in two years.

BEN Really? Well, how did you find it?

AL My daughter drove.

BEN No, I mean, do you find the city different in the two years since you've been here?

AL It's not my New York.

BEN No, I suppose it's not. [*He shoots a glance toward the kitchen.* WILLIE *still hasn't looked in.*] Hey, listen, I'm really very excited about all this. Well, for that matter, everyone in the industry is.

AL [*Nods, noncommittally.*] Well, we'll see.

[*He looks around the room, scrutinizing it.*]

BEN [*He calls out toward the kitchen.*] Uncle Willie, how we doing? [*No answer. Embarrassed, to* AL.] I guess it's not boiling yet . . . Oh, listen, I'd like to arrange to have a car pick you up and take you home after you're through rehearsing.

AL My daughter's going to pick me up.

BEN Oh, I see. What time did you say? Four? Five?

AL She's going to call me every hour.

BEN Right . . .

[*Suddenly* WILLIE *sticks his head out of the kitchen, but looks at* BEN *and not at* AL.]

WILLIE One tea or two teas?

BEN Oh, here he is. Well, Uncle Willie, I guess it's been a long time since you two—

WILLIE One tea or two teas?

BEN Oh. Er, nothing for me, thanks. I'm just about leaving. Mr. Lewis? Some tea?

AL [*Doesn't look toward* WILLIE.] Tea would be nice, thank you.

BEN [*To* WILLIE.] Just the one, Uncle Willie.

WILLIE You're sure? I got two tea balls. I could dunk again.

BEN [*Looks at his watch.*] No, I've got to get back to the office. Honestly.

WILLIE [*Nods.*] Mm-hmm. One tea.

[*On his way back in, he darts a look at* LEWIS, *then goes back into the kitchen. He pulls the curtain shut.*]

BEN [*To* LEWIS.] Well, er . . . Do you have any questions you want to ask about the show? About the studio or rehearsals or the air date? Is there anything on your mind that I could help you with?

AL Like what?

BEN Like, er, the studio? Or the rehearsals? Or air date? Things like that?

AL You got the props?

BEN Which props are those?

AL The props. For the doctor sketch. You gotta have props.

BEN Oh, props. Certainly. What do you need? I'll tell them.

[*Takes out a pad; writes.*]

AL You need a desk. A telephone. A pointer. A blackboard. A piece of white chalk, a piece of red chalk. A skeleton, not too tall, a stethoscope, a thermometer, an "ahh" stick—

BEN What's an "ahh" stick?

AL To put in your mouth to say "ahh."

BEN Oh, right, an "ahh" stick.

AL A look stick, a bottle of pills—

BEN A look stick? What's a look stick?

AL A stick to look in the ears. With cotton on the end.

BEN Right. A look stick.

AL A bottle of pills. Big ones, like for a horse.

BEN [*Makes a circle with his two fingers.*] About this big?

AL That's for a pony. [*Makes a circle using the fingers of both hands.*] For a horse is like this. Some bandages, cotton, and eye chart—

BEN Wait a minute, you're going too fast.

AL [*Slowly.*] A-desk . . . *a*-telephone . . . *a*-pointer . . .

BEN No, I got all that—after the cotton and eye chart.

AL A man's suit. Size forty. Like the one I'm wearing.

BEN Also in blue?

AL What do I need two blue suits— Get me a brown.

BEN A brown suit. Is that all?

AL That's all.

WILLIE [*From the kitchen, without looking in.*] A piece of liver.

AL That's all, plus a piece of liver.

BEN What kind of liver?

AL Regular calves' liver. From the butcher.

BEN Like how much? A pound?

AL A little laugh is a pound. A big laugh is two pounds. Three pounds with a lot of blood'll bring the house down.

BEN Is that it?

AL That's it. And a blonde.

BEN You mean a woman—

AL You know a blonde nurse that's a man? . . . Big! As big as you can find. With a big chest —a forty-five, a fifty—and a nice bottom.

BEN You mean a sexy girl with a full, round, rear end?

AL [*Spreads hands apart.*] About like this. [*Makes a smaller behind with his hands.*] This is too small. [*Makes a bigger one.*] And this is too big. [*Goes back to the original one.*] Like this is perfect.

BEN I know what you mean.

AL If you can bring me pictures, I'll pick out one.

BEN There's a million girls like that around.

AL The one we had was the best. I would call her, but she's maybe fifty-five, sixty.

BEN No, no. I'll get a girl. Anything else?

AL Not for me.

BEN Uncle Willie?

WILLIE [*From the kitchen.*] I wasn't listening.

BEN Well, if either of you thinks of anything, just call me. [*Looks at his watch again.*] Eleven-fifteen—I've got to go. [*He gets up.*] Uncle Willie, I'm going. [*He crosses to* LEWIS *and extends his hand.*] Mr. Lewis, I can't express to you enough how happy I am, and speaking for the millions of young people in this country who never had the opportunity of seeing Lewis and Clark work, I just want to say "thank you." To both of you. [*Calls out.*] To *both of you,* Uncle Willie.

AL [*Nods.*] I hope they won't be disappointed.

BEN Oh, they won't.

AL I know they won't. I'm just saying it.

BEN [*Crosses to the kitchen.*] *Goodbye,* Uncle Willie. I'm going.

WILLIE I'll show you the elevator.

BEN I *know* where it is. I'll call you tonight. I just want to say that this is a very happy moment for me. To see you both together again, reunited . . . The two kings of comedy. [*Big smile.*] I'm sure it must be *very exciting* for the both of you, isn't it? [*No answer. They both just stare at him.*] Well, it looks like we're off to a great start. I'll call you later . . . Goodbye.

[*He leaves and closes the door. They are alone.* WILLIE *carries the two teas to the dining table, where the sugar bowl is. He pours himself a teaspoonful of sugar.*]

WILLIE [*Without looking in* AL*'s direction.*] Sugar?

AL [*Doesn't turn.*] If you got.

WILLIE [*Nods.*] I got sugar. [*He bangs the sugar bowl down in front of* AL, *crosses with his own tea to his leather chair and sits. And then the two drink tea . . . silently and interminably. They blow, they sip, they blow, they sip and they sit. Finally.*] You like a cracker?

AL [*Sips.*] What kind of cracker?

WILLIE Graham, chocolate, coconut, whatever you want.

AL Maybe just a plain cracker.

WILLIE I don't have plain crackers. I got graham, chocolate and coconut.

AL All right, a graham cracker.

WILLIE [*Without turning, points into the kitchen.*] They're in the kitchen, in the closet.

[AL *looks over at him, a little surprised at his uncordiality. He nods in acknowledgment.*]

AL Maybe later.

[*They both sip their tea.*]

WILLIE [*Long pause.*] I was sorry to hear about Lillian.

AL Thank you.

WILLIE She was a nice woman. I always liked Lillian.

AL Thank you.

WILLIE And how about you?

AL Thank God, knock wood—[*Raps knuckles on his cane.*]—perfect.

WILLIE I heard different. I heard your blood didn't circulate.

AL Not true. My blood circulates . . . I'm not saying *everywhere,* but it circulates.

WILLIE Is that why you use the cane?

AL It's not a cane. It's a walking stick . . . Maybe once in a great while it's a cane.

WILLIE I've been lucky, thank God. I'm in the pink.

AL I was looking. For a minute I thought you were having a flush.

WILLIE [*Sips his tea.*] You know Sol Burton died?

AL Go on . . . Who's Sol Burton?

WILLIE You don't remember Sol Burton?

AL [*Thinks.*] Oh, yes. The manager from the Belasco.

WILLIE That was Sol Bernstein.

AL Not Sol Bernstein. Sol *Burton* was the manager from the Belasco.

WILLIE Sol *Bernstein* was the manager from the Belasco, and it wasn't the Belasco, it was the Morosco.

AL Sid *Weinstein* was the manager from the Morosco. Sol *Burton* was the manager from the Belasco. Sol *Bernstein* I don't know *who* the hell was.

WILLIE How can you remember anything if your blood doesn't circulate?

AL It circulates in my *head.* It doesn't circulate in my *feet.*

[*He stomps his foot on the floor a few times.*]

WILLIE Is anything coming down?

AL Wait a minute. Wasn't Sid Weinstein the songwriter?

WILLIE No for chrissakes! That's SOL BURTON!

AL Who wrote "Lady, lady, be my baby"?

WILLIE That's what I'm telling you! Sol Burton, the lousy songwriter.

AL Oh, *that* Sol Burton . . . He died?

WILLIE Last week.

AL Where?

WILLIE [*Points.*] In *Variety.*

AL Sure, now I remember . . . And how is Sol Bernstein?

WILLIE I didn't read anything.

AL Good. I always liked Sol Bernstein. [*They quietly sip their tea.* AL *looks around the room.*] So-o-o . . . this is where you live now?

WILLIE Didn't I always live here?

AL [*Looks again.*] Not in here. You lived in the big suite.

WILLIE This *is* the big suite . . . Now it's five small suites.

[AL *nods, understanding.*]

AL [*Looks around.*] That's what they do today. Anything to squeeze a dollar. What do they charge now for a small suite?

WILLIE The same as they used to charge for the big suite.

[AL *nods, understanding.*]

AL I have a very nice room with my daughter in New Jersey. I have my own bathroom. They don't bother me, I don't bother them.

WILLIE What is it, in the country?

AL Certainly it's in the country. Where do you think New Jersey is, in the city?

WILLIE [*Shrugs.*] New Jersey is what I see from the bench on Riverside Drive. What have they got, a private house?

AL Certainly it's a private house. It's some big place. Three quarters of an acre. They got their own trees, their own bushes, a nice little swimming pool for the kids they blow up in the summertime, a big swing in the back, a little dog house, a rock garden—

WILLIE A what?

AL A rock garden.

WILLIE What do you mean, a rock garden? You mean for rocks?

AL You never saw a rock garden?

WILLIE And I'm not that anxious.

AL It's beautiful. A Chinaman made it. Someday you'll take a bus and you'll come out and I'll show you.

WILLIE I should drive all the way out to New Jersey on a bus to see a rock garden?

AL You don't even know what I'm talking about. You have to live in the country to appreciate it. I never thought it was possible I could be so happy in the country.

WILLIE You don't mind it's so quiet?

AL [*Looks at him.*] They got noise in New

Jersey. But it's a quiet noise. Birds . . . drizzling . . . Not like here with the buses and trucks and screaming and yelling.

WILLIE Well, it's different for you. You like the country better because you're retired. You can sit on a porch, look at a tree, watch a bush growing. You're still not active like me. You got a different temperament, you're a slow person.

AL I'm a slow person?

WILLIE You're here fifteen minutes, you still got a whole cup of tea. I'm finished already.

AL That's right. You're finished, and I'm still enjoying it. That was always the difference with us.

WILLIE You're wrong. I can get up and make a *second* cup of tea and enjoy it twice as much as you. I like a busy life. That's why I love the city. I gotta be near a phone. I never know when a picture's gonna come up, a musical, a commercial . . .

AL When did you do a picture?

WILLIE They're negotiating.

AL When did you do a musical?

WILLIE They're talking.

AL When did you do a commercial?

WILLIE All the time. I did one last week.

AL For what?

WILLIE For, er, for the . . . what's it, the potato chips.

AL What potato chips?

WILLIE The big one. The crispy potato chips . . . er . . . you know.

AL What do I know? I don't eat potato chips.

WILLIE Well, what's the difference what the name is?

AL They hire you to sell potato chips and you can't remember the name?

WILLIE Did you remember Sol Burton?

AL [*Shrugs.*] I'm not selling Sol Burton.

WILLIE Listen, I don't want to argue with you.

AL I didn't come from New Jersey to argue.

[*They sit quietly for a few seconds.* AL *sips his tea;* WILLIE *looks at his empty cup.*]

WILLIE [*Finally.*] So-o-o . . . What do you think? . . . You want to do the doctor sketch?

AL [*Thinks.*] Well, listen, it's very good money. It's only a few days' work, I can be back in New Jersey. If you feel you'd like to do it, then my feeling is I'm agreeable.

WILLIE And my feeling they told you.

AL What?

WILLIE They didn't tell you? My feeling is I'm against it.

AL You're against it?

WILLIE Right. But I'll do it if you want to.

AL I don't want to do it if you're against it. If you're against it, don't do it.

WILLIE What do you care if I'm against it as long as we're doing it? I just want you to know *why* I'm doing it.

AL Don't do me any favors.

WILLIE Who's doing you a favor? I'm doing my nephew a favor. It'll be good for him in the business if we do it.

AL You're sure?

WILLIE Certainly I'm sure. It's a big break for a kid like that to get big stars like us.

AL That's different. In that case, I'm against it too but I'll do it.

WILLIE [*Nods.*] As long as we understand each other.

AL And I want to be sure you know I'm not doing it for the money. The money goes to my grandchildren.

WILLIE The whole thing?

AL The whole thing. But not now. Only if I die. If I don't die, it'll be for my old age.

WILLIE The same with me.

AL You don't have grandchildren.

WILLIE My *nephew's* children. Sidney and Marvin.

AL [*Nods.*] Very good.

WILLIE Okay . . . So-o-o, you wanna rehearse?

AL You're not against rehearsing?

WILLIE Why should I be against rehearsing? I'm only against doing the show. Rehearsing is important.

AL All right, let's rehearse. Why don't we move the furniture, and we'll make the set.

[*They both get up and start to move the furniture around. First each one takes a single chair and moves it into a certain position. Then they both take a table and jointly move it away. Then they each take the chair the other one had moved before, and more it into a different place. Every time one moves something somewhere, the other moves it into a different spot. Finally* WILLIE *becomes aware that they are getting nowhere.*]

WILLIE Wait a minute, wait a minute. What the hell are we doing here?

AL I'm fixing up the set, I don't know what you're doing.

WILLIE You're fixing up the set?

AL That's right.

WILLIE You're fixing up the set for the doctor sketch?

[AL *looks at him for a long time without saying a word. It suddenly becomes clear to him.*]

AL Oh, the *doctor* sketch?

[*He then starts to pick up a chair and move it into another position.* WILLIE *does the same with another chair. They both move the table . . . and then they repeat what they did before. Every time one moves a chair, the other one moves the same chair to a different position.* WILLIE *stops and looks again.*]

WILLIE Wait a minute! Wait a minute! We're doing the same goddamn thing. Are you fixing up for the doctor sketch or are you redecorating my apartment?

AL I'm fixing up for the doctor sketch. If you'd leave what I'm doing alone, we'd be finished.

WILLIE We'd be finished, but we'd be wrong.

AL Not for the doctor sketch. I know what I'm doing. I did this sketch for forty-three years.

WILLIE And where was I all that time, taking a smoke? Who did you think did it with you for forty-three years? That was *me,* mister.

AL Don't call me mister, you know my name. I never liked it when you called me mister.

WILLIE It's not a dirty word.

AL It is when you say it.

WILLIE Forgive me, *sir.*

AL Let's please, for Pete's sakes, fix up for the doctor sketch.

WILLIE You think *you* know how to do it? You fix it up.

AL It'll be my pleasure. [WILLIE *stands aside and watches with arms folded as* AL *proceeds to move table and chairs and stools until he arranges them exactly the way he wants them. Then he stands back and folds his arms the same way.*] There! *That's* the doctor sketch!

WILLIE [*Smiles arrogantly.*] For how much money?

AL I don't want to bet you.

WILLIE You're afraid to lose?

AL I'm afraid to *win.* You don't even have enough to buy a box of plain crackers.

WILLIE —Don't be so afraid you're gonna win —because you're gonna lose! That's not the doctor sketch. That's the gypsy chiropractor sketch.

AL You're positive?

WILLIE I'm *more* than positive. I'm *sure.*

AL All right. Show me the doctor sketch.

WILLIE [*Looks at him confidently, then goes to a chair, picks it up and moves it to the left about four inches, if that much. Then he folds his arms over his chest.*] There, *that's* the doctor sketch!

AL [*Looks at him.*] You know what you are, Willie? You're a lapalooza.

WILLIE [*Nods.*] If I'm a lapalooza, you're a mister.

AL Let's please rehearse the sketch.

WILLIE All right, go outside. I'm in the office.

AL You gonna do the part with the nurse first?

WILLIE You see a nurse here? How can I rehearse with a nurse that's not here?

AL I'm just asking a question. I'm not allowed to ask questions?

WILLIE Ask whatever you want. But try to make them intelligent questions.

AL I beg your pardon. I usually ask the kind of question to the kind of person I'm talking to . . . You get my drift?

WILLIE I get it, mister.

AL All right. Let's skip over the nurse. We'll start from where I come in.

WILLIE All right, from where you come in. First go out.

AL [*Takes a few steps toward the door, stops and turns.*] All right, I'm outside. [*Pantomimes with his fist, knocking on a door.*] Knock, knock, knock! I was looking for the doctor.

WILLIE Wait a minute. You're not outside.

AL Certainly I'm outside.

WILLIE If you were outside, you couldn't see me, could you?

AL No.

WILLIE Can you see me?

AL Yes.

WILLIE So you're not outside. Go *all* the way outside. What the hell kind of a rehearsal is this?

AL It's a rehearsing rehearsal. Can't you make believe I'm all the way out in the hall?

WILLIE I could also make believe you were still in New Jersey, but you're not. You're here. Let's have a professional rehearsal, for chrissakes. We ain't got a nurse, but we got a door. Let's use what we got.

AL [*Sighs deeply.*] Listen, we're not gonna

stop for every little thing, are we? I don't know how many years I got left, I don't wanna spend it rehearsing.

WILLIE We're not gonna stop for the little things. We're gonna stop for the big things . . . The door is a big thing.

AL All right, I'll go through the door, I'll come in, and then we'll run through the sketch once or twice, and that'll be it for today. All right?

WILLIE Right . . . Unless another big thing comes up.

AL [*Glares at him.*] All right, I'm going out. I'll be right back in. [*He crosses to the door, opens it, stops and turns.*] If I'm outside and my daughter calls, tell her to pick me up in an hour.

[*He goes out and closes the door behind him.*]

WILLIE [*Mumbles, half to himself.*] She can pick you up *now* for all I care. [*He puts his hands behind his back, clasps them, and paces back and forth. He calls out.*] All right! Knock, knock, knock!

AL [*From outside.*] Knock, knock, knock!

WILLIE [*Screams.*] *Don't say it,* for God's sakes, *do it!* [*To himself.*] He probably went *crazy* in the country.

AL [*From outside.*] You ready?

WILLIE [*Yells.*] I'm ready. Knock, knock, knock! [AL *knocks three times on the door.*] Come in. [*We see and hear the doorknob jiggle, but it doesn't open. This is repeated.*] All right, come in already.

AL [*From outside.*] It doesn't open—it's stuck.

WILLIE [*Wearily.*] All right, wait a minute. [*He shuffles over to the door and puts his hand on the knob and pulls. It doesn't open.*] Wait a minute.

[*He tries again, to no avail.*]

AL [*From outside.*] What's the matter?

WILLIE Wait a minute.

[*He pulls harder, to no avail.*]

AL Is it locked?

WILLIE It's not locked. Wait a minute. [*He tries again; it doesn't open.*] It's locked. You better get somebody. Call the boy downstairs. Sandy. Tell him it's locked.

AL [*From outside.*] Let me try it again.

WILLIE What are you wasting time? Call the boy. Tell him it's locked.

[AL *tries it again, turning it in the other direction, and the door opens. They stand there face-to-face.*]

AL I fixed it.

WILLIE [*Glares at him.*] You didn't fix it. You just don't know how to open a door.

AL Did my daughter call?

WILLIE You know, I think you went crazy in the country.

AL You want to stand here and insult me, or do you want to rehearse the sketch?

WILLIE I would like to do *both,* but we ain't got the time . . . Let's forget the door. Stand in here and say "Knock, knock, knock."

AL [AL *comes in and closes the door. Sarcastically.*] I hope I can get *out* again.

WILLIE I hope so too. [*He places his hands behind his back and paces.*] All right. "Knock, knock, knock."

AL [*Pantomimes with his fist.*] Knock, knock, knock.

WILLIE [*Singsong.*] Enter!

AL [*Stops and looks at him.*] What do you mean "Enter"? [*He does it in the same singsong way.*] What happened to "Come in"?

WILLIE It's the same thing, isn't it? "Enter" or "come in." What's the difference, as long as you're in?

AL The difference is we've done this sketch twelve thousand times, and you've always said "Come in," and suddenly today it's "Enter." Why today, after all these years, do you suddenly change it to "Enter"?

WILLIE [*Shrugs.*] I'm trying to freshen up the act.

AL Who asked you to freshen up the act? They asked for the doctor sketch, didn't they? The doctor sketch starts with "Come in," not "Enter." You wanna freshen up something, put some flowers in here.

WILLIE It's a new generation today. This is not 1934, you know.

AL No kidding? I didn't get today's paper.

WILLIE What's bad about "Enter" instead of "Come in"?

AL Because it's different. You know why we've been doing it the same way for forty-three years? Because it's good.

WILLIE And you know why we don't do it any more? Because we've been doing it the same way for forty-three years.

AL So, if we're not doing it any more, why are we changing it?

WILLIE Can I make a comment, nothing personal? I think you've been sitting on a New Jersey porch too long.

AL What does that mean?

WILLIE That means I think you've been sitting on a New Jersey porch too long. From my window, I see everything that goes on in the world. I see old people, I see young people, nice people, bad people, I see holdups, drug addicts, ambulances, car crashes, jumpers from buildings—I see everything. You see a lawn mower and a milkman.

AL [*Looks at him for a long moment.*] And that's why you want to say "Enter" instead of "Come in"?

WILLIE Are you listening to me?

AL [*Looks around.*] Why, there's someone else in the room?

WILLIE You don't know the first thing that's going on today?

AL All right, what's going on today?

WILLIE Did you ever hear the expression "That's where it is"? Well, this is where it is, and that's where I am.

AL I see . . . Did you ever hear the expression "You don't know what the hell you're talking about"? It comes right in front of the *other* expression "You *never* knew what the hell you were talking about."

WILLIE *I* wasn't the one who retired. You know why you retired? Because you were tired. You were getting old-fashioned. I was still new-fashioned, and I'll *always* be.

AL I see. That's why you're in such demand. That's why you're such a "hot" property today. That's why you do movies you don't do, that's why you're in musicals you're not in, and that's why you make commercials you don't make—because you can't even remember them to *make* them.

WILLIE You know what I *do* remember? I remember what a pain in the ass you are to work with, that's what I remember.

AL That's right. And when you worked with this pain in the ass, you lived in a *five*-room suite. Now you live in a *one*-room suite . . . And you're still wearing the same goddamn pajamas you wore in the five-room suite.

WILLIE I don't have to take this crap from you.

AL You're lucky you're getting it. No one else wants to give it to you.

WILLIE I don't want to argue with you. After you say "Knock, knock, knock," I'm saying "Enter," and if you don't like it you don't have to come in.

AL You can't say nothing without my permission. I own fifty percent of this act.

WILLIE Then say *your* fifty percent. I'm saying "Enter" in my fifty percent.

AL If you say "Enter" after "Knock, knock, knock" . . . I'm coming in all right. But not alone. I'm bringing a lawyer with me.

WILLIE Where? From New Jersey? You're lucky if a *cow* comes with you.

AL Against *you* in court, I could *win* with a cow.

[*He enunciates each point by poking* WILLIE *in the chest.*]

WILLIE [*Slaps his hand away.*] The *finger?* You're starting with the finger again?

[*He runs into the kitchen and comes out brandishing a knife.*]

AL I'll tell you the truth now. I didn't retire. I *escaped.*

WILLIE [*Wielding the knife.*] The next time you give me the finger, say goodbye to the finger.

AL [*Hiding behind a chair.*] Listen, I got a terrific idea. Instead of working together again, let's never work together again. You're crazy.

WILLIE I'm crazy, heh? I'M CRAZY!

AL Keep saying it until you believe it.

WILLIE I may be crazy, but you're *senile!* You know what that is?

AL I'm not giving you any straight lines.

WILLIE Crazy is when you got a couple of parts that go wrong. Senile is when you went the hell out of business. That's you, mister. [*The phone rings.* AL *moves toward the phone.*] Get away from that phone. [*He drives the knife into the table.* AL *backs away in shock.* WILLIE *picks up the phone.*] Hello?

AL Is that my daughter?

WILLIE Hello . . . How are you?

AL Is that my daughter? Is that her?

WILLIE [*To* AL.] Will you shut up? Will you be quiet? Can't you see I'm talking? Don't you see me on the phone with a person? For God's sakes, behave like a human being for five seconds, will you? WILL YOU BEHAVE

FOR FIVE SECONDS LIKE A HUMAN BEING? [*Into the phone.*] Hello? . . . Yes . . . Just a minute. [*To* AL.] It's your daughter.

[*He sits, opens up* Variety.]

AL [*Takes the phone, turns his back to* WILLIE, *speaks low.*] Hello . . . Hello, sweetheart . . . No . . . No . . . I can't talk now . . . I said I can't talk now . . . Because he's a crazy bedbug, that's why.

WILLIE [*Jumps up.*] Mister is no good but bedbug is all right?? [*Yells into the phone.*] Your father is sick! Come and get your sick father!

AL [*Turns to him.*] Don't you see me on the phone with a person? Will you please be quiet, for God's sakes! [*Back into the phone.*] Listen, I want you to pick me up now . . . I don't want to discuss it. Pick me up now. In front of the hotel. Don't park too close, it's filthy here . . . I *know* what I promised. Don't argue with me. I'm putting on my coat. I'll wait in the street—I'll probably get mugged . . . All right, just a minute. [*He hands the phone to* WILLIE.] She'd like to talk to you for a second.

WILLIE Who is it?

AL [*Glares at him.*] Mrs. Eleanor Roosevelt . . . What do you mean, who is it? Didn't you just say it's my daughter?

WILLIE I know it's your daughter. I forgot her name.

AL Doris.

WILLIE What does she want?

AL [*Yells.*] Am I Doris? She'll tell you.

WILLIE [*Takes the phone.*] Hello? . . . Hello, dear, this is Willie Clark . . . Unpleasantness? There was no unpleasantness . . . There was stupidity maybe but no unpleasantness . . .

AL Tell her I'm getting into my coat. [*He is putting his coat on.*] Tell her I got one sleeve on.

WILLIE [*Into the phone.*] I was hoping it would work out too . . . I bent over backwards and forwards. He didn't even bend sideways . . .

AL I got the other sleeve on . . . Tell her I'm up to my hat and then I'm out the door.

WILLIE It's a question of one word, darling. "Enter!" . . . "Enter"—thats all it comes down to.

AL [*Puts his hat on.*] The hat is on. I'm bundled up, tell her.

WILLIE [*Into the phone.*] Yes . . . Yes, I will . . . I'll tell him myself. I promise . . . Goodbye, Dorothy. [*He hangs up.*] I told her we'll give it one more chance.

AL Not if you say "Enter." "Come in," I'll stay. "Enter," I go.

WILLIE Ask me "Knock, knock, knock."

AL Don't fool around with me. I got enough pains in my neck. Are you going to say "Come in"?

WILLIE Ask me "Knock, knock, knock"!

AL I know you, you bastard!

WILLIE ASK ME "KNOCK, KNOCK, KNOCK"!

AL KNOCK, KNOCK, KNOCK!

WILLIE [*Grinding it in.*] EN-TERRR!

AL BEDBUG! CRAZY BEDBUG!

[*He starts to run out.*]

WILLIE [*Big smile.*] ENNN-TERRRRR!

[*The curtain starts down.*]

AL [*Heading for the door.*] LUNATIC BASTARD!

WILLIE ENNN-TERRRR!

[*Curtain.*]

ACT II

Scene I

The scene is a doctor's office or, rather, an obvious stage "flat" representation of a doctor's office. It has an old desk and chair, a telephone, a cabinet filled with medicine bottles, a human skeleton hanging on a stand, a blackboard with chalk and pointer, an eye chart on the wall.

Overhead television lights surround the top of the set. Two boom microphones extend from either end of the set over the office.

At rise, the set is not fully lit. A thin, frail man in a hat and business suit sits in the chair next to the doctor's desk, patiently waiting.

VOICE OF TV DIRECTOR [*Over the loudspeaker.*] Eddie! *EDDIE!*

[EDDIE, *a young assistant TV director with headset and speaker, trailing wires and carrying a clipboard, steps out on the set. He speaks through his mike.*]

EDDIE Yeah, Phil?

VOICE OF TV DIRECTOR Any chance of doing this today?

EDDIE [*Shrugs.*] We're all set here, Phil. We're just waiting on the actors.

VOICE OF TV DIRECTOR What the hell is happening?

EDDIE I don't know. There's a problem with the makeup. Mr. Clark wants a Number Seven amber or something.

VOICE OF TV DIRECTOR Well, get it for him.

EDDIE Where? They stopped making it thirty-four years ago.

VOICE OF TV DIRECTOR Christ!

EDDIE And Mr. Lewis says the "ahh" sticks are too short.

VOICE OF TV DIRECTOR The what?

EDDIE The "ahh" sticks. Don't ask me. I'm still trying to figure out what a "look" stick is.

VOICE OF TV DIRECTOR What the hell are we making, *Nicholas and Alexandra*? Tell them it's just a dress rehearsal. We'll worry about the props later. Let's get moving, Eddie. Christ Almighty.

[WILLIE'S *nephew* BEN *appears onstage. He talks up into the overhead mike.*]

BEN Mr. Schaefer . . . Mr. Schaefer, I'm awfully sorry about the delay. Mr. Lewis and Mr. Clark have had a few technical problems backstage.

VOICE OF TV DIRECTOR Yeah, well, we've had it all week . . . I'm afraid we're running out of time here. I've got twelve goddamned other numbers to get through today.

BEN I'll get them right out. There's no problem.

VOICE OF TV DIRECTOR Tell them I want to run straight through, no stopping. They can clean up whatever they want afterwards.

BEN Absolutely.

VOICE OF TV DIRECTOR I haven't seen past "Knock, knock, knock"—"Come in" since Tuesday.

BEN [*Looks offstage.*] Right. There they are. [*Into the mike.*] We're ready, Mr. Schaefer. I'll tell them we're going to go straight through, no stopping. Thank you very much.

[BEN *exits very quickly.*]

VOICE OF TV DIRECTOR All right, Eddie, bring in the curtains.

EDDIE What?

VOICE OF TV DIRECTOR Bring in the curtains. Let's run it from the top with the voice over.

EDDIE [*Calls up.*] Let's have the curtains.

[*The curtains come in.*]

VOICE OF TV DIRECTOR Voice over!

ANNOUNCER The golden age of comedy reached its zenith during a fabulous and glorious era known as Vaudeville—Fanny Brice, W. C. Fields, Eddie Cantor, Ed Wynn, Will Rogers and a host of other greats fill its Hall of Fame. There are two other names that belong on this list, but they can never be listed separately. They are more than a team. They are two comic shining lights that beam as one. For, Lewis without Clark is like laughter without joy. We are privileged to present tonight, in their first public performance in over eleven years, for half a century known as "The Sunshine Boys"—Mr. Al Lewis and Mr. Willie Clark, in their beloved scene, "The Doctor Will See You Now."

[*The curtain rises, and the set is fully lit. The frail man in the hat is sitting on the chair as* WILLIE, *the doctor, dressed in a floor-length white doctor's jacket, a mirror attached to his head and a stethoscope around his neck is looking into the* PATIENT'S *mouth, holding his tongue down with an "ahh" stick.*]

WILLIE Open wider and say "Ahh."

PATIENT Ahh.

WILLIE Wider.

PATIENT *Ahhh!*

WILLIE [*Moves with his back to the audience.*] A little wider.

PATIENT Ahhh!

WILLIE [*Steps away.*] Your throat is all right, but you're gonna have some trouble with your stomach.

PATIENT How come?

WILLIE You just swallowed the stick.

[*The* PATIENT *feels his stomach.*]

PATIENT Is that bad?

WILLIE It's terrible. I only got two left.

PATIENT What about getting the stick out?

WILLIE What am I, a tree surgeon? . . . All right, for another ten dollars, I'll take it out.

PATIENT That's robbery.

WILLIE Then forget it. Keep the stick.

PATIENT No, no. I'll pay. Take the stick out.

WILLIE Come back tomorrow. On Thursdays I do woodwork. [*The* PATIENT *gets up and crosses to the door, then exits.* WILLIE *calls out.*] Oh, Nurse! Nursey!

[*The* NURSE *enters. She is a tall, voluptuous and overstacked blonde in a tight dress.*]

NURSE Did you want me, Doctor?

WILLIE [*He looks at her, knowingly.*] Why do

you think I hired you? . . . What's your name again?

NURSE Miss MacKintosh. You know, like the apples.

WILLIE [*Nods.*] The name I forgot, the apples I remembered . . . Look in my appointment book, see who's next.

NURSE It's a Mr. Kornheiser.

WILLIE Maybe you're wrong. Look in the book. It's better that way.

[*She crosses to the desk and bends way over as she looks through the appointment book. Her firm, round rear end faces us and* WILLIE. WILLIE *shakes his head from side to side in wonderful contemplation.*]

NURSE [*Still down.*] No, I was right.

WILLIE So was I.

NURSE [*Straightens up and turns around.*] It's Mr. Kornheiser.

WILLIE Are you sure? Spell it.

NURSE [*Turns, bends and gives us the same wonderful view again.*] K-o-r-n-h-e-i-s-e-r!

[*She turns and straightens up.*]

WILLIE [*Nods.*] What's the first name?

NURSE [*Turns, bends.*] Walter.

WILLIE Stay down for the middle name.

NURSE [*Remains down.*] Benjamin.

WILLIE Don't move and give me the whole thing.

NURSE [*Still rear end up, reading.*] Walter Benjamin Kornheiser.

[*She turns and straightens up.*]

WILLIE Oh, boy. From now on I only want to see patients with long names.

NURSE Is there anything else you want?

WILLIE Yeah. Call a carpenter and have him make my desk lower.

[*The* NURSE *walks sexily right up to* WILLIE *and stands with her chest practically on his, breathing and heaving.*]

NURSE [*Pouting.*] Yes, Doctor.

WILLIE [*Wipes his brow.*] Whew, it's hot in here. Did you turn the steam on?

NURSE [*Sexily.*] No, Doctor.

WILLIE In that case, take a five-dollar raise. Send in the next patient before *I'm* the next patient.

NURSE Yes, Doctor. [*She coughs.*] Excuse me, I think I have a chest cold.

WILLIE Looks more like an epidemic to me.

NURSE Yes, Doctor. [*She wriggles her way to the door.*] Is there anything else you can think of?

WILLIE I can *think* of it, but I'm not so sure I can *do* it.

NURSE Well, if I *can* help you, Doctor, that's what the nurse is for.

[*She exits and closes the door with an enticing look.*]

WILLIE I'm glad I didn't go to law school. [*Then we hear three knocks on the door. "Knock, knock, knock."*] Aha. That must be my next patient. [*Calls out.*] Come in! [*The door starts to open.*]—and *enter!*

[AL *steps in and glares angrily at* WILLIE. *He is in a business suit, wears a wig, and carries a cheap attaché case.*]

AL I'm looking for the doctor.

WILLIE Are you sick?

AL Are *you* the doctor?

WILLIE Yes.

AL I'm not *that* sick.

WILLIE What's your name, please?

AL Kornheiser. Walter Benjamin Kornheiser. You want me to spell it?

WILLIE Never mind. I got a better speller than you . . . [*Takes a tongue depressor from his pocket.*] Sit down and open your mouth, please.

AL There's nothing wrong with my mouth.

WILLIE Then just sit down.

AL There's nothing wrong with that either.

WILLIE Then what are you doing here?

AL I came to examine you.

WILLIE I think you got everything backwards.

AL It's possible. I dressed in a hurry this morning.

WILLIE You mean you came here for me to examine *you.*

AL No, I came here for me to examine *you.* I'm a tax collector.

WILLIE [*Nods.*] That's nice. I'm a stamp collector. What do you do for a living.

AL I find out how much money people make.

WILLIE Oh, a busybody. Make an appointment with the nurse.

AL I did. I'm seeing her Friday night . . .

WILLIE [*Jumps up and down angrily.*] Don't fool around with my nurse. DON'T FOOL AROUND WITH MY NURSE! She's a nice girl. She's a *Virginian!*

AL A what?

WILLIE A *Virginian.* That's where she's from.

AL Well, she ain't going *back,* I can tell you that. [*He sits, opens the attaché case.*] I got some questions to ask you.

WILLIE I'm too busy to answer questions. I'm a doctor. If you wanna see me, you gotta be a patient.

AL But I'm not sick.

WILLIE Don't worry. We'll find something.

AL All right, you examine me and I'll examine you . . . [*Takes out a tax form as* WILLIE *wields the tongue depressor.*] The first question is, How much money did you make last year?

WILLIE Last year I made—

[*He moves his lips mouthing a sum, but it's not audible.*]

AL I didn't hear that.

WILLIE Oh. Hard of hearing. I knew we'd find something. Did you ever have any childhood diseases?

AL Not lately.

WILLIE Father living or deceased?

AL Both.

WILLIE What do you mean, both?

AL First he was living, now he's deceased.

WILLIE What did your father die from?

AL My mother . . . Now it's my turn. Are you married?

WILLIE I'm looking.

AL Looking to get married?

WILLIE No, looking to get out.

[*He looks in* AL*'s ear with a flashlight.*]

AL What are you doing?

WILLIE I'm examining your lower intestines.

AL So why do you look in the ear?

WILLIE If I got a choice of two places to look, I'll take this one.

AL [*Consulting his form.*] Never mind. Do you own a car?

WILLIE Certainly I own a car. Why?

AL If you use it for medical purposes, you can deduct it from your taxes. What kind of car do you own?

WILLIE An ambulance.

AL Do you own a house?

WILLIE Can I deduct it?

AL Only if you use it for medical purposes. Where do you live?

WILLIE In Mount Sinai Hospital . . . Open your shirt, I want to listen to your heartbeat.

AL [*Unbuttons two buttons on his shirt.*] Will this take long?

WILLIE Not if I hear something. [*He puts his ear to* AL*'s chest and listens.*] Uh-huh. I hear something . . . You're all right.

AL Aren't you going to listen with the stethoscope?

WILLIE Oh, sure. I didn't know you wanted a thorough examination. [*Puts the stethoscope to his ears and listens to* AL*'s chest.*] Oh, boy. Ohhh, boyyyy! You know what you got?

AL What?

WILLIE A filthy undershirt.

AL Never mind that. Am I in good health?

WILLIE Not unless you change your undershirt.

AL What is this, a doctor's office or a laundry? I bet you never went to medical school.

WILLIE [*Jumping up and down again.*] What are you talkin'? . . . WHAT ARE YOU TALKIN'? . . . I went to Columbia Medical School.

AL Did you pass?

WILLIE Certainly.

AL Well, you should have gone *in!*

WILLIE Never mind . . . I'm gonna examine your eyes now.

AL They're perfect. I got twenty-twenty eyes.

WILLIE That's too much. All you need is one and one. Look at that chart on the wall. Now put your left hand over your left eye and your right hand over your right eye. [AL *does so.*] Now tell me what you see.

AL I don't see nothing.

WILLIE Don't panic, I can cure you . . . Take your hands away. [AL *does.*] Can you see now?

AL Certainly I can see now.

WILLIE You know, I fixed over two thousand people like that.

AL It's a miracle.

WILLIE Thank you.

AL A miracle you're not in jail . . . What do you charge for a visit?

WILLIE A dollar.

AL A dollar? That's very cheap for an examination.

WILLIE It's not an examination. It's just a visit. "Hello and Goodbye" . . . "Hello and How Are You?" is ten dollars.

AL If you ask me, you're a quack.

WILLIE If I was a duck I would ask you . . .

Now roll up your sleeve, I wanna take some blood.

AL I can't do it.

WILLIE Why not?

AL If I see blood, I get sick.

WILLIE Do what I do. Don't look.

AL I'm sorry. I'm not giving blood. I'm anemic.

WILLIE What's anemic?

AL You're a doctor and you don't know what anemic means?

WILLIE That's because I'm a specialist.

AL What do you specialize in?

WILLIE Everything but anemic.

AL Listen, can I continue my examination?

WILLIE You continue yours, and I'll continue mine. All right, cross your legs. [*He hits* AL'*s knee with a small hammer.*] Does it hurt if I hit you with the hammer?

AL Yes.

WILLIE Good. From now on, try not to get hit with a hammer. [*He throws the hammer over his shoulder. He takes a specimen bottle from the cabinet and returns.*] You see this bottle?

AL Yes.

WILLIE You know what you're supposed to do with this bottle?

AL I think so.

WILLIE You *think* so or you *know* so? If you're not sure, let me know. The girl doesn't come in to clean today.

AL What do you want me to do?

WILLIE I want you to go in this bottle.

AL I haven't got time. I have to go over your books.

WILLIE *The hell you will!*

AL If I don't go over your books, the *government* will come in here and go over your books.

WILLIE Don't they have a place in Washington?

AL Certainly, but they have to go where the books are.

WILLIE The whole government?

AL No, just the Treasury Department.

WILLIE That's a relief.

AL I'm glad you're relieved.

WILLIE I wish *you* were before you came in here.

[*The door opens and the big-chested* NURSE *steps in.*]

NURSE Oh, Doctor. Doctor Klockenmeyer.

WILLIE Yes.

NURSE Mrs. Kolodny is on the phone. She wants you to rush right over and deliver her baby.

WILLIE I'm busy now. Tell her I'll mail it to her in the morning.

NURSE Yes, Doctor.

[*She exits and closes the door.*]

AL Where did you find a couple of nurses like that?

WILLIE She was standing on Forty-third and Forty-fourth Street . . . Let me see your tongue, please.

AL I don't want to.

[WILLIE *squeezes* AL'*s throat, and his tongue comes out.*]

WILLIE Open the mouth . . . How long have you had that white coat on your tongue?

AL Since January. In the spring I put on a gray sports jacket.

WILLIE Now hold your tongue with your fingers and say "shish kabob."

AL [*Tolds his tongue with his fingers.*] Thickabob.

WILLIE Again.

AL Thickabob.

WILLIE I have bad news for you.

AL What is it?

WILLIE If you do that in a restaurant, you'll never get shish kabob.

AL [*Stands with his face close to* WILLIE'*s.*] Never mind that. What about your *t*axes?

[*On the "T," he spits a little.*]

WIILIE [*Wipes his face.*] The what?

AL The *t*axes. It's *t*ime *t*o pay your *t*axes to the *T*reasury.

[*All the "T's" are quite fluid.* WILLIE *wipes his face and glares angrily at* AL.]

WILLIE I'm warning you, don't start in with me.

AL What are you talking about?

WILLIE You know what I'm talking about. [*Illustrates.*] "It's *t*ime *t*o pay the *t*axes." You're speaking with spitting again.

AL I said the right line, didn't I? If it comes out juicy, I can't help that.

WILLIE [*Quite angry.*] It doesn't come out juicy unless you squeeze the "T's." I'm warning you, don't squeeze them on me.

[VOICE OF TV DIRECTOR *is heard over the loudspeaker.*]

VOICE OF TV DIRECTOR Okay, let's hold it a second. Mr. Clark, I'm having trouble with the dialogue. I don't find those last few lines in the script.

WILLIE [*Shouts up.*] It's not in the script, it's in *his mouth.*

AL [*Talking up into the mike.*] I said the right line. Look in the script, you'll find it there.

WILLIE [*Shouting.*] You'll find the words, you won't find the spit. The spit's his own idea. He's doing it on *purpose!*

AL I don't spit on purpose. I spit on accident. I've *always* spitted on accident. It's not possible to say that line without spitting a little.

WILLIE [*Addressing all his remarks to the unseen director.*] *I* can say it. [*He says the line with great delicacy, especially on the "T's".*] "It's time to pay your taxes to the Treasury." [*Back to his normal inflection.*] There wasn't a spit in my entire mouth. Why doesn't he say it like *that?*

AL What am I, an Englishman? I'm talking the same as I've talked for forty-three years.

VOICE OF TV DIRECTOR Gentlemen, can we argue this point after the dress rehearsal and go on with the sketch?

WILLIE I'm not going to stand here and get a shower in the face. If you want me to go on, either take out the line or get me an umbrella.

VOICE OF TV DIRECTOR Can we *please* go on? With all due respect, gentlemen, we have twelve other scenes to rehearse and we cannot spend all day on personal squabbles . . .

WILLIE I'll go on, but I'm moving to a safer spot.

VOICE OF TV DIRECTOR Don't worry about the moves, we'll pick you up on camera. Now, let's skip over this spot and pick it up on "I hope you don't have what Mr. Melnick had." [WILLIE *moves away from* AL.] All right, Mr. Clark, whenever you're ready.

WILLIE [*Waits a minute, then goes back into the doctor character.*] I hope you don't have what Mr. Melnick had.

AL What did Mr. Melnick have?

WILLIE [*Points to standing skeleton.*] Ask him yourself, he's standing right there.

AL That's Mr. Melnick?

WILLIE It could be *Mrs.* Melnick. Without high heels, I can't tell.

AL If he's dead, why do you leave him standing in the office?

WILLIE He's still got one more appointment with me.

AL [*Cross to him.*] You know what you are? You're a charlatan! [*As* AL *says that line, he punctuates each word by poking* WILLIE *in the chest with his finger. It does not go unnoticed by* WILLIE.] Do you know what a charlatan is?

[*More pokes.*]

WILLIE It's a city in North Carolina. And if you're gonna poke me again like that, you're gonna end up in Poughkeepsie.

VOICE OF TV DIRECTOR [*Over the loudspeaker.*] Hold it, hold it. Where does it say, "You're going to end up in Poughkeepsie"?

WILLIE [*Furious.*] Where does it say he can poke me in the chest? He's doing it on purpose. He *always* did it on purpose, just to get my goat.

AL [*Looking up to the mike.*] I didn't poke him, I tapped him. A light little tap, it wouldn't hurt a baby.

WILLIE Maybe a baby elephant. I *knew* I was going to get poked. First comes the spitting, then comes the poking. I know his routine already.

AL [*To the mike.*] Excuse me. I'm sorry we're holding up the rehearsal, but we have a serious problem on our hands. The man I'm working with is a lunatic.

WILLIE [*Almost in a rage.*] *I'm* a lunatic, heh? He breaks my chest and spits in my face and calls *me* a lunatic! I'm gonna tell you something now I never told you in my entire life. I hate your guts.

AL You told it to me on Monday.

WILLIE Then I'm telling it to you again.

VOICE OF TV DIRECTOR Listen, gentlemen, I really don't see any point in going on with this rehearsal.

AL I don't see any point in going on with this *show.* This man is persecuting me. For eleven years he's been waiting to get back at me, only I'm not gonna give him the chance.

[*The assistant director,* EDDIE, *walks out in an attempt to make peace.*]

WILLIE [*Half-hysterical.*] I knew it! I knew it! He planned it! He's been setting me up for eleven years just to walk out on me again.

EDDIE [*Trying to be gentle.*] All right, Mr. Clark, let's settle down. Why don't we all go into the dressing room and talk this out?

AL I didn't want to do it in the first place.

WILLIE [*Apoplectic.*] *Liar! Liar!* His daughter *begged* me on the phone. She *begged* me!

[BEN *rushes out to restrain* WILLIE.]

BEN Uncle Willie, please, that's enough. Come back to the dressing room.

EDDIE Gentlemen, we need the stage. Can we please do this over on the side?

AL [*To the assistant director.*] The man is hysterical, you can see for yourself. He's been doing this to me all week long.

[*He starts taking off the wig and suit jacket.*]

WILLIE Begged me. She begged me. His own daughter begged me.

BEN Uncle Willie, stop it, please.

AL [*To the others.*] I'm sorry we caused everyone so much trouble. I should have stayed in New Jersey in the first place. [*On his way out. To the assistant director.*] He pulled a knife on me last week. In his own apartment he pulled a knife on me. A crazy man.

[*He is gone.*]

WILLIE I don't need you. I *never* needed you. You were nothing when I found you, and that's what you are today.

BEN Come on, Willie. [*Out front.*] I'm sorry about this, Mr. Schaefer.

WILLIE He thinks I can't get work without him. Maybe *his* career is over, but not mine. Maybe he's finished, but not me. You hear? not me! NOT M—

[*He clutches his chest.*]

BEN [*Turns and sees him stagger.*] Grab him, quick! [EDDIE *rushes to* WILLIE, *but it's too late*—WILLIE *falls to the floor.* BEN *rushes to his side.*] All right, take it easy, Uncle Willie, just lie there. [*To* EDDIE.] Get a doctor, please hurry.

[*A bit actor and the* NURSE *rush onstage behind* BEN.]

WILLIE [*Breathing hard.*] I don't need a doctor. Don't get a doctor, I don't trust them.

BEN Don't talk, Willie, you're all right. [*To the* NURSE.] Somebody get a blanket, please.

WILLIE [*Breathing fast.*] Don't tell him. Don't tell him I fell down. I don't want to give him the satisfaction.

BEN Of course, I won't tell him, Willie. There's nothing to tell. You're going to be all right.

WILLIE Frito-Lays . . . That's the name of the potato chip . . . You see? I remembered . . . I remembered the name! Frito-Lays.

[BEN *is holding* WILLIE'*s hand as the lights dim. The curtain falls on the scene. In the dark, we hear the voice of the* ANNOUNCER.]

ANNOUNCER The golden age of comedy reached its zenith during a fabulous and glorious era known as Vaudeville—Fanny Brice, W. C. Fields, Eddie Cantor, Ed Wynn, Will Rogers and a host of other greats fill its Hall of Fame. There are two other names that belong on this list, but they can never be listed separately. They are more than a team. They are two comic shining lights that beam as one. For, Lewis without Clark is like laughter without joy. When these two greats retired, a comic style disappeared from the American scene that will never see its likes again . . . Here, then, in a sketch taped nearly eleven years ago on *The Ed Sullivan Show,* are Lewis and Clark in their classic scene, "The Doctor Will See You Now."

[*We hear* WILLIE'*s voice and that of the first* PATIENT.]

WILLIE Open wider and say "Ahh."

PATIENT Ahh.

WILLIE Wider.

PATIENT Ahh.

WILLIE A little wider.

PATIENT Ahhh!

WILLIE Your throat is all right, but you're gonna have some trouble with your stomach.

PATIENT How come?

WILLIE You just swallowed the stick.

Scene II

The curtain rises. The scene is WILLIE'*s hotel room, two weeks later. It is late afternoon,* WILLIE *is in his favorite pajamas in bed, propped up on the pillows, his head hanging down, asleep.*

The television is droning away—another daytime serial. A black REGISTERED NURSE *in uniform, a sweater draped over her shoulders, and her glasses on a chain around her neck, is sitting in a chair watching the television. She is eating from a big box of chocolates. Two very large vases of flowers are on the bureau.* WILLIE'*s head bobs a few times; then he open his eyes.*

WILLIE What time is it?

NURSE [*Turns off the TV and glances at her watch.*] Ten to one.

WILLIE Ten to one? . . . Who are you?

NURSE Don't give me that. You now who I am.

WILLIE You're the same nurse from yesterday?

NURSE I'm the same nurse from every day for two weeks now. Don't play your games with me.

WILLIE I can't even chew a piece of bread, who's gonna play games? . . . Why'd you turn off the television?

NURSE It's either watching that or watching you sleep—either one ain't too interesting.

WILLIE I'm sorry. I'll try to sleep more entertaining . . . What's today, Tuesday?

NURSE Wednesday.

[*She bites into a piece of chocolate.*]

WILLIE How could this be Wednesday? I went to sleep on Monday.

NURSE Haven't we already seen Mike Douglas twice this week?

WILLIE Once.

NURSE Twice.

WILLIE [*Reluctantly.*] All right, twice . . . I don't even remember. I was all right yesterday?

NURSE We are doing very well.

WILLIE We are? When did *you* get sick?

NURSE [*Deadly serious, no smile.*] That's funny. That is really funny, Mr. Clark. Soon as I get home tonight I'm gonna bust out laughing.

WILLIE You keep eating my candy like that, you're gonna bust out a lot sooner.

NURSE Well, *you* can't eat it and there's no sense throwing it out. I'm just storing up energy for the winter.

WILLIE Maybe you'll find time in between the nougat and the peppermint to take my pulse.

NURSE I took it. It's a little better today.

WILLIE When did you take my pulse?

NURSE When you were sleeping.

WILLIE *Everybody's* pulse is good when they're sleeping. You take a pulse when a person is up. Thirty dollars a day, she takes a sleeping pulse. I'll tell you the truth, I don't think you know what you're doing . . . and I'm not a prejudiced person.

NURSE Well, *I* am: I don't like sick people who tell registered nurses how to do their job. You want your tea now?

WILLIE I don't want to interrupt your candy.

NURSE And don't get fresh with me. You can get fresh with your nephew, but you can't get fresh with me. Maybe *he* has to take it, but I'm not a blood relative.

WILLIE That's for sure.

NURSE That's even funnier than the other one. My *whole* evening's gonna be taken up tonight with nothing but laughing.

WILLIE I don't even eat candy. Finish the whole box. When you're through, I hope you eat the flowers too.

NURSE You know why I don't get angry at anything you say to me?

WILLIE I give up. Why?

NURSE Because I have a good sense of humor. I am *known* for my good sense of humor. That's why I can take anything you say to me.

WILLIE If you nurse as good as your sense of humor, I won't make it to Thursday . . . Who called?

NURSE No one.

WILLIE I thought I heard the phone.

NURSE [*Gets up.*] No one called. [*She crosses and puffs up his pillow.*] Did you have a nice nap?

WILLIE It was a nap, nothing special . . . Don't puff up the pillows, please. [*He swats her hands away.*] It takes me a day and a night to get them the way I like them, and then you puff them up.

NURSE Oh, woke up a little grouchy, didn't we?

WILLIE Stop making yourself a partner all the time. I woke up grouchy. Don't make the bed, please. I'm still sleeping in it. Don't make a bed with a person in it.

NURSE Can't stand to have people do things for you, can you? If you just want someone to sit here and watch you, you're better off getting a dog, Mr. Clark. I'll suggest that to your nephew.

WILLIE Am I complaining? I'm only asking for two things. Don't take my pulse when I'm sleeping and don't make my bed when I'm in it. Do it the other way around and then we're in business.

NURSE It doesn't bother me to do nothing as long as I'm getting paid for it.

[*She sits.*]

WILLIE [*A pause.*] I'm hungry.

NURSE You want your junket?

WILLIE Forget it. I'm not hungry. [*She reads.*] Tell me something, how old is a woman like you?

NURSE That is none of your business.

WILLIE I'm not asking for business.

NURSE I am fifty-four years young.

WILLIE Is that so? . . . You're married?

NURSE My husband passed away four years ago.

WILLIE Oh . . . You were the nurse?

NURSE No, I was not the nurse . . . You could use some sleep and I could use some quiet.

[*She gets up.*]

WILLIE You know something? For a fifty-four-year-old registered widow, you're an attractive woman.

[*He tries to pat her. She swings at him.*]

NURSE And don't try that with me!

WILLIE Who's trying anything?

NURSE You are. You're getting fresh in a way I don't like.

WILLIE What are you worried about? I can't even put on my slippers by myself.

NURSE I'm not worried about your slippers. And don't play on my sympathy. I don't have any, and I ain't expecting any coming in, in the near future.

WILLIE Listen, how about a nice alcohol rub?

NURSE I just gave you one.

WILLIE No, I'll give *you* one.

NURSE I know you just say things like that to agitate me. You like to agitate people, don't you? Well, I am not an agitatable person.

WILLIE You're right. I think I'd be better off with the dog.

NURSE How did your poor wife stand a man like you?

WILLIE Who told you about my poor wife?

NURSE Your poor nephew . . . Did you ever think of getting married again?

[*She takes his pulse.*]

WILLIE What is this, a proposal?

NURSE [*Laughs.*] Not from me . . . I am *not* thinking of getting married again . . . Besides, you're just not my type.

WILLIE Why? It's a question of religion?

NURSE It's a question of age. You'd wear me out in no time.

WILLIE You think I can't support you? I've got Medicare.

NURSE You never stop, do you?

WILLIE When I stop, I won't be here.

NURSE Well, that's where you're gonna be unless you learn to slow up a little.

WILLIE Slow up? I moved two inches in three weeks, she tells me slow up.

NURSE I mean, if you're considering getting well again, you have to stop worrying about telephone calls and messages, and especially about when you're going back to work.

WILLIE I'm an actor—I have to act. It's my profession.

NURSE Your profession right now is being a sick person. And if you're gonna act anywhere, it's gonna be from a sick bed.

WILLIE Maybe I can get a job on Marcus Welby.

NURSE You can turn everything I say into a vaudeville routine if you want, but I'm gonna give you a piece of advice, Mr. Clark . . .

WILLIE What?

NURSE The world is full of sick people. And there just ain't enough doctors or nurses to go around to take care of all these sick people. And all the doctors and all the nurses can do just so much, Mr. Clark. But God, in His Infinite Wisdom, has said He will help those who help themselves.

WILLIE [*Looks at her.*] So? What's the advice?

NURSE *Stop bugging me!*

WILLIE All right, I'll stop bugging you . . . I don't even know what the hell it means.

NURSE That's better. Now you're my type again.

[*The doorbell rings. The* NURSE *crosses to the door.*]

WILLIE Here comes today's candy.

[*She opens the door.* BEN *enters with packages.*]

BEN Hello. How is he?

NURSE Fine. I think we're gonna get married.

BEN Hey, Uncle Willie, you look terrific.

WILLIE You got my *Variety*?

BEN [*Goes over to him, and hands him* Variety.] I also got about two hundred get-well telegrams from just about every star in show business—Lucille Ball, Milton Berle, Bob Hope, the mayor. It'll take you nine months just to answer them.

WILLIE What about a commercial? Did you hear from Alka-Seltzer?

BEN We have plenty of time to talk about that . . . Miss O'Neill, did you have your lunch yet?

NURSE Not yet.

WILLIE She just finished two pounds of appetizers.

BEN Why don't you go out, take an hour or so? I'll be here for a while.

NURSE Thank you. I could use some fresh air. [*Gets her coat. To* WILLIE.] Now, when I'm gone, I don't want you getting all agitated again, you hear?

WILLIE I hear, I hear. Stop bugging me.

NURSE And don't get up to go to the bathroom. Use the you-know-what.

WILLIE [*Without looking up from his* Variety.] And if not, I'll do it you-know-where.

[*The* NURSE *exits.*]

BEN [*Pulling up a chair next to the bed.*] Never mind, she's a very good nurse.

WILLIE [*Looks in the paper.*] Oh, boy, Bernie Eisenstein died.

BEN Who?

WILLIE Bernie Eisenstein. Remember the dance team "Ramona and Rodriguez"? Bernie Eisenstein was Rodriguez. . . . He would have been seventy-eight in August.

BEN [*Sighs.*] Uncle Willie, could you put down *Variety* for a second?

WILLIE [*Still reading.*] Did you bring a cigar?

BEN Uncle Willie, you realize you've had a heart attack, don't you? . . . You've been getting away with it for years—the cigars, the corned beef sandwiches, the tension, the temper tantrums. You can't do it any more, Willie. Your heart's just not going to take it.

WILLIE This is the good news you rushed up with? For this we could have skipped a Wednesday.

BEN [*A pause.*] I talked to the doctor this morning . . . and I'm going to have to be very frank and honest with you, Willie . . . You've got to retire. I mean give it up. Show business is out.

WILLIE Until when?

BEN Until *ever!* Your blood pressure is abnormally high, your heart is weak—if you tried to work again you would kill yourself.

WILLIE All right, let me think it over.

BEN *Think what over?* There's nothing to think over. You can't work any more, there's no decision to be made. Can't you understand that?

WILLIE You decide for Ben Silverman, I'll decide for Willie Clark.

BEN No, *I'll* decide for Willie Clark. I am your closest and *only* living relative, and I am responsible for your welfare . . . You can't live here any more, Willie. Not alone . . . And I can't afford to keep this nurse on permanently. Right now she's making more than I am. Anyway she already gave me her notice. She's leaving Monday. She's going to Buffalo to work for a very wealthy family.

WILLIE Maybe she'll take me. I always did well in Buffalo.

BEN Come on, Willie, face the facts. We have to do something, and we have to do it quickly.

WILLIE I can't think about it today. I'm tired, I'm going to take a nap.

[*He closes his eyes and drops his head to the side on the pillow.*]

BEN You want to hear my suggestion?

WILLIE I'm napping. Don't you see my eyes closed?

BEN I'd like you to move in with me and Helen and the kids. We have the small spare room in the back, I think you would be very comfortable . . . Uncle Willie, did you hear what I said?

WILLIE What's the second suggestion?

BEN What's the matter with the first?

WILLIE It's not as good as the second.

BEN I haven't made any yet.

WILLIE It's still better than the first. Forget it.

BEN Why?

WILLIE I don't like your kids. They're noisy. The little one hit me in the head with a baseball bat.

BEN And I've also seen you talk to them for hours on end about vaudeville and had the time of your life. Right?

WILLIE If I stopped talking, they would hit me with the bat. No offense, but I'm not living with your children. If you get rid of them, then we'll talk . . .

BEN I know the reason you won't come. Because Al Lewis lives with his family, and you're just trying to prove some stupid point about being independent.

WILLIE What's the second suggestion?

BEN [*A long sigh.*] All right . . . Now don't jump when I say this, because it's not as bad as it sounds.

WILLIE Say it.

BEN There's the Actors' Home in New Brunswick—

WILLIE It's as bad as it sounds.

BEN You're wrong. I drove out there last Sunday and they showed me around the whole place. I couldn't believe how beautiful it was.

WILLIE You went out there? You didn't have the decency to wait until I turned down living with you first?

BEN I just went out to investigate, that's all. No commitments.

WILLIE The Old Actors' Home: the first booking you got me in ten years.

BEN It's on a lake, it's got twenty-five acres of beautiful grounds, it's an old converted mansion with a big porch . . .

WILLIE I knew it. You got me on a porch in New Jersey. He put you up to this, didn't he?

BEN You don't have to sit on the porch. There's a million activities there. They put on shows every Friday and Saturday night. I mean, it's all old actors—what could be better for you?

WILLIE Why New Jersey? I hate New Jersey . . . I'm sorry they ever finished the George Washington Bridge.

BEN I couldn't get over how many old actors were there that I knew and remembered. I thought they were all dead.

WILLIE Some recommendation. A house in the swamps with forgotten people.

BEN They're not forgotten. They're well taken care of . . . Uncle Willie, I promise you, if you spend one day there that you're not happy, you can come back and move in with me.

WILLIE That's my choice—New Jersey or the baseball bat.

BEN All right, I feel a lot better about everything.

WILLIE And what about you?

BEN What do you mean what about me?

WILLIE [*A pause; looks away.*] I won't see you no more?

BEN Certainly you'll see me. As often as I can . . . Did you think I wouldn't come to visit you, Uncle Willie?

WILLIE Well, you know . . . People don't go out to New Jersey unless they have to.

BEN Uncle Willie, I'll be there every week. *With* the *Variety*. I'll even bring Helen and the kids.

WILLIE *Don't bring the kids!* Why do you think I'm going to the home for?

BEN You know, this is the first moment since I've known you, that you've treated me like a nephew and not an agent. It's like a whole new relationship.

WILLIE I hope this one works out better than the other one.

BEN I've been waiting for this for fifteen years. You just wouldn't ever let me get close, Uncle Willie.

WILLIE If you kiss me, I call off the whole thing.

BEN No kiss, I promise . . . Now there's just one other thing I'd like you to do for me.

WILLIE With my luck it's a benefit.

BEN In a way it is a benefit. But not for any organization. It's for another human being.

WILLIE What are you talking about?

BEN Al Lewis wants to come and see you.

WILLIE If you wanted to kill me, why didn't you bring the cigars?

BEN He's been heartsick ever since this happened.

WILLIE What do you think I've been? What is this, the mumps?

BEN You know what I mean . . . He calls me twice a day to see how you are. He's worried to death.

WILLIE Tonight tell him I'm worse.

BEN He's not well himself, Willie. He's got diabetes, hardening of the arteries, his eyes are getting very bad . . .

WILLIE He sees good enough to spit in my face.

BEN He's lost seven pounds since you were in the hospital. Who do you think's been sending all the candy and flowers every day? He keeps signing other people's names because he knows otherwise you'd throw them out.

WILLIE They're *his* flowers? Throw 'em out!

BEN Uncle Willie, I've never asked you to do a personal favor for me as long as I've known you. But this is important—for me, and for you, for Al Lewis. He won't even stay. He just wants to come up and say hello . . .

WILLIE Hello, heh?

BEN That's all.

WILLIE And if he pokes me in the chest with the finger, I'm a dead man. That's murder, you know.

BEN Come on, Willie. Give us all a break.

WILLIE Well, if he wants to come up, I won't stop him. But I can't promise a "hello." I may be taking a nap.

BEN [*Starts toward the phone.*] I knew I could

count on you, Willie. He's going to be very happy.

[*He picks up the phone.*]

WILLIE You don't have to call him from here. Why should I pay sixty cents for him to come say hello?

BEN [*He dials "O".*] It's not going to cost you sixty cents. [*To the operator.*] Hello. Would you tell the boy at the desk to send Mr. Lewis up to Mr. Clark's room, please? Thank you.

[*He hangs up.*]

WILLIE [*As near to shouting as he can get.*] You mean he's here now in the hotel?

BEN He's been with me all morning. I knew it would be all right.

WILLIE First you commit me to the Old Man's Home, bring that bastard here and *then* you ask me?

BEN [*All smiles.*] I'm sorry. I apologize. Never speak to me again . . . But just promise you'll be decent to Al Lewis.

WILLIE I'll be wonderful to him. In my will, I'll leave him *you!*

[*He starts to get out of bed.*]

BEN What are you doing? You're not supposed to be out of bed.

WILLIE You think I'm going to give him the satisfaction of seeing me laying in bed like a sick person? I'm gonna sit in my chair and I'm gonna look healthier than he does.

[*He tries weakly to get on his slippers.*]

BEN The doctor said you're not to get out of bed for *anything.*

WILLIE Lewis coming to apologize to Clark is not anything. To me, this is worth another heart attack. Get my coat from the closet.

BEN [*Starting for the closet.*] All right, but just walk slowly, will you, please?

[*He opens the closet.*]

WILLIE And then I want you to move my chair all the way back. I want that son-of-a-bitch to have a long walk.

BEN [*Takes out a bathrobe from the closet.*] Here, put this on.

WILLIE Not the bathrobe, the jacket. The blue sports jacket. This is gonna be a *formal* apology.

BEN [*Puts back the bathrobe and takes out the blue sports jacket.*] He's not coming to apologize. He's just coming to say hello.

WILLIE If he doesn't apologize, I'll drop dead in the chair for spite. And you can tell him that.

[BEN *helps him into the blue sports jacket over the pajamas.*]

BEN Now I'm sorry I started in with this.

WILLIE That's funny. Because now I'm starting to feel good. [*Buttons the jacket.*] Push the chair back. All the way.

[BEN *picks up the chair and carries it to the far side of the room.*]

BEN I thought I was bringing you two together.

WILLIE [*He shuffles over to the chair.* BEN *helps him to sit.*] Put a pillow underneath. Make it two pillows. When I sit, I wanna look down on him.

[BEN *puts a pillow under* WILLIE.]

BEN This is the last time. I'm never going to butt into your lives again.

WILLIE The only thing that could have made today better is if it was raining. I would love to see him apologize dripping wet. [*And then come three knocks on the door: "Knock, knock, knock."*] Aha! This is it! . . . *This* was worth getting sick for! Come on, knock again. [*Points his finger in the air, his crowning moment.* AL *knocks again.*] *En-terrr!*

[BEN *crosses to the door and opens it.* AL LEWIS *timidly steps in, with his hat in his hand.* WILLIE *immediately drops his head to his side, closes his eye and snores, feigning a nap.*]

AL [*Whispers.*] Oh, he's sleeping. I could come back later.

BEN [*Also whispers.*] No, that's all right. He must be dozing. Come on in. [AL *steps in and* BEN *closes the door.*] Can I take your hat?

AL No, I'd like to hold on to something, if you don't mind.

[BEN *crosses over to* WILLIE, *who is still dozing. He bends over and speaks softly in* WILLIE'S *ear.*]

BEN Uncle Willie. There's someone here to see you.

WILLIE [*Opens his eyes, stirs.*] Heh? What?

BEN Look who's here to see you, Uncle Willie.

WILLIE [*Squints.*] I don't have my glasses. Who's that?

AL It's me, Willie, Al . . . Al Lewis.

WILLIE [*Squints harder.*] Al Lewis? You're so far away . . . Walk all the way over here. [AL *sheepishly makes the trek across the room with hat in hand. He squints again.*] Oh, *that* Al Lewis.

AL I don't want to disturb you, Willie. I know you're resting.

WILLIE That's all right. I was just reading my telegrams from Lucille Ball and Bob Hope.

AL Oh, that's nice . . . [*Turns, looks at the vase.*] Oh, look at the beautiful flowers.

WILLIE I'm throwing them out. I don't like the smell. People send them to me every day with boxes of cheap candy. They mean well.

AL [*Nods.*] They certainly do . . . Well, I just came up to see how you're doing. I don't want to take up your time. I just wanted to say hello . . . So "hello"—and goodbye.

[*He starts to put on his hat to go.*]

WILLIE Wait a minute. You got a few minutes before my next nap. Sit down and talk for a while.

AL You're sure it's okay?

WILLIE I'm sure you got a lot more to say than just "hello" . . . Would you like some tea?

AL I would love some.

WILLIE Go in the kitchen and make it.

BEN I've got a better idea. I'll go down and have the kitchen send up a tray. If I call room service it'll take forever.

[*He starts for the door.*]

WILLIE [*To* BEN.] You're going? You don't want to hear what Al has to say?

BEN I don't think it's necessary. I'll be back in ten minutes. [*At the door.*] It's good to see you, Mr. Lewis . . . It's good to see the *both* of you.

[*He nods, then exits, closing the door. There is an awkward silence between the two men for a moment.*]

AL [*Finally.*] He's a nice boy.

WILLIE He's the best . . . Not too bright, but a good boy.

AL [*Nods.*] You've got everything you need here?

WILLIE What could I need here?

AL Some books? Some magazines?

WILLIE No, I got plenty to do. I got all my fan mail to answer.

AL You get fan mail?

WILLIE Don't you?

AL I don't even get jury duty.

WILLIE Sure, plenty of people still remember . . . [*He coughs.*] Excuse me.

AL You're sure it's all right for you to talk like this?

WILLIE I'm not talking. I'm just answering. *You're* talking. [*There is a long pause.*] Why? Is there something special you wanted to talk about?

AL Like what?

WILLIE What do I know like what? How should I know what's on your mind? Do I know why you can't sleep at night?

AL Who said I don't sleep at night! I sleep beautifully.

WILLIE Funny, to me you look tired. A little troubled. Like a person who had something on his conscience, what do I know?

AL I have nothing on my conscience.

WILLIE [*A pause.*] Are you sure you looked good?

AL I have *nothing* on my conscience. The only thing I feel badly about is that you got sick.

WILLIE Thank you. *I accept your apology!*

AL What apology? Who apologized? I just said I'm sorry you got sick.

WILLIE Who do you think *made* me sick?

AL Who? *You* did, that's who! Not me. You yelled and screamed and carried on like a lunatic until you made yourself sick . . . and for that I'm sorry.

WILLIE All right, as long as you're sorry for something.

AL I'm also sorry that people are starving in India, but I'm not going to apologize. I didn't do it.

WILLIE I didn't accuse you of India. I'm just saying you're responsible for making me sick, and since you've come up here to apologize, I am gentleman enough to accept it.

AL Don't be such a gentleman, because there's nothing to accept.

WILLIE You're the one who came up here with your hat in your hand, not me.

AL It's a twenty-five dollar hat, what was I gonna do, fold it up in my pocket?

WILLIE If you didn't come to apologize, why did you send me the candy and flowers?

AL I sent you candy and flowers?

WILLIE Yes. Because it was on your conscience and *that's* why you couldn't sleep at night and *that's* why you came up here with your hat in your hand to apologize, only *this* time I'm not a gentleman any more and I *don't accept the apology!* How do you like that?

[AL *stares at* WILLIE.]

AL I knew there was gonna be trouble when you said "Enter" instead of "Come in."

WILLIE There's no trouble. The trouble is over. I got what I want and now I'm happy.

AL What did you get? You got "no apology" from me, which you didn't accept.

WILLIE I don't want to discuss it any more, I just had a heart attack.

[AL *stares at* WILLIE *silently*.]

AL [*Calmly*.] You know something, Willie. I don't think we get along too good.

WILLIE Well, listen, everybody has their ups and downs.

AL In forty-three years, we had maybe one "up" . . . To tell you the truth, I can't take the "downs" any more.

WILLIE To be honest with you, for the first time I feel a little tired myself. In a way this heart attack was good for me. I needed the rest.

AL So what are you going to do now?

WILLIE Well, my nephew made me two very good offers today.

AL Is that right?

WILLIE I think I'm gonna take the second one.

AL Are you in any condition to work again?

WILLIE Well, it wouldn't be too strenuous . . . Mostly take it easy, maybe do a show on Saturday night, something like that.

AL Is that so? Where, in New York?

WILLIE No, no. Out of town . . .

AL Isn't that wonderful.

WILLIE Well, you know me, I gotta keep busy . . . What's with you?

AL Oh, I'm very happy. My daughter's having another baby. They're gonna need my room, and I don't want to be a burden on them. . . . So we talked it over, and I decided I'm gonna move to the Actors' Home in New Brunswick.

WILLIE [*He sinks back onto his pillow, his head falls over to one side, and he sighs deeply*.] Ohh, God. I got the finger again.

AL What's the matter? You all right? Why are you holding your chest? You got pains?

WILLIE Not yet. But I'm expecting.

AL [*Nervously*.] Can I get you anything? Should I call the doctor?

WILLIE It wouldn't help.

AL It wouldn't hurt.

[*The realization that they slipped accidentally into an old vaudeville joke causes* WILLIE *to smile*.]

WILLIE "It wouldn't hurt" . . . How many times have we done that joke?

AL It always worked . . . Even from you I just got a laugh.

WILLIE You're a funny man, Al . . . You're a pain in the ass, but you're a funny man.

AL You know what your trouble was, Willie? You always took the jokes too seriously. They were just jokes. We did comedy on the stage for forty-three years, I don't think you enjoyed it once.

WILLIE If I was there to enjoy it, I would buy a ticket.

AL Well, maybe now you can start enjoying it . . . If you're not too busy, maybe you'll come over one day to the Actors' Home and visit me.

WILLIE You can count on it.

AL I feel a lot better now that I've talked to you . . . Maybe you'd like to rest now, take a nap.

WILLIE I think so . . . Keep talking to me, I'll fall asleep.

AL [*Looks around*.] What's new in *Variety*?

WILLIE Bernie Eisenstein died.

AL Go on. Bernie Eisenstein? The house doctor at the Palace?

WILLIE That was Sam Hesseltine. Bernie Eisenstein was "Ramona and Rodriguez."

AL Jackie Aaronson was Ramona and Rodriguez. Bernie Eisenstein was the house doctor at the Palace. Sam Hesseltine was Sophie Tucker's agent.

WILLIE Don't argue with me, I'm sick.

AL I know. But why should I get sick too? [*The curtain starts to fall.* WILLIE *moans*.] Bernie Eisenstein was the house doctor when we played for the first time with Sophie Tucker, and that's when we met Sam Hesseltine . . . Jackie Aaronson wasn't Rodriguez yet . . . He was "DeMarco and Lopez" . . . Lopez died, and DeMarco went into real estate, so Jackie became Rodriguez . . .

[*Curtain*.]

[*Curtain Call*.]

AL Don't you remember Big John McCafferey? The Irishman? He owned the Biltmore Theater in Pittsburgh? And the Adams Theater in Syracuse? Always wore a two-pound diamond ring on his finger? He was the one who used to take out Mary Donatto, the cute little Italian girl from the Follies. Well, she used to go with Abe Berkowitz who was then the booker for the Orpheum circuit and Big John hated his guts because of the time when Harry Richman . . .

Comments and Questions

Neil Simon is the most successful and prolific writer of light comedy in America today. He began his career about the time Absurdist plays such as Camus's *Caligula* (p. 619) had taken over many stages both on and off-Broadway. It is doubtful that Simon set out to challenge the doomsday dramatists, but challenge them he did. His well-made witty farces have proved to be effective antidotes for preachments of despair. Few, however, have taken Simon seriously. He writes by formula, his critics say, and besides, he only makes audiences laugh. His defenders reply that if tragedy requires belief in man as consequential, so does comedy, perhaps even more, for laughter is man believing.

1. Compare *The Sunshine Boys* and Molière's *The Physician in Spite of Himself,* p. 486. The plots are quite different, but what about the stage business in both plays? How much of the fun grows out of physical actions of the characters?

2. Are the amusing lines simply wisecracks imposed upon the characters by the author, or do they fit the *individuals* who speak them? Consider Willie in particular.

3. Comment on the overt irony of the title.

4. Humor has been the subject of many heavy treatises. Willie and Al know nothing about theory but much about the art of provoking laughter. Examine their specific observations on what is funny and what is not. Does your taste in humor agree with theirs? Discuss.

5. It is said that humor and pathos are close kin. Is there any pathos in this play?

Appendix of Critical Essays

ARISTOTLE
384–322 B.C.

From *Poetics*[1]

I

I propose to treat of Poetry in itself and of its various kinds, noting the essential quality of each; to inquire into the structure of the plot as requisite to a good poem; into the number and nature of the parts of which a poem is composed; and similarly into whatever else falls within the same inquiry. Following, then, the order of nature, let us begin with the principles which come first.

Epic poetry and Tragedy, Comedy also and Dithyrambic poetry, and the music of the flute and of the lyre in most of their forms, are all in their general conception modes of imitation. They differ, however, from one another in three respects—the medium, the objects, the manner or mode of imitation, being in each case distinct.

For as there are persons who, by conscious art or mere habit, imitate and represent various objects through the medium of colour and form, or again by the voice; so in the arts above mentioned, taken as a whole, the imitation is produced by rhythm, language, or "harmony," either singly or combined. . . .

II

Since the objects of imitation are men in action, and these men must be either of a higher or a lower type (for moral character mainly answers to these divisions, goodness and badness being the distinguishing marks of moral differences), it follows that we must represent men either as better than in real life, or as worse, or as they are. . . . Homer, for example, makes men better than they are; Cleophon as they are; Hegemon the Thasian, the inventor of parodies, and Nicochares, the author of the Deiliad, worse than they are. . . .

[1] Butcher translation, 4th ed.

III

There is still a third difference—the manner in which each of these objects may be imitated. For the medium being the same, and the objects the same, the poet may imitate by narration—in which case he can either take another personality as Homer does, or speak in his own person, unchanged—or he may present all his characters as living and moving before us.

These, then, as we said at the beginning, are the three differences which distinguish artistic imitation—the medium, the objects, and the manner. So that from one point of view, Sophocles is an imitator of the same kind as Homer—for both imitate higher types of character; from another point of view, of the same kind as Aristophanes—for both imitate persons acting and doing. Hence, some say, the name of "drama" is given to such poems, as representing action. . . .

This may suffice as to the number and nature of the various modes of imitation.

IV

Poetry in general seems to have sprung from two causes, each of them lying deep in our nature. First, the instinct of imitation is implanted in man from childhood, one difference between him and other animals being that he is the most imitative of living creatures, and through imitation learns his earliest lessons; and no less universal is the pleasure felt in things imitated. We have evidence of this in the facts of experience. Objects which in themselves we view with pain, we delight to contemplate when reproduced with minute fidelity: such as the forms of the most ignoble animals and of dead bodies. The cause of this again is, that to learn gives the liveliest pleasure, not only to philosophers but to men in general; whose capacity, however, of learning is more limited. Thus the reason why men enjoy seeing a likeness is, that in contemplating it they find themselves learning or inferring, and saying perhaps, "Ah, that is he." For if you happen not to have seen the original, the pleasure will be due not to the imitation as such, but to the execution, the colouring, or some such other cause.

Imitation, then, is one instinct of our nature. Next, there is the instinct for "harmony" and rhythm, metres being manifestly sections of rhythm. Persons, therefore, starting with this natural gift developed by degrees their special aptitudes, till their rude improvisations gave birth to Poetry.

Poetry now diverged in two directions, according to the individual character of the writers. The graver spirits imitated noble actions, and the actions of good men. The more trivial sort imitated the actions of meaner persons, at first composing satires, as the former did hymns to the gods and the praises of famous men. . . . But when Tragedy and Comedy came to light, the two classes of poets still followed their natural bent: the lampooners became writers of Comedy, and the Epic poets were succeeded by Tragedians, since the drama was a larger and higher form of art. . . .

V

Comedy is, as we have said, an imitation of characters of a lower type—not, however, in the full sense of the word bad, the Ludicrous being merely a subdivision of the ugly. It consists in some defect or ugliness which is not painful or destructive. To take an obvious example, the comic mask is ugly and distorted, but does not imply pain. . . .

Epic poetry agrees with Tragedy in so far as it is an imitation in verse of characters of a higher type. They differ, in that Epic poetry admits but one kind of metre, and is narrative in form. They differ, again, in their length: for Tragedy endeavours, as far as possible, to confine itself to a single revolution of the sun, or but slightly to exceed this limit; whereas the Epic action has no limits of time. This, then, is a second point of difference; though at first the same freedom was admitted in Tragedy as in Epic poetry.

Of their constituent parts some are common to both, some peculiar to Tragedy: whoever, therefore, knows what is good or bad Tragedy, knows also about Epic poetry. All the elements of an Epic poem are found in Tragedy, but the elements of a Tragedy are not all found in the Epic poem.

VI

. . . . Let us now discuss Tragedy, resuming its formal definition, as resulting from what has been already said.

Tragedy, then, is an imitation of an action that is serious, complete, and of a certain magnitude; in language embellished with each kind of artistic ornament, the several kinds being found in separate parts of the play; in the form of action, not of narrative; through pity and fear effecting the proper purgation of these emotions. By "language embellished," I mean language into which rhythm, "harmony," and song enter. By "the several kinds in separate parts," I mean, that some parts are rendered through the medium of verse alone, others again with the aid of song.

Now as tragic imitation implies persons acting, it necessarily follows, in the first place, that Spectacular equipment will be a part of Tragedy. Next, Song and Diction, for these are the medium of imitation. By "Diction" I mean the mere metrical arrangement of the words: as for "Song," it is a term whose sense every one understands.

Again, Tragedy is the imitation of an action; and an action implies personal agents, who necessarily possess certain distinctive qualities both of character and thought; for it is by these that we qualify actions themselves, and these—thought and character—are the two natural causes from which actions spring, and on actions again all success or failure depends. Hence, the Plot is the imitation of the action:—for by plot I here mean the arrangement of the incidents. By Character I mean that in virtue of which we ascribe certain qualities to the agents. Thought is required wherever a statement is proved, or, it may be, a general truth enunciated. Every Tragedy, therefore, must have six parts, which parts determine its quality—namely, Plot, Character, Diction, Thought, Spectacle, Song. Two of the parts constitute the medium of imitation, one the manner, and three the objects of imitation. And these complete the list. These elements have been employed, we may say, by the poets to a man; in fact, every play contains Spectacular elements as well as Character, Plot, Diction, Song, and Thought.

But most important of all is the structure of the incidents. For Tragedy is an imitation, not of men, but of an action and of life, and life consists in action, and its end is a mode of action, not a quality. Now character determines men's qualities, but it is by their actions that they are happy or the reverse. Dramatic action, therefore, is not with a view to the representation of character: character comes in as subsidiary to the actions. Hence the incidents and the plot are the end of a tragedy; and the end is the chief thing of all. Again, without action there cannot be a tragedy; there may be without character. . . . Again, if you string together a set of speeches expressive of character, and well finished in point of diction and thought, you will not produce the essential tragic effect nearly so well as with a play which, however deficient in these respects, yet has a plot and artistically constructed incidents. Besides which, the most powerful elements of emotional interest in Tragedy—Peripeteia or Reversal of the Situation, and Recognition scenes—are parts of the plot. A further proof is, that novices in the art attain to finish of diction and precision of portraiture before they can construct the plot. It is the same with almost all the early poets.

The Plot, then, is the first principle, and, as it were, the soul of a tragedy: Character holds the second place. . . .

Third in order is Thought,—that is, the faculty of saying what is possible and pertinent in given circumstances. In the case of oratory, this is the function of the political art and of the art of rhetoric: and so indeed the older poets make their characters speak the language of civic life; the poets of our time, the language of the rhetoricians. Character is that which reveals moral purpose, showing what kind of things a man chooses or avoids. Speeches, therefore, which do not make this manifest, or in which the speaker does not choose or avoid anything whatever, are not expressive of character. Thought, on the other hand, is found where something is proved to be or not to be, or a general maxim is enunciated. . . .

VII

These principles being established, let us now discuss the proper structure of the Plot, since this is the first and most important thing in Tragedy.

Now, according to our definition, Tragedy is an imitation of an action that is complete, and whole, and of a certain magnitude; for there may be a whole that is wanting in magnitude. A whole is that which has a beginning, a middle, and an end. A beginning is that which does not iself follow anything by causal necessity, but after which something naturally is or comes to be. An end, on the contrary, is that which itself naturally follows some other thing, either by necessity, or as a rule, but has nothing following it. A middle is that which follows something as some other thing follows it. A well constructed plot, therefore, must neither begin nor end at haphazard, but conform to these principles.

Again, a beautiful object, whether it be a living organism or any whole composed of parts, must not only have an orderly arrangement of parts, but must also be of a certain magnitude; for beauty depends on magnitude and order. Hence a very small animal organism cannot be beautiful; for the view of it is confused, the object being seen in an almost imperceptible moment of time. Nor, again, can one of vast size be beautiful; for as the eye cannot take it all in at once, the unity and sense of the whole is lost for the spectator; as for instance if there were one a thousand miles long. As, therefore, in the case of animate bodies and organisms a certain magnitude is necessary, and a magnitude which may be easily embraced in one view; so in the plot, a certain length is necessary, and a length which can be easily embraced by the memory. The limit of length in relation to dramatic competition and sensuous presentment, is no part of artistic theory. For had it been the rule for a hundred tragedies to compete together, the performance would have been regulated by the water-clock,—as indeed we are told was formerly done. But the limit as fixed by the nature of the drama itself is this:—the greater the length, the more beautiful will the piece be by reason of its size, provided that the whole be perspicuous. And to define the matter roughly, we may say that the proper magnitude is comprised within such limits, that the sequence of events, according to the law of probability or necessity, will admit of a change from bad fortune to good, or from good fortune to bad.

VIII

Unity of plot does not, as some persons think, consist in the unity of the hero. . . . In composing the Odyssey [Homer] did not include all the adventures of Odysseus—such as his wound on Parnassus, or his feigned madness at the mustering of the host—incidents between which there was no necessary or probable connection: but he made the Odyssey, and likewise the Iliad, to centre round an action that in our sense of the word is one. As therefore, in the other imitative arts, the imitation is one when the object imitated is one, so the plot, being an imitation of an action, must imitate one action and that a whole, the structural union of the parts being such that, if any one of them is displaced or removed, the whole will be disjointed and disturbed. For a thing whose presence or absence makes no visible difference, is not an organic part of the whole.

IX

It is, moreover, evident from what has been said, that it is not the function of the poet to relate what has happened, but what may happen,—what is possible according to the law of probability or necessity. The poet and the historian differ not by writing in verse or in prose. The work of Herodotus might be put into verse, and it would still be a species of history, with metre no less than without it. The true difference is that one relates what has happened, the other what may happen. Poetry, therefore, is a more philosophical and a higher thing than history: for poetry tends to express the universal, history the particular. By the universal I mean how a person of a certain type will on occasion speak or act, according to the law of probability or necessity; and it is this universality at which poetry aims in the names she attaches to the personages. . . .

Of all plots and actions the epeisodic are the worst. I call a plot "epeisodic" in which the episodes or acts succeed one another without probable or necessary sequence. Bad poets compose such pieces by their own fault, good poets, to please the players; for, as they write show pieces for competition, they stretch the plot beyond its capacity, and are often forced to break the natural continuity.

But again, Tragedy is an imitation not only of a complete action, but of events inspiring fear or pity. Such an effect is best produced when the events come on us by surprise; and the effect is heightened when, at the same time, they follow as cause and effect. The tragic wonder will then be greater than if they happened of themselves or by accident; for even coincidences are most striking when they have an air of design. We may instance the statue of Mitys at Argos, which fell upon his murderer while he was a spectator at a festival, and killed him. Such events seem not to be due to mere chance. Plots, therefore, constructed on these principles are necessarily the best.

X

Plots are either Simple or Complex, for the actions in real life, of which the plots are an imitation, obviously show a similar distinction. An action which is one and continuous in the sense above defined, I call Simple, when the change of fortune takes place without Reversal of the Situation and without Recognition.

A Complex action is one in which the change is accompanied by such Reversal, or by Recognition, or by both. These last should arise from the internal structure of the plot, so that what follows should be the necessary or probable result of the preceding action. It makes all the difference whether any given event is a case of *propter hoc* or *post hoc*.

XI

Reversal of the Situation is a change by which the action veers round to its opposite, subject always to our rule of probability or necessity. Thus in the Oedipus the messenger comes to cheer Oedipus and free him from his alarms about his mother, but by revealing who he is, he produces the opposite effect. Again in the Lynceus, Lynceus is being led away to his death, and Danaus goes with him, meaning to slay him; but the outcome of the preceding incidents is that Danaus is killed and Lynceus saved.

Recognition, as the name indicates, is a change from ignorance to knowledge, producing love or hate between the persons destined by the poet for good or bad fortune. The best form of recognition is coincident with a Reversal of the Situation, as in the Oedipus. . . .

XIII

As the sequel to what has already been said, we must proceed to consider what the poet should aim at, and what he should avoid, in constructing his plots; and by what means the specific effect of Tragedy will be produced.

A perfect tragedy should, as we have seen, be arranged not on the simple but on the complex plan. It should, moreover, imitate actions which excite pity and fear, this being the distinctive mark of tragic imitation. It follows plainly, in the first place, that the change of fortune presented must not be the spectacle of a virtuous man brought from prosperity to adversity: for this moves neither pity nor fear; it merely shocks us. Nor, again, that of a bad man passing from adversity to prosperity: for nothing can be more alien to the spirit of Tragedy; it possesses no single tragic quality; it neither satisfies the moral sense nor calls forth pity or fear. Nor, again, should the downfall of the utter villain be exhibited. A plot of this kind would, doubtless, satisfy the moral sense, but it would inspire neither pity nor fear; for pity is aroused by unmerited misfortune, fear by the misfortune of a man like ourselves. Such an event, therefore, will be neither pitiful nor terrible. There remains, then, the character between these two extremes,—that of a man who is not eminently good and just, yet whose misfortune is brought about not by vice or depravity, but by some error or frailty. He must be one who is highly renowned and prosperous—a personage like Oedipus, Thyestes, or other illustrious men of such families.

A well constructed plot should, therefore, be single in its issue, rather than double as some maintain. The change of fortune should be not from bad to good, but, reversely, from good to bad. It should come about as the result not of vice, but of some great error or frailty, in a character either such as we have described, or better rather than worse. The practice of the stage bears out our view. At first the poets recounted any legend that came in their way. Now, the best tragedies are founded on the story of a few houses,—on the fortunes of Alcmaeon, Oedipus, Orestes, Meleager, Thyestes, Telephus, and those others who have done or suffered something terrible. A tragedy, then, to be perfect according to the rules of art should be of this construction. . . .

XIV

Fear and pity may be aroused by spectacular means; but they may also result from the inner structure of the piece, which is the better way, and indicates a superior poet. For the plot ought to be so constructed that, even without the aid of the eye, he who hears the tale told will thrill with horror and melt to pity at what takes place. This is the impression we should receive from hearing the story of the Oedipus. But to produce this effect by the mere spectacle is a less artistic method, and dependent on extraneous aids. Those who employ spectacular means to create a sense not of the terrible but only of the monstrous, are strangers to the purpose of Tragedy; for we must not demand of Tragedy any and every kind of pleasure, but only that which is proper to it. And since the pleasure which the poet should afford is that which comes from pity and fear through imitation, it is evident that this quality must be impressed upon the incidents.

Let us then determine what are the circumstances which strike us as terrible or pitiful.

Actions capable of this effect must happen between persons who are either friends or enemies or indifferent to one another. If an enemy kills an enemy, there is nothing to excite pity either in the act or the intention,—except so far as the suffering in itself is pitiful. So again with indifferent persons. But when the tragic incident occurs between those who are near or dear to one another—if, for example, a brother kills, or intends to kill, a brother, a son his father, a mother her son, a son his mother, or any other deed of the kind is done—these are the situations to be looked for by the poet. He may not indeed destroy the framework of the received legends—the fact, for instance, that Clytemnestra was slain by Orestes and Eriphyle by Alcmaeon—but he ought to show invention of his own, and skillfully handle the traditional material. Let us explain more clearly what is meant by skillful handling.

The action may be done unconsciously and with knowledge of the persons, in the manner of the older poets. It is thus too that Euripides makes Medea slay her children. Or, again, the deed of horror may be done, but done in ignorance, and the tie of kinship or friendship be discovered afterwards. The Oedipus of Sophocles is an example. Here, indeed, the incident is outside the drama proper; but cases occur where it falls within the action of the play: one may cite the Alcmaeon of Astydamas, or Telegonus in the Wounded Odysseus. Again, there is a third case,—to be about to act with knowledge of the persons and then not to act. The fourth case is when some one is about to do an irreparable deed through ignorance, and makes the discovery before it is done. These are the only possible ways. For the deed must either be done or not done,—and that wittingly or unwittingly. But of all these ways, to be about to act knowing the persons, and then not to act, is the worst. It is shocking without being tragic, for no disaster follows. It is, therefore, never, or very rarely, found in poetry. One instance, however, is in the Antigone, where Haemon threatens to kill Creon. The next and better way is that the deed should be perpetrated. Still better, that it should be perpetrated in ignorance, and the discovery made afterwards. There is then nothing to shock us, while the discovery produces a startling effect. The last case is the best, as when in the Cresphontes Merope is about to slay her son, but, recognising who he is, spares his life. So in the Iphigenia, the sister recognises the brother just in time. Again in the Helle, the son recognizes the mother when on the point of giving her up. This, then, is why a few families only, as has been already observed, furnish the subject of tragedy. It was not art, but happy chance, that led the poets in search of subjects to impress the tragic quality upon their plots. They are compelled, therefore, to have recourse to those houses whose history contains moving incidents like these.

Enough has now been said concerning the structure of the incidents, and the right kind of plot.

XV

In respect of Character there are four things to be aimed at. First, and most important, it must be good. Now any speech or action that manifests moral purpose of any kind will be expressive of character: the character will be good if the purpose is good. This rule is relative to each class. Even a woman may be good, and also a slave; though the woman may be said to be an inferior being, and the slave quite worthless. The second thing to aim at is propriety. There is a type of manly valour; but valour in a woman, or unscrupulous cleverness, is inappropriate. Thirdly, character must be true to life: for this is a distinct thing from goodness and propriety, as here described. The fourth point is consistency: for though the subject of the imitation, who suggested the type, be inconsistent, still he must be consistently inconsistent. . . .

As in the structure of the plot, so too in the portraiture of character, the poet should always aim either at the necessary or the probable. Thus a person of a given character should speak or act in a given way, by the rule either of necessity or of probability; just as this event should follow that by necessary or probable sequence. . . .

Again, since Tragedy is an imitation of persons who are above the common level, the example of good portrait-painters should be followed. They, while reproducing the distinctive form of the original, make a likeness which is true to life and yet more beautiful. So too the poet, in representing men who are irascible or indolent, or have other defects of character, should preserve the type and yet ennoble it. In this way Achilles is portrayed by Agathon and Homer. . . .

XVIII

Every tragedy falls into two parts,—Complication and Unravelling or *Dénouement*. Incidents extraneous to the action are frequently combined with a portion of the action proper, to form the Complication; the rest is the Unravelling. By the Complication I mean all that extends from the beginning of the action to the part which marks the turning-point to good or bad fortune. The Unravelling is that which extends from the beginning of the change to the end. . . .

XIX

. . . Under Thought is included every effect which has to be produced by speech, the subdivisions being—proof and refutation; the excitation of the feelings, such as pity, fear, anger, and the like; the suggestion of importance or its opposite. Now, it is evident that the dramatic incidents must be treated from the same points of view as the dramatic speeches, when the object is to evoke the sense of pity, fear, importance, or probability. The only difference is, that the incidents should speak for themselves without verbal exposition; while the effects aimed at in speech should be produced by the speaker, and as a result of the speech. For what were the business of a speaker, if the Thought were revealed quite apart from what he says? . . .

XXII

. . . But the greatest thing by far is to have a command of metaphor. This alone cannot be imported by another; it is the mark of genius, for to make good metaphors implies an eye for resemblances. . . .

XXIII

As to that poetic imitation which is narrative in form and employs a single metre, the plot manifestly ought, as in a tragedy, to be constructed on dramatic principles. It should have for its subject a single action, whole and complete, with a beginning, a middle, and an end. It will thus resemble a living organism in all its unity, and produce the pleasure proper to it. It will differ in structure from historical compositions, which of necessity present not a single action, but a single period, and all that happened within that period to one person or to many, little connected together as the events may be. For as the sea-fight at Salamis and the battle with the Carthaginians in Sicily took place at the same time, but did not tend to any one result, so in the sequence of events, one thing sometimes follows another, and yet no single result is thereby produced. Such is the practice, we may say, of most poets. . . .

XXIV

Again, Epic poetry must have as many kinds as Tragedy: it must be simple, or complex, or "ethical," or "pathetic." The parts also, with the exception of song and spectacle, are the same; for it requires Reversals of the Situation, Recognitions, and Scenes of Suffering. Moreover, the thoughts and the diction must be artistic. In all these respects Homer is our earliest and sufficient model. Indeed each of his poems has a twofold character. The Iliad is at once simple and "pathetic," and the Odyssey complex (for Recognition scenes run through it), and at the same time "ethical." Moreover, in diction and thought they are supreme.

Epic poetry differs from Tragedy in the scale on which it is constructed, and in its metre. As regards scale or length, we have already laid down an adequate limit:—the beginning and the end must be capable of being brought within a single view. This condition will be satisfied by poems on a smaller scale than the old epics, and answering in length to the group of tragedies presented at a single sitting.

Epic poetry has, however, a great—a special—capacity for enlarging its dimensions, and we can see the reason. In Tragedy we cannot imitate several lines of actions carried on at one and the same time; we must confine ourselves to the action on the stage and the part taken by the players. But in Epic poetry, owing to the narrative form, many events simultaneously transacted can be presented; and these, if relevant to the subject, add mass and dignity to the poem. The Epic has here an advantage, and one that conduces to grandeur of effect, to diverting the mind of the hearer, and relieving the story with varying episodes. For sameness of incident soon produces satiety, and makes tragedies fail on the stage. . . .

Homer, admirable in all respects, has the special merit of being the only poet who rightly appreciates the part he should take himself. The poet should speak as little as possible in his own person, for it is not this that makes him an imitator. Other poets appear themselves upon the scene throughout, and imitate but little and rarely. Homer, after a few prefatory words, at once brings in a man, or woman, or other personage; none of them wanting in characteristic qualities, but each with a character of his own.

The element of the wonderful is required in Tragedy. The irrational, on which the wonderful depends for its chief effects, has wider scope in Epic poetry, because there the person acting is not seen. Thus, the pursuit of Hector would be ludicrous if placed upon the stage—the Greeks standing still and not joining in the pursuit, and Achilles waving them back. But in the Epic poem the absurdity passes unnoticed. Now the wonderful is pleasing: as may be inferred from the fact that every one tells a story with some addition of his own, knowing that his hearers like it. . . .

Accordingly, the poet should prefer probable impossibilities to improbable possibilities. The tragic plot must not be composed of irrational parts. Everything irrational should, if possible, be excluded; or, at all events, it should lie outside the action of the play (as, in the Oedipus, the hero's ignorance as to the manner of Laius' death); not within the drama—as in the Electra, the messenger's account of the Pythian games; or, as in the Mysians, the man who has come from Tegea to Mysia and is still speechless. The plea that otherwise the plot would have been ruined, is ridiculous; such a plot should not in the first instance be constructed. But once the irrational has been introduced and an air of likelihood imparted to it, we must accept it in spite of the absurdity. Take even the irrational incidents in the Odyssey, where Odysseus is left upon the shore of Ithaca. How intolerable even these might have been would be apparent if an inferior poet were to treat the subject. As it is, the absurdity is veiled by the poetic charm with which the poet invests it.

The diction should be elaborated in the pauses of the action, where there is no expression of character or thought. For, conversely, character and thought are merely obscured by a diction that is over brilliant.

STEPHEN SPENDER
1909–

On Teaching Modern Poetry

A poem has many levels of meaning, and none of them is prose. Are some of these "righter" than others? Is it altogether "wrong" to think that a poem may be paraphrased? Can an appreciation of poetry be acquired? Does poetry have educational value for the student who is incapable of a complete experience of poetry but who can acquire a limited appreciation which may not seem to survive his years at school or college? This last question, which the reader may be inclined to answer with an immediate "No" is, in practice, not so easy to answer. For students who may never completely understand a poem, can often understand other things through the discussion of poetry. Those who prefer discussing poetry to reading poems, look to poetry for an illumination of some of the problems of living. One cannot afford to dismiss this as irrelevant when one is taking into consideration the whole picture of the education of an individual. Many people look to poetry today as an illumination of religious and philosophic problems. Although poetry is not and cannot be a substitute for religion and philosophy, nevertheless, it may lead people to think seriously about such things. It may lead them through poetry and out of it into their real interest or vocation.

Probably most modern critics would agree that a poem *means* the sum of everything which it *is*, in language used to suggest not just thought but also imagery and sound. It means a thought which can be paraphrased in prose, plus the sound of the words in which this thought is expressed and which add as much to the thought as color does to drawing in a painting, plus the imagery which becomes a sensory experience to the reader as he reads from line to line, plus the energy of the metre, plus the poet's taste or palate in words, plus even such things as the punctuation and spacing of the poem upon the printed page. All these things become an *experience* which the poem is and means.[1]

Most contemporary critics, as I say, would agree about this. On the whole, the tendency today is to judge the poem by the sacred order of the irreplaceable line, and not by the generalized reducible opinions and attitudes of the poet within his poem. This modern appreciation of the concreteness and texture of art is surely one of the characteristics of intellectual life in the twentieth century which we can consider to be an advance of the nineteenth.

Yet, if we do not feel the need to translate poetry into prose, nevertheless the need to explain and annotate it seems to remain. Why else those books explaining the philosophy of T. S. Eliot's *Four Quartets* or of Rilke's *Duino Elegies?* It is all very well for Mr. Robert Graves to declare that his poems are written only for poets, implying that all poems should be that and that only. But evidently, despite the modern purist desire not to lose the poem in the prose translation, poetry expresses complicated ideas and attitudes. This inevitably leads us on from a discussion of the best order of the best words to that of the ideas behind them. Robert Graves may be right in thinking that poetry should be for poets only. But despite his protestations, the overwhelming mass of contemporary criticism of poetry assumes that poetry is written for a reading public who are not just poets: or at least that there is a content of poetry which exists, as it were, apart from the pure esthetic experience which can only be communicated to people who think poetically, as the poet himself thinks.

The teacher of poetry finds that although it is important to stress that a poetry *is*, it is also true that poetry is about things. To a certain type of student the "about" ness will always be more important than the "is" ness: and perhaps this student may learn more from having poetry explained to him than the one who understands poetry intuitively and who therefore scarcely requires to be taught.

The teacher is not a poet teaching poets, nor even a literary critic concerned only with readers whose interest in poetry is "pure." He has to accept, I think, that the interest of most students in poetry, however serious it may be, will not be for the sake of that which is essentially the poetry in poetry. At the same time, poetry itself is ambiguous, and that which it is about is inseparably bound up with that which it is. If a critic as austere as Mr. T. S. Eliot can argue that a poet as pure as Blake is not a great poet because he has a "homemade philosophy," that means that one approach to Blake is certainly by way of his philosophy. And if many of Blake's readers never get beyond his philosophy to the center of his imagination, that does not mean that they have entirely missed the poetry in Blake: because Blake's thought, which can perhaps be paraphrased, nevertheless remains a part of his poetry. What a poem is about, even if it can be expressed in critics' prose, does take us some way toward understanding that which it is.

Many students undoubtedly try to *use* poetry to help them to develop attitudes towards things other than poetry. Sarah Lawrence College provided me with several examples of such a utilitarian attitude. One student, K., had difficulty with certain modern poems at the beginning of the course, because she disapproved of the views which the poets appeared to her to be expressing in their poems; for example, the pessimism of Thomas Hardy, the mysticism of T. S. Eliot, and the insistence on sexuality of D. H. Lawrence. She thought that poetry should in some way express ideas which contributed to the betterment of human society.

Perhaps I should have argued with K. that poetry had nothing to do with the views of poets and still less to do with improving the lot of humanity. But I only partly did this. I also argued against her views in themselves, quite apart from their relevance to poetry. I tried to point out that the search for a meaning in life, even if it seems to neglect the exigencies of social welfare, is not escapism. The result of allowing

[1] The point of view expressed in this paragraph, especially in the first sentence, is demonstrated in some detail in "Poetry Preliminaries," pp. 218 ff.

her to discuss aspects of poetry, such as the opinions and personalities of poets, which seemed on the face of it to have little to do with their work, was that she did, in the course of a year, develop powers of appreciation which I had not thought possible. A block to her appreciation was removed. She learned tolerance through tolerating poets. Having acquired a certain tolerance she experienced a certain release in her imaginative life which brought her to an appreciation of poetry for its own sake. Her prejudices were not just irrelevant: they were barriers which had to be removed before she could understand poetry at all. Her criticism of every poem—that it said something with which she disagreed—implied conviction that poetry ought to have a social message with which she did agree. It would have been useless to say that what a poem *said* was irrelevant to the poetry, because to her the saying something was what really mattered, and ultimately her objection was to the expression of any attitudes of mind which she did not consider socially responsible. To say to her that Thomas Hardy's pessimism was irrelevant to his poetry would only be a way of making her think that Hardy not only had the wrong opinions but also attempted to evade responsibility for them. Therefore it seemed best to accept her view that poetry was about opinions which she could not tolerate and to point out that those opinions, within the contexts in which they were expressed, might have a value which she could come to appreciate. When she had learned to tolerate these opinions she was well on the way to understanding the freedom of the imagination of the poet in his poetry. On the other hand, so long as she could not tolerate what she considered antisocial opinions, she would not tolerate the life of the imagination.

K., it transpired, was using poetry as a means of liberating herself from a narrow application of her social conscience to every situation. Her case was not rare. There is a fairly widespread tendency amongst students today to label a great deal of their reading "escapist," for the most superficial reasons. To them all the poetry of Walter de la Mare is "escapist," Mr. T. S. Eliot is not "escapist" in *The Waste Land* but becomes so in the *Four Quartets,* Mr. W. H. Auden has recently become an "escapist," D. H. Lawrence is escaping from social reality into "personal relationships and mysticism," and so on. Such readers seem to expect that it is the duty of literature to confront them with a social reality, which, in fact, they rarely face themselves in their lives. They wish poets to stop being what is called escapists and become scapegoats, punished and punishing in their work for all the ills of society. One might reasonably argue that if literature did do this, it might indeed be providing a facile escape in imagination from problems which people ought to be facing in their living. In fact, there is a case to be made for saying that people should be social realists in their lives but not in their literature. For living should certainly be pre-occupied with improving conditions, but literature should be concerned with enlarging our ideas of a significance beyond the paraphernalia of living. Without such a significance, improved conditions themselves become a burden. There must be a goal beyond the goal of social improvement—to give significance to better conditions of living when they have been achieved.

In an ideal world I suppose that living would be involved in problems of living, and that literature would be concerned with values which transcend living. It is these values which ultimately give living itself a purpose. Of course, as long as we do not live in an ideal world, some writers will insist on the necessity of using writing as a means of describing the problems of social reality and, if they are so inspired, they will be right to do so. But to call this kind of literature "realistic" and any other kind escapist is to sacrifice the pursuit of permanent values for immediate and pressing ones: and there is danger of the sense of that which endures being lost in the exigencies of the present.

If there is any such thing as "escapism" in poetry, it is the tendency of poets sometimes to assert that experiences contained in certain poems have some kind of consoling application to other experiences of a different nature. That a sunset, a rose, or a landscape can be evoked in language which compensates for poverty, social injustice, or war, is obviously a false proposition. To maintain it is to escape from the greater evil into the lesser prettiness. Poets, even in such a poet as Keats, have occasionally misled themselves and their readers in writing about poetry as though it were a housing project for happy dreamers. The mistake perhaps arises from confusing the objective standards by which poetry is made and judged with the subjective experience it provides. For the fact is that poetry is an art employing an objective medium and technique for the purpose of communicating the subjective insight of the poet to the subjective sensibility of the reader. It can express and communicate an experience which may be of great value to the individual reader, perhaps even providing him with a philosophy and helping him in his life. But this kind of individual experience conveyed from one individual to another by means of the objective medium of art, arises only as a possible rather irrelevant reaction of the reader to the subject matter of the poem. Poetry cannot preach social values as effectively as journalism or propaganda or systematized thought, even though it may indirectly have a social effect. Poetry does not provide a kind of reality which can either, on the one hand, console readers for the ills of society, or, on the other, by being "realistic," make people face up to social problems. All poetry may do, as an incidental effect of its use of language, is to provide the reader with an experience which will affect him according to the laws of his own nature. The propagandist view that poetry can save society is just as irrelevant to the nature of poetry as the one that it can provide an escape from the ills of the modern age.

I have dwelt on "escapism" so long because one of the chief prejudices the teacher of students of poetry today has to fight is indicated by the word "escapist." However, I think the teacher should be sympathetic to the student who wants to know how poetry will be useful to him. After all, utility itself, in connection with poetry, is a somewhat complex concept, and there is every reason to consider it. For one thing, poetry is useful to anyone who appreciates it, in enabling him to enter into complex states of mind which should help him to understand his own nature and that of other people. The reader of a poem has the illusion, through the sensuous use of language, of being in the presence of the event which is the occasion of the poem. The subject of a poem is an event individually experienced; its method (sensuous language) creates the form which is the universal form of all experience for everyone of every event. The reader of a poem is made aware that the experience of every event by every individual is a unique occasion in the universe, and that at the same time, this uniqueness is the universal mode of experiencing all events. Poetry makes one realize that one is alone, and complex; and that to be alone is universal.

The fact that one cannot establish the value of the experience of a poem in a hierarchy of utilitarian values, does not mean that poetry is not useful. On the contrary, one can insist that poetry is of use to the individual who appreciates it, even while one may refuse to measure that utility. The teacher who thinks it is part of his integrity, or of the integrity of his subject, to refuse to admit the utility of spiritual values, may be in the position of offering art to his pupils in the form of significantly formed stones, when they are asking for bread. He should ask himself seriously whether there is not a sense in which poetry is indeed bread for those who can understand it, and even, to a lesser extent, to those who partially misunderstand it.

Poetry, as has often been said, reveals the familiar as unfamiliar. The inspiration of the poet is the moment in which he becomes aware of unfamiliarity. The unfamiliarity, the newness of things, the uniqueness of every contact of a mind with an event, is, indeed, everything. But there are certain experiences in life which are always unfamiliar for everyone, and these form a vast subject matter for poetry, the unfamiliarity of the unfamiliar. Such subjects are death, love, infinity, the idea of God, the smallness of man in relation to the vastness of the universe, the unknown. Religion, philosophy, and morals are also concerned with these fundamentals of the human condition, and it is here that the experiencing of life in poetry brings the poetic experience close to the reasoned processes of philosophers, theologians, and moralists. Thus the teaching of poetry leads the student to a discussion of conditions of human life, where man is alone with the strangeness of his situation in time and space.

Poets can only express their experiences in terms of other experiences, which men have experienced with their senses. Sensuous language means that the poet creates his poem from words which have associations, and these associations are of the experience of things with the senses. A love poem can only be expressed in words which have associations with actual loving, and in the same way a religious poem can only be created in the language of religious experience—however remote this may seem. For this reason, the teacher will find that a great deal of discussion of poetry in class will consist of inquiring into the connection between the poet's experience and his poem. Is the poet sincere? Did he really feel this? are questions often asked by students. When poetry goes beyond personal experience to the experience of belief, we are brought up against a more difficult question of sincerity. Can the poet really believe this? Does he know God? Can he believe in immortality? We are soon confronted with problems of tradition and belief which may seem far removed from a particular poem, but which may really be essential to an understanding of it.

Amongst our contemporaries today one finds that directly a poet ceases to write of some immediate human experience of an occasional nature, for which purposes he can draw on the simple associative language of the physical senses, one is up against the difficulty that a shared language of religious or philosophical experience, with associations which are as easily recognized as those of the senses, does not exist. In reading poetry such as T. S. Eliot's *Four Quartets* with students, one finds that for many of them there is no sensuous language associated with ideas of eternity. God, immortality, heaven, hell, and so on. Eliot's world is for them a world of abstract speculation, his language never, or almost never strikes the note of an experience of eternity in their own minds. Naturally they think of Eliot's preoccupations as "escapism," because they are about an experience of which they know nothing.

If one wishes to teach such students to appreciate the *Four Quartets* the only way to do so seems to be to build up by intellectual arguments the associations with experience on which the poetry is based. One can show that each of the four poems in the *Four Quartets* is connected with real places which have historic associations with certain disciplines of living dependent on certain metaphysical beliefs. One can discuss the use to which Eliot has deliberately put the influence of Dante in his poem, and one can discuss the time-philosophy and the theological ideas of the *Four Quartets.* All this will not give the student the immediate contact with the metaphysical searching which is as much the sensuous experience of this poetry as the color grey is sensuous experience in the line:

> Towards what shores what grey rocks and
> what islands.

Consider such lines as:

> All manner of things shall be well
> When the tongues of flame are infolded
> Into the crowned knot of fire
> And the fire and the rose are one.

Here it is far easier to make the student understand the Dantesque imagery than the sensuous mystical perception of the life of the individual within eternity. Can one understand such writing without having had, consciously or unconsciously, a mystical experience which foreshadows the condition described? This is a baffling question for the teacher. All he can reasonably hope to do is make the student understand the traditional belief within which Eliot's recent poetry exists, and to argue against the view of the student who thinks that mystical experience is "escapist."

Teachers of Latin within the system of a classical education have always taught much poetry, partly because this branch of classical literature is supremely excellent, partly because the language of poetry taught the greatest mastery of all the uses of the language, and partly also because within poetry there exist all the ideas of Roman civilization. These reasons for teaching poetry remain in force today. Insistence on the esthetic aspect should not conceal from us that poetry remains the most instructive of the arts, being rooted in myth, being supremely the exercise by the poet of the historic sense within the tradition of literature, and involving often discussion of general ideas.

The most important thing to teach about modern poetry is that modern poetry is simply poetry, expressing what poets have tried to express at all times, but within modern conditions. The problem of the poet has always been to express inward experience in imagery and sound which communicate the significance of this experience to others. He can only communicate to other minds what is significant to him by involving an outward event symbolizing a significance which corresponds to his inner state of mind. If he is an Elizabethan, certain of his inner experiences may have a significance recognized by others when he attaches to these experiences the symbolism of the rose, the crown, or the cross. For a modern man who, as a human being, has an inner experience exactly similar to that of the Elizabethan, the symbol which corresponds to his experience will be one chosen from modern life, if it is to communicate itself in a way which will awaken the living experience of our time to his contemporaries. To select rose, crown, or cross would be for him to detach his experience from the present and place it in a literary past.

Our expansive, restless, materialist, explosive age does not easily provide us in our environment with outward symbols for inner states of mind. For our outer world has little accessible language of symbols to which we can attach the experiences of our lives. Instead of our minds being able to invade it with their inwardness, it invades us with its outwardness, almost persuading us that not the inner life of man, but non-human, geographical and mechanical events are all that is significant in the universe. However, the fact remains that a man's problem is that everything for him is a mental event in his own mind. This includes the whole extent of the universe, and all the achievements of scientists and generals. The external world is man's inner world and his problem is to organize this inner world within his own mind.

Therefore the eternal problem of poetry—to express inner experiences in terms of outer things—remains, although the apparent unresponsiveness of outer things in the modern world makes this appear difficult. Man has learned, invented, and organized his modern world. It is an object of his awareness, inventiveness, and will. He is not an object of it. Therefore the machine and the spatial distances which appear to impose their vastness on him are the material of his own inner spiritual life. Within his mind they are symbols. Perhaps they are symbols of the apparent powerlessness of his inner life. But his sanity depends on his mastering within himself what he has discovered and invented in his outer world. He has power to imagine the inner mastery of his own situation. Modern poetry is an aspect of the struggle to restore the balance of our inner with our outer world.

In view of this, it is a peculiarity of American education that it makes a division of literature into "creative," "critical," and "reading" functions. Some students will tell you that they expect to learn to write creatively, others to criticize, and others to read. An extreme example of this oversimple approach was given to me by a student who told me that I could not expect her to be interested in any of the poets she read: because she wished to learn to write poetry, not to read it. This was exceptional, but three other students whom I taught were only really interested in those poets whom they considered useful to them in their own writing.

The creative writing classes in the United States must be considered a very interesting educational experiment, but their advantages must be weighed against several disadvantages. One disadvantage is that they tend to divide literary studies into creative and non-creative. If this means also that the student thinks of writing as being an activity which has little to do with reading, or which has the effect of limiting the writer's reading to that which helps him in his own creative work, here is a further disadvantage. For one only has to read the lives of writers to see that an avaricious habit of reading everything that comes his way is the atmosphere in which most writers have developed and lived.

There is certainly a good deal in the writing of poetry which can be taught. Readers of the prose passages in Dante's *Vita Nuova* will see that Dante considered himself a member of a school who were inventing and propagating a particular style of poetry. Baudelaire, Mallarmé, and several other poets have considered the teaching of poetry as a theoretical possibility. At the beginning of this century the imagists held views about the writing of poetry, such as that the poet must concentrate entirely on producing a perfectly clear image, and that this can be taught and learned.

Poetry is written in various forms, and there is no doubt that these can be taught, just as musical technique can be. The parallel with music exists in theory, but actually it does not quite work out in practice. Music is concerned with notes measured in time. A sequence of notes producing the same tune can be invented to produce a slow or fast effect simply by lengthening the duration of each note, or variations can be made by sustaining some notes and quickening others, within the rhythm. Thus a musician can take a tune and produce a great many variations on it without altering the original idea. However, poetry uses words and not notes. A poet cannot alter the speed and mood of an idea simply by adding syllables and emphatic pauses with the ease which is possible to the composer. Thus the idea which in poetry corresponds to tune can only be created in one set of words in which meaning is inseparable from the form in which it is expressed. A poet is not like a composer in search for freedom of expression which he can achieve among a great variety of forms: he is in search for the few forms which correspond most exactly to that which he wishes to say. When he has discovered those forms, he interests himself in no others, except insofar as he is feeling his way towards those which may further his later development. Form in poetry is inseparable from thought: and the only form which the poet needs is that in which he can think. Thus from Walt Whitman, down to T. S. Eliot, one can think of dozens of poets who know far less in general about poetic forms than is taught in the creative writing courses: they are masters of their own particular forms, and probably even avoid thinking in other ones, through an instinctive discipline.

A sonnet, for example, is a poetic form for thinking a thought which is a sonnet. If a poet had no potentiality for thinking in sonnets, to write them may actually confuse him and prevent him from attaining so soon the form which is uniquely his. The poet W. B. Yeats once told me that he had learned to write in an overliterary poetic tradition and that he had spent his life trying to write poems in a simpler manner. To a lesser talent, nothing might seem simpler than Yeats's problem. All he had to do was to leave out some rhymes and prune away his imagery, one might think. But the ornament, the over-poetic style had become his poetic thought, and when he struggled to express ideas which were too bare and harsh for this form, he had great difficulty in adapting his style to his later subject-matter.

Thus, to teach students to write in a variety of poetic techniques would be a doubtful benefit. What one can do, perhaps, is criticize their work, with a view to helping them to discover their own form, teach them to relate as widely as possible the poetry of others to what they themselves are trying to do, teach them to think concretely and with their senses, and develop in their minds a sense of purpose independent of the literary market and literary fashions.

Young writers often forget that a poem should be as well written as a letter or diary or any other piece of prose, that is to say, as well written, considered simply as writing, as they can possibly make it. Perhaps the most reasonable method of writing a poem is first of all to write down rapidly those impressions, that rhythm, that shape which makes it seem a poetic experience, without regard to other considerations. But the second or third stage of writing should certainly be to take out the "bad writing," that is to say, the redundancies, the bad grammar, the linguistic inversions, and write the sense of the poem as well and clearly as possible. A teacher can certainly be of help here, because a good deal of potentially good poetry is lost under sheer bad writing.

A poet discovers his own formal qualities through learning to analyze the qualities of his own sensibility. He must know whether, for example, his gifts are predominantly of the eye or the ear. The visual writer cannot afford to sacrifice his eye to his ear: a preoccupation with rules of rhyme and strict metre could disintegrate the concentration on the image which is necessary to develop his gift.

In relating his own work to that of other poets, the student has to learn to avoid two dangers which have destroyed many talents: on the one hand, the danger of being absorbed into a greater talent; on the other, the danger of shutting out the greater talent for fear of being absorbed. One has to learn to relate one's own work to that of others and to learn from this relation by using other work for purposes of criticising one's own, or sometimes for interpreting the work of other poets in terms of one's own talent. The relation of Keats to Shakespeare, or, in our own time, of Eliot to Dante, is each a classic example of the power of a poet to interpret within his own sensibility the achievement of a past poet. Here it seems to me that the teacher should be of considerable help to the student. For example, I think it would be a good exercise for students to make free translations of poems in a foreign language, interpreting the particular significance for them of a poem which appeals to them into terms of their own technique and sensibility. They should seek in such free renderings, not for accuracy, but to create in their own language the general effect which appeals to them in the foreign poem.

Of course far and away the most important quality of a poet is his power of thinking sensuously in words. The test of sensuous thought is not the occasional striking image or well-sounding line, but the power as it were to *follow through* with the senses, just as in a game a player may have a perception of a whole sequence of moves following from one move, which affect him physically, as though he were at one moment feeling the muscular changes required by all these moves expanding through his blood and muscles. The power of the verbal eye to see the transformation from line to line of the image and sound in a poem: this is the central excitement of poetry, it is the real life, and everything else is fabrication. The teacher cannot of course teach sensuous energy: still less can he explain how this can clothe itself in vital words. But he can at least be an efficient guide; for it is in confused imagery, mixed metaphor, abstract expressions, that by far the greatest number of mistakes are made by poets. If he is able to see with intensity, even for the duration of a phrase or a line, there is the possibility of development. If he is able to understand the necessity of a certain consistency, a poetic logic in the development of imagery and sound, then he may well be capable of poetry.

Too often in schools of creative writing, the student's eye is directed towards the market of magazines and reviews. Perhaps it would be too idealistic to say that creative writing courses should be directed against rather than towards the standards of editorial offices; but at least it may be said that as far as possible independence from such standards should be taught. The period during a student's life when he is writing only for teachers and friends, is not only in itself one of liberty, but it should represent a freedom which he is able to value afterwards, and to which he should always return. In a sense a writer should always remain a student, should be writing only for himself and his friend. But if, when he is a student, he is already considered to be writing for publication, this standard is destroyed in his own mind. Therefore teachers should encourage students to indulge in that kind of writing which cannot be published: for example, the writing of journals and experiments, perhaps even of erotic and obscene poems. The habit of writing for the wastepaper basket is the most valuable one that a writer can acquire.

Despite the creative writing courses, teaching students to read poems seems more useful than teaching them to write them, for various reasons. Although the true readers of poetry are perhaps as rare as the poets themselves, the reading of poetry does lead to many other things. Poetry is, after all, a nerve center of the consciousness of a civilization, with responses to many of the important situations in that civilization. The reading of poetry within an education therefore justifies itself as a discipline of the humanities. Learning to write poetry is an interesting experiment and in some years' time a survey of the results of this education will be interesting. Perhaps it will be found that in place of the creative writing courses there should be a far greater emphasis on writing in all literary courses. It would seem that a very valuable development of the American experiment would be if the conception of written work in all English courses were extended considerably beyond the essay, to include poems and stories.

To sum up: the teacher of poetry has always to remember that he is not only a poet teaching poets or even a critic insisting on the purest and fullest appreciation. He is really filling several roles, of which these two are the easiest and perhaps not the most important, since writers and readers with a true vocation will probably find it without him.

His most important role is to teach poetry as a discipline of the imagination; a discipline which reveals the complexity of the experience of the individual human being isolated in time and place within the universe and experiencing everything at every moment of his life, as no one before or since has experienced or will ever experience it; which, when it has revealed this terrifying uniqueness and complexity, shows how the unique, which is also the universal form of experiencing, can be related through the understanding of poetry to the experiences of other men who have been able to express a similar sense of their isolation within time and space, at other times and other places; which shows that complexity and awareness only become creative when they can be disciplined within a formal pattern.

The student who is unable to attain complete appreciation can learn a great deal from the discipline of poetry. Modern poetry can teach above all that the poetic problem is the same, at all times, though it has to express itself in different forms; the same, because the problem of the poet is to relate his inner significant experiences to the outward world which impresses itself on him. The world of modern phenomena is as much a product of man's spiritual condition as the world in the past has been and the world in the future will be.

WALLACE L. ANDERSON
1917–

An Analysis of "Mr. Flood's Party"[1]

An old man living alone on the outskirts of Tilbury Town has gone into town to fill his jug with liquor. Returning home, he stops along the road and invites himself to have a drink. He accepts the invitation several times until the bottle is empty, after which presumably he makes his way back to his "forsaken upland hermitage." "Turned down for alcoholic reasons" by *Collier's*, "Mr. Flood's Party" was first published in the *Nation*, November 24, 1920. The origin of the poem goes back twenty-five years to the time when Robinson was working on his prose sketches. Harry de Forest Smith had told him of an interesting character that he knew. "I am going to take a change of air," Robinson wrote Smith, "and write a little thing to be called 'Saturday,' of which you will be indirectly the father, as it is founded on the amiable portrait of one Mr. Hutchings in bed with a pint of rum and a pile of dime novels." Mr. Flood is one of Robinson's original "scattered lives," wonderfully transmuted over the years.

"Mr. Flood's Party" is in some ways much like "Miniver Cheevy" and "Richard Cory." It is a character sketch, a miniature drama with hints and suggestions of the past; its tone is a blend of irony, humor, and pathos. Yet it is, if not more sober, at least more serious, and a finer poem. It is more richly conceived and executed, and it contains two worlds, a world of illusion and a world of reality. A longer poem with a more complex stanza pattern and a heightened use of language, its theme fully informs the poem: it is dramatically represented by Mr. Flood and given emotional and intellectual depth by means of interrelated allusions and images focused on a central symbol. The theme is the transience of life; the central symbol is the jug. Both the theme and the symbolic import of the jug are announced in the line "The bird is on the wing, the poet says," though only the theme, implicit in the image, is immediately apparent. Its relationship to the jug goes back to its source in the *Rubáiyát of Omar Khayyám:*

Come, fill the Cup, and in the fire of Spring
Your winter-garment of Repentance fling:
  The Bird of Time has but a little way
To flutter—and the Bird is on the Wing.

Whether at Naishapur or Babylon,
Whether the Cup with sweet or bitter run,
  The Wine of Life keeps oozing drop by
    drop,
The Leaves of Life keep falling one by one.

The transience symbols coupled with the eat-drink-and-be-merry philosophy of the *Rubáiyát* prepare the way for Mr. Flood's party but also intensify the poignance and sharpen the irony. In stanza three, the passage referring to "Roland's ghost winding a silent horn" is the richest in the poem, both in language and in suggestion. It serves a multiple function. The likening of Mr. Flood with lifted jug to Roland, the most courageous of Charlemagne's knights, blowing his magic horn presents a vivid picture, made both striking and humorous by the incongruity. At the same time, however, it is a means of adding pathos and dignity to the figure of Mr. Flood, for there are some similarities. By the time that Roland blew his horn the last time, all his friends were dead; like Mr. Flood he reminisced about the past, and his eyes were dim. Moreover, he had fought valiantly and endured to the end, and these attributes of courage and endurance are transferred to Mr. Flood. The expression "enduring to the end" has a double reference

[1] "Mr. Flood's Party" appears on p. 339.

behind it: it calls to mind the words of Jesus when he sent forth his disciples, "He that endureth to the end shall be saved," a statement that Browning said was the theme of his "Childe Roland to the Dark Tower Came." The Roland allusion is even more subtle. The comparison is not to Roland blowing his horn in broad daylight and surrounded by the newly dead, but to the *ghost* of Roland, and the horn he is winding is a "silent horn." Roland, the last to die, is seeking his phantom friends. So is Mr. Flood. Lighted by the harvest moon glinting on the "valiant armor" of Roland-Flood, this is a world of the past, dim and mute. Fusion of figure and scene is complete. "Amid the silver loneliness/ Of night" Mr. Flood creates his own illusory world with his jug.

The significance of the jug symbol, foreshadowed by the *Rubáiyát* and Roland references, becomes clear in an extended simile at the mid and focal point of the poem:

> Then, as a mother lays her sleeping child
> Down tenderly, fearing it may awake,
> He set the jug down slowly at his feet
> With trembling care, knowing that most
> things break.

The interplay of similarities and dissimilarities in the relationship of *mother:child* and *Mr. Flood:jug* is too delicate and suggestive to be pinned down and spoiled by detailed analysis. Suffice it to say here that in the child the future is contained; in the jug, the past. Memories flood in as Eben drinks, and he lives once more, temporarily secure, among "friends of other days," who "had honored him," opened their doors to him, and welcomed him home. Two moons also keep him company, one real and one illusory. A last drink and the singing of "Auld Lang Syne," with its "auld acquaintance" and "cup o' kindness," and the party is over. And with a shock we and Mr. Flood are back in the harsh world of reality which frames the poem and his present and fleeting life:

> There was not much that was ahead of him,
> And there was nothing in the town below.

The loneliness of an old man, the passing of time; Eben Flood, ebb and flood. There is no comment, and none is needed.

PETER J. STANLIS
1919–

Robert Frost's "A Masque of Reason": An Analysis*

Frost's *A Masque of Reason* is a dramatic explication of Old Testament justice, contained in the forty-two chapters of The Book of Job, as understood by modern man in a modern setting. At the end of the masque Frost wrote: "Here endeth chapter forty-three of Job." This is Frost's bland and ironic way of saying that no one can understand his masque without a complete knowledge of The Book of Job, and also, in light of his theme, that his masque is a prophetic-like satire on modern man's excessive confidence in his own reason.

In the opening scene ("A fair oasis in the purest desert"), Job and his wife, Thyatira, awake to find God caught in the branches of the Burning Bush (the Christmas Tree), which, ironically, gives not a light of Old Testament revelation, but "a strange light" of New Testament Christianity, of spirit entangled in matter, or religion organized and refined by art, so that "the Tree is troubled" by God's being "caught in the branches."[1] Job's comment on the Christmas tree ornaments extends this point through a parody of Yeats' rhetoric in "Sailing to Byzantium" and through a probable allusion to T. S. Eliot's "Sweeney Among the Nightingales":

> The ornaments the Greek artificers
> Made for the Emperor Alexius,
> The Star of Bethlehem, the pomegranates,
> The birds, seem all on fire with Paradise.
> And hark, the gold enameled nightingales
> Are singing.

* The full text of "A Masque of Reason" appears on p. 376. The footnotes that follow are the author's.

[1] Frost believed that the embodiment of spirit in matter was the manifestation of true religion and that the highest reaches of poetry were the attempt to say spirit in terms of matter. . . . Frost's theism, like Abraham Lincoln's, was not sectarian; he believed it could be best fulfilled individually, not through institutions.

In *A Masque of Mercy* Frost again criticized Yeats through a long speech by Paul, condemning Yeats for having

> Once charged the Nazarene with having brought
> A darkness out of Asia that had crossed
> Old Attic grace and Spartan discipline
> With violence.

Frost then defends Christ against Yeats' charge by noting that Christ introduced "The mercy on the Sin against the Sermon," whose "origin was love." But in *A Masque of Reason* Frost omitted consideration of mercy in the conflict between justice and mercy.

When God finally gets disentangled from the Christmas tree Job's wife remarks:

> It's God.
> I'd know Him by Blake's picture anywhere,

to which, later, God responds: "The best, I'm told, I ever have had taken." God sets up a plywood flat, prefabricated throne (obviously a parody on conventional notions of the throne of God, as held by pious literalists, and also in keeping with modern efficiency in construction), and Job's wife guesses the throne is "for an Olympic Tournament,/Or Court of Love," but which Job assumes is for Judgment Day. Job looks for a forthcoming verdict on himself, and being a student of English literature, he bids his wife: "Suffer yourself to be admired, my love/ As Waller says." All these Biblical, classical and courtly love allusions, linked by historical and literary anachronisms and verbal buffooneries, immediately establish the mixed comic-tragic ingredients and tone of the whole masque. It is obvious from the very beginning of the masque that Frost's method involves an ironical, mocking, comic treatment of the serious and tragic theme of Job's suffering of injustice. Throughout the masque the whimsical situational comedy, the witty quips, playful puns and double entendres, indulged in by Job, his wife and even by God, underscore Frost's mock-serious treatment of the Biblical characters, who think and talk like modern Americans, and give an externally light tone to the serious internal discourse at the heart of the theme.

There are many things in both the manner and the matter of Frost's masque deliberately calculated to raise the temperature of sincere and conventional religious believers who are hopelessly humorless—and even more that of sincere and militantly devout agnostics or freethinking atheists who have an undoubting confidence in man's self-sufficient reason. Unfortunately for Frost, his comic and satirical technique has been the chief source of misunderstanding of his masques. Too many readers have ignored Frost's dictum that in good writing "the way of understanding is partly mirth," and that when writing "is with outer humor, it must be with inner seriousness." Frost's statement in the amended preface to E. A. Robinson's *King Jasper,* that "the style is the way a man takes himself," best explains the function of comic wit and irony in his masques. The terrible tragedies that overwhelmed his family—the early deaths of his parents and several of his children, the mental affliction of his sister, the suicide of his son Carol, and other sorrows that pursued him into late life—were enough to make him the modern living embodiment of Job. On August 9, 1947, when his daughter Irma was about to be confined in a mental institution, Frost wrote to Louis Untermeyer: "Cast your eye back over my family luck and perhaps you will wonder if I haven't had pretty near enough." Then he added: "That is for the angels to say."[2]

Frost's implicit religious faith included both evil and good, and therefore both the tragic and comic sense toward life. This belief required him to assume a God-like, cosmic, stoical detachment toward all of life, even in matters in which he was most personally involved and intensely committed, so that he could grasp the tragic as tragic but also in terms of the comic, and understand sorrow in terms of laughter and irony. In this way of taking himself Frost was unique. Louis Untermeyer wrote of this trait in Frost: "His was a high stoicism which could mask unhappiness in playfulness, which could even delight in darkness. . . ." [Frost] was "one who could tease and be tortured, renounce and

[2] *The Letters of Robert Frost to Louis Untermeyer,* ed. Louis Untermeyer (New York: Holt, Rinehart and Winston, 1963), 346.

be reconciled."[3] Certainly, Frost never lost his balance between the tragic and the comic. Although the theme of his masque is centered in the serious tragedy and unhappiness of Job, Frost's method is playful, like the casual, bantering, whimsical, frolicsome, tongue-in-cheek teasing of one who has a lover's quarrel with the world. His masque is ironical in tone, with levity-gravity and light-somber qualities that at once intensify God's arbitrary injustice to Job, and balance it off with the perverse relief of laughter. To Frost, God is a comic wit who cares for man, at once detached and concerned. He is not only the source of revelation but also the master of revels.

Most critics of *A Masque of Reason* have failed to perceive the function of the comic elements, and have dismissed the masque as a serious artistic lapse. According to Randall Jarrell, "*A Masque of Reason* . . . is a frivolous, trivial, and bewilderingly corny affair, full of jokes inexplicable except as the contemptuous patter of an old magician certain that *he* can get away with anything in the world."[4] This singularly obtuse criticism is typical of many critics who cannot understand how comedy, even low comedy, can heighten the sense of high tragedy in Job's affliction. Yvor Winters stated that Frost's comic "details . . . are offered merely for the shock of cleverness; the details are irrelevant to any theme discernible in the poem," and he concluded that the masque is among Frost's "feeblest and least serious efforts."[5] It is ironical that critics who fall far short of Frost's all-inclusive comic-tragic view of the tragedy of man's temporal life should insist from the one-dimensional base of their high seriousness that his wit and humor and comic view of man are sadly misplaced in the masque.[6]

A more valid criticism of Frost's use of comedy in the masque is that it is not always well integrated with the dialogue and dramatic action of the serious theme. This is partly the result of Frost's indiscriminate mixing of things sacred and profane, which has been questioned as bad taste—a sacrilege against the religious sensibility of Christians and Jews. Even here a distinction needs to be made. Frost's comedy is not directed against traditional religious orthodoxy regarding the justice or mercy of God, but against the conventional social respectability of devout but humorless prudes. But it is even more sharply directed against antireligious or nonreligious rationalists. Those readers whose rigid religious faith does not permit spoofing, bantering, and raillery between man and God fail to understand that it is the very intimacy of Job and his wife with God that allows them such liberties in speech. Their dialogue is like gossip, like the fierce spontaneous give and take of a domestic quarrel, where an assumed and intense love allows for great liberties in the expression of resentments or demands. There is nothing unctious or reserved about the faith of Job and his wife. If God is a real person He should be spoken to as a real person, not as a remote and bloodless abstraction.

The whole question in comic relief is whether it fulfills its dramatic purpose artistically. Since most of the comedy is provided by Thyatira, Job's shrewd and sharp-tongued wife, in her remarks to Job, God, and Satan, an examination of her function in the play will clarify Frost's skill in comedy. Clearly, Job's wife is a blood descendant of Mother Eve, by way of the shrew in medieval and Tudor drama. She is proud to acknowledge that the Witch of Endor was a friend of hers. She has the advanced and militant social consciousness of a pre-World War I Bloomer girl or a Women's Liberation advocate. In the modern setting of Frost's masque Job's wife is an emancipated and sophisticated American woman, the prototype of the most ardent member of the League of Women Voters. But she is also a tangled skein of contradictions. She is convinced that God (being Male) has it in for women, and asks Him if it stands to reason (her reason, not God's)

> That women prophets should be burned as witches,
> Whereas men prophets are received with honor.

Her complaint against this injustice is particularly

[3] *Ibid.*, 388. [4] Randall Jarrell, "The Other Frost," in *Robert Frost: An Introduction*, ed. Robert A. Greenberg and James G. Hepburn (New York: Holt, Rinehart and Winston, 1961), 131. [5] Yvor Winters, "Robert Frost: or, the Spiritual Drifter as Poet," in *Robert Frost: A Collection of Critical Essays*, ed. James M. Cox (Englewood Cliffs, N.J.: Prentice-Hall, 1962), 71, 79. [6] See for example Radcliffe Squires, *The Major Themes of Robert Frost* (Ann Arbor: University of Michigan Press, 1963), 80–83.

ludicrous, because it follows immediately after God's long speech to Job on why men have to endure injustices they can't explain, for reasons God does not have to give. Thyatira's complaint is the comic equivalent of Job's serious case against God.

But, it turns out, she wasn't really listening to the exchange between Job and God, because philosophical discourse doesn't interest her. In a tone of disdainful superiority Thyatira says: "You don't catch women trying to be Plato." Job confirms this to God:

> And she's a woman: she's not interested
> In general ideas and principles.

Thyatira's interests are "Witch-women's rights," so that the moment Satan appears, "like a sapphire wasp/That flickers mica wings," she promptly sits up and says:

> Well, if we aren't all here,
> Including me, the only Dramatis
> Personae needed to enact the problem.

After so many eons of time, as Eve's undoubted and unrepentant daughter, she still feels a deep kinship with old Nick. When Satan first speaks she responds:

> That strain again! Give me excess of it!
> As dulcet as a pagan temple gong!

Although this is said in light mock-seriousness, Job's wife is in truth a perverse feminine Romantic to the bitter-sweet end, and says of Satan:

> He's very real to me
> And always will be.—Please don't go. Stay, stay
> But to the evensong, and having played
> Together we will go with you along.
> There are who won't have had enough of you
> If you go now.

Romantic love and sensual delight are supreme for Job's wife. In her rapport with Satan and her emotive anxiety to receive with honor the prince of evil wizards, she has forgotten completely her intellectual concern about witch women's rights and the differences between men and women prophets. Could anything be more charming and disarming than Frost's portrait of Job's wife? Other than a modern naive intellectual critic would any male—pagan or religious—claim that the comedy she provides has no place in the drama of the masque?

Job's wife supplies the comic subplot for the serious theme centered in the dialogue between Job and God. Her comic role adds an ironical dimension to the main theme. It is ironical that Job, the rational and philosophical male, is less virulent in asking God for explanations that satisfy his reason than Thyatira, the nonphilosophical and emotional female, who is quick to insist "to know the reason why" God allows irrational and unjust events to happen:

> All You can seem to do is lose Your temper
> When reason-hungry mortals ask for reasons.
> Of course, in the abstract high singular
> There isn't any universal reason;
> And no one but a man would think there was.
> You don't catch women trying to be Plato.
> Still there must be lots of unsystematic
> Stray scraps of palliative reason
> It wouldn't hurt You to vouchsafe the faithful.

Job's wife is in a profound sense more reasonable and more religious in rejecting hope or belief in an "abstract" or "universal" reason than men philosophers whose very attempt to find a universal reason is itself a kind of irrational madness.

Frost's serious theme in the masque can best be understood by reference to The Book of Job, the most disturbing book to Judaic orthodoxy in the Old Testament. Its challenge to the Mosaic law contained in the first five books (the Pentateuch), through Deuteronomy, puzzled and disturbed the pious among the orthodox. In Deuteronomy, God is angry at men who are incredulous and disobedient against His commandments. But in The Book of Job much discontent against God is expressed by Job, who has been true to God's law yet has suffered many terrible and apparently meaningless afflictions. But in his acceptance of God's injustice Job helped to change God's old relationship to man. Frost has God acknowledge this to Job:

> I have no doubt
> You realize by now the part you played
> To stultify the Deuteronomist
> And change the tenor of religious thought.

In a long speech by God, which contains much that is essential to that part of the theme which is concerned with justifying God's ways to man, and reveals the essence of Frost's own "Old Testament Christianity," Job is made to realize how he stultified the Deuteronomist:

> I've had you on my mind a thousand years
> To thank you someday for the way you helped
> me
> Establish once for all the principle
> There's no connection man can reason out
> Between his just deserts and what he gets.
> Virtue may fail and wickedness succeed.
> 'Twas a great demonstration we put on.
>
> . . .
>
> Too long I've owed you this apology
> For the apparently unmeaning sorrow
> You were afflicted with in those old days.
> But it was of the essence of the trial
> You shouldn't understand it at the time.
> It had to seem unmeaning to have meaning.
>
> . . .
>
> My thanks are to you for releasing me
> From moral bondage to the human race.
> The only free will there at first was man's,
> Who could do good or evil as he chose.
> I had no choice but I must follow him
> With forfeits and rewards he understood—
> Unless I liked to suffer loss of worship.
> I had to prosper good and punish evil.
> You changed all that. You set me free to reign.

Yvor Winters' comment on this vital passage sets it in its correct (religious) historical perspective: "So far as the ideas in this passage are concerned, the passage belongs to the fideistic tradition of New England Calvinism; the ideas can be found in more than one passage in Jonathan Edwards, as well as elsewhere."[7]

In that part of his theme which justifies the mysterious and irrational ways of God to man, Frost added little beyond Scripture or Milton's treatment in *Paradise Lost*. Job's endurance of an apparently meaningless evil which released God from the end of adhering to strict poetic justice was not original with Frost. God's reply to Job's insistence to know "plainly and unequivocally" why God hurt him so is sifted through many delays and witty equivocations, before God gives His shocking reason: "I was just showing off to the Devil." But this aesthetic shock, which is something both more and less than Job can understand, is finally shown to be based on the less shocking idea that "the Devil's . . . God's best inspiration," which in turn rests upon the platitude that God and man cannot exist in a meaningful moral relationship without both good and evil, including evils inexplicable by human finite reason. For mankind this means that spiritual salvation can come only through a perpetual trial by existence, a struggle to endure even unreasonable afflictions and to triumph over them through a personal implicit faith in God. This defense of the ancient ways of God to man comes close to an orthodoxy that is common to both Judaism and historical Christianity.

If Frost's main object had been merely to justify the ways of God's justice to man it would have been more appropriate to call his play *A Masque of Justice*. One excellent critic, Marion Montgomery, has noted that the main thrust of Frost's theme is a criticism of the human error of reading man's own rational nature into God. He asks: "Is man's reason sufficient to overcome the wall between himself and God?" His answer is—not without God's help—which is the traditional answer of Judaism and Christianity in their doctrines of grace. He concludes: "The theme of the poem, then, is that understanding is dependent not only upon reason, but upon faith as well, a faith which helps the finite mind accept the mystery its reason will not completely explain."[8] So far as it goes this is excellent criticism, because it interprets the masque as centered in man's reason rather than in God's justice. But it falls short of a full statement of Frost's theme, which is not merely that man should add faith to his reason, but that modern man's excessive faith in his own reason, his lack of doubt or intellectual skepticism toward his reason, leaves little or no room for any religious faith and ends in the cardinal sin of pride. Frost called his play *A Masque of Reason* not only because he rejected man's finite reason as insufficient to understand and accept the mystery of God's justice, but even more because in essence his masque was a satire on faith in reason as such, a severe condemnation of modern man's proud and delusive Faustian ways toward God.

Frost certainly recognized that there are ra-

[7] Winters, *Ibid.*, 71–72.

[8] Marion Montgomery, "Robert Frost and His Use of Barriers," in Cox, *Frost: Critical Essays*, 142–143.

tional and creative powers in man that give form and meaning through science and art to Nature, and that these probes into the infinite in search of truth are among the chief glories of human nature. In "Neither Out Far nor In Deep," in man's search for "wherever the truth may be—," Frost had written:

> They cannot look out far.
> They cannot look in deep.
> But when was that ever a bar
> To any watch they keep?

Compared to the infinite perfection of God's power and knowledge the rational and creative powers of man are very limited, though the recognition of his limitations does not prevent man from persisting in his search for truth. The satire in *A Masque of Reason* is directed against modern man's failure to recognize the severe limitations of his finite reason.

In light of this interpretation of Frost's main theme, one of the most crucial passages in his masque is this speech by God:

> Job and I together
> Found out the discipline man needed most
> Was to learn his submission to unreason;
> And that for man's own sake as well as mine. . . .

There is nothing in man's "submission to unreason" contrary to Frost's lifelong belief that man should strive to find "truth" wherever it is by all the power of his limited reason. Job finally comes to understand this paradox when he replies to God:

> Yet I suppose what seems to us confusion
> Is not confusion, but the form of forms,
> The serpent's tail stuck down the serpent's throat,
> Which is the symbol of eternity
> And also of the way all things come round,
> Or of how rays return upon themselves,
> To quote the greatest Western poem yet.

The only critic who has interpreted Frost's masque with reference to Emerson, Reuben A. Brower,[9] has made no use of the allusion to Emerson's poem "Uriel" beyond comparing parallel images. Yet this passage, and the lines in "Uriel" to which they allude,

> In vain produced, all rays return;
> Evil will bless, and ice will burn

are crucial to an understanding of Frost's satirical theme.

Several critics have noted that Frost's philosophy has many important points in common with Emerson,[10] particularly his love of seeking truth in "a world of conflicts, clear to the limit," and his ability to contain vast inconsistencies within himself, to perceive "how rays return upon themselves" and finally harmonize in "the form of forms." But much as Frost agreed with Emerson's philosophy, and admired his skill with words, there was one very crucial difference between them concerning the problem of good and evil. In "Uriel" Emerson had written that "The bounds of good and ill were rent;" and that "Uriel's voice" shamed the evil Angels' "veiling wings . . . out of the good of evil born." In a letter to Lawrance Thompson (July 11, 1959), Frost referred directly to these lines and stated concisely how radically he differed from Emerson's optimistic view of good and evil: "Emerson's defect was that he was of the great tradition of Monists. He could see the 'good of evil born' but he couldn't bring himself to say the evil of good born. He was an Abominable Snowman of the top-lofty peaks. . . . Arnold thought him a voice oracular. ('A voice oracular has pealed today.') I couldn't go as far as that because I am a Dualist. . . ."[11] Frost's ethical dualism included a view of reality in which good and evil were both real, so that evil was born of good as well as good of evil. Emerson's ethical monism made good (God) the only reality to man, and he explained evil not as real in itself but only as the absence of good, so that in the end Emerson explained evil by explaining it away altogether. In Frost's masque God, Job and Job's wife all refer to evil (the Devil) as real, though Satan has a very small part in the play.

[9] Reuben A. Brower, *The Poetry of Robert Frost* (New York: Oxford University Press, 1963), 164, 215–218.

[10] See, for example, Reginald L. Cook, "Emerson and Frost: A Parallel of Seers," *New England Quarterly*, XXXI (June 1958), 216–217. [11] *Selected Letters of Robert Frost*, ed. Lawrence Thompson (New York: Holt, Rinehart and Winston, 1964), 584.

Frost's contention that Satan's "originality" in doing evil is "God's best inspiration" implies that great evil provokes God to create an opposing complementary good. In this sense Satan is not only God's great antagonist but also His collaborator in making good and evil meaningful to man. In Judaic and Christian religion Satan's originality, in first defying God, was built upon the false premise that his will and reason were superior to God's and should prevail. This is precisely the same premise upon which the modern rationalist builds his faith in progress through physical science. The evil that comes of good for modern man is his Faustian pride, which is the result of his originality and inventiveness and great success in advancing his knowledge and his power over the laws and processes of physical nature, until he imagines that he can eliminate all temporal evil and achieve salvation through his own self-sufficient reason, without God. This is what from Frost's point of view so frequently underlies modern man's facile optimism, his denial of original sin, that is, of the natural limitations inherent in his finite and fallible nature, and his boundless faith that his private reason is sufficient to create a heaven on earth. Although in religion Frost referred to himself as "an old dissenter,"[12] and wrote "I believe I am safely secular till the last go down. . . ,"[13] he was sharply critical of modern secular rationalists whose dissent made their own private reason a substitute for religion. In a letter written a few days before his death Frost alluded to the combined themes of his two masques, and denied emphatically that man's salvation can come of man: "Why will the quidnuncs always be hoping for a salvation man will never have from anyone but God? I was just saying today how Christ posed Himself the whole problem and died for it. How can we be just in a world that needs mercy and merciful in a world that needs justice?"[14]

In *A Masque of Reason* Frost's Old Testament religious orthodoxy is voiced most explicitly by God, who makes it plain that in any conflict between the old, unchanging moral wisdom of Genesis and the claims of modern science, with its novelty and current change, the ethical norms of traditional revelation are still the fountain of wisdom:

> My forte is truth,
> Or metaphysics, long the world's reproach
> For standing still in one place true forever;
> While science goes self-superseding on.
> Look at how far we've left the current science
> Of Genesis behind. The wisdom there, though,
> Is just as good as when I uttered it.
> Still, novelty has doubtless an attraction.

Frost wrote this passage on the flyleaf of a student's book in 1945, and then added below it: "Really Robert Frost's though by him ascribed to someone higher up."[15] Although Job and even Job's wife express some of Frost's deepest personal convictions, the ideas, viewpoint and tone of God in the masque are practically identical with Frost's philosophy.

Perhaps nothing could be more antithetical than the philosophy of modern secular man, with his faith in reason, and Frost's satire on reason based upon a theology which derives from Old Testament religious orthodoxy. Where the modern rationalist makes man's reason supreme and simply eliminates God as irrelevant to his temporal or spiritual salvation, Frost exalts the omnipotence of God's arbitrary justice and makes man's reason appear peevish and impotent by comparison. To those moderns who are infatuated with the dynamics of an ever-changing society, and believe in the idea of scientific progress through education, politics, and technology, including ethical "progress" for man, Frost's Old Testament theology and insistence that the world is always a hard place in which to save man's soul must appear as an unforgivable heresy against modern man's faith in himself. Perhaps this explains why so many modern critics have gotten so little out of Frost's masque.

Frost accepted completely the superiority of God's mysterious ways and the limitations and

[12] *Letters to Louis Untermeyer,* 340. [13] *Ibid.,* 331.
[14] Frost to G. R. and Alma Elliott, January 12, 1963, in *Selected Letters,* 596.

[15] See Elizabeth S. Sergeant, *Robert Frost: The Trial by Existence* (New York: Holt, Rinehart and Winston, 1960), 372.

fallibility of man's reason. His hard principles are so well fitted to the voices and exploratory dialogue of his characters in the masque that they appear natural and easy in delivery, perhaps even too easy. This is probably what is behind the charge of some critics that Frost is "smug"; he accepts unflinchingly the fact that there are terrible evils in the world about which man can do little. But the charge of smugness can cut both ways; perhaps the critics themselves are smug in assuming that modern man is God and can remove all unreasonable evils from the world. Only a critic victimized by his pride in his own reason would accuse Frost of dramatizing a philosophy of irrational despair. In *A Masque of Reason* Frost's explicit theme is Job's quarrel with God for afflicting him with undeserved evils. But implicit throughout the masque is Frost's own lover's quarrel with smug modern man for not remembering original sin and his fallen state, and for presumptuously assuming the supreme position in the universe. Implicit in Frost's satire against man's presumptuous reason is God's soul-shattering question to Job, in chapter thirty-eight: "Where wast thou when I laid the foundations of the earth?" In this light the humor and comedy in the masque may well be taken as Frost's amusement that men who forget their own finiteness and limitations should at once deny or question the infinite wisdom of God and yet expect heavenly miracles on earth from the manipulation of their social machinery, from their programs of education, science, and government. Far from being frivolous and irresponsible, as so many critics have charged, *A Masque of Reason* is the purest example in the whole of Frost's writings of his serious case against modern man's fondest delusions about himself. In this masque Frost's intellectual skepticism toward man's reason as an instrument adequate to explain the moral mystery at the core of life is as rigorous and profound, within its dramatic medium, as anything found in the philosophical poems of Donne and Dryden and the prose of Swift and Dr. Johnson. Indeed, *A Masque of Reason* places Frost squarely in the great tradition of Pyrrhonism in English thought and literature.

GROVER SMITH
1923–

A Critique of T. S. Eliot's "The Love Song of J. Alfred Prufrock"*

Eliot's Prufrock is a tragic figure. Negligible to others, he suffers in a hell of defeated idealism, tortured by unappeasable desires. He dare not risk the disappointment of seeking actual love, which, if he found it and had energy for it, still could not satisfy him. The plight of this hesitant, inhibited man, an aging dreamer trapped in decayed, shabby-genteel surroundings, aware of beauty and faced with sordidness, mirrors the plight of the sensitive in the presence of the dull. Prufrock, however, has a tragic flaw, which he discloses in the poem: through timidity he is incapable of action. In contrast with the lady in the "Portrait," who feels that she might come alive with lilacs in the spring, he has descended, because of his very idealism, into a winter of passivity. To pursue the tragical analogy, one might call Prufrock's idealism the "curse" which co-operates with his flaw to make him wretched. Alone, neither curse nor flaw would be dangerous; together, they destroy him. Prufrock's responsiveness to ideal values is something theoretically good in itself, an appanage of virtue; yet it partakes of impiety, for it is sentimental instead of ethical. His values are inherited from the romantic-love tradition, a cult of the unreal and consequently of the inapprehensible. But since he is consciously unheroic, as a comparison of his own with Hamlet's dilemma convinces him, Prufrock should seem comic rather than tragic did not precisely his awareness, his sense of proportion, counter laughter with a virtual admission that his case makes much ado about nothing. A comic discovery would set all to rights; Prufrock's discovery of his flaw,

* The text of "The Love Song of J. Alfred Prufrock appears on p. 390. The following footnotes are by Grover Smith.

> I have seen the eternal Footman hold my coat, and snicker,
> And in short, I was afraid,

reminds one that no problem is trifling to the man it grieves and that the more ridiculous its revelation would seem to others, the more it may distress him.

The drama of the poem is presented through soliloquy, the action being limited to the interplay of impressions, including memories, in Prufrock's mind. A rather curious device complicates his reverie. By a distinction between "I" and "you," he differentiates between his thinking, sensitive character and his outward self. It may be that the poem contains traces of a medieval *débat,* as in "The Body and the Soul"; but Prufrock, in saying "you," is not speaking only to his body. He is addressing, as if looking into a mirror, his whole public personality. His motive seems to be to repudiate the inert self, which cannot act, and to assert his will. In a strict sense it is not this mirror image which is a *Doppelgänger* but the ego supervising the *monologue intérieur.* The ego alone "goes" anywhere, even in fantasy; the other, at the risk of being rebuffed with "Oh, do not ask, 'What is it?' " merely originates objections, though unfortunately this self finally decides his failure. Being no image of the heroic Prufrock he would like to be, but his own spindling, wispy frame, it necessitates his refusal of an action in which it, and not he, would be the real agent. The man of feeling can treat with no one except through his physical and psychological mask: through it he is interpreted and by it he is condemned. Nor can the ego survive disgrace of the personality; at the end of the poem it is "we" who drown.

The epigraph to the poem expands the context of Prufrock's frustration. Guido da Montefeltro, tormented in the eighth circle of the *Inferno* (XXVII) for the sin of fraud through evil counsel, replies to Dante's question about his identity:

> If I thought my answer were to one who ever could return to the world, this flame should shake no more;
>
> But since none ever did return alive from this depth, if what I hear be true, without fear of infamy I answer thee.

His crime has been to pervert human reason by guile; like Ulysses he is wrapped in a flame representing his duplicity in his former life, when he knew and practiced "wiles and covert ways"—"Gli accorgimenti e le coperte vie." To Prufrock's own life this reply is also applicable. He, like Guido, is in hell, though, unlike Guido, he has never participated in the active evil of the world, so that this resemblance is as ironic as the resemblance to Hamlet. But in this also there is a core of substantial truth. Prufrock is similar to Guido in having abused intellect; he has done so by channeling it into profitless fantasy. By indulging in daydreams (the soliloquy in the poem itself), he has allowed his ideal conception of woman (the sea-girls at the end) to dominate his transactions with reality. He has neither used human love nor rejected it but has cultivated an illusory notion of it which has paralyzed his will and kept him from turning desire into action. His self-detraction when he confesses that he is only a pompous fool, a Polonius instead of a Hamlet (and recognizing this fact, partly a wise Fool too), accompanies his realization that the dream itself has been only a snare, though he cannot get out of its meshes.

> I have heard the mermaids singing, each to each.
>
> I do not think that they will sing to me.

Failing to abandon the illusion or to be content without physical love, he despairs of life. He has advanced beyond naïve sentimentality in discovering its emptiness, but he has found nothing to replace it. His tragedy remains that of a man for whom love is beyond achievement but still within desire. His age, his shyness, and the somewhat precious and for America, at least, esoteric quality of his name, with its obtrusive initial *J* (recalling the signature T. Stearns-Eliot which Eliot used), underscore his demureness. The name Prufrock, which sounds like the man, was borrowed for him by Eliot from a St. Louis family.[1] It was a good choice.

Prufrock's thoughts start with a command to the self designated as "you" to accompany him

[1] Stephen Stepenchev, "The Origin of J. Alfred Prufrock," *Modern Language Notes,* LXVI (June, 1951), 400–401.

to a distant drawing-room. His object is to declare himself to a lady—though to precisely which one of the roomful, he never specifies and perhaps has not decided. The opening image symbolizes through bathos the helpless Prufrock's subjective impression of the evening, which is like an anesthetized patient because he himself is one. By the meditated visit he might escape from the seclusion, both physical and psychological, oppressing him. That he cannot thus escape, first because of hesitancy and then because of despair, means that he will not stir from his spot at all. As the imagery shows, his world is a closed one. Various oppositions convey Prufrock's sense of impotent inferiority or isolation: the evening against the sky and the patient on the table; the streets and the room; the fog and the house; the women's transfixing eyes and the victim wriggling like a stuck bug; the white, bare arms of cold day and the sensuous arms of lamplight; the proper coat and collar and the informal shirt-sleeves; the clothing and the feeble limbs; the prim manners and the amorous appetite; the prophet and the ignobly severed head; the resurrection and the grave; the prince and the emotional pauper; the bright world of singing mermaids skimming the waves and the buried world of death in the sea-depths of fantasy. These all set down a record of Prufrock's longing to reach out, like grasping claws, and take life into his embrace and of his inhibition by the discrepancy between wishes and facts.

In his tentative urge toward action he betrays the fruitlessness of his search: the streets, stifling "retreats" with cheap hotels and with restaurants ("sawdust restaurants" in more than one sense, perhaps) littered with oyster shells like the sea floor of his emotional submersion, could lead only to a question as overwhelming to the lady as to him. And the women meanwhile are talking, no doubt tediously and ignorantly, of Michelangelo, the sculptor of a strength and magnitude with which Prufrock cannot compete.[2] From the prospect of his visit he distracts himself by considering the yellow fog which sleepily laps the house and then by musing that he has plenty of time to "prepare a face," whether in order to lay a plot of momentous effect or to make small-talk over a teacup. But the recurring thought of the women leads him to speculate on their reaction to him, to the baldness he might betray if he beat too hasty a retreat, and to the ill-disguised thinness of his arms and legs. At this point he admits his first doubt, namely, whether he "dare/Disturb the universe"—a hyperbole illustrating his terrified self-consciousness. Immediately after he thus reveals his want of easy terms with life, he shows his distaste for the women as they are; both circumstances result, it appears later, from absorption in daydreams. Rejecting the voices, the eyes, and the arms (all impersonal, all monotonous, hostile, delusive), he can think of no formula of proposal but one humiliating to himself—a presumptuous obsequiousness:

Shall I say, I have gone at dusk through narrow streets
And watched the smoke that rises from the pipes
Of lonely men in shirt-sleeves, leaning out of windows?

His horror of being dissected, of being "pinned," makes him recoil to the wish that he had been

a pair of ragged claws
Scuttling across the floors of silent seas.[3]

With this image, just before the climax of the dramatic structure, Prufrock perceives his lack of instinct, of mindless appetite, which would have given him a realizable aim and which, of course, would have made him at home in those depths where at present he exists abnormally.

He has already spoken of the fog and smoke as if it were a cat (a Sandburg cat, no doubt) curling round the house. He now refers to the drowsy afternoon (which, correcting himself, he realizes is evening after all), saying, it "sleeps so peacefully," "stretched on the floor"—or, like his etherized self, "malingers." He is again confronting the difficulty of action rather than its unpleasantness. The difficulty lies in dread of personal inadequacy, maybe even of sexual insufficiency—"the strength to force the moment to its crisis." The climax of his reverie is shaped

[2] Roberta Morgan and Albert Wohlstetter, "Observations on 'Prufrock,'" *Harvard Advocate,* CXXV, No. 3 (December, 1938), 30.

[3] Perhaps an allusion to *Hamlet,* Act II, scene 2, lines 204–206.

as he compares himself, in his feeling of being decapitated (perhaps, in effect, of being unmanned), to John the Baptist: and yet at once he disclaims the dignity of a prophet, seeing himself instead as the butt of a lackey's derision, as the butt of snickering Death. Having confessed his cowardice, he knows that it is too late for him to go, and indeed that it always was.

The remainder of the poem moves toward the image of drowning, a counterpart to the undersea image in the "ragged claws" lines. Henceforth Prufrock speaks of what *would have* happened and affirms the improbability of a favorable issue to his suit. He would have had to "bite off" and "spit out" his question in some graceless way; he would have had to "squeeze the universe into a ball" (an image in part borrowed from Marvell's "To His Coy Mistress," where it has sexual value); he would have had to rise like Lazarus from the dead (the comparison was suggested to Eliot by Dostoevsky's *Crime and Punishment*[4]) and "tell all," as Dives implored in the parable of the other Lazarus. And, at that, the answer of the lady might have been a casual rebuff. In view therefore of these impossibilities, of their clash with decorous commonplaceness and, above all, of their unacceptability because they would have brought exposure, "as if a magic lantern threw the nerves in patterns on a screen," he disclaims his pretensions. He cannot even dignify his *accidia* by associating it with that of Hamlet. Consequently he resolves, in the only positive decision he can make, to go down upon the seashore, where for a while he may masquerade in his dandyishly cuffed white-flannel trousers. He will perhaps part his hair to conceal his baldness and risk the solaces of a peach, the sole forbidden fruit he is likely to pluck. The happy mermaids, at least, will not insist that he wear a morning coat and tie. But even the mermaids, alas, will not sing to him. His vision of them has been a delusion into whose waters he has sunk deeper and deeper until, recalled to the intolerable real world by human voices in a drawing-room, he has waked and drowned in his subjective world of dreams. Like legendary sailors lulled asleep by mermaids or sirens and then dragged down to perish in the sea, Prufrock has awakened too late.

[4] John C. Pope, "Prufrock and Raskolnikov," *American Literature,* XVII (November, 1945), 213–230; "Prufrock and Raskolnikov Again: A Letter from Eliot," *American Literature,* XVIII (January, 1947), 319–321.

H. B. CHARLTON
1890–1961

Hamlet

Ostensibly the plot of *Hamlet* is simple. A son is called upon to kill his father's murderer. The son was wellnigh the perfect pattern of manhood, rich in the qualities which make for excellence in the full life of one who in himself is scholar, soldier and courtier. The murdered father, moreover, was dearly loved, one of so much worthiness that the earth seldom has produced his like. The murderer was not only wicked with the common wickedness of murderers; the man he murdered was his brother, and he took to himself not only the murdered man's crown but also his widow. The situation appears even extravagantly simple. The moment the son hears of the murder, he resolves that with "wings as swift as meditation, or the thoughts of love" he will sweep to his revenge. There appears to be no reason on earth why he should not, and could not, do it in the next moment. Yet the whole stuff of the play is that he did not and could not do so. He fails until in the end by an unpremeditated stroke, he kills his uncle by his own last human act. Why then did he fail? What is the inevitability of his doom?

He fails because he is himself, Hamlet, and because the particular circumstance which he is called upon to encounter proves itself to be precisely of the sort which a man such as he cannot surmount. It is obvious that even in this statement of the situation there are elements belonging to the mysteries of life which the drama leaves in their own inscrutable darkness. Why, for instance, was Hamlet the sort of man he was, and why did he chance to be born with such an uncle and in times so very much out of joint? These are questions for all who seek a complete metaphysic; but they are neither raised nor answered in the play: they are *data,* even as in the *Iphigenia* of Euripides certain preliminary acceptances of given conditions are, in the view of Aristotle, to be fully approved: "the fact that the oracle for some reason ordered him [her brother] to go there, is outside the general plan of the play; the purpose, again, of his coming is outside the action proper."[1] Shakespeare takes it for granted as his starting-point that Hamlet is the sort of man he is, and that he was born to such circumstances as those in which we see him move. Round that smaller orb which engrosses Shakespeare's dramatic genius, his poetic imagination throws the sense of more ultimate mysteries, the speculative possibilities undreamed of by philosophy, and the vast dubieties of "thoughts which wander through eternity." But for his human purpose, the play is the thing: and the play is a revelation of how Hamlet, being the man he is, founders on the circumstances which he is called upon to face.

What, then, is there in Hamlet's nature to bring about this disaster? Why does he not kill his uncle forthwith? Teased by the problem, men have propounded many solutions, all of them abstractly possible, and many of them partly warranted by some trait or another in Hamlet's character. Let us look at some of these suggestions.

First of them: Hamlet is clearly a man of fine moral susceptibilities, so exquisite in his sense of right that questions such as that of chastity, and even of the purity of second marriage, touch him profoundly. He is disgusted wellnigh to frenzy by the thought of impurity. Hence, it is held, he was bound to find killing, though the killing of a villain, an immoral deed: still more, he was bound to find the act of killing a loathsome experience from which his sensitiveness would recoil. But though these are qualities commonly associated with to-day's men of fine moral fibre, they are not in themselves, not even now, a necessary adjunct of high morality; how, otherwise, would our war-heroes be fitted into a high moral system? Moreover, the association of these qualities with fineness of soul is of very recent growth: no human sentiment has spread so fruitfully as has the one we call humanitarianism, but its modern form is largely a product of the eighteenth century and after; witness the crusades for penal and social reforms in the last two centuries. In Shakespeare's day, however, a man could be hanged for pilfering, even for wandering without visible means of subsistence. And certainly Hamlet has no squeamishness at the sight of blood, and no abstract compunctions about the taking of life. "Now could I drink hot blood," he says in one of his passions; and a skilled fencer is no more likely to swoon on seeing blood than is a surgeon. Or hear how he talks about the body of Polonius, a body which would still have been alive had not Hamlet just made it a corpse. "I'll lug the guts into the neighbour room." Here, at least, is no antivivisectionist's utterance. Nor is Hamlet's mind preoccupied with the sanctity of individual life. He has killed Polonius, not of intent, but by mistake; and Polonius was once to have been his father-in-law. Yet how easily, complacently, and even callously, he puts the incident aside:

> Thou wretched, rash, intruding fool, farewell!
> I took thee for thy better: take thy fortune;
> Thou find'st to be too busy is some danger.[2]

Further, when he plans the death of Rosencrantz and Guildenstern, there is positive gloating in his anticipation of the condign punishment—execution, in fact—which, by his contrivance, is in store for them:

> For 'tis the sport to have the enginer
> Hoist with his own petar: and 't shall go hard
> But I will delve one yard below their mines
> And blow them at the moon.[3]

Perhaps even more incompatible with Hamlet's alleged humanitarian recoil from bloodshed is his soliloquy, as, passing by the king at prayer, he contemplates killing him, and then desists:

> Now might I do it pat, now he is praying;
> And now I'll do't. And so he goes to heaven;
> And so am I revenged. That would be
> scann'd.[4]

To kill the king in such circumstances, he decides, would be to do the king a favor, "hire and salary," not revenge. And he is eager to defer the killing until its consequences will be fraught with the direst horrors:

[1] *Poetics* XVII. 3.

[2] *Hamlet* III. iv. 31. All succeeding references are to *Hamlet*. [3] III. iv. 206. [4] III. iii. 73.

Am I then revenged,
To take him in the purging of his soul,
When he is fit and season'd for his passage?
No!
Up, sword; and know thou a more horrid hent;
When he is drunk asleep, or in his rage,
Or in the incestuous pleasure of his bed;
At gaming, swearing, or about some act
That has no relish of salvation in 't;
Then trip him, that his heels may kick at heaven,
And that his soul may be as damn'd and black
As hell, whereto it goes.[5]

In the face of these instances, it would seem wrong to detect modern sentiments and susceptibilities about bloodshed in the constraints which obstruct Hamlet's achievement of his object.

Perhaps the intrusion of a present-day point of view is also responsible for the notion that Hamlet is seriously withheld by a growing feeling of some insufficiency in the evidence on which he has pledged himself to avenge his father's murder. He begins really to distrust the testimony of the ghost, we are asked to believe; and, naturally, the suggestion is easily taken in an age like ours which is eminently sceptical about the supernatural. But does Hamlet ever seriously question the ghost's authenticity and the reliability of its intimations? Nominally he does, of course: but are these genuine doubts or are they excuses in the sense that they are his attempts to rationalize his delay after it has occurred?

One thing is certain. When Hamlet sees and listens to the ghost, there is not even the faintest hint of possible deception. He takes the spectre for what it really is, the spirit of his dead father. Moreover, the tale which the ghost tells him fits exactly into his instinctive sense of the wickedness of his uncle. "O, my prophetic soul, my uncle!"[6] is his immediate conviction of the truth of the ghost's evidence. He does not mean that he suspected his uncle of murder; he means that he has always felt that his uncle was a villain, and now the tale of the murder provides him with particular confirmation. Hamlet's acceptance of the ghost is instantaneous and absolute: and in the relative calm following the exacting encounter, he assures his friends, "It is an honest ghost." The first intimation from Hamlet that he is apparently wavering in this confidence comes only after the lapse of considerable time, and therefore when Hamlet must feel self-reproach at his tardiness. The time-lapse is made clear by the introduction of seemingly extraneous incidents. Laertes has gone back to Paris, and Polonius is sending his "spy" there to see how Laertes is settling down. More striking, there is the dull drawn-out tale of the dispute between Denmark and Norway; a dramatically tedious scene is occupied by the instructions to the emissaries. These envoys have now fulfilled their mission and have returned to Denmark. Some time, therefore, some months, it would seem, have elapsed, and Hamlet's uncle still lives. Hamlet surely must needs justify his delay to his own soul. One can almost watch the plea of distrust in the ghost thrusting itself as an excuse into his mind. Chance has brought the players to the court. As Hamlet meets them, his former intellectual interests immediately reassert themselves: he becomes first-nighter and amateur dramatic critic again. There is green-room talk, and an actor or two is asked to go over a familiar speech. At the end, Hamlet asks the troupe to have ready for the morrow a murder play, into which he will insert some dozen or sixteen lines. Of course, the murder is in his mind, and a few lines easily added to a murder play will sharpen its application and will make the murderer writhe. But there is no hint yet that such writhing is being planned for anything more than to submit a murderer to some of the torments which he deserves. Indeed, the moment the players leave Hamlet, he reproaches himself bitterly for a rogue and peasant slave, since a merely fictitious grief can force a player to more passion than real grief seems able to arouse in Hamlet himself. What, thinks Hamlet, what would such a man do,

Had he the motive and the cue for passion
That I have?[7]

That is, he accepts entirely the ghost's tale of his uncle's villainy. Indeed he continues to reprove his inexplicable delay. "Am I a coward?"

[5] III. iii. 84. [6] I. v. 40.

[7] II. ii. 586.

and in bitter scorn of his own apparent inaction, he heaps contempt upon himself:

> 'Swounds, I should take it: for it cannot be
> But I am pigeon-liver'd and lack gall
> To make oppression bitter, or ere this
> I should have fatted all the region kites
> With this slave's offal.

In the heat of his searing self-analysis, he repeats the indictment of his uncle with complete conviction:

> bloody, bawdy villain!
> Remorseless, treacherous, lecherous, kindless
> villain!

It is at that very moment that he first invents a purpose for the play which he has already planned for the morrow. He knows, of course, that instead of dabbling in theatricals, he should be sharpening his sword: and so he tells himself—and us—that the play is really a necessary part of his main plot:

> I have heard
> That guilty creatures sitting at a play
> Have by the very cunning of the scene
> Been struck so to the soul that presently
> They have proclaim'd their malefactions;
> For murder, though it have no tongue, will
> speak
> With most miraculous organ. I'll have these
> players
> Play something like the murder of my father
> Before mine uncle: I'll observe his looks;
> I'll tent him to the quick: if he but blench,
> I know my course. The spirit that I have seen
> May be the devil: and the devil hath power
> To assume a pleasing shape; yea, and perhaps
> Out of my weakness and my melancholy,
> As he is very potent with such spirits,
> Abuses me to damn me: I'll have grounds
> More relative than this: the play's the thing,
> Wherein I'll catch the conscience of the king.[8]

But the plea is specious, too palpable; it is Hamlet excusing himself for dissipating his energies and side-tracking his duty, for the execution of which he had so passionately reiterated the full and entire grounds a moment before. Moreover, how real can the need for confirmation of the ghost's story be when though the plan to provide it is spectacularly successful, the success is not followed by the slightest overt move to complete the alleged scheme? "If he but blench, I know my course." But he knew it already; and the additional item of credit now obtained, like his previous knowledge, leaves him passive.

Further, if the play within the play was devised by Hamlet to give him a really necessary confirmation of the ghost's evidence, why is this the moment he chooses to utter his profoundest expression of despair, "To be, or not to be, that is the question"? For, if his difficulty is what he says it is, this surely is the moment when the strings are all in his own hands. He has by chance found an occasion for an appropriate play, and, as the king's ready acceptance of the invitation to attend shows, he can be morally certain that the test will take place; and so, if one supposes him to need confirmation, within a trice he will really know. Yet this very situation finds him in the depths of despair. Can he really have needed the play within the play? The point is of some importance, because in the 1603 Quarto of *Hamlet,* this "To be, or not to be" speech occurs before Hamlet has devised the incriminating play. In the 1604 and later versions, the speech comes where we now read it. I know no more convincing argument that the 1604 Quarto is a master-dramatist's revision of his own first draft of a play.

Characteristic, too, is the nature of his alleged misgivings: they turn on the function and the nature of devils in general—"the devil hath power to assume a pleasing shape." But no stretch of words could describe Hamlet's encounter with the ghost as an appointment with "a pleasing shape." As we shall see, his account is as philosophically valid and as particularly inept as are so many of his generalizations. The fact is patent. He knew it was an honest ghost; he knew that its tale was true; and, not having fulfilled his promise to act on it, his moral nature could only be contented by plausible excuses.

Similarly one might go over other alleged explanations of Hamlet's inaction. There is the flat suggestion that he was restrained by material difficulties: he did not know how the Danes would look on his uncle's death, and he did not know how he could plan his *coup.* But

[8] II. ii. 636.

these need not take up our time. Hamlet could rely on the people's approval of almost anything which he might choose to do; even Laertes had no trouble in rousing their suspicion of the new king. Moreover, no elaborate *coup* was needed; one stroke of the sword was all that was necessary; and, as we have seen, when Hamlet foregoes the opportunity, it is not for fear of the people's disapproval, it is because to kill the king at prayers would despatch him to heaven and not to the hell which he deserves. He never doubted that he had cause and will and strength and means to do it.

More difficult to set aside is the Freudian or the semi- or pseudo-Freudian explanation that a mother- or a sex-complex is the primary cause of Hamlet's delay. But the difficulty is one of terminology, not one of substance. The Elizabethans believed that a man could love his mother without being in love with her or without unconsciously lusting for her. Hamlet's filial love for his mother is certainly a main cause of his estrangement from the people who inhabit the world in which he lives, the world in which he must build his own soul. Certainly, too, her "o'er hasty" remarriage shatters the pillars of his moral universe. He has lived in an ideal world, that is, a world fashioned in his own idea, a world in which chastity is a main prop: and when he finds that, of all the women in his world, it is his own mother who seems unaware of this mainstay of the moral order, the structure topples over him. The only way to preserve purity is for womankind to seclude themselves from men: "get thee to a nunnery"; and Ophelia becomes a potential source of contagion. "Why wouldst thou be a breeder of sinners?" But sterility is a denial of life; as a moral injunction it is the tragic negation of morality. It is, however, only the young imaginative idealist's intellectual world which is fractured: but so far that is Hamlet's main, if not his only, world.

Consider, for instance, the difference in depth between his first soliloquy, "O, that this too too solid flesh," and the later one, "To be, or not to be." Both are contemplations of suicide. But what immeasurable difference between the constraining sanctions! When Hamlet speaks the first soliloquy, all that he knows to his own grief is that his father has died and that his mother has married again o'er-hastily. Neither he nor anybody else has any suspicion that murder, and murder most foul and most unnatural, has been done. His father has died from natural causes. But this death and, still more, his mother's remarriage, have reduced Hamlet's ideal universe to chaos. His rich and exquisitely sensitive nature, the observed of all observers, has suffered a shock which starts it reeling. A father dead, and untimely dead, though in itself a common experience, may prompt some sceptical scrutiny of divine providence; but worse still, a mother so soon married again seems to reveal an even more immediate despair; for here, not the divine but the human will seems to be working without moral sensibility. Yet the seat of the sorrow is nothing near so deep in human experience as is that which Hamlet utters when later he knows that his father has been murdered by his uncle.

In the first soliloquy, "O that this too too solid flesh," Hamlet is not so much actively contemplating suicide as passively longing to be dead. And the respect which makes it unthinkable to resort to self-slaughter is that the Everlasting has set his canon against it. In a way there is something of a pose in Hamlet's gesture: as if a young poet peering into the waters of a pool should long for the eternal quiet of its depths, but should be kept to the bank for fear that the water might be too cold. How much deeper in human nature are the constraints which withhold the Hamlet of the "To be, or not to be" soliloquy! No merely intellectual recognition of a theological injunction, but a primitive fear of the unknown after-world. "What dreams may come when we have shuffled off this mortal coil." The first speech is that of a sensitive soul in spiritual discomfort, the second is that of a man in profound despair. The discovery of the murder of his father by his uncle, of an act of uttermost human sacrilege, drives him to abysses of grief deeper than those occasioned by his mother's frailty. Something more human, more overt and intelligible than the Freudian hypothesis is the main stress of Hamlet's tragic incapacitation.

So far our explorations of the source of Hamlet's doom have been negative; mere statements of the inadequacy of suggested causes of it. But cannot something positive be propounded? Why cannot Hamlet perform the simple and righteous act of killing his uncle? The root of the trouble is generally agreed. He is too much "sicklied o'er with the pale cast of thought." That's the respect which makes calamity of life; he thinks too much, and conscience, that is (in the use of the word here), persistent rumination, makes cowards of us all:

> some craven scruple
> Of thinking too precisely on the event,
> A thought which, quarter'd, hath but one part wisdom
> And ever three parts coward.[9]

He is, we are told, a philosopher, and the habit of thinking unfits him for the practical needs of doing: and, of course, popular opinion will easily take it that a thinker is a dreamer, and a dreamer is incapable of ready and effective action. But, is this easy assumption sufficient to explain Hamlet's failure? Moreover, if it be true, is it not a proposition which must give us pause, especially those of us who as teachers are mainly bent on encouraging the younger world to think? If thought is but a snare, to what then shall we turn? Thinking, in itself, is surely what we all take to be the world's greatest need: if in itself it is an incapacitating and unpractical activity, then the sooner our schools and our universities are abolished the better.

Nor will it do to say that Hamlet fails, not because he thinks, but because he thinks too much. In one sense, if thought is what will save the world, there cannot be too much of it. In another, if all that is meant is that Hamlet thinks too often, then clearly this is no matter for tragedy: it is merely a question of a revised time-table, more time to be allocated for field sports and other nonintellectual forms of activity.

What is wrong is not that Hamlet thinks or thinks too much or too often, but that his way of thinking frustrates the object of thought. It is the kind of distortion to which cerebration is liable when it is fired by a temperamental emotionalism and guided by an easily excited imagination. The emotion thrusts one factor of the thinker's experience into especial prominence, and the imagination freely builds a speculative universe in which this prominence is a fundamental pillar. Hence, the business of thinking overreaches itself. The mind's function to construct an intellectual pattern of reality becomes merely a capacity to build abstract patterns, and the relation of these patterns to reality is misapprehended, if not discounted entirely. In the main, this way of thinking constructs a cosmic picture which only serves to give apparent validity to what the feeling of the person and of the moment makes most immediately significant. But examples will help to make the effect of it apparent. They will be better, because more certainly characteristic of the more normal working of Hamlet's mind, if they are taken from scenes before Hamlet is given the additional shock of discovery that his uncle is a murderer and has murdered his father. There are sufficient of them in his first soliloquy.

The scene of it is worth recalling to establish other qualities of Hamlet which are easily overlooked. He is the hero: and in our backward rumination when we have come to know him, unconsciously we idealize his earlier appearances. But in this first episode, he is not an altogether attractive person. The Court is in session: he is in the royal train, but not a part of it. In manner, in dress and in place, he is staging his contemptuous aloofness from it. He stands apart, taking no share in the social formalities of the occasion, and he draws attention to his aloofness by an extravagant garb of mourning and by excessive display of the conventional gestures of grief. He is swathed in elaborate black: his "inky cloak," on top of his "customary suits of solemn black" in full funereal fashion prescribed by the sixteenth-century mortician, his incessantly repeated sighs, his perpetual flow of tears, his fixed deflection of gaze: these are trappings and suits of conventional woe whose emphasis reflects suspicion of insincerity on their wearer, or at least, until a relative judgment is possible, mark him as liable to such suspicion. Nor is this possibility of a Pharisaic isolation weakened by memory of his only other words, his earlier sardonic interjections and his affectedly humorous comments on the king's greeting.

Hence, when he soliloquizes, our willingness to sympathize with a son whose father has died and whose mother has hastily married again is suspended by our suspicion of the son's leaning to morbidity. His words appear to justify suspicion to the full:

[9] IV. iv. 40.

O, that this too too solid flesh would melt,
Thaw and resolve itself into a dew!
Or that the Everlasting had not fix'd
His canon 'gainst self-slaughter![10]

We have seen that the utterance of a wish for death in such a phrase lacks the convincing urgency of the constraints expressed in the incalculable fears of the "To be, or not to be" speech. His imagination goes on to explore illimitable stretches of despair; "weary" and "stale" and "flat" and "unprofitable" are the suggestions by which it deprives the uses of the world of all their value. "Things rank and gross in nature possess it merely." Yet the absoluteness of this denunciation prompts our question. Hamlet has hitherto enjoyed a privileged life, and the good things of the world, material and spiritual, have been fully and freely at his disposal: but the passionate sorrow of the moment blots these out of his intellectual picture of the universe. His next remarks let us see how such obliviousness and its consequently distorted sense of reality are natural to Hamlet's mode of speculation. "But two months dead." Much will happen to these two months as Hamlet fits them into their place in his scheme of things; the fact that as a lapse of time they are in themselves a part of physical nature, unalterable and absolute, will be completely forgotten. "That it should come to this": Hamlet's desperate anger heats his mind. "But two months dead"—an incredibly short span wherein such things should have happened. "Nay, not so much, not two." The notion of a real measure of time, and of its unthinkable brevity for such occasion, is caught up by Hamlet's imagination, still further excited by intermitted recollection of the overwhelming difference between the dead husband and his successor, "Hyperion to a satyr." So the nearly two months is seized by the mind, not as a physical fact, but as a concept of brevity, just as thought habitually converts minutes into moments; and the concept is translated into imaginative symbols which will provide the framework of Hamlet's intellectual cosmology. "A little month," little, that is, not objectively in relation to other months, but little in relation to the moral idea of propriety. As his imagination lashes his anger, other symbols still further hide the natural measure of a month:

Or 'ere those shoes were old
With which she follow'd my poor father's body;

the slip of the time-scheme here is perhaps not easily assessable, since we have no exact information as to how long a queen's shoes are held to be wearable. But the final symbolic expression for this "little month,"

Ere yet the salt of most unrighteous tears
Had left the flushing in her galled eyes,

can be estimated more readily, for the world knows how long it takes to remove signs of weeping from the complexion. A month, a real objective month, has been imaginatively caught up and is then imaginatively retranslated into objective reality as an hour. The sequence of ideas and the structure of the argument in the whole speech are symbolic of what Hamlet's mind perpetually does. With the philosopher's genius for intellectual creation, it fashions an image of the universe, but in the fashioning patently distorts fundamental elements of that universe. The world, as his mind builds it, ceases to be a representation of the world as it is.

This very soliloquy includes another striking instance of similar intellectual transformation. As he remembers his mother's lapse, his passion prompts the general condemnation, "Frailty, thy name is woman." As far as one knows, Hamlet, of all the women in the world, has known but two, his mother and Ophelia. His mother has unexpectedly proved "frail," but, in the Elizabethan sense of the word, Ophelia is entirely free of such charge. Yet the generalization: all women are frail. Again, the mind's picture of life is a distortion of real life, of even so much or so little of it as Hamlet really knew.

This does not mean, of course, that Hamlet's thinking is generally or regularly so prone to fallacious conclusions. His philosophic grasp of much of life's riddle is sure and permanent: and imagination has prompted his discoveries. But when the thought springs from a particular incident which moves his own feelings to new depths, imagination leads his speculations awry.

[10] I. ii. 129.

Into the fate of man at large he has a deep and broad view: he holds the macrocosm more securely than the microcosm of his own personal experience. Hence the magnificent appeal of the most famous of all the speeches in the play, "To be, or not to be." Here is a purely philosophical or speculative statement of the general tragedy of man. The problem is a universal, not a particular, one:

> Whether 'tis nobler in the mind to suffer
> The slings and arrows of outrageous fortune,
> Or to take arms against a sea of troubles,
> And by opposing end them?[11]

That is, it is not really a question of whether Hamlet shall commit suicide, but whether all men ought not to do so. For Hamlet is a metaphysician, not a psychologist; he is speculative, but not essentially introspective. The ills of life are the "heartache and the thousand natural shocks that flesh is heir to," all men's flesh, and not Hamlet's in particular. Indeed, when he recites his examples of man's outrageous fortune, there is scarcely one of them by which he himself has been especially afflicted: "the oppressor's wrong, the proud man's contumely, the insolence of office and the spurns that patient merit of the unworthy take"—these are almost everybody's troubles more than they are Hamlet's: and the "pangs of despised love" are no part at all of his relation to Ophelia. Naturally, although the whole problem is seen generally and impersonally, Hamlet's own personality affects his sense of relative values. The major ill—"what dreams may come when we have shuffled off this mortal coil"—is only major to such as Hamlet, though even this peculiar sentiment is only a particular form of the universal dread of something after death, something unpredictable in the limitless range of conjectural agonies. How completely Hamlet's mind is engrossed in the general philosophic problem is superbly revealed by the most familiar lines in the whole speech:

> The undiscover'd country from whose bourn
> No traveller returns.

The phrase has dwelt familiarly on the tongues of men as an indubitable miracle of poetic utterance, and such indeed it is. Hamlet is putting into words his sense of the after-world. He fastens on two of the aspects which belong to it in the minds and sentiments of mankind at large, namely, our complete isolation from it, "from whose bourn no traveller returns," and our entire ignorance of its particular nature, "the undiscover'd country." But choosing these as the symbols by which to suggest the after-world he gathers to the general sense a host of other appropriate associations: our intuitive feeling about the after-world is made more conscious and intelligible. The phrase is, in fact, a statement of the after-world which at some, or at many, or at all moments is true for everybody. But the amazing thing is that what makes it impress all of us, its general truth, is a quality which it cannot have for Hamlet. For mankind at large the after-world is the undiscovered country from whose bourn no traveller returns: and the philosopher Hamlet is absorbed in this general truth so completely that he forgets that for him the general truth is a particular error. A traveller *has* returned to him from the after-world, a ghost, the ghost, moreover, of his dead father, to tell a tale setting his hair on end and completely changing the rest of his life. Yet, philosophizing, he climbs to the world of ideas, of abstract truths; and forgets for the moment the most outstanding experience in his own life.

This flair of Hamlet's for abstract thinking is perpetually liable to make him momentarily indifferent to the concrete world about him. Another speech spoken before his mind is doubly strained by knowledge of the murder will show us how the natural functioning of his brain works. The situation is exciting. A ghost has been seen by Hamlet's friends. They have informed Hamlet that his father's spirit in arms has twice appeared at midnight. Hamlet is agog with excitement. The three of them plan to be in wait for the ghost: they are here on the battlements at midnight. "The air bites shrewdly," "very cold," "a nipping and an eager air," "it has struck twelve"—the whole atmosphere is one of strained excited nerves: suddenly, as they peer in hushed expectation, the silence is broken by the blast of cannon. It is a situation not likely, one would think, to soothe nerves on edge. Horatio, normally calmest of men, is rattled: "What does this mean, my lord?" asking

[11] III. i. 57.

questions more from discomposure than from desire to have repeated what he surely knows. Yet at this very moment, of all moments the most inopportune, unexpected and inappropriate, Hamlet solemnly embarks on a regular professorial disquisition about the nature of habit and its influence on moral character: "So, oft it chances in particular men": a characteristic academic text from the chair of philosophy. The discourse which ensues is typically philosophic in form. It glances round all the related contingencies, seeking to build them into a generalization. As tentative propositions are put forward, the philosopher's mind turns momentarily aside to put their implications into line with the general argument. The very syntax of this speech, with its interrupted and broken structure, is Hamlet's brain in action under our eyes. And again he is so enthralled in its operations that when the ghost does appear, his attention to it has to be called, "Look, my lord, it comes."

But this abstraction is not in itself ominous. When he does see the ghost, he is fully capable of meeting the situation which is immediately presented, and, despite his friends' fear, he follows the ghost without hesitation. So he hears the terrible story. Murder had been suspected by nobody, not even by Hamlet. Now he finds villainy blacker than he had known, villainy infecting both his mother and his uncle. He dedicates himself passionately and immediately to obey the ghost's call to revenge. Nothing, he says, will ever cause him to forget:

> Remember thee!
> Ay, thou poor ghost, while memory holds a seat
> In this distracted globe.[12]

Yet the words he continues to utter arouse our misgivings: they do not seem part of a promising project for sweeping to revenge with wings as swift as meditation:

> Yea, from the table of my memory
> I'll wipe away all trivial fond records,
> All saws of books, all forms, all pressures past,
> That youth and observation copied there.

He is, of course, talking metaphorically; the "table of his memory" is the memorandum book, and whilst it is not inappropriate to symbolize memory by such figure, it is disturbing to connect the recollection of the task which Hamlet must perform with the need to jot it down against forgetfulness even in a metaphorical diary. Disturbance grows as the metaphor usurps reality. Hamlet in his excitement is driven by his imagination; its "table," "book and volume," have become palpable, and subconsciously Hamlet is impelled to take out his actual notebook:

> My tables,—meet it is I set it down.

The action is ominous, and would be even if Hamlet should set down his determination to kill his uncle within a week. But more ominous is what he does set down:

> That one may smile, and smile, and be a villain;

—a mere truism, given, too, the conventional philosophical safeguard by qualification,

> At least I'm sure it may be so in Denmark.

It is absolutely clear, then, that Hamlet's habit of mind will in some way or another complicate his procedure. His tendency to abstraction, his proneness to let imagination stimulate and direct his intellectual voyagings beyond the reaches of the soul, his liability to set the mind awork before the body takes its appropriate complementary posture: these may recurrently obstruct a ready response in action. But in themselves they will not induce a general paralysis: and, in fact, Hamlet is normally very ready to act. As soon as he has seen the ghost, he is planning a means to kill the king, though, characteristically, his mind is apter to long-term plans than to ready improvisations. He tells his friends that he may perchance find it convenient to put an antic disposition on. But there are other significant occasions when his deeds are those of the quick resolute actor rather than of the halting, undetermined hesitator. When pirates attack the vessel on which he is sailing to England, he is the first to jump aboard as they grapple. On an earlier occasion, when he sees a stirring behind the arras, he draws at once and kills Polonius:

[12] I. v. 95.

and it is no explanation to say that this was purely instinctive, for it is obvious that he has suspected eavesdropping and, presumably, has determined beforehand on the proper response. When, towards the end, he comes on Ophelia's funeral, he acts with almost a madman's precipitancy, and jumps into the grave; and though it is a frenzied display, it is not one of a man whose sinews have atrophied in general paralysis. It is, indeed, a very significant action. It has energy, deliberateness, and the application of force on circumstances in the world about him: and these qualities are what distinguish action from mere reflex activities. But its significance for the tragedy is this: it is the wrong action for the actual world in which Hamlet must live; it is proper only to the ideal world (that is, the picture of the world which he has built in his own mind) in which he now lives without knowing that it is a distorted image of reality. If his ideal world were a valid intellectual projection of the real world, his action would be apt and effective. A crucial illustration of this is provided by his treatment of Ophelia.

Nothing is more difficult to reconcile with our impulse to sympathize with Hamlet than are his dealings with Ophelia. However docile she may be to her father (and that has not always been regarded as a sign of weakness; moreover, she stands up triumphantly to her preachifying brother), she cannot hide her love for Hamlet from us. She is not forthcoming in the way of the modern girl, nor even as naturally wise as Shakespeare's comic heroines. But is this a moral defect? And can anybody suppose for a moment that it justifies Hamlet's abominable treatment of her? It is not so much that he determines to break with her. It is the manner of the breaking. He talks to her, at best, as a salvationist preacher would reprove a woman of the street, and then as a roué who is being cynical with an associate in looseness. His remarks are disgusting and even revolting; they offend because they are preposterously out of place, for Ophelia is in no wise deserving of such ineptitudes. But if frailty (that is, immorality) is woman's name, if Ophelia, because a woman, is therefore necessarily frail, then of course everything fits. The serious advice, "get thee to a nunnery," is the only way to save the world; and the smut of the wise-cracks in the play-within-the-play scene is a proper garb. But, of course, these hypotheses are pure fiction. They are real only in Hamlet's "ideal" world, and it is only in that world that his actions would be appropriate. The other and the real world, the one in which he must live and act and succeed or fail, is a different one; and we have seen how Hamlet came to create his ideal world and then to mistake it for a true intellectual projection of the real one.

This, it would appear, is the way of Hamlet's tragedy. His supreme gift for philosophic thought allows him to know the universe better than the little world of which he is bodily a part. But his acts must be in this physical world: and his mind has distorted for him the particular objects of his actual environment. So he cannot act properly within it: or rather, towards those parts of it which the stress of his feeling and the heat of his imagination have made especially liable to intellectual distortion, he cannot oppose the right response. He can kill a Rosencrantz, but not his villainous uncle. Yet though the paralysis is localized at first, it tends to be progressive. The world of action, or the world in which outward act is alone possible, becomes increasingly different from the world as his mind conceives it. Yet the mind increasingly imposes its own picture on him as absolute. The end is despair. The will to act in the one necessary direction it first frustrated and then gradually atrophied. Worst of all, the recognition of the will's impotence is accepted as spiritual resignation; and the resignation is not seen as the moral abnegation, the *gran rifiuto,* which it certainly is; on the contrary, it is phrased as if it were the calm attainment of a higher benignity, whereas it is nothing more than a fatalist's surrender of his personal responsibility. That is the nadir of Hamlet's fall. The temper of Hamlet's converse with Horatio in the graveyard, the placidity of his comments on disinterred bones, his reminiscent ruminations on Yorick's skull, and his assumed hilarity in tracking Alexander's progress till the loam whereto he is converted serves to stop a beer-barrel—these are traits of his final frame of mind and they indicate no ascent to the serenity of philosophic calm. They are only processes which reconcile him to his last stage of failure. His increasing nonchalance, he confesses to Horatio, is really part of his falling off. "Thou wouldst not think how ill all's here about my heart." And his gesture of noble defiance is no firm confession of trust in a benign Providence: it is merely the courage of despair:

> We defy augury: there's a special providence in the fall of a sparrow. . . .
> If it be not now, yet it will come: the readiness is all: since no man has aught of what he leaves, what is't to leave betimes?[13]

This is absolute abdication: if Hamlet's duty is to be done, Providence will occasion its doing, as indeed Providence does in the heat of the fencing match when chance discloses more villainy, and stings Hamlet into a reflex retaliation. But Hamlet has failed. That is the tragedy.

In his own world, Hamlet, this noble mind, has been o'erthrown. But as he has moved on to his undoing, his generous nature, instinctively averse from all contriving, has linked the whole audience with the general gender in great love and veneration for him. Yet when his doom overtakes him, there is neither from him nor from the audience any cry of resentment; no anger against the gods, no challenging of the providence that shapes our ends. The rest is silence. The play done, however, and the deep impression of it remaining, the mind of man remits this *Hamlet*-experience to the cumulative mass of spiritual data which is piling up within it through every channel and every mode of consciousness. *Hamlet* is added to the vast medley of other imprints which every act of our living stamps on our spiritual retina: and the mind strives to find some clue to a form in the enigma, some shape in an apparent confusion, a pattern which, giving full force to tragedy, will not compel despair. . . .

A. ALVAREZ
1929–
August Strindberg

The fiftieth anniversary of Strindberg's death misfired in 1962. Elizabeth Sprigge's lovingly prepared translation of twelve of his plays does not seem to have been ready in time. All we got here was *Inferno,* the record of his breakdown after he separated from his second wife, which is fascinating as a case-history but a non-starter as a work of art. The Royal Shakespeare Company's contribution was a burlesque of his quite good one-acter, *Playing With Fire.* And that was that.

Yet it was typical. Strindberg has nearly always had the wrong kind of success and the wrong kind of failure: both have been scandalous, noisy, racked. He seems only to have been able to stomach public acclaim provided it was accompanied by a proportionate public fury. He was, from the start, a tortured man who exploited his tortures, who chronicled his appalling autobiography as it happened, and wrote to hurt. He was as self-destructive as he was paranoid; conversely, he pitied himself as much as he persecuted himself. He had a flair for disastrous marriages and melodramatic affairs. He quarrelled with everyone—particularly his friends—and had his first collection of stories prosecuted for blasphemy. He fancied himself as an alchemist and dabbled in theosophy and occultism. At his worst, he seems preoccupied by his own sinfulness, his "passions" and the sweet smell of decadence.

But these last *fin de siècle* mannerisms are a mere irritation on the surface of his work. Eliot once remarked that the odd thing about the British writers of the Nineties—Wilde, Dowson, Lionel Johnson—was that they suffered so much and wrote so superficially. They were protected, he thought, by their histrionics. Strindberg lacked that extra thickness of skin. Instead, his genius was directly related to the rawness of his nerves. The state of mind he so meticulously described in *Inferno* is, in the technical sense, psychotic; he shows, I am told, all the symptoms of a paranoid schizophrenic. More simply, he commanded neither the defences nor the sense of reality to keep him in the manageable realm of neurosis. Yet it was from precisely this failing that his power and his curiously contemporary air come. In painting, Expressionism may have gone a long way beyond Edvard Munch, whom Strindberg knew in Paris during his *Inferno* period. On the stage, however, it is still catching up with Strindberg.

He seems to have invented what now passes for the *avant-garde* theatre, and a great deal of

[13] V. ii. 237.

what we take for granted in the cinema. As early as the foreword to *Miss Julie*[1] he had set about the reform of the stage. He wanted to get rid of the footlights, the distractions of orchestra and intervals, the boxes "with their tittering diners and supper-parties," and the heavy encumbrances of elaborate sets. In their place he wanted a fluid stage—of the kind, presumably, which Svoboda has perfected in Prague—and acting fluid enough to include improvisation, ballet and mime; also a fluidity of writing, to avoid

> the symmetrical, mathematical construction of French dialogue, and let people's minds work irregularly, as they do in real life where, during a conversation, no topic is drained to the dregs, and one mind finds in another a chance cog to engage in.

Above all, he was after "a *small* stage and a *small* house" and "total darkness in the auditorium." It sounds like the usual attack on the conventionality, complacency and philistinism of the socialite theatre. But it has little to do with the naturalist programme of Ibsen. Strindberg's brand of realism was more like that of the cinema, where the darkness and the looming black and white images are closer not to life but to dreams.

This fits with Strindberg's preoccupation as an artist. He was continually trying to cut through the polished surface of ideas and manners to examine the springs of action. "We want," he wrote, "to see the wires themselves, to watch the machinery." Perhaps Beckett works in the same way. But he is more limited, more negative; the essence of his people is their isolation, and their most passionate relationship is with Nothingness. Strindberg, on the other hand, was too close to Ibsen to be able to abstract his obsessions so tidily. And the obsessions themselves were all concerned with the destructive complexity of his feelings for women.

He is the master of sexual ambivalence and uncertainty. Pathologically jealous, he was a sensualist who yearned always for "masculine virginity." He courted rejection and reacted savagely to any positive show of love. It is as though he were unable to get over the fact that women have their own sexual desires. That is the chief offence of Miss Julie, of Henriette in *Crime and Crime* and of Alice in *The Dance of Death*. It seemed to open to him menacing perspectives of feminism, lesbianism and a whole world in which embattled women usurped the rights of men. His perfect heroines were all virginal, suffering, bodiless: Swanwhite, Eleanor in *Easter*, Indra's Daughter in *A Dream Play*, and the Girl in his masterpiece, *The Ghost Sonata*. All his heroes, meanwhile, suffered maternal agonies of tenderness for their children, shared even their wives' labour pains and were passionately involved with their wives' former husbands or lovers. The result is an endless and unresolved sense of outrage. His couples destroy each other in acts of what, in *Creditors*, he calls "pure cannibalism." In his works there are no solutions, only at times a grudging acceptance of the horror of the other person's individuality. His talent lay in catching that note of human violence in constricted surroundings. In comparison with his chamber plays, the more ambitious open-scene poetic quests, like *To Damascus* and *The Great Highway*, are diffuse and unconvincing. His genius needed the domestic prison for the full expression of its ferocity. He was the inventor of marital Expressionism.

The core of Expressionism is in an impossible intensity of feeling which lies just behind the work of art but which is never quite expressed by it. You are constantly forced back from the work to its creator. In his famous essay on *Hamlet*, Eliot wrote:

> The only way of expressing emotion in the form of art is by finding an "objective correlative"; in other words, a set of objects, a situation, a chain of events which shall be the formula of that *particular* emotion; such that when the external facts, which must terminate in sensory experience, are given, the emotion is immediately invoked. . . . Hamlet (the man) is dominated by an emotion which is inexpressible, because it is in *excess* of the facts as they appear.

By this reckoning, *Hamlet* is the first Expressionist play. But what is an exception with Shakespeare is the rule with Strindberg. *The Father*, for example, begins with the bullying, insistently masculine hero trapped in a houseful of women and in a heartless, mutually destruc-

[1] For the Foreword, see p. 533.

tive marriage. The situation has all the makings of a piece of Ibsen-like claustrophobia. Then it explodes. His wife has only to drop two hints—that he is mad and that their daughter is not his, both legitimate manoeuvres in the style of battle they are fighting—and he promptly becomes insane. For despite appearances, the madness was already there, though neither in the situation nor in anything you are told of the Captain's character. Instead, it existed in Strindberg's own mind, as a permanent background of horrified anxiety. To understand the play you must understand Strindberg: his history of breakdowns, excesses and frenzies; his love-hatred for his first wife and the man he had taken her from, and for his icy father who had married the housekeeper directly his own first wife died, when Strindberg was at puberty. The play calls for a kind of Method reading, just as it calls for Method acting. The words, in order to make sense of the actions they go with, must imply intensities which they do not in fact define. This is the opposite of Shakespeare's way, where the feelings develop with and through the language, the images releasing layer after layer of meaning. In Strindberg's chamber plays the language and the feeling are always a little apart.

He seems to have been aware of the split. It was, I think, in the hope of mending it that he tried to break down the conventions of his contemporary stage and turned more and more to poetic drama. As he said in the note to *A Dream Play*:

> The Author has sought to reproduce the disconnected but apparently logical form of a dream. Anything can happen; everything is possible and probable. Time and space do not exist . . . And since on the whole, there is more pain than pleasure in the dream, a tone of melancholy, and of compassion for all living things, runs through the swaying narrative.

This is a stage further on from the theatre he postulated in the foreword to *Miss Julie*. In that play Strindberg himself is divided equally between Miss Julie and Jean; in *A Dream Play* he is deliberately fragmented through all the characters. He used the dream convention as a way through to the emotions. The feelings experienced in dreams are both more intense and more direct than any experienced in waking life. So by creating in his "swaying narrative" the condition of dreams, he was able to tap the roots of his obsessions without feeling constricted by that reality which, in his sickness, he was never properly able to face.

Yet the pure dream plays lack the power of his earlier, more firmly localized works. He needed the "objective correlative" of domesticity to fix that tension between love as he felt it should be and marriage as he knew it was. He was possessed by the idea of marriage. But only in *The Ghost Sonata* did he manage to reconcile its constrictions with the imaginative freedom of his dream narrative. The result was a kind of acted-out, personified poetry. "Not reality," as he says in *A Dream Play*, "but more than reality. Not dreams but waking dreams."

ACKNOWLEDGMENTS

(continued from copyright page)

Combine Music Corporation for permission to reprint "Me and Bobby McGee" and "Sunday Mornin' Comin' Down," both copyright © 1969 by Combine Music Corporation. International copyright secured. All rights reserved.

Corinth Books, Inc., for permission to reprint "Preface to a Twenty-Volume Suicide Note," copyright © 1961 by LeRoi Jones.

Curtis Brown, Ltd., for permission to reprint "Miss Julie," copyright © 1955 by Elizabeth Sprigge, and "Self-Portrait as a Bear," copyright © 1969 by Donald Hall.

Frank Marshall Davis for permission to reprint "Roosevelt Smith."

J. M. Dent and Sons, Ltd., and the Trustees for the Copyrights of the late Dylan Thomas for permission to reprint "Do Not Go Gentle into That Good Night" and "The Force That Through the Green Fuse Drives the Flower" from *The Collected Poems of Dylan Thomas.*

Delacorte Press/Seymour Lawrence for permission to reprint "Harrison Bergeron," excerpted from *Welcome to the Monkey House* by Kurt Vonnegut, Jr. Originally published in *Fantasy and Science Fiction.* Copyright © 1961 by Kurt Vonnegut, Jr.

Candida Donadio & Associates, Inc., for permission to reprint "August Strindberg" from *Beyond All This Fiddle* by A. Alvarez, copyright © 1968 by A. Alvarez.

Doubleday & Company, Inc., for permission to reprint "The Colonel's Lady" from *Creatures of Cirstance* by W. Somerset Maugham.

Norma Millay Ellis for permission to reprint "To Jesus on His Birthday" from *Collected Poems* by Edna St. Vincent Millay, Harper & Row, copyright 1928, 1955 by Edna St. Vincent Millay and Norma Millay Ellis.

James A. Emanuel for permission to reprint "Emmett Till."

Faber and Faber Limited for permission to reprint "Lullaby," "Musée des Beaux Arts," and "The Unknown Citizen" from *Collected Shorter Poems* by W. H. Auden; "The Cultivation of Christmas Trees," "The Hollow Men," "The Love Song of J. Alfred Prufrock," and "Morning at the Window" from *Collected Poems 1909–1962* by T. S. Eliot; and "An Elementary School Classroom in a Slum" and "I Think Continually of Those Who Were Truly Great" from *Collected Poems* by Stephen Spender.

Fall River Music, Inc., for permission to reprint lyrics of "Where Have All the Flowers Gone?" by Pete Seeger, copyright © 1961 by Fall River Music, Inc. All rights reserved. Used by permission.

Famous Music Publishing for permission to reprint lyrics of "Gentle on My Mind" by Johnny Hartford, copyright by Ensign Music Corporation.

Farrar, Straus & Giroux, Inc., for permission to reprint "The Bitch" from *Creatures Great and Small* by Colette, translated by Enid MacLeod, copyright 1951 by Martin Secker and Warburg, Ltd.; "A City of Churches" from *Sadness* by Donald Barthelme, copyright © 1970, 1971, 1972 by Donald Barthelme (appeared originally in *The New Yorker*); "Sorrow Is the Only Faithful One" from *Powerful Long Ladder* by Owen Dodson, copyright 1946 by Owen Dodson; "The Cultivation of Christmas Trees" by T. S. Eliot, copyright © 1954, 1956 by Thomas Stearns Eliot; "The Lottery" from *The Lottery* by Shirley Jackson, copyright 1948, 1949 by Shirley Jackson, copyright renewed © 1976 by Laurence Hyman, Barry Hyman, Mrs. Sarah Webster, and Mrs. Joanne Schnurer (appeared originally in *The New Yorker*); "The Emancipators" and "Second Air Force" by Randall Jarrell from *The Complete Poems* by Randall Jarrell, copyright 1943, 1944 by Randall Jarrell, copyright renewed 1971, 1972 by Mary von Schrader Jarrell; "The Magic Barrel" from *The Magic Barrel* by Bernard Malamud, copyright © 1954, 1958 by Bernard Malamud; and "Everything That Rises Must Converge" from *Everything That Rises Must Converge* by Flannery O'Connor, copyright © 1961, 1965 by the Estate of Mary Flannery O'Connor.

Grove Press, Inc., for permission to reprint "What would I do without this world faceless incurious," French and English versions, from *Poems in English* by Samuel Beckett, copyright © 1961 by Samuel Beckett.

Hamish Hamilton Limited for permission to reprint "Caligula" from *Caligula* by Albert Camus, copyright © 1947 in USA by Albert Camus, translation by Stuart Gilbert copyright © by Hamish Hamilton Ltd., London.

Harcourt Brace Jovanovich for permission to reprint "Candles" from *The Complete Poems of Cavafy,* translated by Rae Delven, copyright 1948, 1949, © 1959, 1961 by Rae Delven; "a/mong crum/bling people," copyright 1931, 1959 by E. E. Cummings and "the Cambridge ladies," copyright 1923, 1951 by E. E. Cummings, both from his volume, *Poems 1923–1954*; "pity this busy monster, manunkind," copyright 1944 by E. E. Cummings, renewed 1972 by Nancy Andrews; "The Love Song of J. Alfred Prufrock," "Morning at the Window," and "The Hollow

Men" from *Collected Poems, 1909–1962* by T. S. Eliot, copyright 1936 by Harcourt Brace Jovanovich, Inc., copyright © 1963, 1964 by T. S. Eliot; "As a Plane Tree by the Water" and "The Dead in Europe" from *Lord Weary's Castle* by Robert Lowell, copyright 1946, 1974 by Robert Lowell; selections from *The People, Yes* by Carl Sandburg, copyright 1936 by Harcourt Brace Jovanovich, Inc., renewed © 1964 by Carl Sandburg; and "Edgar A. Guest Considers 'The Old Woman Who Lived in a Shoe' and the Good Old Verities at the Same Time" from *Collected Parodies* by Louis Untermeyer, copyright 1926.

Harper & Row, Publishers, Inc., for permission to reprint "The Ballad of Chocolate Mabbie," p. 14, copyright 1945 by Gwendolyn Brooks Blakely, and "The Children of the Poor," p. 99, copyright 1949 by Gwendolyn Brooks Blakely, both from *The World of Gwendolyn Brooks*; "For John Keats," copyright 1925 by Harper & Row, Publishers, Inc., and "Yet Do I Marvel," copyright 1925 by Harper & Row, Publishers, Inc., from *On These I Stand* by Countee Cullen; "Theology" from *Selected Poems* (1974) by Ted Hughes, copyright © 1961 by Ted Hughes; "What We Said" from *After Experience* by W. D. Snodgrass, copyright © 1958 by W. D. Snodgrass; "Traveling through the Dark" from *Traveling through the Dark* by William Stafford, copyright © 1960 by William Stafford; "The Hour of Letdown" from *The Second Tree from the Corner* by E. B. White, copyright 1951 by E. B. White (originally appeared in *The New Yorker*); and "I Paint What I See" from *The Fox of Peapack* by E. B. White, copyright 1933 by E. B. White.

Harvard University Press and the Trustees of Amherst College for permission to reprint selections from *The Poems of Emily Dickinson*, edited by Thomas H. Johnson, Cambridge, Mass.: The Belknap Press of Harvard University Press, © 1951, 1955 by the President and Fellows of Harvard College.

James Hearst for permission to reprint "Landmark" and "Truth" from *Limited View* by James Hearst (Iowa City, Iowa: Prairie Press), copyright © 1962 by James Hearst.

William Heinemann, Ltd., for permission to reprint "Quality" from *The Inn of Tranquility* by John Galsworthy, copyright 1912 by Charles Scribner's Sons, 1940 by Ada Galsworthy.

Holt, Rinehart and Winston, Publishers, for permission to reprint "Acquainted with the Night," "Departmental," "The Gift Outright," "A Masque of Reason," "Neither Out Far nor In Deep," "The Secret Sits," "Stopping by Woods on a Snowy Evening," "The Strong Are Saying Nothing," and "The Trial by Existence" from *The Poetry of Robert Frost*, edited by Edward Connery Lathem, copyright 1945 by Robert Frost, copyright © 1969 by Holt, Rinehart and Winston, copyright © 1973 by Lesley Frost Ballantine; "The True Lover" and "When I Was One-and-Twenty" from "A Shropshire Lad"—Authorized Edition—from *The Collected Poems of A. E. Housman*, copyright 1939, 1940, © 1965 by Holt, Rinehart and Winston, copyright © 1967, 1968 by Robert E. Symons; and "How You Get Born" from *Half-Lives* by Erica Jong, copyright © 1971, 1972, 1973 by Erica Mann Jong.

Houghton Mifflin Company for permission to reprint "The Dinner-Party" from *Men, Women, and Ghosts* by Amy Lowell; "America Was Promises," "Ars Poetica," "Not Marble nor the Gilded Monuments," "You Also, Gaius Valerius Catullus," and "You, Andrew Marvell" from *The Collected Poems of Archibald MacLeish*, copyright 1962 by Archibald MacLeish; and "The Kiss" from *Love Poems* by Anne Sexton, copyright © 1967, 1968, 1969 by Anne Sexton.

Olwyn Hughes, Literary Agent, for permission to reprint "Suicide off Egg Rock" and "Two Views of a Cadaver Room" from *The Colossus*, published by Faber and Faber Limited, London, copyright 1967 by Ted Hughes.

International Creative Management for permission to reprint "The Portable Phonograph" from *The Portable Phonograph* by Walter Van Tilburg Clark, copyright © 1941, 1969 by Walter Van Tilburg Clark.

Jeffers Literary Properties for permission to reprint "Shine, Empire" by Robinson Jeffers.

Colette de Jouvenel for permission to reprint "The Bitch" from *Creatures Great and Small* by Colette.

Little, Brown and Company for permission to reprint "The Seven Spiritual Ages of Mrs. Marmaduke Moore" from *Verses from 1929 on* by Ogden Nash, copyright 1933 by Ogden Nash.

Liveright Publishing Corporation for permission to reprint "To Brooklyn Bridge" and "North Labrador" from *The Complete Poems and Selected Letters and Prose of Hart Crane*, copyright 1933, ©1958, 1966 by Liveright Publishing Corporation; and "Frederick Douglass" from *Angle of Ascent: New and Selected Poems* by Robert Hayden, copyright © 1975, 1972, 1970, 1966 by Robert Hayden.

Macmillan Publishing Co., Inc., for permission to reprint "On the Road" from *The Chorus Girl and Other Stories* by Anton Chekhov, copyright 1920 by Macmillan Publishing Co., Inc., renewed 1948 by David Garnett; "Hap," "The Last Chrysanthemum," and "The Man He Killed" from *Collected Poems* by Thomas Hardy, copyright 1925 by Macmillan Publishing Co., Inc.; "Eve" from *Poems* by Ralph Hodgson, copyright 1917 by Macmillan Publishing Co., Inc., renewed 1945 by Ralph Hodgson; "Mr. Flood's Party" from *Collected Poems* by Edwin Arlington Robinson, copyright 1921 by Edwin Arlington Robinson, renewed 1949 by Ruth Nivison; "Three Deaths" by Leo Tolstoy from *A Treasury of Great Russian Short Stories,* translated by Constance Garnett, copyright 1944; "Among School Children," copyright 1928 by Macmillan Publishing Co., Inc., renewed 1956 by George Yeats, "The Ballad of Father Gilligan," copyright 1906 by Macmillan Publishing Co., Inc., renewed 1934 by William Butler Yeats, "The Second Coming," copyright 1924 by Macmillan Publishing Co., Inc., renewed 1952 by Bertha Georgie Yeats, and "The Wild Swans at Coole," copyright 1919 by Macmillan Publishing Co., Inc., renewed 1947 by Bertha Georgie Yeats, all four from *Collected Poems* by William Butler Yeats, copyright 1950.

Macmillan Company of Canada for permission to reprint "Hap," "The Last Chrysanthemum," and "The Man He Killed" from *Collected Poems* by Thomas Hardy, copyright 1925 by Macmillan Publishing Co., Inc.; and "Eve" from *Poems* by Ralph Hodgson, copyright 1917 by Macmillan Publishing Co., Inc., renewed 1945 by Ralph Hodgson.

Martin Secker & Warburg Limited for permission to reprint "The Bitch" from *Creatures Great and Small* by Colette, translated by Enid MacLeod.

Harold Matson Company, Inc., for permission to reprint "There Will Come Soft Rains," copyright 1950 by Ray Bradbury.

Mietus Copyright Management for permission to reprint lyrics of "Tennessee Bird Walk," copyright © Back Bay Music. All rights reserved. Used by permission.

Stephen Mooney, *The Beloit Poetry Journal,* and the University of Tennessee Press for permission to reprint "Assassination at Memphis," © 1968 by Stephen Mooney, and "The Garden."

William Morris Agency, Inc., for permission on behalf of the author to reprint "King of the Bingo Game" by Ralph Ellison, copyright © 1944 (renewed) by Ralph Ellison.

New Directions Publishing Corporation for permission to reprint "In Goya's Greatest Scenes" from *A Coney Island of the Mind* by Lawrence Ferlinghetti, copyright © 1958 by Lawrence Ferlinghetti; "Ballad of the Goodly Fere," "Envoi (1919)," and "A Pact" from *Personae* by Ezra Pound, copyright 1926, 1954 by Ezra Pound; "In the Naked Bed, in Plato's Cave" from *Selected Poems: Summer Knowledge* by Delmore Schwartz, copyright 1938 by New Directions Publishing Corporation; "A Walk" from *The Back Country* by Gary Snyder, copyright © 1960 by Gary Snyder; and "Do Not Go Gentle into That Good Night" and "The Force That Through the Green Fuse Drives the Flower" from *The Poems of Dylan Thomas,* copyright 1939 by New Directions Publishing Corporation, copyright 1952 by Dylan Thomas.

The New York Times for permission to reprint "Emmett Till" by James A. Emanuel, copyright © 1963 by The New York Times Company.

W. W. Norton & Company for permission to reprint "Living in Sin" from *Poems, Selected and New* by Adrienne Rich, copyright © 1975, 1973, 1971, 1969, 1966 by W. W. Norton & Company, Inc., copyright © 1967, 1963, 1962, 1961, 1960, 1959, 1958, 1957, 1956, 1955, 1954, 1953, 1952, 1951 by Adrienne Rich.

Harold Ober Associates, Inc., for permission to reprint "I'm a Fool" by Sherwood Anderson, copyright © 1922 by Dial Publishing Company, Inc., renewed 1949 by Eleanor Copenhaver Anderson; "Southern Mansion" by Arna Bontemps, copyright © 1963 by Arna Bontemps; and "On the Road" by Langston Hughes, copyright © 1952 by Langston Hughes.

Oxford University Press for permission to reprint "Spring and Fall" and "The Windhover" by Gerard Manley Hopkins.

Peer–Southern Organization for permission to reprint lyrics of "Hampstead Incident" by Donovan Leitch, copyright © 1967 by Donovan (Music) Ltd., sole selling agent Peer International Corporation, used by permission; and "The Lullaby of Spring" by Donovan Leitch, copyright © 1967 by Donovan (Music) Ltd., sole selling agent Peer International Corporation, used by permission.

A. D. Peters & Company, Limited, for permission to reprint "The Drunkard" from *Stories of Frank O'Connor.*

Nancy Price for permission to reprint "Centennial of Shiloh."

Lora Rackstraw for permission to reprint "The Word" by Richard Rackstraw.

Random House, Inc., Alfred A. Knopf, Inc., for permission to reprint "August Strindberg" from *Beyond All This Fiddle* by A. Alvarez, copyright © 1968 by A. Alvarez; "Lullaby," "Musée des Beaux Arts," and "The Unknown Citizen" from *Collected Shorter Poems 1927–1957* by W. H. Auden, copyright 1940 and renewed 1968 by W. H. Auden; "The Demon Lover" from *Ivy Gripped the Steps and Other Stories* by Elizabeth Bowen, copyright 1946, renewed 1974; "Caligula" from *Caligula and Three Other Plays* by Albert Camus, translated by Stuart Gilbert, copyright © 1958 by Alfred A. Knopf, Inc.; "The Visit" by Friedrich Duerrenmatt (copyright © 1956 by Maurice Valency as an unpublished work entitled "The Old Lady's Visit," adapted by Maurice Valency from *Der Besuch der Alten Dame* by Friedrich Duerrenmatt), copyright © 1958 by Maurice Valency, reprinted from *Masters of Modern Drama* by permission of Random House, Inc.; "Celebration for a Grey Day" from *Long Time Coming and a Long Time Gone* by Richard Fariña, copyright © 1961 by Margarita M. Fariña, Administratrix of the Estate of Richard G. Fariña; "A Rose for Emily" from *Collected Stories of William Faulkner,* copyright 1930, renewed © 1958 by William Faulkner; "The Bloody Sire" from *Selected Poems* by Robinson Jeffers, copyright © 1965 by Donnan Jeffers and Garth Jeffers; "Shine, Republic" from *Solstice* by Robinson Jeffers, copyright 1934, renewed © 1962 by Donnan Jeffers and Garth Jeffers; "Shine, Perishing Republic" and "Science," from *Selected Poetry of Robinson Jeffers,* copyright 1925, renewed 1953 by Robinson Jeffers; "The Drunkard" from *The Stories of Frank O'Connor,* copyright 1951 by Frank O'Connor (first appeared in *The New Yorker*); "Ile" by Eugene O'Neill, copyright 1919, renewed 1947 by Eugene O'Neill, reprinted from *The Long Voyage Home: Seven Plays of the Sea* by Eugene O'Neill by permission of Random House, Inc.; "Suicide off Egg Rock" and "Two Views of a Cadaver Room" from *The Colossus and Other Poems* by Sylvia Plath, copyright © 1960 by Sylvia Plath; "The Wall" by Jean-Paul Sartre, translated by Maria Jolas, copyright 1945 by Random House, Inc., reprinted from *Bedside Book of Famous French Stories* (B. Becker and R. N. Linscott, editors) by permission of New Directions Publishing Corporation and Random House, Inc.; "Movie Actress" from *V-Letter and Other Poems* by Karl Shapiro, copyright 1943 by Karl Shapiro; "The Sunshine Boys" from *The Sunshine Boys* by Neil Simon, copyright © 1973 by Neil Simon; "An Elementary School Classroom in a Slum," copyright 1942, renewed 1970 by Stephen Spender, and "I Think Continually of Those Who Were Truly Great," copyright 1934, renewed 1962 by Stephen Spender, both from *Selected Poems* by Stephen Spender; "Peter Quince at the Clavier" and "Sunday Morning" from *The Collected Poems of Wallace Stevens,* copyright 1923, renewed 1951 by Wallace Stevens; and "The Playboy of the Western World," copyright 1907, renewed 1935 by the Executors of the Estate of John M. Synge, reprinted from *The Complete Works of John M. Synge.*

Schocken Books, Inc., for permission to reprint "A Hunger Artist" from *The Penal Colony* by Franz Kafka, copyright © 1948, renewed © 1975 by Schocken Books, Inc.

Charles Scribner's Sons for permission to reprint "Quality" from *The Inn of Tranquility* by John Galsworthy, copyright 1912 by Charles Scribner's Sons, 1940 by Ada Galsworthy; "A Clean, Well-Lighted Place" from *Winner Take Nothing* by Ernest Hemingway, copyright 1933 by Charles Scribner's Sons, renewed © 1961 by Ernest Hemingway; "Miniver Cheevy" from *The Town Down the River* by Edwin Arlington Robinson, copyright 1910 by Charles Scribner's Sons, 1938 by Ruth Nivison; and "The Poet's Testament" from *The Poet's Testament* by George Santayana, copyright 1952 by Charles Scribner's Sons (first appeared in *Time*).

Simon & Schuster, Inc., for permission to reprint "You, Letting the Trees Stand as My Betrayer" from *The Motorcycle Betrayal Poems* by Diane Wakoski, copyright © 1971 by Diane Wakoski.

The Society of Authors as the literary representative of the Estate of A. E. Housman, and Jonathan Cape Ltd., publishers of A. E. Housman's *Collected Poems,* for permission to reprint "The True Lover" and "When I Was One-and-Twenty."

Stephen Spender and Harold Taylor for permission to reprint "On Teaching Modern Poetry" from *Essays on Teaching* by Stephen Spender, edited by Harold Taylor.

Peter J. Stanlis and the University Press of Mississippi for permission to reprint "Robert Frost's 'A Masque of Reason': An Analysis" from *Frost: Centennial Essays* (Jackson, Miss.: University Press of Mississippi, 1975).

Stranger Music, Inc., for permission to reprint lyrics of "Hey, That's No Way to Say Goodbye" and "Stories of the Street," words and music by Leonard Cohen, both copyright © 1967 by Stranger Music, Inc., used by permission, all rights reserved.

The Swallow Press, Inc., Chicago, for permission to reprint "The Metaphysical Amorist" from *Exclusions of a Rhyme* by J. V. Cunningham.

Twayne Publishers, a Division of G. K. Hall & Co., Boston, for permission to reprint "Harlem Dancer" from *Selected Poems of Claude McKay,* copyright 1953 by Twayne Publishers, Inc.

United Artists Music Co., Inc., for permission to reprint lyrics of "I Give You the Morning" by Tom Paxton, copyright © 1969 by United Artists

Music Co., Inc., New York, N.Y., used by permission.

University of Chicago Press and Grover Smith for permission to reprint excerpt from *T. S. Eliot's Poetry and Plays* by Grover Smith, 2nd edition, copyright 1974.

Vanguard Press, Inc., for permission to reprint "In the Region of Ice" from *The Wheel of Love and Other Stories* by Joyce Carol Oates, copyright © 1970, 1969, 1968, 1967, 1966, 1965 by Joyce Carol Oates.

Vanguard Recording Society for permission to reprint lyrics of "Black Panther" by Carl Oglesby, copyright © 1968 by Fennario Music Publishers, Inc.

The Viking Press, Inc., for permission to reprint "Piano" from *The Complete Poems of D. H. Lawrence,* edited by Vivian de Sola Pinto and F. Warren Roberts, copyright © 1964, 1971 by Angelo Ravagli and C. M. Weekley, Executives of the Estate of Frieda Lawrence Ravagli; "The Day After Sunday" from *Times Three* by Phyllis McGinley, copyright 1952 by Phyllis McGinley; "Resumé" from *The Portable Dorothy Parker,* copyright 1926, 1954 by Dorothy Parker; and "The Chrysanthemums" from *The Long Valley* by John Steinbeck, copyright 1937, © 1965 by John Steinbeck.

Margaret Alexander Walker for permission to reprint "Molly Means" from *For My People* by Margaret Walker, copyright © 1942 by Yale University Press.

A. Watkins, Inc., for permission to reprint "Roman Fever" from *The World Over* by Edith Wharton, copyright 1934 by Edith Wharton, renewed 1962 by William R. Tyler.

A. P. Watt & Son for permission to reprint "On the Road" by Anton Chekhov, translated by Constance Garnett from *The Chorus Girl and Other Stories,* with permission of David Garnett and Chatto & Windus Ltd.; "The Colonel's Lady" from *The Collected Stories of W. Somerset Maugham,* with permission of the Estate of the late W. Somerset Maugham and William Heinemann Ltd.; and "Among School Children," "The Ballad of Father Gilligan," "The Second Coming," and "The Wild Swans at Coole" from *The Collected Poems* of W. B. Yeats, with permission of M. B. Yeats, Miss Anne Yeats, and the Macmillan Company of London & Basingstoke.

Wesleyan University Press for permission to reprint "Adultery" from *Poems 1957–1967* by James Dickey, copyright © 1966 by James Dickey; "Counting the Mad" from *The Summer Anniversaries* by Donald Justice, copyright © 1957 by Donald Justice; "To the Western World" from *A Dream of Governors* by Louis Simpson, copyright © 1957 by Louis Simpson; and "A Blessing" from *The Branch Will Not Break* by James Wright, copyright © 1961 by James Wright (first appeared in *Poetry*).

Robley Wilson, Jr., for permission to reprint "The Great Teachers" and "War."

Yale University Press for permission to reprint "The Lost Pilot" from *The Lost Pilot* by James Tate, copyright © 1967.

INDEX OF AUTHORS AND TITLES

INDEX OF LITERARY AND CRITICAL TERMS